Introduction to Complex Analysis

and

Its Applications

Donald Trim

The University of Manitoba

Winnipeg, Manitoba

Canada, R3T 2N2

Chapter 10   The z-Transform

Appendix A   Answers to Exercises

PREFACE

To the Instructor

This text is written for undergraduate students in science and engineering. At a brisk pace, theory and a selection of applications can be covered in one semester; for complete coverage at a more leisurely pace allow two semesters. The presentation assumes a working knowledge of single-variable real calculus, including infinite series, and familiarity with partial differentiation and line integrals. Discussions are rigorous, but the approach is intuitive.

Chapter 1 introduces complex numbers. We add, subtract, multiply, divide, and find roots of complex numbers. We introduce the Cartesian, polar, and exponential forms for complex numbers, illustrate complex numbers geometrically, and solve polynomial equations. Chapter 2 begins with the algebra of complex functions, discusses limits and continuity, and ends with complex differentiation and analyticity. The complex exponential, trigonometric, hyperbolic, logarithmic, and inverse trigonometric and hyperbolic functions are introduced in Chapter 3. We concentrate on algebraic properties of these functions, and their zeros and singularities, but, in preparation for conformal mapping in Chapter 7, we also stress the importance of visualizing a function $w = f(z)$ as a mapping from the z-plane to the w-plane. The fact that real and imaginary parts of analytic functions are harmonic suggests the use of complex functions to problems in electrostatics, steady-state temperature distributions, and fluid flows. These applications are introduced in Chapter 3.

In Chapter 4 we focus on contour integration. We verify the Cauchy-Goursat theorem, introduce Cauchy's integral formulas and Poisson's integral formulas, and develop modulus principles for complex and harmonic functions. Power series and Laurent series with the subsequent classification of singularities of complex functions are discussed in Chapter 5. Chapters 4 and 5 culminate in the theory of residues in Chapter 6. The power of residues is brought out in the evaluation of real trigonometric and improper integrals, the principle of the argument, Rouche's theorem, and summations of certain types of infinite series.

Although the first six chapters emphasize algebraic consequences of analyticity, and geometric results in the context of conformal mapping are discussed in Chapter 7, we constantly stress the geometric interpretation of a function as a mapping. Having students repeatedly visualize regional mappings by exponential, trigonometric, and hyperbolic functions, and their inverses, we pave the way for the application of conformal mappings to problems in heat flow, fluid flow, and electrostatics. These applications are dealt with in Chapter 7, perhaps with more detail than most texts at this level, but they are introduced in Chapter 3 as illustrations of the fact that families of curves defined by harmonic conjugates are orthogonal trajectories. In this way we give students an early indication that complex functions are indeed useful in physical applications.

In Chapter 8, we discuss Laplace transforms. We develop their elementary properties and show how they can be used to replace ordinary differential equations with algebraic equations. Cauchy's integral formula and residues then lead to a direct formula for inverting Laplace transforms. The transform is used to solve partial differential equations on bounded and semi-infinite domains. Finally, we introduce transfer functions and the notion of stability for systems governed by differential equations.

In Chapter 9, we use the Fourier transform, the Fourier sine transform, and the Fourier cosine transform to reduce partial differential equations on infinite and semi-infinite intervals to ordinary differential equations. We apply the technique to heat conduction, vibration, and potential problems.

In Chapter 10, we discuss the z-transform. The discussion parallels that for the Laplace transform in that we discuss properties of the transform, followed by its use in solving first- and second-order difference equations. Applications are discussed for difference equations as are transfer functions and stability for discrete systems.

We take every opportunity to compare properties of complex functions to those of real functions. Only then can the power and elegance of complex variable theory truly be appreciated. Plenty of exercises, with answers, are provided. Exercises are graded from routine, for reinforcement of fundamentals, to challenging, for the more enterprising reader. A complete solutions manual containing detailed solutions to all problems is available.

To the Student

When the domain and range of a function are sets of complex numbers, we speak of a complex function of a complex variable. This text is an introduction to the properties and applications of such functions; in particular, we develop the *calculus* of complex functions. Your earliest calculus studies involved real-valued functions $f(x)$ of a real variable x. You found their derivatives and integrals, and used these in many geometric and physical applications. Your second exposure to calculus expanded single-variable concepts to functions of many real variables $f(x, y, \ldots)$. Once again you differentiated and integrated these functions, and applied the derivatives and integrals in more complicated, but more realistic applications. It is now time to take the third, and for most, the final step; calculus of functions $f(z)$ of a complex variable z.

You are well aware of the connection between integration and differentiation in real calculus; you will be amazed at the intimate relationships among the three major topics of complex calculus — differentiation, integration, and infinite series. Properties in any one of these topics are reflected in properties in the other two, so much so, that we could commence complex calculus with any one of the three topics. Our preference is to begin with differentiation, it being, perhaps, the easiest of the three topics for most students in real calculus. We follow this with integration and infinite series.

Calculus of complex functions has many similarities to both single-variable (real) calculus and multivariable (real) calculus, and we shall point these out as discussions unfold. But there are also striking differences, and we shall be even more careful to draw these to your attention. For instance, in most applications of real calculus, we are concerned with points where functions are well-behaved. Contrarily, points where complex functions misbehave are often the most valuable in applications. Existence of the first derivative of a real function implies nothing about existence of higher order derivatives, whereas existence of the first derivative of a complex function implies existence of derivatives of all orders.

Complex calculus provides proofs to many results that seem otherwise intractable in real analysis; it also provides a clearer understanding to some topics in real analysis. For example, the often assumed result that every real polynomial has a zero is verified in Chapter 4; why there is a number called the "radius" of convergence of a real power series becomes clear when we study complex series in Chapter 5; and why solutions of Laplace's equation do not have relative extrema is verified in Chapter 4.

We use geometric visualizations to introduce and clarify ideas whenever possible. Visualizations of real functions $f(x)$ as curves and $f(x, y)$ as surfaces are unavailable for complex functions $f(z)$. Instead, we interpret $f(z)$ as a mapping from one complex plane to another. The mapping approach helps us appreciate many of the properties of functions, and in addition, paves the way for the important topic of conformal mapping in Chapter 7 with its applications to problems in electrostatics, heat flow, and fluid flow.

The study of calculus of complex functions can be a very rewarding experience. Topics unfold naturally, and each new topic intimately relates to everything that has gone before. Proofs of most results, even the very profound, are usually quite straightforward, and the material is rich in applications. To aid in recognizing when discussions are complete, we have designated the end of the proof of a theorem by ∎, and the end of an example by a •.

True understanding cannot be achieved simply by reading the text. You must engross yourself in the subject and we have included numerous exercises for this purpose. Try as many as you can; you will not regret the effort. Answers to exercises can be found in Appendix A. A solutions manual with detailed solutions to all problems is available.

Finally, we wish you every success in your studies, and we hope that you will share in our fascination with the subject.

CHAPTER 1   COMPLEX NUMBERS

When the domain and range of a function are sets of complex numbers, we speak of a complex function of a complex variable. In this chapter we study complex numbers in preparation for complex functions. We add, subtract, multiply, and divide complex numbers, and find their roots. We introduce the Cartesian, polar, and exponential forms of complex numbers, illustrate complex numbers in the complex plane, and solve polynomial equations.

§1.1   Introduction

Perhaps the most natural way to introduce complex numbers is through real quadratic equations; equations of the form

$$ax^2 + bx + c = 0, \tag{1.1}$$

where a, b, and c are real numbers. It is well known that when the discriminant $b^2 - 4ac$ is positive, this equation has two real distinct roots given by the quadratic formula

$$x = \frac{-b \pm \sqrt{b^2 - 4ac}}{2a}, \tag{1.2}$$

and when $b^2 - 4ac = 0$, there is a repeated real root $x = -b/(2a)$. But when $b^2 - 4ac < 0$, there are no real numbers that satisfy the equation.

Complex numbers enable us to solve quadratic equations with negative discriminants. The most fundamental complex number is denoted by i; it is defined as a number whose square is -1,

$$i^2 = -1. \tag{1.3}$$

In other words, i is a solution of the quadratic equation

$$z^2 + 1 = 0 \tag{1.4}$$

(with discriminant equal to -4).

The introduction of i is often met with apprehension because it does not conform to our past experience with real numbers. But the transition from real numbers to complex numbers is completely analogous to the transition from rational numbers to real numbers. All rational numbers satisfy linear equations

$$ax + b = 0,$$

with integer coefficients a and b, where $a \neq 0$. For example, $3/2$ satisfies $2x - 3 = 0$. The quadratic equation $x^2 - 3 = 0$, on the other hand, does not have rational solutions. We denote the solutions of $x^2 - 3 = 0$ by $\pm\sqrt{3}$. But what is $\sqrt{3}$? It is not a rational number; it cannot be expressed as an integer divided by an integer, and it does not have a repeating decimal representation. We usually say that $\sqrt{3}$ is a number that multiplies itself to give 3. Over the years, you have accepted this explanation and now regard $\sqrt{3}$ with no trepidation whatsoever. The same is true when we extend the real number system to the complex number system. Equation 1.4 has no real solutions. We denote a solution of the equation by the letter i. But what is i? It is a number that, when multiplied by itself, gives -1. As we see then, the definition of i is much the same as the definition of $\sqrt{3}$, and with a little experience, you will regard i with no more apprehension that $\sqrt{3}$.

EXERCISES 1.1

In these exercises we discuss operations on real numbers of the form $a + b\sqrt{3}$, where a and b are rational numbers. Each operation is analogous to an operation on complex numbers in Section 1.2.

1. Show that $a + b\sqrt{3} = c + d\sqrt{3}$ if and only if $a = c$ and $b = d$.
2. How do we add $a + b\sqrt{3}$ and $c + d\sqrt{3}$?
3. How do we subtract $c + d\sqrt{3}$ from $a + b\sqrt{3}$?
4. How do we multiply $a + b\sqrt{3}$ and $c + d\sqrt{3}$?
5. How do we divide $a + b\sqrt{3}$ by $c + d\sqrt{3}$?

§1.2 Complex Numbers

The fundamental complex number is i, a number whose square is -1. The complete set of complex numbers is introduced in the following definition.

Definition 1.1 The **complex number system** $\mathcal{C}$ consists of all "numbers" of the form

$$z = x + yi, \tag{1.5}$$

where x and y are real, and i satisfies $i^2 = -1$.

Examples are $4+2i$, $3-2i$, $-3+\pi i$, and $-6-3i$. We liken $x+yi$ to numbers of the form $a+b\sqrt{3}$ in Exercises 1.1; corresponding to each of the complex numbers in the previous sentence, we would have $4+2\sqrt{3}$, $3-2\sqrt{3}$, $-3+\pi\sqrt{3}$, and $-6-3\sqrt{3}$. The number $3-2\sqrt{3}$ cannot be written exactly in a simpler form, the 3 and -2 cannot in any way be combined. Likewise, the 3 and -2 in the complex number $3-2i$ are distinct parts, so much so that we give them special names. The number x in equation 1.5 is called the **real part** of the complex number z; it is denoted by $x = \mathrm{Re}\, z$. The number y is called the **imaginary part** of z, denoted by $y = \mathrm{Im}\, z$. For example, $\mathrm{Re}(3-2i) = 3$ and $\mathrm{Im}(3-2i) = -2$. Both the real and imaginary parts of a complex number are themselves real numbers. The real number system is a subset of $\mathcal{C}$ obtained when $y = 0$.

To appreciate many results involving complex numbers, it is helpful to have geometric visualizations. Because a complex number has two distinct parts, its real and imaginary parts, and they are independent, a two-dimensional model is required to specify $\mathcal{C}$. We choose a plane, called the **complex (Argand) plane**. In particular, some fixed point O is chosen to represent the complex number $0 + 0i$. Through O are drawn two mutually perpendicular axes (Figure 1.1), one called the **real axis**, and the other called the **imaginary axis**. The complex number $x + yi$ is then represented by the point x units in the real direction and y units in the imaginary direction. For example, the complex numbers $1+2i$, $-1-i$, $4-3i$, and $-2+2i$ are shown in Figure 1.2. With this geometric representation, there is a one-to-one correspondence between numbers in $\mathcal{C}$ and points in the complex plane. In addition, the real number system (which is a subset of $\mathcal{C}$) is represented by points on the real axis. Complex numbers of the form $z = yi$ are said to be **purely imaginary**. They lie on the imaginary axis.

The point in the complex plane representing the number $x + yi$ is the same as the point (x, y) in the Cartesian plane, and we therefore call $x + yi$ the **Cartesian form** for a complex number.

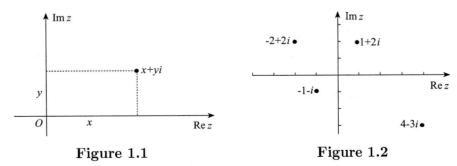

Figure 1.1   Figure 1.2

In order to add, subtract, multiply, and divide complex numbers, we first define what it means for two complex numbers to be equal, and we do so by analogy with Exercise 1 in Section 1.1.

Definition 1.2 Two complex numbers $z_1 = x + yi$ and $z_2 = a + bi$ are said to be equal if their real parts are equal and their imaginary parts are equal; that is,

$$x + yi = a + bi \qquad \Longleftrightarrow \qquad x = a \text{ and } y = b. \tag{1.6}$$

Geometrically, two complex numbers are equal if they correspond to the same point in the complex plane. Do not pass this definition off too lightly; we use it many times in our work. It allows us to replace an equation with complex numbers by a pair of equations with real numbers.

We now learn how to add, subtract, multiply, and divide complex numbers. Addition and subtraction of complex numbers are defined as follows.

Definition 1.3 If $z_1 = x + yi$ and $z_2 = a + bi$, then

$$z_1 + z_2 = (x + a) + (y + b)i, \tag{1.7a}$$
$$z_1 - z_2 = (x - a) + (y - b)i. \tag{1.7b}$$

In words, complex numbers are added and subtracted by adding and subtracting their real parts and adding and subtracting their imaginary parts. (Compare this with the addition and subtraction of numbers of the form $a + b\sqrt{3}$ in Exercises 2 and 3 of Section 1.1.) For example,

$$(3 - 2i) + (6 + i) = (3 + 6) + (-2 + 1)i = 9 - i,$$

$$(3 - 2i) - (6 + i) = (3 - 6) + (-2 - 1)i = -3 - 3i.$$

It is sometimes convenient to consider a complex number z to be represented geometrically by the vector joining O to the point representing z (Figure 1.3), rather than the point itself. The real and imaginary parts of the complex number correspond to the x- and y-components of the vector. It is clear that law 1.7a for addition of complex numbers is the same as the law of addition of vectors. Thus, to add two complex numbers z_1 and z_2 geometrically, we perform vector addition by means of either a triangle (Figure 1.4a) or a parallelogram (Figure 1.4b) on their geometric representations as vectors.

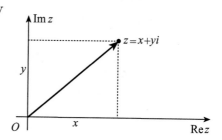

Figure 1.3

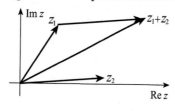

Figure 1.4a

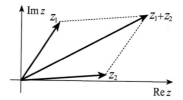

Figure 1.4b

Complex numbers can be subtracted vectorially also. Subtraction by triangles is shown in Figure 1.5a and by parallelograms in Figure 1.5b.

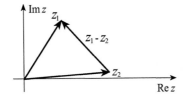 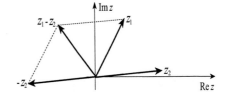

Figure 1.5a   **Figure 1.5b**

Complex numbers are multiplied according to the following definition.

Definition 1.4 If $z_1 = x + yi$ and $z_2 = a + bi$, then

$$z_1 z_2 = (x + yi)(a + bi) = (xa - yb) + (xb + ya)i. \qquad (1.8)$$

For example,

$$(3 - 2i)(6 + i) = [(3)(6) - (-2)(1)] + [(3)(1) + (-2)(6)]i = (18 + 2) + (3 - 12)i = 20 - 9i.$$

It is not necessary to memorize equation 1.8 when we note that this definition is precisely what we would expect if the usual laws for multiplying binomials were applied, together with the fact that $i^2 = -1$:

$$\begin{aligned}
(3 - 2i)(6 + i) &= (3)(6) + (3)(i) + (-2i)(6) + (-2i)(i) \\
&= 18 + 3i - 12i - 2i^2 \\
&= 18 - 9i - 2(-1) \\
&= 20 - 9i.
\end{aligned}$$

With addition, subtraction, and multiplication taken care of, it is natural to turn to division of complex numbers. If we accept that division of any complex number by itself should be equal to 1, and that ordinary rules of algebra should prevail, a definition of division of complex numbers is not necessary. It follows from equation 1.8. When $z_1 = x + yi$ and $z_2 = a + bi$, we calculate

$$\frac{z_1}{z_2} = \frac{x + yi}{a + bi}$$

by multiplying numerator and denominator by $a - bi$. This results in

$$\begin{aligned}
\frac{z_1}{z_2} = \frac{x + yi}{a + bi} &= \frac{(x + yi)(a - bi)}{(a + bi)(a - bi)} = \frac{(xa + yb) + (-xb + ya)i}{a^2 + b^2} \qquad \text{(using 1.8)} \\
&= \left(\frac{xa + yb}{a^2 + b^2} \right) + \left(\frac{ya - xb}{a^2 + b^2} \right) i. \qquad (1.9)
\end{aligned}$$

For example,

$$\frac{3 - 2i}{6 + i} = \frac{(3 - 2i)(6 - i)}{(6 + i)(6 - i)} = \frac{16 - 15i}{37} = \frac{16}{37} - \frac{15}{37}i.$$

In summary, addition, subtraction, multiplication, and division of complex numbers are performed using ordinary rules of algebra with the extra condition that i^2 is always replaced by -1.

Example 1.1 Write the following complex numbers in Cartesian form:

$$\text{(a)} \quad (3+i)(2-i)^2 - i \qquad \text{(b)} \quad \frac{i^3}{2+i} \qquad \text{(c)} \quad \frac{4-3i^2+2i}{(2-2i^{15})^2}$$

Solution (a) $(3+i)(2-i)^2 - i = (3+i)(3-4i) - i = (13-9i) - i = 13-10i$

(b) $\dfrac{i^3}{2+i} = \dfrac{-i(2-i)}{(2+i)(2-i)} = \dfrac{-1-2i}{5} = -\dfrac{1}{5} - \dfrac{2}{5}i$

(c) $\dfrac{4-3i^2+2i}{(2-2i^{15})^2} = \dfrac{4+3+2i}{(2+2i)^2} = \dfrac{7+2i}{8i} = \dfrac{(7+2i)(-i)}{(8i)(-i)} = \dfrac{2-7i}{8} = \dfrac{1}{4} - \dfrac{7}{8}i$ •

Notice in part (c) of this example that we multiplied numerator and denominator by $-i$ rather than $-8i$; the result is the same in either case. Both lead to a real denominator.

Definition 1.5 The **complex conjugate** $\overline{z}$ of a complex number $z = x + yi$ is

$$\overline{z} = x - yi. \tag{1.10}$$

For example, the complex conjugates of $1 + 2i$ and $3 - 4i$ are $\overline{1 + 2i} = 1 - 2i$ and $\overline{3 - 4i} = 3 + 4i$. Geometrically, $\overline{z}$ is the reflection of z in the real axis (Figure 1.6).

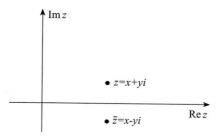

Figure 1.6

The procedure by which two complex numbers are divided (equation 1.9) can be stated as follows. To divide z_1 by z_2, multiply z_1 and z_2 by $\overline{z_2}$,

$$\frac{z_1}{z_2} = \frac{z_1 \overline{z_2}}{z_2 \overline{z_2}}.$$

The denominator will be real, and the Cartesian form is immediate.

Let us now return to the discussion of quadratic equation 1.1. When the discriminant is positive, the equation has two real solutions, and when the discriminant is zero, we regard the quadratic as having two real solutions which are identical. A solution of

$$x^2 + 1 = 0,$$

(which has a negative discriminant) is the complex number i, but so also is $-i$ because $(-i)^2 + 1 = -1 + 1 = 0$. The quadratic equation

$$x^2 + 16 = 0$$

has two solutions $x = \pm 4i$. If we apply quadratic formula 1.2 to the equation

$$x^2 + 2x + 5 = 0,$$

the result is

$$x = \frac{-2 \pm \sqrt{4-20}}{2} = \frac{-2 \pm \sqrt{-16}}{2}.$$

By $\sqrt{-16}$ we would seem to mean the number which multiplied by itself is -16. But there are two such complex numbers, namely $\pm 4i$. We make the agreement that $\sqrt{-16}$ shall denote that complex number whose square is -16, and that has a positive imaginary part. By this agreement,

$$\sqrt{-16} = 4i \qquad \text{and} \qquad -\sqrt{-16} = -4i.$$

The quadratic formula applied to $x^2 + 2x + 5 = 0$ therefore gives the two complex numbers

$$x = \frac{-2 \pm 4i}{2} = -1 \pm 2i.$$

It is straightforward to verify that these two complex conjugates do indeed satisfy the quadratic equation $x^2 + 2x + 5 = 0$.

The agreement made in this last example is worth reiterating as a general principle:

When $a > 0$ (is a real number),

$$\sqrt{-a} = \sqrt{a}\, i. \tag{1.11}$$

We call $\sqrt{a}\, i$ the **principal square root** of $-a$; the other square root is $-\sqrt{a}\, i$.

The above examples lead us to the following result.

Theorem 1.1 Every real quadratic equation

$$ax^2 + bx + c = 0 \tag{1.12a}$$

has two solutions. They are given by the quadratic formula

$$x = \frac{-b \pm \sqrt{b^2 - 4ac}}{2a}. \tag{1.12b}$$

When $b^2 - 4ac > 0$, the roots are real and distinct; when $b^2 - 4ac = 0$, the roots are real and equal; and when $b^2 - 4ac < 0$, the roots are complex conjugates.

That formula 1.12b defines two complex numbers that satisfy equation 1.12a, even when $b^2 - 4ac < 0$, is easily verified by substituting from 1.12b into 1.12a.

Example 1.2 Find all solutions of the following equations:

(a) $x^2 + x + 3 = 0$ (b) $x^2 - 6x + 9 = 0$ (c) $2x^2 + 17x - 2 = 0$ (d) $x^4 + 5x^2 + 4 = 0$

Solution   (a) By quadratic formula 1.12b,

$$x = \frac{-1 \pm \sqrt{1 - 12}}{2} = \frac{-1 \pm \sqrt{-11}}{2} = -\frac{1}{2} \pm \frac{\sqrt{11}}{2}\, i.$$

(b) This quadratic can be factored, $0 = x^2 - 6x + 9 = (x - 3)^2$, and therefore has a double root $x = 3$.
(c) By formula 1.12b,

$$x = \frac{-17 \pm \sqrt{289 + 16}}{4} = \frac{-17 \pm \sqrt{305}}{4},$$

two real roots.

(d) If we set $y = x^2$, then

$$0 = x^4 + 5x^2 + 4 = y^2 + 5y + 4 = (y+4)(y+1).$$

Consequently, y is equal to -1 or -4. Since $y = x^2$, we set $x^2 = -1$ and $x^2 = -4$. These equations have roots $x = \pm i$ and $x = \pm 2i$.●

Theorem 1.1 is valid even when coefficients a, b, and c in equation 1.12a are complex, in which case we speak of a complex quadratic equation. However, formula 1.12b may lead to square roots of complex numbers when a, b, and c are complex. This is not a problem; using equation 1.6 for equality of complex numbers we can find the square roots of any complex number. (Other, and better, methods will be developed in Sections 1.5 and 3.6.)

Finding the square roots of a complex number Z is equivalent to solving the following equation for z,

$$z^2 = Z. \tag{1.13}$$

If X and Y are the real and imaginary parts of Z ($Z = X + Yi$), and we let x and y be the real and imaginary parts of z, then

$$X + Yi = (x + yi)^2 = x^2 - y^2 + 2xyi.$$

But according to equation 1.6, two complex numbers are equal if and only if their real parts are equal and their imaginary parts are equal; that is, we may set

$$x^2 - y^2 = X, \qquad 2xy = Y.$$

We now have two real equations in two real unknowns x and y, the real and imaginary parts of z. Once they are solved, and there should be two solutions, we have the two square roots of Z. We illustrate by finding the square roots of i.

If we set $z = x + yi$ in the equation $z^2 = i$, the result is

$$i = (x + yi)^2 = (x^2 - y^2) + 2xyi.$$

Equating real and imaginary parts of the complex numbers on each side of this equation gives

$$x^2 - y^2 = 0, \qquad 2xy = 1.$$

From the second of these, $y = 1/(2x)$, which we substitute into the first,

$$0 = x^2 - \frac{1}{(2x)^2} = \frac{4x^4 - 1}{4x^2}.$$

This implies that

$$0 = 4x^4 - 1 = (2x^2 + 1)(2x^2 - 1).$$

Because x must be real, we have two solutions $x = \pm 1/\sqrt{2}$; and correspondingly, $y = \pm 1/\sqrt{2}$. Thus, the square roots of i are

$$z = \pm \frac{1}{\sqrt{2}} \pm \frac{1}{\sqrt{2}} i = \pm \left(\frac{1}{\sqrt{2}} + \frac{1}{\sqrt{2}} i \right).$$

One of these would be denoted by $\sqrt{i}$ and the other by $-\sqrt{i}$. The following agreement extends equation 1.11 to all complex numbers:

Definition 1.6   The **principal square root** of $a + bi$, denoted by $\sqrt{a + bi}$, is the square root with nonnegative real part.

With this agreement,

$$\sqrt{i} = \frac{1}{\sqrt{2}} + \frac{1}{\sqrt{2}}\, i \qquad \text{and} \qquad -\sqrt{i} = -\frac{1}{\sqrt{2}} - \frac{1}{\sqrt{2}}\, i.$$

We have uncovered here a most important principle. A complex equation can be replaced by two real equations, the equations obtained by equating real and imaginary parts of each side of the complex equation. Watch for this principle; we use it often.

Unfortunately the above technique for finding square roots of complex numbers does not generalize easily to finding cube roots, fourth roots, etc. For example, consider finding the cube roots of $1 - 2i$. This is equivalent to solving the equation $z^3 = 1 - 2i$, and if we set $z = x + yi$,

$$1 - 2i = (x + yi)^3 = (x^3 - 3xy^2) + (3x^2 y - y^3)i.$$

When we equate real and imaginary parts, we obtain the unattractive, real equations

$$x^3 - 3xy^2 = 1, \quad 3x^2 y - y^3 = -2.$$

But, as we mentioned earlier, Sections 1.5 and 3.6 develop easier methods for finding roots of complex numbers of all orders.

With the ability to find square roots of complex numbers, we can use formula 1.12b to find roots of complex quadratic equations. We illustrate in the following example.

Example 1.3   Find roots of the complex quadratic equation

$$iz^2 + 2z + 3 = 0.$$

Solution   Quadratic formula 1.12b gives

$$z = \frac{-2 \pm \sqrt{4 - 12i}}{2i} = \frac{1}{i}\left(-1 \pm \sqrt{1 - 3i}\right) = -i\left(-1 \pm \sqrt{1 - 3i}\right).$$

To find the square roots of $1 - 3i$, we set $w = x + yi$ in $w^2 = 1 - 3i$,

$$1 - 3i = (x + yi)^2 = (x^2 - y^2) + 2xyi.$$

Equating real and imaginary parts gives

$$x^2 - y^2 = 1, \qquad 2xy = -3.$$

From the second of these, $y = -3/(2x)$, which we substitute into the first,

$$x^2 - \left(\frac{-3}{2x}\right)^2 = 1 \qquad \Longrightarrow \qquad 4x^4 - 4x^2 - 9 = 0.$$

This is essentially a quadratic equation in x^2, namely, $4(x^2)^2 - 4(x^2) - 9 = 0$, and therefore

$$x^2 = \frac{4 \pm \sqrt{16 + 144}}{8} = \frac{1 \pm \sqrt{10}}{2}.$$

Since x^2 must be positive, it follows that

$$x^2 = \frac{1 + \sqrt{10}}{2} \qquad \Longrightarrow \qquad x = \pm \sqrt{\frac{1 + \sqrt{10}}{2}}.$$

Correspondingly,

$$y = \frac{\mp 3}{\sqrt{2 + 2\sqrt{10}}}.$$

Hence, the square roots of $1 - 3i$ are

$$\sqrt{1 - 3i} = \sqrt{\frac{1 + \sqrt{10}}{2}} - \frac{3}{\sqrt{2 + 2\sqrt{10}}}\, i, \qquad -\sqrt{1 - 3i} = -\sqrt{\frac{1 + \sqrt{10}}{2}} + \frac{3}{\sqrt{2 + 2\sqrt{10}}}\, i,$$

and the solutions of the quadratic equation $iz^2 + 2z + 3 = 0$ are

$$z = -i\left[-1 \pm \left(\sqrt{\frac{1 + \sqrt{10}}{2}} - \frac{3}{\sqrt{2 + 2\sqrt{10}}}\, i \right) \right] = \frac{\pm 3}{\sqrt{2 + 2\sqrt{10}}} + \left(1 \pm \sqrt{\frac{1 + \sqrt{10}}{2}} \right) i. \bullet$$

EXERCISES 1.2

1. Show each of the following complex numbers in the complex plane: (a) $2 - i$, (b) $3 + 4i$, (c) $-1 - 5i$, (d) $-3 + 2i$, (e) $5i$, and (f) $2(1 + i)$

In Exercises 2–15 write the complex expression in Cartesian form.

2. $(2 + 4i) - (3 - 2i)$

3. $(1 + 2i)^2$

4. $(-2 + i)(3 - 4i)$

5. $3i(4i - 1)^2$

6. $i^3 - 3i^2 + 2i + 4$

7. $(1 + i)^6$

8. $\dfrac{1 - i}{3 + 2i}$

9. $\dfrac{(3 + i)^2}{2 - i}$

10. $i^{24} - 3i^{13} + 4$

11. $(i - 2)[(2 + i)(1 - i) + 3i - 2]$

12. $6i\left(\dfrac{1 + i}{2 - i}\right) + 3\left(\dfrac{i - 4}{2i + 1}\right)$

13. $\overline{2 + i} - (3 + \overline{4i})$

14. $\overline{1 + i}^2 + \overline{(1 + i)^2}$

15. $\left(\dfrac{1}{2} - \dfrac{\sqrt{3}}{2}i\right)^3$

16. Verify the following properties for the complex conjugation operation:
    (a) $\overline{z_1 + z_2} = \overline{z_1} + \overline{z_2}$
    (b) $\overline{z_1 - z_2} = \overline{z_1} - \overline{z_2}$
    (c) $\overline{z_1 z_2} = \overline{z_1}\,\overline{z_2}$
    (d) $\overline{\left(\dfrac{z_1}{z_2}\right)} = \dfrac{\overline{z_1}}{\overline{z_2}}$
    (e) $\overline{z^n} = \overline{z}^{\,n}$, $\quad n$ a positive integer

17. (a) If $P(z)$ is a polynomial with real coefficients, use the results of Exercise 16 to verify that $\overline{P(z)} = P(\overline{z})$.

(b) Verify that if z is a root of a polynomial equation $P(z) = 0$, with real coefficients, then so also is $\bar{z}$. In other words, complex roots of a real polynomial equation always occur in complex conjugate pairs.

18. Verify that all complex numbers z satisfying the equation $z\bar{z} = r^2$, $r > 0$ a real constant, lie on a circle. What are its centre and radius?

19. Prove that if $z_1 z_2 = 0$, then at least one of z_1 and z_2 must be zero.

20. We have made the agreement that when $a > 0$ is a real number, $\sqrt{-a}$ denotes a complex number with positive imaginary part (see equation 1.11). Show that with this agreement,

$$\sqrt{z_1 z_2} \text{ is not always equal to } \sqrt{z_1}\sqrt{z_2}.$$

Hint: Try $z_1 = z_2 = -1$.

21. Explain the fallacy in

$$-1 = \sqrt{-1}\sqrt{-1} = \sqrt{(-1)(-1)} = \sqrt{1} = 1.$$

In Exercises 22–31 find all solutions of the equation.

22. $x^2 + 5x + 3 = 0$

23. $x^2 + 3x + 5 = 0$

24. $x^2 + 8x + 16 = 0$

25. $x^2 + 2x - 7 = 0$

26. $x^2 + 2x + 7 = 0$

27. $4x^2 - 2x + 5 = 0$

28. $\sqrt{3}x^2 + 5x + \sqrt{15} = 0$

29. $x^4 + 4x^2 - 5 = 0$

30. $x^4 + 4x^2 + 3 = 0$

31. $x^4 + 6x^2 + 3 = 0$

32. Find two numbers whose sum is 6 and whose product is 10.

In Exercises 33–36 find square roots of the complex number.

33. $-7 - 24i$

34. $21 - 20i$

35. $2 + i$

36. $-1 + i$

In Exercises 37–42 use quadratic formula 1.12b to find both solutions of the complex quadratic equation.

37. $z^2 + (2 - i)z + 1 - i = 0$

38. $2iz^2 + 4z + 3 - 2i = 0$

39. $z^2 + 2z + i = 0$

40. $iz^2 + 2iz + 3 = 0$

41. $z^2 + 4iz - 1 + i = 0$

42. $z^2 + (2 - i)z + 1 + i = 0$

43. Show that the solutions of the equation in Exercise 37 can be obtained by letting $z = x + yi$, substituting into the equation, and equating real and imaginary parts.

44. Repeat the procedure of Exercise 43 on the equation in Exercise 38.

45. Show that the line joining the complex numbers z_1 and z_2 is perpendicular to the line joining z_3 and z_4 if and only if $\operatorname{Re}\left[(z_1 - z_2)(\overline{z_3} - \overline{z_4})\right] = 0$.

46. Show that the line joining the complex numbers z_1 and z_2 is parallel to the line joining z_3 and z_4 if and only if $\operatorname{Im}\left[(z_1 - z_2)(\overline{z_3} - \overline{z_4})\right] = 0$.

§1.3   Polar Representation of Complex Numbers

In Section 1.2 we worked with complex numbers in Cartesian form, and this proved sufficient to solve quadratic equations. For other applications, it is often advantageous to have what is called the *polar representation* of a complex number. Even more useful is the *exponential representation* of a complex number; it is developed in Section 1.4. To find the polar representation, we define the modulus and argument of a complex number.

Definition 1.7   The **modulus** of a complex number $z = x + yi$ is

$$r = |z| = \sqrt{x^2 + y^2}. \qquad (1.14)$$

It is the length of the line segment joining the points in the complex plane representing the complex numbers $z = 0$ and $z = x + yi$ (Figure 1.7). It is unique; a complex number has exactly one modulus. For example, $|2 + 3i| = \sqrt{2^2 + 3^2} = \sqrt{13}$ and $|-3 + 4i| = \sqrt{(-3)^2 + 4^2} = 5$. Notice that when z is real, say $z = x$, then $|z| = \sqrt{x^2} = |x|$, where $|x|$ is the absolute value of x. In other words, when z is real, the modulus bars are absolute value bars. Often useful is the fact that

$$|z|^2 = z\overline{z}. \qquad (1.15)$$

Definition 1.8   An **argument** of a nonzero complex number $z = x + yi$, usually denoted by θ or $\arg z$, is an angle of rotation of the positive real axis in a counterclockwise direction to the line segment joining $z = 0$ and $z = x + yi$. Clockwise rotations are regarded as negative.

Notice that in this definition we said "an" argument rather than "the" argument of a complex number. The reason for this is that arguments of complex numbers are not unique. For instance, one possible value for an argument of the complex number $z = 1 - i$ (Figure 1.8) is $\theta = 7\pi/4$, but another is $\theta = -\pi/4$. In fact, there are infinitely many possibilities for θ, namely, $\theta = 2k\pi - \pi/4$, where k is any integer. We call that value of the argument of a nonzero complex number z which satisfies the restriction $-\pi < \theta \le \pi$ the **principal value** of the argument, and denote it with a capital A,

$$-\pi < \operatorname{Arg} z \le \pi. \qquad (1.16)$$

For $z = 1 - i$, the principal value of the argument is $-\pi/4$.

We have a choice to make for an argument of $z = 0$. We could accept that any real number could be used as an argument for $z = 0$, and any number in the interval $(-\pi, \pi]$ could be used as a principal value for its argument. On the other hand, since we eventually wish to regard $\arg z$ and $\operatorname{Arg} z$ as functions, which must therefore be single-valued, we choose instead not to assign an argument to $z = 0$.

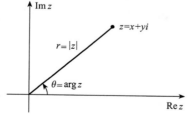

Figure 1.7

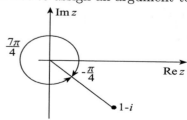

Figure 1.8

The real and imaginary parts of a complex number can be expressed in terms of its modulus and argument. The triangle in Figure 1.9 indicates that

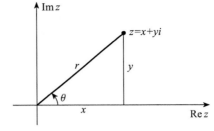

$$x = r\cos\theta, \qquad y = r\sin\theta. \qquad (1.17)$$

It is easy to reverse these equations and express r in terms of x and y; equation 1.14 does this. But the case for θ is more complicated. Certainly we can write that

Figure 1.9

$$\cos\theta = \frac{x}{\sqrt{x^2 + y^2}} \qquad \text{and} \qquad \sin\theta = \frac{y}{\sqrt{x^2 + y^2}}, \qquad (1.18)$$

and these equations do indeed define all arguments of $z = x + yi$. In an attempt to find a single equation defining θ in terms of x and y, there is a tendency to divide the second equation by the first

$$\tan\theta = \frac{y}{x},$$

and take this one step further to

$$\theta = \mathrm{Tan}^{-1}\left(\frac{y}{x}\right). \qquad (1.19)$$

Unfortunately, principal values† of the inverse tangent function are between $\pm\pi/2$, and therefore this equation gives a correct argument only for complex numbers in the first and fourth quadrants.

How then are we to find arguments for given $z = x + yi$? Certainly we can find all angles satisfying equation 1.18. Alternatively, we can find the angle θ defined by equation 1.19. If z is in the first or fourth quadrants $(x > 0)$, then all possible arguments are $\theta + 2k\pi$, where k is an integer. When z is in the second quadrant, arguments are $(\theta + \pi) + 2k\pi = \theta + (2k+1)\pi$; and when z is in the third quadrant, arguments are $(\theta - \pi) + 2k\pi = \theta + (2k-1)\pi$.

Example 1.4   Find all arguments and the principal value of the argument for the following complex numbers:

$$\text{(a)} \quad 1 + \sqrt{3}i \qquad \text{(b)} \quad 2 - 2i \qquad \text{(c)} \quad -4 + 3i \qquad \text{(d)} \quad -3 - 2i$$

Solution We have shown all four complex numbers in Figure 1.10.
(a) Since $\mathrm{Tan}^{-1}(\sqrt{3}/1) = \pi/3$, arguments of $1 + \sqrt{3}i$ are $\pi/3 + 2k\pi = (6k+1)\pi/3$. The principal value of the argument is $\pi/3$.

(b) One argument of $2 - 2i$ is clearly $-\pi/4$, and therefore all arguments are $2k\pi - \pi/4 = (8k-1)\pi/4$. The principal value is $-\pi/4$.

---

† Capital letters on inverse trigonometric functions denote principal values. For the inverse sine, cosine, and tangent functions, capital letters denote the principal values $-\pi/2 \le \mathrm{Sin}^{-1}a \le \pi/2$, $0 \le \mathrm{Cos}^{-1}a \le \pi$, and $-\pi/2 < \mathrm{Tan}^{-1}a < \pi/2$.

(c) Since $\text{Tan}^{-1}[3/(-4)] \approx -0.6435$,
and $-4 + 3i$ is in the second quadrant,
it follows that arguments are
$(\pi - 0.6435) + 2k\pi = (2k + 1)\pi - 0.6435$.
The principal value is $\pi - 0.6435$.

(d) With $\text{Tan}^{-1}[-2/(-3)] \approx 0.5880$ and
$-3 - 2i$ in the third quadrant, arguments
are $(0.5880 - \pi) + 2k\pi = (2k - 1)\pi + 0.5880$.
The principal value is $0.5880 - \pi$.•

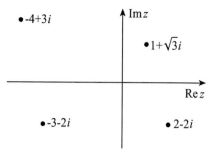

Figure 1.10

If expressions 1.17 are substituted into the Cartesian form $z = x + yi$ for a complex number,

$$z = x + yi = r\cos\theta + (r\sin\theta)i.$$

When r is factored from both terms,

$$z = r(\cos\theta + \sin\theta\, i). \tag{1.20}$$

This expression is called the **polar representation** of a complex number. Realize again that it is not unique. If 1.20 is a polar representation of a complex number, then

$$r[\cos(\theta + 2k\pi) + \sin(\theta + 2k\pi)\, i],$$

for any integer k, is also a polar representation for the same complex number.

Example 1.5   Find polar representations for $-1 + i$ and $2 - 3i$.

Solution   Since the modulus of $-1 + i$
is $\sqrt{2}$, and an argument is $3\pi/4$ (Figure
1.11), a polar representation is
$-1 + i = \sqrt{2}[\cos(3\pi/4) + \sin(3\pi/4)\, i]$.
The modulus of $2 - 3i$ is $\sqrt{13}$, and an
argument is $\text{Tan}^{-1}(-3/2) \approx -0.983$.
Consequently,

$$2 - 3i = \sqrt{13}\{\cos[\text{Tan}^{-1}(-3/2)]$$
$$+ \sin[\text{Tan}^{-1}(-3/2)]\, i\}$$
$$\approx \sqrt{13}[\cos(-0.983) + \sin(-0.983)\, i].•$$

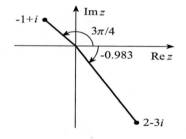

Figure 1.11

Example 1.6   Is $-2[\cos(\pi/4) + \sin(\pi/4)\, i]$ the polar form for a complex number?

Solution   No, because -2 cannot be the modulus of a complex number (moduli must be nonnegative). To express this complex number in polar form, we write

$$-2[\cos(\pi/4) + \sin(\pi/4)\, i] = 2[-\cos(\pi/4) - \sin(\pi/4)\, i] = 2[\cos(5\pi/4) + \sin(5\pi/4)\, i].•$$

Two complex numbers are equal if and only if they have the same real parts and the same imaginary parts. How do we phrase equality in terms of moduli and arguments? Certainly complex numbers can be equal only if they have the same moduli. Their arguments need not be the same, however, but they must differ by a multiple of 2π. In other words, we have:

Two nonzero complex numbers z_1 and z_2 are equal if and only if

$$|z_1| = |z_2|,\tag{1.21a}$$

and

$$\arg z_1 = \arg z_2 + 2k\pi, \ k \text{ an integer.}\tag{1.21b}$$

Since principal values of arguments of complex numbers are unique, an alternative to conditions 1.21 is that nonzero complex numbers z_1 and z_2 are equal if and only if

$$|z_1| = |z_2|,\tag{1.22a}$$

and

$$\text{Arg } z_1 = \text{Arg } z_2.\tag{1.22b}$$

Complex numbers are easily added and subtracted in Cartesian form. Even multiplication and division of two complex numbers is relatively easy in Cartesian form. On the other hand, multiplication and division in polar form lead to properties that are not evident in Cartesian form. For example, if $z_1 = r_1(\cos\theta_1 + \sin\theta_1\, i)$ and $z_2 = r_2(\cos\theta_2 + \sin\theta_2\, i)$ are any two complex numbers, their product is

$$\begin{aligned}
z_1 z_2 &= [r_1(\cos\theta_1 + \sin\theta_1\, i)][r_2(\cos\theta_2 + \sin\theta_2\, i)]\\
&= r_1 r_2[(\cos\theta_1\,\cos\theta_2 - \sin\theta_1\,\sin\theta_2) + (\sin\theta_1\,\cos\theta_2 + \sin\theta_2\,\cos\theta_1)i]\\
&= r_1 r_2[\cos(\theta_1 + \theta_2) + \sin(\theta_1 + \theta_2)\, i].
\end{aligned}\tag{1.23}$$

Because the last expression is the polar representation of $z_1 z_2$, we have proved the following facts:

1. The modulus of the product of two complex numbers is the product of their moduli; that is,

$$|z_1 z_2| = |z_1||z_2|.\tag{1.24a}$$

2. An argument of the product of two complex numbers is the sum of their arguments; that is,

$$\arg(z_1 z_2) = \arg z_1 + \arg z_2.\tag{1.24b}$$

Be wary of how you interpret 1.24b; it is not an equation in the normal sense of equation. Each of the three terms has infinitely many possible values (since the argument of a complex number is determined only to multiples of 2π). What this "equation" says is that given any two terms in 1.24b, there is a value of the third that makes 1.24b an equation. For example, positive arguments of $z_1 = 1 + i$ and $z_2 = 1 - i$ are $\pi/4$ and $7\pi/4$. The product of these complex numbers is $z_1 z_2 = (1+i)(1-i) = 2$. An argument for the complex number 2 is 0, but certainly the arguments $\arg z_1 = \pi/4$, $\arg z_2 = 7\pi/4$, and $\arg z_1 z_2 = 0$ do not satisfy 1.24b. On the other hand, the arguments $\arg z_1 = \pi/4$, $\arg z_2 = 7\pi/4$, and $\arg z_1 z_2 = 2\pi$ do satisfy 1.24b.

Condition 1.24b cannot be replaced by principal values, because, in general, $\text{Arg } z_1 z_2$ may not be equal to $\text{Arg } z_1 + \text{Arg } z_2$. This is the situation when $z_1 = z_2 = -1$. In this case, $\text{Arg } z_1 z_2 = \text{Arg } 1 = 0$, and $\text{Arg } z_1 + \text{Arg } z_2 = \pi + \pi = 2\pi$.

A similar analysis shows that

$$\frac{z_1}{z_2} = \frac{r_1}{r_2}[\cos(\theta_1 - \theta_2) + \sin(\theta_1 - \theta_2)i]. \tag{1.25}$$

In other words, we have the following properties corresponding to equations 1.24:

$$\left|\frac{z_1}{z_2}\right| = \frac{|z_1|}{|z_2|}, \tag{1.26a}$$

$$\arg\left(\frac{z_1}{z_2}\right) = \arg z_1 - \arg z_2. \tag{1.26b}$$

Example 1.7   Find $z_1 z_2$ and z_1/z_2 if $z_1 = 6(\cos 1.1 + \sin 1.1\,i)$ and $z_2 = 3(\cos 2.4 + \sin 2.4\,i)$.

Solution   According to equations 1.23 and 1.25,

$$z_1 z_2 = 18(\cos 3.5 + \sin 3.5\,i) \qquad \text{and} \qquad \frac{z_1}{z_2} = 2[\cos(-1.3) + \sin(-1.3)\,i].\bullet$$

The polar form for a complex number can be very useful when we raise a complex number to a power, say $(1 + \sqrt{3}i)^8$. To do this we derive a simple formula for z^n when n is a positive integer. With $z = r(\cos\theta + \sin\theta\,i)$,

$$z^2 = [r(\cos\theta + \sin\theta\,i)][r(\cos\theta + \sin\theta\,i)] = r^2(\cos 2\theta + \sin 2\theta\,i);$$

$$z^3 = zz^2 = [r(\cos\theta + \sin\theta\,i)][r^2(\cos 2\theta + \sin 2\theta\,i)] = r^3(\cos 3\theta + \sin 3\theta\,i).$$

The pattern emerging (which could be proved by mathematical induction) is

$$z^n = r^n[\cos(n\theta) + \sin(n\theta)\,i]. \tag{1.27}$$

This result is often called **DeMoivre's** theorem.

Example 1.8   Evaluate $(1 + \sqrt{3}i)^8$.

Solution   With $|1+\sqrt{3}i| = \sqrt{(1)^2 + (\sqrt{3})^2} = 2$, and $\text{Arg}(1+\sqrt{3}i) = \text{Tan}^{-1}(\sqrt{3}) = \pi/3$,

$$(1 + \sqrt{3}i)^8 = \{2[\cos(\pi/3) + \sin(\pi/3)\,i]\}^8 = 2^8[\cos(8\pi/3) + \sin(8\pi/3)\,i]$$

$$= 256[\cos(2\pi/3) + \sin(2\pi/3)\,i] = 256\left(-\frac{1}{2} + \frac{\sqrt{3}}{2}i\right) = 128(-1 + \sqrt{3}i).\bullet$$

DeMoivre's theorem can also be used to find roots of complex numbers; that is, find the square roots of $1+i$, the cube roots of $-2+3i$, the fourth roots of $6-2i$, etc. In general, we can find the n n^{th} roots of any given complex number Z. What we are really doing when we find these roots is solving the equation

$$z^n = Z, \tag{1.28}$$

where $n > 1$ is an integer, and Z is a given complex number. As we said, we can use DeMoivre's theorem to find all solutions of 1.28, but there is an easier way. We use what is called the *exponential form* of complex numbers (Section 1.4). It is equivalent to the polar form, using modulus r and argument θ, but it is so much simpler. In fact, we regard the polar form of a complex number as a stepping stone to the preferred exponential form, and only use Cartesian and exponential forms.

EXERCISES 1.3

In Exercises 1–6 express the complex number in polar form.

1. $-1 + i$

2. $-2i$

3. $\sqrt{3} - i$

4. $3 + 4i$

5. $-1 - 2i$

6. $-2[\cos(\pi/3) - \sin(\pi/3)\, i]$

In Exercises 7–10 express the complex number in Cartesian form.

7. $3[\cos(\pi/6) + \sin(\pi/6)\, i]$

8. $\cos(1.4) + \sin(1.4)\, i$

9. $2[\cos(\pi/4) + \sin(\pi/4)\, i]^2$

10. $\dfrac{4[\cos(2\pi/3) + \sin(2\pi/3)\, i]}{\cos(\pi/6) + \sin(\pi/6)\, i}$

In Exercises 11–16 simplify the expression as much as possible.

11. $(1 - i)^4$

12. $[\cos(\pi/5) + \sin(\pi/5)\, i]^{10}$

13. $\dfrac{1}{(\sqrt{3} + i)^6}$

14. $\dfrac{-2[\cos(\pi/3) - \sin(\pi/3)\, i]^3}{3 + i}$

15. $\left(\dfrac{1 + i}{2 - 2i}\right)^5$

16. $\dfrac{(2 + i)^6}{(4 - i)^3}$

17. What are the argument(s) of the complex number $z = 0$?

18. Prove the following properties for moduli of complex numbers:

    (a) $|z_1 + z_2|^2 = |z_1|^2 + 2\operatorname{Re}(z_1\overline{z_2}) + |z_2|^2$

    (b) $|z_1 + z_2|^2 + |z_1 - z_2|^2 = 2(|z_1|^2 + |z_2|^2)$

    (c) $|z_1 - z_2|^2 - |z_1 + \overline{z_2}|^2 = -4(\operatorname{Re} z_1)(\operatorname{Re} z_2)$

19. Verify that for any complex number

$$|\operatorname{Re} z| + |\operatorname{Im} z| \le \sqrt{2}\,|z|.$$

§1.4   Exponential Form for Complex Numbers

As we mentioned at the end of the last section, the *exponential form* for complex numbers is so convenient, that we seldom use the polar form. You can almost see a connection with exponential functions in equations 1.23 and 1.25. If $r_1 = r_2 = 1$ in 1.23, then

$$(\cos\theta_1 + \sin\theta_1\,i)(\cos\theta_2 + \sin\theta_2\,i) = \cos(\theta_1 + \theta_2) + \sin(\theta_1 + \theta_2)\,i.$$

Compare this with $e^{\theta_1}e^{\theta_2} = e^{\theta_1+\theta_2}$. In each case we have something with θ_1 in it, multiplied by the same something with θ_2 in it, giving the same something with $\theta_1 + \theta_2$ in it. Similarly, compare equation 1.25 (with $r_1 = r_2 = 1$),

$$\frac{\cos\theta_1 + \sin\theta_1\,i}{\cos\theta_2 + \sin\theta_2\,i} = \cos(\theta_1 - \theta_2) + \sin(\theta_1 - \theta_2)\,i,$$

with $\dfrac{e^{\theta_1}}{e^{\theta_2}} = e^{\theta_1-\theta_2}$. We exploit this similarity by defining $e^{\theta i}$ for a real number θ as follows

$$e^{\theta i} = \cos\theta + \sin\theta\,i. \qquad (1.29)$$

This is often called **Euler's identity**. From our perspective, it is not an identity; it is the definition of $e^{\theta i}$. We have worked with e^x for real x for many years. We have now defined what it means to take the exponential of a purely imaginary number. In Section 3.2, we will deal with the exponential function e^z for arbitrary z in which case, Euler's identity will be but a special case. However, because the exponential form for complex numbers has so many advantages over the polar representation, it would be a shame to delay its introduction. Using definition 1.29 of $e^{\theta i}$, we can write that

$$e^{\pi i/3} = \cos(\pi/3) + \sin(\pi/3)\,i = \frac{1}{2} + \frac{\sqrt{3}i}{2}, \qquad e^{\pi i/2} = \cos(\pi/2) + \sin(\pi/2)\,i = i.$$

If $z = r(\cos\theta + \sin\theta\,i)$ is the polar form of a complex number, then using 1.29, we may write

$$z = re^{\theta i}. \qquad (1.30)$$

This is called the **exponential form** of a complex number. As for the polar form, it uses the modulus and argument of z, but replaces $\cos\theta + \sin\theta\,i$ with $e^{\theta i}$. In terms of this exponential representation, notice that equations 1.23 and 1.25 can be expressed in the forms

$$z_1 z_2 = \left(r_1 e^{\theta_1 i}\right)\left(r_2 e^{\theta_2 i}\right) = r_1 r_2 e^{(\theta_1+\theta_2)i}, \qquad (1.31a)$$

$$\frac{z_1}{z_2} = \frac{r_1 e^{\theta_1}}{r_2 e^{\theta_2}} = \frac{r_1}{r_2} e^{(\theta_1-\theta_2)i}. \qquad (1.31b)$$

But this is exactly what we would expect if the complex exponential $e^{\theta i}$ were to obey the usual rules for real exponentials, namely that $e^{x_1}e^{x_2} = e^{x_1+x_2}$ and $e^{x_1}/e^{x_2} = e^{x_1-x_2}$. In other words, if we define $e^{\theta i}$ by 1.29, write complex numbers in form 1.30, and demand that $e^{\theta i}$ obey the usual multiplication and division rules, then equations 1.31 follow immediately, and we can forget about rules 1.23 and 1.25 for multiplication and division of complex numbers. DeMoivre's theorem is even more evident with exponential notation; it states that

$$z^n = (re^{\theta i})^n = r^n e^{n\theta i}. \tag{1.32}$$

Example 1.8 would now read as follows: Since $1 + \sqrt{3}i = 2e^{\pi i/3}$,

$$(1 + \sqrt{3}i)^8 = (2e^{\pi i/3})^8 = 2^8 e^{8\pi i/3} = 2^8 e^{2\pi i/3}$$

$$= 256[\cos(2\pi/3)] + \sin(2\pi/3)\, i] = 256\left(-\frac{1}{2} + \frac{\sqrt{3}i}{2}\right) = 128(-1 + \sqrt{3}i).$$

We have replaced $e^{8\pi i/3}$ by $e^{2\pi i/3}$ and two simple arguments justify this. The easiest is to realize that $8\pi/3$ and $2\pi/3$ are arguments of a complex number and as such they are equivalent, $8\pi/3 = 2\pi + 2\pi/3$. Alternatively,

$$e^{8\pi i/3} = e^{(2\pi + 2\pi/3)i} = e^{2\pi i} e^{2\pi i/3} = [\cos(2\pi) + \sin(2\pi)\, i]e^{2\pi i/3} = e^{2\pi i/3}.$$

What we are claiming here is stated more generally as

$$e^{(\theta + 2k\pi)i} = e^{\theta i}, \qquad \text{whenever } k \text{ is an integer.} \tag{1.33}$$

We can also state that

$$e^{2k\pi i} = 1, \qquad \text{whenever } k \text{ is an integer.} \tag{1.34}$$

Example 1.9   Find the imaginary part of $\dfrac{(1 + i)^{10}}{(\sqrt{3} - i)^5}$.

Solution   Since

$$\frac{(1 + i)^{10}}{(\sqrt{3} - i)^5} = \frac{(\sqrt{2}e^{\pi i/4})^{10}}{(2e^{-\pi i/6})^5} = \frac{2^5 e^{5\pi i/2}}{2^5 e^{-5\pi i/6}} = e^{(5\pi/2 + 5\pi/6)i} = e^{10\pi i/3} = e^{4\pi i/3},$$

the imaginary part is $\sin(4\pi/3) = -\sqrt{3}/2$.●

Example 1.10   Describe the position of the complex number $e^{\phi i}z$ in the complex plane relative to the position of z.

Solution   If $z = re^{\theta i}$ is the exponential representation of z, then equation 1.31a gives

$$e^{\phi i}z = re^{(\phi + \theta)i}.$$

The modulus of z does not change, but its argument increases by ϕ. In other words, multiplying a complex number by $e^{\phi i}$ rotates it through angle ϕ about the origin.●

In some applications, it is advantageous to express $\cos n\theta$ and $\sin n\theta$, where $n \geq 2$ is an integer, as polynomials in $\sin\theta$ and $\cos\theta$. This can be done with trigonometric identities, but as the following example shows, DeMoivre's theorem provides an alternative.

Example 1.11   Use DeMoivre's theorem to verify that

$$\cos 3\theta = \cos^3\theta - 3\cos\theta \sin^2\theta.$$

Solution   When the complex number in DeMoivre's theorem 1.32 has modulus $r = 1$,

$$z^n = (e^{\theta i})^n = e^{n\theta i}.$$

For $n = 3$, this becomes

$$(e^{\theta i})^3 = e^{3\theta i}.$$

If we replace the exponentials with their polar counterparts, we obtain

$$(\cos\theta + \sin\theta\, i)^3 = \cos 3\theta + \sin 3\theta\, i.$$

When the left side is expanded (with the binomial theorem), the result is

$$\cos 3\theta + \sin 3\theta\, i = \cos^3\theta + 3\cos^2\theta(\sin\theta\, i) + 3\cos\theta(\sin\theta\, i)^2 + (\sin\theta\, i)^3$$
$$= (\cos^3\theta - 3\cos\theta\sin^2\theta) + (3\cos^2\theta\sin\theta - \sin^3\theta)i.$$

Each side of this equation is a complex number, and two complex numbers are equal if and only if their real and imaginary parts are the same. When we equate real parts, we obtain

$$\cos 3\theta = \cos^3\theta - 3\cos\theta\sin^2\theta.$$

Imaginary parts give the additional trigonometric identity

$$\sin 3\theta = 3\cos^2\theta\sin\theta - \sin^3\theta.\bullet$$

In other applications, it can prove advantageous to express $\cos^n\theta$ and $\sin^n\theta$, where $n \geq 2$ is an integer, as a polynomial in $\cos n\theta$ and $\sin n\theta$. Once again, this can be done with trigonometric identities, but complex exponentials can also be used. When we replace θ by $-\theta$ in Euler's identity 1.29, we obtain

$$e^{-\theta i} = \cos(-\theta) + \sin(-\theta)\, i = \cos\theta - \sin\theta\, i.$$

When this is added to Euler's identity, the result is

$$e^{\theta i} + e^{-\theta i} = 2\cos\theta.$$

In other words,

$$\cos\theta = \frac{e^{\theta i} + e^{-\theta i}}{2}. \tag{1.35a}$$

Similarly,

$$\sin\theta = \frac{e^{\theta i} + e^{-\theta i}}{2}. \tag{1.35b}$$

These can be used in examples such as the following.

Example 1.12   Use equation 1.35(a) to verify that

$$\cos^4\theta = \frac{1}{8}(3 + 4\cos 2\theta + \cos 4\theta).$$

Solution   If we raise both sides of the equation $\cos\theta = \dfrac{e^{\theta i} + e^{-\theta i}}{2}$ to power 4,

$$\cos^4 \theta = \frac{1}{16}(e^{\theta i} + e^{-\theta i})^4 = \frac{1}{16}(e^{4\theta i} + 4e^{2\theta i} + 6 + 4e^{-2\theta i} + e^{-4\theta i})$$

$$= \frac{1}{16}(2\cos 4\theta + 8\cos 2\theta + 6) = \frac{1}{8}(3 + 4\cos 2\theta + \cos 4\theta). \bullet$$

EXERCISES 1.4

In Exercises 1–6 express the complex number in exponential form.

1. $-1 + i$ **2.** $-2i$ **3.** $\sqrt{3} - i$

4. $3 + 4i$ **5.** $-1 - 2i$ **6.** $-2[\cos(\pi/3) - \sin(\pi/3)\,i]$

In Exercises 7–19 express the complex number in simplified Cartesian form.

7. $3e^{\pi i/6}$ **8.** $e^{-\pi i}$ **9.** $(2e^{\pi i/4})^2$

10. $\dfrac{4e^{2\pi i/3}}{e^{\pi i/6}}$ **11.** $(1 - i)^4$ **12.** $[\cos(\pi/5) + \sin(\pi/5)\,i]^{10}$

13. $\dfrac{1}{(\sqrt{3} + i)^6}$ **14.** $\dfrac{-2[\cos(\pi/3) - \sin(\pi/3)\,i]^3}{3 + i}$ **15.** $\left(\dfrac{1+i}{2-2i}\right)^5$

16. $\dfrac{(2+i)^6}{(4-i)^3}$ **17.** $\left(\dfrac{1 + \sqrt{3}i}{1 - \sqrt{3}i}\right)^{10}$ **18.** $\left(\dfrac{\sqrt{3} - i}{\sqrt{3} + i}\right)^4 \left(\dfrac{1+i}{1-i}\right)^5$

19. $\dfrac{(3e^{\pi i/6})(2e^{-5\pi i/4})(6e^{5\pi i/3})}{(4e^{2\pi i/3})^2}$

In Exercises 20–23 use DeMoivre's theorem 1.32 to verify the identity.

20. $\cos 4\theta = \cos^4 \theta - 6\cos^2 \theta \sin^2 \theta + \sin^4 \theta$

21. $\sin 4\theta = 4\cos^3 \theta \sin \theta - 4\cos \theta \sin^3 \theta$

22. $\cos 5\theta = \cos^5 \theta - 10\cos^3 \theta \sin^2 \theta + 5\cos \theta \sin^4 \theta$

23. $\sin 5\theta = 5\cos^4 \theta \sin \theta - 10\cos^2 \theta \sin^3 \theta + \sin^5 \theta$

In Exercises 24–26 use equations 1.35 to verify the identity.

24. $\cos^3 \theta = \dfrac{1}{4}(3\cos \theta + \cos 3\theta)$

25. $\sin^3 \theta = \dfrac{1}{4}(3\sin \theta - \sin 3\theta)$

26. $\sin^4 \theta = \dfrac{1}{8}(3 - 4\cos 2\theta + \cos 4\theta)$

27. Show that if θ is an argument of a complex number z with modulus equal to one, then

$$\cos n\theta = \frac{1}{2}\left(z^n + \frac{1}{z^n}\right), \qquad \sin n\theta = \frac{1}{2i}\left(z^n - \frac{1}{z^n}\right).$$

28. Verify that

$$\left(\frac{1 + i\tan \theta}{1 - i\tan \theta}\right)^n = \frac{1 + i\tan n\theta}{1 - i\tan n\theta}.$$

In Exercises 29–30 use equations 1.35 to verify the identity when $n > 0$ is an integer.

29. $\cos^n \theta = \begin{cases} \dfrac{n!}{2^n[(n/2)!]^2} + \dfrac{1}{2^{n-1}} \displaystyle\sum_{k=0}^{(n-2)/2} \binom{n}{k} \cos(n-2k)\theta, & n \text{ even} \\[4mm] \dfrac{1}{2^{n-1}} \displaystyle\sum_{k=0}^{(n-1)/2} \binom{n}{k} \cos(n-2k)\theta, & n \text{ odd.} \end{cases}$

30. $\sin^n \theta = \begin{cases} \dfrac{(-1)^n n!}{2^n[(n/2)!]^2} + \dfrac{(-1)^{n/2}}{2^{n-1}} \displaystyle\sum_{k=0}^{(n-2)/2} (-1)^k \binom{n}{k} \cos(n-2k)\theta, & n \text{ even} \\[4mm] \dfrac{(-1)^{(n+1)/2}}{2^{n-1}} \displaystyle\sum_{k=0}^{(n-1)/2} (-1)^{k+1} \binom{n}{k} \sin(n-2k)\theta, & n \text{ odd.} \end{cases}$

§1.5 Applications of the Exponential Form for Complex Numbers

Roots of Complex Numbers

An equation of the form

$$a_n z^n + a_{n-1} z^{n-1} + \cdots + a_1 z + a_0 = 0, \qquad (1.36)$$

where $n \geq 1$ is an integer and $a_0, a_1, \ldots, a_n \neq 0$ are constants is called a **polynomial equation** of degree n. When the a_j are real, we speak of a real polynomial equation, and when the a_j are complex, we have a complex polynomial equation. For instance, the quadratic equation $3z^2 + 2z + 5 = 0$ is a real polynomial equation of degree 2; the equation $(4 - i)z^3 - 2z^2 + 3iz + 6 = 0$ is a complex polynomial equation of degree 3 (in short, a complex cubic equation). Early in your calculus studies, or even before, someone quoted to you a theorem called the Fundamental Theorem of Algebra. It was probably stated as follows: Every real polynomial equation of degree $n \geq 1$ has exactly n solutions (counting multiplicities). Recall the meaning of multiplicity. Each root $z = 1$ and $z = 2$ of the quadratic equation $z^2 - 3z + 2 = 0$ has multiplicity 1, but the root $z = 1$ of $z^2 - 2z + 1 = 0$ has multiplicity 2. The sixth degree equation $(z - 1)^2(z - 2)^3(z + 4) = 0$ has three distinct roots, but it has 6 roots counting multiplicities — $z = 1$ is a root of multiplicity 2, $z = 2$ has multiplicity 3, and $z = -4$ has multiplicity 1. The fundamental theorem indicates that when multiplicities are taken into account, the number of solutions is equal to the degree of the equation. The theorem is true for complex polynomial equations as well as real ones. You could not prove the real version when it was first given to you, and you cannot prove either version now, but you will be able to in Chapter 4. This presents no problem, since the theorem does not tell us how to find solutions anyway; it only tells us how many to expect.

Of particular interest are polynomial equations of the form

$$z^n = Z \qquad (1.37)$$

where $n > 1$ is an integer, and Z is a given complex number. The n solutions are called the n n^{th} roots of Z. For example, the two solutions of $z^2 = 1 + i$ are the square roots of $1 + i$, and the three solutions of $z^3 = -1 + 2i$ are the cube roots of $-1 + 2i$. DeMoivre's theorem can be used to advantage here. To illustrate we begin with the example

$$z^3 = 8i.$$

The three solutions are called the cube roots of $8i$. To find them we express z and $8i$ in exponential form, $z = re^{\theta i}$ and $8i = 8e^{\pi i/2}$, and substitute into $z^3 = 8i$,

$$(re^{\theta i})^3 = 8e^{\pi i/2}.$$

Using DeMoivre's theorem on the left we obtain

$$r^3 e^{3\theta i} = 8e^{\pi i/2}.$$

Since conditions 1.21 for equality of complex numbers in polar form are also valid for complex numbers in exponential form, we can state that

$$r^3 = 8 \qquad \text{and} \qquad 3\theta = \frac{\pi}{2} + 2k\pi, \quad k \text{ an integer.}$$

Hence,

$$r = 2 \qquad \text{and} \qquad \theta = \frac{\pi}{6} + \frac{2k\pi}{3}.$$

The values $k = 0$, 1, and 2 lead to distinct complex numbers:

$$z_0 = 2e^{\pi i/6} = 2[\cos(\pi/6) + \sin(\pi/6)\, i] = 2\left(\frac{\sqrt{3}}{2} + \frac{i}{2}\right) = \sqrt{3} + i,$$

$$z_1 = 2e^{(\pi/6 + 2\pi/3)i} = 2[\cos(5\pi/6) + \sin(5\pi/6)\, i] = 2\left(\frac{-\sqrt{3}}{2} + \frac{i}{2}\right) = -\sqrt{3} + i,$$

$$z_2 = 2e^{(\pi/6 + 4\pi/3)i} = 2[\cos(3\pi/2) + \sin(3\pi/2)\, i] = -2i.$$

These are the cube roots of $8i$; the cube of each complex number is equal to $8i$. Other values of k simply repeat these cube roots. It is interesting to plot the cube roots in the complex plane (Figure 1.12). All three lie on a circle centred at the origin with radius 2 (the cube root of the modulus of $8i$). They are equally spaced around the circle with angle $2\pi/3$ between each pair. The argument of z_0 is one-third the principal argument of $8i$.

This process can be used on equation 1.37. If we set $z = re^{\theta i}$ and $Z = Re^{\Theta i}$, then

$$r^n e^{n\theta i} = Re^{\Theta i}.$$

Conditions 1.21 require

$$r^n = R \qquad \text{and} \qquad n\theta = \Theta + 2k\pi, \quad k \text{ an integer.}$$

Consequently,

$$r = R^{1/n} \qquad \text{and} \qquad \theta = \frac{\Theta + 2k\pi}{n}.$$

The n n^{th} roots of $Z = R(\cos\Theta + \sin\Theta\, i)$ are therefore

$$z_k = R^{1/n} e^{(\Theta + 2k\pi)i/n} = R^{1/n}\left[\cos\left(\frac{\Theta + 2k\pi}{n}\right) + \sin\left(\frac{\Theta + 2k\pi}{n}\right) i\right], \quad (1.38)$$

where $k = 0, 1, \ldots, n - 1$. Geometrically they are equally spaced around a circle of radius $R^{1/n}$ with angle $2\pi/n$ between successive pairs (Figure 1.13). The first (z_0) has argument Θ/n.

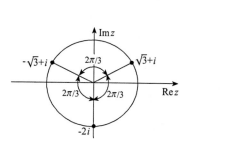

Figure 1.12

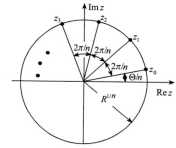

Figure 1.13

In Section 1.2 we found square roots of complex numbers. The above discussion provides a more efficient method. Compare the following discussion for finding the square roots of $2 + i$ with that in Exercise 35 in Section 1.2. To find the square roots of $2 + i$ we set $z = re^{\theta i}$ in $z^2 = 2 + i$,

$$r^2 e^{2\theta i} = 2 + i = \sqrt{5} e^{\Theta i}$$

where $\Theta = \text{Tan}^{-1}(1/2)$. Conditions 1.21 require

$$r^2 = \sqrt{5} \qquad \text{and} \qquad 2\theta = \Theta + 2k\pi, \quad k \text{ an integer.}$$

Hence $r = 5^{1/4}$ and $\theta = \Theta/2 + k\pi$, and we obtain

$$z_0 = 5^{1/4} e^{\Theta i/2}, \qquad z_1 = 5^{1/4} e^{(\Theta/2 + \pi)i} = -z_0.$$

The square roots are $\pm 5^{1/4} e^{\Theta i/2}$. We can use a calculator to approximate real and imaginary parts ($z \approx \pm(1.455 + 0.344i)$), or we can use trigonometry to find exact values. Since $\cos \Theta = 2/\sqrt{5}$ (Figure 1.14), it follows that

$$\sin(\Theta/2) = \sqrt{\frac{1 - \cos \Theta}{2}} = \sqrt{\frac{\sqrt{5} - 2}{2\sqrt{5}}} \quad \text{and} \quad \cos(\Theta/2) = \sqrt{\frac{1 + \cos \Theta}{2}} = \sqrt{\frac{\sqrt{5} + 2}{2\sqrt{5}}}.$$

Thus, the square roots are

$$\pm 5^{1/4} \left(\sqrt{\frac{\sqrt{5} + 2}{2\sqrt{5}}} + \sqrt{\frac{\sqrt{5} - 2}{2\sqrt{5}}} i \right) = \pm(\sqrt{\sqrt{5}/2 + 1} + \sqrt{\sqrt{5}/2 - 1}\, i).$$

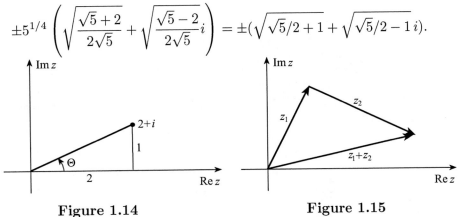

Figure 1.14   **Figure 1.15**

Triangle Inequality

It is a well-known fact that the length of any side of a triangle is less than the sum of the lengths of the other two sides (called the triangle inequality). If the sides of the triangle are represented by the complex numbers z_1, z_2, and $z_1 + z_2$ (Figure 1.15), then the triangle inequality can be expressed in terms of the moduli $|z_1|$, $|z_2|$, and $|z_1 + z_2|$,

$$|z_1 + z_2| < |z_1| + |z_2|. \tag{1.39}$$

When $z_2 = az_1$, where $a < 0$ is a real number (Figure 1.16), z_1, z_2, and $z_1 + z_2$ do not form a triangle, but inequality 1.39 is still valid. When $z_2 = az_1$, where $a > 0$ (Figure 1.17), there is once again no triangle, and in this case

$$|z_1 + z_2| = |z_1| + |z_2|.$$

Hence, we can say that for any two complex numbers z_1 and z_2,

$$|z_1 + z_2| \leq |z_1| + |z_2|. \tag{1.40}$$

This continues to be called the triangle inequality in spite of the fact that when $z_2 = az_1$, there is no triangle. It is proved algebraically in Exercise 36.

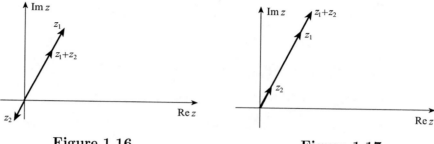

Figure 1.16   **Figure 1.17**

An alternative geometric statement to the triangle inequality (but perhaps not quite so obvious) is that the length of any side of a triangle is greater than the difference between the lengths of the other two sides. When the sides of the triangle are represented by z_1, z_2, and $z_1 + z_2$, this leads to the inequality

$$|z_1 + z_2| \geq \big| |z_1| - |z_2| \big|. \tag{1.41}$$

This result can also be proved algebraically or derived from 1.40 (see Exercises 37 and 38).

Ellipses and Circles

Moduli of complex numbers can be used to advantage in describing circles and ellipses in the complex plane (or the real plane). For example, consider the complex numbers that satisfy the inequality $|z - 2 + 3i| \leq 4$. Vector subtraction suggests that $z - 2 + 3i = z - (2 - 3i)$ may be regarded as the vector from the complex number $2 - 3i$ to the complex number z (Figure 1.18). Because $|z - 2 + 3i|$ is the length of this vector, the inequality $|z - 2 + 3i| \leq 4$ describes all complex numbers z within a distance 4 from $2 - 3i$; that is, all points inside and on a circle centre $2 - 3i$ and radius 4. We can also see this algebraically. If we set $z = x + yi$ in $|z - 2 + 3i| \leq 4$, we obtain

$$4 \geq |(x + yi) - 2 + 3i| = |(x - 2) + (y + 3)i| = \sqrt{(x - 2)^2 + (y + 3)^2}.$$

When both sides are squared, $(x - 2)^2 + (y + 3)^2 \leq 16$. This describes a circle with centre $(2, -3)$ and radius 4, and its interior.

In general, for a fixed complex number z_0, the inequality $|z - z_0| \leq r$ describes all complex numbers inside and on a circle of radius r centred at z_0 (Figure 1.19).

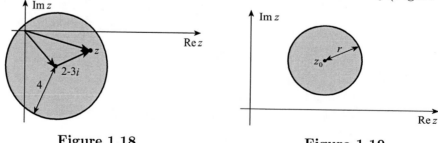

Figure 1.18   **Figure 1.19**

An ellipse is the path traced out by a point that moves so that the sum of its distances from two fixed points called foci is a constant value. If the foci are the complex numbers z_0 and z_1 (Figure 1.20), then the ellipse traced out by a point that moves so that the sum of its distances from z_0 and z_1 is equal to a is

$$|z - z_0| + |z - z_1| = a.$$

Naturally a must be larger than the distance between z_0 and z_1. For example, the equality $|z - 3i| + |z - 4| = 7$ describes the ellipse in Figure 1.21. The inequality $|z - 3i| + |z - 4| > 7$ describes all points outside the ellipse (Figure 1.22). The fact that the ellipse itself is not described by the inequality is indicated with a dashed curve.

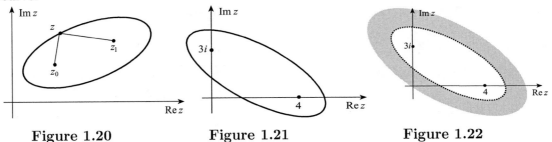

Figure 1.20	Figure 1.21	Figure 1.22

EXERCISES 1.5

In Exercises 1–3 use DeMoivre's theorem 1.32 to find the square roots of the complex number. Compare the results and the difficulty in arriving at these results relative to Exercises 33, 34, and 36 in Section 1.2.

1. $-7 - 24i$ **2.** $21 - 20i$ **3.** $-1 + i$

In Exercises 4–11 find all solutions of the equation.

4. $z^3 = 1$ **5.** $z^4 = i$

6. $z^2 = 2 + 2\sqrt{3}i$ **7.** $z^5 = -32$

8. $z^3 = 4 - 3i$ **9.** $z^6 = -1$

10. $z^4 + 3z^2 + 5 = 0$ **11.** $z^6 - 2z^3 + 4 = 0$

12. (a) The roots of the equation $z^n = 1$, where n is a positive integer, are called the **roots of unity**, often denoted by ω_k, $k = 0, \ldots, n-1$, where $\omega_0 = 1$. Find the other roots.

    (b) Verify that

$$\omega_k \omega_j = \omega_r,$$

where r is the remainder when $j + k$ is divided by n.

    (c) Prove that

$$\omega_0 + \omega_1 + \cdots + \omega_{n-1} = 0.$$

    (d) Verify that for any $k = 1, \ldots, n-1$,

$$1 + \omega_k + \omega_k^2 + \cdots + \omega_k^{n-1} = 0.$$

    (e) Prove that $k = 1, \ldots, n-1$,

$$1 + 2\omega_k + 3\omega_k^2 + 4\omega_k^3 + \cdots + n\omega_k^{n-1} = \frac{-n}{1 - \omega_k}.$$

13. Prove that when $|z_3| > |z_4|$,

$$\left| \frac{z_1 + z_2}{z_3 + z_4} \right| \leq \frac{|z_1| + |z_2|}{|z_3| - |z_4|}.$$

Correct the inequality when $|z_3| < |z_4|$. What inequality encompasses both situations?

In Exercises 14–25 describe the set of points in the complex plane defined by the equation or the inequality.

14. $|z + i| = |z - 2i|$ **15.** $|z + 1| = 3|z + i|$

16. $|z - 2 + i| \leq 3$ **17.** $|z + 3i| > 2$

18. $1 \leq |z + 3| \leq 4$ **19.** $2 < |z - 2 - i| \leq 5$

20. $|z + 1| + |z - 1| \leq 4$ **21.** $|z - 2i| + |z + 3i| \geq 8$

22. $4 \leq |z - 1| + |z + 1| \leq 6$ **23.** $z^2 + \bar{z}^2 = 4$

24. $z^2 + z + 2\bar{z} + 4 = 0$ **25.** $|z| > 1 - \operatorname{Re} z$

In Exercises 26–33 describe the set of points algebraically.

26.   **27.**

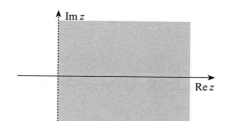 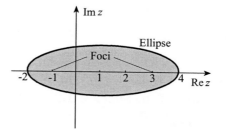

28.   **29.**

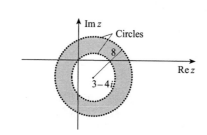 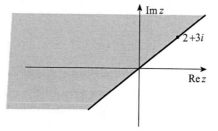

30.   **31.**

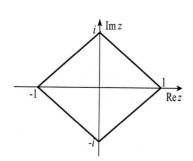 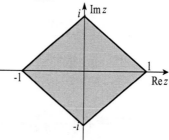

32.   **33.**

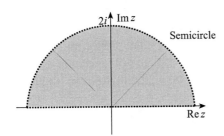

34. Prove that the equation $|z - z_1| = |z - z_2|$ describes a line.

35. Use part (a) of Exercise 18 in Section 1.3 to show that when $\lambda > 0$ and $\lambda \neq 1$, the equation

$$|z - z_1| = \lambda|z - z_2|$$

describes a circle. Find its centre and radius.

36. Give an algebraic proof of triangle inequality 1.40 by setting $z_1 = x_1 + y_1 i$ and $z_2 = x_2 + y_2 i$.

37. Give an algebraic proof of inequality 1.41 by setting $z_1 = x_1 + y_1 i$ and $z_2 = x_2 + y_2 i$.

38. Use inequality 1.40 to prove inequality 1.41.

39. If Z is a given complex number and m and n are relatively prime, positive integers, find all solutions of the equation $z^n = Z^m$.

40. Show that for any real number p and any even, positive integer m,

$$e^{2mi\mathrm{Cot}^{-1}p}\left(\frac{pi + 1}{pi - 1}\right)^m = 1.$$

41. Find all solutions of the equation $(z - 2 + 3i)^4 = z^4$.

42. Find all solutions of the equation $(z + 3)^5 = z^5$. Hint: See Exercise 12.

43. In this exercise, we generalize the results of Exercises 41 and 42. Use Exercise 12 to show that for any nonzero complex number z_0, and any integer $n \geq 2$, solutions of the equation $z^n = (z + z_0)^n$ are

$$z = -\frac{z_0}{2}\left(1 + i \cot \frac{k\pi}{n}\right), \qquad k = 1, \ldots, n - 1.$$

Confirm that this formula gives the solutions in Exercises 41 and 42.

44. Find all solutions of the equation

$$z^4 + z^3 + z^2 + z + 1 = 0.$$

Hint: Multiply the equation by $z - 1$.

45. Extend the result of the previous exercise to find all solutions of the equation

$$z^n + z^{n-1} + \cdots + z^2 + z + 1 = 0,$$

where n is a positive integer.

46. Prove that when $|z| < 1$, then for any positive integer n,

$$|1 + z + z^2 + z^3 + \cdots + z^n| < \frac{2}{1 - |z|}.$$

CHAPTER 2   COMPLEX FUNCTIONS AND THEIR DERIVATIVES

We are now ready to study the calculus of complex functions. In this chapter we introduce functions, limits, and derivatives. A complex function f is a rule that assigns a complex number $w = f(z)$ to each complex number z in some set. Because of the two-dimensional nature of both z and w, it is not possible to visualize a complex function geometrically in the same way that we visualize a real function as a curve in the xy-plane. Instead, we treat functions from a mapping perspective. A function f defines a mapping $w = f(z)$ from points in the z-plane to points in the w-plane. At first, this representation may seem far from adequate but it will pay dividends in the application of conformal mapping to problems in electrostatics, heat flow, and fluid flow in Chapter 7. The definition of the limit of a function $f(z)$ as z approaches a complex number z_0 is identical to the limit of a real function $f(x)$ as x approaches x_0, but once again because of the two-dimensional nature of complex numbers, we find that the geometric interpretation of the limit is more reminiscent of the limit of a real function $f(x, y)$ as (x, y) approaches (x_0, y_0). Algebraically, the derivative $f'(z)$ is defined in exactly the same way as $f'(x)$, but it is interpreted geometrically in the context of mappings (not as the slope of some tangent line). Existence of the derivative $f'(z)$ of a complex function places restrictions on the real and imaginary parts of $f(z)$. These conditions, called the Cauchy-Riemann equations, form the basis for all our studies in complex analysis.

§2.1   Regions of the Complex Plane

An integral part of every real function $f(x)$ is its domain of definition. For example, the functions $f(x) = x^2 + 3$, $x \geq 0$ and $g(x) = x^2 + 3$, $x \leq 0$ perform the same mathematical operations, but because they operate on different sets of values of x, they are regarded as different functions. In spite of this, we seldom pay a great deal of attention to domains of definition of functions in real calculus. We usually say something to the effect that if the domain of definition of a function, specified algebraically as a formula $f(x)$, is not mentioned, it is assumed to be all values of x for which the formula makes sense. For complex functions we must often be more careful. Properties of a complex function may depend on where the function is defined; different domains of definition may lead to different properties. It is therefore important that we not lose sight of the domain of definition of a function. In this section, we describe various possible domains of definition for functions, and fundamental to all of these sets is the *neighbourhood*.

Definition 2.1   An ϵ-**neighbourhood** of a point z_0 is the set of all complex numbers z satisfying

$$|z - z_0| < \epsilon. \tag{2.1}$$

It is the set of all complex numbers interior to a circle of radius ϵ and centre z_0 (Figure 2.1). The fact that the circumference of the circle is not included in the ϵ-neighbourhood is reflected in the dashed curve.

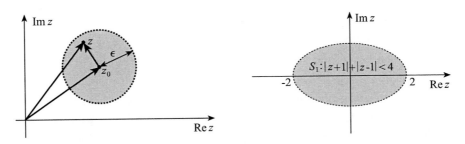

Figure 2.1   **Figure 2.2**

Definition 2.2 A point z of a set S of complex numbers is called an **interior** point of S if there exists an ϵ-neighbourhood of z that contains only points of S; z is a **boundary point** of S if every ϵ-neighbourhood of z contains at least one point of S and at least one point not in S. The set of all boundary points of a set S is called the **boundary** of S.

For example, consider the set of points described by the inequality $S_1 : |z + 1| + |z - 1| < 4$. Equality $|z + 1| + |z - 1| = 4$ describes all points on an ellipse with foci $z = \pm 1$. It follows therefore that S_1 consists of all points inside, but not on, the ellipse (Figure 2.2). Given any point z_0 in S_1, it is possible to draw a circle centred at z_0 that contains only points of S_1 (Figure 2.3). Hence, every point in S_1 is an interior point of S_1. Since every neighbourhood of every point z_1 on the ellipse itself contains points inside and outside S_1 (Figure 2.4), points on the ellipse $|z + 1| + |z - 1| = 4$ are boundary points of S_1; the ellipse is the boundary of S_1.

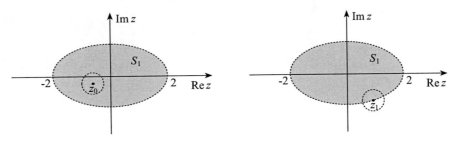

Figure 2.3   **Figure 2.4**

Consider now the set $S_2 : |z + 1| + |z - 1| \geq 4$ of all points on and outside the ellipse (Figure 2.5). Every point outside the ellipse is an interior point of S_2, and every point on the ellipse is a boundary point of S_2. The ellipse $|z + 1| + |z - 1| = 4$ is the boundary for S_2.

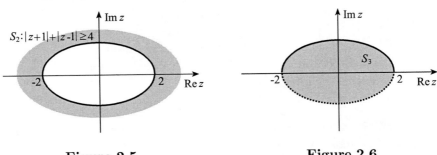

Figure 2.5   **Figure 2.6**

Definition 2.3 A set S of complex numbers is said to be **open** if all points in S are interior points.

Alternatively, a set is open if it contains none of its boundary points.

Definition 2.4 A set S of complex numbers is said to be **closed** if it contains all of its boundary points.

Set S_1 above is open; it contains none of its boundary points (every point is an interior point). Set S_2 is closed, it contains all of its boundary points. Suppose to S_1 we add the points on the upper half of the ellipse (Figure 2.6). This set, call it S_3, is neither open nor closed; it contains some of its boundary points but not all of them.

Definition 2.5 A set S of complex numbers is said to be **bounded** if there exists a positive (real) number R such that $|z| < R$ for all z in S.

Geometrically, a set is bounded if it can be located inside a circle with finite radius. Sets S_1 and S_3 are bounded, set S_2 is not.

Definition 2.6 A set S is said to be **connected** if every pair of points in S can be joined by a finite number of line segments joined end to end that lie entirely within S.

Sets S_1, S_2, and S_3 are all connected. Set S_4 in Figure 2.7 is also connected. Set S_5 in Figure 2.8 is not connected; it consists of two disjoint pieces. It is not possible to join point A to point B by line segments that never leave the set.

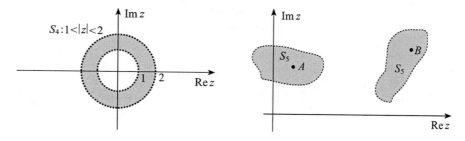

Figure 2.7   **Figure 2.8**

Definition 2.7 A **domain** is an open connected set.

Sets S_1 and S_4 are domains; both are open and connected. Sets S_2, S_3, and S_5 are not domains; S_2 and S_3 fail to be open, and S_5 is not connected.

We might think that the counterpart of a real function being defined on an open interval is a complex function being defined on an open set. Such is not the case; the counterpart of an open interval is a domain. Like an interval, a domain is connected; an open set need not be connected.

It is perhaps unfortunate that the word "domain" was chosen to represent an open, connected set because of its potential confusion with "domain" of definition of a function. We avoid confusion by always using "domain of definition" in the latter context.

Example 2.1 Sketch the following sets in the complex plane and discuss whether each is open, closed, bounded, connected, and a domain:

$$(a)\,|z - i| < 2 \qquad (b)\,|z + 3i| \leq 2 \qquad (c)\,0 < |z + i| < 4$$
$$(d)\,1 < |z - 4 + i| \leq 3 \qquad (e)\,\text{Re}\,z < 3 \qquad (f)\,\text{Im}\,z \leq -2$$

Solution   (a) The set $|z - i| < 2$ is the interior of a circle of radius 2 centred at i (Figure 2.9). It is open, not closed, bounded, and connected. It is therefore a domain.

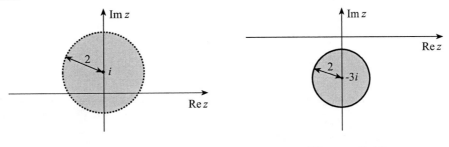

Figure 2.9   Figure 2.10

(b) The set $|z + 3i| \leq 2$ is the interior and edge of a circle with radius 2 and centre $-3i$ (Figure 2.10). The circumference of the circle is solid to indicate that it is included in the set. The set is closed, not open, bounded, and connected. Because the set is not open, it is not a domain.

(c) The set $0 < |z + i| < 4$ is the interior of a circle centred at $-i$ with radius 4, excluding the centre (Figure 2.11). The set is open, but not closed; its boundary $|z + i| = 4$ and $z = -i$ is not contained inside the set. The set is bounded and connected. It is therefore a domain.

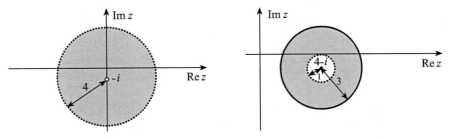

Figure 2.11   Figure 2.12

(d) The set $1 < |z - 4 + i| \leq 3$ is an annulus centred at $4 - i$ with inner and outer radii 1 and 3 (Figure 2.12). It includes the outer edge, but not the inner. Because it includes some of its boundary points, but not all of them, the set is neither open, nor closed. It is bounded and connected, but not a domain.

(e) The set $\operatorname{Re} z < 3$ (Figure 2.13) is open and not closed. It is an unbounded domain.

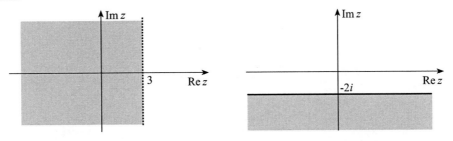

Figure 2.13   Figure 2.14

(f) The set $\operatorname{Im} z \leq -2$ (Figure 2.14) is closed, not open, unbounded, and connected. It is not a domain.•

Example 2.2   Determine whether the set S of complex numbers satisfying $|z| < 1$ or $|z - 2| < 1$ is a domain.

Solution   The set consists of all points interior to either of the circles in Figure 2.15. It is an open set; it contains none of its boundary points on $|z| = 1$ and $|z - 2| = 1$. Because the point $z = 1$ is not contained in S, the set is not connected, and is therefore not a domain. If point $z = 1$ is added to S, the set becomes connected, but it is still not a domain. With $z = 1$ added to S, the set is no longer open.•

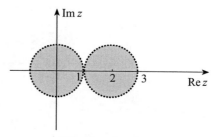

Figure 2.15

EXERCISES 2.1

In Exercises 1–10 sketch the set in the complex plane described by the inequality or inequalities. State whether the set is open, closed, bounded, connected, and/or a domain.

1. $|z - i + 3| \leq 4$

2. $|2z + 4 - 3i| > 5$

3. $|z + i| + |z - 4i| \geq 9$

4. $|z - 1 - i| + |z + 1 + i| < 6$

5. $2 < |z + 3 - 2i| < 4$

6. $\text{Re}\,(z^2 + 2z) \leq 3$

7. $|z|^2 + |z| < 4\text{Im}\,z$

8. $(2\text{Re}\,z + \text{Im}\,z)(\text{Re}\,z - 3\text{Im}\,z) \leq 0$

9. $(2\text{Re}\,z + \text{Im}\,z)(\text{Re}\,z - 3\text{Im}\,z) < 0$

10. $|z| < \text{Arg}\,z + \pi$

11. Prove that the only nonempty set that is both open and closed is $\mathcal{C}$.

12. Is the set of points described by $|z| < 1 - \cos\,(\text{Arg}\,z)$ a domain?

13. Is the set of points described by $|z|^2 < \cos\,(2\text{Arg}\,z)$ a domain?

14. Suppose S is a subset of a domain D. The complement of S in D is the set of all points in D that are not in S. Prove that if the complement of an open set S in a domain D is also open, then $S = D$.

§2.2 Complex Functions

A complex-valued **function** f of a complex variable z is a rule that assigns a complex number $f(z)$ to each complex number z in a set S. For example, the function $f(z) = z^2$ assigns the following complex numbers to $1 + i$ and $2 - 3i$:

$$f(1 + i) = (1 + i)^2 = 2i; \qquad f(2 - 3i) = (2 - 3i)^2 = -5 - 12i.$$

The complex function $g(z) = |z| + 3z$ assigns different numbers to $1 + i$ and $2 - 3i$:

$$g(1 + i) = |1 + i| + 3(1 + i) = (\sqrt{2} + 3) + 3i;$$
$$g(2 - 3i) = |2 - 3i| + 3(2 - 3i) = (\sqrt{13} + 6) - 9i.$$

The set S of complex numbers on which a function operates is called the **domain of definition** of the function. It is often a domain in the sense of Definition 2.7, but it need not be so. When a function is specified algebraically by a formula such as $f(z) = z^3$ or $f(z) = (z + 1)/(1 - z)^2$, and the domain of definition of the function is not mentioned, it is assumed to be the set of all points in the complex plane for which the formula makes sense. For $f(z) = z^3$ this would be all $\mathcal{C}$, and for $f(z) = (z+1)/(1-z)^2$ this would be all $\mathcal{C}$ except $z = 1$. The set of complex numbers $f(z)$ that a function produces as z takes on all values in the domain of definition is called the **range** of the function. For example, when the domain of definition of the function $f(z) = 1/z$ is taken as the complex plane with $z = 0$ deleted, its range is also the complex plane with $0 + 0i$ deleted. If the domain of definition is only the set of points $0 < |z| < 1$, then its range is the set of complex numbers $f(z)$ for which $|f(z)| > 1$.

A real function $f(x)$ of a real variable x is illustrated graphically as the curve $y = f(x)$ in the Cartesian plane. Visualizations of complex functions $f(z)$ are not as revealing. If we set $w = f(z)$, it requires two dimensions to visualize the domain of definition of the function, and another two dimensions to visualize its range. How do we represent four dimensions on a page (or even in space)? One way is to visualize the function as a mapping from the z-plane to the w-plane. Points in the z-plane are mapped by $f(z)$ onto points in the w-plane. By examining images in the w-plane of various regions in the z-plane, we may be able to appreciate the action of a function. We consider a number of simple examples. The function

$$w = z + b, \tag{2.2}$$

where b is a given complex number, is called a **translation**. The reason for this becomes apparent when we draw the z-plane and the w-plane side-by-side (Figure 2.16).

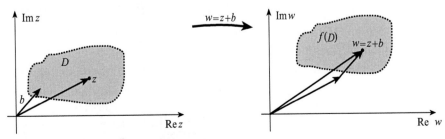

Figure 2.16

Given any point in the z-plane, its image $w = z + b$ in the w-plane is the complex number z translated by the vector corresponding to the complex number b. Any domain D in the z-plane is mapped by $w = z + b$ onto exactly the same domain in the w-plane translated by b.

Consider next the function

$$w = az, \qquad (2.3)$$

where a is a given complex number. If we write a and z in exponential form, $a = \rho e^{\phi i}$ and $z = r e^{\theta i}$, then

$$w = \rho r e^{(\theta + \phi)i}. \qquad (2.4)$$

This indicates that every point z is rotated through an angle ϕ and has its modulus multiplied by ρ (Figure 2.17).

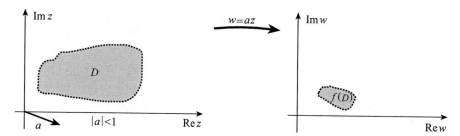

Figure 2.17

The mapping may be considered to be composed of two parts,

$$w^* = e^{\phi i} z, \qquad (2.5a)$$

a **rotation** (see Example 1.10), and

$$w = \rho w^*, \qquad (2.5b)$$

a **magnification**.

Consider now the function

$$w = f(z) = \frac{1}{z}, \qquad (2.6)$$

called a **reciprocation**. When we express z in exponential form $z = re^{\theta i}$,

$$w = f(z) = \frac{1}{re^{\theta i}} = \frac{1}{r}e^{-\theta i}.$$

In this form it is clear that $f(z)$ inverts the modulus of a complex number z and changes the sign of its argument. In Figure 2.18a we have drawn the z- and w-planes side-by-side and shown (via arrows) how three points z_1, z_2, and z_3 are mapped by $f(z)$ to w_1, w_2, and w_3. The circle $|z| = 1$ is important for an appreciation of this function. Points on this circle are mapped by $f(z) = 1/z$ to points on the circle $|w| = 1$. Points on the top half of $|z| = 1$ are mapped to the bottom half of $|w| = 1$, and vice versa (since $f(z)$ changes signs of arguments). Points inside the circle $|z| = 1$ are mapped to points outside $|w| = 1$. This is illustrated in Figure 2.18b.

Points outside $|z| = 1$ are mapped inside $|w| = 1$ (Figure 2.18c). Other regional mappings are shown in Figures 2.18d–f.

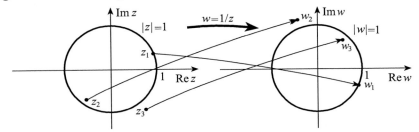

Figure 2.18a

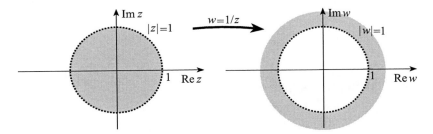

Figure 2.18b

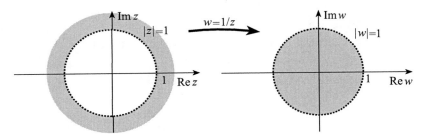

Figure 2.18c

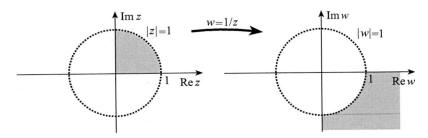

Figure 2.18d

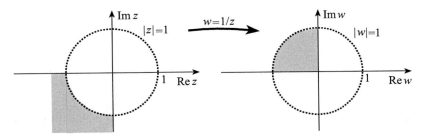

Figure 2.18e

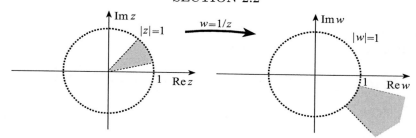

Figure 2.18f

A very important class of functions or mappings are **bilinear** or **linear fractional** or **Mobius** mappings. They are mappings of the form

$$w = \frac{az + b}{cz + d},\tag{2.7}$$

where a, b, c, and d are complex numbers for which $ad - bc \neq 0$. This condition ensures that the mapping is not a constant. To see this, suppose that $ad - bc = 0$. If $a \neq 0$, we may solve for $d = bc/a$, and substitution into 2.7 gives

$$w = \frac{az + b}{cz + \dfrac{bc}{a}} = \frac{a}{c}.$$

a constant. If $ad - bc = 0$ and $a = 0$, then either $b = 0$ or $c = 0$. When $a = b = 0$, it follows that $w = 0$, and when $a = c = 0$, we find $w = b/d$, a constant.

Every bilinear transformation is a succession of rotations, magnifications, reciprocations, and/or translations. If $c = 0$ in 2.7, then d may be absorbed into a and b, with the result that

$$w = az + b.\tag{2.8}$$

This is a rotation and magnification followed by a translation. If $c \neq 0$, then

$$w = \frac{az + b}{cz + d} = \frac{\dfrac{a}{c}(cz + d) + b - \dfrac{ad}{c}}{cz + d} = \frac{a}{c} + \frac{b - \dfrac{ad}{c}}{cz + d}.\tag{2.9}$$

This mapping may be regarded successively as a rotation and magnification, and a translation

$$w_1 = cz + d,$$

a reciprocation,

$$w_2 = \frac{1}{w_1},$$

a rotation and magnification,

$$w_3 = \left(b - \frac{ad}{c}\right) w_2,$$

and finally a translation,

$$w = w_3 + \frac{a}{c}.$$

There are many properties of bilinear transformations that are important in physical problems; in particular, they map circles and straight lines to circles and straight lines, which depending on whether the curve to be mapped passes through the point at which the bilinear mapping is undefined. Here is an illustration; other properties of bilinear mappings are discussed in detail in Section 7.2.

Example 2.3   Show that the points on the circle $|z + 1| = 2$ are mapped to points on a straight line by the bilinear transformation $w = 1/(z - 1)$.

Solution   Real and imaginary parts, x and y, of points on the circle $|z + 1| = 2$ satisfy $|(x + yi) + 1| = 2$ or $(x + 1)^2 + y^2 = 4$. To find the image of this circle under the bilinear mapping, we set $w = u + vi$, and replace x's and y's with u's and v's. To do this, we first find z in terms of w. If $w = 1/(z - 1)$, it follows that $z = 1/w + 1$. Substituting $z = x + yi$ and $w = u + vi$ gives

$$x + yi = \frac{1}{u + vi} + 1 = \frac{1}{u + vi} \frac{u - vi}{u - vi} + 1 = \frac{u - vi}{u^2 + v^2} + 1.$$

Consequently, $x = \dfrac{u}{u^2 + v^2} + 1$ and $y = \dfrac{-v}{u^2 + v^2}$. Images of points on the circle $(x + 1)^2 + y^2 = 4$ therefore satisfy the equation

$$\left(\frac{u}{u^2 + v^2} + 2 \right)^2 + \left(\frac{-v}{u^2 + v^2} \right)^2 = 4 \qquad \Longrightarrow \qquad \frac{(u + 2u^2 + 2v^2)^2}{(u^2 + v^2)^2} + \frac{v^2}{(u^2 + v^2)^2} = 4.$$

This equation simplifies to $u = -1/4$. Thus, points on the circle $|z + 1| = 2$ are mapped to points on the straight line $\operatorname{Re} w = -1/4$.•

Real and Imaginary Parts of Complex Functions

The complex number $w = f(z) = f(x + yi)$ has real and imaginary parts which we denote by u and v. They are functions of x and y, the real and imaginary parts of z,

$$w = u + vi = u(x, y) + v(x, y)i. \tag{2.10}$$

For example, when $w = z^2 = (x + yi)^2 = (x^2 - y^2) + 2xyi$,

$$u(x, y) = x^2 - y^2, \qquad v(x, y) = 2xy,$$

and when $w = |z| + 3z = \sqrt{x^2 + y^2} + 3(x + yi)$,

$$u(x, y) = \sqrt{x^2 + y^2} + 3x, \qquad v(x, y) = 3y.$$

In other words, a complex function can be expressed as a pair of real-valued functions of two independent variables. We find this representation very useful. It was used in Example 2.3.

To find the image C' in the w-plane of a curve C in the z-plane under a mapping $w = f(z)$, there are two procedures that we can follow, and both involve the relations between real and imaginary parts of z and real and imaginary parts of w. Suppose, then, that $g(x, y) = 0$ is the equation of a curve C in the z-plane that is to be mapped by $w = f(z)$.

Procedure 1   If it is convenient to invert $w = f(z)$ and find z in terms of w, $z = h(w)$, then we effectively have x and y in terms of u and v. These can be substituted into $g(x,y) = 0$ to give the equation $g[x(u,v), y(u,v)] = 0$ for C'. This was the procedure followed in Example 2.3. It works well on bilinear mappings and some others.

Procedure 2   When it is inconvenient to find z in terms of w, we represent C parametrically, $x = x(t)$, $y = y(t)$. If we substitute these into $u = u(x,y)$ and $v = v(x,y)$, we obtain parametric equations $u = u[x(t), y(t)]$, $v = v[x(t), y(t)]$ for C'. We use this technique in the next example.

Example 2.4   Find the image of the strip $1 \le \mathrm{Re}\, z \le 2$ under the mapping $w = z^2 + z + 2$.

Solution   It is inconvenient to solve $w = z^2 + z + 2$ for z in terms of w. We therefore adopt Procedure 2. First we find u and v in terms of x and y, from

$$w = u + vi = (x + yi)^2 + (x + yi) + 2 = (x^2 - y^2 + x + 2) + (2xy + y)i.$$

Thus,

$$u(x,y) = x^2 - y^2 + x + 2, \qquad v(x,y) = y(2x + 1).$$

Parametric equations for the vertical line $\mathrm{Re}\, z = x_0$ are $x = x_0$, $y = t$, $-\infty < t < \infty$. Its image in the w-plane has parametric equations

$$u = x_0^2 - t^2 + x_0 + 2, \qquad v = t(2x_0 + 1).$$

These are parametric equations for a parabola, and if we eliminate t, we obtain

$$u = x_0^2 + x_0 + 2 - \frac{v^2}{(2x_0 + 1)^2},$$

(see Figure 2.19).

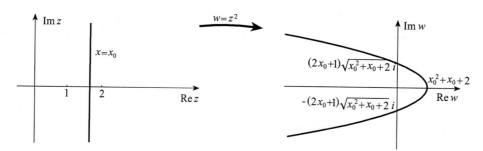

Figure 2.19

Vertical lines $\mathrm{Re}\, z = x_0$ in the z-plane are mapped by $w = z^2 + z + 2$ to parabolas in the w-plane. The vertical line $\mathrm{Re}\, z = 1$ is mapped to the parabola $u = 4 - v^2/9$, and $\mathrm{Re}\, z = 2$ is mapped to $u = 8 - v^2/25$ (Figure 2.20). Images of all vertical lines between $\mathrm{Re}\, z = 1$ and $\mathrm{Re}\, z = 2$ fill the parabolic strip between $u = 4 - v^2/9$ and $u = 8 - v^2/25$.•

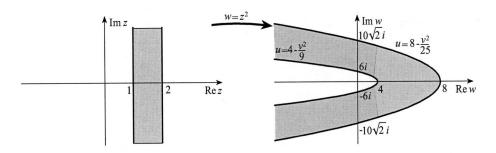

Figure 2.20

A complex function $w = f(z)$ determines a pair of real-valued functions $u(x, y)$ and $v(x, y)$, its real and imaginary parts (equation 2.10). It is important to realize that the converse is not in general true. Given a pair of real-valued functions $u(x, y)$ and $v(x, y)$, we can always define a complex function $u(x, y) + v(x, y)i$ of x and y. However, it is not usually possible to express $u(x, y) + v(x, y)i$ in the form $f(z)$ where $z = x + yi$. Let us illustrate. If $u(x, y) = x^2 - y^2$ and $v(x, y) = 2xy$, then the complex combination $u(x, y) + v(x, y)i = x^2 - y^2 + 2xyi$ can be expressed in terms of z,

$$x^2 - y^2 + 2xyi = (x + yi)^2 = z^2.$$

This cannot be done for $u(x, y) = x^2$ and $v(x, y) = y$. But how do we know this? And if $u(x, y) + v(x, y)i$ can be expressed in terms of z, how in general can we find the expression $f(z)$? One way to proceed is as follows. Given $u(x, y)$ and $v(x, y)$, we can always write $u(x, y) + v(x, y)i$. Now recall that if $z = x + yi$, then its complex conjugate is $\overline{z} = x - yi$. These equations can be solved for x and y in terms of z and $\overline{z}$,

$$x = \frac{z + \overline{z}}{2}, \qquad y = \frac{z - \overline{z}}{2i}. \tag{2.11}$$

When we substitute these into $u(x, y) + v(x, y)i$, we obtain

$$u\left(\frac{z + \overline{z}}{2}, \frac{z - \overline{z}}{2i}\right) + v\left(\frac{z + \overline{z}}{2}, \frac{z - \overline{z}}{2i}\right)i. \tag{2.12}$$

If simplification of this expression leads to a result containing z and not $\overline{z}$, then we shall have proved that $u(x, y) + v(x, y)i$ can be expressed in terms of z and at the same time found $f(z)$. The following two examples demonstrate this procedure.

Example 2.5   Use equations 2.11 to show that $(x^2 - y^2) + 2xyi$ can be expressed as a function of z.

Solution   If we set $x = (z + \overline{z})/2$ and $y = (z - \overline{z})/(2i)$, then

$$(x^2 - y^2) + 2xyi = \left[\left(\frac{z + \overline{z}}{2}\right)^2 - \left(\frac{z - \overline{z}}{2i}\right)^2\right] + 2\left(\frac{z + \overline{z}}{2}\right)\left(\frac{z - \overline{z}}{2i}\right)i$$

$$= \left[\left(\frac{z^2 + 2z\overline{z} + \overline{z}^2}{4}\right) - \left(\frac{z^2 - 2z\overline{z} + \overline{z}^2}{-4}\right)\right] + \frac{1}{2}(z^2 - \overline{z}^2)$$

$$= z^2. \bullet$$

Example 2.6 Use equations 2.11 to show that $x^2 + yi$ cannot be expressed as a function $f(z)$ of $z = x + yi$.

Solution   If we substitute from equations 2.11, then

$$x^2 + yi = \left(\frac{z + \overline{z}}{2}\right)^2 + \left(\frac{z - \overline{z}}{2i}\right) i$$

$$= \frac{1}{4}(z^2 + 2z\overline{z} + \overline{z}^2) + \frac{1}{2}(z - \overline{z}).$$

Unlike Example 2.5, the $\overline{z}$ do not disappear, and therefore $x^2 + yi$ cannot be expressed solely in terms of z.•

In order that the complex combination $u(x, y) + v(x, y)i$ of given functions $u(x, y)$ and $v(x, y)$ be expressible as a function $f(z)$ of $z = x + yi$, these functions must satisfy very stringent conditions. We shall see them in Section 2.4.

In Chapters 2–6, we concentrate on algebraic properties of functions; in Chapter 7, geometric aspects of mappings predominate.

The Point at Infinity

At this juncture in our discussions, we introduce the "point at infinity". We often write $z = \infty$ to represent the point at infinity in the z-plane, but it is really not "a point" as the name suggests. It can be thought of as many points. Let us explain. If we go "infinitely" far out the positive real axis, we say that we are approaching $z = \infty$. But if we go infinitely far out the positive imaginary axis, we also say that we are approaching $z = \infty$. In fact, if we go infinitely far away from the origin in any direction whatsoever, we say that we are approaching $z = \infty$. As you can see then, $z = \infty$ is not a single point, it represents all points that are infinitely far from the origin. There are two ways to describe whether the point at infinity is to be considered a part of the complex plane. When some authors wish to include the point at infinity, they call it the **extended complex plane**. Other authors say that the complex plane includes the point at infinity and the **finite complex plane** excludes the point at infinity. Since we make limited use of the point at infinity, we adopt the former convention, whereby the complex plane does not include the point at infinity, and the extended complex does.

As we approach the origin $z = 0$, images of points in the w-plane under the reciprocation $w = 1/z$ get farther and farther away from $w = 0$. Choosing a specific direction to approach $z = 0$ determines how images get farther and farther from $w = 0$. We say that the origin $z = 0$ is mapped to the point at infinity $w = \infty$. As we take points in the z-plane farther and farther from the origin, images get closer and closer to $w = 0$. The direction in which they approach $w = 0$ is dictated by the manner in which we "approach" $z = \infty$. We say that the point at infinity $z = \infty$ is mapped to the origin $w = 0$.

Although the point at infinity can be brought into many topics in complex variables, we will confine it to situations where it provides a clear advantage to alternatives.

EXERCISES 2.2

In Exercises 1–4 find real and imaginary parts $u(x, y)$ and $v(x, y)$ for the function.

1. $f(z) = z^3 + 2z - 1$

2. $f(z) = (3z + 1)/(1 - z)$

3. $f(z) = z^2 \operatorname{Re} z + 2z$

4. $f(z) = z|z|/(z + i)$

It is sometimes more convenient to express the real and imaginary parts of a complex function $f(z) = u + vi$ in terms of the modulus r and argument θ of z. Do this in Exercises 5–6.

5. $f(z) = z^7 + 3z^6$

6. $f(z) = z^5/(z - 3)$

7. Show that for the function $w = f(z) = z^2 + z$:
   (a) Every vertical line $x = \operatorname{Re} z = x_0$ in the z-plane (except one) is mapped to a parabola in the w-plane. What is the one exception mapped to?
   (b) Every vertical line $u = \operatorname{Re} w = u_0$ in the w-plane (except one) is the image of a hyperbola in the z-plane. What is the exception?

8. Show that under reciprocation 2.6, real and imaginary parts of z and w are related by

$$x = \frac{u}{u^2 + v^2}, \qquad y = \frac{-v}{u^2 + v^2}.$$

In Exercises 9–14 use the expressions in Exercise 8 to verify the results under the reciprocation $w = 1/z$.

9. Points on the circle $|z - 1| = 1$ are mapped to points on the line $\operatorname{Re} w = 1/2$.

10. Points on the circle $|z - 4 + 3i| = 5$ are mapped to points on the line $8 \operatorname{Re} w + 6 \operatorname{Im} w = 1$.

11. Points on the line $2 \operatorname{Re} z + 3 \operatorname{Im} z = 1$ are mapped to points on the circle $|w - 1 + 3i/2| = \sqrt{13}/2$.

12. Points on the line $\operatorname{Re} z + 4 \operatorname{Im} z = 0$ are mapped to points on the line $\operatorname{Re} w - 4 \operatorname{Im} w = 0$.

13. Points on the circle $|z + 1| = 2$ are mapped to points on the circle $|w - 1/3| = 2/3$.

14. Points on the circle $|z - 2 + 3i| = 1$ are mapped to points on the circle $|w - 1/6 - i/4| = 1/12$.

15. Show that points on the circle $|z| = 1$ are mapped to points on a straight line by the bilinear mapping $w = 1/(z + 1)$.

16. Show that points on the circle $|z| = 4$ are mapped to points on a circle by the bilinear mapping $w = 1/(z + 2)$.

17. Show that points on the line $\operatorname{Re} z + 2 \operatorname{Im} z = 4$ are mapped to points on a straight line by the bilinear mapping $w = 3/(z - 4)$.

18. (a) Show that points on the circle $|z| = R$, where $R \neq 1$, are mapped to points on an ellipse by the mapping $w = f(z) = z + 1/z$.
   (b) Verify that points on $R = 1$ are mapped to points on a line segment.

19. Show that points on the circle $|z| = 1$ are mapped to points on two line segments by the mapping $w = z/(1 - z^2)$.

20. Show that points on the circle $|z| = 1$ are mapped to points on two line segments by the mapping $w = z/(1 + z^2)$.

21. Show that the reciprocation $w = 1/z$ maps:

(a) points on a straight line through $z = 0$ to a points on a straight line;

(b) points on a straight line not through $z = 0$ to points on a circle;

(c) points on a circle through $z = 0$ to points on a straight line;

(d) points on a circle not through $z = 0$ to points on a circle.

22. (a) Show that the quadratic function $w = f(z) = a^2 + bz + c$, where a, b, and c are real constants, maps vertical lines in the z-plane to parabolas in the w-plane (with one exception).

(b) Illustrate that part (a) is not generally true if a, b and c are complex, by examining $w = f(z) = (1 + 2i)z^2$.

23. Show that the function $w = f(z) = z^2/a^2 - 1$, where $a > 0$ is a constant, maps the loop of the lemniscate $r^2 = 2a^2 \cos 2\theta$, $-\pi/4 \leq \theta \leq \pi/4$ to the unit circle $|w| = 1$.

24. Show that the function $w = f(z) = z^2$, maps points $z = a + ae^{\theta i}$ on the circle $|z - a| = a$, where $a > 0$ is a constant, to points $w = Re^{\theta i}$ on the cardioid $R = 2a^2(1 + \cos \theta)$.

In Exercises 25–30 determine whether the expression can be written as a function $f(z)$ of $z = x + yi$.

25. $x^2 - 2xyi$

26. $(x^3 - 3xy^2) + (3x^2y - y^3)i$

27. $\dfrac{x}{x^2 + y^2} - \dfrac{yi}{x^2 + y^2}$

28. $\dfrac{x}{x^2 + y^2} + \dfrac{yi}{x^2 + y^2}$

29. $\dfrac{x^2 + x + y^2}{(x + 1)^2 + y^2} + \dfrac{yi}{(x + 1)^2 + y^2}$

30. $(x^2 + y^2)(x + yi)$

31. The Joukowski mapping, important in aeronautics, is

$$w = f(z) = z + \frac{a^2}{z}$$

where $a > 0$ is a constant.

(a) Show that points on circles $|z| = R \neq a$ are mapped to points on ellipses with foci $(\pm 2a, 0)$.

(b) Verify that points on the circle $|z| = a$ are mapped to points on the real axis in the w-plane?

§2.3   Limits and Continuity

Limits of complex functions are defined in exactly the same way as for real functions, but due to the two-dimensional nature of complex numbers, geometric interpretations are more reminiscent of limits of functions $f(x, y)$ of two real variables. Let S be an open set, and let z_0 be a point in S. Suppose that a complex function f is defined at every point in S except possibly at z_0. We say that f has limit L as z approaches z_0 if $f(z)$ can be made arbitrarily close to L by choosing z sufficiently close to z_0, but not equal to z_0. This is stated more precisely in the following definition.

Definition 2.8   A complex function f is said to have **limit** L as z approaches z_0, written

$$\lim_{z \to z_0} f(z) = L,$$

if given any $\epsilon > 0$, there exists a $\delta > 0$ such that $|f(z) - L| < \epsilon$ whenever $0 < |z - z_0| < \delta$.

What this definition demands geometrically is that given any circle of radius ϵ around the complex number L in the $w = f(z)$ plane (Figure 2.21), we must be able to find a circle with radius δ and centre z_0 such that whenever z is inside the circle at z_0, but not equal to z_0, $f(z)$ is defined and its value is inside the circle at L. Provided this can be done, no matter how small ϵ, then $f(z)$ must be getting closer to L as z gets closer to z_0, and $\lim_{z \to z_0} f(z) = L$.

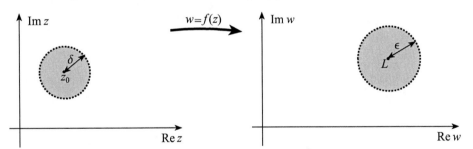

Figure 2.21

The limit of a real function $f(x)$ as x approaches x_0 must be independent of how x approaches x_0 along the x-axis. The same is true for the limit of $f(z)$ as z approaches z_0. Definition 2.8 implies that the limit of $f(z)$ is L as z approaches z_0 if, and only if, $f(z)$ approaches L for every possible mode of approach of z to z_0 (that remains in the domain of the definition of $f(z)$). But z could approach z_0 in many ways — along straight lines, parabolas, cubics, etc.

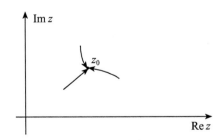

Figure 2.22

(Figure 2.22). Thus, even though $f(z)$ is a function of only one variable, the fact that z requires the complex plane for its specification implies that the geometric interpretation of the limit of $f(z)$ as $z \to z_0$ is analogous to the limit of a real function of two independent variables. It follows therefore that if $f(z)$ can be made to approach two different complex numbers for different modes of approach of z to z_0, then $\lim_{z \to z_0} f(z)$ does not exist.

Example 2.7   Find and verify $\lim\limits_{z\to 4+i}(2z+1+i)$.

Solution   As z approaches $4+i$, we feel that the function approaches $9+3i$, and therefore

$$\lim\limits_{z\to 4+i}(2z+1+i)=9+3i.$$

To verify that this is indeed true, we suppose that $\epsilon>0$ is any given real number, and consider finding $\delta>0$ so that

$$|(2z+1+i)-(9+3i)|<\epsilon$$

whenever $0<|z-(4+i)|<\delta$. Now,

$$|(2z+1+i)-(9+3i)|=|2z-8-2i|=2|z-(4+i)|.$$

Thus, if we choose $\delta=\epsilon/2$, then whenever $0<|z-(4+i)|<\delta$,

$$|(2z+1+i)-(9+3i)|=2|z-(4+i)|<2\left(\frac{\epsilon}{2}\right)=\epsilon.$$

This completes the proof that $\lim_{z\to 4+i}(2z+1+i)=9+3i$.•

Example 2.8   Find and verify $\lim\limits_{z\to 1+i}(z^2+2)$.

Solution   As z approaches $1+i$, it is anticipated that the function z^2+2 approaches $(1+i)^2+2$, and therefore

$$\lim\limits_{z\to 1+i}(z^2+2)=(1+i)^2+2=2+2i.$$

To verify that this is correct, we suppose that $\epsilon>0$ is any given real number, and consider finding $\delta>0$ such that

$$|(z^2+2)-(2+2i)|<\epsilon$$

whenever $0<|z-(1+i)|<\delta$. Now, $|(z^2+2)-(2+2i)|=|z^2-2i|$, and to find δ we must rework the z in z^2-2i into the combination $z-(1+i)$. To do this we note that $(z-1-i)^2=z^2-2(1+i)z+2i$, so that

$$\begin{aligned}
z^2-2i&=(z-1-i)^2+2(1+i)z-2i-2i\\
&=(z-1-i)^2+2(1+i)(z-1-i)+2(1+i)^2-4i\\
&=(z-1-i)^2+2(1+i)(z-1-i).
\end{aligned}$$

With triangle inequality 1.40, we may therefore write that

$$\begin{aligned}
|(z^2+2)-(2+2i)|=|z^2-2i|&=|(z-1-i)^2+2(1+i)(z-1-i)|\\
&\le|z-1-i|^2+2|1+i||z-1-i|\\
&=|z-1-i|^2+2\sqrt{2}|z-1-i|.
\end{aligned}$$

Suppose we set $p=|z-1-i|$, and consider finding p so that $p^2+2\sqrt{2}p<\epsilon$. Since $p^2+2\sqrt{2}p-\epsilon=0$ when

$$p=\frac{-2\sqrt{2}\pm\sqrt{8+4\epsilon}}{2}=\pm\sqrt{2+\epsilon}-\sqrt{2},$$

it follows that $p^2+2\sqrt{2}p<\epsilon$ whenever $0<p<\sqrt{2+\epsilon}-\sqrt{2}$. This means that

$$|z - 1 - i|^2 + 2\sqrt{2}|z - 1 - i| < \epsilon \quad \text{whenever} \quad 0 < |z - 1 - i| < \sqrt{2 + \epsilon} - \sqrt{2}.$$

Thus,

$$|(z^2 + 2) - (2 + 2i)| < \epsilon \quad \text{whenever} \quad 0 < |z - 1 - i| < \delta = \sqrt{2 + \epsilon} - \sqrt{2},$$

and this completes the proof that $\lim_{z \to 1+i} (z^2 + 2) = 2 + 2i.\bullet$

Verification of limits of functions using Definition 2.8 can lead to very complicated calculations — witness Example 2.8 wherein $z^2 + 2$ is a very simple function, yet the calculations were far from trivial. Imagine using Definition 2.8 to verify the limit of $f(z) = (z^2 + 3z + 2)/(z^3 + 3z - 5)$ as z approaches $2 - 3i$. It would also appear that in determining a potential candidate for the limit of $z^2 + 2$ as z approaches $1 + i$ in Example 2.8, we substituted $z = 1 + i$ into $z^2 + 2$. We know (from real calculus) and Definition 2.8 that this should not be done; taking limits and evaluations are distinctly different operations. When a real function $f(x)$ is continuous at $x = a$, we know that the limit of $f(x)$ as x approaches a is equal to $f(a)$. This suggests that we introduce continuity for complex functions. Before doing so, however, we consider an example wherein the function does not have a limit, and a basic theorem concerning limits of sums, differences, products, and quotients.

Example 2.9 Show that $\lim\limits_{z \to 0} \dfrac{\text{Re}(z^2)}{|z|^2}$ does not exist.

Solution If the limit of $\text{Re}(z^2)/|z|^2$ is to exist as $z \to 0$, then the function must approach the limit for all possible modes of approach of z to 0. On the other hand, if $\text{Re}(z^2)/|z|^2$ approaches different values depending on how z approaches 0, then the function has no limit as $z \to 0$. We illustrate that the latter is the case by letting $z \to 0$ along the real and imaginary axes. To approach $z = 0$ along the real axis, we set $z = x$ in which case

$$\lim_{z \to 0} \frac{\text{Re}(z^2)}{|z|^2} = \lim_{x \to 0} \frac{\text{Re}(x^2)}{|x|^2} = \lim_{x \to 0} \frac{x^2}{x^2} = 1.$$

When we approach $z = 0$ along the imaginary axis, we set $z = yi$,

$$\lim_{z \to 0} \frac{\text{Re}(z^2)}{|z|^2} = \lim_{y \to 0} \frac{\text{Re}(-y^2)}{|yi|^2} = \lim_{y \to 0} \frac{-y^2}{y^2} = -1.$$

Because $\text{Re}(z^2)/|z|^2$ approaches different values as $z \to 0$, depending on the mode of approach, we conclude that $\lim_{z \to 0} \text{Re}(z^2)/|z|^2$ does not exist.$\bullet$

The following theorem has its counterpart in real function theory. It allows us to break complicated limits into component parts.

Theorem 2.1 If $\lim\limits_{z \to z_0} f(z) = F$ and $\lim\limits_{z \to z_0} g(z) = G$, then

$$\text{(i)} \ \lim_{z \to z_0} [f(z) \pm g(z)] = F \pm G; \tag{2.13a}$$

$$\text{(ii)} \ \lim_{z \to z_0} [f(z)g(z)] = FG; \tag{2.13b}$$

$$\text{(iii)} \ \lim_{z \to z_0} \frac{f(z)}{g(z)} = \frac{F}{G}, \quad \text{provided } G \neq 0. \tag{2.13c}$$

Proof   We shall prove part (i) in the case of addition. The other three parts are verified in Exercises 44–46. Suppose $\epsilon > 0$ is any given real number. Since $\lim_{z \to z_0} f(z) = F$, there exists a $\delta_1 > 0$ such that whenever $0 < |z - z_0| < \delta_1$,

$$|f(z) - F| < \epsilon/2.$$

Similarly, there exists a $\delta_2 > 0$ such that whenever $0 < |z - z_0| < \delta_2$,

$$|g(z) - G| < \epsilon/2.$$

Now,

$$|[f(z) + g(z)] - (F + G)| = |[f(z) - F] + [g(z) - G]| \le |f(z) - F| + |g(z) - G|.$$

If we choose δ as the smaller of δ_1 and δ_2, then we can say that whenever $0 < |z - z_0| < \delta$,

$$|[f(z) + g(z)] - (F + G)| < \frac{\epsilon}{2} + \frac{\epsilon}{2} = \epsilon.$$

This proves that $\lim_{z \to z_0} [f(z) + g(z)] = F + G$. ∎

Example 2.10   Evaluate $\lim_{z \to 1-i} \dfrac{z - 1}{(z + 2i)\, \text{Im}\, z}$.

Solution   Since

$$\lim_{z \to 1-i} (z - 1) = -i, \qquad \lim_{z \to 1-i} (z + 2i) = 1 + i, \qquad \lim_{z \to 1-i} \text{Im}\, z = -1,$$

it follows by Theorem 2.1 that

$$\lim_{z \to 1-i} \frac{z - 1}{(z + 2i)\, \text{Im}\, z} = \frac{-i}{(1 + i)(-1)} = \frac{i}{1 + i} \frac{1 - i}{1 - i} = \frac{1}{2} + \frac{i}{2}. \bullet$$

The next theorem permits us to examine the limit of a complex function by considering limits of its real and imaginary parts. This has an advantage when the function is defined in the form $u(x, y) + v(x, y)i$ rather than in terms of z.

Theorem 2.2   If $f(z) = u(x, y) + v(x, y)i$, then $\lim_{z \to z_0} f(z)$ exists (where $z_0 = x_0 + y_0 i$) if, and only if,

$$\lim_{(x, y) \to (x_0, y_0)} u(x, y) \qquad \text{and} \qquad \lim_{(x, y) \to (x_0, y_0)} v(x, y)$$

both exist; and when these limits exist,

$$\lim_{z \to z_0} f(z) = \left[\lim_{(x, y) \to (x_0, y_0)} u(x, y) \right] + \left[\lim_{(x, y) \to (x_0, y_0)} v(x, y) \right] i. \qquad (2.14)$$

Proof   Suppose first of all that

$$\lim_{(x, y) \to (x_0, y_0)} u(x, y) = u_0 \qquad \text{and} \qquad \lim_{(x, y) \to (x_0, y_0)} v(x, y) = v_0.$$

Then given any $\epsilon > 0$, there exist constants δ_1 and δ_2 such that

$$|u(x, y) - u_0| < \epsilon/2 \qquad \text{whenever} \qquad 0 < \sqrt{(x - x_0)^2 + (y - y_0)^2} < \delta_1,$$

and

$$|v(x,y) - v_0| < \epsilon/2 \qquad \text{whenever} \qquad 0 < \sqrt{(x-x_0)^2 + (y-y_0)^2} < \delta_2.$$

Now,

$$\begin{aligned}
|f(z) - (u_0 + v_0 i)| &= |u(x,y) + v(x,y)i - u_0 - v_0 i| \\
&= |[u(x,y) - u_0] + [v(x,y) - v_0]i| \\
&\leq |u(x,y) - u_0| + |v(x,y) - v_0|.
\end{aligned}$$

If δ is the smaller of δ_1 and δ_2, then when $0 < |z - z_0| = \sqrt{(x-x_0)^2 + (y-y_0)^2} < \delta$, we can say that

$$|f(z) - (u_0 + v_0 i)| < \frac{\epsilon}{2} + \frac{\epsilon}{2} = \epsilon.$$

This shows that

$$\lim_{z \to z_0} f(z) = u_0 + v_0 i = \left[\lim_{(x,y) \to (x_0, y_0)} u(x,y) \right] + \left[\lim_{(x,y) \to (x_0, y_0)} v(x,y) \right] i.$$

Conversely, suppose that $\lim_{z \to z_0} f(z) = u_0 + v_0 i$. Given any $\epsilon > 0$, there exists a $\delta > 0$ such that whenever $0 < |z - z_0| < \delta$,

$$|f(z) - (u_0 + v_0 i)| = |[u(x,y) + v(x,y)i] - (u_0 + v_0 i)| = |[u(x,y) - u_0] + [v(x,y) - v_0]i| < \epsilon.$$

Thus, whenever $0 < |z - z_0| < \delta$,

$$\sqrt{[u(x,y) - u_0]^2 + [v(x,y) - v_0]^2} < \epsilon.$$

Since $|u(x,y) - u_0| < \sqrt{[u(x,y) - u_0]^2 + [v(x,y) - v_0]^2}$, it follows that whenever $0 < |z - z_0| = \sqrt{(x-x_0)^2 + (y-y_0)^2} < \delta$,

$$|u(x,y) - u_0| < \epsilon;$$

that is, $\lim_{(x,y) \to (x_0, y_0)} u(x,y) = u_0$. Similarly, $\lim_{(x,y) \to (x_0, y_0)} v(x,y) = v_0$. ∎

Example 2.11 Given that $\sin x \cosh y + \cos x \sinh y \, i$ is a function of $z = x + yi$, evaluate its limit as $z \to 2 - 3i$, if it exists.

Solution Since

$$\lim_{(x,y) \to (2,-3)} \sin x \cosh y = \sin 2 \cosh(-3) = \sin 2 \cosh 3,$$

and

$$\lim_{(x,y) \to (2,-3)} \cos x \sinh y = \cos 2 \sinh(-3) = -\cos 2 \sinh 3,$$

it follows by Theorem 2.2 that

$$\lim_{z \to 2-3i} (\sin x \cosh y + \cos x \sinh y \, i) = \sin 2 \cosh 3 - \cos 2 \sinh 3 \, i \approx 9.15 + 4.16i. \bullet$$

Definition 2.9 A complex function f is said to be continuous at $z = z_0$ if

$$\lim_{z \to z_0} f(z) = f(z_0). \tag{2.15}$$

The function is said to be continuous on an open set if it is continuous at each point in the set.

As for real functions, this definition imposes three conditions on the function f:

(1) f must be defined at z_0;

(2) the limit of f as $z \to z_0$ must exist;

(3) the numbers in (1) and (2) must be identical.

According to the following theorem, continuous functions can be added, subtracted, multiplied, and divided; its proof is a straightforward application of Theorem 2.1.

Theorem 2.3   If $f(z)$ and $g(z)$ are continuous at z_0, then so also are the functions

$$f(z) \pm g(z), \quad f(z)g(z), \quad f(z)/g(z),$$

provided in the quotient case that $g(z_0) \neq 0$.

As a result of this theorem, we can state that polynomials, functions of the form $P_n(z) = a_n z^n + a_{n-1} z^{n-1} + \cdots + a_1 z + a_0$ where n is a nonnegative integer and the a_j $(j = 0, \ldots, n)$ are complex constants, are continous functions in the whole complex plane. Rational functions, functions of the form $P(z)/Q(z)$ where $P(z)$ and $Q(z)$ are polynomials, are continuous except where $Q(z) = 0$.

Example 2.12   Find $\lim\limits_{z \to 2-i} \dfrac{z^2 + 3z + i}{2z - 4i}$.

Solution   Since the rational function $(z^2 + 3z + i)/(2z - 4i)$ is continuous at $z = 2 - i$, the limit is equal to the value of the function at $z = 2 - i$,

$$\lim_{z \to 2-i} \frac{z^2 + 3z + i}{2z - 4i} = \frac{(2-i)^2 + 3(2-i) + i}{2(2-i) - 4i} = \frac{9 - 6i}{4 - 6i} = \frac{9 - 6i}{4 - 6i} \frac{4 + 6i}{4 + 6i} = \frac{72 + 30i}{52}$$
$$= \frac{36 + 15i}{26}. \bullet$$

Example 2.13   The function $f(z) = (z^2 + 1)/(z - i)$ is discontinuous at $z = i$. Can it be assigned a value at $z = i$ to make it continuous there?

Solution   Since $\lim\limits_{z \to i} \dfrac{z^2 + 1}{z - i} = \lim\limits_{z \to i} \dfrac{(z+i)(z-i)}{z - i} = \lim\limits_{z \to i} (z + i) = 2i$, if we define $f(i) = 2i$, the function becomes continuous for all z including $z = i$. We say that $f(z)$ has a **removable discontinuity** at $z = i$. $\bullet$

Example 2.14   Find discontinuities of the function $\operatorname{Arg} z$, and determine whether they are removable.

Solution   The function $\operatorname{Arg} z$ takes the principal value of the argument of a complex number. The value of $\operatorname{Arg} z$ at every point on the negative real axis is π, but its limit as z approaches a point on the negative real axis does not exist. As z approaches z_0 along the curve C in Figure 2.23, $\operatorname{Arg} z$ approaches π, whereas it approaches $-\pi$ along the curve C'. Consequently $\operatorname{Arg} z$ is discontinuous at every point on the negative real axis, and these discontinuities are not removable. $\operatorname{Arg} z$

is undefined at $z = 0$. This discontinuity is not removable either since $\lim_{z \to 0} \operatorname{Arg} z$ does not exist. To see this suppose we let z approach 0 along the positive real axis. Then $z = x$, and

$$\lim_{z \to 0} \operatorname{Arg} z = \lim_{x \to 0^+} \operatorname{Arg}(x) = \lim_{x \to 0^+} (0) = 0.$$

But if z approaches 0 along the positive imaginary axis, then $z = yi$ $(y > 0)$, and

$$\lim_{z \to 0} \operatorname{Arg} z = \lim_{y \to 0^+} \operatorname{Arg}(yi) = \lim_{y \to 0^+} (\pi/2) = \pi/2.$$

Other modes of approach lead to other values. Thus, $\operatorname{Arg} z$ is discontinuous at $z = 0$ and every point on the negative real axis, and none of the discontinuities are removable.•

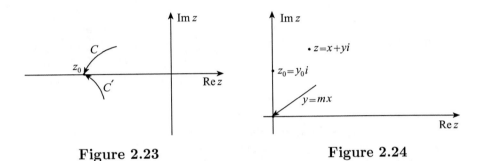

Figure 2.23   **Figure 2.24**

Example 2.15   Determine whether discontinuities of $f(z) = \operatorname{Im} z / \operatorname{Re} z$ are removable.

Solution   The functions $\operatorname{Re} z$ and $\operatorname{Im} z$ which take real and imaginary parts of complex numbers are continuous for all z. It follows (by Theorem 2.3) that $f(z)$ is continuous for all z with $\operatorname{Re} z \neq 0$. The function is discontinuous at all points on the imaginary axis (where $\operatorname{Re} z = 0$) because $f(z)$ is undefined there. Each such discontinuity is removable if $f(z)$ has a limit as z approaches the discontinuity. Consider then whether the limit of $f(z)$ exists as z approaches a point $z_0 = y_0 i$ on the imaginary axis (Figure 2.24). For any point $z = x + yi$ close to z_0,

$$f(z) = \frac{\operatorname{Im} z}{\operatorname{Re} z} = \frac{y}{x}.$$

When $y_0 \neq 0$, the limit of this function as $x \to 0$ does not exist. In other words, discontinuities $z = y_0 i$ where $y_0 \neq 0$ are not removable. Consider now the discontinuity $z = 0$. If we approach $z = 0$ along the line $y = mx$, then

$$\lim_{z \to 0} f(z) = \lim_{x \to 0} \frac{mx}{x} = m.$$

Because $f(z)$ approaches different numbers as $z \to 0$, depending on the mode of approach of z to 0, we conclude that $\lim_{z \to 0} f(z)$ does not exist; that is, $z = 0$ is not a removable discontinuity. Thus, no discontinuity of $f(z)$ is removable.•

Example 2.16   Where is $f(z) = (\operatorname{Arg} z)^2$ discontinuous? Are discontinuities removable?

Solution   Since the only discontinuities of $\operatorname{Arg} z$ are $z = 0$ and points on the negative real axis, these are the only potential discontinuities for $f(z)$. Certainly $z = 0$ is a discontinuity as $f(0)$ is undefined. This discontinuity is not removable since $\lim_{z\to 0}(\operatorname{Arg} z)^2$ does not exist. For any point z_0 on the negative real axis, however,

$$f(z_0) = \pi^2 = \lim_{z\to z_0} f(z),$$

and $f(z)$ is continuous at z_0. •

Example 2.17   Does the function $f(z) = (z+1)\operatorname{Arg} z$ have any discontinuities? Are they removable?

Solution   Because $z + 1$ is continuous for all z, and $\operatorname{Arg} z$ is continuous for all z except $z = 0$ and points on the negative real axis, it follows (by Theorem 2.3) that $f(z) = (z + 1)\operatorname{Arg} z$ is continuous for all z except possibly $z = 0$ and points on the negative real axis. Since $f(0)$ is undefined, $f(z)$ is discontinuous at $z = 0$. This discontinuity is not removable since $\lim_{z\to 0}(z+1)\operatorname{Arg} z$ does not exist. (If $\lim_{z\to 0}(z+1)\operatorname{Arg} z$ were to exist, then part (iii) of Theorem 2.1 could be used with $\lim_{z\to 0}(z+1) = 1$ to prove that $\lim_{z\to 0}\operatorname{Arg} z$ exists, a fact that is not true.) For any point z_0 on the negative real axis, except $z = -1$, $\lim_{z\to z_0}(z+1) = z_0 + 1$, but $\lim_{z\to z_0}\operatorname{Arg} z$ does not exist. It follows that $\lim_{z\to z_0} f(z)$ does not exist, and $f(z)$ has a discontinuity at z_0 that is not removable. This leaves only the point $z = -1$. Because $f(-1) = 0$, continuity of $f(z)$ at $z = -1$ comes down to the existence of $\lim_{z\to -1} f(z)$. Although $\lim_{z\to -1}\operatorname{Arg} z$ does not exist, the fact that $\lim_{z\to -1}(z+1) = 0$ implies that $\lim_{z\to -1} f(z) = 0$. To prove this, we use Definition 2.8. Suppose $\epsilon > 0$ is given. Because the maximum value of $\operatorname{Arg} z$ is π, consider all points z satisfying $0 < |z + 1| < \delta = \epsilon/\pi$ (Figure 2.25). For all such z,

$$|f(z) - 0| = |(z+1)\operatorname{Arg} z| \leq |z+1|\pi < \frac{\epsilon}{\pi}\pi = \epsilon.$$

Thus, $\lim_{z\to -1} f(z) = 0$, and $f(z)$ is continuous at $z = -1$. The function $f(z) = (z + 1)\operatorname{Arg} z$ is therefore discontinuous at $z = 0$ and every point on the negative real axis except $z = -1$. •

Theorem 2.3 implies that continuity of a complex function can be discussed in terms of continuity of its real and imaginary parts.

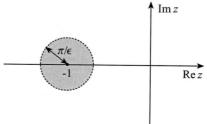

Figure 2.25

Theorem 2.4   A function $f(z) = u(x, y) + v(x, y)i$ is continuous at $z_0 = x_0 + y_0 i$ if and only if $u(x, y)$ and $v(x, y)$ are continuous at (x_0, y_0).

For example, the complex function $f(z) = \cos x \cosh y - \sin x \sinh y\, i$ is continuous at every point in the complex plane since its real and imaginary parts are continuous everywhere in the xy-plane.

Branches, Branch Points, and Branch Cuts

Each of $\operatorname{Re} z$, $\operatorname{Im} z$, $|z|$, and $\operatorname{Arg} z$ is a function. To each value of z in their domains, they assign a single value. Compare this with $f(z) = \arg z$; it is not a (single-valued) function. With every complex number $z \neq 0$, $f(z)$ associates an infinity of values, the arguments of z. We say that $f(z)$ is a **multiple-valued function**. It makes no sense to discuss continuity of multiple-valued functions; nor will it make sense to differentiate them or integrate them. These concepts can only be applied to single-valued functions. As a result, when confronted with a multiple-valued function, it is customary to create single-valued functions from it. This has already been done for $\arg z$. The function $\text{Arg}\, z$ is a single-valued function, derived from $\arg z$, by restricting the range of the function to the interval $-\pi < \text{Arg}\, z \leq \pi$. There are many other ways to do this, however; restrict the range to any half-open interval of length 2π. For example, the function $\arg z$, $0 \leq \arg z < 2\pi$ is single-valued in its domain (all $z \neq 0$). So also is $\arg z$, $\pi/4 < \arg z \leq 9\pi/4$.

To denote some of the most frequently used single-valued functions derived from $\arg z$, we introduce the following notation:

$$\arg_\phi z = \arg z, \quad \text{where } \phi < \arg z \leq \phi + 2\pi. \tag{2.16}$$

We could also define functions where the interval is closed on the left and open on the right. These are not necessary, however, as the functions in equation 2.16 suffice for our purposes, with one exception. When $\phi = 0$, it is commonplace to use the interval $0 \leq \arg z < 2\pi$, and we therefore adopt the convention that $0 \leq \arg_0 z < 2\pi$.

Each of these functions is single-valued. Each has a half-line eminating from the origin along which the function is not continuous. For example, the function $\text{Arg}\, z$ is discontinuous at $z = 0$ and along the negative real axis. The functions $\arg_{\pi/2}(z)$ and $\arg_{5\pi/2}(z)$ are discontinous at $z = 0$ and along the positive imaginary axis.

Each of the functions in 2.16 is called a **branch** of the multiple-valued function $\arg z$. The half-line along which a branch is discontinuous is called the **branch cut** of the branch, and the point $z = 0$ at which all branch cuts meet is called the **branch point** of the multiple-valued function $\arg z$.

In summary, branches of a multiple-valued function are single-valued functions derived from the multiple-valued function by restricting its range. Each branch is continuous except along its branch cut (which includes the branch point).

EXERCISES 2.3

1. Why are the functions $\arg_\phi z$ discontinuous at the branch point $z = 0$?

2. Why are the functions $\arg_\phi z$ discontinuous at points on their branch cuts (excluding the branch point $z = 0$)?

In Exercises 3–22 evaluate the limit, if it exists.

3. $\lim\limits_{z \to 2-i} (z^2 + 3)$

4. $\lim\limits_{z \to i} \dfrac{z^2 - 1}{z + i}$

5. $\lim\limits_{z \to -3i} \dfrac{z^7 + 4}{1 - z}$

6. $\lim\limits_{z \to 0} \dfrac{\text{Im}\, z}{z}$

7. $\lim\limits_{z \to 1} (z - 1)\,\text{Re}\,(z - 1)$

8. $\lim\limits_{z \to 1} \text{Arg}\, z$

9. $\lim\limits_{z \to -1} \text{Arg}\, z$

10. $\lim\limits_{z \to 0} z\,\text{Arg}\, z$

11. $\lim\limits_{z \to 3i} \arg_{\pi/2} z$

12. $\lim\limits_{z \to 3i} \arg_{-3\pi/2} z$

13. $\lim\limits_{z \to 3i} \arg_3 z$

14. $\lim\limits_{z \to 4} \arg_0 z$

15. $\lim_{z \to 4} \arg_{-2\pi} z$

16. $\lim_{z \to 4} \arg_5 z$

17. $\lim_{z \to 1+i} \arg_{\pi/4} z$

18. $\lim_{z \to 1+i} \arg_{9\pi/4} z$

19. $\lim_{z \to 1+i} \arg_{-8} z$

20. $\lim_{z \to 3+i} \arg_0(z - 1)$

21. $\lim_{z \to 1-i} \arg_{2\pi}(3 - z)$

22. $\lim_{z \to (-1+i)/2} \arg_{-2\pi}(2z + 3)$

In Exercises 23–38 find the largest domain (open, connected set) in which the function is continuous.

23. $f(z) = \dfrac{1}{z + 1}$

24. $f(z) = \dfrac{z^2 + 2}{z^2 + 3z + 8}$

25. $f(z) = \dfrac{z^3 + 2z}{z^4 + 1}$

26. $f(z) = e^x(\cos y + \sin y\, i)$

27. $f(z) = \sin x \cosh y + \cos x \sinh y\, i$

28. $f(z) = \cos y \cosh x + \sin y \sinh x\, i$

29. $f(z) = \operatorname{Re} z$

30. $f(z) = |z|$

31. $f(z) = \dfrac{z}{|z|}$

32. $f(z) = \operatorname{Arg} z$

33. $f(z) = \arg_0 z$

34. $f(z) = \arg_{-\pi/2} z$

35. $f(z) = \arg_3(z - 1)$

36. $f(z) = \arg_{-4}(z + 2i)$

37. $f(z) = (z - 2)\arg_0 z$

38. $f(z) = (z^2 + 4)\arg_{\pi/2} z$

39. Show that the function $f(z) = \ln|z| + (\operatorname{Arg} z)\, i$ is discontinuous at $z = 0$ and all points on the negative real axis.

40. Show that the function $f(z) = \sqrt{r}e^{\theta i/2}$, where $z = re^{\theta i}$, $-\pi < \theta \le \pi$, is discontinuous at all points on the negative real axis. Is it continuous at $z = 0$?

41. Can a value be assigned to the function $f(z) = \dfrac{z^2 + 4}{z + 2i}$ at $z = -2i$ in order that the function be continuous for all z?

42. Repeat Exercise 41 for the function $f(z) = \dfrac{z^2 + 9}{z + 2i}$.

43. Find all points at which the function $f(z) = \begin{cases} z + 2, & |z| \le 1 \\ |z|, & |z| > 1 \end{cases}$ is discontinuous.

In Exercises 44–46 we use Definition 2.8 to prove Theorem 2.1. In each exercise assume that $\lim_{z \to z_0} f(z) = F$ and $\lim_{z \to z_0} g(z) = G$.

44. Show that given any $\epsilon > 0$, there exist numbers $\delta_1 > 0$ and $\delta_2 > 0$ such that

$$|f(z) - F| < \epsilon/2 \quad \text{whenever } 0 < |z - z_0| < \delta_1, \quad \text{and}$$
$$|g(z) - G| < \epsilon/2 \quad \text{whenever } 0 < |z - z_0| < \delta_2.$$

Use these results along with inequality 1.40 to prove part (i) of Theorem 2.1 in the subtraction case.

45. (a) Verify that

$$|f(z)g(z) - FG| \le |f(z)||g(z) - G| + |G||f(z) - F|.$$

(b) Show that given any $\epsilon > 0$, there exist numbers $\delta_1 > 0$, $\delta_2 > 0$, and $\delta_3 > 0$ such that

$$|f(z)| < |F| + 1 \quad \text{whenever } 0 < |z - z_0| < \delta_1,$$

$$|g(z) - G| < \frac{\epsilon}{2(|F| + 1)} \quad \text{whenever } 0 < |z - z_0| < \delta_2,$$

$$|f(z) - F| < \frac{\epsilon}{2|G| + 1} \quad \text{whenever } 0 < |z - z_0| < \delta_3.$$

(c) Use these results to prove part (ii) of Theorem 2.1.

46. (a) Verify that when $G \neq 0$,

$$\left| \frac{f(z)}{g(z)} - \frac{F}{G} \right| \leq \frac{|f(z) - F|}{|g(z)|} + \frac{|F||G - g(z)|}{|G||g(z)|}.$$

(b) Show that given any $\epsilon > 0$, there exist numbers $\delta_1 > 0$, $\delta_2 > 0$, and $\delta_3 > 0$ such that

$$|g(z)| > \frac{|G|}{2} \quad \text{whenever } 0 < |z - z_0| < \delta_1,$$

$$|f(z) - F| < \frac{\epsilon |G|}{4} \quad \text{whenever } 0 < |z - z_0| < \delta_2,$$

$$|g(z) - G| < \frac{\epsilon |G|^2}{4|F| + 1} \quad \text{whenever } 0 < |z - z_0| < \delta_3.$$

(c) Now prove part (iii) of Theorem 2.1.

§2.4   Derivatives of Complex Functions

We are now ready to take up the main topic of study in this chapter; differentiation of complex functions. Although the derivative of a complex function has the same algebraic definition as the derivative of a real function, we shall find that existence of the derivative of a complex function has far-reaching consequences that have no counterpart in real analysis. Much of our work in succeeding chapters is an investigation of these consequences.

Definition 2.10   The **derivative** of a complex function f with respect to z at z_0 is defined as

$$f'(z_0) = \lim_{\Delta z \to 0} \frac{f(z_0 + \Delta z) - f(z_0)}{\Delta z}, \tag{2.17}$$

provided the limit exists. If the limit exists, f is said to be **differentiable** at the point z_0.

When a function f is differentiable at a point z_0, then it is continuous at z_0. This is most easily proved by multiplying both sides of equation 2.17 by $\lim_{\Delta z \to 0} \Delta z$,

$$f'(z_0) \left[\lim_{\Delta z \to 0} \Delta z \right] = \left[\lim_{\Delta z \to 0} \frac{f(z_0 + \Delta z) - f(z_0)}{\Delta z} \right] \left[\lim_{\Delta z \to 0} \Delta z \right].$$

Since $\lim_{\Delta z \to 0} \Delta z = 0$, the left side vanishes, and property 2.13b for limits allows us to bring the product of the limits on the right to the limit of a product,

$$0 = \lim_{\Delta z \to 0} \left[\frac{f(z_0 + \Delta z) - f(z_0)}{\Delta z} \Delta z \right] = \lim_{\Delta z \to 0} [f(z_0 + \Delta z) - f(z_0)].$$

This can be rewritten as

$$\lim_{\Delta z \to 0} f(z_0 + \Delta z) = f(z_0),$$

and this is equivalent to condition 2.15 for continuity of $f(z)$ at z_0.

The converse is not necessarily true. Continuous functions need not be differentiable. For example, the function $\operatorname{Re} z$ is continuous everywhere, but we show (in Example 2.20) that it is nowhere differentiable.

In the analysis of limit 2.17, it is necessary to restrict Δz so that $z_0 + \Delta z$ remains within the domain of definition of $f(z)$. For example, suppose $f(z)$ is defined at all points inside and on the rectangle in Figure 2.26. For the derivative at the point z_0 on the upper edge of the rectangle, the imaginary part of Δz must be less than or equal to zero. Only then will $z_0 + \Delta z$ be in the rectangle and $f(z_0 + \Delta z)$ be defined. In other words, special treatment of limit 2.17 is required whenever z_0 is on the edge of the rectangle,

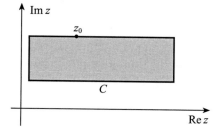

Figure 2.26

be it the sides, the top, or the bottom. To eliminate such discussions, we only calculate derivatives of $f(z)$ at points interior to the rectangle. More generally, if a function $f(z)$ is defined at points interior to and on a curve C, then $f'(z)$ is only considered at points interior to C. This restriction is automatically accomplished if the domain of definition of $f(z)$ is an open set. This is captured in the following definition.

Definition 2.11 A complex function f is said to be **analytic** (regular, or holomorphic) in an open set S if it has a derivative at every point of S.

The theory of complex functions is a study of the properties of analytic functions. In other words, differentiability on a point-by-point basis is replaced by differentiability in open sets.

It is convenient, however, to define analyticity at a point.

Definition 2.12 A complex function f is said to be **analytic at a point** z if it is analytic in some neighbourhood of z.

Differentiability is a point concept; analyticity is differentiability at all points in an open set. Even in Definition 2.12, analyticity at a point means differentiability in a circle around the point.

Definition 2.13 A function which is analytic in the whole complex plane is said to be an **entire** function.

The fact that differentiability implies continuity gives us our first property of analytic functions.

Theorem 2.5 If a complex function f is analytic in an open set S, then f is continuous in S.

When we drop the subscript in equation 2.17, we obtain

$$f'(z) = \lim_{\Delta z \to 0} \frac{f(z + \Delta z) - f(z)}{\Delta z}, \tag{2.18}$$

the derivative of f at the point z. We call the function f' defined by 2.18 the derivative function. As might be expected from equation 2.18, derivatives of complex functions can be calculated in much the same way as derivatives of real functions. In particular, we have the usual rules:

$$[f(z) + g(z)]' = f'(z) + g'(z) \quad \text{(sum rule)}; \tag{2.19a}$$

$$[f(z)g(z)]' = f'(z)g(z) + f(z)g'(z) \quad \text{(product rule)}; \tag{2.19b}$$

$$\left[\frac{f(z)}{g(z)}\right]' = \frac{g(z)f'(z) - f(z)g'(z)}{[g(z)]^2} \quad \text{(quotient rule)}; \tag{2.19c}$$

$$\{[f(z)]^n\}' = n[f(z)]^{n-1}f'(z) \quad \text{(power rule)}; \tag{2.19d}$$

if $w = f(\zeta)$ and $\zeta = g(z)$,

$$\frac{dw}{dz} = \frac{dw}{d\zeta}\frac{d\zeta}{dz} \quad \text{(chain rule)}. \tag{2.19e}$$

The sum and power rules guarantee that polynomials are entire functions. Because of the quotient rule, rational functions are analytic in open sets which do not contain points at which denominators vanish. Other than these functions, we have encountered $\operatorname{Re} z$, $\operatorname{Im} z$, $|z|$, and $\operatorname{Arg} z$. We shall discuss analyticity for these functions shortly. This represents the totality of complex functions with which we are familiar, a very limited source of examples to illustrate the theory of this chapter. In Chapter 3, we rectify this situation when we introduce exponential and logarithm functions, trigonometric and inverse trigonometric, hyperbolic and inverse hyperbolic, and root functions.

Example 2.18 Find derivatives for the following functions:

$$\text{(a)} \quad f(z) = \left(z^2 + \frac{1}{z}\right)^3 \qquad \text{(b)} \quad f(z) = \frac{z^2 + 2}{i - 3z}$$

In what open sets are the functions analytic?

Solution (a) With power rule 2.19d,

$$f'(z) = 3\left(z^2 + \frac{1}{z}\right)^2\left(2z - \frac{1}{z^2}\right).$$

Since this is defined for all $z \neq 0$, the function is analytic in any open set that does not contain the point $z = 0$.
(b) With quotient rule 2.19c,

$$f'(z) = \frac{(i - 3z)(2z) - (z^2 + 2)(-3)}{(i - 3z)^2} = \frac{-3z^2 + 2iz + 6}{(i - 3z)^2}.$$

Since f' exists at all points except $z = i/3$, the function f is analytic in any open set that does not contain the point $z = i/3$.●

Everything seems to be unfolding very smoothly. With the sum, product, quotient, power, and chain rules, it seems that differentiation of complex functions is an easy process; it's just like real calculus. Not so fast; this may not always be the case. For instance, are the functions $\operatorname{Re} z$, $\operatorname{Im} z$, $|z|$, and $\operatorname{Arg} z$ analytic? The differentiation rules in equations 2.19 do not apply to these functions. Certainly we could return to the definition of the derivative to determine whether these functions are differentiable, but we shall find a better way shortly. In addition, a complex function f may be specified in terms of its real and imaginary parts, rather than in terms of z; that is, it may be given in the form $f(z) = u(x, y) + v(x, y)i$. For example, $f(z)$ might be

$$f(z) = \left(x + \frac{x}{x^2 + y^2}\right) + \left(y - \frac{y}{x^2 + y^2}\right)i.$$

When f is defined in this way, how shall we calculate f', or even know that f' exists? One method is to find $f(z)$ in terms of z, and then utilize differentiation rules 2.19; this could be very complicated. In addition, let us not forget a major question that surfaced in Section 2.2. Under what conditions does a complex combination $u(x, y) + v(x, y)i$ of real functions $u(x, y)$ and $v(x, y)$ define a function $f(z)$ of $z = x + yi$? Both of these questions are answered in Theorem 2.6, the most important theorem in this chapter. Because the theorem is quite complicated, intricately using equation 2.18 for the derivative of a function, a few remarks concerning this definition are worthwhile at this juncture.

What is Δz in equation 2.18? Analogous to $x + \Delta x$ in the definition for the real derivative $f'(x) = \lim_{\Delta x \to 0}[f(x + \Delta x) - f(x)]/\Delta x$, we think of $z + \Delta z$ as a complex number close to z (Figure 2.27). Quantity Δz is a complex number, the difference between $z + \Delta z$ and z. It has real and imaginary parts that we denote by $\Delta z = \Delta x + \Delta y\, i$ so that $z + \Delta z = (x + yi) + (\Delta x + \Delta y\, i) = (x + \Delta x) + (y + \Delta y)i$.

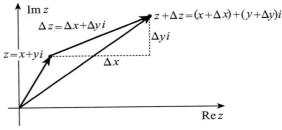

Figure 2.27

For Δz to approach 0 in equation 2.18, we must have $\Delta x \to 0$ and $\Delta y \to 0$. How Δx and Δy approach 0 dictates how $z + \Delta z$ approaches z. For example, if we set $\Delta x = 0$, then $\Delta z = \Delta y\, i$, and $z + \Delta z$ approaches z along the vertical line through z (Figure 2.28a). If we set $\Delta y = 0$, then $\Delta z = \Delta x$, and $z + \Delta z$ approaches z along the horizontal line through z (Figure 2.28b). With $\Delta x = \Delta y$, we have $\Delta z = \Delta x + \Delta x\, i = (1 + i)\Delta x$, and the mode of approach of $z + \Delta z$ to z is along a line through z making an angle of $\pi/4$ radians with the horizontal (Figure 2.28c).

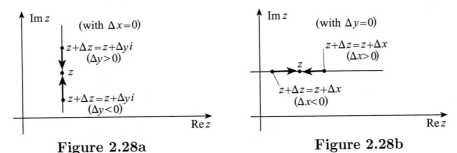

Figure 2.28a   **Figure 2.28b**

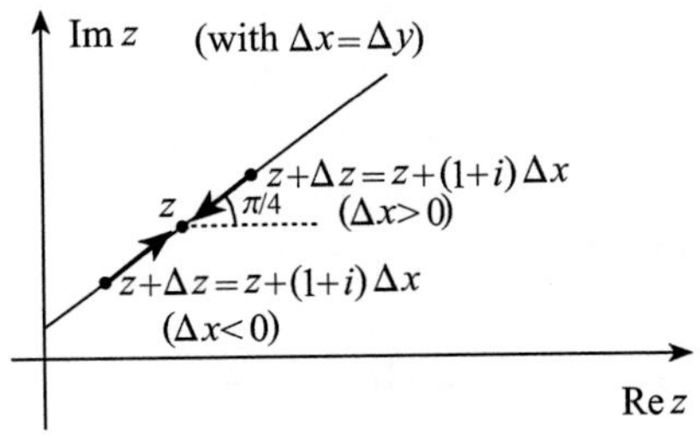

Figure 2.28c

Derivative f' exists if and only if limit 2.18 exists and is the same for all modes of approach of $z + \Delta z$ to z, be it vertical, horizontal, or any other mode, straight line, or otherwise.

The following theorem contains what are perhaps the two most important equations in complex analysis.

Theorem 2.6   A function $f(z) = u(x, y) + v(x, y)i$ is analytic in an open set S if and only if the first partial derivatives of $u(x, y)$ and $v(x, y)$ are continuous in S and satisfy the Cauchy-Riemann equations therein

$$\frac{\partial u}{\partial x} = \frac{\partial v}{\partial y}, \qquad \frac{\partial v}{\partial x} = -\frac{\partial u}{\partial y}. \tag{2.20}$$

Because the proof of this theorem is quite lengthy, we have placed it in Appendix A at the end of the section. Readers who wish to cover it now may do so, and readers who would prefer not to interrupt the flow of the discussion can defer its consideration until later. Do not, however, interpret this to mean that consideration of the proof is optional; it is essential that all readers study the proof before leaving this section.

Theorem 2.6 is most important; the Cauchy-Riemann equations are fundamental to all complex analysis. From the proof of the theorem, we also obtain two formulas for calculating f' when f is specified in terms of its real and imaginary parts.

Corollary   When $f(z) = u(x,y) + v(x,y)i$, and $f'(z)$ exists,

$$f'(z) = \frac{\partial u}{\partial x} + \frac{\partial v}{\partial x}i = \frac{\partial v}{\partial y} - \frac{\partial u}{\partial y}i. \tag{2.21}$$

Thus, when a complex function is specified in terms of z, we calculate its derivative using differentiation rules 2.19; when the function is specified in terms of its real and imaginary parts, we may calculate its derivative with formulas 2.21.

Theorem 2.6 also emphasizes a fact that we pointed out in Section 2.2, namely that real and imaginary parts of a complex function are not independent; they satisfy the Cauchy-Riemann equations. Furthermore, we now have an answer to the question, "Under what conditions does a complex combination $u(x,y) + v(x,y)i$ of real functions $u(x,y)$ and $v(x,y)$ constitute a complex function $f(z)$ of $z = x + yi$?" They constitute an analytic function in some open set S when partial derivatives of $u(x,y)$ and $v(x,y)$ are continuous and satisfy the Cauchy-Riemann equations in S. For example, partial derivatives of the real and imaginary parts of $u(x,y) + v(x,y)i = (x^2 - y^2) + 2xyi$ are continuous and satisfy the Cauchy-Riemann equations in the whole complex plane. This is therefore an entire function of $z = x + yi$. It is in fact the function $f(z) = z^2$. On the other hand, real and imaginary parts of $u + vi = x - yi$ do not satisfy the Cauchy-Riemann equations anywhere. Thus, $u + vi = x - yi$ is a complex-valued function of x and y, but it is not an analytic function of $z = x + yi$.

Example 2.19   Determine all open sets in which $f(z) = \left(x + \dfrac{x}{x^2 + y^2}\right) + \left(y - \dfrac{y}{x^2 + y^2}\right)i$ is analytic.

Solution   For this function, $u(x,y) = x + x/(x^2 + y^2)$ and $v(x,y) = y - y/(x^2 + y^2)$, and therefore

$$\frac{\partial u}{\partial x} = 1 + \frac{1}{x^2 + y^2} + \frac{-2x^2}{(x^2 + y^2)^2} = 1 + \frac{y^2 - x^2}{(x^2 + y^2)^2}; \qquad \frac{\partial u}{\partial y} = \frac{-2xy}{(x^2 + y^2)^2}$$

$$\frac{\partial v}{\partial x} = \frac{2xy}{(x^2 + y^2)^2}; \qquad \frac{\partial v}{\partial y} = 1 - \frac{1}{x^2 + y^2} - \frac{-2y^2}{(x^2 + y^2)^2} = 1 + \frac{y^2 - x^2}{(x^2 + y^2)^2}$$

Since these partial derivatives are continuous and satisfy the Cauchy-Riemann equations at every point except $(0,0)$, $f(z)$ is analytic in any open set not containing $z = 0$. Its derivative is

$$f'(z) = \frac{\partial u}{\partial x} + \frac{\partial v}{\partial x}i = \left[1 + \frac{y^2 - x^2}{(x^2 + y^2)^2}\right] + \frac{2xyi}{(x^2 + y^2)^2}.\bullet$$

Example 2.20 Show that there are no open sets in which the functions

(a) $f(z) = |z|$ (b) $f(z) = \operatorname{Re} z$ (c) $f(z) = \operatorname{Im} z$ (d) $f(z) = \operatorname{Arg} z$ (e) $f(z) = \arg_\phi z$

are analytic.

Solution (a) Even though $f(z) = |z|$ is specified in terms of z, differentiation rules 2.19 are not applicable. We therefore resort to the Cauchy-Riemann equations. With $f(z) = |z| = \sqrt{x^2 + y^2}$, we have $u(x,y) = \sqrt{x^2 + y^2}$ and $v(x,y) = 0$. Thus,

$$\frac{\partial u}{\partial x} = \frac{x}{\sqrt{x^2 + y^2}}; \qquad \frac{\partial u}{\partial y} = \frac{y}{\sqrt{x^2 + y^2}}; \qquad \frac{\partial v}{\partial x} = \frac{\partial v}{\partial y} = 0.$$

Since the Cauchy-Riemann equations are never satisfied, there are no open sets in which $f(z) = |z|$ is analytic.

(b) For $f(z) = \operatorname{Re} z = x$, we obtain $\partial u/\partial x = 1$ and $\partial v/\partial y = 0$, and therefore $f(z)$ is nowhere analytic.

(c) For $f(z) = \operatorname{Im} z = y$, we obtain $\partial u/\partial y = 1$ and $\partial v/\partial x = 0$, and therefore $f(z)$ is nowhere analytic.

(d) The imaginary part of $\operatorname{Arg} z$ is $v(x,y) = 0$. There is no simple formula for its real part; it is $u(x,y) = \operatorname{Tan}^{-1}(y/x)$ with the possible addition of $\pm\pi$ depending on the quadrant for z. Whichever case is involved, partial derivatives of $u(x,y)$ and $v(x,y)$ are

$$\frac{\partial u}{\partial x} = \frac{-y/x^2}{1 + y^2/x^2} = \frac{-y}{x^2 + y^2}, \quad \frac{\partial u}{\partial y} = \frac{1/x}{1 + y^2/x^2} = \frac{x}{x^2 + y^2}, \quad \frac{\partial v}{\partial x} = 0, \quad \frac{\partial v}{\partial y} = 0.$$

Since the Cauchy-Riemann equations are not satisfied at any point, $\operatorname{Arg} z$ is nowhere analytic.

(e) The imaginary part of $\arg_\phi z$ is $v(x,y) = 0$. There is no simple formula for its real part; it can be derived from $u(x,y) = \operatorname{Tan}^{-1}(y/x)$ with the possible addition of a constant depending on ϕ and the quadrant for z. Whichever case is involved, partial derivatives of $u(x,y)$ and $v(x,y)$ are the same as in part (d). Since the Cauchy-Riemann equations are not satisfied at any point, these branches of $\arg z$ are nowhere analytic.$\bullet$

If a real function has a derivative equal to zero on an open interval, the function must be constant on that interval. The complex analogue is also valid.

Theorem 2.7 If $f'(z) = 0$ at every point of a domain D, then $f(z)$ must be constant in D.

Proof If $f'(z) = 0$ at every point in D, then

$$0 = \frac{\partial u}{\partial x} + \frac{\partial v}{\partial x}i = \frac{\partial v}{\partial y} - \frac{\partial u}{\partial y}i,$$

and these imply that $\dfrac{\partial u}{\partial x} = \dfrac{\partial u}{\partial y} = \dfrac{\partial v}{\partial x} = \dfrac{\partial v}{\partial y} = 0$ at every point in D. It follows that u and v must be constant in D, and hence $f(z)$ is constant in D. $\blacksquare$

We demanded that D be a domain,
not just an open set, in this theorem.
The reason for this, as you may recall,
is that a domain in a plane is the counterpart of an open interval on a line.
Were D only an open set, it would
not necessarily be connected; it could
perhaps consist of two disjoint pieces
D_1 and D_2 as in Figure 2.29. In this
case the proof of Theorem 2.7 indicates
that $f(z) = C_1$ in D_1 and $f(z) = C_2$ in
D_2. But it would not be necessary for
$C_1 = C_2$. Thus, Theorem 2.7 can be
generalized to open sets, but it is necessary to distinguish among disjoint parts.

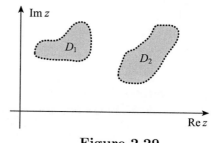

Figure 2.29

An immediate consequence of Theorem 2.7 is the following corollary (see Exercise 17 for a proof).

Corollary   If $f(z) = u + vi$ is analytic in a domain D, and if either $u(x, y)$ or $v(x, y)$ is constant
in D, then $f(z)$ is constant in D.

For some functions, it is easier to express real and imaginary parts in terms
of the modulus r and argument θ of z, $f(z) = u(r, \theta) + v(r, \theta)i$. For example, if
$g(z) = z^{10}$, then DeMoivre's theorem quickly gives $g(z) = (re^{\theta i})^{10} = r^{10}e^{10\theta i} = (r^{10}\cos 10\theta) + (r^{10}\sin 10\theta)i$. Expressing this in terms of x and y is particularly
uninviting. For functions expressed in this way, the Cauchy-Riemann equations
take the form

$$r\frac{\partial u}{\partial r} = \frac{\partial v}{\partial \theta}, \qquad r\frac{\partial v}{\partial r} = -\frac{\partial u}{\partial \theta}, \qquad r \neq 0. \tag{2.22}$$

In addition, when real and imaginary parts of an analytic function $f(z)$ are expressed
in terms of r and θ, the derivative of the function is given by either of the expressions

$$f'(z) = e^{-\theta i}\left(\frac{\partial u}{\partial r} + \frac{\partial v}{\partial r}i\right), \tag{2.23a}$$

or,

$$f'(z) = \frac{e^{-\theta i}}{r}\left(\frac{\partial v}{\partial \theta} - \frac{\partial u}{\partial \theta}i\right). \tag{2.23b}$$

These results are verified in Appendix B at the end of the section.

For example, had we not known that $g(z) = (r^{10}\cos 10\theta) + (r^{10}\sin 10\theta)i$ represents z^{10}, a short calculation shows that it satisfies conditions 2.22 for all z. Hence
the function is entire. It is important to notice here that the value of $g(z)$ is independent of the argument θ of z. If θ is one of the arguments of z, then all possible
arguments of z are $\theta + 2k\pi$, where k is an integer. All such arguments give the same
value to $g(z) = (r^{10}\cos 10\theta) + (r^{10}\sin 10\theta)i$.

Compare this situation with that for the function $f(z) = r^{1/3}e^{\theta i/3}$. It satisfies
conditions 2.22 at every point except $z = 0$ (where $r = 0$). But, there is a difficulty
associated with θ. Different arguments of a complex number can give different values
to the function. For example, arguments 0 and 2π of $z = 1$ lead to different values

for $f(1)$. In other words, $f(z)$ is not single-valued. To remedy this, we could choose θ as the principal value of the argument of z, so that $f(z) = |z|^{1/3}e^{i\operatorname{Arg}z/3}$. This makes $f(z)$ a (single-valued) function (a branch of the multi-valued function), but because $\operatorname{Arg}z$ is discontinuous at points on the negative real axis, so also are the real and imaginary parts of $f(z)$. Theorem 2.4 implies that $f(z)$ is discontinuous at these points and hence $f(z)$ cannot have a derivative there. Thus, the function is analytic in the domain $r > 0$, $-\pi < \theta < \pi$, the complex plane with the origin and negative real axis deleted. Remember our warning that discontinuities of $\operatorname{Arg}z$ would have serious consequences for many functions in Chapter 3. We have just seen an example of this. The function $f(z) = r^{1/3}e^{i\operatorname{Arg}z/3}$ is defined for all $z \neq 0$. It is discontinuous and does not have a derivative at $z = 0$ and points on the negative real axis. This is a direct result of the discontinuities of $\operatorname{Arg}z$.

In Exercise 18 we verify the following analogue of the corollary to Theorem 2.7.

Theorem 2.8 If f is analytic in a domain D, and if $|f(z)|$ is constant in D, then f is constant in D.

Notably absent from our discussions has been a geometric interpretation of the derivative f' of a complex function f. We mention it here, but because justification is delayed until Section 7.4, the geometric interpretation of f' does not play the same fundamental role as for the derivative of a real function in elementary calculus. Naturally the geometric interpretation of f' must be in terms of the geometric interpretation of f as a mapping $w = f(z)$ from the z-plane to the w-plane. Suppose a curve C in the z-plane is mapped by $w = f(z)$ to a curve $f(C)$ in the w-plane (Figure 2.30). A point z_0 on C has image $f(z_0)$ on $f(C)$, and a small length ds along C at z_0 has image $dw = f(ds)$ along $f(C)$. When $f'(z_0) \neq 0$, the modulus $|f'(z_0)|$ is the ratio of the length of dw to that of ds; that is, $|dw| = |f'(z_0)||ds|$. In other words, the modulus of $f'(z_0)$ is a length magnification factor of the mapping $w = f(z)$. Naturally then, $|f'(z_0)|^2$ is an area magnification factor; small area A at z_0 is magnified to $|f'(z_0)|^2 A$ at $f(z_0)$. Furthermore, angles of inclination θ and ϕ of the tangent vectors to C and $f(C)$ with the positive real directions are related by $\phi = \theta + \arg[f'(z_0)]$. Thus, the argument of $f'(z_0)$ is a measure of the rotational effect of the mapping $w = f(z)$. As we said, these geometric interpretations will be discussed more fully in Chapter 7.

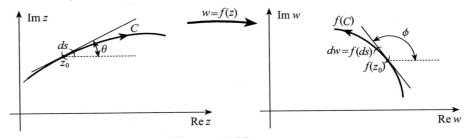

Figure 2.30

Appendix A   Proof of Theorem 2.6

Suppose $f(z)$ is analytic in S and z is any point in S. The limit in equation 2.18 must be independent of the mode of approach of $\Delta z = \Delta x + \Delta y\,i$ to zero. If we set $\Delta y = 0$ and let $\Delta z \to 0$ by letting $\Delta x \to 0$ (Figure 2.28b), then

$$f'(z) = \lim_{\Delta x \to 0} \frac{f(x + yi + \Delta x) - f(x + yi)}{\Delta x}$$

$$= \lim_{\Delta x \to 0} \frac{u(x+\Delta x, y) + v(x+\Delta x, y)i - u(x,y) - v(x,y)i}{\Delta x}.$$

Since $f'(z)$ exists, it follows that limits of real and imaginary parts of the right side both exist (Theorem 2.2); that is,

$$\lim_{\Delta x \to 0} \frac{u(x+\Delta x, y) - u(x,y)}{\Delta x} = \frac{\partial u}{\partial x} \qquad \text{and} \qquad \lim_{\Delta x \to 0} \frac{v(x+\Delta x, y) - v(x,y)}{\Delta x} = \frac{\partial v}{\partial x}$$

both exist, and

$$f'(z) = \frac{\partial u}{\partial x} + \frac{\partial v}{\partial x}i.$$

We now let $\Delta z \to 0$ by setting $\Delta x = 0$ in $\Delta z = \Delta x + \Delta y\, i$, and letting $\Delta y \to 0$ (Figure 2.28a),

$$f'(z) = \lim_{\Delta y \to 0} \frac{f(x+yi+\Delta y\, i) - f(x+yi)}{\Delta y\, i}$$

$$= \lim_{\Delta y \to 0} \frac{u(x, y+\Delta y) + v(x, y+\Delta y)i - u(x,y) - v(x,y)i}{\Delta y\, i}.$$

Once again existence of $f'(z)$ implies existence of real and imaginary parts,

$$\lim_{\Delta y \to 0} \frac{v(x, y+\Delta y) - v(x,y)}{\Delta y} = \frac{\partial v}{\partial y} \qquad \text{and} \qquad \lim_{\Delta y \to 0} \frac{u(x, y+\Delta y) - u(x,y)}{\Delta y} = \frac{\partial u}{\partial y};$$

and therefore

$$f'(z) = \frac{\partial v}{\partial y} - \frac{\partial u}{\partial y}i.$$

If we equate these two expressions for $f'(z)$, we obtain

$$\frac{\partial u}{\partial x} + \frac{\partial v}{\partial x}i = \frac{\partial v}{\partial y} - \frac{\partial u}{\partial y}i.$$

Real and imaginary parts of this equation give the Cauchy-Riemann equations 2.20. Continuity of the partial derivatives will be verified later.

Conversely, suppose that the first partial derivatives of u and v are continuous in S and satisfy the Cauchy-Riemann equations therein. Then for $\Delta z = \Delta x + \Delta y\, i$,

$$\frac{f(z+\Delta z) - f(z)}{\Delta z} = \frac{u(x+\Delta x, y+\Delta y) + v(x+\Delta x, y+\Delta y)i - u(x,y) - v(x,y)i}{\Delta x + \Delta y\, i}.$$

Since $u(x,y)$ and $v(x,y)$ have first partial derivatives in S, Taylor's remainder formula implies that $u(x+\Delta x, y+\Delta y)$ and $v(x+\Delta x, y+\Delta y)$ can be expressed in the forms

$$u(x+\Delta x, y+\Delta y) = u(x,y) + \frac{\partial u}{\partial x}\bigg|_{(x',y')} \Delta x + \frac{\partial u}{\partial y}\bigg|_{(x',y')} \Delta y,$$

$$v(x+\Delta x, y+\Delta y) = v(x,y) + \frac{\partial v}{\partial x}\bigg|_{(x'',y'')} \Delta x + \frac{\partial v}{\partial y}\bigg|_{(x'',y'')} \Delta y,$$

where (x',y') and (x'',y'') are points on the line segment joining (x,y) and $(x+\Delta x, y+\Delta y)$. Since the first partial derivatives are continuous at (x,y), it follows that

$$\frac{\partial u}{\partial x}\bigg|_{(x',y')} = \frac{\partial u}{\partial x}\bigg|_{(x,y)} + \epsilon_1, \qquad \frac{\partial u}{\partial y}\bigg|_{(x',y')} = \frac{\partial u}{\partial y}\bigg|_{(x,y)} + \epsilon_2,$$

$$\frac{\partial v}{\partial x}\bigg|_{(x'',y'')} = \frac{\partial v}{\partial x}\bigg|_{(x,y)} + \epsilon_3, \qquad \frac{\partial v}{\partial y}\bigg|_{(x'',y'')} = \frac{\partial v}{\partial y}\bigg|_{(x,y)} + \epsilon_4,$$

where ϵ_1, $\epsilon_2 \to 0$ as $(x',y') \to (x,y)$ and ϵ_3, $\epsilon_4 \to 0$ as $(x'',y'') \to (x,y)$. Thus, the quotient $[f(z + \Delta z) - f(z)]/\Delta z$ can be written as

$$\frac{f(z + \Delta z) - f(z)}{\Delta z}$$
$$= \frac{1}{\Delta x + \Delta y\, i}\left[\left(\frac{\partial u}{\partial x} + \epsilon_1\right)\Delta x + \left(\frac{\partial u}{\partial y} + \epsilon_2\right)\Delta y + \left(\frac{\partial v}{\partial x} + \epsilon_3\right)\Delta x\, i + \left(\frac{\partial v}{\partial y} + \epsilon_4\right)\Delta y\, i\right]$$
$$= \frac{1}{\Delta x + \Delta y\, i}\left[\left(\frac{\partial u}{\partial x} + \frac{\partial v}{\partial x}\, i\right)\Delta x + \left(\frac{\partial u}{\partial y} + \frac{\partial v}{\partial y}\, i\right)\Delta y + (\epsilon_1 + \epsilon_3 i)\Delta x + (\epsilon_2 + \epsilon_4 i)\Delta y\right],$$

where all partial derivatives are evaluated at (x,y). If we substitute from the Cauchy-Riemann equations,

$$\frac{f(z + \Delta z) - f(z)}{\Delta z}$$
$$= \frac{1}{\Delta x + \Delta y\, i}\left[\left(\frac{\partial u}{\partial x} + \frac{\partial v}{\partial x}\, i\right)\Delta x + \left(-\frac{\partial v}{\partial x} + \frac{\partial u}{\partial x}\, i\right)\Delta y + (\epsilon_1 + \epsilon_3 i)\Delta x + (\epsilon_2 + \epsilon_4 i)\Delta y\right]$$
$$= \frac{1}{\Delta x + \Delta y\, i}\left[\left(\frac{\partial u}{\partial x} + \frac{\partial v}{\partial x}\, i\right)(\Delta x + \Delta y\, i) + (\epsilon_1 + \epsilon_3 i)\Delta x + (\epsilon_2 + \epsilon_4 i)\Delta y\right]$$
$$= \frac{\partial u}{\partial x} + \frac{\partial v}{\partial x}\, i + \frac{(\epsilon_1 + \epsilon_3 i)\Delta x + (\epsilon_2 + \epsilon_4 i)\Delta y}{\Delta x + \Delta y\, i}.$$

Now,

$$\left|\frac{(\epsilon_1 + \epsilon_3 i)\Delta x + (\epsilon_2 + \epsilon_4 i)\Delta y}{\Delta x + \Delta y\, i}\right| \leq \frac{|(\epsilon_1 + \epsilon_3 i)\Delta x|}{|\Delta x + \Delta y\, i|} + \frac{|(\epsilon_2 + \epsilon_4 i)\Delta y|}{|\Delta x + \Delta y\, i|}$$
$$\leq \frac{|(\epsilon_1 + \epsilon_3 i)||\Delta x|}{|\Delta x|} + \frac{|(\epsilon_2 + \epsilon_4 i)||\Delta y|}{|\Delta y|}$$
$$= |\epsilon_1 + \epsilon_3 i| + |\epsilon_2 + \epsilon_4 i|,$$

and the right side approaches zero as Δx, $\Delta y \to 0$. It follows therefore that

$$\lim_{\Delta z \to 0} \frac{f(z + \Delta z) - f(z)}{\Delta z} = \frac{\partial u}{\partial x} + \frac{\partial v}{\partial x}\, i,$$

and $f'(z)$ exists.

Appendix B   Verification of the Polar Form for the Cauchy-Riemann Equations

We give two proofs of the polar form for the Cauchy-Riemann equations. One transforms the Cartesian form of the equations; the other returns to the limit definition of the derivative.

Method 1   Transforming equations 2.20

If $u = u(r, \theta)$ where $r = r(x, y)$ and $\theta = \theta(x, y)$,

$$\frac{\partial u}{\partial x} = \frac{\partial u}{\partial r}\frac{\partial r}{\partial x} + \frac{\partial u}{\partial \theta}\frac{\partial \theta}{\partial x}, \qquad \frac{\partial u}{\partial y} = \frac{\partial u}{\partial r}\frac{\partial r}{\partial y} + \frac{\partial u}{\partial \theta}\frac{\partial \theta}{\partial y}.$$

Differentiation of $x = r\cos\theta$ and $y = r\sin\theta$ with respect to x gives

$$1 = \frac{\partial r}{\partial x}\cos\theta - r\sin\theta\frac{\partial \theta}{\partial x}, \qquad 0 = \frac{\partial r}{\partial x}\sin\theta + r\cos\theta\frac{\partial \theta}{\partial x}.$$

These can be solved for $\partial r/\partial x = \cos\theta$ and $\partial\theta/\partial x = -(1/r)\sin\theta$. Similarly, differentiation of $x = r\cos\theta$ and $y = r\sin\theta$ with respect to y leads to $\partial r/\partial y = \sin\theta$ and $\partial\theta/\partial y = (1/r)\cos\theta$. Hence,

$$\frac{\partial u}{\partial x} = \cos\theta\frac{\partial u}{\partial r} - \frac{\sin\theta}{r}\frac{\partial u}{\partial \theta}, \qquad \frac{\partial u}{\partial y} = \sin\theta\frac{\partial u}{\partial r} + \frac{\cos\theta}{r}\frac{\partial u}{\partial \theta}.$$

Replacing u with v gives

$$\frac{\partial v}{\partial x} = \cos\theta\frac{\partial v}{\partial r} - \frac{\sin\theta}{r}\frac{\partial v}{\partial \theta}, \qquad \frac{\partial v}{\partial y} = \sin\theta\frac{\partial v}{\partial r} + \frac{\cos\theta}{r}\frac{\partial v}{\partial \theta}.$$

When these are substituted into the Cauchy-Riemann equations,

$$\cos\theta\frac{\partial u}{\partial r} - \frac{\sin\theta}{r}\frac{\partial u}{\partial \theta} = \sin\theta\frac{\partial v}{\partial r} + \frac{\cos\theta}{r}\frac{\partial v}{\partial \theta}, \quad \sin\theta\frac{\partial u}{\partial r} + \frac{\cos\theta}{r}\frac{\partial u}{\partial \theta} = -\cos\theta\frac{\partial v}{\partial r} + \frac{\sin\theta}{r}\frac{\partial v}{\partial \theta}.$$

If the first of these is multiplied by $\cos\theta$, the second by $\sin\theta$, and the results added,

$$\frac{\partial u}{\partial r} = \frac{1}{r}\frac{\partial v}{\partial \theta},$$

the first of equations 2.22. The second of equations 2.22 is obtained by adding $-\sin\theta$ times the first of the above equations and $\cos\theta$ times the second.

Before proceeding to the second proof, we verify differentiation formulas 2.23. Substituting the above expressions for $\partial u/\partial x$ and $\partial v/\partial x$ into equation 2.21 gives

$$f'(z) = \frac{\partial u}{\partial x} + \frac{\partial v}{\partial x}i = \left(\cos\theta\frac{\partial u}{\partial r} - \frac{\sin\theta}{r}\frac{\partial u}{\partial \theta}\right) + \left(\cos\theta\frac{\partial v}{\partial r} - \frac{\sin\theta}{r}\frac{\partial v}{\partial \theta}\right)i$$

$$= \cos\theta\left(\frac{\partial u}{\partial r} + \frac{\partial v}{\partial r}i\right) - \frac{\sin\theta}{r}\left(\frac{\partial u}{\partial \theta} + \frac{\partial v}{\partial \theta}i\right)$$

$$= \cos\theta\left(\frac{\partial u}{\partial r} + \frac{\partial v}{\partial r}i\right) - \frac{\sin\theta}{r}\left(-r\frac{\partial v}{\partial r} + r\frac{\partial u}{\partial r}i\right)$$

$$= \cos\theta\left(\frac{\partial u}{\partial r} + \frac{\partial v}{\partial r}i\right) - \sin\theta\left(\frac{\partial u}{\partial r} + \frac{\partial v}{\partial r}i\right)i$$

$$= (\cos\theta - \sin\theta\, i)\left(\frac{\partial u}{\partial r} + \frac{\partial v}{\partial r}i\right)$$

$$= e^{-\theta i}\left(\frac{\partial u}{\partial r} + \frac{\partial v}{\partial r}i\right);$$

or,

$$f'(z) = e^{-\theta i}\left(\frac{1}{r}\frac{\partial v}{\partial \theta} - \frac{1}{r}\frac{\partial u}{\partial \theta}i\right) = \frac{e^{-\theta i}}{r}\left(\frac{\partial v}{\partial \theta} - \frac{\partial u}{\partial \theta}i\right).$$

Method 2   Using the definition of the derivative

Suppose that $f'(z)$ exists. If we set $\Delta z = \Delta r(\cos\theta + \sin\theta\, i)$, so that $z + \Delta z \to z$ radially, then equation 2.18 gives

$$
\begin{aligned}
f'(z) &= \lim_{\Delta z \to 0} \frac{f(z + \Delta z) - f(z)}{\Delta z} \\
&= \lim_{\Delta r \to 0} \frac{[u(r + \Delta r, \theta) + v(r + \Delta r, \theta)i] - [u(r, \theta) + v(r, \theta)i]}{\Delta r(\cos\theta + \sin\theta\, i)} \\
&= \lim_{\Delta r \to 0} \frac{\{[u(r + \Delta r, \theta) - u(r, \theta)] + [v(r + \Delta r, \theta) - v(r, \theta)]i\}(\cos\theta - \sin\theta\, i)}{\Delta r} \\
&= \lim_{\Delta r \to 0} \left\{ \frac{[u(r + \Delta r, \theta) - u(r, \theta)]\cos\theta + [v(r + \Delta r, \theta) - v(r, \theta)]\sin\theta}{\Delta r} \right. \\
&\qquad\qquad \left. + \frac{[v(r + \Delta r, \theta) - v(r, \theta)]\cos\theta - [u(r + \Delta r, \theta) - u(r, \theta)]\sin\theta}{\Delta r} i \right\}.
\end{aligned}
$$

According to Theorem 2.2, existence of this limit implies existence of limits of its real and imaginary parts,

$$
\lim_{\Delta r \to 0} \left\{ \frac{[u(r + \Delta r, \theta) - u(r, \theta)]\cos\theta + [v(r + \Delta r, \theta) - v(r, \theta)]\sin\theta}{\Delta r} \right\},
$$

and

$$
\lim_{\Delta r \to 0} \left\{ \frac{[v(r + \Delta r, \theta) - v(r, \theta)]\cos\theta - [u(r + \Delta r, \theta) - u(r, \theta)]\sin\theta}{\Delta r} \right\}.
$$

When the first of these is muliplied by $\cos\theta$, the second by $\sin\theta$, and the results subtracted, we conclude that the following limit exists,

$$
\begin{aligned}
\lim_{\Delta r \to 0} &\left[\frac{u(r + \Delta r, \theta) - u(r, \theta)}{\Delta r}\cos^2\theta + \frac{u(r + \Delta r, \theta) - u(r, \theta)}{\Delta r}\sin^2\theta \right] \\
&= \lim_{\Delta r \to 0} \frac{u(r + \Delta r, \theta) - u(r, \theta)}{\Delta r} = \frac{\partial u}{\partial r}.
\end{aligned}
$$

Multiplying the first of the above limits by $\sin\theta$, the second by $\cos\theta$, and adding the results leads to existence of $\partial v/\partial r$. It now follows that

$$
\begin{aligned}
f'(z) &= \left(\frac{\partial u}{\partial r}\cos\theta + \frac{\partial v}{\partial r}\sin\theta \right) + \left(\frac{\partial v}{\partial r}\cos\theta - \frac{\partial u}{\partial r}\sin\theta \right) i \\
&= (\cos\theta - \sin\theta\, i)\left(\frac{\partial u}{\partial r} + \frac{\partial v}{\partial r}i \right) = e^{-\theta i}\left(\frac{\partial u}{\partial r} + \frac{\partial v}{\partial r}i \right).
\end{aligned}
$$

Suppose we now set $z + \Delta z = r[\cos(\theta + \Delta\theta) + \sin(\theta + \Delta\theta)\, i]$ so that $z + \Delta z \to z$ along a circular arc. Then,

$$
\begin{aligned}
\Delta z &= r[\cos(\theta + \Delta\theta) + \sin(\theta + \Delta\theta)\, i] - r(\cos\theta + \sin\theta\, i) \\
&= r\{[\cos(\theta + \Delta\theta) - \cos\theta] + [\sin(\theta + \Delta\theta) - \sin\theta]i\} \\
&= r[-2\sin(\theta + \Delta\theta/2)\sin(\Delta\theta/2) + 2\cos(\theta + \Delta\theta/2)\sin(\Delta\theta/2)\, i] \\
&= 2r\sin(\Delta\theta/2)[-\sin(\theta + \Delta\theta/2) + \cos(\theta + \Delta\theta/2)\, i].
\end{aligned}
$$

Now, the derivative $f'(z)$ is defined by the limit

$$\lim_{\Delta z \to 0} \frac{f(z + \Delta z) - f(z)}{\Delta z}$$

$$= \lim_{\Delta \theta \to 0} \frac{[u(r, \theta + \Delta \theta) + v(r, \theta + \Delta \theta)\, i] - [u(r, \theta) + v(r, \theta)\, i]}{2r \sin (\Delta \theta / 2)[- \sin (\theta + \Delta \theta / 2) + \cos (\theta + \Delta \theta / 2)\, i]}$$

$$= \lim_{\Delta \theta \to 0} \left\{ \frac{[u(r, \theta + \Delta \theta) - u(r, \theta)] + [v(r, \theta + \Delta \theta) - v(r, \theta)]i}{2r \sin (\Delta \theta / 2)[- \sin (\theta + \Delta \theta / 2) + \cos (\theta + \Delta \theta / 2)\, i]} \right\} \left\{ \frac{- \sin (\theta + \Delta \theta / 2) - \cos (\theta + \Delta \theta / 2)\, i}{- \sin (\theta + \Delta \theta / 2) - \cos (\theta + \Delta \theta / 2)\, i} \right\}$$

$$= \lim_{\Delta \theta \to 0} \frac{1}{2r \sin (\Delta \theta / 2)} \{ -[u(r, \theta + \Delta \theta) - u(r, \theta)] \sin (\theta + \Delta \theta / 2) + [v(r, \theta + \Delta \theta) - v(r, \theta)] \cos (\theta + \Delta \theta / 2)$$

$$- [v(r, \theta + \Delta \theta) - v(r, \theta)] \sin (\theta + \Delta \theta / 2)\, i - [u(r, \theta + \Delta \theta) - u(r, \theta)] \cos (\theta + \Delta \theta / 2)\, i \}.$$

Existence of this limit implies existence of its real and imaginary parts,

$$\lim_{\Delta \theta \to 0} \frac{[v(r, \theta + \Delta \theta) - v(r, \theta)] \cos (\theta + \Delta \theta / 2) - [u(r, \theta + \Delta \theta) - u(r, \theta)] \sin (\theta + \Delta \theta / 2)}{2r \sin (\Delta \theta / 2)}$$

and

$$\lim_{\Delta \theta \to 0} \frac{[v(r, \theta + \Delta \theta) - v(r, \theta)] \sin (\theta + \Delta \theta / 2) + [u(r, \theta + \Delta \theta) - u(r, \theta)] \cos (\theta + \Delta \theta / 2)}{-2r \sin (\Delta \theta / 2)}.$$

When the first of these is multiplied by $\cos (\theta + \Delta \theta / 2)$, the second by $\sin (\theta + \Delta \theta / 2)$ and the results subtracted, we conclude that the following limit exists

$$\lim_{\Delta \theta \to 0} \frac{[v(r, \theta + \Delta \theta) - v(r, \theta)] \cos^2 (\theta + \Delta \theta / 2) + [v(r, \theta + \Delta \theta) - v(r, \theta)] \sin^2 (\theta + \Delta \theta / 2)}{2r \sin (\Delta \theta / 2)}$$

$$= \lim_{\Delta \theta \to 0} \frac{v(r, \theta + \Delta \theta) - v(r, \theta)}{2r \sin (\Delta \theta / 2)} = \lim_{\Delta \theta \to 0} \left[\frac{\Delta \theta / 2}{r \sin (\Delta \theta / 2)} \frac{v(r, \theta + \Delta \theta) - v(r, \theta)}{\Delta \theta} \right].$$

Since $\displaystyle \lim_{\Delta \theta \to 0} \frac{\Delta \theta / 2}{r \sin (\Delta \theta / 2)} = \frac{1}{r}$, it follows that

$$\lim_{\Delta \theta \to 0} \frac{v(r, \theta + \Delta \theta) - v(r, \theta)}{\Delta \theta} = \frac{\partial v}{\partial \theta}$$

must also exist. In a similar way, we can show that $\partial u / \partial \theta$ exists. In addition, we may write that

$$f'(z) = \frac{1}{r} \lim_{\Delta \theta \to 0} \frac{\Delta \theta / 2}{\sin (\Delta \theta / 2)} \left\{ \left[-\frac{u(r, \theta - \Delta \theta) - u(r, \theta)}{\Delta \theta} \sin (\theta + \Delta \theta / 2) \right. \right.$$

$$\left. + \frac{v(r, \theta + \Delta \theta) - v(r, \theta)}{\Delta \theta} \cos (\theta + \Delta \theta / 2) \right]$$

$$\left. - \left[\frac{v(r, \theta + \Delta \theta) - v(r, \theta)}{\Delta \theta} \sin (\theta + \Delta \theta / 2) + \frac{u(r, \theta + \Delta \theta) - u(r, \theta)}{\Delta \theta} \cos (\theta + \Delta \theta / 2) \right] i \right\}$$

$$= \frac{1}{r} \left\{ \left[-\frac{\partial u}{\partial \theta} \sin \theta + \frac{\partial v}{\partial \theta} \cos \theta \right] - \left[\frac{\partial v}{\partial \theta} \sin \theta + \frac{\partial u}{\partial \theta} \cos \theta \right] i \right\}$$

$$= \frac{\cos \theta - \sin \theta\, i}{r} \left(\frac{\partial v}{\partial \theta} - \frac{\partial u}{\partial \theta} i \right) = \frac{e^{-\theta i}}{r} \left(\frac{\partial v}{\partial \theta} - \frac{\partial u}{\partial \theta} i \right).$$

When we equate these expressions for $f'(z)$,

$$e^{-\theta i}\left(\frac{\partial u}{\partial r}+\frac{\partial v}{\partial r}i\right)=\frac{e^{-\theta i}}{r}\left(\frac{\partial v}{\partial\theta}-\frac{\partial u}{\partial\theta}i\right)$$

and divide by $e^{-\theta i}$,

$$\frac{\partial u}{\partial r}+\frac{\partial v}{\partial r}i=\frac{1}{r}\left(\frac{\partial v}{\partial\theta}-\frac{\partial u}{\partial\theta}i\right).$$

Real and imaginary parts require $\dfrac{\partial u}{\partial r}=\dfrac{1}{r}\dfrac{\partial v}{\partial\theta}$ and $\dfrac{\partial v}{\partial r}=-\dfrac{1}{r}\dfrac{\partial u}{\partial\theta}$.

EXERCISES 2.4

In Exercises 1–6 find $f'(z)$. Determine all open sets in which $f(z)$ is analytic.

1. $f(z)=z^3+1/z^2-2z$

2. $f(z)=z^2(1+z^3)^{10}$

3. $f(z)=(z^3+1)/(z^2-2)$

4. $f(z)=z^3(1-z)^3/(3z+2i)$

5. $f(z)=z|z|^2$

6. $f(z)=\overline{z}$

In Exercises 7–14 determine whether the complex function of x and y is an analytic function $f(z)$ of $z=x+yi$. Find $f'(z)$, if it exists, and determine open sets in which $f(z)$ is analytic.

7. $(2x^2-2y^2+3x)+(4xy+3y+4)i$

8. $(x^3-3xy^2-2x+3)+(3x^2y-y^3-2y)i$

9. $(x+1-yi)/[(x+1)^2+y^2]$

10. $1/x-i/y$

11. $\cos x\cosh y-\sin x\sinh y\,i$

12. $\cos y\sinh x+\sin y\cosh x\,i$

13. $f(z)=(r^8\cos 8\theta+1)+(r^8\sin 8\theta)i$

14. $f(z)=r+\theta\,i$

In Exercises 15–16 verify that the function is analytic in the given domain.

15. $f(z)=\sqrt{r}e^{\theta i/2}$, $r>0$, $-\pi<\theta<\pi$

16. $f(z)=\ln r+\theta\,i$, $r>0$, $-\pi<\theta<\pi$

17. Prove the corollary to Theorem 2.7.

18. Prove Theorem 2.8.

19. Is $f(z)=|z|^2$ analytic at $z=0$? Does $f'(0)$ exist?

20. Show that the complex function $(x^2-y^3)+(x^3+y^2)i$ satisfies the Cauchy-Riemann equations at every point on the line $y=x$. Is it analytic at these points?

21. Prove that if $f(z)=u+vi$ and $\overline{f(z)}=u-vi$ are both analytic in a domain D, then $f(z)$ is constant in D.

22. Suppose the real and imaginary parts of a function $f(z)=u+vi$, analytic in a domain D, are related at every point of D by a linear equation

$$au(x,y)+bv(x,y)+c=0,$$

where a, b, and c are real constants. Show that $f(z)$ must be a constant function.

§2.5 Harmonic Functions

The real and imaginary parts of a complex analytic function f constitute a unique pair of real-valued functions $u(x,y)$ and $v(x,y)$ of two variables x and y that satisfy the Cauchy-Riemann equations. On the other hand, every pair of real-valued functions does not necessarily determine a complex analytic function $f(z) = u(x,y) + v(x,y)i$. They do so only if they have continuous first partial derivatives that satisfy the Cauchy-Riemann equations. What do these equations say about u and v individually? If the second partial derivatives of u and v are continuous, then the Cauchy-Riemann equations can be used to write

$$\frac{\partial^2 u}{\partial x^2} = \frac{\partial}{\partial x}\left(\frac{\partial u}{\partial x}\right) = \frac{\partial}{\partial x}\left(\frac{\partial v}{\partial y}\right) = \frac{\partial}{\partial y}\left(\frac{\partial v}{\partial x}\right) = \frac{\partial}{\partial y}\left(-\frac{\partial u}{\partial y}\right);$$

that is,

$$\frac{\partial^2 u}{\partial x^2} + \frac{\partial^2 u}{\partial y^2} = 0.$$

Similarly,

$$\frac{\partial^2 v}{\partial x^2} + \frac{\partial^2 v}{\partial y^2} = 0.$$

In other words, the real and imaginary parts of an analytic function satisfy Laplace's equation. Laplace's equation is found in many areas of applied mathematics. We shall see it in problems of heat flow, fluid flow, and electrostatics in Sections 3.8, 3.9, and 3.10 of the next chapter, and again in Chapter 7. There are others. What we have shown here is that real and imaginary parts of complex analytic functions are a limitless source of solutions to Laplace's equation. According to the following definition, solutions of Laplace's equation are called harmonic functions.

Definition 2.14 A real-valued function $\phi(x,y)$ is said to be **harmonic** in a domain D if its second partial derivatives are continuous in D and if at each point of D, ϕ satisfies Laplace's equation

$$\frac{\partial^2 \phi}{\partial x^2} + \frac{\partial^2 \phi}{\partial y^2} = 0. \tag{2.24}$$

We have essentially established the following property of analytic functions.

Theorem 2.9 The real and imaginary parts of a function analytic in a domain D are harmonic in D.

The proof of the theorem is not quite complete as the preceding discussion assumed continuity of second partial derivatives of u and v. In Section 4.6 we show that the real and imaginary parts of analytic functions have continuous derivatives not just of second order, but of all orders.

When $u(x,y)$ is harmonic in a domain D, a function $v(x,y)$ such that $u + vi$ is analytic in D is called a **harmonic conjugate** of $u(x,y)$. This definition suggests that given a harmonic function $u(x,y)$ we can always find harmonic conjugates

$v(x,y)$†. Alternatively, given harmonic $v(x,y)$, we can find $u(x,y)$ for which $v(x,y)$ is a harmonic conjugate. We illustrate with an example.

Example 2.21 Find all analytic functions with real part $u(x,y) = x^3 - 3xy^2 + y$.

Solution Since $\partial^2 u/\partial x^2 + \partial^2 u/\partial y^2 = 6x - 6x = 0$, the function $u(x,y)$ is harmonic in the whole complex plane. To find all harmonic conjugates $v(x,y)$, we have by the Cauchy-Riemann equations,

$$\frac{\partial v}{\partial y} = \frac{\partial u}{\partial x} = 3x^2 - 3y^2, \qquad \frac{\partial v}{\partial x} = -\frac{\partial u}{\partial y} = 6xy - 1.$$

When the first of these is integrated with respect to y,

$$v(x,y) = 3x^2 y - y^3 + h(x),$$

where $h(x)$ is an arbitrary function of x. If we assume that $h(x)$ is differentiable and substitute this expression for $v(x,y)$ into the second equation,

$$6xy + h'(x) = 6xy - 1,$$

which implies that $h(x) = -x + k$, where k is a real constant. Thus,

$$v(x,y) = 3x^2 y - y^3 - x + k,$$

and the required analytic functions are

$$f(z) = (x^3 - 3xy^2 + y) + (3x^2 y - y^3 - x + k)i.$$

Should we wish the right side in terms of z, we could write

$$
\begin{aligned}
f(z) &= (x^3 + 3x^2 yi - 3xy^2 - y^3 i) - i(x + yi) + ki \\
&= (x + yi)^3 - (x + yi)i + ki \\
&= z^3 - (z - k)i.
\end{aligned}
$$

Alternatively, by setting $x = (z + \overline{z})/2$ and $y = (z - \overline{z})/(2i)$ (see equations 2.11),

$$
f(z) = \left[\left(\frac{z+\overline{z}}{2} \right)^3 - 3 \left(\frac{z+\overline{z}}{2} \right) \left(\frac{z-\overline{z}}{2i} \right)^2 + \left(\frac{z-\overline{z}}{2i} \right) \right] \\
+ \left[3 \left(\frac{z+\overline{z}}{2} \right)^2 \left(\frac{z-\overline{z}}{2i} \right) - \left(\frac{z-\overline{z}}{2i} \right)^3 - \left(\frac{z+\overline{z}}{2} \right) + k \right] i,
$$

and this simplifies to $z^3 - (z - k)i$.●

---

† This is not quite true. Only if $u(x,y)$ is harmonic in certain kinds of domains can we guarantee the existence of a harmonic conjugate $v(x,y)$. This is discussed in Section 4.8.

An important property of harmonic
functions and their conjugates, especially
when it comes to applications, relates to
orthogonal curves. To derive this property,
suppose that $u(x,y)$ is harmonic in a
domain D of the xy-plane such as that in
Figure 2.31 and $v(x,y)$ is a harmonic
conjugate of $u(x,y)$ in D. The equation
$u(x,y) = C_1$ where C_1 is a constant
defines a 1-parameter family of curves
one of which passes through each point
of D. Similarly, $v(x,y) = C_2$ defines a

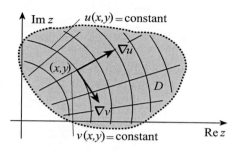

Figure 2.31

family of curves which also covers D. Thus, through each point (x,y) of D there
passes exactly one curve from each family.

A normal vector to $u(x,y) = C_1$ at any point is the gradient of $u(x,y)$, $\nabla u = (\partial u/\partial x)\hat{\mathbf{i}} + (\partial u/\partial y)\hat{\mathbf{j}}$, and a vector perpendicular to $v(x,y) = C_2$ at the same point
is $\nabla v = (\partial v/\partial x)\hat{\mathbf{i}} + (\partial v/\partial y)\hat{\mathbf{j}}$. Since u and v satisfy the Cauchy-Riemann equations,
it follows that the scalar product of these vectors is

$$\nabla u \cdot \nabla v = \frac{\partial u}{\partial x}\frac{\partial v}{\partial x} + \frac{\partial u}{\partial y}\frac{\partial v}{\partial y} = \frac{\partial u}{\partial x}\left(-\frac{\partial u}{\partial y}\right) + \frac{\partial u}{\partial y}\left(\frac{\partial u}{\partial x}\right) = 0.$$

Consequently, at every point (x,y) in D, the curves $u = C_1$ and $v = C_2$ through
(x,y) are perpendicular, or orthogonal. We have shown then that harmonic conjugates define orthogonal families of curves. We shall see the importance of this
property in the applications of harmonic functions. Figures 2.32a–c illustrate this
orthogonality for the analytic function $f(z) = z^2 - z$. Its real and imaginary parts
are $u(x,y) = x^2 - y^2 - x$ and $v(x,y) = 2xy - y$. The one-parameter family of curves
$u(x,y) = C_1$ is shown in Figure 2.32a, and the curves $v(x,y) = C_2$ are shown in
Figure 2.32b. Superposing these curves in Figure 2.32c clearly demonstrates that
each curve from one family intersects each curve from the other family at right
angles.

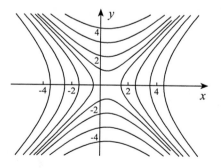

Figure 2.32a

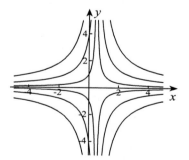

Figure 2.32b

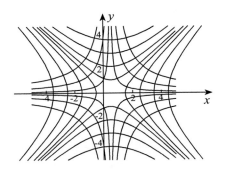

Figure 2.32c

EXERCISES 2.5

In Exercises 1–6 find domains in which $u(x, y)$ is harmonic. Find all harmonic conjugates.

1. $u(x, y) = 4 + x - x^2 + y^2$
2. $u(x, y) = x^3 - 3xy^2 + 2x + 5$
3. $u(x, y) = (x + 1)/[(x + 1)^2 + y^2]$
4. $u(x, y) = \sin x \, \cosh y$
5. $u(x, y) = \cos y \, \cosh x$
6. $u(x, y) = (x^2 + x + y^2)/(x^2 + y^2)$

7. Find all functions $u(x, y)$ to which $v(x, y) = 2xy + 3y$ is conjugate.

8. (a) Find all domains in which $u(x, y) = (2x^2 + 2y^2 - 6y)/(9 + x^2 + y^2 - 6y)$ is harmonic. Find all harmonic conjugates.
   (b) If $f(z) = u + vi$, find $f(z)$ in terms of z.

9. Verify that when $u(x, y)$ and $v(x, y)$ are harmonic conjugates in some domain D, then their product $u(x, y)v(x, y)$ is harmonic in D. Is it true that if $u(x, y)$ and $v(x, y)$ are harmonic in D, then their product is harmonic in D?

10. Find all harmonic conjugates of $u(x, y) = x^2 - y^2$. Draw the orthogonal families of curves defined by $u(x, y)$ and its harmonic conjugates.

11. Harmonic conjugates $u(x, y)$ and $v(x, y)$ define orthogonal families of curves $u(x, y) = C$ and $v(x, y) = C$. Do orthogonal families of curves $u(x, y) = C$ and $v(x, y) = C$ always define harmonic conjugates?

12. Prove that if $v(x, y)$ is the harmonic conjugate of $u(x, y)$ in some domain D, and $u(x, y)$ is the harmonic conjugate of $v(x, y)$ in D, then $u(x, y)$ and $v(x, y)$ are constant functions. Must they be the same constant function?

CHAPTER 3   ELEMENTARY COMPLEX FUNCTIONS

In this chapter we extend definitions of exponential, logarithm, trigonometric, inverse trigonometric, hyperbolic, inverse hyperbolic, and root functions to the complex plane. If $f(x)$ is any one of these functions, we shall want to extend $f(x)$ to a complex function $f(z)$ which agrees with $f(x)$ in the case that z is real, and hopefully has the same properties in the complex plane as does $f(x)$ on the real line. Of particular importance when it comes to applications are *zeros* and *singularities* of functions, and we therefore pay careful attention to zeros and singularities of each newly defined function.

§3.1   Zeros and Singularities

Definition 3.1   A point z_0 is called a **zero** of order m of a complex function f if f is analytic at z_0, and

$$0 = f(z_0) = f'(z_0) = \cdots = f^{(m-1)}(z_0), \quad f^{(m)}(z_0) \neq 0. \tag{3.1}$$

Recall that f is analytic "at z_0" if it is analytic in a neighbourhood of z_0. For a zero of order m, the function and its first $m-1$ derivatives vanish at z_0, but the mth derivative is not zero. If the mth derivative also vanishes, then the order of the zero is greater than m. Zeros of order 1 are often called **simple zeros**.

The polynomial $P(z) = (z - 1 + 2i)^3$ has a zero at $z = 1 - 2i$. Since $P'(z) = 3(z - 1 + 2i)^2$, $P''(z) = 6(z - 1 + 2i)$, and $P'''(z) = 6$, we find that $P(1 - 2i) = P'(1-2i) = P''(1-2i) = 0$, but $P'''(1-2i) \neq 0$. Consequently, the polynomial has a zero of order 3 at $z = 1 - 2i$. The rational function $R(z) = (z+1)^4(z - 4i)^2/(z^2 + 1)$ has zeros at $z = -1$ and $z = 4i$. To use Definition 3.1 to determine the orders of these derivatives would be most inconvenient; it would require calculating five derivatives of the function. The following theorem provides an excellent alternative.

Theorem 3.1   If a function $f(z)$ can be expressed in the form

$$f(z) = (z - z_0)^m g(z), \tag{3.2}$$

valid in some circle $|z - z_0| < R$, where $g(z)$ is analytic at z_0 and $g(z_0) \neq 0$, then $f(z)$ has a zero of order m at z_0.

Proof   If $f(z)$ can be expressed in the form $f(z) = (z - z_0)^m g(z)$ where g is analytic at z_0 and $g(z_0) \neq 0$, then

$f(z_0) \ = 0;$

$f'(z_0) \ = [(z - z_0)^m g'(z) + m(z - z_0)^{m-1} g(z)]_{|z=z_0} = 0;$

$f''(z_0) \ = [(z - z_0)^m g''(z) + 2m(z - z_0)^{m-1} g'(z) + m(m-1)(z - z_0)^{m-2} g(z)]_{|z=z_0} = 0.$

Continuation leads to vanishing derivatives of orders up to and including $m - 1$. Leibnitz's rule for the mth derivative of a product gives

$$f^{(m)}(z_0) = \left\{ (z - z_0)^m g^{(m)}(z) + [m(z - z_0)^{m-1}]g^{(m-1)}(z) + \cdots + m(m-1)\cdots(2)(1)g(z) \right\}_{|z=z_0}$$
$$= m!g(z_0) \neq 0.$$

Thus, z_0 is a zero of order m. ∎

With this theorem, it is straightforward to determine the orders of the zeros $z = -1$ and $z = 4i$ of $R(z) = (z + 1)^4 (z - 4i)^2 / (z^2 + 1)$. To find the order of the zero at $z = -1$, we write $R(z)$ in the form

$$R(z) = (z + 1)^4 \left[\frac{(z - 4i)^2}{z^2 + 1} \right].$$

The function $g(z) = \dfrac{(z - 4i)^2}{z^2 + 1}$ is analytic at $z = -1$ and $g(-1) \neq 0$. Hence, $R(z)$ has a zero of order 4 at $z = -1$. Similarly, to determine the order of the zero at $z = 4i$, we express $R(z)$ in the form

$$R(z) = (z - 4i)^2 \left[\frac{(z + 1)^4}{z^2 + 1} \right].$$

Since the function $h(z) = \dfrac{(z + 1)^4}{z^2 + 1}$ is analytic at $z = 4i$ and $h(4i) \neq 0$, $R(z)$ has a zero of order 2 at $z = 4i$.

We denote zeros of a function with small circles in the complex plane. Those for the rational function $R(z)$ are shown in Figure 3.1.

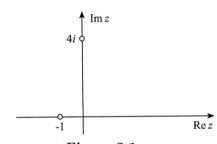

Figure 3.1

Points at which a function fails to be analytic are called "singularities". More precisely, we make the following definitions.

Definition 3.2   A point z_0 is called a **singularity** of a complex function f if f is not analytic at z_0, but every neighbourhood of z_0 contains at least one point at which f is analytic.

Definition 3.3   A singularity z_0 of a complex function f is said to be **isolated** if there exists a neighbourhood of z_0 in which z_0 is the only singularity of f.

Entire functions have no singularities. Rational functions $P(z)/Q(z)$, where $P(z)$ and $Q(z)$ are polynomials, have isolated singularities at points where $Q(z) = 0$. For example, $f(z) = z^2/(z^2 + 4)$ has isolated singularities at $z = \pm 2i$. We denote singularities of a function $f(z)$ graphically with an $\times$. We therefore have $\times$'s at $z = \pm 2i$ for the function $f(z) = z^2/(z^2 + 4)$ (Figure 3.2).

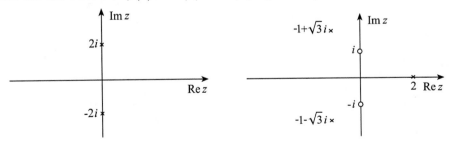

Figure 3.2   **Figure 3.3**

Example 3.1   Find and illustrate the zeros and singularities of the function $f(z) = \dfrac{z^4 + 2z^2 + 1}{z^3 - 8}$.

Solution   Since $z^4 + 2z^2 + 1 = (z^2 + 1)^2 = (z + i)^2(z - i)^2$, $f(z)$ has zeros at $z = \pm i$. By writing the function in the form

$$f(z) = (z - i)^2 \left[\frac{(z + i)^2}{z^3 - 8} \right],$$

and noting that $g(z) = \dfrac{(z + i)^2}{z^3 - 8}$ is analytic at $z = i$ and $g(i) \neq 0$, we conclude that $z = i$ is a zero of order 2. Similarly, $z = -i$ is also a zero of order 2. With $z^3 - 8 = (z - 2)(z^2 + 2z + 4) = (z - 2)(z + 1 - \sqrt{3}i)(z + 1 + \sqrt{3}i)$, we conclude that $f(z)$ has isolated singularities at $z = 2, -1 \pm \sqrt{3}i$. These zeros and singularities are shown in Figure 3.3.●

Example 3.2   What are the singularities of the function $\operatorname{Re} z$, $\operatorname{Im} z$, $|z|$, $\arg_\phi z$, and $\operatorname{Arg} z$?

Solution   According to Example 2.20, these functions are nowhere analytic. Does this mean that every point in the complex plane is a singularity? No! These functions do not have singularities, since every neighbourhood of a singularity of a function must contain a point at which the function is analytic. We will not deny that these functions fail to have a derivative at every point in the complex plane, but we cannot call them singularities according to Definition 3.2.●

EXERCISES 3.1

In Exercises 1–22 identify all zeros and their orders for the function. Locate all singularities and determine which are isolated.

1. $f(z) = 3z - 2$

2. $f(z) = \dfrac{1}{3z - 2}$

3. $f(z) = z^2 + 3z - 2$

4. $f(z) = z^2 + 4$

5. $f(z) = z^3 + 8$

6. $f(z) = z^2 + 2z + 1$

7. $f(z) = \dfrac{1}{z^2 + 2z + 4}$

8. $f(z) = \dfrac{z^2 - 3}{z^2 + 5z + 1}$

9. $f(z) = \dfrac{z^3 + 2z}{z^2 - 2z + 1}$

10. $f(z) = \dfrac{z^3}{3z + 4}$

11. $f(z) = \dfrac{z}{(3z + 1)^3}$

12. $f(z) = \operatorname{Arg} z$

13. $f(z) = |z|$

14. $f(z) = \left(\dfrac{z - 1}{z + 2} \right)^2$

15. $f(z) = \dfrac{z^3 - 3z^2 + 3z - 1}{z + 5}$

16. $f(z) = \dfrac{z^3 + 1}{z^3 - 1}$

17. $f(z) = \dfrac{z^2 + i}{2z - 3}$

18. $f(z) = z^2 + 4iz - 2$

19. $f(z) = \dfrac{z^2 - 2iz + i}{z + 4}$

20. $f(z) = \dfrac{z^3 - 2z^2}{3z^2 + 4z - i}$

21. $f(z) = z^2 + \dfrac{4i}{z}$

22. $f(z) = z^3 + \dfrac{2 + z^2 - 5z^3}{z + 5}$

§3.2 Complex Exponential Function

In this section we define the complex exponential function e^z. Unlike real analysis where the trigonometric, inverse trigonometric, and functions with fractional powers have no relation whatsoever with e^x, we find that in complex analysis, these functions, as well as logarithm, hyperbolic, and inverse hyperbolic functions are all defined in terms of e^z. In other words, complex exponentials are fundamental to our studies; master e^z and its properties before proceeding to further sections in this chapter.

Many approaches lead to a definition of e^z. Although our approach may not be the quickest, it has the advantage of being intuitive and complete. It utilizes differentiation, and it emphasizes once again the importance of the Cauchy-Riemann equations in complex analysis. We shall want to define e^z in such a way that whenever $z = x$ is real, e^z will be e^x as we understand it now. We ask therefore what algebraic and/or differentiation properties characterize the real exponential function e^x from all other real functions. Such properties might then be used to define the complex exponential function e^z. Certainly we cannot forget our first calculus instructor emphasizing the fact that e^x is a function that differentiates to give itself; that is, e^x satisfies the property that $f'(x) = f(x)$. But so also does any constant times e^x. What distinguishes e^x from other solutions of $f'(x) = f(x)$ is the additional requirement that $f(0) = 1$. In other words, e^x is the one and only solution of

$$f'(x) = f(x), \qquad f(0) = 1.$$

It is this characterization that we use to define e^z.

Definition 3.4 The complex exponential function e^z is defined as the solution of the complex differential equation

$$f'(z) = f(z), \quad f(0) = 1. \tag{3.3}$$

(In this way we ensure that $f(z)$ reduces to e^x when z is real.) What do we know about complex differential equations? Nothing, but this can be remedied by separating equation 3.3 into real and imaginary parts. To do this, we set $f(z) = u(x, y) + v(x, y)i$, in which case the equation becomes

$$\frac{\partial u}{\partial x} + \frac{\partial v}{\partial x} i = u + vi, \quad u(0,0) + v(0,0)i = 1.$$

Taking real and imaginary parts gives

$$\frac{\partial u}{\partial x} = u, \quad u(0,0) = 1; \qquad \frac{\partial v}{\partial x} = v, \quad v(0,0) = 0,$$

and we have two separate systems, one in $u(x, y)$ and one in $v(x, y)$. They imply that

$$u(x, y) = p(y)e^x \quad \text{where } p(0) = 1; \qquad v(x, y) = q(y)e^x \quad \text{where } q(0) = 0.$$

Where now; have we not exhausted the information in requirement 3.3? Not quite. The fact that $f'(z)$ must exist (that is, $f(z)$ is analytic) requires u and v to satisfy the Cauchy-Riemann equations. This means that

$$p(y)e^x = q'(y)e^x, \qquad q(y)e^x = -p'(y)e^x,$$

and from these $p = q'$ and $q = -p'$. It follows therefore that

$$p'' = -q' = -p \quad \text{and} \quad q'' = p' = -q.$$

Thus, $p(y)$ and $q(y)$ each satisfy the real differential equation

$$\frac{d^2\phi}{dy^2} + \phi = 0.$$

But all solutions of this differential equation are of the form $A\cos y + B\sin y$ for some constants A and B. Since $p(y)$ satisfies $p(0) = 1$ and $p'(0) = -q(0) = 0$, it follows that $p(y) = \cos y$. Similarly, for $q(0) = 0$ and $q'(0) = p(0) = 1$, we have $q(y) = \sin y$. Hence, the solution of differential equation 3.3, which we have agreed to call e^z, is defined as follows

$$e^z = e^x \cos y + e^x \sin y\, i = e^x(\cos y + \sin y\, i). \tag{3.4}$$

Since this complex exponential function satisfies the Cauchy-Riemann equations (by construction and does so for all z), and first partial derivatives of u and v are clearly continuous, it follows that e^z is an entire function. Based on equation 3.3 we can state that

$$\frac{d}{dz}e^z = e^z. \tag{3.5}$$

Example 3.3 Express e^{3-i} and e^{2i-1} in Cartesian form.

Solution By equation 3.4,

$$e^{3-i} = e^3[\cos(-1) + \sin(-1)\,i] = e^3(\cos 1 - \sin 1\, i)$$
$$= (e^3 \cos 1) - (e^3 \sin 1)i \approx 10.9 - 16.9i,$$

and

$$e^{2i-1} = e^{-1}(\cos 2 + \sin 2\, i) = (e^{-1}\cos 2) + (e^{-1}\sin 2)i$$
$$\approx -0.153 + 0.335i.\bullet$$

Example 3.4 Find $f''(-2 + 4i)$ if $f(z) = e^{3z}$.

Solution The chain rule gives $f''(z) = 9e^{3z}$, and therefore

$$f''(-2 + 4i) = 9e^{3(-2+4i)} = 9e^{-6+12i} = 9e^{-6}(\cos 12 + \sin 12\, i) \approx 0.0188 - 0.0120i.\bullet$$

Algebraic properties of the complex exponential function e^z must be based on equation 3.4. It is straightforward to show that

$$e^{z_1}e^{z_2} = e^{z_1+z_2}, \tag{3.6a}$$
$$e^{z_1}/e^{z_2} = e^{z_1-z_2}. \tag{3.6b}$$

For instance, if $z_1 = x_1 + y_1 i$ and $z_2 = x_2 + y_2 i$, then

$$e^{z_1}e^{z_2} = [e^{x_1}(\cos y_1 + \sin y_1\, i)][e^{x_2}(\cos y_2 + \sin y_2\, i)] \quad \text{(by 3.4)}$$
$$= e^{x_1+x_2}[(\cos y_1 \cos y_2 - \sin y_1 \sin y_2)$$

$$+[\cos y_1 \sin y_2 + \sin y_1 \cos y_2)i] \quad \text{[by ordinary algebra]}$$
$$= e^{x_1+x_2}[\cos(y_1+y_2) + \sin(y_1+y_2)i] \quad \text{[by real trigonometric identities]}$$
$$= e^{x_1+x_2+(y_1+y_2)i} \quad \text{(by 3.4)}$$
$$= e^{z_1+z_2}.$$

We might have expected a third identity to accompany 3.6a,b namely, $(e^{z_1})^{z_2} = e^{z_1 z_2}$. But the left side of this equation is a complex number e^{z_1} raised to a complex number z_2, an operation which as yet is undefined. When it is defined in Section 3.6, we will discuss the identity.

When we set $x = 0$ in equation 3.4, e^z becomes e^{yi}, and therefore

$$e^{yi} = \cos y + \sin y\, i. \tag{3.7}$$

This is Euler's identity that we used as the definition for e^{yi} in developing the exponential form for complex numbers in Section 1.4. In other words, we have now validated the exponential form for complex numbers. The next two examples review this notation.

Example 3.5   Express the complex numbers -1 and $3 - 2i$ in exponential notation.

Solution   Since $|-1| = 1$ and $\text{Arg}(-1) = \pi$, it follows that

$$-1 = (1)e^{\pi i} = e^{\pi i}.$$

With $|3 - 2i| = \sqrt{13}$ and $\theta = \text{Arg}(3 - 2i) = \text{Tan}^{-1}(-2/3) \approx -0.588$,

$$3 - 2i = \sqrt{13}e^{\theta i} = \sqrt{13}e^{i\text{Tan}^{-1}(-2/3)} \approx \sqrt{13}e^{-0.588i}.$$

Neither of these representations is unique; it is not necessary to use principal values of arguments. We could write $-1 = e^{(\pi+2n\pi)i}$ and $3 - 2i \approx \sqrt{13}e^{(2n\pi-0.588)i}$ for any integer n. •

Example 3.6   Find $(1 - 2i)^9 e^{3i}$ in Cartesian form.

Solution   Since $|1 - 2i| = \sqrt{5}$ and $\theta = \text{Arg}(1 - 2i) = \text{Tan}^{-1}(-2) \approx -1.107$, it follows that

$$(1 - 2i)^9 e^{3i} = (\sqrt{5}e^{\theta i})^9 e^{3i} = 5^{9/2}e^{9\theta i}e^{3i} = 5^{9/2}e^{(9\theta+3)i}$$
$$= 5^{9/2}[\cos(9\theta+3) + \sin(9\theta+3)i] \approx 1086.9 - 878.6i \,. •$$

Example 3.7   Find all complex numbers z such such that $e^z = 2 - i$.

Solution   If we set $z = x + yi$, then

$$2 - i = e^z = e^{x+yi} = e^x(\cos y + \sin y\, i).$$

When we equate real and imaginary parts, we obtain

$$e^x \cos y = 2, \qquad e^x \sin y = -1.$$

When these are squared and added, $e^{2x} = 5$, from which $x = (1/2)\ln 5$. It now follows that

$$\sqrt{5}\cos y = 2, \qquad \sqrt{5}\sin y = -1.$$

These imply that $y = 2n\pi - \text{Sin}^{-1}\left(\dfrac{1}{\sqrt{5}}\right)$, where n is an integer, and therefore

solutions are $z = \dfrac{1}{2}\ln 5 + \left[2n\pi - \text{Sin}^{-1}\left(\dfrac{1}{\sqrt{5}}\right)\right]i$. We will be able to provide a more efficient solution to this problem when we introduce the complex logarithm function in Section 3.5.●

In the introduction to this chapter we indicated that we would investigate zeros and singularities of each newly defined function. Being entire, e^z has no singularities. It also has no zeros as can be seen from the fact that

$$|e^z| = |e^x(\cos y + \sin y\, i)| = |e^x||\cos y + \sin y\, i| = e^x,$$

and $e^x \neq 0$. What turns out to have profound significance about e^z are the complex numbers z for which e^z is equal to 1. If $1 = e^z = e^x(\cos y + \sin y\, i)$, then real and imaginary parts imply that

$$e^x \cos y = 1, \qquad e^x \sin y = 0.$$

The second equation requires $y = n\pi$, where n is an integer, which substituted into the first gives $1 = e^x(-1)^n$. Consequently, n must be an even integer, and in this case $x = 0$. Thus, for any integer n, we have

$$e^{2n\pi i} = 1. \tag{3.8}$$

Equation 3.8 indicates that the exponential function $w = e^z$ maps each of the complex numbers $z = 2n\pi i$ onto the real number $w = 1$. Let us examine the mapping further by considering the infinite strip $-\pi < y \leq \pi$ in the complex z-plane (Figure 3.4). Points on the imaginary axis $(x = 0)$ are mapped by $w = e^z$ to points $w = e^z = e^{yi} = \cos y + \sin y\, i$; i.e., to points on the unit circle $|w| = 1$. For points in the strip with negative real parts $(x < 0)$, we find that $|e^z| = e^x < 1$. Hence, points in the left half of the strip are mapped inside the unit circle. Similarly, points with positive real parts $(x > 0)$ are mapped to points outside the unit circle.

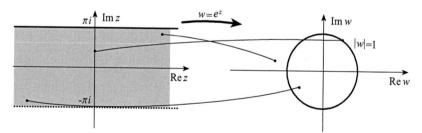

Figure 3.4

We now show that that the mapping $w = e^z$ of the strip $-\pi < y \leq \pi$ to the w-plane is (almost) onto and one-to-one; every point $w = u + vi$ in the w-plane (except $w = 0$) is the image of exactly one point z in the strip $-\pi < y \leq \pi$. To find $z = x + yi$ such that $w = u + vi = e^z$ for given w, we set

$$u + vi = e^z = e^x(\cos y + \sin y\, i).$$

Real and imaginary parts of this equation require

$$e^x \cos y = u \qquad \text{and} \qquad e^x \sin y = v.$$

These imply that $e^{2x} = u^2 + v^2$, or $x = (1/2)\ln(u^2 + v^2)$; and y is then defined by

$$\cos y = \frac{u}{\sqrt{u^2 + v^2}}, \qquad \sin y = \frac{v}{\sqrt{u^2 + v^2}}.$$

Since the value of x is unique, and there is exactly one value of y in the interval $-\pi < y \le \pi$ satisfying these equations, it follows that the image of the strip of Figure 3.4 is the entire w-plane (except for the point $w = 0$), and that the mapping is one-to-one.

Because y is defined only to a multiple of 2π, it also follows that every strip $y_0 < y \le y_0 + 2\pi$ is mapped one-to-one onto the w-plane (less $w = 0$). Another way of saying the same thing is that because

$$e^{z + 2\pi i} = e^z, \tag{3.9}$$

e^z is a periodic complex function with complex period $2\pi i$. The real exponential function e^x is certainly not periodic; but its extension $e^z = e^x(\cos y + \sin y\, i)$ to the complex plane is periodic. Let us examine this periodicity in a slightly different way.

Points $z = x$ on the real z-axis are mapped by $w = e^z$ to $w = e^x$, points on the positive real w-axis. Points on a horizontal line $y = y_0$ where y_0 is just greater than zero are mapped to the points $w = e^x(\cos y_0 + \sin y_0\, i)$; they all lie on the half-line with argument y_0 in the w-plane (Figure 3.5). As we raise the line $y = y_0$, its image in the w-plane rotates. When $y_0 = \pi/2$, its image is the upper half of the imaginary axis in the w-plane. When $y_0 = \pi$, the image is the negative real axis. Finally, when $y_0 = 2\pi$, the image is once again the positive real w-axis. As we see, then, e^z retains the nonperiodic nature of e^x along the real z-axis, but introduces an imaginary period $2\pi i$ with the extension of e^x into the complex plane.

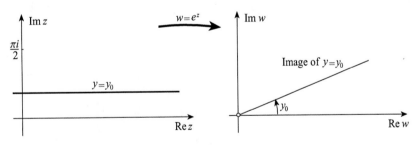

Figure 3.5

Example 3.8   Find the image of the strip $0 \le \text{Im}\, z \le \pi$ under the mapping $w = e^z$.

Solution   The real z-axis C_1 is mapped to the positive real w-axis (Figure 3.6). Points $z = x + \pi i$ on C_2 : $\text{Im}\, z = \pi$ are mapped to $w = e^{x + \pi i} = e^x(\cos \pi + \sin \pi\, i) = -e^x$, points on the negative real axis in the w-plane. When $z = x + yi$, where $0 < y < \pi$, we find that $w = e^{x + yi} = e^x(\cos y + \sin y\, i)$, and the imaginary part $e^x \sin y > 0$. In other words, $w = e^z$ maps the strip $0 \le \text{Im}\, z \le \pi$ to the half-plane $\text{Im}\, w \ge 0$ (less of course the point $w = 0$).

It is straightforward to show that every point in $\text{Im}\, w > 0$ is the image of exactly one point in $0 < \text{Im}\, z < \pi$. Hence, the strip $0 \le \text{Im}\, z \le \pi$ is mapped one-to-one onto the half-plane $\text{Im}\, w \ge 0$ (less $w = 0$).•

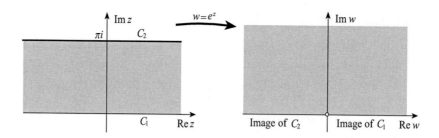

Figure 3.6

Further regional mappings of $w = e^z$ are discussed in Exercise 28. In particular, part (c) shows that the strip $0 \leq \operatorname{Im} z \leq \pi/2$ is mapped onto the quarter plane $\operatorname{Re} w \geq 0$, $\operatorname{Im} w \geq 0$ (Figure 3.7), less again $w = 0$.

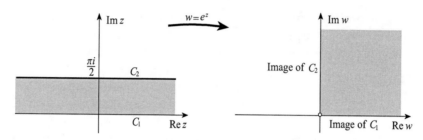

Figure 3.7

EXERCISES 3.2

In Exercises 1–10 express the complex number in exponential form.

1. $1 - i$

2. $-1 + \sqrt{3}i$

3. $(2 + 2i)^2$

4. $3 + 4i$

5. $-2 + 6i$

6. $(1 - 2i)^2$

7. $4[\cos(\pi/3) + \sin(\pi/3)i]$

8. $-4[\cos(-21\pi/10) + \sin(-21\pi/10)i]$

9. $2[\cos(\pi/12) - \sin(\pi/12)i]$

10. $3[\cos(\pi/4) + \sin(\pi/4)i]^3$

In Exercises 11–14 express the complex number in Cartesian form.

11. e^{2+3i}

12. e^{-1-4i}

13. $e^{(2-i)/(3+i)}$

14. e^{i^3+2i}

In Exercises 15–22 find all solutions of the equation.

15. $e^z = 4$

16. $e^z = 4i$

17. $e^z = 4 + 4i$

18. $e^z = 2 - 3i$

19. $e^{2-z} = -1 + i$

20. $e^{2z} + 2e^z + 1 = 0$

21. $e^{2z} + e^z + 1 = 0$

22. $e^{2z} + 3e^z + 5 = 0$

In Exercises 23–26 find the indicated derivative. Express final answers in Cartesian form.

23. $f'(2 + i)$ if $f(z) = e^{3z+2}$

24. $f''(-i)$ if $f(z) = z^2 e^{-z}$

25. $f'(3 + 2i)$ if $f(z) = ze^{-2z}$

26. $f'''(3i + 1)$ if $f(z) = e^{iz}$

27. Based on Definition 3.4 we know that the derivative of e^z is e^z. Show this using equation 3.4 and the Cauchy-Riemann equations.

Mapping Exercises

28. Show that $w = e^z$, regarded as a mapping from the z-plane to the w-plane, performs the mappings indicated in the figures below.

(a)

(b)

(c)

(d)

(e)

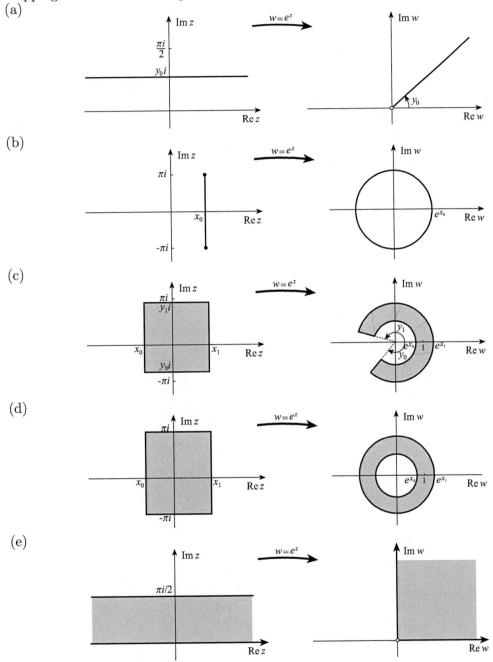

(f)

(g)

(h)

(i)

(j)

(k)

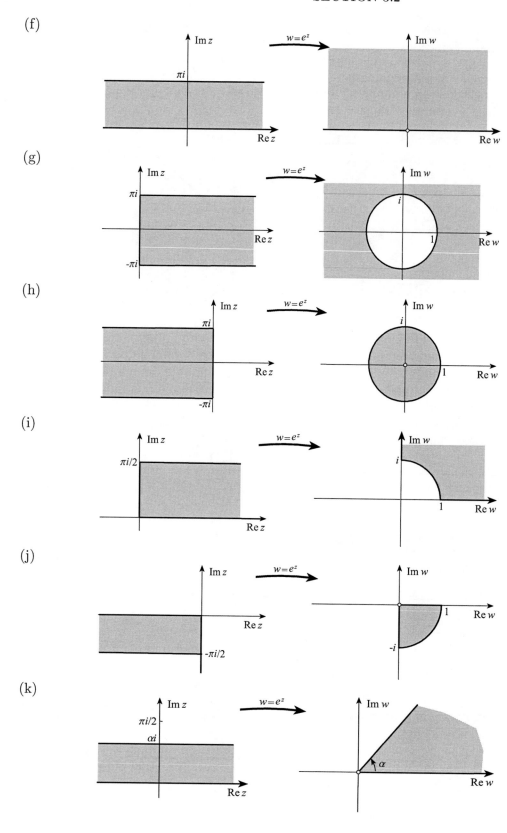

(1)

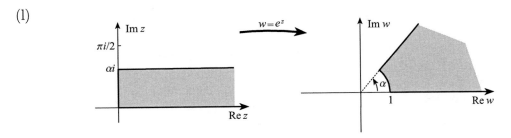

29. Find a function $w = f(z)$ that maps the infinite strip $0 < \operatorname{Im} z < a$ onto the half-plane $\operatorname{Im} w > 0$.

30. Find a function $w = f(z)$ that maps the infinite strip $0 < \operatorname{Im} z < a$ onto the quarter-plane $\operatorname{Re} w > 0$, $\operatorname{Im} w > 0$.

§3.3   Complex Trigonometric Functions

Most introductions to real trigonometric functions begin with trigonometric ratios of sides of right-angled triangles. This leads immediately to a wide variety of applications, and it also provides a straightforward extension to trigonometric ratios of arbitrary angles, the birth of the trigonometric functions. The appeal of this approach is its constant reference to triangles and associated visualizations. We soon realize, however, that trigonometric functions, especially the sine and cosine, enter many, many applications with no associated triangles. We accept that what is important about a function is that it has values, and that we can find these values, and we gradually push into the background ratios of sides of triangles unless they fit naturally into a particular application. But how do we find values for trigonometric functions, say $\sin(1.356)$. As a student, I used tables of trigonometric functions, not particularly accurate and not particularly efficient. You undoubtedly use an electronic calculator, more efficient and definitely more accurate. Is there an alternative? Yes, Maclaurin series for the sine and cosine functions can provide values of these functions with whatever accuracy is required. These series can also be used to verify trigonometric identities, and from many perspectives, the sine and cosine functions should be defined in this way.

What we are suggesting here is that as you acquired more and more mathematical knowledge, you were asked to regard trigonometric functions in a less and less geometric way. In this section, we take the final step. We apply trigonometric functions to complex numbers. There is no geometry. Not that we ask you to suppress it; there just isn't any.

The real trigonometric functions are unrelated to the real exponential function e^x; the trigonometric functions are periodic, e^x is not. Just the opposite is true for complex trigonometric functions. We actually define complex trigonometric functions in terms of the complex exponential function e^z. To see how, recall that Euler's identity implies that $e^{\theta i} = \cos\theta + \sin\theta\, i$ and $e^{-\theta i} = \cos\theta - \sin\theta\, i$ for any real number θ. By adding and subtracting these equations we obtain

$$\cos\theta = \frac{e^{\theta i} + e^{-\theta i}}{2} \quad\text{and}\quad \sin\theta = \frac{e^{\theta i} - e^{-\theta i}}{2i}. \tag{3.10}$$

These equations express the real functions $\sin\theta$ and $\cos\theta$ in terms of the complex exponentials $e^{\theta i}$ and $e^{-\theta i}$. Now, the extension of a real trigonometric function to the complex plane should be done in such a way that when the argument of the complex trigonometric function is real, the function should return to its real form. With this and equations 3.10 in mind, it is natural to extend the sine and cosine functions to the complex plane according to

$$\cos z = \frac{e^{zi} + e^{-zi}}{2} \quad\text{and}\quad \sin z = \frac{e^{zi} - e^{-zi}}{2i}. \tag{3.11}$$

Because e^z is $2\pi i$-periodic, and definitions of $\sin z$ and $\cos z$ involve e^{iz} and e^{-iz}, it follows that $\sin z$ and $\cos z$, like their real counterparts, are 2π-periodic. They also satisfy the usual trigonometric identities. For example,

$$\sin^2 z + \cos^2 z = \left(\frac{e^{zi} - e^{-zi}}{2i}\right)^2 + \left(\frac{e^{zi} + e^{-zi}}{2}\right)^2$$

$$= -\frac{1}{4}(e^{2zi} - 2 + e^{-2zi}) + \frac{1}{4}(e^{2zi} + 2 + e^{-2zi}) = 1;$$

and

$$\sin z \cos w + \cos z \sin w = \frac{e^{zi} - e^{-zi}}{2i} \frac{e^{wi} + e^{-wi}}{2} + \frac{e^{zi} + e^{-zi}}{2} \frac{e^{wi} - e^{-wi}}{2i}$$

$$= \frac{1}{4i}[e^{(z+w)i} - e^{(w-z)i} + e^{(z-w)i} - e^{-(z+w)i}$$

$$+ e^{(z+w)i} - e^{(z-w)i} + e^{(w-z)i} - e^{(z+w)i}]$$

$$= \frac{e^{(z+w)i} - e^{-(z+w)i}}{2i} = \sin(z + w).$$

Example 3.9   Express $\sin(3 + 2i)$ and $\cos(-1 + 4i)$ in Cartesian form.

Solution By definition 3.11,

$$\sin(3 + 2i) = \frac{e^{(3+2i)i} - e^{-(3+2i)i}}{2i} = -\frac{i}{2}[e^{-2+3i} - e^{2-3i}]$$

$$= -\frac{i}{2}[e^{-2}(\cos 3 + \sin 3\, i) - e^{2}(\cos 3 - \sin 3\, i)]$$

$$= \frac{1}{2}\sin 3\,(e^{2} + e^{-2}) + \frac{1}{2}\cos 3\,(e^{2} - e^{-2})i$$

$$\approx 0.531 - 3.59i;$$

and

$$\cos(-1 + 4i) = \frac{e^{(-1+4i)i} + e^{-(-1+4i)i}}{2} = \frac{1}{2}[e^{-4-i} + e^{4+i}]$$

$$= \frac{1}{2}[e^{-4}(\cos 1 - \sin 1\, i) + e^{4}(\cos 1 + \sin 1\, i)]$$

$$= \frac{1}{2}\cos 1\,(e^{4} + e^{-4}) + \frac{1}{2}\sin 1\,(e^{4} - e^{-4})i$$

$$\approx 14.8 + 23.0i. \bullet$$

You may have noticed hyperbolic functions rearing their heads in this example. Trigonometric and hyperbolic functions are intimately related in complex variable work, and we constantly work simultaneously with both sets of functions. It is shown in Exercise 17 that real and imaginary parts of $\sin z$ and $\cos z$ can be expressed as follows:

$$\sin z = \sin(x + yi) = \sin x \cosh y + \cos x \sinh y\, i, \tag{3.12a}$$

$$\cos z = \cos(x + yi) = \cos x \cosh y - \sin x \sinh y\, i. \tag{3.12b}$$

With these we can be more expedient in Example 3.9,

$$\sin(3 + 2i) = \sin 3 \cosh 2 + \cos 3 \sinh 2\, i \approx 0.531 - 3.59i,$$

$$\cos(-1 + 4i) = \cos(-1) \cosh 4 - \sin(-1) \sinh 4\, i \approx 14.8 + 23.0i.$$

According to equation 3.12a, the modulus of $\sin z$ is

$$|\sin z| = \sqrt{\sin^2 x \cosh^2 y + \cos^2 x \sinh^2 y}.$$

This expression becomes arbitrarily large for large positive and negative values of y. In other words, unlike $\sin x$ which satisfies $|\sin x| \le 1$, the modulus of $\sin z$ is unbounded as $y \to \pm\infty$ for any x whatsoever. The modulus of $\cos z$ is also unbounded as $y \to \pm\infty$.

Since $\cos z$ and $\sin z$ are sums of entire functions, they are also entire functions; they have no singularities. It is straightforward to find their derivatives,

$$\frac{d}{dz}(\sin z) = \frac{d}{dz}\left(\frac{e^{zi} - e^{-zi}}{2i}\right) = \frac{ie^{zi} + ie^{-zi}}{2i} = \frac{e^{zi} + e^{-zi}}{2} = \cos z,$$

$$\frac{d}{dz}(\cos z) = \frac{d}{dz}\left(\frac{e^{zi} + e^{-zi}}{2}\right) = \frac{ie^{zi} - ie^{-zi}}{2} = \frac{-e^{zi} + e^{-zi}}{2i} = -\sin z.$$

Zeros of $\sin z$ are defined by

$$0 = \sin z = \sin x \cosh y + \cos x \sinh y\, i.$$

When we equate real and imaginary parts to zero,

$$0 = \sin x \cosh y, \qquad 0 = \cos x \sinh y.$$

The first of these implies that $x = n\pi$, and substitution of this into the second yields $y = 0$. Consequently, the zeros of $\sin z$ are the same as those of $\sin x$, namely, $z = n\pi$. Since the derivative of $\sin z$ at $z = n\pi$ is not zero, these are simple zeros. Similarly, $\cos z$ has simple zeros $z = (2n + 1)\pi/2$. These zeros are illustrated in Figures 3.8 and 3.9. Thus, although we have extended the sine and cosine functions from the real axis to the entire complex plane, no new zeros are introduced.

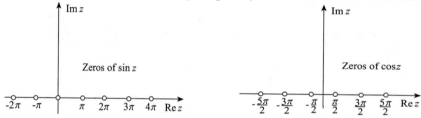

Figure 3.8   **Figure 3.9**

The remaining complex trigonometric functions are defined as usual,

$$\tan z = \frac{\sin z}{\cos z}; \quad \cot z = \frac{\cos z}{\sin z}; \quad \sec z = \frac{1}{\cos z}; \quad \csc z = \frac{1}{\sin z}. \tag{3.13}$$

Derivatives of these functions are as expected,

$$\frac{d}{dz}(\tan z) = \sec^2 z; \qquad \frac{d}{dz}(\cot z) = -\csc^2 z; \tag{3.14a}$$

$$\frac{d}{dz}(\sec z) = \sec z \tan z; \qquad \frac{d}{dz}(\csc z) = -\csc z \cot z. \tag{3.14b}$$

They are analytic functions in the complex plane except where their denominators vanish; in other words, isolated singularities of $\tan z$ and $\sec z$ occur at the zeros $z = (2n + 1)\pi/2$ of $\cos z$, and $\cot z$ and $\csc z$ have isolated singularities at the zeros $z = n\pi$ of $\sin z$.

Example 3.10 Express $\tan i$ in Cartesian form.

Solution Using equations 3.13 and 3.12,

$$\tan i = \frac{\sin i}{\cos i} = \frac{\sinh 1\, i}{\cosh 1} \approx 0.762i.\bullet$$

Example 3.11   Find all solutions of the equation $\sec z = 4i$.

Solution   If $\sec z = 4i$, then $\cos z = -i/4$. If we set $z = x + yi$, then

$$-\frac{i}{4} = \cos x \cosh y - \sin x \sinh y\, i.$$

When we equate real and imaginary parts, x and y satisfy

$$0 = \cos x \cosh y, \qquad -\frac{1}{4} = -\sin x \sinh y.$$

The first requires $x = (2n+1)\pi/2$, where n is an integer, which substituted into the second gives

$$\frac{1}{4} = \sin\left[\frac{(2n+1)\pi}{2}\right] \sinh y = (-1)^n \sinh y.$$

Hence, $y = \text{Sinh}^{-1}[(-1)^n/4] = (-1)^n \text{Sinh}^{-1}(1/4) \approx 0.247(-1)^n$, and the required solutions are $z \approx \dfrac{(2n+1)\pi}{2} + 0.247(-1)^n i$. A more efficient procedure using inverse trigonometric functions is discussed in Section 3.7.●

Example 3.12   Show that $w = \sin z$ maps the semi-infinite strip $-\pi/2 \le \text{Re}\, z \le \pi/2$, $\text{Im}\, z \ge 0$ one-to-one onto the half-plane $\text{Im}\, w \ge 0$.

Solution   Points on $C_2 : z = x$, $-\pi/2 \le x \le \pi/2$, are mapped to $w = \sin x$; that is, to points on the real axis in the w-plane with $-1 \le \text{Re}\, w \le 1$ (Figure 3.10). Points on $C_1 : z = -\pi/2 + yi$, $y \ge 0$ are mapped to

$$w = \sin\left(-\frac{\pi}{2} + yi\right) = \sin\left(-\frac{\pi}{2}\right)\cosh y + \cos\left(-\frac{\pi}{2}\right)\sinh y\, i = -\cosh y.$$

Since $1 \le \cosh y < \infty$ for $y \ge 0$, it follows that the image of C_1 is the real w-axis to the left of $w = -1$. Similarly, the image of C_3 is the real w-axis to the right of $w = 1$. For $z = x + yi$ where $-\pi/2 < x < \pi/2$ and $y > 0$, the imaginary part of $w = \sin z = \sin x \cosh y + \cos x \sinh y\, i$ is positive. We have shown therefore that the semi-infinite strip is mapped into the half-plane $\text{Im}\, w \ge 0$. To show that the strip is mapped one-to-one onto $\text{Im}\, w \ge 0$, we must show that every point $w = u + vi$ in $\text{Im}\, w > 0$ is the image of exactly one point in the semi-infinite strip. Consider, then, solving the equation

$$w = u + vi = \sin z = \sin x \cosh y + \cos x \sinh y\, i$$

for x and y for given u and v. This complex equation is equivalent to the real equations

$$u = \sin x \cosh y, \qquad v = \cos x \sinh y.$$

We can replace these equations with separate ones in x and y,

$$\frac{u^2}{\cosh^2 y} + \frac{v^2}{\sinh^2 y} = 1 \qquad \text{and} \qquad \frac{u^2}{\sin^2 x} - \frac{v^2}{\cos^2 x} = 1.$$

For given y, the first of these equations defines an ellipse in the w-plane, with foci $(\pm 1, 0)$, that increases in size as y increases. Conversely, given u and v, there exists an ellipse that passes through the point (u, v), and hence values of y that satisfy the equation. Similarly, the second equation defines hyperbolas in the w-plane, and given u and v, there exists values of x for which the hyperbola passes through (u, v). This verifies that the mapping is onto. To show that the mapping is one-to-one, suppose that two points z_1 and z_2 of the z-plane map to the same point in the w-plane. Then $\sin z_1 = \sin z_2$, and this is true if and only if

$$\frac{e^{z_1 i} - e^{-z_1 i}}{2i} = \frac{e^{z_2 i} - e^{-z_2 i}}{2i} \qquad \Longleftrightarrow \qquad e^{z_1 i}\left[1 - e^{(z_2 - z_1)i}\right] = -e^{-z_2 i}\left[1 - e^{(z_2 - z_1)i}\right].$$

But this result is valid if and only if $e^{z_1 i} = -e^{-z_2 i} = e^{(\pi - z_2)i}$, or, $1 - e^{(z_2 - z_1)i} = 0$; that is, if and only if $e^{(\pi - z_2 - z_1)i} = 1$, or, $e^{(z_2 - z_1)i} = 1$. According to equation 3.8, these are satisfied if and only if $\pi - z_2 - z_1 = 2n\pi$, or, $z_2 - z_1 = 2n\pi$; that is, if and only if $z_2 = (\pi - z_1) - 2n\pi$ or $z_2 = z_1 + 2n\pi$. No two points in $-\pi/2 < x < \pi/2$ can satisfy either of these, and therefore no two points in $-\pi/2 < x < \pi/2$, $y > 0$ can map to the same point in $w > 0$.$\bullet$

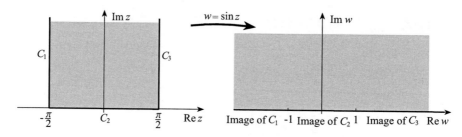

Figure 3.10

EXERCISES 3.3

In Exercises 1–12 express the complex number in Cartesian form.

1. $\sin i$

2. $\cos(1 - i)$

3. $\cos(1.3 + 2i)$

4. $\sin(5.6 + 4.1i)$

5. $e^{2+i}\cos i$

6. $\cos i \sin i$

7. $\cos^2(1 + i)$

8. $(2 - 3i)\sin(2i^2 + 1)$

9. $\tan 2i$

10. $\cot(-i)$

11. $\csc(2/i)$

12. $\sec(2 - 3i)$

In Exercises 13–16 find all solutions of the equation.

13. $\sin z = 2i$

14. $\cos z = 4$

15. $\sin(z + i) = 1$

16. $\tan z = i$

17. Verify equations 3.12.

18. Show that

$$|\sin z|^2 = \sin^2 x + \sinh^2 y, \qquad |\cos z|^2 = \cos^2 x + \sinh^2 y.$$

In Exercises 19–23 find the indicated derivative. Express final answers in Cartesian form.

19. $f'(2 + i)$ if $f(z) = \sin iz$

20. $f''(i)$ if $f(z) = z \tan z$

21. $f'(-i)$ if $f(z) = \csc(2z + i)$

22. $f'(3)$ if $f(z) = \sin(z^2 + i)$

23. $f''(-2i)$ if $f(z) = i \cos^2(2iz)$

24. Verify that $\sin^2 z + \cos^2 z = 1$ by showing that the derivative of the function $f(z) = \sin^2 z + \cos^2 z$ is equal to $f'(z) = 0$ and $f(0) = 1$.

25. For what values of z is $\cos z$ (a) real (b) purely imaginary?

26. For what values of z is $\sin z$ (a) real (b) purely imaginary?

27. Prove that all solutions of the equation $z \tan z = k$, where $k > 0$ is real, must be real.

28. Verify the following extension of Euler's identity 1.29,

$$e^{iz} = \cos z + i \sin z.$$

29. Verify that when $\sin z_1 = \sin z_2$, then either $z_2 = z_1 + 2n\pi$, or, $z_2 = -z_1 + (2n+1)\pi$, where n is an integer.

30. Prove that real and imaginary parts of $\tan z$ are

$$\tan z = \frac{\sin 2x + \sinh 2y\, i}{\cos 2x + \cosh 2y}.$$

31. Prove that when n is a positive integer,

$$\int_0^{\pi/2} \cos^{2n} t\, dt = \int_0^{\pi/2} \sin^{2n} t\, dt = \frac{(2n)!\,\pi}{2^{2n+1}(n!)^2}.$$

Mapping Exercises

32. Show that $w = \sin z$, regarded as a mapping from the z-plane to the w-plane, performs the mappings indicated in the figures below.

(a)

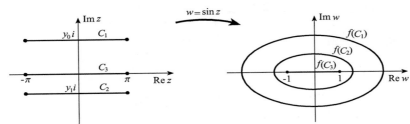

Is each curve mapped one-to-one onto its image?

(b)

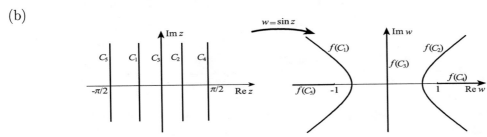

(c)

(d)

(e)

(f)

(g)

(h)

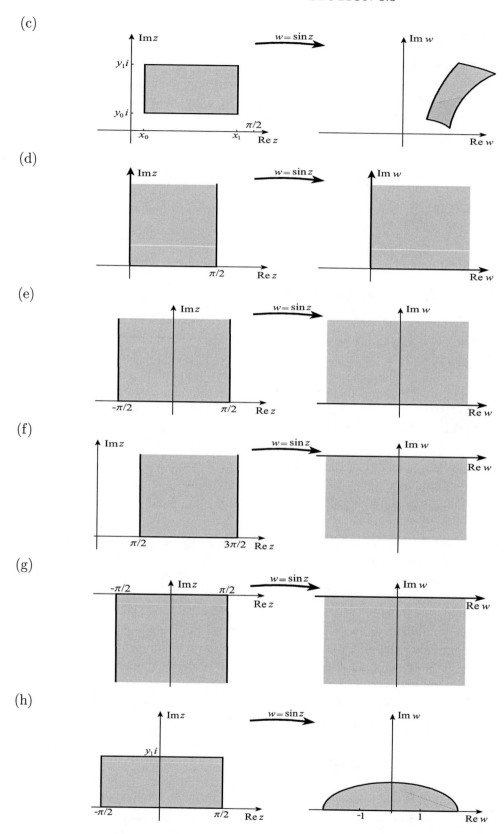

33. Show that $w = \cos z$, regarded as a mapping from the z-plane to the w-plane, performs the mappings indicated in the figures below.

(a)

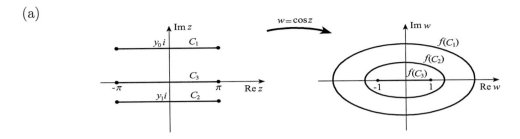

Is each curve mapped one-to-one onto its image?

(b)

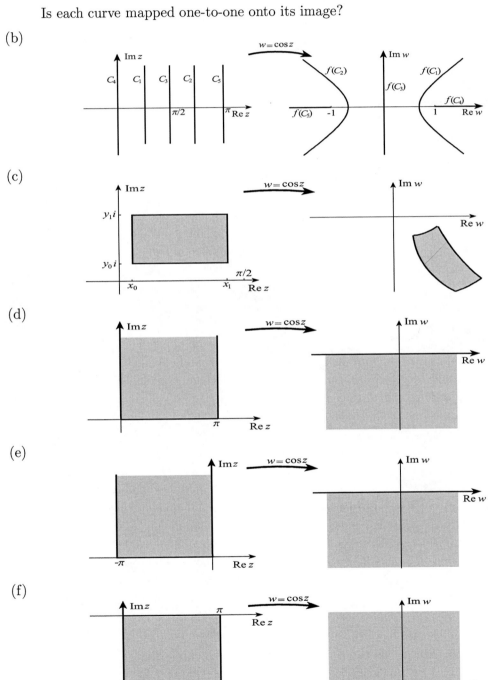

(c)

(d)

(e)

(f)

(g)

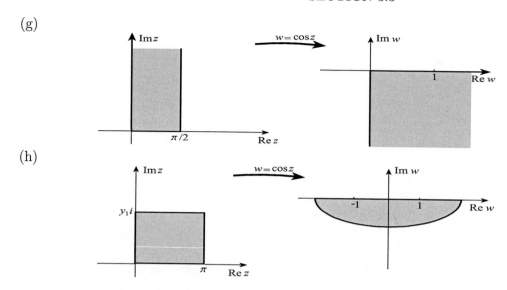

(h)

34. What transformation maps the semi-infinite strip $-a \leq \operatorname{Re} z \leq a$, $\operatorname{Im} z \geq 0$ ($a > 0$ a constant) to the half-plane $\operatorname{Im} w \geq 0$?

§3.4   Complex Hyperbolic Functions

Since the real hyperbolic functions $\sinh x$ and $\cosh x$ are defined in terms of e^x, it is natural to carry these definitions directly into the complex plane,

$$\sinh z = \frac{e^z - e^{-z}}{2}, \qquad \cosh z = \frac{e^z + e^{-z}}{2}. \tag{3.15}$$

They are entire functions with derivatives

$$\frac{d}{dz}\sinh z = \cosh z, \qquad \frac{d}{dz}\cosh z = \sinh z. \tag{3.16}$$

Because these functions have the same definitions as their real counterparts, they satisfy the familiar hyperbolic identities. For example,

$$\cosh^2 z - \sinh^2 z = \left(\frac{e^z + e^{-z}}{2}\right)^2 - \left(\frac{e^z - e^{-z}}{2}\right)^2 = 1.$$

Unlike the real hyperbolic functions, the complex hyperbolic sine and cosine are periodic, the period being $2\pi i$ (the period for e^z). Furthermore, unlike their real counterparts, the complex hyperbolic sine and cosine functions are related to the trigonometric sine and cosine functions according to

$$\sin(iz) = i\sinh z, \qquad \cos(iz) = \cosh z, \tag{3.17a}$$

$$\sinh(iz) = i\sin z, \qquad \cosh(iz) = \cos z. \tag{3.17b}$$

These, or equations 3.15, can be used to find real and imaginary parts of $\sinh z$ and $\cosh z$,

$$\sinh z = \cos y \,\sinh x + \sin y \,\cosh x \, i, \tag{3.18a}$$

$$\cosh z = \cos y \,\cosh x + \sin y \,\sinh x \, i. \tag{3.18b}$$

Example 3.13   Express $3\cosh(2+3i) - 2\sinh(i/2)$ in Cartesian form.

Solution   Using equations 3.18,

$$3\cosh(2+3i) - 2\sinh(i/2) = 3(\cos 3 \,\cosh 2 + \sin 3 \,\sinh 2\, i) - 2i\sin(1/2)$$
$$= 3\cos 3 \,\cosh 2 + [3\sin 3 \,\sinh 2 - 2\sin(1/2)]i$$
$$\approx -11.2 + 0.577i.\bullet$$

Since $\sinh z = -i\sin(iz)$, and $\sin(iz) = 0$ when $iz = n\pi$, it follows that $\sinh z$ vanishes when $z = -n\pi i$; that is, the zeros of $\sinh z$ are $z = n\pi i$ (Figure 3.11). Similarly, the zeros of $\cosh z$ are $z = (2n+1)\pi i/2$ (Figure 3.12). All such zeros are simple ones.

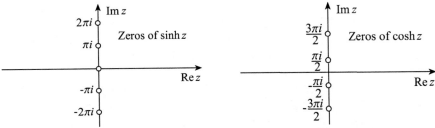

Figure 3.11   **Figure 3.12**

The remaining four hyperbolic functions are defined by

$$\tanh z = \frac{\sinh z}{\cosh z}, \qquad \operatorname{csch} z = \frac{1}{\sinh z}, \qquad (3.19a)$$

$$\operatorname{coth} z = \frac{\cosh z}{\sinh z}, \qquad \operatorname{sech} z = \frac{1}{\cosh z}. \qquad (3.19b)$$

The $\tanh z$ and $\operatorname{sech} z$ functions have isolated singularities at $z = (2n+1)\pi i/2$, the zeros of $\cosh z$ (Figure 3.12), and $\operatorname{coth} z$ and $\operatorname{csch} z$ have isolated singularities at the zeros $z = n\pi i$ of $\sinh z$ (Figure 3.11). Their derivatives are as expected:

$$\frac{d}{dz}(\tanh z) = \operatorname{sech}^2 z; \qquad \frac{d}{dz}(\operatorname{coth} z) = -\operatorname{csch}^2 z; \qquad (3.20a)$$

$$\frac{d}{dz}(\operatorname{sech} z) = -\operatorname{sech} z \ \tanh z; \qquad \frac{d}{dz}(\operatorname{csch} z) = -\operatorname{csch} z \ \operatorname{coth} z. \qquad (3.20b)$$

Example 3.14   Find all solutions of the equation $\cosh z = 5i$.

Solution   Using equation 3.18a,

$$\cos y \cosh x + \sin y \sinh x \, i = 5i.$$

When we equate real and imaginary parts,

$$\cos y \cosh x = 0, \qquad \sin y \sinh x = 5.$$

The first of these implies that $y = (2n+1)\pi/2$, where n is an integer. When this is substituted into the second equation,

$$(-1)^n \sinh x = 5,$$

and therefore

$$5(-1)^n = \frac{e^x - e^{-x}}{2} \qquad \Longrightarrow \qquad e^{2x} - 10(-1)^n e^x - 1 = 0.$$

Solutions of this quadratic equation in e^x are

$$e^x = \frac{10(-1)^n \pm \sqrt{100+4}}{2} = 5(-1)^n \pm \sqrt{26}.$$

Thus, $x = \ln\left[5(-1)^n \pm \sqrt{26}\right]$, but only $x = \ln\left[\sqrt{26} + 5(-1)^n\right]$ is acceptable. Solutions of the given equation are therefore $z = \ln\left[\sqrt{26} + 5(-1)^n\right] + (2n+1)\pi i/2.\bullet$

Example 3.15   Show that $w = \sinh z$ maps the semi-infinite strip $-\pi/2 \le \operatorname{Im} z \le \pi/2$, $\operatorname{Re} z \ge 0$ to the half-plane $\operatorname{Re} w \ge 0$.

Solution   We could verify this result with an analysis parallel to that in Example 3.12. Alternatively, we can use the result of Example 3.12 and the fact that $w = \sinh z = -i\sin(iz)$. The semi-infinite strip $-\pi/2 \le \operatorname{Im} z \le \pi/2$, $\operatorname{Re} z \ge 0$ is mapped by $z^* = iz$ onto the semi-infinite strip $-\pi/2 \le \operatorname{Re} z^* \le \pi/2$, $\operatorname{Im} z^* \ge 0$ (Figure 3.13) since multiplication by i rotates complex numbers $\pi/2$ radians counterclockwise. According to Example 3.12, $w^* = \sin z^*$ maps the semi-infinite strip $-\pi/2 \le \operatorname{Re} z^* \le \pi/2$, $\operatorname{Im} z^* \ge 0$ onto the half-plane $\operatorname{Im} w^* \ge 0$. Finally, $w = -iw^*$ rotates the half-plane $\operatorname{Im} w^* \ge 0$ clockwise through $\pi/2$ radians. Thus,

$$w = -iw^* = -i \sin z^* = -i \sin (iz) = \sinh z$$

maps the semi-infinite strip $-\pi/2 \leq \operatorname{Im} z \leq \pi/2$, $\operatorname{Re} z \geq 0$ to the half-plane $\operatorname{Re} w \geq 0$.•

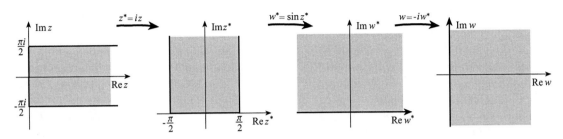

Figure 3.13

EXERCISES 3.4

In Exercises 1–8 express the complex number in Cartesian form.

1. $\sinh 3i$

2. $\cosh (1 - 2i)$

3. $4 \sinh (\pi i/3)$

4. $\coth(3\pi i/4)$

5. $\tanh (1 + i)$

6. $\operatorname{csch}(2i + 1)$

7. $\sinh^2 (-6i)$

8. $\operatorname{sech}(4 + 5i)$

In Exercises 9–12 find all solutions of the equation.

9. $\cosh z = 1$

10. $\sinh z = -3i$

11. $\tanh z = i$

12. $\cosh^2 z + \sinh^2 z = 1$

13. Verify equations 3.18.

14. Show that
$$|\sinh z|^2 = \sinh^2 x + \sin^2 y, \qquad |\cosh z|^2 = \sinh^2 x + \cos^2 y,$$

and hence deduce that $|\sinh z|$ and $|\cosh z|$ are unbounded as $x \to \pm\infty$ for fixed y.

In Exercises 15–18 find the indicated derivative. Express final answers in Cartesian form.

15. $f'(2 + i)$ if $f(z) = \sinh (3z + 1 + i)$

16. $f'(i)$ if $f(z) = \tanh 3z$

17. $f'(1)$ if $f(z) = z \cosh iz$

18. $f''(-2i)$ if $f(z) = \operatorname{sech}(3z + i)$

19. Are $\sinh z$ and $\cosh z$ periodic?

Mapping Exercises

20. Use Exercise 33 in Section 3.3, or otherwise, to find images of horizontal and vertical lines under the mapping $w = \cosh z$.

21. Use Exercise 32 in Section 3.3, or otherwise, to find images of horizontal and vertical lines under the mapping $w = \sinh z$.

22. Find a function that maps the semi-infinite strip $-a < \operatorname{Im} z < a$, $\operatorname{Re} z > 0$ to the half-plane $\operatorname{Im} w > 0$.

§3.5   Complex Logarithm Function

The real logarithm function $\ln x$ is defined as the inverse of the exponential function — $y = \ln x$ is the unique solution of the equation $x = e^y$. This works because e^x is a one-to-one function; if $x_1 \neq x_2$, then $e^{x_1} \neq e^{x_2}$. This is not the case for e^z; we have seen that e^z is $2\pi i$-periodic so that all complex numbers of the form $z + 2n\pi i$ are mapped by $w = e^z$ onto the same complex number as z. To define the logarithm function, $\log z$, as the inverse of e^z is clearly going to lead to difficulties, and these difficulties are much like those encountered when finding the inverse function of $\sin x$ in real-variable calculus. Let us proceed. We call w a logarithm of z, and write $w = \log z$, if $z = e^w$. To find w we let $w = u + vi$ be the Cartesian form for w and $z = re^{\theta i}$ be the exponential form for z. When we substitute these into $z = e^w$,

$$re^{\theta i} = e^{u+vi} = e^u e^{vi}.$$

According to conditions 1.21, equality of these complex numbers implies that

$$e^u = r \quad \text{or} \quad u = \ln r,$$

and

$$v = \theta = \arg z.$$

Thus, $w = \ln r + \theta i$, and a logarithm of a complex number z is

$$\log z = \ln |z| + (\arg z)i. \tag{3.21}$$

We use $\ln$ only for logarithms of real numbers; $\log$ denotes logarithms of complex numbers using base e (and no other base is used).

Because equation 3.21 yields logarithms of every nonzero complex number, we have defined the complex logarithm function. It is defined for all $z \neq 0$, and because $\arg z$ is determined only to a multiple of 2π, each nonzero complex number has an infinite number of logarithms. For example,

$$\log (1 + i) = \ln \sqrt{2} + (\pi/4 + 2k\pi)i = (1/2)\ln 2 + (8k+1)\pi i/4.$$

Thus, to the complex number $1+i$, the logarithm function assigns an infinite number of values, $\log (1 + i) = (1/2)\ln 2 + (8k+1)\pi i/4$. They all have the same real part, but their imaginary parts differ by multiples of 2π. In other words, the logarithm function is a multiple-valued function; to each complex number in its domain, it assigns an infinity of values.

Example 3.16   Express $\log (2 - 3i)$ in Cartesian form.

Solution   Since $|2 - 3i| = \sqrt{13}$, and $\arg (2 - 3i) = 2k\pi - \text{Tan}^{-1}(3/2)$,

$$\log (2 - 3i) = \ln \sqrt{13} + [2k\pi - \text{Tan}^{-1}(3/2)]i = \frac{1}{2}\ln 13 + [2k\pi - \text{Tan}^{-1}(3/2)]i. \bullet$$

Some of the properties of the real logarithm function have counterparts in the complex logarithm. For example, if $z = x + yi = re^{\theta i}$, then

$$e^{\log z} = e^{\ln r + \theta i} = e^{\ln r}e^{\theta i} = re^{\theta i} = z, \tag{3.22a}$$

(as should be expected from the definition of $\log z$), and

$$\log\left(e^z\right) = \log\left(e^{x+yi}\right) = \ln\left(e^x\right) + (y + 2k\pi)i \qquad (k \text{ an integer})$$
$$= x + yi + 2k\pi i$$
$$= z + 2k\pi i. \qquad (3.22b)$$

In real analysis the counterpart of this equation is $\log e^x = x$. The $z + 2k\pi$ on the right side of 3.22b is a reflection of the facts that $\log z$ is multiple-valued and the logarithm is the last operation on the left side of the equation.

If $z_1 = re^{\theta i}$ and $z_2 = Re^{\phi i}$, then

$$\log\left(z_1 z_2\right) = \log\left[rRe^{(\theta+\phi)i}\right] = \ln\left(rR\right) + (\theta + \phi + 2p\pi)i \qquad (p \text{ an integer})$$
$$= (\ln r + \theta i) + (\ln R + \phi i) + 2p\pi i.$$

But $\log z_1 = \ln r + (\theta + 2n\pi)i$ and $\log z_2 = \ln R + (\phi + 2m\pi)i$. Hence,

$$\log\left(z_1 z_2\right) = (\log z_1 - 2n\pi i) + (\log z_2 - 2m\pi i) + 2p\pi i$$
$$= \log z_1 + \log z_2 + 2(p - n - m)\pi i$$
$$= \log z_1 + \log z_2 + 2k\pi i. \qquad (3.23a)$$

Similarly,

$$\log\left(\frac{z_1}{z_2}\right) = \log z_1 - \log z_2 + 2k\pi i. \qquad (3.23b)$$

The last two results must be approached with care. Because the logarithm function is multiple-valued, each equation must be interpreted as saying that given values for the logarithm terms, there is a value of k for which the equation holds. It is also possible to write these equations in the forms

$$\log\left(z_1 z_2\right) = \log z_1 + \log z_2, \qquad (3.24a)$$
$$\log\left(\frac{z_1}{z_2}\right) = \log z_1 - \log z_2. \qquad (3.24b)$$

We interpret them as saying that given values for two of the logarithm terms, there is a value of the third logarithm for which the equation is valid.

Multiple-valued functions cannot be analytic. To see why, consider the derivative of $\log z$,

$$\frac{d}{dz}\log z = \lim_{\Delta z \to 0} \frac{\log\left(z + \Delta z\right) - \log z}{\Delta z}.$$

This limit must exist, be unique, and be independent of the mode of approach of Δz to 0. But this is impossible if there is an infinity of possible choices for $\log z$ and for $\log\left(z + \Delta z\right)$ for each value of Δz. Thus, only single-valued functions can have derivatives. We therefore ask if it is possible to restrict the range of the logarithm function to obtain an analytic function; that is, can we make $\log z$ single-valued in such a way that it will have a derivative. The answer is yes, and there are many ways to do it. The most natural way to make $\log z$ single-valued is to restrict $\arg z$ in equation 3.21 to its principal value $\text{Arg}\, z$. When this is done, we denote the resulting single-valued function by

$$\text{Log}\, z = \ln|z| + (\text{Arg}\, z)i, \quad z \neq 0. \qquad (3.25)$$

Is $\operatorname{Log} z$ an analytic function? The answer is yes in a suitably restricted domain. To see this, we note that at any point on the negative real axis, the imaginary part of $\operatorname{Log} z$ is a discontinuous function. Theorem 2.4 implies therefore that $\operatorname{Log} z$ is discontinuous at points on the negative real axis, and $\operatorname{Log} z$ cannot be differentiable thereon. Suppose we consider the domain $|z| > 0$, $-\pi < \operatorname{Arg} z < \pi$. If we express $\operatorname{Log} z$ in the form

$$\operatorname{Log} z = \ln r + \theta i, \qquad -\pi < \theta < \pi,$$

partial derivatives of its real and imaginary parts are

$$\frac{\partial u}{\partial r} = \frac{1}{r}, \qquad \frac{\partial v}{\partial \theta} = 1, \qquad \frac{\partial u}{\partial \theta} = 0, \qquad \frac{\partial v}{\partial r} = 0.$$

Since these derivatives satisfy Cauchy-Riemann equations 2.22 and are continuous in the domain $|z| > 0$, $-\pi < \operatorname{Arg} z < \pi$, it follows that $\operatorname{Log} z$ is an analytic function in this domain. According to formula 2.23a, the derivative of $\operatorname{Log} z$ is

$$e^{-\theta i}\left(\frac{1}{r}\right) = \frac{1}{re^{\theta i}};$$

that is,

$$\frac{d}{dz}\operatorname{Log} z = \frac{1}{z}. \tag{3.26}$$

Thus, $\operatorname{Log} z$ is analytic in the domain $|z| > 0$, $-\pi < \operatorname{Arg} z < \pi$. It is defined for all $z \neq 0$, but analytic only in the aforementioned domain. Points on the negative real axis and $z = 0$ are singularities of $\operatorname{Log} z$, but they are not isolated singularities (Figure 3.14).

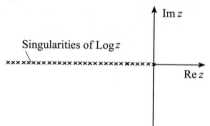

Figure 3.14

The restriction of $\arg z$ to $\operatorname{Arg} z$ in the definition of $\operatorname{Log} z$ produced a branch of the multiple-valued logarithm function called the **principal branch** of $\log z$. Other choices for $\arg z$ lead to different branches. For example, we could restrict $\arg z$ to $\arg_\phi z$. When this is done, we denote the resulting branch of the logarithm function by

$$\log_\phi z = \ln|z| + (\arg_\phi z)i. \tag{3.27}$$

These branches are analytic in any domain that does not contain $z = 0$, the branch point, or points on the branch cut, the half-line through $z = 0$ making an angle of ϕ radians with the positive real axis (Figure 3.15).

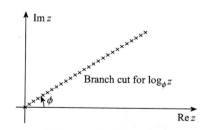

Figure 3.15

In real variable work, the notation $\log_a x$ indicates that a is the base of the logarithm function. This is not the case in complex function theory. Only e is used as the base for logarithms, and ϕ in $\log_\phi z$ indicates a particular branch of the $\log z$ function.

Example 3.17   Express $\text{Log}(-1 + \sqrt{3}i)$, $\log_{\pi/4}(-1 + \sqrt{3}i)$, and $\log_{-3\pi/2}(-1 + \sqrt{3}i)$ in Cartesian form.

Solution   The complex number $-1 + \sqrt{3}i$ is shown in Figure 3.16. We see that

$$\text{Log}(-1 + \sqrt{3}i) = \ln 2 + (2\pi/3)i,$$
$$\log_{\pi/4}(-1 + \sqrt{3}i) = \ln 2 + (2\pi/3)i,$$
$$\log_{-3\pi/2}(-1 + \sqrt{3}i) = \ln 2 + (-4\pi/3)i.\bullet$$

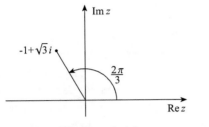

Figure 3.16

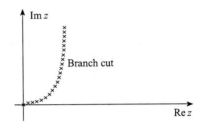

Figure 3.17

Branch cuts for the logarithm function need not be straight lines. We could stipulate that the branch cut of a branch of $\log z$ be the parabolic curve in Figure 3.17. We simply agree that at each point on this curve, arguments of z will be specified in a certain way, perhaps as $0 < \arg z < \pi/2$, that arguments will increase to the left of the curve, and that they will jump by 2π across the curve.

To understand branches of a multiple-valued function f, it is sometimes helpful to visualize ranges of the branches in the $w = f(z)$ plane. The three branches $\text{Log } z$, $\log_0 z$, and $\log_{2\pi} z$ of $\log z$ are illustrated in Figures 3.18–3.20. Each branch maps the z-plane (less $z = 0$) onto a horizontal strip of width 2π.

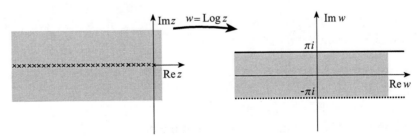

Figure 3.18

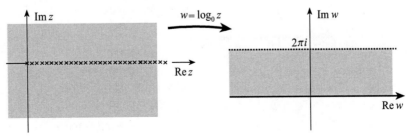

Figure 3.19

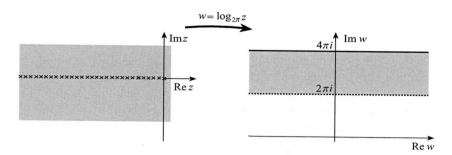

Figure 3.20

Defining branches of $\log z$ is reminiscent of the derivation of the inverse sine function in real-variable work. The situations are very similar. Because $\sin x$ is 2π-periodic, defining $y = \sin^{-1} x$ when $x = \sin y$ results in many values for $\sin^{-1} x$. Principal values $-\pi/2 \le \mathrm{Sin}^{-1} x \le \pi/2$ are chosen in order to create a single-valued function. The difference in the two situations is that we almost always use principal values of $\mathrm{Sin}^{-1} x$; other choices are possible, but they are seldom used. In order that $\log z$ be single-valued, we restrict $\arg z$ to an interval of length 2π. This leads to branches of $\log z$, the principal branch $\mathrm{Log}\, z$, but other branches as well. Because we have taken the effort to discuss other branches of $\log z$, and even given some of them special notations ($\log_\phi z$), the implication is that they are important. This is indeed true. Different problems require different branches of $\log z$.

Quite often in applications, we encounter logarithm functions where arguments are not just z; they are functions $f(z)$ of z. For example, branch points of the function $\mathrm{Log}[f(z)]$ are at the zeros of $f(z)$, and the branch cuts are where $f(z)$ is real and negative. An example follows.

Example 3.18 Find branch points and branch cuts for the function $\mathrm{Log}(z^2 - 1)$.

Solution   Branch points of the function occur at the zeros of $z^2 - 1$, namely $z = \pm 1$. Branch cuts occur where $z^2 - 1$ is real and negative. If we set $z = x + yi$, then $z^2 - 1 = (x^2 - y^2 - 1) + 2xyi$. This is real and negative if $x^2 - y^2 - 1 < 0$ and $2xy = 0$. The second gives $x = 0$ or $y = 0$. When $x = 0$, the inequality requires $-y^2 - 1 < 0$, which is valid for all y. When $y = 0$, the inequality requires $x^2 - 1 < 0$, that part of the real axis between $x = \pm 1$. Branch cuts are therefore the real axis between ± 1, including ± 1, and the imaginary axis (Figure 3.21).•

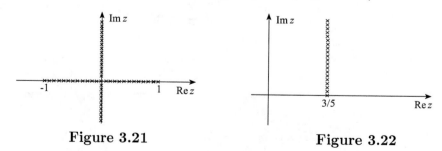

Figure 3.21   **Figure 3.22**

Branch points of the function $\log_\phi[f(z)]$ are once again at the zeros of $f(z)$. Branch cuts are where one of the arguments of $f(z)$ is equal to ϕ. Here is an example.

Example 3.19   Find branch points and branch cuts for the function $\log_{3\pi/2}(3 - 5z)$.

Solution   Branch points occur at the zeros of $3-5z$, there being only one $z = 3/5$. Branch cuts occur where one of the arguments of $3 - 5z$ is equal to $3\pi/2$. If we set $z = x + yi$, then $3 - 5z = (3 - 5x) - 5yi$. If θ is an argument of this complex number, then

$$\cos\theta = \frac{3 - 5x}{\sqrt{(3 - 5x)^2 + 25y^2}}, \qquad \sin\theta = \frac{-5y}{\sqrt{(3 - 5x)^2 + 25y^2}}.$$

For θ to be equal to $3\pi/2$, the first of these requires $x = 3/5$, and then the second implies that

$$-1 = \frac{-5y}{\sqrt{25y^2}} \quad \Longrightarrow \quad 5|y| = 5y \quad \Longrightarrow \quad y > 0.$$

The branch cut is therefore the vertical half-line above $z = 3/5$, including $z = 3/5$, (Figure 3.22).$\bullet$

In Sections 3.3–3.4, we solved equations involving trigonometric and hyperbolic functions by equating real and imaginary parts of both sides of the equation. The logarithm function provides an alternative. The best method for solving such equations is to use inverse trigonometric and hyperbolic functions to be introduced in Section 3.7.

Example 3.20   Use logarithms to solve the equation $\cosh z = 5i$ in Example 3.14.

Solution   We can write that

$$\frac{e^z + e^{-z}}{2} = 5i \quad \Longrightarrow \quad e^{2z} - 10ie^z + 1 = 0.$$

Solutions of this quadratic equation in e^z are

$$e^z = \frac{10i \pm \sqrt{-100 - 4}}{2} = (5 \pm \sqrt{26})i.$$

Thus,

$$z = \log\left[(5 \pm \sqrt{26})i\right] = \begin{cases} \ln(5 + \sqrt{26}) + (2n\pi + \pi/2)i \\ \ln(\sqrt{26} - 5) + (2n\pi - \pi/2)i \end{cases}$$
$$= \begin{cases} \ln(\sqrt{26} + 5) + (4n + 1)\pi i/2 \\ \ln(\sqrt{26} - 5) + (4n - 1)\pi i/2 \end{cases} \bullet$$

Now that we have single-valued logarithm functions, the various branches of the multi-valued logartihm function, we should ask whether equations 3.24 are valid for these single-valued functions; that is, are the following valid

$$\log_\phi z_1 z_2 = \log_\phi z_1 + \log_\phi z_2, \qquad \log_\phi\left(\frac{z_1}{z_2}\right) = \log_\phi z_1 - \log_\phi z_2?$$

The answer is no. Although they may be correct for some values of z_1 and z_2, they are not valid for all z_1 and z_2. For instance, if $z_1 = z_2 = -1$, then

$$\text{Log } z_1 z_2 = \text{Log } 1 = 0, \quad \text{whereas} \quad \text{Log}(-1) + \text{Log}(-1) = 2\text{Log}(-1) = 2(\pi i) = 2\pi i.$$

The special case of division when $z_1 = 1$, namely,

$$\log_\phi \left(\frac{1}{z_2} \right) = -\log_\phi z_2$$

is not true for all ϕ, but it is true for the principal branch of the logarithm function; that is,

$$\text{Log} \left(\frac{1}{z} \right) = -\text{Log}\, z, \qquad (3.28)$$

provided $z \neq 0$ or a negative real. This is verified in Exercise 23.

EXERCISES 3.5

In Exercises 1–4 express the complex number(s) in Cartesian form.

1. $\log i$
2. $\text{Log}\,(2 - 6i)$
3. $\log_{\pi/2}(1 + i)$
4. $\log_{-3}(-2 + 3i)$

In Exercises 5–8 find all solutions of the equation.

5. $\text{Log}\, z = \pi i/2$
6. $\log_1 z = 2 + 3i$
7. $z^4 = i$
8. $e^{z+2} = 4$

Use the complex logarithm function to find all solutions of the equations in Exercises 9–22.

9. Exercise 15 in Section 3.2
10. Exercise 16 in Section 3.2
11. Exercise 17 in Section 3.2
12. Exercise 18 in Section 3.2
13. Exercise 19 in Section 3.2
14. Exercise 20 in Section 3.2
15. Exercise 21 in Section 3.2
16. Exercise 22 in Section 3.2
17. Exercise 13 in Section 3.3
18. Exercise 14 in Section 3.3
19. Exercise 15 in Section 3.3
20. Exercise 9 in Section 3.4
21. Exercise 10 in Section 3.4
22. Exercise 11 in Section 3.4

23. Verify property 3.28 of the principal branch of the logarithm function.

24. You may have noticed that we have not stated the complex analogue of $\ln(x^a) = a\ln x$. The reason for this is that in general

$$\log(z^a) \neq a \log z.$$

Illustrate this with $z = 1 + i$ and $a = 4$.

25. Which branches of $\log z$ have zeros? What are the zeros?

26. Find $f'(3 + i)$ if $f(z) = \text{Log}\,(2z + 3 - i)$.

27. Find $f''(2i)$ if $f(z) = \log_{3\pi/8}(-z + i)$.

28. Is $\text{Log}\, e^z = z$?

The function $\text{Log}\,[f(z)]$ has branch points where $f(z) = 0$ and branch cuts where $f(z)$ is real and negative. In Exercises 29–32 identify branch points and branch cuts for the function.

29. $\text{Log}\,(z + i)$
30. $\text{Log}\,(z - 1)$
31. $\text{Log}\,(3 - 2z)$
32. $\text{Log}\,(3z - 2 + 4i)$

33. (a) What are the branch points for the function $f(z) = \text{Log}\,(z^2 - 4)$?

  (b) Show that the imaginary axis and that part of the real axis between the branch points are branch cuts.

34. Find branch points and branch cuts for $f(z) = \text{Log}\,(z^2 + 1)$.

The function $\log_\phi[f(z)]$ has branch points where $f(z) = 0$ and branch cuts where one of the arguments of $f(z)$ is equal to ϕ. In Exercises 35–38 identify branch points and branch cuts for the function.

35. $\log_0(z - 2i)$ **36.** $\log_{\pi/2}(3 - z)$

37. $\log_{-\pi/2}(4 - 2z)$ **38.** $\log_2(2z + 1)$

39. (a) What are the branch points for the function $f(z) = \log_0(z^2 + 1)$?

  (b) Show that the real axis and the line segment joining the branch points are branch cuts.

40. Find branch points and branch cuts for $f(z) = \log_{3\pi/2}(1 - z^2)$.

41. Compare branch cuts for $f(z) = \text{Log}\,(z^2 - 1)$ and $g(z) = \text{Log}\,(z + 1) + \text{Log}\,(z - 1)$.

42. Compare branch cuts for $f(z) = \text{Log}\,(4 - z^2)$ and $g(z) = \text{Log}\,(2 + z) + \text{Log}\,(2 - z)$.

43. Compare branch cuts for $f(z) = \log_{-\pi/2}(z^2 - 1)$ and $g(z) = \log_{-\pi/2}(z + 1) + \log_{-\pi/2}(z - 1)$.

44. Compare branch cuts for $f(z) = \log_{-\pi/2}(4 - z^2)$ and $g(z) = \log_{-\pi/2}(2 + z) + \log_{-\pi/2}(2 - z)$.

45. (a) Prove that for $b > a > 1$, the function $\text{Log}\left(\dfrac{z - a}{z - b}\right)$ is analytic except for points on the $\text{Re}\,z$ axis for which $a \le \text{Re}\,z \le b$.

  (b) Verify that for $|z| > b$, $\quad \text{Log}\left(\dfrac{z - a}{z - b}\right) = \text{Log}\left(1 - \dfrac{a}{z}\right) - \text{Log}\left(1 - \dfrac{b}{z}\right)$.

Mapping Exercises

46. Show that $w = \text{Log}\,z$, regarded as a mapping from the z-plane to the w-plane, performs the mappings indicated in the figures below.

  (a)

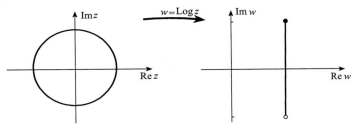

  (b)

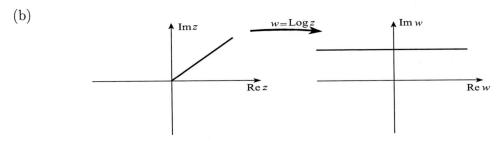

(c)

(d)

(e)

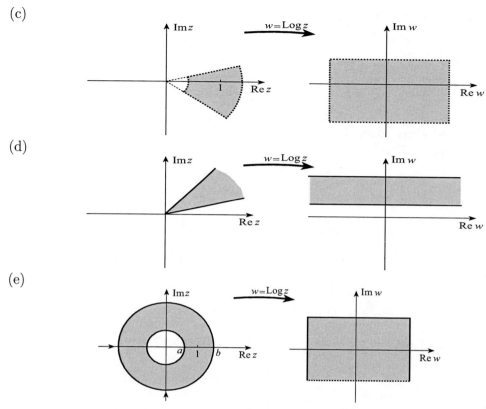

47. Show that the transformation $w = \text{Log}\left[\coth\left(\dfrac{\pi z}{2a}\right)\right]$ maps the semi-infinite strip $-a \leq \text{Im } z \leq a$, $\text{Re } z \geq 0$ to the infinite strip $-\pi/2 \leq \text{Im } w \leq \pi/2$.

§3.6 Complex Powers

The meaning of z^n when n is an integer is clear. When n is a rational number, say $n = 2/3$, we also have no conceptual difficulty. We write $z^{2/3} = (z^{1/3})^2$, and $z^{1/3}$ is interpreted as the cube root of z. There are three cube roots, which can be obtained by methods discussed in Section 1.5, and these should be squared to give values for $z^{2/3}$. Oh, oh. We just said "values", not "value"; that is, we are saying that $z^{2/3}$ is not single-valued. It probably has three values for given z. In this section, we clarify the situation; we define z^α for complex α. When α is a real integer, z^α is single-valued (as is to be expected); when α is not an integer, z^α has many values, sometimes infinitely many, sometimes finitely many.

DeMoivre's theorem 1.32 implies that for any positive integer n,

$$z^n = r^n e^{n\theta i} = e^{n \ln r} e^{n\theta i} = e^{n(\ln r + \theta i)} = e^{n \log z}. \tag{3.29}$$

We use this identity to define the function z^α for complex α, and $z \neq 0$,

$$z^\alpha = e^{\alpha \log z}. \tag{3.30}$$

When it makes sense to do so, we define $0^\alpha = 0$. For example, this would certainly be done when α is a (real) positive integer, but it would be pointless to do so when α is a negative integer.

Since $\log z$ is a multiple-valued function, it follows that so also in general is z^α. We shall show, however, that for certain values of α, z^α is single-valued, double-valued, etc.

Example 3.21 Find all possible values for: (a) $(2i)^i$ (b) $(1-i)^{1/2+i}$

Solution (a) According to equation 3.30,

$$(2i)^i = e^{i \log(2i)} = e^{i[\ln 2 + (\pi/2 + 2k\pi)i]} = e^{-(\pi/2 + 2k\pi)} e^{i \ln 2}$$

where k is an integer. These complex numbers which vary in modulus $(e^{-(\pi/2 + 2k\pi)})$, but have the same argument $(\ln 2)$, are shown in Figure 3.23. What we are saying is that the function z^i has infinitely many values for each value of z.

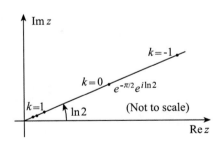

Figure 3.23

(b) Since

$$(1-i)^{1/2+i} = e^{(1/2+i) \log(1-i)} = e^{(1/2+i)[\ln \sqrt{2} + (-\pi/4 + 2k\pi)i]}$$
$$= e^{[(1/2)\ln \sqrt{2} + \pi/4 - 2k\pi] + (\ln \sqrt{2} - \pi/8 + k\pi)i},$$

the function $z^{1/2+i}$ also has infinitely many values for each value of z.•

Example 3.22 When n is an integer, we certainly hope that z^n is single-valued. Verify this.

Solution According to equation 3.30,

$$z^n = e^{n \log z} = e^{n(\ln|z| + i \arg z)}$$
$$= e^{n \ln|z|} e^{in(\operatorname{Arg} z + 2k\pi)} \qquad (k \text{ an integer})$$
$$= |z|^n e^{in \operatorname{Arg} z} e^{2kn\pi i}$$
$$= |z|^n e^{in \operatorname{Arg} z} \qquad (e^{2kn\pi i} = 1),$$

and z^n is single-valued.●

Definition 3.30 for raising complex numbers to complex powers is inconsistent with the exponential function. The exponential function e^z has a unique value for any given z, namely $e^z = e^x(\cos y + \sin y\, i)$. Equation 3.30, on the other hand leads, in general, to multiple values of e^z. To avoid this confusion, many authors use the notation $\exp(z)$ for the exponential function. Since we never use e^z in the sense of 3.30, no confusion can arise, and e^z always denotes the single-valued exponential function.

The Square Root Function

According to equation 3.30, the definition of the function $z^{1/2}$ is

$$z^{1/2} = e^{(1/2)\log z} = e^{(1/2)(\ln|z| + i \arg z)} = e^{(1/2)\ln|z|} e^{(i/2)\arg z} = \sqrt{|z|}\, e^{(i/2)\arg z}. \quad (3.31)$$

Since $\arg z = \operatorname{Arg} z + 2k\pi$, it follows that

$$z^{1/2} = \sqrt{|z|}\, e^{(i/2)(\operatorname{Arg} z + 2k\pi)} = \pm\sqrt{|z|}\, e^{(i/2)\operatorname{Arg} z}, \quad (3.32)$$

since $e^{k\pi i} = \pm 1$. Thus, every nonzero complex number has two square roots, and $z^{1/2}$ is a double-valued function. When $z = 0$, we define $0^{1/2} = 0$, in which case $z^{1/2}$ has only one value at $z = 0$.

Example 3.23 Find, in Cartesian form, the square roots of $3 - 4i$.

Solution According to equation 3.32,
$$(3 - 4i)^{1/2} = \pm\sqrt{|3 - 4i|}\, e^{(i/2)\operatorname{Arg}(3-4i)} = \pm\sqrt{5}\, e^{(i/2)\operatorname{Tan}^{-1}(-4/3)}$$
$$= \pm\sqrt{5}\{\cos[(1/2)\operatorname{Tan}^{-1}(-4/3)] + \sin[(1/2)\operatorname{Tan}^{-1}(-4/3)]\, i\}.$$
A calculator quickly gives $(3 - 4i)^{1/2} = \pm(2 - i)$. We can also show this algebraically. Suppose we let $\theta = \operatorname{Tan}^{-1}(4/3)$ (Figure 3.24). Then

$$\sqrt{5} \cos\left[\frac{1}{2}\operatorname{Tan}^{-1}(-4/3)\right] = \sqrt{5}\cos\left[-\frac{1}{2}\operatorname{Tan}^{-1}(4/3)\right]$$
$$= \sqrt{5}\cos\left(\frac{\theta}{2}\right) = \sqrt{5}\sqrt{\frac{1 + \cos\theta}{2}}$$
$$= \sqrt{5}\sqrt{\frac{1 + 3/5}{2}} = 2.$$

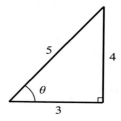

Figure 3.24

In addition,

$$\sqrt{5}\sin\left[\frac{1}{2}\operatorname{Tan}^{-1}(-4/3)\right] = \sqrt{5}\sin\left[-\frac{1}{2}\operatorname{Tan}^{-1}(4/3)\right] = -\sqrt{5}\sin\left(\frac{\theta}{2}\right) = -\sqrt{5}\sqrt{\frac{1 - \cos\theta}{2}}$$
$$= -\sqrt{5}\sqrt{\frac{1 - 3/5}{2}} = -1.$$

Thus, once again $(3 - 4i)^{1/2} = \pm(2 - i)$.●

To create an analytic function from $z^{1/2}$, we first make it single-valued. This can be done by restricting $\arg z$ in equation 3.31 to any interval of length 2π; i.e., by choosing a branch of $\arg z$. When principal values of $\arg z$ are chosen, the resulting single-valued function, denoted by

$$\sqrt{z} = \sqrt{|z|}e^{(i/2)\operatorname{Arg} z}, \tag{3.33}$$

is called the **principal square root function**. This function maps the complex z-plane onto the right half-plane shown in Figure 3.25; that is, it finds that square root of a complex number that has a nonnegative real part. In Section 1.2 we made the agreement that the square root sign over a complex number ($\sqrt{1+i}$ for example) would always denote a number with nonnegative real part. We now see the reason for this; it creates a single-valued function $\sqrt{z}$. This function is continuous at all points in the complex plane with $z = 0$ and the negative real axis deleted. If the function is written in the form $\sqrt{z} = r^{1/2}e^{\theta i/2}$, it is straightforward to show that the function satisfies Cauchy Riemann equations 2.22. In other words, the principal square root function $\sqrt{z}$ is an analytic function in the domain consisting of the complex plane with $z = 0$ and the negative real axis deleted; $z = 0$ and points on the negative real axis are singularities of $\sqrt{z}$, but they are not isolated singularities. They constitute the branch cut of the function.

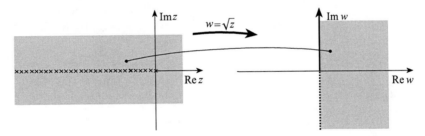

Figure 3.25

The derivative of this function is

$$\frac{d}{dz}\sqrt{z} = \frac{d}{dz}e^{(1/2)\operatorname{Log} z} = e^{(1/2)\operatorname{Log} z}\frac{1}{2z} = \frac{\sqrt{z}}{2z} = \frac{1}{2\sqrt{z}}. \tag{3.34}$$

Other branches of $z^{1/2}$ are obtained by choosing different branches of $\arg z$, say

$$z^{1/2} = \sqrt{|z|}e^{(i/2)\arg_\phi z}.$$

For this branch, the branch cut is the line $\arg z = \phi$ (Figure 3.26).

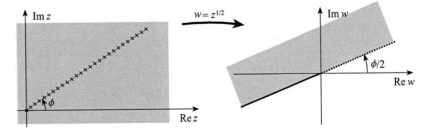

Figure 3.26

The derivative of this square root function is

$$\frac{d}{dz}z^{1/2} = \frac{1}{2z^{1/2}},$$ (3.35)

where $z^{1/2}$ is the same branch on both sides of the equation.

When x_1 and x_2 are nonnegative real numbers, $\sqrt{x_1 x_2} = \sqrt{x_1}\sqrt{x_2}$, and this result is valid whether we interpret the $\sqrt{}$ as the real square root function or the principal branch of the complex root function. Unfortunately, the principal branch of the complex root function does not satisfy this property for all complex numbers; that is, in general

$$\sqrt{z_1 z_2} \neq \sqrt{z_1}\sqrt{z_2}.$$

For example when $z_1 = z_2 = -1$,

$$\sqrt{(-1)(-1)} = \sqrt{1} = 1 \qquad \text{whereas} \qquad \sqrt{-1}\sqrt{-1} = i \cdot i = -1.$$

In other words, we must be careful when performing algebraic manipulations with complex root functions not to assume properties of their real counterparts. For another easy trap, see Exercise 18a.

Example 3.24 Does $\sqrt{z}$ have any zeros?

Solution   The only value of z for which $\sqrt{z} = 0$ is $z = 0$. But $z = 0$ is not a zero since $\sqrt{z}$ is not analytic at $z = 0$. It is a singularity (but not an isolated singularity).●

Example 3.25 Evaluate $f'(-i)$ if $f(z) = -\sqrt{z}$.

Solution   According to equation 3.34, $f'(z) = -1/(2\sqrt{z})$, so that $f'(-i) = -1/(2\sqrt{-i})$. Since

$$\sqrt{-i} = \sqrt{|-i|}e^{(i/2)\text{Arg}(-i)} = e^{(i/2)(-\pi/2)} = e^{-\pi i/4},$$

it follows that

$$f'(-i) = -\frac{1}{2e^{-\pi i/4}} = -\frac{1}{2}e^{\pi i/4} = -\frac{1}{2}\left(\frac{1}{\sqrt{2}} + \frac{i}{\sqrt{2}}\right) = -\frac{\sqrt{2}}{4}(1+i).●$$

Other branches of the square root function are obtained by choosing other branches $\arg_\phi z$ of $\arg z$. We do not have a simple notation to distinguish these branches of the root function as we did for the logarithm function ($\log_\phi z$). This results in two possible interpretations of $z^{1/2}$. It can represent the double-valued square root function. It can also represent a particular branch of the square root function obtained by choosing a branch $\arg_\phi z$ of the argument function, $z^{1/2} = e^{(1/2)\log_\phi z}$. Context will always make it clear which interpretation is expected, but if unspecified, it represents the double-valued root function.

The nth Root Function

When n is a positive integer, the function $z^{1/n}$ is defined by

$$z^{1/n} = e^{(1/n)\log z} = e^{(1/n)[\ln|z| + i\arg z]} = \sqrt[n]{|z|}e^{(i/n)\arg z},$$ (3.36)

provided $z \neq 0$. We define $0^{1/n} = 0$. If we set $\arg z = \text{Arg}\, z + 2k\pi$, where k is an integer, then

$$z^{1/n} = \sqrt[n]{|z|}e^{(i/n)(\operatorname{Arg} z + 2k\pi)} = \sqrt[n]{|z|}e^{(i/n)\operatorname{Arg} z}e^{2k\pi i/n}. \tag{3.37}$$

For given z, the quantity $\sqrt[n]{|z|}e^{(i/n)\operatorname{Arg} z}$ is unique, but as k takes on the values $0, 1, \ldots, n-1$, $e^{2k\pi i/n}$ has n distinct values. In other words, $z^{1/n}$ is an n-valued function; there are n n^{th} roots of a nonzero complex number. For example when $n = 4$ and $z = -16$,

$$(-16)^{1/4} = \sqrt[4]{16}e^{(i/4)(\pi)}e^{2k\pi i/4} = 2e^{(2k+1)\pi i/4}.$$

For $k = 0, 1, 2, 3$, we obtain the four complex numbers

$$2e^{\pi i/4} = \sqrt{2}(1+i), \qquad 2e^{3\pi i/4} = \sqrt{2}(-1+i),$$
$$2e^{5\pi i/4} = \sqrt{2}(-1-i), \qquad 2e^{7\pi i/4} = \sqrt{2}(1-i).$$

Thus, the four fourth roots of -16 are $\sqrt{2}(1 \pm i)$ and $\sqrt{2}(-1 \pm i)$. We have shown these roots in Figure 3.27. They lie on a circle of radius 2 (the fourth root of the modulus of -16). The first $\sqrt{2}(1+i)$ (from $k = 0$) has an argument equal to one-quarter that of -16, and all others are equally spaced around the circle (separated by angles of $\pi/2$ radians).

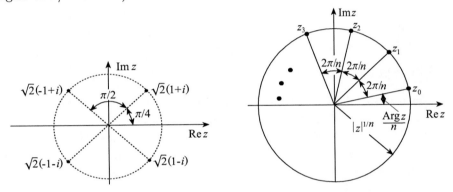

Figure 3.27   **Figure 3.28**

In general, $z^{1/n}$, for given n and z, defines n complex numbers which lie on a circle of radius $|z|^{1/n}$. One has argument equal to $(\operatorname{Arg} z)/n$, and the $n-1$ remaining roots are equally spaced around the circle each pair separated by $2\pi/n$ radians (Figure 3.28).

In Section 1.5 we used exponential representations of complex numbers to find square roots, cube roots, etc. Functions $z^{1/2}$, $z^{1/3}$, etc, perform the same task. The only difference is that we now have a functional representation for the roots, as opposed to simply a procedure by which to find them.

By choosing a branch of the logarithm function, $z^{1/n}$ becomes a single-valued function. When the principal branch $\operatorname{Log} z$ is chosen, we denote the resulting branch of $z^{1/n}$ by

$$\sqrt[n]{z} = \sqrt[n]{|z|}e^{(i/n)\operatorname{Arg} z}, \tag{3.38}$$

and call it the **principal branch** of $z^{1/n}$. It is defined for all z, and it is analytic in the domain $|z| > 0$, $-\pi < \operatorname{Arg} z < \pi$, with derivative

$$\frac{d}{dz}\sqrt[n]{z} = \frac{d}{dz}e^{(1/n)\operatorname{Log} z} = e^{(1/n)\operatorname{Log} z}\left(\frac{1}{nz}\right) = \frac{\sqrt[n]{z}}{n\left(\sqrt[n]{z}\right)^n} = \frac{1}{n\left(\sqrt[n]{z}\right)^{n-1}}. \tag{3.39}$$

In fact, no matter what branch of $z^{1/n}$ is chosen, we may write that

$$\frac{d}{dz}z^{1/n} = \frac{1}{n}z^{1/n-1}. \tag{3.40}$$

The only provision is that branches of $z^{1/n}$ and $z^{1/n-1}$ must correspond; that is, both must use the same branch of $\log z$.

Example 3.26 Find the derivative of $\sqrt[3]{z}$ at $z = -1 - i$.

Solution According to equation 3.39, $\dfrac{d}{dz}\sqrt[3]{z} = \dfrac{1}{3\left(\sqrt[3]{z}\right)^2}$. We use 3.38 to evaluate $\left(\sqrt[3]{z}\right)^2$ at $-1 - i$,

$$\left(\sqrt[3]{-1-i}\right)^2 = \left[(\sqrt{2})^{1/3}e^{(i/3)(-3\pi/4)}\right]^2 = 2^{1/3}e^{-\pi i/2} = -2^{1/3}i.$$

Thus, $\dfrac{d}{dz}\left(\sqrt[3]{z}\right)_{|z=-1-i} = \dfrac{1}{3(-2^{1/3}i)} = \dfrac{i}{3 \cdot 2^{1/3}}. \bullet$

We shall encounter many root functions where the argument is a function $f(z)$ rather than z itself. For example, consider the function $\sqrt{f(z)}$. Its branch points are at the zeros of $f(z)$, and its branch cuts occur where $f(z)$ is real and negative.

Example 3.27 Find branch points and branch cuts for the function $\sqrt{z^2 + 5}$.

Solution Branch points for the function are the zeros of $z^2 + 5$, namely, $z = \pm\sqrt{5}\,i$. Branch cuts occur where $z^2 + 5$ is real and negative. If we set $z = x + yi$, then $z^2 + 5 = (x^2 - y^2 + 5) + 2xyi$. This is real and negative if $x^2 - y^2 + 5 < 0$ and $2xy = 0$. The second gives $x = 0$ or $y = 0$. When $x = 0$, the inequality requires $-y^2 + 5 < 0$, from which $|y| > \sqrt{5}$. When $y = 0$, the inequality requires $x^2 + 5 < 0$, an impossibility. Branch cuts are therefore the imaginary axis above $z = \sqrt{5}\,i$, and the imaginary axis below $z = -\sqrt{5}\,i$, including $z = \pm\sqrt{5}\,i$ (Figure 3.29).$\bullet$

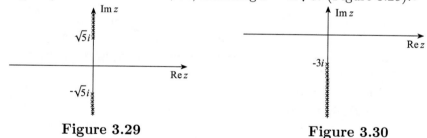

Figure 3.29   **Figure 3.30**

Branch points of the function $[f(z)]^{1/2} = e^{(1/2)\log_\phi f(z)}$ are once again at the zeros of $f(z)$. Branch cuts are where one of the arguments of $f(z)$ is equal to ϕ.

Example 3.28 Find branch points and branch cuts for the function $(z+3i)^{1/2} = e^{(1/2)\log_{3\pi/2}(z+3i)}$.

Solution The only branch point for the function is $z = -3i$, the zero of $z + 3i$. Branch cuts occur where one of the arguments of $z + 3i$ is equal to $3\pi/2$. If we set $z = x + yi$, then $z + 3i = x + (y + 3)i$. If θ is an argument of this complex number, then

$$\cos\theta = \frac{x}{\sqrt{x^2 + (y+3)^2}}, \qquad \sin\theta = \frac{y+3}{\sqrt{x^2 + (y+3)^2}}.$$

For θ to be equal to $3\pi/2$, the first of these requires $x = 0$, and then the second implies that $-1 = \dfrac{y+3}{|y+3|}$. For $|y+3| = -(y+3)$, we must have $y < -3$. The branch cut is therefore the vertical half-line below $z = -3i$, including $z = -3i$ (Figure 3.30).•

EXERCISES 3.6

In Exercises 1–10 express the complex number(s) in Cartesian form.

1. 2^i

2. $(2i)^{3i}$

3. $\sqrt{1+i}$

4. $(1+i)^{1/2}$

5. $\sqrt[3]{8i}$

6. $(8i)^{1/3}$

7. $(\sqrt[4]{i})^3$

8. $i^{3/4}$

9. $(1-i)^{1+i}$

10. $(1+i)^{1-i}$

11. Show that the values of $2^{(4+i)/40}$ are $2^{1/10}e^{-n\pi/20}\left[\cos\left(\dfrac{1}{40}\ln 2 + \dfrac{n\pi}{5}\right) + \sin\left(\dfrac{1}{40}\ln 2 + \dfrac{n\pi}{5}\right)i\right]$, where n is an integer. Plot these values for $n = -10, \ldots, 10$. Do they form a spiral?

12. Find the derivative of $\sqrt{z}$ at $z = i$.

13. Find the derivative of $\sqrt[3]{z}$ at $z = 1 - i$.

14. Is there a difference between $(\sqrt{z})^3$ and $\sqrt{z^3}$?

15. Is there a difference between $(z^{1/2})^3$ and $(z^3)^{1/2}$?

16. Find the second derivative of $(\sqrt{z})^3$ at $z = -2 - 3i$.

17. Evaluate the derivative of $\sqrt{z-i}$ at $z = 2$.

18. (a) When is $\sqrt{z^2} = z$?
(b) Is $(z^2)^{1/2} = z$?

19. Is $(e^{z_1})^{z_2} = e^{z_1 z_2}$?

20. Is $z = 0$ a zero of $\sqrt[n]{z}$?

21. What is $f(1)$ if $f(z) = z^{\sqrt{2}}$?

22. Explain why z^n which is defined as $e^{n\log z}$ does not have a branch cut when n is a positive integer. Is it an entire function?

23. (a) It is a property of reals that $(a^b)^c = a^{bc}$. This property does not in general hold for complex numbers. Illustrate this by calculating $(1^2)^i$ and 1^{2i} using equation 3.30.
(b) Show that when n is an integer, $(z^\alpha)^n = z^{n\alpha}$.

The function $\sqrt{f(z)}$ has branch points where $f(z) = 0$ and branch cuts where $f(z)$ is real and negative. In Exercises 24–32 identify branch points and branch cuts for the function.

24. $\sqrt{z-1}$

25. $\sqrt{2-3z}$

26. $\sqrt{2z+i}$

27. $\sqrt{3z-2+3i}$

28. $\sqrt{z^2-4}$

29. $\sqrt{4-z^2}$

30. $\sqrt{z^2 + 4}$

31. $\sqrt{z^2 + 4z + 5}$

32. $\sqrt{z^4 - 16}$

The function $[f(z)]^{1/2} = e^{(1/2)\log_\phi f(z)}$ has branch points where $f(z) = 0$ and branch cuts where one of the arguments of $f(z)$ is equal to ϕ. In Exercises 33–43 identify branch points and branch cuts for the function.

33. $(z + 3)^{1/2} = e^{(1/2)\log_0(z+3)}$

34. $(2i - z)^{1/2} = e^{(1/2)\log_0(2i-z)}$

35. $(3z + 2)^{1/2} = e^{(1/2)\log_{-\pi/2}(3z+2)}$

36. $(z - 3i)^{1/2} = e^{(1/2)\log_{\pi/2}(z-3i)}$

37. $(2 - i - z)^{1/2} = e^{(1/2)\log_{2\pi}(2-i-z)}$

38. $(z^2 - 1)^{1/2} = e^{(1/2)\log_0(z^2-1)}$

39. $(z^2 + 4)^{1/2} = e^{(1/2)\log_0(z^2+4)}$

40. $(1 - z^2)^{1/2} = e^{(1/2)\log_{\pi/2}(1-z^2)}$

41. $(z^2 + 9)^{1/2} = e^{(1/2)\log_{-\pi/2}(z^2+9)}$

42. $(z^2 + 2z - 3)^{1/2} = e^{(1/2)\log_{3\pi/2}(z^2+2z-3)}$

43. $(z^2 + 4z + 5)^{1/2} = e^{(1/2)\log_0(z^2+4z+5)}$

44. In this exercise we illustrate that care must be taken in combining square root functions.
    (a) Show that in general

$$\sqrt{z^2 - a^2} \neq \sqrt{z+a}\sqrt{z-a}, \quad a > 0 \text{ a constant.}$$

    Illustrate with $z = -2a$.
    (b) Show that branch cuts of $\sqrt{z^2 - a^2}$ are the imaginary axis and the real axis between $z = \pm a$, including $z = \pm a$.
    (c) Show that the branch cut of $\sqrt{z+a}\sqrt{z-a}$ is the real axis between $z = \pm a$, including $z = \pm a$.

45. What are branch cuts for the following functions where $a > 0$ is a constant.
    (a) $\sqrt{z^2 + a^2}$
    (b) $\sqrt{z + ai}\sqrt{z - ai}$
    (c) $(z^2 + a^2)^{1/2} = e^{(1/2)\log_{-\pi/2}(z^2+a^2)}$
    (d) $(z + ai)^{1/2}(z - ai)^{1/2} = e^{(1/2)\log_{-\pi/2}(z+ai)}e^{(1/2)\log_{-\pi/2}(z-ai)}$

46. Show that branches of the functions $(z - z_0)^{1/2}$ and $(z - z_1)^{1/2}$ can be chosen so that $(z - z_0)^{1/2}(z - z_1)^{1/2}$ is discontinuous only along the line segment joining z_0 and z_1.

47. (a) Show that the branch cut of the function $f(z) = \sqrt{1 + \dfrac{1}{z}}$ is the line segment joining $z = -1$ and $z = 0$.
    (b) Verify that arguments of $1 + 1/z$ approach $-\pi$ when complex numbers with positive imaginary parts approach the branch cut.
    (c) Verify that arguments of $1 + 1/z$ approach π when complex numbers with negative imaginary parts approach the branch cut.

48. (a) Show that the branch cut of the function $f(z) = \sqrt{1 - \dfrac{1}{z}}$ is the line segment joining $z = 0$ and $z = 1$.
    (b) Verify that arguments of $1 - 1/z$ approach π when complex numbers with positive imaginary parts approach the branch cut.
    (c) Verify that arguments of $1 - 1/z$ approach $-\pi$ when complex numbers with negative imaginary parts approach the branch cut.

49. (a) Show that the branch cut of the square root function

$$f(z) = \left(\frac{1}{z} - 1\right)^{1/2} = e^{(1/2)\log_0 (1/z-1)}$$

is the line segment joining $z = 0$ and $z = 1$.

(b) Verify that arguments of $1/z-1$ approach 2π when complex numbers with positive imaginary parts approach the branch cut.

(c) Verify that arguments of $1/z-1$ approach 0 when complex numbers with negative imaginary parts approach the branch cut.

50. Prove that z^α has finitely many values only when α is a rational number.

§3.7   Inverse Trigonometric and Hyperbolic Functions

Because the exponential function e^z is $2\pi i$-periodic, defining the logarithm function as its inverse led to a multiple-valued function $\log z$. Branches of $\log z$ evolved as analytic parts of this function. Since the trigonometric and hyperbolic functions are periodic, it should come as no surprise that similar situations arise when we define their inverses.

We call w an inverse sine of z if $z = \sin w$. We find w by solving

$$z = \sin w = \frac{e^{wi} - e^{-wi}}{2i}$$

for w in terms of z. Multiplication by e^{wi} gives a quadratic equation in e^{wi}

$$\left(e^{wi}\right)^2 - 2iz(e^{wi}) - 1 = 0.$$

Application of quadratic formula 1.12b yields

$$e^{wi} = \frac{2iz + (-4z^2 + 4)^{1/2}}{2} = iz + (1 - z^2)^{1/2},$$

where $(1 - z^2)^{1/2}$ has two values. When we take logarithms of both sides, the result is

$$w = -i \log \left[iz + (1 - z^2)^{1/2} \right].$$

This "function" is called the **inverse sine function**, and is denoted by $\sin^{-1} z$,

$$\sin^{-1} z = -i \log \left[iz + (1 - z^2)^{1/2} \right]. \tag{3.41}$$

Because the complex logarithm function is multiple-valued, and $(1 - z^2)^{1/2}$ is double-valued, $\sin^{-1} z$ is multiple-valued; that is, for given z, there is an infinity of values for $\sin^{-1} z$. This is illustrated in the following example.

Example 3.29   Find the values of $\sin^{-1} i$.

Solution   By equation 3.41,

$$\sin^{-1} i = -i \log \left[i(i) + (1 - i^2)^{1/2} \right] = -i \log \left[\pm\sqrt{2} - 1 \right]$$
$$= -i \begin{cases} \ln(\sqrt{2} - 1) + 2n\pi i \\ \ln(\sqrt{2} + 1) + (2n+1)\pi i \end{cases} = \begin{cases} 2n\pi + i \ln(\sqrt{2} + 1) \\ (2n+1)\pi - i \ln(\sqrt{2} + 1) \end{cases} . \bullet$$

The inverse sine function can be made single-valued by choosing a particular branch of the logarithm function and we use this branch both explicitly in equation 3.41 and implicitly in $(1 - z^2)^{1/2}$. When the principal branch $\operatorname{Log} z$ is chosen, the resulting single-valued function is called the **principal branch** of $\sin^{-1} z$, denoted by

$$\operatorname{Sin}^{-1} z = -i \operatorname{Log} \left[iz + \sqrt{1 - z^2} \right]. \tag{3.42}$$

In Exercise 24 it is shown that

$$\sin^{-1} z = \begin{cases} \operatorname{Sin}^{-1} z + 2n\pi \\ (2n+1)\pi - \operatorname{Sin}^{-1} z \end{cases} . \tag{3.43}$$

In other words, all complex numbers $\sin^{-1} z$ whose sines are equal to given z can be obtained from the principal value $\mathrm{Sin}^{-1} z$. (This is the same situation for the inverse sine function in real variable work.)

Example 3.30   Use equation 3.43 to solve Example 3.29.

Solution   Since

$$\mathrm{Sin}^{-1} i = -i\mathrm{Log}\left[i(i) + \sqrt{1 - i^2}\right] = -i\mathrm{Log}\left[\sqrt{2} - 1\right] = -i\ln\left(\sqrt{2} - 1\right) = i\ln\left(\sqrt{2} + 1\right),$$

it follows from equation 3.43 that

$$\sin^{-1} i = \begin{cases} 2n\pi + i\ln\left(\sqrt{2} + 1\right) \\ (2n+1)\pi - i\ln\left(\sqrt{2} + 1\right) \end{cases} \cdot \bullet$$

Example 3.31   Does the value of $\mathrm{Sin}^{-1} z$ coincide with $\mathrm{Sin}^{-1} x$ when z is a real number between -1 and 1?

Solution   When z is a real number say x, and $-1 \le x \le 1$,

$$\begin{aligned} \mathrm{Sin}^{-1} z &= -i\mathrm{Log}\left[iz + \sqrt{1 - z^2}\right] \\ &= -i\mathrm{Log}\left[ix + \sqrt{1 - x^2}\right] \\ &= -i[\ln\sqrt{1 - x^2 + x^2} + i\mathrm{Sin}^{-1} x] \quad \text{(see Figure 3.31)} \\ &= \mathrm{Sin}^{-1} x. \bullet \end{aligned}$$

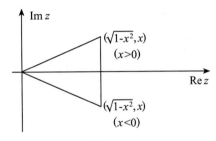

Figure 3.31

This example illustrates that our definition of the inverse sine function adheres to the principle stated in the first paragraph of this chapter — when a function $f(x)$ is extended to a complex function $f(z)$, the values of $f(z)$ for real z should coincide with those of $f(x)$.

Similar derivations lead to the inverse cosine and tangent functions

$$\cos^{-1} z = -i\log\left[z + i(1 - z^2)^{1/2}\right]. \tag{3.44}$$

$$\tan^{-1} z = \frac{i}{2}\log\left(\frac{i + z}{i - z}\right). \tag{3.45}$$

Derivatives of the inverse trigonometric functions can be obtained by direct differentiation of equations 3.41, 3.44, and 3.45, or by implicit differentiation,

$$\frac{d}{dz}\sin^{-1} z = \frac{1}{(1 - z^2)^{1/2}}, \tag{3.46}$$

$$\frac{d}{dz}\cos^{-1} z = \frac{-1}{(1-z^2)^{1/2}}, \tag{3.47}$$

$$\frac{d}{dz}\tan^{-1} z = \frac{1}{1+z^2}. \tag{3.48}$$

These equations are not valid in the strictest sense, since it is not possible to differentiate multiple-valued functions. What we mean is that given a branch for the inverse trigonometric function on the left, its derivative is the corresponding branch of the function on the right; that is, the same branch of $\log z$ must be chosen on the right and left sides of these equations.

The inverse hyperbolic functions are obtained in an analogous way to the inverse trigonometric functions. The inverse hyperbolic sine, cosine, and tangent are

$$\sinh^{-1} z = \log\left[z + (z^2 + 1)^{1/2}\right], \tag{3.49}$$

$$\cosh^{-1} z = \log\left[z + (z^2 - 1)^{1/2}\right], \tag{3.50}$$

$$\tanh^{-1} z = \frac{1}{2}\log\left(\frac{1+z}{1-z}\right). \tag{3.51}$$

Their derivatives are

$$\frac{d}{dz}\sinh^{-1} z = \frac{1}{(z^2 + 1)^{1/2}}, \tag{3.52}$$

$$\frac{d}{dz}\cosh^{-1} z = \frac{1}{(z^2 - 1)^{1/2}}, \tag{3.53}$$

$$\frac{d}{dz}\tanh^{-1} z = \frac{1}{1 - z^2}. \tag{3.54}$$

Example 3.32   Evaluate $\cosh^{-1}(1/2)$.

Solution   From equation 3.50,

$$\cosh^{-1}(1/2) = \log\left[1/2 + (1/4 - 1)^{1/2}\right] = \log\left[1/2 \pm \sqrt{3}i/2\right] = \ln(1) + i(2n\pi \pm \pi/3)$$
$$= (6n \pm 1)\pi i/3. \bullet$$

Example 3.33   What is the derivative of $\mathrm{Sinh}^{-1}z$ at $z = 1 + i$?

Solution   The capital letter "S" indicates the principal branch of the inverse hyperbolic sine function, in which case

$$\frac{d}{dz}\mathrm{Sinh}^{-1} z_{|1+i} = \frac{1}{\sqrt{z^2 + 1}}\Big|_{1+i} = \frac{1}{\sqrt{(1+i)^2 + 1}} = \frac{1}{\sqrt{1 + 2i}}.$$

Since $|1 + 2i| = \sqrt{5}$ and $\mathrm{Arg}\,(1 + 2i) = \mathrm{Tan}^{-1}2$,

$$\frac{d}{dz}\mathrm{Sinh}^{-1} z_{|1+i} = \frac{1}{\sqrt[4]{5}}e^{-(i/2)\mathrm{Tan}^{-1}2} \approx 0.569 - 0.351i. \bullet$$

In Sections 3.3–3.4, we solved equations involving trigonometric and hyperbolic functions by equating real and imaginary parts of both sides of the equation. In Section 3.5, we used the logarithm function as an alternative. The best method for solving such equations is to use inverse trigonometric and hyperbolic functions.

Example 3.34 Solve the equation $\cosh z = 5i$ of Examples 3.14 and 3.20.

Solution   Solutions are

$$z = \cosh^{-1}(5i) = \log\left[5i + (-26)^{1/2}\right] = \log\left(5i \pm \sqrt{26}i\right) = \log\left[(5 \pm \sqrt{26})i\right]$$

$$= \begin{cases} \ln\left(5 + \sqrt{26}\right) + (2n\pi + \pi/2)i \\ \ln\left(\sqrt{26} - 5\right) + (2n\pi - \pi/2)i \end{cases}$$

$$= \begin{cases} \ln\left(\sqrt{26} + 5\right) + (4n + 1)\pi i/2 \\ \ln\left(\sqrt{26} - 5\right) + (4n - 1)\pi i/2 \end{cases} \cdot \bullet$$

EXERCISES 3.7

In Exercises 1–10 express the complex number(s) in Cartesian form.

1. $\sin^{-1}(\sqrt{2})$

2. $\mathrm{Tan}^{-1}(1 - i)$

3. $\mathrm{Cos}^{-1}(4i)$

4. $\sinh^{-1} 2$

5. $\tanh^{-1}(3 + 6i)$

6. $\cosh^{-1}(\sqrt{2}i)$

7. $(2 + i)\sin^{-1} i$

8. $[\tanh^{-1} i]^2$

9. $\tan^{-1}\sqrt{i}$

10. $\sin^{-1} 1 + \cos^{-1} 1$

In Exercise 11–16 find the derivative of the function.

11. $f(z) = \mathrm{Cosh}^{-1}[(2 + i)z]$

12. $f(z) = \mathrm{Log}[\mathrm{Sin}^{-1}(3z)]$

13. $f(z) = \mathrm{Tan}^{-1}\sqrt{z}$

14. $f(z) = e^{\mathrm{Sinh}^{-1}(3iz+6)}$

15. $f(z) = \tan[\mathrm{Cosh}^{-1}(z^2)]$

16. $f(z) = \{\mathrm{Cos}^{-1}[\mathrm{Log}(3z)]\}^2$

In Exercise 17–23 use inverse functions to solve the equation.

17. Exercise 13 in Section 3.3

18. Exercise 14 in Section 3.3

19. Exercise 15 in Section 3.3

20. Exercise 16 in Section 3.3

21. Exercise 9 in Section 3.4

22. Exercise 10 in Section 3.4

23. Exercise 11 in Section 3.4

24. Verify equation 3.43.

25. (a) Verify that $\cos^{-1} z = 2n\pi \pm \mathrm{Cos}^{-1} z$.
    (b) What is the value of $\mathrm{Cos}^{-1} z$ when z is real?
    (c) Verify that when z is a real number x between -1 and 1, the values of $\mathrm{Cos}^{-1} z$ coincide with those of $\mathrm{Cos}^{-1} x$.

26. (a) Verify that $\tan^{-1}z = n\pi + \text{Tan}^{-1}z$.

    (b) What is the value of $\text{Tan}^{-1}z$ when z is real? Does it coincide with the real function $\text{Tan}^{-1}x$?

27. Prove that for any branch of the logarithm function, the derivative of $\sin^{-1}z$ is given by equation 3.46.

28. Find inverse functions for $\csc z$, $\sec z$, and $\cot z$.

29. Find inverse functions for $\text{csch}z$, $\text{sech}z$, and $\coth z$.

30. Verify the following relations among principal branches of the trigonometric and hyperbolic functions:

    (a) $\text{Sin}^{-1}iz = i\,\text{Sinh}^{-1}z$, $\text{Sinh}^{-1}iz = i\,\text{Sin}^{-1}z$,

    (b) $\text{Tan}^{-1}iz = i\,\text{Tanh}^{-1}z$, $\text{Tanh}^{-1}iz = i\,\text{Tan}^{-1}z$,

       but, in general,

    (c) $\text{Cos}^{-1}iz \neq \text{Cosh}^{-1}z$, $\text{Cosh}^{-1}iz \neq \text{Cos}^{-1}z$.

In Exercises 31–37 we investigate branch cuts for principal branches of the inverse trigonometric and inverse hyperbolic functions.

31. Show that branch points of $\sqrt{1-z^2}$ are $z = \pm 1$ and the branch cut consists of the real axis $y = 0$ to the right of $x = 1$ and to the left of $x = -1$; that is, $|x| \geq 1$.

32. Verify that $iz + \sqrt{1-z^2}$ is never zero, and therefore $\text{Sin}^{-1}z = -i\,\text{Log}\,(iz + \sqrt{1-z^2})$ has no further branch points or cuts other than those introduced by $\sqrt{1-z^2}$.

33. Verify that $z + i\sqrt{1-z^2}$ never vanishes, and therefore $\text{Cos}^{-1}z = -i\,\text{Log}\,(z + i\sqrt{1-z^2})$ has no further branch points or cuts other than those introduced by $\sqrt{1-z^2}$.

34. Find branch points and cuts for $\text{Tan}^{-1}z$.

35. Show that $z = \pm i$ are branch points for $\text{Sinh}^{-1}z$ and branch cuts are the imaginary axis above $z = i$ and below $z = -i$, including $z = \pm i$.

36. Show that $z = \pm 1$ are branch points for $\text{Cosh}^{-1}z$ and branch cuts are the imaginary axis and that part of the real axis between $z = \pm 1$, including $z = \pm 1$.

37. Verify that $z = \pm 1$ are branch points for $\text{Tanh}^{-1}z$ and branch cuts are the real axis to the right of $z = 1$ and to the left of $z = -1$, including $z = \pm 1$.

38. In this exercise we derive formulas for the real and imaginary parts of $\text{Sin}^{-1}z$.

    (a) If $w = u + vi = \text{Sin}^{-1}z = \text{Sin}^{-1}(x + yi)$, verify that

$$x = \sin u \cosh v, \qquad y = \cos u \sinh v.$$

    (b) Show that for any fixed value of u, the equations in part (a) are parametric equations for the hyperbola

$$\frac{x^2}{\sin^2 u} - \frac{y^2}{\cos^2 u} = 1.$$

    Verify that $u = \text{Sin}^{-1}\left[\dfrac{\sqrt{(x+1)^2 + y^2} - \sqrt{(x-1)^2 + y^2}}{2}\right]$.

    (c) Show that for any fixed value of v, the equations in part (a) are parametric equations for the ellipse

$$\frac{x^2}{\cosh^2 v} + \frac{y^2}{\sinh^2 v} = 1.$$

Verify that $v = (\operatorname{sgn} y)\operatorname{Cosh}^{-1}\left[\dfrac{\sqrt{(x+1)^2 + y^2} + \sqrt{(x-1)^2 + y^2}}{2}\right]$, where

$\operatorname{sgn} y = \begin{cases} 1 & y \geq 0 \\ -1 & y < 0 \end{cases}$.

39. In this exercise we derive formulas for the real and imaginary parts of $\operatorname{Cos}^{-1}z$.
 (a) If $w = u + vi = \operatorname{Cos}^{-1}z = \operatorname{Cos}^{-1}(x + yi)$, verify that

$$x = \cos u \cosh v, \qquad y = -\sin u \sinh v.$$

 (b) Show that for any fixed value of u, the equations in part (a) are parametric equations for the hyperbola

$$\frac{x^2}{\cos^2 u} - \frac{y^2}{\sin^2 u} = 1.$$

 Verify that $u = \operatorname{Cos}^{-1}\left[\dfrac{\sqrt{(x+1)^2 + y^2} - \sqrt{(x-1)^2 + y^2}}{2}\right]$.

 (c) Show that for any fixed value of v, the equations in part (a) are parametric equations for the ellipse

$$\frac{x^2}{\cosh^2 v} + \frac{y^2}{\sinh^2 v} = 1.$$

 Verify that $v = -(\operatorname{sgn} y)\operatorname{Cosh}^{-1}\left[\dfrac{\sqrt{(x+1)^2 + y^2} + \sqrt{(x-1)^2 + y^2}}{2}\right]$, where

$\operatorname{sgn} y = \begin{cases} 1 & y \geq 0 \\ -1 & y < 0 \end{cases}$.

40. For what values of z is $\operatorname{Sin}^{-1}z$ real? Hint: Use Exercise 38.

Mapping Exercises

41. In Parts (e), (f), and (g) of Exercise 32 in Section 3.3, we showed that vertical half-strips in the z-plane are mapped by $w = \sin z$ onto either the upper or lower half-plane in the w-plane. Show that the principal branch $w = \operatorname{Sin}^{-1}z$ inverts the mapping in part (e); that is, it maps the half-plane $y > 0$ to the semi-infinite strip $-\pi/2 < u < \pi/2$, $v > 0$.

42. In Parts (d), (e), and (f) of Exercise 33 in Section 3.3, we showed that vertical half-strips in the z-plane are mapped by $w = \cos z$ onto either the upper or lower half-plane in the w-plane. Show that the principal branch $w = \operatorname{Cos}^{-1}z$ inverts the mapping in part (f); that is, it maps the half-plane $y > 0$ to the semi-infinite strip $0 < u < \pi$, $v > 0$.

43. Use Exercise 41 to show that $w = \operatorname{Sin}^{-1}z$ maps the z-plane slit along the x-axis between $-\infty < x \leq -1$ and $1 \leq x < \infty$ to the strip $-\pi/2 < u < \pi/2$.

44. Use Exercise 42 to show that $w = \operatorname{Cos}^{-1}z$ maps the z-plane slit along the x-axis between $-\infty < x \leq -1$ and $1 \leq x < \infty$ to the strip $0 < u < \pi$.

§3.8 Steady-state Two-dimensional Heat Conduction

The fact that real and imaginary parts of an analytic function are harmonic suggests the use of complex functions in physical problems involving the two-dimensional Laplace equation. In the following three sections we introduce three such applications — heat flow, fluid flow, and electrostatics. These applications are discussed further in Chapter 7 in the context of conformal mappings.

When temperature $T(x, y, z, t)$ is a function of the coordinates x, y, z in some region V of space, and time t, it must satisfy the three-dimensional heat conduction equation

$$\frac{\partial T}{\partial t} = k \left(\frac{\partial^2 T}{\partial x^2} + \frac{\partial^2 T}{\partial y^2} + \frac{\partial^2 T}{\partial t^2} \right) + \frac{k}{\kappa} g(x, y, z, t), \qquad (3.55)$$

where k is the thermal diffusivity of the material in the region (assumed constant) and κ is another constant, the thermal conductivity of the material. Function $g(x, y, z, t)$ is the amount of heat generated (or absorbed) at point (x, y, z) and time t per unit volume per unit time. Accompanying this equation are boundary conditions that $T(x, y, z, t)$ must satisfy on the surfaces surrounding V, and an initial condition specifying temperature in V at some initial time (usually taken as $t = 0$). Such problems must be specialized considerably before complex variables can be used to advantage. First, we consider partial differential equation 3.55 only in regions that contain no heat sources or sinks in which case $g(x, y, z, t) = 0$. This is not to say that there can be no heat sources or sinks; they must exist or there would be no heat flow. We are simply considering regions V in which they are not to be found. Secondly, we eliminate time by considering steady-state problems; that is, we consider only situations in which temperature in V does not depend on time. Temperature varies from point to point in V, but the temperature at each point remains constant in time. The temperature function $T(x, y, z)$ then satisfies Laplace's equation

$$\frac{\partial^2 T}{\partial x^2} + \frac{\partial^2 T}{\partial y^2} + \frac{\partial^2 T}{\partial z^2} = 0. \qquad (3.56)$$

Finally, we assume that temperature is independent of the z-coordinate; it depends only on x and y. Then $T(x, y)$ satisfies the two-dimensional Laplace equation

$$\frac{\partial^2 T}{\partial x^2} + \frac{\partial^2 T}{\partial y^2} = 0. \qquad (3.57)$$

Although temperature is only a function of two variables x and y, region V can be still regarded as three-dimensional. We visualize this in one of two ways. Think of V as a flat plate lying on the xy-plane (Figure 3.32); its edge is a cylinder standing on the curve C. If perfect insulation is applied to top and bottom faces of the plate, then no heat can enter or leave the plate through these faces. With appropriate boundary conditions on the edges of the plate, heat flows only in the x- and y-directions; temperature does not vary with z, and $T(x, y)$ satisfies equation 3.57. Since temperature is the same in all cross-sections parallel to the xy-plane, we usually draw the cross-section D in the xy-plane (Figure 3.33), and visualize heat flowing in D. However, do not lose sight of the fact that D represents one of many cross-sections all with the same temperature.

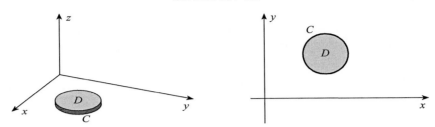

Figure 3.32   **Figure 3.33**

Alternatively, we can think of V as an infinite cylinder in the z-direction with cross-sectional area D (Figure 3.34). Provided boundary conditions on the surface of the cylinder are independent of z, heat does not flow in the z-direction; temperature is identical in all cross-sections parallel to the xy-plane, and we therefore solve equation 3.57 in D.

If $\tilde{T}(x,y)$ is a harmonic conjugate of $T(x,y)$ in D, then $F(z) = T(x,y) + \tilde{T}(x,y)i$ is an analytic function of the complex variable z in D. (Do not confuse the complex variable $z = x + yi$ with the suppressed z-coordinate in space.) This function is called the **complex temperature function** associated with $T(x,y)$.

Curves $T(x,y) = $ constant are called **isothermal curves**. Each curve joins all points in D with the same temperature, and exactly one such curve passes through each point of D. The curves $\tilde{T}(x,y) = $ constant are orthogonal trajectories of isothermal curves; at each point of D, the curves from the two families intersect at right angles (Figure 3.35).

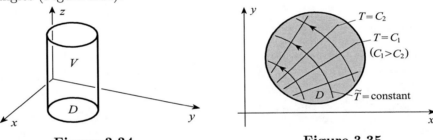

Figure 3.34   **Figure 3.35**

According to Fourier's law of heat conduction, heat flows in the direction opposite to the gradient of $T(x,y)$. Since the gradient of $T(x,y)$ is perpendicular to isothermal curves, it follows that at each point in D, heat flows in the direction of the tangent to $\tilde{T}(x,y) = $ constant. In other words, heat flows along the curves $\tilde{T}(x,y) = $ constant.

Laplace's equation 3.57 will be accompanied by boundary conditions that usually specify either $T(x,y)$, its normal derivative, or a linear combination of these on the boundary of D. A **Dirichlet boundary condition** specifies temperature on the boundary of D

$$T(x,y) = h(x,y), \quad (x,y) \text{ on boundary of } D, \tag{3.58a}$$

where $h(x,y)$ is a given function. A **Neumann boundary condition** specifies the derivative of $T(x,y)$ in the direction perpendicular to the boundary of D. This is often written in the form

$$\nabla T \cdot \hat{\mathbf{n}} = h(x,y), \quad (x,y) \text{ on boundary of } D, \tag{3.58b}$$

where $h(x, y)$ is some given function and $\hat{\mathbf{n}}$ is the unit vector perpendicular to the boundary of D (Figure 3.36). Since heat flows in direction $-\nabla T$, a Neumann boundary condition essentially specifies the amount of heat flowing across the boundary of D. In particular, if the boundary is perfectly insulated (so that no heat can enter or leave D), condition 3.58b takes the form

$$\nabla T \cdot \hat{\mathbf{n}} = 0, \quad (x, y) \text{ on boundary of } D. \tag{3.58c}$$

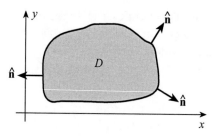

Figure 3.36

In the examples to follow, we illustrate isothermal curves and heat flow lines for some simple problems. More difficult problems will be discussed in Chapter 7.

Example 3.35 Find steady-state temperature $T(x, y)$ in the rectangle $0 < x < a$, $0 < y < b$, given that it must satisfy the boundary conditions in Figure 3.37 where T_0 and T_a are constants. The fact that $\partial T / \partial y$ vanishes on $y = 0$ and $y = b$ means that these edges are perfectly insulated. What are isothermal curves and lines of heat flow? Find the complex temperature function.

Solution Since no heat can pass through $y = 0$ or $y = b$, and edges $x = 0$ and $x = a$ are held at constant temperature, heat flows only in the x-direction. As a result, $T(x, y)$ should only be a function of x, in which case Laplace's equation 3.57 reduces to the ordinary differential equation

$$\frac{d^2 T}{dx^2} = 0.$$

A general solution of this equation is $T = Ax + B$, and boundary conditions on $x = 0$ and $x = a$ require

$$T_0 = B, \qquad T_a = Aa + B.$$

Hence, $T(x) = (T_a - T_0)x/a + T_0$. Isothermal curves $T = $ constant are vertical lines, and heat flows along horizontal lines (Figure 3.38). The temperature function $T(x)$ is the real part of the complex temperature function. The imaginary part $\tilde{T}$ is the complex conjugate of $T(x)$. It satisfies the Cauchy-Riemann equations,

$$\frac{\partial \tilde{T}}{\partial y} = \frac{\partial T}{\partial x} = \frac{T_a - T_0}{a}, \qquad \frac{\partial \tilde{T}}{\partial x} = -\frac{\partial T}{\partial y} = 0.$$

These give $\tilde{T} = \dfrac{(T_a - T_0)y}{a} + C$, where C is a constant. Hence, the complex temperature function is

$$F(z) = \frac{(T_a - T_0)x}{a} + T_0 + \left[\frac{(T_a - T_0)y}{a} + C\right] i = \frac{(T_a - T_0)z}{a} + (T_0 + Ci).$$

The presence of an arbitrary constant is a result of the two Neumann boundary conditions on the upper and lower edges of the rectangle.●

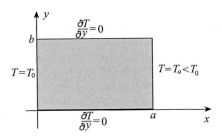

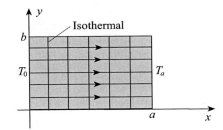

Figure 3.37   **Figure 3.38**

Example 3.36 Find steady-state temperature between two concentric circles $a^2 < x^2 + y^2 < b^2$ given that temperature on inner and outer boundaries are constant values T_a and T_b (Figure 3.39). What are the isothermal curves and lines of heat flow? Find the complex temperature function.

Solution In a steady-state situation with constant inner and outer boundary temperatures, temperature does not vary with polar coordinate angle θ; it depends only on radial distance r from the centre of the concentric circles. Laplace's equation in polar coordinates is

$$\frac{\partial^2 T}{\partial r^2} + \frac{1}{r}\frac{\partial T}{\partial r} + \frac{1}{r^2}\frac{\partial^2 T}{\partial \theta^2} = 0, \tag{3.59}$$

and when T is independent of θ, it reduces to

$$\frac{d^2 T}{dr^2} + \frac{1}{r}\frac{dT}{dr} = 0.$$

When multiplied by r, this equation can be expressed in the form

$$\frac{d}{dr}\left(r\frac{dT}{dr}\right) = 0,$$

and integration gives

$$r\frac{dT}{dr} = C.$$

Hence, $T(r) = C \ln r + D$. The boundary conditions require

$$T_a = C \ln a + D, \quad T_b = C \ln b + D,$$

from which

$$T(r) = T_a + (T_b - T_a)\frac{\ln(r/a)}{\ln(b/a)}.$$

Isothermal curves are concentric circles centred at the origin, and heat flows along radial lines, outwardly when $T_b < T_a$ (Figure 3.40), and inwardly when $T_b > T_a$. We already know that complex functions with $\ln r = \ln\sqrt{x^2 + y^2}$ as real part are $\log_\phi z$. In other words, the complex temperature function is

$$F(z) = T_a + (T_b - T_a)\frac{\log_\phi(z/a)}{\ln(b/a)}.●$$

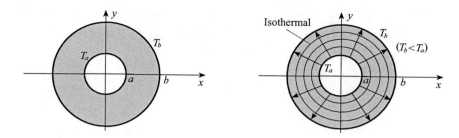

Figure 3.39   **Figure 3.40**

Example 3.37   Steady-state temperature in the half-plane $y > 0$ when temperature on the x-axis between $x = \pm 1$ is a constant value T_0, and zero outside this interval, is

$$T(x, y) = \frac{T_0}{\pi} \left[\text{Tan}^{-1}\left(\frac{1+x}{y} \right) + \text{Tan}^{-1}\left(\frac{1-x}{y} \right) \right].$$

(We derive this function in Chapter 7.)

(a) Show that isothermal curves are circles passing through $(\pm 1, 0)$ with centres on the y-axis.

(b) Show that a harmonic conjugate of $T(x, y)$ is

$$\tilde{T}(x, y) = \frac{T_0}{2\pi} \ln \left[\frac{y^2 + (1+x)^2}{y^2 + (1-x)^2} \right].$$

(c) Find lines of heat flow.

Solution   (a) Isothermal curves are given by

$$C = \frac{T_0}{\pi} \left[\text{Tan}^{-1}\left(\frac{1+x}{y} \right) + \text{Tan}^{-1}\left(\frac{1-x}{y} \right) \right],$$

where C is a constant, and this implies that

$$\frac{\pi C}{T_0} = \text{Tan}^{-1}\left(\frac{1+x}{y} \right) + \text{Tan}^{-1}\left(\frac{1-x}{y} \right).$$

If we take tangents on each side of the equation, we obtain

$$\tan\left(\frac{\pi C}{T_0} \right) = \frac{\dfrac{1+x}{y} + \dfrac{1-x}{y}}{1 - \left(\dfrac{1+x}{y} \right)\left(\dfrac{1-x}{y} \right)} = \frac{2y}{y^2 + x^2 - 1}.$$

Thus, $x^2 + y^2 - 1 = 2y \cot[\pi C/T_0]$, from which

$$x^2 + \left[y - \cot\left(\frac{\pi C}{T_0} \right) \right]^2 = 1 + \cot^2\left(\frac{\pi C}{T_0} \right) = \csc^2\left(\frac{\pi C}{T_0} \right).$$

These are circles with centres on the y-axis that pass through the points $(\pm 1, 0)$.

(b) If $\tilde{T}(x, y)$ is a harmonic conjugate of $T(x, y)$, then the Cauchy-Riemann equations require

$$\frac{\partial \tilde{T}}{\partial y} = \frac{\partial T}{\partial x} = \frac{T_0}{\pi} \left[\frac{1/y}{1 + \left(\dfrac{1+x}{y}\right)^2} + \frac{-1/y}{1 + \left(\dfrac{1-x}{y}\right)^2} \right] = \frac{T_0}{\pi} \left[\frac{y}{(x+1)^2 + y^2} - \frac{y}{(1-x)^2 + y^2} \right],$$

and

$$\frac{\partial \tilde{T}}{\partial x} = -\frac{\partial T}{\partial y} = -\frac{T_0}{\pi} \left[\frac{-(1+x)/y^2}{1 + \left(\dfrac{1+x}{y}\right)^2} + \frac{-(1-x)/y^2}{1 + \left(\dfrac{1-x}{y}\right)^2} \right] = \frac{T_0}{\pi} \left[\frac{1+x}{(x+1)^2 + y^2} + \frac{1-x}{(1-x)^2 + y^2} \right].$$

These imply that

$$\tilde{T}(x,y) = \frac{T_0}{\pi} \left\{ \frac{1}{2} \ln\left[(x+1)^2 + y^2\right] - \frac{1}{2} \ln\left[(1-x)^2 + y^2\right] \right\} = \frac{T_0}{2\pi} \ln\left[\frac{y^2 + (1+x)^2}{y^2 + (1-x)^2}\right],$$

plus perhaps an arbitrary constant.

(c) Heat flow lines are defined by $C = \tilde{T}(x,y) = \dfrac{T_0}{2\pi} \ln\left[\dfrac{y^2 + (1+x)^2}{y^2 + (1-x)^2}\right]$, from which

$$\frac{y^2 + (1+x)^2}{y^2 + (1-x)^2} = e^{2\pi C/T_0} \qquad \Longrightarrow \qquad y^2 + (1+x)^2 = e^{2\pi C/T_0}[y^2 + (1-x)^2].$$

When squared terms are expanded and like terms are combined,

$$y^2(1 - e^{2\pi C/T_0}) + x^2(1 - e^{2\pi C/T_0}) + (1 - e^{2\pi C/T_0}) = -2x(1 + e^{2\pi C/T_0}).$$

This implies that

$$x^2 + y^2 + 1 = \frac{-2x(1 + e^{2\pi C/T_0})}{1 - e^{2\pi C/T_0}} = 2x \coth\left(\frac{\pi C}{T_0}\right)$$

from which

$$\left[x - \coth\left(\frac{\pi C}{T_0}\right)\right]^2 + y^2 = \operatorname{csch}^2\left(\frac{\pi C}{T_0}\right).$$

These are circles with centres on the x-axis. We have shown some isothermals and lines of heat flow in Figure 3.41 in the case that T_0 is positive. Arrows are reversed when T_0 is negative.●

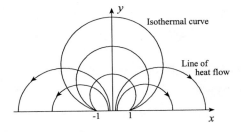

Figure 3.41

EXERCISES 3.8

1. Find steady-state temperature in the half-plane $y > 0$ given that temperature on the negative x-axis is a constant value T_1 and temperature along the positive x-axis is a constant value T_2. Describe isothermal curves and heat flow lines. Hint: Think about radial lines as isothermal curves.

2. Find steady-state temperature in the quarter-plane $x > 0$, $y > 0$ given that temperature on the positive y-axis is a constant value T_1 and temperature on the positive x-axis is a constant value T_2. Describe isothermal curves and heat flow lines.

3. Steady-state temperature in the half-plane $y > 0$ when temperature on the x-axis between $x = \pm 1$ is zero, and a constant value T_0 outside this interval, is

$$T(x,y) = T_0 - \frac{T_0}{\pi}\left[\text{Tan}^{-1}\left(\frac{1+x}{y}\right) + \text{Tan}^{-1}\left(\frac{1-x}{y}\right)\right].$$

(a) Show that isothermal curves are circles passing through $(\pm 1, 0)$ with centres on the y-axis.
(b) Show that harmonic conjugates of $T(x,y)$ are

$$\tilde{T}(x,y) = \frac{T_0}{2\pi}\ln\left[\frac{y^2 + (1-x)^2}{y^2 + (1+x)^2}\right] + C,$$

   where C is a constant.
(c) Show that heat flows along semicircles with centres on the x-axis.

4. Steady-state temperature in a circle $x^2 + y^2 < R^2$ when temperature on the semicircle $y = -\sqrt{R^2 - x^2}$ is a constant value T_1, and temperature on $y = \sqrt{R^2 - x^2}$ is a constant T_2 is

$$T(x,y) = \frac{T_1 + T_2}{2} + \frac{1}{\pi}(T_2 - T_1)\,\text{Tan}^{-1}\left(\frac{2Ry}{R^2 - x^2 - y^2}\right).$$

(a) Show that isothermal curves are circular arcs through the points $(\pm R, 0)$ with centres on the y-axis.
(b) Show that heat flow lines are circular arcs with centres on the x-axis.

5. Steady-state temperature in a semicircle $x^2 + y^2 < R^2$, $y > 0$ when temperature on the semicircle is a constant value T_0, and temperature on the straight edge is zero is

$$T(x,y) = T_0 - \frac{2T_0}{\pi}\,\text{Tan}^{-1}\left(\frac{R^2 - x^2 - y^2}{2Ry}\right).$$

(a) Show that isothermal curves are circular arcs through the points $(\pm R, 0)$ with centres on the y-axis.
(b) Show that heat flow lines are circular arcs with centres on the x-axis.

§**3.9   Electrostatics**

Suppose a distribution of line, surface, or
volume electrostatic charges (but not point
charges) exists in space and is bounded by a
cylinder with axis parallel to a line perpendicular to the xy-plane (Figure 3.42).
Suppose further that the distribution is
in a vacuum and that it is the same in
every plane parallel to the xy-plane.
These charges will create an electric
field inside the cylinder and, due to the
symmetry of their distribution, the
electrostatic potential associated with this electrical field will be a function $V(x,y)$
of x and y only that satisfies the two-dimensional Laplace equation

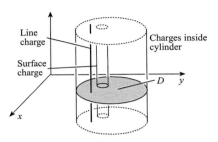

Figure 3.42

$$\frac{\partial^2 V}{\partial x^2} + \frac{\partial^2 V}{\partial y^2} = 0 \tag{3.60}$$

at all points exterior to the charge. Although the physical situation is three-
dimensional, we can think of $V(x,y)$ as being harmonic at points in the cross-section
D of the cylinder with the xy-plane that are free of charge.

If $W(x,y)$ is a harmonic conjugate of $V(x,y)$ in D, then

$$F(z) = V(x,y) + W(x,y)i \tag{3.61}$$

is an analytic function of $z = x + yi$, called the **complex electrostatic potential**.
Thus, with every electrostatic field in a vacuum that is symmetric in one direction,
we associate an analytic complex electrostatic potential $F(z)$.

The electric field intensity due to the charge distribution is given by

$$\mathbf{E} = -\nabla V = -\frac{\partial V}{\partial x}\hat{\mathbf{i}} - \frac{\partial V}{\partial y}\hat{\mathbf{j}}. \tag{3.62}$$

But

$$F'(z) = \frac{\partial V}{\partial x} + \frac{\partial W}{\partial x}i = \frac{\partial V}{\partial x} - \frac{\partial V}{\partial y}i, \tag{3.63}$$

and hence

$$-\overline{F'(z)} = -\frac{\partial V}{\partial x} - \frac{\partial V}{\partial y}i. \tag{3.64}$$

In other words, the real and imaginary parts of $-\overline{F'(z)}$ are the components of the
electric field intensity $\mathbf{E}$.

Curves in the 1-parameter family $V(x,y) = C$ are called **equipotential curves**.
(In actual fact, they represent equipotential cylindrical surfaces.) Since $\mathbf{E} = -\nabla V$,
it follows that at any point in D, $\mathbf{E}$ is perpendicular to the equipotential $V(x,y) = C$
through that point. Curves in the 1-parameter family $W(x,y) = C$ are orthogonal
trajectories of the equipotentials. Consequently, at every point in D, $\mathbf{E}$ is tangent to
the curve $W(x,y) = C$ through that point (Figure 3.43). Because $\mathbf{E}$ is proportional
to the force that would be exerted on a test charge placed at a point, the force field
is always tangent to $W(x,y) = C$, and we therefore call these curves **lines of force**.

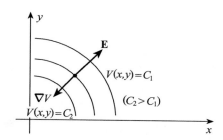

Figure 3.43

Laplace's equation 3.60 will be accompanied by boundary conditions that usually specify either $V(x,y)$ or its normal derivative on the boundary of D. A Dirichlet boundary condition specifies $V(x,y)$ on the boundary of D,

$$V(x,y) = h(x,y), \quad (x,y) \text{ on boundary of } D, \qquad (3.65a)$$

where $h(x,y)$ is a given function. Conducting boundaries give rise to Dirichlet boundary conditions.

A Neumann boundary condition specifies the derivative of $V(x,y)$ in the direction perpendicular to the boundary of D. This is expressed in the form

$$\nabla V \cdot \hat{\mathbf{n}} = h(x,y), \quad (x,y) \text{ on boundary of } D, \qquad (3.65b)$$

where $h(x,y)$ is a given function, and $\hat{\mathbf{n}}$ is the unit vector perpendicular to the boundary of D. Neumann boundary conditions arise when the boundary of D is a dielectric.

In the following examples we illustrate equipotentials and lines of force for some simple problems. More difficult problems will be discussed in Chapter 7.

Example 3.38   An infinite plane perpendicular to the xy-plane contains the x-axis. The left half of the plane ($x < 0$) is held at constant potential V_1 and the potential of the right half ($x > 0$) is a constant value V_2. Find the electrostatic potential in the half-space to the right of the plane. Describe equipotentials and lines of force.

Solution Since electrostatic potential is the same in all planes parallel to the xy-plane, we consider only the xy-plane itself (Figure 3.44), where we have arbitrarily chosen $V_2 < V_1$. The negative and positive x-axis are equipotentials and we might suspect that the y-axis is also an equipotential (perhaps $(V_1 + V_2)/2$). Because these lines are coordinate curves in polar coordinates, we consider solving Laplace's equation 3.60 in polar coordinates

$$\frac{\partial^2 V}{\partial r^2} + \frac{1}{r}\frac{\partial V}{\partial r} + \frac{1}{r^2}\frac{\partial^2 V}{\partial \theta^2} = 0.$$

The fact that $\theta = 0$, $\theta = \pi/2$, and $\theta = \pi$ are equipotential curves (represesnting equipotential surfaces) might suggest further that V is only a function of θ, in which case, Laplace's equation reduces to

$$\frac{d^2 V}{d\theta^2} = 0,$$

a general solution of which is $V(\theta) = A\theta + B$. The boundary conditions on $\theta = 0$ and $\theta = \pi$ require

$$V_2 = B, \qquad V_1 = A\pi + B.$$

Thus, $V(\theta) = \left(\dfrac{V_1 - V_2}{\pi}\right)\theta + V_2$. Equipotentials are radial lines, and lines of force are semicircles centred at the origin (Figure 3.45).•

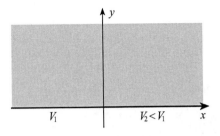

Figure 3.44   **Figure 3.45**

Example 3.39   An infinite plane perpendicular to the xy-plane contains the x-axis. That part of the plane between $x = \pm 1$ is held at constant potential V_0 and the remaining two parts of the plane are grounded, the three parts of the plane being insulated from each other. The electrostatic potential satisfying Laplace's equation in the half-space $y > 0$ is

$$V(x,y) = \frac{V_0}{\pi}\left[\mathrm{Tan}^{-1}\left(\frac{1+x}{y}\right) + \mathrm{Tan}^{-1}\left(\frac{1-x}{y}\right)\right].$$

Find equipotentials and lines of force.

Solution   Since electrostatic potential is the same in all planes parallel to the xy-plane, we consider only the xy-plane itself. Equipotential curves in the xy-plane, which represent equipotential surfaces in space, are given by

$$C = \frac{V_0}{\pi}\left[\mathrm{Tan}^{-1}\left(\frac{1+x}{y}\right) + \mathrm{Tan}^{-1}\left(\frac{1-x}{y}\right)\right],$$

or,

$$\mathrm{Tan}^{-1}\left(\frac{1+x}{y}\right) + \mathrm{Tan}^{-1}\left(\frac{1-x}{y}\right) = \frac{\pi C}{V_0}.$$

If we take tangents of both sides, we obtain

$$\frac{\dfrac{1+x}{y} + \dfrac{1-x}{y}}{1 - \left(\dfrac{1+x}{y}\right)\left(\dfrac{1-x}{y}\right)} = \tan\left(\frac{\pi C}{V_0}\right).$$

This equation simplifies to

$$x^2 + \left[y - \cot\left(\frac{\pi C}{V_0}\right)\right]^2 = \csc^2\left(\frac{\pi C}{V_0}\right).$$

Described are circles that pass through the points $(\pm 1, 0)$ and have centres on the y-axis. Equipotentials for $C = V_0/8$, $3V_0/16$, and $V_0/4$ are shown in Figure 3.46a.

To determine lines of force we find harmonic conjugates $W(x,y)$ of $V(x,y)$. The Cauchy-Riemann equations require

$$\frac{\partial W}{\partial y} = \frac{\partial V}{\partial x} = \frac{V_0}{\pi}\left[\frac{y}{y^2 + (1+x)^2} - \frac{y}{y^2 + (1-x)^2}\right],$$

$$\frac{\partial W}{\partial x} = -\frac{\partial V}{\partial y} = \frac{V_0}{\pi}\left[\frac{1+x}{y^2 + (1+x)^2} + \frac{1-x}{y^2 + (1-x)^2}\right].$$

These give

$$W(x,y) = \frac{V_0}{2\pi}\ln\left[\frac{y^2 + (1+x)^2}{y^2 + (1-x)^2}\right],$$

plus perhaps a constant. Lines of force are therefore defined by

$$C = \frac{V_0}{2\pi}\ln\left[\frac{y^2 + (1+x)^2}{y^2 + (1-x)^2}\right],$$

and this equation can be rewritten in the form

$$\left[x - \coth\left(\frac{\pi C}{V_0}\right)\right]^2 + y^2 = \operatorname{csch}^2\left(\frac{\pi C}{V_0}\right).$$

Described are circles with centres on the x-axis. The circles for $C = \pm V_0/8$, $\pm 3V_0/16$, and $\pm V_0/4$ are shown in Figure 3.46b. Figures 3.46a and 3.46b are superposed in Figure 3.46c illustrating orthogonality of equipotentials and lines of force.●

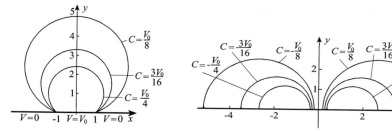

Figure 3.46a   Figure 3.46b

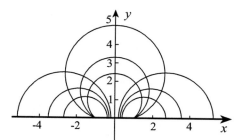

Figure 3.46c

EXERCISES 3.9

For simplicity in formulation, exercises will be posed in the xy-plane. They are, however, the result of three-dimensional problems for which potential is the same in every plane parallel to the xy-plane.

1. Express the potential function in Example 3.38 in terms of x and y.

2. Find electrostatic potential between two concentric circles $a^2 < x^2 + y^2 < b^2$ given that potential on inner and outer boundaries are constant values V_a and V_b. Describe equipotential curves and lines of force.

3. Find electrostatic potential in the quarter-plane $x > 0$, $y > 0$ given that potential on the positive y-axis is a constant value V_1 and potential on the positive x-axis is a constant value V_2. Describe equipotential curves and lines of force.

4. Electrostatic potential in the half-plane $y > 0$ when potential on the x-axis between $x = \pm 1$ is zero, and a constant value V_0 outside this interval, is

$$V(x,y) = V_0 - \frac{V_0}{\pi}\left[\text{Tan}^{-1}\left(\frac{1+x}{y}\right) + \text{Tan}^{-1}\left(\frac{1-x}{y}\right)\right].$$

(a) Show that equipotential curves are circles passing through $(\pm 1, 0)$ with centres on the y-axis.
(b) Show that harmonic conjugates of $V(x,y)$ are

$$W(x,y) = \frac{V_0}{2\pi}\ln\left[\frac{y^2 + (1-x)^2}{y^2 + (1+x)^2}\right] + C,$$

where C is a constant.
(c) Show that lines of force are semicircles with centres on the x-axis.

5. Electrostatic potential in a circle $x^2 + y^2 < R^2$ when potential on the semicircle $y = -\sqrt{R^2 - x^2}$ is a constant value V_1, and potential on $y = \sqrt{R^2 - x^2}$ is a constant V_2 is

$$V(x,y) = \frac{V_1 + V_2}{2} + \frac{1}{\pi}(V_2 - V_1)\,\text{Tan}^{-1}\left(\frac{2Ry}{R^2 - x^2 - y^2}\right).$$

(a) Show that equipotential curves are circular arcs through the points $(\pm R, 0)$ with centres on the y-axis.
(b) Show that lines of force are circular arcs with centres on the x-axis.

6. Electrostatic potential in a semicircle $x^2 + y^2 < R^2$, $y > 0$ when potential on the semicircle is a constant value V_0, and potential on the straight edge is zero is

$$V(x,y) = V_0 - \frac{2V_0}{\pi}\,\text{Tan}^{-1}\left(\frac{R^2 - x^2 - y^2}{2Ry}\right).$$

(a) Show that equipotential curves are circular arcs through the points $(\pm R, 0)$ with centres on the y-axis.
(b) Show that lines of force are circular arcs with centres on the x-axis.

7. Is there a complex electrostatic potential associated with the real electrostatic potential due to a point charge at the origin?

§3.10   Two-dimensional Fluid Flow

Consider fluid flowing over a domain D of the xy-plane in such a way that motion is identical in all planes parallel to the xy-plane. In this situation, it is sufficient to consider motion of the sheet of fluid "in" the xy-plane itself. Velocity of the fluid in this sheet is parallel to the xy-plane, and it is normally a function of position and time. We consider only the case in which the velocity is independent of time, called **steady-state** flow. In this case, velocity of the fluid at point (x, y) can be expressed in the form

$$\mathbf{q} = u(x, y)\hat{\mathbf{i}} + v(x, y)\hat{\mathbf{j}}, \tag{3.66}$$

where, as indicated, u and v depend only on x and y.

Harmonic functions do not fit into the most general of two-dimensional, steady-state flows; further specializations must be made. In the absence of *sources* and *sinks* of fluid, points at which fluid appears or disappears, the equation of continuity for fluid flow is

$$\nabla \cdot (\rho \mathbf{q}) = -\frac{\partial \rho}{\partial t}, \tag{3.67}$$

where ρ is the density of the fluid. The time rate of change of density $\partial \rho / \partial t$ measures how much more mass of fluid enters unit volume in the fluid than leaves it. Since $\rho \mathbf{q}$ is the mass flow rate of the fluid, its divergence $\nabla \cdot (\rho \mathbf{q})$ measures how much more mass leaves unit volume in the fluid than enters. Clearly then, $\partial \rho / \partial t$ and $\nabla \cdot (\rho \mathbf{q})$ measure the same quantity (but in opposite directions), and are therefore related by the equation of continuity.

Fluid flow is said to be **incompressible** if density of the fluid is the same at every point of the fluid and is also independent of time. With constant ρ, the equation of continuity becomes $0 = \nabla \cdot (\rho \mathbf{q}) = \rho \nabla \cdot \mathbf{q}$, or, in terms of u and v,

$$\frac{\partial u}{\partial x} + \frac{\partial v}{\partial y} = 0. \tag{3.68}$$

We also restrict consideration to regions of flow in which

$$\nabla \times \mathbf{q} = \mathbf{0} \tag{3.69}$$

called **irrotational flows**. The x- and y-components of $\nabla \times \mathbf{q}$ vanish identically, and the component perpendicular to the xy-plane yields

$$\frac{\partial v}{\partial x} - \frac{\partial u}{\partial y} = 0. \tag{3.70}$$

It is in the study of incompressible, irrotational, steady-state, two-dimensional flows that complex functions become useful. In suitable domains D, irrotational condition 3.69 or 3.70 implies that there exists a function $\phi(x, y)$, called the **velocity potential** such that

$$u = \frac{\partial \phi}{\partial x}, \qquad v = \frac{\partial \phi}{\partial y}. \tag{3.71}$$

But then equation 3.68 implies that

$$\frac{\partial^2 \phi}{\partial x^2} = \frac{\partial u}{\partial x} = -\frac{\partial v}{\partial y} = -\frac{\partial^2 \phi}{\partial y^2}; \tag{3.72}$$

that is, $\phi(x, y)$ satisfies Laplace's equation. When u and v have continuous first partial derivatives, ϕ has continuous second derivatives, and we conclude that the velocity potential $\phi(x, y)$ is harmonic in D. There therefore exists in D a harmonic conjugate $\psi(x, y)$ such that $\phi + \psi i$ is an analytic function $F(z)$ of the complex variable $z = x + yi$,

$$F(z) = \phi(x, y) + \psi(x, y)i. \tag{3.73}$$

This conjugate function $\psi(x, y)$ is called the **stream function** for the flow, and $F(z)$ is called the **complex potential**.

Analyticity of $F(z)$ in D implies that ϕ and ψ satisfy the Cauchy-Riemann equations

$$\frac{\partial \phi}{\partial x} = \frac{\partial \psi}{\partial y}, \qquad \frac{\partial \phi}{\partial y} = -\frac{\partial \psi}{\partial x}. \tag{3.74}$$

With these we may write

$$F'(z) = \frac{\partial \phi}{\partial x} + \frac{\partial \psi}{\partial x}i = \frac{\partial \phi}{\partial x} - \frac{\partial \phi}{\partial y}i = u - vi, \tag{3.75}$$

or,

$$u + vi = \overline{F'(z)}. \tag{3.76}$$

Thus, with incompressible, irrotational, steady-state, two-dimensional flow, we associate an analytic complex potential $F(z)$ such that the components $u(x, y)$ and $v(x, y)$ of the velocity $\mathbf{q}$ are the real and imaginary parts of $\overline{F'(z)}$. Conversely, given an analytic function $F(z)$, the real and imaginary parts of $\overline{F'(z)}$ define an incompressible, irrotational, steady-state, two-dimensional flow.

Associated with velocity potential $\phi(x, y)$ is a 1-parameter family of curves $\phi(x, y) = C$ called **equipotential curves**. At any point, the velocity of the flow, $\mathbf{q} = \nabla \phi$, is perpendicular to the equipotential curve through that point (Figure 3.47a). But $\psi(x, y) = C$ defines a 1-parameter family of curves which is orthogonal to the family $\phi(x, y) = C$. Thus, at every point in the fluid, $\mathbf{q}$ is tangent to the curve $\psi(x, y) = C$ through that point (Figure 3.47b). In other words, particles of fluid move along the curve $\psi(x, y) = C$, which are therefore called **stream curves**.

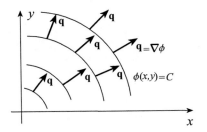

Figure 3.47a

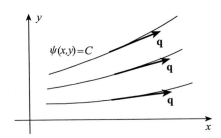

Figure 3.47b

Example 3.40 Find a complex potential for flow with constant velocity field $\mathbf{q} = \alpha\hat{\mathbf{i}} + \beta\hat{\mathbf{j}}$, where α and β are constants.

Solution   If the complex potential for this parallel straightline flow is $F(z) = \phi + \psi i$, then velocity potential $\phi(x, y)$ is defined by

$$\alpha = \frac{\partial \phi}{\partial x}, \qquad \beta = \frac{\partial \phi}{\partial y}.$$

Consequently, $\phi(x, y) = \alpha x + \beta y + C$, where C is a real constant. To find $\psi(x, y)$, the harmonic conjugate of $\phi(x, y)$, we use the Cauchy-Riemann equations,

$$\frac{\partial \psi}{\partial y} = \frac{\partial \phi}{\partial x} = \alpha, \qquad \frac{\partial \psi}{\partial x} = -\frac{\partial \phi}{\partial y} = -\beta.$$

Thus, $\psi(x, y) = -\beta x + \alpha y + D$, where D is a real constant. The complex potential associated with this flow is therefore

$$\begin{aligned} F(z) = \phi + \psi i &= (\alpha x + \beta y + C) + (-\beta x + \alpha y + D)i \\ &= \alpha(x + yi) - \beta i(x + yi) + (C + Di) \\ &= (\alpha - \beta i)(x + yi) + (C + Di) \\ &= (\alpha - \beta i)z + (C + Di). \end{aligned}$$

If δ is the angle of inclination of the flow with the positive x-axis (Figure 3.48), then $\sin\delta = \beta/\sqrt{\alpha^2 + \beta^2}$ and $\cos\delta = \alpha/\sqrt{\alpha^2 + \beta^2}$. Consequently, we may write

$$\begin{aligned} \alpha - \beta i &= \sqrt{\alpha^2 + \beta^2}\cos\delta - \sqrt{\alpha^2 + \beta^2}\sin\delta\, i \\ &= \sqrt{\alpha^2 + \beta^2}(\cos\delta - \sin\delta\, i). \end{aligned}$$

In other words, we may also write $F(z)$ in the form

$$F(z) = |\mathbf{q}|e^{-\delta i}z + C + Di. \bullet$$

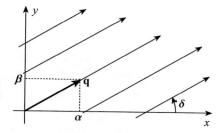

Figure 3.48

Example 3.41 Describe the fluid flow defined by the complex potential

$$F(z) = U\left(z + \frac{a^2}{z}\right), \qquad |z| \geq a,$$

where U and a are positive constants.

Solution   If we set $z = re^{\theta i}$, then

$$F(z) = U\left[re^{\theta i} + \frac{a^2}{r}e^{-\theta i}\right].$$

Stream curves are therefore defined by

$$C = \text{Im}[F(z)] = U\left(r\sin\theta - \frac{a^2}{r}\sin\theta\right), \quad C \text{ a constant.}$$

The $C = 0$ stream curve consists of the circle $r = a$ and those parts of the rays $\theta = 0$ and $\theta = \pi$ for which $r \geq a$ (Figure 3.49). Various other stream curves are also shown. The direction arrows are determined by calculating

$$\overline{F'(z)} = U\left(1 - \frac{a^2}{\bar{z}^2}\right) = U\left[1 - \frac{a^2}{r^2}(\cos 2\theta + \sin 2\theta\, i)\right].$$

It then follows that

$$\mathbf{q} = \mathrm{Re}\left[\overline{F'(z)}\right]\hat{\mathbf{i}} + \mathrm{Im}\left[\overline{F'(z)}\right]\hat{\mathbf{j}} = U\left(1 - \frac{a^2}{r^2}\cos 2\theta\right)\hat{\mathbf{i}} + U\left(-\frac{a^2}{r^2}\sin 2\theta\right)\hat{\mathbf{j}}.$$

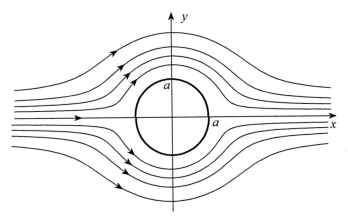

Figure 3.49

Notice that for large r, $\mathbf{q}$ is essentially equal to $U\hat{\mathbf{i}}$, thus corroborating in Figure 3.49 that far from the origin, velocity is essentially parallel to the x-axis. Because $r = a$ is a stream curve, and no stream curves are to be considered inside the circle, we interpret the flow as that due to a circular obstacle (actually a cylinder) placed in a uniform flow.●

Points in the flow where the velocity of the fluid vanishes are called **stagnation points**. They can be found by solving the equation $F'(z) = 0$. In Example 3.41, $(\pm a, 0)$ are stagnation points.

It is important to realize that since fluid flows along stream curves, physical boundaries of the flow must correspond to stream curves $\psi = C$. Such is the case in Example 3.41 where the circular boundary $|z| = a$ to the flow is defined by the stream curve $\psi = 0$. Notice also that by treating a stream curve $\psi = $ constant in a given flow field as a boundary, other flow fields can be obtained. For instance, the stream curve $\psi = 0$ in Example 3.41 corresponds not just to $|z| = a$, but also to the real axis outside the circle. If we treat this stream curve as a boundary to a flow field and consider only that part of the flow above the real axis (Figure 3.50), then $F(z) = U(z + a^2/z)$ is the complex potential for uniform flow in the half-plane $y > 0$ over a semi-circular object of radius a at the origin.

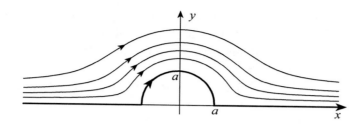

Figure 3.50

Flux and Circulation

When **q** is the velocity of a fluid at each point in space, and ρ is the density of the fluid, the surface integral

$$\iint_S \rho \mathbf{q} \cdot \hat{\mathbf{n}}\, dS \tag{3.77}$$

where $\hat{\mathbf{n}}$ is the unit normal to the surface S (Figure 3.51) is called **flux**. It measures the mass of fluid flowing through the surface in direction $\hat{\mathbf{n}}$ per unit time. If S is a closed surface, and $\hat{\mathbf{n}}$ is the unit outer normal to S, flux is a measure of the net outward flow of fluid through S. It is likely that fluid is flowing into the volume bounded by S at some points on S and flowing out at other points. When the flux is positive there is a net outward flow, and when flux is negative, there is a net inward flow.

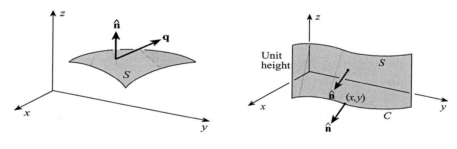

Figure 3.51   **Figure 3.52**

When the flow is two-dimensional, as in this section, surface integral 3.77 can be reduced to a line integral in the xy-plane for certain surfaces. In particular, suppose S is a vertical surface of unit height standing on a curve C in the xy-plane (Figure 3.52). In this case the unit normal at every point on S directly above a point (x,y) on C is equal to the unit normal to C at (x,y). Because ρ is constant, and **q** is only a function of x and y, flux integral 3.77 can be expressed as a line integral

$$\text{Flux} = \rho \int_C \mathbf{q} \cdot \hat{\mathbf{n}}\, ds. \tag{3.78}$$

It measures the mass of fluid flowing through a surface of unit height standing on C. When C is closed and positively oriented (Figure 3.53), $\hat{\mathbf{n}} = (dy/ds, -dx/ds)$, and

$$\text{Flux} = \rho \oint_C u \, dy - v \, dx. \qquad (3.79)$$

This integral measures the net mass flow rate through a surface of unit height standing on C. It is zero if C contains no sources or sinks; it may be nonzero when sources or sinks are interior to C.

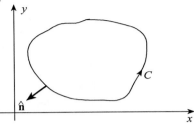

Figure 3.53

Example 3.42   Verify that flux through the curve $C : x^2 + y^2 = 4a^2$ for the flow of Example 3.41 vanishes.

Solution   In Example 3.41, we calculated the velocity

$$\mathbf{q} = U \left(1 - \frac{a^2}{r^2} \cos 2\theta \right) \hat{\mathbf{i}} - U \left(\frac{a^2}{r^2} \sin 2\theta \right) \hat{\mathbf{j}}.$$

Using the polar form $r = 2a$ for C, we calculate the flux as

$$\text{Flux} = \rho \oint_C U \left(1 - \frac{a^2}{r^2} \cos 2\theta \right) dy + U \left(\frac{a^2}{r^2} \sin 2\theta \right) dx$$

$$= \rho U \int_0^{2\pi} \left(1 - \frac{a^2}{r^2} \cos 2\theta \right) (r \cos\theta \, d\theta) + \frac{a^2}{r^2} \sin 2\theta \, (-r \sin\theta \, d\theta)$$

$$= 2\rho a U \int_0^{2\pi} \left[\left(1 - \frac{a^2}{4a^2} \cos 2\theta \right) \cos\theta - \frac{a^2}{4a^2} \sin 2\theta \sin\theta \right] d\theta$$

$$= 2a\rho U \int_0^{2\pi} \frac{3}{4} \cos\theta \, d\theta$$

$$= 0. \bullet$$

A second useful quantity in fluid flow is called circulation. For a closed curve C in a fluid, **circulation** Γ is defined by the line integral

$$\Gamma = \oint_C \mathbf{q} \cdot d\mathbf{r} = \oint_C u \, dx + v \, dy. \qquad (3.80)$$

It is a measure of the tendency of the fluid to circulate around the curve C. If C contains only points at which irrotationality condition 3.70 is satisfied, then circulation vanishes; otherwise, it may not vanish.

Example 3.43   Calculate circulation for the curve and flow in Example 3.41.

Solution   Using definition 3.80,

$$\Gamma = \oint_C U \left(1 - \frac{a^2}{r^2} \cos 2\theta \right) dx - \frac{U a^2}{r^2} \sin 2\theta \, dy$$

$$= U \int_0^{2\pi} \left(1 - \frac{a^2}{r^2} \cos 2\theta \right) (-r \sin\theta \, d\theta) - \frac{a^2}{r^2} \sin 2\theta \, (r \cos\theta \, d\theta)$$

$$= 2aU \int_0^{2\pi} \left[-\left(1 - \frac{a^2}{4a^2} \cos 2\theta \right) \sin \theta - \frac{a^2}{4a^2} \sin 2\theta \, \cos \theta \right] d\theta$$

$$= 2aU \int_0^{2\pi} -\frac{5}{4} \sin \theta \, d\theta$$

$$= 0. \bullet$$

In Chapter 4 we shall see that both flux and circulation integrals can be combined into a single integral of the complex potential function $F(z)$ associated with the flow.

EXERCISES 3.10

In Exercises 1–5 describe the fluid flow defined by the complex potential. Identify any stagnation points in the flow.

1. $F(z) = kz^2$, $\text{Im}\, z \geq 0$, where $k > 0$

2. $F(z) = kz^2$, $\text{Im}\, z \geq 0$, $\text{Re}\, z \geq 0$, where $k > 0$

3. $F(z) = z^2 + 2z$, $\text{Re}\, z \geq -1$

4. $F(z) = z^4$, $0 \leq \text{Arg}\, z \leq \pi/4$

5. $F(z) = V_0 \left(\dfrac{z}{e^{\alpha i}} + \dfrac{a^2 e^{\alpha i}}{z} \right)$,   where a, V_0, and α are positive constants and $|z| \geq a$.

(See Example 3.41.)

6. Consider $F(z) = \sin \dfrac{\pi z}{2a}$, where $a > 0$ is a constant, as the complex potential for a fluid flow.
   (a) What is the velocity of the flow at each point (x, y)?
   (b) Draw the stream curve $\psi(x, y) = 0$.
   (c) Noting that the lines $x = \pm a$ for $y > 0$ and $y = 0$ for $-a \leq x \leq a$ are part of the stream curve in part (b), we can consider flow in the domain $y > 0$, $-a < x < a$ with boundary points of the domain forming the physical boundary for the flow. Describe the flow by drawing stream curves $\psi = \text{constant}$ in the flow domain. What are the stagnation points?

7. Repeat Exercise 6 with $F(z) = \cos \dfrac{\pi z}{2a}$. In part (c) use the domain $y > 0$, $0 < x < 2a$.

8. Consider $F(z) = \text{Cos}^{-1}(z/a)$, where $a > 0$ is a constant, as the complex potential for a fluid flow.
   (a) Show that stream curves are ellipses with foci at $(\pm a, 0)$.
   (b) By choosing a specific ellipse in part (a), say $\psi = \psi_1$ as a physical boundary, the flow may be regarded as that about an elliptic object. Find the velocity and speed of the flow at any point z in terms of values of the velocity potential ϕ and stream function ψ at that point. Is the flow clockwise or counterclockwise?

9. Consider $F(z) = \text{Cosh}^{-1}(z/a)$, where $a > 0$ is a constant, as the complex potential for a fluid flow.
   (a) Show that stream curves are hyperbolas with foci $(\pm a, 0)$.
   (b) By choosing a specific hyperbola in part (a) say $\psi = \psi_1$ as a physical boundary, the flow may be regarded as that through a hyperbolic aperature. Show that the speed of the flow at any point is given by

$$|\mathbf{q}|^2 = \frac{2}{a^2(\cosh 2\phi - \cos 2\psi)}, \quad \text{where } w = \phi + \psi i.$$

(c) Show that by choosing the physical boundary as the limiting hyperbolas $\psi \to 0$ and $\psi \to \pi$, the flow becomes that through a slit $y = 0$, $-a < x < a$ in the x-axis. What is the speed of this flow at $(\pm a, 0)$?

10. (a) What stream curves result by setting $\psi(x, y) = 0$ for the complex potential $F(z) = z^2 + 1/z^2$ defined only for $x^2 + y^2 \geq 1$, $x \geq 0$, $y \geq 0$?

    (b) Show that other stream curves have equations expressible in the form

$$\theta = \begin{cases} \dfrac{1}{2}\text{Sin}^{-1}\left(\dfrac{Cr^2}{r^4 - 1}\right) \\ \dfrac{\pi}{2} - \dfrac{1}{2}\text{Sin}^{-1}\left(\dfrac{Cr^2}{r^4 - 1}\right) \end{cases}.$$

Plot some of these curves to obtain an idea of the flow pattern.

11. Find the complex potential for flow with constant speed U in the positive x-direction over the half-plane $y \geq 0$. Choose $y = 0$ as the stream function $\psi = 0$, and $x = 0$ as the velocity potential $\phi = 0$.

12. Show that flux and circulation for the flow of Exercise 2 vanish around every closed curve.

13. Show that flux and circulation for the flow of Exercise 4 vanish around every closed curve.

14. (a) Show that stream curves for the flow defined by the complex potential $F(z) = 1/z$ are circles with centres on the y-axis that "pass" through the origin.

    (b) Show that velocity potentials are circles with centres on the x-axis that "pass" through the origin.

    (c) Prove that flux and circulation vanish for every curve not containing $z = 0$.

    (d) Find flux and circulation for $x^2 + y^2 = a^2$ directed counterclockwise.

15. Suppose that $F(z) = k \log_\phi z$ is a complex potential for fluid flow. The flow is said to have a line source at the origin if $k > 0$, and a line sink if $k < 0$.

    (a) Show that flow is radially outward for $k > 0$ and radially inward for $k < 0$. Find the speed of the flow at any point.

    (b) Calculate flux and circulation when C is a closed curve not containing the origin.

    (c) Calculate flux and circulation when C is a circle centred at the origin.

16. Suppose that $F(z) = -ki \log_\phi z$ is a complex potential for fluid flow. The flow is said to have a line vortex at the origin.

    (a) Show that stream curves are circles centred at the origin. Find the speed of the flow at any point.

    (b) Calculate flux and circulation when C is a closed curve not containing the origin.

    (c) Calculate flux and circulation when C is a circle centred at the origin.

17. Suppose that the function $F(z) = k[\log_\phi(z + a) - \log_\phi(z - a)]$, $a > 0$, $k > 0$, represents the complex potential for fluid flow. Show that stream curves are circles centred on the y-axis that pass through $z = \pm a$. What is the velocity and speed of the flow?

18. Consider $F(z) = z^{\pi/\alpha}$ (principal branch), where $\pi/2 < \alpha < \pi$, as the complex potential for fluid flow in the domain $0 < \text{Arg } z < \alpha$.

    (a) Describe the stream curve $\psi(x, y) = 0$.

    (b) What is the fluid velocity at every point in the flow? Are there any stagnation points?

    (c) Are the components of the velocity positive or negative for $0 < \text{Arg } z < \alpha/2$?

    (d) Are the components of the velocity positive or negative for $\alpha/2 < \text{Arg } z < \alpha$?

    (e) What is the velocity when $\text{Arg } z = \alpha/2$? Is it perpendicular to the line $\text{Arg } z = \alpha/2$?

19. Repeat Exercise 18 if $0 < \alpha < \pi/2$.

20. Consider $F(z) = e^{-i\pi\alpha/(\pi-\alpha)} z^{\pi/(\pi-\alpha)}$ (principal branch), where $0 < \alpha < \pi/2$, as the complex potential for fluid flow in the domain $\alpha < |\mathrm{Arg}\, z| \le \pi$.

   (a) Describe the stream curve $\psi(x, y) = 0$. Is it consistent with flow past a wedge of angle 2α symmetrically positioned around the positive real z-axis at $z = 0$?

   (b) What is the velocity of the flow? Show that the speed of the flow is the same for all points equidistant from the vertex of the wedge. Is there a stagnation point?

21. Show that when A and B are any two points in a flow and C is a piecewise smooth curve in the flow joining A and B, the flux through C is $\rho[\psi(B) - \psi(A)]$ where $\psi(x, y) = \psi(A)$ is the stream curve through A and $\psi(x, y) = \psi(B)$ is the stream curve through B.

CHAPTER 4   COMPLEX INTEGRALS

We now turn our attention to integration of complex functions. As for real functions we define two kinds of integrals. The antiderivative of a complex function f is completely analogous to that for a real function; it is a complex function whose derivative is f. What corresponds to the definite integral of a real function is called a *contour* integral of a complex function. Because complex numbers are two-dimensional, having real and imaginary parts, the definition of a contour integral more closely resembles that of a line integral in the xy-plane than a definite integral along the x-axis. In spite of this, we find that strategies for evaluating real definite integrals are as prevalent in evaluating contour integrals as are strategies for calculating real line integrals.

Contour integrals lead to a host of properties for analytic functions. These in turn lead to properties of harmonic functions since real and imaginary parts of analytic functions are harmonic.

§4.1   Indefinite Integrals and Antiderivatives

Definition 4.1   A complex function F is said to be an **antiderivative** of a complex function f in a domain D if

$$F'(z) = f(z) \tag{4.1}$$

at every point in D.

For example, since $d(z^4)/dz = 4z^3$, we say that z^4 is an antiderivative of $4z^3$. But so also is $z^4 + 10i$ an antiderivative. In fact, for any complex number C whatsoever, $z^4 + C$ is an antiderivative of $4z^3$.

We have already shown (Theorem 2.7) that if a function F has a derivative equal to zero at every point in some domain D, then F must be a constant function in D. This implies that once we have found one antiderivative of a function, we have essentially found them all.

Theorem 4.1   If F is an antiderivative of f in some domain D, then every antiderivative of f is of the form $F + C$ where C is a complex constant.

When F is an antiderivative of f, we call $F + C$ the **indefinite integral** of f, and write

$$\int f(z)\, dz = F(z) + C. \tag{4.2}$$

It is a simple exercise in differentiation and use of Definition 4.1 to verify the following properties of indefinite integrals.

Theorem 4.2   If $\int f(z)\, dz = F(z) + C$ and $\int g(z)\, dz = G(z) + C$, then

$$\text{(i)} \quad \int [f(z) + g(z)]\, dz = F(z) + G(z) + C, \tag{4.3a}$$

$$\text{(ii)} \quad \int k\, f(z)\, dz = kF(z) + C, \quad k \text{ a complex constant.} \tag{4.3b}$$

Example 4.1   Evaluate $\displaystyle\int \frac{1}{z-3-2i}\,dz.$

Solution   Since
$$\frac{d}{dz}\log_\phi\left(z-3-2i\right)=\frac{1}{z-3-2i},$$
we can say that
$$\int \frac{1}{z-3-2i}\,dz = \log_\phi\left(z-3-2i\right)+C$$
where ϕ is any real number. This indefinite integral is valid at every point of the complex plane except points on the branch cut in Figure 4.1.

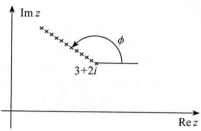

Figure 4.1

EXERCISES 4.1

In Exercises 1–20 evaluate the indefinite integral. Specify the domain of validity of the result.

1. $\displaystyle\int (z^3+3z+2)\,dz$

2. $\displaystyle\int \left(\frac{1}{z^2}-2z\right)dz$

3. $\displaystyle\int z(z^2+3)^4\,dz$

4. $\displaystyle\int z^2(4z^3+2)^6\,dz$

5. $\displaystyle\int \frac{z}{(z^2+1)^2}\,dz$

6. $\displaystyle\int \frac{4z-6}{(z^2-3z+5)^3}\,dz$

7. $\displaystyle\int \cos 3z\,dz$

8. $\displaystyle\int z\sin\left(4z^2\right)dz$

9. $\displaystyle\int \cos^2 z\,dz$

10. $\displaystyle\int \sec^2 z\,dz$

11. $\displaystyle\int \frac{1}{z+5}\,dz$

12. $\displaystyle\int \frac{1}{3z+4i}\,dz$

13. $\displaystyle\int z\sin z\,dz$

14. $\displaystyle\int \sin^3 z\,dz$

15. $\displaystyle\int \frac{z}{(z^2-4)^2}\,dz$

16. $\displaystyle\int \frac{z^2}{z^3-3z+2}\,dz$

17. $\displaystyle\int z^2 e^{2z}\,dz$

18. $\displaystyle\int \frac{z}{\sqrt{1-z}}\,dz$

19. $\displaystyle\int \operatorname{Log} z\,dz$

20. $\displaystyle\int \frac{1}{z^2}\sin\left(\frac{1}{z}\right)dz$

21. Real antidifferentiation would suggest that
$$\int \frac{z}{z^2-4}\,dz = \frac{1}{2}\log_\phi\left(z^2-4\right)+C.$$

Show that partial fractions leads to the antiderivative
$$\int \frac{z}{z^2-4}\,dz = \frac{1}{2}\log_\phi\left(z+2\right)+\frac{1}{2}\log_\psi\left(z-2\right)+C.$$

Are these antiderivatives identical?

§4.2   Curves and Line Integrals

In Section 4.3 we define how to integrate a complex function from one complex number z_0 to another complex number z_1 called a contour integral. Because there are many paths from z_0 to z_1 in the complex plane, it will be necessary to specify the particular curve to be followed. This is reminiscent of line integrals in the real xy-plane. Properties of real line integrals are also prominent in the evaluation of contour integrals in the complex plane. In preparation then for contour integrals we give a quick review of curves, their parametrizations, and real line integrals.

A curve is defined parametrically in the xy-plane if it is specified in the form

$$x = x(t), \quad y = y(t), \qquad \alpha \leq t \leq \beta. \tag{4.4}$$

We regard $\big(x(\alpha), y(\alpha)\big)$ as the initial point on the curve, $\big(x(\beta), y(\beta)\big)$ as the final point, and the direction of the curve is from initial point to final point. For example, the equations

$$x = 2 - 3t, \quad y = 4 + t, \qquad 0 \leq t \leq 1,$$

describe the line segment in Figure 4.2 directed (as shown by the arrowhead) from initial point $(2,4)$ to final point $(-1,5)$. The equations

$$x = 3 \cos t, \quad y = 3 \sin t, \qquad 0 \leq t \leq \pi$$

describe the semicircle from $(3,0)$ to $(-3,0)$ in Figure 4.3.

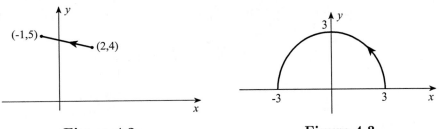

Figure 4.2   **Figure 4.3**

Curves can be parametrized in countless ways. Two additional parametrizations for the semicircle in Figure 4.3 are

$$\begin{array}{ll} x = 3 \cos 2t \\ y = 3 \sin 2t \end{array}, \quad 0 \leq t \leq \pi/2; \qquad \begin{array}{ll} x = -t \\ y = \sqrt{9 - t^2} \end{array}, \quad -3 \leq t \leq 3.$$

A curve is a set of points from some initial point to a final point. Its properties depend only on the set of points, not on the parametric equations that describe the points. All properties discussed in this section are independent of parametric representation of the curve.

Curve 4.4 is **continuous** when both functions $x(t)$ and $y(t)$ are continuous for $\alpha \leq t \leq \beta$. What this means is that at no point is there a separation in the curve. The curves in Figures 4.2 and 4.3 are continuous; the curve in Figure 4.4 is not. All other curves in this chapter are continuous.

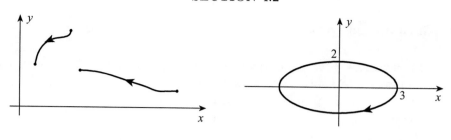

Figure 4.4   Figure 4.5

A curve is said to **closed** if its initial and final points are the same point. Parametric equations $x = 3\cos t$, $y = -2\sin t$, $0 \le t \le 2\pi$, define the ellipse in Figure 4.5. It is a closed curve; initial and final points are both equal to $(3,0)$. The curve in Figure 4.6 has a loop but it is not a closed curve; initial and final points are not the same.

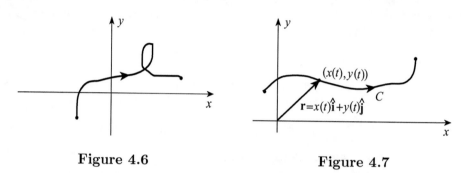

Figure 4.6   Figure 4.7

The position vector of points on a continuous curve C with parametric equations 4.4 is

$$\mathbf{r} = \mathbf{r}(t) = x(t)\hat{\mathbf{i}} + y(t)\hat{\mathbf{j}} \tag{4.5}$$

where $\hat{\mathbf{i}}$ and $\hat{\mathbf{j}}$ are unit vectors in the positive x- and y-directions. It is customary to place the tail of this vector at the origin in which case its tip is at the point on the curve with coordinates $\big(x(t), y(t)\big)$ (Figure 4.7). A tangent vector to C at each point on C is

$$\frac{d\mathbf{r}}{dt} = \frac{dx}{dt}\hat{\mathbf{i}} + \frac{dy}{dt}\hat{\mathbf{j}} \tag{4.6}$$

provided dx/dt and dy/dt both exist and do not simultaneously vanish. This tangent vector always points in the direction in which the parameter increases along the curve. If the parameter increases from initial point to final point (as in 4.4), then $d\mathbf{r}/dt$ points in the direction of motion along C (Figure 4.8).

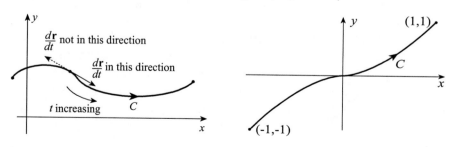

Figure 4.8   Figure 4.9

Example 4.2   Find a tangent vector at each point on the curve

$$C: \; x = t^3, \; y = t^5, \quad -1 \le t \le 1.$$

Solution   According to equation 4.6,

$$\frac{d\mathbf{r}}{dt} = 3t^2\hat{\mathbf{i}} + 5t^4\hat{\mathbf{j}}.$$

This is a tangent vector at each point on C except $(0,0)$ where it vanishes. The curve is shown in Figure 4.9, and it is clear that a tangent vector at $(0,0)$ is $\mathbf{T} = \hat{\mathbf{i}}$. This tangent vector can be obtained from $d\mathbf{r}/dt$ by writing

$$\frac{d\mathbf{r}}{dt} = t^2(3\hat{\mathbf{i}} + 5t^2\hat{\mathbf{j}}).$$

It follows that $\mathbf{T} = 3\hat{\mathbf{i}} + 5t^2\hat{\mathbf{j}}$ is a tangent vector at each point on C (we have simply removed the scale factor t^2 from $d\mathbf{r}/dt$). At $t = 0$, we obtain $\mathbf{T} = 3\hat{\mathbf{i}}$ which is indeed tangent to C at $(0,0)$. •

A curve is said to be **smooth** if it is continuous and there can be assigned a tangent vector at each point on the curve that varies continuously along the curve. By saying that the tangent vector varies "continuously" along the curve, we mean that small changes in t produce small changes in the tangent vector. When the curve is defined by 4.4, this is the case if $x'(t)$ and $y'(t)$ are both continuous for $\alpha < t < \beta$, and $x'(t)$ and $y'(t)$ do not vanish simultaneously for $\alpha < t < \beta$.

Example 4.3   Sketch the curve $C: \; x = 2 \cosh t, \; y = 3 \sinh t, \; -\infty < t < \infty$. Is it smooth?

Solution   Since

$$9x^2 - 4y^2 = 9(4 \cosh^2 t) - 4(9 \sinh^2 t) = 36,$$

and x is always positive, these equations define the right half of the hyperbola in Figure 4.10 directed from fourth quadrant to first quadrant. A tangent vector is

$$\frac{d\mathbf{r}}{dt} = 2 \sinh t \, \hat{\mathbf{i}} + 3 \cosh t \, \hat{\mathbf{j}}.$$

Since components of this vector are continuous, and the y-component never vanishes, the curve is smooth. Figure 4.10 makes this equally clear. The tangent direction to the hyperbola changes continuously from point to point. •

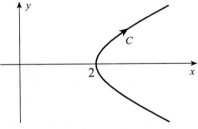

Figure 4.10

Example 4.4   Is the curve in Example 4.2 smooth?

Solution   Figure 4.9 indicates that the curve is indeed smooth. Notice however that the components of $d\mathbf{r}/dt = 3t^2\hat{\mathbf{i}} + 5t^4\hat{\mathbf{j}}$ both vanish at $t = 0$. What this means is that the requirement of simultaneous nonvanishing of $x'(t)$ and $y'(t)$ is a sufficient condition for smoothness of a curve, but it is not necessary. We have already noted that $\mathbf{T} = 3\hat{\mathbf{i}} + 5t^2\hat{\mathbf{j}}$ is also a tangent vector at each point; this vector varies continuously along the curve and does not vanish at $t = 0$. •

Example 4.5   Sketch the curve $C: x = t^3$, $y = t^2$, $-1 \leq t \leq 1$. Is it smooth?

Solution   The curve is shown in Figure 4.11. Due to the "cusp" at $(0,0)$, it is not smooth. Tangent vectors reverse direction at $(0,0)$. Notice that $d\mathbf{r}/dt = 3t^2\hat{\mathbf{i}} + 2t\hat{\mathbf{j}}$ vanishes at $(0,0)$.•

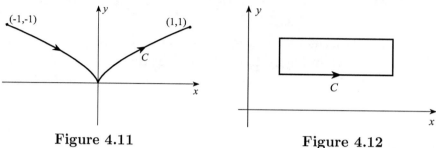

Figure 4.11   Figure 4.12

Most curves that we deal with in this chapter fall into the following category. A curve is said to be **piecewise smooth** if it is continuous and can be divided into a finite number of smooth subcurves. A rectangle is piecewise smooth (Figure 4.12); it can be divided into four smooth subcurves (the sides of the rectangle). The curve in Figure 4.11 is piecewise smooth; parts on either side of the y-axis are smooth. The curve in Figure 4.13 that joins the points $(1/(2n), 1)$ and $(1/(2n-1), -1)$ where $n \geq 1$ is an integer, is not piecewise smooth. It can be divided into smooth line segments, but not a finite number of them.

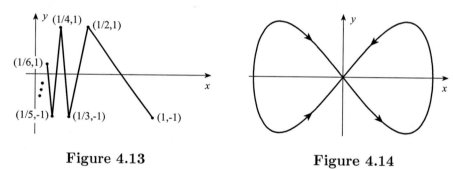

Figure 4.13   Figure 4.14

A continuous curve 4.4 is said to be **simple** if $\mathbf{r}(t_1) = \mathbf{r}(t_2)$ implies that $t_1 = t_2$ for all $\alpha < t_1 < t_2 < \beta$. What this says is that a simple curve cannot cross itself; two different values of t cannot give the same point on the curve, except initial and final point when the curve is closed. The figure eight in Figure 4.14 is not simple, it crosses itself at the origin. The curve in Figure 4.6 is not simple.

Line Integrals in the Plane

Line integrals in the xy-plane that correspond to integrals in the complex plane take the form

$$\int_C P(x,y)\, dx + Q(x,y)\, dy. \qquad (4.7)$$

When $P(x,y)$ and $Q(x,y)$ are continuous and C is smooth, we can calculate the value of the line integral by expressing P, Q, dx, and dy in terms of any parametric representation 4.4 of C and evaluating the resulting definite integral,

$$\int_C P(x,y)\,dx + Q(x,y)\,dy = \int_\alpha^\beta \left\{ P[x(t),y(t)]\frac{dx}{dt} + Q[x(t),y(t)]\frac{dy}{dt} \right\} dt. \quad (4.8)$$

All parametrizations of the curve lead to the same value. When C is piecewise smooth, we evaluate the line integral along each smooth subcurve and add the results.

Example 4.6   Evaluate $\int_C xy\,dx + x^2y\,dy$ where C is the curve $y = x^3$ from $(-1,-1)$ to $(1,1)$.

Solution   Using the parametric representation $x = t$, $y = t^3$, $-1 \le t \le 1$,

$$\int_C xy\,dx + x^2y\,dy = \int_{-1}^1 t(t^3)(dt) + t^2(t^3)(3t^2\,dt) = \int_{-1}^1 (t^4 + 3t^7)\,dt$$

$$= \left\{ \frac{t^5}{5} + \frac{3t^8}{8} \right\}_{-1}^1 = \frac{2}{5}.\bullet$$

Normally the value of line integral 4.7 from one point to another depends on the curve taken between the points. For instance, if we follow the straight line $C' : x = -1 + 2t$, $y = -1 + 2t$, $0 \le t \le 1$ from $(-1,-1)$ to $(1,1)$ in Example 4.6 (Figure 4.15), the value of the line integral is

$$\int_{C'} xy\,dx + x^2y\,dy = \int_0^1 (-1+2t)(-1+2t)(2\,dt) + (-1+2t)^2(-1+2t)(2\,dt)$$

$$= 2\int_0^1 \left[(-1+2t)^2 + (-1+2t)^3 \right] dt$$

$$= 2\left\{ \frac{(-1+2t)^3}{6} + \frac{(-1+2t)^4}{8} \right\}_0^1 = \frac{2}{3}.$$

The integration is simpler if C' is parametrized with $x = t$, $y = t$, $-1 \le t \le 1$,

$$\int_{C'} xy\,dx + x^2y\,dy = \int_{-1}^1 t(t)(dt) + t^2(t)(dt)$$

$$= \int_{-1}^1 (t^2 + t^3)\,dt$$

$$= \left\{ \frac{t^3}{3} + \frac{t^4}{4} \right\}_{-1}^1$$

$$= \frac{2}{3}.$$

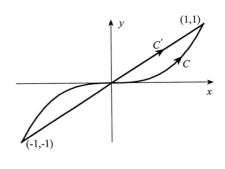

Figure 4.15

For some line integrals, it does not matter what path is taken between two points; the value is always the same. Such line integrals are said to be independent of path. Before making this more formal, we digress to introduce a special kind of domain. Open, closed, and connected sets, and domains were introduced as special regions in the complex plane. But these concepts are equally valid for regions in the xy-plane. A domain in the xy-plane is therefore an open connected set.

Definition 4.2 A domain D in the xy-plane is said to be **simply-connected** if every closed curve in D contains in its interior only points of D.

For example, the domain D_1 in Figure 4.16a is simply-connected. Every closed curve in D_1 contains only points of the set. Examples are curves C_1, C_2, and C_3 in Figure 4.16b.

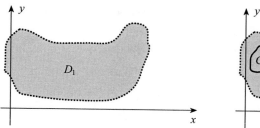

Figure 4.16a   **Figure 4.16b**

Consider the domain $D_2 : 0 < x^2 + y^2 < 1$ in Figure 4.17a. It is not a simply-connected domain. Some curves such as C_1 and C_2 in Figure 4.17b contain only points of D_2, but C_3 contains $z = 0$, and $z = 0$ is not in D_2.

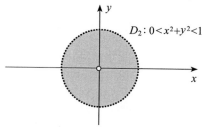

Figure 4.17a   **Figure 4.17b**

In essence, a simply-connected domain has no holes. The domain in Figure 4.18 is not simply-connected; it has two holes. The domain in Figure 4.17a has one hole.

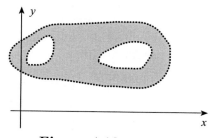

Figure 4.18

We now return to the main discussion — independence of path for line integrals of form 4.7. We say that line integral 4.7 is **independent of path** in a domain D if for any two points A and B in D, the value of the line integral is the same for all piecewise smooth curves in D from A to B. There are two ways to ensure that a line integral is independent of path in a domain D.

1. Show that $P\hat{\mathbf{i}} + Q\hat{\mathbf{j}}$ is the gradient of some function $\phi(x, y)$ at every point of D.

2. If D is simply-connected, show that $\partial Q / \partial x = \partial P / \partial y$.

When a line integral is known to be independent of path, and its value is required along some curve with initial point A and final point B, we can either replace the given curve with a simpler curve, or, take the difference in the values of the function $\phi(x, y)$ at B and A,

$$\int_C P(x,y)\,dx + Q(x,y)\,dy = \left\{\phi(x,y)\right\}_A^B = \phi(x_B, y_B) - \phi(x_A, y_A). \quad (4.9)$$

Example 4.7   Evaluate $\displaystyle\int_C 2xy\,dx + (x^2 + y)\,dy$ where C is $y = x^3 - 2x^2 + 1$ from $(-1,-2)$ to $(3,10)$.

Solution   Since $\nabla(x^2 y + y^2/2) = 2xy\hat{\mathbf{i}} + (x^2 + y)\hat{\mathbf{j}}$, the line integral is independent of path in the whole xy-plane, and

$$\int_C 2xy\,dx + (x^2 + y)\,dy = \left\{x^2 y + \frac{y^2}{2}\right\}_{(-1,-2)}^{(3,10)} = 140.\bullet$$

Example 4.8   Evaluate the line integral $\displaystyle\int_C \frac{x}{x^2 + y^2}\,dx + \frac{y}{x^2 + y^2}\,dy$ where C is that part of the parabola $y = x^2 - 1$ from $(2,3)$ to $(-1,0)$ in Figure 4.19.

Solution   Since $\nabla[(1/2)\ln(x^2 + y^2)] = \dfrac{x}{x^2 + y^2}\hat{\mathbf{i}} + \dfrac{y}{x^2 + y^2}\hat{\mathbf{j}}$ in the domain shown, the line integral is independent of path therein, and

$$\int_C \frac{x}{x^2 + y^2}\,dx + \frac{y}{x^2 + y^2}\,dy = \left\{\frac{1}{2}\ln(x^2 + y^2)\right\}_{(2,3)}^{(-1,0)} = \frac{1}{2}\ln(1) - \frac{1}{2}\ln(13) = -\frac{1}{2}\ln(13).\bullet$$

We could also have verified the existence of a function $\phi(x,y)$ such that

$$\nabla\phi = \frac{x}{x^2 + y^2}\hat{\mathbf{i}} + \frac{y}{x^2 + y^2}\hat{\mathbf{j}}$$

by showing that

$$\frac{\partial}{\partial y}\left(\frac{x}{x^2 + y^2}\right) = \frac{\partial}{\partial x}\left(\frac{y}{x^2 + y^2}\right).$$

The solution would then have proceeded as before.

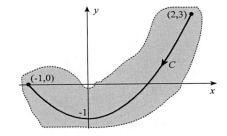

Figure 4.19

If a line integral is independent of path in a domain D, and C is a closed, piecewise smooth curve in D that contains only points of D in its interior, its value is zero,

$$\oint_C P\,dx + Q\,dy = 0. \quad (4.10)$$

The circle on the integral indicates that C is a closed curve.

Example 4.9   Evaluate the line integral of Example 4.8 once counterclockwise around the circle $x^2 + y^2 = 1$.

Solution   In this example it does no good to show that

$$\frac{\partial}{\partial y}\left(\frac{x}{x^2 + y^2}\right) = \frac{\partial}{\partial x}\left(\frac{y}{x^2 + y^2}\right)$$

because this cannot be shown to hold in a simply-connected domain that contains the circle $x^2 + y^2 = 1$. It fails to hold at $(0,0)$, and this point is interior to $x^2 + y^2 = 1$.

On the other hand, we need not follow this line of argument. Parametric equations $x = \cos t$, $y = \sin t$, $0 \leq t \leq 2\pi$ lead to an immediate solution,

$$\oint_C \frac{x}{x^2 + y^2}\, dx + \frac{y}{x^2 + y^2}\, dy = \int_0^{2\pi} \cos t(-\sin t\, dt) + \sin t(\cos t\, dt) = 0. \bullet$$

When a line integral is required around a closed curve, and the line integral is not independent of path, Green's theorem can sometimes be used to advantage. It is stated as follows.

Theorem 4.3   (Green's theorem)   Suppose $P(x, y)$ and $Q(x, y)$ have continuous first partial derivatives in a domain containing a simple, closed, piecewise smooth curve C and its interior R (Figure 4.20). Then

$$\oint_C P\, dx + Q\, dy = \iint_R \left(\frac{\partial Q}{\partial x} - \frac{\partial P}{\partial y} \right) dA. \tag{4.11}$$

The arrowhead on the circle indicates that C is traversed in the counterclockwise direction.

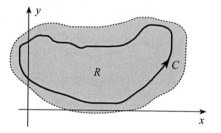

Figure 4.20

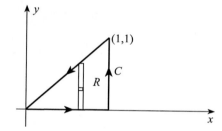

Figure 4.21

Example 4.10   Use Green's theorem to evaluate $\oint_C y^2\, dx + x^2\, dy$ where C is the triangular curve in Figure 4.21.

Solution   Equation 4.11 gives

$$\oint_C y^2\, dx + x^2\, dy = \iint_R (2x - 2y)\, dA = 2\int_0^1 \int_0^x (x - y)\, dy\, dx$$

$$= 2\int_0^1 \left\{ xy - \frac{y^2}{2} \right\}_0^x dx = \int_0^1 x^2\, dx = \left\{ \frac{x^3}{3} \right\}_0^1 = \frac{1}{3}. \bullet$$

EXERCISES 4.2

In Exercises 1–10 find a parametric representation for the curve wherein the parameter increases along the curve. Find a tangent vector at each point on the curve.

1. $x + 2y = 6$ from $(1, 5/2)$ to $(-3, 9/2)$

2. $x^2 + y^2 = 9$ directed counterclockwise with initial point $(3, 0)$

3. $x^2 + y^2 = 9$ directed clockwise with initial point $(0, 3)$

4. $y = x^2 + 2x + 5$ from $(0, 5)$ to $(-2, 5)$

5. $x = y^3 + y$ from $(-2, -1)$ to $(10, 2)$

6. $x^2 + y^2 + 2x - 4y = 0$ directed counterclockwise with initial point $(\sqrt{5} - 1, 2)$

7. $4 - x^2 - 2y^2 = 0$, $y \geq 0$ from $(-2, 0)$ to $(2, 0)$

8. $x + y^3 + xy = 5y^2$ from $(2, 1)$ to $(4, 2)$

9. $x^2 - y^2 = 1$ from $(\sqrt{2}, 1)$ to $\sqrt{5}, -2)$

10. the straight line segment from (x_1, y_1) to (x_2, y_2)

11. Is the curve $x = 3 \cos t$, $y = 3 \sin t$, $0 \leq t \leq 3\pi$ closed?

12. Find parametric equations for the curve in Example 4.2 for which $x'(t)$ and $y'(t)$ are continuous and do not vanish simultaneously at any point on C.

In Exercises 13–27 evaluate the line integral.

13. $\displaystyle\int_C x \, dx + x^2 y \, dy$ where C is the curve $y = x^3$ from $(-1, 1)$ to $(2, 8)$

14. $\displaystyle\int_C xy^2 \, dx + x^2 y \, dy$ where C is the curve $y = x^2$ from $(0, 0)$ to $(1, 1)$

15. $\displaystyle\oint_C y^2 \, dx + x^2 \, dy$ once counterclockwise around $x^2 + y^2 = 1$

16. $\displaystyle\int_C x \, dx + (x + y) \, dy$ where C is the curve $x = 1 + y^2$ from $(2, 1)$ to $(2, -1)$

17. $\displaystyle\int_C (3x^2 + y) \, dx + x \, dy$ where C is the line segment from $(2, 1)$ to $(-3, 2)$

18. $\displaystyle\oint_C (x^2 + 2y^2) \, dy$ once counterclockwise around $x^2 - 4x + y^2 + 3 = 0$

19. $\displaystyle\oint_C x^2 y \, dx + (x - y) \, dy$ once counterclockwise around the curve enclosing the area bounded by
$$x = 1 - y^2 \text{ and } y = x + 1$$

20. $\displaystyle\oint_C y \cos x \, dx + \sin x \, dy$ once clockwise around $x^2 + y^2 - 2x + 4y = 7$

21. $\displaystyle\oint_C x^2 e^y \, dx + (x + y) \, dy$ once clockwise around the square with vertices $(\pm 1, 1)$ and $(\pm 1, -1)$

22. $\displaystyle\int_C y^2 \, dx + x^2 \, dy$ where C is the semicircle $x = \sqrt{1 - y^2}$ from $(0, 1)$ to $(0, -1)$

23. $\displaystyle\int_C 3x^2 y^3 \, dx + 3x^3 y^2 \, dy$ where C is the curve $y = e^x$ from $(0, 1)$ to $(1, e)$

24. $\displaystyle\oint_C (x^2 + y^3) \, dx + (x^3 - y^3) \, dy$ once counterclockwise around the curve enclosing the area
$$\text{bounded by } x = y^2 - 1, \ x = 1 - y^2$$

25. $\displaystyle\oint_C y^2 \, dx + x^2 \, dy$ once clockwise around the curve $|x| + |y| = 1$

26. $\displaystyle\oint_C (x^2 + 2y^2) \, dy$ twice clockwise around the circle $(x - 2)^2 + y^2 = 1$

27. $\int_C -\dfrac{1}{x^2}\text{Tan}^{-1}y\,dx + \dfrac{1}{x + xy^2}\,dy$ where C is the curve $x = y^2 + 1$ from $(2, -1)$ to $(10, 3)$

28. Consider the line integral $\displaystyle\int_C xy\,dx + x^2\,dy$ where C is the quarter circle $x^2 + y^2 = 9$ from $(3, 0)$ to $(0, 3)$. Show that for each of the following parametrizations of C the value of the line integral is the same.

(a) $x = 3\cos t,\ y = 3\sin t,\ 0 \le t \le \pi/2$
(b) $x = \sqrt{9 - y^2},\ 0 \le y \le 3$

29. Evaluate the line integral $\displaystyle\int_C xy\,dx + x\,dy$ from $(-5, 3)$ to $(4, 0)$ along each of the following curves:

(a) the straight line segment joining the points
(b) $x = 4 - y^2$
(c) $3y = x^2 - 16$

30. Evaluate $\displaystyle\oint_C \dfrac{-y\,dx + x\,dy}{x^2 + y^2}$

(a) once counterclockwise around the circle $x^2 + y^2 = 1$
(b) once counterclockwise around the circle $(x - 2)^2 + y^2 = 1$

31. Evaluate $\displaystyle\int_C \dfrac{y}{x^2 + y^2}\,dx - \dfrac{x}{x^2 + y^2}\,dy$ where C is the set of line segments joining successively the points $(1, 0)$, $(1, 1)$, $(-1, 1)$, and $(-1, 0)$

32. Evaluate $\displaystyle\oint_C (2xye^{x^2y} + x^2y)\,dx + x^2e^{x^2y}\,dy$ once clockwise around the ellipse $x^2 + 4y^2 = 4$.

33. Evaluate $\displaystyle\oint_C (3x^2y^3 - x^2y)\,dx + (xy^2 + 3x^3y^2)\,dy$ once counterclockwise around the circle

$$x^2 + y^2 = 9$$

34. Evaluate $\displaystyle\int_C (x - y)(dx + dy)$ where C is the semicircular part of $x^2 + y^2 = 4$ above $y = x$ from

$$(-\sqrt{2}, -\sqrt{2})\ \text{to}\ (\sqrt{2}, \sqrt{2})$$

35. (a) In what domains is the line integral $\displaystyle\int \dfrac{x\,dx + y\,dy}{x^2 + y^2}$ independent of path?

(b) Evaluate the integral clockwise around the curve $x^2 + y^2 - 2y = 1$

36. Find all possible values for the line integral $\displaystyle\oint_C \dfrac{-y\,dx + x\,dy}{x^2 + y^2}$ for curves not passing through the origin.

37. Why is it possible to remove the scale factor t^2 in Example 4.2, but it is not possible to remove a t in Example 4.5?

§4.3   Contour Integrals

In this section we define the integral of a complex function f, with domain D, from a point z_0 in D to a point z_1 in D. Since f is a function of one variable, we might expect the resulting integral to be much like the definite integral of a real function of one variable in elementary calculus. It is not quite this simple, however, due to the fact that specification of z as a complex number requires the two-dimensional complex plane. Unlike the definite integral of $f(x)$ from $x = a$ to $x = b$ where there is only one way to go from $x = a$ to $x = b$ (namely along the x-axis), there is an infinity of ways in the complex plane to proceed from z_0 to z_1 (Figure 4.22). This is reminiscent of line integrals in the plane, which we reviewed in Section 4.2, and we therefore use these results to define the integral of a complex function f from one complex number z_0 to another complex number z_1.

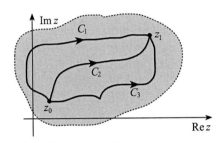

Figure 4.22

Suppose that C is a smooth curve in D with parametric representation

$$C : \; x = x(t), \; y = y(t), \quad \alpha \le t \le \beta. \tag{4.12}$$

Using these, each complex number $z = x + yi$ on C can be expressed in terms of t; that is, we may write

$$C : \; z = z(t) = x(t) + y(t)\,i, \quad \alpha \le t \le \beta. \tag{4.13}$$

If we differentiate this equation with respect to t, we obtain

$$\frac{dz}{dt} = \frac{dx}{dt} + \frac{dy}{dt}i. \tag{4.14}$$

Recalling that dx/dt and dy/dt are the components of a tangent vector to C, we have just shown that at any point on a curve C in the complex plane, the real and imaginary parts of dz/dt are the components of a tangent vector to C.

Suppose now that $f(z) = u(x, y) + v(x, y)i$ is a continuous function defined along C. To define the integral of f along C, denoted by

$$\int_C f(z)\,dz,$$

we first set $f(z) = u + vi$ and $dz = dx + dy\,i$ (see equation 4.14),

$$\int_C f(z)\,dz = \int_C (u + vi)(dx + dy\,i) = \int_C (u\,dx - v\,dy) + (v\,dx + u\,dy)i. \tag{4.15}$$

We now separate this expression into real and imaginary parts,

$$\int_C f(z)\,dz = \int_C u\,dx - v\,dy + i\int_C v\,dx + u\,dy. \tag{4.16}$$

But on the right we have real line integrals along the curve C in the xy-plane. We use equation 4.16 as the definition of the integral on the left; that is, we define the **contour integral** of a continuous function f along a smooth curve C as the complex combination of real line integrals on the right side of equation 4.16. Since these line integrals can be evaluated by expressing u, v, dx, and dy in terms of some parameter along C, we can say that to evaluate a contour integral, express $f(z)$ and dz in terms of any parametric representation of C and evaluate the resulting definite integrals,

$$\int_C f(z)\,dz = \int_\alpha^\beta f[z(t)]\,z'(t)\,dt. \tag{4.17}$$

When C is piecewise smooth rather than smooth, the value of the contour integral is defined as the sum of its values along the smooth parts, each of which can be evaluated as above. Let us illustrate with some examples.

Example 4.11   Evaluate $\displaystyle\int_C z^2\,dz$ where C is one quarter of the circle $|z| = 1$ joining 1 to i.

Solution   With the parametric representation

$$C: \ x = \cos t, \ y = \sin t, \ 0 \le t \le \pi/2,$$

for the curve (Figure 4.23),

$$\int_C z^2\,dz = \int_C (x + yi)^2(dx + dy\,i)$$

$$= \int_C (x^2 - y^2 + 2xyi)(dx + dy\,i)$$

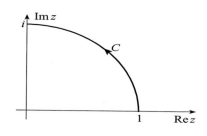

Figure 4.23

$$= \int_0^{\pi/2} (\cos^2 t - \sin^2 t + 2\cos t \sin t\,i)(-\sin t + \cos t\,i)\,dt$$

$$= \int_0^{\pi/2} \left[(-\cos^2 t \sin t + \sin^3 t - 2\cos^2 t \sin t) + (\cos^3 t - \sin^2 t \cos t - 2\sin^2 t \cos t)i\right] dt$$

$$= \int_0^{\pi/2} \left\{[-3\cos^2 t \sin t + \sin t(1 - \cos^2 t)] + [\cos t(1 - \sin^2 t) - 3\sin^2 t \cos t]i\right\} dt$$

$$= \int_0^{\pi/2} \left[(\sin t - 4\cos^2 t \sin t) + (\cos t - 4\sin^2 t \cos t)i\right] dt$$

$$= \left\{\left(-\cos t + \frac{4\cos^3 t}{3}\right) + \left(\sin t - \frac{4\sin^3 t}{3}\right)i\right\}_0^{\pi/2} = -\frac{1+i}{3}.$$

Alternatively, because the modulus of z is constant along C, we could use the argument of z as parameter by writing $C: \ z = e^{\theta i}$, $0 \le \theta \le \pi/2$, in which case

$$\int_C z^2\,dz = \int_0^{\pi/2} e^{2\theta i} i e^{\theta i}\,d\theta = i\int_0^{\pi/2} e^{3\theta i}\,d\theta = i\left\{\frac{e^{3\theta i}}{3i}\right\}_0^{\pi/2} = -\frac{1+i}{3}.\ \bullet$$

When the path of integration in a contour integral is a closed curve, we place a circle on the integral sign,

$$\oint_C f(z)\,dz \qquad \text{or} \qquad \oint_C f(z)\,dz.$$

The arrowheads indicate a clockwise direction (Figure 4.24a) or counterclockwise direction (Figure 4.24b) around the curve.

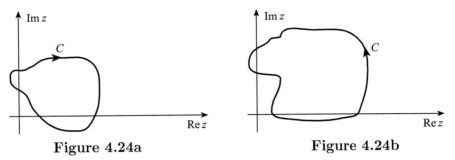

Figure 4.24a   **Figure 4.24b**

Example 4.12 Evaluate $\oint_C e^z \, dz$ where $C = C_1 + C_2 + C_3$ is the closed curve in Figure 4.25.

Solution $\oint_C e^z \, dz = \int_{C_1} e^z \, dz + \int_{C_2} e^z \, dz + \int_{C_3} e^z \, dz$, where

C_1 : $y = 0$, $0 \le x \le 1$;
C_2 : $x = 1$, $0 \le y \le 1$;
C_3 : $x = t$, $y = t$, $1 \ge t \ge 0$.

Thus,

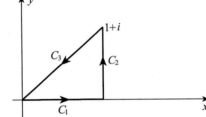

Figure 4.25

$$\oint_C e^z \, dz = \int_0^1 e^x \, dx + \int_0^1 e^{1+yi} \, i \, dy + \int_1^0 e^{t+ti} (dt + dt\,i)$$

$$= \left\{ e^x \right\}_0^1 + \left\{ e^{1+yi} \right\}_0^1 + \left\{ e^{(1+i)t} \right\}_1^0$$

$$= (e - 1) + (e^{1+i} - e) + (1 - e^{1+i}) = 0. \bullet$$

The following properties of contour integrals are immediate consequences of similar properties for line integrals. When $\int_C f(z) \, dz$ and $\int_C g(z) \, dz$ both exist,

$$\int_C [f(z) + g(z)] \, dz = \int_C f(z) \, dz + \int_C g(z) \, dz; \tag{4.18a}$$

$$\int_C k f(z) \, dz = k \int_C f(z) \, dz, \quad k \text{ a complex constant.} \tag{4.18b}$$

Furthermore,

$$\int_C f(z) \, dz = \int_{C_1} f(z) \, dz + \int_{C_2} f(z) \, dz, \quad \text{where } C = C_1 + C_2; \tag{4.19a}$$

$$\int_{-C} f(z) \, dz = - \int_C f(z) \, dz, \quad \text{where } -C \text{ is } C \text{ in the reverse direction.} \tag{4.19b}$$

Expression 4.16 leads to the following two properties:

$$\text{Re} \int_C f(z)\, dz = \int_C \text{Re}\,[f(z)\, dz]; \qquad (4.20\text{a})$$

$$\text{Im} \int_C f(z)\, dz = \int_C \text{Im}\,[f(z)\, dz]. \qquad (4.20\text{b})$$

Integrals on the left sides of 4.20 are contour integrals in the complex z-plane; integrals on the right are real line integrals in the xy-plane.

A much less obvious property of contour integrals, but one that we use extensively, is

$$\left| \int_C f(z)\, dz \right| \le \int_C |f(z)|\,|dz| \le ML, \qquad (4.21)$$

when M is the maximum value of $|f(z)|$ for z on C, and L is the length of C. To verify the left inequality, suppose that r and θ are modulus and argument of the contour integral of $f(z)$ along C,

$$re^{\theta i} = \int_C f(z)\, dz.$$

Then,

$$r = e^{-\theta i} \int_C f(z)\, dz = \int_C e^{-\theta i} f(z)\, dz.$$

Because the real part of any complex number is less than or equal to its modulus, we can state that for any z on C and $dz = dx + dy\, i$,

$$\text{Re}\,[e^{-\theta i} f(z)\, dz] \le |e^{-\theta i} f(z)\, dz| = |f(z)|\,|dz|.$$

Integration of this result along C gives

$$\int_C |f(z)|\,|dz| \ge \int_C \text{Re}\,[e^{-\theta i} f(z)\, dz]$$

$$= \text{Re} \int_C e^{-\theta i} f(z)\, dz \qquad \text{(property 4.20a)}$$

$$= \text{Re}\,(r) = r = \left| \int_C f(z)\, dz \right|.$$

The right inequality in 4.21 is a property of real line integrals when we interpret $|dz| = ds = \sqrt{(dx)^2 + (dy)^2}$ as an element of length along C.

Definite integrals have many geometric and physical interpretations (area, volume, fluid pressure, etc.), as do line integrals (area, work, etc.). Complex contour integrals can also have physical interpretations (see Exercise 13). More importantly, many areas of applied mathematics make use of complex variable theory, and much of this theory is based on contour integration.

EXERCISES 4.3

In Exercises 1–8 evaluate the contour integral.

1. $\displaystyle\int_C z\,dz$ where C is the straight line from $z = 0$ to $z = 1 + 2i$

2. $\displaystyle\int_C (3z^2 + z)\,dz$ where C is the straight line from $z = 1$ to $z = i$

3. $\displaystyle\int_C e^z\,dz$ where C is the broken line from $z = -3i$ to $z = 0$ and then from $z = 0$ to $z = 2$

4. $\displaystyle\oint_C z^2\,dz$ once around the circle $C : |z| = 4$

5. $\displaystyle\oint_C \frac{1}{z^2}\,dz$ once around the circle $C : |z - 2| = 1$

6. $\displaystyle\int_C \sin z\,dz$ where C is the straight line from $z = 2i$ to $z = 2$

7. $\displaystyle\int_C \cosh z\,dz$ where C is the broken line from $z = -2$ to $z = 0$ and then from $z = 0$ to $z = i$

8. $\displaystyle\int_C \operatorname{Log} z\,dz$ where C is the straight line from $z = 1 + i$ to $z = 3 + 3i$

In Exercises 9–12 use inequalities 4.21, 1.40, and 1.41 to verify the result.

9. $\displaystyle\left|\oint_C z^{14}\,dz\right| \le 2^{15}\pi R^{15}$ where C is once around the circle $|z - R| = R$

10. $\displaystyle\left|\int_C (z^2 + 4z + 3)\,dz\right| \le 15\pi$ where C is the semicircle $|z - 1| = 1$, $\operatorname{Im} z \ge 0$ from $z = 0$ to $z = 2$

11. $\displaystyle\left|\oint_C \frac{1}{1 + z^4}\,dz\right| \le \frac{2\pi R}{R^4 - 1}$ where C is once around the circle $|z| = R > 1$

12. $\displaystyle\left|\int_C \frac{e^{zi}}{z^2 + 1}\,dz\right| \le \frac{\pi R}{R^2 - 1}$ where C is the semicircle $|z| = R > 1$, $\operatorname{Im} z \ge 0$ from $z = -R$ to $z = R$

13. Suppose that $F(z)$ is the complex potential associated with fluid flow in some domain D. Show that when ρ is taken as unity, circulation and flux for a closed curve C in D are real and imaginary parts of the contour integral of $F'(z)$ around C; that is,

$$(\text{circulation}) + (\text{flux})i = \oint_C F'(z)\,dz.$$

§4.4   Independence of Path

Since real line integrals can be independent of path, and contour integrals are defined in terms of line integrals, it follows that contour integrals can also be independent of path. Formally we make the following definition.

Definition 4.3   A contour integral $\int_C f(z)\,dz$ is said to be independent of path in a domain D if for any pair of complex numbers z_0 and z_1 in D, the value of the contour integral is the same for all piecewise smooth curves C in D from z_0 to z_1.

According to the following theorem, contour integrals are independent of path when their integrands have antiderivatives.

Theorem 4.4   The contour integral of a continuous function f is independent of path in a domain D if and only if f has an antiderivative in D.

Proof   For the sufficiency part of the theorem, we suppose that f has an antiderivative F in D. Let z_0 and z_1 be any two points in D, and C be any smooth curve in D joining z_0 to z_1. By equation 4.16,

$$\int_C f(z)\,dz = \int_C u\,dx - v\,dy + i\int_C v\,dx + u\,dy.$$

If we set $F(z) = U(x,y) + V(x,y)i$, then

$$F'(z) = \frac{\partial U}{\partial x} + \frac{\partial V}{\partial x}i = u + vi = f(z).$$

Hence, $u = \partial U/\partial x$ and $v = \partial V/\partial x$, and

$$\int_C f(z)\,dz = \int_C \frac{\partial U}{\partial x}dx - \frac{\partial V}{\partial x}dy + i\int_C \frac{\partial V}{\partial x}dx + \frac{\partial U}{\partial x}dy.$$

Since F is analytic in D, it must satisfy the Cauchy-Riemann equations,

$$\frac{\partial U}{\partial x} = \frac{\partial V}{\partial y}, \qquad \frac{\partial V}{\partial x} = -\frac{\partial U}{\partial y},$$

and using these we may express the contour integral in the form

$$\int_C f(z)\,dz = \int_C \frac{\partial U}{\partial x}dx + \frac{\partial U}{\partial y}dy + i\int_C \frac{\partial V}{\partial x}dx + \frac{\partial V}{\partial y}dy.$$

Because each of these line integrals is independent of path in D,

$$\int_C f(z)\,dz = \Big\{U(x,y)\Big\}_{z_0}^{z_1} + i\Big\{V(x,y)\Big\}_{z_0}^{z_1} = \Big\{U+Vi\Big\}_{z_0}^{z_1} = F(z_1) - F(z_0).$$

If now C is any piecewise smooth curve with discontinuities in its tangent vector at n points γ_j along C (Figure 4.26), then on each smooth subcurve C_j joining γ_{j-1} to γ_j,

$$\int_{C_j} f(z)\,dz = F(\gamma_j) - F(\gamma_{j-1}),$$

where $\gamma_0 = z_0$ and $\gamma_{n+1} = z_1$. Addition of these results gives

$$\int_C f(z)\,dz = \sum_{j=1}^{n+1} \int_{C_j} f(z)\,dz = \sum_{j=1}^{n+1} [F(\gamma_j) - F(\gamma_{j-1})] = F(z_1) - F(z_0).$$

We have shown then that the contour integral is independent of path in D.

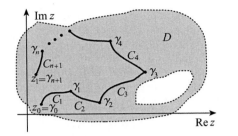

Figure 4.26   **Figure 4.27**

For the necessity part of the theorem, we assume that the contour integral is independent of path in D. If z' is any fixed point in D, then the contour integral

$$F(z) = \int_C f(z)\,dz$$

where C is any piecewise smooth curve in D from z' to z defines a single-valued function F in D. We claim that F is an antiderivative of f. To prove this, we show that $F'(z_0) = f(z_0)$ for any point z_0 in D; that is, we show that

$$\lim_{\Delta z \to 0} \left[\frac{F(z_0 + \Delta z) - F(z_0)}{\Delta z} - f(z_0) \right] = 0.$$

Since D is a domain, there exists a δ-neighbourhood of z_0 which is completely contained in D. Suppose $z_0 + \Delta z$ is contained in this neighbourhood and $C = C'' + C'$ is the curve joining z' to z_0 where C'' is any piecewise smooth curve in D joining z' to $z_0 + \Delta z$, and C' is the straight line segment joining $z_0 + \Delta z$ to z_0 (Figure 4.27). Now

$$F(z_0 + \Delta z) - F(z_0) = \int_{C''} f(z)\,dz - \int_{C''+C'} f(z)\,dz$$

$$= \int_{C''} f(z)\,dz - \int_{C''} f(z)\,dz - \int_{C'} f(z)\,dz$$

$$= -\int_{C'} f(z)\,dz,$$

and $\int_{C'} dz = -\Delta z$. Hence,

$$\frac{F(z_0 + \Delta z) - F(z_0)}{\Delta z} - f(z_0) = -\frac{1}{\Delta z} \int_{C'} f(z)\,dz + \frac{f(z_0)}{\Delta z} \int_{C'} dz = \frac{1}{\Delta z} \int_{C'} [f(z_0) - f(z)]\,dz.$$

Since f is continuous, given any $\epsilon > 0$, there exists a $\delta > 0$ such that $|f(z_0) - f(z)| < \epsilon$ whenever $|z - z_0| < \delta$. By inequality 4.21 then,

$$\left| \frac{F(z_0 + \Delta z) - F(z_0)}{\Delta z} - f(z_0) \right| = \left| \frac{1}{\Delta z} \int_{C'} [f(z_0) - f(z)]\,dz \right| \le \frac{1}{|\Delta z|} \epsilon |\Delta z| = \epsilon.$$

This verifies that $F'(z_0) = f(z_0)$. ∎

This theorem has yielded a very simple and important method for evaluating contour integrals.

Corollary   If f is continuous in a domain D and has an antiderivative F in D, then for any piecewise smooth curve C in D joining point z_0 to point z_1,

$$\int_C f(z)\,dz = F(z_1) - F(z_0). \tag{4.22}$$

Notice the dichotomy that we have here. Because of the two-dimensional nature of the complex plane, contour integrals, although integrals of a function of one variable, are analogous to line integrals. They can be evaluated by substituting from parametric equations of the curve along which integration is performed. But many contour integrals are independent of the path taken between initial point and final point. And how do we know when this is the case — when the integrand has an antiderivative. And in this case, the value of the contour integral is the difference in values of the antiderivative at final and initial points. This is how definite integrals of functions of one real variable are evaluated. What we are saying is that sometimes it is advantageous to think of contour integrals as similar to real definite integrals; sometimes it is better to think of them as analogues of real line integrals. Be prepared to think either way or both ways.

The following theorem is not particularly practical in determining whether a contour integral is independent of path, but it is very important in deriving practical tests for independence of path.

Theorem 4.5   The contour integral of a continuous function f is independent of path in a domain D if and only if the contour integral of f around every closed, piecewise smooth curve C in D vanishes,

$$\oint_C f(z)\,dz = 0. \tag{4.23}$$

Proof   Suppose first of all that the value of the contour integral around every closed, piecewise smooth curve in D vanishes. Let z_0 and z_1 be any two points in D, and C_1 and C_2 be any two piecewise smooth curves in D from z_0 to z_1 (Figure 4.28). The curve $C_1 - C_2$ consisting of C_1 and C_2 in the reverse direction is a closed curve, and therefore the contour integral of $f(z)$ around this curve vanishes,

$$0 = \oint_{C_1-C_2} f(z)\,dz = \int_{C_1} f(z)\,dz + \int_{-C_2} f(z)\,dz$$

$$= \int_{C_1} f(z)\,dz - \int_{C_2} f(z)\,dz.$$

In other words,

$$\int_{C_1} f(z)\,dz = \int_{C_2} f(z)\,dz,$$

and the contour integral is independent of path in D.

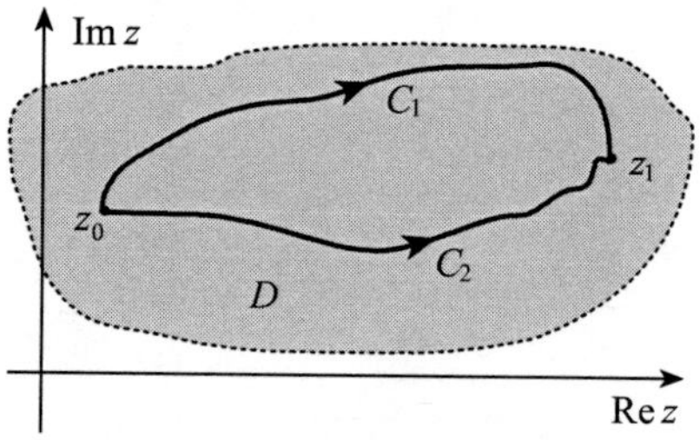

Figure 4.28

Conversely, suppose that the contour integral of f is independent of path in D. Then f has an antiderivative F in D and the value of the contour integral along any curve C from z_0 to z_1 is $F(z_1) - F(z_0)$. When the curve is closed, z_0 and z_1 are identical and $F(z_1) - F(z_0) = 0$. ∎

With Theorem 4.5 and the corollary to Theorem 4.4, Examples 4.11 and 4.12 are trivial. In Example 4.11, $z^3/3$ is an antiderivative of z^2 in the whole complex plane, and therefore

$$\int_C z^2 \, dz = \left\{ \frac{z^3}{3} \right\}_1^i = \frac{1}{3}(i^3 - 1) = -\frac{1+i}{3}.$$

Since e^z is its own antiderivative, the contour integral in Example 4.12 is independent of path. By Theorem 4.5 then, its value around the closed curve in Figure 4.25 vanishes. In fact, the integral of e^z around every closed curve vanishes.

Example 4.13 Evaluate $\int_C \dfrac{1}{z} \, dz$ along the paths in Figures 4.29a and 4.29b.

Solution The integrand $1/z$ is continuous in the domain in Figure 4.29a, and in this domain $d(\text{Log } z)/dz = 1/z$ (the branch cut of $\text{Log } z$ is the negative real axis). Hence,

$$\int_C \frac{1}{z} \, dz = \left\{ \text{Log } z \right\}_{-i}^i = \text{Log}\,(i) - \text{Log}\,(-i) = [\ln 1 + i(\pi/2)] - [\ln 1 + i(-\pi/2)] = \pi i.$$

Once again $1/z$ is continuous in the domain in Figure 4.29b, and in this domain $d(\log_0 z)/dz = 1/z$ (the branch cut of $\log_0 z$ is the positive real axis). Thus,

$$\int_C \frac{1}{z} \, dz = \left\{ \log_0 z \right\}_{-i}^i = \log_0 i - \log_0(-i) = [\ln 1 + i(\pi/2)] - [\ln 1 + i(3\pi/2)] = -\pi i.$$

Many other branches of $\log z$ would have yielded the same result. They must simply have a branch cut that does not pass through the curve C.•

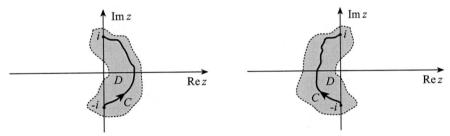

Figure 4.29a   **Figure 4.29b**

Example 4.14 Evaluate $\displaystyle\oint_C \frac{1}{(z - z_0)^n} \, dz$ where n is an integer and $C : |z - z_0| = r$.

Solution If $n \neq 1$, then in the domain $|z - z_0| > 0$ (Figure 4.30), the integrand has antiderivative

$$\int \frac{1}{(z - z_0)^n} \, dz = \frac{1}{(1 - n)(z - z_0)^{n-1}} + k.$$

Consequently, for $n \neq 1$,

$$\oint_C \frac{1}{(z - z_0)^n} \, dz = 0.$$

For $n = 1$, on the other hand, $1/(z - z_0)$ does not have an antiderivative in any domain which contains C. (Every branch of $\log(z - z_0)$ has a branch cut which intersects C.) If we set $z = z_0 + re^{\theta i}$, $-\pi \leq \theta \leq \pi$, on C, however,

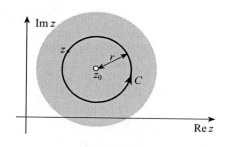

$$\oint_C \frac{1}{z - z_0}\, dz = \int_{-\pi}^{\pi} \frac{1}{re^{\theta i}}\, rie^{\theta i}\, d\theta$$

$$= \Big\{ \theta i \Big\}_{-\pi}^{\pi} = 2\pi i. \bullet$$

Figure 4.30

Theorem 4.5 is not a practical test for independence of path of contour integrals, but it can be useful in proving that a contour integral is not independent of path. For instance, the function $1/z$ is analytic in the domain D consisting of the complex plane with $z = 0$ deleted. According to Example 4.14, the contour integral of $1/z$ counterclockwise around any circle with centre $z = 0$ has value $2\pi i$. By Theorem 4.5, the contour integral of $1/z$ is not independent of path in D, and Theorem 4.4 now implies that $1/z$ does not have an antiderivative in D.

EXERCISES 4.4

For Exercises 1–8 evaluate the contour integrals in Exercises 1–8 of EXERCISES 4.3. In Exercises 9–20 evaluate the contour integral.

9. $\displaystyle\int_C \frac{1}{(z-1)^3}\, dz$ where C is the semicircle $|z - 1| = 1$, $\operatorname{Im} z \geq 0$ from $z = 0$ to $z = 2$

10. $\displaystyle\int_C \frac{z}{z^4 + 2z^2 + 1}\, dz$ where C is the broken straight line joining successively $1+i$, $2i$, and $-1+i$

11. $\displaystyle\int_C e^z \sin z\, dz$ where C is the curve $\operatorname{Im} z = (\operatorname{Re} z)^2$ from $z = 0$ to $z = 1 + i$

12. $\displaystyle\int_C z \sinh 2z\, dz$ where C is the straight line from $z = -1$ to $z = i$

13. $\displaystyle\int_C \sin^2 z\, dz$ where C is the right half of the ellipse $|z - i| + |z + i| = 6$ from $z = -3i$ to $z = 3i$

14. $\displaystyle\int_C \frac{1}{z}\, dz$ where C is the quarter circle $|z - i| = 2$ from $z = -i$ to $z = -2 + i$

15. $\displaystyle\int_C \frac{1}{z^2 - z}\, dz$ where C is any curve from $z = -2$ to $z = -3 + i$ for which $\operatorname{Re} z$ is always negative

16. $\displaystyle\int_C \frac{1}{\sqrt{z}}\, dz$ where C is the quarter circle $|z| = 2$ from $z = \sqrt{2} - \sqrt{2}i$ to $z = \sqrt{2} + \sqrt{2}i$

17. $\displaystyle\int_C \frac{1}{z^2 + 4}\, dz$ where C is the straight line from $z = 1$ to $z = i$

18. $\displaystyle\int_C z^{1/2}\,dz$ where C is the straight line from $z = -2 - 2\sqrt{3}i$ to $z = -2 + 2\sqrt{3}i$ and $z^{1/2}$ is the branch of the square root function $z^{1/2} = e^{(1/2)\log_{-\pi/2} z}$

19. $\displaystyle\oint_C \operatorname{Log} z\,dz$ where C is the square with vertices ± 1, $\pm i$

20. $\displaystyle\oint_C \sqrt{z}\,dz$ where $C : |z| = 3$

21. Use inequality 4.21 to show that if z_1 and z_2 are any two complex numbers with negative real parts, then

$$|e^{z_2} - e^{z_1}| \leq |z_2 - z_1|.$$

§4.5   The Cauchy-Goursat Theorem

The contour integral of a continuous function f is independent of path in a domain D if and only if f has an antiderivative in D, or equivalently, if and only if the contour integral of f around every closed, piecewise smooth curve vanishes. In other words, we have two methods for determining whether the contour integral of a continuous function is independent of path:

(a) prove that f has an antiderivative in D;

(b) prove that the contour integral of f around every closed, piecewise smooth curve in D is equal to zero.

This is not a completely satisfactory situation. Condition (b) clearly is not the easiest to put into practice. Condition (a) may be somewhat difficult also. For instance, if the integrand is given in terms of its real and imaginary parts, it would be necessary to find its definition $f(z)$ in terms of z. Even if f is defined in terms of z, say $f(z) = \sin(1/z)$, how shall we know whether it has an antiderivative, or what the antiderivative is?

What we need then is a condition that guarantees existence of the antiderivative of a function. To find such a condition, suppose that C is a simple, closed, piecewise smooth curve (Figure 4.31), and that f' is continuous in a domain D containing C and its interior R. Since

$$f'(z) = \frac{\partial u}{\partial x} + \frac{\partial v}{\partial x}i = \frac{\partial v}{\partial y} - \frac{\partial u}{\partial y}i,$$

it follows that the first partial derivatives of u and v are continuous inside and on C. We may therefore apply Green's theorem (Theorem 4.3) to each of the real line integrals in equation 4.16,

$$\oint_C f(z)\,dz = \oint_C u\,dx - v\,dy + i\oint_C v\,dx + u\,dy$$

$$= \iint_R \left(-\frac{\partial v}{\partial x} - \frac{\partial u}{\partial y}\right) dA + i\iint_R \left(\frac{\partial u}{\partial x} - \frac{\partial v}{\partial y}\right) dA.$$

But if f' is continuous, then certainly f is analytic (analyticity requiring only existence of f'), and hence f must satisfy the Cauchy-Riemann equations. Consequently, each integrand vanishes in R, and

$$\oint_C f(z)\,dz = 0.$$

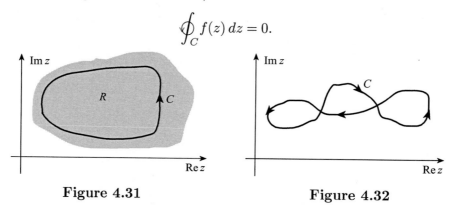

Figure 4.31   **Figure 4.32**

We have just established the following result.

Theorem 4.6 If the derivative f' of a complex function f is continuous in a domain containing a simple, closed, piecewise smooth curve C and its interior, then

$$\oint_C f(z)\,dz = 0.$$

If C is closed but not simple (Figure 4.32), the contour integral in Theorem 4.6 can be expressed as a sum of contour integrals over simple, closed curves, and hence the simple character of C is an unnecessary restriction. The theorem can be generalized even further, but not so trivially. The continuity of f' was required because we wished to use Green's theorem. It can be shown, by completely different methods, that this condition is unnecessary also. We state the result here and prove it at the end of this section.

Theorem 4.7 (**Cauchy-Goursat Theorem**) If f is analytic inside and on a closed, piecewise smooth curve C, then

$$\oint_C f(z)\,dz = 0.$$

Let us illustrate the Cauchy-Goursat theorem with a simple example before indicating its importance in complex variable theory.

Example 4.15 Evaluate $\displaystyle\oint_C \frac{e^z}{z^2 - 9}\,dz$ where $C : |z| = 2$.

Solution Singularities of $e^z/(z^2 - 9)$ occur at $z = \pm 3$ (Figure 4.33). The integrand is therefore analytic inside and on C, and the Cauchy-Goursat theorem implies that the value of the integral is zero.•

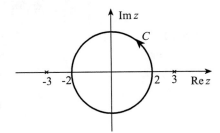

Figure 4.33

Consequences of the Cauchy-Goursat theorem can be developed in two directions. First, it has a straightforward extension that is sometimes useful in the evaluation of contour integrals around closed curves inside of which the integrand is not analytic. Secondly, consequences of the Cauchy-Goursat theorem in the theory of analytic functions cannot be overstated. We discuss the extension of the Cauchy-Goursat theorem to other contour integrals before indicating its impact on analytic functions.

The Cauchy-Goursat theorem yields a value of zero for the contour integral of an analytic function around a closed curve which contains only points at which the function is analytic. If the curve encloses singularities of the function, we might be able to resort to the antiderivative (Theorem 4.4), but not the Cauchy-Goursat theorem. For instance, the integrand of

$$\oint_C \frac{1}{(z-1)^2}\, dz$$

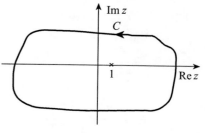

Figure 4.34

has a singularity at $z = 1$ interior to the curve C in Figure 4.34. We cannot therefore use the Cauchy-Goursat theorem. However, $1/(z-1)^2$ has antiderivative $-1/(z-1)$ in the domain $|z-1| > 0$. Consequently, by Theorems 4.4 and 4.5, the value of this contour integral is zero.

Neither Theorem 4.4 nor 4.7 is applicable to the integrals

$$\oint_C \frac{1}{z-1}\, dz, \qquad \oint_C \frac{e^z}{z^2-1}\, dz$$

when C is the curve of Figure 4.34. The Cauchy-Goursat theorem cannot be used because integrands are not analytic at all points interior to C. Theorem 4.4 cannot be applied to the first integral since $1/(z-1)$ does not have an antiderivative in any domain which contains C (any domain which contains C also contains points on the branch cut of every branch of $\log(z-1)$). It is not at all clear whether $e^z/(z^2-1)$ has an antiderivative, and consequently Theorem 4.4 fails on the second integral as well. For such examples the following theorem permits us to simplify the problem by replacing the given curve with another, or others.

Theorem 4.8   Let C be a simple, closed, piecewise smooth curve, and $C_1, C_2, \ldots, C_n$ be disjoint, simple, closed, piecewise smooth curves in the interior of C. If f is analytic at all points that are both inside or on C, and outside or on each C_j, then

$$\oint_C f(z)\, dz = \sum_{j=1}^{n} \oint_{C_j} f(z)\, dz. \qquad (4.24)$$

Proof   Construct $n+1$ piecewise smooth curves γ_j joining C_{j-1} to C_j (γ_1 joins C to C_1, and γ_{n+1} joins C_n to C), so that no two γ_j intersect (Figure 4.35). This divides the region inside C and outside the C_j into two parts. Each part is bounded by a closed, piecewise smooth curve, say L_1 and L_2, inside and on which f is analytic. Thus, by the Cauchy-Goursat theorem, the contour integrals of f around L_1 and L_2 vanish,

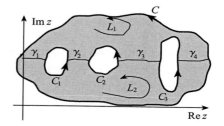

Figure 4.35

$$\oint_{L_1} f(z)\, dz = 0, \qquad \oint_{L_2} f(z)\, dz = 0.$$

Addition of these equations gives

$$\oint_{L_1} f(z)\, dz + \oint_{L_2} f(z)\, dz = 0.$$

But if L_1 and L_2 are traversed in the directions indicated, Figure 4.35 clearly shows that this combination of contour integrals amounts to:

(1) the contour integral around C in the direction shown; plus

(2) the contour integrals around each C_j in the opposite direction shown; plus

(3) the contour integrals over each γ_j, once in each direction.

Consequently,

$$\oint_C f(z)\,dz + \sum_{j=1}^{n} \oint_{-C_j} f(z)\,dz = 0, \quad \text{or} \quad \oint_C f(z)\,dz = \sum_{j=1}^{n} \oint_{C_j} f(z)\,dz. \quad \blacksquare$$

Example 4.16   Evaluate $\displaystyle\oint_C \frac{1}{z-1}\,dz$ where C is the curve in Figure 4.34.

Solution   The integrand $1/(z-1)$ fails to be analytic at the point $z = 1$ inside C, and hence the Cauchy-Goursat theorem is not applicable. With Theorem 4.8, we can replace integration around the somewhat ugly curve C with integration around the much simpler curve $C' : |z - 1| = 1$. The reason for this is that $1/(z-1)$ is analytic at all points that are both inside and on C and outside or on C' (Figure 4.36). Hence,

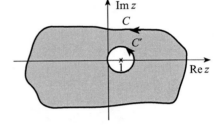

$$\oint_C \frac{1}{z-1}\,dz = \oint_{C'} \frac{1}{z-1}\,dz = 2\pi i,$$

(see Example 4.14).•

Figure 4.36

A slight generalization of this example occurs so often in future work that we state it as a theorem. It is proved in exactly the same way as Example 4.16.

Theorem 4.9   If C is a simple, closed, piecewise smooth curve and z_0 is interior to C, then

$$\oint_C \frac{1}{z - z_0}\,dz = 2\pi i. \tag{4.25}$$

In the next example, the integrand has two singularities inside the contour of integration.

Example 4.17   Evaluate $\displaystyle\oint_C \frac{1}{z^2 - 4}\,dz$ where C is the curve $|z| = 4$.

Solution   Since $1/(z^2 - 4)$ is analytic at all points both inside and on C and outside and on the curves $C' : |z + 2| = 1$ and $C'' : |z - 2| = 1$ in Figure 4.37, Theorem 4.8 allows us to replace integration around C by integrations around C' and C'',

$$\oint_C \frac{1}{z^2 - 4}\,dz = \oint_{C'} \frac{1}{(z+2)(z-2)}\,dz + \oint_{C''} \frac{1}{(z+2)(z-2)}\,dz.$$

The partial fraction decomposition of $1/(z^2 - 4)$ is $\dfrac{1}{z^2 - 4} = \dfrac{-1/4}{z+2} + \dfrac{1/4}{z-2}$. It follows that

$$\oint_C \frac{1}{z^2 - 4}\,dz = \frac{1}{4}\oint_{C'}\left(\frac{1}{z-2} - \frac{1}{z+2}\right)dz + \frac{1}{4}\oint_{C''}\left(\frac{1}{z-2} - \frac{1}{z+2}\right)dz.$$

Since $1/(z - 2)$ is analytic inside and on C', its integral around C' is zero (by the Cauchy-Goursat theorem). Similarly, the contour integral of $1/(z + 2)$ around C'' vanishes. According to Theorem 4.9,

$$\oint_{C'} \frac{1}{z + 2} dz = 2\pi i \quad \text{and} \quad \oint_{C''} \frac{1}{z - 2} dz = 2\pi i.$$

Consequently, $\quad \oint_C \frac{1}{z^2 - 4} dz = \frac{1}{4}(-2\pi i) + \frac{1}{4}(2\pi i) = 0.$ •

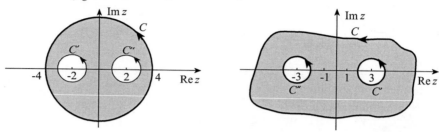

Figure 4.37   **Figure 4.38**

By Theorem 4.8 we could replace the contour integral $\oint_C \dfrac{e^z}{z^2 - 9} dz$ where C is the curve in Figure 4.34 with the integrals

$$\oint_C \frac{e^z}{z^2 - 9} dz = \oint_{C'} \frac{e^z}{z^2 - 9} dz + \oint_{C''} \frac{e^z}{z^2 - 9} dz,$$

where C' and C'' are unit circles centred at $z = \pm 3$ (Figure 4.38). Each of these integrals is evaluated in the next section.

The Cauchy-Goursat theorem is not just a tool for evaluation of contour integrals; it, and its consequences are foremost in the theory of analytic functions. Three immediate implications are discussed below; other consequences are discussed in Section 4.6. Although the three results mentioned here require very little proof, their importance justifies designating them as theorems rather than corollaries to the Cauchy-Goursat theorem.

According to Theorem 4.5, the contour integral of a complex function f is independent of path in a domain D if the contour integral of f around every closed, piecewise smooth curve C in D vanishes,

$$\oint_C f(z) \, dz = 0.$$

According to the Cauchy-Goursat theorem, if f is analytic inside and on C, the contour integral of f around C vanishes. Can we put these two results together and say that when f is analytic in a domain D, its contour integral is independent of path in D? No! We could do this only if we could guarantee that every closed, piecewise smooth curve in D contained points at which f is analytic, and this is not in general possible. Let us illustrate with the function $f(z) = 1/z$ and two different domains. First consider the domain $D^* : 0 < |z| < 1$, the unit circle with centre $z = 0$ deleted. The contour integral of $1/z$ around any closed, piecewise smooth curve in D^* that does not enclose $z = 0$ (Figure 4.39a) has value zero since the curve contains only points of analyticity of $1/z$. However, the contour integral around curves that enclose $z = 0$ (Figure 4.39b) do not all have value zero. For instance, around $|z| = 1/2$ the value is $\pm 2\pi i$ depending on clockwise or counterclockwise orientation. Thus, the contour integral of $1/z$ is not independent of path in $0 < |z| < 1$.

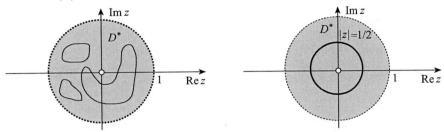

Figure 4.39a   **Figure 4.39b**

Consider now the domain D in Figure 4.40. Every closed, piecewise smooth curve C in this domain contains only points at which $1/z$ is analytic. Hence, for any such curve

$$\oint_C \frac{1}{z}\, dz = 0,$$

and the contour integral of $1/z$ is independent of path in D.

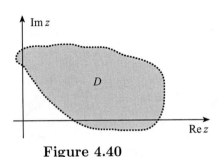

Figure 4.40

Domains D and D^* are different. We can say that every closed curve in D contains only points of D; we cannot say this for D^*. This attribute of D was described in Section 4.2; D is a simply-connected domain, D^* is not. The domains in Figures 4.41 and 4.42 are not simply-connected; the first has two holes, the second has three holes.

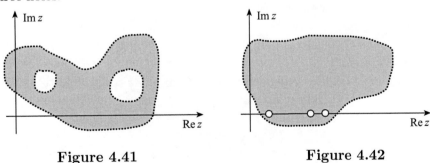

Figure 4.41   **Figure 4.42**

For simply-connected domains, the Cauchy-Goursat theorem implies the following result.

Theorem 4.10   When f is analytic in a simply-connected domain D, the contour integral of f around every closed, piecewise smooth curve in D vanishes.

Theorem 4.5 combines with this result to give the next theorem.

Theorem 4.11   When f is analytic in a simply-connected domain D, the contour integral of f is independent of path in D.

Furthermore, Theorem 4.4 now implies that functions analytic in simply-connected domains have antiderivatives therein.

Theorem 4.12   When f is analytic in a simply-connected domain D, then f has an antiderivative in D.

More important consequences of the Cauchy-Goursat theorem are developed in the next section.

Appendix   (Proof of Cauchy-Goursat theorem)

The Cauchy-Goursat theorem states that when f is analytic inside and on a closed, piecewise smooth curve C, then

$$\oint_C f(z)\,dz = 0.$$

Our discussion leading from Theorem 4.6 to the Cauchy-Goursat theorem indicated that there is no loss in generality in assuming that C is a simple curve (since curves that intersect themselves can be decomposed into simple ones). We therefore assume that C is simple, and we begin with a curve C which is a triangle (Figure 4.43a).

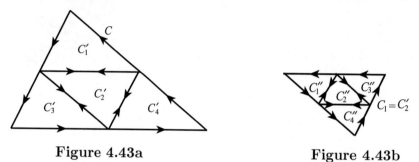

Figure 4.43a   **Figure 4.43b**

To show that the contour integral of f around this curve vanishes, it is sufficient to show that its modulus vanishes,

$$\left| \oint_C f(z)\,dz \right| = 0,$$

and this is true if we can show that given any $\epsilon > 0$, no matter how small,

$$\left| \oint_C f(z)\,dz \right| < \epsilon.$$

Suppose we denote by C_1', C_2', C_3', and C_4' the edges of the four triangles obtained by joining midpoints of the sides of triangle C. Because of internal cancellations,

$$\oint_C f(z)\,dz = \oint_{C_1'} f(z)\,dz + \oint_{C_2'} f(z)\,dz + \oint_{C_3'} f(z)\,dz + \oint_{C_4'} f(z)\,dz.$$

If we take moduli, then inequality 1.40 gives

$$\left| \oint_C f(z)\,dz \right| \le \left| \oint_{C_1'} f(z)\,dz \right| + \left| \oint_{C_2'} f(z)\,dz \right| + \left| \oint_{C_3'} f(z)\,dz \right| + \left| \oint_{C_4'} f(z)\,dz \right|.$$

One of the contour integrals on the right is at least as large as each of the other three. If we denote this contour by C_1 (so that C_1 is one of C_1', C_2', C_3', or C_4', say C_2'), then

$$\left| \oint_C f(z)\,dz \right| \le 4 \left| \oint_{C_1} f(z)\,dz \right|.$$

We now repeat this process on triangle C_1 (Figure 4.43b), yielding a contour C_2 for which

$$\left| \oint_C f(z)\,dz \right| \le 4^2 \left| \oint_{C_2} f(z)\,dz \right|.$$

Continuation leads to a sequence of contours $\{C_n\}$ where the interior of C_n lies in the interior of C_{n-1} and

$$\left| \oint_C f(z)\,dz \right| \le 4^n \left| \oint_{C_n} f(z)\,dz \right|.$$

What seems geometrically clear, but is not easily proved, is the following fact: There is a unique point z_0 that belongs to each and every one of the triangles C_n. Assuming that this is indeed the case, f is analytic at z_0, and we can write that

$$f'(z_0) = \frac{f(z) - f(z_0)}{z - z_0} + g(z)$$

where g is continuous in some δ-neighbourhood of z_0 and where $\lim_{z \to z_0} g(z) = 0$. When this equation is solved for $f(z)$, the result is

$$f(z) = f(z_0) + f'(z_0)(z - z_0) - g(z)(z - z_0).$$

Suppose n is sufficiently large that C_n is contained in the δ-neighbourhood of z_0 (Figure 4.44). Then

$$\oint_{C_n} f(z)\,dz = \oint_{C_n} [f(z_0) + f'(z_0)(z - z_0) - g(z)(z - z_0)]\,dz$$

$$= f(z_0)\oint_{C_n} dz + f'(z_0)\oint_{C_n} (z - z_0)\,dz - \oint_{C_n} g(z)(z - z_0)\,dz$$

$$= -\oint_{C_n} g(z)(z - z_0)\,dz.$$

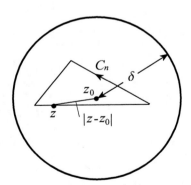

Figure 4.44

We propose to use inequality 4.21 on the modulus of the contour integral on the right. This requires us to know the length of C_n and to have a maximum value for the modulus of the integrand. Clearly the length L_n of C_n is one-half the length of C_{n-1}, and therefore $L_n = L/2^n$ where L is the length of C. Since z_0 is inside or on C_n and z is on C_n, it follows that $|z - z_0|$, the length of the line joining z_0 and z must be less than one-half the length of C_n; i.e., $|z - z_0| < L_n/2 = L/2^{n+1}$. Because $\lim_{z \to z_0} g(z) = 0$, δ can be chosen sufficiently small that for all z in the δ-neighbourhood, $|g(z)| < 2\epsilon/L^2$. With these results, inequality 4.21 applied to the above contour integral gives

$$\left| \oint_{C_n} f(z)\, dz \right| = \left| \oint_{C_n} g(z)(z - z_0)\, dz \right| \le \left(\frac{2\epsilon}{L^2} \right) \left(\frac{L}{2^{n+1}} \right) \left(\frac{L}{2^n} \right) = \frac{\epsilon}{4^n}.$$

Consequently,

$$\left| \oint_C f(z)\, dz \right| \le 4^n \left| \oint_{C_n} f(z)\, dz \right| \le 4^n \left(\frac{\epsilon}{4^n} \right) = \epsilon.$$

As indicated earlier, since ϵ can be made arbitrarily small, this implies that

$$\oint_C f(z)\, dz = 0.$$

Suppose now that C is a polygon rather than a triangle (Figure 4.45). Interior lines can be introduced so that the interior of C is divided into a finite number of triangles. The contour integral of f around each of these triangles is zero, and the sum of the contour integrals around the triangles is equal to the integral around C. Hence the contour integral of f around a polygonal path also vanishes.

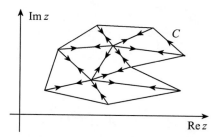

Figure 4.45

The final step in the proof should be to show that any curved path can be approximated arbitrarily closely by a polygonal one. We omit this part of the proof.

EXERCISES 4.5

For Exercises 1–10 evaluate the contour integral.

1. $\oint_C \dfrac{e^z}{z - 5}\, dz$ where $C : |z| = 3$

2. $\oint_C \dfrac{\cosh 2z}{(z + 2)^3}\, dz$ where $C : |z - 2| = 2$

3. $\oint_C \dfrac{1}{z^2 + 4z + 16}\, dz$ where $C : |z| = 1$

4. $\oint_C \dfrac{1}{1 - z^4}\, dz$ where $C : |z + 4i| = 1$

5. $\oint_C \dfrac{1}{z^2 - 1}\, dz$ where $C : |z| = 2$

6. $\oint_C \dfrac{1}{z^2 + 2z}\, dz$ where $C : |z + 1| = 2$

7. $\oint_C \dfrac{z}{z^2 + 1}\, dz$ where C is the square with vertices $z = 0$, $z = \pm 1 + i$, $z = 2i$

8. $\oint_C \dfrac{1}{z^2 \sin z}\, dz$ where $C : |z - 2 - 2i| = 1$

9. $\oint_C \dfrac{1}{z^2 + 4z + 5}\, dz$ where $C : |z + 2 - 2i| = 2$

10. $\oint_C \dfrac{1}{z^3+1}\, dz$ where $C : |z - i| = 1$

In Exercises 11–20 determine whether the set is a simply-connected domain.

11. $1 < |z - 3| < 2$

12. $|z + 1| + |z - 1| < 4$

13. $|\operatorname{Re} z| < 3$

14. $|\operatorname{Re} z| > 3$

15. $2\operatorname{Re} z + 3\operatorname{Im} z < 6$

16. $0 < \operatorname{Arg} z < \pi/2$

17. $|z| < 5,\ z \neq 1, 2, 3$

18. $|z| > 5$

19. The domain of analyticity of $\operatorname{Log} z$

20. $0 < |\operatorname{Im} z| < 1$

21. (a) Prove that when z_1 and z_2 are interior to a simple, closed, piecewise smooth curve C, then

$$\oint_C \frac{1}{(z - z_1)(z - z_2)}\, dz = 0.$$

(b) If $z_1, \ldots, z_n$ are n points interior to C, is

$$\oint_C \frac{1}{(z - z_1) \cdots (z - z_n)}\, dz = 0?$$

22. Evaluate $\displaystyle\int_C z^i\, dz$, where z^i is the principal branch of the function, and C is any contour from $z = -1$ to $z = 1$ that lies in the half-plane $\operatorname{Im} z \geq 0$.

23. Suppose that $P(z)$ is a polynomial of degree $n > 1$, and C is a simple, closed, piecewise smooth curve that contains all zeros of $P(z)$.

(a) Show that

$$\oint_C \frac{1}{P(z)}\, dz = \oint_{C_R} \frac{1}{P(z)}\, dz$$

if C_R is a circle centred at the origin with radius R that contains C.

(b) By writing $P(z)$ in factored form

$$P(z) = A(z - z_1)^{k_1}(z - z_2)^{k_2} \cdots (z - z_m)^{k_m}$$

where A is a constant, z_j are the zeros of $P(z)$ with multiplicities k_j, and $k_1 + k_2 + \cdots + k_m = n$, show that on C_R,

$$\frac{1}{|P(z)|} \leq \frac{1}{|A|(R - |z_1|)^{k_1}(R - |z_2|)^{k_2} \cdots (R - |z_m|)^{k_m}}.$$

(c) Use inequality 4.21 and parts (a) and (b) to show that

$$\oint_C \frac{1}{P(z)}\, dz = 0.$$

§4.6   Cauchy Integral Formulas

In this section we develop the Cauchy integral formulas. They serve two purposes. They provide an additional method for evaluation of contour integrals, but far more importantly, they lead to properties of analytic functions that are without parallel in real calculus.

When f is analytic inside and on a simple, closed, piecewise smooth curve C, the Cauchy-Goursat theorem states that

$$\oint_C f(z)\, dz = 0.$$

When z_0 is a point interior to C, the integrand of

$$\oint_C \frac{f(z)}{z - z_0}\, dz$$

for the same curve C and function f, has an isolated singularity at z_0 (Figure 4.46).

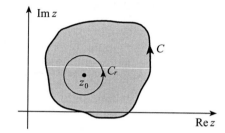

Figure 4.46

Theorem 4.8 (a consequence of the Cauchy-Goursat theorem) implies that when $C_r : |z - z_0| = r$ is a circle with centre z_0 that lies in the interior of C, then the contour integral around C has the same value as the contour integral around C_r,

$$\oint_C \frac{f(z)}{z - z_0}\, dz = \oint_{C_r} \frac{f(z)}{z - z_0}\, dz.$$

We manipulate the integral on the right,

$$\oint_C \frac{f(z)}{z - z_0}\, dz = \oint_{C_r} \frac{f(z)}{z - z_0}\, dz = \oint_{C_r} \frac{f(z_0)}{z - z_0}\, dz + \oint_{C_r} \frac{f(z) - f(z_0)}{z - z_0}\, dz$$

$$= f(z_0) \oint_{C_r} \frac{1}{z - z_0}\, dz + \oint_{C_r} \frac{f(z) - f(z_0)}{z - z_0}\, dz$$

$$= 2\pi i f(z_0) + \oint_{C_r} \frac{f(z) - f(z_0)}{z - z_0}\, dz,$$

(see Theorem 4.9). Since the integral on the left side of this equation has a fixed value, as does $2\pi i f(z_0)$, we may state that for every circle C_r interior to C, the value of the contour integral

$$\oint_{C_r} \frac{f(z) - f(z_0)}{z - z_0}\, dz \tag{4.26}$$

is always the same. We now show that this value must be zero. Suppose M is the maximum value of $|f(z) - f(z_0)|$ on C_r. By property 4.21 for contour integrals,

$$\left| \oint_{C_r} \frac{f(z) - f(z_0)}{z - z_0}\, dz \right| \leq \frac{M}{r}(2\pi r) = 2\pi M.$$

Now M is a function of r, say $M(r)$, and since f is continuous in D, $\lim_{r \to 0} M(r) = 0$. What have we shown? First, the value of contour integral 4.26 is the same for all circles $C_r : |z - z_0| = r$ inside C. Secondly, by choosing r sufficiently small, we can make the value of the integral, in modulus, arbitrarily close to zero. It follows that the value of this contour integral must be zero for all C_r, and consequently

$$\oint_C \frac{f(z)}{z - z_0} \, dz = 2\pi i f(z_0), \quad \text{or} \quad f(z_0) = \frac{1}{2\pi i} \oint_C \frac{f(z)}{z - z_0} \, dz.$$

This result is called Cauchy's integral formula. We restate it in the following theorem replacing z_0 by z and z by ζ.

Theorem 4.13   **(Cauchy Integral Formula)**   When f is analytic inside and on a simple, closed, piecewise smooth curve C, its value at any point z interior to C is given by the contour integral

$$f(z) = \frac{1}{2\pi i} \oint_C \frac{f(\zeta)}{\zeta - z} \, d\zeta. \tag{4.27}$$

This formula states that the values of an analytic function interior to a curve C are completely determined by its values on C. This result is amazingly different compared to the situation for real functions. When a real function $f(x)$ is differentiable on $a \leq x \leq b$, its values at $x = a$ and $x = b$ in no way dictate its values between $x = a$ and $x = b$. Likewise, when a function $f(x, y)$ is differentiable inside and on a simple, closed, piecewise smooth curve C, its values on C do not determine its values inside C. Just the opposite is true for complex analytic functions. Values on a simple, closed, piecewise smooth curve completely determine its values inside C. The following theorem enables us to extend the Cauchy integral formula to an even more startling result.

Theorem 4.14   Let f be continuous on a piecewise smooth curve C (Figure 4.47). At each point z not on C, define the value of a function F by

$$F(z) = \int_C \frac{f(\zeta)}{\zeta - z} \, d\zeta. \tag{4.28a}$$

Then F is analytic in the domain consisting of all points not on C, and

$$F'(z) = \int_C \frac{f(\zeta)}{(\zeta - z)^2} \, d\zeta. \tag{4.28b}$$

Proof   By the definition of the derivative of a complex function,

$$F'(z) = \lim_{\Delta z \to 0} \frac{F(z + \Delta z) - F(z)}{\Delta z} = \lim_{\Delta z \to 0} \frac{1}{\Delta z} \left[\int_C \frac{f(\zeta)}{\zeta - (z + \Delta z)} \, d\zeta - \int_C \frac{f(\zeta)}{\zeta - z} \, d\zeta \right]$$

$$= \lim_{\Delta z \to 0} \int_C \frac{f(\zeta)}{(\zeta - z - \Delta z)(\zeta - z)} \, d\zeta.$$

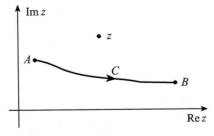

Figure 4.47

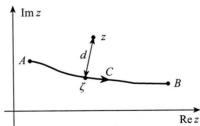

Figure 4.48

To verify 4.28b, we show that

$$0 = \lim_{\Delta z \to 0} \left[\int_C \frac{f(\zeta)}{(\zeta - z - \Delta z)(\zeta - z)} \, dz - \int_C \frac{f(\zeta)}{(\zeta - z)^2} \, d\zeta \right] = \lim_{\Delta z \to 0} \int_C \frac{f(\zeta)\Delta z}{(\zeta - z - \Delta z)(\zeta - z)^2} \, d\zeta.$$

To estimate the maximum value of the modulus of this integral, let M be the maximum value of $|f(\zeta)|$ for ζ on C, and d be the minimum value of $|\zeta - z|$ for ζ on C (Figure 4.48). With inequality 1.41, we may write that $|\zeta - z - \Delta z| \geq |\zeta - z| - |\Delta z| > 0$, provided $|\Delta z|$ is chosen smaller than d. Hence,

$$\left| \frac{f(\zeta)\Delta z}{(\zeta - z - \Delta z)(\zeta - z)^2} \right| \leq \frac{M|\Delta z|}{(|\zeta - z| - |\Delta z|)d^2} \leq \frac{M|\Delta z|}{d^2(d - |\Delta z|)},$$

and therefore using inequality 4.21,

$$\left| \int_C \frac{f(\zeta)\Delta z}{(\zeta - z - \Delta z)(\zeta - z)^2} \, d\zeta \right| \leq \frac{M|\Delta z|}{d^2(d - |\Delta z|)} L,$$

where L is the length of C. Clearly the limit of this expression as $\Delta z \to 0$ is zero, and the proof is complete. ∎

This theorem can be extended in a similar way to show not only that F' exists, but that F has derivatives of all orders. In particular,

$$F^{(n)}(z) = n! \int_C \frac{f(\zeta)}{(\zeta - z)^{n+1}} \, d\zeta. \tag{4.28c}$$

What equation 4.28b and its extension in 4.28c show is that the operations of differentiation and contour integration can be interchanged. When we combine 4.28c with Cauchy's integral formula, we obtain a most startling result.

Theorem 4.15   (**Generalized Cauchy Integral Formula**)   Let f be analytic inside and on a simple, closed, piecewise smooth curve C. Then for any point z interior to C, and $n = 0, 1, 2, \ldots$

$$f^{(n)}(z) = \frac{n!}{2\pi i} \oint_C \frac{f(\zeta)}{(\zeta - z)^{n+1}} \, d\zeta. \tag{4.29}$$

The generalized Cauchy integral formula has the most profound consequences. In particular, we can immediately prove that an analytic function has derivatives of all orders.

Theorem 4.16   If f is analytic in a domain D, then its derivatives f', f'', $\ldots$ are analytic in D.

Proof   Given any point z in D, there exists a circle C centre z which is contained in D, and which contains in its interior only points of D. By the generalized Cauchy integral formula

$$f^{(n)}(z) = \frac{n!}{2\pi i} \oint_C \frac{f(\zeta)}{(\zeta - z)^{n+1}} \, d\zeta, \qquad n = 0, 1, \ldots,$$

and all derivatives of f exist at z. ∎

This situation is totally different than that for real functions. The existence of the first derivative of a real function implies nothing about higher order derivatives. For example, the function $x^{5/3}$ has a first derivative for every value of x including

$x = 0$, but it does not have a second derivative at $x = 0$. The function $(x + 1)^{8/3}$ has a first and second derivative for all x, but no third derivative at $x = -1$. In fact, the existence of no number of derivatives of a function $f(x)$ guarantees another derivative. For complex functions, on the other hand, existence of the first derivative in some domain D implies existence of derivatives of all orders at all points in D.

Existence of all derivatives of a complex function f implies existence of all partial derivatives of its real and imaginary parts. This is proved in the following corollary.

Corollary   If $f(z) = u + vi$ is analytic in a domain D, then all partial derivatives of u and v exist and are continuous in D.

Proof   Theorem 4.16 implies that when f is analytic in D so also is

$$f'(z) = \frac{\partial u}{\partial x} + \frac{\partial v}{\partial x}\, i = \frac{\partial v}{\partial y} - \frac{\partial u}{\partial y}\, i.$$

But analyticity of f' implies continuity of f'; hence each of the first partial derivatives of u and v is continuous in D.

Since f' is analytic in D, we may write (by the corollary to Theorem 2.6)

$$f''(z) = \frac{\partial^2 u}{\partial x^2} + \frac{\partial^2 v}{\partial x^2}\, i = \frac{\partial^2 v}{\partial x \partial y} - \frac{\partial^2 u}{\partial x \partial y}\, i = \frac{\partial^2 v}{\partial y \partial x} - \frac{\partial^2 u}{\partial y \partial x}\, i = -\frac{\partial^2 u}{\partial y^2} - \frac{\partial^2 v}{\partial y^2}\, i.$$

Again, analyticity of f'' implies continuity of f'', and we therefore obtain continuity of all second partial derivatives of u and v. This process may be continued indefinitely to give the corollary. ∎

Theorem 4.10 states that when a function f is analytic in a simply-connected domain, the contour integral of f around every closed, piecewise smooth curve in the domain vanishes. According to the next theorem, the converse is true even when the domain is not simply-connected.

Theorem 4.17   **(Morera's Theorem)**   If f is continuous in a domain D, and if the contour integral of f is zero around every closed, piecewise smooth curve in D, then f is analytic in D.

Proof   If the contour integral of f vanishes around every closed, piecewise smooth curve in D, then by Theorem 4.5, the contour integral is independent of path in D. Consequently, by Theorem 4.4, f has an antiderivative in D, say F. Hence F is analytic in D, and by Theorem 4.16, its derivative $F' = f$ is analytic in D also. ∎

Before discussing further implications of analyticity, we indicate how the generalized Cauchy integral formula can be used to evaluate contour integrals around closed curves. The formula implies that when f is analytic inside and on a closed, piecewise smooth curve C, and n is a nonnegative integer, the value of the contour integral

$$\oint_C \frac{f(z)}{(z - z_0)^{n+1}}\, dz = \begin{cases} 0, & z_0 \text{ outside } C \\ \dfrac{2\pi i}{n!} f^{(n)}(z_0), & z_0 \text{ inside } C. \end{cases} \tag{4.30}$$

Be clear in your mind that certain conditions must be met before using formula 4.30. Firstly, C must be a closed, piecewise smooth curve. Secondly, the integrand must be of the form $f(z)/(z-z_0)^{n+1}$ where f is analytic inside and on C, and z_0 is interior to C.

Example 4.18 Evaluate:

(a) $\displaystyle\oint_C \frac{e^z \sin z}{z-5}\, dz$ where $C : |z| = 6$

(b) $\displaystyle\oint_C \frac{z^2}{(z-1)^n}\, dz$ where $C : |z| = 2$, and n is a positive integer.

Solution   (a) Since $e^z \sin z$ is an entire function, and $z = 5$ is interior to C (Figure 4.49), the Cauchy integral formula gives

$$\oint_C \frac{e^z \sin z}{z-5}\, dz = 2\pi i\, \{e^z \sin z\}_{|z=5} = 2\pi i(e^5 \sin 5).$$

(b) Since z^2 is entire, and $z = 1$ is interior to C (Figure 4.50), we have by the generalized Cauchy integral formula,

$$\oint_C \frac{z^2}{(z-1)^n}\, dz = \frac{2\pi i}{(n-1)!}\frac{d^{n-1}}{dz^{n-1}}\{z^2\}\Big|_{|z=1} = \begin{cases} 2\pi i & n = 1 \\ 4\pi i & n = 2 \\ 2\pi i & n = 3 \\ 0 & n > 3 \end{cases} . \bullet$$

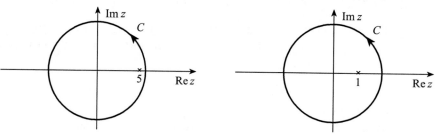

Figure 4.49   Figure 4.50

Example 4.19 Evaluate $\displaystyle\oint_C \frac{z^2}{2z^2+9}\, dz$ where C is the rectangle in Figure 4.51.

Solution   Factoring the denominator of the integrand gives

$$\frac{z^2}{2z^2+9} = \frac{z^2}{2(z+3i/\sqrt{2})(z-3i/\sqrt{2})}.$$

Since $z^2/[2(z-3i/\sqrt{2})]$ is analytic inside and on C, the Cauchy integral formula gives

$$\oint_C \frac{z^2}{2z^2+9}\, dz = -\oint_{-C} \frac{z^2}{2z^2+9}\, dz = -\oint_{-C} \frac{\dfrac{z^2}{2(z-3i/\sqrt{2})}}{z+3i/\sqrt{2}}\, dz$$

$$= -2\pi i\left\{\frac{z^2}{2(z-3i/\sqrt{2})}\right\}_{|z=-3i/\sqrt{2}} = -2\pi i\left[\frac{-9/2}{2(-6i/\sqrt{2})}\right] = \frac{-3\sqrt{2}\pi}{4}. \bullet$$

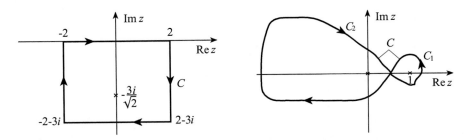

Figure 4.51   **Figure 4.52**

Example 4.20 Evaluate $\displaystyle\oint_C \frac{2z+1}{z(z-1)^2}\,dz$ where C is the curve in Figure 4.52.

Solution If we divide C into C_1 and C_2 as shown, then

$$\oint_C \frac{2z+1}{z(z-1)^2}\,dz = \oint_{C_1}\frac{2z+1}{z(z-1)^2}\,dz + \oint_{C_2}\frac{2z+1}{z(z-1)^2}\,dz.$$

Since $(2z+1)/(z-1)^2$ is analytic inside and on C_2,

$$\oint_{C_2}\frac{2z+1}{z(z-1)^2}\,dz = -\oint_{-C_2}\frac{\frac{2z+1}{(z-1)^2}}{z}\,dz = -2\pi i\left\{\frac{2z+1}{(z-1)^2}\right\}_{|z=0} = -2\pi i.$$

Because $(2z+1)/z$ is analytic inside and on C_1,

$$\oint_{C_1}\frac{2z+1}{z(z-1)^2}\,dz = \oint_{C_1}\frac{\frac{2z+1}{z}}{(z-1)^2}\,dz = 2\pi i\frac{d}{dz}\left\{\frac{2z+1}{z}\right\}_{|z=1}$$

$$= 2\pi i\left[\frac{z(2)-(2z+1)(1)}{z^2}\right]_{|z=1} = -2\pi i.$$

Finally,

$$\oint_C \frac{2z+1}{z(z-1)^2}\,dz = -2\pi i - 2\pi i = -4\pi i.\bullet$$

Example 4.21 Redo Example 4.17 using equation 4.27.

Solution The integrand $1/(z^2-4)$ has two singularities $z=\pm 2$ inside $C:|z|=4$. According to Theorem 4.8, however, we may replace the integral around C with integrals around the curves $C':|z+2|=1$ and $C'':|z-2|=1$ (Figure 4.53),

$$\oint_C\frac{1}{z^2-4}\,dz = \oint_{C'}\frac{1}{(z+2)(z-2)}\,dz + \oint_{C''}\frac{1}{(z+2)(z-2)}\,dz.$$

Since $1/(z+2)$ is analytic inside and on C'', and $z=2$ is interior to C'', 4.27 gives

$$\oint_{C''}\frac{1}{(z+2)(z-2)}\,dz = \oint_{C''}\frac{\frac{1}{z+2}}{z-2}\,dz = 2\pi i\left\{\frac{1}{z+2}\right\}_{|z=2} = \frac{\pi i}{2}.$$

Similarly,

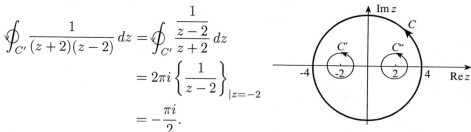

$$\oint_{C'} \frac{1}{(z+2)(z-2)} \, dz = \oint_{C'} \frac{\frac{1}{z-2}}{z+2} \, dz$$

$$= 2\pi i \left\{ \frac{1}{z-2} \right\}_{|z=-2}$$

$$= -\frac{\pi i}{2}.$$

Figure 4.53

Thus,

$$\oint_C \frac{1}{z^2 - 4} \, dz = \frac{\pi i}{2} - \frac{\pi i}{2} = 0. \bullet$$

Example 4.22   Show that if C is a closed, piecewise smooth curve not passing through $z = 0$, the contour integral

$$I = \frac{1}{2\pi i} \oint_C \frac{1}{z} \, dz$$

is equal to the number of times that C encircles $z = 0$ in the counterclockwise direction.

Solution   If C has a loop which does not encircle $z = 0$ (C_1 in Figure 4.54), then

$$\oint_{C_1} \frac{1}{z} \, dz = 0$$

(since $1/z$ is analytic inside and on C_1). Consequently any loops of C which do not encircle $z = 0$ may be removed from C as making no contribution to I. What remains is either no curve at all (Figure 4.55), or a curve C' which encircles $z = 0$ (Figure 4.56).

When no curve remains, I is equal to zero, and this is also the number of times that C encircles $z = 0$.

When C' does encircle $z = 0$, let n represent the number of times ($n = 2$ in Figure 4.56). Then C' can be subdivided into n loops C_j each of which encircles $z = 0$ once. But according to Theorem 4.9, the contour integral around each C_j is equal to $2\pi i$. Thus, if C' encircles $z = 0$ n times in the counterclockwise direction, then $I = n$. If C' encircles $z = 0$ n times in the clockwise direction, $I = -n. \bullet$

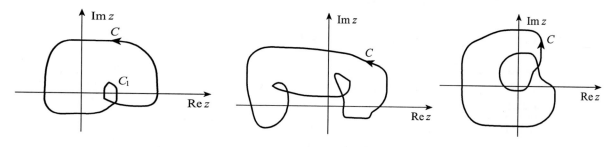

Figure 4.54   **Figure 4.55**   **Figure 4.56**

Example 4.23   Determine whether the functions $f(z) = \dfrac{\sin 3z}{z^6}$ and $f(z) = \dfrac{\sin 3z}{z^5}$ have antiderivative in the domain D consisting of the complex plane with $z = 0$ deleted.

Solution   We first show that $f(z)$ does not have an antiderivative in D. If we take any curve C surrounding $z = 0$, then according to generalized integral formula 4.30,

$$\oint_C f(z)\, dz = \oint_C \frac{\sin 3z}{z^6}\, dz = \frac{2\pi i}{5!} \frac{d^5}{dz^5}(\sin 3z)_{|z=0} = \frac{\pi i}{60}(3^5 \cos 3z)_{|z=0} = \frac{81\pi i}{20}.$$

Because this is nonzero, Theorem 4.5 implies that the contour integral of $f(z)$ is not independent of path in D, and Theorem 4.4 then indicates that $f(z)$ does not have an antiderivative in D. Now we show that $g(z)$ does have an antiderivative in D. Any piecewise smooth, closed curve in D can be decomposed into closed curves that contain $z = 0$ and closed curves that do not enclose $z = 0$. The contour integral of $g(z)$ around any piecewise smooth, closed curve not containing $z = 0$ has value zero, since the curve can be enclosed in a simply-connected domain in which $g(z)$ is analytic. If C is a piecewise smooth, closed curve that encloses $z = 0$, then by generalized integral formula 4.30,

$$\oint_C g(z)\, dz = \oint_C \frac{\sin 3z}{z^5}\, dz = \frac{\pm 2\pi i}{4!} \frac{d^4}{dz^4}(\sin 3z)_{|z=0} = \frac{\pm \pi i}{12}(27 \sin 3z)_{z=0} = 0.$$

Thus, the contour integral of $g(z)$ vanishes around all piecewise smooth, closed curves in D, and by Theorem 4.5, the contour integral is independent of path. Theorem 4.4 implies that $g(z)$ has an antiderivative in D.$\bullet$

As a final consideration in this section, we prove an extension to Cauchy's integral formula 4.27 which will be useful in taking inverse Laplace transforms (Section 8.4).

Theorem 4.18   Suppose that f is analytic in the half-plane $x > \delta > 0$, and that in this half-plane, there exist constants M, R, and $k > 0$ such that

$$|f(z)z^k| < M \text{ for } |z| > R.$$

If z is a point with $\operatorname{Re} z > \gamma > \delta$, then

$$f(z) = -\frac{1}{2\pi i} \lim_{\beta \to \infty} \int_{\gamma - \beta i}^{\gamma + \beta i} \frac{f(\zeta)}{\zeta - z}\, d\zeta. \tag{4.31}$$

Proof   For the given z it is always possible to draw a circular arc centred at $z = 0$ with radius r which, along with the line segment $\operatorname{Re} z = \gamma$ from $z = \gamma - \beta i$ to $z = \gamma + \beta i$, encloses z (Figure 4.57). Since f is analytic inside and on the curve composed of the straight line segment C and the circular arc Γ, Cauchy's integral formula gives

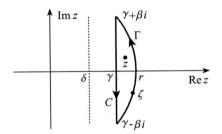

Figure 4.57

$$f(z) = \frac{1}{2\pi i} \int_C \frac{f(\zeta)}{\zeta - z}\, d\zeta + \frac{1}{2\pi i} \int_\Gamma \frac{f(\zeta)}{\zeta - z}\, d\zeta.$$

If r is chosen larger than R, then on Γ,

$$\left| \frac{f(\zeta)}{\zeta - z} \right| \leq \frac{M/|\zeta|^k}{|\zeta - z|} \leq \frac{M}{r^k(r - |z|)}.$$

According to inequality 4.21,

$$\left| \int_\Gamma \frac{f(\zeta)}{\zeta - z}\, d\zeta \right| < \frac{M}{r^k(r - |z|)}(\pi r) = \frac{\pi M}{r^{k-1}(r - |z|)},$$

and this quantity approaches zero as $r \to \infty$. Consequently, we may write that

$$f(z) = \frac{1}{2\pi i} \lim_{\beta \to \infty} \int_C \frac{f(\zeta)}{\zeta - z}\, d\zeta = -\frac{1}{2\pi i} \lim_{\beta \to \infty} \int_{\gamma - \beta i}^{\gamma + \beta i} \frac{f(\zeta)}{\zeta - z}\, d\zeta. \quad \blacksquare$$

EXERCISES 4.6

In Exercises 1–13 evaluate the contour integral.

1. $\oint_C \dfrac{e^z}{z - 2}\, dz$ where $C : |z| = 3$

2. $\oint_C \dfrac{z^3}{z + \pi i/2}\, dz$ where $C : |z + 1| = 5$

3. $\oint_C \dfrac{\sin z}{(z + 2)^3}\, dz$ where $C : |z - 2| + |z + 2| = 10$

4. $\oint_C \dfrac{z^2}{(z + 5i)^4}\, dz$ where $C : |z| = 6$

5. $\oint_C \dfrac{z}{(z^2 + 4)^2}\, dz$ where $C : |z - i| = 2$

6. $\oint_C \dfrac{1}{z^2 + 4z + 16}\, dz$ where $C : |z + 2 - 3i| = 3$

7. $\oint_C \dfrac{\cos z}{(z^2 - 4)^2}\, dz$ where $C : |z - 2| = 2$

8. $\oint_C \dfrac{1}{z^2 + z - 2}\, dz$ where: (a) $C : |z - 1| = 2$ (b) $C : |z + 2| = 1$ (c) $C : |z| = 3$

9. $\oint_C \dfrac{3z - 2}{z^2 - z}\, dz$ where C is the square with vertices $2 \pm 2i$, $-2 \pm 2i$

10. $\oint_C \dfrac{\operatorname{Log} z}{z - 2}\, dz$ where $C : |z - 2| = 1$

11. $\oint_C \dfrac{\sqrt{z}}{(z - 4i)^2}\, dz$ where $C : |z - 5i| + |z - 3i| = 6$

12. $\oint_C \dfrac{z \log_{\pi/2} z}{(z - 2)^2}\, dz$ where C is the square with vertices 1, $2 + i$, 3, and $2 - i$

13. $\oint_C \dfrac{2z^2 - z + 1}{(z - 1)^2(z + 1)}\, dz$ where C is the curve of Figure 4.52

14. Functions f and g are analytic inside and on a simple, closed, piecewise smooth curve C. If $f(z) = g(z)$ on C, is it necessary that $f(z) = g(z)$ inside C?

15. Prove that all derivatives of real and imaginary parts of a function f analytic in a domain D are harmonic in D.

16. The Legendre polynomials for complex arguments are defined by

$$P_m(z) = \frac{1}{2^m m!} \frac{d^m}{dz^m}(z^2 - 1)^m.$$

(a) Show that when C is a simple, closed, piecewise smooth curve, and z_0 is interior to C,

$$P_m(z_0) = \frac{-i}{2^{m+1}\pi} \oint_C \frac{(z^2 - 1)^m}{(z - z_0)^{m+1}} \, dz,$$

called Schlaefli's formula.

(b) Use this result to prove that $P_m(1) = 1$ and $P_m(-1) = (-1)^m$.

(c) Replace z_0 with z and z with ζ to write Schlaefli's formula in the form

$$P_m(z) = \frac{-i}{2^{m+1}\pi} \oint_C \frac{(\zeta^2 - 1)^m}{(\zeta - z)^{m+1}} \, d\zeta.$$

Now set $\zeta = z + \sqrt{z^2 - 1}\, e^{\theta i}$, $-\pi < \theta \le \pi$ to show that

$$P_m(z) = \frac{1}{\pi} \int_0^\pi [z + \sqrt{z^2 - 1} \, \cos\theta]^m \, d\theta.$$

17. Evaluate $\oint_C \dfrac{z}{z^4 - 1} \, dz$ where C is the circle $|z - R| = R$, where $R \ne 1/2$.

18. Show that the function $f(z) = \dfrac{z^n}{(z - 1)^{44}}$, where $0 \le n \le 42$ is an integer, has an antiderivative in any domain in which it is defined.

19. Show that the function $f(z) = \dfrac{z^n}{(z - 1)^{44}}$, where $n \ge 43$ is an integer, has an antiderivative in any simply-connected domain that does not contain the point $z = 1$, but it does not have an antiderivative in the domain $|z - 1| > 0$.

20. Show that the function $f(z) = \dfrac{\sin z}{z^n}$, where $n \ge 1$ is an integer, has an antiderivative in the domain consisting of the complex plane with $z = 0$ deleted if and only if n is odd.

§4.7   Bounds for Moduli of Analytic Functions

We have represented complex functions geometrically as mappings from one plane to another. In some applications, however, it is only the modulus $|f(z)|$ of a function $f(z)$ that is important, and this can be illustrated geometrically by setting $z = x+yi$ and drawing the surface $|w| = |f(x + yi)|$. Three examples are shown in Figures 4.58. Cauchy's generalized integral formulas lead to properties of moduli of analytic functions, properties that are reflected in surfaces like these. They also lead to important facts about harmonic functions.

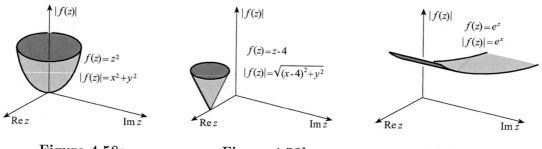

Figure 4.58a   Figure 4.58b   Figure 4.58c

Cauchy's generalized integral formula indicates that when the values of an analytic function are known on a closed curve, its values, and those of its derivatives, are known everywhere inside the curve. The following somewhat weaker result indicates that when the maximum value of the modulus of an analytic function is known on a circle, maximum values for moduli of the derivatives of the function at the centre of the circle are known.

Theorem 4.19   Let f be analytic inside and on a circle C_r of radius r centred at z_0. If $|f(z)| \le M$ for all z on C_r, then

$$|f^{(n)}(z_0)| \le \frac{n!M}{r^n}, \qquad n = 1, 2, \dots. \tag{4.32}$$

Proof   By the generalized Cauchy integral formula,

$$f^{(n)}(z_0) = \frac{n!}{2\pi i} \oint_{C_r} \frac{f(z)}{(z - z_0)^{n+1}}\, dz,$$

and hence using property 4.21,

$$|f^{(n)}(z_0)| \le \frac{n!}{2\pi} \frac{M}{r^{n+1}}(2\pi r) = \frac{n!M}{r^n}. \quad \blacksquare$$

We now use this result to prove that the only functions which are entire and bounded are constant functions. A function f is said to be **bounded** in a domain D if there exists a (real) number $M > 0$ such that $|f(z)| \le M$ for all z in D.

Theorem 4.20   **(Liouville's Theorem)**   If an entire function is bounded, then it is constant.

Proof   Suppose f is entire and bounded. Then there exists a constant M such that $|f(z)| \le M$ for all z. If z_0 is any point in the complex plane, and $C_r : |z - z_0| = r$ is a circle centred at z_0 with radius r, then by Theorem 4.19,

$$|f'(z_0)| \le \frac{M}{r}.$$

Since r can be made arbitrarily large, and therefore $|f'(z_0)|$ arbitrarily small, it follows that $f'(z_0) = 0$, and $f(z)$ is constant. ∎

We saw instances of Liouville's theorem in Chapter 3, but each situation was investigated separately. For example, since $e^z = e^x(\cos y + \sin y\, i)$, it is clear that $|e^z| = e^x$ which is unbounded as $x \to \infty$. Moduli of functions $\sin z$ and $\cos z$ are unbounded as $y \to \pm\infty$ for any fixed x (see Exercise 18 in Section 3.3). Likewise, moduli of $\sinh z$ and $\cosh z$ are unbounded (see Exercise 14 in Section 3.4). Liouville's theorem indicates that every one of these functions must be unbounded since each is entire and not constant.

The modulus of a complex function can be visualized geometrically as a surface such as in Figure 4.58. Liouville's Theorem indicates that such surfaces for non-constant, entire functions must be unbounded in some direction(s). These figures suggest other properties of the modulus of a complex function. In particular, suppose that one of the surfaces in Figure 4.58 is restricted to lie above some domain D. No matter what this domain is, the surface has no maximum point therein; in other words, the modulus $|f(z)|$ does not take on a maximum value in D. Furthermore, when $|f(z)|$ is defined on the region consisting of D and its boundary, its maximum value occurs on the boundary. That these facts are always true is proved in the following theorem.

Theorem 4.21 **(Maximum Modulus Principle)** If f is analytic and not constant in a domain D, then $|f(z)|$ cannot have a maximum value in D.

Proof Suppose to the contrary that there exists a point z_0 in D such that $|f(z)| \leq |f(z_0)|$ for all z in D. Cauchy's integral formula states that when $C_r : |z - z_0| = r$ is a circle which contains only points of D (Figure 4.59),

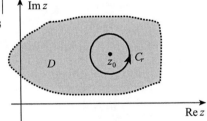

Figure 4.59

$$f(z_0) = \frac{1}{2\pi i} \oint_{C_r} \frac{f(z)}{z - z_0}\, dz.$$

If C_r is represented parametrically by $z = z_0 + re^{\theta i}, \; -\pi \leq \theta \leq \pi$, then

$$f(z_0) = \frac{1}{2\pi i} \int_{-\pi}^{\pi} \frac{f(z_0 + re^{\theta i}) r i e^{\theta i}}{r e^{\theta i}}\, d\theta = \frac{1}{2\pi} \int_{-\pi}^{\pi} f(z_0 + re^{\theta i})\, d\theta.$$

According to inequality 4.21, we may write that

$$|f(z_0)| \leq \frac{1}{2\pi} \int_{-\pi}^{\pi} |f(z_0 + re^{\theta i})|\, d\theta,$$

and notice that the integral on the right is a definite integral, not a contour integral. Suppose at some point on C_r, $|f(z)| < |f(z_0)|$. Then due to the continuity of $f(z)$, there exists an arc of C_r along which $|f(z)| < |f(z_0)|$. This means that there is an interval $-\pi \leq \theta_1 \leq \theta \leq \theta_2 \leq \pi$ in which $|f(z_0 + re^{\theta i})| < |f(z_0)|$, and hence

$$|f(z_0)| \leq \frac{1}{2\pi} \int_{-\pi}^{\pi} |f(z_0 + re^{\theta i})|\, d\theta < \frac{1}{2\pi}|f(z_0)|(2\pi) = |f(z_0)|,$$

a contradiction. It follows therefore that at every point on C_r, $|f(z)| = |f(z_0)|$. But the radius of C_r is arbitrary (except that C_r be in D). Hence $|f(z)| = |f(z_0)|$ for all points in and on C_r.

Let S be the set of all points in D for which $|f(z)| = |f(z_0)|$. If z' is any point in S, then by the foregoing proof, we may construct a circle around z' in which $|f(z)| = |f(z')| = |f(z_0)|$. In other words, S is an open set. If z'' is in $D - S$, then $|f(z'')| \neq |f(z_0)|$. Since $f(z)$ is continuous, there exists a circle centred at z'' in which $|f(z)| \neq |f(z_0)|$; that is, $D - S$ is open also. But the only way for an open subset S of a domain D (in particular a connected set) to have an open complement $D - S$ is for the complement to be empty (see Exercise 14 in Section 2.1). Consequently, $S = D$ and $|f(z)|$ is constant in D. By Theorem 2.8, $f(z)$ is constant in D, a contradiction. No such point z_0 for which $|f(z)| \leq |f(z_0)|$ can therefore exist. ∎

Corollary 1   If f is analytic in a bounded domain D, and continuous on the region consisting of D and its boundary $\beta(D)$, then $|f(z)|$ attains its maximum on $\beta(D)$.

Proof   Since a continuous (real) function on a closed and bounded set must attain a maximum at some point in that set, $|f(z)|$ must attain a maximum in D or on $\beta(D)$. If $f(z) \neq$ constant in D, it cannot attain this maximum in D (by the maximum modulus principle), and must therefore attain it on $\beta(D)$. If $f(z)$ is constant in D, then $|f(z)|$ attains its maximum at every point of D and $\beta(D)$. Thus, in either case, $|f(z)|$ attains its maximum on $\beta(D)$. ∎

Example 4.24   If $f(z) = z/(z^2 + 2)$, find the maximum value of $|f(z)|$ for $|z| \leq 1$.

Solution   Since f is analytic for $|z| < 1$ and continuous for $|z| \leq 1$, $|f(z)|$ attains its maximum value on the boundary $|z| = 1$. For $z = e^{\theta i}$, $-\pi \leq \theta \leq \pi$, on $|z| = 1$,

$$|f(z)| = \left| \frac{e^{\theta i}}{e^{2\theta i} + 2} \right| = \frac{1}{|e^{2\theta i} + 2|} = \frac{1}{\sqrt{(2 + \cos 2\theta)^2 + \sin^2 2\theta}} = \frac{1}{\sqrt{5 + 4\cos 2\theta}}.$$

This expression is a maximum when $5 + 4\cos 2\theta$ is a minimum. But clearly the minimum value is 1 occuring when $\theta = \pm\pi/2$. The maximum value of $|f(z)|$ is therefore 1. ●

There is also a minimum modulus principle. Consider again the surfaces in Figure 4.58. If D is a domain in the complex plane in Figure 4.58b and D does not contain the zero $z = 4$ of $f(z) = z - 4$, then the surface has no relative minimum in D. On the other hand, if the domain contains $z = 4$, then the surface has a minimum at $z = 4$. Similarly, the surface in Figure 4.58a has a relative minimum only when $z = 0$, the zero of $f(z) = z^2$, is contained in D. The surface in Figure 4.58c does not have a relative minimum for any domain, and e^z has no zeros. These are instances of the minimum modulus principle.

Theorem 4.22   **(Minimum Modulus Principle)**   Let f be analytic and not constant in a domain D. If f has no zeros in D, then $|f(z)|$ cannot take on a minimum value in D.

Proof   When f is analytic and never zero in D, then $1/f$ is also analytic in D. By the maximum modulus principle, $|1/f(z)| = 1/|f(z)|$ cannot take on a maximum value in D; that is, $|f(z)|$ cannot take on a minimum value in D. ∎

Further, we may prove the following analogue to the corollary of the maximum modulus principle.

Corollary 1 Let f be analytic in a bounded domain D, and continuous on the region consisting of D and its boundary $\beta(D)$. If f does not vanish in D, then $|f(z)|$ attains its minimum on $\beta(D)$.

EXERCISES 4.7

1. Use Liouville's Theorem to prove the "Fundamental Theorem of Algebra": Every polynomial of degree greater than zero with complex coefficients has at least one zero. In Exercise 44 of Section 5.4, this result is extended to show that every polynomial of degree n has exactly n zeros.

2. Find all functions f analytic in the domain $D : |z| < R$ which satisfy $f(0) = i$ and $|f(z)| \leq 1$ in D.

3. A function f has period T if $f(z+T) = f(z)$ for all z. Prove that if an entire function has both a real and an imaginary period, then it must be a constant function.

4. What is the maximum value of $|z^2/(z^3 - 15)|$ for $|z| \leq 2$?

5. What is the maximum value of $|\sin z|$ on the rectangle $0 \leq \operatorname{Re} z \leq \pi/2$, $0 \leq \operatorname{Im} z \leq a$?

6. What is the maximum value of $|\cos 2z|$ on the rectangle $0 \leq \operatorname{Re} z \leq \pi/2$, $a \leq \operatorname{Im} z \leq b$?

7. What is the minimum value of $|e^{1-2z}|$ on the region $|\operatorname{Re} z| + |\operatorname{Im} z| \leq 4$?

8. What is the minimum value of $|\cos 2z|$ on $|z| \leq 1$?

9. What is the maximum value of $|\operatorname{Log} z|$ on $|z| \leq 2$, $\operatorname{Re} z \geq 1$?

10. What is the minimum value of $|z/(z^2 + 9)|$ on $1 \leq |z| \leq 2$?

11. Let P_1, P_2, ..., P_n be n distinct points in the xy-plane. Let Q be the product of the distances from any point P to the P_j. Show that Q cannot have relative extrema except for relative minima at the P_j.

12. Suppose a nonconstant function f is analytic inside and on a simple, closed, piecewise smooth curve C. If $|f(z) - 1| < 1$ on C, show that $f(z)$ is never zero inside C.

13. Is it possible for an entire function $w = f(z)$ to map the z-plane into the circle $|w| < 1$? Explain.

14. Show that if the nth derivative $f^{(n)}(z)$ of an entire function $f(z)$ is bounded, but not zero, then $f(z)$ is a polynomial of degree n.

15. Show that if an entire function $w = f(z)$ omits an open set in the w-plane, then it is a constant function.

16. Use Exercise 15 to show that if either the real or imaginary part of an entire function is bounded, then the function is a constant function.

§4.8   Applications to Harmonic Functions

In Chapter 2 we showed that the real and imaginary parts of an analytic function are harmonic functions, subject to the provision that these functions have continuous second partial derivatives. This restriction has been removed by the corollary to Theorem 4.16 since the real and imaginary parts of an analytic function have continuous partial derivatives of all orders. We also stated that given a harmonic function $u(x, y)$ defined in a some special kind of domain D, it is possible to find a harmonic function $v(x, y)$, called the harmonic conjugate of $u(x, y)$, such that the function $u(x, y) + v(x, y)i$ is an analytic function f in D. That this cannot always be done for arbitrary domains is illustrated by the function $u(x, y) = (1/2) \ln (x^2 + y^2)$ which is harmonic in the domain consisting of the entire xy-plane with the origin deleted. It is not possible to find a function $v(x, y)$ such that $u + vi$ is analytic in this domain. Indeed, we have already seen that $u(x, y)$ is the real part of the function $\log z = \ln |z| + (\arg z)i$, and $\log z$ cannot be made analytic in any domain that completely surrounds the origin.

The following theorem proves that harmonic conjugates can always be found in simply-connected domains.

Theorem 4.23   If $u(x, y)$ is harmonic in a simply-connected domain D, there exists a harmonic conjugate $v(x, y)$ in D.

Proof   If we define a function $F(z) = \dfrac{\partial u}{\partial x} - \dfrac{\partial u}{\partial y} i$, then the real and imaginary parts of $F(z)$ satisfy the Cauchy-Riemann equations at each point of D:

$$\frac{\partial}{\partial x} \left(\frac{\partial u}{\partial x} \right) = \frac{\partial}{\partial y} \left(-\frac{\partial u}{\partial y} \right) \quad \text{(since } u \text{ satisfies Laplace's equation),}$$

$$\frac{\partial}{\partial x} \left(-\frac{\partial u}{\partial y} \right) = -\frac{\partial}{\partial y} \left(\frac{\partial u}{\partial x} \right) \quad \text{(since second partial derivatives of } u \text{ are continuous).}$$

Consequently, F is analytic in D, and by Theorem 4.12, F has an antiderivative in D. If we denote this antiderivative by $f(z) = \phi + vi$, then

$$f'(z) = \frac{\partial \phi}{\partial x} - \frac{\partial \phi}{\partial y} i = F(z) = \frac{\partial u}{\partial x} - \frac{\partial u}{\partial y} i.$$

But this equation implies that $\phi = u + k$, where k is a complex constant. If we choose $k = 0$, then $f(z) = u + vi$; that is, we have found a function f analytic in D which has $u(x, y)$ as its real part, (and therefore $v(x, y)$ as the harmonic conjugate of $u(x, y)$). ∎

The maximum and minimum modulus principles for analytic functions in Theorems 4.21 and 4.22 and their corollaries imply similar principles about harmonic functions.

Theorem 4.24   If $u(x, y)$ is harmonic and not constant in a domain D, then $u(x, y)$ cannot take on a maximum or minimum value in D.

Proof   We shall prove only the maximum case (the minimum case is similar, see Exercise 1). First suppose that D is simply-connected. Then by Theorem 4.23, there exists a function $f(z) = u + vi$, analytic in D, which has $u(x,y)$ as its real part. Now the function $e^{f(z)}$ is also analytic in D, and by the maximum modulus principle $|e^{f(z)}|$ cannot take on a maximum value in D. But $|e^{f(z)}| = |e^{u+vi}| = e^u$, and therefore e^u cannot take on a maximum value in D. Since e^u is maximized when u is maximized, it follows that $u(x,y)$ cannot take on a maximum value in D.

Take now the case that D is just a domain (and could therefore be multiply-connected). Suppose to the contrary of the theorem that $u(x,y)$ takes on a maximum value at some point (x_0, y_0) in D (Figure 4.60). If we draw an open circle around (x_0, y_0) which contains only points of D, then in this simply-connected domain, $u(x,y)$ takes on a maximum value, contradicting the previous paragraph. Consequently, $u(x,y)$ cannot take on a maximum value in D. ∎

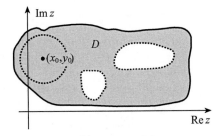

Figure 4.60

Corollaries corresponding to those of Theorems 4.21 and 4.22 can be combined into one.

Corollary 1 If $u(x,y)$ is harmonic in a bounded domain D, and continuous on the region consisting of D and its boundary $\beta(D)$, then $u(x,y)$ attains its maximum and minimum values on $\beta(D)$.

In addition, we can prove the following result.

Corollary 2 If $u(x,y)$ is harmonic in a bounded domain D, and continuous on the region consisting of D and its boundary $\beta(D)$, and if $u(x,y)$ is constant on $\beta(D)$, then $u(x,y)$ is constant in D.

Proof If k is the constant value of $u(x,y)$ on $\beta(D)$, then according to Corollary 1, k must be both the maximum and minimum value of $u(x,y)$ on D and $\beta(D)$. Therefore $u(x,y)$ must be equal to k everywhere in D. ∎

In Sections 3.8–3.10, we saw how important solutions to Laplace's equation are in the fields of heat and fluid flow and electrostatics. An important class of problems in these fields, and one that we deal with extensively in Chapter 7, is to find a solution to Laplace's equation in some domain D that also takes on prescribed values on the boundary $\beta(D)$ of D. The following corollary indicates that there cannot be more than one solution to the problem; that is, if there is a solution, it is unique.

Corollary 3 There cannot be more than one function $u(x,y)$ that is harmonic in a bounded domain D, continuous on the region consisting of D and its boundary $\beta(D)$, and takes on prescribed values on $\beta(D)$.

Proof Suppose to the contrary that $u_1(x,y)$ and $u_2(x,y)$ are two solutions of Laplace's equation in D that are continuous on the region consisting of D and its boundary, and have the same values at each point on $\beta(D)$. Then the function $u(x,y) = u_1(x,y) - u_2(x,y)$ satisfies Laplace's equation in D, is continuous on the region consisting of D and $\beta(D)$, and has value zero on $\beta(D)$. By Corollary 2, $u(x,y)$ must vanish everywhere in D, and hence $u_1(x,y) = u_2(x,y)$ in D. ∎

Theorem 4.24 and its corollaries provide direct implications about the physical phenomena of heat and fluid flow and electrostatics. We shall see them in the detailed discussions of these applications in Sections 7.7–7.9.

Poisson's Integral Formulas

When a function f is analytic inside and on a simple, closed, piecewise smooth curve C, the value of f at any point z interior to C can, according to Cauchy's integral formula, be expressed in terms of its values on C,

$$f(z) = \frac{1}{2\pi i} \oint_C \frac{f(\zeta)}{\zeta - z}\, d\zeta.$$

If we set $f(z) = u + vi$, then it is possible (given parametric equations for C) to take real and imaginary parts of both sides of this equation, and have thereby, line integrals describing the values of u and v at points interior to C in terms of their values on C. The difficulty would be that each integral would contain the values of both u and v on C. We ask now whether it is possible to develop a line integral which describes u at a point interior to C in terms of only the values of u on C. In general this is a very difficult problem, and we therefore consider it with a very simple curve.

In particular, suppose that f is analytic inside and on the circle $C : |z| = R$ (Figure 4.61). When z is interior to C,

$$f(z) = \frac{1}{2\pi i} \oint_C \frac{f(\zeta)}{\zeta - z}\, d\zeta.$$

If we write $z = re^{\theta i}$, then the point $w = (R^2/r)e^{\theta i}$ is clearly exterior to C. As a result, the function $f(z)/(z - w)$ is analytic in a domain containing C, and by the Cauchy-Goursat theorem

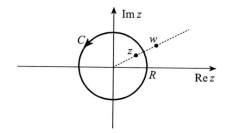

Figure 4.61

$$0 = \frac{1}{2\pi i} \oint_C \frac{f(\zeta)}{\zeta - w}\, d\zeta.$$

If we subtract the second of these equations from the first,

$$f(z) = \frac{1}{2\pi i} \oint_C f(\zeta) \left(\frac{1}{\zeta - z} - \frac{1}{\zeta - w} \right) d\zeta = \frac{1}{2\pi i} \oint_C \frac{f(\zeta)(z - w)}{(\zeta - z)(\zeta - w)}\, d\zeta.$$

On C we set $\zeta = Re^{\phi i}$, $-\pi \le \phi \le \pi$, in which case

$$
\begin{aligned}
f(re^{\theta i}) &= \frac{1}{2\pi i} \int_{-\pi}^{\pi} \frac{f(Re^{\phi i})(re^{\theta i} - R^2 e^{\theta i}/r)}{(Re^{\phi i} - re^{\theta i})(Re^{\phi i} - R^2 e^{\theta i}/r)} Rie^{\phi i}\, d\phi \\
&= \frac{1}{2\pi} \int_{-\pi}^{\pi} \frac{f(Re^{\phi i})(r^2 - R^2)e^{(\theta + \phi)i}}{(Re^{\phi i} - re^{\theta i})(re^{\phi i} - Re^{\theta i})}\, d\phi \\
&= \frac{1}{2\pi} \int_{-\pi}^{\pi} \frac{(R^2 - r^2)f(Re^{\phi i})}{(Re^{\phi i} - re^{\theta i})(Re^{-\phi i} - re^{-\theta i})}\, d\phi \\
&= \frac{1}{2\pi} \int_{-\pi}^{\pi} \frac{(R^2 - r^2)f(Re^{\phi i})}{R^2 + r^2 - rR[e^{(\theta - \phi)i} + e^{-(\theta - \phi)i}]}\, d\phi
\end{aligned}
$$

$$= \frac{1}{2\pi} \int_{-\pi}^{\pi} \frac{(R^2 - r^2)f(Re^{\phi i})}{R^2 + r^2 - 2rR\cos(\theta - \phi)} \, d\phi.$$

This equation

$$f(re^{\theta i}) = \frac{R^2 - r^2}{2\pi} \int_{-\pi}^{\pi} \frac{f(Re^{\phi i})}{R^2 + r^2 - 2rR\cos(\theta - \phi)} \, d\phi,$$

like the Cauchy integral formula, expresses $f(z)$ at points interior to C in terms of its values on C. It does however divide very conveniently into real and imaginary parts. Indeed, if we set $f(z) = f(re^{\theta i}) = u(r, \theta) + v(r, \theta)i$, then

$$u(r, \theta) + v(r, \theta)i = \frac{R^2 - r^2}{2\pi} \int_{-\pi}^{\pi} \frac{u(R, \phi) + v(R, \phi)i}{R^2 + r^2 - 2rR\cos(\theta - \phi)} \, d\phi$$

and real and imaginary parts give

$$u(r, \theta) = \frac{R^2 - r^2}{2\pi} \int_{-\pi}^{\pi} \frac{u(R, \phi)}{R^2 + r^2 - 2rR\cos(\theta - \phi)} \, d\phi, \qquad (4.33\text{a})$$

$$v(r, \theta) = \frac{R^2 - r^2}{2\pi} \int_{-\pi}^{\pi} \frac{v(R, \phi)}{R^2 + r^2 - 2rR\cos(\theta - \phi)} \, d\phi. \qquad (4.33\text{b})$$

Each of these formulas (and they are the same) is called the **Poisson integral formula** for a circle. It expresses the value of a harmonic function at points interior to a circle of radius R centred at the origin, in terms of its values on the circumference of the circle.

Our development of 4.33a was based on the assumption that f is analytic inside and on the circle $|z| < R$. The results are valid with somewhat weaker restrictions, but the proof is correspondingly more difficult. We simply state the result.

Theorem 4.25 **(Poisson Integral Formula)** When U is a piecewise continuous function on the circle $C : r = R$, the function

$$u(r, \theta) = \frac{R^2 - r^2}{2\pi} \int_{-\pi}^{\pi} \frac{U(R, \phi)}{R^2 + r^2 - 2rR\cos(\theta - \phi)} \, d\phi \qquad (4.34)$$

is harmonic inside C. Furthermore, as (r, θ) approaches any point on C where U is continuous, $u(r, \theta)$ approaches the value of U at that point. In particular, if U is continuous on C, so also is $u(r, \theta)$.

Poisson's integral formula defines values for the solution $u(r, \theta)$ of Laplace's equation in $r < R$ in terms of its values $U(R, \phi)$ on $r = R$. Unfortunately, the difficulty in finding an antiderivative for the integrand, even for the simplest of functions $U(R, \phi)$ renders the formula of limited practical use. For example, if

$$U(R, \phi) = \begin{cases} 1 & 0 < \phi < \pi \\ 0 & \pi < \phi < 2\pi \end{cases},$$

then 4.34 becomes

$$u(r, \theta) = \frac{R^2 - r^2}{2\pi} \int_{0}^{\pi} \frac{1}{R^2 + r^2 - 2rR\cos(\theta - \phi)} \, d\phi,$$

not a pleasant integration problem. Notice, however, that the solution of Laplace's equation at the centre of the circle is

$$u(0,\theta) = \frac{R^2}{2\pi} \int_0^\pi \frac{1}{R^2}\,d\phi = \frac{1}{2}.$$

This value $1/2$ also happens to be the average value of $U(R,\phi)$ on the circumference of the circle $r = R$. This is not a peculiarity of this example, but as we now show is a property of all solutions of Laplace's equation in the circle $r = R$. According to Poisson's integral formula 4.34, the value of $u(r,\theta)$ at the centre of the circle $r = R$ is

$$u(0,\theta) = \frac{1}{2\pi} \int_{-\pi}^\pi U(R,\phi)\,d\phi = \frac{1}{2\pi R} \int_{-\pi}^\pi U(R,\phi)\,R\,d\phi; \qquad (4.35a)$$

This is the average value of $U(R,\phi)$ on $r = R$.

In Exercise 16 it is shown that the average value of $u(r,\theta)$ around every circle centred at the origin (not just $r = R$) is equal to its value $u(0,\theta)$ at the centre of the circle. In other words, we can write that

$$u(0,\theta) = \frac{1}{2\pi r} \int_{-\pi}^\pi u(r,\phi) r\,d\phi$$

for every r in $0 < r < R$. If we multiply this equation by r and integrate with respect to r from $r = 0$ to $r = R$,

$$\int_0^R u(0,\theta) r\,dr = \int_0^R \frac{1}{2\pi} \left(\int_{-\pi}^\pi u(r,\phi) r\,d\phi \right) dr,$$

or,

$$\frac{R^2}{2} u(0,\theta) = \frac{1}{2\pi} \int_0^R \int_{-\pi}^\pi u(r,\phi) r\,d\phi\,dr.$$

Multiplication by $2/R^2$ gives

$$u(0,\theta) = \frac{1}{\pi R^2} \int_{-\pi}^\pi \int_0^R u(r,\phi) r\,dr\,d\phi. \qquad (4.35b)$$

Thus, not only is the value of $u(r,\theta)$ at the centre of the circle $r = R$ equal to its average value on the circle $r = R$, it is also equal to its average over the interior of the circle.

Because of the difficulty in performing the integration in formula 4.34, it is of limited utility. A second integral formula, one for a half-space proves more useful. To develop this formula, we suppose that f is an analytic function at all points in the upper half-plane $\text{Im}\, z \geq 0$, and that f is bounded therein. Let C be the curve consisting of the semicircle $\Gamma : |z| = R$ ($\text{Im}\, z \geq 0$) and that part of the real axis $-R \leq \text{Re}\, z \leq R$ (Figure 4.62). When z is interior to C, Cauchy's integral

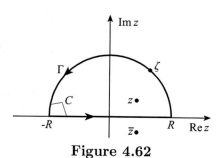

Figure 4.62

formula gives

$$f(z) = \frac{1}{2\pi i} \oint_C \frac{f(\zeta)}{\zeta - z} \, d\zeta.$$

Since $\bar{z}$ is clearly exterior to C, it follows that

$$0 = \frac{1}{2\pi i} \oint_C \frac{f(\zeta)}{\zeta - \bar{z}} \, d\zeta.$$

If we subtract the second of these from the first

$$f(z) = \frac{1}{2\pi i} \oint_C \frac{f(\zeta)}{\zeta - z} \, d\zeta - \frac{1}{2\pi i} \oint_C \frac{f(\zeta)}{\zeta - \bar{z}} \, d\zeta = \frac{1}{2\pi i} \oint_C \frac{(z - \bar{z})f(\zeta)}{(\zeta - z)(\zeta - \bar{z})} \, d\zeta.$$

We now divide this contour integral into two integrals, one along the real axis, and one along Γ. We set $z = x + yi$ and $f(z) = u(x,y) + v(x,y)i$, and on the real axis we set $\zeta = X$,

$$f(z) = \frac{1}{2\pi i} \int_{-R}^{R} \frac{2yi[u(X,0) + v(X,0)]i}{(X - x - yi)(X - x + yi)} \, dX + \frac{1}{2\pi i} \int_{\Gamma} \frac{2yif(\zeta)}{(\zeta - z)(\zeta - \bar{z})} \, d\zeta$$

$$= \frac{y}{\pi} \int_{-R}^{R} \frac{u(X,0) + v(X,0)i}{(X - x)^2 + y^2} \, dX + \frac{y}{\pi} \int_{\Gamma} \frac{f(\zeta)}{(\zeta - z)(\zeta - \bar{z})} \, d\zeta. \qquad (4.36)$$

Since f is bounded for $\operatorname{Im} z \geq 0$, there exists a constant M such $|f(z)| \leq M$ for all such z. As a result, the modulus of the integrand for the contour integral along Γ is

$$\left| \frac{f(\zeta)}{(\zeta - z)(\zeta - \bar{z})} \right| \leq \frac{M}{|\zeta - z||\zeta - \bar{z}|}.$$

Using inequality 1.41, we may write that

$$\left| \frac{f(\zeta)}{(\zeta - z)(\zeta - \bar{z})} \right| \leq \frac{M}{(|\zeta| - |z|)(|\zeta| - |\bar{z}|)} = \frac{M}{(R - |z|)(R - |z|)} = \frac{M}{(R - |z|)^2}.$$

Inequality 4.21 now gives

$$\left| \int_{\Gamma} \frac{f(\zeta)}{(\zeta - z)(\zeta - \bar{z})} \, d\zeta \right| \leq \frac{M}{(R - |z|)^2} (\pi R),$$

and this expression approaches zero as $R \to \infty$. We use this result by taking limits as $R \to \infty$ in equation 4.36,

$$f(z) = \lim_{R \to \infty} \left[\frac{y}{\pi} \int_{-R}^{R} \frac{u(X,0) + v(X,0)i}{(X - x)^2 + y^2} \, dX + \frac{y}{\pi} \int_{\Gamma} \frac{f(\zeta)}{(\zeta - z)(\zeta - \bar{z})} \, d\zeta \right]$$

$$= \frac{y}{\pi} \int_{-\infty}^{\infty} \frac{u(X,0) + v(X,0)i}{(X - x)^2 + y^2} \, dX.$$

When we take real parts (the imaginary parts give a similar formula),

$$u(x,y) = \frac{y}{\pi} \int_{-\infty}^{\infty} \frac{u(X,0)}{(X - x)^2 + y^2} \, dX. \qquad (4.37)$$

This is **Poisson's integral formula** for the half-space $y > 0$. It expresses the values of a bounded function $u(x, y)$ harmonic in the upper half-plane in terms of its values on the x-axis.

Example 4.25 Find the bounded solution of Laplace's equation in the half-plane $y > 0$ that has value -1 on the negative x-axis and value 1 on the positive x-axis.

Solution   By Poisson's integral formula 4.37,

$$u(x, y) = \frac{y}{\pi} \int_{-\infty}^{0} \frac{-1}{(X - x)^2 + y^2} \, dX + \frac{y}{\pi} \int_{0}^{\infty} \frac{1}{(X - x)^2 + y^2} \, dX$$

$$= -\frac{y}{\pi} \left\{ \frac{1}{y} \operatorname{Tan}^{-1}\left(\frac{X - x}{y} \right) \right\}_{-\infty}^{0} + \frac{y}{\pi} \left\{ \frac{1}{y} \operatorname{Tan}^{-1}\left(\frac{X - x}{y} \right) \right\}_{0}^{\infty}$$

$$= -\frac{1}{\pi} \left[\operatorname{Tan}^{-1}\left(-\frac{x}{y} \right) + \frac{\pi}{2} \right] + \frac{1}{\pi} \left[\frac{\pi}{2} - \operatorname{Tan}^{-1}\left(-\frac{x}{y} \right) \right]$$

$$= \frac{2}{\pi} \operatorname{Tan}^{-1}\left(\frac{x}{y} \right).$$

It is interesting to draw curves along which $u(x, y)$ is constant (see Exercise 5).●

This example has illustrated that when the x-axis can be divided into subintervals inside of which a harmonic function takes on constant values, integrations in formula 4.37 are straightforward. We take advantage of this in the following theorem where we develop a formula for such a situation.

Theorem 4.26 The bounded solution of Laplace's equation $\nabla^2 u = 0$ in the domain $\operatorname{Im} z > 0$ subject to the piecewise constant Dirichlet boundary condition in Figure 4.63 is

$$u(x, y) = \frac{a_1 + a_n}{2} + \frac{1}{\pi} \sum_{j=1}^{n-1} (a_j - a_{j+1}) \operatorname{Tan}^{-1}\left(\frac{x_j - x}{y} \right). \qquad (4.38)$$

Proof   According to Poisson's integral formula 4.37,

$$u(x, y) = \frac{y}{\pi} \int_{-\infty}^{x_1} \frac{a_1}{(X - x)^2 + y^2} dX + \frac{y}{\pi} \sum_{j=2}^{n-1} \int_{x_{j-1}}^{x_j} \frac{a_j}{(X - x)^2 + y^2} dX$$

$$+ \frac{y}{\pi} \int_{x_{n-1}}^{\infty} \frac{a_n}{(X - x)^2 + y^2} dX$$

$$= \frac{a_1 y}{\pi} \left\{ \frac{1}{y} \operatorname{Tan}^{-1}\left(\frac{X - x}{y} \right) \right\}_{-\infty}^{x_1} + \frac{a_j y}{\pi} \sum_{j=2}^{n-1} \left\{ \frac{1}{y} \operatorname{Tan}^{-1}\left(\frac{X - x}{y} \right) \right\}_{x_{j-1}}^{x_j}$$

$$+ \frac{a_n y}{\pi} \left\{ \frac{1}{y} \operatorname{Tan}^{-1}\left(\frac{X - x}{y} \right) \right\}_{x_{n-1}}^{\infty}$$

$$= \frac{a_1}{\pi} \left[\operatorname{Tan}^{-1}\left(\frac{x_1 - x}{y} \right) + \frac{\pi}{2} \right] + \frac{a_j}{\pi} \sum_{j=2}^{n-1} \left[\operatorname{Tan}^{-1}\left(\frac{x_j - x}{y} \right) - \operatorname{Tan}^{-1}\left(\frac{x_{j-1} - x}{y} \right) \right]$$

$$+ \frac{a_n}{\pi} \left[\frac{\pi}{2} - \operatorname{Tan}^{-1}\left(\frac{x_{n-1} - x}{y} \right) \right]. \qquad (4.39)$$

Regrouping terms according to inverse tangents gives equation 4.38. ∎

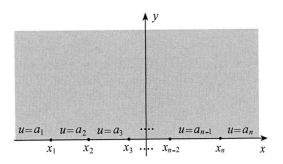

Figure 4.63

The angles represented by the inverse tangents in 4.39 are easily interpreted in Figure 4.64. We may write that

$$u(x,y) = \frac{1}{\pi} \sum_{j=1}^{n} a_j \delta_j. \tag{4.40}$$

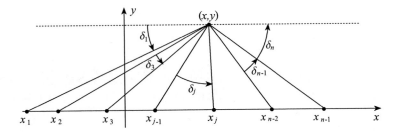

Figure 4.64

Example 4.26   Find the function $u(x,y)$ that is bounded and harmonic in the half-plane $y > 0$ and takes on the values along the x-axis shown in Figure 4.65.

Solution   According to formula 4.38, the solution is

$$u(x,y) = \frac{2+4}{2} + \frac{1}{\pi}\left[\mathrm{Tan}^{-1}\left(\frac{-2-x}{y}\right) + 2\,\mathrm{Tan}^{-1}\left(\frac{1-x}{y}\right) - 5\,\mathrm{Tan}^{-1}\left(\frac{3-x}{y}\right) \right]$$

$$= 3 + \frac{1}{\pi}\left[2\,\mathrm{Tan}^{-1}\left(\frac{1-x}{y}\right) - \mathrm{Tan}^{-1}\left(\frac{2+x}{y}\right) - 5\,\mathrm{Tan}^{-1}\left(\frac{3-x}{y}\right) \right]. \bullet$$

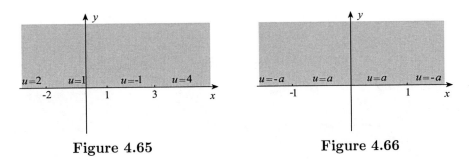

Figure 4.65   **Figure 4.66**

Example 4.27   Find the function $u(x,y)$ that is bounded and harmonic in the half-plane $y > 0$ and takes on the values along the x-axis shown in Figure 4.66.

Solution   According to formula 4.38, the solution is

$$u(x,y) = \frac{-a-a}{2} + \frac{1}{\pi}\left[-2a\,\mathrm{Tan}^{-1}\left(\frac{-1-x}{y}\right) + 2a\,\mathrm{Tan}^{-1}\left(\frac{1-x}{y}\right)\right]$$

$$= -a + \frac{2a}{\pi}\left[\mathrm{Tan}^{-1}\left(\frac{1+x}{y}\right) + \mathrm{Tan}^{-1}\left(\frac{1-x}{y}\right)\right].$$

When there are two inverse tangent functions like this, they can be brought together into a simpler expression as follows. We begin by writing

$$\frac{\pi}{2a}(u+a) = \mathrm{Tan}^{-1}\left(\frac{1+x}{y}\right) + \mathrm{Tan}^{-1}\left(\frac{1-x}{y}\right).$$

We now take tangents of both sides of this equation and use the trigonometric identity $\tan(A+B) = \dfrac{\tan A + \tan B}{1 - \tan A \tan B}$,

$$\tan\left[\frac{\pi}{2a}(u+a)\right] = \frac{\dfrac{1+x}{y} + \dfrac{1-x}{y}}{1 - \left(\dfrac{1+x}{y}\right)\left(\dfrac{1-x}{y}\right)} = \frac{2y}{x^2 + y^2 - 1}.$$

Since $-a < u < a$, it follows that $0 < \dfrac{\pi}{2a}(u+a) < \pi$. If we use $\tan^{-1}$ to denote values of the inverse tangent function between 0 and π, we may write that

$$\frac{\pi}{2a}(u+a) = \tan^{-1}\left(\frac{2y}{x^2+y^2-1}\right) \quad\Longrightarrow\quad u(x,y) = -a + \frac{2a}{\pi}\tan^{-1}\left(\frac{2y}{x^2+y^2-1}\right).\;\bullet$$

EXERCISES 4.8

1. Prove the minimum case for Theorem 4.24.

2. Use the result of Exercise 15 in Section 4.6 to prove that when a function is harmonic in a simply-connected domain, all its derivatives are harmonic therein also.

3. Prove that

$$\int_0^{2\pi} \frac{1}{R^2 + r^2 - 2rR\cos(\theta - \phi)}\,d\phi = \frac{2\pi}{R^2 - r^2}.$$

4. Give an alternative verification of the result in Exercise 16 of Section 4.7.

5. (a) Show that curves along which $u(x,y) = C$ in Example 4.25 are radial lines eminating from the origin.
   (b) What is the limit of $u(x,y)$ as (x,y) approaches a point on the positive x-axis, the negative x-axis, and the origin?

In Exercises 6–14 find a function $u(x,y)$ bounded and harmonic for $y > 0$ that has the given values on the x-axis.

6. $u(x,0) = 1$

7. $u(x,0) = \begin{cases} 1, & |x| < 1 \\ 0, & |x| > 1 \end{cases}$

8. $u(x,0) = \begin{cases} 0, & x < 0 \\ a, & x > 0 \end{cases}$, $\quad a$ a constant

9. $u(x,0) = \begin{cases} -a, & x < 0 \\ a, & x > 0 \end{cases}$, $\quad a$ a constant

10. $u(x,0) = \begin{cases} a, & |x| < c \\ 0, & |x| > c \end{cases}$, $\quad a$ and c constants

11. $u(x,0) = \begin{cases} a, & |x| < c \\ -a, & |x| > c \end{cases}$, $\quad a$ and c constants

12. $u(x,0) = \begin{cases} a|x|/x, & 0 < |x| < c \\ 0, & |x| > c \end{cases}$, $\quad a$ and c constants

13. $u(x,0) = \begin{cases} a|x|/x, & 0 < |x| < c \\ b|x|/x, & |x| > c \end{cases}$, $\quad a$, b, and c constants

14. $u(x,0) = \begin{cases} 0, & |x| < 1 \\ x^{-1}, & |x| > 1 \end{cases}$

15. Suppose $u(x,y)$ is a continuous steady-state temperature distribution in the circle $x^2 + y^2 \leq R^2$. Can $u(x,y)$ have a relative maximum or minimum at any point in $x^2 + y^2 < R^2$?

16. Suppose $u(r,\theta)$ is the solution of Laplace's equation in $r < R$ taking prescribed values on $r = R$. Show that the average value of $u(r,\theta)$ around every circle $r = R_1 < R$ is the same. What is this value?

17. Verify by direct substitution that $u(r,\theta)$ as defined by Poisson's integral formula 4.34 satisfies Laplace's equation

$$\frac{\partial^2 u}{\partial r^2} + \frac{1}{r}\frac{\partial u}{\partial r} + \frac{1}{r^2}\frac{\partial^2 u}{\partial \theta^2} = 0.$$

18. Show that when $u(r,\theta)$ is harmonic in $|z| < R$, the complex conjugate $v(r,\theta)$ of $u(r,\theta)$ can be expressed in the form

$$v(r,\theta) = C + \frac{rR}{\pi}\int_{-\pi}^{\pi} \frac{\sin(\theta-\phi)u(R,\phi)}{R^2 + r^2 - 2rR\cos(\theta-\phi)}\,d\phi,$$

where C is a constant and $u(R,\phi)$ are the values of $u(r,\theta)$ on $|z| = R$.

19. Use Poisson's integral formula 4.34 and the result of Exercise 18 to show that when $u(r,\theta)$ is harmonic in $|z| < R$ and $u(R,\phi)$ are its values on $|z| = R$, then the function $f(z)$ that is analytic in $|z| < R$ and has $u(r,\theta)$ as its real part can be expressed in the form

$$f(z) = Ci + \frac{1}{2\pi}\int_{-\pi}^{\pi} u(R,\phi)\left(\frac{\zeta+z}{\zeta-z}\right)d\phi,$$

where $\zeta = Re^{\phi i}$ and C is a real constant.

20. (a) Show that $u_1(x,y) = y+1$ and $u_2(x,y) = 1$ both satisfy Laplace's equation in the half-plane $y > 0$ and have value 1 on the x-axis.

(b) Do the results in part (a) contradict uniqueness of solutions of Laplace's equation in Corollary 3 to Theorem 4.24?

(c) Which, if either, of these solutions is given by Poisson's integral formula 4.37 (see Exercise 6)? Explain.

CHAPTER 5   POWER SERIES AND LAURENT SERIES

In Chapter 2 we developed properties of analytic functions using derivatives. Contour integrals opened a floodgate of properties in Chapter 4. In this chapter infinite series uncover even more properties of analytic functions. We begin in Sections 5.1 and 5.2 with sequences and series of (complex) constants. These pave the way for power series and Laurent series in Sections 5.3 and 5.4. Laurent series, which have no counterpart in real calculus, provide a classification for isolated singularities of complex functions.

§5.1   Infinite Sequences of Constants

An infinite sequence of constants is a complex-valued function f whose domain is the set of positive integers. It assigns a complex number $f(n)$ to each positive integer n. Quite often we list these numbers as follows

$$f(1),\ f(2),\ \ldots,\ f(n),\ \ldots \tag{5.1}$$

and regard the list as the sequence rather than the rule by which it is formed. We call $f(1)$ the first term of the sequence, $f(2)$ the second term, and $f(n)$ the nth term of the sequence. It is customary to replace $f(1)$ by c_1, $f(2)$ by c_2, etc., so that the sequence is

$$c_1,\ c_2,\ \ldots,\ c_n,\ \ldots. \tag{5.2}$$

To represent this even more compactly, we often write c_n in braces,

$$\{c_n\} = c_1,\ c_2,\ \ldots,\ c_n,\ \ldots. \tag{5.3}$$

Example 5.1   Write out the first 6 terms of the following sequences:

$$\text{(a)} \quad \left\{ \frac{i^{n+1} + n^2 i}{n^2} \right\} \qquad \text{(b)} \quad \left\{ \frac{(1+i)^n}{n!} \right\}$$

Solution   The first six terms of these sequences are

$$-1 + i, \quad \frac{3i}{4}, \quad \frac{1+9i}{9}, \quad \frac{17i}{16}, \quad \frac{-1+25i}{25}, \quad \frac{35i}{36},$$

$$1 + i, \quad i, \quad \frac{-1+i}{3}, \quad -\frac{1}{6}, \quad -\frac{1+i}{30}, \quad -\frac{i}{90}. \bullet$$

Most often we are interested in whether a sequence has a limit; does there exist a number which terms of the sequence get arbitrarily close to, and stay close to, as n gets very large. This is stated precisely in the following definition.

Definition 5.1   A sequence $\{c_n\}$ has limit L if given any $\epsilon > 0$, there exists an integer N such that $|c_n - L| < \epsilon$ for all $n > N$.

The definition for the limit of a real sequence is identical to Definition 5.1, except that in the real case vertical lines in $|c_n - L|$ are interpreted as absolute values instead of moduli.

When L is the limit of a sequence $\{c_n\}$ we write

$$\lim_{n\to\infty} c_n = L, \qquad\qquad (5.4)$$

and we say that the sequence converges to L. For instance, the first sequence in Example 5.1 converges

$$\lim_{n\to\infty} \frac{i^{n+1} + n^2 i}{n^2} = \lim_{n\to\infty} \left(\frac{i^{n+1}}{n^2} + i\right) = 0 + i = i.$$

Convergent sequences can be added, subtracted, multiplied and divided term-by-term.

Theorem 5.1 If sequences $\{c_n\}$ and $\{d_n\}$ have limits C and D, then:

    (i) $\{kc_n\}$ has limit kC;

    (ii) $\{c_n \pm d_n\}$ have limits $C \pm D$;

    (iii) $\{c_n d_n\}$ has limit CD;

    (iv) $\{c_n/d_n\}$ has limit C/D provided $D \neq 0$, and none of the $d_n = 0$.

For example, since

$$\lim_{n\to\infty} \left(1 + \frac{2i}{n}\right) = 1 \qquad \text{and} \qquad \lim_{n\to\infty} \frac{n}{\sin(ni)} = \lim_{n\to\infty} \frac{n}{i \sinh n} = 0,$$

we can say that the sequence $\left\{ \left(1 + \dfrac{2i}{n}\right) \left(\dfrac{n}{\sin(ni)}\right) \right\}$ has limit $1 \cdot 0 = 0$.

The following theorem indicates that, if it is convenient to do so, discussion of the convergence of a sequence $\{c_n\}$ can be separated into discussions of convergence of the real and imaginary parts of c_n.

Theorem 5.2 Suppose $c_n = x_n + y_n i$ and $L = X + Yi$. Then $\lim_{n\to\infty} c_n = L$ if and only if $\lim_{n\to\infty} x_n = X$ and $\lim_{n\to\infty} y_n = Y$.

Proof Suppose first of all that $\lim_{n\to\infty} x_n = X$ and $\lim_{n\to\infty} y_n = Y$. Then given any $\epsilon > 0$, there exists an integer N_1 such that when $n > N_1$, $|x_n - X| < \epsilon/2$. Similarly, there exists an integer N_2 such that when $n > N_2$, $|y_n - Y| < \epsilon/2$. Consequently, when n is greater than the larger of N_1 and N_2,

$$|c_n - L| = |(x_n + y_n i) - (X + Yi)| = |(x_n - X) + (y_n - Y)i| \leq |x_n - X| + |y_n - Y|$$
$$< \frac{\epsilon}{2} + \frac{\epsilon}{2} = \epsilon,$$

and this proves that $\lim_{n\to\infty} c_n = L$.

Conversely, if $\lim_{n\to\infty} c_n = L$, then given any $\epsilon > 0$, there exists an integer N such that for $n > N$,

$$\epsilon > |c_n - L| = |(x_n + y_n i) - (X + Yi)| = |(x_n - X) + (y_n - Y)i|$$
$$= \sqrt{(x_n - X)^2 + (y_n - Y)^2}.$$

It follows from this that for $n > N$,

$$|x_n - X| < \epsilon \qquad \text{and} \qquad |y_n - Y| < \epsilon.$$

Hence, $\lim_{n\to\infty} x_n = X$ and $\lim_{n\to\infty} y_n = Y$. ∎

Example 5.2   Does the sequence $\left\{ \left(1 + \dfrac{1}{n} \right)^n - \left(1 + \dfrac{1}{n} \right)^3 i \right\}$ have a limit?

Solution   Since

$$\lim_{n \to \infty} \left(1 + \frac{1}{n} \right)^n = e \quad \text{and} \quad \lim_{n \to \infty} \left[-\left(1 + \frac{1}{n} \right)^3 \right] = -1,$$

it follows by Theorem 5.2 that $\lim\limits_{n \to \infty} \left[\left(1 + \dfrac{1}{n} \right)^n - \left(1 + \dfrac{1}{n} \right)^3 i \right] = e - i.$ ●

According to Theorem 5.2, sequences of complex converge if, and only if, the sequences of real and imaginary parts converge. This is not the case for moduli and arguments of terms in a complex sequence. Problems can arise with arguments. For example, if we restrict arguments to principal values, then existence of limits of moduli and arguments of terms in a complex sequence imply that the sequence itself must have a limit. This is verified in the next theorem. Even if we restrict arguments to principal values, the converse is not always correct. For example, consider the sequence $\{-1 + (-1)^n i/n\}$. It has limit -1. Moduli of terms in the sequence approach 1, but principal values of the arguments oscillates between numbers close to π and numbers close to $-\pi$.

Theorem 5.3   Suppose $c_n = r_n e^{\theta_n i}$ and $L = R e^{\Theta i}$, where θ_n and Θ are principal values of arguments. Then, $\lim_{n \to \infty} c_n = L$ if $\lim_{n \to \infty} r_n = R$ and $\lim_{n \to \infty} \theta_n = \Theta$.

The following result is an immediate consequence of Theorem 5.3.

Theorem 5.4 $\lim\limits_{n \to \infty} c_n = 0$ if and only if $\lim\limits_{n \to \infty} |c_n| = 0$.

For instance, we can write for the second sequence in Example 5.1,

$$\lim_{n \to \infty} \left| \frac{(1 + i)^n}{n!} \right| = \lim_{n \to \infty} \frac{|1 + i|^n}{n!} = \lim_{n \to \infty} \frac{(\sqrt{2})^n}{n!} = 0,$$

and therefore by Theorem 5.4, $\lim\limits_{n \to \infty} \dfrac{(1 + i)^n}{n!} = 0.$

Example 5.3   Show that $\lim_{n \to \infty} z^n = 0$ if $|z| < 1$, and that the limit does not exist when $|z| > 1$. What can you say if $|z| = 1$?

Solution   If $|z| < 1$,

$$\lim_{n \to \infty} |z^n| = \lim_{n \to \infty} |z|^n = 0,$$

and therefore by Theorem 5.4, $\lim_{n \to \infty} z^n = 0$. On the other hand, if $|z| > 1$, then

$$\lim_{n \to \infty} |z^n| = \lim_{n \to \infty} |z|^n = \infty,$$

and therefore $\lim_{n \to \infty} z^n$ does not exist.

If $z = 1$, then certainly $\lim_{n \to \infty} z^n = 1$. To discuss other points on the circle $|z| = 1$, we use the fact that if a sequence $\{c_n\}$ converges, then $\lim_{n \to \infty} (c_n - c_{n-1}) = 0$, (part (ii) of Theorem 5.1). Theorem 5.4 then implies that $\lim_{n \to \infty} |c_n - c_{n-1}| = 0$. It follows that if $\lim_{n \to \infty} |c_n - c_{n-1}| \neq 0$ for a sequence $\{c_n\}$, then the sequence cannot converge. This is the case for $\{z^n\}$ when $|z| = 1$ and $z \neq 1$,

$$\lim_{n \to \infty} |z^n - z^{n-1}| = \lim_{n \to \infty} |z^{n-1}||z - 1| = \lim_{n \to \infty} |z - 1| = |z - 1| \neq 0.$$

Hence, $\{z^n\}$ diverges for all z on $|z| = 1$ except $z = 1$.•

EXERCISES 5.1

In Exercises 1–10 find the limit of the sequence, if it exists.

1. $\left\{ \dfrac{1 - 2^{n-1}}{2^n} + \dfrac{i}{3^n - 1} \right\}$

2. $\{(1 + i)^n\}$

3. $\left\{ \dfrac{(-1)^n + i^n}{n} \right\}$

4. $\left\{ \sin\left(\dfrac{ni}{n - 1} \right) \right\}$

5. $\left\{ \sinh\left(\dfrac{n^2 + i}{1 - n^2 i} \right) \right\}$

6. $\{\tan^n (i/n)\}$

7. $\left\{ \sqrt[3]{1 - 2e^{(-1+ni)/n}} \right\}$

8. $\left\{ i\mathrm{Log}\left(\dfrac{3i^n - 2n}{n} \right) \right\}$

9. $\left\{ \mathrm{Tan}^{-1}(ni + i) \right\}$

10. $\left\{ \sqrt[n]{i} \right\}$

11. If $\lim_{n \to \infty} c_n = L$, show that $\lim_{n \to \infty} \overline{c_n} = \overline{L}$.

12. Use Theorem 5.3 to prove that $\displaystyle\lim_{n \to \infty} \left(1 + \frac{i}{n} \right)^n = e^i$.

13. Prove that $\displaystyle\lim_{n \to \infty} \left(1 + \frac{z}{n} \right)^n = e^z$.

14. Do the following sequences have limits?

(a) $\left\{ \mathrm{Log}\left(\dfrac{n + i}{2.5 + n} \right) \right\}$ (b) $\left\{ \mathrm{Log}\left(\dfrac{n + i}{2.5 - n} \right) \right\}$ (c) $\left\{ \mathrm{Log}\left(\dfrac{n + (-1)^n i}{2.5 - n} \right) \right\}$

15. Verify Theorem 5.3.

§5.2 Infinite Series of Constants

When the terms of an infinite sequence are added together, we obtain what is called an **infinite series**

$$\sum_{n=1}^{\infty} c_n = c_1 + c_2 + \cdots + c_n + \cdots . \tag{5.5}$$

If the sequence of partial sums $\{S_n\}$, where

$$S_n = c_1 + c_2 + \cdots + c_n,$$

has limit S, we say that the series has sum S or that the series converges to S, and we write

$$\sum_{n=1}^{\infty} c_n = S. \tag{5.6}$$

If $\lim_{n \to \infty} S_n$ does not exist, we say that the series does not have a sum or that it diverges.

For example, the nth partial sum of the **geometric series**

$$a + az + az^2 + \cdots + az^{n-1} + \cdots$$

is

$$S_n = a + az + az^2 + \cdots + az^{n-1}.$$

If we multiply this equation by z,

$$zS_n = az + az^2 + az^3 + \cdots + az^n,$$

and then subtract these equations,

$$S_n - zS_n = a - az^n.$$

This can be solved for

$$S_n = \frac{a(1 - z^n)}{1 - z}, \tag{5.7}$$

provided of course $z \neq 1$. According to Example 5.3, $\lim_{n \to \infty} z^n = 0$ when $|z| < 1$. Hence, $\lim_{n \to \infty} S_n = a/(1 - z)$ when $|z| < 1$. Furthermore, when $|z| > 1$, or $|z| = 1$ (but $z \neq 1$), Example 5.3 also indicates that $\lim_{n \to \infty} z^n$ does not exist. Thus, for all z such that $|z| \geq 1$ and $z \neq 1$, $\lim_{n \to \infty} S_n$ does not exist. Finally when $z = 1$, $S_n = a + a + \cdots + a = na$, and certainly $\lim_{n \to \infty} S_n$ does not exist (unless trivially $a = 0$). To summarize,

$$\lim_{n \to \infty} S_n = \begin{cases} \dfrac{a}{1 - z}, & |z| < 1 \\ \text{does not exist}, & |z| \geq 1 \end{cases}.$$

Thus,

$$\sum_{n=1}^{\infty} az^{n-1} = a + az + az^2 + \cdots = \begin{cases} \dfrac{a}{1 - z}, & |z| < 1 \\ \text{diverges}, & |z| \geq 1 \end{cases}. \tag{5.8}$$

The separation of terms in a sequence into real and imaginary parts in Theorem 5.2 can be extended to series.

Theorem 5.5   A complex series converges if and only if the series of real and imaginary parts converge. To be precise, suppose $c_n = x_n + y_n i$ and $S = X + Y i$. Then

$$\sum_{n=1}^{\infty} c_n = S \quad \text{if and only if} \quad \sum_{n=1}^{\infty} x_n = X \quad \text{and} \quad \sum_{n=1}^{\infty} y_n = Y. \qquad (5.9)$$

Example 5.4   Show that $\displaystyle\sum_{n=1}^{\infty} \frac{1 + \sinh\left(i/n\right)}{2^n}$ converges.

Solution   It is straightforward to identify real and imaginary parts of the nth term of the series

$$\frac{1 + \sinh\left(i/n\right)}{2^n} = \frac{1}{2^n} + \frac{\sin\left(1/n\right)}{2^n} i.$$

Since $\sum_{n=1}^{\infty} 1/2^n$ is a convergent (real) geometric series, and $\sum_{n=1}^{\infty} \sin\left(1/n\right)/2^n$ also converges (being term-by-term less than $\sum_{n=1}^{\infty} 1/2^n$), it follows that the series $\sum_{n=1}^{\infty} [1 + \sinh\left(i/n\right)]/2^n$ converges.$\bullet$

To discuss convergence of a series $\sum_{n=1}^{\infty} c_n$ in terms of its sequence $\{S_n\}$ of partial sums is usually impractical; seldom is it possible to find a simple formula for S_n. Consequently, we must develop alternative ways to decide on the convergence of a series. Before doing this, however, we mention some fairly simple but important results concerning convergence of series. First, if a series $\sum_{n=1}^{\infty} c_n$ has a finite number of terms altered in any fashion whatsoever, the new series converges if and only if the original series converges. The new series may converge to a different sum, but it converges if the original series converges. The following theorem indicates that convergent series can be added and subtracted, and multiplied by constants. These properties can be verified using the definition of the sum of a series as the limit of the sequence of its partial sums.

Theorem 5.6   If $\displaystyle\sum_{n=1}^{\infty} c_n = C$ and $\displaystyle\sum_{n=1}^{\infty} d_n = D$, then:

$$\text{(i)} \quad \sum_{n=1}^{\infty} (c_n \pm d_n) = C \pm D, \qquad (5.10\text{a})$$

$$\text{(ii)} \quad \sum_{n=1}^{\infty} k c_n = k C \quad \text{(when } k \text{ is a constant).} \qquad (5.10\text{b})$$

The following result gives rise to the nth term test for divergence of a series.

Theorem 5.7   If $\displaystyle\sum_{n=1}^{\infty} c_n$ converges, then $\displaystyle\lim_{n \to \infty} c_n = 0$.

Proof   If $\sum_{n=1}^{\infty} c_n$ converges to S, its sequence of partial sums

$$S_1, S_2, \ldots, S_n, \ldots$$

has limit S. But then the sequence

$$0, S_1, S_2, \ldots, S_{n-1}, \ldots$$

also converges to S. When we subtract these sequences term-by-term, the sequence

$$S_1 - 0, S_2 - S_1, \ldots, S_n - S_{n-1}, \ldots$$

has limit $S - S = 0$ (according to Theorem 5.1). Since $S_n - S_{n-1} = c_n$, we have shown that $\lim_{n \to \infty} c_n = 0$. ∎

The contrapositive of this result is the nth term test.

Corollary 1 (n^{th} **term test**)   If $\lim_{n \to \infty} c_n \neq 0$, or does not exist, then $\sum_{n=1}^{\infty} c_n$ diverges.

The nth term test is a test for divergence of a series, not convergence. It states that if $\lim_{n \to \infty} c_n$ exists and is equal to anything but zero, or, if the limit does not exist, then the series $\sum_{n=1}^{\infty} c_n$ diverges. The nth term test never indicates that a series converges. Even if $\lim_{n \to \infty} c_n = 0$, we can conclude nothing about the convergence or divergence of $\sum_{n=1}^{\infty} c_n$; it may converge or diverge.

The concept of convergence of an infinite series is the same whether the terms of the series are real or complex. In other words, everything that we have said in this section (with the exception of Theorem 5.5) is exactly as we would have said it had series 5.5 been real instead of complex.

In real variable theory, two types of series are discussed, those with only non-negative terms, and those with an infinite number of positive and negative terms. To determine whether a series with only nonnegative terms converges or diverges, various tests are developed such as comparison, integral, ratio, and root. To discuss convergence of series with both positive and negative terms, the ideas of absolute and conditional convergence are introduced. The situation for complex series is different but similar. It is different because complex numbers are neither positive nor negative. The situation is similar in that we use absolute convergence as the vehicle to discuss convergence and divergence of most series.

Definition 5.2 A complex series $\sum_{n=1}^{\infty} c_n$ is said to be absolutely convergent (or converge absolutely) if $\sum_{n=1}^{\infty} |c_n|$ converges.

It might seem more appropriate to say "converges in modulus" rather than "converges absolutely" since vertical bars indicate moduli rather than absolute values, but absolute convergence has become the accepted terminology. The importance of absolute convergence is contained in the following theorem.

Theorem 5.8 If a complex series converges absolutely, then it converges.

Proof   Suppose the series $\sum_{n=1}^{\infty} c_n$ converges absolutely where $c_n = a_n + b_n i$. This means that $\sum_{n=1}^{\infty} |c_n| = \sum_{n=1}^{\infty} \sqrt{a_n^2 + b_n^2}$ has a sum, call it S. Now each term in the series $\sum_{n=1}^{\infty} |a_n|$ is nonnegative and is less than the corresponding term in $\sum_{n=1}^{\infty} \sqrt{a_n^2 + b_n^2}$. It follows that $\sum_{n=1}^{\infty} |a_n|$ converges; that is, the real series $\sum_{n=1}^{\infty} a_n$ of real parts of $\sum_{n=1}^{\infty} c_n$ converges absolutely. Similarly, the series of imaginary parts $\sum_{n=1}^{\infty} b_n$ converges absolutely, and by Theorem 5.5, $\sum_{n=1}^{\infty} c_n$ therefore converges. ∎

According to Theorem 5.8, a complex series $\sum_{n=1}^{\infty} c_n$ converges when its series of moduli $\sum_{n=1}^{\infty} |c_n|$ converges. Since the latter series is a series of nonnegative reals, we can utilize the wealth of tests for such series in real variable theory. We describe five of these tests below, but phrase them in the context of complex series and absolute convergence.

Theorem 5.9 **(Comparison Test)** If $|c_n| \leq a_n$ for all $n \geq N$ and $\sum_{n=N}^{\infty} a_n$ converges, then $\sum_{n=1}^{\infty} c_n$ converges absolutely.

Theorem 5.10 **(Limit Comparison Test)** If $\sum_{n=1}^{\infty} b_n$ is a convergent series of positive real numbers, and

$$\lim_{n \to \infty} \frac{|c_n|}{b_n} = l, \quad 0 \leq l < \infty,$$

then $\sum_{n=1}^{\infty} c_n$ converges absolutely.

Theorem 5.11 **(Integral Test)** If $|c_n| = f(n)$ and $f(x)$ is a continuous, decreasing function for $x \geq N$ such that

$$\int_{N}^{\infty} f(x)\, dx < \infty,$$

then $\sum_{n=1}^{\infty} c_n$ converges absolutely.

Theorem 5.12 **(Limit Ratio Test)** Suppose $c_n \neq 0$ and $\lim_{n \to \infty} \left| \dfrac{c_{n+1}}{c_n} \right| = L$. Then

(i) $\sum_{n=1}^{\infty} c_n$ converges absolutely if $L < 1$;

(ii) $\sum_{n=1}^{\infty} c_n$ diverges if $L > 1$ or if $\lim_{n \to \infty} |c_{n+1}/c_n| = \infty$;

(iii) $\sum_{n=1}^{\infty} c_n$ may converge or diverge if $L = 1$.

Theorem 5.13 **(Limit Root Test)** Suppose $\lim_{n \to \infty} \sqrt[n]{|c_n|} = \mathcal{L}$. Then,

(i) $\sum_{n=1}^{\infty} c_n$ converges absolutely if $\mathcal{L} < 1$;

(ii) $\sum_{n=1}^{\infty} c_n$ diverges if $\mathcal{L} > 1$ or if $\lim_{n \to \infty} \sqrt[n]{|c_n|} = \infty$;

(iii) $\sum_{n=1}^{\infty} c_n$ may converge or diverge if $\mathcal{L} = 1$.

The following examples illustrate the application of these tests.

Example 5.5 Determine whether the following series converge or diverge:

(a) $\displaystyle\sum_{n=1}^{\infty} \frac{(n+i)^2}{n^4}$ (b) $\displaystyle\sum_{n=1}^{\infty} \frac{(2+i)^n}{n!}$ (c) $\displaystyle\sum_{n=1}^{\infty} \left(2 + \frac{i}{n^2} \right)^n$ (d) $\displaystyle\sum_{n=1}^{\infty} \frac{1}{n \mathrm{Log}^2 ni}$

Solution (a) Since $l = \lim\limits_{n \to \infty} \dfrac{\left| \frac{(n+i)^2}{n^4} \right|}{\frac{1}{n^2}} = \lim\limits_{n \to \infty} \dfrac{n^2(n^2+1)}{n^4} = 1$, and the real series $\sum_{n=1}^{\infty} 1/n^2$ converges, it follows that $\sum_{n=1}^{\infty} (n+i)^2/n^4$ converges absolutely by the limit comparison test.

(b) Since $L = \lim\limits_{n \to \infty} \left| \dfrac{\frac{(2+i)^{n+1}}{(n+1)!}}{\frac{(2+i)^n}{n!}} \right| = \lim\limits_{n \to \infty} \dfrac{|2+i|}{n+1} = 0$, the limit ratio test implies that the series $\sum_{n=1}^{\infty} (2+i)^n/n!$ converges absolutely.

(c) Since $\mathcal{L} = \lim\limits_{n\to\infty} \sqrt[n]{\left|\left(2 + \dfrac{i}{n^2}\right)^n\right|} = \lim\limits_{n\to\infty}\left|2 + \dfrac{i}{n^2}\right| = \lim\limits_{n\to\infty}\sqrt{4 + 1/n^4} = 2$,

the series diverges by the limit root test.

(d) First we note that $\left|\dfrac{1}{n\text{Log}^2 ni}\right| = \dfrac{1}{n|\ln n + \pi i/2|^2} = \dfrac{1}{n[(\ln n)^2 + \pi^2/4]}$. If we

set $f(x) = 1/\{x[(\ln x)^2 + \pi^2/4]\}$, then for $x \geq 2$, $f(x) < 1/[x(\ln x)^2]$, and

$$\int_2^\infty f(x)\,dx < \int_2^\infty \frac{1}{x(\ln x)^2}\,dx = \left\{\frac{-1}{\ln x}\right\}_2^\infty = \frac{1}{\ln 2}.$$

Thus, the series converges absolutely by the integral test.•

Geometric series along with the fact that the sine and cosine functions are related to the complex exponential function through Euler's identity can be used to find sums of many series of trigonometric functions. Here is a simple example; others can be found in the exercises.

Example 5.6 Verify that when θ is not a multiple of 2π,

(a) $\displaystyle\sum_{k=0}^n \cos k\theta = 1 + \cos\theta + \cos 2\theta + \cdots + \cos n\theta = \dfrac{\sin\dfrac{(n+1)\theta}{2}\cos\dfrac{n\theta}{2}}{\sin\dfrac{\theta}{2}}$

(b) $\displaystyle\sum_{k=1}^n \sin k\theta = \sin\theta + \sin 2\theta + \cdots + \sin n\theta = \dfrac{\sin\dfrac{(n+1)\theta}{2}\sin\dfrac{n\theta}{2}}{\sin\dfrac{\theta}{2}}$

Solution We note that these series can be obtained by taking real and imaginary parts of the geometric series

$$1 + e^{\theta i} + e^{2\theta i} + \cdots + e^{n\theta i}.$$

Using formula 5.7,

$$\sum_{k=0}^n e^{k\theta i} = \frac{1 - e^{(n+1)\theta i}}{1 - e^{\theta i}} = \frac{1 - e^{(n+1)\theta i}}{1 - e^{\theta i}}\frac{1 - e^{-\theta i}}{1 - e^{-\theta i}} = \frac{1 - e^{(n+1)\theta i} - e^{-\theta i} + e^{n\theta i}}{2 - 2\cos\theta}.$$

When we take real parts,

$$\sum_{k=0}^n \cos k\theta = \frac{1 - \cos(n+1)\theta - \cos\theta + \cos n\theta}{2(1 - \cos\theta)}$$

$$= \frac{(1 - \cos\theta) + [\cos n\theta - \cos(n+1)\theta]}{2(1 - \cos\theta)}$$

$$= \frac{2\sin^2\frac{\theta}{2} + 2\sin\frac{(2n+1)\theta}{2}\sin\frac{\theta}{2}}{4\sin^2\frac{\theta}{2}} = \frac{\sin\frac{\theta}{2} + \sin\frac{(2n+1)\theta}{2}}{2\sin\frac{\theta}{2}}$$

$$= \frac{2\sin\frac{(n+1)\theta}{2}\cos\frac{n\theta}{2}}{2\sin\frac{\theta}{2}} = \frac{\sin\frac{(n+1)\theta}{2}\cos\frac{n\theta}{2}}{\sin\frac{\theta}{2}}.$$

A similar calculation with imaginary parts gives the sum of sine functions.•

EXERCISES 5.2

In Exercises 1–20 determine whether the series converges or diverges.

1. $\displaystyle\sum_{n=1}^{\infty} i^n$

2. $\displaystyle\sum_{n=1}^{\infty} \frac{1 + 3^n i}{5^n}$

3. $\displaystyle\sum_{n=1}^{\infty} \frac{n + 2i}{ni - 3}$

4. $\displaystyle\sum_{n=1}^{\infty} \frac{1}{n^2 + i}$

5. $\displaystyle\sum_{n=1}^{\infty} (1 + i)^n$

6. $\displaystyle\sum_{n=2}^{\infty} \left[1 - \left(\frac{3}{2 + 4i} \right)^n \right]$

7. $\displaystyle\sum_{n=2}^{\infty} \left(\frac{1}{2 + 3i} \right)^n$

8. $\displaystyle\sum_{n=1}^{\infty} \left(\frac{2 - i}{3 + i} \right)^{2n}$

9. $\displaystyle\sum_{n=1}^{\infty} \frac{2ni + 3}{n^2 + 4i}$

10. $\displaystyle\sum_{n=1}^{\infty} \frac{e^{ni}}{n^2 - 4i}$

11. $\displaystyle\sum_{n=1}^{\infty} \frac{2^n}{(n + 1)i^n}$

12. $\displaystyle\sum_{n=1}^{\infty} \frac{3 - (2i)^n}{\cos ni}$

13. $\displaystyle\sum_{n=1}^{\infty} \frac{\sin ni}{(1 + i)^n}$

14. $\displaystyle\sum_{n=1}^{\infty} \frac{\sqrt{n + i}}{n^2}$

15. $\displaystyle\sum_{n=1}^{\infty} \left(-2 + \frac{i}{n} \right)^n$

16. $\displaystyle\sum_{n=1}^{\infty} \left(\frac{ni}{n + i} \right)^{n^2}$

17. $\displaystyle\sum_{n=1}^{\infty} \frac{(4 - 3i)^{2n}}{n!}$

18. $\displaystyle\sum_{n=1}^{\infty} \frac{(1 + i)(2 + i) \cdots (n + i)}{n^n}$

19. $\displaystyle\sum_{n=1}^{\infty} \frac{\text{Log}(n + i)}{n^3}$

20. $\displaystyle\sum_{n=1}^{\infty} \frac{\tan (ni)}{n^2 + 1}$

21. The comparison test for real series states that when $c_n \geq d_n \geq 0$ for all n and $\sum_{n=1}^{\infty} d_n$ diverges, so also does $\sum_{n=1}^{\infty} c_n$. Is the following complex analogue valid: If $|c_n| \geq d_n \geq 0$ for all n and $\sum_{n=1}^{\infty} d_n$ diverges, so also does $\sum_{n=1}^{\infty} c_n$.

22. For what values of z does the series $\displaystyle\sum_{n=1}^{\infty} \frac{e^{nz}}{(n + 1)^2}$ converge?

23. Evaluate $\displaystyle\sum_{n=1}^{\infty} \frac{1}{(n + i)(n + i - 1)}$.   Hint: Use partial fractions.

24. Verify the following results for $x < 0$:

$$\sum_{n=0}^{\infty} e^{-nx} \cos ny = \frac{1 - e^{-x} \cos y}{1 + e^{-2x} - 2e^{-x} \cos y} \quad \text{and} \quad \sum_{n=1}^{\infty} e^{-nx} \sin ny = \frac{e^{-x} \sin y}{1 + e^{-2x} - 2e^{-x} \cos y}.$$

25. Verify the following results when θ is not a multiple of π.

(a) $\displaystyle\sum_{k=1}^{n} \cos (2k - 1)\theta = \cos \theta + \cos 3\theta + \cdots + \cos (2n - 1)\theta = \frac{\sin 2n\theta}{2 \sin \theta}$

(b) $\displaystyle\sum_{k=1}^{n} \sin{(2k-1)\theta} = \sin\theta + \sin 3\theta + \cdots + \sin{(2n-1)\theta} = \dfrac{\sin^2 n\theta}{\sin\theta}$

26. Verify that when θ is not a multiple of π,

$$\sin\theta - \sin 2\theta + \cdots + (-1)^{n-1}\sin n\theta = \begin{cases} \dfrac{\sin\dfrac{(n+1)\theta}{2}\cos\dfrac{n\theta}{2}}{\cos\dfrac{\theta}{2}} & n \text{ odd} \\[4mm] -\dfrac{\cos\dfrac{(n+1)\theta}{2}\sin\dfrac{n\theta}{2}}{\cos\dfrac{\theta}{2}} & n \text{ even.} \end{cases}$$

27. Use Example 5.6 to verify the following results when θ is not a multiple of 2π:

(a) $\displaystyle\sum_{k=0}^{n} \cos{(a+k\theta)} = \cos a + \cos{(a+\theta)} + \cdots + \cos{(a+n\theta)} = \dfrac{\sin\dfrac{(n+1)\theta}{2}\cos\left(a+\dfrac{n\theta}{2}\right)}{\sin\dfrac{\theta}{2}}$

(b) $\displaystyle\sum_{k=0}^{n} \sin{(a+k\theta)} = \sin a + \sin{(a+\theta)} + \cdots + \sin{(a+n\theta)} = \dfrac{\sin\dfrac{(n+1)\theta}{2}\sin\left(a+\dfrac{n\theta}{2}\right)}{\sin\dfrac{\theta}{2}}$

28. Use Exercise 25 to verify the following results when θ is not a multiple of π:

(a) $\displaystyle\sum_{k=1}^{n} \cos{[(a+(2k-1)\theta]} = \cos{(a+\theta)} + \cos{(a+3\theta)} + \cdots + \cos{[a+(2n-1)\theta]}$

$$= \dfrac{\sin n\theta \cos{(a+n\theta)}}{\sin\theta}$$

(b) $\displaystyle\sum_{k=1}^{n} \sin{[(a+(2k-1)\theta]} = \sin{(a+\theta)} + \sin{(a+3\theta)} + \cdots + \sin{[a+(2n-1)\theta]}$

$$= \dfrac{\sin n\theta \sin{(a+n\theta)}}{\sin\theta}$$

29. Use Exercise 27 to verify the following results when θ is not a multiple of 2π:

(a) $\displaystyle\sum_{k=0}^{n} k\cos{(a+k\theta)} = \dfrac{\sin\left(a+\dfrac{n\theta}{2}\right)\sin\dfrac{n\theta}{2} + n\sin\dfrac{\theta}{2}\sin\left[a+\dfrac{(2n+1)\theta}{2}\right]}{2\sin^2\dfrac{\theta}{2}}$

(b) $\displaystyle\sum_{k=0}^{n} k\sin{(a+k\theta)} = \dfrac{\cos\left(a+\dfrac{n\theta}{2}\right)\sin\dfrac{n\theta}{2} - n\sin\dfrac{\theta}{2}\cos\left[a+\dfrac{(2n+1)\theta}{2}\right]}{2\sin^2\dfrac{\theta}{2}}$

30. Prove the following results:

(a) $\displaystyle\sum_{k=0}^{n} r^k\sin{(a+k\theta)} = \dfrac{\sin a - r\sin{(a-\theta)} - r^{n+1}\sin{[a+(n+1)\theta]} + r^{n+2}\sin{(a+n\theta)}}{1+r^2-2r\cos\theta}$

(b) $\displaystyle\sum_{k=0}^{n} r^k \cos\left(a+k\theta\right) = \frac{\cos a - r\cos\left(a-\theta\right) - r^{n+1}\cos\left[a+(n+1)\theta\right] + r^{n+2}\cos\left(a+n\theta\right)}{1+r^2-2r\cos\theta}$

31. Use the results of Exercise 30 to prove that when $|r| < 1$,

(a) $\displaystyle\sum_{k=0}^{\infty} r^k \sin\left(a+k\theta\right) = \frac{\sin a - r\sin\left(a-\theta\right)}{1+r^2-2r\cos\theta}$

(b) $\displaystyle\sum_{k=0}^{\infty} r^k \cos\left(a+k\theta\right) = \frac{\cos a - r\cos\left(a-\theta\right)}{1+r^2-2r\cos\theta}$

32. Verify the following results where $\displaystyle\binom{n}{k}$ denote binomial coefficients:

(a) $\displaystyle\sum_{k=0}^{n}\binom{n}{k}\cos\left(a+k\theta\right) = 2^n \cos^n\frac{\theta}{2}\cos\left(a+\frac{n\theta}{2}\right)$

(b) $\displaystyle\sum_{k=0}^{n}\binom{n}{k}\sin\left(a+k\theta\right) = 2^n \cos^n\frac{\theta}{2}\sin\left(a+\frac{n\theta}{2}\right)$

33. Because hyperbolic sine and cosine functions are related to their trigonometric counterparts through equations 3.17, it might seem that series of hyperbolic functions could be summed using the formulas in Example 5.6 and the above exercises. Unfortunately, these results have only been verified for real θ, and therefore they cannot be used to verify similar properties for hyperbolic functions. Results for hyperbolic functions must be verified anew. As an example, verify the following results corresponding to Example 5.6:

(a) $\cosh\theta + \cosh 2\theta + \cdots + \cosh n\theta = \dfrac{\cosh\dfrac{(n+1)\theta}{2}\sinh\dfrac{n\theta}{2}}{\sinh\dfrac{\theta}{2}}$

(b) $\sinh\theta + \sinh 2\theta + \cdots + \sinh n\theta = \dfrac{\sinh\dfrac{(n+1)\theta}{2}\sinh\dfrac{n\theta}{2}}{\sinh\dfrac{\theta}{2}}$

34. In this exercise, we verify that the sequence $\{\sin n\theta\}$ converges only when θ is a multiple of π, and the sequence $\{\cos n\theta\}$ converges only when θ a multiple of 2π.

(a) Demonstrate that $\{\sin n\theta\}$ converges when $\theta = m\pi$, m an integer, and $\{\cos n\theta\}$ converges for $\theta = 2m\pi$, but not $\theta = (2m+1)\pi$.

(b) Prove that if a sequence $\{z_n\}$ has limit Z, then so also does the sequence $\left\{\dfrac{1}{n}\displaystyle\sum_{k=1}^{n} z_k\right\}$.

(c) When θ is not a multiple of 2π, the sequences $\{\sin n\theta\}$ and $\{\cos n\theta\}$ converge or diverge together. Suppose that they both converge. Then so also does the sequence $\{e^{n\theta i}\}$, (its real and imaginary parts being the cosine and sine sequences. Does it follow that the sequence $\left\{\dfrac{1}{n}\displaystyle\sum_{k=0}^{n} e^{k\theta i}\right\}$ converges? What would be its modulus?

(d) Verify the following summation formula:

$$\sum_{k=0}^{n} e^{k\theta i} = \frac{e^{n\theta i/2}\sin\dfrac{(n+1)\theta}{2}}{\sin\dfrac{\theta}{2}}.$$

What does this result say about the limit of the sequence $\left\{\dfrac{1}{n}\displaystyle\sum_{k=0}^{n} e^{k\theta i}\right\}$? Does this contradict part (c)?

§5.3 Complex Power Series

A **complex power series** is a series of the form

$$\sum_{n=0}^{\infty} a_n(z - z_0)^n = a_0 + a_1(z - z_0) + a_2(z - z_0)^2 + \cdots \qquad (5.11)$$

where z_0 is a point in the complex plane and the a_n are complex constants. Such series are called power series in $z - z_0$ or power series about the point z_0. When a complex number z is substituted into 5.11, a series of complex constants results; this series may converge or diverge. It is clear that a complex power series always converges for $z = z_0$, but does it converge for other values of z? We now show that there are exactly three possibilities as far as values of z for which a power series yields a convergent series of constants:

(i) the power series converges only for $z = z_0$;
(ii) the power series converges absolutely for all z;
(iii) there exists a number $R > 0$ such that the power series converges absolutely for $|z - z_0| < R$, diverges for $|z - z_0| > R$, and may or may not converge for $|z - z_0| = R$.

It is helpful to visualize (iii) geometrically. Since $|z - z_0| = R$ is a circle centred at z_0 with radius R (Figure 5.1), situation (iii) says that the power series converges absolutely for all points inside the circle, diverges for points outside the circle, and may or may not converge for points on the circle.

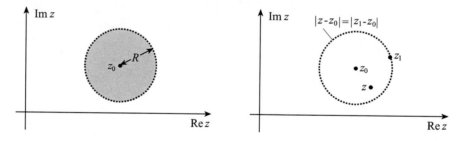

Figure 5.1   **Figure 5.2**

The power series $\sum_{n=0}^{\infty} n!(z - z_0)^n$ and $\sum_{n=0}^{\infty} (z - z_0)^n/n!$ establish (i) and (ii). For any $z \neq z_0$, the limit ratio test on the first series gives

$$L = \lim_{n \to \infty} \left| \frac{(n + 1)!(z - z_0)^{n+1}}{n!(z - z_0)^n} \right| = \lim_{n \to \infty} (n + 1)|z - z_0| = \infty.$$

Hence, $\sum_{n=0}^{\infty} n!(z - z_0)^n$ diverges for all $z \neq z_0$. For the second series we calculate that

$$L = \lim_{n \to \infty} \left| \frac{(z - z_0)^{n+1}/(n + 1)!}{(z - z_0)^n/n!} \right| = \lim_{n \to \infty} \frac{|z - z_0|}{n + 1} = 0,$$

and therefore $\sum_{n=0}^{\infty} (z - z_0)^n/n!$ converges absolutely for all z. To establish that (iii) is the only other possibility we first prove that if a power series converges for z_1, then it converges absolutely for all points closer to z_0 than z_1 (Figure 5.2).

Theorem 5.14 If $\sum_{n=0}^{\infty} a_n(z - z_0)^n$ converges for z_1, then it converges for all z in the circle $|z - z_0| < |z_1 - z_0|$.

Proof If $\sum_{n=0}^{\infty} a_n(z_1 - z_0)^n$ converges, then the terms of the series must be bounded; that is, there exists a number $M > 0$ such that $|a_n(z_1 - z_0)^n| \leq M$ for all $n \geq 0$. For any z in the circle $|z - z_0| < |z_1 - z_0|$,

$$|a_n(z - z_0)^n| = |a_n||z - z_0|^n = |a_n| \left| \frac{z - z_0}{z_1 - z_0} \right|^n |z_1 - z_0|^n \leq M \left| \frac{z - z_0}{z_1 - z_0} \right|^n .$$

Since $\sum_{n=0}^{\infty} M|(z - z_0)/(z_1 - z_0)|^n$ is a geometric series with common ratio $|(z - z_0)/(z_1 - z_0)| < 1$, it follows that $\sum_{n=0}^{\infty} a_n(z - z_0)^n$ converges absolutely in the circle $|z - z_0| < |z_1 - z_0|$ (by the comparison test). ∎

We can now establish that (iii) above is the only possibility besides (i) and (ii). Suppose that S is the set of points for which $\sum_{n=0}^{\infty} a_n(z - z_0)^n$ converges and that S contains more than the point z_0, but S is not the whole complex plane. If S contains a complex number z_1 which is farthest from z_0, then the power series converges absolutely for all z such that $|z - z_0| < |z_1 - z_0|$ and diverges for $|z - z_0| > |z_1 - z_0|$; that is, R in (iii) is equal to $|z_1 - z_0|$. If S does not contain a complex number farthest from z_0, consider the set of all real numbers $d = |z - z_0|$ where z is in S. This set forms an interval $0 \leq d < R$ on the real line. According to Theorem 5.14, the series converges absolutely for all z satisfying $|z - z_0| < R$. Furthermore, it does not converge for any z satisfying $|z - z_0| > R$. Thus, whether or not S has a complex number farthest from z_0, (iii) is established.

In (iii) we call R the **radius of convergence** of the power series. In (i) and (ii) we say that $R = 0$ and $R = \infty$. Every power series then has a radius of convergence. If $R = 0$, the series converges only for $z = z_0$; if $R = \infty$, the series converges absolutely for all z; and if $0 < R < \infty$, the series converges absolutely for all points in the **circle of convergence** $|z - z_0| < R$, diverges for points outside the circle, and may or may not converge for points on the circle. For many power series, the radius of convergence can be calculated according to

$$R = \lim_{n \to \infty} \left| \frac{a_n}{a_{n+1}} \right|, \tag{5.12a}$$

or

$$R = \lim_{n \to \infty} \frac{1}{|a_n|^{1/n}}, \tag{5.12b}$$

provided either limit exists or is equal to infinity. These can be established using the limit ratio and limit root tests in Section 5.2. Formulas 5.12 yield radii of convergence for real power series $\sum_{n=0}^{\infty} a_n(x - x_0)^n$, but in the context of real power series, R represents half the length of the interval of convergence. We now see the reason for calling R the radius of convergence of a power series.

An integral part of the discussion of the interval of convergence of a real power series is consideration of the end points of this interval. The counterpart of these end points for complex series is the circle $|z - z_0| = R$. We do not discuss whether complex power series converge or diverge on $|z - z_0| = R$ in these notes except for the results in Exercises 47–51 at the end of this section.

Example 5.7 Find circles of convergence for the following power series:

(a) $\displaystyle\sum_{n=0}^{\infty} \frac{(n+1)}{(3i)^n}(z-1)^n$ (b) $\displaystyle\sum_{n=0}^{\infty} \left(\frac{n+i}{n-2i}\right)^n (z-i)^n$ (c) $\displaystyle\sum_{n=1}^{\infty} \frac{1}{n2^n}(z-2+i)^{2n}$

Solution (a) Since

$$\lim_{n\to\infty} \left| \frac{\dfrac{n+1}{(3i)^n}}{\dfrac{n+2}{(3i)^{n+1}}} \right| = \lim_{n\to\infty} \frac{3(n+1)}{n+2} = 3,$$

the radius of convergence of the power series is $R = 3$. Its circle of convergence is $|z-1| < 3$ (Figure 5.3). The power series converges for all points inside this circle, diverges for points outside the circle, and may or may not converge for points on the circle.

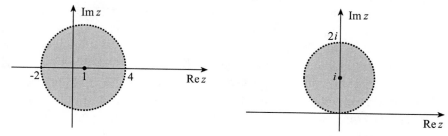

Figure 5.3   **Figure 5.4**

(b) Since

$$\lim_{n\to\infty} \frac{1}{\left[\left|\left(\dfrac{n+i}{n-2i}\right)^n\right|\right]^{1/n}} = \lim_{n\to\infty} \left|\frac{n-2i}{n+i}\right| = 1,$$

the radius of convergence of the power series is $R = 1$. Its circle of convergence is $|z-i| < 1$ (Figure 5.4).

(c) Because the series contains only even powers of $z - 2 + i$ we first set $w = (z-2+i)^2$. Then

$$\sum_{n=1}^{\infty} \frac{1}{n2^n}(z-2+i)^{2n} = \sum_{n=1}^{\infty} \frac{1}{n2^n} w^n.$$

The radius of convergence of this series is

$$R_w = \lim_{n\to\infty} \frac{\dfrac{1}{n2^n}}{\dfrac{1}{(n+1)2^{n+1}}} = \lim_{n\to\infty} \frac{2(n+1)}{n} = 2;$$

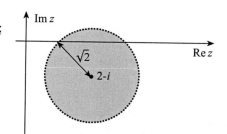

that is, $\sum_{n=1}^{\infty} [1/(n2^n)]w^n$ converges absolutely for $|w| < 2$. It follows that the series $\sum_{n=1}^{\infty} [1/(n2^n)](z-2+i)^{2n}$ converges absolutely for $|z-2+i| < \sqrt{2}$ (Figure 5.5).•

Figure 5.5

When a function f has the same value $f(z)$ as the sum of a power series $\sum_{n=0}^{\infty} a_n(z - z_0)^n$ at every point interior to its circle of convergence, we call f the sum of the series, and write

$$f(z) = \sum_{n=0}^{\infty} a_n(z - z_0)^n, \quad |z - z_0| < R. \tag{5.13}$$

For example, the geometric series $1 + z + z^2 + \cdots$ has sum $1/(1 - z)$ provided z is in modulus less than one, and we express this by writing

$$\frac{1}{1 - z} = 1 + z + z^2 + \cdots, \quad |z| < 1. \tag{5.14}$$

Example 5.8   What is the sum of the power series $\sum_{n=2}^{\infty} \frac{2^n}{3^{2n+1}}(z - 1 - 2i)^n$?

Solution   Since $\sum_{n=2}^{\infty} \frac{2^n}{3^{2n+1}}(z - 1 - 2i)^n = \frac{1}{3}\sum_{n=2}^{\infty} \left[\frac{2}{9}(z - 1 - 2i)\right]^n$, the power series is geometric with sum

$$\frac{1}{3}\left\{ \frac{[(2/9)(z - 1 - 2i)]^2}{1 - (2/9)(z - 1 - 2i)} \right\} = \frac{4(z - 1 - 2i)^2}{27(11 + 4i - 2z)},$$

provided $|(2/9)(z - 1 - 2i)| < 1$, or $|z - 1 - 2i| < 9/2$. •

We might ponder the following question at this point: If f is the sum of a power series $\sum_{n=0}^{\infty} a_n(z - z_0)^n$, what properties does f possess? The following theorem indicates that every convergent power series converges to an analytic function in its circle of convergence.

Theorem 5.15   Suppose that f is the sum of a complex power series $\sum_{n=0}^{\infty} a_n(z - z_0)^n$ inside its circle of convergence $|z - z_0| < R$, where $R > 0$. Then:

(i) f is an analytic function in the circle of convergence.

(ii) The derivative of f can be obtained by term-by-term differentiation of the power series for f,

$$f'(z) = \sum_{n=0}^{\infty} na_n(z - z_0)^{n-1}, \tag{5.15}$$

valid in the same circle of convergence.

(iii) If C is any piecewise smooth curve (in the circle of convergence) joining point A to point B, then

$$\int_C f(z)\,dz = \sum_{n=0}^{\infty} \int_C a_n(z - z_0)^n\,dz = \sum_{n=0}^{\infty} a_n \left\{ \frac{(z - z_0)^{n+1}}{n + 1} \right\}_A^B. \tag{5.16}$$

(iv) Antiderivatives of f can be obtained by term-by-term antidifferentiation of the power series for f,

$$\int f(z)\,dz = \sum_{n=0}^{\infty} \frac{a_n}{n + 1}(z - z_0)^{n+1} + C, \tag{5.17}$$

valid in the same circle of convergence.

The proof of this result is given in the Appendix at the end of the section. It can be omitted, at this point, by those who would prefer not to interrupt the flow of the discussion. The following is an immediate corollary of the theorem.

Corollary 5.15.1   The sum of a power series with infinite radius of convergence is an entire function.

Example 5.9   Use Theorem 5.15 to find a power series about $z = 0$ for $1/(1 - 2z)^2$.

Solution   We may regard $1/(1 - 2z)$ as the sum of a geometric series,

$$\frac{1}{1 - 2z} = 1 + 2z + 4z^2 + \cdots = \sum_{n=0}^{\infty} 2^n z^n,$$

valid for $|2z| < 1$ or $|z| < 1/2$. Term-by-term differentiation gives

$$\frac{2}{(1 - 2z)^2} = \sum_{n=0}^{\infty} 2^n n z^{n-1} = \sum_{n=1}^{\infty} n 2^n z^{n-1},$$

or,

$$\frac{1}{(1 - 2z)^2} = \sum_{n=1}^{\infty} n 2^{n-1} z^{n-1} = \sum_{n=0}^{\infty} (n + 1) 2^n z^n, \quad |z| < 1/2. \bullet$$

Example 5.10   Find the sum of the series $\displaystyle\sum_{n=1}^{\infty} \frac{1}{n}(z - 2)^n$.

Solution   We set $f(z) = \displaystyle\sum_{n=1}^{\infty} \frac{1}{n}(z - 2)^n$, valid for $|z - 2| < 1$. Term-by-term differentiation gives

$$f'(z) = \sum_{n=1}^{\infty} (z - 2)^{n-1} = \frac{1}{1 - (z - 2)} = \frac{1}{3 - z}.$$

Antidifferentiation now gives

$$f(z) = -\log_\phi (3 - z) + C,$$

where the branch cut must lie in the half-plane $\operatorname{Re} z \geq 3$ (Figure 5.6). We require this because $f(z)$ is to be analytic in $|z - 2| < 1$. Since $f(2) = 0$, it follows that

$$0 = -\log_\phi 1 + C,$$

and therefore

$$f(z) = \log_\phi 1 - \log_\phi (3 - z).$$

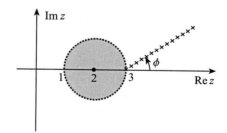

Figure 5.6

For instance, if we choose the principal branch of this logarithm function with branch cut along the positive real axis to the right of $z = 3$, then

$$\sum_{n=1}^{\infty} \frac{1}{n}(z - 2)^n = -\operatorname{Log}(3 - z). \bullet$$

We complete this section with a proof of Theorem 5.15, but before doing so, it is important to point out that our discussions are leading to a new characterization of analytic functions. Theorem 5.15 states that the sum of a convergent power series is an analytic function. The converse result is also valid, that analytic functions can be expressed as convergent power series (and this will be proved in Section 5.4). What this means is that the study of analytic functions is equivalent to the study of convergent power series. Properties of convergent power series are properties of analytic functions.

Appendix

To give a rigorous proof of Theorem 5.15, it is necessary to introduce the idea of uniform convergence. We do so in a more general setting than that of power series. To say that a series of functions $\sum_{n=0}^{\infty} f_n(z)$ has sum f in some domain D is to say that its sequence of partial sums has limit f; that is, given any $\epsilon > 0$, there exists an $\overline{N}$ such that when $N > \overline{N}$,

$$\left| f(z) - \sum_{n=0}^{N} f_n(z) \right| < \epsilon.$$

Now $\overline{N}$ is certainly a function of ϵ, the smaller ϵ, the larger $\overline{N}$. In addition, $\overline{N}$ normally depends on z. For certain values of z (and fixed ϵ), the value of $\overline{N}$ may be larger than it is for other values of z. When $\overline{N}$ can be chosen independent of z, we say that the series converges uniformly to f. This is stated in the following definition.

Definition 5.3   A series $\sum_{n=0}^{\infty} f_n(z)$ is said to converge uniformly to f in a domain D if given any $\epsilon > 0$, there exists an $\overline{N}$ such that for $N > \overline{N}$, and all z in D,

$$\left| f(z) - \sum_{n=0}^{N} f_n(z) \right| < \epsilon.$$

The most common way to verify uniform convergence is with the Weierstrass M-test.

Theorem 5.16   **(Weierstrass M-test)**   A series $\sum_{n=0}^{\infty} f_n(z)$ is uniformly convergent in a domain D if there exists a convergent series of constants $\sum_{n=0}^{\infty} M_n$ such that $|f_n(z)| \leq M_n$ for all $n \geq 0$ and all z in D.

Proof   Since $|f_n(z)| \leq M_n$ for any fixed z in D, it follows by the comparison test that the series $\sum_{n=0}^{\infty} f_n(z)$ converges. Let its sum be f; that is, let $f(z) = \sum_{n=0}^{\infty} f_n(z)$. Since $\sum_{n=0}^{\infty} M_n$ converges, given any $\epsilon > 0$, there exists an $\overline{N}$ such that for $N > \overline{N}$,

$$\sum_{n=N+1}^{\infty} M_n < \epsilon.$$

Since $|f_n(z)| \leq M_n$, it follows that $\displaystyle\sum_{n=N+1}^{\infty} |f_n(z)| \leq \sum_{n=1}^{\infty} M_n < \epsilon$. But this means that for $N > \overline{N}$, and all z in D,

$$\left| f(z) - \sum_{n=0}^{N} f_n(z) \right| = \left| \sum_{n=N+1}^{\infty} f_n(z) \right| \le \sum_{n=N+1}^{\infty} M_n < \epsilon.$$

Thus, $\sum_{n=0}^{\infty} f_n(z)$ converges uniformly to f in D. $\blacksquare$

For example, the power series $\sum_{n=0}^{\infty} z^n$ converges uniformly in the domain $|z| \le R < 1$ since therein $|z|^n \le R^n$ and $\sum_{n=0}^{\infty} R^n$ converges. The series converges in the domain $|z| < 1$, but it does not converge uniformly in this domain.

The importance of knowing that a series of functions converges uniformly is contained in the following theorem.

Theorem 5.17 Suppose that a series $\sum_{n=0}^{\infty} f_n(z)$ of analytic functions converges uniformly to its sum f in a domain D. Then:
(i) f is an analytic function in D.
(ii) The derivative of f in D can be obtained by term-by-term differentiation of the series for f,

$$f'(z) = \sum_{n=0}^{\infty} f_n'(z). \tag{5.18}$$

(iii) If C is any piecewise smooth curve in D, then

$$\int_C f(z)\,dz = \sum_{n=0}^{\infty} \int_C f_n(z)\,dz. \tag{5.19}$$

(iv) Antiderivatives of f in D can be obtained by term-by-term antidifferentiation of the series for f,

$$\int f(z)\,dz = \sum_{n=0}^{\infty} \int f_n(z)\,dz + C, \tag{5.20}$$

where C is a constant of integration.

Proof (i) First we verify that f is continuous in D. If z and z_0 are points in D, then

$$f(z) - f(z_0) = \left[f(z) - \sum_{n=0}^{N} f_n(z) \right] + \left[\sum_{n=0}^{N} f_n(z) - \sum_{n=0}^{N} f_n(z_0) \right] + \left[\sum_{n=0}^{N} f_n(z_0) - f(z_0) \right].$$

When we take moduli and use triangle inequality 1.40,

$$|f(z) - f(z_0)| \le \left| f(z) - \sum_{n=0}^{N} f_n(z) \right| + \left| \sum_{n=0}^{N} f_n(z) - \sum_{n=0}^{N} f_n(z_0) \right| + \left| f(z_0) - \sum_{n=0}^{N} f_n(z_0) \right|.$$

Since $\sum_{n=0}^{\infty} f_n(z)$ converges uniformly to f, given any $\epsilon > 0$, there exists an $\overline{N}$ such that for $N > \overline{N}$ and all z in D (including z_0),

$$\left| f(z) - \sum_{n=0}^{N} f_n(z) \right| < \frac{\epsilon}{3}.$$

Because $\sum_{n=0}^{N} f_n(z)$ is a finite sum of continuous functions, it is continuous. It follows that for fixed N and z_0, there exists a $\delta > 0$ such that when $|z - z_0| < \delta$, and z is in D,

$$\left| \sum_{n=0}^{N} f_n(z) - \sum_{n=0}^{N} f_n(z_0) \right| < \frac{\epsilon}{3}.$$

Hence, for any given $\epsilon > 0$, there exists a δ such that when $|z - z_0| < \delta$, and z is in D,

$$|f(z) - f(z_0)| < \frac{\epsilon}{3} + \frac{\epsilon}{3} + \frac{\epsilon}{3} = \epsilon;$$

that is, f is continuous at z_0.

We now use Morera's theorem to verify that f is analytic in D. Let z_0 be any point in D, and D' be a neighbourhood of z_0 which contains only points of D. Since f_n is analytic in D', if C is any simple, closed, piecewise smooth curve in D' (a simply-connected domain), then by the Cauchy-Goursat theorem,

$$\oint_C f_n(z)\, dz = 0, \quad n = 0, 1, \ldots .$$

Consequently,

$$\left| \oint_C f(z)\, dz \right| = \left| \oint_C f(z)\, dz - \oint_C \sum_{n=0}^{N} f_n(z)\, dz \right| = \left| \oint_C \left[f(z) - \sum_{n=0}^{N} f_n(z) \right] dz \right|.$$

But for given $\epsilon > 0$, there exists $\overline{N}$ such that for $N > \overline{N}$, and all z in D',

$$\left| f(z) - \sum_{n=0}^{N} f_n(z) \right| < \frac{\epsilon}{L}$$

where L is the length of C. Hence, for $N > \overline{N}$, we may use inequality 4.21 to write

$$\left| \oint_C f(z)\, dz \right| < \frac{\epsilon}{L}(L) = \epsilon.$$

Since ϵ can be made arbitrarily small, it follows that

$$\left| \oint_C f(z)\, dz \right| = 0.$$

When C is not simple, it may be decomposed into simple curves so that for any closed piecewise smooth curve in D',

$$\oint_C f(z)\, dz = 0.$$

Morera's theorem implies that f is analytic in D', and therefore at z_0. Hence f is analytic in D.

(ii) To verify equation 5.18 we show that for any point z_0 in D, given any $\epsilon > 0$, there exists an $\overline{N}$ such that for $N > \overline{N}$,

$$\left| f'(z_0) - \sum_{n=0}^{N} f_n'(z_0) \right| < \epsilon.$$

Since f and $\sum_{n=0}^{N} f_n(z)$ are both analytic in a neighbourhood D' of z_0 that is contained in D, Cauchy's generalized integral formula gives

$$f'(z_0) = \frac{1}{2\pi i} \oint_{C_r} \frac{f(z)}{(z - z_0)^2} \, dz \quad \text{and} \quad \sum_{n=0}^{N} f'_n(z_0) = \frac{1}{2\pi i} \oint_{C_r} \frac{\sum_{n=0}^{N} f_n(z)}{(z - z_0)^2} \, dz$$

where $C_r : |z - z_0| = r$ is a circle of radius r centred at z_0 that is contained in D'. Consequently,

$$f'(z_0) - \sum_{n=0}^{N} f'_n(z_0) = \frac{1}{2\pi i} \oint_{C_r} \frac{f(z) - \sum_{n=0}^{N} f_n(z)}{(z - z_0)^2} \, dz.$$

Since $\sum_{n=0}^{\infty} f_n(z)$ converges uniformly to f in D', there exists an $\overline{N}$ such that for all z in D' and $N > \overline{N}$,

$$\left| f(z) - \sum_{n=0}^{N} f_n(z) \right| < \epsilon r.$$

Thus, for $N > \overline{N}$,

$$\left| f'(z_0) - \sum_{n=0}^{N} f'_n(z_0) \right| = \frac{1}{2\pi} \left| \oint_{C_r} \frac{f(z) - \sum_{n=0}^{N} f_n(z)}{(z - z_0)^2} \, dz \right| < \frac{1}{2\pi} \left(\frac{\epsilon r}{r^2} \right) (2\pi r) = \epsilon.$$

(iii) To verify result 5.19 we show that given any $\epsilon > 0$, there exists an $\overline{N}$ such that for $N > \overline{N}$,

$$\left| \int_C f(z) \, dz - \sum_{n=0}^{N} \int_C f_n(z) \, dz \right| < \epsilon.$$

Since $\sum_{n=0}^{\infty} f_n(z)$ converges uniformly to f in D, there exists an $\overline{N}$ such that for all z in D and $N > \overline{N}$,

$$\left| f(z) - \sum_{n=0}^{N} f_n(z) \right| < \frac{\epsilon}{L}$$

where L is the length of C. Then, for $N > \overline{N}$,

$$\left| \int_C f(z) \, dz - \sum_{n=0}^{N} \int_C f_n(z) \, dz \right| = \left| \int_C \left[f(z) - \sum_{n=0}^{N} f_n(z) \right] dz \right| < \frac{\epsilon}{L} (L) = \epsilon.$$

(iv) Equation 5.17 is an immediate consequence of 5.19 when we note that if curve C is from a fixed point z_0 in D to an arbitrary point z in D, then $\int_C f(z) \, dz$ is an antiderivative of $f(z)$.

This completes the proof of Theorem 5.17. ∎

We now use the results of Theorem 5.17 to verify Theorem 5.15.

Proof of Theorem 5.15   Let z^* be any point in the circle of convergence $|z - z_0| < R$ of the power series $\sum_{n=0}^{\infty} a_n(z - z_0)^n$ (Figure 5.7). It is always possible to draw a circle $|z - z_0| = r < R$ centred at z_0 that contains z^*. Since the power series converges absolutely for all points on $|z - z_0| = r$, we can say that $\sum_{n=0}^{\infty} |a_n| r^n$ is a convergent series of constants.

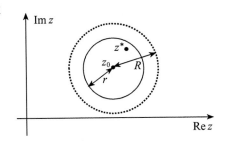

Figure 5.7

Since $|a_n(z - z_0)^n| < |a_n| r^n$ for every point z in $|z - z_0| < r$, the Weierstrass M-test implies that the power series converges uniformly in $|z - z_0| < r$. According to Theorem 5.17 the series is analytic in $|z - z_0| < r$, and in particular at z^*. In addition,

$$f'(z^*) = \sum_{n=0}^{\infty} n a_n (z^* - z_0)^{n-1}.$$

Since z^* is an arbitrary point in the circle of convergence $|z - z_0| < R$, this verifies 5.15. Properties 5.16 and 5.17 follow from equations 5.19 and 5.20.

EXERCISES 5.3

In Exercises 1–20 find the circle of convergence for the power series.

1. $\sum_{n=1}^{\infty} \frac{1}{n} z^n$

2. $\sum_{n=1}^{\infty} n^2 (z - 2)^n$

3. $\sum_{n=1}^{\infty} n^2 i^n (z + i)^n$

4. $\sum_{n=0}^{\infty} \frac{1}{(n + i)^3} z^n$

5. $\sum_{n=1}^{\infty} \frac{1}{n^n} (z + 3i)^n$

6. $\sum_{n=0}^{\infty} (-1)^n (n + 1)^2 (z + 4 + i)^n$

7. $\sum_{n=0}^{\infty} \left(\frac{n-1}{n+1} \right) (2z)^n$

8. $\sum_{n=0}^{\infty} 2^n \left(\frac{n-i}{n+2i} \right) (z - 4)^n$

9. $\sum_{n=0}^{\infty} (-i)^n (z + 4)^{2n}$

10. $\sum_{n=0}^{\infty} (1 + i)^n (z - 4)^{2n}$

11. $\sum_{n=0}^{\infty} \frac{(n!)^3}{(3n)!} (z + 1 - i)^n$

12. $\sum_{n=1}^{\infty} \left(1 + \frac{4}{n} \right)^{n^2} (z - 2 + i)^{2n}$

13. $\sum_{n=0}^{\infty} \frac{1}{(2 + i)^n} (z - i)^{2n+1}$

14. $\sum_{n=0}^{\infty} \frac{(-1)^n}{3^n} (z + 1)^{3n}$

15. $\sum_{n=1}^{\infty} \frac{2 \cdot 4 \cdot 6 \cdots (2n)}{3 \cdot 5 \cdot 7 \cdots (2n+1)} z^n$

16. $\sum_{n=1}^{\infty} \frac{[1 \cdot 3 \cdot 5 \cdots (2n+1)]^2}{2^{2n}(2n)!} (z + 1)^n$

17. $\sum_{n=1}^{\infty} \frac{1}{\sqrt{ni}}(z + 2i - 1)^n$

18. $\sum_{n=0}^{\infty} \frac{1}{\sqrt{n+i}}(z - 2)^n$

19. $\sum_{n=1}^{\infty} \frac{1}{\operatorname{Log} n} z^n$

20. $\sum_{n=1}^{\infty} \frac{1}{\operatorname{Log} ni} z^n$

In Exercises 21–33 find the sum of the power series.

21. $\sum_{n=0}^{\infty} \frac{1}{2^n} z^n$

22. $\sum_{n=2}^{\infty} i^n (z + 1)^n$

23. $\sum_{n=0}^{\infty} \frac{(-1)^{n+1} 3^n}{5^{n+2}}(z + i)^{2n}$

24. $\sum_{n=1}^{\infty} \left(\frac{1+i}{1-i}\right)^n (z - i)^{3n}$

25. $\sum_{n=1}^{\infty} n(z + 2i)^{n-1}$

26. $\sum_{n=2}^{\infty} n(n - 1)(z - 1 - i)^{n-2}$

27. $\sum_{n=1}^{\infty} (n + 1) z^{n-1}$

28. $\sum_{n=1}^{\infty} n^2 z^{n-1}$

29. $\sum_{n=2}^{\infty} \frac{1}{n} z^n$

30. $\sum_{n=1}^{\infty} \frac{n + 1}{n}(z - 2)^n$

31. $\sum_{n=2}^{\infty} n 3^n z^{2n}$

32. $\sum_{n=1}^{\infty} (n^2 + 2n) z^n$

33. $\sum_{n=1}^{\infty} n^{(-1)^n} z^n$

34. Find the circle of convergence for the hypergeometric series

$$1 + \frac{\alpha\beta}{\gamma} z + \frac{\alpha(\alpha+1)\beta(\beta+1)}{\gamma(\gamma+1)2!} z^2 + \frac{\alpha(\alpha+1)(\alpha+2)\beta(\beta+1)(\beta+2)}{\gamma(\gamma+1)(\gamma+2)3!} z^3 + \cdots,$$

where α, β, and γ are constant, and γ is not zero or a negative integer.

35. When m is a nonnegative integer, the Bessel function of the first kind of order m is defined by

$$J_m(z) = \sum_{n=0}^{\infty} \frac{(-1)^n}{2^{2n+m} n!(n + m)!} z^{2n+m}.$$

What is its circle of convergence?

In Exercises 36–41 use formula 5.14 to find the required power series of the function.

36. $f(z) = \dfrac{1}{1 + 3z}$ about $z_0 = 0$

37. $f(z) = \dfrac{z^2}{2 - z}$ about $z_0 = 0$

38. $f(z) = \dfrac{1}{1 + z}$ about $z_0 = 1$

39. $f(z) = \dfrac{1}{1 + z}$ about $z_0 = i$

40. $f(z) = \dfrac{z}{1 + z}$ about $z_0 = 1 + i$

41. $f(z) = \dfrac{z}{(1 - 3z)^2}$ about $z_0 = 0$

The results in Exercises 42–44 are useful in potential theory. Prove them for real x and θ.

42. $\displaystyle\sum_{n=1}^{\infty} x^n \cos n\theta = \frac{x\cos\theta - x^2}{1 + x^2 - 2x\cos\theta}, \quad |x| < 1$

43. $\displaystyle\sum_{n=1}^{\infty} x^n \sin n\theta = \frac{x\sin\theta}{1 + x^2 - 2x\cos\theta}, \quad |x| < 1$

44. $\displaystyle\sum_{n=1}^{\infty} \frac{x^n \cos n\theta}{n} = -\frac{1}{2}\ln\left(1 + x^2 - 2x\cos\theta\right), \quad |x| < 1$

In Exercises 45–46 find the circle of convergence by separating the series into two series each of which has an easily determined radius of convergence.

45. $1 - z + \dfrac{z^2}{4} - \dfrac{z^3}{3!} + \dfrac{z^4}{8} - \dfrac{z^5}{5!} + \dfrac{z^6}{16} + \cdots$ **46.** $\displaystyle\sum_{n=0}^{\infty} [3 - (-1)^n]^n\, z^n$

In Exercises 47–51 we discuss convergence of power series for points on the circle of convergence using the following result attributed to Weierstrass: Suppose the coefficients a_n of a power series $\sum_{n=0}^{\infty} a_n z^n$ are such that for $n \geq N$, N some integer,

$$\frac{a_{n+1}}{a_n} = 1 - \frac{\alpha}{n} + C_n,$$

where $\sum_{n=N}^{\infty} C_n$ converges absolutely, and α is a constant. Then the power series has radius of convergence equal to 1, and

   (i) converges absolutely for all $|z| = 1$ if $\operatorname{Re}\alpha > 1$;
   (ii) converges (but not absolutely) for all $|z| = 1$ if $0 < \operatorname{Re}\alpha \leq 1$, except for $z = 1$ where it diverges;
   (iii) diverges for all $|z| = 1$ if $\operatorname{Re}\alpha \leq 0$.

Use this result to examine convergence of the series on the circle of convergence in Exercises 47–49.

47. $\displaystyle\sum_{n=0}^{\infty} z^n$ **48.** $\displaystyle\sum_{n=1}^{\infty} \frac{z^n}{n}$

49. $\displaystyle\sum_{n=1}^{\infty} \frac{z^n}{n^2}$

To discuss convergence of power series $\sum_{n=0}^{\infty} a_n z^n$ on the circle of convergence $|z| = R$ when $R \neq 1$, we set $\zeta = z/R$, and apply the above result to the series $\sum_{n=0}^{\infty} a_n R^n \zeta^n$. Illustrate this by examining the series for convergence on the circle of convergence in Exercises 50–51.

50. $\displaystyle\sum_{n=0}^{\infty} \frac{z^n}{2^n}$ **51.** $\displaystyle\sum_{n=1}^{\infty} n^2 (3z)^{2n}$

§5.4   Taylor and Maclaurin Series

In Section 5.3 we established the fact that every convergent power series sums to an analytic function in its circle of convergence. The following theorem provides the converse result — analytic functions can be expanded in power series.

Theorem 5.18   **(Taylor Expansion Theorem)**   Let f be analytic in a domain D and z_0 be a point in D. Then f can be expanded in a power series

$$f(z) = f(z_0) + f'(z_0)(z - z_0) + \frac{f''(z_0)}{2!}(z - z_0)^2 + \cdots, \qquad (5.21)$$

valid in all circles $|z - z_0| < r$ containing only points of D.

Proof   When C_r is a circle centre z_0 and radius r which contains only points of D (Figure 5.8), Cauchy's integral formula states that for any point z inside C_r,

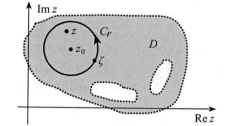

Figure 5.8

$$f(z) = \frac{1}{2\pi i} \oint_{C_r} \frac{f(\zeta)}{\zeta - z}\, d\zeta$$

$$= \frac{1}{2\pi i} \oint_{C_r} \frac{f(\zeta)}{(\zeta - z_0) - (z - z_0)}\, d\zeta$$

$$= \frac{1}{2\pi i} \oint_{C_r} \frac{f(\zeta)}{\zeta - z_0} \left(\frac{1}{1 - \dfrac{z - z_0}{\zeta - z_0}} \right) d\zeta$$

$$= \frac{1}{2\pi i} \oint_{C_r} \frac{f(\zeta)}{\zeta - z_0} \left[1 + \left(\frac{z - z_0}{\zeta - z_0} \right) + \left(\frac{z - z_0}{\zeta - z_0} \right)^2 + \cdots + \left(\frac{z - z_0}{\zeta - z_0} \right)^{n-1} + \frac{\left(\dfrac{z - z_0}{\zeta - z_0} \right)^n}{1 - \left(\dfrac{z - z_0}{\zeta - z_0} \right)} \right] d\zeta.$$

When Cauchy's generalized integral formula is applied to the first n terms, the result is

$$f(z) = f(z_0) + f'(z_0)(z - z_0) + \frac{f''(z_0)}{2!}(z - z_0)^2 + \cdots + \frac{f^{(n-1)}(z_0)}{(n-1)!}(z - z_0)^{n-1} + R_n,$$

where

$$R_n = \frac{(z - z_0)^n}{2\pi i} \oint_{C_r} \frac{f(\zeta)}{(\zeta - z)(\zeta - z_0)^n}\, d\zeta.$$

If M denotes the maximum value of $|f(z)|$ for ζ on C_r, and $|z - z_0| = \rho$, then for all ζ on C_r,

$$\left| \frac{f(\zeta)}{(\zeta - z)(\zeta - z_0)^n} \right| \leq \frac{M}{(r - \rho)r^n}.$$

By inequality 4.21 then,

$$|R_n| \leq \frac{\rho^n}{2\pi} \frac{M}{(r - \rho)r^n}(2\pi r) = \frac{rM}{r - \rho} \left(\frac{\rho}{r} \right)^n.$$

Since $\rho < r$, it follows that $R_n \to 0$ as $n \to \infty$, and we may write for any z inside C_r,

$$f(z) = f(z_0) + f'(z_0)(z - z_0) + \frac{f''(z_0)}{2!}(z - z_0)^2 + \cdots . \; \blacksquare$$

The expansion

$$f(z) = \sum_{n=0}^{\infty} \frac{f^{(n)}(z_0)}{n!}(z - z_0)^n \qquad (5.22)$$

is called the **Taylor series** of f about z_0. The special case in which $z_0 = 0$

$$f(z) = \sum_{n=0}^{\infty} \frac{f^{(n)}(0)}{n!} z^n \qquad (5.23)$$

is called the **Maclaurin series** of f.

Notice the simplicity of Theorem 5.18 compared to its real counterpart. The Taylor series

$$f(a) + f'(a)(x - a) + \frac{f''(a)}{2!}(x - a)^2 + \cdots$$

for a function $f(x)$ converges to $f(x)$ if all derivatives $f^{(n)}(a)$ exist and if Taylor remainders approach zero as $n \to \infty$. For complex analytic functions, there is no necessity to consider "remainders"; analyticity guarantees that remainders approach zero, and that the Taylor series of $f(z)$ converges to $f(z)$. The circle $|z - z_0| < r$ in Theorem 5.18 in which the Taylor series converges to the function is called the **circle of convergence** for the Taylor series.

An immediate consequence of this theorem is the following corollary.

Corollary 5.18.1　Every power series representation of (or, Taylor series for) an entire function has infinite radius of convergence.

Example 5.11　Find Maclaurin series for the following functions and show that their circles of convergence are the entire complex plane:

　　　　　　(a) e^z　　　　　　(b) $\sin z$　　　　　　(c) $\cos z$

Solution　(a) All derivatives of e^z are equal to 1. Hence, formula 5.23 gives

$$e^z = 1 + z + \frac{z^2}{2!} + \frac{z^3}{3!} + \cdots = \sum_{n=0}^{\infty} \frac{1}{n!} z^n.$$

Since e^z is an entire function, the Maclaurin series must converge to e^z for all z.
(b) Derivatives of $f(z) = \sin z$ at $z = 0$ are:

$$f(0) = 0, \quad f'(0) = \cos z_{|z=0} = 1, \quad f''(0) = -\sin z_{|z=0} = 0, \quad f'''(0) = -\cos z_{|z=0} = -1,$$

and the four values now repeat. Formula 5.23 gives the Maclaurin series as

$$\sin z = z - \frac{z^3}{3!} + \frac{z^5}{5!} - \frac{z^7}{7!} + \cdots = \sum_{n=0}^{\infty} \frac{(-1)^n}{(2n+1)!} z^{2n+1},$$

valid for all z. A similar calculation leads to the Maclaurin series for $\cos z$, also valid for all z,

$$\cos z = 1 - \frac{z^2}{2!} + \frac{z^4}{4!} - \frac{z^6}{6!} + \cdots = \sum_{n=0}^{\infty} \frac{(-1)^n}{(2n)!} z^{2n}.\bullet$$

Example 5.12   Find the Taylor series for $f(z) = \dfrac{z}{1 - 2z}$ valid in a circle with centre $z_0 = 1$.

Solution   Since the centre of the circle of convergence is $z_0 = 1$, the series will be in powers of $z - 1$ and we require the derivatives of $f(z)$ at $z = 1$. We calculate that

$$f(1) = -1; \quad f'(1) = \frac{(1 - 2z)(1) - z(-2)}{(1 - 2z)^2}\bigg|_{z=1} = \frac{1}{(1 - 2z)^2}\bigg|_{z=1} = 1,$$

$$f''(1) = \frac{2 \cdot 2}{(1 - 2z)^3}\bigg|_{z=1} = -4, \quad f'''(1) = \frac{2^2(2 \cdot 3)}{(1 - 2z)^4}\bigg|_{z=1} = 2^2(3!),$$

$$f''''(1) = \frac{2^3(3!)4}{(1 - 2z)^5}\bigg|_{z=1} = -2^3(4!).$$

The pattern unfolding is $f^{(n)}(1) = (-2)^{n-1}n!$, except for $f(0)$. Formula 5.22 gives the Taylor series for $f(z)$,

$$\frac{z}{1 - 2z} = -1 + \sum_{n=1}^{\infty} \frac{(-2)^{n-1}n!}{n!}(z - 1)^n = -1 + \sum_{n=1}^{\infty} (-2)^{n-1}(z - 1)^n.$$

Since the only singularity of $f(z)$ is $z = 1/2$, and the series is expanded about $z_0 = 1$, the circle of convergence must be $|z - 1| < 1/2.\bullet$

Using formulas 5.22 and 5.23 to find Taylor and Maclaurin series for functions is not as simple as the previous two examples seem to imply. For many functions, perhaps even most, it is difficult to find a formula for the nth derivative of the function. The following theorem provides an alternative to these formulas; it shows that there is only one power series representation of a function about a given point, its Taylor series about that point.

Theorem 5.19   If f has a power series expansion about a point z_0 with nonzero radius of convergence, it must be the Taylor series about z_0.

Proof   Suppose f has a power series expansion about a point z_0,

$$f(z) = a_0 + a_1(z - z_0) + a_2(z - z_0)^2 + \cdots$$

valid in some circle of convergence $|z - z_0| < R$ with nonzero radius of convergence R. Substitution of $z = z_0$ gives $f(z_0) = a_0$. Differentiation with respect to z (see Theorem 5.15) yields

$$f'(z) = a_1 + 2a_2(z - z_0) + 3a_3(z - z_0)^2 + \cdots ,$$

and when we set $z = z_0$, we obtain $f'(z_0) = a_1$. Another differentiation gives

$$f''(z) = 2a_2 + 3 \cdot 2a_3(z - z_0) + 4 \cdot 3a_4(z - z_0)^2 + \cdots ,$$

and for $z = z_0$,

$$f''(z_0) = 2a_2, \quad \text{or} \quad a_2 = \frac{f''(z_0)}{2!}.$$

Continued differentiation and substitution of $z = z_0$ gives $a_n = f^{(n)}(z_0)/n!$. ∎

What this theorem establishes is that there is only one power series expansion of a given function f about a given point z_0, its Taylor series about z_0. It follows that if we are required to find the Taylor series of f about z_0, we do not necessarily have to use formula 5.22. As we have already noted, it could be very difficult to determine a formula for the nth derivative of a function. Instead, if by any means whatsoever, we can find a power series of the form $\sum_{n=0}^{\infty} a_n(z - z_0)^n$ for f (with nonzero radius of convergence), then this series must be the Taylor series for f about z_0. In Section 5.3, we illustrated a few techniques for finding power series for functions. In light of the previous remarks, these same techniques can now be used to find Taylor series for functions. We discuss them in more detail in the remainder of this section.

Our discussions have established the following equivalence between analytic functions and convergent power series: When a function f is analytic in a domain D and z_0 is a point of D, then f can be expressed in a Taylor series about z_0 which converges to f in every circle $|z - z_0| < r$ interior to D. Conversely, every power series $\sum_{n=0}^{\infty} a_n(z - z_0)^n$ with nonzero radius of convergence R sums to an analytic function in $|z - z_0| < R$, (and is in fact the Taylor series of that function).

When a function f is analytic at a point z_0, it can be expanded in a Taylor series about that point, and the Taylor series converges to f in every circle inside of which the function is analytic. It follows therefore that this circle can be expanded until the radius is equal to the distance from the centre of the circle to the first point at which the function fails to be analytic. In other words, we can state the following theorem.

Theorem 5.20   The radius of convergence of the Taylor series for a function $f(z)$ about a point z_0 is the distance from z_0 to the nearest singularity of $f(z)$.

This is an excellent way to determine the circle of convergence for a Taylor series. We will use it many times. Let us now show, as promised, various techniques for finding Taylor and Maclaurin series for functions that do not use formulas 5.22 and 5.23.

Algebraic Manipulations

By manipulating known Maclaurin and Taylor series algebraically, it is possible to find series representations for other functions. Particularly important in this regard are the Maclaurin series for e^z, $\sin z$, $\cos z$, and $1/(1 - z)$:

$$e^z = 1 + z + \frac{z^2}{2!} + \frac{z^3}{3!} + \cdots = \sum_{n=0}^{\infty} \frac{1}{n!} z^n, \quad |z| < \infty, \tag{5.24a}$$

$$\sin z = z - \frac{z^3}{3!} + \frac{z^5}{5!} - \frac{z^7}{7!} + \cdots = \sum_{n=0}^{\infty} \frac{(-1)^n}{(2n+1)!} z^{2n+1}, \quad |z| < \infty, \tag{5.24b}$$

$$\cos z = 1 - \frac{z^2}{2!} + \frac{z^4}{4!} - \frac{z^6}{6!} + \cdots = \sum_{n=0}^{\infty} \frac{(-1)^n}{(2n)!} z^{2n}, \quad |z| < \infty, \tag{5.24c}$$

$$\frac{1}{1-z} = 1 + z + z^2 + z^3 + \cdots = \sum_{n=0}^{\infty} z^n, \quad |z| < 1. \tag{5.24d}$$

The following examples illustrate some such manipulations.

Example 5.13   Find the Maclaurin series for $f(z) = z/(1 - 4z)$.

Solution We can use formula 5.23 by calculating

$$f(0) \quad = 0,$$

$$f'(0) \quad = \frac{(1 - 4z) - z(-4)}{(1 - 4z)^2}\bigg|_{z=0} = \frac{1}{(1 - 4z)^2}\bigg|_{z=0} = 1,$$

$$f''(0) \quad = \frac{2(4)}{(1 - 4z)^3}\bigg|_{z=0} = 2(4),$$

$$f'''(0) = \frac{2(3)4^2}{(1 - 4z)^4}\bigg|_{z=0} = 3!\, 4^2.$$

The pattern emerging is $f^{(n)}(0) = n!\, 4^{n-1}$ for $n \geq 1$, and therefore

$$\frac{z}{1 - 4z} = \sum_{n=1}^{\infty} 4^{n-1} z^n.$$

Since the nearest singularity of the function to $z = 0$, the point of expansion, is $z = 1/4$, the interval of convergence is $|z| < 1/4$.

Alternatively, we can use formula 5.24d to write

$$\frac{z}{1 - 4z} = z\left[1 + (4z) + (4z)^2 + \cdots\right] = \sum_{n=1}^{\infty} 4^{n-1} z^n,$$

where $|4z| < 1$ or $|z| < 1/4$.●

In the remaining examples of this section, we will avoid using formulas 5.22 and 5.23 for finding Taylor and Maclaurin series. We will concentrate on using alternative procedures. The reader might want to attempt to calculate derivatives of the given function at the point of expansion in order to make comparisons.

Example 5.14   Find the Taylor series about $z_0 = 1$ for e^{2z}.

Solution   Since the point of expansion is $z_0 = 1$, we require a series in powers of $z - 1$. With this in mind, we write

$$e^{2z} = e^{2(z-1)+2} = e^2 e^{2(z-1)}.$$

We now replace z in Maclaurin series 5.24a for e^z with $2(z - 1)$,

$$e^{2z} = e^2 \sum_{n=0}^{\infty} \frac{1}{n!}[2(z-1)]^n = \sum_{n=0}^{\infty} \frac{e^2 2^n}{n!}(z-1)^n.$$

This is valid for $|2(z - 1)| < \infty$, and this implies that $|z| < \infty$.●

Example 5.15   Find the Taylor series for $1/(13 + 2z)$ about $z_0 = -5$.

Solution   Since the point of expansion is $z_0 = -5$, we require a series in powers of $z + 5$. This suggests that we write

$$\frac{1}{13+2z} = \frac{1}{3+2(z+5)} = \frac{1}{3\left[1+\frac{2}{3}(z+5)\right]} = \frac{1}{3}\left[\frac{1}{1+\frac{2}{3}(z+5)}\right].$$

We can now use series 5.24d,

$$\frac{1}{13+2z} = \frac{1}{3}\sum_{n=0}^{\infty}\left[-\frac{2}{3}(z+5)\right]^n, \qquad \left|-\frac{2}{3}(z+5)\right| < 1$$

$$= \sum_{n=0}^{\infty}\frac{(-2)^n}{3^{n+1}}(z+5)^n, \qquad |z+5| < \frac{3}{2}.\bullet$$

It is often expedient to add and/or subtract known power series. According to the following theorem, this can be done in the common circle of convergence of the series provided both are expanded about the same point.

Theorem 5.21   If $f(z) = \sum_{n=0}^{\infty} a_n(z-z_0)^n$ and $g(z) = \sum_{n=0}^{\infty} b_n(z-z_0)^n$ have positive radii of convergence, then

$$f(z) \pm g(z) = \sum_{n=0}^{\infty}(a_n \pm b_n)(z-z_0)^n, \qquad (5.25)$$

valid for every z that is common to the circles of convergence of the two series.

We use this result in the following example.

Example 5.16   Find the Maclaurin series for $f(z) = 5z/(z^2 - 3z - 4)$.

Solution   We decompose $f(z)$ into partial fractions,

$$f(z) = \frac{5z}{z^2 - 3z - 4} = \frac{4}{z-4} + \frac{1}{z+1},$$

and expand each of these terms in a Maclaurin series using equation 5.24d,

$$\frac{4}{z-4} = \frac{-1}{1-\frac{z}{4}} = -\left(1+\frac{z}{4}+\frac{z^2}{4^2}+\cdots\right), \qquad |z| < 4, \qquad \text{and}$$

$$\frac{1}{1+z} = 1 - z + z^2 - z^3 + \cdots, \qquad |z| < 1.$$

Addition of these series within their common circle of convergence gives the Maclaurin series for $f(z)$:

$$\frac{5z}{z^2 - 3z - 4} = \left(-1 - \frac{z}{4} - \frac{z^2}{4^2} - \frac{z^3}{4^3} - \cdots\right) + \left(1 - z + z^2 - z^3 + \cdots\right)$$

$$= \left(-1 - \frac{1}{4}\right)z + \left(1 - \frac{1}{4^2}\right)z^2 + \left(-1 - \frac{1}{4^3}\right)z^3 + \cdots$$

$$= \sum_{n=1}^{\infty}\left[(-1)^n - \frac{1}{4^n}\right]z^n, \qquad |z| < 1.\bullet$$

Differentiation and Integration of Known Series

Perhaps the most powerful technique for generating Taylor series is to differentiate or integrate known expansions according to Theorem 5.15.

Example 5.17   Find the Maclaurin series for $f(z) = \dfrac{z^5}{(2-z)^3}$.

Solution   We begin with the Maclaurin series for $1/(2-z)$,

$$\frac{1}{2-z} = \frac{1}{2\left(1-\dfrac{z}{2}\right)} = \frac{1}{2}\sum_{n=0}^{\infty}\left(\frac{z}{2}\right)^n = \sum_{n=0}^{\infty}\frac{1}{2^{n+1}}z^n,$$

valid for $|z/2| < 1$, from which $|z| < 2$. Since the radius of convergence of this series is positive, we may differentiate term-by-term (twice) to obtain the Maclaurin series

$$\frac{1}{(2-z)^2} = \sum_{n=0}^{\infty}\frac{n}{2^{n+1}}z^{n-1} \quad \text{and} \quad \frac{2}{(2-z)^3} = \sum_{n=0}^{\infty}\frac{n(n-1)}{2^{n+1}}z^{n-2}.$$

Multiplication by $z^5/2$ now gives

$$\frac{z^5}{(2-z)^3} = \sum_{n=0}^{\infty}\frac{n(n-1)}{2^{n+2}}z^{n+3} = \sum_{n=3}^{\infty}\frac{(n-3)(n-4)}{2^{n-1}}z^n = \sum_{n=5}^{\infty}\frac{(n-3)(n-4)}{2^{n-1}}z^n.$$

This is valid for $|z| < 2$.•

Example 5.18   Find the Taylor series for $\operatorname{Log} z$ about $z = 1$.

Solution Term-by-term integration of

$$\frac{1}{z} = \frac{1}{(z-1)+1} = \sum_{n=0}^{\infty}(-1)^n(z-1)^n, \quad |z-1| < 1,$$

gives

$$\operatorname{Log} z = \sum_{n=0}^{\infty}\frac{(-1)^n}{n+1}(z-1)^{n+1} + C, \quad |z-1| < 1.$$

Since $\operatorname{Log}(1) = 0$, we must choose $C = 0$, in which case

$$\operatorname{Log} z = \sum_{n=0}^{\infty}\frac{(-1)^n}{n+1}(z-1)^{n+1} = (z-1) - \frac{1}{2}(z-1)^2 + \frac{1}{3}(z-1)^3 + \cdots,$$

valid for $|z-1| < 1$.•

The Taylor series in Example 5.18 is a representation for other branches of the logarithm function as well. In particular, it represents any branch of $\log z$ for which $\log 1 = 0$ and which does not have a branch cut passing through the interior of the circle of convergence. In other words, we may write

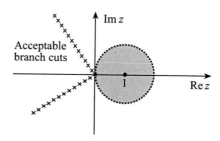

Figure 5.9

$$\log_\phi z = \sum_{n=1}^{\infty} \frac{(-1)^{n-1}}{n}(z-1)^n, \quad |z-1| < 1,$$

provided $-3\pi/2 \leq \phi \leq -\pi/2$ (Figure 5.9).

We associate a circle of convergence with each power series, the radius of which is given by limits 5.12, provided the limits exist or are equal to infinity. Each Taylor series has a circle of convergence inside of which it converges to the function. But Taylor series are power series and power series are Taylor series. Does this mean that the two circles are identical? For most functions, the answer is yes, but not for all functions. In particular, functions for which these circles may differ are branches of multiple-valued functions. In Example 5.13, the radius of convergence of the Maclaurin series for $z/(1-4z)$ was found to be $1/4$, the distance from $z = 0$ to $z = 1/4$, the only singularity of the function. The same radius would be found if we were to apply formula 5.12a to the series. In Example 5.18, the radius of convergence of the Taylor series is 1, the distance from the point of expansion $z = 1$ to the nearest singularity $z = 0$ of $\text{Log}\, z$. Once again, formula 5.12a would give $R = 1$. In the following example, the circle of convergence of the function as a power series is larger than the circle inside of which the series converges to the function.

Example 5.19 Find the Taylor series for the function $\text{Log}\, z$ about the point $z = -1 + i$. Show that the circle inside of which the series converges to the function has radius 1. Show also that the radius of convergence of the series as determined by formula 5.12a is $\sqrt{2}$. Explain this difference.

Solution To find the Taylor series about $z = -1 + i$, we begin with the function $1/z$ and write it in the equivalent forms

$$\frac{1}{z} = \frac{1}{-(1-i)+(z+1-i)} = \frac{-1}{1-i}\left(\frac{1}{1-\dfrac{z+1-i}{1-i}}\right).$$

We can now use equation 5.24d to write

$$\frac{1}{z} = \frac{-1}{1-i}\sum_{n=0}^{\infty}\left(\frac{z+1-i}{1-i}\right)^n = -\sum_{n=0}^{\infty}\frac{1}{(1-i)^{n+1}}(z+1-i)^n,$$

and this is valid for $\left|\dfrac{z+1-i}{1-i}\right| < 1 \implies |z+1-i| < \sqrt{2}.$

When we integrate this series term-by-term, we obtain

$$\text{Log}\, z = -\sum_{n=0}^{\infty}\frac{1}{(n+1)(1-i)^{n+1}}(z+1-i)^{n+1} + C.$$

To evaluate the constant of integration C, we substitute $z = -1+i$ into this equation,

$$\text{Log}\,(-1+i) = \ln\sqrt{2} + \frac{3\pi i}{4} = C.$$

Thus, the Taylor series for $\text{Log}\, z$ about $-1+i$ is

$$\text{Log}\, z = \frac{1}{2}\ln 2 + \frac{3\pi i}{4} - \sum_{n=0}^{\infty}\frac{1}{(n+1)(\sqrt{2}e^{-\pi i/4})^{n+1}}(z+1-i)^{n+1}$$

$$= \frac{1}{2}\ln 2 + \frac{3\pi i}{4} - \sum_{n=0}^{\infty} \frac{1}{(n+1)2^{(n+1)/2}e^{-(n+1)\pi i/4}}(z+1-i)^{n+1}$$

$$= \frac{1}{2}\ln 2 + \frac{3\pi i}{4} - \sum_{n=1}^{\infty} \frac{e^{n\pi i/4}}{n2^{n/2}}(z+1-i)^n.$$

Since the nearest singularity of $\text{Log}\, z$ to $-1+i$ is the point $z=-1$ on the branch cut of the function, it follows that this series converges to $\text{Log}\, z$ in the circle $|z+1-i|<1$. The above derivation shows that the radius of convergence of this series as a power series in $z+1-i$ is $\sqrt{2}$. This is also confirmed by formula 5.12a,

$$R = \lim_{n\to\infty} \left| \frac{e^{-n\pi i/4}(n+1)2^{(n+1)/2}}{n2^{n/2}e^{-(n+1)\pi i/4}} \right| = \sqrt{2}.$$

The reason for this difference is the fact that the logarithm function is multiple-valued. When we integrated the series for $1/z$ term-by-term, the result could represent many branches of the logarithm function, not just the principal branch. Once the principal branch of the logarithm function is chosen to evaluate the constant of integration, the series represents $\text{Log}\, z$ in the largest circle that does not include singularities of $\text{Log}\, z$. This is the circle $|z+1-i|<1$ in Figure 5.10. Had we chosen the branch $\log_{\pi/4} z$, then the nearest singularity of the function would be the origin, in which case the series would represent $\log_{\pi/4} z$ in the circle $|z+1-i|<\sqrt{2}$ (Figure 5.11).•

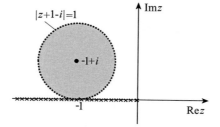

Figure 5.10   Figure 5.11

Multiplication of Power Series

In Example 5.16 we added the Maclaurin series for $4/(z-4)$ and $1/(1+z)$ to obtain the Maclaurin series for $5z/(z^2-3z-4)$. An alternative procedure might be to multiply the two series since

$$\frac{5z}{z^2-3z-4} = 5z\left(\frac{1}{z-4}\right)\left(\frac{1}{z+1}\right)$$

$$= \frac{5z}{-4}\left(1 + \frac{z}{4} + \frac{z^2}{4^2} + \frac{z^3}{4^3} + \cdots\right)\left(1 - z + z^2 - z^3 + \cdots\right).$$

The rules of algebra demand that we multiply every term of the first series by every term of the second. If we do this and group all products with like powers of z, we obtain

$$\frac{5z}{z^2-3z-4} = \frac{5z}{-4}\left[1 + \left(-1+\frac{1}{4}\right)z + \left(1 - \frac{1}{4} + \frac{1}{4^2}\right)z^2\right.$$
$$\left. + \left(-1 + \frac{1}{4} - \frac{1}{4^2} + \frac{1}{4^3}\right)z^3 + \cdots\right].$$

It is clear that the coefficient of z^n is a finite geometric series to which we can apply formula 5.7,

$$(-1)^n \left[1 - \frac{1}{4} + \frac{1}{4^2} - \cdots + \frac{(-1)^n}{4^n} \right] = (-1)^n \left[\frac{1 - \left(-\frac{1}{4}\right)^{n+1}}{1 + \frac{1}{4}} \right] = (-1)^n \frac{4}{5} \left[1 - \left(-\frac{1}{4}\right)^{n+1} \right].$$

Consequently,

$$\frac{5z}{z^2 - 3z - 4} = \frac{5z}{-4} \sum_{n=0}^{\infty} (-1)^n \frac{4}{5} \left[1 - \left(-\frac{1}{4}\right)^{n+1} \right] z^n = \sum_{n=0}^{\infty} (-1)^{n+1} \left[1 - \frac{(-1)^{n+1}}{4^{n+1}} \right] z^{n+1}$$

$$= \sum_{n=0}^{\infty} \left[(-1)^{n+1} - \frac{1}{4^{n+1}} \right] z^{n+1} = \sum_{n=1}^{\infty} \left[(-1)^n - \frac{1}{4^n} \right] z^n.$$

For this example, then, multiplication as well as addition of power series leads to the Maclaurin series. Clearly, addition of power series is much simpler for this example, but we have at least demonstrated that power series can be multiplied together. That this is generally possible is stated in the following theorem.

Theorem 5.22 If $f(z) = \sum_{n=0}^{\infty} a_n(z - z_0)^n$ and $g(z) = \sum_{n=0}^{\infty} b_n(z - z_0)^n$ have positive radii of convergence R_1 and R_2, respectively, then

$$f(z)g(z) = \sum_{n=0}^{\infty} d_n(z - z_0)^n, \qquad (5.26\text{a})$$

where

$$d_n = \sum_{i=0}^{n} a_i b_{n-i} = a_0 b_n + a_1 b_{n-1} + \cdots + a_{n-1} b_1 + a_n b_0, \qquad (5.26\text{b})$$

and the radius of convergence is greater than or equal to the smaller of R_1 and R_2.$\bullet$

Example 5.20 Find the Maclaurin series for $f(z) = \dfrac{1}{z-1} \text{Log}\,(1-z)$.

Solution   If we integrate the Maclaurin series

$$\frac{1}{1-z} = 1 + z + z^2 + z^3 + \cdots, \qquad |z| < 1,$$

we can write that

$$-\text{Log}\,(1-z) = \left(z + \frac{z^2}{2} + \frac{z^3}{3} + \frac{z^4}{4} + \cdots \right) + C.$$

By setting $z = 0$, we obtain $C = -\text{Log}\,1 = 0$, and therefore

$$\text{Log}\,(1-z) = -z - \frac{z^2}{2} - \frac{z^3}{3} - \frac{z^4}{4} - \cdots.$$

The radius of convergence of the series is 1. We now form the Maclaurin series for $f(z)$ and multiply it by this series for $\text{Log}\,z$,

$$\frac{1}{z-1}\text{Log}\,(1-z) = \frac{-1}{1-z}\text{Log}\,(1-z)$$

$$= \left(1 + z + z^2 + z^3 + \cdots\right)\left(z + \frac{z^2}{2} + \frac{z^3}{3} + \cdots\right)$$

$$= z + \left(1 + \frac{1}{2}\right)z^2 + \left(1 + \frac{1}{2} + \frac{1}{3}\right)z^3 + \cdots$$

$$= \sum_{n=1}^{\infty}\left(1 + \frac{1}{2} + \frac{1}{3} + \cdots + \frac{1}{n}\right)z^n.$$

Since both of the multiplied series have radius of convergence 1, so also does the Maclaurin series for $(z-1)^{-1}\text{Log}\,(1-z)$. In other words, its circle of convergence is $|z| < 1$.•

Power series can be divided one by another. Unfortunately, it seldom leads to a recognizable formula for the general term in the power series so that it is useful only when a few terms in the series are required. For example, the long division to the right demonstrates that the first three non-zero terms in the Maclaurin series for $\tan z$ are

$$\tan z = z + \frac{1}{3}z^3 + \frac{2}{15}z^5 + \cdots .$$

$$
\require{enclose}
\begin{array}{r}
z + \dfrac{z^3}{3} + \dfrac{2z^5}{15} + \cdots \\[2pt]
\hline
\end{array}
$$

$$1 - \frac{z^2}{2} + \frac{z^4}{24} - \cdots \enclose{longdiv}{\; z - \frac{z^3}{6} + \frac{z^5}{120} - \cdots}$$

$$\underline{z - \frac{z^3}{2} + \frac{z^5}{24} - \cdots}$$

$$\frac{z^3}{3} - \frac{z^5}{30} - \cdots$$

$$\underline{\frac{z^3}{3} - \frac{z^5}{6} - \cdots}$$

$$\frac{2z^5}{15} - \cdots$$

$$\underline{\frac{2z^5}{15} - \cdots}$$

Binomial Expansion

Most readers will be familiar with the binomial theorem by which expressions of the form $(a+b)^n$ are expanded into $n+1$ terms when n is a positive integer. A similar expansion can be developed in the event that n is a negative integer or a fraction. In these cases, however, the finite sum is replaced by an infinite series. We develop it here by considering the power series

$$1 + mz + \frac{m(m-1)}{2!}z^2 + \frac{m(m-1)(m-2)}{3!}z^3 + \cdots .$$

It is straightforward to use formula 5.12a to verify that the radius of convergence of this series is $R = 1$ so that its circle of convergence is $|z| < 1$. Suppose we denote the sum of the series by $f(z)$,

$$f(z) = 1 + \sum_{n=1}^{\infty}\frac{m(m-1)\cdots(m-n+1)}{n!}z^n.$$

The derivative is

$$f'(z) = \sum_{n=1}^{\infty}\frac{m(m-1)\cdots(m-n+1)}{(n-1)!}z^{n-1}.$$

If we add this series to z times itself, we obtain

$$f'(z) + zf'(z) = \sum_{n=1}^{\infty} \frac{m(m-1)\cdots(m-n+1)}{(n-1)!} z^{n-1} + \sum_{n=1}^{\infty} \frac{m(m-1)\cdots(m-n+1)}{(n-1)!} z^n.$$

We now change the variable of summation in the first sum,

$$f'(z) + zf'(z) = \sum_{n=0}^{\infty} \frac{m(m-1)\cdots(m-n)}{n!} z^n + \sum_{n=1}^{\infty} \frac{m(m-1)\cdots(m-n+1)}{(n-1)!} z^n.$$

When these summations are added over their common range, beginning at $n = 1$, and the $n = 0$ term in the first summation is written out separately, the result is

$$f'(z) + zf'(z) = m + \sum_{n=1}^{\infty} \frac{m(m-1)\cdots(m-n+1)}{(n-1)!} \left(\frac{m-n}{n} + 1 \right) z^n$$

$$= m \left[1 + \sum_{n=1}^{\infty} \frac{m(m-1)\cdots(m-n+1)}{n!} z^n \right]$$

$$= mf(z).$$

In other words, the sum of the series $f(z)$ satisfies this complex differential equation. In addition, we can say that $f(0) = 1$. But if we substitute $(1 + z)^m$ into the left side of the differential equation, we get

$$m(1+z)^{m-1} + mz(1+z)^{m-1} = m(1+z)(1+z)^{m-1} = m(1+z)^m.$$

Since the value of $(1 + z)^m$ at $z = 0$ is 1, we have shown that $(1 + z)^m$ satisfies the differential equation as well as the condition $f(0) = 1$. In other words, this function must be the sum of the series; that is,

$$(1+z)^m = 1 + mz + \frac{m(m-1)}{2!} z^2 + \frac{m(m-1)(m-2)}{3!} z^3 + \cdots, \qquad (5.27)$$

valid for $|z| < 1$. This is called the **binomial expansion** of the function $(1 + z)^m$; it is the Maclaurin series of the function.

Example 5.21 Use the binomial expansion to find the Maclaurin series of the function $\dfrac{z^3}{(2-z)^3}$ in Example 5.17.

Solution Using equation 5.27,

$$\frac{z^5}{(2-z)^3} = \frac{z^5}{2^3 \left(1 - \frac{z}{2} \right)} = \frac{z^5}{2^3} \left(1 - \frac{z}{2} \right)^{-3}$$

$$= \frac{z^5}{2^3} \left[1 + (-3)\left(-\frac{z}{2} \right) + \frac{(-3)(-4)}{2!} \left(-\frac{z}{2} \right)^2 + \frac{(-3)(-4)(-5)}{3!} \left(-\frac{z}{2} \right)^3 + \cdots \right]$$

$$= \frac{z^5}{2^3} \left[1 + \frac{3z}{2} + \frac{3 \cdot 4}{2^2 \, 2!} z^2 + \frac{3 \cdot 4 \cdot 5}{2^3 \, 3!} z^3 + \frac{3 \cdot 4 \cdot 5 \cdot 6}{2^4 \, 4!} z^4 + \cdots \right]$$

$$= \frac{z^5}{2^3} \left[1 + \frac{3z}{2} + \frac{2 \cdot 3 \cdot 4}{2^3 \, 2!} z^2 + \frac{2 \cdot 3 \cdot 4 \cdot 5}{2^4 \, 3!} z^3 + \frac{2 \cdot 3 \cdot 4 \cdot 5 \cdot 6}{2^5 \, 4!} z^4 + \cdots \right]$$

$$= \frac{z^5}{2^3} \left[1 + \frac{3z}{2} + \frac{3 \cdot 4}{2^3} z^2 + \frac{4 \cdot 5}{2^4} z^3 + \frac{5 \cdot 6}{2^5} z^4 + \cdots \right]$$

$$= \frac{z^5}{2^3} \sum_{n=0}^{\infty} \frac{(n+1)(n+2)}{2^{n+1}} z^n = \sum_{n=0}^{\infty} \frac{(n+1)(n+2)}{2^{n+4}} z^{n+5}$$

$$= \sum_{n=5}^{\infty} \frac{(n-4)(n-3)}{2^{n-1}} z^n.$$

It converges for $|-z/2| < 1$ or $|z| < 2.\bullet$

Example 5.22 Find the Maclaurin series for $\operatorname{Sin}^{-1} z$.

Solution   By binomial expansion 5.27, we have

$$\frac{1}{\sqrt{1-z^2}} = 1 + \left(-\frac{1}{2}\right)(-z^2) + \frac{\left(-\frac{1}{2}\right)\left(-\frac{3}{2}\right)}{2!}(-z^2)^2 + \frac{\left(-\frac{1}{2}\right)\left(-\frac{3}{2}\right)\left(-\frac{5}{2}\right)}{3!}(-z^2)^3 + \cdots$$

$$= 1 + \frac{1}{2}z^2 + \frac{3}{2^2 2!}z^4 + \frac{3 \cdot 5}{2^3 3!}z^6 + \frac{3 \cdot 5 \cdot 7}{2^4 4!}z^8 + \cdots, \qquad |z| < 1.$$

Integration gives

$$\operatorname{Sin}^{-1} z = \left(z + \frac{1}{2 \cdot 3}z^3 + \frac{3}{2^2 2! \, 5}z^5 + \frac{3 \cdot 5}{2^3 3! \, 7}z^7 + \frac{3 \cdot 5 \cdot 7}{2^4 4! \, 9}z^9 + \cdots \right) + C.$$

Evaluation of both sides of this equation at $z = 0$ gives $C = 0$. Thus,

$$\operatorname{Sin}^{-1} z = z + \sum_{n=1}^{\infty} \frac{1 \cdot 3 \cdot 5 \cdots \cdot (2n-1)}{2^n n! \, (2n+1)} z^{2n+1}$$

$$= z + \sum_{n=1}^{\infty} \frac{1 \cdot 2 \cdot 3 \cdot 4 \cdot 5 \cdots \cdot (2n-2)(2n-1)(2n)}{2 \cdot 4 \cdots \cdot (2n) 2^n n! \, (2n+1)} z^{2n+1}$$

$$= z + \sum_{n=1}^{\infty} \frac{(2n)!}{(2n+1)2^{2n}(n!)^2} z^{2n+1} = \sum_{n=0}^{\infty} \frac{(2n)!}{(2n+1)2^{2n}(n!)^2} z^{2n+1}.$$

According to Exercises 31 and 32 in Section 3.7, branch points of $\operatorname{Sin}^{-1} z$ are $z = \pm 1$ and branch cuts are the real axis to the right of $z = 1$ and the real axis to the left of $z = -1$. This means that the closest singularities of the function to $z = 0$ are $z = \pm 1$. Theorem 5.20 indicates that the circle of convergence of the series as the Maclaurin series for $\operatorname{Sin}^{-1} z$ is $|z| < 1$. As a power series, the above discussion indicates that the circle of convergence is also $|z| < 1.\bullet$

In Section 3.1, we mentioned the importance of zeros of analytic functions. We used the next theorem extensively in arriving at the orders of the zeros of many functions. In Section 3.1, we proved the sufficiency of the theorem. We are now prepared to prove the necessity.

Theorem 5.23   A function f has a zero of order m at z_0 if and only if it can be written in the form

$$f(z) = (z - z_0)^m g(z), \qquad (5.28)$$

valid in some circle $|z - z_0| < R$, where g is analytic at z_0 and $g(z_0) \neq 0$.

Proof of the necessity   If f has a zero of order m at z_0, it is analytic in a neighbourhood $|z - z_0| < R$ of z_0. In this neighbourhood, it has a convergent Taylor series,

$$f(z) = f(z_0) + f'(z_0)(z - z_0) + \frac{f''(z_0)}{2}(z - z_0)^2 + \cdots .$$

Since $f(z_0) = f'(z_0) = \cdots = f^{(m-1)}(z_0) = 0$, and $f^{(m)}(z_0) \neq 0$, the Taylor series reduces to

$$\begin{aligned} f(z) &= \frac{f^{(m)}(z_0)}{m!}(z - z_0)^m + \frac{f^{(m+1)}(z_0)}{(m+1)!}(z - z_0)^{m+1} + \cdots \\ &= (z - z_0)^m \left[\frac{f^{(m)}(z_0)}{m!} + \frac{f^{(m+1)}(z_0)}{(m+1)!}(z - z_0) + \cdots \right] . \end{aligned}$$

If we define

$$g(z) = \frac{f^{(m)}(z_0)}{m!} + \frac{f^{(m+1)}(z_0)}{(m+1)!}(z - z_0) + \cdots ,$$

then $f(z) = (z - z_0)^m g(z)$ where clearly $g(z_0) = f^{(m)}(z_0)/m! \neq 0$. Further, the series for g converges wherever the series for f converges, and hence g is analytic at z_0.

The sufficiency was proved in Theorem 3.1. ∎

An important consequence of Theorem 5.23 is the following corollary.

Corollary The zeros of a nonconstant analytic function are isolated; that is, every zero has a neighbourhood inside of which it is the only zero.

Proof If z_0 is a zero of f of order m, then $f(z)$ can be written in form 5.28 where g is analytic at z_0 and $g(z_0) \neq 0$. Since g is therefore continuous at z_0, it follows that there exists a neighbourhood of z_0 in which $g(z) \neq 0$. In this neighbourhood, $f(z) \neq 0$ except at $z = z_0$. ∎

We can also use Theorem 5.23 to establish L'Hôpital's rule for complex functions.

Theorem 5.24 Let f and g be functions which are analytic in a domain D but not identically equal to zero. If $f(z_0) = g(z_0) = 0$ at a point z_0 in D, then

$$\lim_{z \to z_0} \frac{f(z)}{g(z)} = \lim_{z \to z_0} \frac{f'(z)}{g'(z)}, \tag{5.29}$$

provided the latter limit exists.

Proof If the orders of the zeros of f and g at z_0 are m and n respectively, then in some neighbourhood of z_0 we may write

$$f(z) = (z - z_0)^m F(z) \quad \text{and} \quad g(z) = (z - z_0)^n G(z),$$

where $F(z_0)G(z_0) \neq 0$. With these,

$$\frac{f(z)}{g(z)} = (z - z_0)^{m-n} \frac{F(z)}{G(z)},$$

and

$$\frac{f'(z)}{g'(z)} = \frac{m(z - z_0)^{m-1}F(z) + (z - z_0)^m F'(z)}{n(z - z_0)^{n-1}G(z) + (z - z_0)^n G'(z)} = (z - z_0)^{m-n} \frac{mF(z) + (z - z_0)F'(z)}{nG(z) + (z - z_0)G'(z)}.$$

When $m = n$, the limit of each of these expressions for $f(z)/g(z)$ and $f'(z)/g'(z)$ as $z \to z_0$ is $F(z_0)/G(z_0)$. When $m > n$, both expressions have limit zero, and when $m < n$, neither limit exists. ∎

EXERCISES 5.4

In Exercises 1–26 find the Taylor series for the function about the given point. In each case determine values of z for which the series converges to the function.

1. $\dfrac{z}{1 + z^2}$ about $z_0 = 0$

2. $\dfrac{3}{1 + z}$ about $z_0 = 1$

3. $\dfrac{z}{(1 - z)^2}$ about $z_0 = 0$

4. e^z about $z_0 = 1 + i$

5. $\sin z$ about $z_0 = i$

6. $\cos z$ about $z_0 = 2 - i$

7. $\sinh z$ about $z_0 = 0$

8. $\cosh z$ about $z_0 = 0$

9. e^{2z} about $z_0 = 1$

10. $\sin^2 z$ about $z_0 = 0$

11. $(z + 1) \cosh 3z$ about $z_0 = 0$

12. $\sin z$ about $z_0 = \pi/4$

13. $\cosh z$ about $z_0 = i$

14. $\dfrac{\cos 2z}{z^2 + 1}$ about $z_0 = 0$

15. $\cos(z^2 - 1)$ about $z_0 = 0$

16. $\sin(3z^2 + 2)$ about $z_0 = 0$

17. $\dfrac{1}{1 + 2z}$ about $z_0 = 3$

18. $\dfrac{1}{1 + z}$ about $z_0 = i$

19. $\dfrac{z}{(1 - 3z)^2}$ about $z_0 = 0$

20. $\dfrac{z}{1 + z}$ about $z_0 = 1 + i$

21. $\sinh 4z$ about $z_0 = -i$

22. $\text{Log } z$ about $z_0 = i$

23. $\text{Tan}^{-1} z$ about $z_0 = 0$

24. $\dfrac{z^2}{3 - 4z}$ about $z_0 = 2$

25. $\sqrt[3]{1 + z^3}$ about $z_0 = 0$

26. $\text{Sin}^{-1} z$ about $z_0 = 0$

In Exercises 27–32 identify all zeros and their orders for the function.

27. $\dfrac{z^2 + 1}{z^2(z + 1)}$

28. $z^3 e^{z+2}$

29. $\dfrac{\sin 3z}{z^5}$

30. $\dfrac{\sinh^2 z}{z + 5i}$

31. $\sqrt{z}$

32. $\text{Log}(z - 1)$

33. Use series to prove Euler's identity 1.29.

34. Use Maclaurin series for $\sin z$ and $\sinh z$ to prove that $|\sin z| \le \sinh |z|$.

In Exercises 35–37 find the Taylor series for the function about the given point. In each case determine values of z for which the series converges to the function.

35. $\sin^3 z$ about $z_0 = 0$

36. $e^z \sin z$ about $z_0 = 0$

37. $\sqrt{z + i}$ about $z_0 = 0$

38. $\sqrt{z + i}$ about $z_0 = -1 + i$

39. Prove that when f has a zero of order m at z_0, and g is analytic at z_0, but $g(z_0) \ne 0$, then fg has a zero of order m at z_0.

40. Find all power series $\sum_{n=0}^{\infty} a_n z^n$ which converge at $z = 4 + 3i$ and diverge at $z = 2 - i$.

41. Find the Taylor series for the function $\log_{\pi/4} z$ about the point $z_0 = i$. Show that the circle inside of which the series converges to the function has radius $1/\sqrt{2}$. Show also that the radius of convergence of the series as determined by formula 5.12a is 1. Explain this difference.

42. Find the Taylor series about the point $z_0 = -1+i$ for the function $(z+i)^{1/2}$ using the branch of the function corresponding to $\log_{\pi/4} z$. Show that the circle inside of which the series converges to the function has radius $3/\sqrt{2}$. Show also that the radius of convergence of the series as determined by formula 5.12a is $\sqrt{5}$. Explain this difference.

43. A function $f(z)$ has Taylor series $\sum_{n=0}^{\infty} a_n(z - z_0)^n$ about z_0, and the circle inside of which the series converges to the function has radius R. Must there exist a point on the circle $|z - z_0| = R$ at which the series diverges?

44. Show that every polynomial of degree n with complex coefficients has exactly n zeros (counting multiplicities). (See Exercise 1 in Section 4.7.)

45. Prove that

$$\sum_{n=0}^{\infty} \frac{\cos n\theta}{n!} = e^{\cos \theta} \cos(\sin \theta) \qquad \text{and} \qquad \sum_{n=0}^{\infty} \frac{\sin n\theta}{n!} = e^{\cos \theta} \sin(\sin \theta).$$

46. (a) Consider the series

$$\sum_{n=0}^{\infty} a_n z^n = 1 + z + 2z^2 + 3z^3 + 5z^4 + 8z^5 + \cdots,$$

where the coefficients a_n are the Fibonacci numbers defined by $a_0 = 1$, $a_1 = 1$, $a_{n+1} = a_n + a_{n-1}$, for $n \geq 2$. Show that the sum of the series is $1/(1 - z - z^2)$.
(b) What is the largest circle inside of which the series converges to this function?
(c) Find an explicit formula for the coefficients a_n.

47. Where is the function $f(z) = \sin(1/z)$ analytic? What are its zeros? Are they isolated?

48. Prove that if f is analytic at z_0, then there exists a neighbourhood of z_0 inside of which f takes on the value $f(z_0)$ only at z_0.

49. If f is analytic inside and on the circle $C : |z - z_0| \leq R$, then its Taylor series $\sum_{n=0}^{\infty} a_n(z - z_0)^n$ is valid inside and on C. Show that

$$\oint_C |f(z)|^2 \, |dz| = 2\pi R \sum_{n=0}^{\infty} |a_n|^2 R^{2n}.$$

50. Verify the following result due to Schwarz: Suppose f is analytic inside and on $C : |z - z_0| \leq R$, and $f(z_0) = 0$. If $|f(z)| \leq M$ on C, then $|f(z)| \leq (M/R)|z - z_0|$ for $|z| < R$. Furthermore, if $|f(z)| \leq (M/R)|z - z_0|$ for some z inside C, then $f(z) = (M/R)e^{\lambda i}(z - z_0)$, where λ is some real constant.

§5.5   Laurent Series

In applications of real variable calculus we are most often concerned with a function near points at which the function is well-behaved, in particular, where it has derivatives. When it has derivatives of all orders, and Taylor remainders approach zero, the function can be represented as its Taylor series. Likewise, a complex function can be represented by its Taylor series around points at which it is analytic. But in many applications of complex functions, it is the function's singularities that prove useful. Laurent series of this section represent complex functions near isolated singularities.

Theorem 5.25   **(Laurent Expansion Theorem)**   Let f be analytic in an annulus $D : r < |z - z_0| < R$. Then $f(z)$ can be expressed in the form

$$f(z) = \sum_{n=-\infty}^{\infty} a_n (z - z_0)^n \qquad (5.30\text{a})$$

which converges and represents $f(z)$ in D. Coefficients can be calculated with the formula

$$a_n = \frac{1}{2\pi i} \oint_C \frac{f(\zeta)}{(\zeta - z_0)^{n+1}} \, d\zeta, \qquad (5.30\text{b})$$

where C is any simple, closed, piecewise smooth curve in D which contains z_0 in its interior.

Proof   Let z be any point in D.
If $\rho = |z - z_0|$, construct two circles
$C_1 : |\zeta - z_0| = R'$ and $C_2 : |\zeta - z_0| = r'$
where $r < r' < \rho < R' < R$, and join C_1
and C_2 by nonintersecting, piecewise
smooth curves Γ_1 and Γ_2 which do
not pass through z (Figure 5.12).
Since f is analytic inside and on the
loop L_1, and z is interior to L_1,
Cauchy's integral formula gives

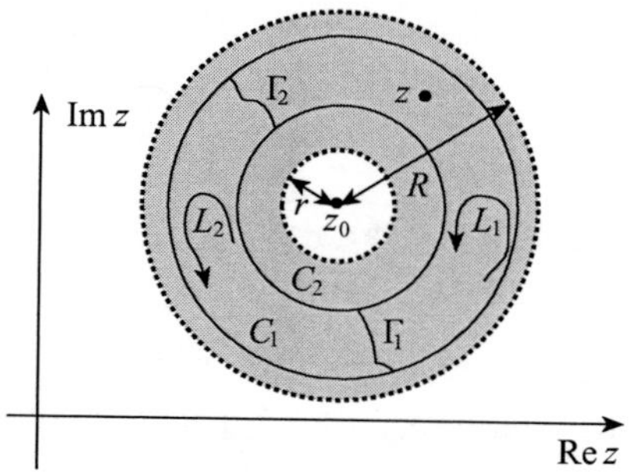

Figure 5.12

$$f(z) = \frac{1}{2\pi i} \oint_{L_1} \frac{f(\zeta)}{\zeta - z} \, d\zeta.$$

Because loop L_2 contains only points of D in its interior, the Cauchy-Goursat theorem requires

$$0 = \frac{1}{2\pi i} \oint_{L_2} \frac{f(\zeta)}{\zeta - z} \, d\zeta.$$

Addition of these equations gives

$$f(z) = \frac{1}{2\pi i} \oint_{L_1} \frac{f(\zeta)}{\zeta - z} \, d\zeta + \frac{1}{2\pi i} \oint_{L_2} \frac{f(\zeta)}{\zeta - z} \, d\zeta.$$

Traversing L_1 and L_2 results in integrations along Γ_1 and Γ_2 twice each, once in one direction and once in the opposite direction. What remains is integrations around C_1 in the counterclockwise direction, and C_2 in the clockwise direction,

$$f(z) = \frac{1}{2\pi i} \oint_{C_1} \frac{f(\zeta)}{\zeta - z} \, d\zeta - \frac{1}{2\pi i} \oint_{C_2} \frac{f(\zeta)}{\zeta - z} \, d\zeta.$$

As in Theorem 5.18, we may write for the integral around C_1,

$$\frac{1}{2\pi i} \oint_{C_1} \frac{f(\zeta)}{\zeta - z} \, d\zeta = \frac{1}{2\pi i} \oint_{C_1} \frac{f(\zeta)}{\zeta - z_0} \left[1 + \left(\frac{z - z_0}{\zeta - z_0} \right) + \left(\frac{z - z_0}{\zeta - z_0} \right)^2 + \cdots \right.$$

$$\left. + \left(\frac{z - z_0}{\zeta - z_0} \right)^{n-1} + \frac{\left(\dfrac{z - z_0}{\zeta - z_0} \right)^n}{1 - \left(\dfrac{z - z_0}{\zeta - z_0} \right)} \right] d\zeta$$

$$= \frac{1}{2\pi i} \oint_{C_1} \frac{f(\zeta)}{\zeta - z_0} \, d\zeta + \frac{1}{2\pi i} (z - z_0) \oint_{C_1} \frac{f(\zeta)}{(\zeta - z_0)^2} \, d\zeta + \cdots$$

$$+ \frac{(z - z_0)^{n-1}}{2\pi i} \oint_{C_1} \frac{f(\zeta)}{(\zeta - z_0)^n} \, d\zeta + R_n,$$

where

$$R_n = \frac{(z - z_0)^n}{2\pi i} \oint_{C_1} \frac{f(\zeta)}{(\zeta - z)(\zeta - z_0)^n} \, d\zeta.$$

If M is the maximum value of $|f(\zeta)|$ for ζ on C_1, then for all ζ on C_1,

$$\left| \frac{f(\zeta)}{(\zeta - z)(\zeta - z_0)^n} \right| \leq \frac{M}{(R' - \rho)(R')^n}.$$

Thus,

$$|R_n| \leq \frac{\rho^n}{2\pi} \frac{M}{(R' - \rho)(R')^n} (2\pi R') = \frac{R'M}{R' - \rho} \left(\frac{\rho}{R'} \right)^n.$$

Since $\rho < R'$, it follows that $R_n \to 0$ as $n \to \infty$, and we may write

$$\frac{1}{2\pi i} \oint_{C_1} \frac{f(\zeta)}{\zeta - z} \, dz = a_0 + a_1(z - z_0) + a_2(z - z_0)^2 + \cdots,$$

where

$$a_n = \frac{1}{2\pi i} \oint_{C_1} \frac{f(\zeta)}{(\zeta - z_0)^{n+1}} \, d\zeta.$$

For the integral around C_2,

$$\frac{-1}{2\pi i} \oint_{C_2} \frac{f(\zeta)}{\zeta - z} \, d\zeta = \frac{-1}{2\pi i} \oint_{C_2} \frac{f(\zeta)}{(\zeta - z_0) + (z_0 - z)} \, d\zeta = \frac{-1}{2\pi i} \oint_{C_2} \frac{f(\zeta)}{(z_0 - z) \left(1 - \dfrac{\zeta - z_0}{z - z_0} \right)} \, d\zeta$$

$$= \frac{-1}{2\pi i} \oint_{C_2} \frac{f(\zeta)}{z_0 - z} \left[1 + \left(\frac{\zeta - z_0}{z - z_0} \right) + \left(\frac{\zeta - z_0}{z - z_0} \right)^2 + \cdots \right.$$

$$\left. + \left(\frac{\zeta - z_0}{z - z_0} \right)^{n-1} + \frac{\left(\dfrac{\zeta - z_0}{z - z_0} \right)^n}{1 - \left(\dfrac{\zeta - z_0}{z - z_0} \right)} \right] d\zeta$$

$$= \frac{1}{2\pi i(z-z_0)} \oint_{C_2} f(\zeta)\,d\zeta + \frac{1}{2\pi i(z-z_0)^2} \oint_{C_2} f(\zeta)(\zeta-z_0)\,d\zeta + \cdots$$

$$+ \frac{1}{2\pi i(z-z_0)^n} \oint_{C_2} f(\zeta)(\zeta-z_0)^{n-1}\,d\zeta + S_n,$$

where

$$S_n = \frac{1}{2\pi i(z-z_0)^n} \oint_{C_2} \frac{f(\zeta)(\zeta-z_0)^n}{z-\zeta}\,d\zeta.$$

If m is the maximum value of $|f(\zeta)|$ for ζ on C_2, then for all ζ on C_2,

$$\left| \frac{f(\zeta)(\zeta-z_0)^n}{z-\zeta} \right| \le \frac{m(r')^n}{\rho-r'}.$$

Thus,

$$|S_n| \le \frac{1}{2\pi\rho^n} \frac{m(r')^n}{\rho-r'} (2\pi r') = \frac{r'm}{\rho-r'} \left(\frac{r'}{\rho} \right)^n.$$

Since $r' < \rho$, it follows that $S_n \to 0$ as $n \to \infty$. Consequently,

$$\frac{-1}{2\pi i} \oint_{C_2} \frac{f(\zeta)}{\zeta-z}\,d\zeta = \frac{a_{-1}}{z-z_0} + \frac{a_{-2}}{(z-z_0)^2} + \cdots + \frac{a_{-n}}{(z-z_0)^n} + \cdots$$

where

$$a_{-n} = \frac{1}{2\pi i} \oint_{C_2} f(\zeta)(\zeta-z_0)^{n-1}\,d\zeta.$$

We have shown that

$$f(z) = \sum_{n=0}^{\infty} a_n(z-z_0)^n + \sum_{n=-1}^{-\infty} a_n(z-z_0)^n$$

where

$$a_n = \frac{1}{2\pi i} \oint_{C_1} \frac{f(\zeta)}{(\zeta-z_0)^{n+1}}\,d\zeta, \quad n \ge 0,$$

$$a_n = \frac{1}{2\pi i} \oint_{C_2} \frac{f(\zeta)}{(\zeta-z_0)^{n+1}}\,d\zeta, \quad n < 0.$$

Suppose now that C is any simple, closed, piecewise smooth curve in D which contains z_0 in its interior. It is always possible to construct C_1 and C_2 as above such that C is contained in the interior of C_1, and C_2 is contained in the interior of C. Since $f(z)/(\zeta-z_0)^{n+1}$ is analytic in D, it follows by Theorem 4.8 that

$$\oint_{C_1} \frac{f(\zeta)}{(\zeta-z_0)^{n+1}}\,d\zeta = \oint_{C} \frac{f(\zeta)}{(\zeta-z_0)^{n+1}}\,d\zeta, \quad n \ge 0,$$

$$\oint_{C_2} \frac{f(\zeta)}{(\zeta-z_0)^{n+1}}\,d\zeta = \oint_{C} \frac{f(\zeta)}{(\zeta-z_0)^{n+1}}\,d\zeta, \quad n < 0,$$

and the proof is complete. ∎

Series 5.30 is called the **Laurent expansion** of f in the annulus D. In the particular case that f is analytic for $|z-z_0| \le r$ as well as in D, we find that:

for $n < 0$, $f(\zeta)/(\zeta - z_0)^{n+1}$ is analytic in $|z - z_0| < R$, and

$$\oint_C \frac{f(\zeta)}{(\zeta - z_0)^{n+1}} \, d\zeta = 0;$$

and for $n \geq 0$, the generalized Cauchy integral formula gives

$$a_n = \frac{1}{2\pi i} \oint_C \frac{f(\zeta)}{(\zeta - z_0)^{n+1}} \, d\zeta = \frac{f^{(n)}(z_0)}{n!}.$$

Thus, in this case, the Laurent series reduces to the Taylor series as expected.

Just as the power series of a function is unique, so also is the Laurent expansion.

Corollary   If f has a Laurent series valid in an annulus $r < |z - z_0| < R$, then it has only one such expansion.

Because of this corollary, we seldom use formula 5.30b to calculate the coefficients a_n in the Laurent expansion. Often we use properties of geometric series and/or Taylor series from Section 5.4. This is illustrated in the following examples.

Example 5.23   Find Laurent series for $f(z) = 1/(z^2 - 3z + 2)$ valid in the domains: (a) $|z| < 1$ (b) $1 < |z| < 2$ (c) $|z| > 2$.

Solution   The singularities of f are $z = 1$ and $z = 2$. Figure 5.13 makes it clear that f is analytic in each of the domains $|z| < 1$, $1 < |z| < 2$, and $|z| > 2$.
(a) Since f is analytic for $|z| < 1$, the Laurent series will be the Maclaurin series. The partial fraction decomposition of $f(z)$ is

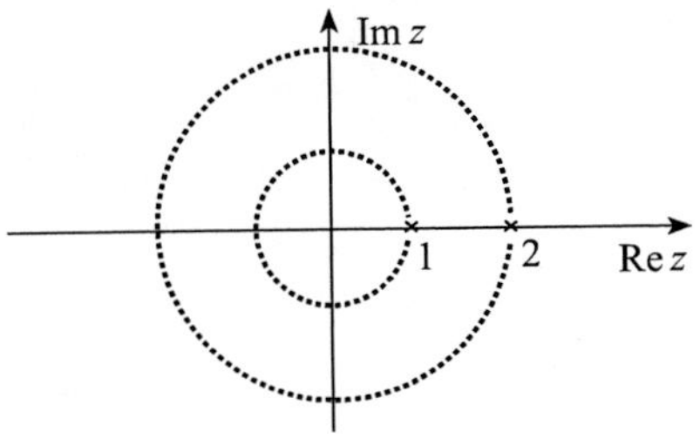

$$f(z) = \frac{1}{z-2} - \frac{1}{z-1}.$$

Since

$$\frac{1}{1-z} = 1 + z + z^2 + z^3 + \cdots, \quad |z| < 1,$$

and

$$\frac{-1}{2-z} = \frac{-1}{2(1-z/2)} = -\frac{1}{2}\left(1 + \frac{z}{2} + \frac{z^2}{4} + \frac{z^3}{8} + \cdots\right), \quad |z| < 2,$$

Figure 5.13

the Maclaurin series is

$$f(z) = (1 + z + z^2 + z^3 + \cdots) - \frac{1}{2}\left(1 + \frac{z}{2} + \frac{z^2}{4} + \frac{z^3}{8} + \cdots\right), \quad |z| < 1$$

$$= \frac{1}{2} + \frac{3}{4}z + \frac{7}{8}z^2 + \frac{15}{16}z^3 + \cdots$$

$$= \sum_{n=0}^{\infty} \frac{2^{n+1} - 1}{2^{n+1}} z^n, \quad |z| < 1.$$

(b) The expansion for $1/(z - 2)$ obtained in part (a) is valid for $|z| < 2$. Since

$$\frac{-1}{z-1} = \frac{-1}{z\left(1-\frac{1}{z}\right)} = -\frac{1}{z}\left(1+\frac{1}{z}+\frac{1}{z^2}+\frac{1}{z^3}+\cdots\right),$$

valid for $|1/z| < 1$ or $|z| > 1$, the Laurent series for $1 < |z| < 2$ is

$$f(z) = -\frac{1}{z}\left(1+\frac{1}{z}+\frac{1}{z^2}+\frac{1}{z^3}+\cdots\right) - \frac{1}{2}\left(1+\frac{z}{2}+\frac{z^2}{4}+\frac{z^3}{8}+\cdots\right)$$

$$= -\sum_{n=1}^{\infty}\frac{1}{z^n} - \sum_{n=0}^{\infty}\frac{1}{2^{n+1}}z^n.$$

(c) The expansion for $-1/(z-1)$ obtained in part (b) is valid for $|z| > 1$. Since

$$\frac{1}{z-2} = \frac{1}{z\left(1-\frac{2}{z}\right)} = \frac{1}{z}\left(1+\frac{2}{z}+\frac{4}{z^2}+\frac{8}{z^3}+\cdots\right),$$

valid for $|2/z| < 1$ or $|z| > 2$, the Laurent series for $|z| > 2$ is

$$f(z) = -\frac{1}{z}\left(1+\frac{1}{z}+\frac{1}{z^2}+\frac{1}{z^3}+\cdots\right) + \frac{1}{z}\left(1+\frac{2}{z}+\frac{4}{z^2}+\frac{8}{z^3}+\cdots\right)$$

$$= \frac{1}{z^2}+\frac{3}{z^3}+\frac{7}{z^4}+\frac{15}{z^5}+\cdots$$

$$= \sum_{n=2}^{\infty}\frac{2^{n-1}-1}{z^n}.\bullet$$

Example 5.24 Find the Laurent series for $f(z) = 1/(z^2+z)$ valid in the domain $0 < |z+1| < 1$.

Solution   Since $z = 0$ and $z = -1$ are singularities (Figure 5.14), f is analytic for $0 < |z+1| < 1$. The Laurent series in this annulus will be in powers of $z+1$. The second term in the partial fraction decomposition $f(z) = \dfrac{1}{z(z+1)} = \dfrac{1}{z} - \dfrac{1}{z+1}$ is therefore of the required form. Since

$$\frac{1}{z} = \frac{1}{(z+1)-1} = \frac{-1}{1-(z+1)} = -[1+(z+1)+(z+1)^2+\cdots], \quad |z+1| < 1,$$

the required Laurent series is

$$f(z) = \frac{-1}{z+1} - [1+(z+1)+(z+1)^2+\cdots] = \sum_{n=-1}^{\infty}-(z+1)^n, \quad 0 < |z+1| < 1.\bullet$$

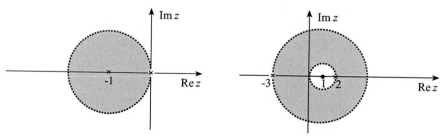

Figure 5.14   **Figure 5.15**

Example 5.25   Find the Laurent series for $f(z) = 5z/(z^2 + z - 6)$ in the annulus $1 < |z - 1| < 4$.

Solution   Since $z = 2$ and $z = -3$ are singularities of f (Figure 5.15), f is analytic in $1 < |z - 1| < 4$. To expand $f(z)$ we first form its partial fraction decomposition

$$f(z) = \frac{3}{z + 3} + \frac{2}{z - 2}.$$

Both terms must be expressed in powers of $z - 1$. For the first we write

$$\frac{3}{z + 3} = \frac{3}{(z - 1) + 4} = \frac{3}{4 \left(1 + \dfrac{z - 1}{4}\right)} = \frac{3}{4} \sum_{n=0}^{\infty} \left(-\frac{z - 1}{4}\right)^n, \quad \left|-\frac{z - 1}{4}\right| < 1$$

$$= \sum_{n=0}^{\infty} \frac{3(-1)^n}{4^{n+1}} (z - 1)^n, \quad |z - 1| < 4.$$

For the second term,

$$\frac{2}{z - 2} = \frac{2}{(z - 1) - 1} = \frac{2}{(z - 1)\left(1 - \dfrac{1}{z - 1}\right)} = \frac{2}{z - 1} \sum_{n=0}^{\infty} \left(\frac{1}{z - 1}\right)^n, \quad \left|\frac{1}{z - 1}\right| < 1$$

$$= \sum_{n=0}^{\infty} \frac{2}{(z - 1)^{n+1}}, \quad |z - 1| > 1.$$

The required Laurent series is therefore

$$f(z) = \sum_{n=0}^{\infty} \frac{2}{(z - 1)^{n+1}} + \sum_{n=0}^{\infty} \frac{3(-1)^n}{4^{n+1}} (z - 1)^n, \quad 1 < |z - 1| < 4. \bullet$$

Example 5.26   Find the Laurent series for $f(z) = z^{-3} \cos 2z$ valid in the domain $|z| > 0$.

Solution   The Maclaurin series for $\cos 2z$, valid for all z, is

$$\cos 2z = \sum_{n=0}^{\infty} \frac{(-1)^n 2^{2n}}{(2n)!} z^{2n}.$$

Multiplication by $1/z^3$ gives the Laurent series for $z^{-3} \cos 2z$ valid when $|z| > 0$,

$$\frac{1}{z^3} \cos 2z = \sum_{n=0}^{\infty} \frac{(-1)^n 2^{2n}}{(2n)!} z^{2n-3}. \bullet$$

Like Taylor series, Laurent series can be differentiated term-by-term within their annuli of convergence. This is stated in the following theorem.

Theorem 5.26   When the Laurent series of a function $f(z) = \displaystyle\sum_{n=-\infty}^{\infty} a_n(z - z_0)^n$, valid in an annulus $r < |z - z_0| < R$, is differentiated term-by-tern, the resulting series converges to $f'(z)$ in the same annulus.

Here is an example to illustrate.

Example 5.27   Find the laurent series for $f(z) = \dfrac{1}{(z - 1)^2(z + 2)}$, valid for $|z + 2| > 3$.

Solution We begin by expanding $1/(z-1)$,

$$\frac{1}{z-1} = \frac{1}{(z+2)-3} = \frac{1}{(z+2)\left(1-\frac{3}{z+2}\right)} = \frac{1}{z+2}\sum_{n=0}^{\infty}\left(\frac{3}{z+2}\right)^n = \sum_{n=0}^{\infty}\frac{3^n}{(z+2)^{n+1}},$$

valid for $\left|\frac{-3}{z+2}\right| < 1$, or $|z+2| > 3$. We differentiate this series to obtain the expansion for $1/(z-1)^2$,

$$\frac{-1}{(z-1)^2} = \sum_{n=0}^{\infty}\frac{-3^n(n+1)}{(z+2)^{n+2}} \quad\Longrightarrow\quad \frac{1}{(z-1)^2} = \sum_{n=0}^{\infty}\frac{3^n(n+1)}{(z+2)^{n+2}}.$$

We now write

$$\frac{1}{(z-1)^2(z+2)} = \sum_{n=0}^{\infty}\frac{3^n(n+1)}{(z+2)^{n+3}} = \sum_{n=3}^{\infty}\frac{3^{n-3}(n-2)}{(z+2)^n}. \bullet$$

EXERCISES 5.5

In Exercises 1–6 find the Laurent series for the function in the given domain.

1. $\dfrac{1}{z-3}$ for $|z| > 3$

2. $\dfrac{1}{z^2+2z}$ for $0 < |z| < 2$

3. $\dfrac{z}{z^2-3z+2}$ for $1 < |z-3| < 2$

4. $\sin\left(\dfrac{1}{z}\right)$ for $|z| > 0$

5. $\dfrac{z}{(z+2)^2(3-z)}$ for $|z-3| > 5$

6. $\dfrac{1}{z^2(z-i)}$ for $1 < |z-1| < \sqrt{2}$

In Exercises 7–17 find the Laurent series for the function about the given point. Indicate the domain of convergence of the series.

7. $\dfrac{1}{z^3-z^2}$ about $z=0$

8. $\dfrac{z}{z^2+4}$ about $z=2i$

9. $\dfrac{z}{z^2+4}$ about $z=2$

10. $\dfrac{e^z}{z+1}$ about $z=-1$

11. $\dfrac{z^2}{(z+1)^2}$ about $z=-1$

12. $\dfrac{z^2+2z}{z^2+4}$ about $z=2i$

13. $\dfrac{1-e^z}{z^3}$ about $z=0$

14. $\dfrac{\sin z}{z-3}$ about $z=3$

15. $\dfrac{e^{4z}}{(z-2)^3}$ about $z=2$

16. $(z-2)\sin\left(\dfrac{1}{z+2}\right)$ about $z=-2$

17. $e^{z/(z-3)}$ about $z=3$

18. Find Laurent series for the function $\dfrac{1}{z^2(z+2)}$ valid in the domains (a) $0 < |z+2| < 2$, and (b) $|z+2| > 2$.

19. Find the first three nonzero terms in the Laurent series of $\csc z$ about $z=0$.

20. Find the Laurent series for $f(z) = (3z-3)/(2z^2-5z+2)$ convergent for $1/2 < |z-1| < 1$.

21. Expand $f(z) = z^3/(-z^2 + 3z - 2)$ in Laurent series valid for:

(a) $|z| < 1$ (b) $1 < |z| < 2$ (c) $|z| > 2$ (d) $|z - 1| > 1$ (e) $0 < |z - 2| < 1$

22. Does the function $f(z) = \operatorname{Re} z$ have a Laurent series valid in some domain $0 < |z| < R$? Explain.

23. Does $\operatorname{Log} z$ have a Laurent series in any annulus centred at $z = 0$? Does it have a Laurent series about any of its singularities?

24. Use long division to obtain the first four nonzero terms in the Laurent series of $\csc 2z$ about $z = 0$. What do you anticipate for a domain of validity of the series?

25. (a) Show that the Laurent series for $e^{t(z-1/z)/2}$ (t a parameter) valid for $|z| > 0$ is

$$e^{t(z-1/z)/2} = \sum_{n=-\infty}^{\infty} J_n(t) z^n,$$

where $J_n(t)$ is the Bessel function of the first kind of order n. We call $e^{t(z-1/z)/2}$ a generating function for the integer order Bessel functions.

(b) Use formula 5.30b to verify the following integral representation for $J_n(t)$,

$$J_n(t) = \frac{1}{2\pi} \int_0^{2\pi} \cos(n\theta - t \sin\theta) \, d\theta.$$

26. Find Laurent series for the function $f(z) = \sqrt{z-1}\sqrt{z+1}$ valid in some annulus about:
(a) $z = 0$ (b) $z = 1$

27. Show that when $b > a > 1$,

$$\operatorname{Log}\left(\frac{z-a}{z-b}\right) = \sum_{n=1}^{\infty} \frac{b^n - a^n}{nz^n}$$

for $|z| > b$. Hint: See Exercise 45 in Section 3.5.

28. Obviously, the sum of the series $\displaystyle\sum_{n=-\infty}^{\infty} z^n$ is not equal zero. Consider the following proof that the sum is zero for all z. Show that both of the following expansion are valid:

$$\frac{z}{1-z} = \sum_{n=1}^{\infty} z^n, \qquad \text{and} \qquad \frac{z}{1-z} = \sum_{n=0}^{\infty} \frac{1}{z^n}.$$

When these are added, the result is $\displaystyle\sum_{n=-\infty}^{\infty} z^n = 0$. Explain the fallacy in the argument.

§5.6 Classification of Singularities

When z_0 is an isolated singularity of an analytic function f, there exists an annulus $0 < |z - z_0| < R$ centred at z_0 in which f is analytic, and therein f has a Laurent expansion. We use this expansion to classify the type of singularity at z_0.

Definition 5.4   Suppose an analytic function f has an isolated singularity at z_0, and

$$f(z) = \sum_{n=-\infty}^{\infty} a_n (z - z_0)^n$$

is the Laurent expansion of f valid in some annulus $0 < |z - z_0| < R$. Then:
(i) if $a_n = 0$ for all $n < 0$, z_0 is called a **removable** singularity;
(ii) if $a_n = 0$ for $n < -m$, m a fixed positive integer, but $a_{-m} \neq 0$, z_0 is called a **pole** of order m;
(iii) if $a_n \neq 0$ for an infinity of negative integers n, z_0 is called an **essential** singularity.

Part (i) of this definition agrees with the definition of removable singularity in Section 2.3. If $a_n = 0$ for all $n < 0$, then the Laurent series of f about z_0 takes the form

$$f(z) = a_0 + a_1 (z - z_0) + a_2 (z - z_0)^2 + \cdots .$$

It follows that $\lim_{z \to z_0} f(z) = a_0$, and existence of the limit is the definition of removable singularity in Section 2.3. Conversely, if $\lim_{z \to z_0} f(z)$ exists, then the Laurent series of f cannot contain terms $(z - z_0)^n$ where $n < 0$. By process of elimination, the Laurent series must satisfy (i).

The classification of singularities in Definition 5.4 is illustrated in the following example.

Example 5.28   Classify singularities for the following functions:

$$\text{(a)} \ \frac{\sin z}{z} \qquad \text{(b)} \ e^{1/z} \qquad \text{(c)} \ \frac{1}{z^3 (z + 3)^2}$$

Solution (a) Since the Maclaurin series for $\sin z$ is

$$\sin z = z - \frac{z^3}{3!} + \frac{z^5}{5!} - \cdots , \quad |z| < \infty,$$

it follows that

$$\frac{\sin z}{z} = 1 - \frac{z^2}{3!} + \frac{z^4}{5!} - \cdots .$$

This is the Laurent series for $z^{-1} \sin z$ in the annulus $0 < |z| < \infty$. It satisfies (i) in Definition 5.4, and therefore $z = 0$ is a removable singularity for $z^{-1} \sin z$. The Laurent series clearly demonstrates that $\lim_{z \to 0} z^{-1} \sin z = 1$.

(b) If we replace each z in the Maclaurin series

$$e^z = 1 + z + \frac{z^2}{2!} + \frac{z^3}{3!} + \cdots , \quad |z| < \infty,$$

by $1/z$, we obtain

$$e^{1/z} = 1 + \frac{1}{z} + \frac{1}{2! \, z^2} + \frac{1}{3! \, z^3} + \cdots,$$

valid for $0 < |z| < \infty$. This is therefore the Laurent series for $e^{1/z}$ about $z = 0$, and $z = 0$ is an essential singularity.

(c) For the singularity at $z = 0$, we first expand

$$\frac{1}{z+3} = \frac{1}{3(1+z/3)} = \frac{1}{3}\left(1 - \frac{z}{3} + \frac{z^2}{9} - \cdots\right), \quad |z| < 3.$$

Term-by-term differentiation with respect to z, gives

$$-\frac{1}{(z+3)^2} = \frac{1}{3}\left(-\frac{1}{3} + \frac{2z}{9} - \frac{3z^2}{27} + \cdots\right), \quad |z| < 3,$$

and therefore

$$\frac{1}{z^3(z+3)^2} = \frac{1}{9z^3} - \frac{2}{27z^2} + \frac{1}{27z} - \cdots, \quad 0 < |z| < 3.$$

This is the Laurent series for $1/[z^3(z+3)^2]$ about the singularity $z = 0$. Since it satisfies part (ii) of Definition 5.4 with $m = 3$, $z = 0$ is a pole of order 3.

For the singularity at $z = -3$, we first expand

$$\frac{1}{z} = \frac{1}{(z+3)-3} = \frac{1}{-3\left(1 - \dfrac{z+3}{3}\right)} = -\frac{1}{3}\left[1 + \frac{z+3}{3} + \left(\frac{z+3}{3}\right)^2 + \cdots\right],$$

valid for $|z+3| < 3$. Term-by-term differentiation gives

$$-\frac{1}{z^2} = -\frac{1}{3}\left[\frac{1}{3} + \frac{2}{9}(z+3) + \frac{3}{27}(z+3)^2 + \cdots\right], \quad |z+3| < 3.$$

A second differentiation yields

$$\frac{2}{z^3} = -\frac{1}{3}\left[\frac{2}{9} + \frac{6}{27}(z+3) + \cdots\right], \quad |z+3| < 3.$$

Hence

$$\frac{1}{z^3(z+3)^2} = -\frac{1}{6}\left[\frac{2}{9(z+3)^2} + \frac{2}{9(z+3)} + \cdots\right], \quad 0 < |z+3| < 3,$$

and $z = -3$ is a pole of order 2.•

In the theory to follow, it is important to be able to determine quickly the poles (and their orders) of a function. The following result allows us to do this.

Theorem 5.27   A function f has a pole of order m at z_0 if and only if it can be written in the form

$$f(z) = \frac{g(z)}{(z-z_0)^m}, \tag{5.31}$$

valid in some annulus $0 < |z - z_0| < R$, where g is analytic at z_0 and $g(z_0) \neq 0$.

Proof   Suppose that $f(z)$ can be expressed in form 5.31 in some annulus $0 < |z - z_0| < R$, and $g(z)$ is expanded in a Taylor series about z_0,

$$g(z) = a_0 + a_1(z - z_0) + \cdots, \quad |z - z_0| < r \quad \text{(for some } r\text{)}$$

where $a_0 = g(z_0) \neq 0$. Then in the annulus $0 < |z - z_0| < \text{minimum}(R, r)$, $f(z)$ can be expressed in the form

$$f(z) = \frac{a_0}{(z - z_0)^m} + \frac{a_1}{(z - z_0)^{m-1}} + \cdots .$$

Since the right side of this equation is the Laurent expansion of f about z_0, z_0 is a pole of order m.

Conversely, if f has a pole of order m at z_0, the Laurent expansion of f about z_0 is of the form

$$f(z) = \frac{a_{-m}}{(z - z_0)^m} + \frac{a_{-m+1}}{(z - z_0)^{m-1}} + \cdots + \frac{a_{-1}}{z - z_0} + a_0 + a_1(z - z_0) + \cdots$$

$$= \frac{1}{(z - z_0)^m} [a_{-m} + a_{-m+1}(z - z_0) + \cdots]$$

valid in some annulus $0 < |z - z_0| < R$. The power series in the braces represents a function which is analytic for $|z - z_0| < R$, and the function clearly does not vanish at z_0. ∎

Notice how this theorem shortens the work in part (c) of Example 5.28. The function $1/(z + 3)^2$ is analytic at $z = 0$, and is nonvanishing there. Consequently, $[z^3(z + 3)^2]^{-1}$ has a pole of order 3 at $z = 0$. Since $1/z^3$ is analytic at $z = -3$ and does not vanish there, $[z^3(z + 3)^2]^{-1}$ has a pole of order 2 at $z = -3$. Further illustrations of Theorem 5.27 are contained in the following example. To appreciate the theorem, try finding the Laurent series for the functions and using Definition 5.4.

Example 5.29   Classify singularities for the following functions:

$$\text{(a)} \quad \frac{\sin 3z}{(z + 1)^4} \qquad \text{(b)} \quad \frac{z^2 + 2z - 1}{z^4 - 3z^3 + 3z^2 - z}$$

Solution (a) Since $\sin 3z$ is entire and does not vanish at $z = -1$, $z = -1$ is a pole of order 4.

(b) The factored form

$$\frac{z^2 + 2z - 1}{z^4 - 3z^3 + 3z^2 - z} = \frac{z^2 + 2z - 1}{z(z - 1)^3}$$

indicates singularities at $z = 0$ and $z = 1$. Since $(z^2 + 2z - 1)/(z - 1)^3$ is analytic at $z = 0$ and does not vanish there, $z = 0$ is a pole of order 1 (also called a simple pole). Because $(z^2 + 2z - 1)/z$ is analytic at $z = 1$ and not zero there, $z = 1$ is a pole of order 3.•

Behaviour of Functions Near Isolated Singularities

The behaviours of a function near a removable singularity, a pole, and an essential singularity are very different. In a nutshell, a function $f(z)$ is bounded near a removable singularity, its modulus $|f(z)| \to \infty$ as z approaches a pole, and any other behaviour constitutes an essential singularity. Obviously a function is well-behaved near a removable singularity; either the function has no value at the singularity, or its limit as z aproaches the singularity differs from its value at the singularity. We summarize the results in the following theorem.

Theorem 5.28   If a function has a removable singularity at z_0 then:

(a) $f(z)$ can be defined, or redefined, at z_0 so that the new function is analytic at z_0; and

(b) $f(z)$ has a limit as z approaches z_0; and

(c) $f(z)$ is bounded in some annulus around z_0.

Conversely, if a function $f(z)$ has an isolated singularity at z_0, and has any one of these properties, then z_0 is a removable singularity.

Proof   If $f(z)$ has a removable singularity at z_0, then its Laurent series around z_0 takes the form

$$f(z) = a_0 + a_1(z - z_0) + a_2(z - z_0)^2 + \cdots,$$

valid in some annulus $0 < |z - z_0| < R$. Suppose we define a function $g(z)$ which is identical to $f(z)$ at all $z \neq z_0$ in $0 < |z - z_0| < R$, but also has value a_0 at z_0; that is, define

$$g(z) = a_0 + a_1(z - z_0) + a_2(z - z_0)^2 + \cdots,$$

for all z in $|z - z_0| < R$. This is the Taylor series for $g(z)$ about z_0, and therefore $g(z)$ is analytic at z_0. This verifies part (a) of the theorem. Since $g(z)$ is analytic at z_0, it is continuous there. It follows that $\lim_{z \to z_0} g(z)$ exists. Since values of $f(z)$ are identical to those of $g(z)$ for all z except z_0, the $\lim_{z \to z_0} f(z)$ must also exist (part (b)). Existence of the limit of $f(z)$ at z_0 certainly implies that $f(z)$ is bounded in some annulus around z_0 (part (c)).

Conversely, suppose that z_0 is an isolated singularity of $f(z)$ and that $f(z)$ is bounded in some annulus $0 < |z - z_0| < R$ around z_0. If C_r is the circle $|z - z_0| = r$, where $r < R$, then coefficients in the Laurent series of $f(z)$ about z_0 are given by formula 5.30b,

$$a_n = \frac{1}{2\pi i} \oint_{C_r} \frac{f(\zeta)}{(\zeta - z_0)^{n+1}} d\zeta.$$

Since $f(z)$ is bounded in $0 < |z - z_0| < R$, there exists an $M > 0$ such that $|f(z)| < M$ for all z in the annulus and therefore on C_r. When $n < 0$, we can use inequality 4.21 to write that

$$|a_n| = \left| \frac{1}{2\pi i} \oint_{C_r} \frac{f(\zeta)}{(\zeta - z_0)^{n+1}} d\zeta \right| \leq \frac{1}{2\pi} \left(\frac{M}{r^{n+1}} \right) (2\pi r) = \frac{M}{r^n}.$$

Since the right side of this inequality must be independent of r, and for $n < 0$, it can be made arbitrarily small, it follows that it must have value zero. Thus, all coefficients of negative of powers of $z - z_0$ in the Laurent series for $f(z)$ about z_0 vanish, and z_0 is a removable singularity. ∎

This theorem has shown that a function is well-behaved around a removable singularity; only its value at the singularity is a problem. Contrast this with the behaviour of a function around a pole in the following theorem; the modulus of the function must become unbounded as the pole is approached.

Theorem 5.29   An isolated singularity z_0 of a function $f(z)$ is a pole if, and only if, $\lim_{z \to z_0} |f(z)| = \infty$.

Proof   If z_0 is a pole of order m of $f(z)$, then $f(z)$ can be expressed in the form

$$f(z) = \frac{g(z)}{(z - z_0)^m},$$

in some annulus $0 < |z - z_0| < R$, where $g(z)$ is analytic at z_0 and $g(z_0) \neq 0$. Since $\lim_{z \to z_0} |g(z)| = |g(z_0)| \neq 0$, it follows that

$$\lim_{z \to z_0} |f(z)| = \lim_{z \to z_0} \left| \frac{g(z)}{(z - z_0)^m} \right| = \infty.$$

Conversely, suppose that $\lim_{z \to z_0} |f(z)| = \infty$. There therefore exists an annulus D : $0 < |z - z_0| < R$ inside of which $|f(z)| > 1$. Consider the function $g(z) = 1/f(z)$. Since $f(z) \neq 0$ inside D, it follows that $g(z)$ is analytic and bounded in D. According to Theorem 5.28, z_0 must be a removable singularity for $g(z)$. Since $\lim_{z \to z_0} |g(z)| = 0$, we define $g(z_0) = 0$, in which case z_0 is a zero of $g(z)$. This zero must have finite order, say m; otherwise, we would have $g^{(n)}(z_0) = 0$ for all n. It would then follow that $g(z)$ would be equal to zero for all z in D, an impossibility. According to Exercise 1, $f(z) = 1/g(z)$ has a pole of order m at z_0. ∎

You may feel that because the Laurent expansion of a function $f(z)$ around a pole z_0 of order m takes the form

$$f(z) = \frac{a_{-m}}{(z - z_0)^m} + \frac{a_{-m+1}}{(z - z_0)^{m-1}} + \cdots,$$

it is obvious that $\lim_{z \to z_0} |f(z)| = \infty$. Why then the need for the proof in Theorem 5.29? If you believe this argument, then you must accept it for the behaviour of a function near an essential singularity since its Laurent series takes a similar form

$$f(z) = \cdots + \frac{a_{-m}}{(z - z_0)^m} + \frac{a_{-m+1}}{(z - z_0)^{m-1}} + \cdots.$$

Nothing could be further from the truth. The limit of the modulus of a function does not become infinite as an essential singularity is approached. In fact, because Theorems 5.28 and 5.29 are complete characterizations of the behaviour of functions near removable singularities and poles, we have the following test for an essential singularity.

Theorem 5.30   A function $f(z)$ has an essential singularity at z_0 if, and only if, $\lim_{z \to z_0} |f(z)|$ does not exist, and $\lim_{z \to z_0} |f(z)| \neq \infty$.

This result describes what a function does not do near an essential singularity; the following theorem describes what it does do.

Theorem 5.31   **(Picard's Theorem)**   If a function $f(z)$ has an essential singularity at z_0, then the function takes on every possible value, with possibly one exception, in every neighbourhood of z_0.

The proof of this theorem is beyond the scope of our text, but it clearly illustrates that the behaviour of a function near an essential singularity is very different than that near a removable singularity or a pole. Here is an example to illustrate Picard's Theorem.

Example 5.30   Show that $e^{1/z}$ has an essential singularity at $z = 0$ and confirm the result of Picard's Theorem.

Solution   The Laurent series for $e^{1/z}$ around $z = 0$ is

$$1 + \frac{1}{z} + \frac{1}{2!\,z^2} + \frac{1}{3!\,z^3} + \cdots,$$

confirming that $z = 0$ is an essential singularity. Since $e^{1/z}$ is never equal to zero, this number would seem to be the exception in Picard's Theorem. Let us show that in every neighbourhood of $z = 0$, the function takes on every other value, say k, at least once. To do this, we must show that in any circle $|z| < r$, no matter how small, there is a solution of the equation $e^{1/z} = k$. Solutions of this equation are given by

$$\frac{1}{z} = \log k \quad \Longrightarrow \quad z = \frac{1}{\ln|k| + (\operatorname{Arg} k + 2n\pi)i}.$$

By choosing n sufficiently large, the modulus of $\ln|k| + (\operatorname{Arg} k + 2n\pi)i$ can be made greater than $1/r$, in which case the modulus of z is less than r and z is inside the circle $|z| < r$.•

A pole z_0 of a function $f(z)$ is characterized by the fact that $\lim_{z \to z_0} |f(z)| = \infty$, the function is unbounded in every circle around z_0. When z_0 is an essential singularity, $\lim_{z \to z_0} |f(z)| \neq \infty$. In spite of this, the following theorem states that a function is unbounded near an essential singularity.

Theorem 5.32   If z_0 is an essential singularity of a function $f(z)$, and the Laurent series of $f(z)$ around z_0 is valid in the annulus $0 < |z - z_0| < R$, then $f(z)$ is unbounded in every circle $|z - z_0| < r < R$.

Proof   This is guaranteed for a pole by Theorem 5.29. Suppose then that z_0 is an essential singularity of $f(z)$, and the Laurent series of the function around z_0 is

$$f(z) = \sum_{n=-\infty}^{\infty} a_n (z - z_0)^n,$$

valid in some annulus $0 < |z - z_0| < R$, where coefficients are given by the integrals

$$a_n = \frac{1}{2\pi i} \oint_C \frac{f(\zeta)}{(\zeta - z_0)^{n+1}} \, d\zeta,$$

and C is any simple, closed, piecewise smooth curve in the annulus. In particular, we can choose C as any circle of radius $r < R$ in the annulus. Suppose that $f(z)$ is bounded in and on the circle so that there exists a constant M such that for all $|z - z_0| = r$, $|f(z)| \leq M$. It follows that for ζ on C,

$$\left| \frac{f(\zeta)}{(\zeta - z_0)^{n+1}} \right| \leq \frac{M}{r^{n+1}}.$$

Consequently,

$$|a_n| \leq \frac{1}{2\pi} \frac{M}{r^{n+1}} (2\pi r) = \frac{M}{r^n}.$$

Consider coefficients a_n where $n < 0$. Since $|a_n|$ can be made arbitrarily small by choosing r small, it follows that $a_n < 0$ for $n < 0$, contradicting the fact that z_0 is an essential singularity. Thus, $f(z)$ must be unbounded in the circle $|z - z_0| < r$.∎

Singularities at Infinity

It is sometimes advantageous to determine whether the point at infinity is a singularity of a function. We define what this means as follows.

Definition 5.5 If a function $f(z)$ is analytic for $|z| > R$, for some R, it is said to have an isolated singularity at the point of infinity. It is a removable singularity, a pole, or an esential singularity of $f(z)$ if $z = 0$ is a removable singularity, a pole, or an essential singularity of $f(1/z)$.

For example, $f(z) = z^2 - 3z + 1$ is entire, and $f(1/z) = 1/z^2 - 3/z + 1$. Since $z = 0$ is a pole of order two for this function, the point at infinity is a pole of order two for $f(z)$. The function $f(z) = 1/(z - z^3)$ is analytic for $|z| > 3$, and $f(1/z) = z^3/(z^2 - 1)$. Since this function is analytic at $z = 0$, we say that $f(z)$ has a removable singularity at infinity. Since $\sin(1/z)$ has an essential singularity at $z = 0$, $\sin z$ has an essential singularity at infinity. There is no annulus $|z| > R$ in which $\csc z$ is analytic (singularities are $z = n\pi$). We do not therefore regard the point at infinity as an isolated singularity for this function. Here are some further examples.

Example 5.31 Determine the nature of the singularity at infinity for the functions:

(a) $f(z) = \dfrac{z^5}{1 + z - z^2}$ (b) $f(z) = \dfrac{e^{2z}}{1 + 3z^2}$ (c) $f(z) = \dfrac{1}{e^z - 1}$

Solution (a) The function is certainly analytic for $|z| > 10$. Since

$$f(1/z) = \frac{1/z^5}{1 + 1/z - 1/z^2} = \frac{1}{z^3(z^2 + z - 1)}$$

has a pole of order three at $z = 0$, so also does $f(z)$ at infinity.

(b) The function is analytic for $|z| > 1/\sqrt{3}$. Since $f(1/z) = \dfrac{e^{2/z}}{1 + 3/z^2} = \dfrac{z^2 e^{2/z}}{z^2 + 3}$ has an essential singularity at $z = 0$, so also does $f(z)$ at infinity.

(c) Since $e^z = 1$ when $z = 2n\pi i$, n an integer, there is no annulus $|z| > R$ in which $f(z)$ is analytic. It does not therefore have an isolated singularity at infinity.●

EXERCISES 5.6

In Exercises 1–2 use Theorems 5.23 and 5.27 (or otherwise) to prove the result.

1. If f is analytic at z_0 and has a zero of order m at z_0, then $1/f$ has a pole of order m at z_0.

2. Suppose that f and g are analytic with zeros of orders m and n, respectively, at z_0. Then the quotient f/g has the following behaviour.
   (a) If $m < n$, then f/g has a pole of order $n - m$ at z_0.
   (b) If $m > n$, then f/g has a removable singularity at z_0. If the quotient function is given value 0 at z_0, then the function has a zero of order $m - n$.
   (c) If $m = n$, then f/g has a removable singularity at z_0. The singularity can be removed by defining the function at z_0 as the limit of f/g as $z \to z_0$.

In Exercises 3–16 find and classify all isolated singularities of the function.

3. $\dfrac{z^2+1}{z^2(z+1)}$

4. $z^3 e^{1/z}$

5. $\dfrac{z^2-4}{z-2}$

6. $\dfrac{\sin 3z}{z^5}$

7. $\operatorname{csch} z$

8. $\operatorname{Log} z$

9. $\dfrac{z^3+3z}{\cos^2 z}$

10. $\cot z$

11. $z \cot z$

12. $\dfrac{1}{(z^2+1)\cosh(z+i)}$

13. $\dfrac{z-\sin z}{z^6}$

14. $\dfrac{1}{\sin z - \sin 2z}$

15. $\sec(1/z)$

16. $\dfrac{z^4(z-1)}{\sin^2 \pi z}$

In Exercises 17–20 classify the singularity at the point of infinity for the function, if it is an isolated singularity.

17. $z^4 + \dfrac{2}{z^2}$

18. $\dfrac{5+z^3}{e^{4z}}$

19. $e^{2z/(1-3z)}$

20. $\tan(3/z)$

21. Classify the singularity $z=0$ of the function $f(z) = \dfrac{1}{(2\cos z - 2 + z^2)^2}$

22. Show that the function $f(z) = \cos(e^{1/z})$ has an essential singularity at $z=0$. Hint: Consider the sequence of points $\{1/\ln(n\pi)\}$.

23. Discuss whether $z=2$ is an isolated singularity of the function $1/[(z-1)^{1/2}-1]$ when $(z-1)^{1/2}$ is the following branch of the double-valued function:
   (a) $\sqrt{z-1}$
   (b) $-\sqrt{z-1}$
   (c) $(z-1)^{1/2} = |z-1|^{1/2} e^{(i/2)\arg(z-1)}, \quad \pi/2 < \arg(z-1) \le 5\pi/2$
   (d) $(z-1)^{1/2} = |z-1|^{1/2} e^{(i/2)\arg(z-1)}, \quad 0 < \arg(z-1) \le 2\pi$

24. Show that $\sin(1/z)$ has an essential singularity at $z=0$ and confirm the result of Picard's Theorem for this singularity.

§5.7 Analytic Continuation

We have seen that the infinite series

$$\frac{1}{1-z} = \sum_{n=0}^{\infty} z^n, \quad |z| < 1,$$

is a valid representation for the function $1/(1-z)$ inside the unit circle $|z| < 1$. By writing

$$\frac{1}{1-z} = \frac{1}{(1-i)-(z-i)} = \frac{1}{1-i}\left[\frac{1}{1-\left(\dfrac{z-i}{1-i}\right)}\right] = \sum_{n=0}^{\infty} \frac{1}{(1-i)^{n+1}}\,(z-i)^n,$$

we obtain a representation of the same function in a different, but overlapping circle $|z - i| < \sqrt{2}$ (Figure 5.16). Inside the overlapping region, values of the two series coincide. We say that each series is an **analytic continuation** of the other. By picking further points of expansion we could continue these representations of $1/(1-z)$ into all parts of the complex plane which do not include the point $z = 1$.

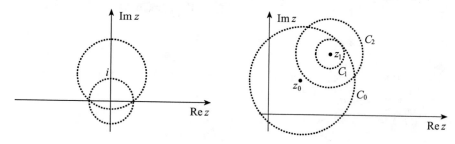

Figure 5.16   Figure 5.17

In practical problems which involve analytic continuation, we may not have a closed form sum for a series; we may have only a series which we know represents an analytic function, call it f, inside its circle of convergence,

$$f(z) = \sum_{n=0}^{\infty} a_n(z-z_0)^n, \quad C_0 : |z - z_0| < R.$$

If z_1 is a point interior to C_0 (Figure 5.17), Theorem 5.18 guarantees that the Taylor series of f about z_1 is analytic inside the largest circle C_1 about z_1 which is interior to C_0. It may happen, however, that this Taylor series about z_1 actually converges inside a larger circle C_2 which includes points exterior to C_0. We say then that the Taylor series about z_1 is an analytic continuation of f from C_0 into C_2. The values of f as calculated by either series are the same inside their common region of convergence. Taylor series about other points in C_0, or in C_2, may lead to further analytic continuations of f into other regions. The following theorem leads to important results about analytic continuations.

Theorem 5.33 Let f_1 and f_2 be analytic in a domain D. If $f_1(z) = f_2(z)$ at all points in a subdomain D' of D, then $f_1(z) = f_2(z)$ in D.

Proof   If z_0 is any point in D'
(Figure 5.18), each of $f_1(z)$ and $f_2(z)$
can be expanded in Taylor series about z_0,
and both series converge in the largest circle
contained in D. Because $f_1(z) = f_2(z)$ in
D', these Taylor series must be identical;
that is, $f_1(z)$ must now be equal to $f_2(z)$
inside C. By expanding $f_1(z)$ and $f_2(z)$
about points inside C and outside D',
the domain in which $f_1(z) = f_2(z)$ can be
extended further, and eventually be made
to coincide with D. ∎

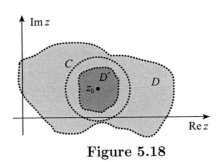

Figure 5.18

The requirement that $f_1(z) = f_2(z)$ in a subdomain D' of D can be relaxed to coincident values along a curve in D, or even a sequence of points having limit in D, but the proof is correspondingly more difficult.

Corollary 1   (Local Uniqueness of Analytic Continuation)   When a function f, analytic in a domain D, is analytically continued to a domain D' which has points in common with D, the continuation is unique.

Corollary 2   If it is possible to analytically continue a function $f(x)$, defined on some interval of the x-axis, into the complex plane, it can be done in only one way.

In essence, this result completes the work on the trigonometric and hyperbolic functions and their inverses in Chapter 3. For example, we defined functions $\sin z = (e^{zi} - e^{-zi})/(2i)$ and $\cosh z = (e^z + e^{-z})/2$ in order that they agree with their real counterparts $\sin x$ and $\cosh x$ on the real axis. The above result indicates that because these complex functions are analytic, they are the only possible analytic functions which continue $\sin x$ and $\cosh x$ into the complex plane.

As a further example, recall that the complex exponential e^z was derived from the differential equation $f'(z) = f(z)$, $f(0) = 1$. Subsequently, it was shown that the Maclaurin series for e^z is $\sum_{n=0}^{\infty} z^n/n!$. Corollary 2 presents an alternative procedure — define

$$e^z = \sum_{n=0}^{\infty} \frac{1}{n!} z^n.$$

Because the function so defined is entire, and coincides with e^z for $z = x$, it is the only possible analytic extension of e^x to the complex plane. Properties of e^z could then be derived from the complex power series representation.

It is important to notice that Corollary 1
is one of local uniqueness. To emphasize this,
suppose a function f, analytic in a domain D
(Figure 5.19), is analytically continued by two
separate chains of circles beginning at z_1 and
z_2 in such a way that they both eventually
define values for f in some common domain R.
Do the continuations yield the same values for
f in R. Corollary 1 does not address this global
problem; it is a local result. To answer the

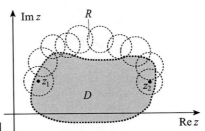

Figure 5.19

question, we note that it is always possible to construct a chain of circles lying completely within D that joins the beginning circles at z_1 and z_2. If the simply-connected domain consisting of points interior to all three chains and all points bounded by the chains is free of singularities of f, it can be shown that the values of f in R are identical for the two continuations. (This result is called the Monodromy Theorem.) When the domain bounded by the chains contains a singularity of f, continuations around opposite sides of the singularity may not lead to identical values for f in overlapping domains. In fact, such continuations may lead to multiple-valued functions with their associated branches. We illustrate this with the following alternative approach to the logarithm function. At the same time notice that in this section we have constantly worked with chains of circles in order to analytically continue a function from one domain into others. To indicate other possible continuation techniques, we consider the complex logarithm function from a contour integral point of view.

It is well known that the real logarithm function can be defined for all $x > 0$ by

$$\ln x = \int_1^x \frac{1}{t}\, dt.$$

We continue this function to the half-plane $D : \operatorname{Re} z > 0$ with the definition

$$\log z = \int_C \frac{1}{\zeta}\, d\zeta,$$

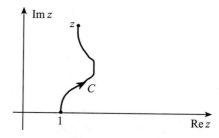

where C is any curve in D from $\zeta = 1$ to $\zeta = z$ (Figure 5.20). In the proof of the necessary part of Theorem 4.4 in Section 4.4, it was shown that $\int_C \zeta^{-1}\, d\zeta$ is an antiderivative of $1/z$

Figure 5.20

in D, and hence $\log z$ is an analytic continuation of $\ln x$ into D. We can continue $\log z$ into the left-half plane $\operatorname{Re} z \le 0$ with essentially the same definition, but C is restricted to not pass through the origin. This continuation, however, does not lead to a single-valued function. For example, the upper half C' of the unit circle leads to the value

$$\log(-1) = \int_{C'} \frac{1}{\zeta}\, d\zeta = \int_0^\pi \frac{1}{e^{\theta i}} i e^{\theta i}\, d\theta = \pi i,$$

whereas the lower half C'' of the same circle yields

$$\log(-1) = \int_{C''} \frac{1}{\zeta}\, d\zeta = \int_{2\pi}^\pi \frac{1}{e^{\theta i}} i e^{\theta i}\, d\theta = -\pi i.$$

Furthermore, according to Example 4.22 in Section 4.6, by taking curves which encircle the origin, it is possible to produce values $\log(-1) = (2n + 1)\pi$ for any integer n whatsoever. Continuation of $\log z$ back to D leads to multiple values there also.

In this way we have continued $\ln x$ to a function $\log z$ which although infinitely-valued, is analytic at every point except $z = 0$; analytic in the sense that about any point z, there exists a neighbourhood inside of which $\log z$ can be assigned values which constitute a single-valued analytic function. Indeed, in every simply-connected domain which does not contain $z = 0$, it is possible to select such values.

When this domain is enlarged as much as possible, we are led to branches and branch cuts of $\log z$.

EXERCISES 5.7

1. In Figure 5.17, what is the largest possible radius for circle C_1?

2. Prove that if a function f is analytic and not constant throughout a domain D, then it cannot be constant over any subdomain of D.

3. In this exercise we show that it is not always possible to analytically continue a function beyond its original domain of analyticity.

   (a) Show that the function $f(z) = \sum_{n=1}^{\infty} z^{n!}$ is analytic in the circle $|z| < 1$.

   (b) If $f(z)$ were continuable beyond the circle $|z| < 1$, there would necessarily be an arc of points on the circle at which $f(z)$ would be analytic. We show that this is impossible. Every arc of $|z| = 1$ contains an infinity of points representable in the form $z^* = e^{2\pi(p/q)i}$ where p and q are positive integers. Consider any one of them, and let $z = az^*$, $0 < a < 1$ be a point on the line joining 0 and z^*. Show that for this z, $f(z)$ can be expressed in the form

$$f(z) = \sum_{n=1}^{q-1} z^{n!} + \sum_{n=q}^{\infty} a^{n!}.$$

   Show that $|f(z)|$ becomes unbounded as $z \to z^*$ along the radial line toward z^*.

   (c) Complete the proof that $f(z)$ cannot be continued analytically beyond $|z| < 1$.

4. In this exercise we prove and illustrate the "Schwarz Reflection Principle". Let f be analytic in some domain D which is symmetric about the real axis, and contains a segment of this axis. If the function is real-valued when z is replaced by x (i.e., if $f(x)$ is real), then

$$\overline{f(\bar{z})} = f(z) \Leftrightarrow \overline{f(z)} = f(\bar{z}).$$

   (a) Prove this result by showing that $F(z) = \overline{f(\bar{z})}$ is analytic in D, and equal to $f(z)$ on that part of the x-axis in D.

   (b) Prove the converse result that if $\overline{f(z)} = f(\bar{z})$, then $f(x)$ is real.

   (c) Illustrate the principle with $\sin x$ and $\cosh x$.

CHAPTER 6   RESIDUE THEORY

In Chapter 4 we developed three methods for evaluating contour integrals around closed curves — the Cauchy-Goursat theorem, the Cauchy integral formulas, and Theorem 4.8. This was not a completely satisfactory situation. The Cauchy-Goursat theorem requires the integrand to be analytic inside and on the curve; Cauchy's integral formulas are only applicable to integrands that have a very special form; and Theorem 4.8 really does not evaluate contour integrals, it replaces a contour integral along a curve enclosing a number of singularities with contour integrals along curves each of which encloses only one singularity. With Laurent series we can develop Cauchy's residue theorem, a technique that encompasses each of these. This theorem is far more powerful than just a synthesis of the above three methods however. It evaluates contour integrals around closed curves that enclose any number of isolated singularities, and it is independent of the form of the integrand. With this theorem we can also evaluate many real integrals that are otherwise intractable (Sections 6.2 and 6.3), find a direct way to evaluate inverse Laplace transforms (Chapter 8), and evaluate Fourier and inverse Fourier transforms (Chapter 9). Finally, residues can be used to develop techniques for finding sums of series of constants (Section 6.5).

§6.1   Cauchy's Residue Theorem

Cauchy's residue theorem is a simple consequence of equation 5.30b for coefficients in Laurent series 5.30a. To illustrate, suppose $f(z) = \sum_{n=-\infty}^{\infty} a_n (z - z_0)^n$ is the Laurent series of a function f valid in some annulus $0 < |z - z_0| < R$ about an isolated singularity z_0. When C is a simple, closed, piecewise smooth curve in this annulus that contains z_0 in its interior (Figure 6.1), coefficient a_{-1} is defined by

$$a_{-1} = \frac{1}{2\pi i} \oint_C f(z)\, dz.$$

Consequently,

$$\oint_C f(z)\, dz = 2\pi i a_{-1};$$

that is, the contour integral of f around the singularity z_0 of f is $2\pi i$ times the coefficient a_{-1} in its Laurent series about z_0.

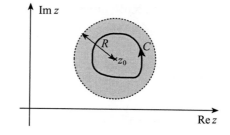

Figure 6.1

Cauchy's residue theorem is a simple extension of this result to the case when C encloses an arbitrary number of isolated singularities. Clearly, coefficient a_{-1} in the Laurent series of a function about an isolated singularity plays a fundamental role in this theory. We give it a name in the following definition.

Definition 6.1   The **residue** of a function f at an isolated singularity z_0 is denoted by $\mathrm{Res}[f, z_0]$. It is the coefficient a_{-1} in the Laurent expansion of f about z_0.

From Example 5.28, we may state that

$$\mathrm{Res}[(\sin z)/z, 0] = 0, \qquad \mathrm{Res}[e^{1/z}, 0] = 1,$$

$$\mathrm{Res}[1/[z^3(z+3)^2], 0] = 1/27, \qquad \mathrm{Res}[1/[z^3(z+3)^2], -3] = -1/27.$$

How residues are used to evaluate contour integrals is contained in the next theorem.

Theorem 6.1 (**Cauchy's Residue Theorem**)   Suppose a function f is analytic inside and on a simple, closed, piecewise smooth curve C, except at singularities $z_1, \ldots, z_n$ in its interior. Then,

$$\oint_C f(z)\, dz = 2\pi i \sum_{j=1}^{n} \text{Res}[f, z_j]. \tag{6.1}$$

Proof   Construct around the z_j disjoint circles $C_j : |z - z_j| = r_j$ such that each C_j is interior to C (Figure 6.2). By Theorem 4.8, the contour integral around C can be replaced by contour integrals around the C_j,

$$\oint_C f(z)\, dz = \sum_{j=1}^{n} \oint_{C_j} f(z)\, dz.$$

Now if f is expanded in a Laurent series about z_j,

$$f(z) = \sum_{n=-\infty}^{\infty} a_n (z - z_j)^n \qquad \text{where} \qquad a_{-1} = \frac{1}{2\pi i} \oint_{C_j} f(z)\, dz.$$

But then $\displaystyle\oint_{C_j} f(z)\, dz = 2\pi i\, a_{-1} = 2\pi i\, \text{Res}[f, z_j]$, and

$$\oint_C f(z)\, dz = 2\pi i \sum_{j=1}^{n} \text{Res}[f, z_j]. \quad\blacksquare$$

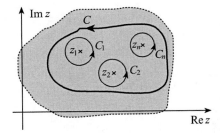

Figure 6.2

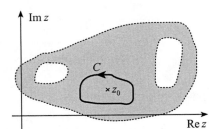

Figure 6.3

We suggested at the beginning of the chapter that Cauchy's residue theorem encompasses the Cauchy-Goursat theorem, the Cauchy integral formulas, and Theorem 4.8. If f is analytic inside a closed, piecewise smooth curve C, then it has no residues interior to C. Hence the contour integral around C must vanish (Cauchy-Goursat theorem). Certainly residue theory encompasses Theorem 4.8; the theorem was instrumental in verifying Theorem 6.1. To illustrate that the generalized Cauchy integral formula is a special case of the Cauchy residue theorem, suppose that f is analytic inside and on a simple, closed, piecewise smooth curve C (Figure 6.3). If z_0 is a point interior to C, then the function $f(z)/(z - z_0)^{n+1}$ is analytic inside C except at z_0. Thus,

$$\oint_C \frac{f(z)}{(z - z_0)^{n+1}}\, dz = 2\pi i\, \text{Res}\left[\frac{f(z)}{(z - z_0)^{n+1}}, z_0\right].$$

If f is expanded in a Taylor series about z_0,

$$f(z) = f(z_0) + f'(z_0)(z - z_0) + \cdots + \frac{f^{(n)}(z_0)}{n!}(z - z_0)^n + \cdots.$$

Thus,

$$\frac{f(z)}{(z - z_0)^{n+1}} = \frac{f(z_0)}{(z - z_0)^{n+1}} + \frac{f'(z_0)}{(z - z_0)^n} + \cdots + \frac{f^{(n)}(z_0)}{n!(z - z_0)} + \cdots,$$

and

$$\operatorname{Res}\left[\frac{f(z)}{(z - z_0)^{n+1}}, z_0\right] = \frac{f^{(n)}(z_0)}{n!}.$$

Consequently,

$$\oint_C \frac{f(z)}{(z - z_0)^{n+1}}\, dz = 2\pi i \frac{f^{(n)}(z_0)}{n!},$$

the Cauchy generalized integral formula.

Example 6.1   Evaluate $\oint_C \dfrac{\sin z}{z^3}\, dz$ where $C : |z| = 1$.

Solution   Since $\sin z$ is entire and $z = 0$ is interior to C, Cauchy's generalized integral formula gives

$$\oint_C \frac{\sin z}{z^3}\, dz = \frac{2\pi i}{2!} \frac{d^2}{dz^2}(\sin z)_{|z=0} = \pi i(-\sin z)_{|z=0} = 0.$$

Alternatively, $z = 0$ is the only singularity of $(\sin z)/z^3$ interior to C. Since

$$\frac{\sin z}{z^3} = \frac{1}{z^3}\left(z - \frac{z^3}{3!} + \frac{z^5}{5!} - \cdots\right) = \frac{1}{z^2} - \frac{1}{3!} + \frac{z^2}{5!} - \cdots,$$

we find that $\operatorname{Res}[(\sin z)/z^3, 0] = 0$, and hence

$$\oint_C \frac{\sin z}{z^3}\, dz = 2\pi i(0) = 0.\bullet$$

Example 6.2   Evaluate $\oint_C e^{1/z}dz$ where $C : |z| = 1$.

Solution   Since the Laurent series for $e^{1/z}$ around $z = 0$ is

$$e^{1/z} = 1 + \frac{1}{z} + \frac{1}{2!z^2} + \frac{1}{3!z^3} + \cdots,$$

(see Example 5.28), the residue of $e^{1/z}$ at $z = 0$ is $\operatorname{Res}[e^{1/z}, 0] = 1$. Thus,

$$\oint_C e^{1/z}dz = 2\pi i(1) = 2\pi i.\bullet$$

In order to use Cauchy's residue theorem effectively, it is essential to be able to calculate residues quickly. Using Laurent series (as in Examples 6.1 and 6.2) is not always efficient. The following theorem gives a formula for calculating residues at poles.

Theorem 6.2 If f has a pole of order m at z_0, then

$$\text{Res}[f, z_0] = \lim_{z \to z_0} \frac{1}{(m-1)!} \frac{d^{m-1}}{dz^{m-1}} [(z - z_0)^m f(z)]. \tag{6.2}$$

Proof When f has a pole of order m at z_0, its Laurent expansion about z_0 takes the form

$$f(z) = \frac{a_{-m}}{(z - z_0)^m} + \frac{a_{-m+1}}{(z - z_0)^{m-1}} + \cdots + \frac{a_{-1}}{z - z_0} + a_0 + \cdots,$$

valid in some annulus $0 < |z - z_0| < R$. Thus,

$$(z - z_0)^m f(z) = a_{-m} + a_{-m+1}(z - z_0) + \cdots + a_{-1}(z - z_0)^{m-1} + \cdots$$

and

$$\frac{d^{m-1}}{dz^{m-1}} [(z - z_0)^m f(z)] = (m-1)! \, a_{-1} + m! a_0 (z - z_0) + \cdots.$$

Finally,

$$\lim_{z \to z_0} \frac{1}{(m-1)!} \frac{d^{m-1}}{dz^{m-1}} [(z - z_0)^m f(z)] = a_{-1}. \quad \blacksquare$$

Example 6.3 Evaluate $\oint_C \frac{1}{(z+5)(z^2-1)^3} \, dz$ where $C : |z| = 2$.

Solution Since the integrand has singularities at $z = -5$ and $z = \pm 1$, only the last two of which are interior to C,

$$\oint_C \frac{1}{(z+5)(z^2-1)^3} \, dz = 2\pi i \left\{ \text{Res}\left[\frac{1}{(z+5)(z^2-1)^3}, -1 \right] + \text{Res}\left[\frac{1}{(z+5)(z^2-1)^3}, 1 \right] \right\}.$$

Now $z = 1$ is a pole of order 3, and therefore

$$\text{Res}\left[\frac{1}{(z+5)(z^2-1)^3}, 1 \right] = \frac{1}{2!} \lim_{z \to 1} \left\{ \frac{d^2}{dz^2} \left[\frac{(z-1)^3}{(z+5)(z+1)^3(z-1)^3} \right] \right\}$$

$$= \frac{1}{2} \lim_{z \to 1} \left[\frac{2}{(z+5)^3(z+1)^3} + \frac{6}{(z+5)^2(z+1)^4} + \frac{12}{(z+5)(z+1)^5} \right]$$

$$= \frac{1}{27}.$$

Similarly, $z = -1$ is a pole of order 3, and

$$\text{Res}\left[\frac{1}{(z+5)(z^2-1)^3}, -1 \right] = \frac{1}{2!} \lim_{z \to -1} \left\{ \frac{d^2}{dz^2} \left[\frac{(z+1)^3}{(z+5)(z+1)^3(z-1)^3} \right] \right\}$$

$$= \frac{1}{2} \lim_{z \to -1} \left[\frac{2}{(z+5)^3(z-1)^3} + \frac{6}{(z+5)^2(z-1)^4} + \frac{12}{(z+5)(z-1)^5} \right]$$

$$= -\frac{19}{512}.$$

Thus,

$$\oint_C \frac{1}{(z+5)(z^2-1)^3} \, dz = 2\pi i \left(\frac{1}{27} - \frac{19}{512} \right) = -\frac{\pi i}{6912}. \quad \bullet$$

One of the most important consequences of the residue theorem is the principle of the argument.

Theorem 6.3 **(Principle of the Argument)**   Let f be analytic in a domain D except at a finite number of poles. If C is a simple, closed, piecewise smooth curve in D which does not pass through any poles or zeros of f, then

$$\oint_C \frac{f'(z)}{f(z)}\, dz = 2\pi i(N - P) \tag{6.3}$$

where N and P are the sums of the orders of the zeros and poles of f inside C.

Proof   According to the residue theorem

$$\oint_C \frac{f'(z)}{f(z)}\, dz = 2\pi i \left\{ \begin{array}{c} \text{sum of residues of } f'/f \\ \text{at its singularities interior to } C \end{array} \right\}.$$

The possible singularities of f'/f occur at the poles and zeros of f. If z_0 is a zero of order m, then according to equation 5.28, f can be written in the form

$$f(z) = (z - z_0)^m g(z)$$

where g is analytic at z_0 and $g(z_0) \neq 0$. Consequently, $f'(z) = m(z - z_0)^{m-1} g(z) + (z - z_0)^m g'(z)$, and

$$\frac{f'(z)}{f(z)} = \frac{m}{z - z_0} + \frac{g'(z)}{g(z)}.$$

Since $g(z_0) \neq 0$, it follows that $g(z) \neq 0$ in some neighbourhood of z_0. As a result, g'/g is analytic therein, and f'/f has a simple pole at z_0 with residue m.

If z_1 is a pole of order m of f, then according to equation 5.31, f can be written in the form

$$f(z) = \frac{g(z)}{(z - z_1)^m}$$

where g is analytic at z_1 and $g(z_1) \neq 0$. Consequently,

$$f'(z) = \frac{-mg(z)}{(z - z_1)^{m+1}} + \frac{g'(z)}{(z - z_1)^m},$$

and

$$\frac{f'(z)}{f(z)} = \frac{-m}{z - z_1} + \frac{g'(z)}{g(z)}.$$

Thus, f'/f has a simple pole at z_1 with residue $-m$. Clearly then, the sum of the residues of f'/f inside C is the sum of the orders of the zeros of f less the sum of the orders of the poles of f. ∎

To see why this theorem is called the Principle of the Argument, we transform contour integral 6.3 from the z-plane to the w-plane with $w = f(z)$. It follows that

$$N - P = \frac{1}{2\pi i} \oint_C \frac{f'(z)}{f(z)}\, dz = \frac{1}{2\pi i} \oint_{f(C)} \frac{1}{w}\, dw,$$

where $f(C)$ is the image of C in the w-plane. But according to Example 4.22, the contour integral on the right is the number of times that $f(C)$ encircles $w = 0$. In other words, $N - P$ measures how many times the curve $f(C)$ encircles $w = 0$ as z traverses C once in the counterclockwise direction; that is, $N - P$ measures how many times the argument of $f(z)$ increases by 2π as z traverses C.

Example 6.4   Use the Principle of the Argument to evaluate $\oint_C \tan z \, dz$ where C is the circle $|z| = 5$.

Solution   If we set $f(z) = \cos z$, then

$$\oint_C \tan z \, dz = -\oint_C \frac{-\sin z}{\cos z} \, dz = -\oint_C \frac{f'(z)}{f(z)} \, dz = -2\pi i (N - P),$$

where N and P are respectively the sums of the orders of the zeros and poles of $f(z)$ inside C. Clearly, $f(z) = \cos z$ has no poles, and its zeros are $z = (2n + 1)\pi/2$ (n an integer), all of order one. Since $\pm\pi/2$ and $\pm 3\pi/2$ are the only zeros interior to C,

$$\oint_C \tan z \, dz = -2\pi i (4 - 0) = -8\pi i. \bullet$$

The principle of the argument leads to Rouche's theorem.

Theorem 6.4   (**Rouche's Theorem**)   Let f and g be analytic in a domain D. If C is a simple, closed, piecewise smooth curve in D which contains in its interior only points of D, and if $|g(z)| < |f(z)|$ on C, then sums of the orders of the zeros of $f + g$ and f inside C are the same.

Proof   The fact that $|g(z)| < |f(z)|$ on C implies that $|f(z)| \neq 0$ and $|f(z) + g(z)| \geq |f(z)| - |g(z)| > 0$ on C. The function $F = [f + g]/f$ does not therefore have any zeros or poles on C. If we apply the principle of the argument to F and C,

$$\frac{1}{2\pi i} \oint_C \frac{F'(z)}{F(z)} \, dz = N - P,$$

and each side may be interpreted as the number of times $w = F(z)$ encircles $w = 0$ as z traverses C. But on C,

$$|F(z) - 1| = \left| \frac{f(z) + g(z)}{f(z)} - 1 \right| = \left| \frac{g(z)}{f(z)} \right| < 1.$$

This implies that the curve $F(C)$ cannot encircle $w = 0$ (Figure 6.4), and therefore $N = P$. Since the zeros of F occur at the zeros of $f + g$ and the poles of F occur at the zeros of f, it follows that the sum of the orders of the zeros of f and $f + g$ inside C must be the same. ∎

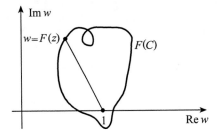

Figure 6.4

Rouche's theorem does not say that f and $f + g$ have the same zeros inside C, but they do have the same number of zeros inside C.

Example 6.5 Show that the equation $e^z = az^n$ has exactly n solutions inside the circle $|z| = 1$ when $a > e$ is real.

Solution On $C : |z| = 1$, the modulus of $-az^n$ is $|-az^n| = a$. On the other hand,

$$|e^z| = |e^{x+yi}| = e^x \le e,$$

since $-1 \le x \le 1$. Hence, $e^z - az^n$ and $-az^n$ have the same number of zeros inside C. Since $-az^n$ has a zero of order n at $z = 0$, it follows that $e^z - az^n$ has n zeros inside C also.●

EXERCISES 6.1

In Exercises 1–11 calculate residues at all isolated singularities of the function.

1. $\dfrac{(z+3)^6}{(z-4i)^4}$

2. $\dfrac{z^2+4}{(z+2)(z^2+1)^2}$

3. $\dfrac{\sin^3 2z}{z^3}$

4. $\dfrac{\sin^3 2z}{z^4}$

5. $\dfrac{\sin^3 2z}{z^5}$

6. $(z-1)^n e^{1/(z-1)}$, $n \ge 1$ an integer

7. $\csc 2z$

8. $\cot z$

9. $\dfrac{z^n}{(z-1)^m}$, m, n positive integers

10. $\dfrac{e^{1/z} z^n}{z+1}$, $n \ge 1$ an integer

11. $e^{z-2/z}$

In Exercises 12–36 use Cauchy's residue theorem to evaluate the contour integral.

12. Exercise 2 in Section 4.5

13. Exercise 3 in Section 4.5

14. Exercise 1 in Section 4.6

15. Exercise 2 in Section 4.6

16. Exercise 3 in Section 4.6

17. Exercise 4 in Section 4.6

18. Exercise 5 in Section 4.6

19. Exercise 6 in Section 4.6

20. Exercise 7 in Section 4.6

21. Exercise 8(c) in Section 4.6

22. Exercise 9 in Section 4.6

23. Exercise 10 in Section 4.6

24. Exercise 11 in Section 4.6

25. Exercise 12 in Section 4.6

26. $\displaystyle\oint_C \frac{\sin z}{z^2-4}\, dz$ where $C : |z| = 5$

27. $\displaystyle\oint_C \frac{e^z}{z(z-2)^3}\, dz$ where $C : |z| = 3$

28. $\displaystyle\oint_C \frac{z^2}{(z-2)^2(z^2-1)}\, dz$ where $C : |z-2| = 2$

29. $\displaystyle\oint_C \left(\frac{z-1}{z+1}\right)^3 dz$ where $C : |z-1| = 1$

30. $\displaystyle\oint_C z e^{3/z}\, dz$ where $C : |z| = 5$

31. $\displaystyle\oint_C \frac{1}{z^2+z+1}\, dz$ where $C : |z| = 8$

32. $\displaystyle\oint_C \frac{1}{z^2 \sin z}\, dz$ where $C : |z| = 1$

33. $\displaystyle\oint_C \frac{e^z - 1}{\sin^2 z}\, dz$ where $C : |z| = 1$

34. $\displaystyle\oint_C \frac{1}{z^2(e^z-1)}\, dz$ where $C : |z| = 1/2$

35. $\oint_C \dfrac{z^{n-1}}{z^n - 1}\, dz$ where $C : |z| = R > 1$, and $n \geq 1$ is an integer

36. $\oint_C e^{1/z} \sin(1/z)\, dz$ where C is the square with vertices ± 1 and $\pm i$

Use the principle of the argument to evaluate the contour integral in Exercises 37–40.

37. $\oint_C \dfrac{2z \sin z + z^2 \cos z}{z^2 \sin z}\, dz$ where $C : |z| = 4$ **38.** $\oint_C \dfrac{z^3}{z^4 + 1}\, dz$ where $C : |z| = 2$

39. $\oint_C \dfrac{z \sinh z + 3 \cosh z}{z \cosh z}\, dz$ where $C : |z - i| = 7$

40. $\oint_C \dfrac{2z \sec^2 z^2}{\tan z^2}\, dz$ where C is the square with vertices ± 2 and $\pm 2i$

41. Use Rouche's theorem to show that $z^4 + 4z + 1$ has exactly one zero inside $|z| = 1$. Hint: Let $f(z) = 4z$ and $g(z) = z^4 + 1$.

42. Use Rouche's theorem to show that $z^5 + 3z^2 + 6z + 1$ has exactly one zero inside $|z| = 1$. Hint: Let $f(z) = 6z + 1$ and $g(z) = z^5 + 3z^2$.

43. Use Rouche's theorem to show that all zeros of $z^5 + 3z^2 + 6z + 1$ are inside $|z| = 2$. Hint: Let $f(z) = z^5$ and $g(z) = 3z^2 + 6z + 1$.

44. Show that all roots of the equation $z^7 - 2z^3 + 8 = 0$ satisfy $1 < |z| < 2$.

45. Show that if g is analytic inside and on $C : |z| = 1$ and if $|g(z)| < 1$ on C, then there is exactly one point z inside C for which $g(z) = z$.

46. (a) Show that the function $f(z) = 1/(4 + z^2)^{10}$ does not have an antiderivative in the domain consisting of the complex plane with the points $\pm 2i$ deleted.

     (b) Show that $f(z)$ does have an antiderivative in the domain consisting of the complex plane with the line segment joining the points $\pm 2i$ deleted.

§6.2 Evaluation of Definite Integrals

We have used definite integrals to evaluate contour integrals. It may come as a surprise to learn that contour integrals and residues can be used to evaluate certain classes of definite integrals that might otherwise prove intractable.

Definite Integrals Involving Trigonometric Functions

Contour integrals and residues can be useful in the evaluation of definite integrals that are rational functions of sines and cosines,

$$\int_a^b \frac{P(\cos\theta, \sin\theta)}{Q(\cos\theta, \sin\theta)}\, d\theta \tag{6.4}$$

where $P(\cos\theta, \sin\theta)$ and $Q(\cos\theta, \sin\theta)$ are polynomials in $\cos\theta$ and $\sin\theta$, provided Q is never equal to zero in the interval. The technique is to set $z = e^{\theta i}$. This transforms the definite integral to a contour integral along an arc of the unit circle in the complex z-plane. When $a = 0$ and $b = 2\pi$, it is the complete circle, and residues are used to evaluate the contour integral. For other intervals of integration, residues may not be applicable, but other techniques for evaluating contour integrals may be advantageous. The integrand for the contour integral is obtained by substituting

$$\cos\theta = \frac{e^{\theta i} + e^{-\theta i}}{2} = \frac{1}{2}\left(z + \frac{1}{z}\right), \qquad \sin\theta = \frac{e^{\theta i} - e^{-\theta i}}{2i} = \frac{1}{2i}\left(z - \frac{1}{z}\right).$$

Example 6.6 Evaluate $\displaystyle\int_0^{2\pi} \frac{1}{2 - \cos\theta}\, d\theta.$

Solution We transform the definite integral to the complex plane by setting $z = e^{\theta i}$ and $dz = ie^{\theta i}d\theta = iz\, d\theta$. As θ traces out the values 0 through 2π, z traces out the circle $C : |z| = 1$ once counterclockwise (Figure 6.5). We replace $\cos\theta$ with $\cos\theta = (z + z^{-1})/2$,

$$\int_0^{2\pi} \frac{1}{2 - \cos\theta}\, d\theta = \oint_C \frac{1}{2 - \left(\frac{z + z^{-1}}{2}\right)} \frac{dz}{iz} = 2i \oint_C \frac{1}{z^2 - 4z + 1}\, dz.$$

The (real) definite integral has been replaced by a (complex) contour integral. Because $z^2 - 4z + 1 = 0$ when $z = (4 \pm \sqrt{16 - 4})/2 = 2 \pm \sqrt{3}$, the integrand

$$\frac{1}{z^2 - 4z + 1} = \frac{1}{(z - 2 - \sqrt{3})(z - 2 + \sqrt{3})}$$

has simple poles at $z = 2 \pm \sqrt{3}$, only one of which is interior to C. Since

$$\text{Res}\left[\frac{1}{z^2 - 4z + 1}, 2 - \sqrt{3}\right] = \lim_{z \to 2 - \sqrt{3}} \frac{z - 2 + \sqrt{3}}{(z - 2 - \sqrt{3})(z - 2 + \sqrt{3})} = -\frac{1}{2\sqrt{3}},$$

Cauchy's residue theorem gives

$$\int_0^{2\pi} \frac{1}{2 - \cos\theta}\, d\theta = 2i\left[2\pi i\left(-\frac{1}{2\sqrt{3}}\right)\right] = \frac{2\pi}{\sqrt{3}}.\bullet$$

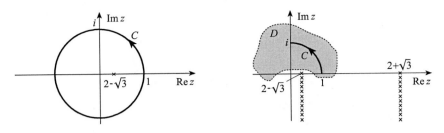

Figure 6.5　　　　　　**Figure 6.6**

The transformation $z = {}^{\theta i}$ from a real definite integral to a contour integral can be applied to integrals over intervals other than $[0, 2\pi]$, but residue theory may not be applicable.

Example 6.7 Evaluate $\displaystyle\int_0^{\pi/2} \frac{1}{2 - \cos\theta}\, d\theta.$

Solution The transformation $z = e^{\theta i}$ transforms the real integral into the contour integral of Example 6.6 over the quarter circle in Figure 6.6. This time we use the partial fraction decomposition of the integrand to write

$$\int_0^{\pi/2} \frac{1}{2 - \cos\theta}\, d\theta = 2i \int_C \frac{1}{z^2 - 4z + 1}\, dz = 2i \int_C \left(\frac{\frac{1}{2\sqrt{3}}}{z - 2 - \sqrt{3}} + \frac{\frac{-1}{2\sqrt{3}}}{z - 2 + \sqrt{3}} \right) dz.$$

In the domain D of Figure 6.6, the integrand has an antiderivative, and hence

$$\int_0^{\pi/2} \frac{1}{2 - \cos\theta}\, d\theta = \frac{i}{\sqrt{3}} \left\{ \log_\phi(z - 2 - \sqrt{3}) - \log_\phi(z - 2 + \sqrt{3}) \right\}_1^i,$$

where we choose branches with cuts $\phi = -\pi/2$. Then

$$\int_0^{\pi/2} \frac{1}{2 - \cos\theta}\, d\theta = \frac{i}{\sqrt{3}} \left[\log_{-\pi/2}(i - 2 - \sqrt{3}) - \log_{-\pi/2}(i - 2 + \sqrt{3}) \right.$$

$$\left. - \log_{-\pi/2}(-1 - \sqrt{3}) + \log_{-\pi/2}(-1 + \sqrt{3}) \right]$$

$$= \frac{i}{\sqrt{3}} \left\{ \left[\ln\sqrt{(-2 - \sqrt{3})^2 + 1} + i\left(\pi - \text{Tan}^{-1}\left(\frac{1}{2 + \sqrt{3}} \right) \right) \right] \right.$$

$$- \left[\ln\sqrt{(-2 + \sqrt{3})^2 + 1} + i\left(\pi - \text{Tan}^{-1}\left(\frac{1}{2 - \sqrt{3}} \right) \right) \right]$$

$$\left. - \left[\ln(1 + \sqrt{3}) + \pi i \right] + \ln(\sqrt{3} - 1) \right\}$$

$$= \frac{i}{\sqrt{3}} \left\{ \left[\ln\sqrt{8 + 4\sqrt{3}} - \ln\sqrt{8 - 4\sqrt{3}} - \ln(1 + \sqrt{3}) + \ln(\sqrt{3} - 1) \right] \right.$$

$$\left. + i\left[-\pi + \text{Tan}^{-1}\left(\frac{1}{2 - \sqrt{3}} \right) - \text{Tan}^{-1}\left(\frac{1}{2 + \sqrt{3}} \right) \right] \right\}.$$

We can bring the inverse tangents together using the identity

$$\text{Tan}^{-1}A - \text{Tan}^{-1}B = \text{Tan}^{-1}\left(\frac{A - B}{1 + AB} \right), \qquad \text{valid when } AB > 0.$$

The result is

$$\int_0^{\pi/2} \frac{1}{2 - \cos\theta}\, d\theta = \frac{i}{2\sqrt{3}} \ln\left[\frac{8 + 4\sqrt{3}}{8 - 4\sqrt{3}}\frac{(\sqrt{3} - 1)^2}{(\sqrt{3} + 1)^2}\right]$$

$$- \frac{1}{\sqrt{3}}\left\{-\pi + \mathrm{Tan}^{-1}\left[\frac{\dfrac{1}{2 - \sqrt{3}} - \dfrac{1}{2 + \sqrt{3}}}{1 + \left(\dfrac{1}{2 - \sqrt{3}}\right)\left(\dfrac{1}{2 + \sqrt{3}}\right)}\right]\right\}$$

$$= \frac{i}{2\sqrt{3}} \ln\left[\frac{8 + 4\sqrt{3}}{8 - 4\sqrt{3}}\frac{4 - 2\sqrt{3}}{4 + 2\sqrt{3}}\right] - \frac{1}{\sqrt{3}}\left[-\pi + \mathrm{Tan}^{-1}\sqrt{3})\right]$$

$$= \frac{2\sqrt{3}\pi}{9}.\ \bullet$$

Real Improper Integrals

Contour integrals can also be effective in evaluation of improper integrals which have infinite upper and/or lower limits.

Improper Integrals of Rational Functions

The first type of improper integral that we consider involve integrands that are rational functions; that is, integrals of the form

$$\int_a^b \frac{P(x)}{Q(x)}\, dx, \tag{6.5}$$

where $P(x)$ and $Q(x)$ are polynomials, and at least one of a and b is infinite. They are simplest when $Q(x)$ does not vanish for any value of x in the interval of integration. We illustrate the procedure to be followed in the next example.

Example 6.8 Evaluate $\displaystyle\int_{-\infty}^{\infty} \frac{1}{1 + x^4}\, dx.$

Solution   It is fairly clear that were we to evaluate the contour integral

$$\oint_C \frac{1}{1 + z^4}\, dz$$

where C is shown in Figure 6.7a, and were we to let $R \to \infty$, then that part of the contour integral along the real axis would give rise to the required improper integral. Let us consider this contour integral then.

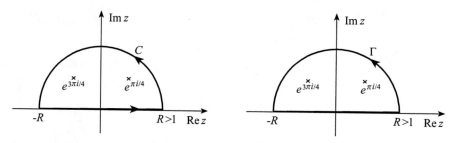

Figure 6.7a   **Figure 6.7b**

The integrand $(1 + z^4)^{-1}$ has simple poles at the four fourth roots of -1,

$$e^{\pi i/4}, \qquad e^{3\pi i/4}, \qquad e^{5\pi i/4}, \qquad e^{7\pi i/4},$$

only the first two of which are interior to C. L'Hôpital's rule (Theorem 5.24) gives

$$\text{Res}\left[\frac{1}{1+z^4}, e^{\pi i/4}\right] = \lim_{z \to e^{\pi i/4}} \frac{z - e^{\pi i/4}}{1 + z^4} = \lim_{z \to e^{\pi i/4}} \frac{1}{4z^3} = \frac{1}{4e^{3\pi i/4}} = -\frac{\sqrt{2}}{8}(1 + i).$$

Similarly, $\text{Res}\left[\dfrac{1}{1+z^4}, e^{3\pi i/4}\right] = \dfrac{\sqrt{2}}{8}(1 - i)$. By Cauchy's residue theorem then,

$$\oint_C \frac{1}{1+z^4}\, dz = 2\pi i \left[-\frac{\sqrt{2}}{8}(1 + i) + \frac{\sqrt{2}}{8}(1 - i)\right] = \frac{\pi}{\sqrt{2}}.$$

Suppose we now divide C into a semicircular part Γ and a straight line part (Figure 6.7b). Then

$$\frac{\pi}{\sqrt{2}} = \int_{-R}^{R} \frac{1}{1+x^4}\, dx + \int_{\Gamma} \frac{1}{1+z^4}\, dz.$$

If we set $z = Re^{\theta i}$, $0 \le \theta \le \pi$, on Γ, then inequality 1.41 on the semicircle gives

$$\left|\frac{1}{1+z^4}\right| \le \frac{1}{|z^4| - 1} = \frac{1}{R^4 - 1}.$$

Hence, by property 4.21,

$$\left|\int_{\Gamma} \frac{1}{1+z^4}\, dz\right| \le \frac{1}{R^4 - 1}(\pi R).$$

It is clear that the limit of this expression is zero as $R \to \infty$, and therefore

$$\frac{\pi}{\sqrt{2}} = \lim_{R \to \infty} \left(\int_{-R}^{R} \frac{1}{1+x^4}\, dx + \int_{\Gamma} \frac{1}{1+z^4}\, dz\right) = \int_{-\infty}^{\infty} \frac{1}{1+x^4}\, dx.\ \bullet$$

This example has illustrated that the contour integral of $1/(1+z^4)$ around the curve C of Figure 6.7 can be used to evaluate the improper integral of $1/(1 + x^4)$ from negative infinity to infinity. When the integrand is a rational function $f(x)$ of x, the integrand for the contour integral is always chosen as $f(z)$.

The most arduous part of the above example, and other similar examples, is establishing that the contour integral along Γ approaches zero as the radius of the semicircle becomes infinite. The following theorem eliminates this task in many examples.

Theorem 6.5 Suppose that $P(x)$ and $Q(x)$ are polynomials of degrees m and n, where $n \ge m+2$, and $Q(x) \ne 0$ for all real x. Then,

$$\int_{-\infty}^{\infty} \frac{P(x)}{Q(x)}\, dx = 2\pi i \left\{ \begin{array}{l} \text{sum of the residues of } P(z)/Q(z) \text{ at} \\ \text{its poles in the half-plane Im } z > 0 \end{array} \right\}. \qquad (6.6)$$

Proof   Consider $\oint_C \dfrac{P(z)}{Q(z)}\, dz$ where
contour C in Figure 6.8 encloses all
singularities of $P(z)/Q(z)$ in the
upper half-plane. (Such singularities
must be poles, provided of course that
all removable singularities have been
removed.) By Cauchy's residue theorem,

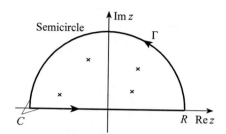

Figure 6.8

$$2\pi i \left\{ \begin{array}{c} \text{sum of the residues of } P(z)/Q(z) \text{ at} \\ \text{the poles inside the curve } C \end{array} \right\} = \oint_C \frac{P(z)}{Q(z)}\, dz = \int_{-R}^{R} \frac{P(x)}{Q(x)}\, dx + \int_{\Gamma} \frac{P(z)}{Q(z)}\, dz.$$

Let $P(z) = a_m z^m + \cdots + a_0$ and $Q(z) = b_n z^n + \cdots + b_0$. On Γ, $|z| = R$, and R can
be chosen so large that $|b_n R^n| \geq |b_{n-1} R^{n-1}| + \cdots + |b_0|$. For such R, we can say
that on Γ,

$$\left| \frac{P(z)}{Q(z)} \right| \leq \frac{|a_m| R^m + \cdots + |a_0|}{|b_n| R^n - \cdots - |b_0|},$$

and therefore using inequality 4.21,

$$\left| \int_{\Gamma} \frac{P(z)}{Q(z)}\, dz \right| \leq \frac{|a_m| R^m + \cdots + |a_0|}{|b_n| R^n - \cdots - |b_0|} (\pi R).$$

This quantity approaches 0 as $R \to \infty$ since $n \geq m + 2$. Thus,

$$2\pi i \left\{ \begin{array}{c} \text{sum of the residues of } P(z)/Q(z) \text{ at} \\ \text{the poles in the upper half-plane Im } z > 0 \end{array} \right\} = \lim_{R \to \infty} \left[\int_{-R}^{R} \frac{P(x)}{Q(x)}\, dx + \int_{\Gamma} \frac{P(z)}{Q(z)}\, dz \right]$$

$$= \int_{-\infty}^{\infty} \frac{P(x)}{Q(x)}\, dx. \blacksquare$$

With this result, it is no longer necessary to introduce the contour of Figure
6.7. The fact that $n \geq m + 2$ guarantees that the contour integral along Γ vanishes
as $R \to \infty$.

Example 6.9   Evaluate the improper integral $\displaystyle\int_0^{\infty} \frac{x^2}{a^4 + x^4}\, dx$, where $a > 0$.

Solution   First, we note that because the integrand is an even function, we can
write that

$$\int_0^{\infty} \frac{x^2}{a^4 + x^4}\, dx = \frac{1}{2} \int_{-\infty}^{\infty} \frac{x^2}{a^4 + x^4}\, dx.$$

The function $z^2/(a^4 + z^4)$ has simple poles at the four fourth roots of $-a^4$,

$$ae^{\pi i/4}, \qquad ae^{3\pi i/4}, \qquad ae^{5\pi i/4}, \qquad ae^{7\pi i/4},$$

only the first two of which are in the upper half of the complex plane. L'Hôpital's
rule (Theorem 5.24) gives

$$\text{Res}\left[\frac{z^2}{a^4+z^4}, ae^{\pi i/4}\right] = \lim_{z\to ae^{\pi i/4}} \frac{z^2(z-ae^{\pi i/4})}{a^4+z^4} = \lim_{z\to ae^{\pi i/4}} \frac{z^2+2z(z-ae^{\pi i/4})}{4z^3}$$

$$= \frac{1}{4ae^{\pi i/4}} = \frac{1}{4a}e^{-\pi i/4}.$$

Similarly, $\text{Res}\left[\dfrac{z^2}{a^4+z^4}, e^{3\pi i/4}\right] = \dfrac{1}{4a}e^{-3\pi i/4}$. By Theorem 6.5 then,

$$\int_0^\infty \frac{x^2}{a^4+x^4}\,dx = \frac{1}{2}(2\pi i)\left[\frac{1}{4a}e^{-\pi i/4} + \frac{1}{4a}e^{-3\pi i/4}\right]$$

$$= \frac{\pi}{4a}\left[\left(\frac{1}{\sqrt{2}}-\frac{i}{\sqrt{2}}\right) + \left(-\frac{1}{\sqrt{2}}-\frac{i}{\sqrt{2}}\right)\right] = \frac{\sqrt{2}\pi}{4a}.\ \bullet$$

When function $Q(x)$ in integral 6.5 has a zero on the real axis, Theorem 6.5 is not applicable and the contour of Example 6.8 must be modified. Consider the following example.

Example 6.10 Evaluate $\displaystyle\int_0^\infty \frac{1}{1+x^3}\,dx$.

Solution   Based on the previous examples, we should perhaps consider

$$\oint_C \frac{1}{1+z^3}\,dz$$

where C is some appropriate contour. Clearly a part of C should be the positive real axis and possibly a circular arc of radius $R > 1$. But we cannot take a semicircle as in Example 6.8 since $1/(1+z^3)$ has a singularity at $z = -1$ on the negative real axis. What we should like to do then is choose some other line eminating from the origin say $z = re^{\phi i}$, $0 < \phi < \pi$, which leads to a simple solution (Figure 6.9). The integrand has simple poles at $z = e^{\pi i/3}$, -1, $e^{5\pi i/3}$.

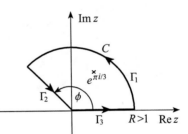

Figure 6.9

Suppose for the moment we stipulate that ϕ be in the interval $\pi/3 < \phi < \pi$, but, for the moment, leave it otherwise arbitrary. Cauchy's residue theorem and L'Hôpital's rule give

$$\oint_C \frac{1}{1+z^3}\,dz = 2\pi i\,\text{Res}\left[\frac{1}{1+z^3}, e^{\pi i/3}\right] = 2\pi i \lim_{z\to e^{\pi i/3}} \frac{z-e^{\pi i/3}}{1+z^3}$$

$$= 2\pi i \lim_{z\to e^{\pi i/3}} \frac{1}{3z^2} = \frac{2\pi i}{3e^{2\pi i/3}} = \frac{(\sqrt{3}-i)\pi}{3}.$$

Thus,

$$\frac{(\sqrt{3}-i)\pi}{3} = \int_{\Gamma_1} \frac{1}{1+z^3}\,dz + \int_{\Gamma_2} \frac{1}{1+z^3}\,dz + \int_{\Gamma_3} \frac{1}{1+z^3}\,dz.$$

If we set $z = Re^{\theta i}$ on Γ_1, then on this arc

$$\left| \frac{1}{1+z^3} \right| \leq \frac{1}{|z|^3 - 1} = \frac{1}{R^3 - 1},$$

and hence

$$\left| \int_{\Gamma_1} \frac{1}{1+z^3} \, dz \right| \leq \frac{1}{R^3 - 1}(R\phi).$$

The limit of this expression is zero as $R \to \infty$. Thus,

$$\frac{(\sqrt{3} - i)\pi}{3} = \lim_{R \to \infty} \left(\int_{\Gamma_1} \frac{1}{1+z^3} \, dz + \int_{\Gamma_2} \frac{1}{1+z^3} \, dz + \int_{\Gamma_3} \frac{1}{1+z^3} \, dz \right)$$

$$= \int_{\Gamma_2} \frac{1}{1+z^3} \, dz + \int_0^\infty \frac{1}{1+x^3} \, dx,$$

where $\Gamma_2 : z = re^{\phi i}$, $\infty > r \geq 0$ (and $\pi/3 < \phi < \pi$). Our problem then is to choose ϕ in order that the contour integral along Γ_2 can be evaluated. Since $z = re^{\phi i}$ on Γ_2,

$$\int_{\Gamma_2} \frac{1}{1+z^3} \, dz = \int_\infty^0 \frac{1}{1+r^3 e^{3\phi i}} e^{\phi i} \, dr = -e^{\phi i} \int_0^\infty \frac{1}{1+r^3 e^{3\phi i}} \, dr.$$

If we choose $\phi = 2\pi/3$, then

$$\int_{\Gamma_2} \frac{1}{1+z^3} \, dz = -e^{2\pi i/3} \int_0^\infty \frac{1}{1+r^3} \, dr,$$

and

$$\frac{(\sqrt{3} - i)\pi}{3} = -e^{2\pi i/3} \int_0^\infty \frac{1}{1+r^3} \, dr + \int_0^\infty \frac{1}{1+x^3} \, dx$$

$$= \left[-\left(-\frac{1}{2} + \frac{\sqrt{3}i}{2} \right) + 1 \right] \int_0^\infty \frac{1}{1+x^3} \, dx.$$

Thus,

$$\int_0^\infty \frac{1}{1+x^3} \, dx = \frac{(\sqrt{3} - i)\pi}{3} \frac{2}{3 - \sqrt{3}i} = \frac{2\pi}{3\sqrt{3}}. \bullet$$

Improper Integrals of Rational Functions Multiplied by Sines and/or Cosines

We now consider improper integrals of the forms

$$\int_{-\infty}^\infty \frac{P(x)}{Q(x)} \cos ax \, dx \quad \text{and} \quad \int_{-\infty}^\infty \frac{P(x)}{Q(x)} \sin ax \, dx, \qquad (6.7)$$

where $a > 0$ is a constant. Based on integrals of type 6.5, it would be natural to replace x's with z's, and consider contour integrals around the contour in Figure 6.7. Unfortunately, this does not work, principally because the sine and cosine functions become unbounded on Γ as the radius of the semicircle gets large. We will illustrate this in the next example. Instead, we replace $\sin ax$ and $\cos ax$ with e^{azi}, and consider the contour integral

$$\int_C \frac{P(z)}{Q(z)} e^{azi} \, dz, \tag{6.8}$$

where C is the contour in Figure 6.7.

Example 6.11   Evaluate $\displaystyle\int_0^\infty \frac{\cos 2x}{x^2 + 1} \, dx.$

Solution   Since the integrand is an even function, we may write that

$$\int_0^\infty \frac{\cos 2x}{x^2 + 1} \, dx = \frac{1}{2} \int_{-\infty}^\infty \frac{\cos 2x}{x^2 + 1} \, dx.$$

Suppose that we consider the contour integral

$$\oint_C \frac{\cos 2z}{z^2 + 1} \, dz$$

around the contour in Figure 6.7. Certainly along the straight line portion of C the integrand reduces to $\cos 2x/(x^2 + 1)$, but if we set $z = x + yi$ along Γ, then on the semicircle

$$\left| \frac{\cos 2z}{z^2 + 1} \right| = \left| \frac{e^{2(x+yi)i} + e^{-2(x+yi)i}}{2(z^2 + 1)} \right| = \left| \frac{e^{-2y+2xi} + e^{2y-2xi}}{2(z^2 + 1)} \right|$$

which becomes infinite as $|z| \to \infty$. We shall not therefore be able to show that the contour integral along Γ approaches zero as $|z| \to \infty$ as in Example 6.8. Consider instead

$$\oint_C \frac{e^{2zi}}{z^2 + 1} \, dz$$

where C is again the contour in Figure 6.7. Since the integrand has simple poles at $z = \pm i$, only $z = i$ being interior to C,

$$\oint_C \frac{e^{2zi}}{z^2 + 1} \, dz = 2\pi i \operatorname{Res}\left[\frac{e^{2zi}}{z^2 + 1}, i \right] = 2\pi i \lim_{z \to i} \left[\frac{(z-i)e^{2zi}}{(z-i)(z+i)} \right] = 2\pi i \frac{e^{2i(i)}}{2i} = \frac{\pi}{e^2}.$$

Thus,

$$\begin{aligned}
\frac{\pi}{e^2} &= \int_{-R}^R \frac{e^{2xi}}{x^2 + 1} \, dx + \int_\Gamma \frac{e^{2zi}}{z^2 + 1} \, dz \\
&= \int_{-R}^R \frac{\cos 2x}{x^2 + 1} \, dx + i \int_{-R}^R \frac{\sin 2x}{x^2 + 1} \, dx + \int_\Gamma \frac{e^{2zi}}{z^2 + 1} \, dz \\
&= \int_{-R}^R \frac{\cos 2x}{x^2 + 1} \, dx + \int_\Gamma \frac{e^{2zi}}{z^2 + 1} \, dz \quad \text{(since } \sin 2x/(x^2 + 1) \text{ is an odd function).}
\end{aligned}$$

If we set $z = x + yi = Re^{\theta i}$ on Γ, then on this semicircle,

$$\begin{aligned}
\left| \frac{e^{2zi}}{z^2 + 1} \right| &\le \frac{|e^{2(x+yi)i}|}{|z^2| - 1} \qquad \text{(by inequality 1.41)} \\
&= \frac{e^{-2y}}{R^2 - 1} \\
&\le \frac{1}{R^2 - 1} \qquad \text{(since } y \ge 0\text{).}
\end{aligned}$$

Hence, by inequality 4.21,

$$\left| \int_\Gamma \frac{e^{2zi}}{z^2 + 1} \, dz \right| \le \frac{1}{R^2 - 1}(\pi R).$$

Since the limit of this expression is zero as $R \to \infty$, it follows that

$$\frac{\pi}{e^2} = \lim_{R \to \infty} \left(\int_{-R}^{R} \frac{\cos 2x}{x^2 + 1} \, dx + \int_\Gamma \frac{e^{2zi}}{z^2 + 1} \, dz \right) = \int_{-\infty}^{\infty} \frac{\cos 2x}{x^2 + 1} \, dx = 2 \int_0^{\infty} \frac{\cos 2x}{x^2 + 1} \, dx.$$

Finally,

$$\int_0^{\infty} \frac{\cos 2x}{x^2 + 1} \, dx = \frac{\pi}{2e^2}. \bullet$$

Theorem 6.5 eliminated the necessity of considering the contour integral along the semicircle Γ in Figure 6.7 for integrals of type 6.5. The following theorem accomplishes the same simplification for integrals of type 6.7.

Theorem 6.6 Suppose that $P(x)$ and $Q(x)$ are polynomials of degrees m and n, where $n \ge m+1$, and $Q(x) \ne 0$ for all real x. When $a > 0$ is a constant,

$$\int_{-\infty}^{\infty} \frac{P(x) \cos ax}{Q(x)} \, dx = -2\pi \, \mathrm{Im} \left\{ \begin{array}{l} \text{sum of the residues of } P(z)e^{azi}/Q(z) \\ \text{at its poles in the half-plane } \mathrm{Im}\, z > 0 \end{array} \right\}, \quad (6.9a)$$

and

$$\int_{-\infty}^{\infty} \frac{P(x) \sin ax}{Q(x)} \, dx = 2\pi \, \mathrm{Re} \left\{ \begin{array}{l} \text{sum of the residues of } P(z)e^{azi}/Q(z) \\ \text{at its poles in the half-plane } \mathrm{Im}\, z > 0 \end{array} \right\}. \quad (6.9b)$$

Proof First we prove a result called Jordan's inequality. It states that for $a > 0$

$$\int_0^{\pi} e^{-aR\sin\theta} \, d\theta = 2 \int_0^{\pi/2} e^{-aR\sin\theta} \, d\theta \le \frac{\pi}{aR}(1 - e^{-aR}). \quad (6.10)$$

We use Figure 6.10. Since the equation of the straight line joining $(0,0)$ to $(\pi/2, 1)$ is $y = 2\theta/\pi$, it follows that $\sin\theta \ge 2\theta/\pi$ for $0 \le \theta \le \pi/2$, and

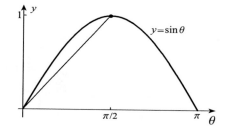

Figure 6.10

$$\int_0^{\pi} e^{-aR\sin\theta} \, d\theta = 2 \int_0^{\pi/2} e^{-aR\sin\theta} \, d\theta \le 2 \int_0^{\pi/2} e^{-aR(2\theta/\pi)} \, d\theta$$

$$= \left\{ \frac{-\pi}{aR} e^{-2aR\theta/\pi} \right\}_0^{\pi/2} = \frac{\pi}{aR}(1 - e^{-aR}).$$

Now consider the contour integral $\oint_C \frac{P(z)}{Q(z)} e^{azi} \, dz$ where C is the contour in the Figure 6.7 and R is sufficiently large for C to contain all singularities of $P(z)/Q(z)$ in the upper half-plane. (Such singularities must be poles, provided that all removable singularities have been removed.) Cauchy's residue theorem gives

$$2\pi i \left\{ \begin{array}{c} \text{sum of the residues of } P(z)e^{azi}/Q(z) \\ \text{at the poles inside } C \end{array} \right\} = \oint_C \frac{P(z)e^{azi}}{Q(z)} \, dz$$

$$= \int_{-R}^{R} \frac{P(x)}{Q(x)} \cos ax \, dx + i \int_{-R}^{R} \frac{P(x)}{Q(x)} \sin ax \, dx$$

$$+ \int_{\Gamma} \frac{P(z)e^{azi}}{Q(z)} \, dz.$$

Let $P(z) = a_m z^m + \cdots + a_0$ and $Q(z) = b_n z^n + \cdots + b_0$. On Γ, $|z| = R$, and R can be chosen so large that $|b_n R^n| \geq |b_{n-1} R^{n-1}| + \cdots + |b_0|$. For such R, we can say that on Γ,

$$\left| \frac{P(z)}{Q(z)} e^{azi} \right| = \frac{|P(z)| e^{a(R\cos\theta + R\sin\theta\, i)i}|}{|Q(z)|} \leq \frac{(|a_m|R^m + \cdots + |a_0|)e^{-aR\sin\theta}}{|b_n|R^n - \cdots - |b_0|}.$$

Inequality 4.21 now gives

$$\left| \int_{\Gamma} \frac{P(z)}{Q(z)} e^{azi} dz \right| \leq \frac{|a_m|R^m + \cdots + |a_0|}{|b_n|R^n - \cdots - |b_0|} \int_0^{\pi} e^{-aR\sin\theta} R \, d\theta$$

$$\leq \frac{|a_m|R^m + \cdots + |a_0|}{|b_n|R^n - \cdots - |b_0|} \frac{\pi}{a}(1 - e^{-aR}).$$

This quantity approaches 0 as $R \to \infty$ since $n \geq m + 1$. Thus,

$$2\pi i \left\{ \begin{array}{c} \text{sum of the residues of } P(z)e^{azi}/Q(z) \text{ at} \\ \text{the poles in the upper half-plane Im } z > 0 \end{array} \right\}$$

$$= \int_{-\infty}^{\infty} \frac{P(x)}{Q(x)} \cos ax \, dx + i \int_{-\infty}^{\infty} \frac{P(x)}{Q(x)} \sin ax \, dx.$$

Real and imaginary parts complete the proof.■

Example 6.12 Evaluate the improper integral $\displaystyle\int_{-\infty}^{\infty} \frac{\cos ax}{x^2 + b^2} \, dx$, where $b > 0$ is a constant.

Solution The function $e^{azi}/(z^2 + b^2)$ has simple poles $z = \pm bi$, only $z = bi$ being in the upper half-plane. The residue at this pole is

$$\text{Res}\left[\frac{e^{azi}}{z^2 + b^2}, bi \right] = \lim_{z \to bi} \frac{(z - bi)e^{azi}}{(z + bi)(z - bi)} = \frac{e^{a(bi)i}}{2bi} = -\frac{e^{-ab}i}{2b}.$$

According to Theorem 6.6,

$$\int_{-\infty}^{\infty} \frac{\cos ax}{x^2 + b^2} \, dx = -2\pi \, \text{Im}\left(-\frac{e^{-ab}i}{2b} \right) = \frac{\pi e^{-ab}}{b}. \bullet$$

EXERCISES 6.2

In Exercises 1–19 use a contour integral to evaluate the definite integral.

1. $\displaystyle\int_0^{2\pi} \frac{1}{3 - \sin\theta}\, d\theta$

2. $\displaystyle\int_0^{2\pi} \frac{1}{3 + 2\cos\theta}\, d\theta$

3. $\displaystyle\int_0^{2\pi} \frac{1}{6 + 5\sin\theta}\, d\theta$

4. $\displaystyle\int_0^{2\pi} \frac{1}{\sin\theta + 2\cos\theta + 4}\, d\theta$

5. $\displaystyle\int_0^{2\pi} \frac{1}{4\cos^2\theta + 3}\, d\theta$

6. $\displaystyle\int_0^{2\pi} \frac{\sin 2\theta}{2 + \cos\theta}\, d\theta$

7. $\displaystyle\int_0^{2\pi} \frac{\sin^2\theta}{5 + 4\cos\theta}\, d\theta$

8. $\displaystyle\int_0^{2\pi} \frac{\cos\theta}{3 + \cos\theta}\, d\theta$

9. $\displaystyle\int_0^{\pi} \frac{1}{3 + 2\cos\theta}\, d\theta$

10. $\displaystyle\int_0^{\pi/2} \frac{1}{6 + 5\sin\theta}\, d\theta$

11. $\displaystyle\int_0^{\pi/2} \frac{1}{3 - \sin\theta}\, d\theta$

12. $\displaystyle\int_{-\pi/2}^{0} \frac{1}{5 + 2\cos\theta}\, d\theta$

13. $\displaystyle\int_0^{2} \frac{1}{3 + 2\sin\theta}\, d\theta$

14. $\displaystyle\int_0^{1} \frac{1}{4 + 3\cos\theta}\, d\theta$

15. $\displaystyle\int_{-\pi}^{0} \frac{1}{4 + \cos\theta}\, d\theta$

16. $\displaystyle\int_{-\pi}^{\pi/2} \frac{1}{5 + 2\sin\theta}\, d\theta$

17. $\displaystyle\int_0^{\pi/2} \frac{\cos\theta}{3 + \cos\theta}\, d\theta$

18. $\displaystyle\int_0^{2\pi} \frac{\cos 3\theta}{5 + 4\cos\theta}\, d\theta$

19. $\displaystyle\int_0^{2\pi} e^{2\cos\theta}\, d\theta$

In Exercises 20–38 use a contour integral to evaluate the improper integral.

20. $\displaystyle\int_0^{\infty} \frac{1}{2 + x^2}\, dx$

21. $\displaystyle\int_{-\infty}^{\infty} \frac{x^2}{(x^2 + 1)(x^2 + 4)}\, dx$

22. $\displaystyle\int_{-\infty}^{\infty} \frac{1}{(x^2 + 4x + 5)^2}\, dx$

23. $\displaystyle\int_{-\infty}^{\infty} \frac{x^2 + 3}{(x^2 + 1)(x^2 - x + 1)}\, dx$

24. $\displaystyle\int_{-\infty}^{\infty} \frac{1}{3 + x^6}\, dx$

25. $\displaystyle\int_0^{\infty} \frac{x}{1 + x^3}\, dx$

26. $\displaystyle\int_0^{\infty} \frac{x^2}{x^4 + a^4}\, dx$

27. $\displaystyle\int_{-\infty}^{\infty} \frac{1}{x^6 + a^6}\, dx$

28. $\displaystyle\int_0^{\infty} \frac{x^3}{x^8 + a^8}\, dx$

29. $\displaystyle\int_0^{\infty} \frac{x}{x^6 + a^6}\, dx$

30. $\displaystyle\int_0^{\infty} \frac{x\sin 2x}{x^2 + 5}\, dx$

31. $\displaystyle\int_{-\infty}^{\infty} \frac{x^2\cos 3x}{x^4 + 4}\, dx$

32. $\displaystyle\int_0^{\infty} \frac{\sin^2 x}{x^2 + 1}\, dx$

33. $\displaystyle\int_0^{\infty} \frac{x^2\cos x}{(x^2 + 9)^2}\, dx$

34. $\displaystyle\int_{-\infty}^{\infty} \frac{\sin x}{x^2 + 2x + 2}\, dx$

35. $\displaystyle\int_{-\infty}^{\infty} \frac{\cos x}{(x + a)^2 + b^2}\, dx,\ a > 0,\ b > 0$

36. $\displaystyle\int_0^{\infty} \frac{\cos ax}{1 + x^4}\, dx,\ a > 0$

37. $\displaystyle\int_{-\infty}^{\infty} \frac{\cos bx}{x^2 + a^2}\, dx,\ a > 0,\ b > 0$

38. $\displaystyle\int_0^{\infty} \frac{\cos bx}{(x^2 + a^2)^2}\, dx$

39. Show that

$$\int_0^{2\pi} \cos^{2n}\theta \, d\theta = \frac{(2n)!\pi}{2^{2n-1}(n!)^2} = \int_0^{2\pi} \sin^{2n}\theta \, d\theta.$$

40. (a) Use the substitution $u = 1/x$ to show that

$$I = \int_0^1 \frac{1+x^2}{1+x^4} \, dx = \int_1^\infty \frac{1+u^2}{1+u^4} \, du,$$

and hence

$$I = \frac{1}{4} \int_{-\infty}^\infty \frac{1+x^2}{1+x^4} \, dx.$$

(b) Now use contour integration to calculate I.

41. Use contour integrals to prove the result of Exercise 3 in Section 4.8.

42. Evaluate $\displaystyle\int_0^{\pi/2} \frac{1}{(3-\sin\theta)^2} \, d\theta.$

In Exercises 43–51 verify the formula for the given values of the parameters.

43. $\displaystyle\int_0^{2\pi} \frac{1}{a+b\sin\theta} \, d\theta = \frac{2\pi}{\sqrt{a^2-b^2}}$, when $0 < |b| < a$

44. $\displaystyle\int_0^{2\pi} \frac{1}{a+b\cos\theta} \, d\theta = \frac{2\pi}{\sqrt{a^2-b^2}}$, when $0 < |b| < a$

45. $\displaystyle\int_0^{2\pi} \frac{1}{a+b\cos^2\theta} \, d\theta = \frac{2\pi}{\sqrt{a^2+ab}}$, when $0 < b < a$

46. $\displaystyle\int_0^{2\pi} \frac{1}{a+b\sin^2\theta} \, d\theta = \frac{2\pi}{\sqrt{a^2+ab}}$, when $0 < b < a$

47. $\displaystyle\int_0^{2\pi} \frac{1}{d+a\cos\theta+b\sin\theta} \, d\theta = \frac{2\pi\operatorname{sgn}d}{\sqrt{d^2-a^2-b^2}}$, where $\operatorname{sgn}d = \begin{cases} 1, & d>0 \\ -1, & d<0 \end{cases}$, when a, b, and d are real with $d^2 > a^2 + b^2$.

48. $\displaystyle\int_{-\infty}^\infty \frac{1}{(1+x^2)^n} \, dx = \frac{(2n-2)!\pi}{2^{2n-2}[(n-1)!]^2}$, $n \geq 1$ an integer

49. $\displaystyle\int_{-\infty}^\infty \frac{1}{1+x^n} \, dx = \frac{\frac{\pi}{n}}{\sin\frac{\pi}{n}}$, $n \geq 2$ an integer

50. $\displaystyle\int_{-\infty}^\infty \frac{x^{2m}}{1+x^{2n}} \, dx = \frac{\frac{\pi}{n}}{\sin\frac{(2m+1)\pi}{2n}}$, $n \geq 1$ an integer, and m an integer with $0 \leq m < n$

51. $\displaystyle\int_0^\infty \frac{x^m}{a^n+x^n} \, dx = \frac{\frac{\pi}{n}}{a^{n-m-1}\sin\frac{(m+1)\pi}{n}}$, $a > 0$, $n \geq 2$ an integer, and $0 < m < n-1$ an integer

52. From results like those in Exercises 43–47, many other results can be obtained by differentiation. For instance, by differentiating the formula in Exercise 43 with respect to a, obtain

$$\int_0^{2\pi} \frac{1}{(a+b\sin\theta)^2} \, d\theta = \frac{2\pi a}{(a^2-b^2)^{3/2}}, \qquad 0 < |b| < a.$$

53. Use the idea of Exercise 52 and the result of Exercise 44 to calculate

$$\int_0^{2\pi} \frac{1}{(4 - 3\cos\theta)^3} \, d\theta.$$

§6.3 More Improper Integrals by Residues

In this section we use residues to evaluate more difficult improper integrals. Before doing so, however, we discuss the concept of Cauchy's principal value for an improper integral. The improper integral of a continuous function $f(x)$ over the real line is defined by

$$\int_{-\infty}^{\infty} f(x)\,dx = \lim_{a \to -\infty} \int_{a}^{0} f(x)\,dx + \lim_{b \to \infty} \int_{0}^{b} f(x)\,dx, \qquad (6.11)$$

provided both limits exist. The **Cauchy principal value** of the integral is defined as

$$\fint_{-\infty}^{\infty} f(x)\,dx = \lim_{b \to \infty} \int_{-b}^{b} f(x)\,dx, \qquad (6.12)$$

provided this limit exists. When an improper integral has a value in the ordinary sense 6.11, it must have an identical Cauchy principal value. However, an improper integral may have a Cauchy principal value, but no value in the ordinary sense. For example, the first of the integrals

$$\int_{-\infty}^{\infty} \frac{x}{x^4 + 1}\,dx, \qquad \int_{-\infty}^{\infty} \frac{x}{x^2 + 1}\,dx$$

has value zero in both senses; the second has a Cauchy principal value of zero, but does not converge in the sense of 6.11.

Cauchy principal values are also defined for improper integrals due to discontinuities in integrands. When the only discontinuity of a function $f(x)$ in the interval $a < x < b$ is $x = d$, its improper integral over the interval $a \le x \le b$ is defined by

$$\int_{a}^{b} f(x)\,dx = \lim_{\epsilon \to 0^{+}} \int_{a}^{d-\epsilon} f(x)\,dx + \lim_{\epsilon \to 0^{+}} \int_{d+\epsilon}^{b} f(x)\,dx, \qquad (6.13)$$

provided both limits exist. The integral is said to have a **Cauchy principal value** when the limit

$$\fint_{a}^{b} f(x)\,dx = \lim_{\epsilon \to 0^{+}} \left[\int_{a}^{d-\epsilon} f(x)\,dx + \int_{d+\epsilon}^{b} f(x)\,dx \right] \qquad (6.14)$$

exists. Once again existence of 6.13 implies that of 6.14, but not conversely. The integral of $1/x$ from $x = -1$ to $x = 1$ has a Cauchy principal value of zero, but no value in the sense of 6.13.

In this section we are careful to distinguish those improper integrals which converge in the sense of Cauchy's principal value, but do not converge in the ordinary sense.

Improper Integrals of Rational Functions With Simple Poles

The first type of integral we consider is

$$\int_{-\infty}^{\infty} \frac{P(x)}{Q(x)}\,dx \qquad (6.15)$$

where $P(x)$ and $Q(x)$ are polynomials, and $Q(x)$ has real, simple zeros. We illustrate with the following example.

Example 6.13   Evaluate $\displaystyle\int_{-\infty}^{\infty} \frac{x}{x^3-1}\, dx.$

Solution   This integral does not have a value in the ordinary sense as can be seen by writing

$$\int_{-\infty}^{\infty} \frac{x}{x^3-1}\, dx = \int_{-\infty}^{0} \frac{x}{x^3-1}\, dx + \int_{0}^{1} \frac{x}{x^3-1}\, dx + \int_{1}^{2} \frac{x}{x^3-1}\, dx + \int_{2}^{\infty} \frac{x}{x^3-1}\, dx.$$

When the partial fraction decomposition of the integrand is substituted into the second of these,

$$\int_{0}^{1} \frac{x}{x^3-1}\, dx = \frac{1}{3}\int_{0}^{1} \left(\frac{1}{x-1} + \frac{1-x}{x^2+x+1} \right) dx,$$

and the integral of $1/(x-1)$ diverges at $x=1$. So also will the third integral diverge at $x=1$, but the first and last integrals converge. In other words, the Cauchy principal value in this example is only in the sense of the discontinuity at $x=1$, not as regards the infinite limits. To evaluate Cauchy principal value of the integral, consider the contour integral

$$\oint_C \frac{z}{z^3-1}\, dz$$

where C is the contour in Figure 6.11.

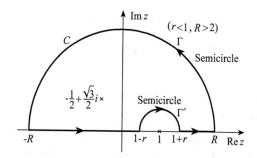

Figure 6.11

The integrand has a simple pole at $z=1$ (on the real axis), and two other simple poles at $z = (-1/2) \pm (\sqrt{3}/2)i$, but only $-1/2 + \sqrt{3}i/2$ is inside C. By Cauchy's residue theorem,

$$\oint_C \frac{z}{z^3-1}\, dz = 2\pi i \, \text{Res}\left[\frac{z}{z^3-1}, -\frac{1}{2} + \frac{\sqrt{3}i}{2} \right] = 2\pi i \lim_{z \to -1/2+\sqrt{3}i/2} \frac{(z+1/2-\sqrt{3}i/2)z}{z^3-1}.$$

When we use L'Hôpital's rule on this limit,

$$\oint_C \frac{z}{z^3-1}\, dz = 2\pi i \lim_{z \to -1/2+\sqrt{3}i/2} \frac{(z+1/2-\sqrt{3}i/2)+z}{3z^2} = 2\pi i \lim_{z \to -1/2+\sqrt{3}i/2} \frac{1}{3z}$$

$$= \frac{2\pi i}{3(-1/2+\sqrt{3}i/2)} = \frac{\pi}{3}(\sqrt{3}-i).$$

On the semicircle Γ of radius $R > 2$, $\left| \dfrac{z}{z^3 - 1} \right| \le \dfrac{R}{R^3 - 1}$, and it follows that

$$\left| \int_\Gamma \frac{z}{z^3 - 1}\, dz \right| \le \frac{R}{R^3 - 1}(\pi R).$$

The limit of this expression as $R \to \infty$ is zero. Now consider the integral along Γ'. The partial fraction decomposition of $z/(z^3 - 1)$ gives

$$\int_{\Gamma'} \frac{z}{z^3 - 1}\, dz = \frac{1}{3} \int_{\Gamma'} \frac{1}{z - 1}\, dz + \frac{1}{3} \int_{\Gamma'} \frac{1 - z}{z^2 + z + 1}\, dz.$$

If we set $z = 1 + re^{\theta i}$, $\pi \ge \theta \ge 0$, on Γ',

$$\frac{1}{3} \int_{\Gamma'} \frac{1}{z - 1}\, dz = \frac{1}{3} \int_\pi^0 \frac{1}{re^{\theta i}} rie^{\theta i} d\theta = -\frac{\pi i}{3}.$$

Because $(1 - z)/(z^2 + z + 1)$ is analytic in the domain $|z - 1| < 1$, it must be bounded therein; that is, there exists a constant M such that for z in $|z - 1| < 1$, $|(1 - z)/(z^2 + z + 1)| \le M$. Since Γ' lies within this domain, it follows that

$$\left| \int_{\Gamma'} \frac{1 - z}{z^2 + z + 1}\, dz \right| \le M\pi r,$$

and this expression approaches zero as $r \to 0$. Consequently,

$$\lim_{r \to 0} \int_{\Gamma'} \frac{z}{z^3 - 1}\, dz = -\frac{\pi i}{3}.$$

We now return to the equation $\displaystyle\oint_C \frac{z}{z^3 - 1}\, dz = \frac{\pi}{3}(\sqrt{3} - i)$, break the contour integral into its constituent parts, take limits as $r \to 0$ and $R \to \infty$, and use the above results,

$$\frac{\pi}{3}(\sqrt{3} - i) = \lim_{\substack{r \to 0 \\ R \to \infty}} \oint_C \frac{z}{z^3 - 1}\, dz$$

$$= \lim_{\substack{r \to 0 \\ R \to \infty}} \left(\int_{-R}^{1-r} \frac{x}{x^3 - 1}\, dx + \int_{1+r}^R \frac{x}{x^3 - 1}\, dx + \int_\Gamma \frac{z}{z^3 - 1}\, dz + \int_{\Gamma'} \frac{z}{z^3 - 1}\, dz \right)$$

$$= \int_{-\infty}^\infty \frac{x}{x^3 - 1}\, dx + 0 - \frac{\pi i}{3},$$

and therefore $\displaystyle\int_{-\infty}^\infty \frac{x}{x^3 - 1}\, dx = \frac{\pi}{\sqrt{3}}.$ $\bullet$

Obviously the laborious part of this example was showing that integrals along Γ and Γ' vanish as $R \to \infty$ and $r \to 0$, respectively. The following theorem eliminates the necessity for doing this in future examples.

Theorem 6.7   When $P(x)$ and $Q(x)$ are polynomials of degrees m and n where $n \ge m + 2$, and the only zeros of $Q(x)$ on the real axis are simple zeros,

$$\int_{-\infty}^\infty \frac{P(x)}{Q(x)}\, dx = 2\pi i \left\{ \begin{array}{l} \text{sum of the residues of } P(z)/Q(z) \text{ at} \\ \text{its poles in the half-plane } \operatorname{Im} z > 0 \end{array} \right\}$$

$$+\pi i \left\{ \begin{array}{c} \text{sum of the residues of } P(z)/Q(z) \text{ at} \\ \text{its simple poles on the real axis} \end{array} \right\}.$$

Proof   Let $x_1, \ldots, x_n$ be the simple
zeros of $Q(x)$ on the x-axis, and $z_1, \ldots, z_m$
be the zeros of $Q(z)$ with positive
imaginary parts. Consider the contour
integral of $P(z)/Q(z)$ around the contour
in Figure 6.12. Radius R of the outer
semicircle is chosen so large and radius r
of the semicircles Γ_k around x_k is
chosen so small that the semicircles
are disjoint, and all z_k are interior to C.

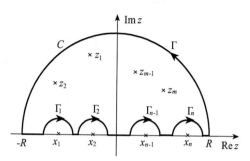

Figure 6.12

Cauchy's residue therorem states that

$$\oint_C \frac{P(z)}{Q(z)} dz = 2\pi i \sum_{j=1}^{m} \text{Res}\left[\frac{P(z)}{Q(z)}, z_j\right].$$

Because x_k is a simple pole of $P(z)/Q(z)$, the Laurent series of $P(z)/Q(z)$ about
x_k must be of the form

$$\frac{P(z)}{Q(z)} = \frac{\text{Res}[P(z)/Q(z), x_k]}{z - x_k} + g_k(z),$$

where $g_k(z)$ is analytic in a domain containing Γ_k. Integration gives

$$\int_{\Gamma_k} \frac{P(z)}{Q(z)} dz = \int_{\Gamma_k} \frac{\text{Res}[P(z)/Q(z), x_k]}{z - x_k} dz + \int_{\Gamma_k} g_k(z) \, dz$$

$$= -\text{Res}[P(z)/Q(z), x_k] \int_{-\Gamma_k} \frac{1}{z - x_k} dz + \int_{\Gamma_k} g_k(z) \, dz.$$

If we set $z = x_k + re^{\theta i}$, $0 \leq \theta \leq \pi$ on $-\Gamma_k$,

$$\int_{-\Gamma_k} \frac{1}{z - x_k} dz = \int_0^\pi \frac{rie^{\theta i}}{re^{\theta i}} d\theta = \pi i.$$

Because $g_k(z)$ is analytic in a domain containing Γ_k, it must be bounded therein;
that is, there exists a constant M_k such that for z on Γ_k, $|g_k(z)| \leq M_k$. It follows
that

$$\left| \int_{\Gamma_k} g_k(z) \, dz \right| \leq M_k(\pi r) \to 0 \quad \text{as } r \to 0,$$

and we conclude that

$$\lim_{r \to 0} \int_{\Gamma_k} \frac{P(z)}{Q(z)} dz = -\pi i \, \text{Res}[P(z)/Q(z), x_k].$$

Let $P(z) = a_m z^m + \cdots + a_0$ and $Q(z) = b_n z^n + \cdots + b_0$. On Γ, $|z| = R$, and R can
be chosen so large that $|b_n z^n| = |b_n R^n| \geq |b_{n-1} R^{n-1}| + \cdots + |b_0|$. For such R, we
can say that on Γ,

$$\left| \frac{P(z)}{Q(z)} \right| \leq \frac{|a_m| R^m + \cdots + |a_0|}{|b_n| R^n - \cdots - |b_0|},$$

and therefore using inequality 4.21,

$$\left| \int_\Gamma \frac{P(z)}{Q(z)} \, dz \right| \le \frac{|a_m| R^m + \cdots + |a_0|}{|b_n| R^n - \cdots - |b_0|} (\pi R).$$

This quantity approaches 0 as $R \to \infty$ since $n \ge m + 2$. It now follows that

$$2\pi i \sum_{j=1}^{m} \text{Res}\left[\frac{P(z)}{Q(z)}, z_j \right] = \lim_{\substack{r \to 0 \\ R \to \infty}} \oint_C \frac{P(z)}{Q(z)} \, dz = \int_{-\infty}^{\infty} \frac{P(x)}{Q(x)} \, dx + \sum_{k=1}^{n} -\pi i \, \text{Res}\left[\frac{P(z)}{Q(z)}, x_k \right],$$

or,

$$\int_{-\infty}^{\infty} \frac{P(x)}{Q(x)} \, dx = 2\pi i \sum_{j=1}^{m} \text{Res}\left[\frac{P(z)}{Q(z)}, z_j \right] + \pi i \sum_{k=1}^{n} \text{Res}\left[\frac{P(z)}{Q(z)}, x_k \right]. \blacksquare$$

Example 6.14 Evaluate the improper integral $\displaystyle \int_{-\infty}^{\infty} \frac{x^2}{x^4 - 1} \, dx$. The Cauchy principal value is in the sense of the discontinuities at $x = \pm 1$.

Solution The function $z^2/(z^4 - 1)$ has simple poles at $z = \pm 1$, and $z = \pm i$. Residues at $z = \pm 1$ and $z = i$ are

$$\text{Res}\left[\frac{z^2}{z^4 - 1}, -1 \right] = \lim_{z \to -1} \frac{(z+1)z^2}{(z-1)(z+1)(z^2+1)} = -\frac{1}{4},$$

$$\text{Res}\left[\frac{z^2}{z^4 - 1}, 1 \right] = \lim_{z \to 1} \frac{(z-1)z^2}{(z-1)(z+1)(z^2+1)} = \frac{1}{4},$$

$$\text{Res}\left[\frac{z^2}{z^4 - 1}, i \right] = \lim_{z \to i} \frac{(z-i)z^2}{(z-i)(z+i)(z^2-1)} = -\frac{i}{4}.$$

According to Theorem 6.7,

$$\int_{-\infty}^{\infty} \frac{x^2}{x^4 - 1} \, dx = 2\pi i \left(-\frac{i}{4} \right) + \pi i \left(\frac{1}{4} - \frac{1}{4} \right) = \frac{\pi}{2}. \bullet$$

Improper Integrals of Rational Functions With Simple Poles Multiplied by Sines and/or Cosines

We now consider integrals of the form

$$\int_{-\infty}^{\infty} \frac{P(x)}{Q(x)} \cos ax \, dx \qquad \text{and} \qquad \int_{-\infty}^{\infty} \frac{P(x)}{Q(x)} \sin ax \, dx, \qquad (6.16)$$

where $P(x)$ and $Q(x)$ are polynomials, and $Q(x)$ has simple, real zeros. We first look at an example.

Example 6.15 Evaluate $\displaystyle \int_0^{\infty} \frac{\cos 3x}{16 - x^4} \, dx$.

Solution Because the integrand is an even function, we may write that

$$\int_0^{\infty} \frac{\cos 3x}{16 - x^4} \, dx = \frac{1}{2} \int_{-\infty}^{\infty} \frac{\cos 3x}{16 - x^4} \, dx.$$

Improper integrals for the discontinuities of the latter integral at $x = \pm 2$ do not converge in the ordinary sense, so that this integral must be regarded in the sense of

Cauchy's principal value. (The integral does exist in the ordinary sense as regards the infinite limits.) We consider the contour integral

$$\oint_C \frac{e^{3zi}}{16 - z^4} \, dz,$$

where C is the curve in Figure 6.13.

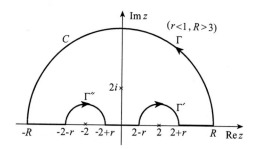

Figure 6.13

The integrand has simple poles at $z = \pm 2$ and $z = \pm 2i$, but only $2i$ is interior to C. By Cauchy's residue theorem,

$$\oint_C \frac{e^{3zi}}{16 - z^4} \, dz = 2\pi i \, \text{Res}\left[\frac{e^{3zi}}{16 - z^4}, 2i \right] = 2\pi i \lim_{z \to 2i} \frac{e^{3zi}(z - 2i)}{16 - z^4}$$

$$= 2\pi i \lim_{z \to 2i} \frac{e^{3zi} + 3i(z - 2i)e^{3zi}}{-4z^3} = 2\pi i \lim_{z \to 2i} \frac{e^{3zi}}{-4z^3} = 2\pi i \frac{e^{-6}}{-4(2i)^3} = \frac{\pi}{16e^6}.$$

On the semicircle Γ of radius $R > 3$,

$$\left| \frac{e^{3zi}}{16 - z^4} \right| = \left| \frac{e^{3(x+yi)i}}{z^4 - 16} \right| \leq \frac{e^{-3y}}{R^4 - 16} \leq \frac{1}{R^4 - 16},$$

and it follows that

$$\left| \int_\Gamma \frac{e^{3zi}}{16 - z^4} \, dz \right| \leq \frac{\pi R}{R^4 - 16}.$$

The limit of this expression as $R \to \infty$ is zero. Now consider the integral along Γ'. Because

$$\text{Res}\left[\frac{e^{3zi}}{16 - z^4}, 2 \right] = \lim_{z \to 2} \frac{(z - 2)e^{3zi}}{(2 - z)(2 + z)(4 + z^2)} = -\frac{e^{6i}}{32},$$

$e^{3zi}/(16 - z^4)$ has a Laurent expansion about $z = 2$ of the form

$$\frac{e^{3zi}}{16 - z^4} = \frac{-e^{6i}/32}{z - 2} + g(z),$$

where g is analytic in the domain $|z - 2| < 1$. (This expression takes the place of the partial fraction decomposition in Example 6.13.) The contour integral along Γ' can therefore be expressed in the form

$$\int_{\Gamma'} \frac{e^{3zi}}{16 - z^4} \, dz = \int_{\Gamma'} \frac{-e^{6i}/32}{z - 2} \, dz + \int_{\Gamma'} g(z) \, dz = -\frac{e^{6i}}{32} \int_{\Gamma'} \frac{1}{z - 2} \, dz + \int_{\Gamma'} g(z) \, dz.$$

If we set $z = 2 + re^{\theta i}$, $\pi \geq \theta \geq 0$, on Γ', then

$$-\frac{e^{6i}}{32} \int_{\Gamma'} \frac{1}{z-2} \, dz = -\frac{e^{6i}}{32} \int_{\pi}^{0} \frac{1}{re^{\theta i}} ire^{\theta i} \, d\theta = \frac{\pi i e^{6i}}{32}.$$

Since g is analytic in $|z-2| < 1$, it is bounded therein; that is, there exists a constant M such that for z in $|z - 2| < 1$, $|g(z)| < M$. Thus,

$$\left| \int_{\Gamma'} g(z) \, dz \right| \le M\pi r,$$

and this expression approaches zero as $r \to 0$. Consequently,

$$\lim_{r \to 0} \int_{\Gamma'} \frac{e^{3zi}}{16 - z^4} \, dz = \frac{\pi i e^{6i}}{32}.$$

It can be shown similarly that

$$\lim_{r \to 0} \int_{\Gamma''} \frac{e^{3zi}}{16 - z^4} \, dz = \frac{-\pi i e^{-6i}}{32}.$$

We now return to the equation $\oint_C \dfrac{e^{3zi}}{16 - z^4} \, dz = \dfrac{\pi e^{-6}}{16}$, break the contour integral into its constituent parts, take limits as $r \to 0$ and $R \to \infty$, and use the above results,

$$\frac{\pi}{16e^6} = \lim_{\substack{r \to 0 \\ R \to \infty}} \oint_C \frac{e^{3zi}}{16 - z^4} \, dz$$

$$= \lim_{\substack{r \to 0 \\ R \to \infty}} \left(\int_{-R}^{-2-r} \frac{e^{3xi}}{16 - x^4} \, dx + \int_{-2+r}^{2-r} \frac{e^{3xi}}{16 - x^4} \, dx + \int_{2+r}^{R} \frac{e^{3xi}}{16 - x^4} \, dx \right.$$

$$\left. + \int_{\Gamma} \frac{e^{3zi}}{16 - z^4} \, dz + \int_{\Gamma'} \frac{e^{3zi}}{16 - z^4} \, dz + \int_{\Gamma''} \frac{e^{3zi}}{16 - z^4} \, dz \right)$$

$$= \fint_{-\infty}^{\infty} \frac{e^{3xi}}{16 - x^4} \, dx + 0 + \frac{\pi i e^{6i}}{32} - \frac{\pi i e^{-6i}}{32}.$$

When we take real parts, we obtain

$$\frac{\pi}{16e^6} = \fint_{-\infty}^{\infty} \frac{\cos 3x}{16 - x^4} \, dx - \frac{\pi}{16} \sin 6.$$

Thus,

$$\fint_{0}^{\infty} \frac{\cos 3x}{16 - x^4} \, dx = \frac{1}{2} \fint_{-\infty}^{\infty} \frac{\cos 3x}{16 - x^4} \, dx = \frac{\pi}{32} (e^{-6} + \sin 6). \bullet$$

To simmplfy future examples, we verify the following theorem.

Theorem 6.8 When $P(x)$ and $Q(x)$ are polynomials of degrees m and n where $n \ge m + 1$, and the only zeros of $Q(x)$ on the real axis are simple zeros, then for $a > 0$,

$$\fint_{-\infty}^{\infty} \frac{P(x) \cos ax}{Q(x)} \, dx = -2\pi \operatorname{Im} \left\{ \begin{array}{l} \text{sum of the residues of } P(z)e^{azi}/Q(z) \\ \text{at its poles in the half-plane Im } z > 0 \end{array} \right\}$$

$$-\pi \operatorname{Im} \left\{ \begin{array}{l} \text{sum of the residues of } P(z)e^{azi}/Q(z) \\ \text{at its simple poles on the real axis} \end{array} \right\},$$

and

$$\int_{-\infty}^{\infty} \frac{P(x)\sin ax}{Q(x)}\, dx = 2\pi \,\mathrm{Re} \left\{ \begin{array}{l} \text{sum of the residues of } P(z)e^{azi}/Q(z) \\ \text{at its poles in the half-plane } \mathrm{Im}\, z > 0 \end{array} \right\}$$

$$+ \pi \,\mathrm{Re} \left\{ \begin{array}{l} \text{sum of the residues of } P(z)e^{azi}/Q(z) \\ \text{at its simple poles on the real axis} \end{array} \right\}.$$

Proof   Let $x_1, \ldots, x_n$ be the simple zeros of $Q(x)$ on the real axis, and $z_1, \ldots, z_m$ be the zeros of $Q(z)$ with positive imaginary parts. Consider the contour integral of $P(z)e^{azi}/Q(z)$ around the contour in Figure 6.12. Cauchy's residue therorem states that

$$\oint_C \frac{P(z)e^{azi}}{Q(z)}\, dz = 2\pi i \sum_{j=1}^{m} \mathrm{Res}\left[\frac{P(z)}{Q(z)} e^{azi}, z_j \right].$$

Because x_k is a simple pole of $P(z)e^{azi}/Q(z)$, the Laurent series of $P(z)e^{azi}/Q(z)$ about x_k must be of the form

$$\frac{P(z)}{Q(z)} e^{azi} = \frac{\mathrm{Res}[P(z)e^{azi}/Q(z), x_k]}{z - x_k} + g_k(z),$$

where $g_k(z)$ is analytic in a domain containing Γ_k. Integration gives

$$\int_{\Gamma_k} \frac{P(z)}{Q(z)} e^{azi} dz = \int_{\Gamma_k} \frac{\mathrm{Res}[P(z)e^{azi}/Q(z), x_k]}{z - x_k} dz + \int_{\Gamma_k} g_k(z)\, dz$$

$$= -\mathrm{Res}[P(z)e^{azi}/Q(z), x_k] \int_{-\Gamma_k} \frac{1}{z - x_k} dz + \int_{\Gamma_k} g_k(z)\, dz.$$

If we set $z = x_k + re^{\theta i}$, $0 \le \theta \le \pi$ on $-\Gamma_k$,

$$\int_{-\Gamma_k} \frac{1}{z - x_k} dz = \int_0^\pi \frac{rie^{\theta i}}{re^{\theta i}} d\theta = \pi i.$$

Because $g_k(z)$ is analytic in a domain containing Γ_k, it must be bounded therein; that is, there exists a constant M_k such that for z on Γ_k, $|g_k(z)| \le M_k$. It follows that

$$\left| \int_{\Gamma_k} g_k(z)\, dz \right| \le M_k(\pi r) \to 0 \quad \text{as } r \to 0,$$

and we conclude that

$$\lim_{r \to 0} \int_{\Gamma_k} \frac{P(z)e^{azi}}{Q(z)} dz = -\pi i\, \mathrm{Res}[P(z)e^{azi}/Q(z), x_k].$$

In Theorem 6.6, it was shown that

$$\lim_{R \to \infty} \int_{\Gamma_k} \frac{P(z)}{Q(z)} e^{azi} dz = 0.$$

It now follows that

$$2\pi i \sum_{j=1}^{m} \mathrm{Res}\left[\frac{P(z)}{Q(z)} e^{azi}, z_j \right] = \lim_{\substack{r \to 0 \\ R \to \infty}} \oint_C \frac{P(z)}{Q(z)} e^{azi} dz$$

$$= \int_{-\infty}^{\infty} \frac{P(x)}{Q(x)} e^{axi} dx - \pi i \sum_{k=1}^{n} \mathrm{Res}\left[\frac{P(z)}{Q(z)} e^{azi}, x_k \right].$$

Real and imaginary parts give

$$\int_{-\infty}^{\infty} \frac{P(x)}{Q(x)} \cos ax \, dx = -2\pi \operatorname{Im} \left\{ \sum_{j=1}^{m} \operatorname{Res} \left[\frac{P(z)}{Q(z)} e^{azi}, z_j \right] \right\} - \pi \operatorname{Im} \left\{ \sum_{k=1}^{n} \operatorname{Res} \left[\frac{P(z)}{Q(z)} e^{azi}, x_k \right] \right\},$$

and

$$\int_{-\infty}^{\infty} \frac{P(x)}{Q(x)} \sin ax \, dx = 2\pi \operatorname{Re} \left\{ \sum_{j=1}^{m} \operatorname{Res} \left[\frac{P(z)}{Q(z)} e^{azi}, z_j \right] \right\} + \pi \operatorname{Re} \left\{ \sum_{k=1}^{n} \operatorname{Res} \left[\frac{P(z)}{Q(z)} e^{azi}, x_k \right] \right\}. \blacksquare$$

Example 6.16 Evaluate the improper integral $\displaystyle\int_{-\infty}^{\infty} \frac{\cos 2x}{1 - 3x^2} \, dx$.

Solution Simple poles of $e^{2zi}/(1 - 3z^2)$ occur at $z = \pm 1/\sqrt{3}$, with residues

$$\operatorname{Res} \left[\frac{e^{2zi}}{1 - 3z^2}, \frac{1}{\sqrt{3}} \right] = \lim_{z \to 1/\sqrt{3}} \frac{-(z - 1/\sqrt{3})e^{2zi}}{3(z + 1/\sqrt{3})(z - 1/\sqrt{3})} = -\frac{e^{2(1/\sqrt{3})i}}{3(2/\sqrt{3})} = -\frac{e^{2i/\sqrt{3}}}{2\sqrt{3}},$$

and similarly, $\operatorname{Res} \left[\dfrac{e^{2zi}}{1 - 3z^2}, \dfrac{-1}{\sqrt{3}} \right] = \dfrac{e^{-2i/\sqrt{3}}}{2\sqrt{3}}$. According th Theorem 6.8, then,

$$\int_{-\infty}^{\infty} \frac{\cos 2x}{1 - 3x^2} dx = -\pi \operatorname{Im} \left(\frac{e^{-2i/\sqrt{3}}}{2\sqrt{3}} - \frac{e^{2i/\sqrt{3}}}{2\sqrt{3}} \right) = \frac{\pi}{\sqrt{3}} \sin \left(\frac{2}{\sqrt{3}} \right). \bullet$$

Suppose that any singularities of an even function $f(x)$ are removable. If the improper integral of $f(x)$ on the interval $(-\infty, \infty)$ exists, then so also does the improper integral on the interval $[0, \infty)$, and, in fact, is equal to half the value on $(-\infty, \infty)$. Furthermore, the Cauchy principal value of the integral of the function on the interval $(-\infty, \infty)$ also exists. In general, the converse is not true; existence of the Cauchy principal value of an integral does not guarantee existence of the integral in the ordinary sense. But, when the function is even with only removable singularities, existence of the Cauchy principal value of the function on the interval $(-\infty, \infty)$ guarantees existence of the integral in the ordinary sense. We use this principle in the next example.

Example 6.17 Evaluate the improper integral $\displaystyle\int_{0}^{\infty} \frac{\sin ax}{x} \, dx$.

Solution We should first verify that the integral converges. Since $\displaystyle\lim_{x \to 0} \frac{\sin ax}{x} = 1$, the singularity at $x = 0$ is removable. When we note that the function is even, we can use the principle in the above paragraph to say that the improper integral converges if the Cauchy principal of the integral

$$\int_{-\infty}^{\infty} \frac{\sin ax}{x} \, dx$$

converges. The residue of e^{azi}/z at $z = 0$ is

$$\operatorname{Res} \left[\frac{e^{azi}}{z}, 0 \right] = \lim_{z \to 0} e^{azi} = e^{0i} = 1.$$

According to Theorem 6.8, then,

$$\int_{-\infty}^{\infty} \frac{\sin ax}{x} dx = \pi \operatorname{Re}(1) = \pi.$$

It now follows that

$$\int_{0}^{\infty} \frac{\sin ax}{x} dx = \frac{1}{2} \int_{-\infty}^{\infty} \frac{\sin ax}{x} dx = \frac{\pi}{2}. \bullet$$

We now consider improper integrals which lead to branch points and cuts of multiple-valued functions.

Improper Integrals Involving Logarithms

Example 6.18 Evaluate $\displaystyle\int_{0}^{\infty} \frac{\ln x}{x^2 + a^2} dx$, when $a > 0$.

Solution This integral exists in the ordinary sense since both integrals on the right side of the following equation converge

$$\int_{0}^{\infty} \frac{\ln x}{x^2 + a^2} dx = \int_{0}^{1} \frac{\ln x}{x^2 + a^2} dx + \int_{1}^{\infty} \frac{\ln x}{x^2 + a^2} dx.$$

Because

$$\int_{0}^{\infty} \frac{\ln x}{x^2 + a^2} dx = \int_{-\infty}^{0} \frac{\ln(-x)}{x^2 + a^2} dx,$$

we are led to consider

$$\oint_{C} \frac{\log_{-\pi/2} z}{z^2 + a^2} dz$$

where C is the contour in Figure 6.14. The integrand has simple poles at $z = \pm ai$, so that

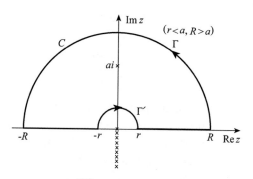

Figure 6.14

$$\oint_{C} \frac{\log_{-\pi/2} z}{z^2 + a^2} dz = 2\pi i \operatorname{Res}\left[\frac{\log_{-\pi/2} z}{z^2 + a^2}, ai\right] = 2\pi i \lim_{z \to ai} \frac{(z - ai)\log_{-\pi/2} z}{(z - ai)(z + ai)}$$

$$= \frac{\pi}{a} \log_{-\pi/2}(ai) = \frac{\pi}{a}[\ln a + \pi i/2].$$

On the semicircle Γ, we set $z = Re^{\theta i}$, $0 \leq \theta \leq \pi$, in which case

$$\left|\frac{\log_{-\pi/2} z}{z^2 + a^2}\right| \leq \frac{|\ln R + \theta i|}{R^2 - a^2} \leq \frac{\ln R + \pi}{R^2 - a^2},$$

(provided $R > a$ and $R > 1$). Consequently,

$$\left|\int_{\Gamma} \frac{\log_{-\pi/2} z}{z^2 + a^2} dz\right| \leq \frac{\ln R + \pi}{R^2 - a^2}(\pi R),$$

and this expression has limit zero as $R \to \infty$. On the semicircle Γ', we set $z = re^{\theta i}$, $\pi \geq \theta \geq 0$, in which case

$$\left|\frac{\log_{-\pi/2} z}{z^2 + a^2}\right| \leq \frac{|\ln r + \theta i|}{a^2 - r^2} \leq \frac{|\ln r| + \pi}{a^2 - r^2}.$$

Thus,

$$\left| \int_{\Gamma'} \frac{\log_{-\pi/2} z}{z^2 + a^2} \, dz \right| \le \frac{|\ln r| + \pi}{a^2 - r^2} (\pi r),$$

and this value has limit zero as $r \to 0$. We now return to the equation following Figure 6.14, break the contour integral into its constituent parts, take limits as $r \to 0$ and $R \to \infty$, and use the above results,

$$\frac{\pi}{a} [\ln a + \pi i/2] = \lim_{\substack{r \to 0 \\ R \to \infty}} \oint_C \frac{\log_{-\pi/2} z}{z^2 + a^2} \, dz = \int_{-\infty}^{\infty} \frac{\log_{-\pi/2} x}{x^2 + a^2} \, dx$$

$$= \int_{-\infty}^{0} \frac{\ln(-x) + \pi i}{x^2 + a^2} \, dx + \int_{0}^{\infty} \frac{\ln x}{x^2 + a^2} \, dx$$

$$= 2 \int_{0}^{\infty} \frac{\ln x}{x^2 + a^2} \, dx + \int_{-\infty}^{0} \frac{\pi i}{x^2 + a^2} \, dx.$$

Real parts give $\quad \displaystyle\int_{0}^{\infty} \frac{\ln x}{x^2 + a^2} \, dx = \frac{\pi}{2a} \ln a.\bullet$

Improper Integrals Involving Fractional Powers

Example 6.19 Evaluate $\displaystyle\int_{0}^{\infty} \frac{1}{x^a(x+1)} \, dx$, where $0 < a < 1$.

Solution To evaluate this improper integral by contour integration it would seem reasonable to replace the real integrand with the complex one $[z^a(z+1)]^{-1}$. Because z^a, for fractional a, is multiple-valued, we must choose some branch of the function. This will be dictated by the choice of contour. To obtain the required real improper integral, part of the contour should consist of a portion of the positive real axis. To avoid the branch point, we include a small circle (of radius r) around $z = 0$. In addition, we should have a circle of large radius R centred at $z = 0$. So far we have the curves in Figure 6.15a, but they do not form a closed contour. Our choice for contour C is that shown in Figure 6.15b. It consists of a portion of the circle of radius $r < 1$ centred at the origin, two horizontal lines segments joining this circle to a portion of the large circle with radius $R > 1$. We choose the branch $z^a = e^{a \log_0 z}$ with branch cut along the positive real axis. To retrieve the required real integral we will eventually take limits as $r \to 0$ and $R \to \infty$.

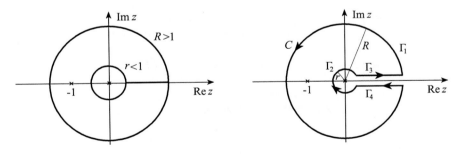

Figure 6.15a   **Figure 6.15b**

Since the integrand has a simple pole $z = -1$ interior to C, Cauchy's residue theorem gives

$$\oint_C \frac{1}{z^a(z+1)} \, dz = 2\pi i \operatorname{Res}\left[\frac{1}{z^a(z+1)}, -1 \right] = \frac{2\pi i}{(-1)^a} = \frac{2\pi i}{e^{a \log_0(-1)}} = \frac{2\pi i}{e^{a \pi i}} = 2\pi i e^{-a\pi i}.$$

When we break C into its four component parts, we have

$$2\pi i e^{-a\pi i} = \int_{\Gamma_1} \frac{1}{z^a(z+1)}dz + \int_{\Gamma_2} \frac{1}{z^a(z+1)}dz + \int_{\Gamma_3} \frac{1}{z^a(z+1)}dz + \int_{\Gamma_4} \frac{1}{z^a(z+1)}dz.$$

On Γ_1,

$$\left| \frac{1}{z^a(z+1)} \right| = \left| \frac{1}{(z+1)e^{a\log_0 z}} \right| = \left| \frac{1}{(z+1)e^{a(\ln R + \arg_0 z\, i)}} \right| \leq \frac{1}{R^a(R-1)},$$

so that

$$\left| \int_{\Gamma_1} \frac{1}{z^a(z+1)}dz \right| \leq \frac{1}{R^a(R-1)}(2\pi R).$$

This expression approaches zero as $R \to \infty$. On Γ_2,

$$\left| \frac{1}{z^a(z+1)} \right| = \left| \frac{1}{(z+1)e^{a\log_0 z}} \right| = \left| \frac{1}{(z+1)e^{a(\ln r + \arg_0 z\, i)}} \right| \leq \frac{1}{r^a(1-r)},$$

so that

$$\left| \int_{\Gamma_2} \frac{1}{z^a(z+1)}\, dz \right| \leq \frac{1}{r^a(1-r)}(2\pi r).$$

This also approaches zero as $r \to 0$. When limits are taken on the result of Cauchy's residue theorem as $r \to 0$ and $R \to \infty$, and the above two limits are taken into account,

$$2\pi i e^{-a\pi i} = \lim_{\substack{r \to 0 \\ R \to \infty}} \int_{\Gamma_3} \frac{1}{z^a(z+1)}\, dz + \lim_{\substack{r \to 0 \\ R \to \infty}} \int_{\Gamma_4} \frac{1}{z^a(z+1)}\, dz$$

$$= \lim_{\substack{r \to 0 \\ R \to \infty}} \int_{\Gamma_3} \frac{1}{(z+1)e^{a\log_0 z}}\, dz + \lim_{\substack{r \to 0 \\ R \to \infty}} \int_{\Gamma_4} \frac{1}{(z+1)e^{a\log_0 z}}\, dz.$$

In the limit, each of these integrals is along the positive real axis. Since the integral along Γ_3 is in the first quadrant, the limit of the argument in $\log_0 z$ is 0. On the other hand, since Γ_4 is in the fourth quadrant, the limit of the argument of $\log_0 z$ is 2π. In other words, when limits are taken,

$$2\pi i e^{-a\pi i} = \int_0^\infty \frac{1}{(x+1)e^{a\ln x}}dx + \int_\infty^0 \frac{1}{(x+1)e^{a(\ln x + 2\pi i)}}dx$$

$$= \int_0^\infty \frac{1}{x^a(x+1)}dx - \int_0^\infty \frac{1}{x^a(1+x)e^{2a\pi i}}dx = (1 - e^{-2a\pi i})\int_0^\infty \frac{1}{x^a(x+1)}dx.$$

We can solve this equation for the required integral,

$$\int_0^\infty \frac{1}{x^a(x+1)}dx = \frac{2\pi i e^{-a\pi i}}{1 - e^{-2a\pi i}} = \frac{2\pi i}{e^{a\pi i} - e^{-a\pi i}} = \frac{2\pi i}{2i\sin a\pi} = \frac{\pi}{\sin a\pi}. \bullet$$

EXERCISES 6.3

In Exercise 1–22 evaluate the improper integral.

1. $\displaystyle\oint_{-\infty}^{\infty} \frac{x+1}{x(x^2+4)^2}\,dx$

2. $\displaystyle\oint_{-\infty}^{\infty} \frac{1}{x^5+x^4+x+1}\,dx$

3. $\displaystyle\oint_{-\infty}^{\infty} \frac{x^2+2x}{(x-1)(x^3+1)}\,dx$

4. $\displaystyle\oint_{-\infty}^{\infty} \frac{x^2\cos x}{x^4-1}\,dx$

5. $\displaystyle\oint_{-\infty}^{\infty} \frac{\cos ax}{b^2-x^2}\,dx$

6. $\displaystyle\oint_{-\infty}^{\infty} \frac{\sin ax}{b^2-x^2}\,dx$

7. $\displaystyle\oint_{-\infty}^{\infty} \frac{\sin x\cos x}{x^3-8}\,dx$

8. $\displaystyle\int_{0}^{\infty} \frac{\ln x}{(x^2+a^2)^2}\,dx, \quad a>0$

9. $\displaystyle\int_{0}^{\infty} \frac{\ln x}{x^4+a^4}\,dx, \quad a>0$

10. $\displaystyle\int_{0}^{\infty} \frac{(\ln x)^2}{x^2+a^2}\,dx, \quad a>0$

11. $\displaystyle\int_{0}^{\infty} \frac{\ln x}{(x^2+a^2)(x^2+b^2)}\,dx,\, a>0,\, b>0$

12. $\displaystyle\int_{0}^{\infty} \frac{\ln(x^2+a^2)}{x^2+a^2}\,dx \quad a>0$ Hint: Use the integrand $f(z)=\dfrac{\log_{-\pi/2}(z+ai)}{z^2+a^2}$.

13. $\displaystyle\int_{-\infty}^{\infty} \frac{\cos ax-\cos bx}{x^2}\,dx \quad a\ge 1,\ b\ge 1 \text{ integers}$

14. $\displaystyle\int_{0}^{\infty} \frac{1}{\sqrt{x}(x^2+a^2)}\,dx, \quad a>0$

15. $\displaystyle\int_{0}^{\infty} \frac{x^a}{(x+b)^2}\,dx, \quad -1<a<1,\quad a\ne 0,\quad b>0$

16. $\displaystyle\int_{0}^{\infty} \frac{x^a}{x^2+b^2}\,dx, \quad -1<a<1,\quad b>0$

17. $\displaystyle\int_{0}^{\infty} \frac{1}{x^a(x+b)}\,dx, \quad 0<a<1,\quad b>0$

18. $\displaystyle\int_{0}^{\infty} \frac{x^a}{(x+b)(x+c)}\,dx, \quad -1<a<1,\quad b>0,\, c>0$

19. $\displaystyle\int_{0}^{\infty} \frac{x^a}{(x^2+b^2)^2}\,dx, \quad 0<a<3,\quad b>0$

20. $\displaystyle\int_{0}^{\infty} \frac{x^a}{x^4+b^4}\,dx, \quad -1<a<3,\quad b>0$

21. $\displaystyle\oint_{0}^{\infty} \frac{1}{x^a(x-b)}\,dx, \quad 0<a<1,\quad b>0$

22. $\displaystyle\oint_{0}^{\infty} \frac{x^a}{x^2-b^2}\,dx, \quad -1<a<1,\quad a\ne 0,\quad b>0$

23. Use the result in Exercise 15 to prove that
$$\int_{0}^{\infty} \frac{x^a\ln x}{(x+b)^2}\,dx = \pi b^{a-1}\left(\frac{1+a\ln b}{\sin a\pi} - \frac{a\pi\cos a\pi}{\sin^2 a\pi}\right).$$

24. Use the result in Exercise 12 to prove that
$$\int_{0}^{\pi/2} \ln(\cos\theta)\,d\theta = \int_{0}^{\pi/2} \ln(\sin\theta)\,d\theta = -\frac{\pi}{2}\ln 2.$$

25. The free-space Green's function for the one-dimensional Helmholtz operator is sometimes quoted as

$$U = \frac{1}{2\pi} \int_{-\infty}^{\infty} \frac{\cos \omega |x - X|}{k^2 - \omega^2} \, d\omega,$$

where $k > 0$ and X are constants. Show that a simpler expression is

$$U = \frac{1}{2k} \sin k|x - X|.$$

26. Prove that for $0 < a < 1$,

$$\int_{-\infty}^{\infty} \frac{e^{ax}}{1 + e^x} \, dx = \frac{\pi}{\sin a\pi}.$$

Hint: Integrate $e^{az}/(1 + e^z)$ around the rectangle with vertices $z = \pm R$ and $z = \pm R + 2\pi i$.

27. (a) Use Cauchy's residue theorem to evaluate

$$\oint_C \frac{e^{az}}{\cosh z} \, dz$$

where C is the contour in the diagram to the right and $-1 < a < 1$.

(b) Show that contributions to the contour integral along the two vertical lines vanish in the limit as $R \to \infty$.

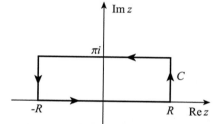

(c) Take limits as $R \to \infty$ on the contour integral in part (a) to obtain

$$\int_{-\infty}^{\infty} \frac{e^{ax}}{\cosh x} \, dx = \frac{\pi}{\cos (\pi a/2)}.$$

(d) Now evaluate $\displaystyle\int_0^{\infty} \frac{\cosh ax}{\cosh x} \, dx$, $-1 < a < 1$.

28. Show that

$$\int_0^{\infty} e^{-x^2} \cos 2bx \, dx = \frac{\sqrt{\pi}}{2} e^{-b^2}$$

by integrating $f(z) = e^{-z^2}$ around the edge of the rectangle $|x| \le R$, $0 \le y \le b$, and using the fact that

$$\int_{-\infty}^{\infty} e^{-x^2} \, dx = \sqrt{\pi}.$$

29. The Fresnel integrals

$$\int_0^{\infty} \sin x^2 \, dx \qquad \text{and} \qquad \int_0^{\infty} \cos x^2 \, dx$$

are important in optics. Evaluate them using the contour integral of $e^{z^2 i}$ around the boundary of the sector $0 \le r \le R$, $0 \le \theta \le \pi/4$.

30. Use the contour integral of $e^{-z^2(1-i)}$ around the boundary of the sector $0 \le r \le R$, $0 \le \theta \le \pi/8$ to evaluate the improper integrals:

$$(a) \int_0^\infty e^{-t^2} \cos t^2 \, dt, \qquad (b) \int_0^\infty e^{-t^2} \cos t^2 \, dt$$

31. Show that

$$\int_0^\infty \frac{\cos ax}{\sqrt{x}} \, dx = \sqrt{\frac{\pi}{2a}} \qquad \text{and} \qquad \int_0^\infty \frac{\sin ax}{\sqrt{x}} \, dx = \sqrt{\frac{\pi}{2a}}.$$

32. Show that

$$\int_0^\infty \frac{\cos x}{x^a} \, dx = \Gamma(1-a)\sin\frac{\pi a}{2} \qquad \text{and} \qquad \int_0^\infty \frac{\sin x}{x^a} \, dx = \Gamma(1-a)\cos\frac{\pi a}{2},$$

where $\Gamma(\nu)$ is the gamma function with values defined by $\Gamma(\nu) = \int_0^\infty x^{\nu-1} e^{-x} \, dx$.

33. In this exercise, we consider evaluation of the improper integral $\int_0^\infty \left(\frac{\sin ax}{x}\right)^n dx$, where $a > 0$,
for $n = 2, 3, 4$. The case $n = 1$ was dealt with in Example 6.17. Evaluation with $a = 1$ simplifies calculations, and a change of variable of integration can generalize the result to the case when $a \neq 1$. The technique is to express $\sin^n x$ in terms of $\sin nx$ and/or $\cos nx$ and replace the trigonometric functions with complex exponentials.

(a) For $n = 2$, the trigonometric identity $\sin^2 x = \dfrac{1 - \cos 2x}{2}$ suggests considering the contour integral of $\dfrac{1 - e^{2zi}}{z^2}$ around the curve in Figure 6.14. Do this.

(b) For $n = 3$, prove that $\sin^3 x = \dfrac{1}{4}(3\sin x - \sin 3x)$, which suggests the contour integral of $\dfrac{3e^{zi} - e^{3zi}}{z^3}$.

(c) For $n = 4$, prove that $\sin^4 x = \dfrac{1}{8}(3 - 4\cos 2x + \cos 4x)$, which suggests the contour integral of $\dfrac{3 - 4e^{2zi} + e^{4zi}}{z^4}$.

The following two exercises evaluate improper integrals that are useful in the solution of initial boundary value problems by Fourier transforms in Chapter 9.

34. (a) To evaluate the improper integrals

$$\int_0^\infty \frac{\cosh \alpha x}{\cosh \beta x} \cos \omega x \, dx \qquad \text{and} \qquad \int_0^\infty \frac{\sinh \alpha x}{\cosh \beta x} \sin \omega x \, dx,$$

where $0 < \alpha < \beta$, consider the contour integral

$$\oint_C \frac{e^{\alpha z}}{\cosh \beta z} e^{i\omega z} \, dz = \oint_C \frac{e^{(\alpha + \omega i)z}}{\cosh \beta z} \, dz,$$

where C is the contour in the figure to the right. Use residues to show that the value of the contour integral is

$$\frac{2\pi}{\beta} e^{\pi(-\omega + \alpha i)/(2\beta)}.$$

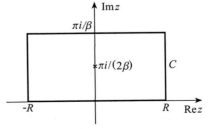

(b) Verify that integrals along the vertical line segments approach zero as $R \to \infty$.

(c) Combine integrals along the horizontal line segments and take limits as $R \to \infty$ to show that

$$\int_0^\infty \frac{\cosh(\alpha+\omega i)x}{\cosh\beta x}\,dx = \frac{\pi e^{\pi(-\omega+\alpha i)/(2\beta)}}{\beta[1+e^{\pi(-\omega+\alpha i)/\beta}]}.$$

(d) Finally, take real and imaginary parts to obtain

$$\int_0^\infty \frac{\cosh\alpha x}{\cosh\beta x}\cos\omega x\,dx = \frac{\pi\cos\frac{\pi\alpha}{2\beta}\cosh\frac{\pi\omega}{2\beta}}{\beta\left(\cosh\frac{\pi\omega}{\beta}+\cos\frac{\pi\alpha}{\beta}\right)}, \qquad \int_0^\infty \frac{\sinh\alpha x}{\cosh\beta x}\sin\omega x\,dx = \frac{\pi\sin\frac{\pi\alpha}{2\beta}\sinh\frac{\pi\omega}{2\beta}}{\beta\left(\cosh\frac{\pi\omega}{\beta}+\cos\frac{\pi\alpha}{\beta}\right)}.$$

35. (a) To evaluate the improper integrals

$$\int_0^\infty \frac{\sinh\alpha x}{\sinh\beta x}\cos\omega x\,dx \qquad \text{and} \qquad \int_0^\infty \frac{\cosh\alpha x}{\sinh\beta x}\sin\omega x\,dx,$$

where $0<\alpha<\beta$, consider the contour integral

$$\oint_C \frac{e^{\alpha z}}{\sinh\beta z}e^{i\omega z}\,dz = \oint_C \frac{e^{(\alpha+\omega i)z}}{\sinh\beta z}\,dz,$$

where C is the contour in the figure
to the right. Use residues to show that
the value of the contour integral is

$$-\frac{2\pi i}{\beta}e^{\pi(-\omega+\alpha i)/\beta}.$$

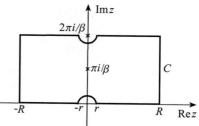

(b) Verify that integrals along the vertical line
segments approach zero as $R\to\infty$.

(c) Prove that in the limit as $r\to 0$, the integrals over the semicircles at $z=0$ and $z=2\pi i/\beta$
have values

$$\frac{-\pi i}{\beta}, \qquad \text{and} \qquad -\frac{\pi i e^{2\pi(-\omega+\alpha i)/\beta}}{\beta}, \qquad \text{respectively.}$$

(d) Combine integrals along the horizontal line segments and the two semicircles, and take limits
as $R\to\infty$ and $r\to 0$ to show that

$$\int_0^\infty \frac{\sinh(\alpha+\omega i)x}{\sinh\beta x}\,dx = \frac{\pi i[1-e^{\pi(-\omega+\alpha i)/\beta}]}{2\beta[1+e^{\pi(-\omega+\alpha i)/\beta}]}.$$

(e) Finally, take real and imaginary parts to obtain

$$\int_0^\infty \frac{\sinh\alpha x}{\sinh\beta x}\cos\omega x\,dx = \frac{\pi\sin\frac{\pi\alpha}{\beta}}{2\beta\left(\cosh\frac{\pi\omega}{\beta}+\cos\frac{\pi\alpha}{\beta}\right)}, \qquad \int_0^\infty \frac{\cosh\alpha x}{\sinh\beta x}\sin\omega x\,dx = \frac{\pi\sinh\frac{\pi\omega}{\beta}}{2\beta\left(\cosh\frac{\pi\omega}{\beta}+\cos\frac{\pi\alpha}{\beta}\right)}.$$

§6.4   Residues at Infinity

In Section 5.6, we defined what it means for a function to have an isolated singularity at the point of infinity. We now define residues associated with this singularity.

Definition 6.2   When the point at infinity is an isolated singularity of a function $f(z)$, the **residue at infinity** is defined as

$$\text{Res}\,[f(z), \infty] = -\text{Res}\left[\frac{1}{z^2}f\left(\frac{1}{z}\right), 0\right]. \tag{6.17}$$

Based on the fact that the nature of the singularity at infinity is based on the nature of the singularity $z = 0$ of $f(1/z)$, it might seem more natural to define the residue at infinity as the resdiue of $f(1/z)$ at $z = 0$, without therefore the factor $1/z^2$ and the negative sign. The above definition turns out to be far more useful, and we shall see why shortly.

Example 6.20   Calculate residues at infinity for the following functions:

(a) $f(z) = \dfrac{z^5}{1 + z - z^2}$ (b) $f(z) = z^n \sin(1/z)$, n an integer

Solution   (a) The function $f(z) = \dfrac{z^5}{1 + z - z^2}$ has a pole of order three at infinity (see Example 5.31). Its residue at this pole is

$$\text{Res}\left[\frac{z^5}{1+z-z^2}, \infty\right] = -\text{Res}\left[\frac{1}{z^2}\left(\frac{1/z^5}{1 + 1/z - 1/z^2}\right), 0\right] = -\text{Res}\left[\frac{1}{z^5(z^2 + z - 1)}, 0\right].$$

The function $1/[z^5(z^2 + z - 1)]$ has a pole of order 5 at $z = 0$. To use formula 6.2 to calculate the residue involves four differentiations of $1/(z^2 + z - 1)$. Instead, we write

$$\frac{1}{z^5(1 - z - z^2)} = \frac{1}{z^5[1 - (z + z^2)]} = \frac{1}{z^5}\left[1 + (z + z^2) + (z + z^2)^2 + (z + z^2)^3 + \cdots\right]$$

$$= \frac{1}{z^5}\left[1 + (z + z^2) + (z^2 + 2z^3 + z^4)\right.$$

$$\left. + (z^3 + 3z^4 + 3z^5 + z^6) + (z^4 + \cdots) + \cdots\right]$$

$$= \frac{1}{z^5}\left[1 + z + 2z^2 + 3z^3 + 5z^4 + \cdots\right].$$

This shows that the residue of $1/[z^5(z^2 + z - 1)]$ at $z = 0$ is 5. Hence,

$$\text{Res}\left[\frac{z^5}{1+z-z^2}, \infty\right] = 5.$$

(b) Since

$$\frac{1}{z^2}f\left(\frac{1}{z}\right) = \frac{1}{z^{n+2}}\sin z,$$

$f(z)$ has a removable singularity or a pole at $z = \infty$, depending on the value of n. If we replace $\sin z$ by its Maclaurin series, we get

$$\frac{1}{z^2}f\left(\frac{1}{z}\right) = \frac{1}{z^{n+2}}\sum_{k=0}^{\infty}\frac{(-1)^k}{(2k+1)!}z^{2k+1} = \sum_{k=0}^{\infty}\frac{(-1)^k}{(2k+1)!}z^{2k-n-1}.$$

If $n \leq 0$, or n is an odd positive integer, there is no term in $1/z$ in this series. Hence, the residue in this case is zero. When n is an even positive integer, then the term in $1/z$ occurs for $k = 2n$. In other words, the residue in this case is $\dfrac{(-1)^{n/2}}{(n+1)!}$. •

The residue of a function $f(z)$ at an isolated singularity z_0 in the (finite) plane is defined by integral 5.30b, (although we seldom calculate it this way),

$$\operatorname{Res}\left[\, f(z), z_0 \right] = \frac{1}{2\pi i} \oint_C f(z)\, dz, \tag{6.18}$$

where C can be taken as any circle centred at z_0 that contains no other singularity of $f(z)$. The residue at infinity is given by the same integral, but traversed in the opposite direction.

Theorem 6.9 If a function $f(z)$ is analytic on and exterior to a circle C of radius $R > 1$, then the residue at infinity of $f(z)$ is given by the integral

$$\operatorname{Res}\left[f(z), \infty \right] = \frac{1}{2\pi i} \oint_C f(z)\, dz. \tag{6.19}$$

Proof According to equation 6.17, the residue at infinity is

$$\operatorname{Res}\left[f(z), \infty \right] = -\operatorname{Res}\left[\frac{1}{z^2} f\left(\frac{1}{z}\right), 0 \right] = \frac{-1}{2\pi i} \oint_{C'} \frac{1}{z^2} f\left(\frac{1}{z}\right) dz,$$

where C' is any circle that contains only the singularity $z = 0$ of the integrand. The circle with radius $r = 1/R$ satisfies this requirement; all (finite) singularities of $f(z)$ are inside C, and for them, $1/z$ is outside C'. If we parametrize C' with $z = re^{\theta i}$, $0 \leq \theta \leq 2\pi$, then,

$$\operatorname{Res}\left[f(z), \infty \right] = \frac{-1}{2\pi i} \int_0^{2\pi} \frac{1}{r^2 e^{2\theta i}} f\left(\frac{1}{re^{\theta i}}\right) rie^{\theta i} d\theta = \frac{-1}{2\pi} \int_0^{2\pi} f(Re^{-\theta i}) Re^{-\theta i}\, d\theta.$$

If we set $\phi = -\theta$, then

$$\operatorname{Res}\left[f(z), \infty \right] = \frac{-1}{2\pi} \int_0^{-2\pi} f(Re^{\phi i}) Re^{\phi i}(-d\phi) = \frac{-1}{2\pi} \int_{-2\pi}^0 f(Re^{\phi i}) Re^{\phi i} d\phi$$

$$= \frac{-1}{2\pi} \int_0^{2\pi} f(Re^{\phi i}) Re^{\phi i} d\phi \qquad (\text{since } e^{\phi i} \text{ is } 2\pi\text{-periodic})$$

$$= \frac{-1}{2\pi i} \int_0^{2\pi} f(Re^{\phi i}) i Re^{\phi i} d\phi = \frac{-1}{2\pi i} \oint_C f(z)\, dz = \frac{1}{2\pi i} \oint_C f(z)\, dz. \blacksquare$$

To calculate the residue of a function $f(z)$ at a finite singularity, we traverse the circle C in equation 6.18 in the positive sense which means that the singularity will be on our left as we move along C. Similarly, in traversing C in integral 6.19 in the negative sense, the singularity at infinity is once again on the left. It is worthwhile pointing out that without the z^2-factor, and the negative sign, in definition 6.17, this result would not be valid.

Although we like to draw parallels between singularities at finite points in the complex plane and those at infinity, do not attempt to carry this too far. If $z = z_0$ is a removable singularity of a function $f(z)$, then the residue at this singularity is zero. Such may not be the case when $z = \infty$ is a removvble singularity. For instance, $f(z) = 1/z$ has a removable singularity at $z = \infty$ (since $f(1/z) = z$), but the residue at infinity is

$$\text{Res}\,[1/z, \infty] = -\text{Res}\left[\frac{1}{z^2}(z), 0\right] = -\text{Res}\left[\frac{1}{z}, 0\right] = -1.$$

Residues at infinity can be useful in the evaluation of contour integrals as the following theorem shows.

Theorem 6.10 Suppose that a function $f(z)$ is analytic on a simple, closed, piecewise smooth curve C, with only a finite number of singularities outside of C. Then,

$$\oint_C f(z)\,dz = -2\pi i \big[\text{Sum of residues of } f(z) \text{ at its singularities exterior to } C,$$

$$\text{including infinity}\big]. \tag{6.20}$$

Proof Because there is only a finite number of singularities outside of C, they can be enclosed in a circle C' that also contains C (Figure 6.16). Suppose that Γ is a piecewise smooth curve that joins C and C' that does not pass through any of the singularities exterior to C. This creates a loop L to which we can apply Cauchy's residue theorem,

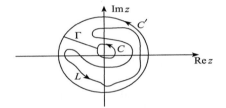

Figure 6.16

$$\oint_L f(z)\,dz = 2\pi i \left[\text{Sum of residues of } f(z) \text{ at its singularities interior to } L\right].$$

In traversing L, curve Γ is followed twice, once in each direction, so that its contribution to the integral vanish. This leaves clockwise integration along C and counterclockwise integration along C',

$$\oint_C f(z)\,dz + \oint_{C'} f(z)\,dz = 2\pi i \left[\text{Sum of residues of } f(z) \text{ at its finite singularities}\right.$$

$$\left.\text{exterior to } C\right].$$

Thus,

$$\oint_C f(z)\,dz = \oint_{C'} f(z)\,dz - 2\pi i \big[\text{Sum of residues of } f(z) \text{ at its finite singularities}$$

$$\text{exterior to } C\big]$$

$$= -2\pi i \,\text{Res}\,[f(z), \infty] - 2\pi i \big[\text{Sum of residues of } f(z) \text{ at its finite}$$

$$\text{singularities exterior to } C\big]$$

$$= -2\pi i \big[\text{Sum of residues of } f(z) \text{ at its singularities exterior to } C,$$

$$\text{including infinity}\big]. \blacksquare$$

We can use this result to provide an alternative solution to many of the contour integrals to which we applied Cauchy's residue theorem. Here are two examples.

Example 6.21   Use Theorem 6.10 to evaluate the contour integral in Example 6.3.

Solution   Since the singularity $z = -5$ is exterior to C, equation 6.20 gives

$$\oint_C \frac{1}{(z+5)(z^2-1)^3}\, dz = -2\pi i \left\{ \text{Res}\left[\frac{1}{(z+5)(z^2-1)^3}, -5\right] + \text{Res}\left[\frac{1}{(z+5)(z^2-1)^3}, \infty\right] \right\}.$$

Since $z = -5$ is a simple pole,

$$\text{Res}\left[\frac{1}{(z+5)(z^2-1)^3}, -5\right] = \lim_{z\to -5}\left[\frac{z+5}{(z+5)(z^2-1)^3}\right] = \frac{1}{24^3}.$$

The residue at infinity is

$$\text{Res}\left[\frac{1}{(z+5)(z^2-1)^3}, \infty\right] = -\text{Res}\left[\frac{1}{z^2}\left(\frac{1}{(1/z+5)(1/z^2-1)^3}\right), 0\right]$$

$$= -\text{Res}\left[\frac{z^5}{(1+5z)(1-z^2)^3}, 0\right] = 0.$$

Thus,

$$\oint_C \frac{1}{(z+5)(z^2-1)^3}\, dz = -2\pi i \left(\frac{1}{24^3}\right) = -\frac{\pi i}{6912}. \bullet$$

Example 6.22   Show how much easier it is to use the point at infinity to verify the result in Exercise 23 of Section 4.5.

Solution   Let the polynomial be $P(z) = a_0 + a_1 z + \cdots + a_n z^n$, where $n \geq 2$, and $a_n \neq 0$. Since curve C contains all singularities of $1/P(z)$, equation 6.20 implies that

$$\oint_C \frac{1}{P(z)}\, dz = 2\pi i \text{Res}\left[\frac{1}{P(z)}, \infty\right] = -2\pi i\, \text{Res}\left[\frac{1}{z^2 P(1/z)}, 0\right]$$

$$= -2\pi i\, \text{Res}\left[\frac{1}{z^2(a_0 + a_1/z + \cdots + a_n/z^n)}, 0\right]$$

$$= -2\pi i\, \text{Res}\left[\frac{z^{n-2}}{a_0 z^n + a_1 z^{n-1} + \cdots + a_n}, 0\right].$$

Since $a_n \neq 0$, and $n \geq 2$, $z = 0$ is not a singularity of this function, and therefore the residue, and the value of the integral, is zero. An even more general result is proved in Exercise 26. $\bullet$

The above examples did not require the use of the point at infinity, but it did facilitate the results. The following examples can only be done with the point at infinity.

Example 6.23   In Exercise 42 of Section 6.1, it was shown that all zeros of the function $f(z) = z^5 + 3z^2 + 6z + 1$ are inside the circle $C : |z| = 2$. Use this fact to evaluate the contour integral

$$\oint_C \frac{z^4}{z^5 + 3z^2 + 6z + 1}\, dz.$$

Solution   Since there are no finite singularities exterior to C, we can use Theorem 6.10 to write

$$\oint_C \frac{z^4}{z^5 + 3z^2 + 6z + 1}\, dz = -2\pi i\, \text{Res}\left[\frac{z^4}{z^5 + 3z^2 + 6z + 1}, \infty\right]$$

$$= 2\pi i\, \text{Res}\left[\frac{1}{z^2}\frac{1/z^4}{1/z^5 + 3/z^2 + 6/z + 1}, 0\right]$$

$$= 2\pi i\, \text{Res}\left[\frac{1}{z(1 + 3z^3 + 6z^4 + z^5)}, 0\right]$$

$$= 2\pi i \lim_{z \to 0}\left[\frac{z}{z(1 + 3z^2 + 6z^4 + z^5)}\right] = 2\pi i.\ \bullet$$

Example 6.24 Evaluate the integral $\displaystyle\int_0^1 \frac{\sqrt{1 - x^2}}{1 + x^2}\, dx$.

Solution   Because the integrand is an even function , we can write that

$$\int_0^1 \frac{\sqrt{1 - x^2}}{1 + x^2}\, dx = \frac{1}{2}\int_{-1}^1 \frac{\sqrt{1 - x^2}}{1 + x^2}\, dx.$$

It would seem natural to replace the integrand with $\sqrt{1 - z^2}/(1 + z^2)$ around some appropriate contour. However, a suitable contour cannot be found because $\sqrt{1 - z^2}$ has two branch cuts, the real axis to the left of $z = -1$ and to the right of $z = 1$. Instead consider the function

$$f(z) = \frac{z}{1 + z^2}\sqrt{1 + \frac{1}{z}}\sqrt{1 - \frac{1}{z}}.$$

Notice that if $z = x$, $-1 < x < 1$, is real, this reduces to

$$\frac{x}{1 + x^2}\sqrt{1 + \frac{1}{x}}\sqrt{1 - \frac{1}{x}} = \frac{x}{1 + x^2}\sqrt{1 - \frac{1}{x^2}} = \pm\frac{\sqrt{1 - x^2}}{1 + x^2}.$$

According to Exercises 47 and 48 in Section 3.6, branch points of $f(z)$ are $z = \pm 1$, and the branch cut is the line segment joining these points. Suppose we consider the contour integral of $f(z)$ around the contour C in Figure 6.17. Be cause the only finite singularities of $f(z)$ outside C are $\pm i$, we can write that

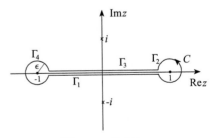

Figure 6.17

$$\oint_C f(z)\, dz = -2\pi i\left\{\text{Res}[f(z), i] + \text{Res}[f(z), -i] + \text{Res}[f(z), \infty]\right\}.$$

Residues at $z = \pm i$ are

$$\text{Res}[f(z), i] = \lim_{z \to i}\left[\frac{z(z - i)}{(z + i)(z - i)}\sqrt{1 + \frac{1}{z}}\sqrt{1 - \frac{1}{z}}\right] = \frac{i}{2i}\sqrt{1 + \frac{1}{i}}\sqrt{1 - \frac{1}{i}}$$

$$= \frac{1}{2}\sqrt{1 - i}\sqrt{1 + i} = \frac{1}{2}e^{(1/2)\text{Log}(1 - i)}e^{(1/2)\text{Log}(1 + i)}$$

$$= \frac{1}{2}e^{(1/2)(\ln\sqrt{2}-\pi i/4)}e^{(1/2)(\ln\sqrt{2}+\pi i/4)} = \frac{1}{\sqrt{2}},$$

$$\text{Res}[f(z),-i] = \lim_{z\to -i}\left[\frac{z(z+i)}{(z+i)(z-i)}\sqrt{1+\frac{1}{z}}\sqrt{1-\frac{1}{z}}\right] = \frac{-i}{-2i}\sqrt{1+\frac{1}{-i}}\sqrt{1-\frac{1}{-i}}$$

$$= \frac{1}{2}\sqrt{1+i}\sqrt{1-i} = \frac{1}{\sqrt{2}}.$$

The residue at infinity is

$$\text{Res}[f(z),\infty] = -\text{Res}\left[\frac{1}{z^2}\frac{1/z}{1+1/z^2}\sqrt{1+z}\sqrt{1-z},0\right] = -\text{Res}\left[\frac{\sqrt{1+z}\sqrt{1-z}}{z(1+z^2)},0\right].$$

If we expand these terms in Maclaurin series,

$$\frac{\sqrt{1+z}\sqrt{1-z}}{z(1+z^2)} = \frac{1}{z}\left(1-z^2+\cdots\right)\left(1+\frac{z}{2}+\cdots\right)\left(1-\frac{z}{2}+\cdots\right),$$

the coefficient of $1/z$ is 1. Thus, $\text{Res}[f(z),\infty] = -1$, and

$$\oint_C f(z)\,dz = -2\pi i\left[\frac{1}{\sqrt{2}}+\frac{1}{\sqrt{2}}-1\right] = 2\pi i(1-\sqrt{2}).$$

When we break C into its four component parts, we have

$$2\pi i(1-\sqrt{2}) = \int_{\Gamma_1}f(z)\,dz + \int_{\Gamma_2}f(z)\,dz + \int_{\Gamma_3}f(z)\,dz + \int_{\Gamma_4}f(z)\,dz. \quad (6.21)$$

Since the only singularities of $f(z)$ off the branch cut are $\pm i$, the function must be bounded on Γ_2; that is, there exists a constant $M>0$ such that $|f(x)|\le M$ on Γ_2. It follows that

$$\left|\int_{\Gamma_2}f(z)\,dz\right| \le M(2\pi\epsilon),$$

and this approaches zero as $\epsilon\to 0$. Similarly, the integral along Γ_4 approaches zero as $\epsilon\to 0$. If we now let $\epsilon\to 0$ in equation 6.21, and take into account that integrals along Γ_2 and Γ_4 approach zero, we obtain

$$2\pi i(1-\sqrt{2}) = \lim_{\epsilon\to 0}\int_{\Gamma_1}f(z)\,dz + \lim_{\epsilon\to 0}\int_{\Gamma_3}f(z)\,dz$$

$$= \lim_{\epsilon\to 0}\int_{\Gamma_1}\frac{x}{1+x^2}\sqrt{1+\frac{1}{x}}\sqrt{1-\frac{1}{x}}\,dx + \lim_{\epsilon\to 0}\int_{\Gamma_3}\frac{x}{1+x^2}\sqrt{1+\frac{1}{x}}\sqrt{1-\frac{1}{x}}\,dx$$

$$= \lim_{\epsilon\to 0}\int_{\Gamma_1}\frac{x}{1+x^2}e^{(1/2)\text{Log}(1+1/x)}e^{(1/2)\text{Log}(1-1/x)}\,dx$$

$$+ \lim_{\epsilon\to 0}\int_{\Gamma_3}\frac{x}{1+x^2}e^{(1/2)\text{Log}(1+1/x)}e^{(1/2)\text{Log}(1-1/x)}\,dx.$$

Suppose we denote these limits I_1 and I_3. To calculate I_1, we divide the integration into two and use the results of Exercises 47 and 48 in Section 3.6.

$$I_1 = \int_{-1}^{0} \frac{x}{1+x^2} e^{(1/2)(\ln|1+1/x|+\pi i)} e^{(1/2)\ln|1-1/x|} \, dx$$

$$+ \int_{0}^{1} \frac{x}{1+x^2} e^{(1/2)\ln|1+1/x|} e^{(1/2)(\ln|1-1/x|-\pi i)} \, dx$$

$$= \int_{-1}^{0} \frac{x}{1+x^2} \sqrt{\left|1+\frac{1}{x}\right|} \sqrt{\left|1-\frac{1}{x}\right|} e^{\pi i/2} \, dx$$

$$+ \int_{0}^{1} \frac{x}{1+x^2} \sqrt{\left|1+\frac{1}{x}\right|} \sqrt{\left|1-\frac{1}{x}\right|} e^{-\pi i/2} \, dx$$

$$= \int_{-1}^{0} \frac{ix}{1+x^2} \sqrt{\left|1-\frac{1}{x^2}\right|} \, dx + \int_{0}^{1} \frac{-ix}{1+x^2} \sqrt{\left|1-\frac{1}{x^2}\right|} \, dx$$

$$= i \int_{-1}^{0} \frac{x}{1+x^2} \frac{\sqrt{1-x^2}}{|x|} \, dx - i \int_{0}^{1} \frac{x}{1+x^2} \frac{\sqrt{1-x^2}}{|x|} \, dx$$

$$= -i \int_{-1}^{0} \frac{\sqrt{1-x^2}}{1+x^2} \, dx - i \int_{0}^{1} \frac{\sqrt{1-x^2}}{1+x^2} \, dx = -i \int_{-1}^{1} \frac{\sqrt{1-x^2}}{1+x^2} \, dx.$$

A similar calculation shows that I_3 has the same value. Thus,

$$2\pi i(1-\sqrt{2}) = -2i \int_{-1}^{1} \frac{\sqrt{1-x^2}}{1+x^2} \, dx \quad \Longrightarrow \quad \int_{-1}^{1} \frac{\sqrt{1-x^2}}{1+x^2} \, dx = \pi(\sqrt{2}-1).$$

Finally,

$$\int_{0}^{1} \frac{\sqrt{1-x^2}}{1+x^2} \, dx = \frac{\pi}{2}(\sqrt{2}-1). \bullet$$

EXERCISES 6.4

In Exercises 1–10 find the residue at infinity for the function.

1. $\dfrac{z^2}{(z+1)(z^2-4)}$

2. $\dfrac{z^4}{(z^2+1)(z-5)}$

3. $z^4 \sin\left(\dfrac{2}{z}\right)$

4. $\dfrac{1}{z^4} \tan z$

5. $z^2 e^{3/z}$

6. $\dfrac{1}{z^5} e^{4z}$

7. $\dfrac{e^{3z}}{1-z}$

8. $\dfrac{1}{z^3} \sin^2 z \cos z$

9. $\dfrac{z^n}{1-z}$, n a positive integer

10. $\dfrac{e^{1/z} z^n}{z+1}$, $n \geq 1$ an integer

11. Does $\operatorname{Log} z$ have a residue at infinity?

In Exercises 12–20 use Theorem 6.10 to evaluate the contour integral.

12. $\displaystyle\oint_C \frac{1}{z^2+z^6} \, dz$ where $C: |z| = 2$

13. $\displaystyle\oint_C \frac{z^2}{(1+z)^3(z^2+4)^2} \, dz$ where $C: |z-1| = 10$

14. $\displaystyle\oint_C \frac{\sin(2/z)}{(z^2+5)^4}\,dz$ where $C: |z| = 5$

15. $\displaystyle\oint_C \frac{z^8 \sin(2/z)}{(z^2+5)^4}\,dz$ where $C: |z| = 5$

16. $\displaystyle\oint_C \frac{z^{10} \sin(2/z)}{(z^2+5)^4}\,dz$ where $C: |z| = 5$

17. Exercise 35 in Section 6.1

18. $\displaystyle\oint_C ze^{2/z}\,dz$ where $C: |z| = 2$

19. $\displaystyle\oint_C \frac{z}{z^n-1}\,dz$, where $C: |z| = 4$ and $n \geq 1$ is an integer

20. $\displaystyle\oint_C \frac{z^{n-1}}{3z^n - 10^n}\,dz$, where $C: |z| = 10$ and $n \geq 1$ is an integer

21. Evaluate the contour integral $\displaystyle\oint_C \frac{z^2}{(z-10)(z^2+1)(z+1)}\,dz$ where C is the circle $|z| = 2$ using (a) Cauchy's residue theorem, (b) Theorem 6.10.

22. Repeat Example 6.23 if the integrand is $\displaystyle\frac{z^5}{z^5 + 3z^2 + 6z + 1}$.

23. Use Exercise 44 from Section 6.1 and Theorem 6.10 to evaluate the contour integral

$$\oint_C \frac{z^6}{z-5)(z^7 - 2z^3 + 8)}\,dz,$$

where C is the square with vertices ± 4 and $\pm 4i$.

24. Show that

$$\text{Res}\,[f(z), \infty] = \lim_{z\to\infty}\,[-z\,f(z)],$$

provided that the limit exists.

25. Prove that when a function $f(z)$ has only a finite number of singularities, then the sum of the residues at these singularities, including the point at infinity, is zero.

26. Suppose that $P(z) = a_0 + a_1 z + \cdots + a_m z^m$ and $Q(z) = b_0 + b_1 z + \cdots + b_n z^n$, and C is a curve that encloses all finite singularities of $P(z)/Q(z)$. Show that

$$\oint_C \frac{P(z)}{Q(z)}\,dz = \begin{cases} \dfrac{2\pi a_m i}{b_{m+1}}, & \text{when } n = m+1 \\ 0, & n \geq m+2. \end{cases}$$

27. Evaluate

$$\int_0^1 x^{n-2}\sqrt{x(1-x)}\,dx$$

when $n \geq 2$ is an integer. Hint: Evaluate the contour integral of $f(z) = z^{n-1}\left(\dfrac{1}{z} - 1\right)^{1/2}$, where the square root function is the branch resulting from $\log_0 z$, around a contour like that in Figure 6.17. But with circles at $z = 0$ and $z = 1$. See also Exercise 49 in Section 3.6.

28. Use Exercises 47 and 48 in Section 3.6 to evaluate

$$\int_0^1 \frac{x^2\sqrt{1-x^2}}{1+x^2}\,dx.$$

§6.5   Summation of Real Series

In Sections 6.2 and 6.3, we saw how residues can be used to evaluate real definite integrals. In this section we show that they can be used to find sums of many series of real constants that would otherwise seem intractable. For instance, how would you find the sum of the series $\sum_{n=1}^{\infty} \frac{1}{n^2 + a^2}$? The following theorem describes the method.

Theorem 6.11   Suppose that $f(z) = P(z)/Q(z)$ is a rational function where $\deg Q \geq 2 + \deg P$. Suppose further that poles of $f(z)$ do not occur at the points $z = 0, \pm 1, \pm 2, \ldots$. Then

$$\sum_{n=-\infty}^{\infty} f(n) = - \{\text{sum of the residues of } \pi f(z) \cot \pi z \text{ at the poles of } f(z)\}. \quad (6.22)$$

Proof   Notice that the condition on the degrees of P and Q ensures convergence of the series $\sum_{n=-\infty}^{\infty} f(n)$. To verify the theorem, we consider the contour integral of the function $\pi f(z) \cot \pi z$ around the square Γ_n in Figure 6.18 with corners $\pm(n + 1/2)(1 + i)$ and $\pm(n + 1/2)(1 - i)$. We choose n so large that Γ_n encloses all poles of $f(z)$. Since singularities of the function occur at the poles of $f(z)$ and $z = n$, (n an integer), the zeros of $\sin \pi z$, Cauchy's residue theorem gives

$$\oint_{\Gamma_n} \pi f(z) \cot \pi z \, dz = \{\text{sum of the residues of } \pi f(z) \cot \pi z \text{ at its singularities inside } \Gamma_n\}$$

$$= \{\text{sum of the residues of } \pi f(z) \cot \pi z \text{ at the poles of } \cot \pi z \text{ inside } \Gamma_n\}$$
$$+ \{\text{sum of the residues } \pi f(z) \cot \pi z \text{ at the poles of } f(z)\}.$$

Using L'Hôpital's rule, the residue at $z = n$ is

$$\text{Res}\,[\pi f(z) \cot \pi z, n] = \lim_{z \to n} \frac{(z - n)\pi f(z) \cos \pi z}{\sin \pi z} = \lim_{z \to n} \frac{\pi f(z) \cos \pi z}{\pi \cos \pi z} = f(n).$$

Consequently, we can write that

$$\oint_{\Gamma_n} \pi f(z) \cot \pi z \, dz = \sum_{j=-n}^{n} f(j) + \{\text{sum of the residues } \pi f(z) \cot \pi z \text{ at the poles of } f(z)\}.$$

$$(6.23)$$

On the right side of Γ_n, $z = (n + 1/2) + yi$, where $-(n + 1/2) \leq y \leq n + 1/2$. If we use the result of Exercise 18 in Section 3.3 for moduli of the sine and cosine functions, we can write that

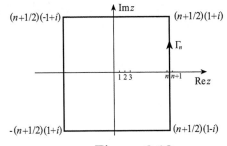

Figure 6.18

$$|\cot \pi z|^2 = \frac{|\cos \pi z|^2}{|\sin \pi z|^2} = \frac{\cosh^2 \pi y - \sin^2 (n + 1/2)\pi}{\cosh^2 \pi y - \cos^2 (n + 1/2)\pi} = \frac{\cosh^2 \pi y - 1}{\cosh^2 \pi y} \leq 1.$$

Thus, on the right side of Γ_n, $|\pi \cot \pi z| \leq \pi$. A similar analysis shows that this inequality is also true on the left side of the square. On the upper side of Γ_n, $z = x + (n + 1/2)i$, where $-(n + 1/2) \leq x \leq n + 1/2$. For z on this side of the square, we have

$$|\cot \pi z|^2 = \frac{|\cos \pi z|^2}{|\sin \pi z|^2} = \frac{\cosh^2 (n + 1/2)\pi - \sin^2 \pi x}{\cosh^2 (n + 1/2)\pi - \cos^2 \pi x} \leq \frac{\cosh^2 (n + 1/2)\pi}{\cosh^2 (n + 1/2)\pi - 1}$$

$$= \frac{\cosh^2 (n + 1/2)\pi}{\sinh^2 (n + 1/2)\pi} = \coth^2 (n + 1/2)\pi.$$

For positive arguments the hyperbolic cotangent function is decreasing, and for $n = 0$, we find that $\coth \pi/2 < 2$. Consequently, we can say that on the upper side of the square Γ_n, $|\pi \cot \pi z| \leq 2\pi$. A similar analysis shows that this inequality is also true on the lower side of the square. We have shown therefore that on all four sides of Γ_n, $|\pi \cot \pi z| \leq 2\pi$.

Consider now the function $f(z)$ on Γ_n. Let $P(z) = a_m z^m + \cdots + a_0$ and $Q(z) = b_k z^k + \cdots + b_0$. Using inequalities 1.40 and 1.41, we can write that

$$|f(z)| = \frac{|a_m z^m + \cdots + a_0|}{|b_k z^k + \cdots + b_0|} \leq \frac{|a_m||z|^m + \cdots + |a_0|}{||b_k||z|^k - |b_{k-1}||z|^{k-1} - \cdots - |b_0||}.$$

For points sufficiently far from the origin, say $|z| > R$, $|b_k||z|^k > |b_{k-1}||z|^{k-1} + \cdots + |b_0|$, in which case

$$|f(z)| \leq \frac{|a_m||z|^m + \cdots + |a_0|}{|b_k||z|^k - |b_{k-1}||z|^{k-1} - \cdots - |b_0|}.$$

It follows that for all points on Γ_n when $n + 1/2 > R$,

$$|f(z)| \leq \frac{|a_m|(n + 1/2)^m 2^{m/2} + \cdots + |a_0|}{|b_k|(n + 1/2)^k 2^{k/2} - |b_{k-1}|(n + 1/2)^{k-1} 2^{(k-1)/2} - \cdots - |b_0|}.$$

Using inequality 4.21, we can say that when $n + 1/2 > R$,

$$\left| \oint_{\Gamma_n} \pi f(z) \cot \pi z \, dz \right|$$

$$\leq 2\pi \left[\frac{|a_m|(n + 1/2)^m 2^{m/2} + \cdots + |a_0|}{|b_k|(n + 1/2)^k 2^{k/2} - |b_{k-1}|(n + 1/2)^{k-1} 2^{(k-1)/2} - \cdots - |b_0|} \right] (8)(n + 1/2).$$

Since $k \geq m + 2$, it follows that the limit of this expression is zero as $n \to \infty$. When we take the limit as $n \to \infty$ in equation 6.23, and use this result, we obtain

$$0 = \lim_{n \to \infty} \sum_{j=-n}^{n} f(j) + \{\text{sum of the residues of } \pi f(z) \cot \pi z \text{ at the poles of } f(z)\}.$$

In other words,

$$\sum_{n=-\infty}^{\infty} f(n) = -\{\text{sum of the residues of } \pi f(z) \cot \pi z \text{ at the poles of } f(z)\}. \quad \blacksquare$$

Example 6.25 Find the sum of the series $\displaystyle\sum_{n=1}^{\infty} \frac{1}{n^2 + a^2}$.

Solution First we note that

$$\sum_{n=-\infty}^{\infty} \frac{1}{n^2 + a^2} = \sum_{n=-\infty}^{-1} \frac{1}{n^2 + a^2} + \frac{1}{a^2} + \sum_{n=1}^{\infty} \frac{1}{n^2 + a^2}$$

$$= \frac{1}{a^2} + 2\sum_{n=1}^{\infty} \frac{1}{n^2 + a^2}.$$

Consequently,

$$\sum_{n=1}^{\infty} \frac{1}{n^2 + a^2} = \frac{1}{2}\sum_{n=-\infty}^{\infty} \frac{1}{n^2 + a^2} - \frac{1}{2a^2}.$$

We now use Theorem 6.11 to evaluate the sum on the right. It is the negative of the sum of the residues of $\dfrac{\pi \cot \pi z}{z^2 + a^2}$ at the poles $z = \pm ai$ of $1/(z^2 + a^2)$. The residue at $z = ai$ is

$$\operatorname{Res}\left[\frac{\pi \cot \pi z}{z^2 + a^2}, ai\right] = \lim_{z \to ai} \frac{(z - ai)\pi \cot \pi z}{(z - ai)(z + ai)} = \frac{\pi \cot (\pi a i)}{2ai} = -\frac{\pi \coth(\pi a)}{2a}.$$

The residue at $z = -ai$ is the same. Hence,

$$\sum_{n=1}^{\infty} \frac{1}{n^2 + a^2} = \frac{\pi}{2a}\coth(\pi a) - \frac{1}{2a^2}.\;\bullet$$

There is a similar result for alternating series. It is contained in the following theorem.

Theorem 6.12 Suppose that $f(z) = P(z)/Q(z)$ is a rational function where $\deg Q \geq 2 + \deg P$. Suppose further that poles of $f(z)$ do not occur at the points $z = 0, \pm 1, \pm 2, \ldots$. Then

$$\sum_{n=-\infty}^{\infty} (-1)^{n+1} f(n) = \{\text{sum of the residues of } \pi f(z)\csc \pi z \text{ at the poles of } f(z)\}. \quad (6.24)$$

The proof is similar to that for Theorem 6.11.

Example 6.26 Find the sum of the series $\displaystyle\sum_{n=-\infty}^{\infty} \frac{(-1)^{n+1}}{(n + a)^2}$ where a is a real number not equal to an integer.

Solution According to Theorem 6.12, the sum of the series is the residue of $\dfrac{\pi \csc \pi z}{(z + a)^2}$ at the double pole $z = -a$ of $1/(z + a)^2$. Hence,

$$\sum_{n=-\infty}^{\infty} \frac{(-1)^{n+1}}{(n + a)^2} = \lim_{z \to -a}\left[\frac{d}{dz}\frac{(z + a)^2 \pi \csc \pi z}{(z + a)^2}\right]$$

$$= \lim_{z \to -a}\left(-\pi^2 \csc \pi z \cot \pi z\right) = -\frac{\pi^2 \cos (\pi a)}{\sin^2 (\pi a)}.\;\bullet$$

EXERCISES 6.5

In Exercises 1–4 find the sum of the series.

1. $\displaystyle\sum_{n=-\infty}^{\infty} \frac{1}{(n+a)^2}$ $(a \neq \text{integer})$

2. $\displaystyle\sum_{n=1}^{\infty} \frac{n^2 - a^2}{(n^2 + a^2)^2}$

3. $\displaystyle\sum_{n=1}^{\infty} \frac{1}{(n^2 + a^2)^2}$

4. $\displaystyle\sum_{n=1}^{\infty} \frac{n^2}{n^4 + a^4}$

When the conditions of Theorem 6.11 are satisfied but $f(z)$ has a pole at the origin, equation 6.22 must be modified. An examination of the theorem indicates that the modification is

$$\sum_{\substack{n=-\infty \\ n\neq 0}}^{\infty} f(n) = -\{\text{sum of the residues of } \pi f(z) \cot \pi z \text{ at the poles of } f(z)\}.$$

Use this result to find the sum of the series in Exercises 5–8.

5. $\displaystyle\sum_{n=1}^{\infty} \frac{1}{n^2}$

6. $\displaystyle\sum_{n=1}^{\infty} \frac{1}{n^4}$

7. $\displaystyle\sum_{\substack{n=-\infty \\ n\neq 0}}^{\infty} \frac{1}{n(n+a)}$ $(a \neq \text{integer})$

8. $\displaystyle\sum_{n=1}^{\infty} \frac{1}{n^2(n^2 + a^2)}$

In Exercises 9–10 find the sum of the alternating series.

9. $\displaystyle\sum_{n=-\infty}^{\infty} \frac{(-1)^{n+1}}{(n+a)^3}$ $(a \neq \text{integer})$

10. $\displaystyle\sum_{n=1}^{\infty} \frac{(-1)^n}{n^2 + a^2}$

When the conditions of Theorem 6.12 are satisfied but $f(z)$ has a pole at the origin, equation 6.24 must be modified. An examination of the theorem indicates that the modification is

$$\sum_{\substack{n=-\infty \\ n\neq 0}}^{\infty} (-1)^{n+1} f(n) = \{\text{sum of the residues of } \pi f(z) \csc \pi z \text{ at the poles of } f(z)\}.$$

Use this result to find the sum of the series in Exercises 11–12.

11. $\displaystyle\sum_{n=1}^{\infty} \frac{(-1)^{n+1}}{n^2}$

12. $\displaystyle\sum_{n=1}^{\infty} \frac{(-1)^{n+1}}{n^4}$

CHAPTER 7   CONFORMAL MAPPING

In Chapters 4–6 we concentrated on algebraic properties of analytic functions. In this chapter we concentrate on functions $w = f(z)$ as mappings from the z-plane to the w-plane, and uncover geometric consequences of analyticity. We confirm what was suggested in Section 2.4, namely that the modulus of $f'(z)$ is a length magnification factor of the mapping, and the argument of $f'(z)$ is the rotational effect of the mapping. In Sections 3.8–3.10 we indicated how complex variables, through harmonic functions, fit into discussions on two-dimensional heat and fluid flow and electrostatics. The power of complex variables in these applications is brought out in this chapter.

§7.1   One-to-one Mappings

We have already seen that a function f can be regarded as a mapping from the z-plane to the w-plane where $w = f(z)$. Of particular importance to our discussion are mappings which are "one-to-one".

Definition 7.1   A mapping $w = f(z)$ is said to be **one-to-one** (1-1) in a domain D if for any two points $z_1 \neq z_2$ in D, $f(z_1) \neq f(z_2)$.

What this implies is that given any point w in the image $f(D)$ of D, there is exactly one point z in D which is mapped by $f(z)$ to w. We may therefore define an inverse mapping f^{-1} which maps points w in $f(D)$ to points in D,

$$z = f^{-1}(w) \qquad \text{if} \qquad w = f(z). \tag{7.1}$$

The following four examples indicate that a mapping may be 1-1 in some domains but not in others.

Example 7.1   Discuss the mapping $w = f(z) = z^2$. Is it one-to-one?

Solution   If we set $z = re^{\theta i}$ in the mapping, then $w = r^2 e^{2\theta i}$. Consequently, the modulus of w is the square of the modulus of z, and the argument of w is double that of z. It follows therefore that the angle in a sector-shaped domain (Figure 7.1) is doubled under $w = z^2$.

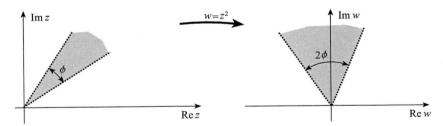

Figure 7.1

In particular, any half-space formed by a line through $z = 0$ (Figure 7.2) maps to the entire w-plane. Another way of saying the same thing is to note that since $(-z)^2 = z^2$, the mapping is 2-1 on some domains. It is in fact 2-1 on any open circle $|z| < R$ centred at $z = 0$. On the other hand, for any open circle $|z - z_0| < R$, which does not contain $z = 0$ (Figure 7.3), the mapping is 1-1. Thus, $z = 0$ is the only point about which it is impossible to construct a neighbourhood in which $w = z^2$ is 1-1.•

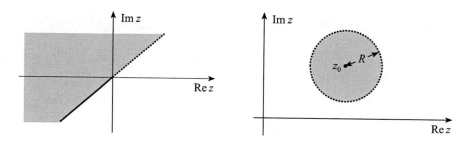

Figure 7.2   **Figure 7.3**

Example 7.2 Discuss the mapping $w = f(z) = e^z$. Is it one-to-one?

Solution   We have already seen that the
function $f(z) = e^z$ is $2\pi i$-periodic so
that each point in the w-plane is the
image of an infinite number of points
in the z-plane. The discussion in
Section 3.2 indicated that $w = e^z$ is 1-1
on any strip $y_0 < \operatorname{Im} z \le y_0 + 2\pi$
(Figure 7.4). It follows then that $w = e^z$
is 1-1 on any open circle $|z - z_0| < R$ with
radius $R \le \pi$. In other words, about any
point z_0, we can construct a neighbourhood
in which $w = e^z$ is 1-1.●

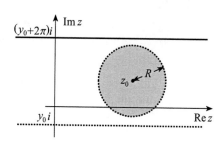

Figure 7.4

Example 7.3 Discuss the mapping $w = f(z) = \log_\phi z$. Is it one-to-one?

Solution   The branch

$$\log_\phi z = \ln|z| + \arg z\, i, \quad z \ne 0, \quad \phi < \arg z \le \phi + 2\pi,$$

of the logarithm function maps the z-plane to the horizontal strip in the w-plane
shown in Figure 7.5. It maps circles $|z| = R$ to vertical line segments, and radial lines
$\arg z = $ constant to horizontal lines in the w-plane. When $z_1 \ne z_2$, either $|z_1| \ne |z_2|$,
or $\arg z_1 \ne \arg z_2$, or both. In any case, $\log_\phi z_1 \ne \log_\phi z_2$, and $w = \log_\phi z$ is 1-1.●

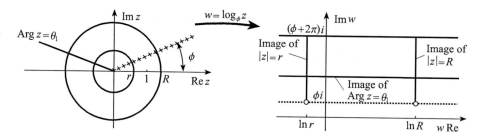

Figure 7.5

Example 7.4 Discuss the mapping $w = f(z) = |z|$. Is it one-to-one?

Solution   The function $w = |z|$ maps the entire z-plane to the nonnegative real
axis. All points on the circle $|z| = R$ are mapped by $w = |z|$ to the single point
$w = R$ (Figure 7.6). Furthermore, it is impossible to construct about any point z a
circle inside of which the mapping is 1-1.●

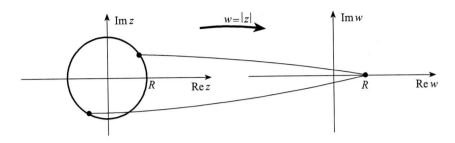

Figure 7.6

We have just seen that about any point $z \neq 0$ we can find circles inside of which z^2 is 1-1; about any point we can find circles inside of which e^z and $\log_\phi z$ are 1-1. On the other hand, about no point can we find circles inside of which $|z|$ is 1-1. If we note that $d(z^2)/dz = 0$ at $z = 0$, $d(e^z)/dz$ never vanishes, and $d(\log_\phi z)/dz$ never vanishes, we might suspect the following result.

Theorem 7.1   If f is analytic at z_0 and $f'(z_0) \neq 0$, then there is a neighbourhood of z_0 in which f is 1-1.

We now establish that analytic functions map domains to domains.

Theorem 7.2   If f is analytic and not constant in a domain D, then the image $f(D)$ of D in the $w = f(z)$ plane is a domain.

Proof   We first establish that $f(D)$ is an open set by showing that every point w_0 in $f(D)$ has a neighbourhood that is contained in $f(D)$. Let z_0 be any point in D for which $w_0 = f(z_0)$. The function $F(z) = w_0 - f(z)$ has an isolated zero at z_0, $F(z)$ being analytic and nonconstant (see the corollary to Theorem 5.23). There therefore exists a circle $C : |z - z_0| = \epsilon$ in D such that $F(z)$ does not vanish on C and the only point inside C at which it vanishes is z_0 (Figure 7.7).

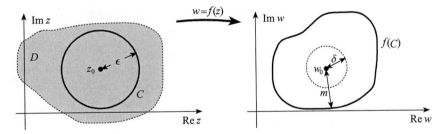

Figure 7.7

It follows that $f(C)$ cannot pass through w_0, and we let m be the distance from w_0 to the point on $f(C)$ closest to w_0,

$$m = \mathop{\text{minimum}}_{w \text{ on } f(C)} |w - w_0| = \mathop{\text{minimum}}_{z \text{ on } C} |f(z) - f(z_0)|.$$

Let $\delta < m$ and consider the open set $|w - w_0| < \delta$. We show that the open set $|w - w_0| < \delta < m$ is contained in the image of $|z - z_0| < \epsilon$. To do this we show that for any point w^* in $|w - w_0| < \delta$, there exists a point z in $|z - z_0| < \epsilon$ for which $w^* = f(z)$.

Consider the function

$$f(z) - w^* = [f(z) - w_0] + [w_0 - w^*].$$

For any point on C, we have

$$|w_0 - w^*| < \delta < |f(z) - w_0|.$$

By Rouche's theorem (Theorem 6.4), the functions $f(z) - w^*$ and $f(z) - w_0$ have the same number of zeros inside C. Since $f(z) - w_0$ has at least one zero inside C (counting multiplicities it could be more than one), it follows that $f(z) - w^*$ has at least one zero inside C; that is, there exists at least one point inside C at which $w^* = f(z)$. This completes the proof that $f(D)$ is an open set.

We now prove that $f(D)$ is connected. Let $w_1 = f(z_1)$ and $w_2 = f(z_2)$ be any two points in $f(D)$. Since D is connected, there is a continuous curve C joining z_1 and z_2 that lies entirely within D (Figure 7.8).

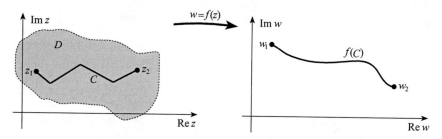

Figure 7.8

Since a differentiable mapping always maps a curve to a curve, it follows that the image $f(C)$ of C is a curve in $f(D)$ joining w_1 and w_2. ∎

To summarize Theorems 7.1 and 7.2, suppose $w = f(z)$ where f is analytic in some domain D, and z_0 is a point in D at which $f'(z_0) \neq 0$. Then about z_0 we can find a neighbourhood $N : |z - z_0| < \delta$ in which $w = f(z)$ is 1-1. The image $f(N)$ of N is a domain in the w-plane (Figure 7.9), and the inverse mapping f^{-1} which maps points w in $f(N)$ to their pre-images z in N exists,

$$z = f^{-1}(w) \qquad \text{if} \qquad w = f(z).$$

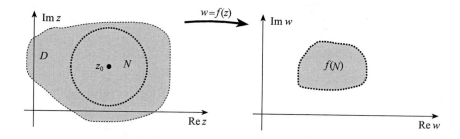

Figure 7.9

These are local properties; they indicate what can be done in a neighbourhood around a point at which $f'(z_0) \neq 0$.

When mappings are used in the solution of boundary-value problems associated with the two-dimensional Laplacian (and we shall see how in Section 7.4), the following global problem always arises: Given a domain D_z in the z-plane, is it possible to find a 1-1 mapping $w = f(z)$ which maps D_z to a prescribed domain D_w in the w-plane? Fortunately, there exist theorems which reply affirmatively. One such is

Theorem 7.3 (**Riemann's Mapping Theorem**) If D is a simply-connected domain in the z-plane (but not the z-plane itself), there exist 1-1 mappings $w = f(z)$ of D to the unit circle $|w| < 1$.

With the unit circle as a reference domain, this theorem indicates that there are 1-1 mappings that map any simply-connected domain to any other simply-connected domain.

EXERCISES 7.1

1. Find images under the mapping $w = z^2 = (x + yi)^2$ of the following domains:
   (a) $x > 0, y > 0$
   (b) $0 < \text{Arg } z < 3\pi/4, |z| < 2$
   (c) $0 < \text{Arg } z < \pi/2, xy < 1$
   (d) $x^2 - y^2 > 4, x > 0$

2. Find images under the mapping $w = e^z = e^{x+yi}$ of the following domains:
   (a) $1 < x < 2, -\pi/2 < y < \pi/2$
   (b) $|x| < 1, 0 < y < 2$
   (c) $0 < y < \pi$
   (d) $x > 0, 0 < y < 2\pi$
   (e) $x > 0, 0 < y < \pi$

3. Find images under the mapping $w = \text{Log } z = \text{Log } (x + yi)$ of the following domains:
   (a) $x > 0, y > 0$
   (b) $y > x, y > -x, x^2 + y^2 < 4$
   (c) $1 < x^2 + y^2 < 3, y \neq 0$ when $x < 0$

4. Illustrate that the mapping $w = \log_\phi z$ maps an open sector centred at $z = 0$ to two rectangles in the w-plane only one of which is open when the sector contains the branch cut.

5. Give a discussion of the mapping $w = z^n$, where $n \geq 3$ is an integer, which parallels Example 7.1.

6. Find images under the mapping $w = z^{\pi/\alpha} \ (0 < \alpha < 2\pi)$ of the following domains:
   (a) $0 < \text{Arg } z < \alpha, |z| < 1$
   (b) $0 < \text{Arg } z < \alpha$

7. Find images under the mapping $w = \sqrt{z}$ of the following domains:
   (a) $x^2 + y^2 < R^2, y \neq 0$ when $x \leq 0$
   (b) $y > 0$
   (c) $x > 0, x^2 + y^2 > 4$
   (d) $x > 1$
   (e) $y > 1$

8. Illustrate that the mapping $w = \sin z$ maps:
   (a) a vertical line to one-half a hyperbola
   (b) a horizontal line to an ellipse
   (c) the rectangular domain $-\pi < x < \pi$, $1 < y < 2$ to an elliptic domain
   (d) the half-strip $-\pi/2 < x < \pi/2$, $y > 0$ to the half-plane $v > 0$

9. Illustrate that the mapping $w = \cosh z$ maps:
   (a) a vertical line to an ellipse
   (b) a horizontal line to one-half a hyperbola
   (c) the rectangular domain $0 < x < 2$, $0 < y < 2\pi$ to an elliptic domain with a slit

10. (a) What is the branch cut for $\operatorname{Log}(z - 2i)$?
   (b) What is the image of the domain $y > 2$ when $w = \operatorname{Log}(z - 2i)$?

11. (a) Show that the function $w = \cos^2 z$ maps the semi-infinite strip $0 < x < \pi/2$, $y > 0$ to the half-plane $v < 0$.
   (b) What does $w = \sin^2 z$ do to the same strip?

12. Show that the Joukowski transformation $w = z + a^2/z$, where $a > 0$ is a constant, maps:
   (a) circles $|z| = R$ ($R \neq a$) to ellipses with foci at $(\pm 2a, 0)$,
   (b) line segments $\theta = \alpha$ to hyperbolas with foci at $(\pm 2a, 0)$,
   (c) the circle $|z| = a$ to that part of the $\operatorname{Re} w$ axis for which $-2a \leq u \leq 2a$,
   (d) the domain $|z| > a$ to the w-plane slit along the line segment $-2a < u < 2a$ (that is, points on the slit are not images of points outside the circle),
   (e) the circle $|z| < a$ to the w-plane slit along the line segment $-2a < u < 2a$.

§7.2   Bilinear Transformations

We introduced bilinear (linear fractional, or Mobius) mappings in Section 2.2, transformations of the form

$$w = f(z) = \frac{az + b}{cz + d},$$ (7.2)

where a, b, c, and d are complex constants for which $ad - bc \neq 0$. The condition $ad - bc \neq 0$ guarantees that $f(z)$ is not a constant. Since

$$f'(z) = \frac{(cz + d)(a) - (az + b)(c)}{(cz + d)^2} = \frac{ad - bc}{(cz + d)^2}$$

never vanishes, Theorem 7.1 indicates that every point except the pole $z = -d/c$ has a neighbourhood in which the function is one-to-one. The function is globally 1-1 also. We can solve equation 7.2 for z in terms of w,

$$z = \frac{-dw + b}{cw - a},$$

so that $f^{-1}(w)$ is defined for all $w \neq a/c$. In other words, bilinear transformations are globally invertible.

Every bilinear transformation is a composition of translations,

$$w = z + b,$$ (7.3)

magnifications,

$$w = az, \quad a \text{ real},$$ (7.4)

rotations,

$$w = e^{\phi i} z, \quad \phi \text{ real},$$ (7.5)

and reciprocations,

$$w = \frac{1}{z}.$$ (7.6)

If $c = 0$ in equation 7.2, we may absorb d into a and b, and the transformation becomes

$$w = f(z) = az + b,$$ (7.7)

a combination of a magnification, rotation, and translation. When $c \neq 0$, equation 7.2 can be expressed in the form

$$w = f(z) = \frac{az + b}{cz + d} = \frac{\dfrac{a}{c}(cz + d) + b - \dfrac{ad}{c}}{cz + d} = \frac{a}{c} + \frac{b - \dfrac{ad}{c}}{cz + d},$$ (7.8)

and $f(z)$ may be regarded successively as a rotation and magnification, and a translation

$$w_1 = cz + d,$$

a reciprocation,

$$w_2 = \frac{1}{w_1},$$

a rotation and magnification,

$$w_3 = \left(b - \frac{ad}{c}\right)w_2,$$

and finally a translation,

$$w = w_3 + \frac{a}{c}.$$

Bilinear transformations have properties that make them very useful in solving problems in heat conduction, electrostatics, and fluid flow. We discuss some of these properties in the following theorems and examples. Firstly, if you look back at the bilinear transformations of Exercises 9–17 in Section 2.2, you were asked to map circles and straight lines by reciprocations. In every case, the result was a circle or a straight line. These were special cases of the following general result.

Theorem 7.4   Circles and straight lines in the z-plane are mapped by bilinear transformations to circles and straight lines in the w-plane.

Proof   Every bilinear transformation can be expressed as a finite sequence of translations, rotations, magnifications, and/or reciprocations. Clearly, translations, rotations, and magnifications map circles to circles and lines to lines. The only question concerns that of a reciprocation $w = 1/z$. If we set $w = u + vi$ and $z = x + yi$, then

$$z = x + yi = \frac{1}{w} = \frac{1}{u + vi} = \frac{u - vi}{u^2 + v^2}.$$

Thus,

$$x = \frac{u}{u^2 + v^2}, \qquad y = \frac{-v}{u^2 + v^2}.$$

All circles in the z-plane have real and imaginary parts satisfying equations of the form

$$x^2 + y^2 + Ax + By + C = 0,$$

where $A^2 + B^2 > 4C$. Consequently, the real and imaginary parts of the image of such a circle under $w = 1/z$ must satisfy

$$\frac{u^2}{(u^2 + v^2)^2} + \frac{v^2}{(u^2 + v^2)^2} + \frac{Au}{u^2 + v^2} - \frac{Bv}{u^2 + v^2} + C = 0,$$

or,

$$C(u^2 + v^2) + Au - Bv + 1 = 0.$$

If $C \neq 0$ (so that the circle in the z-plane does not pass through the pole of the reciprocation), then

$$u^2 + v^2 + \frac{A}{C}u - \frac{B}{C}v + \frac{1}{C} = 0,$$

a circle in the w-plane. If $C = 0$ (so that the circle in the z-plane does pass through the pole),

$$Au - Bv + 1 = 0,$$

a straight line in the w-plane. Circles in the z-plane are therefore mapped by the reciprocation $w = 1/z$ either to circles or straight lines in the w-plane.

Straight lines in the z-plane have real and imaginary parts satisfying equations of the form

$$Ax + By + C = 0,$$

where $A^2 + B^2 > 0$. Consequently, the real and imaginary parts of the image of such a straight line under $w = 1/z$ must satisfy

$$A\left(\frac{u}{u^2 + v^2}\right) + B\left(\frac{-v}{u^2 + v^2}\right) + C = 0,$$

or,

$$Au - Bv + C(u^2 + v^2) = 0.$$

If $C \neq 0$ (in which case the line does not pass through the pole),

$$u^2 + v^2 + \frac{A}{C}u - \frac{B}{C}v = 0,$$

a circle in the w-plane. If $C = 0$ (so that the line passes through the pole),

$$Au - Bv = 0,$$

a straight line in the w-plane. Straight lines in the z-plane are therefore mapped by $w = 1/z$ either to circles or straight lines in the w-plane. ∎

This theorem has shown that circles and straight lines are mapped by bilinear transformations to circles and straight lines. In particular, when a circle or straight line in the z-plane does not pass through the pole of the transformation, it is mapped to a circle in the w-plane; when a circle or straight line in the z-plane passes through the pole of the transformation, it is mapped to a straight line in the w-plane. The following example is an illustration of this point.

Example 7.5   Find images of the following curves under the reciprocation $w = 1/z$:

(a) $2x + 3y = 5$ (b) $y = 4x$ (c) $x^2 + y^2 + 2x = 3$ (d) $x^2 + y^2 + 2x = 0$

Solution   If we set $w = u + vi = \dfrac{1}{z} = \dfrac{1}{x + yi}$, then $x + yi = \dfrac{1}{u + vi} = \dfrac{u - vi}{u^2 + v^2}$.

Thus,

$$x = \frac{u}{u^2 + v^2}, \qquad y = \frac{-v}{u^2 + v^2}.$$

(a) The line $2x + 3y = 5$ does not pass through the pole of the reciprocation. Its image has equation

$$2\left(\frac{u}{u^2 + v^2}\right) + 3\left(\frac{-v}{u^2 + v^2}\right) = 5 \qquad \Longrightarrow \qquad 5(u^2 + v^2) = 2u - 3v.$$

This is a circle in the w-plane.

(b) The line $y = 4x$ passes through the pole of the mapping. Its image has equation

$$\frac{-v}{u^2 + v^2} = 4\left(\frac{u}{u^2 + v^2}\right) \qquad \Longrightarrow \qquad v = -4u.$$

This is a line in the w-plane.

(c) The circle $x^2 + y^2 + 2x = 3$ does not pass through the pole of the reciprocation. Its image has equation

$$\left(\frac{u}{u^2 + v^2}\right)^2 + \left(\frac{-v}{u^2 + v^2}\right)^2 + 2\left(\frac{u}{u^2 + v^2}\right) = 3 \qquad \Longrightarrow \qquad 1 + 2u = 3(u^2 + v^2).$$

This is a circle in the w-plane.

(d) The circle $x^2 + y^2 + 2x = 0$ passes through the pole. Its image has equation

$$\left(\frac{u}{u^2 + v^2}\right)^2 + \left(\frac{-v}{u^2 + v^2}\right)^2 + 2\left(\frac{u}{u^2 + v^2}\right) = 0 \qquad \Longrightarrow \qquad 1 + 2u = 0.$$

This is a straight line.●

So far we have concerned ourselves with finding images of various curves when given a bilinear transformation. In practice, we must find a bilinear transformation that maps a given curve in the z-plane (say line or circle) to a given curve in the w-plane. We shall find that the *cross-ratio* in the following definition can be instrumental in doing this, and the next theorem indicates why.

Definition 7.2   The **cross-ratio** of four points z, z_1, z_2, and z_3 in the z-plane is defined as the quotient

$$\frac{(z - z_1)(z_2 - z_3)}{(z - z_3)(z_2 - z_1)}. \tag{7.9}$$

Theorem 7.5   The cross-ratio is invariant under a bilinear mapping; that is, if w, w_1, w_2, and w_3 are the images of z, z_1, z_2, and z_3, respectively, under a bilinear mapping, then

$$\frac{(w - w_1)(w_2 - w_3)}{(w - w_3)(w_2 - w_1)} = \frac{(z - z_1)(z_2 - z_3)}{(z - z_3)(z_2 - z_1)}. \tag{7.10}$$

Proof   If $w = f(z) = (az + b)/(cz + d)$, then the cross-ratio of $w = f(z)$, $w_1 = f(z_1)$, $w_2 = f(z_2)$, and $w_3 = f(z_3)$ is

$$
\frac{(w - w_1)(w_2 - w_3)}{(w - w_3)(w_2 - w_1)} = \frac{\left(\dfrac{az + b}{cz + d} - \dfrac{az_1 + b}{cz_1 + d}\right)\left(\dfrac{az_2 + b}{cz_2 + d} - \dfrac{az_3 + b}{cz_3 + d}\right)}{\left(\dfrac{az + b}{cz + d} - \dfrac{az_3 + b}{cz_3 + d}\right)\left(\dfrac{az_2 + b}{cz_2 + d} - \dfrac{az_1 + b}{cz_1 + d}\right)}
$$

$$
= \frac{[(az + b)(cz_1 + d) - (az_1 + b)(cz + d)][(az_2 + b)(cz_3 + d) - (cz_2 + d)(az_3 + b)]}{[(az + b)(cz_3 + d) - (cz + d)(az_3 + b)][(az_2 + b)(cz_1 + d) - (az_1 + b)(cz_2 + d)]}
$$

$$
= \frac{[(ad - bc)(z - z_1)][(ad - bc)(z_2 - z_3)]}{[(ad - bc)(z - z_3)][(ad - bc)(z_2 - z_1)]}
$$

$$
= \frac{(z - z_1)(z_2 - z_3)}{(z - z_3)(z_2 - z_1)}. \qquad \blacksquare
$$

Although the general bilinear transformation $w = (az + b)/(cz + d)$ contains four constants, only three are independent. This is most easily seen by dividing numerator and denominator either by a or c (since at least one of them must be nonzero),

$$w = \frac{z + b/a}{cz/a + d/a}, \qquad \text{or} \qquad w = \frac{az/c + b/c}{z + d/c}.$$

As a result, it should only be necessary to specify the images w_1, w_2, and w_3 in the w-plane of three points z_1, z_2, and z_3 in the z-plane to determine the three independent constants. If they are substituted into $w = (az + b)/(cz + d)$, the resulting equations

$$w_1 = \frac{az_1 + b}{cz_1 + d}, \qquad w_2 = \frac{az_2 + b}{cz_2 + d}, \qquad w_3 = \frac{az_3 + b}{cz_3 + d}$$

can then be solved for three of the constants in terms of the fourth. Setting the fourth constant equal to 1 then gives the bilinear transformation. An alternative is to use cross-ratios. They can be used to map any three points in the z-plane to any three points in the w-plane. In effect, equation 7.10 implicitly defines the unique bilinear transformation that maps any three given points z_1, z_2, and z_3 in the z-plane to any three given points w_1, w_2, and w_3 in the w-plane. This is shown in the next theorem.

Theorem 7.6 Any three distinct points z_1, z_2, and z_3 in the z-plane can be mapped by a bilinear transformation to any three distinct points w_1, w_2, and w_3 in the w-plane.

Proof Bilinear transformations preserve the cross-ratios of z, z_1, z_2, and z_3 and their images w, w_1, w_2, and w_3; that is,

$$\frac{(w - w_1)(w_2 - w_3)}{(w - w_3)(w_2 - w_1)} = \frac{(z - z_1)(z_2 - z_3)}{(z - z_3)(z_2 - z_1)},$$

or,

$$(w - w_1)(w_2 - w_3)(z - z_3)(z_2 - z_1) = (w - w_3)(w_2 - w_1)(z - z_1)(z_2 - z_3).$$

If we define

$$W_{23} = w_2 - w_3, \qquad W_{21} = w_2 - w_1, \qquad Z_{23} = z_2 - z_3, \qquad Z_{21} = z_2 - z_1,$$

then,

$$W_{23}Z_{21}(w - w_1)(z - z_3) = W_{21}Z_{23}(w - w_3)(z - z_1),$$

from which

$$[W_{23}Z_{21}(z - z_3) - W_{21}Z_{23}(z - z_1)]w = W_{23}Z_{21}w_1(z - z_3) - W_{21}Z_{23}w_3(z - z_1).$$

Thus,

$$w = \frac{(W_{23}Z_{21}w_1 - W_{21}Z_{23}w_3)z + (W_{21}Z_{23}w_3z_1 - W_{23}Z_{21}w_1z_3)}{(W_{23}Z_{21} - W_{21}Z_{23})z + (W_{21}Z_{23}z_1 - W_{23}Z_{21}z_3)}.$$

This equation defines a transformation $w = f(z)$ which is bilinear (provided that it is not a constant mapping). From the equality of cross-ratios (from which the transformation was derived), it is clear that if $z = z_1$, then

$$0 = \frac{(w - w_1)(w_2 - w_3)}{(w - w_3)(w_2 - w_1)},$$

and this implies that $w = w_1$. If $z = z_2$, then

$$1 = \frac{(w - w_1)(w_2 - w_3)}{(w - w_3)(w_2 - w_1)},$$

and hence

$$ww_2 - ww_3 - w_1 w_2 + w_1 w_3 = ww_2 - ww_1 - w_3 w_2 + w_3 w_1,$$

or,

$$0 = (w - w_2)(w_1 - w_3).$$

But this implies that $w = w_2$. Finally if $z = z_3$, the only way equality of cross-ratios can hold is if $w = w_3$. Consequently the transformation defined by the equality of the cross-ratios is bilinear (since we have now established that $f(z) \neq$ constant), and maps z_1, z_2, and z_3 to w_1, w_2, and w_3. ∎

A most important consequence of Theorems 7.4 and 7.6 is that any circle in the z-plane can be mapped to any circle in the w-plane by a bilinear transformation. Indeed, let C be any circle in the z-plane (Figure 7.10). The circle is characterized by any three distinct points z_1, z_2, and z_3 on it. Suppose it is desired to map C to some circle C' in the w-plane which is also characterized by any three points w_1, w_2 and w_3. By Theorem 7.6, the cross-ratio defines a bilinear transformation that carries z_1, z_2, and z_3 to w_1, w_2, and w_3, respectively. But according to Theorem 7.4, bilinear transformations always map circles to either circles or straight lines. Consequently, C must be mapped to a circle (or line) in the w-plane. But there is only one circle in the w-plane containing w_1, w_2, and w_3 (and certainly no line) and this circle is C'. Thus C is mapped to C' by the bilinear transformation which takes z_1, z_2, and z_3 to w_1, w_2, and w_3.

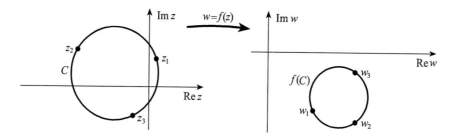

Figure 7.10

It is also true that particular straight lines in the z-plane can be mapped to particular circles in the w-plane, particular circles to particular lines, and particular lines to particular lines.

Three points z_1, z_2, and z_3 on a circle C (or line) specify a direction along the circle, the direction if we proceed from z_1 to z_2 to z_3 along the circle. The same is true for the images w_1, w_2, and w_3 on the image curve $f(C)$ of these points under a bilinear transformation. It can be shown that under a bilinear transformation, the region to the left of C is mapped to the region to the left of $f(C)$. For example, if the points z_1, z_2, and z_3 on the circle in Figure 7.11 are mapped to the points w_1,

w_2, and w_3 on the line, then the interior of the circle is mapped to the half-plane to the right of the line.

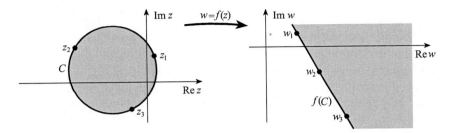

Figure 7.11

Example 7.6 Find a bilinear transformation that maps the interior of the circle $|z - 1 + 2i| = 2$ to the exterior of the circle $|w| = 1$.

Solution   The first thing that we should note is that there is an infinite number of bilinear transformations that will accomplish the task. To map the interior of $|z - 1 + 2i| = 2$, we pick three points in counterclockwise order on the circle to be mapped. Suppose we choose $z_1 = 3 - 2i$, $z_2 = 1$, and $z = -1 - 2i$ (Figure 7.12). For the image to be the exterior of $|w| = 1$, we choose three points in clockwise order, say $w_1 = -1$, $w_2 = i$, and $w_3 = 1$. We can find the bilinear mapping by either setting up equations to solve for a, b, c, and d, or by using cross-ratios. We illustrate both methods. The equations to solve for a, b, c, and d are

$$-1 = \frac{(3 - 2i)a + b}{(3 - 2i)c + d}, \quad i = \frac{a + b}{c + d}, \quad 1 = \frac{(-1 - 2i)a + b}{(-1 - 2i)c + d}.$$

By cross multiplying, we obtain three linear equations in the unknown coefficients,

$$(3 - 2i)a + b + (3 - 2i)c + d = 0, \quad a + b - ic - id = 0, \quad (-1 - 2i)a + b + (1 + 2i)c - d = 0.$$

When these are solved for a, b, and d in terms of c, the result is $a = 0$, $b = -2c$ and $d = (-1 + 2i)c$. If we set $c = 1$, the required bilinear mapping is

$$w = \frac{-2}{z + (-1 + 2i)}.$$

Alternatively, the mapping is defined implicitly by the equality of cross-ratios 7.10. When we substitute the chosen points, we get

$$\frac{(w + 1)(i - 1)}{(w - 1)(i + 1)} = \frac{(z - 3 + 2i)(2 + 2i)}{(z + 1 + 2i)(-2 + 2i)}.$$

When this is solved for w in terms of z, the above result is obtained.●

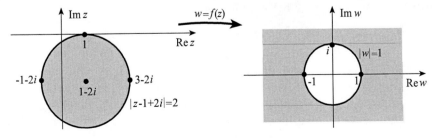

Figure 7.12

The next example maps a circle to a straight line.

Example 7.7 Find a bilinear transformation that maps the circle $|z| = R$ to the real axis in the w-plane.

Solution As in the previous example, we note that there is an infinite number of transformations that will do this. We give three solutions to the problem.

Method 1: In this method we pick three arbitrary points on $|z| = R$ to map to three arbitrary points on $\text{Im}\, w = 0$. Suppose we choose to map the points $z_1 = R$, $z_2 = Ri$, and $z_3 = -R$ to the three points $w_1 = -1$, $w_2 = 0$, and $w_3 = 1$. Using cross-ratios, we can say that the transformation is defined implicitly by the equation

$$\frac{(w+1)(0-1)}{(w-1)(0+1)} = \frac{(z-R)(Ri+R)}{(z+R)(Ri-R)}.$$

When this is solved for w in terms of z, the result is

$$w = \frac{z - Ri}{iz - R}.$$

Method 2: In this method, we take advantage of the fact that the pole of the transformation must be on the circle. If we choose $z = R$ as the pole, then the transformation must be of the form

$$w = \frac{az + b}{z - R}.$$

Suppose we now choose $z_2 = Ri$ and $z_3 = -R$ to map to $w_2 = 0$ and $w_3 = 1$. Then,

$$0 = \frac{aRi + b}{Ri - R}, \qquad 1 = \frac{-aR + b}{-R - R}.$$

When these are solved for a and b, we find that $a = 1 - i$ and $b = -R(1+i)$. Hence, the bilinear transformation is

$$w = \frac{(1-i)z - R(1+i)}{z - R}.$$

Method 3: In this method we rephrase Method 2 using the point at infinity ($w = \infty$) instead of the pole of the transformation, and bring in cross-ratios. Suppose we specify that $z_1 = R$, $z_2 = Ri$, and $z_3 = -R$ map to $w_1 = \infty$, $w_2 = 0$, and $w_3 = 1$. The normal cross-ratio that we would use to find the transformation is

$$\frac{(w - w_1)(w_2 - w_3)}{(w - w_3)(w_2 - w_1)} = \frac{(z - z_1)(z_2 - z_3)}{(z - z_3)(z_2 - z_1)}.$$

With $w_1 = \infty$, we delete the terms $\dfrac{w - w_1}{w_2 - w_1}$, implying that their ratio is 1. When this is done, and we substitute for the remaining points, we obtain

$$\frac{0 - 1}{w - 1} = \frac{(z - R)(Ri + R)}{(z + R)(Ri - R)}.$$

This gives

$$w = 1 - \frac{(z + R)(Ri - R)}{(z - R)(Ri + R)} = \frac{(1-i)z - R(1+i)}{z - R},$$

the transformation in Method 2.●

In the next example, we use the point at infinity in the z-plane.

Example 7.8   Find a bilinear transformation that maps the straight line $\operatorname{Re} z = \operatorname{Im} z$ to the circle $|w - R - Ri| = R$.

Solution   The line and circle are shown in Figure 7.13.

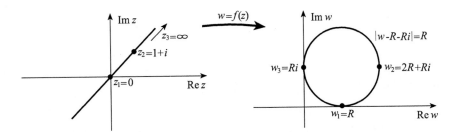

Figure 7.13

Suppose we choose to map the points $z_1 = 0$, $z_2 = 1 + i$, and $z_3 = \infty$ on the line to the points $w_1 = R$, $w_2 = 2R + Ri$, and $w_3 = Ri$. We use the cross-ratio to define the transformation implicitly, but expunge the two terms that involve z_3. The result is

$$\frac{(w - R)(2R + Ri - Ri)}{(w - Ri)(2R + Ri - R)} = \frac{z - 0}{1 + i - 0}.$$

When we solve for w, the transformation is

$$w = \frac{R(iz - 2)}{z - 2}. \bullet$$

Example 7.9   Find all bilinear transformations that map the circle $|z| = 1$ to the right half-plane $\operatorname{Re} w < 0$.

Solution   According to Theorem 7.4, circles are mapped by bilinear transformations to either circles or straight lines, and a circle is mapped to a straight line when the circle passes through the pole of the transformation. Suppose we take $z_0 = e^{\theta_0 i}$, any point on $|z| = 1$, as the pole of the required bilinear transformation $w = f(z)$ (Figure 7.14). Then the bilinear mapping must have the form $w = \dfrac{az + b}{z - z_0}$.

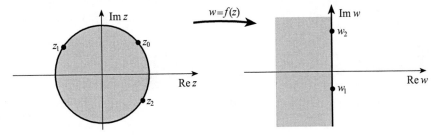

Figure 7.14

Let $z_1 = e^{\theta_1 i}$ and $z_2 = e^{\theta_2 i}$, $0 < \theta_1 < \theta_2 \neq \theta_0$ be any two other points on $|z| = 1$, and $w = v_1 i$ and $w_2 = v_2 i$ be any two points on the v-axis for which $v_2 > v_1$. For $w_1 = f(z_1)$ and $w_2 = f(z_2)$,

$$w_1 = \frac{az_1 + b}{z_1 - z_0}, \qquad w_2 = \frac{az_2 + b}{z_2 - z_0}.$$

If these equations are solved for a and b, the result is

$$a = \frac{w_2(z_2 - z_0) - w_1(z_1 - z_0)}{z_2 - z_1}, \qquad b = \frac{w_1 z_2(z_1 - z_0) - w_2 z_1(z_2 - z_0)}{z_2 - z_1}.$$

Thus, any bilinear transformation of the form

$$w = \frac{[w_2(z_2 - z_0) - w_1(z_1 - z_0)]z + [w_1 z_2(z_1 - z_0) - w_2 z_1(z_2 - z_0)]}{(z_2 - z_1)(z - z_0)}$$

maps $|z| < 1$ to $\operatorname{Re} w < 0$. For example, if we choose $z_0 = 1$, $z_1 = i = -z_2$, $w_2 = i = -w_1$, then

$$w = \frac{[i(-i-1) - (-i)(i-1)]z + [(-i)(-i)(i-1) - i(i)(-i-1)]}{(-i-i)(z-1)} = \frac{z+1}{z-1}. \bullet$$

We now define what it means for points to be inverses with respect to lines and circles. Some authors refer to inverse points as *symmetric* points. Inverse (or symmetric) points are useful in finding certain types of mappings.

Definition 7.3 Two points z_1 and z_2 are said to be **inverses** with respect to a straight line if they are mirror images of one another in the line.

It should be clear that inverse points with respect the real axis are complex conjugates. It is straightforward to check whether points are inverses with respect to a straight line. Quite often a diagram can give a quick answer.

Example 7.10 Determine whether the following pairs of points are inverses with respect to the line that passes through the points $z = -3$ and $z = 2i$:

(a) $z = 3 + 3i$ and $z = 2 + 4i$ \qquad (b) $z = 6 + 9i$ and $z = 8 + 6i$

Solution (a) The equation of the line that passes through the points $z = -3$ and $z = 2i$ is $3y - 2x = 6$; it has slope $2/3$. Since the slope of the line joining $3 + 3i$ and $2 + 4i$ is -1, and this is not the negative reciprocal of $2/3$, the points cannot be inverses.

(b) The slope of the line joining $6 + 9i$ and $8 + 6i$ is $-3/2$, the negative reciprocal of $2/3$. Since distances from these points to the line are

$$\frac{|3(9) - 2(6) - 6|}{\sqrt{13}} = \frac{9}{\sqrt{13}} \qquad \text{and} \qquad \frac{|3(6) - 2(8) - 6|}{\sqrt{13}} = \frac{4}{\sqrt{13}},$$

the points are not inverses. $\bullet$

Definition 7.4 Two points z_1 and z_2 are said to be inverses with respect to the circle $|z - z_0| = R$ if they lie on the same half-line through the centre of the circle and the product of their distances from the centre of the circle is equal to the square of the radius of the circle. We say that the centre of the circle and the point at infinity are inverses.

Inverse points are illustrated in Figure 7.15. Obviously one of the points is inside the circle and the other is outside. The closer one of them is to the centre of the circle, the farther the other is away from the centre. We can develop a formula for the inverse z_2 of a point z_1 with respect to the circle $|z - z_0| = R$. Thinking of vectors, we can write that

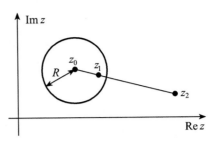

Figure 7.15

$$z_2 = z_0 + (z_2 - z_0) = z_0 + \frac{z_1 - z_0}{|z_1 - z_0|}|z_2 - z_0|.$$

Since $|z_2 - z_0||z_1 - z_0| = R^2$,

$$z_2 = z_0 + \frac{z_1 - z_0}{|z_1 - z_0|}\frac{R^2}{|z_1 - z_0|}$$
$$= z_0 + \frac{R^2(z_1 - z_0)}{|z_1 - z_0|^2} = z_0 + \frac{R^2(z_1 - z_0)}{(z_1 - z_0)(\overline{z_1} - \overline{z_0})} = z_0 + \frac{R^2}{\overline{z_1} - \overline{z_0}}. \qquad (7.11)$$

Example 7.11 Find the inverse of the point $z = 2 - 3i$ with respect to the circle $|z - 4 + i| = 2$.

Solution With formula 7.11, the inverse point is

$$z = 4 - i + \frac{4}{(2 + 3i) - (4 + i)} = 3 - 2i. \bullet$$

The next example makes use of inverse points. It depends on the following property of bilinear mappings. The result is proved in Exercise 24.

Theorem 7.7 Under a bilinear mapping, inverse points are mapped to inverse points.

Example 7.12 Find a bilinear transformation that maps the half-plane $\operatorname{Im} z > 0$ outside the circle $|z - 3 + 3i| = \sqrt{5}$ to an annulus centred at the origin.

Solution We solve this problem by first finding a pair of points that are simultaneously inverses with respect to the x-axis and to the circle (Figure 7.16a). The inverse of a point z_1 with respect to the x-axis is its conjugate $\overline{z_1}$. According to equation 7.11, z_1 and $\overline{z_1}$ are inverses with respect to the circle if

$$\overline{z_1} = 3 - 3i + \frac{5}{\overline{z_1} - (3 + 3i)}.$$

Solutions of this equation are $z_1 = 3 \pm 2i$. Consider the bilinear transformation $w = f(z) = \dfrac{z - 3 + 2i}{z - 3 - 2i}$. Since the circle $C : |z - 3 + 3i| = \sqrt{5}$ does not pass through the pole of the mapping, its image $f(C)$ in the w-plane is a circle. Because points $z = 3 \pm 2i$ are mapped to "infinity" and the origin, respectively, and inverse points are preserved under a bilinear mapping, it follows that the origin and "infinity" must be inverse points with respect to $f(C)$. But this means that $w = 0$ must be the centre of $f(C)$. Similarly, the image of the x-axis must be a circle centred at the origin (Figure 7.16b). The radius r of $f(C)$ is the modulus of the image of any point on the circle; in particular,

$$r = |f(3 + \sqrt{5} - 3i)| = \left| \frac{(3 + \sqrt{5} - 3i) - 3 + 2i}{(3 + \sqrt{5} - 3i) - 3 - 2i} \right| = \frac{1}{\sqrt{5}}.$$

The radius R of the image of the x-axis is the modulus of the image of any point on the axis; in particular,

$$R = |f(0)| = \left| \frac{-3 + 2i}{-3 - 2i} \right| = 1.$$

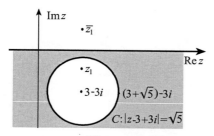

Figure 7.16a

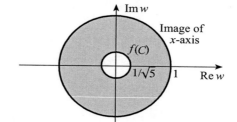

Figure 7.16b

EXERCISES 7.2

In Exercises 1–4 find the bilinear transformation that maps the circle passing through the points z_j to the circle passing through the corresponding points w_j.

1. $z_1 = 1$, $z_2 = i$, $z_3 = -1$; $w_1 = 2i$, $w_2 = -2$, $w_3 = -2i$

2. $z_1 = 2$, $z_2 = 1 + i$, $z_3 = 0$; $w_1 = 1$, $w_2 = i$, $w_3 = -i$

3. $z_1 = -1 + 2i$, $z_2 = -i$, $z_3 = 3 + 4i$; $w_1 = 0$, $w_2 = 1 + i$, $w_3 = -1 + i$

4. $z_1 = -1 - i$, $z_2 = 4 + 5i$, $z_3 = 1 - i$; $w_1 = 3 - 2i$, $w_2 = -1$, $w_3 = -1 + 3i$

In Exercises 5–8 find the bilinear transformation that maps the straight line passing through the points z_1, z_2, and z_3 to the line passing through w_1 and w_2 in such a way that z_3 is the pole of the transformation.

5. $z_1 = 0$, $z_2 = 1 + i$, $z_3 = 2 + 2i$; $w_1 = 3$, $w_2 = 3 + 4i$

6. $z_1 = 2 - i$, $z_2 = -1 + 2i$, $z_3 = 1$; $w_1 = -1$, $w_2 = 1$

7. $z_1 = -3 + i$, $z_2 = 3 + i$, $z_3 = i$; $w_1 = i$, $w_2 = -i$

8. $z_1 = 2 + 5i$, $z_2 = -1 + i$, $z_3 = -4 - 3i$; $w_1 = 1 - 3i$, $w_2 = -3 + 6i$

9. What bilinear transformation results in Exercise 3 if w_2 and w_3 are interchanged? How does it differ from the result in Exercise 3?

In Exercises 10–13 find a bilinear transformation that performs the indicated mapping.

10. maps the interior of the circle in the z-plane defined by $1 + i$, $-1 + i$, and $-\sqrt{2}i$ to the half-plane $\operatorname{Im} w > 0$

11. maps the exterior of the circle $|z + 1| = 2$ to the interior of the circle $|w| = 1$

12. maps the left half-plane $\operatorname{Re} z < 0$ to the circle $|w| < 1$

13. maps the exterior of the circle $|z + 1 - 2i| = 3$ to the half-plane $\operatorname{Re} w > 0$

14. Show that the bilinear mapping $w = (1+z)/(1-z)$ maps the half-plane $\text{Re}\, z < 0$ to the circle $|w| < 1$.

15. For what value of R will the image of the circle $|z - 5| = R$ under the bilinear transformation $w = (z + 4 + 2i)/(3z + i)$ be a line?

16. A bilinear transformation maps a circle to a straight line when the pole of the transformation is on the circle. If two circles (one inside the other) share a common tangent line, and the point of tangency is chosen as pole for a bilinear transformation, then the crescent shaped domain between the circles is mapped to an infinite strip. Illustrate this by finding a bilinear transformation that maps the circle $|z - 1| = 1$ to the u-axis in the w-plane and has $z = 0$ as pole. Now show that any other circle $|z - R| = R$ is mapped by your transformation to a line parallel to the u-axis.

17. If the bilinear transformation $w = R(1 - z)/(1 + z)$ maps the half-plane $\text{Re}\, z > 0$ to the circle $|w| < R$, what bilinear transformation maps $|z| < R$ to $\text{Re}\, w > 0$?

18. Show that the composition of two bilinear transformations is a bilinear transformation.

19. When a bilinear transformation maps a circle to a circle, is the centre of the circle mapped to the centre of the circle?

20. Find a bilinear mapping that maps the region bounded by the circles $|z - R| < R$ and $|z - Ri| < R$ to the first quadrant of the w-plane. Hint: Consider a bilinear transformation with $z = 0$ as zero and $z = R + Ri$ as pole, followed by a rotation.

21. (a) Show that bilinear transformations that map the circle $|z| < R$ to the half-plane $\text{Im}\, w > 0$ so that z_0 on $|z| = R$ is mapped to $w = 0$ and $-z_0$ is the pole of the transformation are of the form $w = a(z - z_0)/(z + z_0)$. Is a arbitrary?
(b) What is a if a point z_1 on $|z| = R$ is to map to w_1? Are there any restrictions on z_1 and w_1?
(c) What is the transformation when $z_0 = R$, $z_1 = Ri$, and $w_1 = 1$?

22. Determine whether the following pairs of points are inverses with respect to the given line:
(a) $3i$ and $2 + i$ with respect to the line through -1 and i
(b) $3i$ and $2 + i$ with respect to the line through -1 and $-i$
(c) 2 and $-2 + 2i$ with respect to the line through 1 and $2i$

23. In each of the following, find the inverse of the given point with respect to the circle.
(a) $z = 2 + i$ with respect to $|z - 1 + 3i| = 2$
(b) $z = 4 - i$ with respect to $|z + 2 + 2i| = 1$
(c) $z = i$ with respect to $|z + 2 + i| = 3$

24. Bilinear mappings preserve inverse points; that is, they map inverse points to inverse points. Prove this for translations, rotations and magnifications.

25. (a) Show that all bilinear transformations that map the half-plane $\text{Im}\, z > 0$ to the circle $|w| < R$ so that some given point z_0 maps to $w = 0$ can be expressed in the form $w = Re^{\lambda i}(z - z_0)/(z - \overline{z_0})$, where λ is a real number. Hint: Use the fact that bilinear transformations preserve inverse points.
(b) Show that all bilinear transformations that map the circle $|z| < R$ to the half-plane $\text{Im}\, w > 0$ so that the centre $z = 0$ of the circle maps to $w = w_0$ can be expressed in the form $w = (\overline{w_0}z - w_0 Re^{\lambda i})/(z - Re^{\lambda i})$.
(c) What form does the transformation in part (b) take if w_0 is purely imaginary?

26. Show that all bilinear transformations that map the unit circle $|z| = 1$ to the unit circle $|w| = 1$ so that some given point z_0 maps to $w = 0$ can be expressed in the form $w = e^{\lambda i}(z - z_0)/(1 - \overline{z_0}z)$, where λ is a real number. Hint: Use the fact that bilinear transformations preserve inverse points.

27. (a) If a bilinear transformation 7.2 maps the unit circle $|z| < 1$ to some simply-connected domain D, what transformation maps $|z| < R$ to D?

(b) What transformation maps the circle $|z - z_0| < R$ to D?

In the applications later in this chapter, it is sometimes advantageous to map regions bounded by two circles, or by a circle and a line, to an annulus bounded by circles centred at the origin. In the remaining problems, we consider some such situations. Properties of inverse points are crucial to solutions. See Theorem 7.7 and Example 7.12.

28. Find a bilinear transformation that maps the half-plane $\text{Im } z > 0$ outside the circle $|z - 4i| = 3$ to an annulus centred at the origin. Determine the inner and outer radii of the annulus.

29. Repeat Exercise 28 with the circle $|z - ai| = R$, where $a > R$.

30. Use a technique similar to that in Example 7.12 to find a bilinear transformation that maps the region between the nonconcentric circles $|z| = 4$ and $|z - i| = 1$ to an annulus centred at the origin.

31. Repeat Exercise 30 with the circles $|z| = R$ and $|z - ai| = a$, where $R > 2a$.

32. Use a technique similar to that in Example 7.12 to find a bilinear transformation that maps the region between the nonconcentric circles $|z| = 4$ and $|z - 2i| = 1$ to an annulus centred at the origin.

33. Repeat Exercise 32 with the circles $|z| = R$ and $|z - ai| = r$, where $R > a + r$ and $r \neq a$.

34. (a) The left figure below shows two circles with equal radii R and centres $(-a, 0)$ and $(a, 0)$, where $a > R$. Show that the domain outside the circles can be mapped by a bilinear transformation to the domain between the concentric circles in the right figure provided that ρ is chosen as

$$\rho = \frac{2a^2}{R^2} - 1 + \frac{2a}{R}\sqrt{\frac{a^2}{R^2} - 1}.$$

Hint: Map z_1, z_2, z_3, and z_4 to w_1, w_2, w_3, and w_4, as shown, and demand that cross-ratios be equal.

(b) Show that the bilinear transformation is

$$w = \frac{[R\rho(1 - \rho) + 2\rho(a - R)]z + [R\rho(1 - \rho)(a - R) - 2\rho(a^2 - R^2)]}{[R(1 - \rho) - 2\rho(a - R)]z + [R(1 - \rho)(a - R) + 2\rho(a^2 - R^2)]}.$$

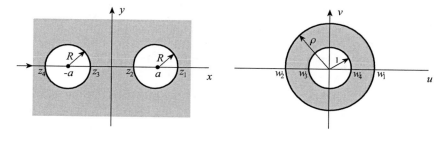

§7.3   Mappings to the Half-plane $\mathrm{Im}\,w > 0$

Frequently in applications it is advantageous to map a domain D in the z-plane to the half-plane $\mathrm{Im}\,w > 0$. Figures 7.17–7.22 illustrate mappings that do this.

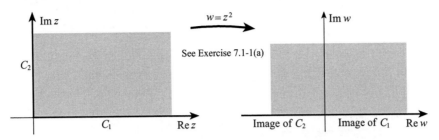

Figure 7.17

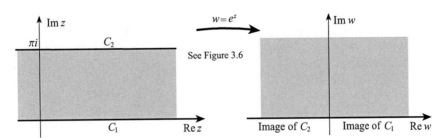

Figure 7.18

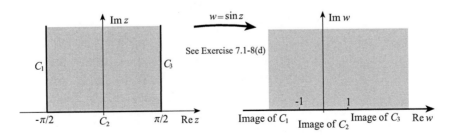

Figure 7.19

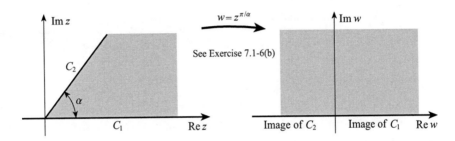

Figure 7.20

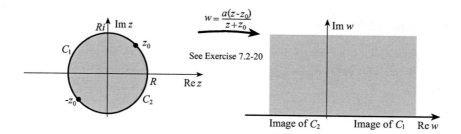

Figure 7.21

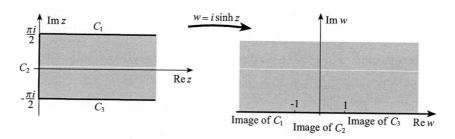

Figure 7.22

Compositions of these transformations with others lead to further mappings of domains in the z-plane to the half-plane $\operatorname{Im} w > 0$. We illustrate in the following examples.

Example 7.13 Find a transformation that maps the semi-infinite strip between $-a$ and a in Figure 7.23 to the half-plane $\operatorname{Im} w > 0$.

Solution   The magnification $z^* = \pi z/(2a)$ maps the given semi-infinite strip to the semi-infinite strip $-\pi/2 < \operatorname{Re} z^* < \pi/2$, $\operatorname{Im} z^* > 0$. When this is composed with the mapping in Figure 7.20, we obtain the mapping

$$w = \sin z^* = \sin\left(\frac{\pi z}{2a}\right).$$

It maps the given semi-infinite strip to the upper half-plane.●

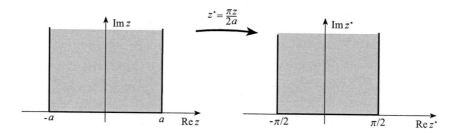

Figure 7.23

Example 7.14 Find a transformation that maps the wedge in Figure 7.24 to the half-plane $\operatorname{Im} w > 0$.

Solution   The rotation $z^* = e^{-\alpha i}z$ rotates the wedge clockwise through angle α. When this is composed with the mapping in Figure 7.18, the result is

$$w = (z^*)^{\pi/(\beta-\alpha)} = (e^{-\alpha i}z)^{\pi/(\beta-\alpha)} = e^{-\alpha\pi i/(\beta-\alpha)}z^{\pi/(\beta-\alpha)}.$$

It maps the given wedge to the half-plane $\operatorname{Im} w > 0.\bullet$

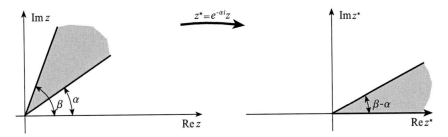

Figure 7.24

Example 7.15   Find a transformation that maps the channel $0 < \operatorname{Im} z < a$ to the half-plane $\operatorname{Im} w > 0$.

Solution   The magnification $z^* = \pi z/a$ maps the channel $0 < \operatorname{Im} z < a$ to the channel $0 < \operatorname{Im} z^* < \pi$ (Figure 7.25). When this is composed with the function $w = e^z$ (Figure 7.19), the result is

$$w = e^{z^*} = e^{\pi z/a}.$$

It maps the channel $0 < \operatorname{Im} z < a$ to $\operatorname{Im} w > 0.\bullet$

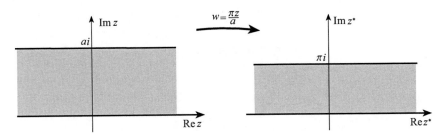

Figure 7.25

EXERCISES 7.3

In Exercises 1–13 show that the transformation maps the domain D to the half-plane $\operatorname{Im} w > 0$.

1. $w = e^{iz}, \quad D: 0 < \operatorname{Re} z < \pi$

2. $w = e^{\pi z}, \quad D: 0 < \operatorname{Im} z < 1$

3. $w = \sin(\pi z/6), \quad D: -3 < \operatorname{Re} z < 3, \operatorname{Im} z > 0$

4. $w = \sin^2 z, \quad D: 0 < \operatorname{Re} z < \pi/2, \operatorname{Im} z > 0$

5. $w = i \sinh[\pi z/(2a)], \quad D: -a < \operatorname{Im} z < a, \operatorname{Re} z > 0$

6. $w = \sinh^2[\pi z/(2a)], \quad D: 0 < \operatorname{Im} z < a, \operatorname{Re} z > 0$

7. $w = z^4, \quad D: 0 < \operatorname{Arg} z < \pi/4$

8. $w = z^{2/3}, \quad D: 0 < \operatorname{Arg} z < 3\pi/2$

9. $w = i(R - z)/(R + z), \quad D: |z| < R$

10. $w = i(z - R)/(z + R), \quad D: |z| > R$

11. $w = (R + z)^2/(R - z)^2, \quad D: |z| < R, \operatorname{Im} z > 0$

12. $(R + z^{\pi/\alpha})^2/(R - z^{\pi/\alpha})^2, \quad |z| < R, 0 < \operatorname{Arg} z < \alpha < \pi$

13. $w = z + R^2/z, \quad D: |z| > R, \operatorname{Im} z > 0$

In Exercises 14–20 find a transformation that maps the domain D to the half-plane $\operatorname{Im} w > 0$.

14. $D: -1 < \operatorname{Re} z < 1, \operatorname{Im} z > 0$

15. $D: 0 < \operatorname{Re} z < a, \operatorname{Im} z > 0$

16. $D: -1 < \operatorname{Im} z < 1, \operatorname{Re} z > 0$

17. $D: -1 < \operatorname{Im} z < 1, \operatorname{Re} z < 0$

18. $D: 0 < \operatorname{Im} z < 4$

19. $D: 0 < \operatorname{Re} z < 2$

20. $D: 1 < \operatorname{Im} z < 2$

21. (a) Show that the transformation
$$w = \sqrt{z - \frac{1}{4a}} - \frac{i}{2\sqrt{a}},$$
where $a > 0$ is a constant, maps the domain to the right to the quarter-plane $\operatorname{Re} w > 0, \operatorname{Im} w > 0$.
(b) Find a transformation that maps D to the half-plane $\operatorname{Im} w > 0$.

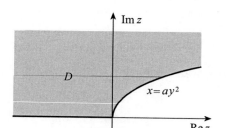

22. Show that $w = \coth(\pi a/z)$ maps the half-plane $\operatorname{Im} z > 0$ outside the circle $|z - ai| = a$ to the half-plane $\operatorname{Im} w > 0$.

23. Find a transformation that maps that part of the first quadrant outside the circle $x^2 + y^2 = a^2$ to the half-plane $\operatorname{Im} w > 0$. Hint: See Exercise 13.

24. Show that the mapping $w = (z + ai)^{1/2}(z - ai)^{1/2}$, where $a > 0$ is a constant, and branches of the square root functions are chosen as $(z + ai)^{1/2} = e^{(1/2)\log_{-\pi/2}(z+ai)}$ and $(z - ai)^{1/2} = e^{(1/2)\log_{-\pi/2}(z-ai)}$, maps the half-plane $\operatorname{Im} z \geq 0$ slit along the imaginary axis from $z = 0$ to $z = ai$ to the half-plane $\operatorname{Im} w \geq 0$.

§7.4 Conformal Mappings

Suppose that f is analytic in a domain D and C is a smooth curve in D passing through a point z_0 at which $f'(z_0) \neq 0$ (Figure 7.26). If C is defined parametrically by

$$C: \quad z(t) = x(t) + y(t)i, \quad t_A \leq t \leq t_B, \tag{7.12}$$

then real and imaginary parts of $z'(t_0) = x'(t_0) + y'(t_0)i$ define the components of a tangent vector to C at z_0. We assume that $z'(t_0)$ does not vanish.

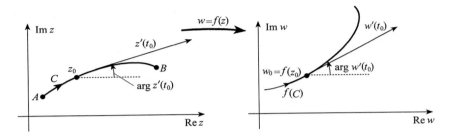

Figure 7.26

Under the mapping $w = f(z)$, C is mapped to a curve $f(C)$ in the w-plane defined by $w(t) = f[z(t)]$. The components of a tangent vector to $f(C)$ at $f(z_0)$ are the real and imaginary parts of

$$w'(t_0) = \left(\frac{df}{dz} \frac{dz}{dt} \right)_{|z_0} = f'(z_0)z'(t_0), \tag{7.13}$$

which cannot vanish since both terms on the right are nonzero. When we take arguments of both sides of this equation

$$\arg\left[w'(t_0)\right] = \arg\left[f'(z_0)\right] + \arg[z'(t_0)], \tag{7.14}$$

which relates the angle of inclination of the tangent vector to C at z_0 to that of the tangent vector to $f(C)$ at $w_0 = f(z_0)$. Because C is any curve whatsoever through z_0, we have shown that every curve through z_0 is rotated by an amount $\arg\left[f'(z_0)\right]$ under the mapping $w = f(z)$. Consequently, if C_1 and C_2 are two curves through z_0, the angle between their images $f(C_1)$ and $f(C_2)$ is exactly the same as the angle between C_1 and C_2 (Figure 7.27).

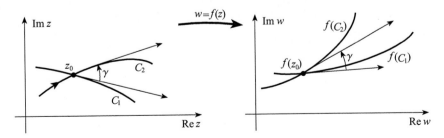

Figure 7.27

Mappings which preserve angles between curves and their orientation are said to be **conformal**. We have shown the following result.

Theorem 7.8 An analytic function f is conformal at every point z_0 at which $f'(z_0) \neq 0$.

We have just illustrated that at a point z_0 where an analytic function f has a nonvanishing derivative, curves are all rotated through an angle $\arg[f'(z_0)]$. We now give a geometric interpretation of $|f'(z_0)|$. Length along the curve C defined by 7.12 as measured from z_0 is given by

$$s = \int_{z_0}^{z} \sqrt{(dx)^2 + (dy)^2}.$$

But $dz = dx + dy\, i$, so that

$$s = \int_{z_0}^{z} |dz|.$$

Similarly, if $f(C)$ is the image of C under $w = f(z) = u + vi$, length along $f(C)$ measured from $w_0 = f(z_0)$ is

$$s' = \int_{w_0}^{w} |dw| = \int_{w_0}^{w} \sqrt{(du)^2 + (dv)^2}.$$

But $dw/dz = f'(z)$, and hence $|dw| = |f'(z)||dz|$. In particular, at z_0,

$$|dw| = |f'(z_0)||dz|; \tag{7.15}$$

that is, at w_0 the element of length $|dw|$ along $f(C)$ is $|f'(z_0)|$ times that at z_0 along C. In other words, the modulus $|f'(z_0)|$ is the length magnification factor at z_0 for the mapping $w = f(z)$.

We now have a geometric interpretation for $f'(z)$ in terms of the mapping $w = f(z)$ — its modulus is a length magnification factor, and its argument represents the rotational effect of the mapping.

The mapping $w = z^2$ of Example 7.1 is conformal at every point except $z = 0$. At $z = 0$, $w = z^2$ preserves the sense of angles but doubles them. The functions e^z and $\log_\phi z$ of Examples 7.2 and 7.3 are conformal at every point at which they are differentiable. In particular, notice that in Example 7.2, vertical and horizontal lines (which intersect at right angles) are mapped to circles and radial lines (which also intersect orthogonally). In Example 7.3, circles and radial lines are mapped by $\log_\phi z$ (the inverse of e^z) to vertical and horizontal lines.

Example 7.16 Illustrate the conformality of the mapping $w = z^2$ at every point (except $z = 0$) by showing that horizontal and vertical lines, which intersect at right angles, are mapped to curves which also intersect at right angles.

Solution If we set $w = u + vi$, then $u + vi = (x + yi)^2$, implying that

$$u = x^2 - y^2, \qquad v = 2xy.$$

A horizontal line $y = y_0$ in the z-plane is mapped by $w = z^2$ to a curve defined parametrically by

$$u = x^2 - y_0^2, \qquad v = 2xy_0.$$

If x is eliminated,

$$u = \frac{v^2}{4y_0^2} - y_0^2, \qquad (y_0 \neq 0),$$

a parabola (Figure 7.28).

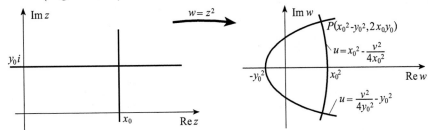

Figure 7.28

A vertical line $x = x_0$ is mapped by $w = z^2$ to the curve

$$u = x_0^2 - y^2, \quad v = 2x_0 y,$$

or,

$$u = x_0^2 - \frac{v^2}{4x_0^2}, \quad (x_0 \neq 0).$$

This is also a parabola. The two parabolas intersect at the points $(x_0^2 - y_0^2, \pm 2x_0 y_0)$, and the point $P(x_0^2 - y_0^2, 2x_0 y_0)$ is the image of (x_0, y_0) under $w = z^2$. The slope dv/du of the former parabola at any point is defined by

$$1 = \frac{2v}{4y_0^2} \frac{dv}{du},$$

and hence the slope of this parabola at P is

$$\frac{dv}{du}\Big|_P = \frac{2y_0^2}{v}\Big|_P = \frac{2y_0^2}{2x_0 y_0} = \frac{y_0}{x_0}.$$

Similarly, the slope of $u = x_0^2 - v^2/(4x_0^2)$ at P is

$$\frac{dv}{du}\Big|_P = -\frac{2x_0^2}{v}\Big|_P = -\frac{2x_0^2}{2x_0 y_0} = -\frac{x_0}{y_0}.$$

Clearly then, these parabolas intersect at right angles at P.

We have shown that horizontal and vertical lines in the z-plane are mapped by $w = z^2$ to parabolas in the w-plane which also intersect orthogonally. Notice however that the argument is not valid at $z = 0$ (where $x_0 = 0$ and $y_0 = 0$). The real z-axis $y = 0$ is mapped to the positive part of the real w-axis ($y = 0$ implies $u = x^2$, $v = 0$), and the imaginary z-axis $x = 0$ is mapped to the negative part of the real w-axis. Thus, the right angle between the axes at $z = 0$ is doubled to an angle of π radians at $w = 0$.●

EXERCISES 7.4

1. Prove that if the argument of $f'(z)$ is constant along a straight line segment in the z-plane, then the image of the line segment in the $w = f(z)$ plane is also a straight line segment.

In Exercises 2–5 illustrate conformality of the mapping $w = f(z)$ by showing that horizontal and vertical lines, which intersect at right angles, are mapped to curves that also intersect at right angles.

2. $f(z) = e^{2z}$

3. $f(z) = 2z^2 + 1$

4. $f(z) = \cos z$

5. $f(z) = \sinh z$

6. Illustrate conformality of the mapping $w = \text{Log}\,(z - 2 - i)$ by showing that circles centred at $2 + i$ and radial lines from this point are mapped to vertical and horizontal lines.

7. Verify that $w = \cos z$ is not a conformal mapping in any neighbourhood of the points $z = n\pi$ where n is an integer.

In Exercises 8–11 find the length magnification factor of the mapping at the point.

8. $f(z) = 3z^2 + 2z$ at $z = 1 - i$

9. $f(z) = (z + 1)/(2z - i)$ at $z = 3i$

10. $f(z) = \cosh\,(3z - 1)$ at $z = 1 - i$

11. $f(z) = z \sin z$ at $z = -2i$

12. When a certain curve C is mapped by a conformal mapping $w = f(z)$ to a curve C', its length is doubled. Does this imply that every curve with the same length as C has its length doubled under the mapping? Explain.

13. If $|f'(z)|$ is a length magnification factor for a conformal mapping, then $|f'(z)|^2$ is an area magnification factor. To illustrate this consider the mapping $w = e^{2z}$.
   (a) What is the length magnification factor of $f(z)$ at $z = 0$?
   (b) The area of the rectangle $-a \le x \le a$, $-b \le y \le b$ is $4ab$. Find the area of the image of this rectangle in the w-plane when $a < 1$ and $b < \pi/2$.
   (c) Show that the limit of the ratio of the areas in part (b) as $a \to 0$ and $b \to 0$ is 4.
   (d) Does this mean that regions in the z-plane have their areas quadrupled when mapped to the w-plane by $w = e^{2z}$?

14. Conformal mappings preserve angles and their orientations between intersecting curves. Consider the crescent shaped region in the figure to the right. Since the circles are tangent to each other at the origin, the angle between their tangent lines there is zero.

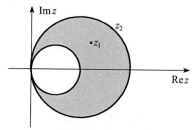

   (a) If a bilinear transformation $w = f(z)$ maps the z-plane to the w-plane and z_1 is the pole of the transformation, what can you say about the images of the circles at the point $w = f(0)$?
   (b) If a bilinear transformation $w = f(z)$ maps the z-plane to the w-plane and z_2 is the pole of the transformation, what can you say about the images of the circles at the point $w = f(0)$?
   (c) If a bilinear transformation $w = f(z)$ maps the z-plane to the w-plane and $z = 0$ is the pole of the transformation, what can you say about the images of the circles at the point $w = f(0)$?

15. A mapping $w = f(z)$ that is analytic is not conformal at a point z_0 at which $f'(z_0) = 0$. Show that when z_0 is a zero of order $m - 1$ of $f'(z)$, then curves with angle β between their tangents at z_0 are mapped to curves with angle $m\beta$ between their tangents at $w_0 = f(z_0)$.

16. In this exercise, we have you illustrate conformality of the reciprocation $w = 1/z$ for a pair of specific curves. One of the points of intersection of the circle $|z - 4| = \sqrt{2}$ and the line $2\,\text{Re}\,z + \text{Im}\,z = 11$ is $z = 5 + i$.

(a) Find the angle between the circle and line at $z = 5 + i$.

(b) Find images of the circle and the line in the w-plane, and use them to show that the angle between these images at the image of $z = 5 + i$ is the same as that in part (a).

17. Is it possible for a bilinear transformation to map the first quadrant of the z-plane to the interior of the unit circle in the w-plane?

18. Show that if $w = f(z)$ is 1-1 and conformal in a domain D, then $z = f^{-1}(w)$ is conformal in $f(D)$.

§7.5   Conformal Mappings and Harmonic Functions

Conformal mappings are important in the solution of boundary-value problems for the two-dimensional Laplace equation. To see why, suppose that $\phi(x, y)$ is harmonic in some domain D of the xy-plane. Let $w = f(z)$ be a 1-1 conformal mapping from D to $f(D)$. We set $f(z) = u + vi$, where as usual

$$u = u(x, y), \quad v = v(x, y). \tag{7.16}$$

Since the mapping is 1-1, the inverse function $f^{-1}(w)$ is defined throughout $f(D)$, and it follows that equations 7.16 can be solved for x and y in terms of u and v,

$$x = x(u, v), \quad y = y(u, v). \tag{7.17}$$

We use $\phi(x, y)$ to define a function $\psi(u, v)$ in $f(D)$ according to

$$\psi(u, v) = \phi[x(u, v), y(u, v)]. \tag{7.18}$$

Alternatively, $\psi(u, v)$ is that function satisfying

$$\psi[u(x, y), v(x, y)] = \phi(x, y). \tag{7.19}$$

Now $\phi(x, y)$ is harmonic in D so that in D

$$\frac{\partial^2 \phi}{\partial x^2} + \frac{\partial^2 \phi}{\partial y^2} = 0. \tag{7.20}$$

By chain rules for partial derivatives, we may write

$$\frac{\partial \phi}{\partial x} = \frac{\partial \psi}{\partial u}\frac{\partial u}{\partial x} + \frac{\partial \psi}{\partial v}\frac{\partial v}{\partial x},$$

and

$$\frac{\partial^2 \phi}{\partial x^2} = \left(\frac{\partial^2 \psi}{\partial u^2}\frac{\partial u}{\partial x} + \frac{\partial^2 \psi}{\partial v \partial u}\frac{\partial v}{\partial x}\right)\frac{\partial u}{\partial x} + \frac{\partial \psi}{\partial u}\frac{\partial^2 u}{\partial x^2} + \left(\frac{\partial^2 \psi}{\partial u \partial v}\frac{\partial u}{\partial x} + \frac{\partial^2 \psi}{\partial v^2}\frac{\partial v}{\partial x}\right)\frac{\partial v}{\partial x} + \frac{\partial \psi}{\partial v}\frac{\partial^2 v}{\partial x^2}.$$

Similarly,

$$\frac{\partial^2 \phi}{\partial y^2} = \left(\frac{\partial^2 \psi}{\partial u^2}\frac{\partial u}{\partial y} + \frac{\partial^2 \psi}{\partial u \partial v}\frac{\partial v}{\partial y}\right)\frac{\partial u}{\partial y} + \frac{\partial \psi}{\partial u}\frac{\partial^2 u}{\partial y^2} + \left(\frac{\partial^2 \psi}{\partial u \partial v}\frac{\partial u}{\partial y} + \frac{\partial^2 \psi}{\partial v^2}\frac{\partial v}{\partial y}\right)\frac{\partial v}{\partial y} + \frac{\partial \psi}{\partial v}\frac{\partial^2 v}{\partial y^2}.$$

Consequently,

$$0 = \frac{\partial^2 \phi}{\partial x^2} + \frac{\partial^2 \phi}{\partial y^2} = \frac{\partial^2 \psi}{\partial u^2}\left[\left(\frac{\partial u}{\partial x}\right)^2 + \left(\frac{\partial u}{\partial y}\right)^2\right] + 2\frac{\partial^2 \psi}{\partial u \partial v}\left(\frac{\partial u}{\partial x}\frac{\partial v}{\partial x} + \frac{\partial u}{\partial y}\frac{\partial v}{\partial y}\right)$$
$$+ \frac{\partial^2 \psi}{\partial v^2}\left[\left(\frac{\partial v}{\partial x}\right)^2 + \left(\frac{\partial v}{\partial y}\right)^2\right] + \frac{\partial \psi}{\partial u}\left(\frac{\partial^2 u}{\partial x^2} + \frac{\partial^2 u}{\partial y^2}\right) + \frac{\partial \psi}{\partial v}\left(\frac{\partial^2 v}{\partial x^2} + \frac{\partial^2 v}{\partial y^2}\right).$$

Because $f(z) = u + vi$ is analytic, u and v are harmonic and satisfy the Cauchy-Riemann equations in D; that is, in D,

$$0 = \frac{\partial^2 u}{\partial x^2} + \frac{\partial^2 u}{\partial y^2}; \quad 0 = \frac{\partial^2 v}{\partial x^2} + \frac{\partial^2 v}{\partial y^2}; \quad \frac{\partial u}{\partial x} = \frac{\partial v}{\partial y}; \quad \frac{\partial u}{\partial y} = -\frac{\partial v}{\partial x}.$$

We may write therefore that

$$0 = \frac{\partial^2\psi}{\partial u^2}\left[\left(\frac{\partial u}{\partial x}\right)^2 + \left(\frac{\partial v}{\partial x}\right)^2\right] + 2\frac{\partial^2\psi}{\partial u\partial v}\left(\frac{\partial u}{\partial x}\frac{\partial v}{\partial x} - \frac{\partial v}{\partial x}\frac{\partial u}{\partial x}\right) + \frac{\partial^2\psi}{\partial v^2}\left[\left(\frac{\partial v}{\partial x}\right)^2 + \left(\frac{\partial u}{\partial x}\right)^2\right]$$

$$= \left(\frac{\partial^2\psi}{\partial u^2} + \frac{\partial^2\psi}{\partial v^2}\right)\left[\left(\frac{\partial u}{\partial x}\right)^2 + \left(\frac{\partial v}{\partial x}\right)^2\right].$$

Since $f'(z) = \dfrac{\partial u}{\partial x} + \dfrac{\partial v}{\partial x}\, i \neq 0$ in D,

$$0 \neq |f'(z)|^2 = \left(\frac{\partial u}{\partial x}\right)^2 + \left(\frac{\partial v}{\partial x}\right)^2,$$

and therefore in $f(D)$,

$$0 = \frac{\partial^2\psi}{\partial u^2} + \frac{\partial^2\psi}{\partial v^2}. \tag{7.21}$$

Thus, $\psi(u,v)$ is harmonic in $f(D)$. We have shown therefore that conformal mappings carry harmonic functions to harmonic functions.

But why is this so important? To answer this, consider the problem of finding a function $\phi(x,y)$ satisfying Laplace's equation 7.20 in the domain D of the xy-plane in Figure 7.29.

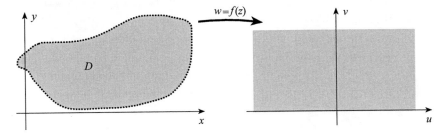

Figure 7.29

Suppose we interpret this plane as the complex z-plane, and that we can find a 1-1 conformal mapping $w = f(z) = u + vi$ which takes D to a simpler domain, say perhaps the half-plane $\operatorname{Im} w > 0$. Then the function

$$\psi(u,v) = \phi[x(u,v), y(u,v)]$$

where $x = x(u,v)$ and $y = y(u,v)$ are the inverses of $u = u(x,y)$ and $v = v(x,y)$ satisfies Laplace's equation in $\operatorname{Im} w > 0$. Further, any conditions that $\phi(x,y)$ satisfies on the boundary of D impose conditions that $\psi(u,v)$ must satisfy on $\operatorname{Im} w = 0$. Consequently, the problem of finding $\phi(x,y)$ harmonic in D and satisfying conditions on the rather unpleasant boundary of D can be replaced by the problem of finding $\psi(u,v)$ harmonic in $\operatorname{Im} w > 0$ and satisfying conditions on the line $\operatorname{Im} w = 0$. If we solve the latter problem, then the solution of the original problem is

$$\phi(x,y) = \psi[u(x,y), v(x,y)].$$

Clearly then, the ability to map a domain D in the z-plane to a simpler domain in the w-plane under a conformal mapping $w = f(z)$ could be very useful in solving boundary-value problems involving Laplace's equation. We have some examples to illustrate this shortly.

Boundary conditions always accompany Laplace's equation in a domain D of the xy-plane, the most common being Dirichlet and Neumann conditions. A Dirichlet boundary condition specifies the value of the harmonic function $\phi(x, y)$ on the boundary $\beta(D)$ of D,

$$\phi(x, y) = F(x, y), \quad (x, y) \text{ on } \beta(D). \tag{7.22a}$$

Transformation 7.17 induced by a conformal mapping $w = f(z)$, which maps D to $f(D)$, replaces condition 7.22a on $\phi(x, y)$ with the following condition on the harmonic function $\psi(u, v) = \phi[x(u, v), y(u, v)]$,

$$\psi(u, v) = F[x(u, v), y(u, v)], \quad (u, v) \text{ on } \beta[f(D)]. \tag{7.22b}$$

In other words, conformal mappings transform Dirichlet boundary conditions to Dirichlet boundary conditions.

A Neumann boundary condition specifies the directional derivative of $\phi(x, y)$ in the direction outwardly normal to $\beta(D)$ (Figure 7.30),

$$\nabla\phi \cdot \hat{\mathbf{n}} = \frac{\partial\phi}{\partial n} = F(x, y), \quad (x, y) \text{ on } \beta(D). \tag{7.23a}$$

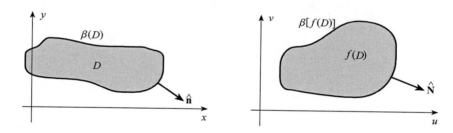

Figure 7.30

We now investigate the effect of a conformal mapping $w = f(z)$ on such a boundary condition. When s measures length counterclockwise around $\beta(D)$, the unit normal vector is defined by $\hat{\mathbf{n}} = (dy/ds)\hat{\mathbf{i}} - (dx/ds)\hat{\mathbf{j}}$, and therefore

$$\nabla\phi \cdot \hat{\mathbf{n}} = \frac{\partial\phi}{\partial x}\frac{dy}{ds} - \frac{\partial\phi}{\partial y}\frac{dx}{ds}.$$

Chain rules based on equation 7.19 give

$$\frac{\partial\phi}{\partial x} = \frac{\partial\psi}{\partial u}\frac{\partial u}{\partial x} + \frac{\partial\psi}{\partial v}\frac{\partial v}{\partial x}, \qquad \frac{\partial\phi}{\partial y} = \frac{\partial\psi}{\partial u}\frac{\partial u}{\partial y} + \frac{\partial\psi}{\partial v}\frac{\partial v}{\partial y}.$$

Furthermore, based on transformation 7.17 and the fact that x and y can be expressed in terms of length s along $\beta(D)$, we can write that $x = x[u(s), v(s)]$ and $y = y[u(s), v(s)]$. Chain rules for these give

$$\frac{dx}{ds} = \frac{\partial x}{\partial u}\frac{du}{ds} + \frac{\partial x}{\partial v}\frac{dv}{ds}, \qquad \frac{dy}{ds} = \frac{\partial y}{\partial u}\frac{du}{ds} + \frac{\partial y}{\partial v}\frac{dv}{ds}.$$

When these are all substituted into the expression for $\nabla\phi \cdot \hat{\mathbf{n}}$,

$$\nabla \phi \cdot \hat{\mathbf{n}} = \frac{\partial \phi}{\partial x} \frac{dy}{ds} - \frac{\partial \phi}{\partial y} \frac{dx}{ds}$$

$$= \left(\frac{\partial \psi}{\partial u} \frac{\partial u}{\partial x} + \frac{\partial \psi}{\partial v} \frac{\partial v}{\partial x} \right) \left(\frac{\partial y}{\partial u} \frac{du}{ds} + \frac{\partial y}{\partial v} \frac{dv}{ds} \right) - \left(\frac{\partial \psi}{\partial u} \frac{\partial u}{\partial y} + \frac{\partial \psi}{\partial v} \frac{\partial v}{\partial y} \right) \left(\frac{\partial x}{\partial u} \frac{du}{ds} + \frac{\partial x}{\partial v} \frac{dv}{ds} \right)$$

$$= \frac{\partial \psi}{\partial u} \frac{du}{ds} \left(\frac{\partial u}{\partial x} \frac{\partial y}{\partial u} - \frac{\partial u}{\partial y} \frac{\partial x}{\partial u} \right) + \frac{\partial \psi}{\partial u} \frac{dv}{ds} \left(\frac{\partial u}{\partial x} \frac{\partial y}{\partial v} - \frac{\partial u}{\partial y} \frac{\partial x}{\partial v} \right)$$

$$+ \frac{\partial \psi}{\partial v} \frac{du}{ds} \left(\frac{\partial v}{\partial x} \frac{\partial y}{\partial u} - \frac{\partial v}{\partial y} \frac{\partial x}{\partial u} \right) + \frac{\partial \psi}{\partial v} \frac{dv}{ds} \left(\frac{\partial v}{\partial x} \frac{\partial y}{\partial v} - \frac{\partial v}{\partial y} \frac{\partial x}{\partial v} \right).$$

Differentiation of $u = u[x(u,v), y(u,v)]$ with respect to u gives $1 = \dfrac{\partial u}{\partial x} \dfrac{\partial x}{\partial u} + \dfrac{\partial u}{\partial y} \dfrac{\partial y}{\partial u}$, and if we use the Cauchy-Riemann equations,

$$1 = \left(\frac{\partial v}{\partial y} \right) \frac{\partial x}{\partial u} + \left(-\frac{\partial v}{\partial x} \right) \frac{\partial y}{\partial u}.$$

Similar results for the other three terms in parentheses lead to

$$\nabla \phi \cdot \hat{\mathbf{n}} = \frac{\partial \psi}{\partial u} \frac{dv}{ds} - \frac{\partial \psi}{\partial v} \frac{du}{ds} = \left(\frac{\partial \psi}{\partial u} \frac{dv}{dS} - \frac{\partial \psi}{\partial v} \frac{du}{dS} \right) \frac{dS}{ds} = \nabla \psi \cdot \hat{\mathbf{N}} \left(\frac{dS}{ds} \right),$$

or

$$\nabla \psi \cdot \hat{\mathbf{N}} = |f'(z)|^{-1} \nabla \phi \cdot \hat{\mathbf{n}},$$

where $\hat{\mathbf{N}}$ is the unit outward pointing normal to $f[\beta(D)]$, and S is length thereon. Neumann condition 7.23a along $\beta(D)$ is therefore transformed by $w = f(z)$ to a Neumann condition along $\beta[f(D)]$,

$$\nabla \psi \cdot \hat{\mathbf{N}} = \frac{\partial \psi}{\partial N} = \frac{F[x(u,v), y(u,v)]}{|f'[z(w)]|}, \quad (u,v) \text{ on } \beta[f(D)]. \tag{7.23b}$$

Very often in applications it is required to solve Laplace's equation in a domain D together with a Dirichlet boundary condition that is piecewise constant on $\beta(D)$. Suppose for example, that $\phi(x,y)$, harmonic in the simply-connected domain of Figure 7.31, is to have constant values a_j $(j = 1, \ldots, n)$ on the n parts C_j of the boundary $\beta(D)$.

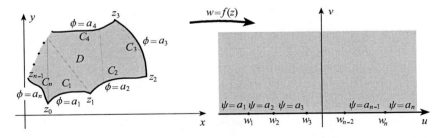

Figure 7.31

We can solve this problem very easily if a 1–1 conformal mapping $w = f(z)$ can be found that maps D to the half-plane $\operatorname{Im} w > 0$. Indeed, suppose z_0 is the pole of the mapping (so that z_0 is mapped infinitely far out the $\operatorname{Re} w$ axis), and the z_j

$(j = 1, \ldots, n - 1)$ are mapped to points $w_1, \ldots, w_{n-1}$. Once we find the function $\psi(u, v)$ satisfying Laplace's equation in $\operatorname{Im} w > 0$ and the boundary conditions along $\operatorname{Im} w = 0$, the solution of the original problem in D is $\phi(x, y) = \psi[u(x, y), v(x, y)]$. In other words, function $\psi(u, v)$ together with the conformal mapping $w = f(z)$ that maps D to $\operatorname{Im} w > 0$ provide $\phi(x, y)$. We can find $\psi(u, v)$ using formula 4.38 developed specifically for this purpose in Section 4.8. We give two examples here to illustrate these ideas. More are found in the exercises and many more will be given in Sections 7.7–7.9.

Example 7.17   Find the solution of Laplace's equation in the circle $x^2 + y^2 < 1$ that has value 0 on the semi-circle $x^2 + y^2 = 1$, $y > 0$, and value 1 on the semi-circle $x^2 + y^2 = 1$, $y < 0$.

Solution   According to Poisson's integral formula 4.34, the solution can be expressed in polar coordinates

$$\phi(r, \theta) = \frac{1 - r^2}{2\pi} \int_{-\pi}^{0} \frac{1}{1 + r^2 - 2r \cos(\theta - \zeta)} \, d\zeta.$$

It is difficult, but not impossible, to evaluate this integral in closed form.

Instead, we map the unit circle $|z| \leq 1$ to the half-plane $v = \operatorname{Im} w \geq 0$ with a bilinear transformation in such a way that the upper semicircle is mapped to the positive $u = \operatorname{Re} w$ axis and the lower semicircle to the negative u-axis. If we choose to map $z = 1$ onto $w = 0$, then $z = -1$ maps to points infinitely far out the real u-axis (Figure 7.32). Since $z = -1$ is the pole of the mapping, the transformation takes the form

$$w = \frac{a(z - 1)}{z + 1}.$$

(See also Figure 7.21 with $z_0 = 1$.) If we arbitrarily demand that $z = i$ map to $w = 1$, then $1 = a(i - 1)/(i + 1)$, and this requires that $a = -i$. The bilinear transformation is therefore

$$w = \frac{i(1 - z)}{1 + z}.$$

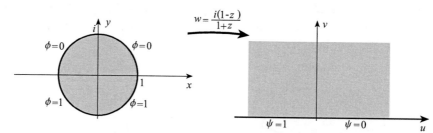

Figure 7.32

According to formula 4.38, the solution for the function $\psi(u, v)$ harmonic in $v > 0$ is

$$\psi(u, v) = \frac{1}{2} + \frac{1}{\pi} \operatorname{Tan}^{-1}\left(\frac{-u}{v}\right) = \frac{1}{2} - \frac{1}{\pi} \operatorname{Tan}^{-1}\left(\frac{u}{v}\right).$$

Because

$$w = u + vi = i\left(\frac{1-z}{1+z}\right) = \frac{2y + i(1 - x^2 - y^2)}{(1+x)^2 + y^2},$$

it follows that $u = 2y/[(1+x)^2 + y^2]$ and $v = (1 - x^2 - y^2)/[(1+x)^2 + y^2]$, and therefore

$$\phi(x,y) = \psi[u(x,y), v(x,y)] = \frac{1}{2} - \frac{1}{\pi}\,\mathrm{Tan}^{-1}\left(\frac{2y}{1 - x^2 - y^2}\right). \bullet$$

Example 7.18   Find the solution of Laplace's equation in the semi-infinite strip $-\pi/2 < x < \pi/2$, $y > 0$ (Figure 7.33) given that its values along the edges are

$$\phi(-\pi/2, y) = \phi(\pi/2, y) = -1, \quad y > 0,$$

$$\phi(x,0) = 1, \quad -\pi/2 < x < \pi/2.$$

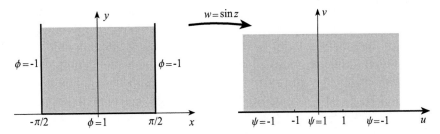

Figure 7.33

Solution   The transformation $w = \sin z$ maps the semi-infinite strip to the half-plane $\mathrm{Im}\, w > 0$ (see Figure 7.20). According to formula 4.38, the solution of Laplace's equation $\psi(u,v)$ with boundary conditions $\psi(u,0) = \begin{cases} -1 & |u| > 1 \\ 1 & |u| < 1 \end{cases}$ is

$$\psi(u,v) = \frac{1}{2}(-1 - 1) + \frac{1}{\pi}\left[-2\,\mathrm{Tan}^{-1}\left(\frac{-1-u}{v}\right) + 2\,\mathrm{Tan}^{-1}\left(\frac{1-u}{v}\right)\right]$$

$$= -1 + \frac{2}{\pi}\left[\mathrm{Tan}^{-1}\left(\frac{1+u}{v}\right) + \mathrm{Tan}^{-1}\left(\frac{1-u}{v}\right)\right].$$

Since $w = u + vi = \sin z = \sin x \cosh y + \cos x \sinh y\, i$, it follows that $u = \sin x \cosh y$ and $v = \cos x \sinh y$. The solution of Laplace's equation in the strip is therefore

$$\phi(x,y) = -1 + \frac{2}{\pi}\left[\mathrm{Tan}^{-1}\left(\frac{1 + \sin x \cosh y}{\cos x \sinh y}\right) + \mathrm{Tan}^{-1}\left(\frac{1 - \sin x \cosh y}{\cos x \sinh y}\right)\right].$$

We can simplify this solution by bringing the inverse tangents together. We return to the expression for $\psi(u,v)$ and rewrite it in the form

$$\frac{\pi}{2}(\psi + 1) = \mathrm{Tan}^{-1}\left(\frac{1+u}{v}\right) + \mathrm{Tan}^{-1}\left(\frac{1-u}{v}\right).$$

When we take tangents on both sides,

$$\tan\left[\frac{\pi}{2}(\psi + 1)\right] = \frac{\dfrac{1+u}{v} + \dfrac{1-u}{v}}{1 - \left(\dfrac{1+u}{v}\right)\left(\dfrac{1-u}{v}\right)} = \frac{2v}{u^2 + v^2 - 1}.$$

Because $-1 \leq \psi \leq 1$, it follows that $0 \leq \pi(\psi + 1)/2 \leq \pi$. If we use the notation $\tan^{-1}$ to denote values of the inverse tangent function between 0 and π (whereas Tan^{-1} denotes values between $\pm\pi/2$), then

$$\frac{\pi}{2}(\psi + 1) = \tan^{-1}\left(\frac{2v}{u^2 + v^2 - 1}\right),$$

and

$$\psi(u, v) = -1 + \frac{2}{\pi}\tan^{-1}\left(\frac{2v}{u^2 + v^2 - 1}\right).$$

Hence,

$$\phi(x, y) = -1 + \frac{2}{\pi}\tan^{-1}\left(\frac{2\cos x \sinh y}{\sin^2 x \cosh^2 y + \cos^2 x \sinh^2 y - 1}\right)$$

$$= -1 + \frac{2}{\pi}\tan^{-1}\left(\frac{2\cos x \sinh y}{\sinh^2 y - \cos^2 x}\right)$$

$$= -1 + \frac{2}{\pi}\tan^{-1}\left(\frac{\dfrac{2\cos x}{\sinh y}}{1 - \dfrac{\cos^2 x}{\sinh^2 y}}\right).$$

If we set $\alpha = \tan^{-1}\left(\dfrac{\cos x}{\sinh y}\right)$, then

$$\phi(x, y) = -1 + \frac{2}{\pi}\tan^{-1}\left(\frac{2\tan\alpha}{1 - \tan^2\alpha}\right) = -1 + \frac{2}{\pi}\tan^{-1}(\tan 2\alpha)$$

$$= -1 + \frac{4\alpha}{\pi} = -1 + \frac{4}{\pi}\tan^{-1}\left(\frac{\cos x}{\sinh y}\right)$$

$$= -1 + \frac{4}{\pi}\text{Tan}^{-1}\left(\frac{\cos x}{\sinh y}\right),$$

since $\cos x / \sinh y > 0$.$\bullet$

EXERCISES 7.5

In Exercises 1–18 map the domain D to the half-plane $\text{Im}\, w > 0$. Then use formula 4.38 to find the solution $\phi(x, y)$ of Laplace's equation in D subject to the given boundary conditions. Appropriate mappings are suggested at the end of the exercises. Try to discover them yourself; failing this, consult the list.

1.

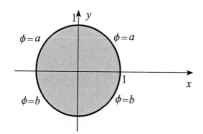

2.

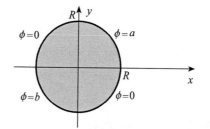

3.

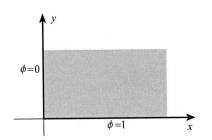

4.

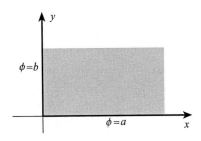

5.

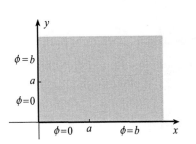

6.

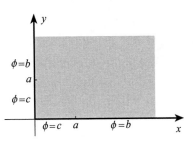

7.

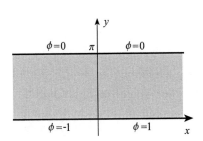

8.

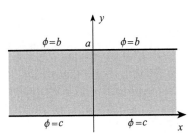

9.

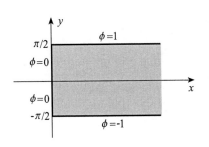

10.

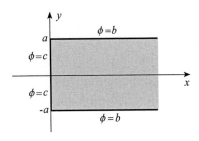

11.

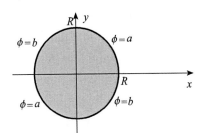

12.

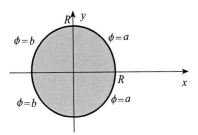

13.

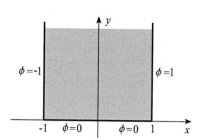

14.

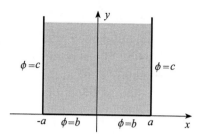

15.

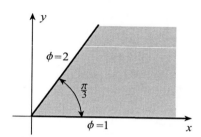

16.

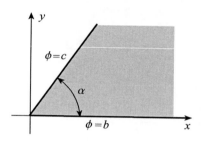

17.

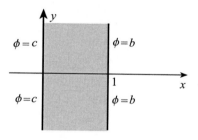

18.

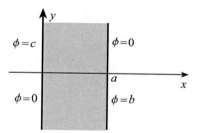

19. Consider finding the function $\phi(x, y)$ that is harmonic in the quarter plane $x > 0$, $y > 0$ and satisfies

$$\phi(0, y) = b, \quad y > 0,$$

$$\phi(x, 0) = a, \quad x > 0.$$

(a) Use the transformation $w = \text{Log } z$ to derive the solution $\phi(x, y) = a + \dfrac{2}{\pi}(b - a) \text{Tan}^{-1}\left(\dfrac{y}{x}\right)$.

(b) See Exercise 6 for the solution $\phi(x, y) = \dfrac{a + b}{2} + \left(\dfrac{a - b}{\pi}\right) \text{Tan}^{-1}\left(\dfrac{x^2 - y^2}{2xy}\right)$ when the transformation $w = z^2$ is used. Verify that the solutions are identical.

20. Consider finding the function $\phi(x, y)$ that is harmonic in the semicircle $|z| < R$, $\text{Im } z > 0$ and satisfies

$$\phi(x, y) = a \quad \text{on } |z| = R, \ \text{Im } z > 0,$$
$$\phi(x, y) = b \quad \text{on } y = 0, \ -R < x < R.$$

(a) Use the transformation $w = (R + z)^2/(R - z)^2$ of Exercise 11 in Section 7.3 to derive the solution

$$\phi(x,y) = \frac{a+b}{2} + \left(\frac{b-a}{\pi}\right) \text{Tan}^{-1}\left[\frac{(R^2-x^2)^2 + y^4 + 2y^2(x^2-3R^2)}{4Ry(R^2-x^2-y^2)}\right].$$

(b) Use the transformation $w = i(R-z)/(R+z)$ and the result of Exercise 19 to derive the solution

$$\phi(x,y) = a + \frac{2}{\pi}(b-a)\text{Tan}^{-1}\left(\frac{R^2-x^2-y^2}{2Ry}\right).$$

21. Find the function $\phi(x,y)$ that is harmonic in the half-plane $y > 0$ outside the circle $x^2 + (y-4)^2 = 4$ and has value b on the x-axis and value a on the circle. Hint: See Example 7.12 to map the region to an annulus, and then consider functions of the form $c + d\ln(u^2 + v^2)$.

22. Find the function $\phi(x,y)$ that is harmonic in the region between the circles $x^2 + (y-1)^2 = 1$ and $x^2 + y^2 = 16$ and has constant values a and b on the circles, respectively. Hint: See Exercise 30 in Section 7.2 to map the region to an annulus, and then consider functions of the form $c + d\ln(u^2 + v^2)$.

Transformations: 1. $w = i(1-z)/(1+z)$ **2.** $i(R-z)/(R+z)$ **3.** $i(R-z)/(R+z)$
4. $i(R-z)/(R+z)$ **5.** $w = z^2$ **6.** $w = z^2$ **7.** $w = z^2$ **8.** $w = z^2$ **9.** $w = e^z$
10. $w = e^{\pi z/a}$ **11.** $w = i\sinh z$ **12.** $w = i\sinh[\pi z/(2a)]$ **13.** $w = \sin\pi z/2$
14. $w = \sin[\pi z/(2a)]$ **15.** $w = z^3$ **16.** $w = z^{\pi/\alpha}$ **17.** $w = e^{\pi zi}$ **18.** $w = e^{\pi zi/a}$

§7.6   The Schwarz-Christoffel Transformation

In this section we consider the problem of mapping the interior of a polygon in the
z-plane to the half-plane $\operatorname{Im} w > 0$ (Figure 7.34).

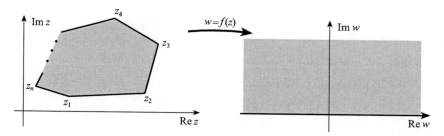

Figure 7.34

Riemann's mapping theorem (Theorem 7.3) essentially guarantees existence of such
mappings. Unfortunately, as we shall see, the mappings cannot be found in terms
of standard elementary functions even for the simplest of polygons —triangles and
rectangles. In spite of this, the information that we uncover in attempting to find
such mappings, proves very useful in closely related problems.

It is easier to begin discussions by considering the inverse mapping, but in a
less specific sense. Given n points $w_1, \ldots, w_n$ on the real axis in the w-plane, what
mappings $z = f^{-1}(w)$ map the upper half-plane $\operatorname{Im} w > 0$ to a polygon with the
images of the w_j as vertices. For the moment, we do not specify positions of the
vertices, we simply require that the mapping produce a polygon with the w_j mapped
to its vertices. To find such mappings, we first discuss the transformation

$$z = f^{-1}(w) = A(w - w_1)^{\alpha/\pi} + B, \tag{7.24}$$

where A and B are complex constants, and w_1 and $\alpha > 0$ are real. (The branch
cut may be anywhere in $\operatorname{Im} w < 0$.) Points on Γ_2, that part of the real w-axis to
the right of w_1 (Figure 7.35), are mapped to points on the half-line Γ'_2, and those
to the left of w_1 are mapped to

$$\Gamma'_1 : \quad z = A(w - w_1)^{\alpha/\pi} + B$$
$$= A[(w_1 - w)e^{\pi i}]^{\alpha/\pi} + B = A(w_1 - w)^{\alpha/\pi} e^{\alpha i} + B.$$

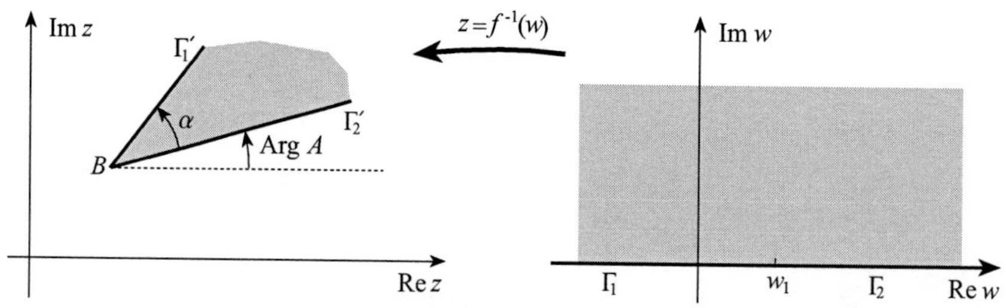

Figure 7.35

In other words, the half-space $\operatorname{Im} w > 0$ is mapped to a sector with angle α at $z = B$.
The effect of A is to rotate the sector by $\arg A$ and to introduce an expansion
(or contraction) equal to $|A|$. Functions of form 7.24 result from integrations of
differential equations of the form

$$\frac{dz}{dw} = A(w - w_1)^{\alpha/\pi - 1}. \tag{7.25}$$

With this in mind, we now consider a mapping that results from integration of a differential equation containing the product of two such factors,

$$\frac{dz}{dw} = A(w - w_1)^{\alpha_1/\pi - 1}(w - w_2)^{\alpha_2/\pi - 1}, \tag{7.26}$$

where $w_1 < w_2$ and $\alpha_1 > 0$ and $\alpha_2 > 0$ are all real constants. We can express the solution as an antiderivative

$$z = A \int (w - w_1)^{\alpha_1/\pi - 1}(w - w_2)^{\alpha_2/\pi - 1} dw + B \tag{7.27a}$$

(but in general, the integration is impossible), or as a contour integral,

$$z = A \int_{w_0}^{w} (\zeta - w_1)^{\alpha_1/\pi - 1}(\zeta - w_2)^{\alpha_2/\pi - 1} d\zeta + B, \tag{7.27b}$$

where w_0 is constant. Suppose that such a mapping carries w_1 and w_2 to points z_1 and z_2 in the z-plane (Figure 7.36).

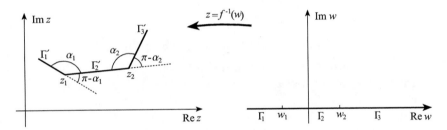

Figure 7.36

If we take arguments in equation 7.26,

$$\arg \frac{dz}{dw} = \arg A + \left(\frac{\alpha_1}{\pi} - 1\right) \arg(w - w_1) + \left(\frac{\alpha_2}{\pi} - 1\right) \arg(w - w_2). \tag{7.28}$$

For points on Γ_1, that part of the real w-axis to the left of w_1, we find

$$\arg \frac{dz}{dw} = \arg A + \left(\frac{\alpha_1}{\pi} - 1\right)(\pi) + \left(\frac{\alpha_2}{\pi} - 1\right)(\pi) = \arg A + \alpha_1 + \alpha_2 - 2\pi. \tag{7.29a}$$

The fact that this is constant implies that the image Γ_1' of Γ_1 is a straight line (see Exercise 1 in Section 7.4). For points on Γ_2,

$$\arg \frac{dz}{dw} = \arg A + \left(\frac{\alpha_1}{\pi} - 1\right)(0) + \left(\frac{\alpha_2}{\pi} - 1\right)(\pi) = \arg A + \alpha_2 - \pi. \tag{7.29b}$$

This is also constant, and differs from 7.29a by $\pi - \alpha_1$. In other words, Γ_2' is a straight line at angle $\pi - \alpha_1$ relative to Γ_1'. Similarly, for points on Γ_3,

$$\arg \frac{dz}{dw} = \arg A + \left(\frac{\alpha_1}{\pi} - 1\right)(0) + \left(\frac{\alpha_2}{\pi} - 1\right)(0) = \arg A, \tag{7.29c}$$

indicating that Γ_3' is a straight line at angle $\pi - \alpha_2$ relative to Γ_2'.

In general, any mapping $z = f^{-1}(w)$ defined by the differential equation

$$\frac{dz}{dw} = A(w - w_1)^{\alpha_1/\pi - 1} \cdots (w - w_n)^{\alpha_n/\pi - 1} \tag{7.30}$$

maps the real axis in the w-plane to a succession of straight line segments joining the images z_j of w_j in such a way that the angle between the segments at z_j is α_j. We can express the solution of differential equation 7.30 in antiderivative form

$$z = A \int (w - w_1)^{\alpha_1/\pi - 1} \cdots (w - w_n)^{\alpha_n/\pi - 1} dw + B, \tag{7.31a}$$

or as a contour integral

$$z = A \int_{w_0}^{w} (\zeta - w_1)^{\alpha_1/\pi - 1} \cdots (\zeta - w_n)^{\alpha_n/\pi - 1} d\zeta + B. \tag{7.31b}$$

For such a mapping to take the real axis in the w-plane to a polygon in the z-plane, the straight lines must close. Since the sum of the interior angles of a polygon with n sides is $(n - 2)\pi$ radians, we require that

$$\sum_{j=1}^{n} \alpha_j = (n - 2)\pi. \tag{7.32}$$

The shape of the polygon is dictated by solution 7.31 with $A = 1$ and $B = 0$. Constant A rotates and expands (or contracts) this polygon, and B translates it.

Suppose now that we are given a polygon in the z-plane with vertices $z_1, \ldots, z_n$, and it is required to find a mapping $z = f^{-1}(w)$ that maps the half-plane $\operatorname{Im} w > 0$ to the interior of the polygon. Such a mapping is called a **Schwarz–Christoffel** transformation. In view of the above remarks, this would entail solving 7.30 so that $\operatorname{Im} w = 0$ maps to the sides of a polygon similar to the given polygon, similar in the sense that the interior angles of the polygons are identical, as are ratios of corresponding sides. Naturally then we would choose the α_j in 7.30 to be the interior angles of the given polygon. Can we choose the w_j arbitrarily? If the polygon is a triangle, then the fact that equality of angles implies equality of ratios of sides, means that w_1, w_2, and w_3 can be chosen arbitrarily. But for a quadrilateral, say a rectangle, equality of interior angles is not sufficient to guarantee equality of ratios of corresponding sides. We must specify the ratio of lengths of two adjacent sides. This means that only three of the four constants w_1, w_2, w_3, and w_4 can be assigned arbitrarily. The fourth must be chosen to guarantee similarity to the given quadrilateral. In general, for an n-sided polygon, only three of the points w_j can be chosen arbitrarily; the remaining $n - 3$ must be determined in order to guarantee the required similarity. Considerable ingenuity is often required in arriving at the remaining w_j. We illustrate this in the following example.

Example 7.19   Find a Schwarz-Christoffel transformation $z = f^{-1}(w)$ that maps the half-plane $\operatorname{Im} w > 0$ to the interior of the rectangle with vertices $z = \pm 1, \pm 1 + i$.

Solution   According to the above discussion only three of the points w_1, w_2, w_3, and w_4 that map to the vertices of the rectangle can be assigned arbitrarily; the fourth must be chosen so that the ratio of sides is 2 to 1. Because of the symmetry of the rectangle, it seems likely that we may choose the w_j as shown in Figure 7.37 for some value $0 < a < 1$.

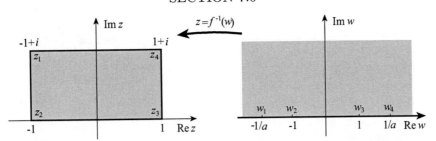

Figure 7.37

With interior angles of $\pi/2$ radians, equation 7.30 for the transformation gives

$$\frac{dz}{dw} = A(w + 1/a)^{-1/2}(w + 1)^{-1/2}(w - 1)^{-1/2}(w - 1/a)^{-1/2}$$

$$= \frac{A}{(w + 1)^{1/2}(w - 1)^{1/2}(w + 1/a)^{1/2}(w - 1/a)^{1/2}}.$$

We cannot integrate this equation analytically, but we can express the solution as a contour integral,

$$z = A \int_0^w \frac{1}{(\zeta + 1)^{1/2}(\zeta - 1)^{1/2}(\zeta + 1/a)^{1/2}(\zeta - 1/a)^{1/2}} d\zeta + B$$

$$= aA \int_0^w \frac{1}{(\zeta + 1)^{1/2}(\zeta - 1)^{1/2}(a\zeta + 1)^{1/2}(a\zeta - 1)^{1/2}} d\zeta + B.$$

Since integrations are in the half-plane $\text{Im}\, w > 0$, branch cuts for the root functions are chosen in the lower half-plane such as in Figure 7.38.

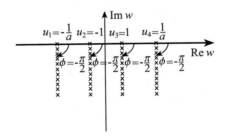

Figure 7.38

To determine a, A, and B, we specify the conditions for the u_j to map to the vertices of the rectangle,

$$-1 + i = aA \int_0^{-1/a} \frac{1}{(\zeta + 1)^{1/2}(\zeta - 1)^{1/2}(a\zeta + 1)^{1/2}(a\zeta - 1)^{1/2}} d\zeta + B, \quad \text{(a)}$$

$$-1 = aA \int_0^{-1} \frac{1}{(\zeta + 1)^{1/2}(\zeta - 1)^{1/2}(a\zeta + 1)^{1/2}(a\zeta - 1)^{1/2}} d\zeta + B, \quad \text{(b)}$$

$$1 = aA \int_0^1 \frac{1}{(\zeta + 1)^{1/2}(\zeta - 1)^{1/2}(a\zeta + 1)^{1/2}(a\zeta - 1)^{1/2}} d\zeta + B, \quad \text{(c)}$$

$$1 + i = aA \int_0^{1/a} \frac{1}{(\zeta + 1)^{1/2}(\zeta - 1)^{1/2}(a\zeta + 1)^{1/2}(a\zeta - 1)^{1/2}} d\zeta + B. \quad \text{(d)}$$

A change of variable of integration in (b) together with (c) shows that $B = 0$. Condition (c) can then be expressed in the form

$$1 = aA \int_0^1 \frac{1}{\sqrt{\zeta+1}\left(\sqrt{1-\zeta i}\right)\sqrt{a\zeta+1}\left(\sqrt{1-a\zeta i}\right)}d\zeta = aA \int_0^1 \frac{-1}{\sqrt{(1-\zeta^2)(1-a^2\zeta^2)}}d\zeta,$$

where all square roots are applied to positive real numbers. For real ζ,

$$F(a) = \int_0^1 \frac{1}{\sqrt{(1-\zeta^2)(1-a^2\zeta^2)}}d\zeta$$

is the well-known and tabulated complete elliptic integral of the first kind. In terms of this function, a and A must satisfy

$$-1 = aA\,F(a). \qquad (e)$$

Condition (d) can be expressed as

$$1 + i = aA\left[\int_0^1 \frac{1}{(\zeta+1)^{1/2}(\zeta-1)^{1/2}(a\zeta+1)^{1/2}(a\zeta-1)^{1/2}}d\zeta \right.$$
$$\left. + \int_1^{1/a} \frac{1}{(\zeta+1)^{1/2}(\zeta-1)^{1/2}(a\zeta+1)^{1/2}(a\zeta-1)^{1/2}}d\zeta\right].$$

When we substitute from (c),

$$1 + i = 1 + aA \int_1^{1/a} \frac{-i}{\sqrt{(\zeta^2-1)(1-a^2\zeta^2)}}d\zeta.$$

Hence,

$$-1 = aA \int_1^{1/a} \frac{1}{\sqrt{(\zeta^2-1)(1-a^2\zeta^2)}}d\zeta, \qquad \text{or,} \qquad -1 = aA\,G(a), \qquad (f)$$

where

$$G(a) = \int_1^{1/a} \frac{1}{\sqrt{(\zeta^2-1)(1-a^2\zeta^2)}}d\zeta.$$

Equations (e) and (f) require $G(a) = F(a)$, which can be solved numerically for a. Either (e) or (f) now yields A, and the Schwarz-Christoffel transformation is essentially defined.●

Example 7.20 Illustrate, but do not find, the Schwarz-Christoffel transformation $z = f^{-1}(w)$ that maps the half-plane $\operatorname{Im} w > 0$ to the interior of the equilateral triangle with vertices $z = \pm 1$ and $z = \sqrt{3}i$ in such a way that $w = -1$, 0, and 1 are mapped to $z = -1$, 1, and $\sqrt{3}i$, respectively (Figure 7.39). As suggested earlier, we may, and have assigned the three points on the $\operatorname{Re} w$ axis that map to the vertices of the triangle.

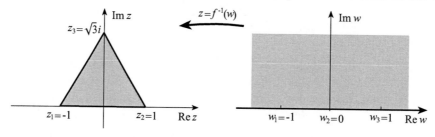

Figure 7.39

Solution   Since the interior angles of the triangle are $\pi/3$ radians, the mapping can be found by solving

$$\frac{dz}{dw} = A(w+1)^{1/3-1}w^{1/3-1}(w-1)^{1/3-1} = \frac{A}{w^{2/3}(w+1)^{2/3}(w-1)^{2/3}}.$$

We cannot integrate this equation analytically, but we can express the solution as a contour integral

$$z = A\int_i^w \frac{1}{\zeta^{2/3}(\zeta+1)^{2/3}(\zeta-1)^{2/3}}d\zeta + B.$$

To determine A and B we use the fact that $w = -1, 0$, and 1 are mapped to $z = -1$, 1, and $\sqrt{3}i$,

$$-1 = A\int_i^{-1} \frac{1}{\zeta^{2/3}(\zeta+1)^{2/3}(\zeta-1)^{2/3}}d\zeta + B,$$

$$1 = A\int_i^0 \frac{1}{\zeta^{2/3}(\zeta+1)^{2/3}(\zeta-1)^{2/3}}d\zeta + B,$$

$$\sqrt{3}i = A\int_i^1 \frac{1}{\zeta^{2/3}(\zeta+1)^{2/3}(\zeta-1)^{2/3}}d\zeta + B.$$

We shall not attempt to solve these for A and B. Using the "point at infinity" in the w-plane in place of $w = 0$ leads to a much simpler transformation (Example 7.21).●

It is often more convenient to map the "point at infinity" on the real axis in the w-plane to one of the vertices of a polygon. This leaves $n-1$ finite points w_j to map to the remaining vertices. We claim that a mapping defined by

$$\frac{dz}{dw} = A(w-w_1)^{\alpha_1/\pi-1}\cdots(w-w_{n-1})^{\alpha_{n-1}/\pi-1}, \qquad (7.33)$$

maps the real axis in the w-plane to a polygon in the z-plane with the point at infinity mapped to one of the vertices of the polygon. To verify this we suppose that a transformation defined by this equation maps the w_j $(j = 1, \ldots, n-1)$ to points z_j and maps $w = \infty$ to z_n. If we take arguments of 7.33,

$$\arg\frac{dz}{dw} = \arg A + \sum_{j=1}^{n-1}\left(\frac{\alpha_j}{\pi}-1\right)\arg(w-w_j).$$

The difference between limits of this expression as $w \to \pm\infty$ for real w represents the angle of rotation, β, of the sides of the polygon at z_n (Figure 7.40),

$$\beta = \lim_{w\to-\infty}\arg\frac{dz}{dw} - \lim_{w\to\infty}\arg\frac{dz}{dw} = \sum_{j=1}^{n-1}\left(\frac{\alpha_j}{\pi}-1\right)(\pi) - \sum_{j=1}^{n-1}\left(\frac{\alpha_j}{\pi}-1\right)(0)$$

$$= \sum_{j=1}^{n-1}\alpha_j - (n-1)\pi.$$

If α_n is the angle that satisfies equation 7.32, then $\sum_{j=1}^{n-1}\alpha_j = (n-2)\pi - \alpha_n$, and $\beta = (n-2)\pi - \alpha_n - (n-1)\pi = -(\alpha_n + \pi)$. Rotationally, this angle is equivalent to

$2\pi - (\alpha_n + \pi) = \pi - \alpha_n$, and therefore the polygon has a vertex at z_n with interior angle α_n.

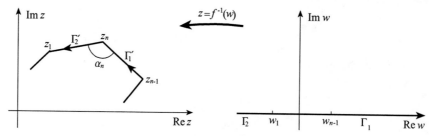

Figure 7.40

When the point at infinity maps to a vertex of the polygon, there is one less term in the product 7.33 as compared to 7.30. The resulting integration may be simplified considerably. We illustrate by repeating Example 7.20 using the point at infinity as one of the source points in the w-plane.

Example 7.21   Repeat Example 7.20 using the points $w = -1$, 1, and ∞ to map to $z = -1$, 1 and $\sqrt{3}i$ (Figure 7.41).

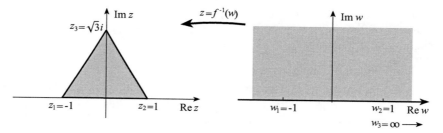

Figure 7.41

Solution   Since interior angles are $\pi/3$ radians, we consider

$$\frac{dz}{dw} = A(w+1)^{1/3-1}(w-1)^{1/3-1} = \frac{A}{(w+1)^{2/3}(w-1)^{2/3}}.$$

The solution can be expressed in the form

$$z = A \int_0^w \frac{1}{(\zeta+1)^{2/3}(\zeta-1)^{2/3}} d\zeta + B.$$

To determine A and B, we use that fact that $w = \pm 1$ and ∞ are mapped to $z = \pm 1$, and $\sqrt{3}i$,

$$1 = A \int_0^1 \frac{1}{(\zeta+1)^{2/3}(\zeta-1)^{2/3}} d\zeta + B,$$

$$-1 = A \int_0^{-1} \frac{1}{(\zeta+1)^{2/3}(\zeta-1)^{2/3}} d\zeta + B,$$

$$\sqrt{3}i = A \int_0^\infty \frac{1}{(\zeta+1)^{2/3}(\zeta-1)^{2/3}} d\zeta + B.$$

A change of variable of integration on the second of these, combined with the first, implies that $B = 0$. From the first condition,

$$1 = A \int_0^1 \frac{1}{(\zeta+1)^{2/3}[(1-\zeta)e^{\pi i}]^{2/3}} d\zeta = A \int_0^1 \frac{1}{(1-\zeta^2)^{2/3}e^{2\pi i/3}} d\zeta$$

$$= A e^{-2\pi i/3} \int_0^1 \frac{1}{(1-\zeta^2)^{2/3}} d\zeta.$$

If we set $\zeta = \sqrt{t}$ in this definite integral,

$$\int_0^1 \frac{1}{(1-\zeta^2)^{2/3}} d\zeta = \frac{1}{2}\int_0^1 t^{-1/2}(1-t)^{-2/3}\, dt = \frac{1}{2}\mathrm{B}(1/2, 1/3),$$

where $\mathrm{B}(p, q)$ is the beta function

$$\mathrm{B}(p, q) = \int_0^1 t^{p-1}(1-t)^{q-1}\, dt.$$

In other words, $A = 2e^{2\pi i/3}/\mathrm{B}(1/2, 1/3)$.•

Degenerate Polygons

Quite often in applications it is required to map a "degenerate" polygon in the z-plane to the half-plane $\operatorname{Im} w > 0$. A polygon is degenerate if one or more of its vertices is "at infinity". Examples of this are the infinite strip and the semi-infinite strip in Figure 7.42. The infinite strip can be thought of as the limit of the polygon $OABC$ as $d \to \infty$. The semi-infinite strip is the limit of triangle OAB as $d \to \infty$.

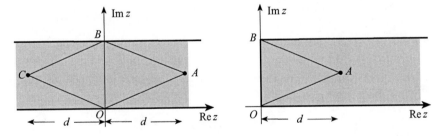

Figure 7.42

What we have just learned about Schwarz-Christoffel transformations can be used to advantage in such problems. We illustrate with the following examples.

Example 7.22 The transformation $w = \sin\dfrac{\pi z}{2a}$ maps the semi-infinite strip in Figure 7.43 to the half-plane $\operatorname{Im} w > 0$. (see Example 7.13). Show that this transformation can be obtained from a Schwarz-Christoffel transformation.

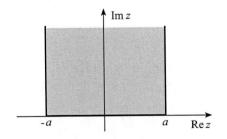

Figure 7.43

Solution   The semi-infinite strip can be regarded as a degenerate isosceles triangle with vertex infinitely far up the imaginary axis (Figure 7.44).

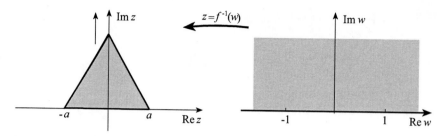

Figure 7.44

Let us choose to map vertices $w = \pm 1$ to $z = \pm a$, and regard the point at infinity in the w-plane as mapped to the vertex up the imaginary z-axis. To obtain changes in direction of $\pi/2$ radians at $z = \pm a$, equation 7.33 suggests that we solve

$$\frac{dz}{dw} = A(w-1)^{-1/2}(w+1)^{-1/2},$$

and since A is as yet undetermined, we write

$$\frac{dz}{dw} = \frac{A}{(1-w^2)^{1/2}}.$$

Integration gives $z = A\,\mathrm{Sin}^{-1}w + B$, or

$$w = \sin\left[\frac{1}{A}(z-B)\right].$$

For $z = \pm a$ to map to $w = \pm 1$, we require

$$1 = \sin\left(\frac{a-B}{A}\right), \qquad -1 = \sin\left(\frac{-a-B}{A}\right).$$

These can be solved for $A = 2a/\pi$ and $B = 0$, and therefore the required Schwarz-Christoffel transformation is

$$w = \sin\left(\frac{\pi z}{2a}\right).$$

Notice that we did not concern ourselves with the fact that branch cuts of the functions $1/[(w-1)^{1/2}(w+1)^{1/2}]$ and $1/(1-w^2)^{1/2}$ may not agree. Ultimately we invert the function $z = f^{-1}(w)$ for $w = f(z)$, and $w = f(z)$ has no branch cuts. What we normally do is verify that the final transformation $w = f(z)$ satisfies the original mapping requirements. In this case, it means checking that $w = \sin[\pi z/(2a)]$ maps the semi-infinite strip in Figure 7.43 to $\mathrm{Im}\,w > 0$.•

Example 7.23   Find a Schwarz-Christoffel transformation that maps the half-plane $\mathrm{Im}\,z > 0$, slit along the imaginary axis from $z = 0$ to $z = ai$ $(a > 0)$, to the half-plane $\mathrm{Im}\,w > 0$ (Figure 7.45).

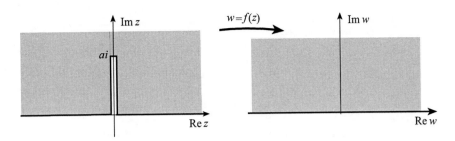

Figure 7.45

Solution   Consider the transformation that maps the half-plane $\text{Im } w > 0$ to the degenerate quadrilateral in Figure 7.46 where $w = \pm 1$ and $w = 0$ are mapped to $z = \pm b$ and $z = ai$. Angles at $z = \pm b$ and $z = ai$ require

$$\frac{dz}{dw} = A(w+1)^{\alpha/\pi - 1} w^{\beta/\pi - 1}(w-1)^{\alpha/\pi - 1}.$$

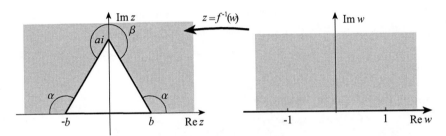

Figure 7.46

To obtain the slit in Figure 7.45, we let $\alpha \to \pi/2$ and $\beta \to 2\pi$. The limit of the derivative is

$$\frac{dz}{dw} = A(w+1)^{-1/2} w (w-1)^{-1/2}, \qquad \text{or} \qquad \frac{dz}{dw} = \frac{Aw}{(w^2 - 1)^{1/2}}.$$

Integration gives $z = A(w^2 - 1)^{1/2} + B$. The fact that $w = 0$ and $w = \pm 1$ are mapped to $z = ai$ and $z = 0$ requires

$$ai = A(-1)^{1/2} + B, \qquad 0 = B.$$

We must choose a branch of the square root function for which $(-1)^{1/2} = i$ (since upper half-plane is mapped to upper half-plane), in which case these equations give $A = a$ and $B = 0$; that is $z = a(w^2 - 1)^{1/2}$. When this equation is solved for w, the result is $w = (1 + z^2/a^2)^{1/2}$. We must choose a branch of this multivalued function. In order to restrict the branch cut to the imaginary axis below $z = ai$, we separate the function in the form

$$w = \frac{1}{a}(z + ai)^{1/2}(z - ai)^{1/2}$$

and choose branches of the root functions corresponding to $\log_{-\pi/2} z$.●

We have not verified that it is acceptable to take limits on angles in equation 7.30 in order to produce degenerate polygons. Once again if we verify that the mapping obtained does indeed produce the desired effect, then justification of limits is unnecessary. This is done for Example 7.23 in Exercise 1.

EXERCISES 7.6

1. Verify that the transformation $w = f(z) = a^{-1}(z + ai)^{1/2}(z - ai)^{1/2}$ in Example 7.23 maps the half-plane $\operatorname{Im} z > 0$, slit along the imaginary axis from $z = 0$ to $z = ai$ $(a > 0)$, to the half-plane $\operatorname{Im} w > 0$. Do this by showing that:

   (a) points $z = x < 0$ are mapped to $w = u < -1$;
   (b) points $z = x > 0$ are mapped to $w = u > 1$;
   (c) in the limit as $x \to 0^+$, the point z_2 to the right of the imaginary axis in the diagram to the right is mapped to a point $w = u$ where $0 < u < 1$;
   (d) in the limit as $x \to 0^-$, the point z_1 to the left of the imaginary axis in the diagram to the right is mapped to a point $w = u$ where $-1 < u < 0$.

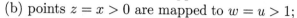

2. In this exercise we use a Schwarz-Christoffel transformation to derive the mapping $w = e^{\pi z/a}$ for the infinite channel $0 < \operatorname{Im} z < a$ to the half-plane $\operatorname{Im} w > 0$.

   (a) Regard the infinite channel as a degeneration of the rhombus shown below as $b \to \infty$. Choose images of z_1, z_2, z_3, and z_4 as $w_1 < 0$ (but as yet undetermined), $w_2 = 0$, $w_3 = 1$, and w_4 at infinity. Show that using differential equation 7.33 and letting $\alpha \to \pi$ and $\beta \to 0$, the mapping $z = f^{-1}(w)$ must satisfy

   $$\frac{dz}{dw} = \frac{A}{w}.$$

   (b) Integrate the differential equation in part (a), determine A and u_1, and hence show that $z = (a/\pi) \log_\phi w$ for appropriately chosen ϕ. This can be solved for $w = e^{\pi z/a}$.

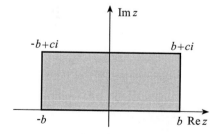

3. Repeat Example 7.19 for the rectangle shown below.

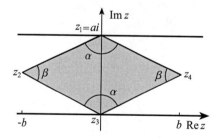

4. In this exercise we use the Schwarz-Christoffel transformation to derive the mapping $w = z^2$ from a quarter-plane to a half-plane.

   (a) Show that differential equation 7.33 takes the form

$$\frac{dz}{dw} = Aw^{-1/2}(w+1)^{\alpha_1/\pi-1}(w-1)^{\alpha_2/\pi-1}$$

when the quadrilateral with vertices 0, 1, i, and $x + yi$ where $x > 0$ and $y > 0$ is mapped to the half-plane $\operatorname{Im} w > 0$ if these vertices map to the points 0, 1, -1, ∞ respectively.

(b) To map the quarter-plane $x > 0$, $y > 0$ to $\operatorname{Im} w > 0$, take limits of the differential equation as $\alpha_1 \to \pi$ and $\alpha_2 \to \pi$.

(c) Solve the differential equation in part (b) and show that $w = z^2$.

5. Derive the transformation $z = a(w + \log_{-\pi/2} w)$ that maps the half-plane $\operatorname{Im} w > 0$ to the half-plane $\operatorname{Im} z > 0$ slit along the line $y = a > 0$, $x \le -a$ (left diagram below). Hint: Regard the slit z-plane as the limit of the polygon $EFCD$ as $C \to -\infty$ along the real axis (right diagram). Points E and D are at infinity. Hint: Map $w = -1$ to F and $w = 0$ to C with angles α and β as shown. Let $\alpha \to 0$ and $\beta \to 2\pi$.

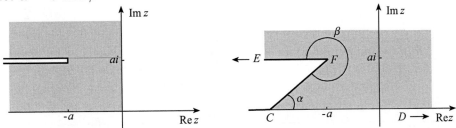

6. Use the technique of Exercise 5 to find the Schwarz-Christoffel transformation that maps the half-plane $\operatorname{Im} w > 0$ to the half-plane $\operatorname{Im} z > 0$ slit along the line $y = a > 0$, $x \le 0$.

7. Derive the transformation

$$z = \frac{a}{\pi}(\sqrt{w^2-1} + \operatorname{Cosh}^{-1} w) - ai$$

that maps the half-plane $\operatorname{Im} w > 0$ to the half-plane with a step shown in the left figure below. Hint: Regard the step in the z-plane as the limit of the polygon $EFCD$ as E and D move to infinity in the right diagram. Map $w = -1$ to F and $w = 1$ to C.

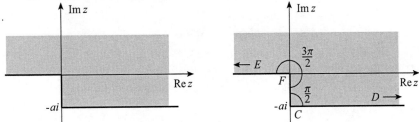

8. Derive the transformation $z = \frac{ia}{2}\sqrt{w}(3 - w)$ that maps the half-plane $\operatorname{Im} w > 0$ to the domain in the left figure below — quadrants 1, 2, and 4 with the y-axis slit to height a. Hint: Regard the slit z-plane as the limit of the polygon CDE as $C \to 0$ along the real axis (right figure). Point E is at infinity. Map C and D to $w = 0$ and $w = 1$, respectively. Let $\alpha \to 2\pi$ and $\beta \to \pi/2$. To evaluate the constant A and B in equation 7.31, use the fact that D is mapped to $w = 1$, and let $z = 0$ map to $w = \sqrt{3}$.

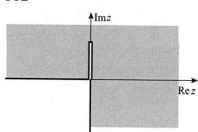

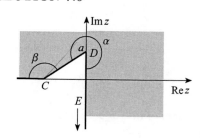

9. Derive the transformation $z = \dfrac{(a+b)+(b-a)i}{2\pi}\left[\mathrm{Sin}^{-1}w + i\,\mathrm{Sin}^{-1}\left(\dfrac{1}{w}\right)\right] + \dfrac{a+bi}{2}$ that maps the half-plane $\mathrm{Im}\,w > 0$ to the channel in the left figure below. Hint: Regard the channel as the limit as $C \to \infty$ of the degenerate polygon $OCDE$ in the right figure below. Vertex E is at infinity. Map $w = -1$, $w = 0$, and $w = 1$ to $z = 0$, $z = C$, and $z = a + bi$, respectively. Let $\alpha \to 3\pi/2$ and $\beta \to 0$.

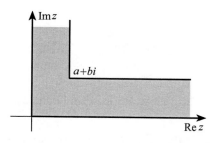

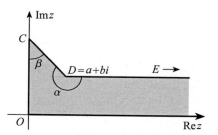

10. Derive the transformation $z = b(w-1)^{\alpha/\pi}\left(1 + \dfrac{\alpha w}{\pi - \alpha}\right)^{1-\alpha/\pi}$ that maps the half-plane $\mathrm{Im}\,w > 0$ to the half-plane $\mathrm{Im}\,z > 0$ slit along the line segment joining the origin to the point $be^{\alpha i}$ in the left figure below. Hint: Regard the slit z-plane as the limit as $d \to 0$ of the degenerate polygon $EDCO$ in the right figure. Map the points $w = -(\pi - \alpha)/\alpha$, $w = 0$, and $w = 1$ to $z = 0$, $z = C$, and $z = D$, respectively.

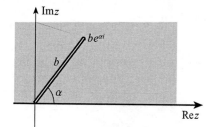

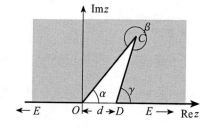

§7.7 Steady-state Two-dimensional Heat Flow

§7.7.1 Heat Flow Without Sources

In Section 3.8 we indicated that when a thin plate occupying a domain D in the xy-plane is insulated top and bottom, any steady-state temperature distribution $T(x,y)$ in the plate must satisfy Laplace's equation

$$\frac{\partial^2 T}{\partial x^2} + \frac{\partial^2 T}{\partial y^2} = 0. \qquad (7.34a)$$

Accompanying 7.34a will be Dirichlet and/or Neumann boundary conditions specifying values of temperature or its normal derivative along the boundary $\beta(D)$ of D. Curves $T(x,y) = $ constant are isothermal curves, curves joining all points with the same temperature (Figure 7.47). The harmonic conjugate $\tilde{T}(x,y)$ defines a one-parameter family of curves $\tilde{T}(x,y) = $ constant that are orthogonal trajectories of the isothermal curves. They represent curves along which heat flows. The analytic function $F(z) = T(x,y) + \tilde{T}(x,y)i$ is the complex temperature function associated with $T(x,y)$.

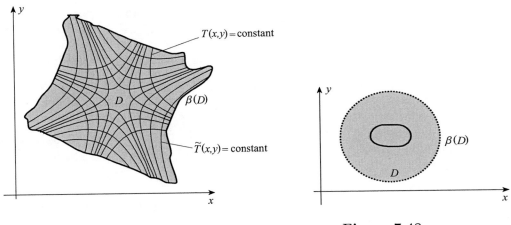

Figure 7.47   **Figure 7.48**

Suppose for the moment that D is a bounded domain (as shown in Figure 7.47), and it is required to solve 7.34a subject to prescribed values for temperature on the boundary $\beta(D)$ of D,

$$T(x,y) = h(x,y), \qquad (x,y) \text{ on } \beta(D), \qquad (7.34b)$$

where $h(x,y)$ is a given function. According to Corollary 3 of Theorem 4.24 in Section 4.8, there is one and only one steady-state temperature distribution $T(x,y)$ satisfying this Dirichlet problem. We have mathematical confirmation of what we would expect physically. The theorem itself states that there can be no relative maxima or minima for temperature inside the plate; hottest and coldest points of the plate must be on the edge of the plate. Because the domain shown is simply-connected, this means that no isothermal could be a closed curve as shown in Figure 7.48; all isothermals must begin and end on the edge of the plate such as in Figure 7.47.

In our first example, we derive the temperature function that we simply stated in Example 3.37.

Example 7.24   Find steady-state temperature $T(x,y)$ in a thin semi-infinite plate $y > 0$ with insulated surfaces, given that the temperature along its edge $y = 0$ is

$$T(x,0) = \begin{cases} T_0 > 0 & |x| < 1 \\ 0 & |x| > 1 \end{cases}.$$

Identify isothermal curves and curves along which heat flows.

Solution   Formula 4.38 gives

$$T(x,y) = \frac{1}{\pi}\left[-T_0 \operatorname{Tan}^{-1}\left(\frac{-1-x}{y}\right) + T_0 \operatorname{Tan}^{-1}\left(\frac{1-x}{y}\right) \right]$$

$$= \frac{T_0}{\pi}\left[\operatorname{Tan}^{-1}\left(\frac{1+x}{y}\right) + \operatorname{Tan}^{-1}\left(\frac{1-x}{y}\right) \right].$$

Using the technique in Example 7.18 of Section 7.5, we can bring the inverse tangent functions together. If we take tangents of both sides of

$$\frac{\pi T}{T_0} = \operatorname{Tan}^{-1}\left(\frac{1+x}{y}\right) + \operatorname{Tan}^{-1}\left(\frac{1-x}{y}\right),$$

and use the trigonometric identity $\tan(A + B) = \dfrac{\tan A + \tan B}{1 - \tan A \tan B}$, we obtain

$$\tan\frac{\pi T}{T_0} = \frac{\dfrac{1+x}{y} + \dfrac{1-x}{y}}{1 - \left(\dfrac{1+x}{y}\right)\left(\dfrac{1-x}{y}\right)} = \frac{2y}{x^2 + y^2 - 1}.$$

Since $0 < T < T_0$, it follows that $0 < \pi T/T_0 < \pi$. If we use the notation $\tan^{-1}$ to denote values of the inverse tangent function between 0 and π, the solution can be written in the form

$$\frac{\pi T}{T_0} = \tan^{-1}\left(\frac{2y}{x^2 + y^2 - 1}\right) \quad \Longrightarrow \quad T(x,y) = \frac{T_0}{\pi}\tan^{-1}\left(\frac{2y}{x^2 + y^2 - 1}\right).$$

Isothermal curves have equations

$$C = \frac{T_0}{\pi}\tan^{-1}\left(\frac{2y}{x^2 + y^2 - 1}\right).$$

If we multiply by π/T_0, and take tangents,

$$\tan\left(\frac{\pi C}{T_0}\right) = \frac{2y}{x^2 + y^2 - 1}.$$

Cross multiplication gives

$$x^2 + y^2 - 1 = 2y\cot\left(\frac{\pi C}{T_0}\right).$$

When the square of the y-terms is completed, isothermals are

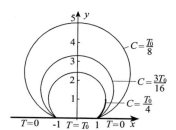

Figure 7.49

$$x^2 + \left[y - \cot\left(\frac{\pi C}{T_0}\right)\right]^2 = \csc^2\left(\frac{\pi C}{T_0}\right).$$

These are circles through the points $(\pm 1, 0)$ with centres on the y-axis. Isothermals for $T = T_0/8$, $3T_0/16$, and $T_0/4$ are shown in Figure 7.49.

To determine curves along which heat flows, we find the harmonic conjugate $\tilde{T}(x,y)$ of $T(x,y)$. The Cauchy-Riemann equations require

$$\frac{\partial \tilde{T}}{\partial y} = \frac{\partial T}{\partial x} = \frac{T_0}{\pi}\left[\frac{y}{y^2+(1+x)^2} - \frac{y}{y^2+(1-x)^2}\right],$$

$$\frac{\partial \tilde{T}}{\partial x} = -\frac{\partial T}{\partial y} = \frac{T_0}{\pi}\left[\frac{1+x}{y^2+(1+x)^2} + \frac{1-x}{y^2+(1-x)^2}\right].$$

These give

$$\tilde{T}(x,y) = \frac{T_0}{2\pi}\ln\left[\frac{y^2+(1+x)^2}{y^2+(1-x)^2}\right].$$

Heat flow lines are defined by

$$C = \frac{T_0}{2\pi}\ln\left[\frac{y^2+(1+x)^2}{y^2+(1-x)^2}\right],$$

and this equation can be written in the form

$$\left[x-\coth\left(\frac{\pi C}{T_0}\right)\right]^2 + y^2 = \operatorname{csch}^2\left(\frac{\pi C}{T_0}\right).$$

Described are circles with centres on the x-axis. Heat flow lines for $C = \pm T_0/8$, $\pm 3T_0/16$, and $\pm T_0/4$ are shown in Figure 7.50.

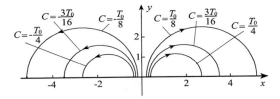

Figure 7.50

Superposition of Figures 7.49 and 7.50 in Figure 7.51 illustrates orthogonality of isothermals and heat flow lines.●

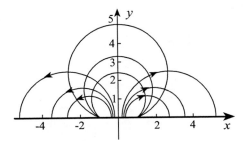

Figure 7.51

When the domain D of a heat flow problem is complicated, it may be possible to use a conformal mapping to map D onto a simpler domain, solve the simple problem, and then invert the transformation to obtain the solution to the original problem. We illustrate in the following examples.

Example 7.25   Find steady-state temperature $T(x, y)$ in a thin plate in the form of a semi-infinite strip $-a < x < a$, $y > 0$ (Figure 7.52), that satisfies the Dirichlet boundary conditions

$$T(\pm a, y) = T_0 > 0, \ y > 0; \qquad T(x, 0) = 0, \ -a < x < a.$$

Identify and plot isothermal curves.

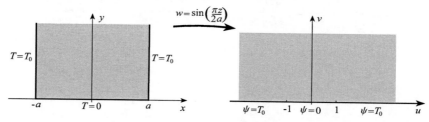

Figure 7.52

Solution   In Examples 7.13 and 7.22 we derived the mapping $w = \sin\left[\pi z/(2a)\right]$ that maps the strip to the half-plane $\operatorname{Im} w > 0$ in such a way that $z = \pm a$ are mapped to $w = \pm 1$. Formula 4.38 gives the solution $\psi(u, v)$ of Laplace's equation in $\operatorname{Im} w > 0$ subject to the piecewise constant boundary condition along $\operatorname{Im} w = 0$,

$$\psi(u, v) = \frac{1}{2}(T_0 + T_0) + \frac{1}{\pi}\left[T_0 \operatorname{Tan}^{-1}\left(\frac{-1 - u}{v}\right) - T_0 \operatorname{Tan}^{-1}\left(\frac{1 - u}{v}\right)\right]$$

$$= T_0 - \frac{T_0}{\pi}\left[\operatorname{Tan}^{-1}\left(\frac{1 + u}{v}\right) + \operatorname{Tan}^{-1}\left(\frac{1 - u}{v}\right)\right].$$

Since $w = u + vi = \sin\dfrac{\pi z}{2a} = \sin\dfrac{\pi x}{2a}\cosh\dfrac{\pi y}{2a} + \cos\dfrac{\pi x}{2a}\sinh\dfrac{\pi y}{2a}\,i$, it follows that

$$T(x, y) = \psi[u(x, y), v(x, y)]$$

$$= T_0 - \frac{T_0}{\pi}\left[\operatorname{Tan}^{-1}\left(\frac{1 + \sin\dfrac{\pi x}{2a}\cosh\dfrac{\pi y}{2a}}{\cos\dfrac{\pi x}{2a}\sinh\dfrac{\pi y}{2a}}\right) + \operatorname{Tan}^{-1}\left(\frac{1 - \sin\dfrac{\pi x}{2a}\cosh\dfrac{\pi y}{2a}}{\cos\dfrac{\pi x}{2a}\sinh\dfrac{\pi y}{2a}}\right)\right].$$

As in Example 7.24, we can simplify this solution by bringing the inverse tangents together. If we take tangents of both sides of

$$\frac{\pi}{T_0}(T_0 - \psi) = \operatorname{Tan}^{-1}\left(\frac{1 + u}{v}\right) + \operatorname{Tan}^{-1}\left(\frac{1 - u}{v}\right),$$

we obtain

$$\tan\left[\frac{\pi}{T_0}(T_0 - \psi)\right] = \frac{\dfrac{1 + u}{v} + \dfrac{1 - u}{v}}{1 - \left(\dfrac{1 + u}{v}\right)\left(\dfrac{1 - u}{v}\right)} = \frac{2v}{u^2 + v^2 - 1}.$$

Since $0 < \psi < T_0$, it follows that $0 < \pi(T_0 - \psi)/T_0 < \pi$. With $\tan^{-1}$ denoting values of the inverse tangent function between 0 and π, the solution can be written in the form

$$\frac{\pi}{T_0}(T_0 - \psi) = \tan^{-1}\left(\frac{2v}{u^2 + v^2 - 1}\right) \quad \Longrightarrow \quad \psi(u, v) = T_0 - \frac{T_0}{\pi}\tan^{-1}\left(\frac{2v}{u^2 + v^2 - 1}\right).$$

Since $u = \sin\dfrac{\pi x}{2a}\,\cosh\dfrac{\pi y}{2a}$ and $v = \cos\dfrac{\pi x}{2a}\,\sinh\dfrac{\pi y}{2a}$,

$$T(x,y) = T_0 - \frac{T_0}{\pi}\tan^{-1}\left[\frac{2\cos\dfrac{\pi x}{2a}\,\sinh\dfrac{\pi y}{2a}}{\sin^2\dfrac{\pi x}{2a}\,\cosh^2\dfrac{\pi y}{2a} + \cos^2\dfrac{\pi x}{2a}\,\sinh^2\dfrac{\pi y}{2a} - 1}\right]$$

$$= T_0 - \frac{T_0}{\pi}\tan^{-1}\left[\frac{2\cos\dfrac{\pi x}{2a}\,\sinh\dfrac{\pi y}{2a}}{\sin^2\dfrac{\pi x}{2a} + \sinh^2\dfrac{\pi y}{2a} - 1}\right]$$

$$= T_0 - \frac{T_0}{\pi}\tan^{-1}\left[\frac{2\cos\dfrac{\pi x}{2a}\,\sinh\dfrac{\pi y}{2a}}{\sinh^2\dfrac{\pi y}{2a} - \cos^2\dfrac{\pi x}{2a}}\right].$$

Isothermals (Figure 7.53) are defined implicitly by

$$C = T_0 - \frac{T_0}{\pi}\tan^{-1}\left[\frac{2\cos\dfrac{\pi x}{2a}\,\sinh\dfrac{\pi y}{2a}}{\sinh^2\dfrac{\pi y}{2a} - \cos^2\dfrac{\pi x}{2a}}\right],$$

or,

$$\tan\left[\frac{\pi(T_0 - C)}{T_0}\right] = \frac{2\cos\dfrac{\pi x}{2a}\,\sinh\dfrac{\pi y}{2a}}{\sinh^2\dfrac{\pi y}{2a} - \cos^2\dfrac{\pi x}{2a}}.\ \bullet$$

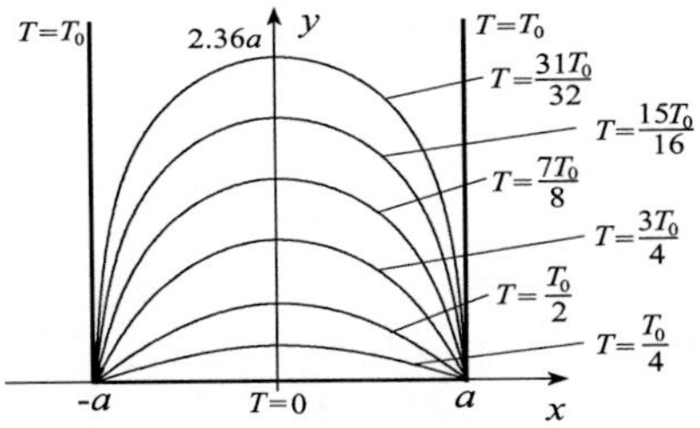

Figure 7.53

Example 7.26   Find steady-state temperature $T(x,y)$ in a thin plate in the form of a quarter-plane $x > 0$, $y > 0$ given that edge temperatures $T(0,y) = T_1$ and $T(x,0) = T_2$. Identify isothermal curves and lines of heat flow.

Solution   We give two solutions to this problem. First, the conformal mapping $w = \text{Log}\,z$ maps the first quadrant in the z-plane to the infinite strip $0 < v < \pi/2$ in the w-plane (Figure 7.54).

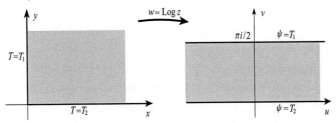

Figure 7.54

The solution of Laplace's equation in this strip subject to constant conditions on the horizontal boundaries is

$$\psi(u,v) = T_2 + \frac{2(T_1 - T_2)}{\pi}v.$$

Since $v = \text{Tan}^{-1}(y/x)$, temperature in the plate is given by

$$T(x,y) = T_2 + \frac{2}{\pi}(T_1 - T_2)\,\text{Tan}^{-1}\!\left(\frac{y}{x}\right).$$

Alternatively, the conformal mapping $w = z^2$ maps the first quadrant in the z-plane to the half-plane $v > 0$ (Figure 7.55).

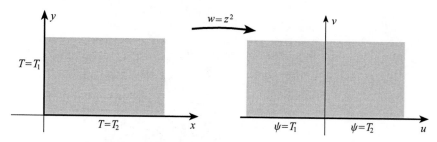

Figure 7.55

According to formula 4.38, the solution of Laplace's equation in the uv-plane subject to the boundary conditions $\psi(u,0) = T_1$ for $u < 0$ and $\psi(u,0) = T_2$ for $u > 0$ is

$$\psi(u,v) = \frac{1}{2}(T_1 + T_2) + \frac{1}{\pi}(T_1 - T_2)\operatorname{Tan}^{-1}\left(\frac{u}{v}\right).$$

Since $u = x^2 - y^2$ and $v = 2xy$, it follows that

$$T(x,y) = \frac{1}{2}(T_1 + T_2) + \frac{1}{\pi}(T_2 - T_1)\operatorname{Tan}^{-1}\left(\frac{x^2 - y^2}{2xy}\right).$$

The former solution is simpler. (They are shown to be the same in Exercise 21.) Isothermal curves are radial lines and lines of heat flow are quarter circles centred at $(0,0)$.●

Example 7.27   Find steady-state temperature $T(x,y)$ in a thin plate $y > 0$ with insulated faces, given that temperature along the edge $y = 0$ is T_2 for $x > 1$; it is $T_1 < T_2$ for $x < -1$; and that part of the x-axis between $x = -1$ and $x = 1$ is insulated (Figure 7.56). Identify isothermal curves and plot them in the case that $T_1 = 1$ and $T_2 = 2$.

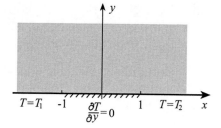

Figure 7.56

Solution   It is advantageous to map the plate to a region such that the Neumann condition falls on a boundary perpendicular to the boundaries with Dirichlet conditions. Recall from Example 7.13 in Section 7.3 that the function $w = \sin[\pi z/(2a)]$ maps the semi-infinite strip in Figure 7.57 to the upper half-plane with $z = \pm a$ mapped to $w = \pm 1$.

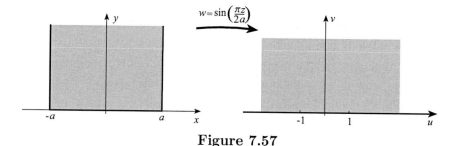

Figure 7.57

This suggests that for the present problem we consider the mapping $w = \text{Sin}^{-1} z$; it maps the half-plane $y > 0$ to the semi-infinite strip in Figure 7.58.

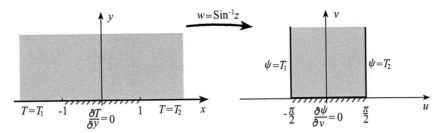

Figure 7.58

The solution $\psi(u, v)$ of Laplace's equation in the strip is

$$\psi(u, v) = T_1 + \frac{1}{\pi}(T_2 - T_1)\left(u + \frac{\pi}{2}\right) = \frac{T_1 + T_2}{2} + \frac{1}{\pi}(T_2 - T_1)u.$$

In Exercise 38 of Section 3.7, it was shown that the real part u of the mapping $w = u + vi = \text{Sin}^{-1}(x + yi)$ is

$$u = \text{Sin}^{-1}\left[\frac{\sqrt{(x+1)^2 + y^2} - \sqrt{(x-1)^2 + y^2}}{2}\right].$$

Steady-state temperature in the half-plane $y > 0$ is therefore

$$T(x, y) = \frac{T_1 + T_2}{2} + \frac{1}{\pi}(T_2 - T_1)\,\text{Sin}^{-1}\left[\frac{\sqrt{(x+1)^2 + y^2} - \sqrt{(x-1)^2 + y^2}}{2}\right].$$

Isothermal curves are defined implicitly by

$$C = \frac{T_1 + T_2}{2} + \frac{1}{\pi}(T_2 - T_1)\,\text{Sin}^{-1}\left[\frac{\sqrt{(x+1)^2 + y^2} - \sqrt{(x-1)^2 + y^2}}{2}\right],$$

where C is a constant between T_1 and T_2. If we set

$$k = \left(\frac{\pi}{T_2 - T_1}\right)\left(C - \frac{T_1 + T_2}{2}\right),$$

this equation simplifies to

$$\frac{x^2}{\sin^2 k} - \frac{y^2}{\cos^2 k} = 1,$$

(see Exercise 22). Some of these hyperbolas are plotted in Figure 7.59 in the case that $T_1 = 1$ and $T_2 = 2$.●

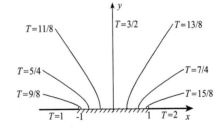

Figure 7.59

EXERCISES 7.7.1

In Exercises 1–17 find steady-state temperature $T(x, y)$ in the thin plate with insulated faces and edge conditions shown. Describe isothermal curves. Appropriate mappings are suggested at the end of the exercises. Try to discover them yourself; failing this, consult the list.

1.

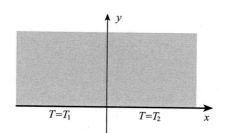

2.

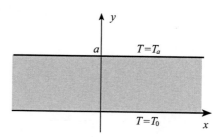

3.

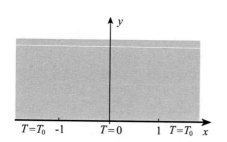

4.

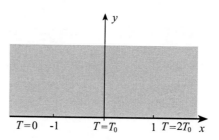

5.

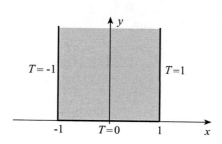

6.

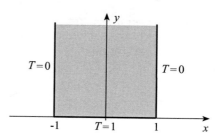

7.

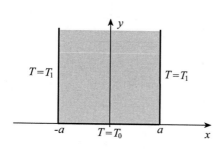

8.

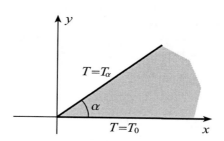

9.

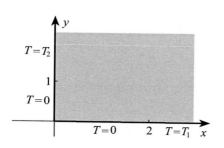

10.

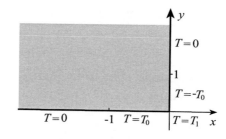

11.

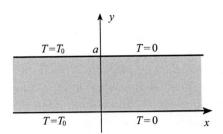

12.

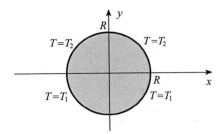

13.

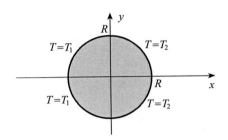

14.

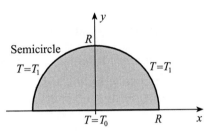

15.

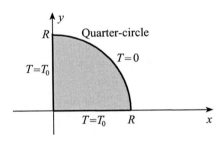

16.

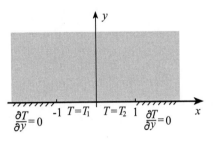

17.

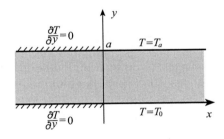

18. Find temperature $T(x, y)$ in the semicircle $x^2 + y^2 < R^2$, $y > 0$ if temperature on the quarter-circle in the first quadrant is T_0, temperature on the quarter-circle in the second quadrant is T_1, and the diameter is insulated. Hint: Use the mapping $w = i(R - z)/(R + z)$.

19. Find temperature $T(x, y)$ in the semicircle $x^2 + y^2 < R^2$, $y > 0$ that satisfies the boundary conditions

$$T(x, 0) = T_0, \quad 0 < x < R,$$
$$T(x, 0) = T_1, \quad -R < x < 0,$$

$$\frac{\partial T(x,y)}{\partial n} = 0, \quad \text{on } x^2 + y^2 = R^2, \ y > 0.$$

Hint: Use the mapping $w = \log_{-\pi/2} z$.

20. Find steady-state temperature in the quarter-plane $x > 0$, $y > 0$ when boundary conditions are as shown in the figure to the right. Hint: Use $w = \text{Sin}^{-1} z$ and see Example 7.27.

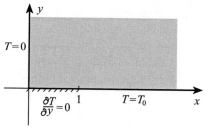

21. Verify that the solutions in Example 7.26 are the same.

22. Verify the simplification for isothermal curves in Example 7.27.

23. A steady-state temperature situation exists in a circular plate $x^2 + y^2 \leq R^2$. Is it possible for heat to flow along circles $x^2 + y^2 = r^2$?

24. Find steady-state temperature in the half-plane $y > 0$ exterior to $x^2 + y^2 = 1$ if temperature on the linear boundary is $100°$ C while that on the semicircle is $0°$ C by:
    (a) using the transformation $w = z + 1/z$;
    (b) using the transformation $w = (z - 1)/(1 + z)$.
    (c) Confirm that the solutions give equal values.

25. Repeat Exercise 24(b) if the radius of the circle is R, and temperature on the linear boundary is T_1 while that on the semicircle is T_0.

26. Steady-state temperature between concentric circles at constant temperatures was derived using a differential equation in Example 3.36. Derive the solution using the transformation $w = \text{Log } z$.

27. A plate is bounded by the two circles $(x - a)^2 + y^2 = a^2$ and $(x - b)^2 + y^2 = b^2$ where $b > a$. The edge of the inner circle is held at constant temperature T_0 and the outer edge at temperature $T_1 > T_0$, the point of contact of the circles being separated by perfect insullation.
    (a) Find temperature at all points in the plate.
    (b) Find and draw isothermal curves in the plate.

28. A circle with radius 2 has its centre 4 units away from a line. The circle is held at temperature T_1 while the line is at temperature T_0. Find temperature at all points outside the circle on the same side of the line as the circle. Hint: Use a bilinear transformation like that in Exercise 28 of Section 7.2 to map the problem to that in an annulus.

29. Generalize Exercise 28 to a circle with radius R and centre $a > R$ units away from a line. Hint: Use the bilinear transformation in Exercise 29 of Section 7.2 to map the problem to that in an annulus.

30. The circles $x^2 + (y - 2)^2 = 4$ and $x^2 + y^2 = 25$ are held at temperatures T_0 and T_1, respectively. Find the temperature between the circles. Hint: Use a bilinear transformation like that in Exercise 30 of Section 7.2 to map the region to an annulus.

31. Use the transformation of Exercise 34 in Section 7.2 to show that temperature in the region exterior to the circles in the figure below can be expressed in the form

$$T(x,y) = T_a + \frac{T_b - T_a}{2\ln\rho}\ln\left|\frac{[R\rho(1-\rho) + 2\rho(a-R)]z + [R\rho(1-\rho)(a-R) - 2\rho(a^2 - R^2)]}{[R(1-\rho) - 2\rho(a-R)]z + R(1-\rho)(a-R) + 2\rho(a^2 - R^2)]}\right|^2.$$

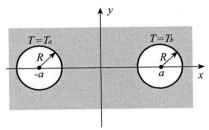

Transformations: 5. $w = \sin(\pi z/2)$ **6.** $w = \sin(\pi z/2)$ **7.** $w = \sin[\pi z/(2a)]$ **8.** $w = z^{\pi/\alpha}$ **9.** $w = z^2$ **10.** $w = -z^2$ **11.** $w = e^{\pi z/a}$ **12.** $w = i(R-z)/(R+z)$ **13.** $w = i(R - iz)/(R + iz)$ **14.** $w = i(R-z)/(R+z)$ **15.** $w = i(R^2 - z^2)/(R^2 + z^2)$ **16.** $w = 1/z$ **17.** $w = e^{\pi z/a}$

§7.7.2 Heat Flow With Sources

In this subsection we discuss heat flow problems wherein there are sources and sinks of heat. This is not to say that previous problems did not have sources and sinks; every problem had sources and sinks, otherwise there would have been no flow of heat. For instance, consider the semi-infinite plate in Example 7.24. Heat flows from points in the interval $-1 < x < 1$ to points on the rest of the x-axis in the case that $T_0 > 0$ (see Figure 7.50). In effect, the interval $-1 < x < 1$ is a source of heat, and the remainder of the x-axis is a sink. What was important in subsection 7.7.1 was that all sources and sinks were distributed over the boundary of the plate.

Our interest in this subsection is "point" or "line" sources, (depending on the physical model that we use to describe heat flow), interior to the flow region. When we use the physical model of subsection 7.7.1 of a thin flat plate insulated top and bottom, a **point source** of heat at a point (x_0, y_0) is a device that radiates heat equally in all directions. When we use the physical model of a very long cylinder in a direction perpendicular to the xy-plane in which temperature is the same in all cross-sections parallel to the xy-plane, a **line source** parallel to the axis of the cylinder and through the point (x_0, y_0) radiates heat equally in all radial directions. We might think of a thin wire radiating heat due to its carrying an electric current. The line model is more conducive to early discussions, but we will often revert to the point model later.

Consider then a line source through the origin and perpendicular to the xy-plane that radially emits h joules of heat per second per metre of length of the source (called the **strength** of the source). Clearly, isothermal surfaces should be right-circular cylinders surrounding the source; that is, they should have equations of the form $x^2 + y^2 = C$. In other words, temperature $T(x, y)$ due to the source should be a function of the radial coordinate $r = \sqrt{x^2 + y^2}$ only; that is, in polar coordinates, $T = f(r)$. In Example 3.36, we saw that the only solutions of Laplace's equation of this form are $f(r) = C \ln r + D$, where C and D are constants. Thus, the temperature function due to a line source at the origin perpendicular to the xy-plane must be of the form

$$T(x, y) = C \ln \sqrt{x^2 + y^2} + D = E \ln (x^2 + y^2) + D. \qquad (7.35)$$

We can relate constant E to strength h. The theory of heat conduction is based on Fourier's law of heat conduction which relates heat flow to temperature gradient. The **heat flux density** is a vector $\mathbf{q}$ that points in the direction in which heat flows and its magnitude is the amount of heat per second crossing one square metre perpendicular to $\mathbf{q}$. It is usually a function of position and time, but in our steady-state problems, it is a function of x and y only; $\mathbf{q} = \mathbf{q}(x, y)$. Fourier's law of heat conduction states that heat flows in the direction in which temperature decreases most rapidly. Since this is the direction opposite ∇T, we have

$$\mathbf{q} = -\kappa \nabla T, \qquad (7.36)$$

where κ is a constant of proportionality called the *thermal conductivity* of the medium through which heat is being propogated. In general, it is a function of position, but we will assume a homogeneous medium so that κ is a numerical constant. If S is a surface in the medium, and $\hat{\mathbf{n}}$ is a unit normal vector on one side of S (Figure 7.60), the following surface integral is called the flux for S; it is the amount of heat (joules per second) passing though S in direction $\hat{n}$,

$$\text{Flux} = \iint_S \mathbf{q} \cdot \hat{n} \, dS. \tag{7.37}$$

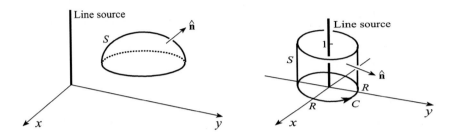

Figure 7.60   **Figure 7.61**

Suppose now that S is that part of the cylinder $x^2 + y^2 = R^2$ of radius R with height one metre beginning on the xy-plane (Figure 7.61) and $\hat{n}$ is the outward pointing normal to S. Because $\mathbf{q}$ is a function of x and y only, and the surface has height one metre, we can replace the surface integral with a line integral around the circle C: $x^2 + y^2 = R^2$,

$$\iint_S \mathbf{q} \cdot \hat{n} \, dS = \oint_C \mathbf{q} \cdot \hat{n} \, ds,$$

where $\hat{n}$ is now the outward unit normal to C. It is an established fact from calculus that when C is positively oriented (counterclockwise), a unit outward normal to C is $\hat{n} = (dy/ds, -dx/ds)$. If we use Fourier's law 7.36 for the components of $\mathbf{q}$, then flux through cylinder S becomes

$$\text{Flux} = \oint_C \left(-\kappa \frac{\partial T}{\partial x} \hat{i} - \kappa \frac{\partial T}{\partial y} \hat{j} \right) \cdot \left(\frac{dy}{ds} \hat{i} - \frac{dx}{ds} \hat{j} \right) ds = \kappa \oint_C -\frac{\partial T}{\partial x} dy + \frac{\partial T}{\partial y} dx.$$

Using formula 7.35 for the partial derivatives of $T(x, y)$, we obtain

$$\text{Flux} = \kappa \oint_C \frac{-2Ex}{x^2 + y^2} dy + \frac{2Ey}{x^2 + y^2} dx = 2\kappa E \oint_C \frac{y \, dx - x \, dy}{x^2 + y^2}.$$

When we use parametric equations $x = R \cos t$ and $y = R \sin t$, $-\pi \leq t \leq \pi$, to evaluate this integral, we get

$$\text{Flux} = 2\kappa E \int_{-\pi}^{\pi} \frac{R \sin t (-R \sin t \, dt) - R \cos t (R \cos t \, dt)}{R^2} = -4\pi\kappa E.$$

Notice that this is independent of R, as it should be; the amount of heat passing through every cylinder of unit height coaxial with the line source should be the same. But this flux should be equal to h, the amount of heat radiated by the line source per metre per second; that is, $h = -4\pi\kappa E$. Temperature function 7.35 due to a line source with strength h at the origin is therefore

$$T(x, y) = \frac{-h}{4\pi\kappa} \ln (x^2 + y^2) + D. \tag{7.38}$$

We know that $\ln \sqrt{x^2 + y^2}$ is the real part of the complex function $\log_\phi z$ so that the complex temperature function associated with a line source of strength h at the origin is

$$F(z) = \frac{-h}{2\pi\kappa} \log_\phi z + (D + Ei). \tag{7.39}$$

When the line source is at the point (x_0, y_0), equations 7.38 and 7.39 are replaced, respectively, by

$$T(x, y) = \frac{-h}{4\pi\kappa} \ln\left[(x - x_0)^2 + (y - y_0)^2\right] + D, \tag{7.40}$$

and

$$F(z) = \frac{-h}{2\pi\kappa} \log_\phi (z - z_0) + (D + Ei), \tag{7.41}$$

where $z_0 = x_0 + y_0 i$.

Example 7.28 A line source emits h joules of heat per metre per second. If temperature at a distance R from the source is T_R, find temperature at a distance r from the source.

Solution If the source is at the point (x_0, y_0), then according to equation 7.40, the temperature at a point (x, y) is

$$T(x, y) = \frac{-h}{4\pi\kappa} \ln\left[(x - x_0)^2 + (y - y_0)^2\right] + D.$$

Since temperature on the circle $(x - x_0)^2 + (y - y_0)^2 = R^2$ is T_R,

$$T_R = \frac{-h}{4\pi\kappa} \ln\left(R^2\right) + D \qquad \Longrightarrow \qquad D = T_R + \frac{h}{2\pi\kappa} \ln R.$$

Thus,

$$T(x, y) = \frac{-h}{4\pi\kappa} \ln\left[\frac{(x - x_0)^2 + (y - y_0)^2}{R^2}\right] + T_R.$$

If $T(r)$ represents temperature at a distance r from the source, then

$$T(r) = T_R - \frac{h}{2\pi\kappa} \ln(r/R). \bullet$$

It is important to realize that the development of equations 7.38–7.41 and the discussion in Example 7.28 took place in all space. There were no boundaries to consider that might affect temperature; temperature was due only to a line source of heat. In the presence of boundaries at designated temperatures, equations 7.38–7.41 might, or might not, be a correct description of temperature. For instance, suppose that in Example 7.28, a circular cylinder of radius R at temperature T_R has the line source of heat along its axis. Because the cylinder is coincident with an equipotential surface for the source, temperature inside the cylinder is exactly as in the example. In other words, this particular bounding surface does not affect the temperature function, only its domain of definition. The next example is a further illustration of this. On the other hand, if the line source is outside the cylinder, finding temperature outside the cylinder is more difficult (see Exercise 4).

Example 7.29   Find the strength of a line source at the origin that would maintain the temperature situation in Example 3.36.

Solution   Equation 7.38 gives the temperature function for a source of strength h at the origin in the absence of boundaries. However, because the boundaries in this example are coincident with equipotentials for the source, equation 7.38 also represents the temperature between the boundaries. For the source to maintain temperatures T_a and T_b at distances a and b from the source, we must have

$$T_a = \frac{-h}{4\pi\kappa} \ln\left(a^2\right) + D, \qquad T_b = \frac{-h}{4\pi\kappa} \ln\left(b^2\right) + D.$$

When these are solved for h, the strength of the source is $h = \dfrac{2\pi\kappa(T_a - T_b)}{\ln(b/a)}$. The strength increases as the the conductivity of the medium increases, as the difference between T_a and T_b increases, and as the proximity of the circles decreases.●

In preparation for the next example, we note that the real (or complex) temperature function due to multiple line sources or sinks (in space) is simply the sum of their real (or, complex) temperature functions. This is not usually the case for sources in the presence of boundaries. The example leads to a technique that is often useful in handling line sources in the presence of boundaries.

Example 7.30   A line source with strength h is located at the point (x_0, y_0) and is perpendicular to the xy-plane. A plane containing the x-axis, and perpendicular to the xy-plane, is held at temperature T_0. Find temperature in the half space $y > 0$. Find and plot isothermal curves and lines of heat flow.

Solution   To make visualization easier, we reduce the three-dimensional situation to two dimensions by replacing the line source with a point source at (x_0, y_0), and replacing the plane at temperature T_0 by the x-axis at temperature T_0 (Figure 7.62). To make use of complex temperature function 7.39 for temperature due to a source in the absence of boundaries, we map the half-plane $y > 0$ to the interior of the unit circle $|w| = 1$ in such a way that the source is mapped to the origin and the x-axis is mapped to the unit circle. Although the circle $|w| = 1$ is a boundary for the region, the fact that it is at constant temperature makes it compatible with a source at the origin with no boundary where isothermals are also circles centred at the origin. A bilinear transformation will perform the mapping. According to Exercise 25 in Section 7.2, all bilinear transformations that map the half-plane $y > 0$ to the unit circle and take a point z_0 to $w = 0$ are of the form $w = e^{\lambda i}(z - z_0)/(z - \overline{z_0})$, for some real constant λ. If we arbitrarily set $\lambda = 0$ and choose $z_0 = x_0 + y_0 i$, then $w = (z - z_0)/(z - \overline{z_0})$.

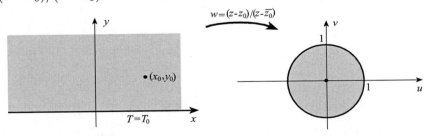

Figure 7.62

The complex temperature function in the w-plane due to the source at the origin must be of the form

$$G(w) = -\frac{h}{2\pi\kappa} \log_\phi w + (D + Ei),$$

and therefore the complex temperature function in the z-plane is

$$F(z) = -\frac{h}{2\pi\kappa} \log_\phi \left(\frac{z - z_0}{z - \overline{z_0}}\right) + (D + Ei).$$

The real temperature function is

$$T(x, y) = \mathrm{Re}\,[F(z)] = -\frac{h}{2\pi\kappa} \ln \left|\frac{z - z_0}{z - \overline{z_0}}\right| + D.$$

Since temperature along $y = 0$ is T_0, we must have

$$T_0 = -\frac{h}{2\pi\kappa} \ln \left|\frac{x - (x_0 + y_0 i)}{x - (x_0 - y_0 i)}\right| + D = D.$$

Thus,

$$T(x, y) = T_0 - \frac{h}{4\pi\kappa} \ln \left[\frac{(x - x_0)^2 + (y - y_0)^2}{(x - x_0)^2 + (y + y_0)^2}\right].$$

Isothermal curves are defined implicitly by

$$C = T_0 - \frac{h}{4\pi\kappa} \ln \left[\frac{(x - x_0)^2 + (y - y_0)^2}{(x - x_0)^2 + (y + y_0)^2}\right].$$

If we define $k = e^{2\pi\kappa(C-T_0)/h}$, it is a straightforward exercise in algebra to show that this equation can be written in the form

$$(x - x_0)^2 + (y - y_0 \coth k)^2 = y_0^2 \mathrm{csch}^2 k.$$

These are circles with centres at $(x_0, y_0 \coth k)$, some of which are shown in Figure 7.63.

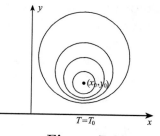

Figure 7.63

Lines along which heat flows are defined implicitly by

$$\begin{aligned}
C = \mathrm{Im}\,[F(z)] &= E - \frac{h}{2\pi\kappa} \arg_\phi \left[\frac{(x - x_0) + (y - y_0)i}{(x - x_0) + (y + y_0)i}\right] \\
&= E - \frac{h}{2\pi\kappa} \arg_\phi \left[\frac{(x - x_0) + (y - y_0)i}{(x - x_0) + (y + y_0)i} \frac{(x - x_0) - (y + y_0)i}{(x - x_0) - (y + y_0)i}\right] \\
&= E - \frac{h}{2\pi\kappa} \arg_\phi \left[\frac{(x - x_0)^2 + y^2 - y_0^2 - 2y_0(x - x_0)i}{(x - x_0)^2 + (y + y_0)^2}\right] \\
&= E - \frac{h}{2\pi\kappa} \tan^{-1} \left[\frac{-2y_0(x - x_0)}{(x - x_0)^2 + y^2 - y_0^2}\right],
\end{aligned}$$

where due account must be taken for ϕ and the quadrant of (x, y). If we transpose E, multiply both sides of the equation by $-2\pi\kappa/h$, and take tangents,

$$\tan\left[\frac{2\pi\kappa(C-E)}{h}\right] = \frac{2y_0(x-x_0)}{(x-x_0)^2 + y^2 - y_0^2}.$$

When we set $k = 2\pi\kappa(C-E)/h$, this equation can be written in the form

$$(x - x_0 - y_0\cot k)^2 + y^2 = y_0^2\csc^2 k.$$

These are semicircle with centres on the x-axis, some of which are shown in the Figure 7.64. Notice that they intersect the x-axis at right angles as indeed they should since the x-axis is an isothermal curve.●

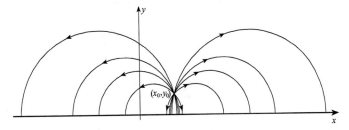

Figure 7.64

It is instructive to write the complex temperature function in this example in the form

$$F(z) = T_0 - \frac{h}{2\pi\kappa}\log_\phi(z - z_0) + \frac{h}{2\pi\kappa}\log_\phi(z - \overline{z_0}) + Ei.$$

It is T_0 plus the sum of two complex temperature functions, one due to a source at z_0 and the other due to a sink of equal strength at $\overline{z_0}$. The source and sink, by themselves, result in a temperature of zero along the x-axis. This suggests an alternative technique for solving Example 7.29 that generalizes to many other problems, a technique called the *method of images*. The given problem with a source and a boundary with prescribed temperature is replaced by a problem with the original source and a second source (or sink) so that the two sources yield temperature $T = 0$ on the boundary. In the example, the sink is at the image of the source in the x-axis. In some configurations, more than one image may be required, or the image may be in some other line, or even a circle (see Exercise 3 for the case of a circle).

EXERCISES 7.7.2

1. Use the method of images to find temperature in the half-space $y > 0$ if a source with strength h is located a metres from an insulated x-axis. Find and plot isothermal curves and lines of heat flow.

2. The positive x-axis and a half-line from the origin at a positive rotation of angle α are both held at temperature T_0. A source with strength h is at the point $z_0 = Re^{\phi i}$ between the lines. Show that the temperature between the lines is

$$T(r,\theta) = T_0 + \frac{h}{4\pi\kappa}\ln\left[\frac{r^{2\pi/\alpha} + R^{2\pi/\alpha} - 2r^{\pi/\alpha}R^{\pi/\alpha}\cos\dfrac{\pi(\theta+\phi)}{\alpha}}{r^{2\pi/\alpha} + R^{2\pi/\alpha} - 2r^{\pi/\alpha}R^{\pi/\alpha}\cos\dfrac{\pi(\theta-\phi)}{\alpha}}\right].$$

3. A source with strength h is located at the point $x = a$ in the xy-plane. Surrounding the source is a circle of radius R, centred at the origin, that is held at temperature T_0.

(a) Find the temperature inside the circle by mapping the situation to a circle with the source at the centre of the circle.

(b) Show that if a negative source is placed at the inverse point of the source in the circle (see equation 7.11 in Section 7.2), then their combination leads to the required temperature. This is an example of the method of images where the image is the inverse point in a circle.

4. A source with strength h is at $x = a$ on the x-axis. A circle of radius R ($R < a$), centred at the origin, is held at temperature T_0. Show that temperature outside the circle is

$$T(x, y) = T_0 + \frac{h}{4\pi\kappa} \ln\left\{ \frac{(ax - R^2)^2 + a^2 y^2}{R^2[(x-a)^2 + y^2]} \right\}.$$

5. A semi-infinite channel consists of the region bounded by the x-axis, $-a \leq x \leq a$, and the lines $x = \pm a$, $y \geq 0$. Each of the lines is at temperature T_0. A source with strength h is located at the point $(0, b)$. Show that temperature in the channel is

$$T(x, y) = T_0 + \frac{h}{4\pi\kappa} \ln\left(\frac{\sin^2\frac{\pi x}{2a} + \sinh^2\frac{\pi y}{2a} + \sinh^2\frac{\pi b}{2a} + 2\cos\frac{\pi x}{2a}\sinh\frac{\pi y}{2a}\sinh\frac{\pi b}{2a}}{\sin^2\frac{\pi x}{2a} + \sinh^2\frac{\pi y}{2a} + \sinh^2\frac{\pi b}{2a} - 2\cos\frac{\pi x}{2a}\sinh\frac{\pi y}{2a}\sinh\frac{\pi b}{2a}} \right).$$

6. The positive x- and y-axes have temperature T_0. A source with strength h is at the point (x_0, y_0).

(a) Use the method of images with an equal source at $(-x_0, -y_0)$ and negative sources of the same strength at the points $(-x_0, y_0)$ and $(x_0, -y_0)$ to show that temperature in the first quadrant can be expresed in the form

$$T(x, y) = T_0 + \frac{h}{4\pi\kappa} \ln\left\{ \frac{[(x - x_0)^2 + (y + y_0)^2][(x + x_0)^2 + (y - y_0)^2]}{[(x - x_0)^2 + (y - y_0)^2][(x + x_0)^2 + (y + y_0)^2]} \right\}.$$

(b) Use the mapping $w = z^2$ and Example 7.30 to write the temperature in the form

$$T(r, \theta) = T_0 + \frac{h}{4\pi\kappa} \ln\left\{ \frac{r^4 + R^4 - 2r^2 R^2 \cos[2(\theta + \phi)]}{r^4 + R^4 - 2r^2 R^2 \cos[2(\theta - \phi)]} \right\},$$

where $z_0 = Re^{\phi i}$.

(c) Show that the results in parts (a) and (b) are the same.

7. The semicircle $x^2 + y^2 = R^2$, $y > 0$ and the x-axis for $|x| \geq R$ are at temperature T_0. A source with strength h is at the point $z_0 = ae^{\phi i}$, where $a > R$ and $0 < \phi < \pi$. Show that the temperature in the half-plane $y > 0$ outside the semicircle is

$$T(r, \theta) = T_0 + \frac{h}{4\pi\kappa} \ln\left\{ \frac{[r^2 + a^2 - 2ar\cos(\theta + \phi)][a^2 R^2 + 1 - 2ar\cos(\theta - \phi)]}{[r^2 + a^2 - 2ar\cos(\theta - \phi)][a^2 R^2 + 1 - 2ar\cos(\theta + \phi)]} \right\}.$$

Hint: Map the region of interest to the half-plane $v > 0$ with $w = z + 1/z$ and use Example 7.30.

8. The positive x-axis is held at temperature T_0, and there is a source with strength h at the point $z_0 = Re^{\phi i}$. Use Exercise 2 to find temperature in the xy-plane.

§7.8 Electrostatic Potential

§7.8.1 Electrostatic Potential Without Sources

In Section 3.9, we associated an analytic complex potential $F(z) = V(x,y) + W(x,y)i$ with two-dimensional electrostatic fields $V(x,y)$ that were the result of three-dimensional problems in which potential was identical in every plane parallel to the xy-plane. The components of the electric field intensity $\mathbf{E}$ are the real and imaginary parts of $-\overline{F'(z)}$. Curves (cylinders) in the one-parameter family $V(x,y) = C$ are equipotentials, and curves $W(x,y) = C$ are lines of force.

In domains D which are free of charge, the potential satisfies Laplace's equation

$$\frac{\partial^2 V}{\partial x^2} + \frac{\partial^2 V}{\partial y^2} = 0. \tag{7.42a}$$

What completes the characterization of $V(x,y)$ is specification of a boundary condition on the boundary $\beta(D)$ of D, usually a Dirichlet or Neumann condition (see equations 7.22a and 7.23a).

Suppose for the moment that D is a bounded domain as shown in Figure 7.65, and it is required to solve 7.42a subject to a Dirichlet condition on $\beta(D)$,

$$V(x,y) = h(x,y), \qquad (x,y) \text{ on } \beta(D), \tag{7.42b}$$

where $h(x,y)$ is a given function. According to Corollary 3 to Theorem 4.24 in Section 4.8, the solution of this problem is unique; there cannot be two different solutions. Furthermore, Theorem 4.24 indicates that $V(x,y)$ cannot have a relative maximum or minimum inside D; maximum and minimum potentials must occur on $\beta(D)$.

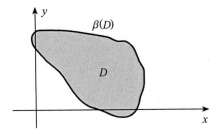

Figure 7.65

When D is a complicated domain, it may be possible to use a conformal mapping to map D onto a simpler domain, solve the simple problem, and then invert the transformation to obtain the solution to the original problem. We illustrate in the following examples.

Example 7.31 A cylindrical conductor of infinite length and radius R is centred around a line through the origin of the xy-plane and perpendicular to the plane. One half is held at potential V_1, and the other half at V_2, the parts being separated by thin pieces of insulation. Find the potential interior to the cylinder. Describe the equipotential surfaces and lines of force interior to the cylinder.

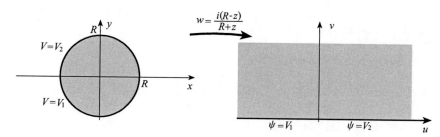

Figure 7.66

Solution   Since potential in all planes parallel to the xy-plane is the same, we rephrase the problem as finding the potential inside the circle $x^2 + y^2 < R^2$, given that its values on the upper and lower halves are V_2 and V_1, respectively (Figure 7.66). We begin by mapping the circle to the half-plane $\operatorname{Im} w > 0$ with a bilinear transformation in such a way that the upper semicircle is mapped to the positive $u = \operatorname{Re} w$ axis and the lower semicircle is mapped to the negative u-axis. If we choose to map $z = R$ to $w = 0$, then $z = -R$ maps to points infinitely far out the real u-axis. Since $z = -R$ is the pole of the mapping, the transformation takes the form $w = a(z - R)/(z + R)$. If we arbitrarily demand that $z = Ri$ map to $w = 1$, then $1 = a(Ri - R)/(Ri + R)$, and this requires that $a = -i$. The bilinear transformation is therefore

$$ w = \frac{i(R - z)}{R + z}. $$

According to equation 4.38, the solution $\psi(u, v)$ of Laplace's equation in the domain $\operatorname{Im} w > 0$ subject to the boundary conditions in Figure 7.66 is

$$ \psi(u, v) = \frac{V_1 + V_2}{2} + \frac{1}{\pi}(V_1 - V_2) \operatorname{Tan}^{-1}\left(-\frac{u}{v}\right) $$
$$ = \frac{V_1 + V_2}{2} + \frac{1}{\pi}(V_2 - V_1) \operatorname{Tan}^{-1}\left(\frac{u}{v}\right). $$

If we set $w = u + vi$ and $z = x + yi$ in the bilinear transformation,

$$ u + vi = \frac{i(R - x - yi)}{R + x + yi} = \frac{i[(R - x) - yi]}{(R + x) + yi} \frac{(R + x) - yi}{(R + x) - yi} = \frac{2yR + (R^2 - x^2 - y^2)i}{(R + x)^2 + y^2}. $$

Thus,

$$ u = \frac{2yR}{(R + x)^2 + y^2}, \qquad v = \frac{R^2 - x^2 - y^2}{(R + x)^2 + y^2}, $$

and the electrostatic potential is

$$ V = \frac{V_1 + V_2}{2} + \frac{1}{\pi}(V_2 - V_1) \operatorname{Tan}^{-1}\left(\frac{2Ry}{R^2 - x^2 - y^2}\right). $$

Equipotential surfaces are defined implicitly by

$$ C = \frac{V_1 + V_2}{2} + \frac{V_2 - V_1}{\pi} \operatorname{Tan}^{-1}\left(\frac{2Ry}{R^2 - x^2 - y^2}\right) \quad \Longrightarrow \quad \operatorname{Tan}^{-1}\left(\frac{2Ry}{R^2 - x^2 - y^2}\right) = k, $$

where C is a constant and $k = \pi(2C - V_1 - V_2)/(2V_2 - 2V_1)$. When we take tangents on both sides of the latter equation,

$$\frac{2Ry}{R^2 - x^2 - y^2} = \tan k \qquad \Longrightarrow \qquad R^2 - x^2 - y^2 = 2Ry \cot k.$$

This can be rearranged into the form

$$x^2 + (y + R \cot k)^2 = R^2 + R^2 \cot^2 k = R^2 \csc^2 k.$$

These are circular arcs through $(\pm R, 0)$ with centres on the y-axis ((Figure 7.67). If we set $K = \cot k$, then equipotentials are given by $x^2 + y^2 + 2KRy = R^2$. Lines of force are orthogonal trajectories of these curves. They can be derived by finding harmonic conjugates $W(x, y)$ of $V(x, y)$, but this turns out to be a formidable task. Instead, we use differential equations to find the orthogonal trajectories of $x^2 + y^2 + 2KRy = R^2$. If we

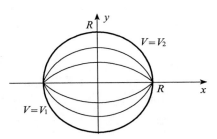

Figure 7.67

differentiate this equation with respect to x, we obtain $2x + 2y\dfrac{dy}{dx} + 2KR\dfrac{dy}{dx} = 0$. Thus,

$$\frac{dy}{dx} = \frac{-x}{y + KR} = \frac{-x}{y + (R^2 - x^2 - y^2)/(2y)} = \frac{-2xy}{R^2 - x^2 + y^2}.$$

The differential equation for orthogonal trajectories is

$$\frac{dy}{dx} = \frac{R^2 - x^2 + y^2}{2xy} \qquad \Longrightarrow \qquad \frac{dy}{dx} - \frac{y}{2x} = \frac{R^2 - x^2}{2xy}.$$

We substitute $z = y^2$ and $dz/dx = 2y\, dy/dx$ into this Bernoulli equation,

$$\frac{1}{2y}\frac{dz}{dx} - \frac{y}{2x} = \frac{R^2 - x^2}{2xy} \qquad \Longrightarrow \qquad \frac{dz}{dx} - \frac{z}{x} = \frac{R^2 - x^2}{x}.$$

An integrating factor for this linear first-order differential equation is $e^{\int (-1/x)\, dx} = 1/x$. When the differential equation is multiplied by $1/x$,

$$\frac{1}{x}\frac{dz}{dx} - \frac{z}{x^2} = \frac{R^2 - x^2}{x^2} \qquad \Longrightarrow \qquad \frac{d}{dx}\left(\frac{z}{x}\right) = \frac{R^2 - x^2}{x^2}.$$

Integration gives

$$\frac{z}{x} = -\frac{R^2}{x} - x + 2C \qquad \Longrightarrow \qquad y^2 = -R^2 - x^2 + 2Cx,$$

where C is a constant. Lines of force are therefore $(x - C)^2 + y^2 = C^2 - R^2$. These are circular arcs with centres on the x-axis.●

Example 7.32 Find potential in the semi-infinite strip $-1 < x < 1$, $y > 0$ if potential on the horizontal side is 0 and that on the vertical sides is $V_0 > 0$. Identify and plot equipotentials.

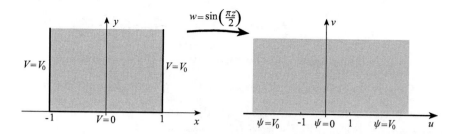

Figure 7.68

Solution   In Examples 7.13 and 7.22 we derived the mapping $w = \sin\left[\pi z/(2)\right]$ that maps the strip to the half-plane $\operatorname{Im} w > 0$ in such a way that $z = \pm 1$ are mapped to $w = \pm 1$. Formula 4.38 gives the solution $\psi(u, v)$ of Laplace's equation in $\operatorname{Im} w > 0$ subject to the piecewise constant boundary condition along $\operatorname{Im} w = 0$,

$$\psi(u, v) = \frac{1}{2}(V_0 + V_0) + \frac{1}{\pi}\left[V_0 \operatorname{Tan}^{-1}\left(\frac{-1 - u}{v}\right) - V_0 \operatorname{Tan}^{-1}\left(\frac{1 - u}{v}\right)\right]$$

$$= V_0 - \frac{V_0}{\pi}\left[\operatorname{Tan}^{-1}\left(\frac{1 + u}{v}\right) + \operatorname{Tan}^{-1}\left(\frac{1 - u}{v}\right)\right].$$

Since $w = u + vi = \sin\dfrac{\pi z}{2} = \sin\dfrac{\pi x}{2}\cosh\dfrac{\pi y}{2} + \cos\dfrac{\pi x}{2}\sinh\dfrac{\pi y}{2}\,i$, it follows that

$V(x, y) = \psi[u(x, y), v(x, y)]$

$$= V_0 - \frac{V_0}{\pi}\left[\operatorname{Tan}^{-1}\left(\frac{1 + \sin\dfrac{\pi x}{2}\cosh\dfrac{\pi y}{2}}{\cos\dfrac{\pi x}{2}\sinh\dfrac{\pi y}{2}}\right) + \operatorname{Tan}^{-1}\left(\frac{1 - \sin\dfrac{\pi x}{2}\cosh\dfrac{\pi y}{2}}{\cos\dfrac{\pi x}{2}\sinh\dfrac{\pi y}{2}}\right)\right].$$

We can simplify this solution by bringing the inverse tangents together. If we take tangents of both sides of

$$\frac{\pi}{V_0}(V_0 - \psi) = \operatorname{Tan}^{-1}\left(\frac{1 + u}{v}\right) + \operatorname{Tan}^{-1}\left(\frac{1 - u}{v}\right),$$

we obtain

$$\tan\left[\frac{\pi}{V_0}(V_0 - \psi)\right] = \frac{\dfrac{1 + u}{v} + \dfrac{1 - u}{v}}{1 - \left(\dfrac{1 + u}{v}\right)\left(\dfrac{1 - u}{v}\right)} = \frac{2v}{u^2 + v^2 - 1}.$$

Since $0 < \psi < V_0$, it follows that $0 < \pi(V_0 - \psi)/V_0 < \pi$. With $\tan^{-1}$ denoting values of the inverse tangent function between 0 and π, the solution can be written in the form

$$\frac{\pi}{V_0}(V_0 - \psi) = \tan^{-1}\left(\frac{2v}{u^2 + v^2 - 1}\right) \quad \Longrightarrow \quad \psi(u, v) = V_0 - \frac{V_0}{\pi}\tan^{-1}\left(\frac{2v}{u^2 + v^2 - 1}\right).$$

Since $u = \sin\dfrac{\pi x}{2}\cosh\dfrac{\pi y}{2}$ and $v = \cos\dfrac{\pi x}{2}\sinh\dfrac{\pi y}{2}$,

$$V(x, y) = V_0 - \frac{V_0}{\pi}\tan^{-1}\left[\frac{2\cos\dfrac{\pi x}{2}\sinh\dfrac{\pi y}{2}}{\sin^2\dfrac{\pi x}{2}\cosh^2\dfrac{\pi y}{2} + \cos^2\dfrac{\pi x}{2}\sinh^2\dfrac{\pi y}{2} - 1}\right]$$

$$= V_0 - \frac{V_0}{\pi} \tan^{-1} \left[\frac{2 \cos \frac{\pi x}{2} \sinh \frac{\pi y}{2}}{\sin^2 \frac{\pi x}{2} + \sinh^2 \frac{\pi y}{2} - 1} \right]$$

$$= V_0 - \frac{V_0}{\pi} \tan^{-1} \left[\frac{2 \cos \frac{\pi x}{2} \sinh \frac{\pi y}{2}}{\sinh^2 \frac{\pi y}{2} - \cos^2 \frac{\pi x}{2}} \right].$$

Equipotentials are defined implicitly by

$$C = V_0 - \frac{V_0}{\pi} \tan^{-1} \left[\frac{2 \cos \frac{\pi x}{2} \sinh \frac{\pi y}{2}}{\sinh^2 \frac{\pi y}{2} - \cos^2 \frac{\pi x}{2}} \right],$$

or,

$$\tan \left[\frac{\pi (V_0 - C)}{V_0} \right] = \frac{2 \cos \frac{\pi x}{2} \sinh \frac{\pi y}{2}}{\sinh^2 \frac{\pi y}{2} - \cos^2 \frac{\pi x}{2}}.$$

They are shown in Figure 7.69.●

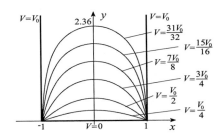

Figure 7.69

Example 7.33 An infinite conducting cylinder with radius 2 has its centre 4 units away from a plane that is parallel to the axis of the cylinder. The cylinder is held at potential V_1 while the plane is at potential V_0. Find potential at all points outside the cylinder on the same side of the plane as the cylinder.

Solution Figure 7.70 shows a cross-section of the cylinder which therefore has its axis perpendicular to the xy-plane. The plane at potential V_0 is represented by the x-axis. To find the potential above the x-axis and outside the circle, we use the technique of Example 7.12 to map the region to an annulus. Consider finding a pair of points z_1 and z_2 that are simultaneously inverses with respect to the x-axis and to the circle . The inverse of z_1 with respect to the x-axis is its conjugate $\overline{z_1}$. According to equation 7.11, z_1 and $\overline{z_1}$ are inverses with respect to the circle if

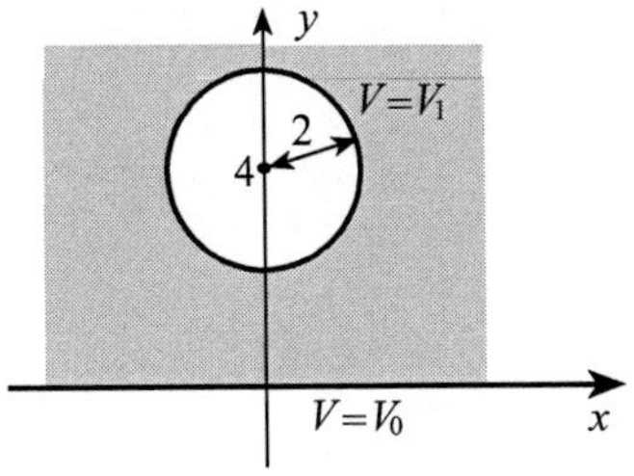

$$\overline{z_1} = 4i + \frac{4}{\overline{z_1} - (-4i)}.$$

Figure 7.70

Solutions of this equation are $z_1 = \pm 2\sqrt{3} i$. The bilinear transformation

$w = f(z) = \dfrac{z - 2\sqrt{3} i}{z + 2\sqrt{3} i}$ maps the region outside the cylinder to an annulus (Figure 7.71). The radius of the image of the circle $|z - 4i| = 2$ is the modulus of the image of any point on the circle; in particular,

$$|f(2i)| = \left| \frac{2i - 2\sqrt{3} i}{2i + 2\sqrt{3} i} \right| = 2 - \sqrt{3}.$$

The radius of the image of the x-axis is the modulus of the image of any point on the axis; in particular,

$$|f(0)| = \left| \frac{-2\sqrt{3}i}{2\sqrt{3}i} \right| = 1.$$

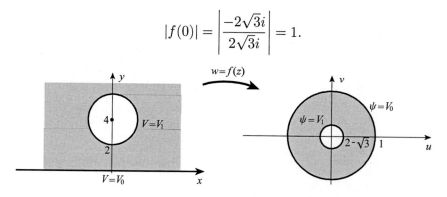

Figure 7.71

Any function of the form $c + d \ln(u^2 + v^2)$ satisfies Laplace's equation, and this function is constant along any circle centred at the origin. If $\psi(u, v) = c + d \ln(u^2 + v^2)$ is to be the solution of Laplace's equation in the annulus satisfying the specified boundary conditions, then c and d are given by the equations

$$V_1 = c + d \ln(2 - \sqrt{3})^2, \quad V_0 = c \quad \Longrightarrow \quad d = \frac{V_1 - V_0}{2 \ln(2 - \sqrt{3})}.$$

Thus,

$$\psi(u, v) = V_0 + \frac{V_1 - V_0}{2 \ln(2 - \sqrt{3})} \ln(u^2 + v^2).$$

To express this in terms of x and y, we could find u and v in terms of x and y. A simpler expression is obtained if we note that $u^2 + v^2 = |w|^2$, and therefore

$$V(x, y) = V_0 + \frac{V_1 - V_0}{2 \ln(2 - \sqrt{3})} \ln|w|^2 = V_0 + \frac{V_1 - V_0}{2 \ln(2 - \sqrt{3})} \ln \left| \frac{z - 2\sqrt{3}i}{z + 2\sqrt{3}i} \right|^2$$

$$= V_0 + \frac{V_1 - V_0}{2 \ln(2 - \sqrt{3})} \ln \left[\frac{x^2 + (y - 2\sqrt{3})^2}{x^2 + (y + 2\sqrt{3})^2} \right]. \bullet$$

Example 7.34   In Figure 7.72a, the horizontal lines $y = \pm d$ for $x < 0$ represent the cross-section of a semi-infinite parallel plate capacitor. If potentials on top and bottom plates are V_0 and $-V_0$, respectively, find equipotentials and lines of force.

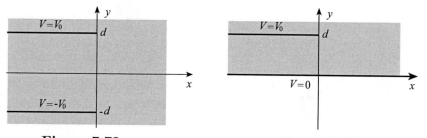

Figure 7.72a   **Figure 7.72b**

Solution   Symmetry indicates that potential along the x-axis is zero for $x < 0$ and $x > 0$, and that potential below the x-axis is the negative of that above the x-axis. We therefore solve the problem in Figure 7.72b where potential is V_0 along the half-line $y = d$ $(x < 0)$ and is 0 along $y = 0$ $(-\infty < x < \infty)$. We begin by mapping the region onto the upper half-plane $\operatorname{Im} \tilde{w} > 0$ with a Schwarz-Christoffel transformation. We regard the region in the z-plane as a degenerate triangle with vertices z_1, z_2, and z_3 in Figure 7.73.

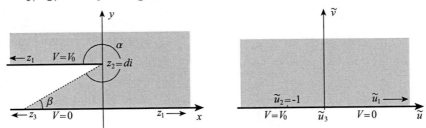

Figure 7.73

Angles α and β at z_2 and z_3 must be made to approach 2π and 0 respectively. Difficulty with the angle at z_1 is eliminated by choosing $\tilde{u}_1$, the pre-image of z_1 as the point at infinity, in which case the angle does not enter the Schwarz-Christoffel transformation. If we choose $\tilde{u}_2 = -1$ and $\tilde{u}_3 = 0$, then taking limits of

$$\frac{dz}{d\tilde{w}} = A(\tilde{w} + 1)^{\alpha/\pi - 1} \tilde{w}^{\beta/\pi - 1}$$

as $\alpha \to 2\pi$ and $\beta \to 0$ gives

$$\frac{dz}{d\tilde{w}} = A\left(\frac{\tilde{w} + 1}{\tilde{w}}\right) = A\left(1 + \frac{1}{\tilde{w}}\right).$$

Integration gives

$$z = A(\tilde{w} + \log_\phi \tilde{w}) + B.$$

If we choose $\phi = -\pi/2$, then for $\tilde{u}_2 = -1$ to map to $z_2 = di$, A and B must satisfy

$$di = A[-1 + \log_{-\pi/2}(-1)] + B = A(-1 + \pi i) + B.$$

This is satisfied if we choose $A = B = d/\pi$, in which case

$$z = \frac{d}{\pi}(1 + \tilde{w} + \log_{-\pi/2} \tilde{w}).$$

It is straightforward to check that this transformation maps the positive $\tilde{u}$-axis to the x-axis, and maps both parts $-\infty < \tilde{u} < -1$ and $-1 < \tilde{u} < 0$ of the negative $\tilde{u}$-axis to the half-line $y = d$, $x < 0$.

We could now use equation 4.38 to find potential in the half-plane $\operatorname{Im} \tilde{w} > 0$ with value V_0 on the negative $\tilde{u}$-axis and value 0 on the positive $\tilde{u}$-axis. Unfortunately, it would not yield a convenient representation for equipotentials and/or lines of force. Instead, we map $\operatorname{Im} \tilde{w} > 0$ to the infinite strip in Figure 7.74 in such a way that the negative $\tilde{u}$-axis is mapped to the line $V = V_0 i$ and the positive $\tilde{u}$-axis is mapped to the u-axis. A mapping that will do this is $w = (V_0/\pi) \log_{-\pi/2} \tilde{w}$.

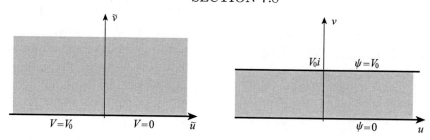

Figure 7.74

Since $\tilde{w} = e^{\pi w/V_0}$, the transformation

$$z = \frac{d}{\pi}\left[1 + e^{\pi w/V_0} + \log_{-\pi/2}\left(e^{\pi w/V_0}\right)\right] = \frac{d}{\pi}\left(1 + e^{\pi w/V_0} + \frac{\pi w}{V_0}\right)$$

therefore maps the strip in Figure 7.74 to the half-space, with u-axis mapped to x-axis, and line $V_0 i$ mapped to half-line $y = d$, $x < 0$.

The solution of Laplace's equation in the strip is $\psi(u,v) = v$. To find potential $V(x,y)$, we would set

$$x + yi = z = \frac{d}{\pi}\left[1 + e^{\pi(u+vi)/V_0} + \frac{\pi(u+vi)}{V_0}\right],$$

and solve for v in terms of x and y, an impossibility. We can, however, find equations for equipotential curves and lines of force. If we take take real and imaginary parts of the above equation,

$$x = \frac{d}{\pi}\left[1 + e^{\pi u/V_0}\cos\frac{\pi v}{V_0} + \frac{\pi u}{V_0}\right], \quad \text{and} \quad y = \frac{d}{\pi}\left[e^{\pi u/V_0}\sin\frac{\pi v}{V_0} + \frac{\pi v}{V_0}\right].$$

Equipotential curves for $y \geq 0$ are therefore defined parametrically by

$$x = \frac{d}{\pi}\left[1 + e^{\pi u/V_0}\cos\frac{\pi V}{V_0} + \frac{\pi u}{V_0}\right], \quad y = \frac{d}{\pi}\left[e^{\pi u/V_0}\sin\frac{\pi V}{V_0} + \frac{\pi V}{V_0}\right],$$

for fixed $V \geq 0$ and u as parameter.

Orthogonal trajectories in the strip are $u = U = $ constant, and therefore lines of force in the xy-plane are given parametrically by

$$x = \frac{d}{\pi}\left[1 + e^{\pi U/V_0}\cos\frac{\pi v}{V_0} + \frac{\pi U}{V_0}\right], \quad y = \frac{d}{\pi}\left[e^{\pi U/V_0}\sin\frac{\pi v}{V_0} + \frac{\pi v}{V_0}\right],$$

for fixed U and v as parameter. Both sets of curves are shown in Figure 7.75.●

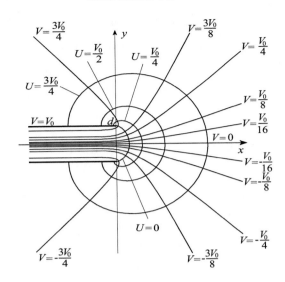

Figure 7.75

EXERCISES 7.8.1

For simplicity in formulation, exercises will be posed in the xy-plane. They are, however, the result of three-dimensional problems for which potential is the same in every plane parallel to the xy-plane.

1. Find potential interior to the wedge $0 \leq \theta \leq \alpha < 2\pi$ if potential along $\theta = 0$, $r > 0$ is V_0, and along $\theta = \alpha$, $r > 0$, potential is V_α.

2. Find potential in the semicircle $x^2 + y^2 < R^2$, $y > 0$ when $V = V_1$ on $y = 0$ and $V = V_0$ on $x^2 + y^2 = R^2$. Hint: Use the mapping $w = i(R - z)/(R + z)$.

3. Find potential in the circle $x^2 + y^2 < R^2$ when potential on that part of the circle in the first quadrant is V_0 and potential on the remainder of the circle is zero. Hint: Use a bilinear transformation that maps the points $z = Ri$, $z = -R$, and $z = R$ to $w = 0$, $w = 1$, and $w = \infty$. What is the potential at the centre of the circle?

4. Find potential in the half-plane $y > 0$ outside the circle $x^2 + y^2 = R^2$ given that potential on the semicircle is V_0 and potential on the x-axis for $|x| > R$ is zero. Hint: Use the bilinear transformation $w = (z - R)/(R + z)$ and Exercise 1.

5. Find potential in the half-plane $y > 0$ outside the circle $x^2 + y^2 = R^2$ given that potential on the semicircle is V_1 and potential on the x-axis for $|x| > R$ is V_0. Hint: Use the bilinear transformation $w = (z - R)/(R + z)$ and Exercise 1.

6. Find potential in the semi-infinite strip $-a < x < a$, $y > 0$ if potential on the horizontal side is V_0 and that on the vertical sides is V_1.

7. Find potential in the semi-infinite strip $-a < y < a$, $x > 0$ if potential on the horizontal sides is V_0 and that on the vertical side is V_1. Hint: Use the transformation $w = i \sinh [\pi z/(2a)]$.

8. Find potential in the domain bounded by that part of $x^2 + y^2 = a^2$ above the x-axis and that part of $x^2 + (y - a)^2 = 2a^2$ below the x-axis. Potential on $x^2 + y^2 = a^2$ is V_0, and potential on

$x^2 + (y-a)^2 = 2a^2$ is V_1. Hint: First map the domain to the sector $\pi/2 < \arg w^* < 5\pi/4$ by $w^* = (z-a)/(z+a)$, and then map the sector to an infinite strip with $w = \log_{-\pi/2} w^* - \pi i/2$.

9. Find potential at points in the half-plane $y > 0$ that are outside the circle $x^2 + (y-a)^2 = a^2$ given that potential on the circle is a constant V_0 and potential on $y = 0$ is a constant V_1. Hint: Try $w = -2a/z$. Find equipotential curves.

10. A circle with radius R has its centre $a > R$ units away from a line. The circle is held at potential V_1 while the line is at potential V_0. Find potential at all points outside the circle on the same side of the line as the circle. Hint: Use the bilinear transformation in Exercise 29 of Section 7.2 to map the problem to that in an annulus.

11. Two conducting circles have equations $x^2 + (y-2)^2 = 4$ and $x^2 + y^2 = 25$. The inner circle is held at potential V_0, and the outer one is held at potential V_1. Find the potential between the circles. Hint: Use a bilinear transformation like that in Exercise 30 of Section 7.2 to map the region to an annulus.

12. Two arcs are parts of the circles
$x^2 + (y-R)^2 = R^2$ and $(x-R)^2 + y^2 = R^2$
(figure to the right). The lower arc is held
at potential V_0, and the upper one is held
at potential V_1. Find the potential
between the arcs. Hint: First, use a bilinear
transformation with $z = R(1+i)$ as pole
and $z = 0$ as zero. Then map the image to
the first quadrant and use Exercise 19 of
Section 7.5.

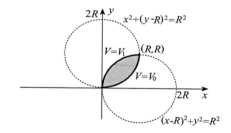

13. Two circles $(x-a)^2 + y^2 = a^2$ and $(x-b)^2 + y^2 = b^2$, where $b > a$, are held at constant potentials V_0 and $V_1 > V_0$, respectively. The point of contact of the circles is separated by perfect insullation.
(a) Find potential between the circles.
(b) Find and draw equipotential curves.

14. The x-axis to the left of $x = -1$ is held at constant potential $V = V_0$, and the x-axis to the right of $x = 1$ is held at potential $V = 0$. Find the resulting potential in the xy-plane. Hint: Consider the mapping $w = \mathrm{Cos}^{-1} z$, and see Exercises 44 and 39 in Section 3.7. Find and draw equipotential curves.

15. Use the transformation of Exercise 34 in Section 7.2 to show that the potential in the region exterior to the two circles in the figure below can be expressed in the form

$$V(x,y) = V_a + \frac{V_b - V_a}{\ln \rho} \ln \left| \frac{[R\rho(1-\rho) + 2\rho(a-R)]z + [R\rho(1-\rho)(a-R) - 2\rho(a^2 - R^2)]}{[R(1-\rho) - 2\rho(a-R)]z + R(1-\rho)(a-R) + 2\rho(a^2 - R^2)]} \right|.$$

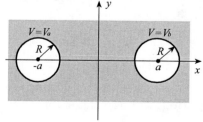

§7.8.2 Electrostatic Potential With Sources

In the previous subsection, electrostatic potential in a domain D was the result of surfaces bounding D being held at constant potentials. In this subsection we introduce line charges as additional factors affecting potential. To begin with, consider a line of charge q coulombs per metre perpendicular to the xy-plane at the origin (Figure 7.76). We use Coulomb's law to find the potential in space due to the line of charge rather than working with Laplace's equation.

The electric field intensity $\mathbf{E}$ due to this line of charge is always parallel to the xy-plane, and is therefore a function of x and y only. By definition, $\mathbf{E}$ is the force on a unit positive charge placed in the field. With Coulomb's law, we obtain for the magnitude of $\mathbf{E}$ at (x, y),

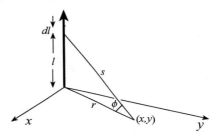

Figure 7.76

$$|\mathbf{E}| = 2 \int_0^\infty \cos\phi \, \frac{q(1)}{4\pi\epsilon_0 s^2} dl = \frac{rq}{2\pi\epsilon_0} \int_0^\infty \frac{1}{(r^2 + l^2)^{3/2}} dl.$$

Since $l = r \tan\phi$, we change variables of integration,

$$|\mathbf{E}| = \frac{rq}{2\pi\epsilon_0} \int_0^{\pi/2} \frac{r\sec^2\phi}{r^3 \sec^3\phi} d\phi = \frac{q}{2\pi\epsilon_0 r} \int_0^{\pi/2} \cos\phi \, d\phi = \frac{q}{2\pi\epsilon_0 r} = \frac{q}{2\pi\epsilon_0 \sqrt{x^2 + y^2}}.$$

Since $\mathbf{E}$ is directed radially away from the line of charge,

$$\mathbf{E} = \frac{q}{2\pi\epsilon_0 \sqrt{x^2 + y^2}} \frac{x\hat{\mathbf{i}} + y\hat{\mathbf{j}}}{\sqrt{x^2 + y^2}} = \frac{q}{2\pi\epsilon_0 (x^2 + y^2)} (x\hat{\mathbf{i}} + y\hat{\mathbf{j}}).$$

Because the electric field is the negative of the gradient of the potential ($\mathbf{E} = -\nabla V$, see equation 3.62), it follows that

$$\frac{\partial V}{\partial x} = -\frac{qx}{2\pi\epsilon_0 (x^2 + y^2)}, \qquad \frac{\partial V}{\partial y} = -\frac{qy}{2\pi\epsilon_0 (x^2 + y^2)}.$$

These give

$$V(x, y) = \frac{-q}{4\pi\epsilon_0} \ln(x^2 + y^2) + D, \tag{7.43}$$

where D is a real constant, as the real potential due to a line of charge q coulombs per metre at the origin. We know that the function $\ln\sqrt{x^2 + y^2}$ is the real part of the complex function $\log_\phi z$. Hence, the complex potential function associated with a line charge q coulombs per metre at the origin is

$$F(z) = \frac{-q}{2\pi\epsilon_0} \log_\phi z + (D + Ei). \tag{7.44}$$

When the line of charge is at the point (x_0, y_0), the real potential is

$$V(x, y) = \frac{-q}{4\pi\epsilon_0} \ln[(x - x_0)^2 + (y - y_0)^2] + D, \tag{7.45}$$

and the complex electrostatic potential is

$$F(z) = \frac{-q}{2\pi\epsilon_0} \log_\phi (z - z_0) + (D + Ei), \qquad (7.46)$$

where $z_0 = x_0 + y_0 i$. In the following examples, we introduce multiple line charges into space and/or the presence of bounding surfaces.

Example 7.35   A line charge has q coulombs per metre. If potential at a distance R from the charge is V_R, find potential at a distance r from the charge.

Solution   According to equation 7.45, potential at a point (x, y) due to a line charge at (x_0, y_0) is

$$V(x, y) = \frac{-q}{4\pi\epsilon_0} \ln[(x - x_0)^2 + (y - y_0)^2] + D.$$

Since potential on the circle $(x - x_0)^2 + (y - y_0)^2 = R^2$ is V_R,

$$V_R = \frac{-q}{4\pi\epsilon_0} \ln(R^2) + D \qquad \Longrightarrow \qquad D = V_R + \frac{k}{2\pi\epsilon_0} \ln R.$$

Thus,

$$V(x, y) = \frac{-q}{4\pi\epsilon_0} \ln\left[\frac{(x - x_0)^2 + (y - y_0)^2}{R^2}\right] + V_R.$$

If $V(r)$ represents potential at a distance r from the source, then

$$V(r) = V_R - \frac{q}{2\pi\epsilon_0} \ln(r/R). \bullet$$

It is important to realize that the development of equations 7.43–7.46 and the discussion in Example 7.35 took place in all space. There were no boundaries to consider that might affect potential; potential was due only to a line of charge. In the presence of boundaries at designated potentials, equations 7.43–7.46 might, or might not, be a correct description of potential. For instance, suppose that in Example 7.35, a circular cylinder of radius R at potential V_R has the line charge along its axis. Because the cylinder is coincident with an equipotential surface for the line charge, potential inside the cylinder is exactly as in the example. In other words, the presence of this particular bounding surface does not affect the potential function, only its domain of definition. On the other hand, if the line charge is outside the cylinder, finding potential outside the cylinder is more difficult (see Exercise 3).

In preparation for the next example, we note that the real (or complex) potential function due to multiple line charges (in space) is simply the sum of their real (or, complex) potential functions.

Example 7.36   Find the real electrostatic potential due to a line of charge q coulombs per metre perpendicular to the xy-plane at (x_0, y_0), and a line of charge $-q$ coulombs per metre perpendicular to the xy-plane at (x_1, y_1). Find equipotentials and lines of force when $y_0 = y_1 = 0$ and $x_0 = -x_1 = a > 0$.

Solution   If we add potentials due to the line charges, and set $z_0 = x_0 + y_0 i$ and $z_1 = x_1 + y_1 i$, equation 7.46 gives the complex electrostatic potential as

$$F(z) = \frac{q}{2\pi\epsilon_0}[\log_\psi (z - z_1) - \log_\phi (z - z_0)] + (D + Ei).$$

The real electrostatic potential is

$$V(x,y) = \mathrm{Re}[F(z)] = \frac{q}{2\pi\epsilon_0}[\ln \sqrt{(x - x_1)^2 + (y - y_1)^2} - \ln \sqrt{(x - x_0)^2 + (y - y_0)^2}] + D$$

$$= \frac{q}{4\pi\epsilon_0} \ln \left[\frac{(x - x_1)^2 + (y - y_1)^2}{(x - x_0)^2 + (y - y_0)^2}\right] + D.$$

Equipotentials are defined by

$$\frac{q}{4\pi\epsilon_0} \ln \left[\frac{(x - x_1)^2 + (y - y_1)^2}{(x - x_0)^2 + (y - y_0)^2}\right] = C = \text{constant},$$

and this equation can be expressed in the form

$$\frac{(x - x_1)^2 + (y - y_1)^2}{(x - x_0)^2 + (y - y_0)^2} = A, \qquad A = e^{4\pi\epsilon_0 C/q}.$$

For $y_0 = y_1 = 0$ and $x_0 = -x_1 = a$, this equation reduces to

$$\frac{(x + a)^2 + y^2}{(x - a)^2 + y^2} = A.$$

When $A = 1$, the equipotential becomes the line $x = 0$. When $A > 1$, the equipotential can be written in the form

$$\left[x - a\left(\frac{A + 1}{A - 1}\right)\right]^2 + y^2 = \left[\left(\frac{A + 1}{A - 1}\right)^2 - 1\right]a^2,$$

a circle with centre on the positive x-axis enclosing charge q at $(a, 0)$. When $A < 1$, the equipotential reduces to

$$\left[x + a\left(\frac{1 + A}{1 - A}\right)\right]^2 + y^2 = \left[\left(\frac{1 + A}{1 - A}\right)^2 - 1\right]a^2,$$

a circle with centre on the negative x-axis enclosing charge $-q$ at $(-a, 0)$. We have shown some of these equipotentials in Figure 7.77.

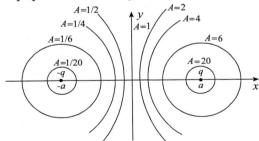

Figure 7.77

Lines of force are the orthogonal trajectories of these two families of circles. They are defined by $\mathrm{Im}\,[F(z)] = $ constant; that is

$$\frac{q}{2\pi\epsilon_0}[\arg_\psi(z - z_1) - \arg_\phi(z - z_0)] = \text{constant}.$$

This equation can be expressed in the form

$$\tan^{-1}\left(\frac{y-y_1}{x-x_1}\right) - \tan^{-1}\left(\frac{y-y_0}{x-x_0}\right) = \text{constant} = B.$$

For $y_0 = y_1 = 0$ and $x_0 = -x_1 = a$,

$$\tan^{-1}\left(\frac{y}{x+a}\right) - \tan^{-1}\left(\frac{y}{x-a}\right) = B.$$

Taking tangents of both sides of this equation gives

$$\frac{\dfrac{y}{x+a} - \dfrac{y}{x-a}}{1 + \dfrac{y^2}{x^2-a^2}} = \tan B,$$

and this simplifies to $D(x^2 + y^2 - a^2) = -2ay$, where $D = \tan B$. When $D = 0$, we obtain $y = 0$. When $D \neq 0$, we rewrite the equation in the form

$$x^2 + \left(y + \frac{a}{D}\right)^2 = \frac{a^2}{D^2}(D^2 + 1).$$

These are circles passing through q and $-q$ (Figure 7.78).●

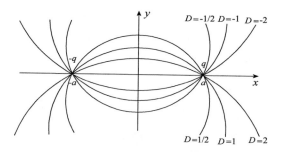

Figure 7.78

The following example leads to a technique that is often useful in handling line charges in the presence of conducting boundaries.

Example 7.37 A line charge of q coulombs per metre is located at the point (x_0, y_0) and is perpendicular to the xy-plane. A plane containing the x-axis, and perpendicular to the xy-plane, is held at potential V_0. Find potential in the half space $y > 0$. Find and draw equipotentials.

Solution We model the three-dimensional situation with the x-axis representing the plane and a point source at (x_0, y_0) (Figure 7.79). To make use of complex potential function 7.44 for potential due to a source in the absence of boundaries, we map the half-plane $y > 0$ to the interior of the unit circle $|w| = 1$ in such a way that the source is mapped to the origin and the x-axis is mapped to the unit circle. Although the circle $|w| = 1$ is a boundary for the region, the fact that it is at constant potential makes it compatible with a source at the origin with no boundary where equipotentials are circles centred at the origin. A bilinear transformation will perform the mapping. According to Exercise 25 in Section 7.2, all bilinear transformations that map the half-plane $y > 0$ to the unit circle and take a point z_0 to $w = 0$ are of the form $w = e^{\lambda i}(z - z_0)/(z - \overline{z_0})$, for some real constant λ. If we arbitrarily set $\lambda = 0$ and choose $z_0 = x_0 + y_0 i$, then

$$w = \frac{z - z_0}{z - \overline{z_0}}.$$

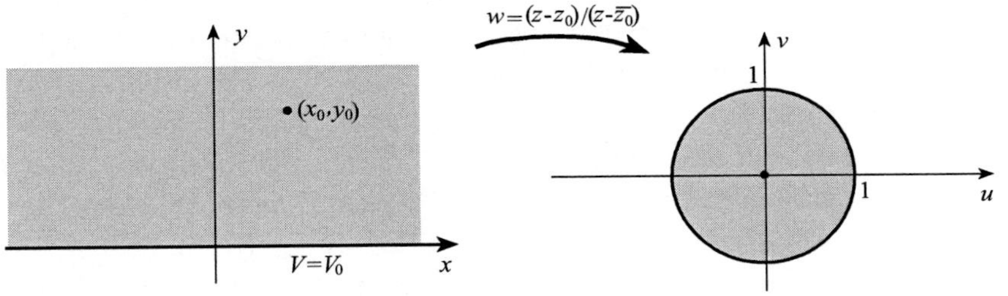

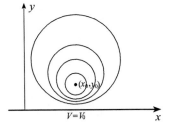

$w=(z-z_0)/(z-\overline{z_0})$

Figure 7.79

The complex potential function in the w-plane due to the source at the origin must be of the form

$$G(w) = -\frac{q}{2\pi\epsilon_0}\log_\phi w + (D + Ei),$$

and therefore the complex potential function in the z-plane is

$$F(z) = -\frac{q}{2\pi\epsilon_0}\log_\phi\left(\frac{z - z_0}{z - \overline{z_0}}\right) + (D + Ei).$$

The real potential function is

$$V(x, y) = \text{Re}\,[F(z)] = \frac{q}{2\pi\epsilon_0}\ln\left|\frac{z - \overline{z_0}}{z - z_0}\right| + D.$$

Since potential along $y = 0$ is V_0, we must have

$$V_0 = \frac{q}{2\pi\epsilon_0}\ln\left|\frac{x - x_0 + y_0 i}{x - x_0 - y_0 i}\right| + D = D.$$

Thus,

$$V(x, y) = V_0 + \frac{q}{4\pi\epsilon_0}\ln\left[\frac{(x - x_0)^2 + (y + y_0)^2}{(x - x_0)^2 + (y - y_0)^2}\right].$$

Equipotential curves are defined implicitly by

$$C = V_0 + \frac{q}{4\pi\epsilon_0}\ln\left[\frac{(x - x_0)^2 + (y + y_0)^2}{(x - x_0)^2 + (y - y_0)^2}\right].$$

If we define $k = e^{2\pi\epsilon_0(C - V_0)/q}$, it is a straightforward exercise in algebra to show that this equation can be rewritten in the form

$$(x - x_0)^2 + (y - y_0\coth k)^2 = y_0^2\text{csch}^2 k.$$

These are circles with centres at $(x_0, y_0\coth k)$ some of which are shown in Figure 7.80.•

Figure 7.80

It is instructive to write the complex potential function in this example in the following form

$$F(z) = V_0 - \frac{q}{2\pi\epsilon_0} \log_\phi (z - z_0) + \frac{q}{2\pi\epsilon_0} \log_\phi (z - \overline{z_0}) + Ei.$$

It is V_0 plus the sum of two complex potential functions, one due to a positive line charge at z_0 and the other due to a negative line charge at $\overline{z_0}$. The two charges result in a potential of zero along the x-axis. This suggests an alternative technique for solving Example 7.37, a technique called the *method of images*. The given problem with a charge and a boundary with prescribed potential is replaced by a problem with the original charge and a second charge so that the two together yield potential zero on the boundary. To this is added the constant potential V_0. In the example, the negative charge is at the image of the positive charge in the x-axis. In some configurations, more than one image charge may be required, or the image may be in some other line, or even a circle (see Exercise 2 for the case of a circle). We use a conformal mapping and the method of images in the following example.

Example 7.38   Two infinite parallel plates separated by a distance a are both at potential V_0. If a line charge of q coulombs per metre is a distance b from one of the plates, determine the electrostatic potential between the plates. Find and plot equipotentials.

Solution   We reduce the problem to two dimensions by modelling the plates as the lines $y = 0$ and $y = a$. The line charge passes through the point $(0, b)$ on the y-axis (Figure 7.81).

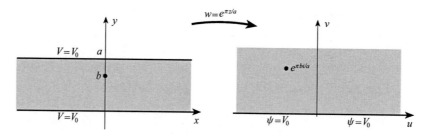

Figure 7.81

The transformation $w = e^{\pi z/a}$ maps the strip between the plates to the half-plane $\operatorname{Im} w > 0$, with the point $z = b$ mapped to $w = e^{\pi bi/a}$. To solve the potential problem in the w-plane, we mometarily replace the boundary condition $\psi = V_0$ with $\psi = 0$. A charge configuration of q at $w = e^{\pi bi/a}$ and $-q$ at the complex conjugate point $w = e^{-\pi bi/a}$ produces zero potential on the real w-axis. Consequently, the complex electrostatic potential in the upper-half of the w-plane when the boundary condition is $V = 0$ is

$$G(w) = -\frac{q}{2\pi\epsilon_0} \log_\phi (w - e^{\pi bi/a}) + \frac{q}{2\pi\epsilon_0} \log_\psi (w - e^{-\pi bi/a}) + (D + Ei).$$

The complex potential when the boundary condition is $V = V_0$ is then

$$G(w) = V_0 - \frac{q}{2\pi\epsilon_0} \log_\phi (w - e^{\pi bi/a}) + \frac{q}{2\pi\epsilon_0} \log_\psi (w - e^{-\pi bi/a}) + (D + Ei).$$

The complex electrostatic potential between the parallel lines in the z-plane is

$$F(z) = V_0 - \frac{q}{2\pi\epsilon_0} \log_\phi (e^{\pi z/a} - e^{\pi bi/a}) + \frac{q}{2\pi\epsilon_0} \log_\psi (e^{\pi z/a} - e^{-\pi bi/a}) + (D + Ei).$$

The real potential is

$$V(x,y) = \operatorname{Re}\left[F(z)\right] = V_0 + \frac{q}{2\pi\epsilon_0}\operatorname{Re}\left[\log_\psi\left(e^{\pi z/a} - e^{-\pi bi/a}\right) - \log_\phi\left(e^{\pi z/a} - e^{\pi bi/a}\right)\right] + D$$

$$= V_0 + \frac{q}{2\pi\epsilon_0}\operatorname{Re}\left[\log_\psi\left(e^{\pi(x+yi)/a} - e^{-\pi bi/a}\right) - \log_\phi\left(e^{\pi(x+yi)/a} - e^{\pi bi/a}\right)\right] + D$$

$$= V_0 + \frac{q}{2\pi\epsilon_0}\operatorname{Re}\left\{\log_\psi\left[\left(e^{\pi x/a}\cos\frac{\pi y}{a} - \cos\frac{\pi b}{a}\right) + \left(e^{\pi x/a}\sin\frac{\pi y}{a} + \sin\frac{\pi b}{a}\right)i\right]\right.$$

$$\left. - \log_\phi\left[\left(e^{\pi x/a}\cos\frac{\pi y}{a} - \cos\frac{\pi b}{a}\right) + \left(e^{\pi x/a}\sin\frac{\pi y}{a} - \sin\frac{\pi b}{a}\right)i\right]\right\} + D$$

$$= V_0 + \frac{q}{2\pi\epsilon_0}\left\{\ln\sqrt{\left(e^{\pi x/a}\cos\frac{\pi y}{a} - \cos\frac{\pi b}{a}\right)^2 + \left(e^{\pi x/a}\sin\frac{\pi y}{a} + \sin\frac{\pi b}{a}\right)^2}\right.$$

$$\left. - \ln\sqrt{\left(e^{\pi x/a}\cos\frac{\pi y}{a} - \cos\frac{\pi b}{a}\right)^2 + \left(e^{\pi x/a}\sin\frac{\pi y}{a} - \sin\frac{\pi b}{a}\right)^2}\right\} + D$$

$$= V_0 + \frac{q}{4\pi\epsilon_0}\ln\left[\frac{\left(e^{\pi x/a}\cos\frac{\pi y}{a} - \cos\frac{\pi b}{a}\right)^2 + \left(e^{\pi x/a}\sin\frac{\pi y}{a} + \sin\frac{\pi b}{a}\right)^2}{\left(e^{\pi x/a}\cos\frac{\pi y}{a} - \cos\frac{\pi b}{a}\right)^2 + \left(e^{\pi x/a}\sin\frac{\pi y}{a} - \sin\frac{\pi b}{a}\right)^2}\right] + D$$

$$= V_0 + \frac{q}{4\pi\epsilon_0}\ln\left[\frac{e^{2\pi x/a} + 1 + 2e^{\pi x/a}\left(\sin\frac{\pi y}{a}\sin\frac{\pi b}{a} - \cos\frac{\pi y}{a}\cos\frac{\pi b}{a}\right)}{e^{2\pi x/a} + 1 - 2e^{\pi x/a}\left(\cos\frac{\pi y}{a}\cos\frac{\pi b}{a} + \sin\frac{\pi y}{a}\sin\frac{\pi b}{a}\right)}\right] + D$$

$$= V_0 + \frac{q}{4\pi\epsilon_0}\ln\left[\frac{e^{2\pi x/a} + 1 - 2e^{\pi x/a}\cos\frac{\pi(y+b)}{a}}{e^{2\pi x/a} + 1 - 2e^{\pi x/a}\cos\frac{\pi(y-b)}{a}}\right] + D$$

$$= V_0 + \frac{q}{4\pi\epsilon_0}\ln\left[\frac{\cosh\frac{\pi x}{a} - \cos\frac{\pi(y+b)}{a}}{\cosh\frac{\pi x}{a} - \cos\frac{\pi(y-b)}{a}}\right] + D.$$

Either of the conditions that $V = V_0$ along $y = 0$ or $y = a$ leads to $D = 0$. Equipotentials are defined implicitly by the equation

$$C = V_0 + \frac{q}{4\pi\epsilon_0}\ln\left[\frac{\cosh\frac{\pi x}{a} - \cos\frac{\pi(y+b)}{a}}{\cosh\frac{\pi x}{a} - \cos\frac{\pi(y-b)}{a}}\right].$$

They are shown in Figure 7.82.•

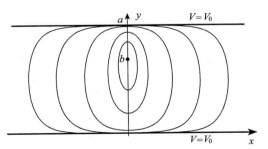

Figure 7.82

EXERCISES 7.8.2

1. The positive x-axis and a half-line from the origin at a positive rotation of angle α are both held at potential V_0. A line charge of q coulombs per metre, perpendicular to the xy-plane, is at the point $z_0 = Re^{\phi i}$ between the lines. Show that the electrostatic potential between the lines is

$$V(r,\theta) = V_0 + \frac{q}{4\pi\epsilon_0} \ln \left[\frac{r^{2\pi/\alpha} + R^{2\pi/\alpha} - 2r^{\pi/\alpha}R^{\pi/\alpha} \cos\dfrac{\pi(\theta+\phi)}{\alpha}}{r^{2\pi/\alpha} + R^{2\pi/\alpha} - 2r^{\pi/\alpha}R^{\pi/\alpha} \cos\dfrac{\pi(\theta-\phi)}{\alpha}} \right].$$

2. A line charge of q coulombs per metre of length is located at the point $x = a$ in the xy-plane. Surrounding the charge is a circle of radius R, centred at the origin, that is held at potential V_0.

   (a) Find the potential inside the circle by mapping the situation to a circle with the line charge at the centre of the circle.

   (b) Show that if a negative line charge is placed at the inverse point of the positive one in the circle (see equation 7.11 in Section 7.2), then their combination leads to the required potential. This is an example of the method of images where the image is the inverse point in a circle.

3. A line charge of q coulombs per metre is at $x = a$ on the x-axis. A conducting circle of radius R $(R < a)$, centred at the origin, is held at potential V_0. Show that the electrostatic potential outside the circle is

$$V(x,y) = V_0 + \frac{q}{4\pi\epsilon_0} \ln \left\{ \frac{(ax - R^2)^2 + a^2 y^2}{R^2[(x-a)^2 + y^2]} \right\}.$$

4. A semi-infinite channel consists of the region bounded by the x-axis, $-a \le x \le a$, and the lines $x = \pm a$, $y \ge 0$. Each of the lines is at potential V_0. A line charge of q coulombs per metre perpendicular to the xy-plane is located at the point $(0,b)$. Show that the potential in the channel is

$$V(x,y) = V_0 + \frac{q}{4\pi\epsilon_0} \ln \left(\frac{\sin^2\dfrac{\pi x}{2a} + \sinh^2\dfrac{\pi y}{2a} + \sinh^2\dfrac{\pi b}{2a} + 2\cos\dfrac{\pi x}{2a}\sinh\dfrac{\pi y}{2a}\sinh\dfrac{\pi b}{2a}}{\sin^2\dfrac{\pi x}{2a} + \sinh^2\dfrac{\pi y}{2a} + \sinh^2\dfrac{\pi b}{2a} - 2\cos\dfrac{\pi x}{2a}\sinh\dfrac{\pi y}{2a}\sinh\dfrac{\pi b}{2a}} \right).$$

5. The positive x- and y-axes have potential V_0. A line charge of q coulombs per metre, at the point (x_0, y_0), is perpendicular to the xy-plane.

   (a) Use the method of images with an equal line charge at $(-x_0, -y_0)$ and negative line charges of the same strength at the points $(-x_0, y_0)$ and $(x_0, -y_0)$ to show that potential in the first quadrant can be expresed in the form

$$V(x,y) = V_0 + \frac{q}{4\pi\epsilon_0} \ln \left\{ \frac{[(x-x_0)^2 + (y+y_0)^2][(x+x_0)^2 + (y-y_0)^2]}{[(x-x_0)^2 + (y-y_0)^2][(x+x_0)^2 + (y+y_0)^2]} \right\}.$$

   (b) Use the mapping $w = z^2$ and Example 7.37 to write the potential in the form

$$V(r,\theta) = V_0 + \frac{q}{4\pi\epsilon_0} \ln \left\{ \frac{r^4 + R^4 - 2r^2 R^2 \cos[2(\theta+\phi)]}{r^4 + R^4 - 2r^2 R^2 \cos[2(\theta-\phi)]} \right\},$$

where $z_0 = Re^{\phi i}$.

(c) Show that the results in parts (a) and (b) are the same.

6. The semicircle $x^2 + y^2 = R^2$, $y > 0$ and the x-axis for $|x| \geq R$ are at potential V_0. A line charge of q coulombs per metre perpendicular to the xy-plane is at the point $z_0 = ae^{\phi i}$, where $a > R$. Show that the potential in the half-plane $y > 0$ outside the semicircle is

$$V(r,\theta) = V_0 + \frac{q}{4\pi\epsilon_0} \ln \left\{ \frac{[r^2 + a^2 - 2ar\cos(\theta + \phi)][a^2 R^2 + 1 - 2ar\cos(\theta - \phi)]}{[r^2 + a^2 - 2ar\cos(\theta - \phi)][a^2 R^2 + 1 - 2ar\cos(\theta + \phi)]} \right\}.$$

Hint: Map the region of interest to the half-plane $v > 0$ with $w = z + 1/z$ and use Example 7.37.

7. The positive x-axis is held at potential V_0, and there is a line of charge q coulombs per metre, perpendicular to the xy-plane, at the point $z_0 = Re^{\phi i}$. Use Exercise 1 to find electrostatic potential in the xy-plane.

§7.9   Fluid Flow

§7.9.1 Fluid Flow Without Sources

In Section 3.10 we associated a complex potential

$$F(z) = \phi(x, y) + \psi(x, y)i \tag{7.47}$$

in domains of incompressible, irrotational, steady-state, two-dimensional flow. The function $\phi(x, y)$ is the velocity potential, and velocity $\mathbf{q}$ of the flow at any point is the gradient of $\phi(x, y)$,

$$\mathbf{q} = \frac{\partial \phi}{\partial x}\hat{\mathbf{i}} + \frac{\partial \phi}{\partial y}\hat{\mathbf{j}}. \tag{7.48}$$

Alternatively, components of $\mathbf{q}$ are real and imaginary parts of $\overline{F'(z)}$. The harmonic conjugate $\psi(x, y)$ of $\phi(x, y)$ is the stream function. Motion of the fluid is along stream curves $\psi(x, y) = C$. In this section, we use conformal mappings to discuss flow patterns associated with various geometries. Fundamental to our discussions is the complex potential for uniform flow over a half-plane. When fluid flows with

constant speed U in the positive x-direction over the half-plane $y > 0$, its velocity is $\mathbf{q} = U\hat{\mathbf{i}}$ (Figure 7.83). The velocity potential is $\phi(x, y) = Ux + A$, A a real constant, and the stream function is $\psi(x, y) = Uy + B$, B a real constant. The complex potential is

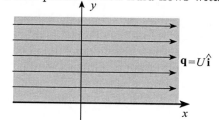

$$F(z) = \phi + \psi i = Uz + A + Bi.$$

Figure 7.83

By choosing $B = 0$ we obtain the natural situation where the boundary $y = 0$ of the flow corresponds to the stream function $\psi = 0$. With $A = 0$, the velocity equipotential $\phi = 0$ corresponds to the line $x = 0$. The complex potential for uniform flow in the positive x-direction over the half-plane $y > 0$ can therefore be taken as

$$F(z) = Uz. \tag{7.49}$$

This is also the complex potential for uniform flow in the positive x-direction for the whole xy-plane.

In solving heat flow and electrostatic problems, the emphasis is on finding a function that satisfies Laplace's equation in some domain, and also satisfies Dirichlet and/or Neumann conditions on the boundary of the domain. In the above discussion for uniform flow for a half-plane, we did not solve Laplace's equation for $\phi(x, y)$ or $\psi(x, y)$. Is this what we should expect in all fluid flow problems? The answer is yes and no. A typical flow problem would be flow around an object in a channel (Figure 7.84).

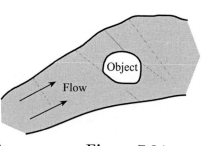

Figure 7.84

The problem is to find stream curves for this geometry; that is, find curves $\psi(x,y) = C$ along which particles of the fluid flow. Certainly, the stream function $\psi(x,y)$ must be harmonic, a solution of Laplace's equation. Furthermore, each distinct part of the boundary of the flow must be a stream curve; that is, along each part of the boundary, $\psi(x,y)$ must be equal to a constant, $\psi(x,y) = C$. In effect, we are saying that to solve the flow problem, we must find the solution $\psi(x,y)$ of Laplace's equation such that parts of the boundary of the flow have equations of the form $\psi(x,y) = C$. We see then, that Laplace's equation is a part of flow problems. Having said this, we do not deal with Laplace's equation in solving flow problems; we take a completely different tact. We use conformal mappings because they map flows to flows. By this we mean the following. Suppose that $F(z)$ is the complex potential for flow in some domain D. Suppose that $w = f(z)$ is a 1-1 analytic function conformally mapping D to $f(D)$, the boundary $\beta(D)$ of D to the boundary $\beta[f(D)]$ of $f(D)$, and the interior of D to the interior of $f(D)$. Then the function $F[f^{-1}(w)]$ is the complex potential for flow in $f(D)$. We state this formally.

Theorem 7.9   If $F(z)$ is a complex potential for flow in a domain D, and $w = f(z)$ is a conformal mapping of D to $f(D)$, then $F[f^{-1}(w)]$ is a complex potential for flow in $f(D)$.

Proof   To verify this we must show that $F[f^{-1}(w)]$ is analytic in $f(D)$, and that the boundary $\beta[f(D)]$ is a stream curve. Since $f(z)$ is conformal, its derivative does not vanish in D, and therefore the derivative of $f^{-1}(w)$ exists at each point in $f(D)$. Since $F(z)$ is analytic, it follows that $F[f^{-1}(w)]$ is analytic in $f(D)$. To verify that $\beta[f(D)]$ is a stream curve, we prove that the imaginary part of $F[f^{-1}(w)]$ is constant along parts of $\beta[f(D)]$. Suppose $F(z) = \phi(x,y) + \psi(x,y)i$ so that the stream function $\psi(x,y)$ is constant along parts of $\beta(D)$. Let its value along a part C_j of the boundary be $\psi(x,y) = k$. We may regard $\psi(x,y) = k$ as the equation of C_j, and therefore the image $f(C_j)$ of C_j under $w = f(z)$ has equation $\psi[x(u,v), y(u,v)] = k$. But the real and imaginary parts of $F(f^{-1}(w)]$ can be expressed in terms of real and imaginary parts of w as follows,

$$F[f^{-1}(w)] = \phi[x(u,v), y(u,v)] + \psi[x(u,v), y(u,v)]i.$$

Hence, the imaginary parts of $F[f^{-1}(w)]$ is constant along $f(C_j)$. ∎

We illustrate these ideas in the following example.

Example 7.39   Use the transformation $w = \sqrt{z}$ to map uniform flow left to right in the half-plane $y > 0$ with speed U to flow in a quarter plane. Draw stream curves and find the velocity and speed of the flow.

Solution   The transformation $w = \sqrt{z}$ maps the half-plane $y > 0$ to the quarter plane $u > 0$, $v > 0$ as shown in Figure 7.85.

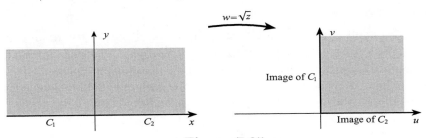

Figure 7.85

Since the complex potential for uniform flow in the z-plane is $F(z) = Uz$, the complex potential for flow in the w-plane is $G(w) = Uw^2$. Stream curves are $C = \psi(u,v) = \operatorname{Im}(Uw^2) = 2Uuv$, rectangular hyperbolas asymptotic to the positive u- and v-axes (Figure 7.86). Notice that the stream curve $\psi(u,v) = 0$ defines the boundary of the flow, the x- and y-axes. Since $\overline{G'(w)} = 2U\overline{w} = 2U(u - vi)$, the velocity of the flow at any point is

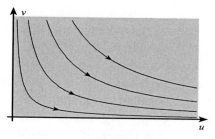

Figure 7.86

$$\mathbf{q} = 2U(u\hat{\mathbf{i}} - v\hat{\mathbf{j}}).$$

The u-component is always positive and the v-component is always negative. In other words, flow is always downward and to the right. The speed of the flow is $|\mathbf{q}| = 2U\sqrt{u^2 + v^2}$; it is proportional to the distance from the origin. The origin is a stagnation point of the flow.•

Conformal transformations map flows to flows; they map stream curves to stream curves and complex potentials to complex potentials. To use this in applications, we need one additional fact, that for a given geometry, flow and its mathematical description by means of the complex potential are in some sense unique. Clearly flow itself is not unique for a given geometry. For example, uniform flow left to right in the xy-plane is not unique; it is always along horizontal lines, but the speed of the flow is arbitrary. Speed is constant, but arbitrary. In other words, for given geometry, the flow "pattern" is unique; variability lies in some overall "strength" factor. For uniform flow in the positive x-direction, this is manifested as far as the complex potential $F(z) = Uz$ is concerned in the multiplicative factor U. Thus, the complex potential for a given flow geometry is subject to the variability of the strength of the flow. A complex constant may also be added to the complex potential. It has no effect on the flow pattern (or its strength) since velocity of the flow is related to the real and imaginary parts of the derivative of $F(z)$. Customarily this constant is determined by specifying that the stream function vanish on some boundary of the flow, and also specifying that one of the equipotentials be identified by $\phi = 0$.

Consider now the problem of finding the flow pattern in a given domain D of the xy-plane, which, based on the above discussion is unique. The flow itself is subject to a strength factor and an additive constant, but the pattern is unique. Suppose that we can find a conformal transformation $w = f(z)$ mapping D onto a domain $f(D)$ in the w-plane, and that the flow pattern, through the complex potential $G(w)$, is known in $f(D)$. It follows then that the flow pattern for D is described by the complex potential $F(z) = G[f(z)]$.

In many practical problems we have the situation where an otherwise uniform flow in the z-plane is interrrupted by an object. To determine the flow pattern around the obstacle, we find a conformal transformation $w = f(z)$ that maps the flow domain in the z-plane to a known flow pattern. The transformation must map any boundaries of the flow in the z-plane to boundaries of the flow in the w-plane. Quite often the image is uniform flow left to right over the half-plane $\operatorname{Im} w > 0$. Since formula 7.49 gives $G(w) = \tilde{U}w$ as a complex potential for uniform flow in the

w-plane, a complex potential for the flow pattern in the z-plane is $\tilde{U}f(z)$. Constant $\tilde{U}$ must be related to the speed of the flow in the z-plane (usually as $|z| \to \infty$). We illustrate this in the following two examples.

Example 7.40   Uniform flow of a fluid from left to right with speed U is interrupted by a circle $x^2 + y^2 = a^2$ (Figure 7.87). Find the resulting flow pattern and stagnation points in the flow.

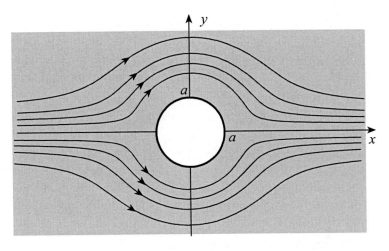

Figure 7.87

Solution   By symmetry, flow is the same above and below the x-axis. We therefore treat the x-axis exterior to the circle and the upper semicircle as a boundary and consider only the upper half of the flow (Figure 7.88).

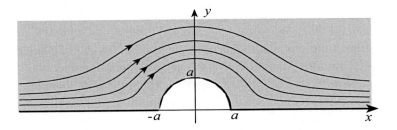

Figure 7.88

It is straightforward to show that

$$w = u + vi = z + \frac{a^2}{z}$$

maps the upper flow region to $v > 0$, with the boundary of the flow mapped to the u-axis in the w-plane (see Exercise 13 in Section 7.3). In particular, $x \le -a$ is mapped to $u \le -2a$; $x \ge a$ is mapped to $u \ge 2a$; and points on the semicircle $x^2 + y^2 = a^2$, $y \ge 0$ are mapped to $v = 0$, $-2a \le u \le 2a$ (Figure 7.89).

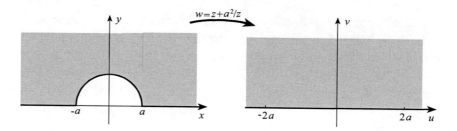

Figure 7.89

Uniform flow over the half-plane $v > 0$ is described by the complex potential $G(w) = \tilde{U}w$. Consequently, a complex potential for the flow in the xy-plane is

$$F(z) = \tilde{U}\left(z + \frac{a^2}{z}\right).$$

For large $|z|$, this function is approximated by $\tilde{U}z$. Because flow in the z-plane far from $z = 0$ should essentially be uniform, with complex potential Uz, we identify $\tilde{U}$ and U, and

$$F(z) = U\left(z + \frac{a^2}{z}\right).$$

Stream curves for this complex potential were discussed in Example 3.41. If we set $z = re^{\theta i}$, then stream curves are defined by

$$C = \operatorname{Im}\left[U\left(re^{\theta i} + \frac{a^2}{r}e^{-\theta i}\right)\right], \qquad C \text{ a constant}$$

$$= U\left(r\sin\theta - \frac{a^2}{r}\sin\theta\right) = \frac{U}{r}(r^2 - a^2)\sin\theta.$$

The stream curve corresponding to $C = 0$ consists of the upper half of the circle $r = a$ and those parts of the lines $\theta = 0$ and $\theta = \pi$ for which $r \geq a$. Other stream curves are shown in Figure 7.88. Stream curves below the x-axis are obtained by symmetry. Stagnation points in the flow can be found by solving

$$0 = F'(z) = 1 - \frac{a^2}{z^2} \qquad \Longrightarrow \qquad z = \pm a. \bullet$$

In the above example, the x-axis outside the circle was a stream curve of the flow. We replaced it by a rigid boundary in order to consider flow in the upper half of the z-plane over the semicircle $x^2 + y^2 = a^2$, $y \geq 0$. This is a general principle: If a stream curve in a flow is replaced by a rigid boundary, then the flow on either side of the boundary remains unchanged.

Example 7.41 Find equations for stream curves for the flow pattern due to uniform flow with speed U left to right across the upper half of the xy-plane which is interrupted by a vertical barrier of height a at $x = 0$ (Figure 7.90).

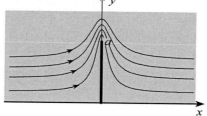

Figure 7.90

Solution   In Example 7.23, we derived the transformation $w = a^{-1}(z+ai)^{1/2}(z-ai)^{1/2}$ that maps the half-plane $\operatorname{Im} z > 0$, slit along the y-axis for $0 \le y \le a$, onto the half-plane $\operatorname{Im} w > 0$ (see also Exercise 24 in Section 7.3). (Branches of the root functions use $\log_{-\pi/2} z$.) With $G(w) = \tilde{U}w$ representing uniform flow over the w-plane, a complex potential for the required flow is

$$F(z) = \frac{\tilde{U}}{a}(z+ai)^{1/2}(z-ai)^{1/2}.$$

For large $|z|$, this flow can be approximated by $\tilde{U}z/a$. We must therefore identify $\tilde{U}/a$ with U, and

$$F(z) = U(z+ai)^{1/2}(z-ai)^{1/2}.$$

The stream function is

$$\psi(x,y) = \operatorname{Im}\left[U(z+ai)^{1/2}(z-ai)^{1/2}\right] = U\operatorname{Im}\left[(x+yi+ai)^{1/2}(x+yi-ai)^{1/2}\right].$$

When $x > 0$ we may write

$$\psi(x,y) = U\operatorname{Im}\left\{\sqrt[4]{x^2+(y+a)^2}\,e^{(i/2)\operatorname{Tan}^{-1}[(y+a)/x]}\sqrt[4]{x^2+(y-a)^2}\,e^{(i/2)\operatorname{Tan}^{-1}[(y-a)/x]}\right\}$$

$$= U\sqrt[4]{x^2+(y+a)^2}\sqrt[4]{x^2+(y-a)^2}\sin\left[\frac{\operatorname{Tan}^{-1}\left(\dfrac{y+a}{x}\right)+\operatorname{Tan}^{-1}\left(\dfrac{y-a}{x}\right)}{2}\right].$$

Consequently, for $x > 0$, stream curves are defined implicitly by the equation

$$C = \psi(x,y) = U[x^2+(y+a)^2]^{1/4}[x^2+(y-a)^2]^{1/4}\sin\left[\frac{\operatorname{Tan}^{-1}\left(\dfrac{y+a}{x}\right)+\operatorname{Tan}^{-1}\left(\dfrac{y-a}{x}\right)}{2}\right].$$

To find a simpler representation, we note that stream curves in the w-plane are horizontal lines $v = C$. We can represent each one parametrically in the form $w = u + Ci$, $-\infty < u < \infty$. The corresponding stream curve in the z-plane can be found by solving

$$u + Ci = U(z+ai)^{1/2}(z-ai)^{1/2}$$

for z in terms of u. If we set $z = x + yi$ and square both sides,

$$\frac{1}{U^2}(u+Ci)^2 = (x+yi+ai)(x+yi-ai).$$

Equating real and imaginary parts gives

$$\frac{1}{U^2}(u^2-C^2) = x^2-(y^2-a^2), \qquad \frac{2uC}{U^2} = 2xy.$$

If we solve the second for u and substitute into the first,

$$\frac{1}{U^2}\left(\frac{x^2y^2U^4}{C^2}-C^2\right) = x^2-y^2+a^2,$$

and this can be solved for y in terms of x, $\quad y = \dfrac{C}{U}\sqrt{\dfrac{x^2 + a^2 + C^2/U^2}{x^2 + C^2/U^2}}$.

This is the equation for the stream curves in Figure 7.90. Notice that for large x, $y \approx C/U$ indicating that the stream curve corresponding to C is asymptotic to the line $y = C/U$; that is, far from the barrier, stream curves are essentially horizontal, as indeed they should be.●

We are primarily interested in finding stream curves for a given flow geometry, and we have stressed the idea of solving a flow problem in the z-plane by mapping it to the uniform flow problem in the upper half of the w-plane. Stream curves are then obtained by setting the imaginary part of the complex potential $\psi(x, y)$ equal to a constant. Unfortunately, as in Example 7.40, it can sometimes be difficult or even impossible to determine $\psi(x, y)$ in a suitable form. There are alternatives. If the complex potential is the result of mapping the flow domain to the half-plane $\operatorname{Im} w > 0$ with a conformal mapping $w = f(z)$, then the complex potential in the z-plane is $\tilde{U} f(z)$. Stream curves in the w-plane are $w = u + Ci$, where C is a constant. In the z-plane, they have equations $u + Ci = \tilde{U} f(z)$. It may be possible to manipulate this equation into a form that is more suitable for separation into real and imaginary parts, yielding thereby implicitly defined, parametric equations for the stream curves for flow in the z-plane. This was the situation in Example 7.40. It may also happen that the mapping $w = f(z)$ is not known, but its inverse is $z = f^{-1}(w)$. Schwarz-Christoffel transformations lead to such representations. In this case, we set $x + yi = f^{-1}((u + Ci)/\tilde{U})$. Separation of this equation into real and imaginary parts leads directly to parametric equations for stream curves in the z-plane.

EXERCISES 7.9.1

1. What is a complex potential for uniform flow with speed U at angle α with the positive x-direction (left figure below)?

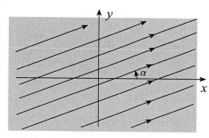 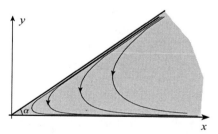

2. (a) Fluid flows closely along the side $\theta = \alpha$ of the wedge $0 < \theta < \alpha$ toward the origin (see right figure above). It then flows away from the corner. Find the flow pattern.
(b) What is the fluid velocity for $\theta = \alpha$?
(c) What is the fluid velocity for $\theta = \alpha/2$? Is it perpendicular to the line $\theta = \alpha/2$?
(d) Are components of the fluid velocity negative for $\theta > \alpha/2$?
(e) Is the x-component of the fluid velocity positive for $\theta < \alpha/2$? Is the y-component negative?

3. (a) Show that a complex potential for the flow resulting from placing a circle of radius a at the origin in an otherwise uniform flow with speed U making angle α ($0 < \alpha < \pi$) with the positive x-axis is

$$F(z) = U\left(e^{-\alpha i}z + \frac{a^2 e^{\alpha i}}{z}\right).$$

(b) Find equations for stream curves and plot a few to verify the left figure below.

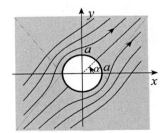 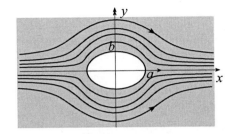

4. (a) According to Exercise 12 in Section 7.1, the Joukowski transformation $w = z + c^2/z$ maps the exterior of the circle $|z| = R$ to the exterior of an ellipse. Use this result to find c and R so that the transformation maps the exterior of $|z| = R$ to the exterior of $u^2/a^2 + v^2/b^2 = 1$ for given a and b.

   (b) Use Example 7.40 to find a complex potential when uniform flow from left to right with speed U in the xy-plane is interrupted by an ellipse $x^2/a^2 + y^2/b^2 = 1$ (right figure above).

5. (a) Use Exercises 3 and 4 to show that a complex potential for the flow due to the ellipse $x^2/a^2 + y^2/b^2 = 1$ in an otherwise uniform flow with speed U making angle α ($0 < \alpha < \pi$) with the positive x-axis (see left figure below) is

$$F(z) = \frac{U(a+b)}{2}\left[\frac{e^{-\alpha i}(z + \sqrt{z^2 + b^2 - a^2})}{a + b} + \frac{e^{\alpha i}(z - \sqrt{z^2 + b^2 - a^2})}{a - b}\right].$$

   (b) Take the limit of the potential in part (a) as $b \to 0$. Would you expect it to represent angular flow past a thin plate of length $2a$ (right figure below)?

   (c) What is the speed of the flow at the ends of the plate?

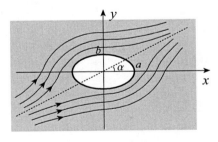 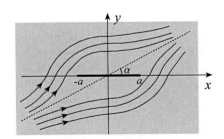

6. (a) Use the mapping in Exercise 20 of Section 7.3 to find a complex potential when uniform flow with speed U in the x-direction is deflected by a parabolic wall as shown to the right.

   (b) Show that $z = 0$ is the only stagnation point of the flow.

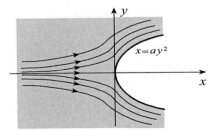

7. Use the transformation in Exercise 22 of Section 7.3 to find a complex potential for uniform flow left to right with speed U in the half-plane $y > 0$ over the circle $x^2 + (y - a)^2 = a^2$.

8. Fluid flows down the left side of the semi-infinite channel $-a < x < a$, $y > 0$ is deflected at $y = 0$ and flows up the right side. Find the stream function for the flow. What is the velocity and speed of the flow?

9. Uniform flow with speed U in the positive x-direction is deflected by a wedge with angle 2α as shown in the figure below. Find a complex potential for the flow.

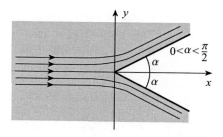

10. Find, and draw, stream curves for the flow with complex potential $F(z) = Ua^3/(2z^2)$ where U and a are positive constants.

11. Find a complex potential for first quadrant flow around the quarter circle $x^2 + y^2 = a^2$ (left figure below). Hint: See Exercise 23 in Section 7.3. Are there any stagnation points?

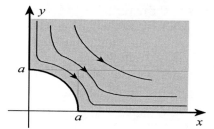
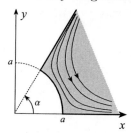

12. (a) Find a complex potential for first quadrant flow in the wedge and outside the circle in the right figure above.
    (b) Find equations for stream curves and plot a few to verify the figure.

13. Use Exercise 7 of Section 7.6 to show that a complex potential for uniform flow left to right with speed U over the step in the left figure below is $F(z) = (aU/\pi)f^{-1}(z)$, where $f^{-1}(z)$ is the inverse of the function

$$z = f(w) = \frac{a}{\pi}[\sqrt{w^2 - 1} + 4\operatorname{Cosh}^{-1}w] - ai.$$

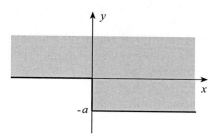
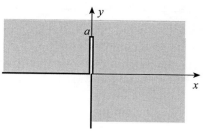

14. Use Exercise 8 of Section 7.6 to show that a complex potential for uniform flow left to right over the barrier in the right figure above must be of the form $F(z) = \tilde{U}f^{-1}(z)$, where $f^{-1}(z)$ is the inverse of the function

$$z = f(w) = \frac{ia}{2}\sqrt{w}(3 - w).$$

15. Use Exercise 9 of Section 7.6 to show that a complex potential for uniform flow down the channel in the left figure below must be of the form $F(z) = \tilde{U}f^{-1}(z)$, where $f^{-1}(z)$ is the inverse of the

function

$$z = f(w) = \frac{(a+b) + (b-a)i}{2\pi} \left[\text{Sin}^{-1} w + i \, \text{Sin}^{-1} \left(\frac{1}{w} \right) \right] + \frac{a+bi}{2}.$$

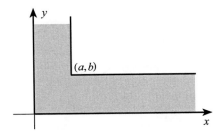

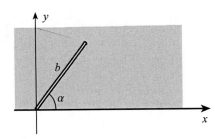

16. Use Exercise 10 of Section 7.6 to show that a complex potential for uniform flow left to right over the slanted barrier in the right figure above is of the form $F(z) = \tilde{U} f^{-1}(z)$, where $f^{-1}(z)$ is the inverse of the function

$$z = b(w-1)^{\alpha/\pi} \left(1 + \frac{\alpha w}{\pi - \alpha} \right)^{1-\alpha/\pi}.$$

17. Uniform flow with speed U in the positive y-direction is interrupted by a wall on the x-axis with an aperture between $x = \pm 1$ (left figure below). Find a complex potential for the flow and stream curves. Hint: Use $w = \text{Cos}^{-1} z$ to map the flow to channel flow bounded by walls $u = 0$ and $u = \pi$. (See Exercises 44 and 39 in Section 3.7.)

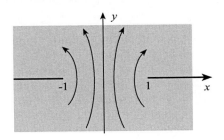

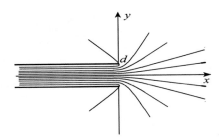

18. Fluid with uniform speed U exits from the channel in the right figure above. Find equations for the stream curves. Hint: See Example 7.34.

§7.9.2 Fluid Flow With Sources

Sources and Sinks in Flows Without Boundaries

If motion of a fluid is radially outward from a point (x_0, y_0), symmetric in all directions, (x_0, y_0) is called a **source** (Figure 7.91). When motion is radially toward (x_0, y_0), we speak of a **sink** at (x_0, y_0).

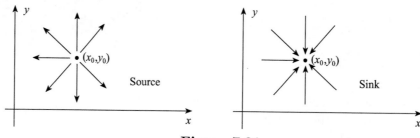

Figure 7.91

Suppose that a source at the origin emits σ units of mass per unit time equally in all directions, called the **strength** of the source. To find a complex potential $F(z) = \phi + \psi i$ associated with the source, we note that stream curves are radial lines from the origin and equipotentials (the orthogonal trajectories of stream curves) are circles centred at the origin. Since equipotentials are obtained by setting ϕ equal to a constant, it follows that ϕ must be a function only of the radial coordinate $r = \sqrt{x^2 + y^2}$; that is, $\phi = \phi(r)$, and this function must satisfy Laplace's equation. Laplace's equation in polar coordinates for a function $\phi(r)$ of r only reduces to

$$\frac{d^2\phi}{dr^2} + \frac{1}{r}\frac{d\phi}{dr} = 0.$$

When multiplied by r, this equation can be expressed in the form

$$\frac{d}{dr}\left(r\frac{d\phi}{dr}\right) = 0,$$

and integration gives

$$r\frac{d\phi}{dr} = k.$$

Hence, $\phi(r) = k \ln r + D$. We know that $\ln \sqrt{x^2 + y^2}$ is the real part of the complex function $\log_\mu z$ so that a complex potential function associated with a source at the origin is

$$F(z) = k \log_\mu z + D. \tag{7.50}$$

Since a flow is characterized by its velocity field, and components of velocity are real and imaginary parts of the complex conjugate of the derivative of the complex potential, we may dispense with constant D. In addition, because branches of the logarithm function differ only by an additive constant, every branch of $k \log_\mu z$ leads to the same velocity field for the flow. We therefore write

$$F(z) = k \log z \tag{7.51}$$

as the complex potential for a source at $z = 0$ (when $k > 0$), or a sink (when $k < 0$), without specifying the particular branch. But we regard $\log z$ as a single-valued function (with unspecified branch). We can relate constant k to the strength σ of the source. If C is a circle centred at $z = 0$ with radius R, then flux (mass flow rate) through C is given by integral 3.79. Since

$$F'(z) = \frac{k}{z} = \frac{k}{x + yi} = \frac{k(x - yi)}{x^2 + y^2},$$

velocity at each point in the flow is $\mathbf{q} = \dfrac{k}{x^2 + y^2}(x\hat{\mathbf{i}} + y\hat{\mathbf{j}})$. Consequently,

$$\text{Flux} = \rho \int_C u\,dy - v\,dx = \rho k \int_C \frac{x\,dy - y\,dx}{x^2 + y^2}.$$

If we set $x = R\cos t$, $y = R\sin t$, $-\pi \le t \le \pi$ on C,

$$\text{Flux} = \rho k \int_{-\pi}^{\pi} \frac{R\cos t(R\cos t\,dt) - (R\sin t)(-R\sin t\,dt)}{R^2} = 2\pi\rho k. \quad (7.52)$$

Alternatively, using the result in Exercise 13 of Section 4.3,

$$\text{Flux} = \text{Im}\left[\rho \int_C F'(z)\,dz\right] = \rho\,\text{Im}\int_C \frac{k}{z}dz = \rho k\,\text{Im}\,(2\pi i) = 2\pi\rho k. \quad (7.53)$$

No matter how small the circle, flux is $2\pi\rho k$. This quantity is therefore the rate σ at which fluid is emitted by the source; that is, $\sigma = 2\pi\rho k$, or $k = \sigma/(2\pi\rho)$. Consequently, a complex potential for a source with strength σ is

$$F(z) = \frac{\sigma}{2\pi\rho}\log z. \quad (7.54)$$

When $\sigma < 0$, we say that the sink has strength $-\sigma$. Notice that the speed of the flow at any point on a circle of radius R centred at the source is $|\mathbf{q}| = \sigma/(2\pi\rho R)$. As expected, it is constant on the circle and it decreases as R increases. This is consistent with the fact that mass flow rate is the same through any circle centred at z_0; since the circumference of the circle increases as R increases, the speed of the flow must decrease as R increases in order to maintain constant flow rate.

When the source is at the point (x_0, y_0), the complex potential is

$$F(z) = \frac{\sigma}{2\pi\rho}\log(z - z_0), \quad (7.55)$$

where $z_0 = x_0 + y_0 i$.

We now introduce sources and sinks into flows without boundaries.

Example 7.42 Uniform flow left to right with speed U parallel to the x-axis fills the xy-plane. Describe the flow when a source of strength σ is placed at the origin.

Solution Since there are no boundaries to the flow, we add complex potentials of the uniform flow and source, $F(z) = Uz + \dfrac{\sigma}{2\pi\rho}\log z$. The stream function is

$$\psi(x, y) = \text{Im}\,[F(z)] = Uy + \frac{\sigma}{2\pi\rho}\tan^{-1}\left(\frac{y}{x}\right),$$

where $-\pi < \tan^{-1}(y/x) \le \pi$. Setting $\psi(x, y)$ equal to a constant gives stream curves,

$$C = Uy + \frac{\sigma}{2\pi\rho}\tan^{-1}\left(\frac{y}{x}\right) \quad \Longrightarrow \quad y = x\tan\left[\frac{2\pi\rho(C - Uy)}{\sigma}\right].$$

They are plotted in Figure 7.92. It would certainly appear that there is a stagnation point for the flow. It occurs when $0 = F'(z) = U + \sigma/(2\pi\rho z)$. Hence, the stagnation point is $z = -\sigma/(2\pi\rho U)$. At this point uniform stream velocity and source neutralize one another.●

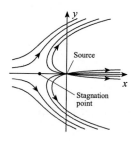

Figure 7.92

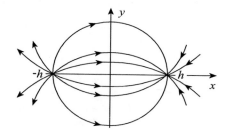

Figure 7.93

Source-Sink Pairs and Doublets

A complex potential for the flow resulting from a source of strength σ at the point $(-h, 0)$ on the negative x-axis, and a sink of equal strength at $(h, 0)$ on the positive x-axis is

$$F(z) = \frac{\sigma}{2\pi\rho}\log(z + h) - \frac{\sigma}{2\pi\rho}\log(z - h).$$

Stream curves are

$$C = \operatorname{Im}[F(z)] = \frac{\sigma}{2\pi\rho}\tan^{-1}\left(\frac{y}{x + h}\right) - \frac{\sigma}{2\pi\rho}\tan^{-1}\left(\frac{y}{x - h}\right),$$

where values of $\tan^{-1}$ are between $\pm\pi$. If we take tangents, then

$$\tan\left(\frac{2\pi\rho C}{\sigma}\right) = \frac{\dfrac{y}{x + h} - \dfrac{y}{x - h}}{1 + \left(\dfrac{y}{x + h}\right)\left(\dfrac{y}{x - h}\right)} = -\frac{2hy}{x^2 + y^2 - h^2}.$$

This equation can be simplified to

$$x^2 + \left[y + h\cot\left(\frac{2\pi\rho C}{\sigma}\right)\right]^2 = h^2\csc^2\left(\frac{2\pi\rho C}{\sigma}\right).$$

Stream curves are therefore circles through the source and sink with centres on the y-axis. Fluid flows from source to sink along circular arcs (Figure 7.93).

Suppose we move the source and sink further and further apart by letting $h \to \infty$. At the same time, suppose strengths of the source and sink increase linearly as h increases. In particular, suppose $\sigma = U\pi\rho h$ where U is a constant. The resulting configuration is called a **doublet at infinity**. This one is oriented horizontally. We calculate the complex potential for the doublet using L'Hôpital's rule,

$$\lim_{h \to \infty} \left[\frac{Uh}{2} \log \left(\frac{z+h}{z-h} \right) \right] = \frac{U}{2} \lim_{h \to \infty} \left[\frac{\log \left(\dfrac{z+h}{z-h} \right)}{1/h} \right]$$

$$= \frac{U}{2} \lim_{h \to \infty} \left[\frac{\dfrac{z-h}{z+h} \left(\dfrac{(z-h)+(z+h)}{(z-h)^2} \right)}{-1/h^2} \right]$$

$$= Uz.$$

This is the complex potential for left to right uniform flow. We have shown that uniform flow can be considered to be the result of a horizontally oriented doublet at infinity. A source at infinity in the negative real direction produces the fluid and a sink of equal strength at infinity in the positive real direction gathers the fluid.

Suppose now that the source and sink in Figure 7.93 have strengths $4\pi\rho/h$ and the source and sink are brought closer and closer together. The resulting configuration is called a **doublet or dipole at the origin**. It is oriented horizontally. Once again, we use L'Hôpital's rule to calculate the complex potential,

$$\lim_{h \to 0} \left[\frac{2}{h} \log \left(\frac{z+h}{z-h} \right) \right] = 2 \lim_{h \to 0} \left[\frac{z-h}{z+h} \frac{(z-h)+(z+h)}{(z-h)^2} \right] = \frac{1}{z}.$$

Stream curves for the dipole are given by

$$C = \text{Im} \left(\frac{1}{z} \right) = \frac{-y}{x^2+y^2} \qquad \Longrightarrow \qquad x^2 + \left(y - \frac{1}{2C} \right)^2 = \frac{1}{4C^2}.$$

These are circle with centres on the y-axis, tangent to the x-axis at the doublet (Figure 7.94).

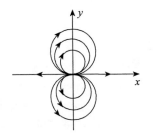

Figure 7.94

Sources and Sinks in Flows With Boundaries

When a source is inserted into an existing flow that has no boundary, a complex potential for the resulting flow is the sum of the complex potentials for the existing flow and the source (see Example 7.42). When the existing flow has boundaries, however, a complex potential for the resulting flow may or may not be the sum of complex potentials for the existing flow and the source. For example, uniform horizontal flow past a circle of radius a has complex potential $U(z + a^2/z)$. If to this is added $[\sigma/(2\pi\rho)] \log(z - z_0)$, where $|z_0| > a$, the result $U(z + a^2/z) + [\sigma/(2\pi\rho)] \log(z - z_0)$ is the complex potential for some flow, but it is not that due to insertion of a source into the flow $U(z + a^2/z)$ (see Example 7.43 below). It would be only if the circle $|z| = a$ continued to be a stream curve of the flow. In other words, complex potentials can be added only when boundaries continue to be stream curves.

Example 7.43   Uniform horizontal flow past a circle of radius a has complex potential $U(z + a^2/z)$. Show that when a source of strength σ is placed at position $(-h, 0)$, where $h > a$, the complex potential for the combined flow is not $F(z) = U\left(z + \dfrac{a^2}{z}\right) + \dfrac{\sigma}{2\pi\rho}\log(z + h)$.

Solution   Function $F(z)$ is a complex potential for the flow if the boundary of the flow, the circle $|z| = a$ is a stream curve for $F(z)$. Stream curves are given by

$$C = \operatorname{Im}\left[U\left(z + \frac{a^2}{z}\right) + \frac{\sigma}{2\pi\rho}\log(z + h)\right] = U\left(r\sin\theta - \frac{a^2}{r}\sin\theta\right) + \frac{\sigma\phi}{2\pi\rho},$$

where θ and ϕ are shown in Figure 7.95. When the equation of the circle $r = a$ is substituted into this equation, $C = \sigma\phi/(2\pi\rho)$, which is not constant. Hence $F(z)$ is not a complex potential for the flow.•

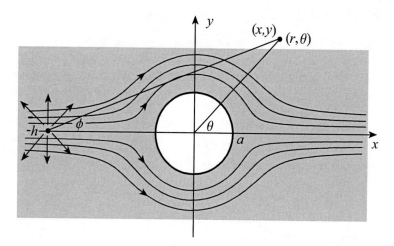

Figure 7.95

We will find potential for this flow in Example 7.44.

When a source occurs on the boundary of a flow, it does not emit fluid in all directions. For example, a source on the x-axis for half-plane flow $y > 0$ emits fluid only into the half-plane; a source at the origin in quarter-plane flow $x > 0$, $y > 0$ emits fluid only into the quarter plane. In these situations, the complex potential for the flow is not given by formulas 7.54 and 7.55.

A more general situation is for a source to emit fluid into a sector with angle α from its vertex (Figure 7.96). Since flow continues to be radially away from the source and equipotentials are circular arcs, a complex potential for the flow is still of form 7.51. The mass flow rate σ of fluid from the source is equal to the flux through any equipotential C. Using equation 7.51, and a calculation similar to that leading to equation 7.53, we find

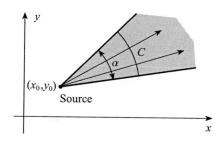

Figure 7.96

that flux through C is

$$\text{Flux} = \sigma = \rho \alpha k.$$

Thus, complex potential for a source of strength σ emitting fluid into a wedge with angle α at z_0 is

$$F(z) = \frac{\sigma}{\alpha \rho} \log (z - z_0). \tag{7.56}$$

When $\alpha = 2\pi$, we have the case of a source emitting fluid in all directions. We now return to Example 7.43 and find a potential for the flow in Figure 7.95.

Example 7.44   Uniform left to right horizontal flow past a circle of radius a has complex potential $U(z + a^2/z)$. Find a complex potential when a source of strength σ is inserted into the flow at position $(-h, 0)$, where $h > a$.

Solution   To find a complex potential for the flow we note that because the flow pattern is symmetric about the x-axis, we may treat the x-axis exterior to the circle as a flow boundary and consider only flow in the half-plane $y > 0$ exterior to the circle (Figure 7.97). The strength of the source at $z = -h$ in this situation is $\sigma/2$ since only half the original flow is emitted into the upper half-plane. The transformation $w = z + a^2/z$, which maps the flow domain to the half-plane $\text{Im}\, w > 0$, maps the source at $z = -h$ to a source at $w_1 = -(h + a^2/h)$ with strength $\sigma/2$.

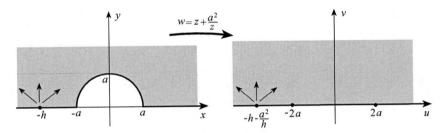

Figure 7.97

Using formula 7.56 with $\alpha = \pi$, a complex potential for the flow pattern in the w-plane is

$$G(w) = \tilde{U} w + \frac{\sigma}{2\pi\rho} \log (w - w_1).$$

(It is straightforward to show that $v = 0$ is a stream curve for this potential.) A complex potential for the flow pattern in the z-plane is therefore

$$F(z) = \tilde{U} \left(z + \frac{a^2}{z} \right) + \frac{\sigma}{2\pi\rho} \log \left(z + \frac{a^2}{z} + h + \frac{a^2}{h} \right).$$

Since $F'(z)$ can be approximated by $\tilde{U}$ for large $|z|$, it follows that we may identify $\tilde{U}$ and U, and

$$F(z) = U \left(z + \frac{a^2}{z} \right) + \frac{\sigma}{2\pi\rho} \log \left(z + \frac{a^2}{z} + h + \frac{a^2}{h} \right). \bullet$$

Because stream curves of a flow can be replaced by rigid boundaries without affecting the flow, it follows that $F(z) = Uz$ is not only a complex potential for left-right, uniform horizontal flow over the xy-plane, it is also a complex potential for uniform flow in a horizontal channel. We use this to show that the "ends" of a channel should be considered as a source and a sink for the flow, and we determine the strengths of the source and sink.

Example 7.45   An infinitely long channel bounded by the horizontal lines $y = 0$ and $y = a$ (Figure 7.98) has uniform flow left to right with speed U. Show that the ends of the channel should be considered as source and sink with strengths $\rho U a$.

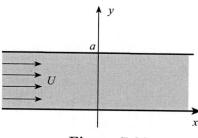

Figure 7.98

Solution   Equipotentials for flow along the channel are vertical line segments between $y = 0$ and $y = a$. The flux through every such equipotential must be strength of the flow. Using equation 3.79, we find the flux to be

$$\text{Flux} = \rho \int_0^a u\, dy - v\, dx = \rho \int_0^a U\, dy = \rho U a.$$

Consequently, the left end of the channel must be considered as a source for the flow with strength $\sigma = \rho U a$ and the right end must be a sink with the same strength.●

We consider one more example of conformal mapping in conjunction with sources.

Example 7.46   A source at the origin with strength σ emits fluid into the channel $0 < y < a$ (Figure 7.99). Find a complex potential for the flow. Is there a stagnation point in the flow? Find and plot stream curves for the flow.

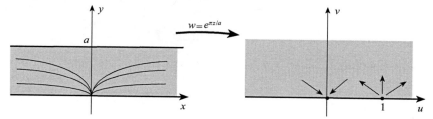

Figure 7.99

Solution   The transformation $w = e^{\pi z/a}$ maps the channel to the half-plane $\text{Im}\, w > 0$ with the source at $z = 0$ mapped to $w = 1$. In addition, it maps the sink at the left end of the channel to the origin $w = 0$. A complex potential for the source at $w = 1$ is $[\sigma/(\pi\rho)]\log(w - 1)$. Symmetry of the flow in the channel indicates that the strength of the sink at the left end of the channel is $\sigma/2$. A complex potential for the sink at $w = 0$ is therefore $-[\sigma/(2\pi\rho)]\log w$. The sum of these potentials is

$$G(w) = \frac{\sigma}{\pi\rho}\log(w - 1) - \frac{\sigma}{2\pi\rho}\log w.$$

This is a complex potential for flow in the w-plane if the u-axis is a stream curve. This is indeed the case, the u-axis is the stream curve $\psi(u, v) = 0$. A complex potential in the channel is therefore

$$F(z) = \frac{\sigma}{\pi\rho} \log\left(e^{\pi z/a} - 1\right) - \frac{\sigma}{2\pi\rho} \log\left(e^{\pi z/a}\right) = \frac{\sigma}{\pi\rho} \log\left[\frac{e^{\pi z/a} - 1}{e^{\pi z/(2a)}}\right]$$

$$= \frac{\sigma}{\pi\rho} \log\left[e^{\pi z/(2a)} - e^{-\pi z/(2a)}\right] = \frac{\sigma}{\pi\rho} \log\left(\sinh\frac{\pi z}{2a}\right),$$

where we have omitted the constant $(\sigma \log 2)/(\pi\rho)$. Stagnation points occur where

$$0 = F'(z) = \frac{\sigma\pi}{2a\rho}\coth\frac{\pi z}{2a},$$

and this yields $z = ai$, as expected. Stream curves are defined by

$$C = \psi(x,y) = \text{Im}\left[F(z)\right] = \frac{\sigma}{\pi\rho} \text{Im}\left[\log\left(\cos\frac{\pi y}{2a}\sinh\frac{\pi x}{2a} + \sin\frac{\pi y}{2a}\cosh\frac{\pi x}{2a}i\right)\right]$$

$$= \frac{\sigma}{\pi\rho}\tan^{-1}\left(\frac{\sin\dfrac{\pi y}{2a}\cosh\dfrac{\pi x}{2a}}{\cos\dfrac{\pi y}{2a}\sinh\dfrac{\pi x}{2a}}\right).$$

If we multiply by $\pi\rho/\sigma$ and take tangents,

$$\tan\frac{\pi\rho C}{\sigma} = \frac{\sin\dfrac{\pi y}{2a}\cosh\dfrac{\pi x}{2a}}{\cos\dfrac{\pi y}{2a}\sinh\dfrac{\pi x}{2a}} \qquad\Longrightarrow\qquad \tan\frac{\pi y}{2a} = \tan\frac{\pi\rho C}{\sigma}\tanh\frac{\pi x}{2a}.$$

Explicitly, then

$$y = \frac{2a}{\pi}\tan^{-1}\left(\tan\frac{\pi\rho C}{\sigma}\tanh\frac{\pi x}{2a}\right).$$

They are plotted in Figure 7.100.●

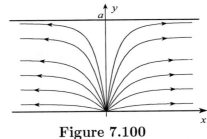

Figure 7.100

EXERCISES 7.9.2

1. Find a complex potential for flow due to a source with strength σ at the origin into a semi-infinite channel $x > 0$, $0 < y < a$ by:
   (a) noting that in Example 7.46, the y-axis inside the channel is a stream curve,
   (b) using the transformation $w = \sinh^2\left[\pi z/(2a)\right]$.

2. (a) What is a complex potential from two sources of equal strengths σ located at the real points $z = \pm a$.
   (b) Find and plot stream curves for the flow. Is there a stagnation point in the flow?
   (c) Find and plot equipotentials for the flow.

3. Into uniform flow in the positive x-direction is placed a source of strength σ at position $(-a, 0)$, where $a > 0$, and a sink of equal strength at $(a, 0)$. Show that stagnation points in the flow are always on the x-axis.

4. Use the result in Exercise 2 to find a complex potential for the flow in the half-plane $x > 0$ due to a source with strength σ at the point $z = a$ ($a > 0$), the y-axis being a boundary for the flow.

Considering only points on the wall $x = 0$, at which points is the speed of the flow smallest and greatest?

5. Show that a complex potential for flow in a wedge $0 < \text{Arg}\, z < \alpha < \pi/2$ due to a source of strength σ at z_0 (figure to ethe right) is

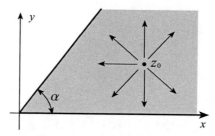

$$F(z) = \frac{\sigma}{2\pi\rho} \log\left(z^{\pi/\alpha} - z_0^{\pi/\alpha}\right)$$
$$+ \frac{\sigma}{2\pi\rho} \log\left(z^{\pi/\alpha} - \overline{z_0}^{\pi/\alpha}\right).$$

Hint: Map the wedge to the half-plane $\text{Im}\, w > 0$ and place an equal source at $w = \overline{z_0}^{\pi/\alpha}$.

6. (a) Find a complex potential for flow due to a source of strength σ at position $x = c > a > 0$ on the x-axis in the presence of a circular obstacle $x^2 + y^2 \le a^2$.

   (b) Show that the same complex potential is obtained if a second source of equal strength is placed at the inverse point of $x = c$ in the circle as well as a sink of equal strength at the origin.

7. Two sources of equal strength σ are placed at points $(0, \pm a)$ in uniform flow left to right with speed U. Find the stagnation points of the resulting flow. When is there only one stagnation point? When are they on the x-axis?

8. If source and sink in Exercise 3 are reversed, show that stagnation points are either on the x-axis or the y-axis.

9. The positive x- and y-axes are boundaries for first-quadrant flow due to a source of strength σ at a distance a from the origin on the line $y = x$. Show that a complex potential for the flow is $[\sigma/(2\pi\rho)] \log (z^4 + a^4)$. Hint: Consider flow in the xy-plane from sources at the points $(\pm a/\sqrt{2}, \pm a/\sqrt{2})$ and $(\pm a/\sqrt{2}, \mp a/\sqrt{2})$.

10. Sources of equal strength σ emit fluid into the semi-infinite channel $|x| < a$, $y > 0$ from its corners. Find a complex potential for the flow. Find and plot stream curves for the flow.

11. A source with strength σ is placed at position $(0,0)$ in the infinite channel $-a/2 < y < a/2$. Find a complex potential for the flow. Find and plot stream curves for the flow. Hint: Exercise 4 may be useful.

12. A source and sink of equal strengths σ are located at $(-a, 0)$ and $(a, 0)$ between the parallel lines $y = \pm b/2$. Find a complex potential for the flow.

13. A source and sink of equal strengths σ at $(0, -a/2)$ and $(0, a/2)$ emit fluid into the channel bounded by the lines $y = \pm a/2$. Find a complex potential for the flow. Find and plot stream curves for the flow.

14. Show that the complex potential function for flow due to sources of strength σ at the points $(0, 0)$, $(0, \pm a)$, $(0, \pm 2a)$, ... is $F(z) = [\sigma/(2\pi\rho)] \log [\sinh (\pi z/a)]$. Find and plot stream curves. Hint:

   The hyperbolic sine function has the infinite product representation $\sinh z = z \displaystyle\prod_{n=1}^{\infty} \left(1 + \frac{z^2}{n^2\pi^2}\right)$.

§7.9.3 Fluid Flow With Vortices

When constant k in equation 7.51 for a source is purely imaginary, a completely different flow pattern results. We shall maintain k has a real constant and write

$$F(z) = -ik \log z. \tag{7.57}$$

The source is called a **vortex** at $z = 0$ and stream curves associated with the vortex are defined by

$$C = \psi(x, y) = \text{Im}\left[-ik \log z\right] = -k\,\text{Re}\left[\log z\right] = -\frac{k}{2}\ln\left(x^2 + y^2\right).$$

They are circles centred at the origin. Equipotentials, being orthogonal trajectories, are radial lines (Figure 7.101). Since

$$\overline{F'(z)} = \frac{-ik}{\overline{z}} = \frac{k(-y + ix)}{x^2 + y^2},$$

velocity of the flow is

$$\mathbf{q} = \frac{k(-y\hat{\mathbf{i}} + x\hat{\mathbf{j}})}{x^2 + y^2}.$$

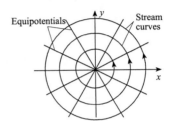

This shows that when k is positive flow is counterclockwise around the origin.

Figure 7.101

We can relate k to circulation of the flow. According to equation 3.80, circulation of the flow for a curve C is

$$\Gamma = \oint_C u\,dx + v\,dy = \oint_C \frac{-ky\,dx + kx\,dy}{x^2 + y^2}.$$

When C is a circle of radius R centred at the source of the vortex with parametric equations $x = R\cos t$, $y = R\sin t$, $-\pi \leq t \leq \pi$,

$$\Gamma = k \int_{-\pi}^{\pi} \frac{-R\sin t(-R\sin t\,dt) + R\cos t(R\cos t\,dt)}{R^2} = 2k\pi.$$

It is independent of the radius of the circle. When we write the complex potential in terms of the circulation of the flow, equation 7.57 is replaced by

$$F(z) = -\frac{i\Gamma}{2\pi}\log z. \tag{7.58}$$

Example 7.47 A vortex with circulation Γ is a units from a straight line boundary. Find the complex potential for the flow. Find stream curves for the flow and identify any stagnation points.

Solution We take the x-axis as the boundary for the flow and place the centre of the vortex at $y = a$ (Figure 7.102). Since the x-axis must be a stream curve for the flow, we use the *method of images* to find the complex potential for the flow. We remove the physical boundary $y = 0$ and insert a vortex of opposite circulation at $y = -a$. It has a clockwise flow around $y = -a$. The result of combining the vortices is a flow that has $y = 0$ as a stream curve. Consequently, the complex potential due to both vortices

$$F(z) = -\frac{i\Gamma}{2\pi}[\log(z - ai) - \log(z + ai)]$$

must be a complex potential for the vortex at $y = a$ with $y = 0$ as a physical boundary. Stream curves for the flow are defined implicitly by

$$C = \mathrm{Im}\,[F(z)] = -\frac{\Gamma}{4\pi}\ln\left[\frac{x^2 + (y - a)^2}{x^2 + (y + a)^2}\right].$$

This equation can be rewritten in the fom

$$x^2 + \left[y - a\coth\left(\frac{2\pi C}{\Gamma}\right)\right]^2 = a^2\mathrm{csch}^2\left(\frac{2\pi C}{\Gamma}\right).$$

Stream curves are circles with centres on the y-axis (Figure 7.103). Stagnation points are given by

$$0 = F'(z) = -\frac{i\Gamma}{2\pi}\left(\frac{1}{z - ai} - \frac{1}{z + ai}\right) = \frac{\Gamma a}{\pi(z^2 + a^2)}.$$

As anticipated, there are no stagnation points.●

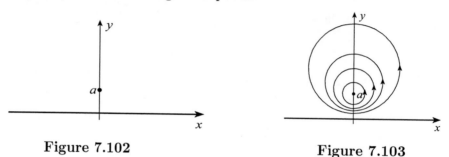

Figure 7.102   **Figure 7.103**

In the next example, we superimpose vortex flow on uniform flow around a circular object.

Example 7.48   Discuss the motion of fluid with complex potential

$$F(z) = U\left(z + \frac{a^2}{z}\right) + \frac{i\Gamma}{2\pi}\log z.$$

Solution   We have a clockwise vortex with circulation Γ at the origin superimposed on uniform left-right flow with speed U around a circular object of radius a. If we set $z = re^{\theta i}$, then stream curves are defined implicitly by

$$C = \mathrm{Im}\,[F(z)] = U\left(r\sin\theta - \frac{a^2}{r}\sin\theta\right) + \frac{\Gamma}{2\pi}\ln r = U\sin\theta\left(r - \frac{a^2}{r}\right) + \frac{\Gamma}{2\pi}\ln r.$$

As might be expected, the flow pattern depends on the relative sizes of Γ and U. In particular, stagnation points of the flow are given by

$$0 = F'(z) = U\left(1 - \frac{a^2}{z^2}\right) + \frac{i\Gamma}{2\pi z}.$$

The number of the stagnation points and their positions in the flow depend on the discriminant of the quadratic equation

$$2\pi U z^2 + i\Gamma z - 2\pi U a^2 = 0 \qquad \text{with solutions} \qquad z = \frac{-i\Gamma \pm \sqrt{16\pi^2 U^2 a^2 - \Gamma^2}}{4\pi U}.$$

Case 1: $\Gamma < 4\pi U a$

In this case of a relatively weak vortex, the discriminant is real, and the solutions have moduli $|z|^2 = \dfrac{\Gamma^2 + (16\pi^2 U^2 a^2 - \Gamma^2)}{16\pi^2 U^2} = a^2$. In other words, stagnation points are on the circular boundary in the third and fourth quadrants (Figure 7.104).

Case 2: $\Gamma = 4\pi U a$

In this case, the discriminant vanishes, and there is one stagnation point $z = -ia$ (Figure 7.105).

Case 3: $\Gamma > 4\pi U a$

This stronger vortex has two purely imaginary solutions of the quadratic equation, but only one is in the flow (the other is inside the circle) (Figure 7.106).

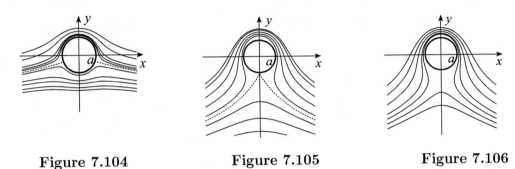

Figure 7.104   Figure 7.105   Figure 7.106

EXERCISES 7.9.3

1. A vortex with circulation Γ is placed at the point (a, a). If the positive x- and y-axes are boundaries for the resulting flow, find a complex potential for the flow. Find and plot stream curves.

2. Find and plot stream curves for the flow due to vortices with equal circulations at the points $(0, -a)$ and $(0, a)$. Determine whether there are any stagnation points in the flow.

3. Find and plot stream curves for the flow due to vortices with opposite circulations at the points $(0, -a)$ and $(0, a)$. Determine whether there are any stagnation points in the flow.

4. Find and plot stream curves for the flow due to a source of strength σ and a vortex with circulation Γ both at the origin.

5. Find and plot stream curves for the flow due to a source of strength σ at $(-a, 0)$ and a vortex with circulation Γ at $(a, 0)$.

§7.9.4 The Joukowski Transformation

The Joukowski transformation, which we have mentioned previously in exercises, is used extensively in the design of aircraft wings. In this section we show why this is true. The transformation is

$$w = J(z) = z + \frac{a^2}{z}, \tag{7.59}$$

where $a > 0$ is a constant. We begin be finding the image of the circle $|z| = a$ under the transformation. With $z = ae^{\theta i}$,

$$w = J(ae^{\theta i}) = ae^{\theta i} + \frac{a^2}{ae^{\theta i}} = ae^{\theta i} + qe^{-\theta i} = 2a \cos\theta.$$

The image of the circle is the real w-axis between $\pm 2a$ (Figure 7.107).

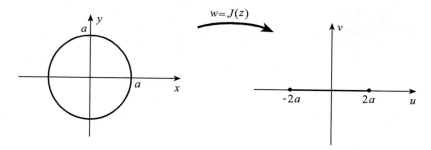

Figure 7.107

Next consider the image of the circle $|z+b| = a+b$, where $b < a$, a circle that passes through $z = a$ and contains $z = -a$ in its interior (Figure 7.108).

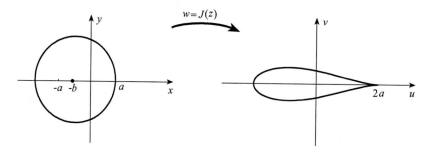

Figure 7.108

We can find parametric equations for the image of the circle by setting $z = -b + (a+b)e^{\theta i}$,

$$w = -b + (a+b)e^{\theta i} + \frac{a^2}{-b + (a+b)e^{\theta i}}$$

$$= -b + (a+b)e^{\theta i} + \frac{a^2}{[-b + (a+b)\cos\theta] + (a+b)\sin\theta\, i} \frac{-b + (a+b)\cos\theta] - (a+b)\sin\theta\, i}{-b + (a+b)\cos\theta] - (a+b)\sin\theta\, i}$$

$$= -b + (a+b)(\cos\theta + \sin\theta\, i) + \frac{a^2[-b + (a+b)\cos\theta - (a+b)\sin\theta\, i]}{[-b + (a+b)\cos\theta]^2 + (a+b)^2\sin^2\theta}.$$

Thus, parametric equations for the image of the circle are

$$u = -b + (a+b)\cos\theta + \frac{a^2[-b + (a+b)\cos\theta]}{[-b + (a+b)\cos\theta]^2 + (a+b)^2\sin^2\theta},$$

$$v = (a+b)\sin\theta - \frac{a^2(a+b)\sin\theta}{[-b + (a+b)\cos\theta]^2 + (a+b)^2\sin^2\theta}.$$

A plot of this curve in Figure 7.108 indicates a sharp point at $w = 2a$. To determine the angle interior or exterior to the point, we note that because $J'(z) = 1 - a^2/z^2$, the derivative vanishes at $z = \pm a$. Since $z = a$ is a zero of order 1 for $f'(z)$, it follows that angles between curves are doubled at $z = a$ (see Exercise 15 in Section 7.4). The angle between the upper and lower semicircles at $z = a$ is π radians. The angle between their images in the w-plane must therefore be 2π. In other words, the image has a cusp at $w = 2a$.

Consider now the image of the circle $|z + b - ci| = (a+b)^2 + c^2$, where $b < a$, and $c > 0$. Once again, the circle passes through $z = a$ and contains $z = -a$ in its interior. The image of the circle is shown in (Figure 7.109); it resembles the cross-section of an airplane wing, an airfoil. The shape of the airfoil is determined by a, b, and c.

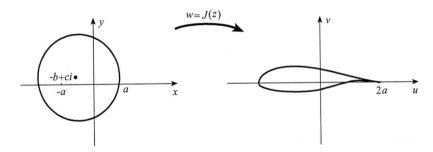

Figure 7.109

What is important in practice is flow around the airfoil. If $F(z)$ is a complex potential for flow around the circle in Figure 7.109, then $F[J(z)]$ is a complex potential for flow around the airfoil in the same figure. Stream curves can be obtained from the imaginary part of this function.

CHAPTER 8   LAPLACE TRANSFORMS

The Laplace transform is a mathematical operation which replaces differentiation problems with algebraic ones, an important simplification for ordinary and partial differential equations. In most elementary approaches to Laplace transforms, discussions are restricted to real variables. As a result, finding inverse Laplace transforms usually requires the practioner to be proficient at calculating partial fraction decompositions of rational functions, and have a table of transforms and/or their inverses. We follow this approach in Sections 8.1–8.3, but in Section 8.4 we show how complex variables lead to a direct method for finding inverse transforms. In Sections 8.2–8.3, we demonstrate how Laplace transforms reduce ordinary differential equations to algebraic equations, and in Section 8.5, partial differential equations are reduced to ordinary differential equations. In Section 8.6, we use Laplace transforms to study the stability of various types of systems, mechanical, electrical, and others.

§8.1   The Laplace Transform

When f is a function of t, its Laplace transform, denoted by $\tilde{f} = \mathcal{L}\{f\}$ is a function of s with values defined by

$$\tilde{f}(s) = \mathcal{L}\{f\}(s) = \int_0^\infty e^{-st} f(t)\, dt \tag{8.1}$$

provided the improper integral converges. In Sections 8.1–8.3, variable s is real; in Section 8.4, it is complex. When f is piecewise continuous† on every finite interval $0 \le t \le T$, and f is of exponential order α, its Laplace transform exists for $s > \alpha$. A function f is said to be of exponential order α, written $O(e^{\alpha t})$, if there exist constants T and M such that $|f(t)| < M e^{\alpha t}$ for all $t > T$. For example, e^{2t} is $O(e^{2t})$, $\sin t$ is $O(e^{0t})$, and t^n, n a positive integer, is $O(e^{\epsilon t})$ for arbitrarily small ϵ.

The following Laplace transforms are fundamental to applications of the transform to ordinary and partial differential equations; more extensive tables are contained in many mathematical reference texts. All entries are straightforward applications of definition 8.1.

$f(t)$	$\tilde{f}(s)$	$f(t)$	$\tilde{f}(s)$
t^n	$\dfrac{n!}{s^{n+1}}$	e^{at}	$\dfrac{1}{s-a}$
$\sin at$	$\dfrac{a}{s^2 + a^2}$	$\cos at$	$\dfrac{s}{s^2 + a^2}$
$\sinh at$	$\dfrac{a}{s^2 - a^2}$	$\cosh at$	$\dfrac{s}{s^2 - a^2}$
$t \sin at$	$\dfrac{2as}{(s^2 + a^2)^2}$	$t \cos at$	$\dfrac{s^2 - a^2}{(s^2 + a^2)^2}$
$t \sinh at$	$\dfrac{2as}{(s^2 - a^2)^2}$	$t \cosh at$	$\dfrac{s^2 + a^2}{(s^2 - a^2)^2}$

Table 8.1

---

† A function is piecewise continuous on $a \le t \le b$ if it has, at most, a finite number of discontinuities in the interval, and left- and right-limits both exist at each discontinuity. Only the right limit must exist at $t = a$, and the left limit at $t = b$.

When $\tilde{f}$ is the Laplace transform of f, we call f the inverse Laplace transform of $\tilde{f}$, and write

$$f = \mathcal{L}^{-1}\{\tilde{f}\}. \tag{8.2}$$

Because the Laplace transform is an integral transform, $\tilde{f}$ is unique for given f, but there exist many functions f having the same transform $\tilde{f}$. For example, the functions defined by

$$f(t) = t^2 \quad \text{and} \quad g(t) = \begin{cases} 0 & t = 1 \\ t^2 & t \neq 1, 2 \\ 0 & t = 2 \end{cases},$$

which are identical except for their values at $t = 1$ and $t = 2$ both have the same transform $2/s^3$. What we are saying is that because the Laplace transform is not a one-to-one operation, the inverse transform $\mathcal{L}^{-1}\{\tilde{f}\}$ in equation 8.2 is not an inverse in the true sense of inverse. In Section 8.4, we derive a formula for calculating inverse transforms, and this formula always yields a continuous function f, if this is possible. In the event that this is not possible, the formula gives a piecewise continuous function whose value is the average of right- and left-limits at discontinuities, namely $[f(t+) + f(t-)]/2$. The importance of this formula is that it defines $f = \mathcal{L}^{-1}\{\tilde{f}\}$ in a unique way. Other functions which have the same transform $\tilde{f}$ differ from f only in their values at isolated points; they cannot differ from f over an entire interval $a \leq t \leq b$. In compliance with this anticipated formula, we adopt the procedure of always choosing a continuous function $\mathcal{L}^{-1}\{\tilde{f}\}$ for given $\tilde{f}$, or when this is not possible, a piecewise continuous function.

The Laplace transform and its inverse are linear operators. Some of their simple properties are summarized below.

Shifting Properties of the Laplace Transform

One of two shifting properties is contained in the following theorem.

Theorem 8.1   If $f(t)$ is piecewise continuous on every interval $0 \leq t \leq T$ and of exponential order α, then

$$\mathcal{L}\{e^{at} f(t)\}(s) = \tilde{f}(s - a), \quad s > a + \alpha, \tag{8.3a}$$
$$\mathcal{L}^{-1}\{\tilde{f}(s - a)\}(t) = e^{at} f(t). \tag{8.3b}$$

(See Exercise 1 for a proof). The theorem states that multiplication by an exponential e^{at} in the t-domain is equivalent to a translation by a in the s-domain.

Example 8.1   Find the Laplace transform of the function $e^{3t} \sin 4t$.

Solution   Using property 8.3a and the transform of $\sin 4t$ from Table 8.1, we find

$$\mathcal{L}\{e^{3t} \sin 4t\} = \frac{4}{(s - 3)^2 + 16}. \bullet$$

Example 8.2   Find the inverse Laplace transform of $\dfrac{s}{s^2 + 4s + 7}$.

Solution   By completing the square on the quadratic expression in the denominator, we may write that

$$\mathcal{L}^{-1}\left\{\frac{(s+2)-2}{(s+2)^2+3}\right\} = e^{-2t}\mathcal{L}^{-1}\left\{\frac{s-2}{s^2+3}\right\} = e^{-2t}\left(\cos\sqrt{3}t - \frac{2}{\sqrt{3}}\sin\sqrt{3}t\right).\bullet$$

The notation in these two examples does not comply with that in properties 8.3. In the first example, we should write $\mathcal{L}\{e^{3t}\sin 4t\}(s)$ rather than $\mathcal{L}\{e^{3t}\sin 4t\}$. In the second example, proper notation is $\mathcal{L}^{-1}\left\{\frac{(s+2)-2}{(s+2)^2+3}\right\}(t)$, not $\mathcal{L}^{-1}\left\{\frac{(s+2)-2}{(s+2)^2+3}\right\}$. We will continue to use this abbreviated notation in specific examples, but full notation will always be used in the display of general properties of the Laplace transforms.

The next theorem contains the second shifting property of the Laplace transform.

Theorem 8.2   If $f(t)$ is piecewise continuous on every interval $0 \le t \le T$ and of exponential order α, then

$$\mathcal{L}\{f(t-a)h(t-a)\}(s) = e^{-as}\tilde{f}(s), \tag{8.4a}$$
$$\mathcal{L}^{-1}\{e^{-as}\tilde{f}(s)\}(t) = f(t-a)h(t-a). \tag{8.4b}$$

Function $h(t-a)$ is the Heaviside unit step function shown in Figure 8.1. It has value 0 when $t < a$ and value 1 when $t > a$. See Exercise 2 for a proof of properties 8.4. They imply that multiplication by an exponential e^{-as} in the s-domain is equivalent to a translation in the t-domain. Graphs of $f(t)$ and $f(t-a)h(t-a)$ are shown in Figure 8.2.

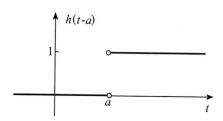

Figure 8.1

Equation 8.4(b) is very useful in its present form; equation 8.4a is more useful if written in the form

$$\mathcal{L}\{f(t)h(t-a)\}(s) = e^{-as}\mathcal{L}\{f(t+a)\}(s). \tag{8.4c}$$

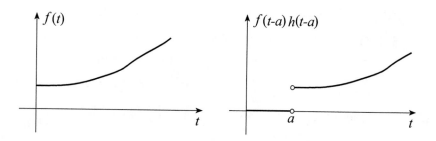

Figure 8.2

For example, the Laplace transform of the
function in Figure 8.3 is

$$\tilde{f}(s) = \mathcal{L}\left\{(t-4)^2 h(t-3)\right\}$$
$$= e^{-3s}\mathcal{L}\left\{(t+3-4)^2\right\}$$
$$= e^{-3s}\mathcal{L}\left\{t^2 - 2t + 1\right\}$$
$$= e^{-3s}\left(\frac{2}{s^3} - \frac{2}{s^2} + \frac{1}{s}\right).$$

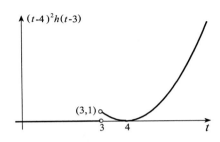

Figure 8.3

Example 8.3 Find the inverse transform for $\tilde{f}(s) = \dfrac{e^{-s} - e^{-2s}}{s}$.

Solution Since $\mathcal{L}^{-1}\{1/s\} = 1$,
property 8.4b gives

$$f(t) = \mathcal{L}^{-1}\left\{\frac{e^{-s}}{s}\right\} - \mathcal{L}^{-1}\left\{\frac{e^{-2s}}{s}\right\}$$
$$= h(t-1) - h(t-2).$$

This function is shown in Figure 8.4.●

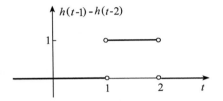

Figure 8.4

Multiplication by t^n

The following theorem indicates that multiplying a function $f(t)$ by t^n results in its
transform being differentiated n times.

Theorem 8.3 If $f(t)$ is piecewise continuous on every finite interval and of exponential order α,
and n is a positive integer, then

$$\mathcal{L}\{t^n f(t)\}(s) = (-1)^n \frac{d^n}{ds^n}[\mathcal{L}\{f\}(s)], \tag{8.5a}$$

$$\mathcal{L}^{-1}\{\tilde{f}^{(n)}(s)\}(t) = (-1)^n t^n \mathcal{L}^{-1}\{\tilde{f}\}(t). \tag{8.5b}$$

(See Exercise 3 for a proof.)

Example 8.4 Confirm the Laplace transform for $t\sin at$ in Table 8.1.

Solution According to equation 8.5a,

$$\mathcal{L}\{t\sin at\} = -\frac{d}{ds}[\mathcal{L}\{\sin at\}] = -\frac{d}{ds}\left(\frac{a}{s^2 + a^2}\right) = \frac{2as}{(s^2 + a^2)^2}.●$$

Example 8.5 Find the inverse Laplace transform for $\tilde{f}(s) = \dfrac{s+1}{(z^2 + 2 + 5)^2}$.

Solution We note that

$$\frac{d}{ds}\left(\frac{1}{s^2 + 2s + 5}\right) = \frac{-(2s+2)}{(s^2 + 2s + 5)^2}.$$

Consequently, using equation 8.5b,

$$\mathcal{L}^{-1}\left\{\frac{s+1}{(s^2+2s+5)^2}\right\} = \mathcal{L}^{-1}\left\{-\frac{1}{2}\frac{d}{ds}\left(\frac{1}{s^2+2s+5}\right)\right\} = -\frac{1}{2}(-t)\mathcal{L}^{-1}\left\{\frac{1}{s^2+2s+5}\right\}$$

$$= \frac{t}{2}\mathcal{L}^{-1}\left\{\frac{1}{(s+1)^2+4}\right\} = \frac{t}{2}e^{-t}\mathcal{L}^{-1}\left\{\frac{1}{s^2+4}\right\} = \frac{t}{4}e^{-t}\sin 2t.\bullet$$

Laplace Transforms of Periodic Functions

When a function f is periodic with period p, the improper integral in equation 8.1 may be replaced by an integral over $0 \le t \le p$,

$$\tilde{f}(s) = \frac{1}{1-e^{-ps}}\int_0^p e^{-st}f(t)\,dt, \tag{8.6}$$

(see Exercise 4). For example, the function in Figure 8.5 has period 2, and therefore

$$\tilde{f}(s) = \frac{1}{1-e^{-2s}}\int_0^2 (1-t)e^{-st}\,dt.$$

Integration now gives

$$\tilde{f}(s) = \frac{1}{1-e^{-2s}}\left\{\frac{(t-1)}{s}e^{-st} + \frac{1}{s^2}e^{-st}\right\}_0^2 = \frac{1+e^{-2s}}{s(1-e^{-2s})} - \frac{1}{s^2}.$$

We can even avoid this integration by interpreting it as the Laplace transform of the function in Figure 8.6. With the algebraic definition $g(t) = (1-t)[h(t) - h(t-2)]$ of this function, we use property 8.4c to write

$$\tilde{f}(s) = \frac{1}{1-e^{-2s}}\mathcal{L}\{(1-t)[h(t)-h(t-2)]\} = \frac{1}{1-e^{-2s}}\left[\mathcal{L}\{1-t\} - \mathcal{L}\{(1-t)h(t-2)\}\right]$$

$$= \frac{1}{1-e^{-2s}}\left[\left(\frac{1}{s}-\frac{1}{s^2}\right) - e^{-2s}\mathcal{L}\{1-(t+2)\}\right]$$

$$= \frac{1}{1-e^{-2s}}\left[\frac{1}{s}-\frac{1}{s^2} - e^{-2s}\left(-\frac{1}{s}-\frac{1}{s^2}\right)\right]$$

$$= \frac{1+e^{-2s}}{s(1-e^{-2s})} - \frac{1}{s^2}.$$

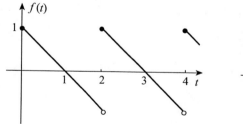

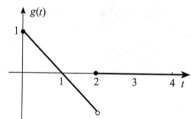

Figure 8.5   Figure 8.6

Convolutions and the Laplace Transform

It is often necessary in applications to find the inverse transform of the product of two functions $\tilde{f}\tilde{g}$ when inverse transforms f and g of $\tilde{f}$ and $\tilde{g}$ are known. We shall see shortly that the inverse of $\tilde{f}\tilde{g}$ is what is called the convolution of f and g. The **convolution** of two functions f and g is defined as

$$(f * g)(t) = \int_0^t f(v)g(t-v)\,dv. \tag{8.7}$$

The following properties of convolutions are easily verified using definition 8.7:

$$f * g = g * f, \tag{8.8a}$$
$$f * (kg) = (kf) * g = k(f * g), \quad k \text{ a constant} \tag{8.8b}$$
$$(f * g) * h = f * (g * h), \tag{8.8c}$$
$$f * (g + h) = f * g + f * h. \tag{8.8d}$$

The importance of convolutions lies in the following theorem.

Theorem 8.4   If f and g are $O(e^{\alpha t})$ and piecewise continuous on every finite interval $0 \le t \le T$, then

$$\mathcal{L}\{f * g\} = \mathcal{L}\{f\}\mathcal{L}\{g\}, \quad s > \alpha. \tag{8.9a}$$

Proof   If $\tilde{f} = \mathcal{L}\{f\}$ and $\tilde{g} = \mathcal{L}\{g\}$, then

$$\tilde{f}(s)\tilde{g}(s) = \int_0^\infty e^{-sv} f(v)\,dv \int_0^\infty e^{-s\tau} g(\tau)\,d\tau = \int_0^\infty \int_0^\infty e^{-s(v+\tau)} f(v)g(\tau)\,d\tau\,dv.$$

Suppose we change variables of integration in the inner integral with respect to τ by setting $t = v + \tau$. Then

$$\tilde{f}(s)\tilde{g}(s) = \int_0^\infty \int_v^\infty e^{-st} f(v)g(t-v)\,dt\,dv = \lim_{T \to \infty} \int_0^T \int_u^\infty e^{-st} f(v)g(t-v)\,dt\,dv.$$

We would like to interchange orders of integration, but to do so requires that the inner integral converge uniformly with respect to v. To verify that this is indeed the case we note that since f and g are $O(e^{\alpha t})$ and piecewise continuous on every finite interval $0 \le t \le T$, there exists a constant M such that for all $t \ge 0$, $|f(t)| < Me^{\alpha t}$ and $|g(t)| < Me^{\alpha t}$. For each $v \ge 0$, we therefore have $|e^{-st} f(v)g(t-v)| < M^2 e^{-st} e^{\alpha v} e^{\alpha(t-v)} = M^2 e^{-t(s-\alpha)}$. Thus,

$$\left| \int_v^\infty e^{-st} f(v)g(t-v)\,dt \right| < M^2 \int_v^\infty e^{-t(s-\alpha)}\,dt = M^2 \left\{ \frac{e^{-t(s-\alpha)}}{\alpha - s} \right\}_u^\infty$$

$$= \frac{M^2 e^{-v(s-\alpha)}}{s - \alpha} < \frac{M^2}{s - \alpha},$$

provided $s > \alpha$, and the improper integral is uniformly convergent with respect to v. The order of integration in the expression for $\tilde{f}(s)\tilde{g}(s)$ may therefore be interchanged (Figure 8.7), and we obtain

$$\tilde{f}(s)\tilde{g}(s) = \lim_{T \to \infty} \left[\int_0^T e^{-st} \int_0^t f(v)g(t-v)\,dv\,dt + \int_T^\infty e^{-st} \int_0^T f(v)g(t-v)\,dv\,dt \right].$$

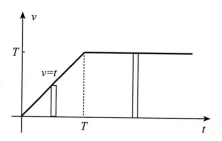

Figure 8.7

Since

$$\left| \int_T^\infty e^{-st} \int_0^T f(v)g(t-v)\, dv dt \right| < \int_T^\infty \int_0^T M^2 e^{-t(s-\alpha)}\, dv\, dt$$

$$= M^2 T \left\{ \frac{e^{-t(s-\alpha)}}{\alpha - s} \right\}_T^\infty = \frac{M^2 T e^{-T(s-\alpha)}}{s - \alpha}$$

provided $s > \alpha$, it follows that

$$\lim_{T \to \infty} \int_T^\infty e^{-st} \int_0^T f(v)g(t-v)\, dv\, dt = 0.$$

Thus,

$$\tilde{f}(s)\tilde{g}(s) = \lim_{T \to \infty} \int_0^T e^{-st} \int_0^t f(v)g(t-v)\, dv\, dt = \lim_{T \to \infty} \int_0^T e^{-st} f * g\, dt = \mathcal{L}\{f * g\}. \quad \blacksquare$$

More important in practice is the inverse of property 8.9a.

Corollary   If $\mathcal{L}^{-1}\{\tilde{f}\} = f$ and $\mathcal{L}^{-1}\{\tilde{g}\} = g$, where f and g are $O(e^{\alpha t})$ and piecewise continuous on every finite interval, then

$$\mathcal{L}^{-1}\{\tilde{f}\tilde{g}\}(t) = \int_0^t f(v)g(t-v)\, dv. \tag{8.9b}$$

The following example illustrates this corollary.

Example 8.6   Find the inverse transform of $\tilde{f}(s) = \dfrac{2}{s^2(s^2 + 4)}$.

Solution   Since $\mathcal{L}^{-1}\{2/(s^2+4)\} = \sin 2t$ and $\mathcal{L}^{-1}\{1/s^2\} = t$, convolution propery 8.9b gives

$$\mathcal{L}^{-1}\left\{ \frac{2}{s^2(s^2+4)} \right\} = \int_0^t v \sin 2(t-v)\, dv = \left\{ \frac{v}{2}\cos 2(t-v) + \frac{1}{4}\sin 2(t-v) \right\}_0^t$$

$$= \frac{t}{2} - \frac{1}{4}\sin 2t. \bullet$$

There are other algebraic properties of the Laplace transform and its inverse, but the ones discussed here suffice for our purposes. In the context of ordinary differential equations, finding inverse transforms is often a matter of finding the partial fraction decomposition of a rational function, together with the above properties and a set of tables. We illustrate in the following example.

Example 8.7 Find inverse Laplace transforms for the following functions:

$$\text{(a)} \quad \tilde{f}(s) = \frac{s^2 - 9s + 9}{s^3(s^2 + 9)} \qquad \text{(b)} \quad \tilde{f}(s) = \frac{e^{-s}}{s^2 - s} \qquad \text{(c)} \quad \tilde{f}(s) = \frac{s + 1}{s^2(s^2 - 4)}$$

Solution   (a) The partial fraction decomposition of $\tilde{f}(s)$ is

$$\tilde{f}(s) = \frac{1}{s^3} - \frac{1}{s^2} + \frac{s}{s^2 + 9}.$$

Table 8.1 therefore gives $f(t) = \dfrac{t^2}{2} - t + \cos 3t$.

(b) Partial fractions give $\dfrac{1}{s(s-1)} = \dfrac{1}{s-1} - \dfrac{1}{s}$, and therefore

$$\mathcal{L}^{-1}\left\{\frac{1}{s(s-1)}\right\} = e^t - 1.$$

Property 8.4b now gives $\mathcal{L}^{-1}\{\tilde{f}(s)\} = (e^{t-1} - 1)h(t - 1)$.

(c) Partial fractions give $\dfrac{s+1}{s^2(s^2 - 4)} = \dfrac{1/4}{s^2 - 4} - \dfrac{1/4}{s^2}$, and therefore

$$\mathcal{L}^{-1}\left\{\frac{s+1}{s^2(s^2 - 4)}\right\} = \frac{1}{4}\left(\frac{1}{2}\sinh 2t\right) - \frac{1}{4}(t) = \frac{1}{8}\sinh 2t - \frac{t}{4}. \bullet$$

EXERCISES 8.1

1. (a) Verify shifting property 8.3a.
   (b) Use 8.3a and Table 8.1 to calculate Laplace transforms for:

   (i) $f(t) = t^3 e^{-5t}$ (ii) $f(t) = e^{-t}\cos 2t + e^{3t}\sin 2t$ (iii) $f(t) = e^{at}\cosh 4t - e^{-at}\sinh 4t$

   (c) Use 8.3b and Table 8.1 to calculate inverse Laplace transforms for:

   $$\text{(i)} \quad \tilde{f}(s) = \frac{1}{s^2 - 2s + 5} \qquad \text{(ii)} \quad \tilde{f}(s) = \frac{s}{s^2 + 4s + 1}$$

2. (a) Verify shifting property 8.4c.
   (b) Use 8.4c and Table 8.1 to calculate Laplace transforms for:

   $$\text{(i)} \quad f(t) = \begin{cases} 0 & 0 < t < 3 \\ t - 2 & t > 3 \end{cases} \qquad \text{(ii)} \quad f(t) = \begin{cases} 0 & 0 < t < a \\ 1 & t > a \end{cases}$$

   $$\text{(iii)} \quad f(t) = \begin{cases} 1 & 0 < t < a \\ 0 & t > a \end{cases} \qquad \text{(iv)} \quad f(t) = \begin{cases} 0 & 0 < t < a \\ 1 & a < t < b \\ 0 & t > b \end{cases}$$

   (c) Use 8.4b and Table 8.1 to calculate inverse Laplace transforms for:

   $$\text{(i)} \quad \tilde{f}(s) = \frac{e^{-2s}}{s^2} \qquad \text{(ii)} \quad \tilde{f}(s) = \frac{e^{-3s}}{s^2 + 1} \qquad \text{(iii)} \quad \tilde{f}(s) = \frac{se^{-5s}}{s^2 - 2}$$

3. (a) Verify equation 8.5a.
   (b) Find Laplace transforms for the following functions:

$$\text{(i) } f(t) = t^2 \cos at \qquad\qquad \text{(ii) } f(t) = te^{2t} \sin 3t$$

(c) Find inverse transforms for the following functions:

$$\text{(i) } \tilde{f}(s) = \frac{s-3}{(s^2 - 6s + 15)^2} \qquad\qquad \text{(ii) } \tilde{f}(s) = \frac{se^{-2s}}{(s^2 + 19)^2}$$

4. (a) Verify equation 8.6.
   (b) Find Laplace transforms for the following functions:

$$\text{(i) } \quad f(t) = t, \quad 0 < t < a, \quad f(t+a) = f(t)$$

$$\text{(ii) } \quad f(t) = \begin{cases} 1 & 0 < t < a \\ -1 & a < t < 2a \end{cases} \qquad f(t+2a) = f(t)$$

$$\text{(iii) } f(t) = |\sin at|$$

In Exercises 5–8 use convolutions to find inverse transforms for the function.

5. $\tilde{f}(s) = \dfrac{1}{s(s+1)}$

6. $\tilde{f}(s) = \dfrac{1}{(s^2+1)(s^2+4)}$

7. $\tilde{f}(s) = \dfrac{s}{(s+4)(s^2-2)}$

8. $\tilde{f}(s) = \dfrac{s}{(s^2-4)(s^2-9)}$

In Exercises 9–14 find the Laplace transform of the function.

9. $f(t) = \begin{cases} 2t & 0 \le t \le 1 \\ t & t > 1 \end{cases}$

10. $f(t) = \begin{cases} t^2 & 0 \le t \le 1 \\ 2t & t > 1 \end{cases}$

11. $f(t) = \begin{cases} t & 0 < t < a \\ 2a - t & a < t < 2a \end{cases} \qquad f(t+2a) = f(t)$

12. $f(t) = \begin{cases} 1 & 0 < t < a \\ 0 & a < t < 2a \end{cases} \qquad f(t+2a) = f(t)$

13. $f(t) = \begin{cases} 0 & 0 < t < a \\ 1 & t > a \end{cases}$

14. $f(t) = \begin{cases} 0 & 0 < t < a \\ 1 & a < t < a+1 \\ 0 & t > a+1 \end{cases}$

Find the inverse Laplace transform in Exercises 15–24.

15. $\tilde{f}(s) = \dfrac{s}{s^2 - 3s + 2}$

16. $\tilde{f}(s) = \dfrac{4s+1}{(s^2+s)(4s^2-1)}$

17. $\tilde{f}(s) = \dfrac{e^{-3s}}{s+5}$

18. $\tilde{f}(s) = \dfrac{e^{-2s}}{s^2 + 3s + 2}$

19. $\tilde{f}(s) = \dfrac{1}{s^3 + 1}$

20. $\tilde{f}(s) = \dfrac{5s-2}{3s^2 + 4s + 8}$

21. $\tilde{f}(s) = \dfrac{e^{-s}(1 - e^{-s})}{s(s^2+1)}$

22. $\tilde{f}(s) = \dfrac{s}{(s+1)^5}$

23. $\tilde{f}(s) = \dfrac{s^2 + 2s + 3}{(s^2 + 2s + 2)(s^2 + 2s + 5)}$

24. $\tilde{f}(s) = \dfrac{s^2}{(s^2 - 4)^2}$

25. Verify that the Laplace transform of a function f which is piecewise continuous on every finite interval $0 \le t \le T$ and is $O(e^{\alpha t})$ exists for $s > \alpha$.

26. (a) Prove that when n is a nonnegative integer, t^n is $O(e^{\epsilon t})$ for every $\epsilon > 0$.
(b) Prove that when f is $O(e^{\alpha t})$, then $t^n f(t)$ is $O(e^{(\alpha+\epsilon)t})$ for every $\epsilon > 0$.

27. Let $f(t)$ be piecewise continuous on every finite interval and of exponential order. Verify that

$$\lim_{s \to \infty} \tilde{f}(s) = 0.$$

28. Let f and f' be $O(e^{\alpha t})$, f' be piecewise continuous on every finite interval $0 \le t \le T$, and f have only a finite number of finite discontinuities for $t \ge 0$. Use the result of Exercise 27 to verify the "initial-value-theorem",

$$\lim_{s \to \infty} s\tilde{f}(s) = \lim_{t \to 0^+} f(t).$$

§8.2   Application of Laplace Transforms to Ordinary Differential Equations

Laplace transforms are a powerful technique for solving ordinary and partial differential equations. They replace differentiations with algebraic operations. The following theorem and its corollary simplify the process.

Theorem 8.5   Suppose f is continuous with a piecewise continuous first derivative on every finite interval $0 \leq t \leq T$. If f is $O(e^{\alpha t})$, then $\mathcal{L}\{f'\}$ exists for $s > \alpha$, and

$$\mathcal{L}\{f'\}(s) = s\tilde{f}(s) - f(0). \tag{8.10a}$$

Proof   If t_j, $j = 1, \ldots, n$ denote the discontinuities of f' in $0 \leq t \leq T$, then

$$\int_0^T e^{-st} f'(t)\, dt = \sum_{j=0}^n \int_{t_j}^{t_{j+1}} e^{-st} f'(t)\, dt,$$

where $t_0 = 0$ and $t_{n+1} = T$. Since f' is continuous on each subinterval, we may integrate by parts on these subintervals,

$$\int_0^T e^{-st} f'(t)\, dt = \sum_{j=0}^n \left[\{e^{-st} f(t)\}_{t_j}^{t_{j+1}} + s \int_{t_j}^{t_{j+1}} e^{-st} f(t)\, dt \right].$$

Because f is continuous, $f(t_j+) = f(t_j-)$, $j = 1, \ldots, n$, and therefore

$$\int_0^T e^{-st} f'(t)\, dt = -f(0) + e^{-sT} f(T) + s \int_0^T e^{-st} f(t)\, dt.$$

Thus,

$$\mathcal{L}\{f'\}(s) = \int_0^\infty e^{-st} f'(t)\, dt = \lim_{T \to \infty} \int_0^T e^{-st} f'(t)\, dt$$

$$= \lim_{T \to \infty} \left[-f(0) + e^{-sT} f(T) + s \int_0^T e^{-st} f(t)\, dt \right]$$

$$= s\tilde{f}(s) - f(0) + \lim_{T \to \infty} e^{-sT} f(T),$$

provided the limit on the right exists. Since f is $O(e^{\alpha t})$, there exists M and $\overline{T}$ such that for $t > \overline{T}$, $|f(t)| < Me^{\alpha t}$. Thus, for $T > \overline{T}$,

$$e^{-sT} |f(T)| < e^{-sT} Me^{\alpha T} = Me^{(\alpha - s)T}$$

which approaches 0 as $T \to \infty$ (provided $s > \alpha$). Consequently,

$$\mathcal{L}\{f'\}(s) = s\tilde{f}(s) - f(0). \ \blacksquare$$

This result is easily extended to second order derivatives. The extension is stated in the following corollary and verified in Exercise 1. For extensions when f is only piecewsie continuous, see Exercise 39.

Corollary   Suppose f and f' are continuous and f'' is piecewise continuous on every finite interval $0 \leq t \leq T$. If f and f' are $O(e^{\alpha t})$, then $\mathcal{L}\{f''\}$ exists for $s > \alpha$, and

$$\mathcal{L}\{f''\}(s) = s^2 \tilde{f}(s) - sf(0) - f'(0). \tag{8.10b}$$

The following examples use these properties and at the same time indicate how Laplace transforms reduce ordinary differential equations to algebraic equations.

Example 8.8   Solve the initial value problem

$$y'' - 2y' + y = 2e^t, \quad y(0) = y'(0) = 0.$$

Solution   When we take Laplace transforms of both sides of the differential equation and use linearity of the operator,

$$\mathcal{L}\{y''\} - 2\mathcal{L}\{y'\} + \mathcal{L}\{y\} = 2\mathcal{L}\{e^t\}.$$

Properties 8.10a,b yield

$$[s^2\tilde{y}(s) - sy(0) - y'(0)] - 2[s\tilde{y}(s) - y(0)] + \tilde{y}(s) = \frac{2}{s-1}.$$

We now use the initial conditions $y(0) = y'(0) = 0$,

$$s^2\tilde{y}(s) - 2s\tilde{y}(s) + \tilde{y}(s) = \frac{2}{s-1},$$

and solve this equation for $\tilde{y}(s)$,

$$\tilde{y}(s) = \frac{2}{(s-1)^3}.$$

The required function $y(t)$ can now be obtained by taking the inverse transform of $\tilde{y}(s)$,

$$y(t) = \mathcal{L}^{-1}\left\{\frac{2}{(s-1)^3}\right\} = 2\mathcal{L}^{-1}\left\{\frac{1}{(s-1)^3}\right\} \qquad \text{(by linearity)}$$

$$= 2e^t\mathcal{L}^{-1}\left\{\frac{1}{s^3}\right\} \qquad \text{(by 8.3b)}$$

$$= 2e^t\left(\frac{t^2}{2}\right) \qquad \text{(from Table 8.1)}$$

$$= t^2e^t. \bullet$$

Example 8.9   Solve the initial value problem

$$y'' + 4y = 3\cos 2t, \qquad y(0) = 1, \quad y'(0) = 0.$$

Solution   When we take Laplace transforms of the differential equation and use the initial conditions

$$[s^2\tilde{y} - s(1) - 0] + 4\tilde{y} = \frac{3s}{s^2 + 4}.$$

For simplicity of notation, we have written $\tilde{y}$ for $\tilde{y}(s)$. The solution of this equation for $\tilde{y}(s)$ is

$$\tilde{y}(s) = \frac{3s}{(s^2+4)^2} + \frac{s}{s^2+4},$$

and Table 8.1 gives

$$y(t) = 3\left(\frac{t}{4}\sin 2t\right) + \cos 2t. \bullet$$

Laplace transforms are particularly adept at handling initial value problems as in the previous two examples. They can also handle boundary value problems as shown in the next example.

Example 8.10   Solve the boundary value problem

$$y'' + 9y = t + 2, \quad y(0) = 1, \quad y(\pi/2) = 4.$$

Solution   Since the Laplace transform of the second derivative of a function involves the first derivative at $t = 0$, and this was not given, we denote it by $A = y'(0)$. When we take Laplace transforms of the differential equation and use the initial conditions

$$[s^2\tilde{y} - s(1) - A] + 9\tilde{y} = \frac{1}{s^2} + \frac{2}{s}.$$

The solution of this equation for $\tilde{y}(s)$ is

$$\tilde{y}(s) = \frac{2s + 1}{s^2(s^2 + 9)} + \frac{s + A}{s^2 + 9}.$$

Partial fractions lead to

$$\tilde{y}(s) = \frac{2/9}{s} + \frac{1/9}{s^2} + \frac{7s/9 + (A - 1/9)}{s^2 + 9}.$$

Inverse transforms give

$$y(t) = \frac{2}{9} + \frac{t}{9} + \frac{7}{9}\cos 3t + \frac{1}{3}\left(A - \frac{1}{9}\right)\sin 3t.$$

We now impose the condition $y(\pi/2) = 4$ to find A,

$$4 = y(\pi/2) = \frac{2}{9} + \frac{\pi}{18} - \frac{1}{3}\left(A - \frac{1}{9}\right).$$

This yields A, and

$$y(t) = \frac{2}{9} + \frac{t}{9} + \frac{7}{9}\cos 3t + \left(\frac{\pi - 68}{18}\right)\sin 3t. \bullet$$

Laplace transforms can also be used to find general solutions of differential equations.

Example 8.11   Find a general solution of the differential equation

$$y'' + 4y' + 5y = te^{2t}.$$

Solution   If we denote the value of $y(t)$ and its derivative $y'(t)$ at $t = 0$ by $y(0) = A$ and $y'(0) = B$, then we can take Laplace transforms of the differential equation,

$$[s^2\tilde{y} - As - B] + 4[s\tilde{y} - A] + 5\tilde{y} = \frac{1}{(s - 2)^2}.$$

The solution of this equation for $\tilde{y}(s)$ is

$$\tilde{y}(s) = \frac{1}{(s - 2)^2(s^2 + 4s + 5)} + \frac{As + (B + 4A)}{s^2 + 4s + 5}.$$

Partial fractions on the first term gives

$$\tilde{y}(s) = \frac{-8/289}{s-2} - \frac{1/17}{(s-2)^2} + \frac{8s/289 + 31/289}{s^2 + 4s + 5} + \frac{As + (B+4A)}{s^2 + 4s + 5}.$$

If we are not concerned that the solution should maintain the character of constants A and B, we can say that this decomposition is of the form

$$\tilde{y}(s) = \frac{-8/289}{s-2} - \frac{1/17}{(s-2)^2} + \frac{Cs + D}{s^2 + 4s + 5},$$

for unknown constants C and D. The inverse transform now gives

$$\begin{aligned}
y(t) &= -\frac{8}{289}e^{2t} - \frac{t}{17}e^{2t} + \mathcal{L}^{-1}\left\{\frac{C(s+2) + E}{(s+2)^2 + 1}\right\} \qquad (E = D - 2C) \\
&= -\frac{8}{289}e^{2t} - \frac{t}{17}e^{2t} + e^{-2t}\mathcal{L}^{-1}\left\{\frac{Cs + E}{s^2 + 1}\right\} \\
&= -\frac{8}{289}e^{2t} - \frac{t}{17}e^{2t} + e^{-2t}(C\cos t + E\sin t).\bullet
\end{aligned}$$

Convolutions are particularly useful when solving linear differential equations that contain unspecified nonhomogeneities.

Example 8.12 Find the solution of the problem

$$y'' + 2y' - y = f(t), \qquad y(0) = A, \quad y'(0) = B,$$

for arbitrary constants A and B and an arbitrary function $f(t)$.

Solution When we take Laplace transforms,

$$[s^2\tilde{y} - As - B] + 2[s\tilde{y} - A] - \tilde{y} = \tilde{f}(s),$$

and solve for $\tilde{y}$,

$$\tilde{y}(s) = \frac{\tilde{f}(s)}{s^2 + 2s - 1} + \frac{As + B + 2A}{s^2 + 2s - 1}.$$

To find the inverse transform of this function, we first note that

$$\mathcal{L}^{-1}\left\{\frac{1}{s^2 + 2s - 1}\right\} = \mathcal{L}^{-1}\left\{\frac{1}{(s+1)^2 - 2}\right\} = e^{-t}\mathcal{L}^{-1}\left\{\frac{1}{s^2 - 2}\right\} = \frac{1}{\sqrt{2}}e^{-t}\sinh\sqrt{2}t.$$

Convolution property 8.9b on the first term of $\tilde{y}(s)$ now yields

$$\begin{aligned}
y(t) &= \int_0^t f(v)\frac{1}{\sqrt{2}}e^{-(t-v)}\sinh\sqrt{2}(t-v)\,dv + \mathcal{L}^{-1}\left\{\frac{A(s+1) + (B+A)}{(s+1)^2 - 2}\right\} \\
&= \frac{1}{\sqrt{2}}\int_0^t f(v)e^{-(t-v)}\sinh\sqrt{2}(t-v)\,dv + e^{-t}\mathcal{L}^{-1}\left\{\frac{As + (B+A)}{s^2 - 2}\right\} \\
&= \frac{1}{\sqrt{2}}\int_0^t f(v)e^{-(t-v)}\sinh\sqrt{2}(t-v)\,dv + e^{-t}\left(A\cosh\sqrt{2}t + \frac{B+A}{\sqrt{2}}\sinh\sqrt{2}t\right).\bullet
\end{aligned}$$

EXERCISES 8.2

1. Verify property 8.10b.

In Exercises 2–20 use Laplace transforms to solve the differential equation subject to the initial or boundary conditions.

2. $y'' + 2y' - y = e^t$, $\quad y(0) = 1$, $\quad y'(0) = 2$

3. $y'' + y = 2e^{-t}$, $\quad y(0) = y'(0) = 0$

4. $y'' + 2y' + y = t$, $\quad y(0) = 0$, $\quad y'(0) = 1$

5. $y'' - 2y' + y = t^2 e^t$, $\quad y(0) = 1$, $\quad y'(0) = 0$

6. $y'' + y = t$, $\quad y(0) = 1$, $\quad y'(0) = -2$

7. $y'' + 2y' + 5y = e^{-t} \sin t$, $\quad y(0) = 0$, $\quad y'(0) = 1$

8. $y'' + 6y' + y = \sin 3t$, $\quad y(0) = 2$, $\quad y'(0) = 1$

9. $y'' + y' - 6y = t + \cos t$, $\quad y(0) = 1$, $\quad y'(0) = -2$

10. $y'' - 4y' + 5y = te^{-3t}$, $\quad y(0) = -1$, $\quad y'(0) = 2$

11. $y'' + 4y = f(t)$, $\quad y(0) = 0$, $\quad y'(0) = 1$, where $f(t) = \begin{cases} 1 & 0 < t < 1 \\ 0 & t > 1 \end{cases}$

12. $y'' + 2y' - 4y = \cos^2 t$, $\quad y(0) = 0$, $\quad y'(0) = 0$

13. $y'' - 3y' + 2y = 8t^2 + 12e^{-t}$, $\quad y(0) = 0$, $\quad y'(0) = 2$

14. $y'' + 4y' - 2y = \sin 4t$, $\quad y(0) = 0$, $\quad y'(0) = 0$

15. $y'' + 8y' + 41y = e^{-2t} \sin t$, $\quad y(0) = 0$, $\quad y'(0) = 1$

16. $y'' + 2y' + y = f(t)$, $\quad y(0) = 0$, $\quad y'(0) = 0$, where $f(t) = \begin{cases} t & 0 < t < 1 \\ 0 & t > 1 \end{cases}$

17. $y'' + 9y = \cos 2t$, $\quad y(0) = 1$, $\quad y(\pi/2) = -1$

18. $y'' + 3y' - 4y = 2e^{-4t}$, $\quad y(0) = 1$, $\quad y(1) = 1$

19. $y'' + 2y' + 5y = e^{-t} \sin t$, $\quad y(0) = 0$, $\quad y(\pi/4) = 1$

20. $y'' - 4y' + 3y = f(t)$, $\quad y(0) = 1$, $\quad y'(0) = 0$

In Exercises 21–26 use Laplace transforms to find a general solution of the differential equation.

21. $y'' - 2y' + 4y = t^2$

22. $y'' - 2y' + y = t^2 e^t$

23. $y'' + y = f(t)$

24. $y'' + 2y' + 5y = e^{-t} \sin t$

25. $y'' + 4y' + y = t + 2$

26. $y'' - 4y = f(t)$

27. To find a general solution of $y'' + 9y = t \sin t$, replace $t \sin t$ by te^{ti}, solve the equation, and then take imaginary parts.

28. To find a general solution of $y'' - 2y' + 3y = t \cos 2t$, replace $t \cos 2t$ by te^{2ti}, solve the equation, and then take real parts.

29. Verify that

$$\mathcal{L}\{f'''\}(s) = s^3 \tilde{f}(s) - s^2 f(0) - s f'(0) - f''(0)$$

when f, f', and f'' are continuous and f''' is piecewise continuous on every finite interval $0 \le t \le T$, and f, f', and f'' are $O(e^{\alpha t})$.

Use the result of Exercise **29** to solve the differential equation in Exercises **30–31**.

30. $y''' - 3y'' + 3y' - y = t^2 e^t$, $\quad y(0) = 1$, $\quad y'(0) = 0$, $\quad y''(0) = -2$

31. $y''' - 3y'' + 3y' - y = t^2 e^t$

One end of a spring with constant k newtons per metre is attached to a mass of M kilograms and the other end is attached to a wall (see figure below).

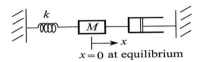

$x = 0$ at equilibrium

Attached to the mass is a dashpot — a device that provides, or represents, a resistive force on the mass directly proportional to the velocity of the mass. If all other forces are grouped into a function denoted by $f(t)$, the differential equation governing motion of the mass is

$$M\frac{d^2 x}{dt^2} + \beta\frac{dx}{dt} + kx = f(t),$$

where $\beta > 0$ is a constant. The position of M when the spring is unstretched corresponds to $x = 0$. Accompanying the differential equation will be two initial conditions $x(0) = A$ and $x'(0) = B$ representing the initial position and velocity of M. In Exercises **32–38**, solve the differential equation with the given information.

32. $M = 1/5$, $\quad \beta = 0$, $\quad k = 10$, $\quad f(t) = 0$, $\quad x(0) = -0.03$, $\quad x'(0) = 0$

33. $M = 1/5$, $\quad \beta = 3/2$, $\quad k = 10$, $\quad f(t) = 0$, $\quad x(0) = -0.03$, $\quad x'(0) = 0$

34. $M = 1/5$, $\quad \beta = 3/2$, $\quad k = 10$, $\quad f(t) = 4\sin 10t$, $\quad x(0) = 0$, $\quad x'(0) = 0$

35. $M = 2$, $\quad \beta = 0$, $\quad k = 16$, $\quad f(t) = 0$, $\quad x(0) = 0.1$, $\quad x'(0) = 0$

36. $M = 1/10$, $\quad \beta = 1/20$, $\quad k = 5$, $\quad f(t) = 0$, $\quad x(0) = -1/20$, $\quad x'(0) = 2$

37. $M = 1/10$, $\quad \beta = 0$, $\quad k = 4000$, $\quad f(t) = 3\cos 200t$, $\quad x(0) = 0$, $\quad x'(0) = 10$

38. $M = 1$, $\quad \beta = 0$, $\quad k = 64$, $\quad f(t) = 2\sin 8t$, $\quad x(0) = 0$, $\quad x'(0) = 0$

39. (a) Let f be $O(e^{\alpha t})$ and be continuous for $t \geq 0$ except for a finite discontinuity at $t = t_0 > 0$; and let f' be piecewise continuous on every finite interval $0 \leq t \leq T$. Show that

$$\mathcal{L}\{f'\}(s) = s\tilde{f}(s) - f(0) - e^{-st_0}[f(t_0+) - f(t_0-)].$$

(b) What is the result in (a) if $t_0 = 0$?

8.3 Discontinuous Nonhomogeneities

Nonhomogeneities for the linear differential equations in Section 8.2 were all continuous. As a result, Laplace transforms did not prove overly advantageous compared to other methods customarily used on such equations. In this section we show that Laplace transforms are exceptional for handling discontinuities. We begin by illustrating the awkwardness of other techniques on the initial-value problem

$$y'' + 2y' + y = f(t), \quad y(0) = 1, \quad y'(0) = 0,$$

where the nonhomogeneity is the discontinuous function

$$f(t) = \begin{cases} t, & 0 < t < 1 \\ 0, & t > 1. \end{cases}$$

Basically what we do is solve the differential equation on the intervals $0 < t < 1$ and $t > 1$ and then match the solutions at $t = 1$. The auxiliary equation $m^2 + 2m + 1 = 0$ has double root $m = -1$. On the interval $0 < t < 1$, a particular solution of the differential equation is $y_p = t - 2$, and hence a general solution on this interval is $y_1(t) = (C_1 + C_2 t)e^{-t} + t - 2$. The initial conditions require

$$1 = y(0) = C_1 - 2, \qquad 0 = y'(0) = C_2 - C_1 + 1,$$

the solutions of which are $C_1 = 3$ and $C_2 = 2$. On the interval $0 < t < 1$, then,

$$y_1(t) = (3 + 2t)e^{-t} + t - 2.$$

For $t > 1$, the general solution of the differential equation is $y_2(t) = (D_1 + D_2 t)e^{-t}$.

The solution of a second-order, linear differential equation must be continuous and have a continuous first derivative, and this must be true even at the point of discontinuity $(t = 1)$ of $f(t)$. This means that $\lim_{t \to 1-} y_1(t) = \lim_{t \to 1+} y_2(t)$ and $\lim_{t \to 1-} y_1'(t) = \lim_{t \to 1+} y_2'(t)$, and therefore

$$5e^{-1} - 1 = (D_1 + D_2)e^{-1}, \qquad -3e^{-1} + 1 = -D_1 e^{-1}.$$

These can be solved for $D_1 = 3 - e$ and $D_2 = 2$, and therefore the solution of the initial-value problem is

$$y(t) = \begin{cases} (3 + 2t)e^{-t} + t - 2, & 0 \le t \le 1 \\ (3 - e + 2t)e^{-t}, & t > 1. \end{cases}$$

Let us now solve the problem by taking Laplace transforms of both sides of the differential equation,

$$[s^2 \tilde{y} - s] + 2[s\tilde{y} - 1] + \tilde{y} = \mathcal{L}\{f(t)\},$$

where

$$\mathcal{L}\{f(t)\} = \mathcal{L}\{t\,[h(t) - h(t-1)]\} = \mathcal{L}\{t\,h(t)\} - \mathcal{L}\{[t\,h(t-1)\}$$
$$= \frac{1}{s^2} - e^{-s}\mathcal{L}\{t + 1\} = \frac{1}{s^2} - e^{-s}\left(\frac{1}{s^2} + \frac{1}{s}\right).$$

Thus,

$$\tilde{y}(s) = \frac{1}{(s+1)^2}\left[s+2+\frac{1}{s^2}-e^{-s}\left(\frac{1}{s^2}+\frac{1}{s}\right)\right]$$

$$= \frac{(s+1)+1}{(s+1)^2}+\frac{1}{s^2(s+1)^2}-\frac{e^{-s}}{s^2(s+1)}.$$

Partial fractions on the second and third terms lead to

$$\tilde{y}(s) = \left[\frac{1}{s+1}+\frac{1}{(s+1)^2}\right]+\left[-\frac{2}{s}+\frac{1}{s^2}+\frac{2}{s+1}+\frac{1}{(s+1)^2}\right]+e^{-s}\left[\frac{1}{s}-\frac{1}{s^2}-\frac{1}{s+1}\right]$$

$$= -\frac{2}{s}+\frac{1}{s^2}+\frac{3}{s+1}+\frac{2}{(s+1)^2}+e^{-s}\left(\frac{1}{s}-\frac{1}{s^2}-\frac{1}{s+1}\right).$$

Consequently,

$$y(t) = -2+t+3e^{-t}+2te^{-t}+\left[1-(t-1)-e^{-(t-1)}\right]h(t-1)$$

$$= (3+2t)e^{-t}+t-2+(2-t-e^{1-t})h(t-1).$$

This solution is identical to that obtained previously, but the Heaviside representation is clearly simpler, and arriving at it with Laplace transforms was less work.

As we use Laplace transforms to solve other differential equations with discontinuous nonhomogeneities, we invite the reader to make comparisons to solutions obtained with other techniques.

Example 8.13 A 2-kg mass is suspended from a spring with constant 512 N/m. It is set into motion by pulling it 10 cm above its equilibrium position and then releasing it. A sinusoidal force $A\sin 8t$ acts on the mass but only for $t > 1$. Find the position of the mass as a function of time if damping is negligible.

Solution We choose $x = 0$ at the equilibrium position of the mass (the position where the mass would hang motionless), with x positive upward (Figure 8.8). If the stretch in the spring at this position is $s > 0$, then $512s - 2g=0$, where $g = 9.81$. When the mass is a distance x from equilibrium, the force of the spring on it is $k(s - x)$. When gravity and the sinusoidal force are added to this, Newton's second law gives

$$2\frac{d^2x}{dt^2} = 512(s-x)-2g+A\sin 8t\,h(t-1).$$

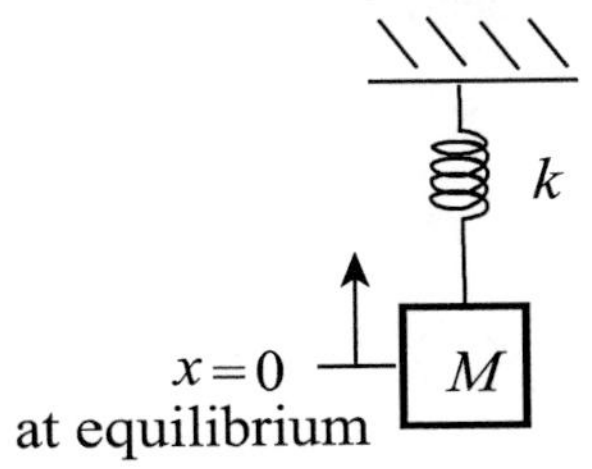

Because $512s - 2g = 0$, this equation simplifies to

$$2\frac{d^2x}{dt^2}+512x = A\sin 8t\,h(t-1).$$

Figure 8.8

Since the mass is released 10 cm above its equilibrium position, $x(t)$ must also satisfy the initial conditions $x(0) = 1/10$ and $x'(0) = 0$. When we take Laplace transforms of the differential equation and use the initial conditions

$$2\left(s^2\tilde{x} - \frac{s}{10}\right) + 512\tilde{x} = Ae^{-s}\mathcal{L}\{\sin 8(t+1)\}$$

$$= Ae^{-s}\mathcal{L}\{\cos 8\,\sin 8t + \sin 8\,\cos 8t\}$$

$$= Ae^{-s}\left[\frac{8\cos 8}{s^2+64} + \frac{(\sin 8)s}{s^2+64}\right].$$

Hence,

$$\tilde{x}(s) = \frac{s}{10(s^2+256)} + \frac{Ae^{-s}[8\cos 8 + (\sin 8)s]}{2(s^2+256)(s^2+64)}.$$

Partial fractions on the second term gives

$$\tilde{x}(s) = \frac{s}{10(s^2+256)} + \frac{Ae^{-s}}{384}\left[\frac{8\cos 8 + (\sin 8)s}{s^2+64} - \frac{8\cos 8 + (\sin 8)s}{s^2+256}\right],$$

and therefore

$$x(t) = \frac{1}{10}\cos 16t + \frac{A}{384}\Big[\cos 8\,\sin 8(t-1) + \sin 8\,\cos 8(t-1)$$

$$- \frac{1}{2}\cos 8\,\sin 16(t-1) - \sin 8\,\cos 16(t-1)\Big]h(t-1).$$

This has been graphed in Figure 8.9 for $A = 100$. Notice the smoothness of the graph even at $t = 1$ when the force is discontinuous.●

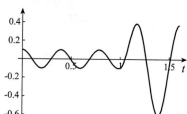

Figure 8.9

The delayed sinusoidal nonhomogeneity presented no problem in Example 8.13. When the nonhomogeneity is periodic, but not sinusoidal, additional difficulties arise. Compared to a solution by other methods, however, Laplace transforms are still superior. We illustrate in the following example.

Example 8.14   Solve the initial-value problem

$$y'' + 4y = f(t), \qquad y(0) = 0, \qquad y'(0) = 0,$$

where $f(t)$ is the periodic function

$$f(t) = \begin{cases} 1, & 0 < t < 1 \\ 0, & 1 < t < 2 \end{cases} \qquad f(t+2) = f(t).$$

Solution   When we take Laplace transforms of both sides of the differential equation,

$$s^2\tilde{y} + 4\tilde{y} = \mathcal{L}\{f(t)\} = \frac{1}{1-e^{-2s}}\int_0^1 e^{-st}\,dt = \frac{1}{1-e^{-2s}}\mathcal{L}\{h(t) - h(t-1)\}$$

$$= \frac{1}{(1+e^{-s})(1-e^{-s})}\left(\frac{1}{s} - \frac{e^{-s}}{s}\right) = \frac{1}{s(1+e^{-s})}.$$

Thus,

$$\tilde{y}(s) = \frac{1}{s(s^2+4)(1+e^{-s})}.$$

Partial fractions gives

$$\frac{1}{s(s^2+4)} = \frac{1/4}{s} - \frac{s/4}{s^2+4}.$$

Now, $1/(1+e^{-s})$ can be interpreted as the sum of a geometric series with common ratio $-e^{-s}$ so that we may write

$$\frac{1}{1+e^{-s}} = 1 - e^{-s} + e^{-2s} - e^{-3s} + \cdots.$$

In other words, $\tilde{y}(s)$ can be expressed as an infinite series

$$\tilde{y}(s) = \frac{1}{4}\left(\frac{1}{s} - \frac{s}{s^2+4}\right)\left(1 - e^{-s} + e^{-2s} - e^{-3s} + \cdots\right).$$

Each term in the series has an easily calculated inverse transform,

$$y(t) = \frac{1}{4}(1 - \cos 2t) - \frac{1}{4}[1 - \cos 2(t-1)]h(t-1) + \frac{1}{4}[1 - \cos 2(t-2)]h(t-2) - \cdots.$$

In sigma notation,

$$y(t) = \frac{1}{4}\sum_{n=0}^{\infty}(-1)^n[1 - \cos 2(t-n)]\,h(t-n).$$

To evaluate $y(t)$ for any given t, it is necessary to include only those terms in the series for which $n < t$. For example, the solution at $t = 2.4$ is given by

$$y(2.4) = \frac{1}{4}[1 - \cos 2(2.4)] - \frac{1}{4}[1 - \cos 2(2.4-1)] + \frac{1}{4}[1 - \cos 2(2.4-2)] = -0.182.$$

Once again the graph of the solution in Figure 8.10 demonstrates that $y(t)$ and $y'(t)$ are continuous, even at the discontinuities $t = 1, 2, \ldots$ of $f(t)$.●

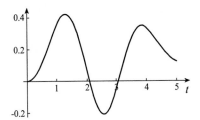

Figure 8.10

Consider using other techniques to find $y(2.4)$ in this example. It would be necessary to solve the differential equation on the intervals $0 < t < 1$, $1 < t < 2$, $2 < t < 3$, match at $t = 1$ and $t = 2$, and then find $y(2.4)$ from the solution for $2 < t < 3$. Try it. You will be convinced that Laplace transforms are superior.

Important in applications are nonhomogeneities called *unit pulses* and *unit impulses*. We discuss them in the context of the vibrating mass-spring system in Figure 8.11. When damping and surface friction are negligible, the differential equation describing the position of the mass relative to its equilibrium position is $M\,d^2x/dt^2 + kx = f(t)$ where $f(t)$ represents all forces on M other than the spring.

The external force is called a **unit pulse** at time $t = t_0$ when it is of the form in Figure 8.12. It can be represented in terms of Heaviside unit step functions as

$$p(t_0, a, t) = \frac{1}{a}[h(t - t_0) - h(t - t_0 - a)]. \tag{8.11}$$

The value of t_0 identifies the time at which the pulse begins and a represents its width. The area under the graph is unity (hence the name *unit* pulse).

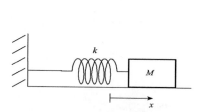

Figure 8.11

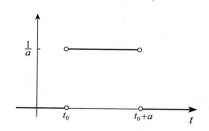

Figure 8.12

The Laplace transform of the unit pulse at $t = t_0$ is

$$\mathcal{L}\{p(t_0, a, t)\}(s) = \frac{1}{as}\left[e^{-t_0 s} - e^{-(t_0 + a)s}\right]. \tag{8.12}$$

Let us determine the reaction of the mass-spring system to a unit pulse at time $t = 0$. We assume that the mass is motionless at its equilibrium position when this force is applied. The initial-value problem for the position of M is

$$M\frac{d^2 x}{dt^2} + kx = p(0, a, t), \qquad x(0) = 0, \qquad x'(0) = 0.$$

If we take Laplace transforms of both sides of the differential equation, and use formula 8.12 with $t_0 = 0$,

$$M s^2 \tilde{x} + k\tilde{x} = \frac{1}{as}(1 - e^{-as}) \quad \Longrightarrow \quad \tilde{x}(s) = \frac{1 - e^{-as}}{as(Ms^2 + k)}.$$

Partial fractions give

$$\tilde{x}(s) = \frac{1}{ka}\left(\frac{1}{s} - \frac{s}{s^2 + k/M}\right)(1 - e^{-as}),$$

from which

$$x(t) = \frac{1}{ka}\left(1 - \cos\sqrt{\frac{k}{M}}t\right) - \frac{1}{ka}\left[1 - \cos\sqrt{\frac{k}{M}}(t - a)\right]h(t - a).$$

At time $t = a$, when the unit pulse ceases, the position of the mass is given by $(1 - \cos\sqrt{k/M}\,a)/(ka)$ and its velocity is $[1/(a\sqrt{kM})]\sin\sqrt{k/M}\,a$. For most applications, a is very small; in particular, sufficiently small that $\sqrt{k/M}\,a < \pi/2$. In this case, the displacement of the mass from equilibrium increases for $0 < t < a$, and its velocity at time $t = a$ is positive.

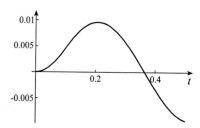

Figure 8.13

A graph of this function for parameter values $k = 100$, $M = 1$, and $a = 1/10$ is shown in Figure 8.13.

Even more important in practice is the response of a system to what is called the *unit impulse* force. It is defined to be the limit of the unit pulse $p(t_0, a, t)$ as the time interval $t_0 < t < t_0 + a$ becomes indefinitely short. As a gets smaller and smaller in Figure 8.12, the area under the curve remains unity; the force simply acts over shorter and shorter time intervals. We have shown the situation for $a = 1/10$, $1/20$, $1/40$, and $1/80$ in Figure 8.14.

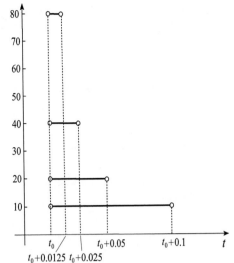

Figure 8.14

The limit of this function as $a \to 0$ is not a function in the normal sense of function. It has value 0 for all t except $t = t_0$ where its value is "infinite". Such functions, called *generalized functions*, are discussed in advanced mathematics. This particular one is called the **unit impulse** or the **Dirac delta** function. It is denoted by

$$\delta(t - t_0) = \lim_{a \to 0} \frac{1}{a} [h(t - t_0) - h(t - t_0 - a)]. \qquad (8.13)$$

The Dirac delta function can be defined in other ways; they are essentially equivalent and lead to identical properties. Two such formulations are limits of the sequences of functions in Figures 8.15 and 8.16. In both cases, the area under each curve is unity. Like the functions in Figure 8.14, those in Figure 8.15 are discontinuous, but they are symmetric around t_0. The functions in Figure 8.16 are continuous and symmetric around t_0.

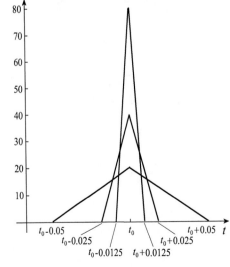

Figure 8.15   **Figure 8.16**

In our vibrating mass-spring system, the Dirac delta function represents a unit force instantaneously applied at time $t = t_0$. It is a function that is of exponential order, but it is not piecewise-continuous on every finite interval. It does, however, have a Laplace transform. If we write

$$\mathcal{L}\{\delta(t - t_0)\} = \mathcal{L}\left\{\lim_{a \to 0} p(t_0, a, t)\right\},$$

it might seem natural to interchange limit and Laplace transform operations,

$$\mathcal{L}\{\delta(t - t_0)\} = \lim_{a \to 0} \mathcal{L}\{p(t_0, a, t)\}.$$

Unfortunately, it not possible to justify the validity of the interchange, but it does lead to a correct formula for the Laplace transform of $\delta(t - t_0)$, and we shall therefore proceed. Substituting from equation 8.12 and using L'Hopital's rule on the limit gives

$$\mathcal{L}\{\delta(t - t_0)\}(s) = \lim_{a \to 0}\left(\frac{e^{-t_0 s} - e^{-(t_0 + a)s}}{as}\right) = \lim_{a \to 0}\left(\frac{se^{-(t_0 + a)s}}{s}\right) = e^{-t_0 s}. \quad (8.14)$$

An alternative way to arrive at equation 8.14 is to develop the operational property of the Dirac delta function. Suppose that $f(t)$ is a continuous function and $F(t)$ is an antiderivative of $f(t)$. Then

$$\int_{-\infty}^{\infty} f(t)p(t_0, a, t)\, dt = \frac{1}{a}\int_{t_0}^{t_0 + a} f(t)\, dt = \frac{1}{a}[F(t_0 + a) - F(t_0)].$$

If we take limits on both sides of this as $a \to 0$ and interchange limit and integration on the left, we get

$$\int_{-\infty}^{\infty} f(t)\left[\lim_{a \to 0} p(t_0, a, t)\right] dt = \lim_{a \to 0}\left[\frac{F(t_0 + a) - F(t_0)}{a}\right].$$

But the limit on the left is the Dirac delta function $\delta(t - t_0)$ and the limit on the right is $F'(t_0) = f(t_0)$. In other words, we have

$$\int_{-\infty}^{\infty} f(t)\delta(t - t_0)\, dt = f(t_0). \quad (8.15)$$

This is the defining property of the Dirac delta function $\delta(t - t_0)$. It is not a stand alone function as we know functions; that is, we cannot assign values to $\delta(t - t_0)$ for every real value of t. It is an operator that operates on functions to yield the value of the function $f(t)$ at t_0. Although we shall use the function to model instantaneous forces (impulse forces), and other "point" entities in ODEs and PDEs, the differential equation will always be integrated to bring property 8.15 into play. The limits of integration in equation 8.15 need not be infinite. More generally, if $f(t)$ is continuous at t_0,

$$\int_a^b f(t)\delta(t - t_0)\, dt = \begin{cases} f(t_0), & \text{if } a < t_0 < b \\ 0, & \text{otherwise.} \end{cases} \quad (8.16)$$

This property of the Dirac delta function immediately yields its Laplace transform,

$$\mathcal{L}\{\delta(t - t_0)\}(s) = \int_0^{\infty} \delta(t - t_0)e^{-st}\, dt = e^{-t_0 s}.$$

Let us determine the response of the mass-spring system in Figure 8.11 to a unit impulse at time $t = 0$. To do so we solve the initial-value problem

$$M\frac{d^2x}{dt^2} + kx = \delta(t), \qquad x(0) = 0, \qquad x'(0) = 0.$$

When we take Laplace transforms and use formula 8.14 with $t_0 = 0$,

$$Ms^2\tilde{x} + k\tilde{x} = 1 \qquad \Longrightarrow \qquad \tilde{x}(s) = \frac{1}{Ms^2 + k}.$$

The inverse transform is

$$x(t) = \frac{1}{M}\mathcal{L}^{-1}\left\{\frac{1}{s^2 + k/M}\right\} = \frac{1}{\sqrt{kM}}\sin\sqrt{\frac{k}{M}}t.$$

A graph of this function for $k = 400$ and $M = 2$ is shown in Figure 8.17. It is straightforward to show that the same displacement results from giving the mass an initial velocity of $1/M$ and applying no impulse. In other words, the solution does not satisfy the initial condition $x'(0) = 0$. This is a result of specifying initial conditions and Dirac delta function simultaneously at $t = 0$. There would be no problem if the impulse force occured at any other time. This is illustrated in the following example.

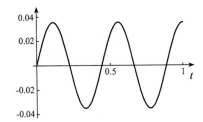

Figure 8.17

Example 8.15 A 100-gm mass is suspended from a spring with constant 50 N/m. It is set into motion by raising it 10 cm above its equilibrium position and giving it a velocity of 1 m/s downward. During the subsequent motion a damping force acts on the mass and the magnitude of this force is twice the velocity of the mass. If an impulse force of magnitude 2 N is applied vertically upward to the mass at $t = 3$ s, find the position of the mass for all time.

Solution If we choose $x = 0$ at the equilibrium position of the mass (the position where the mass would hang motionless), the initial-value problem for displacement is

$$\frac{1}{10}\frac{d^2x}{dt^2} + 2\frac{dx}{dt} + 50x = 2\delta(t-3), \qquad x(0) = \frac{1}{10}, \qquad x'(0) = -1.$$

When we multiply the differential equation by 10, and take Laplace transforms,

$$\left(s^2\tilde{x} - \frac{s}{10} + 1\right) + 20\left(s\tilde{x} - \frac{1}{10}\right) + 500\tilde{x} = 20e^{-3s}.$$

Thus,

$$\tilde{x}(s) = \frac{s/10 + 1}{s^2 + 20s + 500} + \frac{20e^{-3s}}{s^2 + 20s + 500}$$

$$= \frac{1}{10}\left[\frac{s+10}{(s+10)^2 + 400}\right] + \frac{20e^{-3s}}{(s+10)^2 + 400}.$$

The inverse transform is

$$x(t) = \frac{1}{10}e^{-10t}\mathcal{L}^{-1}\left\{\frac{s}{s^2+400}\right\} + \mathcal{L}^{-1}\left\{\frac{20e^{-3s}}{(s+10)^2+400}\right\}.$$

Since $\mathcal{L}^{-1}\{20/[(s+10)^2+400]\} = e^{-10t}\mathcal{L}^{-1}\{20/(s^2+400)\} = e^{-10t}\sin 20t$, it follows that

$$x(t) = \frac{1}{10}e^{-10t}\cos 20t + e^{-10(t-3)}\sin 20(t-3)\, h(t-3).$$

It is straightforward to show that this solution satisfies the initial conditions $x(0) = 1/10$ and $x'(0) = -1$. A graph of the function is shown in Figure 8.18. Due to excessive damping, oscillations essentially disappear after 1 second, but the impulse force restores them at $t = 3$ seconds. Notice the abrupt change in slope (velocity) at $t = 3$ due to the impulse force. Damping again brings the mass essentially to rest after another second.●

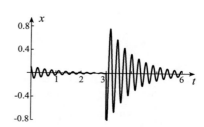

Figure 8.18

When nonhomogeneities are piecewise-continuous functions, we know that solutions are continuous and have continuous first derivatives. This example illustrates that impulse forces, not being piecewise-continuous, lead to solutions with discontinuous first derivatives at the instant of the impulse.

EXERCISES 8.3

In Exercises 1–10 solve the initial-value problem.

1. $y'' + 9y = f(t)$, $y(0) = 1$, $y'(0) = 2$, where $f(t) = \begin{cases} 0, & 0 < t < 4 \\ 1, & t > 4 \end{cases}$

2. $y'' + 9y = f(t)$, $y(0) = 1$, $y'(0) = 2$, where $f(t) = \begin{cases} 2, & 0 < t < 4 \\ 0, & t > 4 \end{cases}$

3. $y'' + 4y' + 4y = f(t)$, $y(0) = 0$, $y'(0) = -1$, where $f(t) = \begin{cases} t, & 0 < t < 1 \\ 1, & t > 1 \end{cases}$

4. $y'' + 4y' + 4y = f(t)$, $y(0) = -1$, $y'(0) = 0$, where $f(t) = \begin{cases} 2-t, & 0 < t < 2 \\ t-2, & t > 2 \end{cases}$

5. $y'' + 4y' + 3y = f(t)$, $y(0) = 1$, $y'(0) = 2$, where $f(t) = \begin{cases} 0, & 0 < t < \pi \\ \sin t, & t > \pi \end{cases}$

6. $y'' + 4y' + 3y = f(t)$, $y(0) = 1$, $y'(0) = 2$, where $f(t) = \begin{cases} \sin t, & 0 < t < \pi \\ 0, & t > \pi \end{cases}$

7. $y'' + 2y' + 5y = f(t)$, $y(0) = 0$, $y'(0) = 0$, where $f(t) = \begin{cases} 3, & 0 < t < 1 \\ -3, & t > 1 \end{cases}$

8. $y'' + 2y' + 5y = f(t)$, $y(0) = 0$, $y'(0) = 0$, where $f(t) = \begin{cases} 4, & 0 < t < 1 \\ -4, & 1 < t < 2 \\ 0, & t > 2 \end{cases}$

9. $y'' + 16y = f(t)$, $y(0) = 2$, $y'(0) = 0$, where $f(t) = \begin{cases} t, & 0 < t < 1 \\ 0, & 1 < t < 2 \end{cases}$ $f(t+2) = f(t)$

10. $y'' + 16y = f(t)$, $y(0) = 2$, $y'(0) = 0$, where $f(t) = \begin{cases} t, & 0 < t < 1 \\ 2-t, & 1 < t < 2 \end{cases}$ $f(t+2) = f(t)$

11. A 100-gm mass is suspended from a spring with constant 40 N/m. The mass is pulled 10 cm above its equilibrium position and given velocity 2 m/s downward. If a force of 100 N acts vertically upward for the first 4 seconds, find the position of the mass as a function of time. Ignore all damping.

12. Repeat Exercise 11 if the force is turned on after 4 seconds.

13. Repeat Exercise 11 if a damping force with constant $\beta = 5$ also acts on the mass.

14. Repeat Exercise 12 if a damping force with constant $\beta = 5$ also acts on the mass.

15. Repeat Exercise 11 if a damping force with constant $\beta = 1$ also acts on the mass.

16. Repeat Exercise 12 if a damping force with constant $\beta = 1$ also acts on the mass.

17. A 2-kg mass is suspended from a spring with constant 512 N/m. It is set into motion with a unit impulse force at time $t = 0$. Find the position of the mass as a function of time. Ignore all damping.

18. Repeat Exercise 17 if a damping force with constant $\beta = 80$ also acts on the mass.

19. Repeat Exercise 18 if $\beta = 8$.

20. A 2-kg mass is suspended from a spring with constant 512 N/m. It is set into motion by moving it to position x_0 and then releasing it. If a unit impulse force is applied at $t_0 > 0$, find the position of the mass for all time.

21. Repeat Exercise 20 if motion is initiated by giving the mass velocity v_0 at time $t = 0$ and position $x = 0$.

22. Repeat Exercise 20 if motion is initiated by giving the mass velocity v_0 from position x_0 at time $t = 0$.

23. A 1-kg mass is suspended from a spring with constant 100 N/m. It is subjected to a unit impulse force at $t = 0$ and again at $t = 1$. Find the position of the mass as a function of time.

24. Repeat Exercise 23 if unit impulse forces are applied one each second beginning at time $t = 0$. Express the solution in sigma notation.

25. Repeat Exercise 24 if unit impulse forces are $\pi/5$ seconds apart, the first at time $t = 0$. Is there resonance?

§8.4   The Complex Inversion Integral

Finding the inverse Laplace transform in Sections 8.1–8.3 was a matter of organization and tables; use properties 8.3b and 8.4b, and partial fractions to organize a given transform $\tilde{f}(s)$ into a form for which the inverse transform can be found in tables. In many applications, transform functions are so complicated, they cannot be found in tables; this is especially true in partial differential equations. What we need is a direct method for inverting the Laplace transform. In this section, we derive such a formula.

We first note that the results in equations 8.3–8.10 remain valid when s is complex; the complex derivation may be somewhat different than its real counterpart, but each result is valid when s is complex.

The following theorem shows that Laplace transforms are analytic functions of the complex variable s.

Theorem 8.6   If f is $O(e^{\alpha t})$ and piecewise continuous on every finite interval $0 \leq t \leq T$, then the Laplace transform $\tilde{f}(s) = \tilde{f}(x+yi)$ of f is an analytic function of s in the half-plane $x > \alpha$.

Proof   If the real and imaginary parts of $\tilde{f}(s)$ are denoted by $u(x,y)$ and $v(x,y)$,

$$\tilde{f}(s) = u + vi = \int_0^\infty e^{-(x+yi)t} f(t)\, dt,$$

then,

$$u(x,y) = \int_0^\infty e^{-xt} \cos yt\, f(t)\, dt, \qquad v(x,y) = \int_0^\infty -e^{-xt} \sin yt\, f(t)\, dt.$$

To verify analyticity of $\tilde{f}$, we show that $u(x,y)$ and $v(x,y)$ have continuous first partial derivatives that satisfy the Cauchy-Riemann equations when $x > \alpha$. Now,

$$\left\{ \begin{array}{l} |e^{-xt} \cos yt\, f(t)| \\ |e^{-xt} \sin yt\, f(t)| \end{array} \right\} \leq e^{-xt} |f(t)|,$$

and since f is $O(e^{\alpha t})$, there exist constants M and T such that for all $t > T$, $|f(t)| < Me^{\alpha t}$. Consequently, whenever $x > \alpha' > \alpha$ and $t > T$,

$$\left\{ \begin{array}{l} |e^{-xt} \cos yt\, f(t)| \\ |e^{-xt} \sin yt\, f(t)| \end{array} \right\} < e^{-xt} Me^{\alpha t} \leq Me^{(\alpha - \alpha')t},$$

and

$$\left\{ \begin{array}{l} |u(x,y)| \\ |v(x,y)| \end{array} \right\} < \int_0^T e^{-xt} |f(t)|\, dt + \int_T^\infty Me^{(\alpha-\alpha')t} dt$$

$$\leq \int_0^T e^{-\alpha' t} |f(t)|\, dt + M \left\{ \frac{e^{(\alpha-\alpha')t}}{\alpha - \alpha'} \right\}_0^\infty$$

$$= \int_0^T e^{-\alpha' t} |f(t)|\, dt + \frac{M}{\alpha' - \alpha}.$$

Thus, the integrals representing u and v converge absolutely and uniformly with respect to x and y in the half-plane $x > \alpha' > \alpha$. Since f is piecewise continuous, u and v are continuous functions for $x > \alpha'$. Now,

$$\int_0^\infty \frac{\partial}{\partial x}\left[e^{-xt}\cos yt\, f(t)\right] dt = \int_0^\infty -te^{-xt}\cos yt\, f(t)\, dt$$

and

$$\int_0^\infty \frac{\partial}{\partial y}\left[-e^{-xt}\sin yt\, f(t)\right] dt = \int_0^\infty -te^{-xt}\cos yt\, f(t)\, dt.$$

Since $tf(t)$ is $O(e^{(\alpha+\epsilon)t})$ for any $\epsilon > 0$ (see Exercise 26 in Section 8.1), and piecewise continuous on every finite interval $0 < t < T$, a similar argument to that above shows that this integral is absolutely and uniformly convergent with respect to x and y for $x > \alpha' > \alpha$. Because $\alpha' > \alpha$ is arbitrary, it follows that this integral converges to a continuous function which is equal to both $\partial u/\partial x$ and $\partial v/\partial y$ for $x > \alpha$. We have shown then that the first of the Cauchy-Riemann equations $\partial u/\partial x = \partial v/\partial y$ is satisfied for $x > \alpha$. In a similar way, we can show that $\partial u/\partial y = -\partial v/\partial x$, and therefore $\tilde{f}(s)$ is analytic for $x > \alpha$. ∎

To obtain the complex inversion integral for $\mathcal{L}^{-1}\{\tilde{f}(s)\}$ we use the extension of Cauchy's integral formula contained in Theorem 4.18 of Section 4.6.

When a function f is $O(e^{\alpha t})$, we know that its transform $\tilde{f}(s)$ is analytic for $x > \alpha$ (Theorem 8.6). Suppose further that in some half-plane $x > \delta > 0$, there exist constants M, R, and $k > 0$ such that $|\tilde{f}(s)s^k| < M$ for $|s| > R$ (Figure 8.19). Then according to Theorem 4.18, if s is a point with $\text{Re}\, s > \gamma > \delta$, $\tilde{f}(s)$ may be expressed in the form

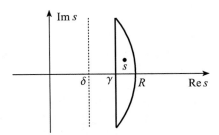

Figure 8.19

$$\tilde{f}(s) = -\frac{1}{2\pi i}\lim_{\beta\to\infty}\int_{\gamma-\beta i}^{\gamma+\beta i}\frac{\tilde{f}(\zeta)}{\zeta - s}\, d\zeta.$$

If we formally take inverse transforms of both sides of this equation and interchange the order of integration and $\mathcal{L}^{-1}$, we obtain

$$f(t) = -\frac{1}{2\pi i}\lim_{\beta\to\infty}\int_{\gamma-\beta i}^{\gamma+\beta i} -\tilde{f}(\zeta)\mathcal{L}^{-1}\left(\frac{1}{s-\zeta}\right) d\zeta = \frac{1}{2\pi i}\lim_{\beta\to\infty}\int_{\gamma-\beta i}^{\gamma+\beta i} e^{\zeta t}\tilde{f}(\zeta)\, d\zeta.$$

This expression

$$f(t) = \frac{1}{2\pi i}\lim_{\beta\to\infty}\int_{\gamma-\beta i}^{\gamma+\beta i} e^{st}\tilde{f}(s)\, ds, \tag{8.17}$$

is called the **complex inversion integral** for the Laplace transform. In the event that $f(t)$ has a discontinuity at a value of t, the integral converges to the average of left- and right-limits; that is,

$$\frac{f(t+) + f(t-)}{2} = \frac{1}{2\pi i}\lim_{\beta\to\infty}\int_{\gamma-\beta i}^{\gamma+\beta i} e^{st}\tilde{f}(s)\, ds. \tag{8.18}$$

Although the integral in equations 8.17 and 8.18 is along the line $x = \gamma$ in the complex plane, it can be written as a complex combination of real improper integrals. But even for very simple functions $\tilde{f}(s)$, the integrations involved in this real form are difficult (see Exercise 18). Fortunately, in Theorem 8.7 we prove that residues of $e^{st}\tilde{f}(s)$ may be used to evaluate the integral.

Theorem 8.7   Let $\tilde{f}$ be a function for which the inversion integral along a line $x = \gamma$ represents the inverse function f, and let $\tilde{f}$ be analytic except for isolated singularities s_n $(n = 1, \ldots)$ in the half-plane $x < \gamma$. Then the series of residues of $e^{st}\tilde{f}(s)$ at $s = s_n$ converges to f for each positive t,

$$f(t) = \text{sum of residues of } e^{st}\tilde{f}(s) \text{ at its singularities,}$$

provided a sequence C_n of contours can be found which satisfies the following properties:

1. C_n consists of the straight line $x = \gamma$ from $\gamma - \beta_n i$ to $\gamma + \beta_n i$, and some curve Γ_n at $\gamma + \beta_n i$, ending at $\gamma - \beta_n i$, and lying in $x \leq \gamma$ (Figure 8.20);

2. C_n encloses $s_1, s_2, \ldots, s_n$;

3. $\displaystyle\lim_{n \to \infty} \beta_n = \infty$;

4. $\displaystyle\lim_{n \to \infty} \int_{\Gamma_n} e^{st}\tilde{f}(s)\,ds = 0$.

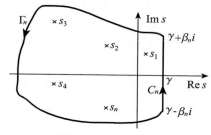

Figure 8.20

Proof   Since $e^{st}\tilde{f}(s)$ is analytic in C_n except at $s_1, \ldots, s_n$, the residue theorem states that

$$\begin{pmatrix} \text{sum of residues of} \\ e^{st}\tilde{f}(s) \text{ at } s_1, \ldots, s_n \end{pmatrix} = \frac{1}{2\pi i}\oint_{C_n} e^{st}\tilde{f}(s)\,ds = \frac{1}{2\pi i}\int_{\gamma - \beta_n i}^{\gamma + \beta_n i} e^{st}\tilde{f}(s)\,ds + \int_{\Gamma_n} e^{st}\tilde{f}(s)\,ds.$$

When we take limits on n, (and use conditions 3 and 4 in the statement of the theorem),

$$\begin{pmatrix} \text{sum of residues of} \\ e^{st}\tilde{f}(s) \text{ at } s_1, \ldots, s_n, \ldots \end{pmatrix} = \frac{1}{2\pi i}\lim_{n \to \infty}\int_{\gamma - \beta_n i}^{\gamma + \beta_n i} e^{st}\tilde{f}(s)\,ds = f(t). \quad\blacksquare$$

It is not essential, as condition 2 requires, that C_n contain precisely the first n singularities of $\tilde{f}(s)$. In fact, this could be difficult to accomplish depending on how singularities are enumerated. What is essential is that as n increases, the C_n expand to eventually include all singularities.

There is a problem using this theorem. For instance, suppose the Laplace transform is applied to an ordinary differential equation in $y(t)$, and some analysis is performed leading to an expression for $\tilde{y}(s)$. To use residues to find $y(t)$, we must satisfy the requirements of Theorem 8.7. In particular, the theorem requires that $y(t)$ be representable by complex inversion integral 8.17. This is unverifiable. Since $y(t)$ is the unknown of the problem, how could we know that it is representable by the complex inversion integral? What we do is ignore the conditions of the theorem, and use residues of $e^{st}\tilde{y}(s)$ to obtain a function $y(t)$, a function that we hope is both the inverse transform of $\tilde{y}(s)$ and a solution of the differential equation. To verify that this is indeed the case, we can proceed in two ways. First, we can take the Laplace transform of $y(t)$; and if we obtain $\tilde{y}(s)$, then there is no question that $y(t)$ is the inverse of $\tilde{y}(s)$. Alternatively, we can set aside Laplace transforms completely and verify that $y(t)$ is a solution of the original differential equation with which we began.

Example 8.16 Use residues to find inverse transforms when $\tilde{f}(s)$ is equal to:

(a) $\dfrac{1}{s^m}$, $m \geq 2$ an integer   (a) $\dfrac{1}{s^2 + 9}$ (c) $\dfrac{s^2}{(s^2 + 1)^2}$

Solution (a) The function $\tilde{f}(s) = 1/s^m$ has a pole of order m at $s = 0$. According to equation 6.2, the residue of $e^{st}\tilde{f}(s)$ at $s = 0$ is

$$\lim_{s \to 0} \frac{1}{(m-1)!} \frac{d^{m-1}}{ds^{m-1}}\left[s^m e^{st}\tilde{f}(s)\right] = \frac{1}{(m-1)!} \lim_{s \to 0} \frac{d^{m-1}}{ds^{m-1}}(e^{st}) = \frac{t^{m-1}}{(m-1)!}.$$

The contours Γ_n in Figure 8.21 are arcs of circles with radius n meeting the straight line $\operatorname{Re} s = 1$ at the points $1 \pm \beta_n i$. They clearly satisfy conditions 1 and 3 in Theorem 8.7. Furthermore, on Γ_n,

$$\left|\frac{e^{st}}{s^m}\right| = \left|\frac{e^{(x+yi)t}}{n^m e^{m\theta i}}\right| = \frac{e^{xt}}{n^m} \leq \frac{e^t}{n^m}.$$

According to inequality 4.21, we may write that

$$\left|\int_{\Gamma_n} \frac{e^{st}}{s^m}\,ds\right| < \frac{2\pi n e^t}{n^m} = \frac{2\pi e^t}{n^{m-1}}.$$

This expression approaches zero as $n \to \infty$. Consequently, the Γ_n satisfy condition 4 in Theorem 8.7, and by this theorem,

$$\mathcal{L}^{-1}\left\{\frac{1}{s^m}\right\} = \frac{t^{m-1}}{(m-1)!}.$$

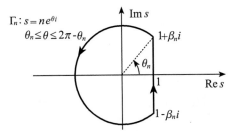

Figure 8.21

(b) The function $\tilde{f}(s) = 1/(s^2 + 9)$ has poles of order one at $s = \pm 3i$. The residue of $e^{st}\tilde{f}(s)$ at $3i$ is

$$\operatorname{Res}\left[e^{st}\tilde{f}(s), 3i\right] = \lim_{s \to 3i} \frac{(s - 3i)e^{st}}{(s + 3i)(s - 3i)} = \frac{e^{3ti}}{6i} = -\frac{i}{6}e^{3ti}.$$

Similarly, $\operatorname{Res}\left[e^{st}\tilde{f}(s), -3i\right] = (i/6)e^{-3ti}$. On the contour Γ_n ($n \geq 4$) in Figure 8.21,

$$\left|\frac{e^{st}}{s^2 + 9}\right| \leq \frac{|e^{(x+yi)t}|}{|s|^2 - 9} = \frac{e^{xt}}{n^2 - 9} \leq \frac{e^t}{n^2 - 9}.$$

Thus,

$$\left|\int_{\Gamma_n} \frac{e^{st}}{s^2 + 9}\,ds\right| < \frac{2\pi n e^t}{n^2 - 9},$$

and this expression approaches zero as $n \to \infty$. By Theorem 8.7 then,

$$\mathcal{L}^{-1}\left\{\frac{1}{s^2 + 9}\right\} = -\frac{i}{6}e^{3ti} + \frac{i}{6}e^{-3ti} = \frac{1}{3}\sin 3t.$$

(c) The function $\tilde{f}(s) = s^2/(s^2+1)^2$ has poles of order two at $s = \pm i$. The residue of $e^{st}\tilde{f}(s)$ at i is

$$\mathrm{Res}\left[e^{st}\tilde{f}(s), i\right] = \lim_{s \to i} \frac{d}{ds}\left[\frac{(s-i)^2 e^{st} s^2}{(s+i)^2(s-i)^2}\right]$$

$$= \lim_{s \to i}\left[\frac{(s+i)^2(2se^{st} + ts^2 e^{st}) - s^2 e^{st}(2)(s+i)}{(s+i)^4}\right]$$

$$= \frac{1}{4}(t-i)e^{ti}.$$

Similarly, $\mathrm{Res}\left[e^{st}\tilde{f}(s), -i\right] = (1/4)(t+i)e^{-ti}$. On the contour Γ_n $(n \geq 2)$ in Figure 8.21,

$$\left|\frac{s^2 e^{st}}{(s^2+1)^2}\right| \leq \frac{|s|^2 e^{xt}}{(|s|^2 - 1)^2} \leq \frac{n^2 e^t}{(n^2-1)^2}.$$

Thus,

$$\left|\int_{\Gamma_n} \frac{s^2 e^{st}}{(s^2+1)^2}\, ds\right| < \frac{2\pi n^3 e^t}{(n^2-1)^2},$$

and this expression approaches zero as $n \to \infty$. By Theorem 8.7 then

$$\mathcal{L}^{-1}\left\{\frac{s^2}{(s^2+1)^2}\right\} = \frac{1}{4}(t-i)e^{ti} + \frac{1}{4}(t+i)e^{-ti} = \frac{t}{2}\cos t + \frac{1}{2}\sin t. \bullet$$

More complicated illustrations of residues are contained in Example 8.17. This example is more typical of problems when Laplace transforms are used to solve partial differential equations.

Example 8.17   Find inverse transforms for:

$$\text{(a)} \quad \tilde{f}(s) = \frac{1}{s^3}(1 - \cosh sx) + \frac{\sinh s \sinh sx}{s^3 \cosh s} \qquad \text{(b)} \quad \tilde{f}(s) = \frac{\sinh\sqrt{s}x}{s \sinh\sqrt{s}}$$

where contrary to previous notation we use $\sqrt{s}$ here to represent the branch of $s^{1/2}$ defined by

$$s^{1/2} = |s|^{1/2}e^{(1/2)\arg s}, \quad 0 \leq \arg s < 2\pi.$$

Omit verification of the existence of contours C_n satisfying the conditions of Theorem 8.17.

Solution (a) This transform has singularities at $s = 0$ and $s = (2n-1)\pi i/2$, n an integer (the zeros of $\cosh s$). The Laurent series of $\tilde{f}(s)$ about $s = 0$ can be found by expanding the hyperbolic functions in Maclaurin series,

$$\tilde{f}(s) = \frac{1}{s^3}\left(1 - 1 - \frac{s^2 x^2}{2!} - \frac{s^4 x^4}{4!} - \cdots\right) + \frac{1}{s^3}\left(\frac{s + \frac{s^3}{3!} + \frac{s^5}{5!} + \cdots}{1 + \frac{s^2}{2!} + \frac{s^4}{4!} + \cdots}\right)\left(sx + \frac{s^3 x^3}{3!} + \cdots\right)$$

$$= \left(-\frac{x^2}{2s} - \frac{x^4 s}{24} - \cdots\right) + \left(s - \frac{s^3}{3} + \cdots\right)\left(\frac{x}{s^2} + \frac{x^3}{6} + \cdots\right)$$

$$= \frac{x}{2s}(2 - x) + \frac{xs}{24}(-x^3 + 4x^2 - 8) + \cdots.$$

Consequently, $\tilde{f}(s)$ has a pole of order one at $s = 0$, as does $e^{st}\tilde{f}(s)$. Multiplication of this series by the Maclaurin series for e^{st} gives

$$e^{st}\tilde{f}(s) = \left[1 + st + \frac{(st)^2}{2!} + \cdots\right]\left[\frac{x}{2s}(2 - x) + \frac{xs}{24}(-x^3 + 4x^2 - 8) + \cdots\right]$$

$$= \frac{x}{2s}(2 - x) + \frac{xt}{2}(2 - x) + \cdots,$$

and therefore the residue of $e^{st}\tilde{f}(s)$ at $s = 0$ is $x(2 - x)/2$.

Because the derivative of $\cosh s$ does not vanish at $s = (2n - 1)\pi i/2$, these singularities are also poles of order one, and the residues of $e^{st}\tilde{f}(s)$ at these poles are given by the limits

$$\lim_{s\to(2n-1)\pi i/2}\left[s - \frac{(2n-1)\pi i}{2}\right]e^{st}\left[\frac{1}{s^3}(1 - \cosh sx) + \frac{\sinh s \sinh sx}{s^3 \cosh s}\right]$$

$$= \frac{e^{(2n-1)\pi ti/2}}{-(2n-1)^3\pi^3 i/8}\sinh\frac{(2n-1)\pi i}{2}\sinh\frac{(2n-1)\pi x i}{2}\lim_{s\to(2n-1)\pi i/2}\frac{s - (2n-1)\pi i/2}{\cosh s}$$

$$= \frac{8e^{(2n-1)\pi ti/2}}{(2n-1)^3\pi^3 i}\sin\frac{(2n-1)\pi}{2}\sin\frac{(2n-1)\pi x}{2}\lim_{s\to(2n-1)\pi i/2}\frac{1}{\sinh s} \quad \text{(using L'Hôpital's rule)}$$

$$= \frac{8(-1)^{n+1}e^{(2n-1)\pi ti/2}}{(2n-1)^3\pi^3 i}\sin\frac{(2n-1)\pi x}{2}\frac{1}{\sinh\frac{(2n-1)\pi i}{2}}$$

$$= -\frac{8e^{(2n-1)\pi ti/2}}{(2n-1)^3\pi^3}\sin\frac{(2n-1)\pi x}{2}.$$

The sum of the residues of $e^{st}\tilde{f}(s)$ at its singularities is therefore

$$f(x,t) = \frac{x}{2}(2 - x) - \frac{8}{\pi^3}\sum_{n=-\infty}^{\infty}\frac{e^{(2n-1)\pi ti/2}}{(2n-1)^3}\sin\frac{(2n-1)\pi x}{2}.$$

To simplify this expression we separate it into two summations, one over positive n and the other over nonpositive n, and in the latter we set $m = 1 - n$,

$$f(x,t) = \frac{x}{2}(2 - x) - \frac{8}{\pi^3}\sum_{n=1}^{\infty}\frac{e^{(2n-1)\pi ti/2}}{(2n-1)^3}\sin\frac{(2n-1)\pi x}{2} - \frac{8}{\pi^3}\sum_{n=-\infty}^{0}\frac{e^{(2n-1)\pi ti/2}}{(2n-1)^3}\sin\frac{(2n-1)\pi x}{2}$$

$$= \frac{x}{2}(2 - x) - \frac{8}{\pi^3}\sum_{n=1}^{\infty}\frac{e^{(2n-1)\pi ti/2}}{(2n-1)^3}\sin\frac{(2n-1)\pi x}{2}$$

$$- \frac{8}{\pi^3}\sum_{m=1}^{\infty}\frac{e^{[2(1-m)-1]\pi ti/2}}{[2(1-m)-1]^3}\sin\frac{[2(1-m)-1]\pi x}{2}.$$

If we now replace m by n in the second summation and combine it with the first

$$f(x,t) = \frac{x}{2}(2 - x) - \frac{8}{\pi^3}\sum_{n=1}^{\infty}\frac{e^{(2n-1)\pi ti/2}}{(2n-1)^3}\sin\frac{(2n-1)\pi x}{2} - \frac{8}{\pi^3}\sum_{n=1}^{\infty}\frac{e^{-(2n-1)\pi ti/2}}{(2n-1)^3}\sin\frac{(2n-1)\pi x}{2}$$

$$= \frac{x}{2}(2 - x) - \frac{8}{\pi^3}\sum_{n=1}^{\infty}\frac{e^{(2n-1)\pi ti/2} + e^{-(2n-1)\pi ti/2}}{(2n-1)^3}\sin\frac{(2n-1)\pi x}{2}$$

$$= \frac{x}{2}(2 - x) - \frac{16}{\pi^3}\sum_{n=1}^{\infty}\frac{1}{(2n-1)^3}\cos\frac{(2n-1)\pi t}{2}\sin\frac{(2n-1)\pi x}{2}.$$

Transforms of this type occur in vibration problems.

(b) The function $\tilde{f}(s)$ has singularities along its branch cut (the positive real axis), and also at the zeros of $\sinh \sqrt{s}$; that is, when $\sqrt{s} = n\pi i$, or, $s = -n^2\pi^2$, $n \geq 0$ an integer. To determine the nature of the singularity at $s = 0$, we substitute $\sqrt{s}x$ and $\sqrt{s}$ into the Maclaurin series for $\sinh s$; the result is

$$\tilde{f}(s) = \frac{1}{s}\left[\frac{\sqrt{s}x + \frac{1}{3!}(\sqrt{s}x)^3 + \cdots}{\sqrt{s} + \frac{1}{3!}(\sqrt{s})^3 + \cdots}\right] = \frac{1}{s}\left[x + \frac{s}{6}(x^3 - x) + \cdots\right].$$

This must be the Laurent series for $\tilde{f}(s)$ about $s = 0$. It shows that, notwithstanding the fact that $\sqrt{s}$ has a branch point at $s = 0$, and a branch cut along the positive real axis, as do $\sinh \sqrt{s}x$ and $\sinh \sqrt{s}$, $\tilde{f}(s)$ has a pole of order one at $s = 0$. The following expansion shows that the residue of $e^{st}\tilde{f}(s)$ at this pole is x,

$$e^{st}\tilde{f}(s) = \left[1 + st + \frac{(st)^2}{2!} + \cdots\right]\left(\frac{1}{s}\right)\left[x + \frac{s}{6}(x^3 - x) + \cdots\right]$$

$$= \frac{1}{s}\left[x + \frac{s}{6}(6xt + x^3 - x) + \cdots\right].$$

Because the derivative of $\sinh \sqrt{s}$ does not vanish at the remaining singularities $s = -n^2\pi^2$ $(n > 0)$, these are also poles of order one, and the residues of $e^{st}\tilde{f}(s)$ at these poles are given by

$$\lim_{s \to -n^2\pi^2} (s + n^2\pi^2)e^{st}\frac{\sinh \sqrt{s}x}{s \sinh \sqrt{s}} = e^{-n^2\pi^2 t}\frac{\sinh n\pi x i}{-n^2\pi^2} \lim_{s \to -n^2\pi^2} \frac{s + n^2\pi^2}{\sinh \sqrt{s}}.$$

L'Hôpital's rule can be used to evaluate this limit, which gives for these residues

$$-\frac{i}{n^2\pi^2}e^{-n^2\pi^2 t}\sin n\pi x \lim_{s \to -n^2\pi^2} \frac{1}{\frac{1}{2\sqrt{s}}\cosh \sqrt{s}} = -\frac{2i}{n^2\pi^2}e^{-n^2\pi^2 t}\sin n\pi x \frac{n\pi i}{\cosh n\pi i}$$

$$= \frac{2}{n\pi}e^{-n^2\pi^2 t}\sin n\pi x \frac{1}{\cos n\pi}$$

$$= \frac{2(-1)^n}{n\pi}e^{-n^2\pi^2 t}\sin n\pi x.$$

Thus, the sum of the residues of $e^{st}\tilde{f}(s)$ at its singularities is

$$f(x,t) = x + \frac{2}{\pi}\sum_{n=1}^{\infty}\frac{(-1)^n}{n}e^{-n^2\pi^2 t}\sin n\pi x.$$

Transforms of this type arise in heat conduction problems.●

EXERCISES 8.4

In Exercises 1–16 use residues to find the inverse Laplace transform of the given function. Omit verification of contours C_n satisfying the conditions of Theorem 8.7 in Exercises 11–16.

1. $\tilde{f}(s) = \dfrac{s}{(s-1)^3}$

2. $\tilde{f}(s) = \dfrac{s}{(s^2+4)^2}$

3. $\tilde{f}(s) = \dfrac{1}{s^2(s+3)}$

4. $\tilde{f}(s) = \dfrac{s^2+2}{(s+1)^2(s-3)^3}$

5. $\tilde{f}(s) = \dfrac{s^2}{(s^2+1)(s^2+4)}$

6. $\tilde{f}(s) = \dfrac{s}{s^4-1}$

7. $\tilde{f}(s) = \dfrac{s^3}{(s^2-4)^3}$

8. $\tilde{f}(s) = \dfrac{1}{(s^2-2s+2)^2}$

9. $\tilde{f}(s) = \dfrac{s-1}{(s^2-2s+2)^2}$

10. $\tilde{f}(s) = \dfrac{s^2}{(s^2-2s+2)^2}$

11. $\tilde{f}(x,s) = \dfrac{1}{s}\left(x - \dfrac{\sinh\sqrt{s}x}{\sinh\sqrt{s}}\right)$, where $\sqrt{s} = |s|^{1/2}e^{(1/2)\arg s}$, $0 \le \arg s < 2\pi$

12. $\tilde{f}(x,u,s) = \dfrac{\sinh sx \, \sinh s(1-u)}{s \sinh s}$

13. $\tilde{f}(x,s) = \dfrac{2\sinh sx}{s^3 \sinh s}(1 - \cosh s) + \dfrac{2}{s^3}(\cosh sx - 1) + \dfrac{x}{s}(1-x)$

14. $\tilde{f}(x,s) = \dfrac{1}{s^3} + \dfrac{\cosh sx}{s^2 \sinh s}$

15. $\tilde{f}(x,s) = \dfrac{\sinh sx}{(4s^2 + \pi^2)\sinh s}$

16. $\tilde{f}(x,s) = \dfrac{\sinh sx}{(s^2 + \pi^2)\sinh s}$

17. (a) What is the inverse transform of $\tilde{f}(s) = e^{-as}/s$, where $a > 0$ is a constant.

  (b) What do you get when you try to find the inverse by residues? Can you explain the difficulty?

18. We have claimed that to use inversion integral 8.17 directly is usually impossible. Set up the complex combination of real improper integrals for 8.17 when $\tilde{f}(s) = 1/s^2$; that is, express 8.17 in the form

$$\mathcal{L}^{-1}\{1/s^2\} = I_1 + I_2 i$$

where I_1 and I_2 are real improper integrals. Use the line $\gamma = 1$.

§8.5   Application of Laplace Transforms to Partial Differential Equations

In Sections 8.2 and 8.3, we illustrated the effective use of Laplace transforms in solving ordinary differential equations. The transform replaces a differential equation in $y(t)$ with an algebraic equation in its transform $\tilde{y}(s)$. It is then a matter of finding the inverse transform of $\tilde{y}(s)$ either by partial fractions and tables (Section 8.1) or by residues (Section 8.4). Laplace transforms also provide a potent technique for solving partial differential equations. When the transform is applied to the variable t in a partial differential equation for a function $y(x,t)$, the result is an ordinary differential equation for the transform $\tilde{y}(x,s)$. The ordinary differential equation is solved for $\tilde{y}(x,s)$ and the function is inverted to yield $y(x,t)$. We illustrate this procedure with five physical examples. The first two examples are on unbounded spatial intervals; inverse transforms are found in tables. The last three examples are on bounded spatial intervals; inverse transforms are calculated with residues.

Problems on Unbounded Intervals

Example 8.18   A very long cylindrical rod is placed along the positive x-axis with one end at $x = 0$ (Figure 8.22). The rod is so long that any effects due to its right end may be neglected. Its sides are covered with perfect insulation so

Figure 8.22

that no heat can enter or escape therethrough. At time $t = 0$, the temperature of the rod is $0°C$ throughout. Suddenly the left end of the rod has its temperature raised to U_0, and maintained at this temperature thereafter. The initial, boundary-value problem describing temperature $U(x,t)$ at points in the rod is

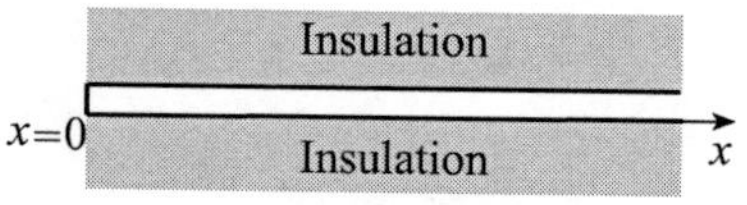

$$\frac{\partial U}{\partial t} = k\frac{\partial^2 U}{\partial x^2}, \quad x > 0, \quad t > 0, \tag{8.19a}$$

$$U(0,t) = U_0, \quad t > 0, \tag{8.19b}$$

$$U(x,0) = 0, \quad x > 0, \tag{8.19c}$$

where k is a constant called the *thermal diffusivity* of the material in the rod. Use Laplace transforms on variable t to find $U(x,t)$.

Solution   When we apply the Laplace transform to the partial differential equation, and use property 8.10a,

$$s\tilde{U}(x,s) - U(x,0) = k\mathcal{L}\left\{\frac{\partial^2 U}{\partial x^2}\right\}.$$

Since the integration with respect to t in the Laplace transform and the differentiation with respect to x are independent, we interchange the order of operations on the right,

$$s\tilde{U}(x,s) = k\frac{\partial^2 \tilde{U}}{\partial x^2},$$

where we have also used initial condition 8.19c. Because only derivatives with respect to x remain, we replace the partial derivative with an ordinary derivative,

$$s\tilde{U} = k\frac{d^2\tilde{U}}{dx^2}, \quad x > 0. \tag{8.20a}$$

When we take Laplace transforms of boundary condition 8.19b, we obtain

$$\tilde{U}(0,s) = \frac{U_0}{s}, \tag{8.20b}$$

a boundary condition to accompany differential equation 8.20a. A general solution of 8.20a is

$$\tilde{U}(x,s) = Ae^{\sqrt{s/k}x} + Be^{-\sqrt{s/k}x}.$$

Because $U(x,t)$ must remain bounded as x becomes infinite, so also must $\tilde{U}(x,s)$. We must therefore set $A = 0$, in which case 8.20b requires $B = U_0/s$. Thus,

$$\tilde{U}(x,s) = \frac{U_0}{s}e^{-\sqrt{s/k}x}. \tag{8.21}$$

The inverse transform of this function can be found in tables,

$$U(x,t) = U_0 \mathcal{L}^{-1}\left\{\frac{e^{-\sqrt{s/k}x}}{s}\right\} = U_0 \,\mathrm{erfc}\left(\frac{x}{2\sqrt{kt}}\right), \tag{8.22a}$$

where $\mathrm{erfc}\,(x)$ is the complementary error function

$$\mathrm{erfc}\,(x) = 1 - \mathrm{erf}\,(x) = 1 - \frac{2}{\sqrt{\pi}}\int_0^x e^{-u^2}\,du = \frac{2}{\sqrt{\pi}}\int_x^\infty e^{-u^2}\,du. \tag{8.22b}$$

Notice that for any $x > 0$ and any $t > 0$, temperature $U(x,t)$ is positive. This indicates that the abrupt change in temperature at the end $x = 0$ from 0°C to U_0 is felt instantaneously at every point in the rod. We have shown a plot of $U(x,t)$ for various fixed values of t in Figure 8.23.•

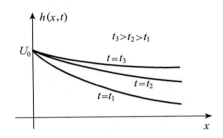

Figure 8.23

Example 8.19 A very long taut string is supported from below so that it lies motionless on the positive x-axis. At time $t = 0$, the support is removed and gravity is permitted to act on the string. If the end $x = 0$ is fixed at the origin, the initial, boundary-value problem describing displacements $y(x,t)$ of points in the string is

$$\frac{\partial^2 y}{\partial t^2} = c^2\frac{\partial^2 y}{\partial x^2} - g, \quad x > 0, \quad t > 0, \tag{8.23a}$$

$$y(0,t) = 0, \quad t > 0, \tag{8.23b}$$

$$y(x,0) = 0, \quad x > 0, \tag{8.23c}$$

$$y_t(x,0) = 0, \quad x > 0, \tag{8.23d}$$

where $g = 9.81$ and $c > 0$ is a constant depending on the material and tension of the string. Initial condition 8.23d expresses the fact that the initial velocity of the string is zero. Use Laplace transforms to solve this problem.

Solution   When we apply Laplace transforms to the partial differential equation, and use property 8.10b,

$$s^2\tilde{y}(x,s) - sy(x,0) - y_t(x,0) = c^2 \mathcal{L}\left\{\frac{\partial^2 y}{\partial x^2}\right\} - \frac{g}{s}.$$

We now use initial conditions 8.23c,d, and interchange operations on the right,

$$s^2\tilde{y} = c^2 \frac{d^2\tilde{y}}{dx^2} - \frac{g}{s},$$

or,

$$\frac{d^2\tilde{y}}{dx^2} - \frac{s^2}{c^2}\tilde{y} = \frac{g}{c^2 s}, \quad x > 0. \tag{8.24a}$$

This ordinary differential equation is subject to the transform of 8.23b,

$$\tilde{y}(0,s) = 0. \tag{8.24b}$$

A general solution of differential equation 8.24a is

$$\tilde{y}(x,s) = Ae^{sx/c} + Be^{-sx/c} - \frac{g}{s^3}.$$

For this function to remain bounded as $x \to \infty$, we must set $A = 0$, in which case condition 8.24b implies that $B = g/s^3$. Thus,

$$\tilde{y}(x,s) = -\frac{g}{s^3} + \frac{g}{s^3}e^{-sx/c}. \tag{8.25}$$

Property 8.4b gives

$$y(x,t) = -\frac{gt^2}{2} + \frac{g}{2}\left(t - \frac{x}{c}\right)^2 h\left(t - \frac{x}{c}\right) \tag{8.26}$$

where $h(t - x/c)$ is the Heaviside unit step function. What this says is that a point x in the string falls freely under gravity for $0 < t < x/c$, after which it falls with constant velocity $-gx/c$ [since for $t > x/c$, $y(x,t) = (g/2)(-2xt/c + x^2/c^2)$]. A picture of the string at any given time t_0 is shown in Figure 8.24. It is parabolic for $0 < x < ct_0$ and horizontal for $x > ct_0$. As t_0 increases, the parabolic portion lengthens and the horizontal section drops.●

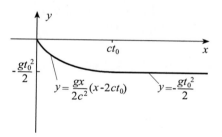

Figure 8.24

Problems on Bounded Intervals

The next three examples are on bounded intervals; we use residues to find inverse transforms.

Example 8.20   A cylindrical rod of length L has its ends at $x = 0$ and $x = L$ on the x-axis. Its sides are insulated so that no heat can enter or escape therethrough. At time $t = 0$, the left end ($x = 0$) has temperature $0°$C, and the right end ($x = L$) has temperature $L°$C, and the temperature rises linearly between the ends. Suddenly at time $t = 0$, the temperature of the right end is reduced to $0°$C, and both ends are held at temperature zero thereafter. The initial, boundary-value problem describing temperature $U(x,t)$ at points in the rod is

$$\frac{\partial U}{\partial t} = k\frac{\partial^2 U}{\partial x^2}, \quad 0 < x < L, \quad t > 0, \tag{8.27a}$$

$$U(0, t) = 0, \quad t > 0, \tag{8.27b}$$

$$U(L, t) = 0, \quad t > 0, \tag{8.27c}$$

$$U(x, 0) = x, \quad 0 < x < L, \tag{8.27d}$$

k again being the thermal diffusivity of the material in the rod. Use Laplace transforms to find $U(x, t)$.

Solution   When we take Laplace transforms of 8.27a, and use property 8.10a,

$$s\tilde{U}(x, s) - x = k\frac{d^2\tilde{U}}{dx^2},$$

or,

$$\frac{d^2\tilde{U}}{dx^2} - \frac{s}{k}\tilde{U} = -\frac{x}{k}, \quad 0 < x < L. \tag{8.28a}$$

This ordinary differential equation is subject to the transforms of 8.27b,c,

$$\tilde{U}(0, s) = 0, \tag{8.28b}$$

$$\tilde{U}(L, s) = 0. \tag{8.28c}$$

A general solution of differential equation 8.28a is

$$\tilde{U}(x, s) = A \cosh\sqrt{\frac{s}{k}}x + B \sinh\sqrt{\frac{s}{k}}x + \frac{x}{s}.$$

For Example 8.17 on an unbounded interval, we used exponentials in the solution of 8.20a. On bounded intervals, hyperbolic functions are preferable. Boundary conditions 8.28b,c require

$$0 = A, \qquad 0 = A \cosh\sqrt{\frac{s}{k}}L + B \sinh\sqrt{\frac{s}{k}}L + \frac{L}{s}.$$

From these,

$$\tilde{U}(x, s) = \frac{1}{s}\left(x - \frac{L \sinh\sqrt{s/k}x}{\sinh\sqrt{s/k}L} \right). \tag{8.29}$$

Although $\sqrt{s/k}$ denotes the principal square root function, $\tilde{U}(x, s)$ in 8.29 is a solution of problem 8.28 for any branch of the root function.

It remains now to find the inverse transform of $\tilde{U}(x, s)$. We do this by calculating residues of $e^{st}\tilde{U}(x, s)$ at its singularities. To discover the nature of the singularity at $s = 0$, we expand $\tilde{U}(x, s)$ in a Laurent series around $s = 0$. Provided we use the same branch for the root function in numerator and denominator of 8.29, we may write that

$$\tilde{U}(x,s) = \frac{1}{s} \left\{ x - \frac{L[\sqrt{s/k}\,x + (\sqrt{s/k}\,x)^3/3! + \cdots]}{\sqrt{s/k}\,L + (\sqrt{s/k}\,L)^3/3! + \cdots} \right\}$$

$$= \frac{1}{s} \left[x - \frac{x + sx^3/(6k) + \cdots}{1 + sL^2/(6k) + \cdots} \right]$$

$$= \frac{1}{s} \left[\frac{sx(L^2 - x^2)}{6k} + \cdots \right]$$

$$= \frac{x(L^2 - x^2)}{6k} + \text{ terms in } s,\, s^2,\, \cdots.$$

Since this is the Laurent series of $\tilde{U}(x,s)$ valid in some annulus around $s = 0$, it follows that $\tilde{U}(x,s)$ has a removable singularity at $s = 0$.

To invert $\tilde{U}(x,s)$ with residues, the function cannot have a branch cut in the left half-plane $\operatorname{Im} s < 0$. Suppose we choose a branch of $\sqrt{s/k}$ in 8.29 with branch cut along the positive real axis. We continue to denote this branch by $\sqrt{s/k}$ notwithstanding the fact that it is no longer the principal branch. Singularities of $\tilde{U}(x,s)$ in the left half-plane then occur at the zeros of $\sinh\sqrt{s/k}L$; that is, when $\sqrt{s/k}L = n\pi i$, or, $s = -n^2\pi^2 k/L^2$, n a positive integer. Because the derivative of $\sinh\sqrt{s/k}L$ does not vanish at $s = -n^2\pi^2 k/L^2$, this function has zeros of order 1 at $s = -n^2\pi^2 k/L^2$. It follows that $\tilde{U}(x,s)$ has simple poles at these singularities. Residues of $e^{st}\tilde{U}(x,s)$ at these poles are

$$\operatorname{Res}\left[e^{st}\tilde{U}(x,s), -\frac{n^2\pi^2 k}{L^2} \right] = \lim_{s \to -n^2\pi^2 k/L^2} \left(s + \frac{n^2\pi^2 k}{L^2} \right) \frac{e^{st}}{s} \left(x - \frac{L\sinh\sqrt{s/k}\,x}{\sinh\sqrt{s/k}\,L} \right)$$

$$= -\frac{e^{-n^2\pi^2 kt/L^2}}{-n^2\pi^2 k/L^2} L \sinh\frac{n\pi x i}{L} \lim_{s \to -n^2\pi^2 k/L^2} \frac{s + n^2\pi^2 k/L^2}{\sinh\sqrt{s/k}\,L}.$$

L'Hôpital's rule yields

$$\operatorname{Res}\left[e^{st}\tilde{U}(x,s), -\frac{n^2\pi^2 k}{L^2} \right] = \frac{iL^3}{n^2\pi^2 k} e^{-n^2\pi^2 kt/L^2} \sin\frac{n\pi x}{L} \lim_{s \to -n^2\pi^2 k/L^2} \frac{1}{\frac{L}{2\sqrt{ks}}\cosh\sqrt{s/k}\,L}$$

$$= \frac{2iL^2}{n^2\pi^2 k} e^{-n^2\pi^2 kt/L^2} \sin\frac{n\pi x}{L} \frac{1}{\frac{L}{n\pi k i}\cosh n\pi i}$$

$$= \frac{2L}{n\pi}(-1)^{n+1} e^{-n^2\pi^2 kt/L^2} \sin\frac{n\pi x}{L}.$$

We sum these residues to find the inverse transform of $\tilde{U}(x,s)$,

$$U(x,t) = \frac{2L}{\pi} \sum_{n=1}^{\infty} \frac{(-1)^{n+1}}{n} e^{-n^2\pi^2 kt/L^2} \sin\frac{n\pi x}{L}.\bullet \tag{8.30}$$

Readers familiar with other methods for solving partial differential equations will be well aware that this solution can also be obtained by separation of variables. Exponentials enhance convergence for large values of t. For instance, suppose the rod is $1/5$ m in length and is made from stainless steel with thermal diffusivity

$k = 3.87 \times 10^{-6}$ m^2/s. Consider finding the temperature at the midpoint $x = 1/10$ m of the rod at the four times $t = 2, 5, 30,$ and 100 minutes. Series 8.30 gives

$$U(1/10, 120) = \frac{2}{5\pi} \sum_{n=1}^{\infty} \frac{(-1)^{n+1}}{n} e^{-0.1145861n^2} \sin \frac{n\pi}{2} \approx 0.100°\text{C};$$

$$U(1/10, 300) = \frac{2}{5\pi} \sum_{n=1}^{\infty} \frac{(-1)^{n+1}}{n} e^{-0.28646526n^2} \sin \frac{n\pi}{2} \approx 0.092°\text{C};$$

$$U(1/10, 1800) = \frac{2}{5\pi} \sum_{n=1}^{\infty} \frac{(-1)^{n+1}}{n} e^{-1.7187915n^2} \sin \frac{n\pi}{2} \approx 0.023°\text{C};$$

$$U(1/10, 6000) = \frac{2}{5\pi} \sum_{n=1}^{\infty} \frac{(-1)^{n+1}}{n} e^{-5.7293052n^2} \sin \frac{n\pi}{2} \approx 0.0004°\text{C}.$$

To obtain these approximations we used four nonzero terms in the first series, three in the second, and one in each of the third and fourth.

Laplace transforms also yield a representation for temperature in the rod that is particularly valuable when t is small. This representation is not available through separation of variables. We write transform 8.29 in the form

$$\tilde{U}(x, s) = \frac{x}{s} - \frac{L \sinh \sqrt{s/k}x}{s \sinh \sqrt{s/k}L} = \frac{x}{s} - \frac{L}{s} \frac{e^{\sqrt{s/k}x} - e^{-\sqrt{s/k}x}}{e^{\sqrt{s/k}L} - e^{-\sqrt{s/k}L}}$$

$$= \frac{x}{s} - \frac{L}{s} \frac{e^{-\sqrt{s/k}L}(e^{\sqrt{s/k}x} - e^{-\sqrt{s/k}x})}{1 - e^{-2\sqrt{s/k}L}}.$$

If we regard $1/(1 - e^{-2\sqrt{s/k}L})$ as the sum of an infinite geometric series with common ratio $e^{-2\sqrt{s/k}L}$, then

$$\tilde{U}(x, s) = \frac{x}{s} - \frac{L}{s} \left[e^{\sqrt{s/k}(x-L)} - e^{-\sqrt{s/k}(x+L)}\right] \sum_{n=0}^{\infty} e^{-2n\sqrt{s/k}L}$$

$$= \frac{x}{s} - L \sum_{n=0}^{\infty} \left[\frac{e^{-\sqrt{s/k}[(2n+1)L-x]}}{s} - \frac{e^{-\sqrt{s/k}[(2n+1)L+x]}}{s}\right].$$

Tables of Laplace transforms indicate that

$$\mathcal{L}^{-1}\left\{\frac{e^{-a\sqrt{s}}}{s}\right\} = \text{erfc}\left(\frac{a}{2\sqrt{t}}\right)$$

where erfc (x) is the complementary error function in equation 8.22b. Hence $U(x, t)$ may be expressed as a series of complementary error functions,

$$U(x, t) = x - L \sum_{n=0}^{\infty} \left\{\text{erfc}\left[\frac{(2n+1)L-x}{2\sqrt{kt}}\right] - \text{erfc}\left[\frac{(2n+1)L+x}{2\sqrt{kt}}\right]\right\}$$

$$= x - L \sum_{n=0}^{\infty} \left\{\text{erf}\left[\frac{(2n+1)L+x}{2\sqrt{kt}}\right] - \text{erf}\left[\frac{(2n+1)L-x}{2\sqrt{kt}}\right]\right\},$$

where we have used the fact that erfc $(x) = 1 - \text{erf}(x)$. This series converges rapidly for small values of t (as opposed to solution 8.30 which converges rapidly for large t). To see this consider temperature at the midpoint of the stainless steel rod at $t = 300$ s:

$$U(1/10, 300) = \frac{1}{10} - \frac{1}{5}\sum_{n=0}^{\infty}\left\{\text{erf}\left[\frac{(2n+1)/5 + 1/10}{2\sqrt{3.87 \times 10^{-6}(300)}}\right] - \text{erf}\left[\frac{(2n+1)/5 - 1/10}{2\sqrt{3.87 \times 10^{-6}(300)}}\right]\right\}.$$

For $n > 0$, all terms essentially vanish, and

$$U(1/10, 300) \approx \frac{1}{10} - \frac{1}{5}[\text{erf}(4.402) - \text{erf}(1.467)] = 0.092°\text{C}.$$

For $t = 1800$,

$$U(1/10, 1800) = \frac{1}{10} - \frac{1}{5}\sum_{n=0}^{\infty}\left\{\text{erf}\left[\frac{(2n+1)/5 + 1/10}{2\sqrt{3.87 \times 10^{-6}(1800)}}\right] - \text{erf}\left[\frac{(2n+1)/5 - 1/10}{2\sqrt{3.87 \times 10^{-6}(1800)}}\right]\right\}.$$

Once again, only the $n = 0$ term is required; it yields

$$U(1/10, 1800) \approx \frac{1}{10} - \frac{1}{5}[\text{erf}(0.1797) - \text{erf}(0.5991)] = 0.023°\text{C}.$$

Even for t as large as 6000, we need only the $n = 0$ and $n = 1$ terms to give

$$U(1/10, 6000) = \frac{1}{10} - \frac{1}{5}\sum_{n=0}^{\infty}\left\{\text{erf}\left[\frac{(2n+1)/5 + 1/10}{2\sqrt{3.87 \times 10^{-6}(6000)}}\right] - \text{erf}\left[\frac{(2n+1)/5 - 1/10}{2\sqrt{3.87 \times 10^{-6}(6000)}}\right]\right\}$$

$$\approx \frac{1}{10} - \frac{1}{5}[\text{erf}(0.9843) - \text{erf}(0.3281) + \text{erf}(2.297) - \text{erf}(1.641)]$$

$$= 0.0004°\text{C}.$$

Example 8.21 The ends of a taut string are fixed at $x = 0$ and $x = L$ on the x-axis. The string is initially at rest along the axis and then at time $t = 0$, it is allowed to drop under its own weight. The initial, boundary-value problem describing displacements $y(x, t)$ of points in the string is

$$\frac{\partial^2 y}{\partial t^2} = c^2\frac{\partial^2 y}{\partial x^2} - g, \quad 0 < x < L, \quad t > 0, \tag{8.31a}$$

$$y(0, t) = 0, \quad t > 0, \tag{8.31b}$$

$$y(L, t) = 0, \quad t > 0, \tag{8.31c}$$

$$y(x, 0) = 0, \quad 0 < x < L, \tag{8.31d}$$

$$y_t(x, 0) = 0, \quad 0 < x < L, \tag{8.31e}$$

where $g = 9.81$ and $c > 0$ is a constant depending on the material and tension of the string. Initial condition 8.31e expresses the fact that the initial velocity of the string is zero. Use Laplace transforms to solve this problem.

Solution When we take Laplace transforms of 8.31a, and use initial conditions 8.31d,e,

$$s^2\tilde{y}(x, s) = c^2\frac{\partial^2\tilde{y}}{\partial x^2} - \frac{g}{s},$$

or,

$$\frac{d^2\tilde{y}}{dx^2} - \frac{s^2}{c^2}\tilde{y} = \frac{g}{c^2 s}, \quad 0 < x < L. \tag{8.32a}$$

This ordinary differential equation is subject to the transforms of 8.31b,c,

$$\tilde{y}(0, s) = 0, \tag{8.32b}$$

$$\tilde{y}(L, s) = 0. \tag{8.32c}$$

A general solution of 8.32a is

$$\tilde{y}(x, s) = A \cosh\frac{sx}{c} + B \sinh\frac{sx}{c} - \frac{g}{s^3}.$$

Boundary conditions 8.32b,c require

$$0 = A - \frac{g}{s^3}, \quad 0 = A \cosh\frac{sL}{c} + B \sinh\frac{sL}{c} - \frac{g}{s^3}.$$

Thus,

$$\tilde{y}(x, s) = \frac{g}{s^3}\cosh\frac{sx}{c} - \frac{g}{s^3 \sinh sL/c}\left(-1 + \cosh\frac{sL}{c}\right)\sinh\frac{sx}{c} - \frac{g}{s^3}. \tag{8.33}$$

We invert this transform function by finding residues of $e^{st}\tilde{y}(x, s)$ at its singularities. To determine the type of singularity at $s = 0$, we expand $\tilde{y}(x, s)$ in a Laurent series around $s = 0$:

$$\tilde{y}(x, s) = -\frac{g}{s^3}\left[1 - \left(1 + \frac{s^2 x^2}{2c^2} + \frac{s^4 x^4}{24c^4} + \cdots\right) + \left(\frac{s^2 L^2}{2c^2} + \frac{s^4 L^4}{24c^4} + \cdots\right)\left(\frac{\frac{sx}{c} + \frac{s^3 x^3}{6c^3} + \cdots}{\frac{sL}{c} + \frac{s^3 L^3}{6c^3} + \cdots}\right)\right]$$

$$= -\frac{g}{s^3}\left[-\left(\frac{s^2 x^2}{2c^2} + \frac{s^4 x^4}{24c^4} + \cdots\right) + \left(\frac{s^2 L^2}{2c^2} + \frac{s^4 L^4}{24c^4} + \cdots\right)\left(\frac{x}{L} + \frac{s^2 x(x - L)}{6Lc^2} + \cdots\right)\right]$$

$$= -\frac{gx(L - x)}{2c^2 s} + \cdots$$

This shows that $\tilde{y}(x, s)$ has a simple pole at $s = 0$, and from the product

$$e^{st}\tilde{y}(x, s) = \left(1 + st + \frac{s^2 t^2}{2!} + \cdots\right)\left[-\frac{gx(L - x)}{2c^2 s} + \cdots\right]$$

$$= -\frac{gx(L - x)}{2c^2 s} + \cdots,$$

the residue of $e^{st}\tilde{y}(x, s)$ at $s = 0$ is $-gx(L - x)/(2c^2)$.

The remaining singularities of $\tilde{y}(x, s)$ occur at the zeros of $\sinh(sL/c)$; that is, when $sL/c = n\pi i$, or, $s = n\pi ci/L$, n an integer. Because the derivative of $\sinh(sL/c)$ does not vanish at $s = n\pi ci/L$, this function has zeros of order one at $s = n\pi ci/L$. When n is even, $s = n\pi ci/L$ is a simple zero of $-1 + \cosh(sL/c)$, and therefore these are removable singularities of $\tilde{y}(x, s)$. When n is odd, $s = n\pi ci/L$ is not a zero of $-1 + \cosh(sL/c)$, and these are therefore simple poles of $\tilde{y}(x, s)$. Residues of $e^{st}\tilde{y}(x, s)$ at these poles are

$$\text{Res}\left[e^{st}\tilde{y}(x,s),\frac{n\pi ci}{L}\right] = \lim_{s\to n\pi ci/L}\left(s-\frac{n\pi ci}{L}\right)\frac{-ge^{st}}{s^3}\left[1-\cosh\frac{sx}{c}+\left(-1+\cosh\frac{sL}{c}\right)\frac{\sinh(sx/c)}{\sinh(sL/c)}\right]$$

$$-\frac{g}{(n\pi ci/L)^3}e^{n\pi cti/L}(-1+\cosh n\pi i)\sinh\frac{n\pi xi}{L}\lim_{s\to n\pi ci/L}\frac{s-n\pi ci/L}{\sinh(sL/c)}$$

$$=-\frac{gL^3 i}{n^3\pi^3 c^3}e^{n\pi cti/L}(-1+\cos n\pi)i\sin\frac{n\pi x}{L}\lim_{s\to n\pi ci/L}\frac{1}{(L/c)\cosh(sL/c)}$$

$$=-\frac{gL^3}{n^3\pi^3 c^3}e^{n\pi cti/L}[1+(-1)^{n+1}]\sin\frac{n\pi x}{L}\frac{1}{(L/c)\cosh n\pi i}$$

$$=\frac{gL^2}{n^3\pi^3 c^2}e^{n\pi cti/L}[1+(-1)^{n+1}]\sin\frac{n\pi x}{L}.$$

Since n is odd, we may write that residues of $e^{st}\tilde{y}(x,s)$ at the poles $s=(2n-1)\pi ci/L$ are

$$\text{Res}\left[e^{st}\tilde{y}(x,s),\frac{(2n-1)\pi ci}{L}\right]\frac{2gL^2}{(2n-1)^3\pi^3 c^2}e^{(2n-1)\pi cti/L}\sin\frac{(2n-1)\pi x}{L}.$$

Displacements of points in the string are given by

$$y(x,t)=-\frac{gx(L-x)}{2c^2}+\sum_{n=-\infty}^{\infty}\frac{2gL^2}{(2n-1)^3\pi^3 c^2}e^{(2n-1)\pi cti/L}\sin\frac{(2n-1)\pi x}{L}.$$

We separate the summation into two parts, one over positive n and the other over nonpositive n, and in the latter we set $m=1-n$,

$$y(x,t)=-\frac{gx(L-x)}{2c^2}+\frac{2gL^2}{\pi^3 c^2}\sum_{n=1}^{\infty}\frac{1}{(2n-1)^3}e^{(2n-1)\pi cti/L}\sin\frac{(2n-1)\pi x}{L}$$

$$+\frac{2gL^2}{\pi^3 c^2}\sum_{n=-\infty}^{0}\frac{1}{(2n-1)^3}e^{(2n-1)\pi cti/L}\sin\frac{(2n-1)\pi x}{L}$$

$$=-\frac{gx(L-x)}{2c^2}+\frac{2gL^2}{\pi^3 c^2}\sum_{n=1}^{\infty}\frac{1}{(2n-1)^3}e^{(2n-1)\pi cti/L}\sin\frac{(2n-1)\pi x}{L}$$

$$+\frac{2gL^2}{\pi^3 c^2}\sum_{m=1}^{\infty}\frac{1}{[2(1-m)-1]^3}e^{[2(1-m)-1]\pi cti/L}\sin\frac{[2(1-m)-1]\pi x}{L}.$$

If we now replace m by n in the second summation, and combine it with the first,

$$y(x,t)=-\frac{gx(L-x)}{2c^2}+\frac{2gL^2}{\pi^3 c^2}\sum_{n=1}^{\infty}\frac{1}{(2n-1)^3}e^{(2n-1)\pi cti/L}\sin\frac{(2n-1)\pi x}{L}$$

$$+\frac{2gL^2}{\pi^3 c^2}\sum_{n=1}^{\infty}\frac{1}{(2n-1)^3}e^{-(2n-1)\pi cti/L}\sin\frac{(2n-1)\pi x}{L}$$

$$=-\frac{gx(L-x)}{2c^2}+\frac{2gL^2}{\pi^3 c^2}\sum_{n=1}^{\infty}\frac{e^{(2n-1)\pi cti/L}+e^{-(2n-1)\pi cti/L}}{(2n-1)^3}\sin\frac{(2n-1)\pi x}{L}$$

$$=-\frac{gx(L-x)}{2c^2}+\frac{4gL^2}{\pi^3 c^2}\sum_{n=1}^{\infty}\frac{1}{(2n-1)^3}\cos\frac{(2n-1)\pi ct}{L}\sin\frac{(2n-1)\pi x}{L}.\quad(8.34)$$

The first term is the static position that the string would occupy were it slowly lowered under the force of gravity. The series represents oscillations about this position due to the fact that the string was dropped from a horizontal position.

The technique of separation of variables and eigenfunction expansions leads to the following solution of problem 8.31

$$y(x,t) = -\frac{2gL^2}{\pi^3 c^2} \sum_{n=1}^{\infty} \frac{[1+(-1)^{n+1}]}{n^3} \left(1 - \cos\frac{n\pi ct}{L}\right) \sin\frac{n\pi x}{L}.$$

We can see the advantage of Laplace transforms. They have rendered part of the series solution in closed form, namely the term $gx(L-x)/(2c^2)$ in solution 8.34.●

Examples 8.17 and 8.21 contained specific nonhomogeneities and/or initial conditions. Although Laplace transforms can handle nonhomogeneities and initial conditions with arbitrary functions, they do not do so particularly efficiently. Our final example is an illustration of this.

Example 8.22 Solve the following heat conduction problem in a rod of length L when the initial temperature distribution is an unspecified function $f(x)$,

$$\frac{\partial U}{\partial t} = k\frac{\partial^2 U}{\partial x^2}, \quad 0 < x < L, \quad t > 0, \tag{8.35a}$$

$$U(0,t) = 0, \quad t > 0, \tag{8.35b}$$

$$U(L,t) = 0, \quad t > 0, \tag{8.35c}$$

$$U(x,0) = f(x), \quad 0 < x < L. \tag{8.35d}$$

Solution When we take Laplace transforms of both sides of PDE 8.35a,

$$s\tilde{U} - f(x) = k\frac{d^2\tilde{U}}{dx^2},$$

or,

$$\frac{d^2\tilde{U}}{dx^2} - \frac{s}{k}\tilde{U} = -\frac{f(x)}{k}, \quad 0 < x < L,$$

subject to transforms of 8.35b,c,

$$\tilde{U}(0,s) = 0, \qquad \tilde{U}(L,s) = 0.$$

Variation of parameters leads to the following general solution of the differential equation

$$\tilde{U}(x,s) = A\cosh\sqrt{\frac{s}{k}}x + B\sinh\sqrt{\frac{s}{k}}x - \frac{1}{\sqrt{ks}}\int_0^x f(u)\sinh\sqrt{\frac{s}{k}}(x-u)\,du.$$

The boundary conditions require

$$0 = A, \qquad 0 = A\cosh\sqrt{\frac{s}{k}}L + B\sinh\sqrt{\frac{s}{k}}L - \frac{1}{\sqrt{ks}}\int_0^L f(u)\sinh\sqrt{\frac{s}{k}}(L-u)\,du.$$

Thus,

$$\tilde{U}(x,s) = \frac{\sinh\sqrt{\frac{s}{k}}x}{\sqrt{ks}\sinh\sqrt{\frac{s}{k}}L}\int_0^L f(u)\sinh\sqrt{\frac{s}{k}}(L-u)\,du - \frac{1}{\sqrt{ks}}\int_0^x f(u)\sinh\sqrt{\frac{s}{k}}(x-u)\,du$$

$$= \frac{1}{\sqrt{k}} \int_0^L f(u) \tilde{p}(x, u, s) \, du - \frac{1}{\sqrt{ks}} \int_0^x f(u) \sinh \sqrt{\frac{s}{k}}(x - u) \, du$$

where

$$\tilde{p}(x, u, s) = \frac{\sinh \sqrt{\frac{s}{k}}x \, \sinh \sqrt{\frac{s}{k}}(L - u)}{\sqrt{s} \sinh \sqrt{\frac{s}{k}}L}.$$

The second integral in $\tilde{U}(x, s)$ has a removable singularity at $s = 0$, and therefore this term may be ignored in taking inverse transforms by residues. The function $\tilde{p}(x, u, s)$ has singularities when $\sqrt{s/k}L = n\pi i$, or, $s = -n^2\pi^2 k/L^2$. Since

$$\tilde{p}(x, u, s) = \frac{\left[\frac{\sqrt{s}x}{\sqrt{k}} + \frac{1}{6}\left(\frac{\sqrt{s}x}{\sqrt{k}}\right)^3 + \cdots \right] \left[\frac{\sqrt{s}(L-u)}{\sqrt{k}} + \frac{1}{6}\left(\frac{\sqrt{s}(L-u)}{\sqrt{k}}\right)^3 + \cdots \right]}{\sqrt{s} \left[\frac{\sqrt{s}L}{\sqrt{k}} + \frac{1}{6}\left(\frac{\sqrt{s}L}{\sqrt{k}}\right)^3 + \cdots \right]} = \frac{x(L - u)}{L\sqrt{k}} + \cdots,$$

it follows that $\tilde{p}(x, u, s)$ has a removable singularity at $s = 0$. The singularities $s = -n^2\pi^2 k/L^2$ are poles of order one, and residues of $e^{st}\tilde{p}(x, u, s)$ at these poles are

$$\lim_{s \to -n^2\pi^2 k/L^2} \left(s + \frac{n^2\pi^2 k}{L^2} \right) e^{st} \frac{\sinh \sqrt{\frac{s}{k}}x \, \sinh \sqrt{\frac{s}{k}}(L - u)}{\sqrt{s} \sinh \sqrt{\frac{s}{k}}L}$$

$$= \frac{e^{-n^2\pi^2 kt/L^2}}{n\pi\sqrt{k}i/L} \sinh \frac{n\pi x i}{L} \sinh \frac{n\pi i(L - u)}{L} \lim_{s \to -n^2\pi^2 k/L^2} \frac{1}{\frac{L}{2\sqrt{ks}} \cosh \sqrt{\frac{s}{k}}L}$$

$$= \frac{-2}{n\pi i} e^{-n^2\pi^2 kt/L^2} \sin \frac{n\pi x}{L} \sin \frac{n\pi(L - u)}{L} \frac{1}{\frac{L}{n\pi\sqrt{k}i} \cosh n\pi i}$$

$$= \frac{-2\sqrt{k}}{L} e^{-n^2\pi^2 kt/L^2} \sin \frac{n\pi x}{L} (-1)^{n+1} \sin \frac{n\pi u}{L} \frac{1}{(-1)^n}$$

$$= \frac{2\sqrt{k}}{L} e^{-n^2\pi^2 kt/L^2} \sin \frac{n\pi x}{L} \sin \frac{n\pi u}{L}.$$

Residues of e^{st} times the first integral in $\tilde{U}(x, s)$ can now be calculated by interchanging limits and integration in

$$\lim_{s \to -\frac{n^2\pi^2 k}{L^2}} \left(s + \frac{n^2\pi^2 k}{L^2} \right) \frac{e^{st}}{\sqrt{k}} \int_0^L f(u) \tilde{p}(x, u, s) \, du$$

to obtain

$$\frac{1}{\sqrt{k}} \int_0^L \left[\lim_{s \to -\frac{n^2\pi^2 k}{L^2}} \left(s + \frac{n^2\pi^2 k}{L^2} \right) e^{st} f(u) \tilde{p}(x, u, s) \right] du$$

$$= \frac{1}{\sqrt{k}} \int_0^L f(u) \left[\lim_{s \to -\frac{n^2\pi^2 k}{L^2}} \left(s + \frac{n^2\pi^2 k}{L^2} \right) e^{st} \tilde{p}(x, u, s) \right] du$$

$$= \frac{1}{\sqrt{k}} \int_0^L f(u) \left[\frac{2\sqrt{k}}{L} e^{-n^2\pi^2 kt/L^2} \sin \frac{n\pi x}{L} \sin \frac{n\pi u}{L} \right] du$$

$$= \frac{2}{L} e^{-n^2\pi^2 kt/L^2} \left[\int_0^L f(u) \sin \frac{n\pi u}{L} \, du \right] \sin \frac{n\pi x}{L}.$$

The inverse transform of $\tilde{U}(x,s)$ is therefore

$$U(x,t) = \frac{2}{L} \sum_{n=1}^{\infty} \left[\int_0^L f(u) \sin \frac{n\pi u}{L} du \right] e^{-n^2 \pi^2 kt/L^2} \sin \frac{n\pi x}{L}. \bullet$$

Readers who are familiar with the method of separation of variables for solving PDEs will attest to the fact that separation of variables is more efficient than Laplace transforms in obtaining the above solution. Similar complications arise when non-homogeneities involve arbitrary functions. In general, Laplace transforms are less appealing as an alternative to separation of variables when nonhomogeneities and initial conditions contain unspecified functions. As a result exercises on bounded intervals will be confined to problems containing specific nonhomogeneities and initial conditions.

EXERCISES 8.5

In these exercises use Laplace transforms to solve the initial, boundary-value problem.

1. A very long cylindrical rod is placed along the positive x-axis with one end at $x = 0$. Its curved sides are perfectly insulated so that no heat can enter or escape therethrough. At time $t = 0$, the temperature of the rod is $0°$ C throughout. For $t > 0$, heat is added at a constant rate to the left end. The initial, boundary-value problem for temperature $U(x,t)$ in the rod is

$$\frac{\partial U}{\partial t} = k \frac{\partial^2 U}{\partial x^2}, \quad x > 0, \quad t > 0,$$
$$U_x(0,t) = C, \quad t > 0,$$
$$U(x,0) = 0, \quad x > 0,$$

   where $k > 0$ and $C < 0$ are constants.

2. A very long cylindrical rod is placed along the positive x-axis with one end at $x = 0$. Its curved sides are perfectly insulated so that no heat can enter or escape therethrough. At time $t = 0$, the temperature of the rod is a constant $\overline{U}$ throughout. For $t > 0$, the left end has temperature U_0. The initial, boundary-value problem for temperature $U(x,t)$ in the rod is

$$\frac{\partial U}{\partial t} = k \frac{\partial^2 U}{\partial x^2}, \quad x > 0, \quad t > 0,$$
$$U(0,t) = U_0, \quad t > 0,$$
$$U(x,0) = \overline{U}, \quad x > 0,$$

   where $k > 0$ is a constant.

3. Use convolutions to express the solution to Exercise 1 in integral form when the boundary condition at $x = 0$ is $U_x(0,t) = f(t)$, $t > 0$.

4. Use convolutions to express the solution to Exercise 2 in integral form when the boundary condition at $x = 0$ is $U(0,t) = f(t)$, $t > 0$.

5. A very long string lies motionless along the positive x-axis. If the left end ($x = 0$) is subjected to vertical motion described by $f(t)$ for $t > 0$, subsequent displacements $y(x,t)$ of the string are described by the initial, boundary-value problem

$$\frac{\partial^2 y}{\partial t^2} = c^2 \frac{\partial^2 y}{\partial x^2}, \quad x > 0, \quad t > 0,$$
$$y(0, t) = f(t), \quad t > 0,$$
$$y(x, 0) = 0, \quad x > 0,$$
$$y_t(x, 0) = 0, \quad x > 0,$$

where $c > 0$ is a constant.

6. A very long string lies motionless along the positive x-axis. At time $t = 0$, the support is removed and gravity is permitted to act on the string. If the left end ($x = 0$) is subjected to periodic vertical motion described by $\sin \omega t$ for $t > 0$, subsequent displacements $y(x, t)$ of the string are described by the initial, boundary-value problem

$$\frac{\partial^2 y}{\partial t^2} = c^2 \frac{\partial^2 y}{\partial x^2} - g, \quad x > 0, \quad t > 0,$$
$$y(0, t) = \sin \omega t, \quad t > 0,$$
$$y(x, 0) = 0, \quad x > 0,$$
$$y_t(x, 0) = 0, \quad x > 0,$$

where $g = 9.81$ and $c > 0$ is a constant.

7. A cylindrical rod of length L has its ends at $x = 0$ and $x = L$ on the x-axis. Its curved sides are perfectly insulated so that no heat can enter or escape therethrough. At time $t = 0$, the temperature of the rod is given by $f(x) = \sin(m\pi x/L)$, $0 \leq x \leq L$, where $m > 0$ is an integer. For $t > 0$, both ends of the rod are held at temperature $0°$ C. The initial, boundary-value problem for temperature $U(x, t)$ in the rod is

$$\frac{\partial U}{\partial t} = k \frac{\partial^2 U}{\partial x^2}, \quad 0 < x < L, \quad t > 0,$$
$$U(0, t) = 0, \quad t > 0,$$
$$U(L, t) = 0, \quad t > 0,$$
$$U(x, 0) = \sin \frac{m\pi x}{L}, \quad 0 < x < L,$$

where $k > 0$ is a constant.

8. A cylindrical rod of length L has its ends at $x = 0$ and $x = L$ on the x-axis. Its curved sides are perfectly insulated so that no heat can enter or escape therethrough. At time $t = 0$, the temperature of the rod is given by $f(x) = x$, $0 \leq x \leq L$. For $t > 0$, both ends of the rod are insulated. The initial, boundary-value problem for temperature $U(x, t)$ in the rod is

$$\frac{\partial U}{\partial t} = k \frac{\partial^2 U}{\partial x^2}, \quad 0 < x < L, \quad t > 0,$$
$$U_x(0, t) = 0, \quad t > 0,$$
$$U_x(L, t) = 0, \quad t > 0,$$
$$U(x, 0) = x, \quad 0 < x < L,$$

where $k > 0$ is a constant.

9. A cylindrical rod of length L has its ends at $x = 0$ and $x = L$ on the x-axis. Its curved sides are perfectly insulated so that no heat can enter or escape therethrough. At time $t = 0$, the temperature of the rod is $0°$ C throughout. For $t > 0$, its left end $(x = 0)$ is kept at $0°$ C, and its right end $(x = L)$ is kept at a constant $U_L°$ C. The initial, boundary-value problem for temperature $U(x, t)$ in the rod is

$$\frac{\partial U}{\partial t} = k \frac{\partial^2 U}{\partial x^2}, \quad 0 < x < L, \quad t > 0,$$
$$U(0, t) = 0, \quad t > 0,$$
$$U(L, t) = U_L, \quad t > 0,$$
$$U(x, 0) = 0, \quad 0 < x < L,$$

where $k > 0$ is a constant.

10. A cylindrical rod of length L has its ends at $x = 0$ and $x = L$ on the x-axis. Its curved sides are perfectly insulated so that no heat can enter or escape therethrough. At time $t = 0$, the temperature of the rod is a constant $U_0°$ C. For $t > 0$, its end $x = 0$ is insulated, heat is added to the end $x = L$ at a constant rate. The initial, boundary-value problem for temperature $U(x, t)$ in the rod is

$$\frac{\partial U}{\partial t} = k \frac{\partial^2 U}{\partial x^2}, \quad 0 < x < L, \quad t > 0,$$
$$U_x(0, t) = 0, \quad t > 0,$$
$$U_x(L, t) = C, \quad t > 0,$$
$$U(x, 0) = U_0, \quad 0 < x < L,$$

where $k > 0$ and $C > 0$ are constants.

11. A cylindrical rod of length L has its ends at $x = 0$ and $x = L$ on the x-axis. Its curved sides are perfectly insulated so that no heat can enter or escape therethrough. At time $t = 0$, the temperature of the rod is a constant $100°$ C. For $t > 0$, its end $x = 0$ is kept at temperature $0°$, and end $x = L$ has temperature $100e^{-t}$. The initial, boundary-value problem for temperature $U(x, t)$ in the rod is

$$\frac{\partial U}{\partial t} = k \frac{\partial^2 U}{\partial x^2}, \quad 0 < x < L, \quad t > 0,$$
$$U(0, t) = 0, \quad t > 0,$$
$$U(L, t) = 100e^{-t}, \quad t > 0,$$
$$U(x, 0) = 100, \quad 0 < x < L,$$

where $k > 0$ is a constant. Assume that $k \neq L^2/(n^2\pi^2)$ for any integer n.

12. A cylindrical rod of length L has its ends at $x = 0$ and $x = L$ on the x-axis. Its curved sides are perfectly insulated so that no heat can enter or escape therethrough. At time $t = 0$, the temperature of the rod is $0°$ C, and for $t > 0$ the ends of the rod continue to be held at $0°$ C. When heat generation at each point of the rod is described by the function $e^{-\alpha t}$, where α is a positive constant, the initial, boundary-value problem for temperature $U(x, t)$ in the rod is

$$\frac{\partial U}{\partial t} = k \frac{\partial^2 U}{\partial x^2} + e^{-\alpha t}, \quad 0 < x < L, \quad t > 0,$$
$$U(0, t) = 0, \quad t > 0,$$
$$U(L, t) = 0, \quad t > 0,$$
$$U(x, 0) = 0, \quad 0 < x < L,$$

where $k > 0$ is a constant. Assume that $\alpha \neq n^2\pi^2/L^2$ for any integer n.

13. A taut string has its ends fixed at $x = 0$ and $x = L$ on the x-axis. If it is given an initial displacement at time $t = 0$ of $f(x) = kx(L - x)$, where $k > 0$ is a constant, and no initial velocity, the initial boundary-value problem for displacements $y(x, t)$ of points in the string is

$$\frac{\partial^2 y}{\partial t^2} = c^2 \frac{\partial^2 y}{\partial x^2}, \quad 0 < x < L, \quad t > 0,$$
$$y(0, t) = 0, \quad t > 0,$$
$$y(L, t) = 0, \quad t > 0,$$
$$y(x, 0) = f(x), \quad 0 < x < L,$$
$$y_t(x, 0) = 0, \quad x > 0,$$

where $c > 0$ is a constant.

14. Repeat Exercise 13 if the initial displacement is zero and $f(x)$ is the initial velocity of the string.

15. A taut string initially at rest along the x-axis has its ends fixed at $x = 0$ and $x = L$ on the x-axis. If gravity is taken into account, the initial boundary-value problem for displacements $y(x, t)$ of points in the string is

$$\frac{\partial^2 y}{\partial t^2} = c^2 \frac{\partial^2 y}{\partial x^2} - g, \quad 0 < x < L, \quad t > 0,$$
$$y(0, t) = 0, \quad t > 0,$$
$$y(L, t) = 0, \quad t > 0,$$
$$y(x, 0) = 0, \quad 0 < x < L,$$
$$y_t(x, 0) = 0, \quad 0 < x < L,$$

where $g = 9.81$.

16. A taut string initially at rest along the x-axis has its ends at $x = 0$ and $x = L$ fixed on the axis. For $t \geq 0$, it is subjected to a force per unit x-length $F = F_0 \sin \omega t$, where F_0 is a constant, as is $\omega \neq n\pi/L$ for any positive integer n. The initial boundary-value problem for displacements $y(x, t)$ of points in the string is

$$\frac{\partial^2 y}{\partial t^2} = c^2 \frac{\partial^2 y}{\partial x^2} + \frac{F_0}{\rho} \sin \omega t, \quad 0 < x < L, \quad t > 0,$$
$$y(0, t) = 0, \quad t > 0,$$
$$y(L, t) = 0, \quad t > 0,$$
$$y(x, 0) = 0, \quad 0 < x < L,$$
$$y_t(x, 0) = 0, \quad 0 < x < L,$$

where $c > 0$ and $\rho > 0$ are constants.

17. A cylindrical rod of length L has its ends at $x = 0$ and $x = L$ on the x-axis. Its curved sides are perfectly insulated so that no heat can enter or escape therethrough. At time $t = 0$, the temperature of the rod is $0°$ C, and for $t > 0$, the ends $x = 0$ and $x = L$ of the rod are held at

temperature $100°$ C and $0°$ C respectively. The initial boundary-value problem for temperature $U(x,t)$ in the rod is

$$\frac{\partial U}{\partial t} = k\frac{\partial^2 U}{\partial x^2}, \quad 0 < x < L, \quad t > 0,$$
$$U(0,t) = 100, \quad t > 0,$$
$$U(L,t) = 0, \quad t > 0,$$
$$U(x,0) = 0, \quad 0 < x < L,$$

where $k > 0$ is a constant. Find two solutions, one in terms of error functions, and the other in terms of time exponentials.

18. A cylindrical rod of length L has its ends at $x = 0$ and $x = L$ on the x-axis. Its curved sides are perfectly insulated so that no heat can enter or escape therethrough. At time $t = 0$, the temperature of the rod is $0°$ C, and for $t > 0$, its left end $x = 0$ continues to be kept at temperature $0°$ C. If heat is added to the end $x = L$ at a constant rate, the initial boundary-value problem for temperature $U(x,t)$ in the rod is

$$\frac{\partial U}{\partial t} = k\frac{\partial^2 U}{\partial x^2}, \quad 0 < x < L, \quad t > 0,$$
$$U(0,t) = 0, \quad t > 0,$$
$$U_x(L,t) = C, \quad t > 0,$$
$$U(x,0) = 0, \quad 0 < x < L,$$

where $k > 0$ and $C > 0$ are constants. Find two solutions, one in terms of error functions, and the other in terms of time exponentials.

§8.6   Transfer Functions and Stability

Systems designed by engineers must be stable.
In this section, we show how Laplace transforms
are used to analyze stability of various types
of mechanical, electrical, and environmental
systems. We use a mechanical system that is
familiar to most everyone to introduce the
ideas. Consider a mass M vibrating
vertically on the end of a spring with
constant k. Suppose a damping force
proportional to velocity also acts on the
mass. This is often modeled by a dashpot as

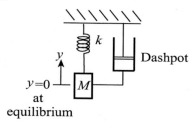

Figure 8.25

shown in Figure 8.25. If $y(t)$ measures distance of M from its equilibrium position
(the position where it would hang motionless on the end of the spring), then the
differential equation describing $y(t)$ is

$$M\frac{d^2y}{dy^2} + \beta\frac{dy}{dt} + ky = f(t), \quad y(0) = y_0, \quad y'(0) = y_0', \tag{8.36}$$

where $\beta > 0$ is a constant. The initial conditions specify the initial displacement of
the mass from its equilibrium position and its initial velocity. Forces due to gravity,
the spring, and the dashpot have been taken into account; any other forces would
be grouped into $f(t)$. We shall present various results here with a minimum of
calculation; we do not want excessive calculations obscuring central ideas.

First consider the situation when the dashpot is absent and a periodic, external
force $f(t) = A\sin\omega t$ acts on the mass. Differential equation 8.36 becomes

$$M\frac{d^2y}{dt^2} + ky = A\sin\omega t, \quad y(0) = 0, \quad y'(0) = 0. \tag{8.37}$$

The altered initial conditions specify that the initial energy of the mass is zero, no
potential energy due to stretch or compression in the spring beyond its equilibrium
position, nor kinetic energy due to initial velocity. When we apply the Laplace
transform to this equation and solve the equation for $\tilde{y}(s)$, we obtain

$$\tilde{y}(s) = \frac{A\omega}{(Ms^2 + k)(s^2 + \omega^2)}. \tag{8.38}$$

When the frequency ω of the applied force is not equal to the natural frequency
$\sqrt{k/M}$ of the system, $\tilde{y}(s)$ has simple poles at $s = \pm\omega i$ and $s = \pm\sqrt{k/M}i$. Oscil-
lation are defined by the bounded function

$$y(t) = \frac{A\sqrt{M/k}}{M\omega^2 - k}\left(\omega\sin\sqrt{\frac{k}{M}}t - \sqrt{\frac{k}{M}}\sin\omega t\right).$$

If $\omega = \sqrt{k/M}$, $\tilde{y}(s)$ has a pole of order two, and the solution is

$$y(t) = \frac{A}{2M\omega^2}(\sin\omega t - \omega t\cos\omega t).$$

Oscillations are unbounded, resonance occurs.

Suppose now that a damping force also acts on the mass. If the initial energy of the mass is again zero, then the Laplace transform of equation 8.36 leads to

$$\tilde{y}(s) = \frac{A\omega}{(Ms^2 + \beta s + k)(s^2 + \omega^2)}. \tag{8.39}$$

Independent of the value of ω, transform $\tilde{y}(s)$ has simple poles, two at the zeros of $Ms^2 + \beta s + k$ and two at $s = \pm \omega i$, and there is no possibility of poles of order two. Because the poles $s = \pm \omega i$ are purely imaginary, and the poles at the zeros of $Ms^2 + \beta s + k$ have negative real parts, the solution $y(t)$ will be bounded for all t. The presence of damping therefore results in bounded solutions for any applied frequency ω.

Transforms 8.38 and 8.39 can both be expressed in the form

$$\tilde{y}(s) = \tilde{H}(s)\tilde{x}(s), \tag{8.40}$$

where $\tilde{x}(s) = A\omega/(s^2 + \omega^2)$ is the transform of the input $A\sin\omega t$, and $\tilde{H}(s) = 1/(Ms^2 + k)$ in the case of equation 8.38, and $\tilde{H}(s) = 1/(Ms^2 + \beta s + k)$ in the case of 8.39. The function $\tilde{H}(s)$ is called the **transfer function** of the system; it is independent of the input, depending only on the parameters of the system (M, β, and k). Multiplication of the input transform $\tilde{x}(s)$ by $\tilde{H}(s)$ gives the output transform $\tilde{y}(s)$. It is worthwhile noting that if the input is the unit impulse function $\delta(t)$, which has transform $\tilde{x}(s) = 1$, then $\tilde{y}(s) = \tilde{H}(s)$. In other words, the transfer function is the Laplace transform of the response of the system to the unit impulse $\delta(t)$ when there is no initial energy in the system.

We now generalize these considerations to the situation where the differential equation governing the system is n^{th}-order with constant coefficients, and once again we assume that the initial energy of the system is zero. The differential equation is

$$a_n\frac{d^n y}{dx^n} + a_{n-1}\frac{d^{n-1}y}{dx^{n-1}} + \cdots + a_1\frac{dy}{dx} + a_0 y = x(t). \tag{8.41}$$

If we take Laplace transforms, we find

$$\tilde{y}(s) = \frac{\tilde{x}(s)}{a_n s^n + a_{n-1}s^{n-1} + \cdots + a_1 s + a_0}. \tag{8.42}$$

The function

$$\tilde{H}(s) = \frac{1}{a_n s^n + a_{n-1}s^{n-1} + \cdots + a_1 s + a_0}, \tag{8.43}$$

is the transfer function for the system. It is the Laplace transform of the response $H(t)$ of the system to the unit impulse $\delta(t)$ (when there is no initial energy in the system). Because the denominator of $\tilde{H}(s)$ is a (real) polynomial, it has n zeros (counting multiplicities) that are poles of $\tilde{H}(s)$. Positions and multiplicities of these poles determine the form of $H(t)$, the response of the system to a unit impulse. We single out three situations for special consideration:

1. If $\tilde{H}(s)$ has a real pole $a \neq 0$ of multiplicity k, then $H(t)$ contains terms of the form

$$(C_0 + C_1 t + \cdots + C_{k-1}t^{k-1})e^{at}.$$

This function approaches zero as $t \to \infty$ if and only if $a < 0$.

2. If $\tilde{H}(s)$ has complex conjugate poles $a \pm bi$, where $a \neq 0$, each of multiplicity k, then $H(t)$ contains terms of the form

$$e^{at}[(C_0 + C_1 t + \cdots + C_{k-1}t^{k-1})\cos bt + (D_0 + D_1 t + \cdots + D_{k-1}t^{k-1})\sin bt)].$$

This function approaches zero as $t \to \infty$ if and only if $a < 0$.

3. If $\tilde{H}(s)$ has complex conjugate poles $\pm bi$ each of multiplicity k (which lie on the imaginary axis), then $H(t)$ contains terms of the form

$$(C_0 + C_1 t + \cdots + C_{k-1}t^{k-1})\cos bt + (D_0 + D_1 t + \cdots + D_{k-1}t^{k-1})\sin bt.$$

This function is bounded as $t \to \infty$ if and only if $k = 1$; that is, if and only if poles on the imaginary axis are simple.

The following three definitions describe the stability of a system in terms of the poles of its transfer function.

Definition 8.1 A system is said to be **stable** if all poles of its transfer function have negative real parts.

Definition 8.2 A system is said to be **marginally stable** if its transfer function has simple poles on the imaginary axis and all other poles have negative real parts.

Definition 8.3 A system is said to be **unstable** if its transfer function has poles with positive real parts or poles on the imaginary axis with order greater than one.

It follows that a system is stable when its impulse response $H(t)$ approaches zero as $t \to \infty$; it is marginally stable when $H(t)$ is bounded as $t \to \infty$; and it is unstable when $H(t)$ is unbounded as $t \to \infty$.

Consider again our introductory mass-spring system. When there is no damping in the system, the transfer function $\tilde{H}(s) = 1/(Ms^2 + k)$ has simple poles at $s = \pm\sqrt{k/M}\,i$. It is therefore marginally stable. The impulse response is

$$H(t) = C_1 \cos\sqrt{\frac{k}{M}}t + C_2 \sin\sqrt{\frac{k}{M}}t,$$

a bounded function as $t \to \infty$. When there is damping in the system, the transfer function $\tilde{H}(s) = 1/(Ms^2 + \beta s + k)$ has poles

$$s = \frac{-\beta \pm \sqrt{\beta^2 - 4kM}}{2M}.$$

If $\beta^2 - 4kM > 0$, then both poles are negative real numbers

$$z_1 = \frac{-\beta + \sqrt{\beta^2 - 4kM}}{2M} \quad \text{and} \quad z_2 = \frac{-\beta - \sqrt{\beta^2 - 4kM}}{2M}.$$

The impulse response is

$$H(t) = C_1 e^{z_1 t} + C_2 e^{z_2 t}$$

which approaches zero as $t \to \infty$. If $\beta^2 - 4kM = 0$, then $\tilde{H}(s)$ has a pole of multiplicity two on the negative real axis $z_1 = -\beta/(2M)$. The impulse response is

$$H(t) = (C_1 + C_2 t)e^{-\beta t/(2M)}$$

which also approaches zero as $t \to \infty$. Finally, if $\beta^2 - 4kM < 0$, then poles are complex conjugates with negative real parts

$$z = \frac{-\beta \pm \sqrt{4kM - \beta^2}i}{2M} = \frac{-\beta}{2M} \pm \theta i, \quad \text{where } \theta = \frac{\sqrt{4kM - \beta^2}}{2M}.$$

The impulse response is

$$H(t) = e^{-\beta t/(2M)}(C_1 \cos \theta t + C_2 \sin \theta t)$$

which approaches zero as $t \to \infty$. Thus, the damped mass-spring system is always stable.

Example 8.23   Determine whether a system with transfer function $\tilde{H}(s) = \dfrac{1}{s^3 + s^2 + s + 1}$ is stable, marginally stable, or unstable.

Solution   Since $s^3 + s^2 + s + 1 = (s+1)(s^2+1)$, poles of $\tilde{H}(s)$ are $s = -1$ and $s = \pm i$. Since the pole $s = -1$ is in the left half-plane, and the poles $s = \pm i$ on the imaginary axis are simple, the system is marginally stable.•

Example 8.24   When a car with mass M is traveling at speed v_0, the driver removes his foot from the accelerator and allows the car to coast to a rest. If air resistance proportional to velocity and friction F bring the car to rest, the differential equation describing position $x(t)$ of the car, relative to its position when it started to slow down, is

$$M\frac{d^2x}{dt^2} + \beta\frac{dx}{dt} = F, \quad x(0) = 0, \quad x'(0) = v_0.$$

Show that the system is marginally stable and find its impulse response.

Solution   To find the transfer function of the system, we take Laplace transforms of the differential equation when F is replaced by $\delta(t)$, and the initial energy of the system is zero; that is, we take transforms of

$$M\frac{d^2H}{dt^2} + \beta\frac{dH}{dt} = \delta(t), \quad H(0) = 0, \quad H'(0) = 0.$$

The result is

$$Ms^2\tilde{H} + \beta s\tilde{H} = 1 \quad \Longrightarrow \quad \tilde{H}(s) = \frac{1}{s(Ms + \beta)}.$$

Because the poles of $\tilde{H}(s)$ are $s = 0$ (on the imaginary axis) and $s = -\beta/M$ (in the left half-plane), the system is marginally stable. Its impulse response is

$$H(t) = \mathcal{L}^{-1}\{\tilde{H}(s)\} = \mathcal{L}^{-1}\left\{ \frac{1/\beta}{s} - \frac{M/\beta}{Ms + \beta} \right\} = \frac{1}{\beta} - \frac{1}{\beta}e^{-\beta t/M}.$$

It is bounded as $t \to \infty$. In fact, $\displaystyle\lim_{t \to \infty} H(t) = \frac{1}{\beta}$. This is the distance that the car, at rest, would travel were it subjected to a unit impulse.•

When a system is stable, every bounded input results in a bounded output. This is sometimes used as the definition of stability of a sytem. When a system is marginally stable, certain inputs produce unbounded outputs. For example, the mass-spring system discussed earlier is marginally stable when damping is absent.

Inputs with frequency equal to the natural frequency of the system lead to unbounded oscillations.

The transfer function associated with differential equation 8.41 is the reciprocal of a polynomial in s. Transfer functions associated with other kinds of systems lead to transfer functions that are rational functions for which the numerator is not unity. For example, transfer functions derived from feedback systems in control theory are rational functions of s with nonconstant numerators, as are transfer functions associated with integral and integrodifferential equations. This changes nothing in our above discussions since stability is strictly determined by the poles of the denominator.

The Nyquist Stability Criterion

A system is stable if all poles of its transfer function, which we take as a rational function $\tilde{H}(s) = P(s)/Q(s)$, are in the left half-plane $\text{Re}(s) < 0$. If it is easy to determine the poles of $\tilde{H}(s)$, then we have an immediate decision on whether the system is stable, marginally stable, or unstable. There are methods to determine whether a system is unstable when it is difficult to actually determine the poles of $\tilde{H}(s)$. One of these is the *Nyquist stability criterion*, a technique that uses the principle of the argument (see Theorem 6.3 in Section 6.1). The principle of the argument states that when a function $Q(s)$ is analytic in a domain D except at a finite number of poles, and when C is a simple, closed, piecewise smooth curve in D which does not pass through any poles or zeros of $Q(s)$, then

$$\oint_C \frac{Q'(s)}{Q(s)}\, ds = 2\pi i (N - P),$$

where N and P are the sums of the orders of the zeros and poles of $Q(s)$ inside C. Since $Q(s)$ is a polynomial, it is entire, and therefore $P = 0$. Thus,

$$\oint_C \frac{Q'(s)}{Q(s)}\, ds = 2\pi i N.$$

Suppose that C is the limit of the curve in Figure 8.26 as the radius R of the semicircle becomes infinite. If the value of the contour integral is positive, then there are zeros of $Q(s)$ in the right half-plane $\text{Re}(s) > 0$. This means that $\tilde{H}(s)$ has poles in the right half-plane, and the system is unstable. Thus, to determine whether $\tilde{H}(s)$ is unstable, we could evaluate the contour integral of $Q'(s)/Q(s)$ around the limit of curve C as $R \to \infty$.

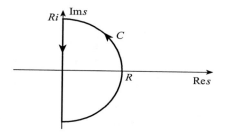

Figure 8.26

But, the principle of the argument indicates that if $w = Q(s)$ is regarded as a mapping from the s-plane to the w-plane, then the value of the integral is $2\pi i$ times the number of times that the curve $Q(C)$ encircles the origin $w = 0$. Thus, what we can do is follow $Q(C)$ as s traces C to determine how many times it encircles the origin, if any. This is the **Nyquist stability criterion**: It states that if, as s traces the limit of the curve in Figure 8.26 as $R \to \infty$, the image $Q(C)$ in the w-plane encircles the origin a nonzero number of times, then the system is unstable. What we do is find how much the argument of w changes as s traces C; each change of

2π represents one encirclement. We can reduce the work involved by developing a simple formula giving the change in argument when s traverses just the semicircle $C_1 : s = Re^{\theta i}$, $-\pi/2 \leq \theta \leq \pi/2$ as $R \to \infty$. It then remains to determine the change in argument as s traverses the imaginary axis. Suppose that $Q(s)$ is an nth-degree polynomial

$$Q(s) = a_n s^n + a_{n-1}s^{n-1} \cdots + a_1 s + a_0.$$

Then, the quotient $Q'(s)/Q(s)$ is

$$\frac{Q'(s)}{Q(s)} = \frac{na_n s^{n-1} + (n-1)a_{n-1}s^{n-2} + \cdots + a_1}{a_n s^n + a_{n-1}s^{n-1} \cdots + a_1 s + a_0}.$$

With long division, we can write this in the form

$$\frac{Q'(s)}{Q(s)} = \frac{n}{s} + \frac{b_{n-2}s^{n-2} + b_{n-3}s^{n-3} + \cdots + b_0}{a_n s^n + a_{n-1}s^{n-1} \cdots + a_1 s + a_0}.$$

Consider first the integral

$$\int_{C_1} \frac{n}{s} ds = n\left\{\text{Log } s\right\}_{-Ri}^{Ri} = n\left[\left(\ln R + \frac{\pi i}{2}\right) - \left(\ln R - \frac{\pi i}{2}\right)\right] = n\pi i.$$

Now, the radius R of the semicircle can be always be chosen sufficiently large so that on C_1,

$$|a_n R^n| \geq |a_{n-1}|R^{n-1} + |a_{n-2}|R^{n-2} + \cdots + |a_1|R + |a_0|.$$

On such a semicircle, we can say that

$$\left|\frac{b_{n-2}s^{n-2} + b_{n-3}s^{n-3} + \cdots + b_0}{a_n s^n + a_{n-1}s^{n-1} \cdots + a_1 s + a_0}\right| \leq \frac{|b_{n-2}|R^{n-2} + |b_{n-3}|R^{n-3} + \cdots + |b_0|}{|a_n|R^n - |a_{n-1}|R^{n-1} - \cdots - |a_1|R - |a_0|}.$$

Using property 4.21, we can write that

$$\left|\int_{C_1} \frac{b_{n-2}s^{n-2} + b_{n-3}s^{n-3} + \cdots + b_0}{a_n s^n + a_{n-1}s^{n-1} \cdots + a_1 s + a_0} ds\right| \leq \left(\frac{|b_{n-2}|R^{n-2} + |b_{n-3}|R^{n-3} + \cdots + |b_0|}{|a_n|R^n - |a_{n-1}|R^{n-1} - \cdots - |a_1|R - |a_0|}\right)(\pi R).$$

The limit of this is zero as $R \to \infty$. We have shown therefore that

$$\lim_{R\to\infty} \int_{C_1} \frac{Q'(s)}{Q(s)} ds = n\pi i;$$

that is, the change in the argument of $w = Q(C)$ as s traverses the limit of the semicircle, itself, is $n\pi$, where n is the degree of $Q(s)$. For the total change in the argument of $w = Q(s)$ as s traverses all of C, we must add to this the change in argument as s traverses the imaginary axis. If the total change is nonzero, then the system is unstable. If the total change is zero, then either the system is stable or marginally stable. We can sometimes tell which. If the image of that part of $Q(C)$ passes through $w = 0$, then it does so because of a zero of $Q(s)$ on the imaginary axis. In such a case, we are unable to determine whether the system is stable or marginally stable (it depends on the order of the zero). If, on the other hand, this part of $Q(C)$ does not pass through $w = 0$, then $Q(s)$ does not have zeros on the imaginary axis; the system is stable. Here are two examples to illustrate these ideas.

Example 8.25   Use the Nyquist stability criterion to determine, if possible, whether the system with transfer function $\tilde{H}(s) = \dfrac{3s - 2}{s^3 + s^2 + 2s + 1}$ is stable, unstable, or marginally stable.

Solution   In Exercise 18, it is shown, with some difficulty, that the poles of this function are in the left half-plane, and therefore the system is stable. To use the Nyquist stability criterion, we calculate the change in the argument of $Q(s)$ as we follow the limit of curve C in Figure 8.26 as $R \to \infty$ and $Q(s) = s^3 + s^2 + 2s + 1$. We know that the change in the argument as s traverses the semicircle is 3π. What remains is to determine the change in the argument as s traverses the imaginary axis. If we set $s = yi$, $\infty > y > -\infty$ along the imaginary axis, then

$$w = Q(yi) = (yi)^3 + (yi)^2 + 2(yi) + 1 = (1 - y^2) + (2y - y^3)i.$$

Parametric equations for this part of $Q(C)$ are therefore

$$u = 1 - y^2, \quad v = 2y - y^3.$$

The curve is plotted in Figure 8.27. What is important is to notice that because u is a quadratic function of y, whereas v is cubic, the principal value of the argument of w approaches $-\pi/2$ for $y \to \infty$, and it approaches $\pi/2$ for $y \to -\infty$. Let us now follow the curve to see the change in the argument of w. The curve begins far down in the third quadrant where the

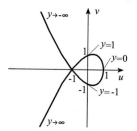

Figure 8.27

argument is $-\pi/2$. As the curve approaches the u-axis, the argument approaches $-\pi$. So far, then, the argument has decreased by $-\pi/2$. The curve then makes a clockwise loop around the origin so that the argument decreases by 2π more. Finally the curve ends high in the second quadrant so that the argument has decreased $-\pi/2$ more. The total change in the argument as s traverses the imaginary axis is -3π. When this is added to 3π, the change from the semicircle, the total change is zero. The Nyquist stability criterion implies that the system is either stable or marginally stable. Because the curve in Figure 8.27 does not pass through $w = 0$, the system is stable.●

Before doing another example, it is perhaps important to point out that the curve in Figure 8.27 was plotted with a software package. The software package could also have calculated the zeros of $Q(s)$ to any degree of accuracy required, and hence the Nyquist discussion would have been unnecessary. It is a matter of how much technology we wish to use. There are also mathematical packages that deal with the Nyquist stability criterion. Again how much are we willing to do by hand, and how much do we send to the computer.

Example 8.26   Use the Nyquist stability criterion to determine, if possible, whether the system with transfer function $\tilde{H}(s) = \dfrac{2s + 1}{s^3 - s^2 + s + 3}$ is stable, unstable, or marginally stable.

Solution   To use the Nyquist stability criterion, we calculate the change in the argument of $Q(s)$ as we follow the limit of curve C in Figure 8.26 as $R \to \infty$ and $Q(s) = s^3 - s^2 + s + 3$. We know that the change in the argument as s traverses the semicircle is 3π. What remains is to determine the change in the argument as s traverses the imaginary axis. If we set $s = yi$, $\infty > y > -\infty$ along the imaginary axis, then

$$w = Q(yi) = (yi)^3 - (yi)^2 + (yi) + 3 = (3 + y^2) + (y - y^3)i.$$

Parametric equations for this part of $Q(C)$ are therefore

$$u = 3 + y^2, \quad v = y - y^3.$$

The curve is plotted in Figure 8.28. Because u is a quadratic function of y, whereas v is cubic, the principal value of the argument of w approaches $-\pi/2$ for $y \to \infty$, and it approaches $\pi/2$ for $y \to -\infty$. Let us now follow the curve to see the change in the argument of w. The curve begins far down in the fourth quadrant where the

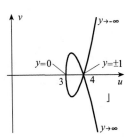

Figure 8.28

argument is $-\pi/2$. As the curve approaches the u-axis, the argument approaches 0. So far, then, the argument has increased by $\pi/2$. The curve then makes a counterclockwise loop but because it does not surround the origin, the change in the argument is zero. Finally the curve ends high in the first quadrant so that the argument has increased $\pi/2$ more. The total change in the argument as s traverses the imaginary axis is π. When this is added to 3π, the change from the semicircle, the total change is 4π. The Nyquist stability criterion implies that the system is unstable.●

There are other ways to determine whether poles of a transfer function are all in the left half-plane. Two of them, the Routh stability criterion and the Hurwitz stability criterion are introduced in the exercises. There is also a method that uses continued fractions.

EXERCISES 8.6

In Exercise 1–10 determine whether a system with given transfer function is stable, marginally stable, or unstable by finding poles of the transfer function.

1. $\tilde{H}(s) = \dfrac{1}{s^2 + s + 2}$

2. $\tilde{H}(s) = \dfrac{1}{s^2 - 3s + 6}$

3. $\tilde{H}(s) = \dfrac{1}{s^2 + 4s + 3}$

4. $\tilde{H}(s) = \dfrac{1}{s^2 - 4s - 12}$

5. $\tilde{H}(s) = \dfrac{1}{s^3 + s^2 + 4s + 4}$

6. $\tilde{H}(s) = \dfrac{1}{s^4 + 5s^2 + 4}$

7. $\tilde{H}(s) = \dfrac{1}{s^3 - s^2 + 4s - 4}$

8. $\tilde{H}(s) = \dfrac{1}{s^4 + 5s^2 - 36}$

9. $\tilde{H}(s) = \dfrac{1}{s^4 + 2s^2 + 1}$

10. $\tilde{H}(s) = \dfrac{1}{s^4 + 6s^3 + 17s^2 + 28s + 20}$

In Exercises 11–14 use the Nyquist stability criterion to determine, if possible, whether the system with given transfer function is stable, unstable, or marginally stable.

11. $\tilde{H}(s) = \dfrac{1}{s^4 + 6s^3 + 17s^2 + 28s + 20}$

12. $\tilde{H}(s) = \dfrac{1}{s^3 - 3s^2 + 2s + 1}$

13. $\tilde{H}(s) = \dfrac{1}{s^4 + s^3 + 2s^2 + s + 1}$

14. $\tilde{H}(s) = \dfrac{1}{s^5 + 2s^4 + s + 2}$

15. Suppose that the input $x(t)$ and output $y(t)$ of a system are related by the equation

$$\frac{dy}{dt} = k\frac{d}{dt}[h(t-T)x(t-T)];$$

that is, dy/dt at time t is proportional to the derivative of $x(t)$ at time $t-T$. For $0 < t < T$, the derivative of $y(t)$ will be zero. Show that the transfer function for this system is not a rational function of s.

16. The differential equation for charge Q on the capacitor in the LCR-circuit in the figure below is

$$L\frac{d^2Q}{dt^2} + R\frac{dQ}{dt} + \frac{1}{C}Q = E(t), \quad Q(0) = Q_0, \quad Q'(0) = I_0.$$

(a) Find the transfer function for the system.

(b) Determine values of L, C, and R for which the system is stable, marginally stable, and unstable.

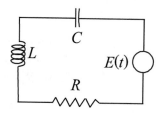

17. Determine values of constant b such that a system with transfer function $\tilde{H}(s) = \dfrac{1}{2s^2 + bs + 3}$ is stable, marginally stable, and unstable.

18. (a) Verify that polynomial $\tilde{f}(s) = s^3 + s^2 + 2s + 1$ has exactly one real zero between -1 and 0.

(b) Let the real zero in part (a) be $s = a$, where $-1 < a < 0$. Show that the remaining two zeros of the polynomial are

$$s = \frac{-(a+1) \pm \sqrt{-3a^2 - 2a - 7}}{2},$$

and conclude that they are complex with negative real parts.

(c) Is the system with transfer function $1/\tilde{f}(s)$ stable, marginally stable, or unstable?

The **Routh criterion** is an alternative to the Nyquist criterion for determining the stability of a system. If $\tilde{H}(s) = P(s)/Q(s)$ is the transfer function for the system, stability is determined by the locations of the zeros of $Q(s) = a_n s^n + a_{n-1}s^{n-1} + \cdots + a_1 s + a_0$. The following table is constructed.

s^n	a_n	a_{n-2}	a_{n-4}	$\cdots$
s^{n-1}	a_{n-1}	a_{n-3}	a_{n-5}	$\cdots$
s^{n-2}	b_{n-2}	b_{n-4}	b_{n-6}	$\cdots$
s^{n-3}	c_{n-3}	c_{n-5}	c_{n-7}	$\cdots$
$\vdots$	$\vdots$	$\vdots$	$\vdots$	
s^2	d_2	d_0	0	$\cdots$
s^1	e_1	0	0	$\cdots$
s^0	f_0	0	0	$\cdots$

The rules for entries are:

1. For entries in the third row:

$$b_{n-2} = \frac{a_{n-1}a_{n-2} - a_n a_{n-3}}{a_{n-1}}, \qquad b_{n-4} = \frac{a_{n-1}a_{n-4} - a_n a_{n-5}}{a_{n-1}}, \qquad \text{etc.}$$

2. For entries in the fourth row:

$$c_{n-3} = \frac{b_{n-2}a_{n-3} - a_{n-1}b_{n-4}}{b_{n-2}}, \qquad c_{n-5} = \frac{b_{n-2}a_{n-5} - a_{n-1}b_{n-6}}{b_{n-2}}, \qquad \text{etc.}$$

3. Entries in succeeding rows are calculated with similar formulas.

4. If any entry in the second column turns out to be equal to 0, set it equal to a very small number ϵ and continue.

5. Each row is continued until a zero is obtained.

The Routh criterion states that all zeros of $Q(s)$ are in the left half-plane $\text{Re}(s) < 0$, and therefore the system is stable, if and only if all entries in the first column are positive. Furthermore, $Q(s)$ has a single pair of complex zeros on the imaginary axis, and therefore the system is marginally stable, if and only if all entries in the first column are positive except that the entry e_1 next to s^1 is 0.

In Exercises 19–22 use the Routh criterion to determine whether the transfer function is stable, unstable, or marginally stable.

19. $\tilde{H}(s) = \dfrac{1}{s^3 + 4s^2 + 8s + 12}$

20. $\tilde{H}(s) = \dfrac{1}{s^3 - 3s^2 + 2s + 1}$

21. $\tilde{H}(s) = \dfrac{1}{s^4 + s^3 - s - 1}$

22. $\tilde{H}(s) = \dfrac{1}{6s^5 + 5s^4 + 4s^3 + 3s^2 + 2s + 1}$

23. What conditions on b and c guarantee that $\tilde{H}(s) = 1/(s^2 + bs + c)$ is the transfer function for a stable system?

24. What conditions on a, b, and c guarantee that $\tilde{H}(s) = 1/(s^3 + as^2 + bs + c)$ is the transfer function for a stable system?

25. For what values of the constant k is a system with transfer function $\tilde{H}(s) = 1/(s^4 + 6s^3 + 11s^2 + 6s + k)$ stable?

The **Hurwitz criterion** is an alternative to the Nyquist and Routh criteria for determining the stability of a system. If $\tilde{H}(s) = P(s)/Q(s)$ is the transfer function for the system, stability is determined by the locations of the zeros of $Q(s) = a^n s^n + a_{n-1}s^{n-1} + \cdots + a_1 s + a_0$. The following $n \times n$ determinant is constructed.

$$\Delta_n = \begin{vmatrix} a_{n-1} & a_{n-3} & \cdots & \begin{bmatrix} a_0 \text{ if } n \text{ is odd} \\ a_1 \text{ if } n \text{ is even} \end{bmatrix} & 0 & \cdots & 0 \\ a_n & a_{n-2} & \cdots & \begin{bmatrix} a_1 \text{ if } n \text{ is odd} \\ a_0 \text{ if } n \text{ is even} \end{bmatrix} & 0 & \cdots & 0 \\ 0 & a_{n-1} & a_{n-3} & & \cdots & \cdots & 0 \\ 0 & a_n & a_{n-2} & & \cdots & \cdots & 0 \\ \vdots & \vdots & \vdots & & \vdots & \cdots & \vdots \\ 0 & \cdots & \cdots & \cdots & \cdots & \cdots & a_0 \end{vmatrix}$$

The n principal minor determinants of this determinant are

$$\Delta_1 = a_{n-1}, \quad \Delta_2 = \begin{vmatrix} a_{n-1} & a_{n-2} \\ a_n & a_{n-2} \end{vmatrix}, \quad \Delta_3 = \begin{vmatrix} a_{n-1} & a_{n-3} & a_{n-5} \\ a_n & a_{n-2} & a_{n-4} \\ 0 & a_{n-1} & a_{n-3} \end{vmatrix},$$

and so on up to Δ_n. The Hurwitz criterion states that all zeros of $Q(s)$ are in the left half-plane $\text{Re}(s) < 0$, and therefore the system is stable, if and only if all principal minor determinants are positive.

In Exercises 26–29 use the Hurwitz criterion to determine whether the transfer function is stable, unstable, or marginally stable.

26. $\tilde{H}(s) = \dfrac{1}{s^3 + 4s^2 + 8s + 12}$

27. $\tilde{H}(s) = \dfrac{1}{s^3 - 3s^2 + 2s + 1}$

28. $\tilde{H}(s) = \dfrac{1}{s^4 + s^2 + s + 4}$

29. $\tilde{H}(s) = \dfrac{1}{6s^5 + 5s^4 + 4s^3 + 3s^2 + 2s + 1}$

30. Repeat Exercise 23 using the Hurwitz criterion.

31. Repeat Exercise 24 using the Hurwitz criterion.

32. Repeat Exercise 25 using the Hurwitz criterion.

33. Prove that a system with transfer function $\tilde{H}(s)$ given by equation 8.43 is stable only if all coefficients in the polynomial $1/\tilde{H}(s)$ are nonzero. It follows therefore that if at least one of the coefficients in $1/\tilde{H}(s)$ is equal to zero, then the system is either unstable or marginally stable.

34. Prove that a system with transfer function $\tilde{H}(s)$ given by equation 8.43 is stable only if all coefficients in the polynomial $1/\tilde{H}(s)$ have the same sign. It follows therefore that if the coefficients in $1/\tilde{H}(s)$ are not of the same sign, then the system is either unstable or marginally stable.

CHAPTER 9   FOURIER TRANSFORMS

In Chapter 8, we saw how Laplace transforms remove time derivatives from partial differential equations, thus reducing them to ordinary differential equations in the space variable. Fourier transforms are also integral transforms, but they remove spatial derivatives from partial differential equations, thereby reducing them to ordinary differential equations in time. In Section 9.1, we introduce the Fourier transform along with its operational properties, and in Section 9.2, we use it to solve partial differential equations. We repeat this procedure in Sections 9.3 and 9.4 for the Fourier sine and cosine transforms.

§9.1   The Fourier Transform

Readers familiar with the method of separation of variables for PDEs may be aware of *finite Fourier transforms*. They are used to solve nonhomogeneous problems on bounded intervals, but are seldom used on homogeneous problems. Fourier transforms, on the other hand, are useful for PDEs defined on infinite intervals, but they are advantageous on both homogeneous and nonhomogeneous problems.

Definition 9.1   When f is a function of x, its **Fourier transform**, denoted by $\tilde{f} = \mathcal{F}\{f\}$ is a complex-valued function of a real variable ω with values defined by

$$\tilde{f}(\omega) = \mathcal{F}\{f\}(\omega) = \int_{-\infty}^{\infty} f(x)e^{-i\omega x}dx, \tag{9.1}$$

provided the improper integral converges.

Convergence of the integral is guaranteed when $f(x)$ is *piecewise smooth* on every finite interval and *absolutely integrable* on $-\infty < x < \infty$. A function $f(x)$ is **piecewise smooth** on an interval $a \leq x \leq b$ if $f(x)$ and $f'(x)$ are both piecewise continuous therein. A function $f(x)$ is **absolutely integrable** (on $-\infty < x < \infty$) if the improper integral

$$\int_{-\infty}^{\infty} |f(x)|\, dx \tag{9.2}$$

converges. When these conditions are satisfied, definition 9.1 leads to a continuous Fourier transform function. We state this as the first of many properties of Fourier transforms.

Theorem 9.1   The Fourier transform of a function that is piecewise smooth on every finite interval and absolutely integrable for $-\infty < x < \infty$ is a continuous function.

Integrability of $f(x)$ is a much more demanding condition than being of exponential order for existence of the Laplace transform of a function $f(t)$. This is due to the fact that in the definition of the Laplace transform, the factor e^{-st} suppresses $f(t)$ substantially for large t, but the factor $e^{-i\omega x} = \cos \omega x - i \sin \omega x$ in definition 9.1 has no such effect, the function $f(x)$ must be integrable on its own. This effectively eliminates most of the functions that we worked with in Chapter 8 such as polynomials, sines and cosines, and exponentials; they are not absolutely integrable on the real line.

Absolute integrability of $f(x)$ on $-\infty < x < \infty$ implies that the integral of $f(x)$ itself must also exist. In fact, definition 9.1 implies that the (signed) area bounded by $f(x)$ and the x-axis is the value of the transform at $\omega = 0$,

$$\tilde{f}(0) = \int_{-\infty}^{\infty} f(x)\,dx. \tag{9.3}$$

Although we have used the tilde notation, $\tilde{f}$, for both the Laplace transform and the Fourier transform, and we will also use it for Fourier sine and cosine transforms in Section 9.3, context always makes it clear which transform is appropriate. In addition, none of the problems that we consider in this chapter simultaneously use more than one type of transform.

It is straightforward to identify the real and imaginary parts of $\tilde{f}(\omega)$,

$$\tilde{f}(\omega) = \int_{-\infty}^{\infty} f(x)e^{-i\omega x}dx = \int_{-\infty}^{\infty} f(x)(\cos\omega x - i\sin\omega x)\,dx$$

$$= \int_{-\infty}^{\infty} f(x)\cos\omega x\,dx - i\int_{-\infty}^{\infty} f(x)\sin\omega x\,dx. \tag{9.4}$$

If $f(x)$ is an even function, then the second of these integrals vanishes; and if $f(x)$ is odd, the first vanishes.

Theorem 9.2   When $f(x)$ is an even function, its Fourier transform is a real function, given by

$$\tilde{f}(\omega) = \int_{-\infty}^{\infty} f(x)\cos\omega x\,dx = 2\int_{0}^{\infty} f(x)\cos\omega x\,dx; \tag{9.5a}$$

and when $f(x)$ is an odd function, its Fourier transform is purely imaginary, given by

$$\tilde{f}(\omega) = -i\int_{-\infty}^{\infty} f(x)\sin\omega x\,dx = -2i\int_{0}^{\infty} f(x)\sin\omega x\,dx. \tag{9.5b}$$

Example 9.1   Find the Fourier transform of the function in Figure 9.1 where $a > 0$ is a constant.

Solution   Because the function is continuous and absolutely integrable on the real line, its Fourier transform exists. Furthermore, since the function is odd, its Fourier transform is given by equation 9.5b,

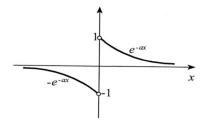

Figure 9.1

$$\tilde{f}(\omega) = -2i\int_{0}^{\infty} e^{-ax}\sin\omega x\,dx$$

We could integrate this by parts, but it is easier to use a complex integral,

$$\tilde{f}(\omega) = -2i\,\text{Im}\left[\int_{0}^{\infty} e^{-ax}e^{i\omega x}dx\right] = -2i\,\text{Im}\left[\int_{0}^{\infty} e^{(-a+\omega i)x}dx\right]$$

$$= -2i\,\text{Im}\left[\left\{\frac{e^{(-a+\omega i)x}}{-a+\omega i}\right\}_{0}^{\infty}\right] = -2i\,\text{Im}\left[\frac{1}{a-\omega i}\right] = \frac{-2\omega i}{a^2+\omega^2}.\,\bullet$$

Because the real and imaginary parts of the Fourier transform are improper integrals (see equation 9.4), they can often be calculated using residues. This is especially so when $f(x)$ is a rational function of x. We illustrate this in the next example.

Example 9.2   Find the Fourier transform of the function $f(x) = \dfrac{1}{a^2 + x^2}$, where $a > 0$ is a constant.

Solution   Because the function is continuous and absolutely integrable on the real line, its Fourier transform exists. Furthermore, since the function is even, its Fourier transform is given by

$$\tilde{f}(\omega) = \int_{-\infty}^{\infty} \frac{\cos \omega x}{a^2 + x^2}\, dx.$$

We use residues to evaluate this integral. According to Theorem 6.6 in Section 6.2,

$$\tilde{f}(\omega) = -2\pi \operatorname{Im}\left\{ \operatorname{Res}\left[\frac{e^{i\omega z}}{a^2 + z^2}, ai \right] \right\},$$

provided $\omega > 0$. For $\omega > 0$ then,

$$\tilde{f}(\omega) = -2\pi \operatorname{Im}\left\{ \lim_{z \to ai} \left[\frac{(z - ai)e^{i\omega z}}{(z + ai)(z - ai)} \right] \right\} = \frac{\pi}{a} e^{-a\omega}.$$

The integral definition of $\tilde{f}(\omega)$ makes it clear that $\tilde{f}(\omega)$ is an even function of ω. Consequently, when $\omega < 0$, we write that

$$\tilde{f}(\omega) = \tilde{f}(-\omega) = \frac{\pi}{a} e^{a\omega}.$$

Both cases $\omega > 0$ and $\omega < 0$ are contained in

$$\tilde{f}(\omega) = \frac{\pi}{a} e^{-a|\omega|}.$$

This result is also valid for $\omega = 0$ since

$$\tilde{f}(\omega) = \int_{-\infty}^{\infty} \frac{1}{a^2 + x^2}\, dx = \frac{\pi}{a}.\; \bullet$$

In our third example, the function $f(x)$ is defined only over a finite interval so that the improper integral in definition 9.1 reduces to an ordinary integral.

Example 9.3   Find the Fourier transform for the function in Figure 9.2.

Solution   Since the function is even, continuous, and absolutely integrable, its Fourier transform is given by equation 9.5a,

$$\tilde{f}(\omega) = 2 \int_{0}^{\infty} f(x) \cos \omega x\, dx$$

$$= 2 \int_{0}^{1} (1 - x) \cos \omega x\, dx.$$

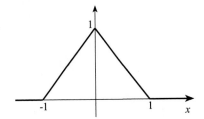

Figure 9.2

Integration by parts gives

$$\tilde{f}(\omega) = 2 \left\{ \frac{1}{\omega}(1 - x) \sin \omega x \right\}_{0}^{1} - 2 \int_{0}^{1} -\frac{1}{\omega} \sin \omega x\, dx \quad \text{(provided } \omega \neq 0\text{)}$$

$$= \frac{2}{\omega} \left\{ -\frac{1}{\omega} \cos \omega x \right\}_{0}^{1} = \frac{2}{\omega^2}(1 - \cos \omega) = \frac{4}{\omega^2} \sin^2 \frac{\omega}{2}.$$

When $\omega = 0$,

$$\tilde{f}(0) = 2 \int_0^\infty f(x)\,dx = 2 \int_0^1 (1-x)\,dx = 2 \left\{ x - \frac{x^2}{2} \right\}_0^1 = 1.$$

Theorem 9.1 promised continuity of the Fourier transform. The only value of ω at which continuity could be questioned is $\omega = 0$. Since $\tilde{f}(0)$ is defined, continuity is established if $\lim_{\omega \to 0} \tilde{f}(\omega) = 1$ also. This is easily verified

$$\lim_{\omega \to 0} \tilde{f}(\omega) = \lim_{\omega \to 0} \left(\frac{4}{\omega^2} \sin^2 \frac{\omega}{2} \right) = \lim_{\omega \to 0} \left[\frac{\sin(\omega/2)}{\omega/2} \right]^2 = 1.$$

In other words, we can write that for all ω,

$$\tilde{f}(\omega) = \frac{4}{\omega^2} \sin^2 \frac{\omega}{2},$$

knowing that the limit as $\omega \to 0$ gives the value of the transform at $\omega = 0$. $\bullet$

One of the most important functions in the application of Fourier transforms to heat conduction problems is contained in the following example.

Example 9.4   Find the Fourier transform of e^{-ax^2}.

Solution   The function is continuous and absolutely integrable since it is a well known result from statistics that

$$\int_{-\infty}^\infty e^{-ax^2}\,dx = \sqrt{\frac{\pi}{a}}. \tag{9.6}$$

Once again the function is even, and therefore its Fourier transform is given by equation 9.5a,

$$\tilde{f}(\omega) = 2 \int_0^\infty e^{-ax^2} \cos \omega x \, dx.$$

We evaluate this integral in two ways. First, if we differentiate the equation with respect to ω, we get

$$\tilde{f}'(\omega) = 2 \int_0^\infty -x e^{-ax^2} \sin \omega x \, dx.$$

Integration by parts with respect to x now gives

$$\tilde{f}'(\omega) = 2 \left\{ \frac{e^{-ax^2}}{2a} \sin \omega x \right\}_0^\infty - 2 \int_0^\infty \frac{e^{-ax^2}}{2a} \omega \cos \omega x \, dx = -\frac{\omega}{2a} \tilde{f}(\omega).$$

In other words, $\tilde{f}(\omega)$ must satisfy the separable differential equation

$$\frac{d\tilde{f}}{d\omega} + \frac{\omega}{2a} \tilde{f} = 0.$$

An initial condition for this differential equation is

$$\tilde{f}(0) = 2 \int_0^\infty e^{-ax^2}\,dx = \sqrt{\frac{\pi}{a}}.$$

The solution of this problem is

$$\tilde{f}(\omega) = \sqrt{\frac{\pi}{a}} e^{-\omega^2/(4a)}.$$

Alternatively, we can use residues to evaluate the integral for $\tilde{f}(\omega)$. Consider the contour integral

$$\oint_C e^{-az^2} dz$$

where C is the contour in Figure 9.3. Along C_1,

$$\int_{C_1} e^{-az^2} dz = \int_{-R}^{R} e^{-ax^2} dx.$$

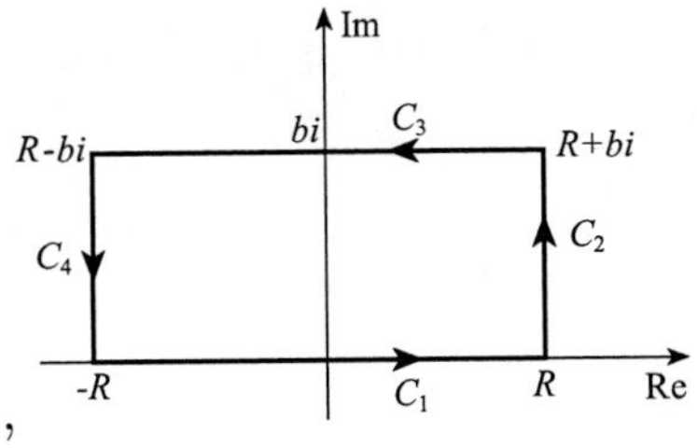

Figure 9.3

Along C_2, we set $z = R + yi$, $0 \le y \le b$, so that

$$\int_{C_2} e^{-az^2} dz = \int_0^b e^{-a(R+yi)^2} i\, dy = ie^{-aR^2} \int_0^b e^{a(y^2 - 2Ryi)}\, dy.$$

Along C_3, we set $z = x + bi$, $R \ge x \ge -R$, so that

$$\int_{C_3} e^{-az^2} dz = \int_R^{-R} e^{-a(x+bi)^2} dx = -e^{ab^2} \int_{-R}^{R} e^{-a(x^2 + 2bxi)}\, dx.$$

Along C_4, we set $z = -R + yi$, $b \ge y \ge 0$, so that

$$\int_{C_4} e^{-az^2} dz = \int_b^0 e^{-a(-R+yi)^2} i\, dy = -ie^{-aR^2} \int_0^b e^{a(y^2 + 2Ryi)}\, dy.$$

Since e^{-az^2} has no singularities inside C, it follows that

$$0 = \int_{-R}^{R} e^{-ax^2} dx + ie^{-aR^2} \int_0^b e^{a(y^2 - 2Ryi)}\, dy - e^{ab^2} \int_{-R}^{R} e^{-a(x^2 + 2bxi)}\, dx$$

$$\quad - ie^{-aR^2} \int_0^b e^{a(y^2 + 2Ryi)}\, dy$$

$$= \int_{-R}^{R} e^{-ax^2} dx + ie^{-aR^2} \int_0^b e^{ay^2} \cos 2aRy\, dy - ie^{-aR^2} \int_0^b e^{ay^2} \sin 2aRy\, dy$$

$$\quad - e^{ab^2} \int_{-R}^{R} e^{-ax^2} \cos 2abx\, dx + i\, e^{ab^2} \int_{-R}^{R} e^{-ax^2} \sin 2abx\, dx$$

$$\quad - ie^{-aR^2} \int_0^b e^{ay^2} \cos 2aRy\, dy + e^{-aR^2} \int_0^b e^{ay^2} \sin 2aRy\, dy.$$

If we take limits as $R \to \infty$, the second, third, sixth, and seventh integrals approach 0. Since the integrand of the fifth integral is an odd function, we obtain

$$0 = \int_{-\infty}^{\infty} e^{-ax^2} dx - e^{ab^2} \int_{-\infty}^{\infty} e^{-ax^2} \cos 2abx\, dx;$$

that is,

$$\int_{-\infty}^{\infty} e^{-ax^2} \cos 2abx\, dx = e^{-ab^2} \int_{-\infty}^{\infty} e^{-ax^2} dx = \sqrt{\frac{\pi}{a}} e^{-ab^2}.$$

If we now set $\omega = 2ab$, we obtain

$$\int_{-\infty}^{\infty} e^{-ax^2} \cos \omega x \, dx = \sqrt{\frac{\pi}{a}} e^{-\omega^2/(4a)}.\,\bullet$$

The Inverse Fourier Transform

When $\tilde{f}$ is the Fourier transform of f, we say that f is the inverse Fourier transform of $\tilde{f}$, and we write $f = \mathcal{F}^{-1}\{\tilde{f}\}$. It can be retrieved from its transform with the following improper integral

$$f(x) = \mathcal{F}^{-1}\{\tilde{f}\}(x) = \frac{1}{2\pi} \int_{-\infty}^{\infty} \tilde{f}(\omega) e^{i\omega x} d\omega. \tag{9.7}$$

Should convergence difficulties be associated with this integral, it should be interpreted as its Cauchy's principal value,

$$f(x) = \frac{1}{2\pi} \fint_{-\infty}^{\infty} \tilde{f}(\omega) e^{i\omega x} d\omega = \frac{1}{2\pi} \lim_{R \to \infty} \int_{-R}^{R} \tilde{f}(\omega) e^{i\omega x} d\omega. \tag{9.8}$$

In actual fact, equations 9.7 and 9.8 are valid only at points of continuity of $f(x)$. Like the inverse Laplace transform, the inverse Fourier transform converges to average of right- and left-hand limits at points of discontinuity; that is, equation 9.7 should be written

$$\frac{f(x+) + f(x-)}{2} = \frac{1}{2\pi} \int_{-\infty}^{\infty} \tilde{f}(\omega) e^{i\omega x} d\omega, \tag{9.9}$$

and likewise for equation 9.8. We can always use equation 9.7 instead of 9.9 if we agree that at a point of discontinuity of $f(x)$, the function is always defined, or redefined, so that its value there is $[f(x+) + f(x-)]/2$.

Contour integral 8.17 for the inverse Laplace transform was unusable, but fortunately, it was replaced by residues. The improper integral in equation 9.7 for the inverse Fourier transform is calculationally viable, but there are often more efficient ways to evaluate the inverse transform.

In order that definitions of Fourier transform and inverse Fourier transforms be more symmetric, some authors multiply each of the integrals in equations 9.1 and 9.7 by $1/\sqrt{2\pi}$. Others interchange the exponentials using $e^{i\omega x}$ for the Fourier transform and $e^{-i\omega x}$ for the inverse transform. Whichever convention is adopted, solutions of initial boundary value problems are ultimately identical.

Corresponding to Theorem 9.2 for the Fourier transform, we have the following for the inverse transform.

Theorem 9.3 When $\tilde{f}(\omega)$ is a (real and) even function, its inverse Fourier transform is given by

$$f(x) = \frac{1}{2\pi} \int_{-\infty}^{\infty} \tilde{f}(\omega) \cos \omega x \, d\omega = \frac{1}{\pi} \int_{0}^{\infty} \tilde{f}(\omega) \cos \omega x \, d\omega; \tag{9.10a}$$

and when $\tilde{f}(\omega)$ is a (real and) odd function, its inverse Fourier transform is given by

$$f(x) = \frac{i}{2\pi} \int_{-\infty}^{\infty} \tilde{f}(\omega) \sin \omega x \, d\omega = \frac{i}{\pi} \int_{0}^{\infty} \tilde{f}(\omega) \sin \omega x \, d\omega. \tag{9.10b}$$

Example 9.5   Find the inverse Fourier transform of $\tilde{f}(\omega) = \dfrac{1}{(a^2 + \omega^2)^2}$, where $a > 0$ is a constant.

Solution   Because the transform is even, we can use equation 9.10a,

$$f(x) = \frac{1}{2\pi} \int_{-\infty}^{\infty} \frac{\cos \omega x}{(a^2 + \omega^2)^2} d\omega.$$

We use residues to evaluate this integral. According to Theorem 6.6 in Section 6.2,

$$\tilde{f}(\omega) = \frac{1}{2\pi} \left\{ -2\pi \operatorname{Im} \left\{ \operatorname{Res} \left[\frac{e^{ixz}}{(a^2 + z^2)^2}, ai \right] \right\} \right\},$$

provided $x > 0$. For $x > 0$ then,

$$f(x) = -\operatorname{Im} \left\{ \operatorname{Res} \left[\frac{e^{ixz}}{(a^2 + z^2)^2}, ai \right] \right\} = -\operatorname{Im} \left\{ \lim_{z \to ai} \frac{d}{dz} \left[\frac{(z - ai)^2 e^{ixz}}{(z + ai)^2 (z - ai)^2} \right] \right\}$$

$$= -\operatorname{Im} \left\{ \lim_{z \to ai} \left[\frac{ix(z + ai)^2 e^{ixz} - 2e^{ixz}(z + ai)}{(z + ai)^4} \right] \right\}$$

$$= -\operatorname{Im} \left\{ \frac{ix(2ai)e^{-ax} - 2e^{-ax}}{(2ai)^3} \right\} = \frac{1}{4a^3}(1 + ax)e^{-ax}.$$

The integral representation of $f(x)$ makes it clear that $f(x)$ is an even function of x. Consequently, when $x < 0$, we write that

$$f(x) = f(-x) = \frac{1}{4a^3}(1 - ax)e^{ax}.$$

Both cases $x > 0$ and $x < 0$ are contained in

$$f(x) = \frac{1}{4a^3}(1 + a|x|)e^{-a|x|}.$$

In addition, this formula is also valid at $x = 0$ since

$$f(0) = \frac{1}{2\pi} \int_{-\infty}^{\infty} \frac{1}{(a^2 + \omega^2)^2} d\omega = \frac{1}{4a^3}. \bullet$$

Example 9.6   Find the inverse Fourier transform of $\tilde{f}(\omega) = e^{-a\omega^2}$?

Solution   We could evaluate the improper integral in equation 9.7, but it is easier to use the result of Example 9.4,

$$\mathcal{F}\left\{ e^{-kx^2} \right\} = \sqrt{\frac{\pi}{k}} e^{-\omega^2/(4k)}.$$

If we set $a = 1/(4k)$, then

$$\mathcal{F}\left\{ \sqrt{\frac{1}{4a\pi}} e^{-x^2/(4a)} \right\} = e^{-a\omega^2} \quad \text{and therefore} \quad \mathcal{F}^{-1}\left\{ e^{-a\omega^2} \right\} = \frac{1}{2\sqrt{a\pi}} e^{-x^2/(4a)}. \bullet$$

Example 9.7 Find the Fourier transform for the function $f(x) = h(x+a) - h(x-a)$ (Figure 9.4a) and illustrate graphically that integral 9.9 converges to $[f(x+) + f(x-)]/2$.

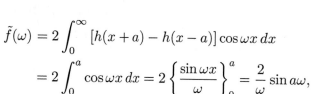

Figure 9.4a

Solution   Because the function is even, its Fourier transform is given by equation 9.5a,

$$\tilde{f}(\omega) = 2 \int_0^\infty [h(x+a) - h(x-a)] \cos \omega x \, dx$$

$$= 2 \int_0^a \cos \omega x \, dx = 2 \left\{ \frac{\sin \omega x}{\omega} \right\}_0^a = \frac{2}{\omega} \sin a\omega,$$

provided $\omega \neq 0$. But

$$\tilde{f}(0) = 2 \int_0^\infty [h(x+a) - h(x-a)] \, dx = 2 \int_0^a dx = 2a.$$

This is the limit of $\tilde{f}(\omega)$ as $\omega \to 0$, and therefore we write for all ω,

$$\tilde{f}(\omega) = \frac{2}{\omega} \sin a\omega.$$

Since $\tilde{f}(\omega)$ is an even function and $f(x)$ has discontinuities, we use formula 9.10a to write

$$\frac{f(x+) + f(x-)}{2} = \frac{2}{\pi} \int_0^\infty \frac{1}{\omega} \sin a\omega \cos \omega x \, d\omega.$$

We have shown approximations to this improper integral with $a = 1$ in Figures 9.4b,c using upper limits of integration equal to 50 and 100, respectively.●

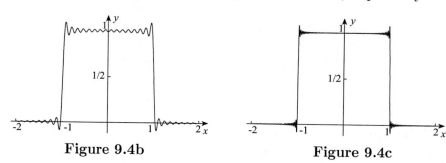

Figure 9.4b   **Figure 9.4c**

We use Fourier transforms to solve (initial) boundary value problems on infinite domains. We shall show how to do this in Section 9.2. We prepare the way by developing properties of the transform and its inverse that make it unnecessary to return to integral definitions 9.1 and 9.7 each time a Fourier transform and its inverse are required. Many of these properties are sufficiently easy to verify that proofs are relegated to the exercises. First, we note that the Fourier transform and its inverse are linear operators; that is,

$$\mathcal{F}\{c_1 f_1 + c_2 f_2\} = c_1 \mathcal{F}\{f_1\} + c_2 \mathcal{F}\{f_2\}, \tag{9.11a}$$

$$\mathcal{F}^{-1}\{c_1 \tilde{f}_1 + c_2 \tilde{f}_2\} = c_1 \mathcal{F}^{-1}\{\tilde{f}_1\} + c_2 \mathcal{F}^{-1}\{\tilde{f}_2\}. \tag{9.11b}$$

(See Exercise 1 for verification.)

Shifting Properties of the Fourier Transform

Like shifting property 8.3 for the Laplace transform, we have the following shifting property for the Fourier transform.

Theorem 9.4 When $f(x)$ is piecewise smooth on every finite interval, and $f(x)$ and $e^{-ax}f(x)$ are absolutely integrable on the real line,

$$\mathcal{F}\{e^{-ax}f(x)\}(\omega) = \tilde{f}(\omega - ai), \qquad (9.12a)$$

$$\mathcal{F}^{-1}\{\tilde{f}(\omega - ai)\}(x) = e^{-ax}f(x). \qquad (9.12b)$$

(See Exercise 3 for a proof).

Example 9.8 Find the Fourier transform of the function $f(x) = e^{-bx}[h(x+a) - h(x-a)]$, where a and b are positive constants.

Solution Example 9.7 derived the transform of $h(x+a) - h(x-a)$,

$$\mathcal{F}\{h(x+a) - h(x-a)\} = \frac{2}{\omega}\sin a\omega.$$

Equation 9.12a now gives

$$\tilde{f}(\omega) = \frac{2}{\omega - bi}\sin a(\omega - bi).\bullet$$

Example 9.9 Find the Fourier transform of the function $f(x) = e^{-ax}h(x)$, where a is a positive constant. Can you use property 9.12a?

Solution We cannot use property 9.12a since $h(x)$ is not absolutely integrable on the real line. We return to definition 9.1,

$$\tilde{f}(\omega) = \int_{-\infty}^{\infty} e^{-ax}h(x)e^{-i\omega x}\,dx = \int_{0}^{\infty} e^{-(a+\omega i)x}\,dx = \left\{\frac{e^{-(a+\omega i)x}}{-(a+\omega i)}\right\}_{0}^{\infty} = \frac{1}{a+\omega i}.\bullet$$

We cannot help but notice the similarity of this result to the Laplace transform $1/(s+a)$ for the function e^{-at}. The function e^{-ax} does not have a Fourier transform (since it is not absolutely integrable on the real line), but $e^{-ax}h(x)$ is absolutely integrable. General discussions of this situation can be found in Exercise 31.

The second shifting property is contained in the next theorem. It should be compared to property 8.4 of the Laplace transform.

Theorem 9.5 When $f(x)$ is piecewise smooth on every finite interval and absolutely integrable on the real line,

$$\mathcal{F}\{f(x-a)\}(\omega) = e^{-ia\omega}\mathcal{F}\{f\}(\omega), \qquad (9.13a)$$

$$\mathcal{F}^{-1}\{e^{-ia\omega}\tilde{f}\}(x) = \mathcal{F}^{-1}\{\tilde{f}\}(x-a). \qquad (9.13b)$$

(See Exercise 2 for verification).

Example 9.10 Find the Fourier transform of the function in Figure 9.5.

Solution This is the function in Figure 9.2 translated 3 units to the right. Hence,

$$\tilde{f}(\omega) = \frac{4e^{-3\omega i}}{\omega^2}\sin^2\frac{\omega}{2}.\bullet$$

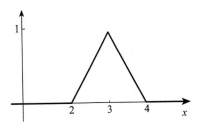

Figure 9.5

Multiplication by x^n

The following theorem indicates that multiplying a function $f(x)$ by x^n results in its Fourier transform being differentiated n times. Compare this to the analogous property 8.5 for the Laplace transform.

Theorem 9.6   If $f(x)$ is piecewise smooth on every finite interval and $f(x)$ and $x^n f(x)$, $n > 0$ an integer, are absolutely integrable on the real line, then

$$\mathcal{F}\{x^n f(x)\}(\omega) = i^n \frac{d^n}{d\omega^n}[\mathcal{F}\{f\}(\omega)], \tag{9.14a}$$

$$\mathcal{F}^{-1}\{\tilde{f}^{(n)}(\omega)\}(x) = (-ix)^n \mathcal{F}^{-1}\{\tilde{f}\}(x). \tag{9.14b}$$

(See Exercise 4 for a proof.)

Example 9.11   Find the Fourier transform of $f(x) = x^2 e^{-ax^2}$.

Solution   Since $\mathcal{F}\{e^{-ax^2}\} = \sqrt{\pi/a}\, e^{-\omega^2/(4a)}$ (see Example 9.4), property 9.14a gives

$$\mathcal{F}\{x^2 e^{-ax^2}\} = i^2 \frac{d^2}{d\omega^2}\left[\sqrt{\frac{\pi}{a}}e^{-\omega^2/(4a)}\right] = \frac{\sqrt{\pi}}{2a^{3/2}}\left(1 - \frac{\omega^2}{2a}\right)e^{-\omega^2/(4a)}.\bullet$$

Convolutions and the Fourier Transform

In applications of Fourier transforms to initial boundary value problems, it is often necessary to find the inverse transform of the product of two functions $\tilde{f}$ and $\tilde{g}$, both of whose inverse transforms are known; that is, we require $\mathcal{F}^{-1}\{\tilde{f}\tilde{g}\}$, knowing that $\mathcal{F}^{-1}\{\tilde{f}\} = f$ and $\mathcal{F}^{-1}\{\tilde{g}\} = g$. In Theorem 9.7, it is shown that

$$\mathcal{F}^{-1}\{\tilde{f}(\omega)\tilde{g}(\omega)\} = \int_{-\infty}^{\infty} f(v)g(x-v)\,dv.$$

This integral, called the **convolution** of the functions $f(x)$ and $g(x)$, is often given the notation $(f * g)(x)$ or $f(x) * g(x)$:

$$(f * g)(x) = f(x) * g(x) = \int_{-\infty}^{\infty} f(v)g(x-v)\,dv. \tag{9.15}$$

Comparison of convolutions 8.7 for Laplace transforms and 9.15 for Fourier transforms indicates that integrands are identical, only limits of integration change.

Theorem 9.7   Suppose that $f(x)$ and $g(x)$ are piecewise smooth on every finite interval and absolutely integrable on $-\infty < x < \infty$. If either $\tilde{f}(\omega)$ or $\tilde{g}(\omega)$ is absolutely integrable on $-\infty < \omega < \infty$, then

$$\mathcal{F}^{-1}\{\tilde{f}\tilde{g}\} = f * g. \tag{9.16}$$

Proof   Let us assume that $\tilde{g}(\omega)$ is absolutely integrable. (The proof is similar if $\tilde{f}(\omega)$ is absolutely integrable.) By equation 9.7,

$$\mathcal{F}^{-1}\{\tilde{f}(\omega)\tilde{g}(\omega)\}(x) = \frac{1}{2\pi}\int_{-\infty}^{\infty} \tilde{f}(\omega)\tilde{g}(\omega)e^{i\omega x}d\omega,$$

and when we substitute the integral definition of $\tilde{f}(\omega)$,

$$\mathcal{F}^{-1}\{\tilde{f}(\omega)\tilde{g}(\omega)\}(x) = \frac{1}{2\pi}\int_{-\infty}^{\infty}\left[\int_{-\infty}^{\infty}f(v)e^{-i\omega v}dv\right]\tilde{g}(\omega)e^{i\omega x}d\omega.$$

The fact that $f(x)$ and $\tilde{g}(\omega)$ are both absolutely integrable permits us to interchange the order of integration and write

$$\mathcal{F}^{-1}\{\tilde{f}(\omega)\tilde{g}(\omega)\}(x) = \int_{-\infty}^{\infty}\left[\frac{1}{2\pi}\int_{-\infty}^{\infty}\tilde{g}(\omega)e^{i\omega(x-v)}d\omega\right]f(v)\,dv$$

$$= \int_{-\infty}^{\infty}f(v)g(x-v)\,dv. \blacksquare$$

The simplicity of the proof of Theorem 9.7 is a direct result of the assumption that $\tilde{g}(\omega)$ is absolutely integrable. This condition can be weakened, but because functions that we encounter satisfy this condition, we pursue the discussion no further.

By making a change of variable of integration in equation 9.15, it is easily shown that convolutions are symmetric; that is, $f * g = g * f$. Other properties of convolutions are discussed in Exercise 5. An example of convolutions that we encounter in heat conduction problems is finding the inverse transform of $\tilde{f}(\omega)e^{-k\omega^2 t}$ where $\tilde{f}(\omega)$ is the transform of an initial temperature distribution, k is thermal diffusivity, and t is time. According to Example 9.6, $\mathcal{F}^{-1}\{e^{-k\omega^2 t}\} = [1/(2\sqrt{k\pi t})]e^{-x^2/(4kt)}$, and hence convolutions yield

$$\mathcal{F}^{-1}\{\tilde{f}(\omega)e^{-k\omega^2 t}\} = \int_{-\infty}^{\infty}f(v)\frac{1}{2\sqrt{k\pi t}}e^{-(x-v)^2/(4kt)}dv$$

$$= \frac{1}{2\sqrt{k\pi t}}\int_{-\infty}^{\infty}f(v)e^{-(x-v)^2/(4kt)}dv.$$

In Section 8.3, we used the Dirac delta function to model instantaneous forces (impulse forces). In this chapter, we use them to model other "point" entities such as a heat source at a point, and a force applied to a vibrating string at a single point. As a result, we need its Fourier transform. With defining relation 8.15,

$$\mathcal{F}\{\delta(x-x_0)\}(\omega) = \int_{-\infty}^{\infty}\delta(x-x_0)e^{-i\omega x}\,dx = e^{-i\omega x_0}. \qquad (9.17)$$

EXERCISES 9.1

1. Verify that the Fourier transform and its inverse are linear operators.

2. Verify property 9.13a.

3. Verify property 9.12a.

4. Verify property 9.14a.

5. Verify the following properties for convolutions:

$$f * g = g * f \qquad (9.18a)$$
$$f * (kg) = (kf) * g = k(f * g), \quad k = \text{constant}, \qquad (9.18b)$$
$$(f * g) * h = f * (g * h) \qquad (9.18c)$$
$$f * (g + h) = f * g + f * h \qquad (9.18d)$$

6. Verify the following shifting properties for the Fourier transform $\tilde{f}(\omega) = \mathcal{F}\{f\}(\omega)$:

$$\mathcal{F}\{f(x)\cos ax\}(\omega) = \frac{\tilde{f}(\omega - a) + \tilde{f}(\omega + a)}{2}, \qquad (9.19a)$$

$$\mathcal{F}\{f(x)\sin ax\}(\omega) = \frac{\tilde{f}(\omega - a) - \tilde{f}(\omega + a)}{2i}, \qquad (9.19b)$$

$$\mathcal{F}^{-1}\{\tilde{f}(\omega)\cos a\omega\}(x) = \frac{f(x - a) + f(x + a)}{2}, \qquad (9.19c)$$

$$\mathcal{F}^{-1}\{\tilde{f}(\omega)\sin a\omega\}(x) = \frac{f(x + a) - f(x - a)}{2i}. \qquad (9.19d)$$

7. (a) Show that

$$\mathcal{F}\{\mathcal{F}\{f\}\}(\omega) = 2\pi f(-\omega). \qquad (9.20)$$

(b) Illustrate the property in part (a) with the function $f(x) = e^{-ax^2}$.

(c) Use equation 9.20 and Example 9.7 to find the Fourier transform of $f(x) = \dfrac{\sin ax}{x}$.

(d) Does the result in part (c) violate Theorem 9.1? Explain.

In Exercises 8–11 use residues to find the Fourier transform of the function.

8. $f(x) = \dfrac{1}{a^4 + x^4}, \quad a > 0$ constant

9. $f(x) = \dfrac{1}{(a^2 + x^2)^2}, \quad a > 0$ constant

10. $f(x) = \dfrac{x}{(a^2 + x^2)^2}, \quad a > 0$ constant

11. $f(x) = \dfrac{1}{1 + x + x^2}$

In Exercises 12–13 use residues to find the inverse Fourier transform of the function.

12. $\tilde{f}(\omega) = \dfrac{i\omega}{(a^2 + \omega^2)^2}, \quad a > 0$ constant

13. $\tilde{f}(\omega) = \dfrac{a^2 - \omega^2}{(a^2 + \omega^2)^2}, \quad a > 0$ constant

In Exercises 14–27 find the Fourier transform of the function.

14. $f(x) = e^{-a|x|}, \quad a > 0$ constant

15. $f(x) = xe^{-a|x|}, \quad a > 0$ constant

16. $f(x) = xe^{-ax^2}, \quad a > 0$ constant

17. $f(x) = \dfrac{x}{a^2 + x^2}, \quad a > 0$ constant

18. $f(x) = |x|e^{-a|x|}, \quad a > 0$ constant

19. $f(x) = x^n e^{-ax} h(x), \quad a > 0$ constant, $n \geq 0$ an integer

20. $f(x) = h(x - a) - h(x - b), \quad b > a$ constants

21. $f(x) = x[h(x + a) - h(x - a)], \quad a > 0$ constant

22. $f(x) = \begin{cases} (b/a)(a - |x|), & |x| < a \\ 0, & |x| > a \end{cases}, \quad a > 0, b > 0$ constants

23. $f(x) = \begin{cases} b(a^2 - x^2)/a^2, & |x| < a \\ 0, & |x| > a \end{cases}, \quad a > 0, b > 0$ constants

24. $f(x) = e^{-kx^2}\cos ax, \quad a > 0, k > 0$ constants

25. $f(x) = e^{-kx^2}\sin ax, \quad a > 0, k > 0$ constants

26. $f(x) = \cos ax\left[h\left(x + \dfrac{\pi}{2a}\right) - h\left(x - \dfrac{\pi}{2a}\right)\right], \quad a > 0$ constant

27. $f(x) = \sin ax\left[h\left(x + \dfrac{\pi}{a}\right) - h\left(x - \dfrac{\pi}{a}\right)\right], \quad a > 0$ constant

28. Use Exercises 34 and 35 in Section 6.3 to show that when $0 < \alpha < \beta$,

$$\mathcal{F}\left\{\frac{\cosh \alpha x}{\cosh \beta x}\right\}(\omega) = \frac{2\pi \cos \frac{\pi \alpha}{2\beta} \cosh \frac{\pi \omega}{2\beta}}{\beta \left(\cosh \frac{\pi \omega}{\beta} + \cos \frac{\pi \alpha}{\beta}\right)}, \qquad \mathcal{F}\left\{\frac{\sinh \alpha x}{\cosh \beta x}\right\}(\omega) = \frac{-2\pi i \sin \frac{\pi \alpha}{\beta} \sinh \frac{\pi \omega}{2\beta}}{\beta \left(\cosh \frac{\pi \omega}{\beta} + \cos \frac{\pi \alpha}{\beta}\right)},$$

$$\mathcal{F}\left\{\frac{\sinh \alpha x}{\sinh \beta x}\right\}(\omega) = \frac{\pi \sin \frac{\pi \alpha}{\beta}}{\beta \left(\cosh \frac{\pi \omega}{\beta} + \cos \frac{\pi \alpha}{\beta}\right)}, \qquad \mathcal{F}\left\{\frac{\cosh \alpha x}{\sinh \beta x}\right\}(\omega) = \frac{\pi \sinh \frac{\pi \omega}{\beta}}{\beta \left(\cosh \frac{\pi \omega}{\beta} + \cos \frac{\pi \alpha}{\beta}\right)}.$$

29. (a) Show that

$$\mathcal{F}^{-1}\{f(-\omega)\}(x) = \frac{1}{2\pi}\mathcal{F}\{f\}(x). \tag{9.21}$$

(b) Illustrate the property in part (a) with the function $f(x) = e^{-ax^2}$.

(c) Use equation 9.21 and Exercise 28 to show that when $0 < \alpha < \beta$,

$$\mathcal{F}^{-1}\left\{\frac{\cosh \alpha \omega}{\cosh \beta \omega}\right\}(x) = \frac{\cos \frac{\pi \alpha}{2\beta} \cosh \frac{\pi x}{2\beta}}{\beta \left(\cosh \frac{\pi x}{\beta} + \cos \frac{\pi \alpha}{\beta}\right)}, \qquad \mathcal{F}^{-1}\left\{\frac{\sinh \alpha \omega}{\cosh \beta \omega}\right\}(x) = \frac{-i \sin \frac{\pi \alpha}{\beta} \sinh \frac{\pi x}{2\beta}}{\beta \left(\cosh \frac{\pi x}{\beta} + \cos \frac{\pi \alpha}{\beta}\right)},$$

$$\mathcal{F}^{-1}\left\{\frac{\sinh \alpha \omega}{\sinh \beta \omega}\right\}(x) = \frac{\sin \frac{\pi \alpha}{\beta}}{2\beta \left(\cosh \frac{\pi x}{\beta} + \cos \frac{\pi \alpha}{\beta}\right)}, \qquad \mathcal{F}^{-1}\left\{\frac{\cosh \alpha \omega}{\sinh \beta \omega}\right\}(x) = \frac{\sinh \frac{\pi x}{\beta}}{2\beta \left(\cosh \frac{\pi x}{\beta} + \cos \frac{\pi \alpha}{\beta}\right)}.$$

30. Verify formally each of the following results, often called **Parseval's relations**:

$$\int_{-\infty}^{\infty} \tilde{f}(x)g(x)\,dx = \int_{-\infty}^{\infty} f(x)\tilde{g}(x)\,dx \tag{9.22a}$$

$$2\pi \int_{-\infty}^{\infty} f(x)g(x)\,dx = \int_{-\infty}^{\infty} \tilde{f}(\omega)\tilde{g}(-\omega)\,d\omega \tag{9.22b}$$

$$2\pi \int_{-\infty}^{\infty} [f(x)]^2\,dx = \int_{-\infty}^{\infty} |\tilde{f}(\omega)|^2\,d\omega \tag{9.22c}$$

The following exercises should be attempted only by readers who are already familiar with the Laplace transform. In these exercises, $\mathcal{L}\{f(x)\}$ denotes the Laplace transform of a function $f(x)$.

31. (a) Show that when $f(x)$ is absolutely integrable on $0 < x < \infty$, and $f(x) = 0$ for $x < 0$,

$$\mathcal{F}\{f\}(\omega) = \mathcal{L}\{f\}(i\omega). \tag{9.23}$$

(b) Use the result in part (a) to calculate Fourier transforms for the functions in Exercise 19, and in Exercise 20 (when $a > 0$).

32. (a) The inverse result of property 9.23 can be stated as follows: Suppose that when ω in the Fourier transform $\tilde{f}(\omega)$ is replaced by $-is$, the function $\tilde{f}(-is)$ has no poles on the imaginary s-axis or in the right half-plane. If $\tilde{f}(-is)$ has an inverse Laplace transform, this is also the inverse Fourier transform of $\tilde{f}(\omega)$,

$$\mathcal{F}^{-1}\{\tilde{f}(\omega)\}(x) = \begin{cases} \mathcal{L}^{-1}\{\tilde{f}(-is)\}(x), & x > 0 \\ 0, & x < 0. \end{cases} \tag{9.24}$$

Use this result to find inverse Fourier transforms for the following:

(i) $\tilde{f}(\omega) = \dfrac{1}{(8 + i\omega)^3}$ (ii) $\tilde{f}(\omega) = \dfrac{b}{a}\left[\left(\dfrac{1 - e^{-i\omega a}}{\omega^2}\right) - \dfrac{ia}{\omega}\right]$, $a > 0$, $b > 0$ constants

(b) Can the result in part (a) be used to find $\mathcal{F}^{-1}\left\{\dfrac{i}{\omega}e^{-ia\omega}\right\}$?

33. (a) Show that when $f(x)$ is absolutely integrable on $-\infty < x < 0$, and $f(x) = 0$ for $x > 0$,

$$\mathcal{F}\{f(x)\}(\omega) = \mathcal{L}\{f(-x)\}(-i\omega). \tag{9.25}$$

(b) Use the result in part (a) to find Fourier transforms for the following:

(i) $f(x) = \begin{cases} -x(x + L), & -L \le x \le 0 \\ 0, & \text{otherwise} \end{cases}$ (ii) $f(x) = e^{cx}[h(x - a) - h(x - b)]$, $a < b < 0$,

$c > 0$

34. (a) Let $f(x)$ be a function that has a Fourier transform. Denote by $f^+(x)$ and $f^-(x)$ the right and left halves respectively, of $f(x)$:

$$f^+(x) = \begin{cases} 0, & x < 0 \\ f(x), & x > 0 \end{cases} ; \qquad f^-(x) = \begin{cases} f(x), & x < 0 \\ 0, & x > 0 \end{cases}.$$

Show that

$$\mathcal{F}\{f\}(\omega) = \mathcal{F}\{f^+\}(\omega) + \mathcal{F}\{f^-\}(\omega).$$

(b) Use the result in part (a) in conjunction with equations 9.23 and 9.25 to find Fourier transforms for the following:

(i) $f(x)$ in Exercise 22

(ii) $f(x) = \sin ax[h(x + 2n\pi/a) - h(x - 2n\pi/a)]$, $n > 0$ an integer, $a > 0$

§9.2 Application of the Fourier Transform to Partial Differential Equations

The following theorem facilitates the application of Fourier transforms to partial differential equations.

Theorem 9.8 Suppose $f(x)$ is continuous for $-\infty < x < \infty$ and $f'(x)$ is piecewise continuous on every finite interval. If both functions are absolutely integrable on $-\infty < x < \infty$, then

$$\mathcal{F}\{f'\}(\omega) = i\omega\mathcal{F}\{f\}(\omega), \tag{9.26a}$$

$$\mathcal{F}^{-1}\{i\omega\tilde{f}\}(x) = \frac{d}{dx}[\mathcal{F}^{-1}\{\tilde{f}\}(x)]. \tag{9.26b}$$

Proof When integration by parts is used on the definition of $\mathcal{F}\{f'\}(\omega)$,

$$\mathcal{F}\{f'\}(\omega) = \int_{-\infty}^{\infty} f'(x)e^{-i\omega x}dx = \left\{f(x)e^{-i\omega x}\right\}_{-\infty}^{\infty} - \int_{-\infty}^{\infty} f(x)(-i\omega)e^{-i\omega x}dx$$

$$= i\omega \int_{-\infty}^{\infty} f(x)e^{-i\omega x}dx = i\omega\mathcal{F}\{f\}(\omega). \blacksquare$$

It is straightforward to extend this result to second derivatives (see the corollary below) and higher-order derivatives (see Exercise 1). In addition, see Exercise 2 for the situation when $f(x)$ has discontinuities.

Corollary Suppose $f(x)$ and $f'(x)$ are continuous for $-\infty < x < \infty$ and $f''(x)$ is piecewise continuous on every finite interval. If all three functions are absolutely integrable on $-\infty < x < \infty$, then

$$\mathcal{F}\{f''\}(\omega) = -\omega^2\mathcal{F}\{f\}(\omega), \tag{9.27a}$$

$$\mathcal{F}^{-1}\{\omega^2\tilde{f}\}(x) = -\frac{d^2}{dx^2}[\mathcal{F}^{-1}\{\tilde{f}\}(x)]. \tag{9.27b}$$

Example 9.12 Find the Fourier transform of the function $f(x) = xe^{-ax^2}$.

Solution If we take Fourier transforms of $\dfrac{d}{dx}e^{-ax^2} = -2axe^{-ax^2}$, and use property 9.26a, we obtain

$$i\omega\mathcal{F}\{e^{-ax^2}\} = -2a\mathcal{F}\{xe^{-ax^2}\}.$$

But from Example 9.4,

$$\mathcal{F}\{e^{-ax^2}\} = \sqrt{\frac{\pi}{k}}e^{-\omega^2/(4a)}.$$

Consequently,

$$i\omega\sqrt{\frac{\pi}{k}}e^{-\omega^2/(4a)} = -2a\mathcal{F}\{xe^{-ax^2}\}, \quad \text{or,} \quad \mathcal{F}\{xe^{-ax^2}\} = -\frac{i\omega}{2a}\sqrt{\frac{\pi}{k}}e^{-\omega^2/(4a)}. \bullet$$

We now illustrate how Fourier transforms are used to solve homogeneous and nonhomogeneous PDEs on infinite intervals, beginning with a homogeneous, heat conduction problem.

Example 9.13   Solve the homogeneous heat conduction problem

$$\frac{\partial U}{\partial t} = k\frac{\partial^2 U}{\partial x^2}, \quad -\infty < x < \infty, \quad t > 0, \tag{9.28a}$$

$$U(x,0) = f(x), \quad -\infty < x < \infty. \tag{9.28b}$$

Solution   When we apply Fourier transform 9.1 to the PDE, we obtain

$$\mathcal{F}\left\{\frac{\partial U}{\partial t}\right\} = k\mathcal{F}\left\{\frac{\partial^2 U}{\partial x^2}\right\}.$$

Since differentiation with respect to t and integration with respect to x in the Fourier transform on the left are independent of each other, we interchange these operations. We use property 9.27a for the transform on the right,

$$\frac{d\tilde{U}}{dt} = -k\omega^2\tilde{U}(\omega,t).$$

A general solution of this ODE is

$$\tilde{U}(\omega,t) = Ce^{-k\omega^2 t}.$$

The Fourier transform of initial condition 9.28b is $\tilde{U}(\omega,0) = \tilde{f}(\omega)$, and this condition requires $C = \tilde{f}(\omega)$. Thus,

$$\tilde{U}(\omega,t) = \tilde{f}(\omega)e^{-k\omega^2 t},$$

and the inverse Fourier transform now gives

$$U(x,t) = \frac{1}{2\pi}\int_{-\infty}^{\infty} \tilde{f}(\omega)e^{-k\omega^2 t}e^{i\omega x}\,d\omega. \tag{9.29a}$$

For heat conduction problems like this, a much more useful form of the solution, which expresses $U(x,t)$ as a real integral involving $f(x)$, rather than a complex integal in $\tilde{f}(\omega)$, can be obtained with convolutions. Because the inverse transform of $e^{-k\omega^2 t}$ is $1/(2\sqrt{k\pi t})e^{-x^2/(4kt)}$ (see Example 9.6), convolution property 9.16 yields

$$U(x,t) = \int_{-\infty}^{\infty} f(v)\frac{1}{2\sqrt{k\pi t}}e^{-(x-v)^2/(4kt)}\,dv$$

$$= \frac{1}{2\sqrt{k\pi t}}\int_{-\infty}^{\infty} f(v)e^{-(x-v)^2/(4kt)}\,dv.\bullet \tag{9.29b}$$

Representation 9.29b clearly indicates the dependence of $U(x,t)$ on the initial temperature distribution $f(x)$. It also has another advantage. Because representation 9.29b does not contain the Fourier transform of $f(x)$, it may represent a solution to problem 9.28 even when $f(x)$ has no Fourier transform. Indeed, provided $f(x)$ is piecewise continuous on some bounded interval, and continuous and bounded outside this interval, it can be shown that $U(x,t)$ so defined satisfies problem 9.28. This is illustrated in the first two special cases that follow. As a general rule then, it is preferable to express the solution of an initial boundary value problem in terms of initial and boundary data, as opposed to their transforms, and we shall endeavour to achieve such representations whenever possible.

Case 1: $f(x) = U_0$, a constant

In this case, we would expect that $U(x,t) = U_0$ for all x and t. That representation 9.29b gives this result is easily demonstrated by setting $u = (x-v)/(2\sqrt{kt})$ and $du = -dv/(2\sqrt{kt})$,

$$U(x,t) = \frac{U_0}{2\sqrt{k\pi t}} \int_{\infty}^{-\infty} e^{-u^2}(-2\sqrt{kt}\,du) = \frac{U_0}{\sqrt{\pi}} \int_{-\infty}^{\infty} e^{-u^2}\,du = U_0$$

(see equation 9.6 for the value of this integral). Thus, integral 9.29b has given the correct solution in spite of the fact that the function $f(x) = U_0$ does not have a Fourier transform.

Case 2: $f(x) = U_0 h(x)$

In this case, we set $u = (x-v)/(2\sqrt{kt})$ and $du = -dv/(2\sqrt{kt})$ in

$$U(x,t) = \frac{U_0}{2\sqrt{k\pi t}} \int_{0}^{\infty} e^{-(x-v)^2/(4kt)}\,dv$$

to obtain

$$
\begin{aligned}
U(x,t) &= \frac{U_0}{2\sqrt{k\pi t}} \int_{x/(2\sqrt{kt})}^{-\infty} e^{-u^2}(-2\sqrt{kt}\,du) = \frac{U_0}{\sqrt{\pi}} \int_{-\infty}^{x/(2\sqrt{kt})} e^{-u^2}\,du \\
&= \frac{U_0}{\sqrt{\pi}} \left[\int_{-\infty}^{0} e^{-u^2}\,du + \int_{0}^{x/(2\sqrt{kt})} e^{-u^2}\,du \right] \\
&= \frac{U_0}{\sqrt{\pi}} \left[\frac{\sqrt{\pi}}{2} + \frac{\sqrt{\pi}}{2}\mathrm{erf}\left(\frac{x}{2\sqrt{kt}}\right) \right] = \frac{U_0}{2}\left[1 + \mathrm{erf}\left(\frac{x}{2\sqrt{kt}}\right) \right]
\end{aligned}
$$

where $\mathrm{erf}(x) = \frac{2}{\sqrt{\pi}} \int_{0}^{x} e^{-u^2}\,du$ is the error function. This solution indicates how heat that is concentrated in one-half of a rod diffuses into the other half. It indicates, in particular, that temperature at every point in the left half of the rod $(x < 0)$ is positive for every $t > 0$. In other words, heat propagates with infinite speed. We have plotted this function for $t = 10^6$ and $t = 10^7$, and the initial temperature distribution $U_0 h(x)$, in Figure 9.6 for $k = 10^{-6}$. They show that although heat propagates with infinite speed, the amount is very small so that it takes a very long time for temperature to approach its steady state value $U_0/2$ throughout the rod.

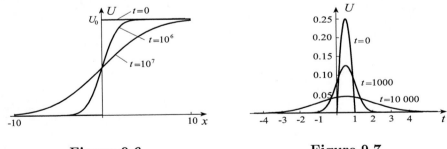

Figure 9.6   Figure 9.7

Case 3: $f(x) = x(L - x), 0 \le x \le L$, and vanishes otherwise

In this case, representation 9.29b gives

$$U(x,t) = \frac{1}{2\sqrt{k\pi t}} \int_0^L v(L-v)e^{-(x-v)^2/(4kt)}dv.$$

It is plotted in Figure 9.7 at $t = 1000$ and $t = 10\,000$ using $L = 1$ and $k = 114 \times 10^{-6}$ for copper.

In the following nonhomogeneous problem, heat is generated over the interval $-a \le x \le a$ at a constant rate.

Example 9.14   Solve the heat conduction problem

$$\frac{\partial U}{\partial t} = k\frac{\partial^2 U}{\partial x^2} + \frac{k}{\kappa}[h(x+a) - h(x-a)], \quad -\infty < x < \infty, \quad t > 0, \quad (9.30a)$$

$$U(x,0) = f(x), \quad -\infty < x < \infty. \tag{9.30b}$$

Solution   When we take Fourier transforms of the PDE (and use property 9.27a and Example 9.7 in Section 9.1),

$$\frac{d\tilde{U}}{dt} = -k\omega^2\tilde{U} + \frac{2k}{\kappa\omega}\sin a\omega.$$

The transform $\tilde{U}(\omega, t)$ must satisfy this ODE subject to the transform of initial condition 9.30b,

$$\tilde{U}(\omega, 0) = \tilde{f}(\omega).$$

A general solution of the ODE is

$$\tilde{U}(\omega, t) = Ce^{-k\omega^2 t} + \frac{2}{\kappa\omega^3}\sin a\omega,$$

and the initial condition requires

$$\tilde{f}(\omega) = C + \frac{2}{\kappa\omega^3}\sin a\omega.$$

Thus,

$$\tilde{U}(\omega, t) = \left[\tilde{f}(\omega) - \frac{2}{\kappa\omega^3}\sin a\omega\right]e^{-k\omega^2 t} + \frac{2}{\kappa\omega^3}\sin a\omega,$$

and $U(x,t)$ is the inverse transform thereof. According to convolution property 9.16, the inverse transform of $\tilde{f}(\omega)e^{-k\omega^2 t}$ can be expressed as

$$\frac{1}{2\sqrt{k\pi t}} \int_{-\infty}^{\infty} f(v)e^{-(x-v)^2/(4kt)}dv,$$

and therefore

$$U(x,t) = \frac{1}{2\sqrt{k\pi t}} \int_{-\infty}^{\infty} f(v)e^{-(x-v)^2/(4kt)}dv$$

$$- \frac{1}{\kappa\pi}\int_{-\infty}^{\infty}\frac{1}{\omega^3}(1 - e^{-k\omega^2 t})\sin a\omega\, e^{i\omega x}d\omega. \bullet \tag{9.31}$$

Example 9.15 The following problem describes displacements of an infinitely long string stretched tightly along the x-axis,

$$\frac{\partial^2 y}{\partial t^2} = c^2 \frac{\partial^2 y}{\partial x^2}, \quad -\infty < x < \infty, \quad t > 0, \tag{9.32a}$$

$$y(x, 0) = f(x), \quad -\infty < x < \infty, \tag{9.32b}$$

$$y_t(x, 0) = 0, \quad -\infty < x < \infty. \tag{9.32c}$$

Constant $c^2 = \tau/\rho$, where τ is the tension in the string and ρ is its linear density (mass per unit length). No other forces act on the string other than its tension. Initial condition 9.32b states that the string is given displacement $f(x)$ at time $t = 0$, and condition 9.32c indicates that the string has velocity zero when it is released at time $t = 0$. Solve the problem for subsequent displacements of the string.

Solution When we apply the Fourier transform to the PDE and use property 9.27a,

$$\frac{d^2 \tilde{y}}{dt^2} = -c^2 \omega^2 \tilde{y},$$

subject to

$$\tilde{y}(\omega, 0) = \tilde{f}(\omega), \quad \tilde{y}'(\omega, t) = 0.$$

A general solution of the differential equation is $\tilde{y}(\omega, t) = A \cos c\omega t + B \sin c\omega t$, and the initial conditions require

$$\tilde{y}(\omega, t) = \tilde{f}(\omega) \cos c\omega t.$$

Displacements are therefore given by

$$y(x, t) = \frac{1}{2\pi} \int_{-\infty}^{\infty} \tilde{f}(\omega) \cos c\omega t \, e^{i\omega x} d\omega.$$

We can express this in closed form by writing

$$y(x, t) = \frac{1}{2\pi} \int_{-\infty}^{\infty} \tilde{f}(\omega) \cos c\omega t e^{i\omega x} d\omega = \frac{1}{2\pi} \int_{-\infty}^{\infty} \tilde{f}(\omega) \left(\frac{e^{ic\omega t} + e^{-ic\omega t}}{2} \right) e^{i\omega x} d\omega$$

$$= \frac{1}{2\pi} \int_{-\infty}^{\infty} \frac{1}{2} \tilde{f}(\omega) [e^{i\omega(x+ct)} + e^{i\omega(x-ct)}] d\omega$$

$$= \frac{1}{2} [f(x + ct) + f(x - ct)].$$

This is called the d'Alembert form of the solution.●

Example 9.16 Consider solving the boundary value problem

$$\frac{\partial^2 U}{\partial x^2} + \frac{\partial^2 U}{\partial y^2} = 0, \quad -\infty < x < \infty, \quad y > 0,$$

$$U(x, 0) = f(x), \quad -\infty < x < \infty,$$

for steady-state temperature in the half-space $y > 0$ given that temperature along the x-axis is $f(x)$.
(a) Show that if $f(x) = h(x)$, Fourier transforms cannot be used.

(b) Show that when $f(x)$ is piecewise smooth on every finite interval and absolutely integrable on the real line, Fourier transforms lead to the solution

$$U(x,y) = \frac{y}{\pi} \int_{-\infty}^{\infty} \frac{f(v)}{(x-v)^2 + y^2} \, dv.$$

Do you recognize this result?

(c) Does this formula lead to a solution when $f(x) = h(x)$?

Solution (a) Since $h(x)$ is not absolutely integrable on the real line, we cannot use Fourier transforms to solve the problem.

(b) If we apply the Fourier transform with respect to x and use property 9.27a,

$$\frac{d^2\tilde{U}}{dy^2} = -\mathcal{F}\left\{\frac{\partial^2 U}{\partial x^2}\right\} = \omega^2 \tilde{U}(\omega, y) \quad \text{or} \quad \frac{d^2\tilde{U}}{dy^2} - \omega^2 \tilde{U} = 0, \quad y > 0,$$

subject to $\tilde{U}(\omega, 0) = \tilde{f}(\omega)$. A general solution of the differential equation is

$$\tilde{U}(\omega, y) = Ae^{\omega y} + Be^{-\omega y}.$$

For $\tilde{U}(\omega, y)$ to remain bounded for large y, we must set $A = 0$ when $\omega > 0$ and $B = 0$ when $\omega < 0$; that is,

$$\tilde{U}(\omega, y) = \begin{cases} Ae^{\omega y}, & \omega < 0 \\ Be^{-\omega y}, & \omega > 0 \end{cases} \quad \Longleftrightarrow \quad \tilde{U}(\omega, y) = Ae^{-|\omega|y}.$$

The boundary condition requires $A = \tilde{f}(\omega)$, and therefore $\tilde{U}(\omega, y) = \tilde{f}(\omega)e^{-|\omega|y}$. According to Exercise 14 in Section 9.1,

$$\mathcal{F}\left\{e^{-a|x|}\right\}(\omega) = \frac{2a}{\omega^2 + a^2},$$

and hence by property 9.20,

$$\mathcal{F}\left\{\frac{2a}{x^2 + a^2}\right\}(\omega) = 2\pi e^{-a|-\omega|} = 2\pi e^{-a|\omega|}.$$

Thus,

$$\mathcal{F}^{-1}\left\{e^{-|\omega|y}\right\}(x) = \frac{y/\pi}{x^2 + y^2}.$$

Alternatively, by definition 9.7,

$$\mathcal{F}^{-1}\left\{e^{-|\omega|y}\right\}(x) = \frac{1}{2\pi} \int_{-\infty}^{\infty} e^{-|\omega|y} e^{i\omega x} \, d\omega$$

$$= \frac{1}{2\pi}\left[\int_{-\infty}^{0} e^{\omega(y+ix)} \, d\omega + \int_{0}^{\infty} e^{\omega(-y+ix)} \, d\omega\right] = \frac{y/\pi}{x^2 + y^2}.$$

By convolution property 9.16, we may write

$$U(x,y) = \int_{-\infty}^{\infty} f(v) \frac{y/\pi}{(x-v)^2 + y^2} \, dv = \frac{y}{\pi} \int_{-\infty}^{\infty} \frac{f(v)}{(x-v)^2 + y^2} \, dv.$$

This is Poisson's integral formula 4.37 for a half space that we developed in Section 4.8.

(c) When $f(x) = h(x)$, the result in part (b) gives

$$U(x, y) = \frac{y}{\pi} \int_{-\infty}^{\infty} \frac{h(v)}{(x - v)^2 + y^2} \, dv = \frac{y}{\pi} \int_{0}^{\infty} \frac{1}{(x - v)^2 + y^2} \, dv$$

$$= \frac{y}{\pi} \left\{ \frac{-1}{y} \text{Tan}^{-1} \left(\frac{x - v}{y} \right) \right\}_{0}^{\infty} = \frac{1}{2} + \frac{1}{\pi} \text{Tan}^{-1} \left(\frac{x}{y} \right).$$

Once again, we have a problem wherein $h(x)$ is not absolutely integrable, but Fourier transforms have led to the solution.•

EXERCISES 9.2

1. (a) Extend the result of Theorem 9.8 to n^{th} derivatives.

(b) Verify the transform in equation 9.27a.

2. Show that when $f(x)$ in Theorem 9.8 has a finite discontinuity at $x = x_0$, then equation 9.26a is replaced with

$$\mathcal{F}\{f'\}(\omega) = i\omega \mathcal{F}\{f\}(\omega) - e^{-i\omega x_0}[f(x_0+) - f(x_0-)].$$

3. Solve the heat conduction problem that has a unit heat source at the point x_0 for $t > 0$,

$$\frac{\partial U}{\partial t} = k\frac{\partial^2 U}{\partial x^2} + \frac{k}{\kappa}\delta(x - x_0), \quad -\infty < x < \infty, \quad t > 0,$$

$$U(x, 0) = f(x), \quad -\infty < x < \infty.$$

4. (a) Use a Fourier transform to find an integral representation for the solution of the heat conduction problem

$$\frac{\partial U}{\partial t} = k\frac{\partial^2 U}{\partial x^2} + \frac{k}{\kappa}g(x, t), \quad -\infty < x < \infty, \quad t > 0,$$

$$U(x, 0) = f(x), \quad -\infty < x < \infty.$$

(b) Simplify the solution in part (a) in the case that $g(x, t) \equiv 0$ and

$$\text{(i)} \quad f(x) = \begin{cases} 1, & |x| < a \\ 0, & |x| > a \end{cases}; \qquad \text{(ii)} \quad f(x) = \begin{cases} 0, & |x| < a \\ 1, & |x| > a \end{cases}.$$

Plot the solutions on the interval $-5 \leq x \leq 5$ with $k = 10^{-6}$ and $a = 1$ for $t = 10^5$ and $t = 10^6$.

5. Express the solution of the following initial value problem as a real improper integral,

$$\frac{\partial U}{\partial t} = k\frac{\partial^2 U}{\partial x^2} + \alpha\frac{\partial U}{\partial x}, \quad -\infty < x < \infty, \quad t > 0,$$

$$U(x, 0) = f(x), \quad -\infty < x < \infty,$$

where k and α are positive constants.

6. Solve the following problem for displacement of an infinitely long string where it is given both an initial displacement and an initial velocity,

$$\frac{\partial^2 y}{\partial t^2} = c^2 \frac{\partial^2 y}{\partial x^2}, \quad -\infty < x < \infty, \quad t > 0,$$
$$y(x,0) = f(x), \quad -\infty < x < \infty,$$
$$y_t(x,0) = g(x), \quad -\infty < x < \infty.$$

Determine the d'Alembert form of the solution.

7. When a restoring force proportional to displacement acts on all points of the string in Exercise 6, PDE 9.32a is replaced with

$$\frac{\partial^2 y}{\partial t^2} = c^2 \frac{\partial^2 y}{\partial x^2} - \frac{ky}{\rho}.$$

Solve Exercise 6 with this differential equation.

8. Solve the following problem for displacement of an infinite string when a unit force acts at the point $x = x_0$ for $t > 0$,

$$\frac{\partial^2 y}{\partial t^2} = c^2 \frac{\partial^2 y}{\partial x^2} + \frac{1}{\rho}\delta(x - x_0), \quad -\infty < x < \infty, \quad t > 0,$$
$$y(x,0) = f(x), \quad -\infty < x < \infty,$$
$$y_t(x,0) = g(x), \quad -\infty < x < \infty.$$

Constant ρ is the linear density of the string.

9. Solve the following problem for displacement of an infinite string when an unspecified force acts on the string,

$$\frac{\partial^2 y}{\partial t^2} = c^2 \frac{\partial^2 y}{\partial x^2} + \frac{1}{\rho}F(x,t), \quad -\infty < x < \infty, \quad t > 0,$$
$$y(x,0) = f(x), \quad -\infty < x < \infty,$$
$$y_t(x,0) = g(x), \quad -\infty < x < \infty.$$

Constant ρ is the linear density of the string.

The following boundary value problems can be interpreted as steady-state temperature problems or potential problems.

10. Solve the boundary value problem

$$\frac{\partial^2 V}{\partial x^2} + \frac{\partial^2 V}{\partial y^2} = 0, \quad -\infty < x < \infty, \quad 0 < y < L,$$
$$V(x,0) = f(x), \quad -\infty < x < \infty,$$
$$V(x,L) = g(x), \quad -\infty < x < \infty.$$

11. Repeat Exercise 10 if the boundary condition along $y = 0$ is Neumann $\partial V(x,0)/\partial y = f(x)$.

12. Repeat Exercise 10 if the boundary condition along $y = L$ is Neumann $\partial V(x,L)/\partial y = g(x)$.

§9.3   The Fourier Sine and Cosine Transforms

Fourier transforms are also associated with functions that are defined only for non-negative values of x. They are defined as follows.

Definition 9.2   The **Fourier cosine transform** of a function $f(x)$ defined for $0 < x < \infty$ is denoted by $\tilde{f} = \mathcal{F}_c\{f\}$ with values given by

$$\tilde{f}(\omega) = \mathcal{F}_c\{f\}(\omega) = \int_0^\infty f(x) \cos \omega x \, dx, \qquad (9.33a)$$

and inverse transform

$$f(x) = \mathcal{F}_c^{-1}\{\tilde{f}\}(x) = \frac{2}{\pi} \int_0^\infty \tilde{f}(\omega) \cos \omega x \, d\omega. \qquad (9.33b)$$

The **Fourier sine transform** of a function $f(x)$ defined for $0 < x < \infty$ is denoted by $\tilde{f} = \mathcal{F}_s\{f\}$ with values given by

$$\tilde{f}(\omega) = \mathcal{F}_s\{f\}(\omega) = \int_0^\infty f(x) \sin \omega x \, dx, \qquad (9.34a)$$

and inverse transform

$$f(x) = \mathcal{F}_s^{-1}\{\tilde{f}\}(x) = \frac{2}{\pi} \int_0^\infty \tilde{f}(\omega) \sin \omega x \, d\omega. \qquad (9.34b)$$

Fourier sine and cosine transforms exist when $f(x)$ is piecewise smooth on every finite interval $0 \le x \le X$ and absolutely integrable on $0 < x < \infty$.

Example 9.17   Find the Fourier cosine and sine transforms of the function $f(x) = e^{-ax}$ $(a > 0)$, defined for $x \ge 0$?

Solution   The Fourier cosine and sine transforms are given by the integrals

$$\mathcal{F}_c\{e^{-ax}\}(\omega) = \int_0^\infty e^{-ax} \cos \omega x \, dx \quad \text{and} \quad \mathcal{F}_s\{e^{-ax}\}(\omega) = \int_0^\infty e^{-ax} \sin \omega x \, dx.$$

We can evaluate both of these by considering the improper integral

$$\int_0^\infty e^{-ax} e^{i\omega x} \, dx = \int_0^\infty e^{(-a+\omega i)x} \, dx = \left\{ \frac{e^{(-a+\omega i)x}}{-a+\omega i} \right\}_0^\infty = \frac{1}{a - \omega i} = \frac{a + \omega i}{a^2 + \omega^2}.$$

Real and imaginary parts of this equation give

$$\mathcal{F}_c\{e^{-ax}\}(\omega) = \frac{a}{\omega^2 + a^2} \quad \text{and} \quad \mathcal{F}_s\{e^{-ax}\}(\omega) = \frac{\omega}{a^2 + \omega^2}.$$

With these transforms, we may write the function e^{-ax}, for $x > 0$, in either of the forms

$$e^{-ax} = \frac{2}{\pi} \int_0^\infty \frac{a}{\omega^2 + a^2} \cos \omega x \, d\omega = \frac{2a}{\pi} \int_0^\infty \frac{\cos \omega x}{\omega^2 + a^2} d\omega$$

or

$$e^{-ax} = \frac{2}{\pi} \int_0^\infty \frac{\omega}{\omega^2 + a^2} \sin \omega x \, d\omega. \bullet$$

When $f(x)$ is an even, rational function with a Fourier cosine transform, the transform can be calculated with residues.

Example 9.18 Find the Fourier cosine transform of the even, rational function $f(x) = \dfrac{1}{a^2 + x^2}$, where $a > 0$ is a constant.

Solution The Fourier cosine transform is

$$\tilde{f}(\omega) = \int_0^\infty \frac{\cos \omega x}{a^2 + x^2} \, dx.$$

If we express this in the form

$$\tilde{f}(\omega) = \frac{1}{2} \int_{-\infty}^\infty \frac{\cos \omega x}{a^2 + x^2} \, dx,$$

then we could use residues to evaluate the integral. This was done in Example 9.2,

$$\tilde{f}(\omega) = \frac{\pi}{2a} e^{-a\omega}. \bullet$$

When $f(x)$ is an odd, rational function with a Fourier sine transform, the transform can be calculated with residues.

Example 9.19 Find the Fourier sine transform of the odd, rational function $f(x) = \dfrac{x}{(a^2 + x^2)^2}$, where $a > 0$ is a constant.

Solution The Fourier sine transform is

$$\tilde{f}(\omega) = \int_0^\infty \frac{x \sin \omega x}{(a^2 + x^2)^2} \, dx.$$

If we express this in the form

$$\tilde{f}(\omega) = \frac{1}{2} \int_{-\infty}^\infty \frac{x \sin \omega x}{(a^2 + x^2)^2} \, dx,$$

then we can use residues to evaluate the integral. According to Theorem 6.6 in Section 6.2,

$$\tilde{f}(\omega) = \pi \operatorname{Re} \left\{ \operatorname{Res} \left[\frac{z e^{i\omega z}}{(a^2 + z^2)^2}, ai \right] \right\} = \pi \operatorname{Re} \left\{ \lim_{z \to ai} \left\{ \frac{d}{dz} \left[\frac{(z - ai)^2 z e^{i\omega z}}{(z + ai)^2 (z - ai)^2} \right] \right\} \right\}$$

$$= \pi \operatorname{Re} \left\{ \lim_{z \to ai} \left[\frac{(z + ai)^2 (e^{i\omega z} + i\omega z e^{i\omega z}) - 2 z e^{i\omega z} (z + ai)}{(z + ai)^4} \right] \right\}$$

$$= \pi \operatorname{Re} \left\{ \frac{(2ai)[e^{i\omega(ai)} + i\omega(ai) e^{i\omega(ai)}] - 2(ai) e^{i\omega(ai)}}{(2ai)^3} \right\}$$

$$= \frac{\pi \omega}{4a} e^{-a\omega}. \bullet$$

The Fourier sine and cosine transforms are linear operators (Exercise 1). They have properties similar to those for the Fourier transform. In particular, corresponding to shifting property 9.13, we have

$$\mathcal{F}_s\{f(x - a) h(x - a)\}(\omega) = (\cos a\omega) \mathcal{F}_s\{f\}(\omega) + (\sin a\omega) \mathcal{F}_c\{f\}(\omega), \quad (9.35\text{a})$$

$$\mathcal{F}_c\{f(x - a) h(x - a)\}(\omega) = (\cos a\omega) \mathcal{F}_c\{f\}(\omega) - (\sin a\omega) \mathcal{F}_s\{f\}(\omega). \quad (9.35\text{b})$$

The presence of $h(x - a)$ is due to the fact that $f(x)$ need not be defined for $x < 0$ and therefore $f(x - a)$ may not be defined for $x < a$. (See Exercise 3 for verification of these.)

Results corresponding to 9.26a and 9.27a for the sine and cosine transforms are

$$\mathcal{F}_c\{f'\}(\omega) = \omega \mathcal{F}_s\{f\}(\omega) - f(0+), \tag{9.36a}$$

$$\mathcal{F}_c\{f''\}(\omega) = -\omega^2 \mathcal{F}_c\{f\}(\omega) - f'(0+), \tag{9.36b}$$

$$\mathcal{F}_s\{f'\}(\omega) = -\omega \mathcal{F}_c\{f\}(\omega), \tag{9.36c}$$

$$\mathcal{F}_s\{f''\}(\omega) = -\omega^2 \mathcal{F}_s\{f\}(\omega) + \omega f(0+). \tag{9.36d}$$

(See Exercise 5 for verification.) The limits in 9.36a,b,d allow for the possibility of $f(x)$ being undefined at $x = 0$ (but its right-hand limit must exist). The fact that the sine transform of the first derivative of a function involves the cosine transform of the function implies that the transform is not useful in differential equations involving both first and second derivatives. The same is true for the cosine transform.

The following convolution properties for sine and cosine transforms are verified in Exercise 7. When $f = \mathcal{F}_c^{-1}\{\tilde{f}\}$ and $g = \mathcal{F}_c^{-1}\{\tilde{g}\}$,

$$\mathcal{F}_c^{-1}\{\tilde{f}\tilde{g}\}(x) = \frac{1}{2} \int_0^\infty f(v)[g(x - v) + g(x + v)] \, dv, \tag{9.37a}$$

$$= \frac{1}{2} \int_0^\infty g(v)[f(x - v) + f(x + v)] \, dv, \tag{9.37b}$$

provided $f(x)$ and $g(x)$ are extended as even functions for $x < 0$.

When $f = \mathcal{F}_s^{-1}\{\tilde{f}\}$ and $g = \mathcal{F}_c^{-1}\{\tilde{g}\}$ (note that $\tilde{g}$ is a Fourier cosine transform),

$$\mathcal{F}_s^{-1}\{\tilde{f}\tilde{g}\}(x) = \frac{1}{2} \int_0^\infty f(v)[g(x - v) - g(x + v)] \, dv, \tag{9.37c}$$

$$= \frac{1}{2} \int_0^\infty g(v)[f(x + v) + f(x - v)] \, dv, \tag{9.37d}$$

provided $f(x)$ and $g(x)$, respectively, are extended as odd and even functions for $x < 0$. There are other convolution results, but these prove the most useful in applications.

EXERCISES 9.3

1. Verify that the Fourier sine and cosine transforms and their inverses are linear operators.

2. What are the results corresponding to equation 9.14a for $\mathcal{F}_s$ and $\mathcal{F}_c$ when $n = 1$ and $n = 2$?

3. Verify equations 9.35.

4. (a) Prove that when $f(x)$ is an even function with a Fourier transform,

$$\mathcal{F}\{f\} = 2\mathcal{F}_c\{f\}. \tag{9.38a}$$

(b) Prove that when $f(x)$ is an odd function with a Fourier transform,

$$\mathcal{F}\{f\} = -2i\mathcal{F}_s\{f\}. \tag{9.38b}$$

5. Verify equations 9.36.

6. Verify the following results for Fourier sine and cosine transforms, corresponding to equation 9.20,

$$\mathcal{F}_c\{\mathcal{F}_c\{f\}\}(\omega) = \frac{\pi}{2}f(\omega), \tag{9.39a}$$

$$\mathcal{F}_s\{\mathcal{F}_s\{f\}\}(\omega) = \frac{\pi}{2}f(\omega). \tag{9.39b}$$

7. (a) Verify convolution properties 9.37a,b for the Fourier cosine transform.
(b) Verify convolution properties 9.37c,d for the Fourier sine transform.

In Exercises 8–12 find the Fourier sine and cosine transforms of the function.

8. $f(x) = \delta(x - x_0)$, $x_0 > 0$

9. $f(x) = e^{-ax^2}$, $a > 0$ constant

10. $f(x) = xe^{-ax}$, $a > 0$ constant

11. $f(x) = h(x - a) - h(x - b)$, $b > a > 0$ constants

12. $f(x) = \begin{cases} (b/a)(a - |x - c|), & |x - c| < a \\ 0, & |x - c| > a \end{cases}$, a, b, and c all positive constants with $c > a$

13. Find the Fourier sine transform of the function $f(x) = xe^{-ax^2}$.

In Exercises 14–15 use residues to find the Fourier sine transform of the function.

14. $f(x) = \dfrac{x}{a^2 + x^2}$, $a > 0$ constant

15. $f(x) = \dfrac{1}{x(a^2 + x^2)}$, $a > 0$ constant

In Exercises 16–17 use residues to find the Fourier cosine transform of the function.

16. $f(x) = \dfrac{x^2}{a^4 + x^4}$, $a > 0$ constant

17. $f(x) = \dfrac{x^2}{(a^2 + x^2)^2}$, $a > 0$ constant

18. Use Exercises 34 and 35 in Section 6.3 to show that when $0 < \alpha < \beta$,

$$\mathcal{F}_s\left\{\frac{\sinh \alpha x}{\cosh \beta x}\right\}(\omega) = \frac{\pi \sin \frac{\pi\alpha}{2\beta} \sinh \frac{\pi\omega}{2\beta}}{\beta\left(\cosh \frac{\pi\omega}{\beta} + \cos \frac{\pi\alpha}{\beta}\right)}, \qquad \mathcal{F}_s\left\{\frac{\cosh \alpha x}{\sinh \beta x}\right\}(\omega) = \frac{\pi \sinh \frac{\pi\omega}{\beta}}{2\beta\left(\cosh \frac{\pi\omega}{\beta} + \cos \frac{\pi\alpha}{\beta}\right)},$$

$$\mathcal{F}_c\left\{\frac{\cosh \alpha x}{\cosh \beta x}\right\}(\omega) = \frac{\pi \cos \frac{\pi\alpha}{2\beta} \cosh \frac{\pi\omega}{2\beta}}{\beta\left(\cosh \frac{\pi\omega}{\beta} + \cos \frac{\pi\alpha}{\beta}\right)}, \qquad \mathcal{F}_c\left\{\frac{\sinh \alpha x}{\sinh \beta x}\right\}(\omega) = \frac{\pi \sin \frac{\pi\alpha}{\beta}}{2\beta\left(\cosh \frac{\pi\omega}{\beta} + \cos \frac{\pi\alpha}{\beta}\right)}.$$

19. (a) Show that

$$\mathcal{F}_c^{-1}\{f\}(x) = \frac{2}{\pi}\mathcal{F}_c\{f\}(x), \tag{9.40a}$$

$$\mathcal{F}_s^{-1}\{f\}(x) = \frac{2}{\pi}\mathcal{F}_s\{f\}(x). \tag{9.40b}$$

(b) Use the results in part (a) and Exercise 18 to verify that, when $0 < \alpha < \beta$,

$$\mathcal{F}_s^{-1}\left\{\frac{\sinh \alpha\omega}{\cosh \beta\omega}\right\}(x) = \frac{2 \sin \frac{\pi\alpha}{2\beta} \sinh \frac{\pi x}{2\beta}}{\beta\left(\cosh \frac{\pi x}{\beta} + \cos \frac{\pi\alpha}{\beta}\right)}, \qquad \mathcal{F}_s^{-1}\left\{\frac{\cosh \alpha\omega}{\sinh \beta\omega}\right\}(x) = \frac{\sinh \frac{\pi x}{\beta}}{\beta\left(\cosh \frac{\pi x}{\beta} + \cos \frac{\pi\alpha}{\beta}\right)},$$

$$\mathcal{F}_c^{-1}\left\{\frac{\cosh \alpha\omega}{\cosh \beta\omega}\right\}(x) = \frac{2 \cos \frac{\pi\alpha}{2\beta} \cosh \frac{\pi x}{2\beta}}{\beta\left(\cosh \frac{\pi x}{\beta} + \cos \frac{\pi\alpha}{\beta}\right)}, \qquad \mathcal{F}_c^{-1}\left\{\frac{\sinh \alpha\omega}{\sinh \beta\omega}\right\}(x) = \frac{\sin \frac{\pi\alpha}{\beta}}{\beta\left(\cosh \frac{\pi x}{\beta} + \cos \frac{\pi\alpha}{\beta}\right)}.$$

20. The **error function**, erf(x), is defined as

$$\text{erf}(x) = \frac{2}{\sqrt{\pi}} \int_0^x e^{-u^2}\, du.$$

Because this function is increasing for $x > 0$ and $\lim_{x\to\infty} \text{erf}(x) = 1$, it does not have Fourier transforms. The **complementary error function**, erfc(x), defined by

$$\text{erfc}(x) = 1 - \text{erf}(x) = \frac{2}{\sqrt{\pi}} \int_x^\infty e^{-u^2}\, du,$$

does have Fourier transforms. Use properties 9.36 and Exercise 9 to derive the following results:

(a) $\mathcal{F}_s\{\text{erfc}(ax)\} = \dfrac{1 - e^{-\omega^2/(4a^2)}}{\omega}$, $a > 0$ constant

(b) $\mathcal{F}_c\left\{ ax\,\text{erfc}(ax) - \dfrac{1}{\sqrt{\pi}} e^{-a^2x^2} \right\} = \dfrac{a}{\omega^2}[-1 + e^{-\omega^2/(4a^2)}]$, $a > 0$ constant

The following exercise should be attempted only by readers who are already familiar with the Laplace transform. In this exercise, $\mathcal{L}\{f(x)\}$ denotes the Laplace transform of a function $f(x)$.

21. (a) Show that when $f(x)$ is absolutely integrable on $0 < x < \infty$, and $f(x) = 0$ for $x < 0$,

$$\mathcal{F}_s\{f(x)\}(\omega) = -\text{Im}[\mathcal{L}\{f(x)\}(i\omega), \tag{9.41a}$$
$$\mathcal{F}_c\{f(x)\}(\omega) = \text{Re}[\mathcal{L}\{f(x)\}(i\omega). \tag{9.41b}$$

(b) Use the results in part (a) to calculate Fourier sine and cosine transforms for the functions in Exercises 11 and 12.

§9.4 Application of the Fourier Sine and Cosine Transforms to Partial Differential Equations

Fourier sine and cosine transforms are used to solve initial boundary value problems associated with second order partial differential equations on the semi-infinite interval $x > 0$. Because property 9.36d for the Fourier sine transform utilizes the value of the function at $x = 0$, the sine transform is applied to problems with a Dirichlet boundary condition at $x = 0$. Similarly, property 9.36b indicates that the cosine transform should be used when the boundary condition at $x = 0$ is of Neumann type.

Example 9.20   Solve the vibration problem

$$\frac{\partial^2 y}{\partial t^2} = c^2 \frac{\partial^2 y}{\partial x^2}, \quad x > 0, \quad t > 0, \tag{9.42a}$$

$$y(0,t) = f_1(t), \quad t > 0, \tag{9.42b}$$

$$y(x,0) = f(x), \quad x > 0, \tag{9.42c}$$

$$y_t(x,0) = g(x), \quad x > 0, \tag{9.42d}$$

for displacement of a semi-infinite string with prescribed motion at its left end $x = 0$.

Solution   Because the boundary condition at $x = 0$ is Dirichlet, we apply the Fourier sine transform to the PDE and use property 9.36d for the transform of $\partial^2 y / \partial x^2$,

$$\frac{d^2 \tilde{y}}{dt^2} = -\omega^2 c^2 \tilde{y}(\omega, t) + \omega c^2 f_1(t).$$

Thus, the Fourier sine transform $\tilde{y}(\omega, t)$ of $y(x,t)$ must satisfy the ODE

$$\frac{d^2 \tilde{y}}{dt^2} + \omega^2 c^2 \tilde{y} = \omega c^2 f_1(t)$$

subject to transforms of initial conditions 9.42c,d,

$$\tilde{y}(\omega, 0) = \tilde{f}(\omega), \quad \tilde{y}'(\omega, 0) = \tilde{g}(\omega).$$

Variation of parameters leads to the following general solution of the ODE

$$\tilde{y}(\omega, t) = A \cos c\omega t + B \sin c\omega t + c \int_0^t f_1(u) \sin c\omega(t - u) \, du.$$

The initial conditions require A and B to satisfy

$$\tilde{f}(\omega) = A, \qquad \tilde{g}(\omega) = c\omega B.$$

Hence,

$$\tilde{y}(\omega, t) = \tilde{f}(\omega) \cos c\omega t + \frac{\tilde{g}(\omega)}{c\omega} \sin c\omega t + c \int_0^t f_1(u) \sin c\omega(t - u) \, du, \tag{9.43}$$

and $y(x,t)$ is the inverse transform of this function

$$y(x,t) = \frac{2}{\pi} \int_0^\infty \tilde{y}(\omega, t) \sin \omega x \, d\omega. \tag{9.44}$$

The first term in this integral is

$$\frac{2}{\pi} \int_0^\infty \tilde{f}(\omega) \cos c\omega t \sin \omega x \, d\omega = \frac{2}{\pi} \int_0^\infty \frac{1}{2}\tilde{f}(\omega)[\sin \omega(x - ct) + \sin \omega(x + ct)] \, d\omega$$

$$= \frac{1}{2}[f(x - ct) + f(x + ct)],$$

provided $f(x)$ is extended as an odd function.

According to Exercise 11 in Section 9.3, the Fourier cosine transform of $h(x + ct) - h(x - ct)$ is $(\sin c\omega t)/\omega$. Consequently, convolution identity 9.37d implies that the inverse sine transform of $[\tilde{g}(\omega)/(c\omega)]\sin c\omega t$ is

$$\frac{1}{2c}\int_0^\infty [h(v) - h(v - ct)][g(x + v) + g(x - v)]\, dv = \frac{1}{2c}\left[\int_0^{ct} g(x + v)\, dv + \int_0^{ct} g(x - v)\, dv\right],$$

provided $g(x)$ is extended as an odd function for $x < 0$. When we set $u = x + v$ and $u = x - v$, respectively, in these integrals, the result is

$$\frac{1}{2c}\left[\int_x^{x+ct} g(u)\, du + \int_x^{x-ct} g(u)(-du)\right] = \frac{1}{2c}\int_{x-ct}^{x+ct} g(u)\, du.$$

The inverse transform of the integral term in $\tilde{y}(\omega, t)$ can also be expressed in closed form if we set $u = c(t - v)$,

$$c\int_0^t f_1(v) \sin c\omega(t - v)\, dv = c\int_{ct}^0 f_1\left(t - \frac{u}{c}\right)\sin \omega u \left(-\frac{du}{c}\right) = \int_0^{ct} f_1\left(t - \frac{u}{c}\right)\sin \omega u \, du.$$

But this is the Fourier sine transform of the function

$$\begin{cases} f_1\left(t - \dfrac{x}{c}\right), & x < ct \\ 0, & x > ct \end{cases}$$

or

$$\begin{cases} 0, & t < x/c \\ f_1\left(t - \dfrac{x}{c}\right), & t > x/c \end{cases} = f_1\left(t - \frac{x}{c}\right) h\left(t - \frac{x}{c}\right).$$

The solution is therefore

$$y(x, t) = \frac{1}{2}[f(x - ct) + f(x + ct)] + \frac{1}{2c}\int_{x-ct}^{x+ct} g(u)\, du + f_1\left(t - \frac{x}{c}\right) h\left(t - \frac{x}{c}\right). \quad (9.45)$$

The first two terms are the d'Alembert part of the solution. The last term is due to the nonhomogeneity at the end $x = 0$; it can be interpreted physically, and this is most easily done when $f(x) = g(x) = 0$. In this case, the complete solution is

$$y(x, t) = f_1\left(t - \frac{x}{c}\right) h\left(t - \frac{x}{c}\right).$$

A point x on the string remains at rest until time $t = x/c$, when it begins to execute the same motion as the end $x = 0$. The time x/c taken by the disturbance to reach x is called **retarded time**. The disturbance $f_1(t)$ at $x = 0$ travels down the string with velocity c.

The solution of the original problem is a superposition of the d'Alembert displacement and the displacement due to the end effect at $x = 0.\bullet$

Example 9.21   The temperature of a semi-infinite rod at time $t = 0$ is $f(x)$, $x \geq 0$. For time $t > 0$, heat is added to the rod uniformly over the end $x = 0$ at a variable rate $f_1(t)$ W/m^2. The initial boundary value problem for temperature $U(x,t)$ in the rod is

$$\frac{\partial U}{\partial t} = k \frac{\partial^2 U}{\partial x^2}, \quad x > 0, \quad t > 0, \tag{9.46a}$$

$$U_x(0,t) = -\kappa^{-1} f_1(t), \quad t > 0, \tag{9.46b}$$

$$U(x,0) = f(x), \quad x > 0. \tag{9.46c}$$

Find $U(x,t)$.

Solution   Because the boundary condition at $x = 0$ is Neumann, we apply the Fourier cosine transform to the PDE and use property 9.36b,

$$\frac{d\tilde{U}}{dt} = -k\omega^2 \tilde{U}(\omega,t) + \frac{k}{\kappa} f_1(t).$$

Thus, the Fourier cosine transform $\tilde{U}(\omega,t)$ must satisfy the ODE

$$\frac{d\tilde{U}}{dt} + k\omega^2 \tilde{U} = \frac{k}{\kappa} f_1(t)$$

subject to the transform of initial condition 9.46c,

$$\tilde{U}(\omega,0) = \tilde{f}(\omega).$$

A general solution of the ODE is

$$\tilde{U}(\omega,t) = Ce^{-k\omega^2 t} + \frac{k}{\kappa} \int_0^t e^{-k\omega^2(t-u)} f_1(u)\, du,$$

and the initial condition requires $\tilde{f}(\omega) = C$. Consequently,

$$\tilde{U}(\omega,t) = \tilde{f}(\omega)e^{-k\omega^2 t} + \frac{k}{\kappa} \int_0^t e^{-k\omega^2(t-u)} f_1(u)\, du, \tag{9.47}$$

and the required temperature is the inverse cosine transform of this function. According to Exercise 9 in Section 9.3, the Fourier cosine transform of the exponential e^{-ax^2} is $\frac{1}{2}\sqrt{\frac{\pi}{a}} e^{-\omega^2/(4a)}$, or, conversely, the inverse Fourier cosine transform of $e^{-k\omega^2 t}$ is $\frac{1}{\sqrt{k\pi t}} e^{-x^2/(4kt)}$. Convolution property 9.37a therefore gives the inverse cosine transform of $\tilde{f}(\omega)e^{-k\omega^2 t}$ as

$$\frac{1}{2} \int_0^\infty f(v) \frac{1}{\sqrt{k\pi t}} [e^{-(x-v)^2/(4kt)} + e^{-(x+v)^2/(4kt)}]\, dv$$

$$= \frac{1}{2\sqrt{k\pi t}} \int_0^\infty f(v)[e^{-(x-v)^2/(4kt)} + e^{-(x+v)^2/(4kt)}]\, dv.$$

Furthermore, the inverse cosine transform of $e^{-k\omega^2(t-u)}$ is $\dfrac{1}{\sqrt{k\pi(t-u)}} e^{-x^2/[4k(t-u)]}$, and therefore the inverse transform of the integral term can be expressed in the form

$$\mathcal{F}_c^{-1} \left\{ \int_0^t e^{-k\omega^2(t-u)} f_1(u)\, du \right\} = \int_0^t \frac{f_1(u)}{\sqrt{k\pi(t-u)}} e^{-x^2/[4k(t-u)]}\, du.$$

Thus, the temperature function is

$$U(x,t) = \frac{1}{2\sqrt{k\pi t}} \int_0^\infty f(v)[e^{-(x-v)^2/(4kt)} + e^{-(x+v)^2/(4kt)}]\,dv$$

$$+ \frac{\sqrt{k}}{\kappa\sqrt{\pi}} \int_0^t \frac{f_1(u)}{\sqrt{t-u}} e^{-x^2/[4k(t-u)]}\,du. \bullet \qquad (9.48)$$

Example 9.22 Solve the following potential problem in the quarter plane $x > 0$, $y > 0$,

$$\frac{\partial^2 V}{\partial x^2} + \frac{\partial^2 V}{\partial y^2} = 0, \quad x > 0, \quad y > 0, \qquad (9.49\text{a})$$

$$V(0,y) = g(y), \quad y > 0, \qquad (9.49\text{b})$$

$$V_y(x,0) = f(x), \quad x > 0. \qquad (9.49\text{c})$$

Solution Superposition can be used to express $V(x,y)$ as the sum of functions $V_1(x,y)$ and $V_2(x,y)$ satisfying

$$\frac{\partial^2 V_1}{\partial x^2} + \frac{\partial^2 V_1}{\partial y^2} = 0, \quad x > 0, \quad y > 0, \qquad\qquad \frac{\partial^2 V_2}{\partial x^2} + \frac{\partial^2 V_2}{\partial y^2} = 0, \quad x > 0, \quad y > 0,$$

$$V_1(0,y) = g(y), \quad y > 0, \qquad\qquad\qquad V_2(0,y) = 0, \quad y > 0,$$

$$\frac{\partial V_1(x,0)}{\partial y} = 0, \quad x > 0, \qquad\qquad\qquad \frac{\partial V_2(x,0)}{\partial y} = f(x), \quad x > 0.$$

To find $V_1(x,y)$ we apply Fourier cosine transform 9.33a (with respect to y) to its PDE and use property 9.36b,

$$\frac{d^2 \tilde{V}_1}{dx^2} - \omega^2 \tilde{V}_1(x,\omega) = 0, \quad x > 0.$$

This transform function $\tilde{V}_1(x,\omega)$ is also subject to

$$\tilde{V}_1(0,\omega) = \tilde{g}(\omega).$$

A general solution of the ODE is

$$\tilde{V}_1(x,\omega) = Ae^{\omega x} + Be^{-\omega x}.$$

For $\tilde{V}_1(x,\omega)$ to remain bounded as $x \to \infty$, A must be zero, and the boundary condition then implies that $B = \tilde{g}(\omega)$. Hence,

$$\tilde{V}_1(x,\omega) = \tilde{g}(\omega)e^{-\omega x}.$$

To invert this transform, first recall from to Example 9.17 that

$$\mathcal{F}_c\{e^{-ay}\}(\omega) = \frac{a}{a^2 + \omega^2} \qquad \text{when } a > 0.$$

With Exercise 19 in Section 9.3, we can say that

$$\mathcal{F}_c^{-1}\{e^{-a\omega}\}(y) = \frac{2}{\pi}\frac{a}{a^2 + y^2}.$$

Convolution property 9.37c, now gives

$$V_1(x,y) = \frac{1}{2}\int_0^\infty g(v)\left(\frac{2}{\pi}\right)\left[\frac{x}{(y-v)^2 + x^2} + \frac{x}{(y+v)^2 + x^2}\right]dv$$

$$= \frac{x}{\pi}\int_0^\infty g(v)\left[\frac{1}{x^2 + (y-v)^2} + \frac{1}{x^2 + (y+v)^2}\right]dv.$$

Taking Fourier sine transforms with respect to x in order to find $V_1(x,y)$ leads to a nonhomogeneous ODE in $\tilde{V}_1(\omega,y)$ that is more difficult to solve.

To find $V_2(x,y)$ we apply the Fourier sine transform with respect to x to its PDE and use property 9.36d,

$$\frac{d^2\tilde{V}_2}{dy^2} - \omega^2 \tilde{V}_2(\omega,y) = 0.$$

The transform must also satisfy

$$\frac{d\tilde{V}_2(\omega,0)}{dy} = \tilde{f}(\omega).$$

A general solution of the ODE is

$$\tilde{V}_2(\omega,y) = Ae^{\omega y} + Be^{-\omega y}.$$

For $\tilde{V}_2(\omega,y)$ to remain bounded as $y \to \infty$, A must be zero, and the boundary condition on $\tilde{V}_2$ then implies that $B = -\tilde{f}(\omega)/\omega$. Hence,

$$\tilde{V}_2(\omega,y) = -\frac{\tilde{f}(\omega)}{\omega}e^{-\omega y}$$

and

$$V_2(x,y) = \frac{2}{\pi}\int_0^\infty -\frac{\tilde{f}(\omega)}{\omega}e^{-\omega y}\sin\omega x\, d\omega.$$

The final solution is

$$V(x,y) = \frac{x}{\pi}\int_0^\infty g(v)\left[\frac{1}{x^2+(y-v)^2} + \frac{1}{x^2+(y+v)^2}\right]dv$$
$$+ \frac{2}{\pi}\int_0^\infty -\frac{\tilde{f}(\omega)}{\omega}e^{-\omega y}\sin\omega x\, d\omega.\bullet$$

EXERCISES 9.4

1. Use a Fourier transform to solve the heat conduction problem

$$\frac{\partial U}{\partial t} = k\frac{\partial^2 U}{\partial x^2}, \quad x>0, \quad t>0,$$
$$U(0,t) = \overline{U} = \text{constant}, \quad t>0,$$
$$U(x,0) = 0, \quad x>0.$$

(Hint: See Exercise 20 in Section 9.3 when inverting the transform.) Plot the solutions on the interval $0 \le x \le 5$ with $k = 10^{-6}$ and $\overline{U} = 1$ for $t = 10^5$ and $t = 10^6$.

2. (a) Use a Fourier transform to solve the heat conduction problem

$$\frac{\partial U}{\partial t} = k\frac{\partial^2 U}{\partial x^2}, \quad x>0, \quad t>0,$$
$$U_x(0,t) = -\kappa^{-1}Q_0 = \text{constant}, \quad t>0,$$
$$U(x,0) = 0, \quad x>0.$$

(Hint: See Exercise 20 in Section 9.3 when inverting the transform.) Plot the solutions on the interval $0 \le x \le 5$ with $k = 10^{-6}$, $\kappa = 10$, and $Q_0 = 1000$ for $t = 10^5$ and $t = 10^6$.

   (b) Describe the temperature of the left end of the rod.

3. (a) Use a Fourier transform to find an integral representation for the solution of the heat conduction problem

$$\frac{\partial U}{\partial t} = k\frac{\partial^2 U}{\partial x^2} + \frac{k}{\kappa}g(x,t), \quad x > 0, \quad t > 0,$$
$$U(0,t) = f_1(t), \quad t > 0,$$
$$U(x,0) = f(x), \quad x > 0.$$

   (b) Simplify the solution in part (a) when $g(x,t) \equiv 0$, $f_1(t) \equiv 0$, and $f(x) = U_0 = $ constant.

   (c) Simplify the solution in part (a) when $g(x,t) \equiv 0$, $f(x) \equiv 0$, and $f_1(t) = \overline{U} = $ constant. Is it the solution of Exercise 1?

4. (a) Use a Fourier transform to find an integral representation for the solution of the heat conduction problem

$$\frac{\partial U}{\partial t} = k\frac{\partial^2 U}{\partial x^2} + \frac{k}{\kappa}g(x,t), \quad x > 0, \quad t > 0,$$
$$U_x(0,t) = -\kappa^{-1}f_1(t), \quad t > 0,$$
$$U(x,0) = f(x), \quad x > 0.$$

   (b) Simplify the solution in part (a) when $g(x,t) \equiv 0$, $f_1(t) \equiv 0$, and $f(x) = U_0 = $ constant.

   (c) Simplify the solution in part (a) when $g(x,t) \equiv 0$, $f(x) \equiv 0$, and $f_1(t) = Q_0 = $ constant. Is it the solution of Exercise 2?

5. Solve the vibration problem of Example 9.20 if a unit force acts at the point $x = x_0$ on the string for all $t > 0$.

6. Repeat Example 9.20 if the Dirichlet boundary condition at $x = 0$ is replaced by the Neumann condition

$$y_x(0,t) = -\tau^{-1}f_1(t).$$

Constant τ is the tension in the string. This boundary condition describes the situation where the end $x = 0$ of the string, taken as massless, moves vertically with tension and an external force $f_1(t)$ acting on the end.

The following boundary value problems can be interpreted as steady-state temperature problems or potential problems.

7. Solve the boundary value problem

$$\frac{\partial^2 V}{\partial x^2} + \frac{\partial^2 V}{\partial y^2} = 0, \quad x > 0, \quad 0 < y < L,$$
$$V(0,y) = 0, \quad 0 < y < L,$$
$$V(x,0) = f(x), \quad x > 0,$$
$$V(x,L) = g(x), \quad x > 0.$$

8. Solve the boundary value problem in Exercise 7 if the boundary condition along the x-axis is Neumann $V_y(x,0) = f(x)$.

9. Solve the boundary value problem in Exercise 7 if the boundary condition along $y = L$ is Neumann $V_y(x, L) = g(x)$.

10. Solve the boundary value problem in Exercise 7 if the boundary condition along $x = 0$ is homogeneous Neumann $V_x(0, y) = 0$.

11. Solve the boundary value problem

$$\frac{\partial^2 V}{\partial x^2} + \frac{\partial^2 V}{\partial y^2} = 0, \quad x > 0, \quad y > 0,$$
$$V(0, y) = g(y), \quad y > 0,$$
$$V(x, 0) = f(x), \quad x > 0.$$

CHAPTER 10   THE z-TRANSFORM

In Chapters 8 and 9, we saw how Laplace and Fourier transforms reduce ordinary differential equations to algebraic equations, and reduce partial differential equations to ordinary differential equations. In many applications, particularly in engineering, difference equations replace differential equations. In this chapter, we develop the z-transform as a tool to reduce difference equations to algebraic ones. We define the transform in Section 10.1 and develop some of its more important properties. In Sections 10.2 and 10.4 we demonstrate how to use the transform to find solutions to difference equations. Applications are discussed in Sections 10.3 and 10.5. In Section 10.6, we discuss transfer functions and stability for systems that are defined by difference equations.

§10.1   The z-transform

The z-transform is often considered to be a discrete version of the Laplace transform. The Laplace transform is an integral transform that operates on functions $f(t)$ defined for $t \geq 0$ to give functions $\tilde{f}(s)$ of a complex variable s. The z-transform replaces integration by its discrete version, a summation, to transform functions $f(n)$ defined for nonnegative integers n to functions $\tilde{f}(z)$ of a complex variable z. The reader who is familiar with the Laplace transform should compare each result in this chapter with the corresponding result in Chapter 8.

Definition 10.1   The z-**transform** of a function $f(n)$, defined for integers $n \geq 0$, is denoted by $\tilde{f} = \mathcal{Z}\{f\}$ with values given by

$$\tilde{f}(z) = \mathcal{Z}\{f\}(z) = \sum_{n=0}^{\infty} f(n)z^{-n} = f(0) + \frac{f(1)}{z} + \frac{f(2)}{z^2} + \frac{f(3)}{z^3} + \cdots , \quad (10.1)$$

provided the series on the right converges in some annulus $|z| > R$.

Definition 10.1 does not give the z-transform $\tilde{f}(z)$ of $f(n)$ in closed form; it gives the Laurent series for $\tilde{f}(z)$. Whenever possible, we find $\tilde{f}(z)$ in closed form by summing the series. By setting $w = 1/z$, transform 10.1 is replaced by a power series in w,

$$\sum_{n=0}^{\infty} f(n)w^n.$$

Its radius of convergence R can be calculated with formulas 5.12 with a_n replaced by $f(n)$, provided either limit exists. It then follows that the z-transform converges for $|z| > 1/R$.

Example 10.1   What is the z-transform of the function $\delta(n - k)$ whose value is 1 for $n = k$ and whose value is 0 for every other value of n?

Solution   The transform of this function is

$$\mathcal{Z}\{\delta(n - k)\} = \frac{1}{z^k},$$

valid for $|z| > 0$.•

The discrete Heaviside unit step function $h(n - k)$ has value 0 for $n < k$ and value 1 for $n \geq k$,

$$h(n-k) = \begin{cases} 0, & n < k \\ 1, & n \geq k. \end{cases} \qquad (10.2)$$

Its transform is calculated in the following example.

Example 10.2 Find the z-transform of $h(n-k)$. What is the transform in the special case that $k = 0$?

Solution   The transform of the function is

$$\mathcal{Z}\{h(n-k)\} = \sum_{n=0}^{\infty} h(n-k)z^{-n} = \frac{1}{z^k} + \frac{1}{z^{k+1}} + \frac{1}{z^{k+2}} + \cdots .$$

This is a geometric series with sum

$$\mathcal{Z}\{h(n-k)\} = \frac{1/z^k}{1 - 1/z} = \frac{1}{z^{k-1}(z-1)}, \quad \text{provided } |1/z| < 1 \implies |z| > 1.$$

When $k = 0$, this reduces to

$$\mathcal{Z}\{h(n)\} = \mathcal{Z}\{1\} = \frac{z}{z-1}.\bullet$$

Example 10.3 Find the z-transform of the function $f(n) = a^n$, where $a > 0$ is a constant.

Solution   The transform of the function is

$$\mathcal{Z}\{a^n\} = \sum_{n=0}^{\infty} a^n z^{-n} = \sum_{n=0}^{\infty} \frac{a^n}{z^n} = \frac{1}{1 - a/z} = \frac{z}{z-a},$$

valid for $|a/z| < 1$ or $|z| > a$. As would be expected, this reduces to the result of Example 10.2 when $a = 1$.$\bullet$

Example 10.4 Find the z-transform of the function $f(n) = n$.

Solution   The transform of the function is

$$\mathcal{Z}\{n\} = \tilde{f}(z) = \sum_{n=0}^{\infty} n z^{-n} = \frac{1}{z} + \frac{2}{z^2} + \frac{3}{z^3} + \cdots .$$

The series converges for $|z| > 1$. If we divide both sides of the equation by z and integrate,

$$\int \frac{\tilde{f}(z)}{z} dz = \int \left(\frac{1}{z^2} + \frac{2}{z^3} + \frac{3}{z^4} + \cdots \right) dz = \left(-\frac{1}{z} - \frac{1}{z^2} - \frac{1}{z^3} - \cdots \right) + C.$$

This series is geometric so that

$$\int \frac{\tilde{f}(z)}{z} dz = \frac{-1/z}{1 - 1/z} + C = \frac{1}{1-z} + C.$$

Differentiation now gives

$$\frac{\tilde{f}(z)}{z} = \frac{1}{(1-z)^2} \qquad \implies \qquad \tilde{f}(z) = \frac{z}{(1-z)^2}.\bullet$$

Example 10.5 Find the domain of convergence of the z-transform of $f(n) = \left(\dfrac{2n^2 + 3}{3n^2 - 1}\right) 3^n$.

Solution Since

$$\lim_{n \to \infty} \frac{\left(\dfrac{2n^2 + 3}{3n^2 - 1}\right) 3^n}{\left[\dfrac{2(n+1)^2 + 3}{3(n+1)^2 - 1}\right] 3^{n+1}} = \frac{1}{3},$$

the z-transform converges for $|z| > 3$.•

There are many approaches to the z-transform, and even more notations to represent it; most are intimately connected to the particular application in which they are to be used. Perhaps the biggest user of the transform is the electrical engineer in digital signal processing, and the functional notation in this context can be such that it disguises the simplicity of the mathematics. The other extreme is to recall that an infinite sequence of constants is a function $f(n)$ whose domain is the set of positive integers, and in Section 5.1, we used the notation $\{c_n\}$ to represent a sequence. It follows that the z-transform maps a sequence $\{c_n\}$ of constants to a complex function

$$\tilde{f}(z) = \sum_{n=0}^{\infty} c_n z^{-n}.$$

We have chosen a middle of the road notation. Using $f(n)$ in place of $\{c_n\}$ does not disguise the simplicity of the mathematics, and the functional notation is not too far removed from that in many applications.

When $\tilde{f}(z)$ is the z-transform of $f(n)$, we say that $f(n)$ is the inverse transform of $\tilde{f}(z)$ and write

$$f = \mathcal{Z}^{-1}\{\tilde{f}(z)\}. \tag{10.3}$$

For instance, based on the Examples 10.2 and 10.4, we can write that

$$\mathcal{Z}^{-1}\left\{\frac{z}{z - 1}\right\} = 1, \qquad \text{and} \qquad \mathcal{Z}^{-1}\left\{\frac{z}{(1 - z)^2}\right\} = n.$$

To find the inverse z-transform of a given function $\tilde{f}(z)$, we expand the function in a Laurent series valid in some infinite annulus $|z| > R$. If the expansion contains only nonnegative powers of z, these coefficients constitute the inverse transform; if the expansion contains positive powers of z, then the function does not have an inverse z-transform in terms of ordinary functions. It might have an inverse in terms of "generalized functions". For instance, we can obtain the Laurent series for the function $\tilde{f}(z) = z^2/(z - 1)$ by writing

$$\frac{z^2}{z - 1} = z + 1 + \frac{1}{z - 1} = z + 1 + \frac{1}{z(1 - 1/z)} = z + 1 + \frac{1}{z} \sum_{n=0}^{\infty} \left(\frac{1}{z}\right)^n$$

$$= z + 1 + \sum_{n=0}^{\infty} \frac{1}{z^{n+1}} = z + 1 + \sum_{n=1}^{\infty} \frac{1}{z^n}.$$

This is the Laurent series series of the function valid for $|1/z| < 1 \implies |z| > 1$. Since it contains a term with a positive power of z, the function does not have an inverse z-transform; it cannot be the z-transform of a function $f(n)$.

Example 10.6   Find the inverse z-transform of the function $\tilde{f}(z) = \dfrac{z}{z^2 - 3z - 4}$.

Solution   We require the Laurent series for $\tilde{f}(z)$ valid in some annulus $|z| > R$. With partial fractions, we write

$$
\tilde{f}(z) = \frac{z}{(z-4)(z+1)} = \frac{4/5}{z-4} + \frac{1/5}{z+1} = \frac{4/5}{z(1-4/z)} + \frac{1/5}{z(1+1/z)}
$$

$$
= \frac{4}{5z} \sum_{n=0}^{\infty} \left(\frac{4}{z}\right)^n + \frac{1}{5z} \sum_{n=0}^{\infty} \left(-\frac{1}{z}\right)^n = \sum_{n=0}^{\infty} \frac{4^{n+1}}{5z^{n+1}} + \sum_{n=0}^{\infty} \frac{(-1)^n}{5z^{n+1}}
$$

$$
= \sum_{n=0}^{\infty} \frac{4^{n+1} + (-1)^n}{5z^{n+1}} = \sum_{n=1}^{\infty} \frac{4^n + (-1)^{n+1}}{5z^n}.
$$

This expansion is valid for $|z| > 4$. The inverse transform of $\tilde{f}(z)$ is therefore

$$
f(n) = \begin{cases} 0, & n = 0 \\ \dfrac{4^n + (-1)^{n+1}}{5}, & n > 0. \end{cases}
$$

Since the formula for $f(n)$ for $n > 0$ also gives 0 when $n = 0$, we can write that $f(n) = [4^n + (-1)^{n+1}]/5$ for all n.●

Expanding $\tilde{f}(z)$ in a Laurent series around $z = 0$ is one way of finding the inverse transform of $\tilde{f}(z)$. Here is an alternative. According to Theorem 5.25, coefficients in the Laurent expansion of $\tilde{f}(z)$ about $z = 0$ are given by the contour integral in equation 5.30b where $z_0 = 0$ and C is any curve in the annulus of convergence $|z| > R$ of the Laurent series that contains $z = 0$ in its interior. In other words, the inverse z-transform of $\tilde{f}(z)$ is given by the contour integral

$$
f(n) = \frac{1}{2\pi i} \oint_C \frac{\tilde{f}(z)}{z^{-n+1}} dz = \frac{1}{2\pi i} \oint_C \tilde{f}(z)\, z^{n-1}\, dz, \tag{10.4}
$$

where C is any simple, closed, piecewise smooth curve in $|z| > R$ that contains $z = 0$ in its interior. When we use residues to evaluate the integral, we obtain

$$
\mathcal{Z}^{-1}\{\tilde{f}(z)\} = \text{Sum of residues of } z^{n-1}\tilde{f}(z) \text{ at its singularities.} \tag{10.5}
$$

Example 10.7   Use formula 10.5 to find the inverse of the function $\tilde{f}(z)$ in Example 10.6.

Solution   Since $z^{n-1}\tilde{f}(z)$ has simple poles at $z = -1$ and $z = 4$, the inverse transform is

$$
f(n) = \text{Res}\left[\frac{z^n}{z^2 - 3z - 4}, -1\right] + \text{Res}\left[\frac{z^n}{z^2 - 3z - 4}, 4\right]
$$

$$
= \lim_{z \to -1}\left[\frac{(z+1)z^n}{(z+1)(z-4)}\right] + \lim_{z \to 4}\left[\frac{(z-4)z^n}{(z+1)(z-4)}\right]
$$

$$
= \frac{(-1)^n}{-5} + \frac{4^n}{5} = \frac{4^n + (-1)^{n+1}}{5}.
$$

When $n = 0$, $z^{-1}\tilde{f}(z)$ has a removable singularity at $z = 0$ with residue zero. Since the above expression also has value zero when $n = 0$, it is the inverse transform for all n.•

The z-transform and its inverse are linear operators; that is, for constants c_1 and c_2,

$$\mathcal{Z}\{c_1 f(n) + c_2 g(n)\} = c_1 \mathcal{Z}\{f(n)\} + c_2 \mathcal{Z}\{g(n)\}, \tag{10.6a}$$

$$\mathcal{Z}^{-1}\{c_1 \tilde{f}(z) + c_2 \tilde{g}(z)\} = c_1 \mathcal{Z}^{-1}\{\tilde{f}(z)\} + c_2 \mathcal{Z}^{-1}\{\tilde{g}(z)\}. \tag{10.6b}$$

The following properties of z-transforms should be compared to properties 8.3 for Laplace transforms,

$$\mathcal{Z}\{a^n f(n)\}(z) = \tilde{f}(z/a), \tag{10.7a}$$
$$\mathcal{Z}^{-1}\{\tilde{f}(z/a)\}(n) = a^n f(n). \tag{10.7b}$$

See Exercise 29 for a proof of the first of these. Compare the following with properties 8.4 for the Laplace transform,

$$\mathcal{Z}\{f(n-k)h(n-k)\}(z) = z^{-k}\tilde{f}(z), \tag{10.8a}$$
$$\mathcal{Z}^{-1}\{z^{-k}\tilde{f}(z)\}(n) = f(n-k)h(n-k). \tag{10.8b}$$

See Exercise 30 for a proof of the first. It is often more useful in the form

$$\mathcal{Z}\{f(n)h(n-k)\}(z) = z^{-k}\tilde{f}(z+k). \tag{10.8c}$$

Convolutions

The convolution of two functions $f(n)$ and $g(n)$ is defined as

$$(f * g)(n) = \sum_{k=0}^{n} f(k)g(n-k). \tag{10.9}$$

The following theorem relates the z-transform of $f * g$ to transforms of $f(n)$ and $g(n)$.

Theorem 10.1 If $\tilde{f} = \mathcal{Z}\{f\}$ and $\tilde{g} = \mathcal{Z}\{g\}$, then

$$\mathcal{Z}\{f * g\}(z) = \tilde{f}(z)\tilde{g}(z). \tag{10.10a}$$

Proof: The z-transform of $f * g$ is

$$\mathcal{Z}\{f * g\} = \sum_{n=0}^{\infty} \left[\sum_{k=0}^{n} f(k)g(n-k) \right] \frac{1}{z^n}$$
$$= f(0)g(0) + \frac{f(0)g(1) + f(1)g(0)}{z} + \frac{f(0)g(2) + f(1)g(1) + f(2)g(0)}{z^2} + \cdots .$$

On the other hand, if we multiply the transforms of $f(n)$ and $g(n)$, we get

$$\tilde{f}(z)\tilde{g}(z) = \left[\sum_{n=0}^{\infty}\frac{f(n)}{z^n}\right]\left[\sum_{m=0}^{\infty}\frac{g(m)}{z^m}\right]$$

$$= \left[f(0) + \frac{f(1)}{z} + \frac{f(2)}{z^2} + \cdots\right]\left[g(0) + \frac{g(1)}{z} + \frac{g(2)}{z^2} + \cdots\right]$$

$$= f(0)g(0) + \frac{f(0)g(1) + f(1)g(0)}{z} + \frac{f(0)g(2) + f(1)g(1) + f(2)g(0)}{z^2} + \cdots .$$

These expressions are the same. ∎

More useful in practice is the inverse of this result.

Corollary   If $\mathcal{Z}^{-1}\{\tilde{f}(z)\} = f$ and $\mathcal{Z}^{-1}\{\tilde{g}(z)\} = g$, then

$$\mathcal{Z}^{-1}\{\tilde{f}(z)\tilde{g}(z)\} = f * g. \tag{10.10b}$$

Example 10.8   Find the inverse z-transform for $\tilde{f}(z) = \dfrac{z^2}{(1-z)^4}$.

Solution   Since $\mathcal{Z}^{-1}\left\{\dfrac{z}{(1-z)^2}\right\} = n$, convolutions give

$$\mathcal{Z}^{-1}\left\{\frac{z^2}{(1-z)^4}\right\} = \mathcal{Z}^{-1}\left\{\left[\frac{z}{(1-z)^2}\right]\left[\frac{z}{(1-z)^2}\right]\right\} = n * n$$

$$= \sum_{k=0}^{n}k(n-k) = n\sum_{k=0}^{n}k - \sum_{k=0}^{n}k^2 = n\left[\frac{n(n+1)}{2}\right] - \frac{n(n+1)(2n+1)}{6}$$

$$= \frac{n(n-1)(n+1)}{6}. \bullet$$

EXERCISES 10.1

In Exercises 1–10 find the z-transform of the function $f(n)$. **Determine its domain of validity.**

1. $f(n) = a,$ a constant
2. $f(n) = h(n-2)$
3. $f(n) = h(n) - h(n-a),$ $a > 0$ an integer
4. $f(n) = h(n-a) - h(n-b),$ $b > a > 0$ integers
5. $f(n) = \delta(n-5)$
6. $f(n) = \delta(n-a) + \delta(n-b),$ $a > 0, b > 0$ integers
7. $f(n) = e^n$
8. $f(n) = a^n h(n-k),$ $a > 0$ a constant
9. $f(n) = a^n[h(n) - h(n-b)],$ $a > 0,$ $b > 0$ an integer
10. $f(n) = n\,h(n-k)$

In Exercises 11–24 find the inverse z-transform of the function $\tilde{f}(z)$, if it exists.

11. $\tilde{f}(z) = 1/z^3$
12. $\tilde{f}(z) = 4/z^6$
13. $\tilde{f}(z) = \dfrac{1}{z^3(z-1)}$
14. $\tilde{f}(z) = \dfrac{4}{3z^2(z-1)}$
15. $\tilde{f}(z) = \dfrac{4z}{(z-1)^2}$
16. $\tilde{f}(z) = \dfrac{z}{3+z}$

17. $\tilde{f}(z) = \dfrac{1}{z^2 + 5z}$

18. $\tilde{f}(z) = \dfrac{z^2}{(z-9)^3}$

19. $\tilde{f}(z) = \dfrac{z}{z^2 - 2z - 8}$

20. $\tilde{f}(z) = \dfrac{z^2 + 3}{z^3 - z^2 - 8z + 12}$

21. $\tilde{f}(z) = \dfrac{2z^2}{z - 1}$

22. $\tilde{f}(z) = \dfrac{3z^4}{2z^2 + z + 4}$

23. $\tilde{f}(z) = \dfrac{z^2 + 2}{z^4 - 1}$

24. $\tilde{f}(z) = \dfrac{z + 1}{z(z-1)^3}$

In Exercises 25–28 use residues to find the inverse z-transform of the function.

25. $\tilde{f}(z) = \dfrac{z}{z^2 - 2z - 8}$

26. $\tilde{f}(z) = \dfrac{z^2 + 3}{z^3 - z^2 - 8z + 12}$

27. $\tilde{f}(z) = \dfrac{z^2 + 2}{z^4 - 1}$

28. $\tilde{f}(z) = \dfrac{z + 1}{z(z-1)^3}$

29. Prove property 10.7a.

30. Prove property 10.8a.

31. If $f(n) = \begin{cases} 0, & n = 0 \\ 1/n, & n \geq 1, \end{cases}$ show that

$$\mathcal{Z}\{f(n)\} = \text{Log}\left(\dfrac{z}{z-1}\right).$$

§10.2   Application of the *z*-transform to First-order Difference Equations

Just as the Laplace transform reduces an ordinary differential equation to an algebraic equation, the *z*-transform reduces a difference equation to an algebraic equation. The following theorem allows us to do this for first-order equations.

Theorem 10.2   If $\tilde{f}(z) = \mathcal{Z}\{f(n)\}$, then the transform of the function $f(n+1)$ is

$$\mathcal{Z}\{f(n+1)\} = z\tilde{f}(z) - f(0)z. \tag{10.11}$$

Proof   By Definition 10.1,

$$\mathcal{Z}\{f(n+1)\} = \sum_{n=0}^{\infty} f(n+1)z^{-n} = \sum_{n=1}^{\infty} f(n)z^{-(n-1)}$$

$$= z\left[\sum_{n=0}^{\infty} f(n)z^{-n} - f(0)\right] = z[\tilde{f}(z) - f(0)]. \quad\blacksquare$$

Before doing some examples, we introduce terminology associated with difference equations. Because it parallels terminology for differential equations, we shall remind you of the terminology for differential equations and then state the correspondent for difference equations. The unknown in a differential equation is a function $f(x)$ of a continuous variable x; the unknown in a difference equation is a function $f(n)$ of the integer variable $n \geq 0$. A differential equation in $f(x)$ contains derivatives of the function like $f'(x)$ and $f''(x)$. An example of a second-order differential equation is $xf''(x) - 3f'(x) + 2x^2 f(x) = \sin x$. A difference equation in $f(n)$ contains differences of the function like $f(n+1) - f(n)$ and $f(n+2) - f(n+1)$. An example of a second-order difference equation might be

$$[f(n+2) - f(n+1)] - 3n[f(n+1) - f(n)] = n^2.$$

Values of the function with equal arguments are always brought together so that we would write

$$f(n+2) - (3n+1)f(n+1) + 3nf(n) = n^2.$$

In doing so we lose the differences, but the resemblance to the form for a second-order differential equation is unmistakable. The general linear first-order differential equation is

$$p(x)f'(x) + q(x)f(x) = g(x). \tag{10.12}$$

The general linear first-order difference equation is

$$p(n)f(n+1) + q(n)f(n) = g(n). \tag{10.13}$$

The general linear second-order differential equation is

$$p(x)f''(x) + q(x)f'(x) + r(x)f(x) = g(x). \tag{10.14}$$

The general linear second-order difference equation is

$$p(n)f(n+2) + q(n)f(n+1) + r(n)f(n) = g(n). \tag{10.15}$$

Equations 10.12–10.15 are said to be **homogeneous** if the function on the right side of the equation is identically equal to zero; they are said to be **nonhomogeneous** if this function is not the zero function. Most of our discussions centre around difference equations in which the coefficients $p(n)$ and $q(n)$ in equation 10.13, and the coefficients $p(n)$, $q(n)$ and $r(n)$ in equation 10.15 are constants. The general linear, first-order difference equation with constant coefficients is

$$p\,f(n+1) + q\,f(n) = g(n). \tag{10.16}$$

The following examples illustrate how property 10.11 of the z-transform reduces this difference equation to an algebraic equation. In many applications, it is important to know whether the solution $f(n)$ of a difference equation has a limit as $n \to \infty$. We therefore determine whether this limit exists in each example. In effect, we are discussing stability of the difference equation, a topic that we deal with in detail in Section 10.6.

Example 10.9   Solve the homogeneous, linear, first-order difference equation

$$f(n+1) = \frac{1}{3}f(n), \quad f(0) = 2.$$

Does the solution have a limit as $n \to \infty$?

Solution   When we take z-transforms of both sides of the difference equation and use equation 10.11, we obtain

$$z\tilde{f}(z) - f(0)z = \frac{1}{3}\tilde{f}(z) \qquad \Longrightarrow \qquad z\tilde{f}(z) - 2z = \frac{1}{3}\tilde{f}(z).$$

We solve this equation for $\tilde{f}(z)$,

$$\tilde{f}(z) = \frac{6z}{3z - 1}.$$

The solution of the difference equation is the inverse transform of this function; the coefficients in the Laurent series of this function valid in some infinite annulus $|z| > R$. This is straightforward,

$$\tilde{f}(z) = \frac{6z}{3z\left(1 - \dfrac{1}{3z}\right)} = \frac{2}{1 - \dfrac{1}{3z}} = 2\sum_{n=0}^{\infty}\left(\frac{1}{3z}\right)^n = \sum_{n=0}^{\infty}\frac{2}{3^n z^n},$$

valid for $|1/(3z)| < 1 \implies |z| > 1/3$. Consequently, $f(n) = 2/3^n$. The solution has limit 0 as $n \to \infty$. We could have obtained the same result by calculating the first few values of $f(n)$:

$$f(1) = \frac{1}{3}f(0) = \frac{2}{3}, \quad f(2) = \frac{1}{3}f(1) = \frac{2}{3^2}, \quad f(3) = \frac{1}{3}f(2) = \frac{2}{3^3}, \ldots.$$

The pattern emerging is $f(n) = 2/3^n$, and this could be verified by mathematical induction.●

Example 10.10   Solve the nonhomogeneous, linear, first-order difference equation

$$f(n+1) + 4f(n) = 25n, \quad f(0) = 0.$$

Does the solution have a limit as $n \to \infty$?

Solution When we take z-transforms of both sides of the difference equation and use equation 10.11 and Example 10.4, we obtain

$$z\tilde{f}(z) + 4\tilde{f}(z) = \frac{25z}{(1-z)^2} \quad \Longrightarrow \quad \tilde{f}(z) = \frac{25z}{(1-z)^2(z+4)}.$$

The solution of the difference equation is the inverse transform of this function; the coefficients in the Laurent series of this function valid in some infinite annulus $|z| > R$. We begin with the partial fraction decomposition of $\tilde{f}(z)$,

$$\tilde{f}(z) = \frac{-4}{1-z} + \frac{5}{(1-z)^2} - \frac{4}{z+4}.$$

Geometric series can be used to expand each of these in powers of $1/z$,

$$\frac{1}{1-z} = \frac{1}{-z(1-1/z)} = -\frac{1}{z}\sum_{n=0}^{\infty}\left(\frac{1}{z}\right)^n = -\sum_{n=0}^{\infty}\frac{1}{z^{n+1}},$$

$$\frac{1}{(1-z)^2} = -\sum_{n=0}^{\infty}\frac{-(n+1)}{z^{n+2}} = \sum_{n=0}^{\infty}\frac{n+1}{z^{n+2}},$$

$$\frac{1}{z+4} = \frac{1}{z(1+4/z)} = \frac{1}{z}\sum_{n=0}^{\infty}\left(-\frac{4}{z}\right)^n = \sum_{n=0}^{\infty}\frac{(-4)^n}{z^{n+1}}.$$

The first two are valid for $|z| > 1$ and the last for $|z| > 4$. When these are substituted into $\tilde{f}(z)$, the result is

$$\tilde{f}(z) = 4\sum_{n=0}^{\infty}\frac{1}{z^{n+1}} + 5\sum_{n=0}^{\infty}\frac{n+1}{z^{n+2}} - 4\sum_{n=0}^{\infty}\frac{(-4)^n}{z^{n+1}}$$

$$= \sum_{n=1}^{\infty}\frac{4}{z^n} + \sum_{n=2}^{\infty}\frac{5(n-1)}{z^n} + \sum_{n=1}^{\infty}\frac{(-4)^n}{z^n}$$

$$= \sum_{n=2}^{\infty}\frac{4 + 5(n-1) + (-4)^n}{z^n}.$$

The solution of the difference equation is therefore

$$f(n) = \begin{cases} 0, & n = 0 \\ 0, & n = 1 \\ 4 + (-4)^n + 5(n-1), & n \geq 2. \end{cases}$$

Since the formula $4 + (-4)^n + 5(n-1)$ gives 0 for $n = 0$ and $n = 1$, the solution of the difference equation can be written simply as $f(n) = 4 + (-4)^n + 5(n-1)$. There is no limit as $n \to \infty$. •

When $g(n)$ in difference equation 10.16 is a constant as well as p and q, it is straightforward to derive a general solution. Because p cannot be zero, we can divide each term by it and write the equation in the form

$$f(n+1) = r\,f(n) + g.$$

Theorem 10.3 The solution of the linear, first-order difference equation

$$f(n+1) = r\,f(n) + g, \qquad f(0) = f_0, \tag{10.17}$$

is

$$f(n) = \begin{cases} f_0 r^n + g\left(\dfrac{1 - r^n}{1 - r}\right), & r \neq 1 \\ f_0 + ng, & r = 1. \end{cases} \tag{10.18}$$

The limit of the solution is

$$\lim_{n \to \infty} f(n) = \begin{cases} \dfrac{g}{1 - r}, & |r| < 1 \\ \text{does not exist,} & |r| \geq 1. \end{cases} \tag{10.19}$$

A proof is developed in Exercise 22.

EXERCISES 10.2

In Exercises 1–5 use equation 10.11 to find the solution of the first-order difference equation. Determine whether the solution has a limit as $n \to \infty$.

1. $f(n+1) = 3f(n), \quad f(0) = 2$

2. $f(n+1) = \dfrac{1}{5}f(n), \quad f(0) = 1$

3. $f(n+1) = -\dfrac{2}{3}f(n), \quad f(0) = -2$

4. $f(n+1) = \dfrac{3}{2}f(n), \quad f(0) = 4$

5. $f(n+1) = -\dfrac{3}{7}f(n), \quad f(0) = 2$

In Exercises 6–9 use equation 10.18 to find the solution of the first-order difference equation. Determine whether the solution has a limit as $n \to \infty$.

6. $f(n+1) = \dfrac{5}{3}f(n) - 2, \quad f(0) = 0$

7. $f(n+1) = -\dfrac{1}{2}f(n) + 4, \quad f(0) = -1$

8. $f(n+1) = \dfrac{5}{12}f(n) - \dfrac{1}{3}, \quad f(0) = 2$

9. $f(n+1) = -f(n) + 5, \quad f(0) = -2$

In Exercises 10–13 use z-transforms and Example 10.3 in Section 10.1 to solve the difference equation. Determine whether the solution has a limit as $n \to \infty$.

10. $f(n+1) = f(n) + \dfrac{1}{3^n}, \quad f(0) = 1$

11. $f(n+1) = f(n) - \left(\dfrac{2}{3}\right)^n, \quad f(0) = -1$

12. $f(n+1) = 2f(n) + \dfrac{1}{(-2)^n}, \quad f(0) = 1$

13. $f(n+1) = \dfrac{1}{3}f(n) - 2^{n-2}, \quad f(0) = -1$

Instead of using the z-transform to solve a difference equation, it is sometimes easier to iterate the recursive definition and recognize the pattern of terms. Do this in Exercises 14–18.

14. $f(n+1) = (n+1)f(n), \quad f(0) = 1$

15. $f(n+1) = \dfrac{f(n)}{n+1}, \quad f(0) = 3$

16. $f(n+1) = \dfrac{(n+2)f(n)}{n+1}, \quad f(0) = 1$

17. $f(n+1) = \dfrac{-3f(n)}{(n+1)^2}, \quad f(0) = -1,$

18. $f(n+1) = f(n) + n, \quad f(0) = 0$

19. Find the solution of the linear, first-order difference equation

$$f(n+1) = rf(n) + a^n, \quad f(0) = f_0,$$

where a is a constant.

20. The first seven terms of a sequence are $-1, 1, 5, 11, 19, 29$, and 41. Show that the terms satisfy the first-order difference equation $f(n+1) - f(n) = 2(n+1)$, and use it to find an explicit formula for the general term of the sequence.

21. Prove that the solution of the difference equation

$$f(n+1) = rf(n) + g(n), \quad f(0) = a,$$

where r is a constant and $g(n)$ is a given function is

$$f(n) = ar^n + \sum_{k=1}^{n} r^{k-1} g(n-k).$$

22. Prove Theorem 10.3.

§10.3 Applications of First-order Difference Equations

In this section, we give examples and exercises that illustrate applications of first-order difference equations.

Example 10.11 For some insects, one generation dies out before the next generation is born. It is sometimes assumed that the increase in size of the population from one generation to the next is proportional to the size of the former generation. If $f(0)$ is the size of the first generation, find the size of the nth generation.

Solution If $f(n-1)$ is the size of the nth generation, the fact that the increase in population from one generation to the next is proportional to the size of the former generation is expressed as

$$f(n+1) - f(n) = kf(n),$$

where k is a constant. This linear difference equation can be expressed in form 10.17 with $g = 0$,

$$f(n+1) = (k+1)f(n),$$

and therefore its solution, according to equation 10.18, is

$$f(n) = f(0)(k+1)^n.$$

The size of the nth generation is therefore $f(n-1) = f(0)(k+1)^{n-1}$.•

Example 10.12 When a certain drug is injected into the body, the body uses up 5% of the remaining drug each hour. If equal injections P of the drug are given every two hours, find a formula for the amount of drug in the body immediately before the nth injection.

Solution Suppose we denote by $f(n)$ the amount of drug in the body immediately before the nth injection. Then the amount immediately after this injection is $f(n) + P$. During the next two hours, this amount of drug will decrease to $(0.95)^2[f(n)+P]$. Consequently, the amount of drug in the body immediately before the next injection is $f(n+1) = (0.95)^2[f(n) + P]$. When we add the initial condition that $f(0) = 0$, we obtain the linear, first-order difference equation

$$f(n+1) = 0.9025[f(n) + P], \qquad f(0) = 0.$$

Equation 10.18 yields the solution

$$f(n) = (0.9025)P\left(\frac{1 - 0.9025^{n-1}}{1 - 0.9025}\right) = 9.256P(1 - 0.9025^{n-1}).•$$

Using differential equations, it is possible to find the amount of drug in the body at any time t; it is a matter of solving many differential equations, one between each pair of injections. The above analysis is much simpler, but it does not give us the amount of drug in the body at every instant of time. We have it only at specific times, immediately before and after each injection. But this may be entirely adequate for whatever questions might be appropriate. Notice for example that $\lim_{n\to\infty} f(n) = 9.256P$. In other words, after many, many injections, the drug accumulates in the body to a point where the amount after each injection is approximately $10.256P$. During the subsequent two hours, the amount in the body decreases to $9.256P$. The body essentially maintains a constant level of $9.256P$ and each injection is used up over the next two hours.

Example 10.13 You borrow $5000 from the bank. You agree to repay the loan by paying $150 installments on the first day of each month. The bank charges 6% per year, compounded monthly, on the outstanding principal, subtracts this from the $150, and applies the difference to the principal. Find a formula for the amount owing after each payment.

Solution Suppose we let $f(n)$ represent the outstanding debt immediately after the nth payment. Interest on this debt at the end of the next month is $0.005f(n)$, leaving an oustanding balance of $f(n) + 0.005f(n) = 1.005f(n)$ immediately before the next payment. Hence, the amount owing immediately after the next payment is $f(n+1) = 1.005f(n) - 150$. When this is combined with $f(0) = 5000$, the function $f(n)$ is defined by the difference equation

$$f(n+1) = 1.005f(n) - 150, \quad f(0) = 5000.$$

According to equation 10.18, the solution of this difference equation is

$$f(n) = 5000(1.005)^n - 150\left(\frac{1 - 1.005^n}{1 - 1.005}\right) = 30\,000 - 25\,000(1.005)^n.\bullet$$

EXERCISES 10.3

1. The size of one generation of a certain insect is $i\%$ greater than the previous generation. If the first generation has size P_0, find the size of the nth generation.

2. Each month you deposit $50 into an account, called an annuity, that earns interest at 5% compounded monthly. How much money is in the annuity immediately after the (a) 20th (b) 40th (c)60th deposits?

3. At the beginning of each interest period, of which there are m per year, $P is deposited into an annuity that earns $i\%$, compounded m times per year. Find a formula for the amount in the annuity immediately after the nth deposit.

4. You borrow $10,000 from the bank. You agree to repay the loan by paying $200 installments on the first day of each month. The bank charges 6% per year, compounded monthly, on the outstanding principal, subtracts this from the $200, and applies the difference to the principal. Find a formula for the amount owing after each payment.

5. A loan of $A is to be repaid with equal monthly installments of $P. Interest at the rate of $i\%$ per year, compounded monthly, on the remaining principal is subtracted from the installment, and the balance is applied to the principal. Find a formula for the amount owing after each payment. What is the minimum monthly payment in order that the loan can be paid off some day?

6. When morphine is injected into the body, the body uses up 10% of the remainder each hour. If doses in the amount P are given every three hours, find a formula for the amount in the body immediately before the nth dose. What minimal amount resides in the body after a very long time?

7. A lake is to be stocked with a new species of fish by adding 1000 new fish each spring. During the year whatever fish are in the lake increase in number by 10%. How many fish are in the lake immediately after the nth batch has been added?

8. Oysters multiply in such a way that each year their number increases by 5%. There are an estimated 1 000 000 oysters just prior to the first harvest. If a company harvests (a) 40,000, (b) 60,000 oysters each spring, find the number of oysters just before the nth harvest? Find the limit as $n \to \infty$ of each answer.

§10.4   Application of the z-transform to Second-order Difference Equations

In Section 10.2, we showed how z-transforms reduce first-order difference equations to algebraic equations. For second-order equations, we require the following extension of Theorem 10.2.

Theorem 10.4   If $\tilde{f}(z) = \mathcal{Z}\{f(n)\}$, then,

$$\mathcal{Z}\{f(n+2)\} = z^2 \tilde{f}(z) - f(0)z^2 - f(1)z. \qquad (10.20)$$

Proof   By equation 10.11,

$$\begin{aligned}
\mathcal{Z}\{f(n+2)\} &= z\mathcal{Z}\{f(n+1)\} - f(1)z = z[z\tilde{f}(z) - f(0)z] - f(1)z \\
&= z^2 \tilde{f}(z) - f(0)z^2 - f(1)z. \quad \blacksquare
\end{aligned}$$

For higher order difference equations, we would require $\mathcal{Z}\{f(n+p)\}$ for integers $p \geq 3$, but our discussions will be confined to first- and second-order equations.

Example 10.14   The Fibonacci sequence $\{c_n\}$ is defined recursively by

$$c_0 = 0, \qquad c_1 = 1, \qquad c_{n+2} = c_{n+1} + c_n, \quad n \geq 0.$$

Use the z-transform to find an explicit formula for c_n.

Solution   Equivalent to this recursive definition of the sequence is the second-order difference equation

$$f(n+2) = f(n+1) + f(n), \quad f(0) = 0, \quad f(1) = 1.$$

When we take z-transforms of both sides of the difference equation and use equations 10.11 and 10.20, we obtain

$$z^2 \tilde{f}(z) - f(0)z^2 - f(1)z = z\tilde{f}(z) - f(0)z + \tilde{f}(z) \quad \Longrightarrow \quad z^2 \tilde{f}(z) - z = z\tilde{f}(z) + \tilde{f}(z).$$

We solve this for $\tilde{f}(z)$,

$$\tilde{f}(z) = \frac{z}{z^2 - z - 1}.$$

The solution of the difference equation is the inverse transform of this function; the coefficients in the Laurent series of this function valid in some infinite annulus $|z| > R$. We use partial fractions to write

$$\begin{aligned}
\tilde{f}(z) &= \frac{z}{\left(z - \dfrac{1+\sqrt{5}}{2}\right)\left(z - \dfrac{1-\sqrt{5}}{2}\right)} = \frac{\dfrac{1+\sqrt{5}}{2\sqrt{5}}}{z - \dfrac{1+\sqrt{5}}{2}} - \frac{\dfrac{1-\sqrt{5}}{2\sqrt{5}}}{z - \dfrac{1-\sqrt{5}}{2}} \\[2em]
&= \frac{1+\sqrt{5}}{2\sqrt{5}z}\left(\frac{1}{1 - \dfrac{1+\sqrt{5}}{2z}}\right) - \frac{1-\sqrt{5}}{2\sqrt{5}z}\left(\frac{1}{1 - \dfrac{1-\sqrt{5}}{2z}}\right) \\[2em]
&= \frac{1+\sqrt{5}}{2\sqrt{5}z}\sum_{n=0}^{\infty}\left(\frac{1+\sqrt{5}}{2z}\right)^n - \frac{1-\sqrt{5}}{2\sqrt{5}z}\sum_{n=0}^{\infty}\left(\frac{1-\sqrt{5}}{2z}\right)^n
\end{aligned}$$

$$= \frac{1}{\sqrt{5}} \sum_{n=0}^{\infty} \left[\frac{(1+\sqrt{5})^{n+1} - (1-\sqrt{5})^{n+1}}{2^{n+1} z^{n+1}} \right]$$

$$= \frac{1}{\sqrt{5}} \sum_{n=1}^{\infty} \left[\frac{(1+\sqrt{5})^{n} - (1-\sqrt{5})^{n}}{2^{n} z^{n}} \right].$$

Thus, the solution of the difference equation, and the term c_n of the Fibonacci sequence is

$$f(n) = \frac{(1+\sqrt{5})^{n} - (1-\sqrt{5})^{n}}{\sqrt{5} \cdot 2^{n}}.$$

The sequence does not have a limit as $n \to \infty$. •

Example 10.15   Find the solution of the second-order difference equation

$$9f(n+2) - 6f(n+1) + f(n) = 0, \quad f(0) = 1, \quad f(1) = 2.$$

Solution   When we take z-transforms of both sides of the difference equation and use equations 10.11 and 10.20, we obtain

$$9[z^2 \tilde{f}(z) - f(0)z^2 - f(1)z] - 6[z\tilde{f}(z) - f(0)z] + \tilde{f}(z) = 0,$$

from which

$$9[z^2 \tilde{f}(z) - z^2 - 2z] - 6[z\tilde{f}(z) - z] + \tilde{f}(z) = 0.$$

We solve this for $\tilde{f}(z)$,

$$\tilde{f}(z) = \frac{9z^2 + 12z}{9z^2 - 6z + 1} = \frac{9z^2 + 12z}{(3z-1)^2}.$$

The solution of the difference equation is the inverse transform of this function; the coefficients in the Laurent series of this function valid in some infinite annulus $|z| > R$. We begin by writing

$$\tilde{f}(z) = 1 + \frac{18z - 1}{(3z-1)^2},$$

and expand $1/(3z-1)$ in negative powers of z,

$$\frac{1}{3z-1} = \frac{1}{3z\left(1 - \dfrac{1}{3z}\right)} = \frac{1}{3z} \sum_{n=0}^{\infty} \left(\frac{1}{3z}\right)^n = \sum_{n=0}^{\infty} \frac{1}{3^{n+1} z^{n+1}},$$

valid for $|z| > 1/3$. Differentiation gives

$$\frac{-3}{(3z-1)^2} = \sum_{n=0}^{\infty} \frac{-(n+1)}{3^{n+1} z^{n+2}} \quad \Longrightarrow \quad \frac{1}{(3z-1)^2} = \sum_{n=0}^{\infty} \frac{(n+1)}{3^{n+2} z^{n+2}}.$$

Substituting this into $\tilde{f}(z)$ gives

$$\tilde{f}(z) = 1 + 18 \sum_{n=0}^{\infty} \frac{(n+1)}{3^{n+2} z^{n+1}} - \sum_{n=0}^{\infty} \frac{(n+1)}{3^{n+2} z^{n+2}} = 1 + \sum_{n=1}^{\infty} \frac{2n}{3^{n-1} z^{n}} - \sum_{n=2}^{\infty} \frac{(n-1)}{3^{n} z^{n}}$$

$$= 1 + \frac{2}{z} + \sum_{n=2}^{\infty} \frac{5n+1}{3^{n} z^{n}}.$$

Thus, the solution of the difference equation is

$$f(n) = \begin{cases} 1, & n = 0 \\ 2, & n = 1 \\ \dfrac{5n + 1}{3^n}, & n \geq 2 \end{cases}$$

Since the formula $(5n + 1)/3^n$ gives 1 when $n = 0$, and 2 when $n = 1$, the solution can be written in the form $f(n) = (5n + 1)/3^n$. The limit of the solution as $n \to \infty$ is 0.●

Example 10.16 Find the solution of the second-order difference equation

$$f(n + 2) - 2f(n + 1) + 2f(n) = 0, \quad f(0) = 2, \quad f(1) = 1.$$

Solution When we take z-transforms of both sides of the difference equation and use equations 10.11 and 10.20, we obtain

$$[z^2 \tilde{f}(z) - f(0)z^2 - f(1)z] - 2[z\tilde{f}(z) - f(0)z] + 2\tilde{f}(z) = 0,$$

from which

$$[z^2 \tilde{f}(z) - 2z^2 - z] - 2[z\tilde{f}(z) - 2z] + 2\tilde{f}(z) = 0.$$

We solve this for $\tilde{f}(z)$,

$$\tilde{f}(z) = \frac{2z^2 - 3z}{z^2 - 2z + 2}.$$

The solution of the difference equation is the inverse transform of this function; the coefficients in the Laurent series of this function valid in some infinite annulus $|z| > R$. We begin with the partial fraction decomposition of $\tilde{f}(z)$,

$$\tilde{f}(z) = 2 + \frac{z - 4}{z^2 - 2z + 2} = 2 + \frac{z - 4}{(z - 1 - i)(z - 1 + i)} = 2 + \frac{(1 + 3i)/2}{z - 1 - i} + \frac{(1 - 3i)/2}{z - 1 + i}.$$

If we expand each term in negative powers of z, we obtain

$$\tilde{f}(z) = 2 + \frac{(1 + 3i)/2}{z\left(1 - \dfrac{1 + i}{z}\right)} + \frac{(1 - 3i)/2}{z\left(1 - \dfrac{1 - i}{z}\right)}$$

$$= 2 + \frac{1 + 3i}{2z} \sum_{n=0}^{\infty} \left(\frac{1 + i}{z}\right)^n + \frac{1 - 3i}{2z} \sum_{n=0}^{\infty} \left(\frac{1 - i}{z}\right)^n$$

$$= 2 + \frac{1}{z} + \sum_{n=1}^{\infty} \frac{(1 + 3i)(1 + i)^n + (1 - 3i)(1 - i)^n}{2z^{n+1}}.$$

We now substitute the exponential forms $1 + i = \sqrt{2}e^{\pi i/4}$, $1 - i = \sqrt{2}e^{-\pi i/4}$, $1 + 3i = \sqrt{10}e^{\theta i}$, $1 - 3i = \sqrt{10}e^{-\theta i}$, where $\theta = \text{Tan}^{-1}3$,

$$\tilde{f}(z) = 2 + \frac{1}{z} + \sum_{n=1}^{\infty} \frac{\sqrt{10}e^{\theta i}(\sqrt{2}e^{\pi i/4})^n + \sqrt{10}e^{-\theta i}(\sqrt{2}e^{-\pi i/4})^n}{2z^{n+1}}$$

$$= 2 + \frac{1}{z} + \sum_{n=1}^{\infty} \frac{\sqrt{10} \cdot 2^{n/2}[e^{(\theta + n\pi/4)i} + e^{-(\theta + n\pi/4)i}]}{2z^{n+1}}$$

$$= 2 + \frac{1}{z} + \sum_{n=1}^{\infty} \frac{\sqrt{10} \cdot 2^{n/2} \cos\left(\theta + n\pi/4\right)}{z^{n+1}}$$

$$= 2 + \frac{1}{z} + \sum_{n=2}^{\infty} \frac{\sqrt{10} \cdot 2^{(n-1)/2} \cos\left[\theta + (n-1)\pi/4\right]}{z^{n}}.$$

This simplifies to

$$\tilde{f}(z) = 2 + \frac{1}{z} + \sum_{n=2}^{\infty} \frac{2^{n/2}}{z^{n}} \left(2\cos\frac{n\pi}{4} - \sin\frac{n\pi}{4}\right).$$

Thus, the solution of the difference equation is

$$f(n) = \begin{cases} 2, & n = 0 \\ 1, & n = 1 \\ 2^{n/2}\left(2\cos\dfrac{n\pi}{4} - \sin\dfrac{n\pi}{4}\right), & n \geq 2. \end{cases}$$

Since the formula for the $n \geq 2$ case also gives $f(0) = 2$ and $f(1) = 1$, the solution for all n is

$$f(n) = 2^{n/2}\left(2\cos\frac{n\pi}{4} - \sin\frac{n\pi}{4}\right).$$

This solution does not have a limit as $n \to \infty$. •

The last three examples contained linear, homogeneous, second-order, constant coefficient difference equations, equations that can always be expressed in the form

$$f(n+2) + pf(n+1) + qf(n) = 0, \quad f(0) = f_0, \quad f(1) = f_1, \qquad (10.21)$$

where p and q are constants. When we apply the z-transform to this difference equation, and solve for $\tilde{f}(z)$, the transform is always of the form

$$\tilde{f}(z) = \frac{R(z)}{z^2 + pz + q}.$$

The quadratic equation

$$z^2 + pz + q = 0 \qquad (10.22)$$

is called the **characteristic equation** associated with equation 10.21. Its roots dictate the form of the solution of the difference equation. The following theorem contains the results.

Theorem 10.5 Let z_1 and z_2 be the roots of characteristic equation 10.22 associated with difference equation 10.21. Then,
   (i) If $z_1 \neq z_2$ are real, a solution of the difference equation in 10.21 is

$$f(n) = Az_1{}^n + Bz_2{}^n \qquad (10.23a)$$

for arbitrary constants A and B.
   (ii) If $z = z_1 = z_2$, a solution of the difference equation in 10.21 is

$$f(n) = (A + Bn)z^n \qquad (10.23b)$$

for arbitrary constants A and B.

(iii) If $z_{1,2} = a \pm bi$, where $b > 0$, a solution of the difference equation in 10.21 is

$$f(n) = r^n (A \cos n\theta + B \sin n\theta), \qquad (10.23c)$$

where r and θ are the modulus and argument of $a + bi$, and A and B are arbitrary constants.

Constants A and B are determined by the conditions $f(0) = f_0$ and $f(1) = f_1$.

We illustrate the third case in the following example. Examples of the other two cases can be found in the exercises.

Example 10.17 Find the solution of the difference equation

$$f(n+2) = \frac{3}{5} f(n+1) - \frac{1}{4} f(n), \quad f(0) = -1, \quad f(1) = 1.$$

Solution The characteristic equation

$$0 = z^2 - \frac{3z}{5} + \frac{1}{4} = \frac{1}{20}(20z^2 - 12z + 5),$$

has solutions

$$z = \frac{12 \pm \sqrt{144 - 400}}{40} = \frac{3 \pm 4i}{10}.$$

Since the modulus and principal value of the argument of $(3 + 4i)/10$ are $r = 1/2$ and $\theta = \text{Tan}^{-1}(4/3)$, equation 10.23c gives

$$f(n) = \frac{1}{2^n}(A \cos n\theta + B \sin n\theta).$$

For $f(0) = -1$ and $f(1) = 1$, A and B must satisfy

$$-1 = A, \qquad 1 = \frac{1}{2}(A \cos\theta + B \sin\theta).$$

With $\sin\theta = 4/5$ and $\cos\theta = 3/5$, these give $A = -1$ and $B = 13/4$, and therefore

$$f(n) = \frac{1}{2^n}\left(-\cos n\theta + \frac{13}{4}\sin n\theta\right) = \frac{1}{2^{n+2}}(13\sin n\theta - 4\cos n\theta).$$

This function approaches zero for large n.•

We now turn our attention to nonhomogeneous equations. Like differential equations, the solution is composed of two parts, one being the solution of the associated, homogeneous equation, and the other a particular solution of the non-homogeneous equation. We shall not develop the corresponding theory for difference equations, but we should at least examine the final solution to see that it takes this form.

Example 10.18 Solve the nonhomogeneous linear, second-order difference equation

$$f(n+2) + 4f(n+1) - 5f(n) = 2n - 3, \quad f(0) = 0, \quad f(1) = 0.$$

Solution When we take z-transforms of both sides of the difference equation and use $f(0) = 0$ and $f(1) = 0$, we obtain

$$z^2 \tilde{f}(z) + 4z\tilde{f}(z) - 5\tilde{f}(z) = \mathcal{Z}\{2n - 3\}.$$

Transforms of the terms on the right were calculated in Examples 10.2 and 10.4,

$$z^2 \tilde{f}(z) + 4z\tilde{f}(z) - 5\tilde{f}(z) = \frac{2z}{(z-1)^2} - \frac{3z}{z-1}.$$

We solve this for $\tilde{f}(z)$,

$$\tilde{f}(z) = \frac{2z}{(z-1)^2(z^2 + 4z - 5)} - \frac{3z}{(z-1)(z^2 + 4z - 5)} = \frac{5z - 3z^2}{(z-1)^3(z+5)}.$$

The solution of the difference equation is the inverse transform of this function. We begin with the partial fraction decomposition of $\tilde{f}(z)$,

$$\tilde{f}(z) = \frac{-25/54}{z-1} - \frac{2/9}{(z-1)^2} + \frac{1/3}{(z-1)^3} + \frac{25/54}{z+5}.$$

If we expand each term in negative powers of z, we obtain

$$\frac{1}{z-1} = \frac{1}{z(1 - 1/z)} = \frac{1}{z}\sum_{n=0}^{\infty}\left(\frac{1}{z}\right)^n = \sum_{n=0}^{\infty}\frac{1}{z^{n+1}},$$

$$\frac{-1}{(z-1)^2} = \sum_{n=0}^{\infty}\frac{-(n+1)}{z^{n+2}} = -\sum_{n=0}^{\infty}\frac{n+1}{z^{n+2}},$$

$$\frac{2}{(z-1)^3} = -\sum_{n=0}^{\infty}\frac{-(n+1)(n+2)}{z^{n+3}} = \sum_{n=0}^{\infty}\frac{(n+1)(n+2)}{z^{n+3}},$$

$$\frac{1}{z+5} = \frac{1}{z(1 + 5/z)} = \frac{1}{z}\sum_{n=0}^{\infty}\left(-\frac{5}{z}\right)^n = \sum_{n=0}^{\infty}\frac{(-5)^n}{z^{n+1}},$$

valid for $|z| > 5$. We substitute these into the partial fraction decomposition,

$$\tilde{f}(z) = \frac{1}{54}\left[-25\sum_{n=0}^{\infty}\frac{1}{z^{n+1}} - 12\sum_{n=0}^{\infty}\frac{n+1}{z^{n+2}} + 18\sum_{n=0}^{\infty}\frac{(n+1)(n+2)}{2z^{n+3}} + 25\sum_{n=0}^{\infty}\frac{(-5)^n}{z^{n+1}}\right]$$

$$= \frac{1}{54}\left[\sum_{n=1}^{\infty}\frac{-25}{z^n} + \sum_{n=2}^{\infty}\frac{-12(n-1)}{z^n} + \sum_{n=3}^{\infty}\frac{9(n-2)(n-1)}{z^n} + \sum_{n=1}^{\infty}\frac{(-5)^{n+1}}{z^n}\right]$$

$$= \frac{1}{54}\left[-\frac{25}{z} - \frac{25}{z^2} - \frac{12}{z^2} + \frac{25}{z} - \frac{125}{z^2} + \sum_{n=3}^{\infty}\frac{-25 - 12(n-1) + 9(n-2)(n-1) + (-5)^{n+1}}{z^n}\right]$$

$$= \frac{1}{54}\left[-\frac{162}{z^2} + \sum_{n=3}^{\infty}\frac{9n^2 - 39n + 5 + (-5)^{n+1}}{z^n}\right].$$

The solution of the difference equation is therefore

$$f(n) = \begin{cases} 0, & n = 0 \\ 0, & n = 1 \\ -3, & n = 2 \\ \dfrac{9n^2 - 39n + 5 + (-5)^{n+1}}{54}, & n \geq 3. \end{cases}$$

Since the formula for $n \geq 3$ also gives the values for $f(0)$, $f(1)$, and $f(2)$, we can write that the solution is

$$f(n) = \frac{9n^2 - 39n + 5 + (-5)^{n+1}}{54}.$$

The characteristic equation for the difference equation is $z^2 + 4z - 5 = 0$ with solutions $z = 1, -5$. The solution of the difference equation should therefore contain terms of the form $A + B(-5)^n$, as indeed it does.●

EXERCISES 10.4

In Exercises 1–10 find the solution of the linear, homogeneous, second-order difference equation.

1. $f(n+2) + 2f(n+1) - 3f(n) = 0$, $\quad f(0) = 1$, $\quad f(1) = 2$

2. $2f(n+2) - f(n+1) - f(n) = 0$, $\quad f(0) = 1$, $\quad f(1) = 2$

3. $f(n+2) - \frac{1}{3}f(n+1) - \frac{1}{9}f(n) = 0$, $\quad f(0) = 1$, $\quad f(1) = 1$

4. $f(n+2) - 2f(n+1) - 2f(n) = 0$, $\quad f(0) = 0$, $\quad f(1) = 2$

5. $f(n+2) + 4f(n+1) + 4f(n) = 0$, $\quad f(0) = -3$, $\quad f(1) = 2$

6. $9f(n+2) - 6f(n+1) + f(n) = 0$, $\quad f(0) = 1$, $\quad f(1) = 1$

7. $f(n+2) - f(n+1) + 4f(n) = 0$, $\quad f(0) = 0$, $\quad f(1) = 1$

8. $9f(n+2) + 30f(n+1) + 25f(n) = 0$, $\quad f(0) = -1$, $\quad f(1) = 1$

9. $3f(n+2) + 3f(n+1) + f(n) = 0$, $\quad f(0) = 0$, $\quad f(1) = 2$

10. $f(n+2) + 2f(n+1) + 2f(n) = 0$, $\quad f(0) = 1$, $\quad f(1) = 2$

11. Find the solution of the difference equation

$$2f(n+2) - f(n+1) - f(n) = 0, \quad f(0) = a, \quad f(1) = b,$$

where a and b are arbitrary numbers.

12. Prove that for any values of $f(0)$ and $f(1)$, the solution of the difference equation

$$f(n+2) = \frac{2}{3}f(n+1) - \frac{1}{9}f(n)$$

has limit zero.

13. Repeat Exercise 12 for the diference equation

$$f(n+2) = \frac{1}{6}[f(n+1) + f(n)].$$

14. Repeat Exercise 12 for the difference equation

$$f(n+2) = \frac{1}{6}[f(n+1) - f(n)].$$

15. Show that when roots of characteristic equation 10.22 have moduli less than 1, the solution of problem 10.21 has limit 0 as $n \to \infty$.

16. Show that the solution of problem 10.21 has a nonzero limit if and only if its characteristic equation has exactly one root equal to 1 and a second root with absolute value less than 1.

17. The first seven terms of a sequence are 0, -2, 2, 18, 52, 110, and 198. Show that the terms satisfy the second-order difference equation $f(n+2) - 2f(n+1) + f(n) = 6(n+1)$, and use it to find an explicit formula for the general term of the sequence.

§10.5 Applications of Second-order Difference Equations

In this section we consider applications of linear, second-order difference equations.

Gambler's Ruin

A gambler begins with \$$n$, where n is a positive integer. Each time an unbiased coin is tossed, the gambler bets \$1 that it will come up heads. If it does, he wins \$1; if it doesn't, he loses the dollar he bet. The gambler quits when he loses all his money or when he has \$N where $N > n$ is a value decided in advance. We would like to calculate the probability $P(n)$ that the gambler runs out of money when he begins with \$$n$. Certainly we can say that $P(0) = 1$ and $P(N) = 0$. What about $P(n)$ for $1 \leq n \leq N - 1$? When the gambler has \$$n$, and the coin is tossed, it can come up heads or tails, each with probability $1/2$. If it comes up heads, then he has \$$(n + 1)$, and the probability that he runs out of money is $P(n + 1)$. If it comes up tails, then he has \$$(n - 1)$, and the probability that he loses his money is $P(n - 1)$. It follows that

$$P(n) = \frac{1}{2}P(n + 1) + \frac{1}{2}P(n - 1) \quad \Longrightarrow \quad P(n + 1) = 2P(n) - P(n - 1).$$

In other words, $P(n)$ satisfies

$$P(0) = 1, \quad P(N) = 0, \quad P(n + 1) = 2P(n) - P(n - 1).$$

Notice the difference between the situation here and that in Section 10.4. The function $P(n)$ is defined only for $n = 0, 1, \ldots, N$. Instead of specifying values $P(0)$ and $P(1)$ as in Section 10.4, we know $P(0)$ and $P(N)$. The characteristic equation associated with the difference equation is $z^2 - 2z + 1 = 0$ with double root $z = 1$. According to equation 10.23b,

$$P(n) = (A + Bn)1^n = A + Bn.$$

Since $P(0) = 1$ and $P(N) = 0$,

$$1 = A, \qquad 0 = A + BN,$$

and therefore

$$P(n) = 1 - \frac{n}{N} = \frac{N - n}{N}, \quad 0 \leq n \leq N.$$

For instance, if the gambler starts with \$20 and sets his goal as \$50, then the probability that he runs our of money is $(50 - 20)/50 = 0.6$. If he sets his sights on \$40, his probability of ruin is $(40 - 20)/40 = 0.5$. The closer N is to n, the more likely he is to achieve his goal; the further N is from n, the less likely he is to reach N. In particular if $N > 2n$, he has less than a 50% chance of reaching \$N.

Proportional Growth Problems

Insect populations sometimes increase in such a way that the growth in some time period is proportional to its growth in the previous time period of the same length. If $N(n)$ denotes the number of insects after n time periods, then

$$N(n + 2) - N(n + 1) = r[N(n + 1) - N(n)], \tag{10.24}$$

where $r > 1$ is a constant. Thus, $N(n)$ must satisfy the second-order linear difference equation

$$N(n + 2) = (1 + r)N(n + 1) - rN(n).$$

The characteristic equation for this difference equation is

$$0 = z^2 - (r + 1)z + r = (z - r)(z - 1),$$

with solutions $z = r$ and $z = 1$. In the case that $r \neq 1$, equation 10.23a gives

$$N(n) = A + Br^n.$$

If $N(0) = N_0$ is the initial population and $N(1) = N_1$ is the population after the first time period, then

$$N_0 = A + B, \qquad N_1 = A + Br.$$

These can be solved for $A = (rN_0 - N_1)/(r - 1)$ and $B = (N_1 - N_0)/(r - 1)$, and therefore

$$N(n) = \frac{rN_0 - N_1}{r - 1} + \left(\frac{N_1 - N_0}{r - 1}\right) r^n = \frac{N_0 r - N_1 - (N_1 - N_0)r^n}{r - 1}.$$

For example, if there is a 25% growth factor, then $r = 5/4$. If $N_1 = 3N_0/2$, then

$$N(n) = \frac{N_0(5/4) - 3N_0/2 + (3N_0/2 - N_0)(5/4)^n}{5/4 - 1} = \left[2\left(\frac{5}{4}\right)^n - 1\right] N_0.$$

You should carefully distinguish between "growth" in this example (being synonymous with $N(n + 1) - N(n)$), and "size" in Example 10.11. Proportional growth situations lead to second-order difference equations, whereas size descriptions result in first-order equations.

EXERCISES 10.5

1. The increase in the size of an insect population in any given time period is 10% larger than its increase in the previous time period. If the initial number of insects is 1000 and the number after the first time period is 1500, find the number after the nth time period.

2. Repeat the previous exercise if the initial population is 1000 and the number after the first time period is 2000, and the increase in the size of the population over any given time period is 20% larger than in the previous period.

3. What is the solution of growth problem 10.24 when $r = 1$, $N(0) = N_0$, and $N(1) = N_1$?

4. In a study of the spread of measles in a school, it was estimated that the probability $P(n)$ of at least one new case in the nth week after an outbreak satisfied the difference equation $P(n + 2) = P(n + 1) - P(n)/5$. If $P(0) = 0$ and $P(1) = 1$, determine $P(n)$.

5. A gambler plays a game with two outcomes, win or lose. He forfeits a $1 bet if he loses, and he gains $1 if he wins. There is a constant probability p that he wins each game and probability $q = 1 - p$ that he loses. Suppose he begins with n, and quits when he is out of money or reaches N.

   (a) Show that the probability $P(n)$ of the gambler running out of money when he begins with n satisfies

   $$P(0) = 1, \quad P(N) = 0, \quad P(n + 1) = pP(n + 2) + qP(n).$$

(b) What is the characteristic equation associated with the difference equation in part (a)?

(c) Show that solutions of the characteristic equation are $z = 1$ and $z = (1 - p)/p$. Use these to determine that

$$P(n) = \frac{r^n - r^N}{1 - r^N} \qquad \text{where} \qquad r = \frac{1 - p}{p}.$$

6. Does the result of Exercise 5 reduce to the Gambler's ruin discussed in the text when $p = 1/2$? Explain.

7. We saw in the Gambler's ruin discussion in the text that when $p = 1/2$, the probability of the gambler doubling any amount of money is equal to $1/2$. Use the result in Exercise 5 to find the probability of the gambler doubling (a) \$10 (b) \$20 (c) \$30 if $p = 0.48$.

8. Your chances of winning a game of blackjack are slightly less than 50%, say 49%. You have \$100 which you would like to double. What are your chances of doing so in the following three scenarios:

(a) Bet \$1 on each game   (b) Bet \$5 on each game   (c) Bet the entire \$100 on one game

9. You are in a game in which the probability of your winning is 0.49. You want to leave with \$100. What amount should you begin with to have a 50% chance of attaining your goal? Each bet is \$1.

§10.6 Transfer Functions and Stability for Discrete Systems

In Section 8.6, we used Laplace transforms to define transfer functions and stability for continuous systems. We give a parallel discussion in this section for discrete systems. Consider a system described by the Nth-order difference equation

$$a_N f(n+N) + a_{N-1} f(n+N-1) + \cdots + a_1 f(n+1) + a_0 f(n) = x(n),$$

$$f(0) = f_0, \quad f(1) = f_1, \quad \cdots f(N-1) = f_{N-1}. \tag{10.25}$$

If $f_0 = f_1 = f_2 = \cdots = f_{N-1} = 0$, called the zero initial state, and we take z-transforms, we obtain

$$\tilde{f}(z) = \frac{X(z)}{a_N z^N + a_{N-1} z^{N-1} + \cdots + a_1 z + a_0}. \tag{10.26}$$

The function

$$\tilde{H}(z) = \frac{1}{a_N z^N + a_{N-1} z^{N-1} + \cdots + a_1 z + a_0}, \tag{10.27}$$

is the **transfer function** for the system. It is the z-transform of the response $H(n)$ of the system to the unit step function $\delta(0)$ (with zero initial state). Because the denominator of $\tilde{H}(z)$ is a (real) polynomial, it has n zeros (counting multiplicities) that are poles of $\tilde{H}(z)$. Positions and multiplicities of these poles determine the form of $H(n)$. We single out three situations for special consideration:

1. If $\tilde{H}(z)$ has a real pole $a \neq 0$ of multiplicity k, then $H(n)$ contains terms of the form

$$(C_0 + C_1 n + \cdots + C_{k-1} n^{k-1}) a^n.$$

This function approaches zero as $n \to \infty$ if and only if $|a| < 1$.

2. If $\tilde{H}(z)$ has complex conjugate poles $a \pm bi$, where $a \neq 0$, and $b > 0$, each of multiplicity k, then $H(n)$ contains terms of the form

$$r^n[(C_0 + C_1 n + \cdots + C_{k-1} n^{k-1}) \cos n\theta + (D_0 + D_1 n + \cdots + D_{k-1} n^{k-1}) \sin n\theta)],$$

where r and θ are modulus and argument of $a + bi$. This function approaches zero as $n \to \infty$ if and only if $r < 1$.

3. If $\tilde{H}(z)$ has complex conjugate poles $\pm bi$, where $b > 0$, each of multiplicity k (which lie on the imaginary axis), then $H(n)$ contains terms of the form

$$b^n \left[(C_0 + C_1 n + \cdots + C_{k-1} n^{k-1}) \cos \frac{n\pi}{2} + (D_0 + D_1 n + \cdots + D_{k-1} n^{k-1}) \sin \frac{n\pi}{2} \right].$$

This function is bounded as $n \to \infty$ if and only if $b < 1$ and $k = 1$; that is, if and only if poles on the imaginary axis are simple and lie within the unit circle $|z| < 1$.

The following three definitions describe the stability of a system in terms of the poles of its transfer function.

Definition 10.2 A system is said to be **stable** if all poles of its transfer function are inside the unit circle $|z| < 1$.

Definition 10.3 A system is said to be **marginally stable** if its transfer function has simple poles on the unit circle $|z| = 1$ and all other poles are inside the circle.

Definition 10.4   A system is said to be **unstable** if its transfer function has poles outside the unit circle $|z| = 1$ or poles on the circle with order greater than one.

It follows that a system is stable when its step function response $H(n)$ approaches zero as $n \to \infty$; it is marginally stable when $H(n)$ is bounded as $n \to \infty$; and it is unstable when $H(n)$ is unbounded as $n \to \infty$. In the case of systems that are functions of a continuous variable t, the boundary of the region of stability is the imaginary axis; for discrete systems, the boundary is the unit circle $|z| = 1$.

Example 10.19   Determine whether a system with transfer function $\tilde{H}(z) = \dfrac{1}{2z^3 - z^2 + 2z - 1}$ is stable, marginally stable, or unstable.

Solution   Since $z^3 - z^2 + 2z - 1 = (2z + 1)(s^2 + 1)$, poles of $\tilde{H}(z)$ are $z = -1/2$ and z=$\pm i$. Since the pole $z = -1/2$ is interior to the unit circle $|z| < 1$, and the poles $z = \pm i$ on the circle are simple, the system is marginally stable.•

Example 10.20   Determine whether a system with transfer function $\tilde{H}(z) = \dfrac{1}{3z^3 + z^2 + 7z - 6}$ is stable, marginally stable, or unstable.

Solution   Since $3z^3 + z^2 + 7z - 6 = (3z - 2)(z^2 + z + 3)$, poles of $\tilde{H}(z)$ are

$$z = \frac{2}{3} \quad \text{and} \quad z = \frac{-1 \pm \sqrt{1 - 12}}{2} = \frac{-1 \pm \sqrt{11}i}{2}.$$

Since the last two are outside the unit circle $|z| = 1$, the system is unstable.•

For continuous systems, we discussed alternative methods for determining stability such Nyquist, Routh, and Hurwitz criteria. There are alternatives for discrete systems as well, but we shall not discuss them.

EXERCISES 10.6

In Exercise 1–10 determine whether a system with given transfer function is stable, marginally stable, or unstable by finding poles of the transfer function.

1. $\tilde{H}(z) = \dfrac{1}{z^2 + 2z + 5}$

2. $\tilde{H}(z) = \dfrac{1}{3z^2 + 2z + 1}$

3. $\tilde{H}(z) = \dfrac{1}{8z^3 + 2z^2 + 3z - 1}$

4. $\tilde{H}(z) = \dfrac{1}{3z^3 + 14z^2 + 11z + 2}$

5. $\tilde{H}(z) = \dfrac{1}{3z^4 + 7z^2 + 2}$

6. $\tilde{H}(z) = \dfrac{1}{4z^4 + 3z^2 - 1}$

7. $\tilde{H}(z) = \dfrac{1}{z^6 + 3z^4 + 3z^2 + 1}$

8. $\tilde{H}(z) = \dfrac{1}{z^4 + 1}$

9. $\tilde{H}(z) = \dfrac{1}{4z^4 + 1}$

10. $\tilde{H}(z) = \dfrac{1}{2z^4 + 2z^3 + 3z^2 + z + 1}$

11. Verify that "proportional growth problems" described by difference equation 10.24 are marginally stable when $r < 1$ and unstable when $r \geq 1$.

12. (a) Verify that the polynomial $f(z) = z^3 + z^2 + 2z + 1$ has exactly one real zero between -1 and 0.

(b) Let the real zero in part (a) be $z = a$, where $-1 < a < 0$. Show that the remaining two zeros of the polynomial are

$$z = \frac{-(a+1) \pm \sqrt{-3a^2 - 2a - 7}}{2},$$

and conclude that they are complex with moduli greater than 1.

(c) Is the system with transfer function $1/f(z)$ stable, marginally stable, or unstable?

APPENDIX A   Answers to Exercises

Exercises 1.1

2. $(a+c)+(b+d)\sqrt{3}$ **3.** $(a-c)+(b-d)\sqrt{3}$ **4.** $(ac+3bd)+(ad+bc)\sqrt{3}$
5. $\left(\dfrac{ac-3bd}{c^2-3d^2}\right)+\left(\dfrac{bc-ad}{c^2-3d^2}\right)\sqrt{3}$

Exercises 1.2

1.

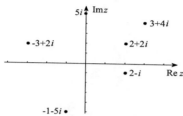

2. $-1+6i$ **3.** $-3+4i$ **4.** $-2+11i$ **5.** $24-45i$ **6.** $7+i$ **7.** $-8i$ **8.** $(1/13)-(5/13)i$ **9.** $2+4i$
10. $5-3i$ **11.** $-4-3i$ **12.** $(-24/5)+(33/5)i$ **13.** $-1+3i$ **14.** $-4i$ **15.** -1 **18.** $z=0,\ r$
22. $(-5\pm\sqrt{13})/2$ **23.** $-3/2\pm\sqrt{11}i/2$ **24.** $-4,\ -4$ **25.** $-1\pm2\sqrt{2}$ **26.** $-1\pm\sqrt{6}i$
27. $1/4\pm\sqrt{19}i/4$ **28.** $-[5/(2\sqrt{3})]\pm[\sqrt{12\sqrt{5}-25}/(2\sqrt{3})]i$ **29.** $\pm\sqrt{5}i,\ \pm1$ **30.** $\pm i,\ \pm\sqrt{3}i$
31. $\pm\sqrt{3-\sqrt{6}i},\ \pm\sqrt{3+\sqrt{6}i}$ **32.** $3\pm i$ **33.** $\pm(3-4i)$ **34.** $\pm(5-2i)$
35. $\pm\left[\sqrt{(2+\sqrt{5})/2}+\sqrt{(\sqrt{5}-2)/2}i\right]$ **36.** $\pm(\sqrt{\sqrt{2}-1}/\sqrt{2}+\sqrt{\sqrt{2}+1}\,i/\sqrt{2})$
37. $-1,\ -1+i$ **38.** $\pm\sqrt{3}/2+(1\pm\sqrt{3}/2)i$ **39.** $\left(-1\pm\sqrt{(\sqrt{2}+1)/2}\right)\mp\sqrt{(\sqrt{2}-1)/2}i$
40. $(-1\pm3/\sqrt{2\sqrt{10}-2})\pm\sqrt{\sqrt{10}-1}\,i/\sqrt{2}$ **41.** $\pm\sqrt{(\sqrt{10}-3)/2}+\left(-2\mp\sqrt{(\sqrt{10}+3)/2}\right)i$
42. $[-1\pm\sqrt{\sqrt{65}-1}/(2\sqrt{2})]+[1/2\mp\sqrt{\sqrt{65}+1}/(2\sqrt{2})]i$

Exercises 1.3

1. $\sqrt{2}[\cos(3\pi/4)+\sin(3\pi/4)i]$ **2.** $2[\cos(-\pi/2)+\sin(-\pi/2)i]$ **3.** $2[\cos(-\pi/6)+\sin(-\pi/6)i]$
4. $5[\cos(0.927)+\sin(0.927)i]$ **5.** $\sqrt{5}[\cos(-2.03)+\sin(-2.03)i]$ **6.** $2[\cos(2\pi/3)+\sin(2\pi/3)i]$
7. $3\sqrt{3}/2+3i/2$ **8.** $0.170+0.985i$ **9.** $2i$ **10.** $4i$ **11.** -4 **12.** 1 **13.** $-1/64$
14. $(3/5)-(1/5)i$ **15.** $i/32$ **16.** $-1.66-0.654i$ **17.** It doesn't have one.

Exercises 1.4

1. $\sqrt{2}e^{3\pi i/4}$ **2.** $2e^{-\pi i/2}$ **3.** $2e^{-\pi i/6}$ **4.** $5e^{i\text{Tan}^{-1}(4/3)}$ **5.** $\sqrt{5}e^{(-\pi+\text{Tan}^{-1}2)i}$ **6.** $2e^{2\pi i/3}$
7. $3\sqrt{3}/2+3i/2$ **8.** -1 **9.** $4i$ **10.** $4i$ **11.** -4 **12.** 1 **13.** $-1/64$ **14.** $3/5-i/5$ **15.** $i/32$
16. $-1.66-0.654i$ **17.** $-1/2+\sqrt{3}i/2$ **18.** $-\sqrt{3}/2-i/2$ **19.** $-9\sqrt{2}/8-9\sqrt{2}i/8$

Exercises 1.5

1. $\pm(3-4i)$ **2.** $\pm(5-2i)$ **3.** $\pm\left[\sqrt{(\sqrt{2}-1)/2}+\sqrt{(\sqrt{2}+1)/2}i\right]$ **4.** $1,\ -1/2\pm\sqrt{3}i/2$
5. $\pm(0.924+0.383i),\ \pm(0.383-0.924i)$ **6.** $\pm(\sqrt{3}+i)$ **7.** $-2,\ 1.618\pm1.176i,\ -0.618\pm1.902i$
8. $1.671-0.364i,\ -0.520+1.629i,\ -1.151-1.265i$ **9.** $\pm i,\ \sqrt{3}/2\pm i/2,\ -\sqrt{3}/2\pm i/2$
10. $\pm(0.607+1.367i),\ \pm(0.607-1.367i)$ **11.** $1.184\pm0.431i,\ -0.965\pm0.810i,\ -0.219\pm1.241i$

12. (a)$\cos(2k\pi/n) + \sin(2k\pi/n)i$, $k = 0, \dots, n-1$

13. $\left|\dfrac{z_1 + z_2}{z_3 + z_4}\right| \leq \dfrac{|z_1| + |z_2|}{|z_4| - |z_3|}$, $\left|\dfrac{z_1 + z_2}{z_3 + z_4}\right| \leq \dfrac{|z_1| + |z_2|}{||z_4| - |z_3||}$

14. Horizontal line $\operatorname{Im} z = 1/2$

15. Circle with radius $3\sqrt{2}/8$ and centre $z = 1/8 - 9i/8$

16. Circle with radius 3 and centre $z = 2 - i$, and its interior

17. Exterior of circle with radius 2 and centre $-3i$

18. Region between concentric circles with centre $z = -3$ and radii 1 and 4, including the circles

19. Region between concentric circles with centre $2 + i$ and radii 2 and 5, including outer circle

20. Ellipse with foci $z = \pm 1$ and major axis of length 4, and its interior

21. Ellipse with foci $2i$ and $-3i$ and major axis of length 8, and its exterior

22. Region between, and including, two ellipses with foci $z = \pm 1$, one with major axis of length 4, the other with major axis of length 6

23. Hyperbola $(\operatorname{Re} z)^2 - (\operatorname{Im} z)^2 = 2$ **24.** $z = 1/2 \pm \sqrt{23}i/2$

25. $\operatorname{Re} z \geq 1$, and $\operatorname{Re} z > [1 - (\operatorname{Im} z)^2]/2$ when $\operatorname{Re} z \leq 1$ **26.** $\operatorname{Re} z > 0$

27. $|z + 1| + |z - 3| \leq 6$ **28.** $5 < |z - 3 + 4i| < 8$ **29.** $3\operatorname{Re} z - 2\operatorname{Im} z \leq 0$

30. $|\operatorname{Re} z| + |\operatorname{Im} z| = 1$ **31.** $|\operatorname{Re} z| + |\operatorname{Im} z| \leq 1$ **32.** $|z| < 2$, $\operatorname{Im} z > 0$

33. $2\operatorname{Im} z \geq 3[(\operatorname{Re} z)^2 - \operatorname{Re} z]$ **35.** $(z_1 - \lambda^2 z_2)/(1 - \lambda^2)$, $\lambda|z_1 - z_2|/|1 - \lambda^2|$

39. $R^{m/n}[\cos(m\Theta/n + 2k\pi/n) + \sin(m\Theta/n + 2k\pi/n)i]$ where R and Θ are modulus and principal argument of Z

41. $1 - 3i/2$, $-1/2 - 5i/2$, $5/2 - i/2$ **42.** $-(3/2)[1 + \cot(k\pi/5)i]$, $k = 1, 2, 3, 4$

44. $\cos\left(\dfrac{2k\pi}{5}\right) + i\sin\left(\dfrac{2k\pi}{5}\right)$, for $k = 1, \dots, 4$

45. $\cos\left(\dfrac{2k\pi}{n+1}\right) + i\sin\left(\dfrac{2k\pi}{n+1}\right)$, for $k = 1, \dots, n$

Exercises 2.1

1. Closed, not open, bounded, connected, not a domain

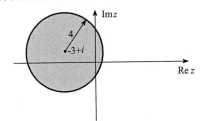

2. Open, not closed, unbounded, connected, domain

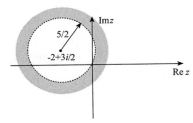

3. Closed, not open, connected, unbounded, not a domain

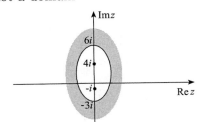

4. Open, not closed, connected, bounded, domain

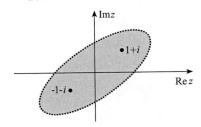

5. open, not closed, bounded, connected, domain

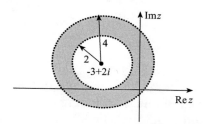

6. closed, not open, unbounded, connected, not a domain

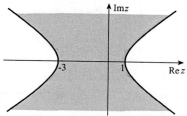

7. open, not closed, bounded, connected, domain

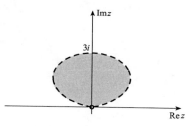

8. closed, not open, unbounded, connected, not a domain

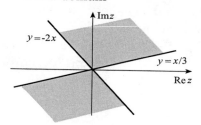

9. open, not closed, unbounded, not connected, not a domain

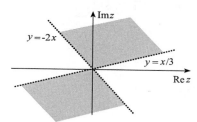

10. not open, not closed, bounded, connected, not a domain

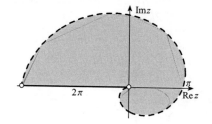

12. Yes   **13.** No

Exercises 2.2

1. $x^3 - 3xy^2 + 2x - 1$, $3x^2y - y^3 + 2y$
2. $[(3x+1)(1-x) - 3y^2]/[(1-x)^2 + y^2]$, $4y/[(1-x)^2 + y^2]$
3. $x^3 - xy^2 + 2x$, $2x^2y + 2y$
4. $\sqrt{x^2 + y^2}(x^2 + y^2 + y)/[x^2 + (y+1)^2]$, $-x\sqrt{x^2 + y^2}/[x^2 + (y+1)^2]$
5. $r^7 \cos 7\theta + 3r^6 \cos 6\theta$, $r^7 \sin 7\theta + 3r^6 \sin 6\theta$
6. $r^5(r \cos 4\theta - 3 \cos 5\theta)/(r^2 - 6r \cos \theta + 9)$, $r^5(r \sin 4\theta - 3 \sin 5\theta)/(r^2 - 6r \cos \theta + 9)$
7. (a) $v = 0$, $u \le -1/4$ (b) $u = -1/4$ **15.** $\mathrm{Re}\, w = 1/2$ **16.** $|w+1/6| = 1/3$ **17.** $\mathrm{Re}\, w = 2\,\mathrm{Im}\, w$
18. (a) $u^2/(R^2+1)^2 + v^2/(R^2-1)^2 = 1/R^2$ (b) Real axis between $w = \pm 2$
19. $u = 0$, $v \ge 1/2$ **20.** $v = 0$, $|u| \ge 1/2$ **25.** No   **26.** z^3 **27.** $1/z$ **28.** $z/|z|^2$ **29.** $z/(z+1)$
30. $z|z|^2$ **31.** (b) Real axis between $w = \pm 2a$

Exercises 2.3

1. Functions are undefined at $z = 0$
2. Limits of functions do not exist at points on branch cut.
3. $6 - 4i$ **4.** i **5.** $(1313 + 435i)/2$ **6.** Does not exist   **7.** 0 **8.** 0 **9.** Does not exist   **10.** 0
11. Does not exist   **12.** Does not exist   **13.** $5\pi/2$ **14.** Does not exist   **15.** Does not exist
16. 2π **17.** Does not exist   **18.** Does not exist   **19.** $-7\pi/4$ **20.** $\mathrm{Tan}^{-1}(1/2)$

21. $2\pi + \text{Tan}^{-1}(1/2)$ **22.** $\text{Tan}^{-1}(1/2) - 2\pi$ **23.** $\mathcal{C}$ with $z = -1$ deleted
24. $\mathcal{C}$ with $z = -3/2 \pm (\sqrt{23}/2)i$ deleted
25. $\mathcal{C}$ with $z = (1 \pm i)/\sqrt{2}$ and $z = -(1 \pm i)/\sqrt{2}$ deleted
26. $\mathcal{C}$ **27.** $\mathcal{C}$ **28.** $\mathcal{C}$ **29.** $\mathcal{C}$ **30.** $\mathcal{C}$ **31.** $\mathcal{C}$ with $z = 0$ deleted
32. $\mathcal{C}$ with $z = 0$ and negative real axis deleted
33. $\mathcal{C}$ with $z = 0$ and positive real axis deleted
34. $\mathcal{C}$ with $z = 0$ and negative imaginary axis deleted
35. $\mathcal{C}$ with $z = 1$ and line $y = (\tan 3)(x - 1)$, $x < 1$ deleted
36. $\mathcal{C}$ with $z = -2i$ and half-line $y = -2 - (\tan 4)x$, $x < 0$ deleted
37. $\mathcal{C}$ with $z = 0$ and positive real axis deleted
38. $\mathcal{C}$ with $z = 0$ and positive imaginary axis deleted **40.** Only if we define $f(0) = 0$.
41. $-4i$ **42.** No **43.** All points on $|z| = 1$ except $z = -1$

Exercises 2.4

1. $3z^2 - 2/z^3 - 2$, any open set not containing $z = 0$ **2.** $2z(1 + z^3)^9(1 + 16z^3)$, entire
3. $z(z^3 - 6z - 2)/(z^2 - 2)^2$, any open set not containing $z = \pm\sqrt{2}$
4. $3z^2(1 - z)^2(-5z^2 + 2z + 2i - 4iz)/(3z + 2i)^2$, any open set not containing $z = -2i/3$
5. Nowhere analytic **6.** Nowhere analytic **7.** $(4x + 3) + 4yi$, entire
8. $(3x^2 - 3y^2 - 2) + 6xyi$, entire
9. $\dfrac{y^2 - (x + 1)^2}{[(x + 1)^2 + y^2]^2} + \dfrac{2y(x + 1)i}{[(x + 1)^2 + y^2]^2}$, any open set not containing $z = -1$
10. Nowhere analytic **11.** $-\sin x \cosh y - \cos x \sinh y\, i$, entire
12. $\cos y \cosh x + \sin y \sinh x\, i$, entire **13.** $8z^7$, entire **14.** Nowhere analytic
15. $1/(2\sqrt{r})e^{-\theta i/2}$ **16.** $(1/r)e^{-\theta i}$ **19.** No, $f'(0) = 0$ **20.** No

Exercises 2.5

1. $\mathcal{C}$, $-2xy + y + C$ **2.** $\mathcal{C}$, $3x^2 y - y^3 + 2y + C$
3. $\mathcal{C}$ with $z = -1$ deleted, $-y/[(x + 1)^2 + y^2] + C$ **4.** $\mathcal{C}$, $\cos x \sinh y + C$ **5.** $\mathcal{C}$, $\sin y \sinh x + C$
6. $\mathcal{C}$ with $z = 0$ deleted, $-y/(x^2 + y^2) + C$ **7.** $x^2 + 3x - y^2 + C$
8. (a) $\mathcal{C}$ with $z = 3i$ deleted, $6x/(9 + x^2 + y^2 - 6y) + C$ (b) $2z/(z - 3i) + Ci$ **9.** No
10. $2xy + C$

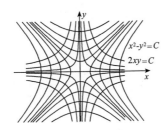

11. No **12.** No

Exercises 3.1

1. Zero of order 1 at $z = 2/3$; no singularities **2.** No zeros; isolated singularity at $z = 2/3$
3. Zeros of order 1 at $z = (-3 \pm \sqrt{17})/2$; no singularities
4. Zeros of order 1 at $z = \pm 2i$; no singularities
5. Zeros of order 1 at $z = -2, 1 \pm \sqrt{3}i$; no singularities
6. Zero of order 2 at $z = -1$; no singularities
7. No zeros; isolated singularities at $z = -1 \pm \sqrt{3}i$

8. Zeros of order 1 at $z = \pm\sqrt{3}$; isolated singularities at $z = (-5 \pm \sqrt{21})/2$

9. Zeros of order 1 at $z = 0, \pm\sqrt{2}i$; isolated singularity at $z = 1$

10. Zero of order 3 at $z = 0$; isolated singularity at $z = -4/3$

11. Zero of order 1 at $z = 0$; isolated singularity at $z = -1/3$ **12.** No zeros or singularities

13. No zeros or singularities **14.** Zero of order 2 at $z = 1$; isolated singularity at $z = -2$

15. Zero of order 3 at $z = 1$; isolated singularity at $z = -5$

16. Zeros of order 1 at $z = -1, (1 \pm \sqrt{3}i)/2$; isolated singularities at $z = 1, (-1 \pm \sqrt{3}i)/2$

17. Zeros of order 1 at $z = \pm(1 - i)/\sqrt{2}$; isolated singularity at $z = 3/2$

18. Zeros of order 1 at $z = (-2 \pm \sqrt{2})i$; no singularities

19. Zeros of order 1 at $\pm\sqrt{(\sqrt{2} - 1)/2} + \left[1 \mp \sqrt{(\sqrt{2} + 1)/2}\right]i$; isolated singularity at $z = -4$

20. Zeros of orders 2 and 1 at $z = 0$ and $z = 2$; isolated singularities at $z = (-2/3 \pm 1/\sqrt{2})$ $\pm i/(3\sqrt{2})$

21. Zeros of order 1 at $z = 2^{2/3}i$, $2^{-1/3}(\pm\sqrt{3} - i)$; isolated singularity at $z = 0$

22. Zeros of order 1 at $z = \pm(0.676 + 0.978i), \pm(0.676 - 0.978i)$; isolated singularity at $z = -5$

Exercises 3.2

1. $\sqrt{2}e^{-\pi i/4}$ **2.** $2e^{2\pi i/3}$ **3.** $8e^{\pi i/2}$ **4.** $5e^{i\operatorname{Tan}^{-1}(4/3)}$ **5.** $2\sqrt{10}e^{(\pi - \operatorname{Tan}^{-1}3)i}$ **6.** $5e^{[\operatorname{Tan}^{-1}(4/3) - \pi]i}$
7. $4e^{\pi i/3}$ **8.** $4e^{9\pi i/10}$ **9.** $2e^{-\pi i/12}$ **10.** $3e^{3\pi i/4}$ **11.** $e^2 \cos 3 + e^2 \sin 3\, i$
12. $(e^{-1} \cos 4) - (e^{-1} \sin 4)\, i$ **13.** $\sqrt{e} \cos(1/2) - \sqrt{e} \sin(1/2)\, i$ **14.** $\cos 1 + (\sin 1)\, i$
15. $\ln 4 + 2n\pi i$ **16.** $\ln 4 + (4n + 1)\pi i/2$ **17.** $(5/2)\ln 2 + (8n + 1)\pi i/4$
18. $(1/2)\ln 13 + [2n\pi - \operatorname{Sin}^{-1}(3/\sqrt{13})]i$ **19.** $(1/2)(4 - \ln 2) + (8n - 3)\pi i/4$ **20.** $(2n + 1)\pi i$
21. $2(3n \pm 1)\pi i/3$ **22.** $(1/2)\ln 5 + [2n\pi \pm \operatorname{Cos}^{-1}(-3\sqrt{5}/10)]i$ **23.** $3e^8 \cos 3 + 3e^8 \sin 3\, i$
24. $(\cos 1 - 4\sin 1) + (\sin 1 + 4\cos 1)i$ **25.** $-e^{-6}(5\cos 4 + 4\sin 4) + e^{-6}(5\sin 4 - 4\cos 4)i$
26. $e^{-3}\sin 1 - e^{-3}\cos 1\, i$ **29.** $w = e^{\pi z/a}$ **30.** $w = e^{\pi z/(2a)}$

Exercises 3.3

1. $\sinh 1\, i$ **2.** $\cos 1 \cosh 1 + \sin 1 \sinh 1\, i$ **3.** $\cos 1.3 \cosh 2 - \sin 1.3 \sinh 2\, i$
4. $\sin 5.6 \cosh 4.1 + \cos 5.6 \sinh 4.1\, i$ **5.** $e^2 \cosh 1 \cos 1 + e^2 \cosh 1 \sin 1\, i$ **6.** $(1/2)\sinh 2\, i$
7. $\frac{1}{2}(1 + \cos 2 \cosh 2) - \frac{1}{2}\sin 2 \sinh 2\, i$ **8.** $-2\sin 1 + 3\sin 1\, i$ **9.** $(\tanh 2)i$ **10.** $\coth 1\, i$
11. $(\operatorname{csch} 2)i$ **12.** $-0.0417 - 0.0906i$ **13.** $n\pi + \ln[2(-1)^n + \sqrt{5}]i$ **14.** $2n\pi + \ln(4 \pm \sqrt{15})i$
15. $(4n + 1)\pi/2 - i$ **16.** No solution **19.** $-\sin 1 \sinh 2 + \cos 1 \cosh 2\, i$ **20.** $2\operatorname{sech}^2 1(1 - \tanh 1)$
21. $2\operatorname{csch} 1 \coth 1$ **22.** $6\cos 9 \cosh 1 - 6\sin 9 \sinh 1\, i$ **23.** $8\cos 8\, i$
25. (a) z real and $z = n\pi + yi$ (b) $z = (2n + 1)\pi/2 + yi$
26. (a) z real and $z = (2n + 1)\pi/2 + yi$, (b) $z = n\pi + yi$ **34.** $w = \sin[\pi z/(2a)]$

Exercises 3.4

1. $(\sin 3)i$ **2.** $\cos 2 \cosh 1 - \sin 2 \sinh 1\, i$ **3.** $2\sqrt{3}i$ **4.** i
5. $(\sinh 1 \cosh 1 + \sin 1 \cos 1\, i)/(\cos^2 1 + \sinh^2 1)$
6. $(\cos 2 \sinh 1 - \sin 2 \cosh 1\, i)/(\sinh^2 1 + \sin^2 2)$ **7.** $-\sin^2 6$
8. $(\cos 5 \cosh 4 - \sin 5 \sinh 4\, i)/(\sinh^2 4 + \cos^2 5)$ **9.** $2n\pi i$ **10.** $\ln(3 \pm 2\sqrt{2}) + (4n + 3)\pi i/2$
11. $(4n + 1)\pi i/4$ **12.** $n\pi i$ **15.** $(3\cos 4 \cosh 7) + (3\sin 4 \sinh 7)i$ **16.** $3\sec^2 3$ **17.** $\cos 1 - \sin 1$
18. $-9\sec 5(1 + 2\tan^2 5)$ **19.** Yes **22.** $i \sinh[\pi z/(2a)]$

Exercises 3.5

1. $(4n + 1)\pi i/2$ **2.** $(1/2)\ln 40 - (\operatorname{Tan}^{-1}3)i$ **3.** $(1/2)\ln 2 + 9\pi i/4$
4. $(1/2)\ln 13 + [\pi - \operatorname{Tan}^{-1}(3/2)]i$ **5.** i **6.** $e^2(\cos 3 + \sin 3\, i)$

7. $\cos{(\pi/8)} + \sin{(\pi/8)}i$, $\cos{(5\pi/8)} + \sin{(5\pi/8)}i$, $\cos{(9\pi/8)} + \sin{(9\pi/8)}i$, $\cos{(13\pi/8)} + \sin{(13\pi/8)}i$

8. $(-2 + \ln 4) + 2n\pi i$ **9.** $\ln 4 + 2n\pi i$ **10.** $\ln 4 + (4n+1)\pi i/2$ **11.** $(5/2)\ln 2 + (8n+1)\pi i/4$

12. $(1/2)\ln 13 + [2n\pi - \text{Tan}^{-1}(3/2)]i$ **13.** $[2 - (1/2)\ln 2] - (8n+3)\pi i/4$ **14.** $(2n+1)\pi i$

15. $2(3n \pm 1)\pi i/3$ **16.** $(1/2)\ln 5 + [2n\pi \pm \text{Cos}^{-1}(-3\sqrt{5}/10)]i$

17. $2n\pi - i\ln{(\sqrt{5} - 2)}$, $(2n+1)\pi - i\ln{(\sqrt{5} + 2)}$ **18.** $2n\pi - \ln{(4 \pm \sqrt{15})}i$ **19.** $(4n+1)\pi/2 - i$

20. $2n\pi i$ **21.** $\ln{(3 \pm 2\sqrt{2})} + (4n-1)\pi i/2$ **22.** $(4n+1)\pi i/4$

25. $z = 1$ for $-2\pi < \phi < 0$ **26.** $(9 - i)/41$ **27.** 1   **28.** only if $-\pi < y \le \pi$

29. $z = -i$; $\text{Im}\,z = -1$, $\text{Re}\,z \le 0$ **30.** $z = 1$; $\text{Im}\,z = 0$, $\text{Re}\,z \le 1$

31. $z = 3/2$; $\text{Im}\,z = 0$, $\text{Re}\,z \ge 3/2$ **32.** $z = 2/3 - 4i/3$; $\text{Im}\,z = -4/3$, $\text{Re}\,z \le 2/3$

33. (a) $z = \pm 2$ **34.** $z = \pm i$; $\text{Re}\,z = 0$ for $\text{Im}\,z \ge 1$ and $\text{Im}\,z \le -1$

35. $z = 2i$; $\text{Im}\,z = 2$, $\text{Re}\,z \ge 0$ **36.** $z = 3$; $\text{Re}\,z = 3$, $\text{Im}\,z \le 0$

37. $z = 2$; $\text{Re}\,z = 2$, $\text{Im}\,z \ge 0$ **38.** $z = -1/2$; $y = (\tan 2)(x + 1/2)$, $y \ge 0$ **39.** (a) $z = \pm i$

40. $z = \pm 1$; parts of $x^2 - y^2 = 1$ in first and third quadrants including $z = \pm 1$

41. For $f(z)$, imaginary axis, and real axis between $z = \pm 1$, including $z = \pm 1$ For $g(z)$, real axis to left of $z = 1$, including $z = 1$

42. For $f(z)$, real axis to the right of $z = 2$ and to the left of $z = -2$, including $z = \pm 2$ Same for $g(z)$

43. For $f(z)$, parts of $x^2 - y^2 = 1$ in second and fourth quadrants, including $z = \pm 1$ For $g(z)$, vertical half-lines below $z = \pm 1$, including $z = \pm 1$

44. For $f(z)$, parts of $x^2 - y^2 = 4$ in first and third quadrants, including $z = \pm 2$ For $g(z)$, vertical half-lines below $z = -2$ and above $z = 2$, including $z = \pm 2$

Exercises 3.6

1. $e^{-2n\pi}\cos{(\ln 2)} + e^{-2n\pi}\sin{(\ln 2)}\,i$ **2.** $e^{-3(4n+1)\pi/2}\cos{(3\ln 2)} + e^{-3(4n+1)\pi/2}\sin{(3\ln 2)}\,i$

3. $\sqrt[4]{2}\cos{(\pi/8)} + \sqrt[4]{2}\sin{(\pi/8)}\,i$ **4.** $\pm[\sqrt[4]{2}\cos{(\pi/8)} + \sqrt[4]{2}\sin{(\pi/8)}]\,i$

5. $\sqrt{3} + i$ **6.** $\pm\sqrt{3} + i$, $-2i$ **7.** $\cos{(3\pi/8)} + \sin{(3\pi/8)}\,i$

8. $\pm[\cos{(3\pi/8)} + \sin{(3\pi/8)}\,i]$, $\pm[\cos{(7\pi/8)} + \sin{(7\pi/8)}\,i]$

9. $\sqrt{2}e^{\pi/4-2n\pi}\cos{(\ln\sqrt{2} - \pi/4)} + \sqrt{2}e^{\pi/4-2n\pi}\sin{(\ln\sqrt{2} - \pi/4)}\,i$

10. $\sqrt{2}e^{(8n+1)\pi/4}\cos{(\pi/4 - \ln\sqrt{2})} + \sqrt{2}e^{(8n+1)\pi/4}\sin{(\pi/4 - \ln\sqrt{2})}i$ **11.** Yes   **12.** $\sqrt{2}(1 - i)/4$

13. $2^{-4/3}(\sqrt{3} + i)/3$ **14.** Sometimes   **15.** No   **16.** $0.186 + 0.348i$ **17.** $0.325 + 0.0768i$

18. (a) When $-\pi/2 < \text{Arg}\,z \le \pi/2$ (b) No   **19.** Not necessarily   **20.** No

21. $\cos{(2\sqrt{2}n\pi)} + \sin{(2\sqrt{2}n\pi)}\,i$ **22.** Yes

24. $z = 1$; $\text{Im}\,z = 0$, $\text{Re}\,z \le 1$ **25.** $z = 2/3$; $\text{Im}\,z = 0$, $\text{Re}\,z \ge 2/3$

26. $z = -i/2$; $\text{Im}\,z = -1/2$, $\text{Re}\,z \le 0$ **27.** $z = 2/3 - i$; $\text{Im}\,z = -1$, $\text{Re}\,z \le 2/3$

28. $z = \pm 2$; imaginary axis and $\text{Im}\,z = 0$, $-2 \le \text{Re}\,z \le 2$ **29.** $z = \pm 2$; $\text{Im}\,z = 0$, $|\text{Re}\,z| \ge 2$

30. $z = \pm 2i$; $\text{Re}\,z = 0$, $|\text{Im}\,z| \ge 2$ **31.** $z = -2 \pm i$; $\text{Re}\,z = -2$, $|\text{Im}\,z| \ge 1$

32. $z = \pm 2$, $z = \pm 2i$; $\text{Re}\,z = \pm\text{Im}\,z$, $\text{Im}\,z = 0$ for $-2 \le \text{Re}\,z \le 2$, $\text{Re}\,z = 0$ for $-2 \le \text{Im}\,z \le 2$

33. $z = -3$; $\text{Im}\,z = 0$, $\text{Re}\,z \ge -3$ **34.** $z = 2i$; $\text{Im}\,z = 2$, $\text{Re}\,z \le 0$

35. $z = -2/3$; $\text{Re}\,z = -2/3$, $\text{Im}\,z \le 0$ **36.** $z = 3i$; $\text{Re}\,z = 0$, $\text{Im}\,z \ge 3$

37. $z = 2 - i$; $\text{Im}\,z = -1$, $\text{Re}\,z \le 2$ **38.** $z = \pm 1$; $\text{Im}\,z = 0$, $|\text{Re}\,z| \ge 1$

39. $z = \pm 2i$; real axis and $\text{Re}\,z = 0$, $|\text{Im}\,z| \le 2$

40. $z = \pm 1$; parts of $x^2 - y^2 = 1$ in second and fourth quadrants, including $z = \pm 1$

41. $z = \pm 3i$; parts of $y^2 - x^2 = 9$ in second and fourth quadrants, including $z = \pm 3i$

42. $z = 1$ and $z = -3$; parts of $(x + 1)^2 - y^2 = 4$ in second and fourth quadrants, including $z = 1$ and $z = -3$

43. $z = -2 \pm i$; real axis and $\text{Re}\,z = -2$, $-1 \le \text{Im}\,z \le 1$

45. (a) $\text{Re}\,z = 0$, $|\text{Im}\,z| \ge a$ (b) $\text{Im}\,z = \pm a$, $\text{Re}\,z \le 0$

(c) Parts of $y^2 - x^2 = a^2$ in second and fourth quadrants, including $z = \pm ai$

(d) $\operatorname{Re} z = 0$, $|\operatorname{Im} z| \leq a$

Exercises 3.7

1. $(4n+1)\pi/2 \pm \ln(\sqrt{2}+1)\,i$ **2.** $\pi/2 - (1/2)\operatorname{Tan}^{-1}2 - (1/4)\ln 5\,i$

3. $\pi/2 - \ln(\sqrt{17}+4)\,i$ **4.** $\ln(2+\sqrt{5}) + 2n\pi i$, $\ln(\sqrt{5}-2) + (2n+1)\pi i$

5. $(1/4)\ln 1.3 + i[(2n+1)\pi - \operatorname{Tan}^{-1}(3/11)]/2$ **6.** $\ln(\sqrt{3} \pm \sqrt{2}) + (4n \pm 1)\pi i/2$

7. $[\ln(\sqrt{2}-1)+4n\pi]+[2n\pi-2\ln(\sqrt{2}-1)]i$, $[\ln(\sqrt{2}+1)+2(2n+1)\pi]+[(2n+1)\pi-2\ln(\sqrt{2}+1)]i$

8. $-(4n+1)^2\pi^2/16$ **9.** $(1-4n)\pi/4 + \ln(\sqrt{2}+1)i/2$ **10.** $(4n+1)\pi/2$

11. $(2+i)/\sqrt{(2+i)^2z^2-1}$ **12.** $3/[\sqrt{1-9z^2}\operatorname{Sin}^{-1}(3z)]$ **13.** $1/[2(1+z)\sqrt{z}]$

14. $3ie^{\operatorname{Sinh}^{-1}(3iz+6)}/\sqrt{37+36iz-9z^2}$ **15.** $2z\sec^2[\operatorname{Cosh}^{-1}(z^2)]/\sqrt{z^4-1}$

16. $-2\operatorname{Cos}^{-1}[\operatorname{Log}(3z)]/[z\sqrt{1-\operatorname{Log}^2(3z)}]$

17. $(2n+1)\pi - \ln(\sqrt{5}+2)i$, $2n\pi - \ln(\sqrt{5}-2)i$ **18.** $2n\pi - \ln(4 \pm \sqrt{15})i$

19. $(4n+1)\pi/2 - i$ **20.** No solution   **21.** $2n\pi i$ **22.** $\ln(3 \pm 2\sqrt{2}) + (4n-1)\pi i/2$

23. $(4n+1)\pi i/4$

25. (b) $\operatorname{Cos}^{-1}x$ when $|x| \leq 1$; $-i\ln(x-\sqrt{x^2-1})$ when $x > 1$; $\pi - i\ln(\sqrt{x^2-1}-x)$ when $x < -1$

26. (b) Yes

28. $-i\log[i/z + (1-1/z^2)^{1/2}]$, $-i\log[1/z + i(1-1/z^2)^{1/2}]$, $(i/2)\log[(z-i)/(z+i)]$

29. $\log[1/z + (1+1/z^2)^{1/2}]$; $\log[1/z + (1/z^2-1)^{1/2}]$; $(1/2)\log[(z+1)/(z-1)]$

34. $z = \pm i$; $\operatorname{Re} z = 0$, $|\operatorname{Im} z| \geq 1$ **40.** $z = x$, real, with $|x| \leq 1$

Exercises 3.8

1. $T_2 + (1/\pi)(T_1-T_2)\operatorname{Arg}(x+yi)$ Isothermals are radial lines $y = mx$; heat flow lines are circular arcs $x^2 + y^2 = r^2$

2. $T_2 + (2/\pi)(T_1-T_2)\operatorname{Tan}^{-1}(y/x)$ Isothermals are radial lines $y = mx$; heat flow lines are circular arcs $x^2 + y^2 = r^2$

Exercises 3.9

1. $V_2 + (1/\pi)(V_1 - V_2)\tan^{-1}(y/x)$, $0 \leq \tan^{-1}(y/x) \leq \pi$

2. $V_a + (V_b - V_a)\dfrac{\ln(r/a)}{\ln(b/a)}$ Equipotentials are circles centred at the origin; lines of force are radial lines.

3. $V_2 + (2/\pi)(V_1 - V_2)\operatorname{Tan}^{-1}(y/x)$ Equipotentials are radial lines; lines of force are circular arcs.

7. No

Exercises 3.10

1.   Stagnation point at $z = 0$ **2.**   Stagnation point at $z = 0$

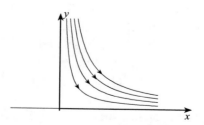

3.   Stagnation point at $z = -1$

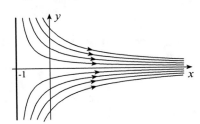

4.   Stagnation point at $z = 0$

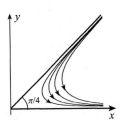

5. Uniform flow making angle α with the positive x-axis past a circular object of radius a at $z = 0$. Stagnation points at $z = \pm ae^{\alpha i}$

6. (a) $\dfrac{\pi}{2a}\left(\cos\dfrac{\pi x}{2a}\cosh\dfrac{\pi y}{2a}\hat{\mathbf{i}} + \sin\dfrac{\pi x}{2a}\sinh\dfrac{\pi y}{2a}\hat{\mathbf{j}}\right)$

(b)

(c) Stagnation points at $(\pm a, 0)$

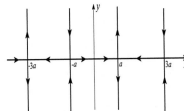

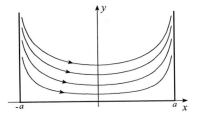

7. (a) $\dfrac{\pi}{2a}\left(-\sin\dfrac{\pi x}{2a}\cosh\dfrac{\pi y}{2a}\hat{\mathbf{i}} + \cos\dfrac{\pi x}{2a}\sinh\dfrac{\pi y}{2a}\hat{\mathbf{j}}\right)$

(b)

(c) Stagnation points at $(0, 0)$ and $(2a, 0)$

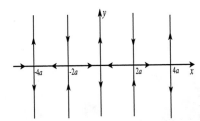

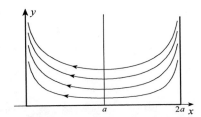

8. (b) $-(2/a)(\sin\phi\cosh\psi\,\hat{\mathbf{i}} + \cos\phi\sinh\psi\,\hat{\mathbf{j}})/(\cosh 2\psi - \cos 2\phi)$, $\sqrt{2}/(a\sqrt{\cosh 2\psi - \cos 2\phi})$, clockwise

9. (c) Infinite

10. (a) Circle $r = 1$ and positive x- and y-axes

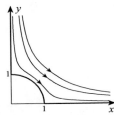

11. Uz **14.** (d) $0,0$ **15.** (a) $|k|/\sqrt{x^2 + y^2}$ (b) $0,0$ (c) $2\pi\rho k$, 0

16. (a) $|k|/\sqrt{x^2 + y^2}$ (b) $0,0$ (c) 0, $2\pi k$

17. $\dfrac{-2ak(x^2 - y^2 - a^2)}{(x^2 - y^2 - a^2)^2 + 4x^2y^2}\hat{\mathbf{i}} - \dfrac{4akxy}{(x^2 - y^2 - a^2)^2 + 4x^2y^2}\hat{\mathbf{j}}$, $\dfrac{2ak}{\sqrt{(x^2 - y^2 - a^2)^2 + 4x^2y^2}}$

18. (a) $\theta = 0$, $\theta = \alpha$ (b) $(\pi/\alpha)r^{\pi/\alpha-1}\{\cos\left[\theta(\pi/\alpha - 1)\right]\hat{\mathbf{i}} - \sin\left[\theta(\pi/\alpha - 1)\right]\hat{\mathbf{j}}$, $z = 0$

(c) x-component positive, y-component negative (d) x-component positive, y-component negative

(e) $(\pi/\alpha)r^{\pi/\alpha-1}[\sin{(\alpha/2)}\hat{\mathbf{i}} - \cos{(\alpha/2)}\hat{\mathbf{j}}]$, yes

19. (a) $\theta = 0$, $\theta = \alpha$ (b) $(\pi/\alpha)r^{\pi/\alpha-1}\{\cos{[\theta(\pi/\alpha - 1)]}\hat{\mathbf{i}} - \sin{[\theta(\pi/\alpha - 1)]}\hat{\mathbf{j}}$, $z = 0$
   (c) x-component positive, y-component negative (d) x-component sometimes positive and sometimes negative, y-component negative (e) $(\pi/\alpha)r^{\pi/\alpha-1}[\sin{(\alpha/2)}\hat{\mathbf{i}} - \cos{(\alpha/2)}\hat{\mathbf{j}}]$, yes

20. (a) $\theta = \alpha$, $\theta = \pi$, and $\theta = 2\pi - \alpha$ (b) $\dfrac{\pi}{\pi - \alpha}r^{\alpha/(\pi-\alpha)}\left[\cos{\dfrac{\alpha(\theta - \pi)}{\pi - \alpha}}\hat{\mathbf{i}} - \sin{\dfrac{\alpha(\theta - \pi)}{\pi - \alpha}}\hat{\mathbf{j}}\right]$, $z = 0$

Exercises 4.1

1. $z^4/4 + 3z^2/2 + 2z + C$, all z **2.** $-1/z - z^2 + C$, $z \neq 0$ **3.** $(z^2 + 3)^5/10 + C$, all z
4. $(4z^3 + 2)^7/84 + C$, all z **5.** $-1/[2(z^2 + 1)] + C$, $z \neq \pm i$
6. $-1/(z^2 - 3z + 5)^2 + C$, $z \neq (3 \pm \sqrt{11}i)/2$ **7.** $(1/3)\sin{3z} + C$, all z
8. $-(1/8)\cos{(4z^2)} + C$, all z **9.** $z/2 + (1/4)\sin{2z} + C$, all z
10. $\tan{z} + C$, $z \neq (2n + 1)\pi/2$ **11.** $\log_\phi{(z + 5)} + C$, z except on branch cut
12. $(1/3)\log_\phi{(3z + 4i)} + C$, except on branch cut **13.** $-z\cos{z} + \sin{z} + C$, all z
14. $-\cos{z} + (1/3)\cos^3{z} + C$, all z **15.** $-1/[2(z^2 - 4)] + C$, $z \neq \pm 2$
16. $(4/9)\log_\phi{(z + 2)} + (5/9)\log_\psi{(z - 1)} - (1/3)/(z - 1) + C$, except on branch cuts
17. $(z^2/2)e^{2z} - (z/2)e^{2z} + (1/4)e^{2z} + C$, all z
18. $-2\sqrt{1 - z} + (2/3)(\sqrt{1 - z})^3 + C$, except on branch cut Im $z = 0$, Re $z \geq 1$
19. $z\text{Log } z - z + C$, except on branch cut Im $z = 0$, Re $z \leq 0$ **20.** $\cos{(1/z)} + C$, $z \neq 0$ **21.** No

Exercises 4.2

1. $x = 6 - 2t$, $y = t$, $5/2 \leq t \leq 9/2$; $-2\hat{\mathbf{i}} + \hat{\mathbf{j}}$
2. $x = 3\cos{t}$, $y = 3\sin{t}$, $0 \leq t \leq 2\pi$; $-3\sin{t}\hat{\mathbf{i}} + 3\cos{t}\hat{\mathbf{j}}$
3. $x = 3\cos{t}$, $y = -3\sin{t}$, $-\pi/2 \leq t \leq 3\pi/2$; $-3\sin{t}\hat{\mathbf{i}} - 3\cos{t}\hat{\mathbf{j}}$
4. $x = -t$, $y = t^2 - 2t + 5$, $0 \leq t \leq 2$; $-\hat{\mathbf{i}} + (2t - 2)\hat{\mathbf{j}}$
5. $x = t^3 + t$, $y = t$, $-1 \leq t \leq 2$; $(3t^2 + 1)\hat{\mathbf{i}} + \hat{\mathbf{j}}$
6. $x = -1 + \sqrt{5}\cos{t}$, $y = 2 + \sqrt{5}\sin{t}$, $0 \leq t \leq 2\pi$; $-\sqrt{5}\sin{t}\hat{\mathbf{i}} + \sqrt{5}\cos{t}\hat{\mathbf{j}}$
7. $x = 2\cos{t}$, $y = -\sqrt{2}\sin{t}$, $-\pi \leq t \leq 0$; $-2\sin{t}\hat{\mathbf{i}} - \sqrt{2}\cos{t}\hat{\mathbf{j}}$
8. $x = (5t^2 - t^3)/(t + 1)$, $y = t$, $1 \leq t \leq 2$; $[(10t + 2t^2 - 2t^3)/(t + 1)^2]\hat{\mathbf{i}} + \hat{\mathbf{j}}$
9. $x = \sqrt{1 + t^2}$, $y = -t$, $-1 \leq t \leq 2$; $(t/\sqrt{1 + t^2})\hat{\mathbf{i}} - \hat{\mathbf{j}}$
10. $x = x_1 + (x_2 - x_1)t$, $y = y_1 + (y_2 - y_1)t$, $0 \leq t \leq 1$; $(x_2 - x_1)\hat{\mathbf{i}} + (y_2 - y_1)\hat{\mathbf{j}}$ **11.** No
12. $x = t$, $y = t^{5/3}$, $-1 \leq t \leq 1$ **13.** $777/8$ **14.** $1/2$ **15.** 0 **16.** $-8/3$ **17.** -43 **18.** 4π
19. $-99/140$ **20.** 0 **21.** $(4/3)\sinh{1} - 4$ **22.** $-4/3$ **23.** e^3 **24.** $8/35$ **25.** 0 **26.** -8π
27. $\pi/8 + (1/10)\text{Tan}^{-1}{3}$ **28.** 9 **29.** (a) $-51/2$ (b) $-141/5$ (c) $141/4$ **30.** (a) 2π (b) 0
31. $-\pi$ **32.** 2π **33.** $81\pi/2$ **34.** -4π
35. (a) Any domain not containing the origin (b) 0
36. $2n\pi$, where n is the number of times the curve encircles the origin

Exercises 4.3

1. $-3/2 + 2i$ **2.** $-2 - i$ **3.** $(e^2 - \cos{3}) + \sin{3}i$ **4.** 0 **5.** 0 **6.** $\cosh{2} - \cos{2}$ **7.** $\sinh{2} + \sin{1}i$
8. $(3\ln{3} + \ln{2} - 2 - \pi/2) + (3\ln{3} + \ln{2} - 2 + \pi/2)i$

Exercises 4.4

9. 0 **10.** $-2i/5$
11. $1/2 + (e/2)\{[\cos{1}\cosh{1}(\sin{1} - \cos{1}) - \sin{1}\sinh{1}(\cos{1} + \sin{1})]$
    $+ [\cos{1}\sinh{1}(\cos{1} + \sin{1}) + \sin{1}\cosh{1}(\sin{1} - \cos{1})]i\}$

12. $(2\cosh 2 - \sinh 2)/4 + (2\cos 2 - \sin 2)i/4$ **13.** $[3 - (1/2)\sinh 6]i$
14. $(1/2)\ln 5 - [\pi/2 + \mathrm{Tan}^{-1}(1/2)]i$ **15.** $\ln(\sqrt{170}/15) + [\mathrm{Tan}^{-1}(1/3) - \mathrm{Tan}^{-1}(1/4)]i$
16. $4\sqrt{2}\sin(\pi/8)\,i$ **17.** $-(1/2)\mathrm{Tan}^{-1}(1/2) + (1/4)\ln 3\,i$ **18.** $-32/3$ **19.** $-2\pi i$ **20.** $-4\sqrt{3}i$

Exercises 4.5

1. 0   **2.** 0   **3.** 0   **4.** 0   **5.** 0   **6.** 0   **7.** $-\pi i$ **8.** 0   **9.** π **10.** $\pi(\sqrt{3} - i)/3$ **11.** No   **12.** Yes
13. Yes   **14.** No   **15.** Yes   **16.** Yes   **17.** No   **18.** No   **19.** Yes   **20.** No   **21.** (b) Yes
22. $(1 + e^{-\pi})(1 - i)/2$

Exercises 4.6

1. $2\pi e^2 i$ **2.** $-\pi^4/4$ **3.** $(\pi\sin 2)i$ **4.** 0   **5.** 0   **6.** $-\sqrt{3}\pi/6$ **7.** $\pi(2\sin 2 + \cos 2)i/16$
8. (a) $-2\pi i/3$ (b) $2\pi i/3$ (c) 0   **9.** $6\pi i$ **10.** $(2\pi\ln 2)i$ **11.** $-\sqrt{2}\pi(1 + i)/4$
12. $4\pi^2 - 2\pi(1 + \ln 2)i$ **13.** 0   **14.** Yes   **17.** $\pi i/2$ when $R > 1/2$; 0 when $R < 1/2$

Exercises 4.7

2. $f(z) = i$ **4.** 4/7   **5.** $\cosh a$ **6.** larger of $\cosh 2a$ and $\cosh 2b$ **7.** e^{-7} **8.** 0
9. $\sqrt{(\ln 2)^2 + \pi^2/9}$ **10.** 1/10
13. Only if it is a constant function with $f(z) = k$ where $|k| < 1$

Exercises 4.8

5. (b) $1, -1$, Does not exist   **6.** 1   **7.** $(1/\pi)\tan^{-1}[2y/(x^2 + y^2 - 1)]$ **8.** $a/2 + (a/\pi)\mathrm{Tan}^{-1}(x/y)$
9. $(2a/\pi)\mathrm{Tan}^{-1}(x/y)$ **10.** $(a/\pi)\tan^{-1}[2cy/(x^2 + y^2 - c^2)]$
11. $-a + (2a/\pi)\tan^{-1}[2cy/(x^2 + y^2 - c^2)]$
12. $\dfrac{a}{\pi}\left[\mathrm{Tan}^{-1}\left(\dfrac{c - x}{y}\right) + 2\,\mathrm{Tan}^{-1}\left(\dfrac{x}{y}\right) - \mathrm{Tan}^{-1}\left(\dfrac{c + x}{y}\right)\right]$
13. $\dfrac{1}{\pi}\left[(a - b)\,\mathrm{Tan}^{-1}\left(\dfrac{c - x}{y}\right) + 2a\,\mathrm{Tan}^{-1}\left(\dfrac{x}{y}\right) - (a - b)\,\mathrm{Tan}^{-1}\left(\dfrac{c + x}{y}\right)\right]$
14. $\dfrac{1}{x^2 + y^2}\left\{x + \dfrac{y}{2\pi}\ln\left[\dfrac{(1 - x)^2 + y^2}{(1 + x)^2 + y^2}\right] - \dfrac{x}{\pi}\mathrm{Tan}^{-1}\left(\dfrac{1 + x}{y}\right) - \dfrac{x}{\pi}\mathrm{Tan}^{-1}\left(\dfrac{1 - x}{y}\right)\right\}$
15. No   **16.** $u(0, \theta)$ **20.** (b) No (c) $u_2(x, y)$

Exercises 5.1

1. $-1/2$ **2.** Does not exist   **3.** 0   **4.** $(\sinh 1)i$ **5.** $(\sin 1)i$ **6.** 0   **7.** $1.02 - 0.611i$
8. $-\pi + (\ln 2)i$ **9.** $-\pi/2$ **10.** 1   **14.** (a) 0 (b) $-\pi i$ (c) Does not exist

Exercises 5.2

1. Diverges   **2.** Converges   **3.** Diverges   **4.** Converges   **5.** Diverges   **6.** Diverges
7. Converges   **8.** Converges   **9.** Diverges   **10.** Converges   **11.** Diverges   **12.** Converges
13. Diverges   **14.** Converges   **15.** Diverges   **16.** Diverges   **17.** Converges   **18.** Converges
19. Converges   **20.** Converges   **21.** No   **22.** $\mathrm{Re}\,z \leq 0$ **23.** $-i$ **34.** (c) Yes, 1

Exercises 5.3

1. $|z| < 1$ **2.** $|z - 2| < 1$ **3.** $|z + i| < 1$ **4.** $|z| < 1$ **5.** all z **6.** $|z + 4 + i| < 1$ **7.** $|z| < 1/2$
8. $|z - 4| < 1/2$ **9.** $|z + 4| < 1$ **10.** $|z - 4| < 2^{-1/4}$ **11.** $|z + 1 - i| < 27$ **12.** $|z - 2 + i| < e^{-2}$
13. $|z - i| < 5^{1/4}$ **14.** $|z + 1| < 3^{1/3}$ **15.** $|z| < 1$ **16.** $|z + 1| < 4$ **17.** $|z - 1 + 2i| < 1$
18. $|z - 2| < 1$ **19.** $|z| < 1$ **20.** $|z| < 1$ **21.** $2/(2 - z), |z| < 2$

22. $-(z+1)^2/[1-i(z+1)]$, $|z+1| < 1$ **23.** $-1/[5(2+6iz+3z^2)]$, $|z+i| < \sqrt{5/3}$

24. $(1+i)(z-i)^3/[(1-i)-(1+i)(z-i)^3]$, $|z-i| < 1$ **25.** $1/(1-2i-z)^2$, $|z+2i| < 1$

26. $2/(2+i-z)^3$, $|z-1-i| < 1$ **27.** $(2-z)/(1-z)^2$, $|z| < 1$

28. $(1+z)/(1-z)^3$, $|z| < 1$ **29.** $-z - \text{Log}\,(1-z)$, $|z| < 1$

30. $(z-2)/(3-z) - \text{Log}\,(3-z)$, $|z-2| < 1$ **31.** $9z^4(2-3z^2)/(1-3z^2)^2$, $|z| < 1/\sqrt{3}$

32. $(3z-z^2)/(1-z)^3$, $|z| < 1$

33. $2z^2/(1-z^2)^2 + (1/2)\text{Log}\,(1+z) - (1/2)\text{Log}\,(1-z)$, $|z| < 1$ **34.** $|z| < 1$

35. $|z| < \infty$ **36.** $\displaystyle\sum_{n=0}^{\infty} (-1)^n 3^n z^n$, $|z| < 1/3$ **37.** $\displaystyle\sum_{n=2}^{\infty} \frac{z^n}{2^{n-1}}$, $|z| < 2$

38. $\displaystyle\sum_{n=0}^{\infty} \frac{(-1)^n}{2^{n+1}}(z-1)^n$, $|z-1| < 2$ **39.** $\displaystyle\sum_{n=0}^{\infty} \frac{(-1)^n}{(1+i)^{n+1}}(z-i)^n$, $|z-i| < \sqrt{2}$

40. $\displaystyle\frac{3+i}{5} + \sum_{n=1}^{\infty} \frac{(-1)^{n+1}}{(2+i)^{n+1}}(z-1-i)^n$, $|z-1-i| < \sqrt{5}$ **41.** $\displaystyle\sum_{n=1}^{\infty} n 3^{n-1} z^n$, $|z| < 1/3$

45. $|z| < \sqrt{2}$ **46.** $|z| < 1/4$ **47.** Diverges for all $|z| = 1$

48. Converges for all $|z| = 1$ except $z = 1$ **49.** Converges for all $|z| = 1$

50. Diverges for all $|z| = 2$ **51.** Diverges for all $|z| = 1/3$

Exercises 5.4

1. $\displaystyle\sum_{n=0}^{\infty} (-1)^n z^{2n+1}$, $|z| < 1$ **2.** $\displaystyle\sum_{n=0}^{\infty} \frac{3(-1)^n}{2^{n+1}}(z-1)^n$, $|z-1| < 2$

3. $\displaystyle\sum_{n=1}^{\infty} n z^n$, $|z| < 1$ **4.** $\displaystyle\sum_{n=0}^{\infty} \frac{e^{1+i}}{n!}(z-1-i)^n$, $|z| < \infty$

5. $\displaystyle\cosh 1 \sum_{n=0}^{\infty} \frac{(-1)^n}{(2n+1)!}(z-i)^{2n+1} + i \sinh 1 \sum_{n=0}^{\infty} \frac{(-1)^n}{(2n)!}(z-i)^{2n}$, $|z| < \infty$

6. $\displaystyle\cos\,(2-i) \sum_{n=0}^{\infty} \frac{(-1)^n}{(2n)!}(z-2+i)^{2n} + \sin\,(2-i) \sum_{n=0}^{\infty} \frac{(-1)^{n+1}}{(2n+1)!}(z-2+i)^{2n+1}$, $|z| < \infty$

7. $\displaystyle\sum_{n=0}^{\infty} \frac{1}{(2n+1)!} z^{2n+1}$, $|z| < \infty$ **8.** $\displaystyle\sum_{n=0}^{\infty} \frac{1}{(2n)!} z^{2n}$, $|z| < \infty$ **9.** $\displaystyle\sum_{n=0}^{\infty} \frac{e^2 2^n}{n!}(z-1)^n$, $|z| < \infty$

10. $\displaystyle\sum_{n=1}^{\infty} \frac{(-1)^{n+1}2^{2n-1}}{(2n)!} z^{2n}$, $|z| < \infty$ **11.** $\displaystyle\sum_{n=0}^{\infty} \frac{3^{2n}}{(2n)!} z^{2n+1} + \sum_{n=0}^{\infty} \frac{3^{2n}}{(2n)!} z^{2n}$, $|z| < \infty$

12. $\displaystyle\sum_{n=0}^{\infty} \frac{(-1)^n}{\sqrt{2}(2n)!}(z-\pi/4)^{2n} + \sum_{n=0}^{\infty} \frac{(-1)^n}{\sqrt{2}(2n+1)!}(z-\pi/4)^{2n+1}$, $|z| < \infty$

13. $\displaystyle\cos 1 \sum_{n=0}^{\infty} \frac{1}{(2n)!}(z-i)^{2n} + (\sin 1)i \sum_{n=0}^{\infty} \frac{1}{(2n+1)!}(z-i)^{2n+1}$, $|z| < \infty$

14. $\displaystyle\sum_{n=0}^{\infty} (-1)^n \left[1 + \frac{2^2}{2!} + \frac{2^4}{4!} + \cdots + \frac{2^{2n}}{(2n)!} \right] z^{2n}$, $|z| < 1$

15. $\displaystyle\cos 1 \sum_{n=0}^{\infty} \frac{(-1)^n}{(2n)!} z^{4n} + \sin 1 \sum_{n=0}^{\infty} \frac{(-1)^n}{(2n+1)!} z^{4n+2}$, $|z| < \infty$

16. $\displaystyle\cos 2 \sum_{n=0}^{\infty} \frac{(-1)^n 3^{2n+1}}{(2n+1)!} z^{4n+2} + \sin 2 \sum_{n=0}^{\infty} \frac{(-1)^n 3^{2n}}{(2n)!} z^{4n}$, $|z| < \infty$

17. $\displaystyle\sum_{n=0}^{\infty} \frac{(-1)^n 2^n}{7^{n+1}}(z-3)^n,\ |z-3| < 7/2$ **18.** $\displaystyle\sum_{n=0}^{\infty} \frac{(-1)^n}{(1+i)^{n+1}}(z-i)^n,\ |z-i| < \sqrt{2}$

19. $\displaystyle\sum_{n=1}^{\infty} n3^{n-1}z^n,\ |z| < 1/3$ **20.** $\displaystyle\frac{3+i}{5} + \sum_{n=1}^{\infty} \frac{(-1)^{n+1}}{(2+i)^{n+1}}(z-1-i)^n,\ |z-1-i| < \sqrt{5}$

21. $\displaystyle\sum_{n=0}^{\infty} \frac{4^{2n+1}\cos 4}{(2n+1)!}(z+i)^{2n+1} - \sum_{n=0}^{\infty} \frac{4^{2n}\sin 4\,i}{(2n)!}(z+i)^{2n},\ |z| < \infty$

22. $\displaystyle\frac{\pi i}{2} + \sum_{n=1}^{\infty} \frac{i^{n+2}}{n}(z-i)^n,\ |z-i| < 1$ **23.** $\displaystyle\sum_{n=0}^{\infty} \frac{(-1)^n}{2n+1}z^{2n+1},\ |z| < 1$

24. $\displaystyle-\frac{4}{5} - \frac{4}{25}(z-2) + \sum_{n=2}^{\infty} \frac{9(-1)^{n+1}4^{n-2}}{5^{n+1}}(z-2)^n,\ |z-2| < \frac{5}{4}$

25. $\displaystyle 1 + \frac{z^3}{3} + \sum_{n=2}^{\infty} \frac{(-1)^{n+1}[2\cdot 5\cdot 8\cdots(3n-4)]}{3^n n!}z^{3n},\ |z| < 1$

26. $\displaystyle\sum_{n=0}^{\infty} \frac{(2n)!}{2^{2n}(n!)^2(2n+1)}z^{2n+1},\ |z| < 1$ **27.** $z = \pm i$ of order 1 **28.** $z = 0$ of order 3

29. $z = n\pi/3,\ n \neq 0$ of order 1 **30.** $z = n\pi i$ of order 2 **31.** No zeros **32.** $z = 2$ of order 1

35. $\displaystyle\sum_{n=1}^{\infty} \frac{3(-1)^n(1-3^{2n})}{4(2n+1)!}z^{2n+1},\ |z| < \infty$ **36.** $\displaystyle\sum_{n=1}^{\infty} \frac{2^{n/2}\sin(n\pi/4)}{n!}z^n,\ |z| < \infty$

37. $\displaystyle e^{\pi i/4} + \sum_{n=1}^{\infty} \frac{(2n-2)!e^{(2n+5)\pi i/4}}{2^{2n-1}(n-1)!\,n!}z^n,\ |z| < 1$

38. $\displaystyle 5^{1/4}e^{\theta i/2} + \sum_{n=1}^{\infty} \frac{(-1)^{n+1}(2n-2)!5^{(1-2n)/4}e^{(1-2n)\theta i/2}}{2^{2n-1}n!(n-1)!}(z+1-i)^n,$ where $\theta = \pi - \text{Tan}^{-1}2$,

$|z+1-i| < 2$

40. There are none. **41.** $\displaystyle\frac{\pi i}{2} + \sum_{n=1}^{\infty} \frac{i^{n+2}}{n}(z-i)^n$

42. $\displaystyle 5^{1/4}e^{\theta i/2} + \sum_{n=1}^{\infty} \frac{(-1)^{n+1}(2n-2)!5^{(1-2n)/4}e^{(1-2n)\theta i/2}}{2^{2n-1}n!(n-1)!}(z+1-i)^n,$ where $\theta = \pi - \text{Tan}^{-1}2$

43. Not always **46.** (b) $|z| < (\sqrt{5}-1)/2$ (c) $a_n = \dfrac{1}{\sqrt{5}}\left[\left(\dfrac{1+\sqrt{5}}{2}\right)^{n+1} - \left(\dfrac{1-\sqrt{5}}{2}\right)^{n+1}\right]$

47. $|z| > 0$, Isolated zeros at $z = 1/(n\pi),\ n \neq 0$

Exercises 5.5

1. $\displaystyle\sum_{n=1}^{\infty} \frac{3^{n-1}}{z^n}$ **2.** $\displaystyle\sum_{n=-1}^{\infty} \frac{(-1)^{n+1}}{2^{n+2}}z^n$ **3.** $\displaystyle\sum_{n=1}^{\infty} \frac{2(-1)^{n+1}}{(z-3)^n} + \sum_{n=0}^{\infty} \frac{(-1)^{n+1}}{2^{n+1}}(z-3)^n$

4. $\displaystyle\sum_{n=0}^{\infty} \frac{(-1)^n}{(2n+1)!\,z^{2n+1}}$ **5.** $\displaystyle\sum_{n=2}^{\infty} \frac{(-1)^n 5^{n-3}(2n+1)}{(z-3)^n}$

6. $\displaystyle\sum_{n=2}^{\infty} \frac{(-1)^n[-1+i(n-1)]}{(z-1)^n} + \frac{1}{z-1} + \sum_{n=0}^{\infty} \frac{(-1)^{n+1}}{(1-i)^{n+1}}(z-1)^n$

7. $\displaystyle\sum_{n=-2}^{\infty} -z^n,\ 0 < |z| < 1$ **8.** $\displaystyle\frac{1/2}{z-2i} + \sum_{n=0}^{\infty} \frac{i^{n-1}}{2^{2n+3}}(z-2i)^n,\ 0 < |z-2i| < 4$

9. $\displaystyle\sum_{n=0}^{\infty} \frac{(-1)^n}{2^{3(n+1)/2}} \cos\frac{(n+1)\pi}{4}(z-2)^n$, $|z-2| < 2\sqrt{2}$ **10.** $\displaystyle\sum_{n=-1}^{\infty} \frac{1}{e(n+1)!}(z+1)^n$, $|z+1| > 0$

11. $1 - 2/(z+1) + 1/(z+1)^2$ $|z+1| > 0$

12. $\displaystyle\frac{1-i}{z+2i} + \frac{1}{4}(3+i) + \sum_{n=1}^{\infty} \frac{-1+i}{4^{n+1}i^n}(z+2i)^n$, $0 < |z+2i| < 4$ **13.** $\displaystyle\sum_{n=-2}^{\infty} \frac{(-1)^n}{(n+3)!}z^n$ $|z| > 0$

14. $\displaystyle\cos 3\sum_{n=0}^{\infty} \frac{(-1)^n}{(2n+1)!}(z-3)^{2n} + \sin 3\sum_{n=0}^{\infty} \frac{(-1)^n}{(2n)!}(z-3)^{2n-1}$, $|z-3| > 0$

15. $\displaystyle\sum_{n=-3}^{\infty} \frac{e^8 4^{n+3}}{(n+3)!}(z-2)^n$, $|z-2| > 0$

16. $\displaystyle\sum_{n=0}^{\infty} \frac{(-1)^n}{(2n+1)!(z+2)^{2n}} + \sum_{n=0}^{\infty} \frac{4(-1)^{n+1}}{(2n+1)!(z+2)^{2n+1}}$, $|z+2| > 0$

17. $\displaystyle\sum_{n=0}^{\infty} \frac{e3^n}{n!(z-3)^n}$, $|z-3| > 0$ **18.** (a) $\displaystyle\sum_{n=-1}^{\infty} \frac{n+2}{2^{n+3}}(z+2)^n$ (b) $\displaystyle\sum_{n=3}^{\infty} \frac{2^{n-3}(n-2)}{(z+2)^n}$

19. $\displaystyle\frac{1}{z} + \frac{z}{6} + \frac{7z^3}{360}$ **20.** $\displaystyle\sum_{n=0}^{\infty} \frac{(-1)^{n+1}}{2^n(z-1)^n} + \sum_{n=1}^{\infty} -(z-1)^n$

21. (a) $\displaystyle\sum_{n=2}^{\infty} \left(\frac{1-2^{n-2}}{2^{n-2}}\right)z^n$ (b) $\displaystyle\sum_{n=1}^{\infty} \frac{1}{z^n} + 1 + z + \sum_{n=2}^{\infty} \frac{1}{2^{n-2}}z^n$ (c) $\displaystyle\sum_{n=-1}^{\infty} \frac{1-2^{n+2}}{z^n}$

(d) $\displaystyle -(z-1) - 4 - \frac{7}{z-1} + \sum_{n=2}^{\infty} \frac{-8}{(z-1)^n}$ (e) $\displaystyle -\frac{8}{z-2} - 4 - 2(z-2) + \sum_{n=2}^{\infty} (-1)^n(z-2)^n$

22. No   **23.** No; No   **24.** $\displaystyle\frac{1}{2z} + \frac{z}{3} + \frac{7z^3}{45} + \frac{74z^5}{945}$, $0 < |z| < \pi/2$

26. (a) $\displaystyle z - \sum_{n=1}^{\infty} \frac{(2n-2)!}{2^{2n-1}n!(n-1)!z^{2n-1}}$, $|z| > 1$ (b) $\displaystyle 1 + (z-1) + \sum_{n=1}^{\infty} \frac{(-1)^n(2n)!}{2^n n!(n+1)!(z-1)^n}$

Exercises 5.6

3. $z = 0$, pole of order 2; $z = -1$, pole of order 1   **4.** $z = 0$, essential   **5.** $z = 2$, removable
6. $z = 0$, pole of order 4   **7.** $z = n\pi i$, poles of order 1   **8.** None
9. $z = (2n+1)\pi/2$, poles of order 2   **10.** $z = n\pi$, poles of order 1
11. $z = 0$, removable; $z = n\pi$, $n \neq 0$, poles of order 1
12. $z = \pm i$, $[(2n+1)\pi/2 - 1]i$, poles of order 1   **13.** $z = 0$, pole of order 3
14. $z = n\pi$, $(6n \pm 1)\pi/3$, poles of order 1   **15.** $z = 2/[(2n+1)\pi]$, poles of order 1
16. $z = 0$, removable; $z = 1$, pole of order 1; $z = n$ for $n \neq 0, 1$, poles of order 2
17. pole of order 4   **18.** essential   **19.** removable   **20.** removable   **21.** $z = 0$ pole of order 8
23. (a) Yes (b) No (c) No (d) No

Exercises 5.7

1. $|z_1 - z_0| + R$ where R is the radius of C_0

Exercises 6.1

1. $-2340 + 880i$ at $z = 4i$ **2.** $8/25$ at $z = -2$; $-(8+31i)/50$ at $z = i$; $-(8-31i)/50$ at $z = -i$
3. 0 at $z = 0$ **4.** 8 at $z = 0$ **5.** 0 at $z = 0$ **6.** $1/(n+1)!$ at $z = 1$ **7.** $(-1)^n/2$ at $z = n\pi/2$
8. 1 at $z = n\pi$

9. At $z = 1$, residue is 0 when $n < m - 1$, 1 when $n = m - 1$, and $n!/[(m-1)!(n-m+1)!]$ when $n < m - 1$

10. $\dfrac{(-1)^n}{e}$ at $z = -1$, $\displaystyle\sum_{k=0}^{\infty} \dfrac{(-1)^k}{(n+k+1)!}$ at $z = 0$ **11.** $\displaystyle\sum_{n=1}^{\infty} \dfrac{(-1)^n 2^n}{n!(n-1)!}$ at $z = 0$

12. 0   **13.** 0   **14.** $2\pi i e^2$ **15.** $-\pi^4/4$ **16.** $(\pi\sin 2)i$ **17.** 0   **18.** 0   **19.** $-\sqrt{3}\pi/6$

20. $\pi(2\sin 2 + \cos 2)i/16$ **21.** 0   **22.** $6\pi i$ **23.** $(2\pi\ln 2)i$ **24.** $-\pi(1+i)/(2\sqrt{2})$

25. $4\pi^2 - 2\pi(1+\ln 2)i$ **26.** $(\pi\sin 2)i$ **27.** $\pi(e^2-1)i/4$ **28.** $\pi i/9$ **29.** 0   **30.** $-9\pi i$ **31.** 0

32. $-\pi i/3$ **33.** $2\pi i$ **34.** $\pi i/6$ **35.** $2\pi i$ **36.** $2\pi i$ **37.** $10\pi i$ **38.** $2\pi i$ **39.** $16\pi i$ **40.** $-4\pi i$

Exercises 6.2

1. $\pi/\sqrt{2}$ **2.** $2\pi/\sqrt{5}$ **3.** $2\pi/\sqrt{11}$ **4.** $2\pi/\sqrt{11}$ **5.** $2\pi/\sqrt{21}$ **6.** 0   **7.** $\pi/4$ **8.** $(4-3\sqrt{2})\pi/2$

9. $\pi/\sqrt{5}$ **10.** $(1/\sqrt{11})\mathrm{Tan}^{-1}(\sqrt{11}/5)$ **11.** $\sqrt{2}[\pi - \mathrm{Tan}^{-1}(2\sqrt{2})]/4$ **12.** $(1/\sqrt{21})\mathrm{Tan}^{-1}(\sqrt{21}/2)$

13. $\dfrac{1}{\sqrt{5}}\left[\mathrm{Tan}^{-1}\left(\dfrac{\sqrt{5}}{2}\right) - \mathrm{Tan}^{-1}\left(\dfrac{\sqrt{5}\cos 2}{2 + 3\sin 2}\right)\right]$ **14.** $(1/\sqrt{7})\mathrm{Tan}^{-1}[\sqrt{7}\sin 1/(3+4\cos 1)]$

15. $\pi/\sqrt{15}$ **16.** $(1/\sqrt{21})[2\pi - \mathrm{Tan}^{-1}(\sqrt{21}/2)]$ **17.** $\pi/2 - (3\sqrt{2}/4)\mathrm{Tan}^{-1}(2\sqrt{2})$ **18.** $-\pi/12$

19. $2\pi\sum_{n=0}^{\infty} 1/(n!)^2$ **20.** $\sqrt{2}\pi/4$ **21.** $\pi/3$ **22.** $\pi/2$ **23.** $4\sqrt{3}\pi/3$ **24.** $2\pi/3^{11/6}$

25. $2\pi\sqrt{3}/9$ **26.** $\pi/(2\sqrt{2}a)$ **27.** $\pi/(3a^5)$ **28.** $\pi/(8a^4)$ **29.** $\sqrt{3}\pi/(9a^4)$ **30.** $(\pi/2)e^{-2\sqrt{5}}$

31. $\pi(\cos 3 - \sin 3)/(2e^3)$ **32.** $\pi(e^2-1)/(4e^2)$ **33.** $-\pi/(3e^3)$ **34.** $-(\pi\sin 1)/e$

35. $(\pi e^{-b}\cos a)/b$ **36.** $(\sqrt{2}/4)\pi e^{-a/\sqrt{2}}[\sin(a/\sqrt{2}) + \cos(a/\sqrt{2})]$ **37.** $(\pi/a)e^{-ab}$

38. $\pi(1+ab)e^{-ab}/(4a^3)$ **40.** (b) $\sqrt{2}\pi/4$ **42.** $1/24 + [3/(16\sqrt{2})][\pi - \mathrm{Tan}^{-1}(2\sqrt{2})]$

53. $41\pi/7^{5/2}$

Exercises 6.3

1. $\pi/16$ **2.** $\pi/\sqrt{2}$ **3.** $\pi/\sqrt{3}$ **4.** $\pi/(2e) - (\pi/2)\sin 1$ **5.** $(\pi/b)\sin ab$ **6.** 0

7. $(\pi/24)\cos 4 - (\pi/24)e^{-2\sqrt{3}}(\cos 2 - \sqrt{3}\sin 2)$ **8.** $\pi(\ln a - 1)/(4a^3)$ **9.** $\sqrt{2}\pi(2\ln a - \pi/2)/(8a^3)$

10. $\pi^3/(8a) + [\pi/(2a)](\ln a)^2$ **11.** $\pi(b\ln a - a\ln b)/[2ab(b^2-a^2)]$ **12.** $(\pi/a)\ln(2a)$ **13.** $(b-a)\pi$

14. $\pi/(\sqrt{2}a^{3/2})$ **15.** $ab^{a-1}\pi\csc(a\pi)$ **16.** $(\pi/2)b^{a-1}\sec(a\pi/2)$ **17.** $\pi b^{-a}\csc a\pi$

18. $\pi(c^a - b^a)\csc a\pi/(c-b)$ **19.** $(\pi/4)(1-a)b^{a-3}\sec(a\pi/2)$ **20.** $(\pi/4)b^{a-3}\csc(a+1)\pi/4$

21. $\pi b^{-a}\cot a\pi$ **22.** $(\pi/2)b^{a-1}\csc(a\pi)(1-\cos a\pi)$ **27.** (a) $2\pi e^{a\pi i/2}$ (d) $(\pi/2)\sec(a\pi/2)$

29. $\sqrt{2}\pi/4$ **30.** $(\sqrt{\pi}/4)\sqrt{\sqrt{2}+1}$, $(\sqrt{\pi}/4)\sqrt{\sqrt{2}-1}$ **33.** (a) $\pi a/2$ (b) $3\pi a^2/8$ (c) $\pi a^3/3$

Exercises 6.4

1. -1 **2.** -24 **3.** $-4/15$ **4.** $-1/3$ **5.** $-9/2$ **6.** $-32/3$ **7.** e^3 **8.** -1 **9.** 1

10. $\sum_{k=0}^{n} (-1)^{k+1}/(n-k)!$ **11.** No   **12.** 0   **13.** 0   **14.** 0   **15.** $4\pi i$ **16.** $-242\pi i/3$ **17.** $2\pi i$

18. $4\pi i$ **19.** 0   **20.** $2\pi i/3$ **21.** $-200\pi i/1111$ **22.** 0   **23.** $-4516\pi i/17883$

27. $\pi(2n-2)!/[2^{2n-1}n!(n-1)!]$ **28.** $\pi(3-2\sqrt{2})/4$

Exercises 6.5

1. $\pi^2\csc^2\pi a$ **2.** $1/(2a^2) - (\pi^2/2)\mathrm{csch}^2\pi a$ **3.** $(\pi^2 a\,\mathrm{csch}^2\pi a + \pi\coth\pi a)/(4a^3) - 1/(2a^4)$

4. $\dfrac{\sqrt{2}\pi}{4a}\left[\dfrac{\sinh(\sqrt{2}\pi a) - \sin\sqrt{2}\pi a}{\cosh\sqrt{2}\pi a - \cos\sqrt{2}\pi a}\right]$ **5.** $\pi^2/6$ **6.** $\pi^4/90$ **7.** $(1 - \pi a\cot\pi a)/a^2$

8. $[1/(2a^2)](\pi^3/3 + 1/a^2) - [\pi/(2a^3)]\coth\pi a$ **9.** $-\pi^3(1 + \cos^2\pi a)/(2\sin^3\pi a)$

10. $[\pi/(2a)]\mathrm{csch}\pi a - 1/(2a^2)$ **11.** $\pi^2/12$ **12.** $7\pi^4/720$

Exercises 7.1

1. (a) $\operatorname{Im} w > 0$ (b) $0 < \operatorname{Arg} w < 3\pi/2$, $|w| < 4$ (c) $0 < \operatorname{Im} w < 2$ (d) $\operatorname{Re} w > 4$

2. (a) $e < |w| < e^2$, $-\pi/2 < \operatorname{Arg} w < \pi/2$ (b) $1/e < |w| < e$, $0 < \operatorname{Arg} w < 2$ (c) $\operatorname{Im} w > 0$
(d) $|w| > 1$ (e) $|w| > 1$, $\operatorname{Im} w > 0$

3. (a) $0 < \operatorname{Im} w < \pi/2$ (b) $\pi/4 < \operatorname{Im} w < 3\pi/4$ (c) $0 < \operatorname{Re} w < (1/2)\ln 3$, $-\pi < \operatorname{Im} w < \pi$

6. (a) $|w| < 1$, $0 < \operatorname{Arg} w < \pi$ (b) $\operatorname{Im} w > 0$

7. (a) $|w| < \sqrt{R}$, $\operatorname{Re} w > 0$ (b) $\operatorname{Re} w > 0$, $\operatorname{Im} w > 0$ (c) $|w| > \sqrt{2}$, $-\pi/4 < \operatorname{Arg} w < \pi/4$
(d) $(\operatorname{Re} w)^2 - (\operatorname{Im} w)^2 > 1$, $\operatorname{Re} w > 1$ (e) $2(\operatorname{Re} w)(\operatorname{Im} w) > 1$, $\operatorname{Re} w > 0$

10. (a) $\operatorname{Im} z = 2$, $\operatorname{Re} z \leq 0$ (b) $0 < \operatorname{Im} w < \pi$ **11.** (b) $\operatorname{Im} w > 0$

Exercises 7.2

1. $w = 2iz$ **2.** $w = [(1+2i)z - 2i]/(iz+2)$ **3.** $w = [(3+5i)z + 13 - i]/[-iz + 8 - 11i]$

4. $w = [-(18+9i)z - 25 + 27i]/[(14+i)z + 1 + 25i]$ **5.** $w = [(3-4i)z - 6(1+i)]/[z - 2(1+i)]$

6. $w = (z - 5 + 4i)/(3z - 3)$ **7.** $w = -3i/(z-i)$ **8.** $w = [(5-12i)z - 40 - 11i]/(z + 4 + 3i)$

9. $w = [-(3+5i)z - 13 + i]/[(-5+2i)z + 9 + 2i]$ **10.** $w = -[(1+\sqrt{2})iz + 2 + \sqrt{2}]/(z + \sqrt{2}i)$

11. $w = (iz + 4 + 3i)/[(1+2i)z + 3 + 2i]$ **12.** $w = (z+1)/(1-z)$

13. $w = (z - 2 - 2i)/(z + 4 - 2i)$ **15.** $\sqrt{226}/3$ **16.** $w = [(1-i)z + 2i]/z$ **17.** $w = (R-z)/(R+z)$

19. Not necessarily

20. $w = e^{-3\pi i/4}z/(z - R - Ri)$ **21.** (b) $w_1(z_1 + z_0)/(z_1 - z_0)$ (c) $w = i(R-z)/(z+R)$

22. (a) Yes (b) No (c) No **23.** (a) $(21 - 35i)/17$ (b) $-(68 + 73i)/37$ (c) $(1 + 5i)/4$

25. (c) $w = -\mu i(z + Re^{\lambda i})/(z - Re^{\lambda i})$

27. (a) $w = (az + bR)/(cz + dR)$ (b) $w = (az + bR - az_0)/(cz + dR - cz_0)$

28. $w = (z - \sqrt{7}i)/(z + \sqrt{7}i)$; $(4 - \sqrt{7})/3$, 1

29. $w = (z - \sqrt{a^2 - R^2}i)/(z + \sqrt{a^2 - R^2}i)$; $(a - \sqrt{a^2 - R^2})/R$, 1

30. $w = [z - (8 - 4\sqrt{3})i]/[z - (8 + 4\sqrt{3})i]$ **31.** $w = \dfrac{2az - (R^2 - R\sqrt{R^2 - 4a^2})i}{2az - (R^2 + R\sqrt{R^2 - 4a^2})i}$

32. $w = [4z - (19 - \sqrt{105})i]/[4z - (19 + \sqrt{105})i]$

33. $w = \dfrac{2az - [R^2 - r^2 + a^2 - \sqrt{(R^2 - r^2 + a^2)^2 - 4a^2 R^2}]i}{2az - [R^2 - r^2 + a^2 + \sqrt{(R^2 - r^2 + a^2)^2 - 4a^2 R^2}]i}$

Exercises 7.3

14. $w = \sin(\pi z/2)$ **15.** $w = \sin^2[\pi z/(2a)]$ **16.** $w = i\sinh(\pi z/2)$ **17.** $w = -i\sinh(\pi z/2)$

18. $w = e^{\pi z/4}$ **19.** $w = e^{\pi zi/2}$ **20.** $w = -e^{\pi z}$ **21.** (b) $w = z - 1/(2a) - [i/(2a)]\sqrt{4az - 1}$

23. $w = z^2 + a^4/z^2$

Exercises 7.4

8. 10 **9.** $\sqrt{5}/25$ **10.** $3\sqrt{\sinh^2 2 + \sin^2 3}$ **11.** $2\cosh 2 + \sinh 2$ **12.** No

13. (a) 2 (b) $4b\sinh 4a$ (d) No **16.** (a) $\operatorname{Cos}^{-1}(3/\sqrt{10})$ **17.** No

Exercises 7.5

1. $\dfrac{a+b}{2} + \dfrac{a-b}{\pi}\operatorname{Tan}^{-1}\left(\dfrac{2y}{1 - x^2 - y^2}\right)$

2. $\dfrac{b}{2} + \dfrac{1}{\pi}\left\{ a\operatorname{Tan}^{-1}\left(\dfrac{2Ry}{R^2 - x^2 - y^2}\right) - b\operatorname{Tan}^{-1}\left[\dfrac{(R+x)^2 + y^2 + 2Ry}{R^2 - x^2 - y^2}\right]\right.$

$\left. + a\operatorname{Tan}^{-1}\left[\dfrac{(R+x)^2 + y^2 - 2Ry}{R^2 - x^2 - y^2}\right]\right\}$

3. $\dfrac{a+b}{2} + \dfrac{a-b}{\pi}\left\{\text{Tan}^{-1}\left(\dfrac{2Ry}{R^2-x^2-y^2}\right) - \text{Tan}^{-1}\left[\dfrac{(R+x)^2+y^2+2Ry}{R^2-x^2-y^2}\right]\right.$

$\left.+\,\text{Tan}^{-1}\left[\dfrac{(R+x)^2+y^2-2Ry}{R^2-x^2-y^2}\right]\right\}$

4. $b + \dfrac{a-b}{\pi}\left\{\text{Tan}^{-1}\left[\dfrac{(R+x)^2+y^2+2Ry}{R^2-x^2-y^2}\right] + \text{Tan}^{-1}\left[\dfrac{(R+x)^2+y^2-2Ry}{R^2-x^2-y^2}\right]\right\}$

5. $\dfrac{1}{2} + \dfrac{1}{\pi}\text{Tan}^{-1}\left(\dfrac{x^2-y^2}{2xy}\right)$ **6.** $\dfrac{a+b}{2} + \left(\dfrac{a-b}{\pi}\right)\text{Tan}^{-1}\left(\dfrac{x^2-y^2}{2xy}\right)$

7. $b - \dfrac{b}{\pi}\tan^{-1}\left[\dfrac{4a^2xy}{(x^2+y^2)^2-a^4}\right]$ **8.** $b - \dfrac{b-c}{\pi}\tan^{-1}\left[\dfrac{4a^2xy}{(x^2+y^2)^2-a^4}\right]$

9. $\dfrac{y}{\pi} - \dfrac{2}{\pi}\text{Tan}^{-1}\left(\dfrac{1-e^x\cos y}{e^x\sin y}\right)$ **10.** $c + (b-c)y/a$

11. $\dfrac{1}{\pi}\left[\text{Tan}^{-1}\left(\dfrac{1+\sin y\cosh x}{\cos y\sinh x}\right) - \text{Tan}^{-1}\left(\dfrac{1-\sin y\cosh x}{\cos y\sinh x}\right)\right]$

12. $b + \left(\dfrac{c-b}{\pi}\right)\left[\text{Tan}^{-1}\left(\dfrac{1-\sin\frac{\pi y}{2a}\cosh\frac{\pi x}{2a}}{\cos\frac{\pi y}{2a}\sinh\frac{\pi x}{2a}}\right) + \text{Tan}^{-1}\left(\dfrac{1+\sin\frac{\pi y}{2a}\cosh\frac{\pi x}{2a}}{\cos\frac{\pi y}{2a}\sinh\frac{\pi x}{2a}}\right)\right]$

13. $\dfrac{1}{\pi}\left[\text{Tan}^{-1}\left(\dfrac{1+\sin\frac{\pi x}{2}\cosh\frac{\pi y}{2}}{\cos\frac{\pi x}{2}\sinh\frac{\pi y}{2}}\right) - \text{Tan}^{-1}\left(\dfrac{1-\sin\frac{\pi x}{2}\cosh\frac{\pi y}{2}}{\cos\frac{\pi x}{2}\sinh\frac{\pi y}{2}}\right)\right]$

14. $c + \left(\dfrac{b-c}{\pi}\right)\left[\text{Tan}^{-1}\left(\dfrac{1+\sin\frac{\pi x}{2a}\cosh\frac{\pi y}{2a}}{\cos\frac{\pi x}{2a}\sinh\frac{\pi y}{2a}}\right) + \text{Tan}^{-1}\left(\dfrac{1-\sin\frac{\pi x}{2a}\cosh\frac{\pi y}{2a}}{\cos\frac{\pi x}{2a}\sinh\frac{\pi y}{2a}}\right)\right]$

15. $1 + \dfrac{3}{\pi}\text{Tan}^{-1}\left(\dfrac{y}{x}\right)$ **16.** $b + \left(\dfrac{c-b}{\alpha}\right)\text{Tan}^{-1}\left(\dfrac{y}{x}\right)$ **17.** $c + (b-c)x$

18. $\dfrac{b+c}{2} - \dfrac{cx}{a} + \dfrac{1}{\pi}\left[c\,\text{Tan}^{-1}\left(\dfrac{1-e^{-\pi y/a}\cos\frac{\pi x}{a}}{e^{-\pi y/a}\sin\frac{\pi x}{a}}\right) - b\,\text{Tan}^{-1}\left(\dfrac{1+e^{-\pi y/a}\cos\frac{\pi x}{a}}{e^{-\pi y/a}\sin\frac{\pi x}{a}}\right)\right]$

21. $b + \dfrac{a-b}{2\ln(2-\sqrt{3})}\ln\left[\dfrac{x^2+(y-2\sqrt{3})^2}{x^2+(y+2\sqrt{3})^2}\right]$

22. $(2b-a) + \dfrac{a-b}{2\ln(2-\sqrt{3})}\ln\left[\dfrac{x^2+(y-8+4\sqrt{3})^2}{x^2+(y-8-4\sqrt{3})^2}\right]$

Exercises 7.6

6. $z = (a/\pi)(1 + w + \log_{-\pi/2} w)$

Exercises 7.7.1

1. $\dfrac{1}{2}(T_2+T_1) + \left(\dfrac{T_2-T_1}{\pi}\right)\text{Tan}^{-1}\left(\dfrac{x}{y}\right)$ **2.** $T_0 + \dfrac{(T_a-T_0)y}{a}$

3. $T_0 - \dfrac{T_0}{\pi}\tan^{-1}\left(\dfrac{2y}{x^2+y^2-1}\right)$ **4.** $T_0 + \dfrac{T_0}{\pi}\left[\text{Tan}^{-1}\left(\dfrac{1+x}{y}\right) - \text{Tan}^{-1}\left(\dfrac{1-x}{y}\right)\right]$

5. $\dfrac{1}{\pi}\left[\text{Tan}^{-1}\left(\dfrac{1+\sin\frac{\pi x}{2}\cosh\frac{\pi y}{2}}{\cos\frac{\pi x}{2}\sinh\frac{\pi y}{2}}\right) - \text{Tan}^{-1}\left(\dfrac{1-\sin\frac{\pi x}{2}\cosh\frac{\pi y}{2}}{\cos\frac{\pi x}{2}\sinh\frac{\pi y}{2}}\right)\right]$ **6.** $\dfrac{2}{\pi}\text{Tan}^{-1}\left(\dfrac{\cos\frac{\pi x}{2}}{\sinh\frac{\pi y}{2}}\right)$

7. $T_1 + \dfrac{2(T_0-T_1)}{\pi}\text{Tan}^{-1}\left(\dfrac{\cos\frac{\pi x}{2a}}{\sinh\frac{\pi y}{2a}}\right)$ **8.** $T_0 + \left(\dfrac{T_\alpha-T_0}{\alpha}\right)\text{Tan}^{-1}\left(\dfrac{y}{x}\right)$

9. $\dfrac{T_1+T_2}{2} - \dfrac{1}{\pi}\left[T_2\,\text{Tan}^{-1}\left(\dfrac{x^2-y^2+1}{2xy}\right) + T_1\,\text{Tan}^{-1}\left(\dfrac{4-x^2+y^2}{2xy}\right)\right]$

10. $\dfrac{T_0}{\pi}\left[\text{Tan}^{-1}\left(\dfrac{1+x^2-y^2}{2xy}\right) - \text{Tan}^{-1}\left(\dfrac{1-x^2+y^2}{2xy}\right) - 2\,\text{Tan}^{-1}\left(\dfrac{x^2-y^2}{2xy}\right)\right]$

11. $\dfrac{T_0}{\pi}\tan^{-1}\left(\dfrac{\sin\frac{\pi y}{a}}{\sinh\frac{\pi x}{a}}\right)$ **12.** $\dfrac{T_1+T_2}{2}+\left(\dfrac{T_2-T_1}{\pi}\right)\text{Tan}^{-1}\left(\dfrac{2Ry}{R^2-x^2-y^2}\right)$

13. $\dfrac{T_1+T_2}{2}+\left(\dfrac{T_2-T_1}{\pi}\right)\text{Tan}^{-1}\left(\dfrac{2Rx}{R^2-x^2-y^2}\right)$ **14.** $T_1+\dfrac{2}{\pi}(T_0-T_1)\text{Tan}^{-1}\left(\dfrac{R^2-x^2-y^2}{2Ry}\right)$

15. $\dfrac{2T_0}{\pi}\text{Tan}^{-1}\left[\dfrac{R^4-(x^2+y^2)^2}{4R^2xy}\right]$

16. $\dfrac{T_1+T_2}{2}+\left(\dfrac{T_2-T_1}{\pi}\right)\text{Sin}^{-1}\left[\dfrac{\sqrt{(x^2+y^2+x)^2+y^2}-\sqrt{(x^2+y^2-x)^2+y^2}}{2(x^2+y^2)}\right]$

17. $\dfrac{T_a+T_0}{2}+\dfrac{1}{\pi}(T_0-T_a)\text{Sin}^{-1}\left[\dfrac{\sqrt{e^{2\pi x/a}+2e^{\pi x/a}\cos\frac{\pi y}{a}+1}-\sqrt{e^{2\pi x/a}-2e^{\pi x/a}\cos\frac{\pi y}{a}+1}}{2}\right]$

18. $T_1+\left(\dfrac{T_0-T_1}{\pi}\right)\tan^{-1}\left\{\dfrac{2(R^2-x^2-y^2)[(R+x)^2+y^2]}{4R^2y^2+(R^2-x^2-y^2)^2-[(R+x)^2+y^2]^2}\right\}$

19. $T_0+\dfrac{T_1-T_0}{\pi}\tan^{-1}(y/x)$ **20.** $\dfrac{2T_0}{\pi}\text{Sin}^{-1}\left[\dfrac{\sqrt{(x+1)^2+y^2}-\sqrt{(x-1)^2+y^2}}{2}\right]$ **23.** No

24. (a) $100-\dfrac{100}{\pi}\tan^{-1}\left[\dfrac{4y(x^2+y^2-1)}{(x^2+y^2)^2-2x^2-6y^2+1}\right]$ (b) $100-\dfrac{200}{\pi}\text{Tan}^{-1}\left(\dfrac{2y}{x^2+y^2-1}\right)$

25. $T_1+\left[\dfrac{2(T_0-T_1)}{\pi}\right]\text{Tan}^{-1}\left(\dfrac{2Ry}{x^2+y^2-R^2}\right)$ **27.** (a) $\dfrac{bT_1-aT_0}{b-a}-\dfrac{2ab(T_1-T_0)x}{(b-a)(x^2+y^2)}$

28. $T_0+\dfrac{T_1-T_0}{2\ln(2-\sqrt{3})}\ln\left[\dfrac{x^2+(y-2\sqrt{3})^2}{x^2+(y+2\sqrt{3})^2}\right]$

29. $T_0+\dfrac{T_1-T_0}{2\ln[(a-\sqrt{a^2-R^2})/R]}\ln\left[\dfrac{x^2+(y-\sqrt{a^2-R^2})^2}{x^2+(y+\sqrt{a^2-R^2})^2}\right]$

30. $(2T_1-T_0)+\left(\dfrac{T_1-T_0}{\ln 4}\right)\ln\left[\dfrac{4x^2+(2y-5)^2}{4x^2+(2y-20)^2}\right]$

Exercises 7.7.2

1. $-\dfrac{h}{4\pi\kappa}\ln[x^2+(y-a)^2][x^2+(y+a)^2]+\text{Re}\,(D)$

3. (a) $T_0-\dfrac{h}{4\pi\kappa}\ln\left\{\dfrac{R^2[(x-a)^2+y^2]}{(R^2-ax)^2+a^2y^2}\right\}$ **8.** $T_0+\dfrac{h}{4\pi\kappa}\ln\left[\dfrac{r+R-2\sqrt{rR}\cos\left(\frac{\theta+\phi}{2}\right)}{r+R-2\sqrt{rR}\cos\left(\frac{\theta-\phi}{2}\right)}\right]$

Exercises 7.8.1

1. $V_0+(V_\alpha-V_0)\theta/\alpha$ **2.** $V_0+\dfrac{2}{\pi}(V_1-V_0)\text{Tan}^{-1}\left(\dfrac{R^2-x^2-y^2}{2Ry}\right)$

3. $\dfrac{V_0}{\pi}\tan^{-1}\left[\dfrac{R^2-x^2-y^2}{(x-R)^2+(y-R)^2-R^2}\right]$, $V_0/4$ **4.** $\dfrac{2V_0}{\pi}\text{Tan}^{-1}\left(\dfrac{2Ry}{x^2+y^2-R^2}\right)$

5. $V_0+\left[\dfrac{2(V_1-V_0)}{\pi}\right]\text{Tan}^{-1}\left(\dfrac{2Ry}{x^2+y^2-R^2}\right)$ **6.** $V_1+\dfrac{2}{\pi}(V_0-V_1)\text{Tan}^{-1}\left(\dfrac{\cos\frac{\pi x}{2a}}{\sinh\frac{\pi y}{2a}}\right)$

7. $V_0+\dfrac{2(V_1-V_0)}{\pi}\text{Tan}^{-1}\left(\dfrac{\cos\frac{\pi y}{2a}}{\sinh\frac{\pi x}{2a}}\right)$ **8.** $V_0+\dfrac{4(V_1-V_0)}{3\pi}\left\{\arg_{-\pi/2}\left[\dfrac{(x-a)+yi}{(x+a)+yi}\right]-\dfrac{\pi}{2}\right\}$

9. $V_1 + \dfrac{2a(V_0 - V_1)y}{x^2 + y^2}$ **10.** $V_0 + \dfrac{V_1 - V_0}{2\ln\left[(a - \sqrt{a^2 - R^2})/R\right]}\ln\left[\dfrac{x^2 + (y - \sqrt{a^2 - R^2})^2}{x^2 + (y + \sqrt{a^2 - R^2})^2}\right]$

11. $(2V_1 - V_0) + \dfrac{V_1 - V_0}{\ln 4}\ln\left[\dfrac{4x^2 + (2y - 5)^2}{4x^2 + (2y - 20)^2}\right]$ **12.** $V_0 + \dfrac{2}{\pi}(V_1 - V_0)\mathrm{Tan}^{-1}\left(\dfrac{x^2 + y^2 - 2Ry}{x^2 + y^2 - 2Rx}\right)$

13. (a) $\dfrac{bV_1 - aV_0}{b - a} - \dfrac{2ab(V_1 - V_0)x}{(b - a)(x^2 + y^2)}$ **14.** $\dfrac{V_0}{\pi}\mathrm{Cos}^{-1}\left[\dfrac{\sqrt{(x + 1)^2 + y^2} - \sqrt{(x - 1)^2 + y^2}}{2}\right]$

Exercises 7.8.2

2. (a) $V_0 - \dfrac{q}{4\pi\epsilon_0}\ln\left\{\dfrac{R^2[(x - a)^2 + y^2]}{(R^2 - ax)^2 + a^2y^2}\right\}$ **7.** $V_0 + \dfrac{q}{4\pi\epsilon_0}\ln\left[\dfrac{r + R - 2\sqrt{rR}\cos\left(\dfrac{\theta + \phi}{2}\right)}{r + R - 2\sqrt{rR}\cos\left(\dfrac{\theta - \phi}{2}\right)}\right]$

Exercises 7.9.1

1. $Ue^{-\alpha i}z$

2. (a) Stream curves are $r = [(C/\tilde{U})\csc(\pi\theta/\alpha)]^{\alpha/\pi}$, C and $\tilde{U}$ constants

(b) $(\tilde{U}\pi/\alpha)r^{\pi/\alpha - 1}(-\cos\alpha\,\hat{\mathbf{i}} - \sin\alpha\,\hat{\mathbf{j}})$ (c) $(\tilde{U}\pi/\alpha)r^{\pi/\alpha - 1}[\sin(\alpha/2)\,\hat{\mathbf{i}} - \cos(\alpha/2)\,\hat{\mathbf{j}}]$, yes

(d) y-component negative; x-component sometimes negative and sometimes positive (e) Yes

3. (b) $C = U(y\cos\alpha - x\sin\alpha)\left(1 - \dfrac{a^2}{x^2 + y^2}\right)$

4. (a) $c^2 = (a^2 - b^2)/4$, $R = (a + b)/2$

(b) $[U(a + b)/2][(z + \sqrt{z^2 + b^2 - a^2})/(a + b) + (z - \sqrt{z^2 + b^2 - a^2})/(a - b)]$

5. (b) $U(z\cos\alpha - \sqrt{z^2 - a^2}\sin\alpha\,i)$, Yes (c) Infinite

6. (a) $U[z - 1/(2a) - i\sqrt{4az - 1}/(2a)]$

7. $\pi aU\coth(\pi a/z)$

8. $\psi(x, y) = \tilde{U}\cos(\pi x/a)\sinh(\pi y/a)$; $\mathbf{q} = (\tilde{U}\pi/a)[\cos(\pi x/a)\cosh(\pi y/a)\,\hat{\mathbf{i}} + \sin(\pi x/a)\sinh(\pi y/a)\,\hat{\mathbf{j}}]$; $|\mathbf{q}| = (\tilde{U}\pi/a)\sqrt{\cosh^2(\pi y/a) - \sin^2(\pi x/a)}$

9. $\tilde{U}e^{-\alpha\pi i/(\pi - \alpha)}z^{\pi/(\pi - \alpha)}$ **10.** Lemniscates $r^2 = -(Ua^3\sin 2\theta)/(2C)$, C a constant

11. $\tilde{U}(z^2 + a^4/z^2)$; $(0, a)$ and $(a, 0)$ **12.** (a) $\tilde{U}(z^{\pi/\alpha} + a^2 z^{-\pi/\alpha})$

17. $iU\mathrm{Cos}^{-1}z$, $\dfrac{x^2}{\cos^2(C/U)} - \dfrac{y^2}{\sin^2(C/U)} = 1$

18. $x = (d/\pi)\{1 + e^{\pi u/(\rho U d)}\cos[\pi C/(\rho U d)] + \pi u/(\rho U d)\}$,

$y = (d/\pi)\{e^{\pi u/(\rho U d)}\sin[\pi C/(\rho U d)] + \pi C/(\rho U d)\}$

Exercises 7.9.2

1. $\dfrac{2\sigma}{\pi\rho}\log\left(\sinh\dfrac{\pi z}{2a}\right)$ **2.** (a) $\dfrac{\sigma}{2\pi\rho}[\log(z + a) + \log(z - a)]$ (b) $z = 0$

4. $\dfrac{\sigma}{2\pi\rho}[\log(z + a) + \log(z - a)]$; $y = 0$, $y = \pm a$

6. (a) $\dfrac{\sigma}{2\pi\rho}\log\left(z + \dfrac{a^2}{z} - c - \dfrac{a^2}{c}\right)$ **7.** $\dfrac{-\sigma \pm \sqrt{\sigma^2 - 4\pi^2\rho^2U^2a^2}}{2\pi\rho U}$; $\sigma = 2\pi\rho Ua$; $\sigma > 2\pi\rho Ua$

10. $\dfrac{2\sigma}{\pi\rho}\log\left(\cos\dfrac{\pi z}{2a}\right)$ **11.** $\dfrac{\sigma}{2\pi\rho}\log\left(\sinh\dfrac{\pi z}{a}\right)$ **12.** $\dfrac{\sigma}{2\pi\rho}\log\left[\dfrac{e^{2\pi(z+a)/b} - 1}{e^{2\pi(z-a)/b} - 1}\right]$

13. $\dfrac{\sigma}{\pi\rho}\log\left(\dfrac{ie^{\pi z/a} - 1}{ie^{\pi z/a} + 1}\right)$

Exercises 7.9.3

1. $-\dfrac{i\Gamma}{2\pi}[\log(z-a-ai)+\log(z+a+ai)-\log(z+a-ai)-\log(z-a+ai)]$

2. $z=0$ **3.** None

Exercises 8.1

1. (b)(i) $3!/(s+5)^4$ (ii) $(s+1)/[(s+1)^2+4]+2/[(s-3)^2+4]$
  (iii) $(s-a)/[(s-a)^2-16]-4/[(s+a)^2-16]$
  (c)(i) $(1/2)e^t\sin 2t$ (ii) $e^{-2t}[\cosh\sqrt{3}t-(2/\sqrt{3})\sinh\sqrt{3}t]$

2. (b)(i) $e^{-3s}(s+1)/s^2$ (ii) $(1/s)e^{-as}$ (iii) $(1-e^{-as})/s$ (iv) $(e^{-as}-e^{-bs})/s$
  (c)(i) $(t-2)h(t-2)$ (ii) $\sin(t-3)h(t-3)$ (iii) $\cosh\sqrt{2}(t-5)h(t-5)$

3. (b)(i) $2s(s^2-3a^2)/(s^2+a^2)^3$ (ii) $6(s-2)/(s^2-4s+13)^2$
  (c)(i) $\dfrac{t}{2\sqrt{6}}e^{3t}\sin\sqrt{6}t$ (ii) $\dfrac{t-2}{2\sqrt{19}}\sin\sqrt{19}(t-2)\,h(t-2)$

4. (b)(i) $\dfrac{1}{1-e^{-as}}\left[\dfrac{1}{s^2}-e^{-as}\left(\dfrac{1}{s^2}+\dfrac{a}{s}\right)\right]$ (ii) $\dfrac{1-e^{-as}}{s(1+e^{-as})}$ (iii) $\dfrac{a(1+e^{-\pi s/a})}{(s^2+a^2)(1-e^{-\pi s/a})}$

5. $1-e^{-t}$ **6.** $(2\sin t-\sin 2t)/6$ **7.** $-(2/7)e^{-4t}+(2/7)\cosh\sqrt{2}t-(\sqrt{2}/14)\sinh\sqrt{2}t$

8. $(\cosh 3t-\cosh 2t)/5$ **9.** $2/s^2-(1/s+1/s^2)e^{-s}$ **10.** $2/s^3+e^{-s}(s^2-2)/s^3$

11. $(1-e^{-as})/[s^2(1+e^{-as})]$ **12.** $1/[s(1+e^{-as})]$ **13.** $(1/s)e^{-as}$ **14.** $e^{-as}(1-e^{-s})/s$

15. $2e^{2t}-e^t$ **16.** $-1+e^{-t}-e^{-t/2}+e^{t/2}$ **17.** $e^{-5(t-3)}h(t-3)$ **18.** $[e^{-(t-2)}-e^{-2(t-2)}]h(t-2)$

19. $(1/3)e^{-t}+(1/3)e^{t/2}[\sqrt{3}\sin(\sqrt{3}t/2)-\cos(\sqrt{3}t/2)]$

20. $(1/3)e^{-2t/3}[5\cos(2\sqrt{5}t/3)-(8\sqrt{5}/5)\sin(2\sqrt{5}t/3)]$

21. $[1-\cos(t-1)]h(t-1)-[1-\cos(t-2)]h(t-2)$ **22.** $e^{-t}(t^3/6-t^4/24)$

23. $(1/3)e^{-t}(\sin t+\sin 2t)$ **24.** $(\sinh 2t+2t\cosh 2t)/4$

Exercises 8.2

2. $(1/2)e^t+(1/2)e^{-t}(\cosh\sqrt{2}t+2\sqrt{2}\sinh\sqrt{2}t)$ **3.** $e^{-t}-\cos t+\sin t$ **4.** $2(1+t)e^{-t}+t-2$

5. $e^t(1-t+t^4/12)$ **6.** $\cos t-3\sin t+t$ **7.** $e^{-t}(\sin 2t+\sin t)/3$

8. $-(9/194)\cos 3t-(2/97)\sin 3t+(1/194)e^{-3t}[397\cosh 2\sqrt{2}t+[1397/(2\sqrt{2})]\sinh 2\sqrt{2}t]$

9. $-1/36-t/6+(377/450)e^{-2t}+(33/100)e^{2t}-(7/50)\cos t+(1/50)\sin t$

10. $(1/338)[(5+13t)e^{-3t}+e^{2t}(1364\sin t-343\cos t)]$

11. $1/4+(1/2)\sin 2t-(1/4)\cos 2t+(1/4)[\cos 2(t-1)-1]h(t-1)$

12. $-1/8+(\sin 2t-2\cos 2t)/40+(1/40)e^{-t}(7\cosh\sqrt{5}t+\sqrt{5}\sinh\sqrt{5}t)$

13. $14+12t+4t^2+2e^{-t}+8e^{2t}-24e^t$

14. $-(8\cos 4t+9\sin 4t)/290+[2/(145\sqrt{6})]e^{-2t}(2\sqrt{6}\cosh\sqrt{6}t+13\sinh\sqrt{6}t)$

15. $e^{-4t}(\cos 5t+39\sin 5t)/200+e^{-2t}(7\sin t-\cos t)/200$

16. $(t+2)e^{-t}+t-2+(2-t-e^{1-t})h(t-1)$ **17.** $(\cos 2t+4\cos 3t+4\sin 3t)/5$

18. $-(2t/5)e^{-4t}+[(5e^5-5e^4-2)/(5e^5-5)]e^{-4t}+[(5e^4-3)/(5e^5-5)]e^t$

19. $(1/3)e^{-t}\sin t+(e^{\pi/4}-\sqrt{2}/6)e^{-t}\sin 2t$

20. $(3/2)e^t-(1/2)e^{3t}+(1/2)\int_0^t f(v)[e^{3(t-v)}-e^{t-v}]dv$

21. $t/4+t^2/4+e^t(C_1\cos\sqrt{3}t+C_2\sin\sqrt{3}t)$ **22.** $(C_1+C_2 t)e^t+(t^4/12)e^t$

23. $C_1\cos t+C_2\sin t+\int_0^t f(v)\sin(t-v)\,dv$

24. $e^{-t}(C_1\cos 2t+C_2\sin 2t)+(1/3)e^{-t}\sin t$

25. $t-2+e^{-2t}(C_1\cosh\sqrt{3}t+C_2\sinh\sqrt{3}t)$

26. $C_1\cosh 2t+C_2\sinh 2t+(1/2)\int_0^t f(v)\sinh 2(t-v)\,dv$

27. $(t/8)\sin t-(1/32)\cos t+C_1\cos 3t+C_2\sin 3t$

28. $e^t(C_1\cos\sqrt{2}t+C_2\sin\sqrt{2}t)-(t/17)\cos 2t-(4t/17)\sin 2t-(62/289)\cos 2t-(44/289)\sin 2t$

30. $e^t(t^5 - 30t^2 - 60t + 60)/60$ **31.** $(C_1 + C_2t + C_3t^2 + t^5/60)e^t$ **32.** $-0.03 \cos 5\sqrt{2}t$ m
33. $-(3/200)e^{-15t/4}[2\cos(5\sqrt{23}t/4) - (6/\sqrt{23})\sin(5\sqrt{23}t/4)]$ m
34. $-(12\cos 10t + 8\sin 10t)/65 + (4/65)e^{-15t/4}[3\cos(5\sqrt{23}t/4) + (25/\sqrt{23})\sin(5\sqrt{23}t/4)]$ m
35. $(1/10)\cos 2\sqrt{2}t$ m   **36.** $(1/20)e^{-t/4}[(159/\sqrt{799})\sin(\sqrt{799}t/4) - \cos(\sqrt{799}t/4)]$ m
37. $(2\sin 200t + 3t\sin 200t)/40$ m   **38.** $(\sin 8t - 8t\cos 8t)/64$ m

Exercises 8.3

1. $\cos 3t + (2/3)\sin 3t + (1/9)[1 - \cos 3(t-4)]h(t-4)$
2. $2/9 + (7/9)\cos 3t + (2/3)\sin 3t - (2/9)[1 - \cos 3(t-4)]h(t-4)$
3. $(t - 1 + e^{-2t} - 3te^{-2t})/4 + (1/4)(2 - t - te^{2-2t})h(t-1)$
4. $(3 - t - 7e^{-2t} - 13te^{-2t})/4 + (1/2)(-3 + t - e^{4-2t} + te^{4-2t})h(t-2)$
5. $(5/2)e^{-t} - (3/2)e^{-3t} + [(1/20)e^{3\pi-3t} - (1/4)e^{\pi-t} + (1/10)\sin t - (1/5)\cos t]h(t-\pi)$
6. $(1/20)(55e^{-t} - 31e^{-3t}) + (1/10)(\sin t - 2\cos t) + (1/20)[5e^{\pi-t} - e^{3\pi-3t} - 2\sin t + 4\cos t]h(t-\pi)$
7. $3/5 - (3/5)e^{-t}\cos 2t - (3/10)e^{-t}\sin 2t - [(6/5) - (6/5)e^{1-t}\cos(2t-2)$
$\quad -(3/5)e^{1-t}\sin(2t-2)]h(t-1)$
8. $(4/5)(1 - e^{-t}\cos 2t) - (2/5)e^{-t}\sin 2t - [8/5 - (8/5)e^{1-t}\cos(2t-2)$
$\quad -(4/5)e^{1-t}\sin(2t-2)]h(t-1) + [4/5 - (4/5)e^{2-t}\cos(2t-4) - (2/5)e^{2-t}\sin(2t-4)]h(t-2)$
9. $2\cos 4t + (1/16)\sum_{n=0}^{\infty}(-1)^n[(t-n) - (1/4)\sin 4(t-n)]h(t-n)$
$\quad +(1/16)\sum_{n=0}^{\infty}[\cos 4(t-2n-1) - 1]h(t-2n-1)$
10. $2\cos 4t + (1/16)\sum_{n=0}^{\infty}(-1)^n[(t-n) - (1/4)\sin 4(t-n)]h(t-n)$
$\quad +(1/16)\sum_{n=0}^{\infty}(-1)^{n+1}[(t-n-1) - (1/4)\sin 4(t-n-1) - 1]h(t-n-1)$
11. $5/2 - (12/5)\cos 20t - (1/10)\sin 20t - (5/2)[1 - \cos 20(t-4)]h(t-4)$ m
12. $(\cos 20t - \sin 20t)/10 + (5/2)[1 - \cos 20(t-4)]h(t-4)$ m
13. $5/2 - (49/15)e^{-10t} + (13/15)e^{-40t} - (5/6)[3 - 4e^{-10(t-4)} + e^{-40(t-4)}]h(t-4)$ m
14. $(e^{-40t} + 2e^{-10t})/30 + (5/2)\left[1 + (1/3)e^{-40(t-4)} - (4/3)e^{-10(t-4)}\right]h(t-4)$ m
15. $(1/50)e^{-5t}(5\cos 5\sqrt{15}t - \sqrt{15}\sin 5\sqrt{15}t) + (5/2)\left[1 - e^{-5t}\left(\cos 5\sqrt{15}t + \frac{1}{\sqrt{15}}\sin 5\sqrt{15}t\right)\right]$
$\quad -(5/2)\left\{1 - e^{-5(t-4)}\left[\cos 5\sqrt{15}(t-4) + \frac{1}{\sqrt{15}}\sin 5\sqrt{15}(t-4)\right]\right\}h(t-4)$ m
16. $(5/2)\left\{1 - e^{-5(t-4)}\left[\cos 5\sqrt{15}(t-4) + (1/\sqrt{15})\sin 5\sqrt{15}(t-4)\right]\right\}h(t-4)$
$\quad +(1/50)e^{-5t}(5\cos 5\sqrt{15}t - \sqrt{15}\sin 5\sqrt{15}t)$ m
17. $(1/32)\sin 16t$ m   **18.** $(e^{-8t} - e^{-32t})/48$ m   **19.** $(\sqrt{7}/84)e^{-2t}\sin 6\sqrt{7}t$ m
20. $x_0\cos 16t + (1/32)\sin 16(t-t_0)h(t-t_0)$ m
21. $(v_0/16)\sin 16t + (1/32)\sin 16(t-t_0)h(t-t_0)$ m
22. $x_0\cos 16t + (v_0/16)\sin 16t + (1/32)\sin 16(t-t_0)h(t-t_0)$ m
23. $(1/10)\sin 10t + (1/10)\sin 10(t-1)h(t-1)$ m
24. $(1/10)\sum_{n=0}^{\infty}\sin 10(t-n)h(t-n)$ m
25. $(1/10)\sin 10t\sum_{n=0}^{\infty}h(t-n\pi/5)$ m   Yes

Exercises 8.4

1. $t(t+2)e^t/2$ **2.** $(t/4)\sin 2t$ **3.** $(3t-1)/9 + (1/9)e^{-3t}$ **4.** $[(1+8t+88t^2)e^{3t} - (1+12t)e^{-t}]/256$
5. $(2\sin 2t - \sin t)/3$ **6.** $(\cosh t - \cos t)/2$ **7.** $(2t^2\cosh 2t + 3t\sinh 3t)/16$ **8.** $e^t(\sin t - t\cos t)/2$

9. $(t/2)e^t\sin t$ **10.** $(t+1)e^t\sin t$ **11.** $\dfrac{2}{\pi}\sum_{n=1}^{\infty}\dfrac{(-1)^{n+1}}{n}e^{-n^2\pi^2t}\sin n\pi x$

12. $\dfrac{2}{\pi}\sum_{n=1}^{\infty}\dfrac{1}{n}\sin n\pi t \sin n\pi u \sin n\pi x$

13. $\dfrac{8}{\pi^3} \displaystyle\sum_{n=1}^{\infty} \dfrac{1}{(2n-1)^3} \cos(2n-1)\pi t \sin(2n-1)\pi x$

14. $t^2 + \dfrac{x^2}{6} - \dfrac{1}{6} + \dfrac{2}{\pi^2} \displaystyle\sum_{n=1}^{\infty} \dfrac{(-1)^{n+1}}{n^2} \cos n\pi t \cos n\pi x$

15. $\dfrac{1}{2\pi} \sin \dfrac{\pi t}{2} \sin \dfrac{\pi x}{2} + \dfrac{2}{\pi^2} \displaystyle\sum_{n=1}^{\infty} \dfrac{(-1)^n}{4n^2-1} \sin n\pi t \sin n\pi x$

16. $\dfrac{1}{2\pi^2} [\sin \pi t (\sin \pi x - 2\pi x \cos \pi x) - 2\pi t \cos \pi t \sin \pi x] + \dfrac{2}{\pi^2} \displaystyle\sum_{n=2}^{\infty} \dfrac{(-1)^n}{n^2-1} \sin n\pi t \sin n\pi x$

17. (a) $h(t-a)$ (b) 1   The sequence of contours of Theorem 8.7 cannot be constructed when $t < a$.

18. $\dfrac{e^t}{2\pi} \displaystyle\int_{-\infty}^{\infty} \dfrac{(1-y^2)\cos yt + 2y \sin yt}{(1+y^2)^2} dy + \dfrac{ie^t}{2\pi} \displaystyle\int_{-\infty}^{\infty} \dfrac{-2y \cos yt + (1-y^2)\sin yt}{(1+y^2)^2} dy$

Exercises 8.5

1. $C\left[-2\sqrt{\dfrac{kt}{\pi}} e^{-x^2/(4kt)} + x \operatorname{erfc}\left(\dfrac{x}{2\sqrt{kt}} \right) \right]$ **2.** $\overline{U} + (U_0 - \overline{U}) \operatorname{erfc}[x/(2\sqrt{kt})]$

3. $-\sqrt{\dfrac{k}{\pi}} \displaystyle\int_0^t \dfrac{f(v)}{\sqrt{t-v}} e^{-x^2/[4k(t-v)]} dv$

4. $\overline{U} - \overline{U} \operatorname{erfc}[x/(2\sqrt{kt})] + \dfrac{2}{\sqrt{\pi}} \displaystyle\int_{x/(2\sqrt{kt})}^{\infty} f\left(t - \dfrac{x^2}{4kv^2} \right) e^{-v^2} dv$

5. $f(t - x/c)h(t - x/c)$ **6.** $-\dfrac{gt^2}{2} + \left[\sin\omega\left(t - \dfrac{x}{c} \right) + \dfrac{g}{2}\left(t - \dfrac{x}{c} \right)^2 \right] h(t - x/c)$

7. $e^{-m^2\pi^2 kt/L^2} \sin \dfrac{m\pi x}{L}$ **8.** $\dfrac{L}{2} - \dfrac{4L}{\pi^2} \displaystyle\sum_{n=1}^{\infty} \dfrac{1}{(2n-1)^2} e^{-(2n-1)^2\pi^2 kt/L^2} \cos \dfrac{(2n-1)\pi x}{L}$

9. $U_L\left[\dfrac{x}{L} + \dfrac{2}{\pi} \displaystyle\sum_{n=1}^{\infty} \dfrac{(-1)^n}{n} e^{-n^2\pi^2 kt/L^2} \sin \dfrac{n\pi x}{L} \right]$

10. $U_0 + \dfrac{C(3x^2 - L^2)}{6L} + \dfrac{Ckt}{L} + \dfrac{2LC}{\pi^2} \displaystyle\sum_{n=1}^{\infty} \dfrac{(-1)^{n+1}}{n^2} e^{-n^2\pi^2 kt/L^2} \cos \dfrac{n\pi x}{L}$

11. $100e^{-t} \dfrac{\sin(x/\sqrt{k})}{\sin(L/\sqrt{k})} + \dfrac{200}{\pi} \displaystyle\sum_{n=1}^{\infty} \dfrac{1}{n} \left[1 + \dfrac{(-1)^{n+1}L^2}{L^2 - n^2\pi^2 k} \right] e^{-n^2\pi^2 kt/L^2} \sin \dfrac{n\pi x}{L}$

12. $\dfrac{e^{-\alpha t}}{\alpha} \left[-1 + \dfrac{\cos\sqrt{\frac{\alpha}{k}}\left(\frac{L}{2} - x \right)}{\cos\sqrt{\frac{\alpha}{k}}\frac{L}{2}} \right] + \dfrac{4L^2}{\pi} \displaystyle\sum_{n=1}^{\infty} \dfrac{e^{-(2n-1)^2\pi^2 kt/L^2}}{(2n-1)[\alpha L^2 - (2n-1)^2\pi^2 k]} \sin \dfrac{(2n-1)\pi x}{L}$

13. $\dfrac{8kL^2}{\pi^3} \displaystyle\sum_{n=1}^{\infty} \dfrac{1}{(2n-1)^3} \cos \dfrac{(2n-1)\pi ct}{L} \sin \dfrac{(2n-1)\pi x}{L}$

14. $\dfrac{8kL^3}{\pi^4 c} \displaystyle\sum_{n=1}^{\infty} \dfrac{1}{(2n-1)^4} \sin \dfrac{(2n-1)\pi ct}{L} \sin \dfrac{(2n-1)\pi x}{L}$

15. $-\dfrac{gx(L-x)}{2c^2} + \dfrac{4gL^2}{\pi^3 c^2} \displaystyle\sum_{n=1}^{\infty} \dfrac{1}{(2n-1)^3} \cos \dfrac{(2n-1)\pi ct}{L} \sin \dfrac{(2n-1)\pi x}{L}$

16. $\dfrac{F_0}{\rho\omega^2 \sin(\omega L/c)} \left[\sin \dfrac{\omega x}{c} - \sin \dfrac{\omega L}{c} + \sin \dfrac{\omega(L-x)}{c} \right] \sin \omega t$

$$+\frac{4F_0\omega L^3}{\rho c\pi^2}\sum_{n=1}^{\infty}\frac{1}{(2n-1)^2[\omega^2 L^2-(2n-1)^2\pi^2 c^2]}\sin\frac{(2n-1)\pi ct}{L}\sin\frac{(2n-1)\pi x}{L}$$

17. $100\sum_{n=0}^{\infty}\left\{\text{erf}\left[\frac{2(n+1)L-x}{2\sqrt{kt}}\right]-\text{erf}\left(\frac{2nL+x}{2\sqrt{kt}}\right)\right\};$

$$100\left(1-\frac{x}{L}\right)-\frac{200}{\pi}\sum_{n=1}^{\infty}\frac{1}{n}e^{-n^2\pi^2 kt/L^2}\sin\frac{n\pi x}{L}$$

18. $\sqrt{k}C\sum_{n=0}^{\infty}(-1)^n\left\{4\sqrt{\frac{t}{\pi}}e^{-[(2n+1)^2 L^2+x^2]/(4kt)}\sinh\frac{(2n+1)Lx}{2kt}\right.$

$$+\frac{(2n+1)L}{\sqrt{k}}\left\{\text{erf}\left[\frac{(2n+1)L-x}{2\sqrt{kt}}\right]-\text{erf}\left[\frac{(2n+1)L+x}{2\sqrt{kt}}\right]\right\}$$

$$\left.-\frac{x}{\sqrt{k}}\left\{\text{erf}\left[\frac{(2n+1)L-x}{2\sqrt{kt}}\right]+\text{erf}\left[\frac{(2n+1)L+x}{2\sqrt{kt}}\right]\right\}+\frac{2x}{\sqrt{k}}\right\};$$

$$Cx+\frac{8CL}{\pi^2}\sum_{n=1}^{\infty}\frac{(-1)^n}{(2n-1)^2}e^{-(2n-1)^2\pi^2 kt/(4L^2)}\sin\frac{(2n-1)\pi x}{2L}$$

Exercises 8.6

1. Stable **2.** Unstable **3.** Stable **4.** Unstable **5.** Marginally stable **6.** Marginally stable
7. Unstable **8.** Unstable **9.** Unstable **10.** Stable **11.** Stable **12.** Unstable
13. Stable or marginally stable **14.** Unstable **16.** $1/(Ls^2+Rs+1/C)$
17. Unstable when $b<0$, marginally stable when $b=0$, stable when $b>0$
18. (c) Stable **19.** Stable **20.** Unstable or marginally stable
21. Unstable or marginally stable **22.** Unstable or marginally stable **23.** $b>0,\,c>0$
24. $a>0,\,c>0,\,ab>c$ **25.** $0<k<10$ **26.** Stable **27.** Unstable or marginally stable
28. Unstable or marginally stable **29.** Unstable or marginally stable **30.** $b>0,\,c>0$
31. $a>0,\,c>0,\,ab>c$ **32.** $0<k<10$

Exercises 9.1

7. (c) $\pi[h(\omega+a)-h(\omega-a)]$ **8.** $\frac{\pi}{\sqrt{2}a^3}e^{-a|\omega|/\sqrt{2}}\left(\cos\frac{a\omega}{\sqrt{2}}+\sin\frac{a|\omega|}{\sqrt{2}}\right)$ **9.** $\frac{\pi}{4a^3}(1+a|\omega|)e^{-a|\omega|}$

10. $-\frac{\pi\omega i}{2a}e^{-a|\omega|}$ **11.** $\frac{2\pi}{\sqrt{3}}e^{-\sqrt{3}|\omega|/2}\left(\cos\frac{\omega}{2}+i\sin\frac{\omega}{2}\right)$ **12.** $-\frac{xe^{-a|x|}}{4a}$ **13.** $\frac{|x|e^{-a|x|}}{2}$

14. $\frac{2a}{\omega^2+a^2}$ **15.** $\frac{-4a\omega i}{(\omega^2+a^2)^2}$ **16.** $-(i\omega/2)\sqrt{\frac{\pi}{a^3}}e^{-\omega^2/(4a)}$ **17.** $-\pi i e^{-a|\omega|}\,\text{sgn}\,\omega$

18. $\frac{2(a^2-\omega^2)}{(a^2+\omega^2)^2}$ **19.** $\frac{n!}{(a+i\omega)^{n+1}}$ **20.** $\frac{2}{\omega}e^{-i\omega(a+b)/2}\sin\frac{\omega(b-a)}{2}$

21. $\frac{2i}{\omega^2}(a\omega\cos a\omega-\sin a\omega)$ **22.** $\frac{4b}{a\omega^2}\sin^2\frac{a\omega}{2}$ **23.** $\frac{4b}{a^2\omega^3}(\sin a\omega-a\omega\cos a\omega)$

24. $\frac{1}{2}\sqrt{\frac{\pi}{k}}\left[e^{-(\omega-a)^2/(4k)}+e^{-(\omega+a)^2/(4k)}\right]$ **25.** $\frac{1}{2i}\sqrt{\frac{\pi}{k}}\left[e^{-(\omega-a)^2/(4k)}-e^{-(\omega+a)^2/(4k)}\right]$

26. $\frac{2a}{a^2-\omega^2}\cos\frac{\omega\pi}{2a}$ **27.** $\frac{-2ai}{a^2-\omega^2}\sin\frac{\omega\pi}{a}$

32. (a)(i) $\begin{cases}(x^2/2)e^{-8x}, & x>0\\ 0, & x<0\end{cases}$ (ii) $\begin{cases}(b/a)(x-a)[h(x-a)-1], & x>0\\ 0, & x<0\end{cases}$ (b) No

33. (b)(i) $-\frac{L}{\omega^2}(1+e^{i\omega L})-\frac{2i}{\omega^3}(e^{i\omega L}-1)$ (ii) $\frac{e^{b(c-i\omega)}-e^{a(c-i\omega)}}{c-i\omega}$

34. (b)(ii) $\dfrac{2ia}{a^2 - \omega^2} \sin\left(\dfrac{2\pi n\omega}{a}\right)$

Exercises 9.2

1. (a) $\mathcal{F}\{f^{(n)}(x)\}(\omega) = (i\omega)^n \mathcal{F}\{f\}(\omega)$

3. $\dfrac{1}{2\sqrt{k\pi t}} \displaystyle\int_{-\infty}^{\infty} f(v)e^{-(x-v)^2/(4kt)}\,dv + \dfrac{1}{2\pi\kappa}\int_{-\infty}^{\infty}\left[\dfrac{e^{i\omega(x-x_0)}}{\omega^2}(1 - e^{-k\omega^2 t})\right]d\omega$

4. (b)(i) $\dfrac{1}{2}\operatorname{erf}\left(\dfrac{x+a}{2\sqrt{kt}}\right) - \dfrac{1}{2}\operatorname{erf}\left(\dfrac{x-a}{2\sqrt{kt}}\right)$,   (ii) $1 - \dfrac{1}{2}\operatorname{erf}\left(\dfrac{x+a}{2\sqrt{kt}}\right) + \dfrac{1}{2}\operatorname{erf}\left(\dfrac{x-a}{2\sqrt{kt}}\right)$

5. $\dfrac{1}{2\sqrt{k\pi t}}\displaystyle\int_{-\infty}^{\infty} f(v)e^{-(x-v+\alpha t)^2/(4kt)}\,dv$ **6.** $\dfrac{1}{2}[f(x+ct) + f(x-ct)] + \dfrac{1}{2c}\displaystyle\int_{x-ct}^{x+ct} g(v)\,dv$

7. $\dfrac{1}{2\pi}\displaystyle\int_{-\infty}^{\infty}\left[\tilde{f}(\omega)\cos\sqrt{k/\rho + c^2\omega^2}\,t + \dfrac{\tilde{g}(\omega)}{\sqrt{k/\rho + c^2\omega^2}}\sin\sqrt{k/\rho + c^2\omega^2}\,t\right]e^{i\omega x}\,d\omega$

8. $\dfrac{1}{2}[f(x+ct) + f(x-ct)] + \dfrac{1}{2c}\displaystyle\int_{x-ct}^{x+ct} g(v)\,dv - \dfrac{1}{2\pi\rho c^2}\int_{-\infty}^{\infty}\dfrac{1}{\omega^2}e^{i\omega(x-x_0)}\cos c\omega t\,d\omega$

9. $\dfrac{1}{2}[f(x+ct) + f(x-ct)] + \dfrac{1}{2c}\displaystyle\int_{x-ct}^{x+ct} g(v)\,dv + \dfrac{1}{2\pi\rho c}\int_{-\infty}^{\infty}\dfrac{e^{i\omega x}}{\omega}\int_0^t \tilde{F}(\omega, u)\sin c\omega(t-u)\,du\,d\omega$

10. $\dfrac{1}{2L}\sin\dfrac{\pi y}{L}\displaystyle\int_{-\infty}^{\infty}\dfrac{g(v)}{\cosh\frac{\pi(x-v)}{L} + \cos\frac{\pi y}{L}}\,dv + \dfrac{1}{2L}\sin\dfrac{\pi y}{L}\int_{-\infty}^{\infty}\dfrac{f(v)}{\cosh\frac{\pi(x-v)}{L} - \cos\frac{\pi y}{L}}\,dv$

11. $\dfrac{1}{L}\cos\dfrac{\pi y}{2L}\displaystyle\int_{-\infty}^{\infty}\dfrac{g(v)\cosh\frac{\pi(x-v)}{2L}}{\cosh\frac{\pi(x-v)}{L} + \cos\frac{\pi y}{L}}\,dv - \dfrac{1}{2\pi}\int_{-\infty}^{\infty}\dfrac{\tilde{f}(\omega)\sinh\omega(L-y)}{\omega\cosh\omega L}e^{i\omega x}\,d\omega$

12. $\dfrac{1}{L}\sin\dfrac{\pi y}{2L}\displaystyle\int_{-\infty}^{\infty}\dfrac{f(v)\cosh\frac{\pi(x-v)}{2L}}{\cosh\frac{\pi(x-v)}{L} - \cos\frac{\pi y}{L}}\,dv + \dfrac{1}{2\pi}\int_{-\infty}^{\infty}\dfrac{\tilde{g}(\omega)\sinh\omega y}{\omega\cosh\omega L}e^{i\omega x}\,d\omega$

Exercises 9.3

2. $\mathcal{F}_c\{xf(x)\}(\omega) = \dfrac{d}{d\omega}[\mathcal{F}_s\{f\}(\omega)], \quad \mathcal{F}_s\{xf(x)\}(\omega) = -\dfrac{d}{d\omega}[\mathcal{F}_c\{f\}(\omega)]$

$\mathcal{F}_c\{x^2 f(x)\}(\omega) = -\dfrac{d^2}{d\omega^2}[\mathcal{F}_c\{f\}(\omega)], \quad \mathcal{F}_s\{x^2 f(x)\}(\omega) = -\dfrac{d^2}{d\omega^2}[\mathcal{F}_s\{f\}(\omega)]$

8. $\sin\omega x_0$, $\cos\omega x_0$ **9.** $e^{-\omega^2/(4a)}\displaystyle\int_0^{\omega/(2a)} e^{ax^2}\,dx$, $\dfrac{1}{2}\sqrt{\dfrac{\pi}{a}}e^{-\omega^2/(4a)}$

10. $\dfrac{2a\omega}{(a^2 + \omega^2)^2}$, $\dfrac{a^2 - \omega^2}{(a^2 + \omega^2)^2}$ **11.** $\dfrac{1}{\omega}(\cos a\omega - \cos b\omega)$, $\dfrac{1}{\omega}(\sin b\omega - \sin a\omega)$

12. $\dfrac{4b}{a\omega^2}\sin c\omega\sin^2\dfrac{a\omega}{2}$, $\dfrac{4b}{a\omega^2}\cos c\omega\sin^2\dfrac{a\omega}{2}$ **13.** $\dfrac{\sqrt{\pi}\omega}{4a^{3/2}}e^{-\omega^2/(4a)}$ **14.** $\dfrac{\pi}{2}e^{-a\omega}$

15. $\dfrac{\pi}{2a^2}(1 - e^{-a\omega})$ **16.** $\dfrac{\pi}{2\sqrt{2}a}e^{-a\omega/\sqrt{2}}\left(\cos\dfrac{a\omega}{\sqrt{2}} - \sin\dfrac{a\omega}{\sqrt{2}}\right)$ **17.** $\dfrac{\pi}{4a}e^{-a\omega}$

Exercises 9.4

1. $\overline{U}\operatorname{erfc}\left(\dfrac{x}{2\sqrt{kt}}\right)$

2. (a) $\dfrac{Q_0}{\kappa}\left[-x\operatorname{erfc}\left(\dfrac{x}{2\sqrt{kt}}\right) + 2\sqrt{\dfrac{kt}{\pi}}e^{-x^2/(4kt)}\right]$ (b) $\dfrac{\sqrt{t}}{5\sqrt{\pi}}$

3. (b) $U_0\operatorname{erf}\left(\dfrac{x}{2\sqrt{kt}}\right)$ (c) $\overline{U}\operatorname{erfc}\left(\dfrac{x}{2\sqrt{kt}}\right)$

4. (b) U_0 (c) $\dfrac{Q_0}{\kappa}\left[-x\operatorname{erfc}\left(\dfrac{x}{2\sqrt{kt}}\right)+\dfrac{2\sqrt{kt}}{\sqrt{\pi}}e^{-x^2/(4kt)}\right]$

5. $\dfrac{1}{2}[f(x+ct)+f(x-ct)]+\dfrac{1}{2c}\displaystyle\int_{x-ct}^{x+ct}g(u)\,du+f_1(t-x/c)h(t-x/c)$

$$-\frac{2}{\pi\rho c^2}\int_0^\infty\frac{1}{\omega^2}\sin\omega x_0\cos c\omega t\sin\omega x\,dx$$

6. $\dfrac{1}{2}[f(x+ct)+f(x-ct)]+\dfrac{1}{2c}\displaystyle\int_{x-ct}^{x+ct}g(u)\,du+\dfrac{c}{\tau}F_1(t-x/c)h(t-x/c),$

where $F_1(t)$ is an antiderivative of $f_1(t)$

7. $\dfrac{1}{2L}\sin\dfrac{\pi y}{L}\displaystyle\int_0^\infty\left[\dfrac{g(v)}{\cosh\frac{\pi(x-v)}{L}+\cos\frac{\pi y}{L}}-\dfrac{g(v)}{\cosh\frac{\pi(x+v)}{L}+\cos\frac{\pi y}{L}}\right]dv$

$$+\frac{1}{2L}\sin\frac{\pi y}{L}\int_0^\infty\left[\frac{f(v)}{\cosh\frac{\pi(x-v)}{L}-\cos\frac{\pi y}{L}}-\frac{f(v)}{\cosh\frac{\pi(x+v)}{L}-\cos\frac{\pi y}{L}}\right]dv$$

8. $\dfrac{1}{L}\cos\dfrac{\pi y}{2L}\displaystyle\int_0^\infty\left[\dfrac{g(v)\cosh\frac{\pi(x-v)}{2L}}{\cosh\frac{\pi(x-v)}{L}+\cos\frac{\pi y}{L}}-\dfrac{g(v)\cosh\frac{\pi(x+v)}{2L}}{\cosh\frac{\pi(x+v)}{L}+\cos\frac{\pi y}{L}}\right]dv$

$$-\frac{2}{\pi}\int_0^\infty\frac{\tilde f(\omega)}{\omega}\frac{\sinh\omega(L-y)}{\cosh\omega L}\sin\omega x\,d\omega$$

9. $\dfrac{1}{L}\sin\dfrac{\pi y}{2L}\displaystyle\int_0^\infty\left[\dfrac{g(v)\cosh\frac{\pi(x-v)}{2L}}{\cosh\frac{\pi(x-v)}{L}-\cos\frac{\pi y}{L}}-\dfrac{g(v)\cosh\frac{\pi(x+v)}{2L}}{\cosh\frac{\pi(x+v)}{L}-\cos\frac{\pi y}{L}}\right]dv$

$$+\frac{2}{\pi}\int_0^\infty\frac{\tilde g(\omega)}{\omega}\frac{\sinh\omega y}{\cosh\omega L}\sin\omega x\,d\omega$$

10. $\dfrac{1}{2L}\sin\dfrac{\pi y}{L}\displaystyle\int_0^\infty\left[\dfrac{g(v)}{\cosh\frac{\pi(x-v)}{L}+\cos\frac{\pi y}{L}}+\dfrac{g(v)}{\cosh\frac{\pi(x+v)}{L}+\cos\frac{\pi y}{L}}\right]dv$

$$+\frac{1}{2L}\sin\frac{\pi y}{L}\int_0^\infty\left[\frac{f(v)}{\cosh\frac{\pi(x-v)}{L}-\cos\frac{\pi y}{L}}+\frac{f(v)}{\cosh\frac{\pi(x+v)}{L}-\cos\frac{\pi y}{L}}\right]dv$

11. $\dfrac{y}{\pi}\displaystyle\int_0^\infty f(v)\left[\dfrac{1}{(x-v)^2+y^2}-\dfrac{1}{(x+v)^2+y^2}\right]dv$

$$+\frac{x}{\pi}\int_0^\infty g(v)\left[\frac{1}{x^2+(y-v)^2}-\frac{1}{x^2+(y+v)^2}\right]dv$$

Exercises 10.1

1. $az/(z-1)$, $|z|>1$ **2.** $1/(z^2-z)$, $|z|>1$ **3.** $(z^{a-1}-1)/[z^{a-1}(z-1)]$, $|z|>1$
4. $(z^{b-a}-1)/[z^{b-1}(z-1)]$, $|z|>1$ **5.** $1/z^5$, $|z|>0$ **6.** $1/z^a+1/z^b$, $|z|>0$
7. $z/(z-e)$, $|z|>e$ **8.** $a^k/[z^{k-1}(z-a)]$, $|z|>a$ **9.** $(z^b-a^b)/[z^{b-1}(z-a)]$, $|z|>a$
10. $[k(z-1)+1]/[z^{k-1}(1-z)^2]$, $|z|>1$ **11.** $\delta(n-3)$ **12.** $4\delta(n-6)$ **13.** $h(n-4)$
14. $(4/3)h(n-3)$ **15.** $4n$ **16.** $(-3)^n$ **17.** $(-5)^{n-2}h(n-2)$ **18.** $n(n+1)(-9)^{n-1}/2$
19. $[(-2)^{n-1}+2^{2n-1}]/3$ **20.** 0, $n=0$; $[12(-3)^{n-1}+2^{n-2}(35n-9)]/25$, $n\ge1$
21. No inverse   **22.** No inverse
23. 0 if n is odd and if $n=0$; 2 if $n=4m$, $m\ge1$ an integer; 1 if $n=4m+2$, $m\ge0$ an integer
24. $(n-2)^2h(n-3)$ **25.** $[2^{2n-1}+(-2)^{n-1}]/3$
26. 0 if $n=0$; $[12(-3)^{n-1}+2^{n-2}(35n-9)]/25$ if $n\ge1$
27. 0 if n is odd and if $n=0$; 2 if $n=4m$, $m\ge1$ an integer; 1 if $n=4m+2$, $m\ge0$ an integer
28. $(n-2)^2h(n-2)$

Exercises 10.2

1. $2(3^n)$, No limit   **2.** $1/5^n$, limit $= 0$ **3.** $(-2)^{n+1}/3^n$, limit $= 0$ **4.** $3^n/2^{n-2}$, No limit
5. $2(-3)^n/7^n$, limit $= 0$ **6.** $3 - 5^n/3^{n-1}$, No limit   **7.** $8/3 + 11(-1)^{n+1}/[3(2^n)]$, limit $= 8/3$
8. $-4/7 + (3/14)5^n/12^{n-1}$, limit $= -4/7$ **9.** $5/2 + (9/2)(-1)^{n+1}$, No limit
10. $5/2 - 1/[2(3^{n-1})]$, limit $= 5/2$ **11.** $2^n/3^{n-1} - 4$, limit $= -4$
12. $(1/5)[7(2^n) + (-1)^{n+1}/2^{n-1}]$, No limit   **13.** $-(1/20)[3(2^n) + 17/3^n]$, No limit   **14.** $n!$
15. $3/n!$ **16.** $n+1$ **17.** $(-1)^{n+1}3^n/(n!)^2$ **18.** $n(n-1)/2$
19. $a^{n-1}(f_0 a + n)$ if $r = a$; $f_0 r^n + (r^n - a^n)/(r - a)$ if $r \neq a$ **20.** $n^2 + n - 1$

Exercises 10.3

1. $P_0(1 + i/100)^n$ **2.** (a) \$1040.59 (b) \$2171.42 (c) \$3400.30
3. $P\left[\left(1 + \dfrac{i}{100m}\right)^n - 1\right]/[i/(100m)]$ **4.** $40,000 - 30,000(1.005)^n$

5. $\dfrac{1200P}{i} - \left(\dfrac{1200P}{i} - A\right)\left(1 + \dfrac{i}{1200}\right)^n$, $Ai/1200$ **6.** $9P[1 - 0.9^n]$, $9P$

7. $10\,000[(1.1)^n - 1]$ **8.** (a) $840,000 + 160,000(1.05)^n$ (b) $1,260,000 - 260,000(1.05)^n$

Exercises 10.4

1. $[5 - (-3)^n]/4$ **2.** $[5 + (-2)^{1-n}]/3$ **3.** $(1/2)6^{-n}[(1 + \sqrt{5})^{n+1} + (1 - \sqrt{5})^{n+1}]$
4. $(1/\sqrt{3})[(1 + \sqrt{3})^n - (1 - \sqrt{3})^n]$ **5.** $(2n - 1)(-2)^n$ **6.** $(1 + 2n)3^{-n}$
7. $(2^{n+1}/\sqrt{15})\sin n\theta$, where $\theta = \text{Tan}^{-1}\sqrt{15}$ **8.** $(-1 + 2n/5)(-5/3)^n$
9. $4/[3^{(n-1)/2}]\sin(5n\pi/6)$ **10.** $2^{n/2}[\cos(3n\pi/4) + 3\sin(3n\pi/4)]$
11. $(a + 2b)/3 + 2(a - b)(-1/2)^n/3$ **17.** $n^3 - 3n$

Exercises 10.5

1. $-4000 + 5000(11/10)^n$ **2.** $-4000 + 5000(6/5)^n$ **3.** $N_0 + (N_1 - N_0)n$
4. $\sqrt{5}\{[(5 + \sqrt{5})/10]^n - [(5 - \sqrt{5})/10]^n\}$ **5.** (b) $z = pz^2 + q$ **6.** No
7. (a) 0.31 (b) 0.17 (c) 0.083   **8.** (a) 0.018 (b) 0.310 (c) 0.49   **9.** \$84

Exercises 10.6

1. Unstable   **2.** Stable   **3.** Stable   **4.** Unstable   **5.** Unstable   **6.** Marginally stable
7. Unstable   **8.** Marginally stable   **9.** Stable   **10.** Marginally stable   **12.** (c) Unstable